THE FABER BOOK OF EXPLORATION

The Faber Book of
EXPLORATION

*

AN ANTHOLOGY OF WORLDS
REVEALED BY EXPLORERS
THROUGH THE AGES

BENEDICT ALLEN

faber and faber

First published in 2002
by Faber and Faber Limited
3 Queen Square London WC1N 3AU

Photoset by RefineCatch Ltd, Bungay, Suffolk
Printed in England by Clays Ltd, St Ives plc

A CIP record for this book
is available from the British Library

ISBN 0–571–20696–4

2 4 6 8 10 9 7 5 3 1

To Yasha and Tolia, who guided me through Siberia –
and to all the other indigenous guides who, often at great cost,
helped so many in this book explore their lands.

Contents

PART III: Hot Deserts

PART IV: Cold Deserts

PART V: Forests

PART VI: Mountains

Introduction

Why am I telling you all these examples of exploration and adventure?
Because we are all explorers in life, whichever path we follow.
Nansen, *Spirit of Adventure*, 1926

We are all explorers. Our desire to discover, and then share that new-found knowledge, is part of what makes us human – indeed, has played an important part in our success as a species. Long before the first caveman ever slumped down beside the fire and grunted news that there were plenty of wildebeest – or something – over yonder, our ancestors had learnt the value of sending out scouts to investigate the unknown. This questing nature of ours undoubtedly helped our species spread around the globe, just as it nowadays no doubt helps the last nomadic Penan maintain their existence in the depleted forests of Borneo, and a visitor negotiate the subways of New York.

Over the years, we've come to think of explorers as a peculiar breed – different from the rest of us, different from those of us who are merely 'well travelled' even; and perhaps there *is* a type of person more suited to seeking out the new, a type of caveman more inclined to risk venturing out. That, however, doesn't take away from the fact that we all have this enquiring urge, even today; and that in all sorts of professions – that of the artist or poet, marine biologist or astronomer – borders of the unknown are being tested each day.

Consider the following description of a deserted landscape:

'The place became full of a watchful intentness now; for when other things sank brooding to sleep the heath appeared slowly to awake and listen. Every night its Titanic form seemed to await something . . . It was at present a place perfectly accordant with man's nature – neither ghastly, hateful, nor ugly: neither commonplace, unmeaning, nor tame; but, like man, slighted and enduring; and withal singularly colossal and mysterious in its swarthy monotony. As with some persons who have long lived apart, solitude seemed to look out of its countenance. It had a lonely face, suggesting tragical possibilities.'

It's Egdon Heath, from Thomas Hardy's *The Return of the Native* – a piece of fiction. The author uses this landscape to explore the desires and fears of his characters; it matters not that this Wessex heath doesn't actually exist. He is delving into matters we all recognize because they are, of course, common to humanity. This is surely an act of exploration, and into a world as remote as the author chooses. And what of Robert Byron's *Road to Oxiana*? This was never considered a work of geographical discovery, and furthermore was at times an obvious pastiche of that grandee of travel books, Kinglake's *Eothen* of 1844. However, by the time of Byron's return home, the reader is in no doubt that the author has successfully engaged himself in another, very remote world:

'At Paddington I began to feel dazed, dazed at the prospect of coming to a stop, at the impending collision between eleven months' momentum and the immobility of a beloved home. The collision happened; it was 19 and a half days since we left Kabul. Our dogs ran up. And then my mother . . .'

This is the moment that Peter Fleming talks of when the home-comer recovers the existence he has left behind with his loved ones. The traveller 'who has for weeks or months seen himself only as a puny and irrelevant alien crawling laboriously over a country in which he has no roots and no back-ground, suddenly encounters his other self, a relatively solid and considerable figure, with a place in the minds of certain people'.

For the purposes of this book about the exploration of the earth's surface I have confined myself to those whose journeys were non-fiction but also aimed at more than personal discovery. But that still left me with another problem: the word 'explorer' has become associated with a past era: we think back to a Golden Age, as if exploration peaked somehow in the Victorian era – with Livingstone and Stanley perhaps – as if the process of discovery is now on the decline, though the truth is that we have named only one and a half million of this planet's species, and there may be more than 10 million – and that's not including the largest group of all, bacteria. We have studied only 5 per cent of the species we do know. We have scarcely mapped the ocean floors, and know even less about ourselves; you could say we fully understand the workings of only 10 per cent of our brains. Over the last ten years or more in which I've gradually researched this book, I've asked, whenever I've been among the elite group thought of as today's 'explorers', how they would define the word. Here's a range of responses from the British lot:

Ran Fiennes, the first to reach both North and South Poles overland (and whom the *Guinness Book of Records* dubbed the 'greatest living explorer') answered the question on a crackly line from Punta Arenas as he was about to launch himself on another Antarctic journey: 'An explorer is someone who has done something that no human has done before – and also done some-thing scientifically useful.'

Chris Bonington, one of the leading mountaineers of the post-war generation, felt exploration was to be found in the act of physically touching the unknown: 'You have to have gone somewhere new,' he said, simply.

Then there was Robin Hanbury-Tenison, many of whose remote journeys have been on behalf of Survival International, an organization campaigning on behalf of remote so-called 'tribal' peoples. 'A traveller', he said, 'simply records information about some far off world, and reports back; but an explorer *changes* the world.'

Wilfred Thesiger, who crossed the Empty Quarter in 1946, and belongs to an era of unmechanized travel now lost to the rest of us, told me years ago, sitting in a mud hut in Kenya, 'If I'd gone across by camel when I could have gone by car, it would have been a stunt.' Exploration meant bringing back information from a remote place regardless of any great self-discovery.

Each definition was slightly different – and tended to reflect the field of endeavour of each pioneer. It was the same whoever I asked: the prominent historian would say exploration was a thing of the past, the cutting-edge scientist would say it was of the present. Deep-sea explorers would say that the exploration of land masses was over, astronauts that the whole of Planet Earth was pretty well charted. They each set their own particular criteria, the common factor in their approach being that they all had, unlike many of us who simply enjoy travel or discovering new things, both a very definite objective from the outset and also a desire to record their findings.

I'd best declare my own bias. I'm a writer, so my interest is skewed towards the exploration of ideas. I've done a great many expeditions over the last twenty years – traversed the Amazon Basin, the Gobi, the Namib – and each journey was unique. I've lived months alone with remote peoples all around the world. I've even contacted two 'uncontacted tribes'; but none of these things is of the slightest interest to anyone (except perhaps me, and a handful of anthropologists) unless, through my books, I've found a new slant, explored a new idea. Why? Because the world has moved on. The time has long passed for the great continental voyages – another walk to the Poles, another crossing of the Empty Quarter. We know how the land surface of our planet lies; exploration of it is now down to the details, the minutiae of existence – the habits of a microbe or, say, the grazing behaviour of a buffalo. Aside from the deep sea and deep underground, it's the era of the specialist. However, this is to disregard one factor: the role the human mind has in conveying remote places; and this is what interests me: how even a well-travelled route might, if travelled again in the right way, allow us to interpret a land anew.

Take an experience of mine in New Guinea, where I embarked, without even leaving my jungle village, on what I would certainly call an act of exploration. In order to understand more of how the Niowra saw their world, I underwent an initiation ceremony there in the steamy lowlands of the swampy Sepik. I was secluded with a group of young Niowra men in what was called the *waark dumba*, or crocodile nest; and we weren't allowed to leave until the elders judged us to be 'men as strong as crocodiles', which meant being beaten every day – all part of the process of bonding, as we were prepared for taking up our positions as responsible members of the community. In our case, the process of man-making took six weeks – we were lucky. In a neighbouring village the ceremony apparently 'overran by a year'. Eventually, we emerged from the crocodile nest, our chests and backs now embossed with hundreds of permanent 'crocodile' scars that were the tribal badge.

Of course, there was no hope of me becoming a Niowra myself, a member of some New Guinea crocodile cult, equipped for life in a mosquito-governed swampland; but, just for a moment, I was able to glimpse, I felt, the forest world seen by the young men who shared such an intimate and traumatic time with me. It was an unpenetrated world, one all but overlooked by the great European explorers who had hacked their way on through the forest, 'opening up' the interior, and I was privileged to be offered a window into it – doubly privileged, because these non-Western slants on life are disappearing all around the globe. More than a hundred 'tribal' groups have become extinct in the Amazon alone over the last century.

This, then, is the formula that my own expeditions follow. By sinking into the alien territory of an indigenous people, the theory goes, you let go of your own world and absorb something of another. It's about fighting Chateaubriand's dictum: 'Every man carries within himself a world made up of all that he has seen and loved,' he wrote in *Voyage en Italie*, 'and it is to this world that he returns incessantly, though he may pass through, and seem to inhabit, a world quite foreign to it.'

Let's agree at least that, however people do it, exploration is about pushing back a frontier of knowledge, mental or physical; crucial to the process is the reporting back of that new information. And for the purposes of this book, I am interested in the investigation of our planet's surface through time. For if, as the great Arctic explorer Nansen wrote, 'In the beginning, the world appeared to mankind like a fairy tale . . .', then the most graphic acts of exploration have occurred while investigating that particular fairy tale.

So, which of these great discoverers should I find room for in the book?

First candidates for inclusion were those who have been key players in the charting of the earth's surface, whether I liked them or not. Where would the world be without Columbus, for example? A better place, as far as the Caribbean Indians were concerned – 'The inhabitants could be made slaves,' he reported back, summing up just one exploitable asset of the New World. However, in accidentally encountering America, Columbus also gave Europe its first good idea of the layout of our planet. More importantly, though he never even knew that he hadn't found Asia, within decades Central and South America were reeling from the impact of those in his wake. In time, the Amazon's population would plummet from 3 million to 250,000 – a twelfth of the original.

Many great scenes in the history of exploration also helped the participants find a way into the book. These moments have somehow captured our imagination back in the West, and therefore defined the nature of the far land in our minds – the 'awful place' that was the South Pole to Scott on his arrival there; and, of course, that handshake of Stanley and Livingstone in Africa – 'Dr Livingstone, I presume' – which reinforced the idea of the white man being alone civilized in a land of darkness.

Other frontiersmen pushed back territories with unfeeling, blunt instruments such as armies – Pizarro, Cortés – but still, I feel, tell us much about the world they crushed. There's also Xenophon, one of the leaders of a march by ten thousand Greek mercenaries fleeing across upland Armenia in 401 BC – 'Cast your eyes upon those mountains, and observe how impassable they are.' He, I thought, was particularly good on details, including that of his own world of baggage trains, slaves and booty – the latter taken from foot-soldiers by generals as they filed by, though those 'smitten with desire of a handsome boy or woman, conveyed them past secretly'.

In this book, women would be better represented than traditionally – so I'd thought, when I began reading though the Royal Geographical Society library. Normally deemed merely 'travellers' because they rarely preceded men, they were generally less concerned with planting flags, establishing records; they simply quietly observed, perhaps from a mission station, perhaps from a mule. Yet again and again they seemed the first really to glean the essence of places that European men had trampled through, even a whole generation or two previously. Thus Freya Stark seems only ever to be whimsically trundling along, while – the reader imagines – men hurry on by, intent on some heroic feat. Master of the vignette, she catches the world they miss in their haste:

'The routine of our journey had begun [she writes in *Southern Gates of*

Arabia], unexpected in its small incidents, immutable in its unchanging lines; this interplay of accident and law, the surprises of everyday worked into a constant pattern by physical necessities . . . this surely is the charm of travel in the open; and when our human methods of transport are so perfect that physical laws no longer regulate our journeys by land or sea or air, why then we shall have outgrown our planet: and that delightful feeling of oneness with its animals and plants and stones, oneness in the grip of the same compulsion will have gone from our wanderings forever.'

However, some very renowned female travellers did fail to make it into this book, often falling at the last hurdle because their male counterparts also evoked the same hidden valleys and forbidden cities and simply outnumbered them ten or twenty to one. The odds were stacked against women from the start, as Abigail Adams, wife of the second American president, observed: 'Women you know Sir are considered as Domestick Beings, and altho they inherit an Eaquel Share of curiosity with the other Sex . . . the Natural tenderness and Delicacy of our Constitutions, added to the many dangers we are subject too from your Sex, renders it almost impossible for a Single Lady to travel without injury to her character.' Of course, more women have been free to travel in modern times, and this is reflected in my selection, notably in the 'Cold Deserts' category, where Sara Wheeler manages to cap centuries' worth of male antics on the polar ice.

On the other hand, there were others too who, though not conventionally seen as explorers, made it into this collection for their ability to reinterpret an 'explored' terrain. In *Songlines*, Bruce Chatwin works his treatise on nomads into the red soil and spinifex of central Australia. The musician/novelist Paul Bowles, in simple, powerful prose, gave an unusual voice to the Sahara, while Peter Matthiessen seems to me to have the gift of saying something new without a single 'false note' – to borrow the phrase one reviewer of Matthiessen's *Cloud Forest* used – whether in the Amazon, the New Guinea highlands or (in the extracts I've included here) in the African savannah where, in the midday, 'heat and silence become one'. A modern-day naturalist, he brings us Africa as it is now, reminding us that the world needs to be continually re-examined, making a nonsense of the conventional idea that exploration belongs to the bygone age of Stanley and Speke. That landscape is long gone; Matthiessen describes another that, being post-colonial, equally needs exploring.

In the spirit of my belief that 'exploration' should be regarded as something that can take place at home as well as in some scorching, kiln-like desert,

I've included the eighteenth-century pioneering naturalist the Reverend Gilbert White, who pottered about the village of Selborne in Hampshire. Equally, I might have chosen a tutor of mine at the University of East Anglia who was also a pioneer, investigating as he did the unknown ways of the humble woodlouse. In investigating this creature's kingdom, he was venturing into territory as remote as any South American jungle. The problem with including such work is that it is generally written for academia. A boffin may be an explorer but his writing rarely evokes the remote world he grapples with. The difficulty of translating discoveries to non-specialists becomes more acute as science becomes ever more specialized and its language ever more remote from the everyday. On the other hand, how hard to resist – though in the end I did, because others were writing of more significant matters – Owen Lattimore, 1920s explorer of Turkestan, Mongolia and other parts of the further east. 'He was built in ovoid curves,' he wrote of one local. 'The smaller end of this fleshy ellipse was decorated . . . with an embroidered skullcap of mulberry plush, while the lower outlines were veiled more with hangings than clothes . . . his shirt hung out like a wilted sporran. He spoke fluent – nay copious – Chinese of a high-flown sort in a saccharine voice like a nightingale choked with Turkish Delight . . .'

As my research for this book went on, I began to wonder if some of the great heroes of exploration were actually . . . well, exploring very much at all. Of course, they saw new territory, but very often they failed to listen and learn from locals, concentrating instead of extending our Western values, our scientific, rationalizing culture – if not our physical territory. They opened up geographical doors – and closed others, creating myths of Dark Continents and Lands of Promise, of Jungles thick with killer snakes and barbaric or (just as false) innocent, 'unspoiled' natives – myths still strong today. Although often unable to see beyond the confines of their officer's mess or gentlemen's club, these pioneers do represent progressive waves of human thought and endeavour. As they stumble and stagger along, penetrating their unknown world, they say something about the way we all go about analysing what we don't know.

Having at last compiled my list of explorers I was still left with a fundamental problem. Despite my best endeavours I had a collection dominated by Europeans, though, frankly, we were rather late on the world scene. Until almost 1500 years after Christ we hardly ventured anywhere much – at least compared to the Chinese and Arabs, who conducted widespread trade through the East. Much of this emphasis on the West I was simply stuck with; even now, early Oriental and Islamic documents remain relatively inaccessible to the West. Thankfully, the most digestible material appears after the Middle Ages, when Europe was at last in the ascendant.

I did slightly better representing the outlook of the natives, the inhabitants of the lands Europeans encountered; though generally only a passive backdrop, these characters are telling shadows, throwing into starker relief the activities of the European protagonists. Sometimes I've been able to include indigenous people as explorers in their own right, and whether Sioux Indian, or Huichol shaman, they then seem to stand like isolated and doomed figures as the great scientists and settlers march on through their lands.

The lack of an indigenous perspective is not the only distortion in our chronicles of exploration; there are also to be found here tales of others traditionally left out of the story – those not of the officer class, those not controlling the official record: there's Peary's long-suffering wife; there's the army captain Orde-Lees, left on an icy shore to await rescue by Shackleton. To these are added an assortment of menial scientists, settlers and sailors who suffered miserable fates, and paid the price of the urge to leave home.

As I've said, the impulse to explore has been with us from our early past; in the Bible, displacement, exile and survival alone in the wilderness are important themes. 'Soon after The Fall,' wrote Mary Campbell, 'human beings took their first journey – in this case, into exile from Paradise. We are, all of us, a displaced people.' What's more, the voyage has always been an essential element of storytelling, a way of describing the human life cycle. Our journey from birth to the grave is symbolized in fairy tales, fables, and the quests of mythical heroes.

The first known voyage of exploration was recorded in Egyptian hieroglyphics in 3200 BC – followed almost 1,000 years later by Harkhuf's expeditions up the Nile to Yam (Southern Nubia) in around 2300 BC. Harkhuf is perhaps the first known explorer whose tomb (in Elephantine, Aswan) is inscribed with proud records of his journeys. After an absence of seven months, we learn, Harkhuf returned to Egypt laden with 'all kinds of gifts', including a dancing dwarf, panthers, ebony and ivory, all of which indicate that he must have travelled up the Nile into Nubia.

Another motive was religious – indeed, until the sixteenth century, the only non-commercial or military travel that took place on a global scale was the pilgrimage, where travellers supported themselves by begging for alms. In medieval days Hejaz, the western coast of Arabia, became one of the most travelled-to locations in the world, as the *hajjis*, or Islamic pilgrims, disembarked on their way to Mecca. Commercial gain ultimately became the greatest of all motivators, spurring on rival nations, principally to control the spice trade routes to the East.

Although Marco Polo's account of his travels would later come in for careful scrutiny and criticism, the medieval world was astounded and intrigued by his descriptions of Kublai Khan's rich and well-ordered empire. Two hundred years later, it was to find a short cut for trade to Cathay and Cipangu (Japan) that Columbus sailed west. When natives in what is now Cuba responded to his queries for gold by mentioning a place called 'Cubanacan', he was sure they were referring to Kublai Khan.

Meanwhile, centuries before they first sailed to the Americas, Europeans were dreaming of unknown lands to the west, places inhabited by the 'fabulous races of mankind', men and women unlike any seen in the known world. There was the belief that, though the people might be frightening, their world would surely be a paradise. Horace wrote of these mystical lands that must exist over the horizon:

> *See before us the distant glow,*
> *Through the thin dawn – mists of the West,*
> *Rich sunlit plains and hilltops gemmed with snow,*
> *The Islands of the Blest.*

Columbus longed to see the mythical western isles 'of which so many marvels are told' and on his third voyage, as his ship coasted the shores of modern Trinidad, he believed he was skirting the Garden of Eden, 'because all men say that it is at the end of the Orient, and that's where we are'.

There are many manuscripts depicting these fantastic peoples and places, such as the Nuremberg Chronicle of 1493, with its collection of 'unknown peoples, weird and fantastical'; but with the Renaissance, things changed. Europeans established a dominance over other parts of the world that was to last for centuries. Their physical presence around the globe stems from the extraordinary voyages of exploration and discovery undertaken from the mid-fifteenth to the mid-sixteenth century, by the Portuguese and Spanish in particular. Portugal's search for direct access to the spices and luxury commodities of the East led to Vasco da Gama's famous journey to India around the Cape of Good Hope.

Since Africa had been known, at least along its northern and western fringes, early on, it was only with the discovery of the Americas that Europeans were brought into contact with a whole world – complete with its own set of beliefs – that they had never known before. Europeans were shocked into re-assessing what it meant to be civilized, and even to be human. The experience also introduced into the history of European colonialism the contrasting themes of the arrogance of conquest and the corresponding guilt at having wreaked so much destruction.

The 'discovery' of the Americas profoundly altered European consciousness. The great French essayist of the period, Michel de Montaigne, wrote of his sadness that the French, who were so critical of the savages, were so blind to their own faults. Comparing the activities of the Inquisition to those of cannibals, he suggested that it was more barbarous to torture a man while he was still alive and able to feel, than to eat him when he was already dead. A number of Brazilian Indians, thought to be cannibals, were shipped to France: 'They said that they had noticed there were rich men among us, with more than they could possibly need, and there were others begging at their doors, desperately thin with hunger and poverty. They found it strange that these poor could bear such injustice, that they did not take the others by the throat or set fire to their houses.'

Montaigne drew an important conclusion: 'Every man calls "barbarous" anything he is not accustomed to. We have no other criterion of truth or right reason than the example and form of the opinion of our own country. There we also find the perfect religion, the perfect political arrangements, the most developed and perfect way of doing anything.'

Up to this point, however, for the European royal courts and the traders bankrolling pioneers such as Cortés and Champlain, geographical discovery *per se* was incidental and sometimes irrelevant. The watershed between exploration motivated by greed and exploration motivated by scientific enquiry occurs only in the eighteenth century and owes much to the Enlightenment. Commercial and colonial interests certainly featured in the instructions issued in 1725 by Peter the Great to Vitus Bering before he set out to discover if the Asian and American land-masses were joined. With its rejection of dogma and its emphasis on reason and experiment, the Enlightenment gave humans a new perspective on their world and a new purpose in it. The apparently 'primitive' societies could no longer be regarded as amongst the raw materials for Christendom. Above all, the Enlightenment encouraged the individual to think and act for himself. The solitary and often hazardous wanderings of James Bruce and Mungo Park in Africa, sponsored or otherwise, were undertaken to a significant degree in a spirit of plain curiosity. It was an investigation into our place in the order of things. As the Enlightenment polymath Sir William Jones put it: 'Man and Nature, whatever is performed by one or produced by the other.'

With Rousseau and the birth of Romanticism there emerged the notion of travel as a way to appreciate natural beauty – the cult of nature. The modern era of professional travellers – and of tourists – had arrived, and with it an increase in documentation. The Industrial Revolution had given rise to a prosperous middle class, who had the time, intellectual inclination and the finance to travel. Many people who travel today search for authenticity, a pure culture that has somehow managed to remain untainted by the mechanization and globalization of our world back home.

Robert Byron justifies his travelling by reminding us that it is a way to knowledge: 'Admittedly there are other ways of making the world's acquaintance. But the traveller is slave to his senses; his grasp of fact can only be complete when reinforced by sensory evidence; he can know the world, in fact, only when he sees, hears and smells it.'

Others find 'out there' a space in which to begin anew. 'Everything must be re-learnt before life can be truly gauged,' Ella Maillart wrote in her *Turkestan Solo* (1934). 'What life is worth is a conception we have all lost, more or less. But in contact with primitive, simple peoples, mountain dwellers, nomads, and sailors it is impossible to ignore the elemental laws. Life finds its equilibrium again . . .'

Elta Close would have agreed: 'Looking with a disinterested spinster eye on the world, I notice that even when women have the health and the money to be free, they seem to like the feeling of being anchored . . . for those who do not marry a man seem inevitably to marry themselves to a garden, or a house, or a dog, and then having forged their own chains say pathetically, "If only I were free, how I would love to travel and see the world." In the year of our Lord 1922 I was free, and realized it . . .'

Freya Stark, in her *Baghdad Sketches*, clearly found satisfaction in the detachment from her sedentary world: 'everything which belongs to your everyday life is a hindrance'. For others, such as the anthropologist Claude Lévi-Strauss, travel was an intellectual challenge, as he tried in vain to piece together the 'idea of the exotic'. He wanted to find people as yet untouched by his world: 'I should have liked to live in the age of *real* travel, when the spectacle on offer had not yet been blemished, contaminated, and confounded.' It was an impossible quest, as he acknowledged himself, for humans are never isolated from visitors, or their effects, and therefore are always changing. 'At what point would the study of the Brazilian savage have yielded the purest satisfaction and the savage himself been at his peak?'

Laurens Van der Post, like many before and since, found his satisfaction in the seemingly unpromising wilderness. 'Ever since I can remember I have been attracted by deserts in a way I do not properly understand . . . I know of nothing more exciting to my imagination than discovery in the waste land which the established world rejects as ugly and sterile, a beauty and promise of rare increase not held out anywhere else in life.' His focus became the inhabitants; time and again he would go on another journey, 'into my mind and the mind of the vanished bushman'. He quotes D. H. Lawrence: 'In the dust where we have buried the silent races and their abominations we have buried so much of the delicate magic of life.'

But whatever the official excuse for an expedition – and the explorers in this book proffer the whole gamut – all those whom I know personally share an internal, silent longing to be back out there – whether in a desert death zone or leechy swamp. Among the explorer fraternity it's something understood, unquestioned, unspoken. Most – and I'd include myself in this – feel a little at a loss back here in the West. We know what Wilfred Thesiger meant when he said, 'I went there to find peace in the hardship of desert travel and the company of desert peoples . . .' There's not much solace to be had from metaphysical poets such as Henry Vaughan and George Herbert, who propose that restlessness is the crucial attribute that distinguishes the human race from other aspects of the natural world – that it's a perpetual torment that might lead mankind to God.

That is not to say that explorers always share common insights, gain some sort of common eternal truth, or even appreciate each others' different spirits of enquiry. 'Interesting,' Thesiger once said to me, 'every single traveller you admire, I simply loathe.' A man who is as if from Edwardian times – and dressed as such even in the 1980s, in Central Africa, where I was then chatting to him – he was referring among others to Bruce Chatwin, whose literary excursions on the theme of the nomadic state he thought just pretentious ramblings – 'imbecilic', I think, was the actual word. In turn, I noted that I didn't much like James Bruce, the first modern scientific explorer of Africa, whose account *Travels to Discover the Source of the Nile* was a childhood solace to Thesiger when at boarding school.

However, Thesiger too felt that all humans, deep down, share the same exploring instinct. 'Everyone knew that there was nothing to be found on the top of Everest,' he said, 'but even in this materialistic age few people asked, "What point is there in climbing Everest? What good will it do anyone when they get there?" They recognized that even today there are experiences that do not need to be justified in terms of material profit.'

The history of exploration has not been a happy one – often, not even for the explorers themselves – and perhaps, as Pascal said, our troubles stem from our inability to sit still in a room. Whatever the root of the restlessness, the useful explorers are those able both to fulfil the needs of those who sponsor them back home, and also to loosen themselves from the shackles of their people's expectations. The pre-Socratic philosopher Xenophanes, born on the Greek-speaking coast of Asia Minor in the sixth century BC, saw that experience of other people's customs could create doubts at home about accepted lore: 'The Ethiopians say that their gods are snub-nosed and black, the Thracians that theirs have light eyes and red hair ... But if cattle and horses or lions had hands and did the works that men do, horses would draw the forms of the gods like horses, and cattle like cattle, and they would make their bodies such as they had themselves.' Whether setting forth in the hope of expanding Christianity, or our rational, scientific understanding of the planet, or in order to conquer lands and snatch their gold, these are the explorers who, in the spirit of Xenophanes, have accommodated the strange and exotic. They do not change the terrain they are exploring; they themselves are changed by it. To me, these are the ones who shine out in this collection.

This book aims to present the new worlds seen by conquistadors, missionary ladies, mountaineers and many more. By bringing this unlikely array of explorers together, side by side in similar terrain, whether traversing deserts or negotiating sweltering forests, we can see how they tick, what drives them on – even how well they match up to each other.

In the end, these people – I suppose that means people like me – are able to launch out because they are maintained by the payers of taxes, the buyers of books, the congregations of churches. For good or bad, they are the hands, eyes and ears of the rest of society: those without the time, specialized skills or, frankly, the desire to go themselves. The pity is when individuals set out, undertake the most extraordinary venture, but never leave a record. Such a one was Ney Elias (1844–1897), a British Civil Servant who in 1872, accompanied by only one Chinese attendant, left Peking and crossed western Mongolia 2,500 miles to the Russian frontier, then travelled 2,300 miles to the then railhead at Nijni Novgorod. He never wrote a book of reminiscences, and is remembered chiefly through his obituaries; but even if he had scribbled it all down, how would we have judged his new information if he had not also given his personal tale? As Voltaire said in 1764, 'If you have nothing to tell us but that on the banks of the Oxus and Jaxartes, one barbarian has been succeeded by another barbarian, in what respect do you benefit the public?'

PART I

Seas and Landfalls

*

In the beginning the world appeared to mankind like a fairytale; everything that lay beyond the circle of familiar experience was a shifting cladland of the fancy; a playground for all the fabled beings of mythology. Out of this fairy world, in course of time, the calm and sober lines of the northern landscape appeared.
Nansen, *In Northern Mists*, 1911

The early navigators were the fingers with which we, from the shores of the known, first reached out and grasped at the horizon and beyond. Western Europeans first stretched out across the world by way of cold, northern waters. They did so blindly, often helplessly – but in that way discovered a new continent: America. Eventually, they would dominate all the world's oceans; but for now they were, in world terms, backward. A thousand years before, there had been other great seafarers – and a thousand years before that.

The Phoenicians were perhaps the first to develop sea-borne commerce, and though 3000 years ago the Chinese conducted as large a coastal trade, the surviving records show the Phoenicians to be the greatest sailors of the Ancient World. As early as the fourteenth century BC, the Eastern Mediterranean was a hive of activity. Phoenician city states such as Tyre and Sidon spread their influence beyond the home shores of Canaan. They were manufacturers, producing metalware, glassware and textiles, but their real wealth was built on their ability to trade these things at sea; by the ninth century BC colonies had been founded along the north coast of Africa, notably the Tyrian settlement of Carthage. The Old Testament talks in Ezekiel of the linen for ships' sails coming from Egypt, deck planks from Amanus, cedar for masts from Lebanon, and oars from Bashan. They were the first to sail out through the Strait of Gibraltar; and according to Herodotus, when Pharaoh Necho sent a ship around Africa in c.620 BC, he naturally chose to crew her with Phoenicians.

Though the great seafaring nations changed through history, the actual business of negotiating the sea remained the same. It was only when winds, tides, currents, rocks, reefs or ice blocks had been navigated that any enterprise inland could begin.*

My own experience of near-destruction by sea is limited to one unhappy venture – I've been determined ever since to keep it that way, and so have stuck to dry land. With two New Guinean friends, I took a seafaring canoe across the Torres Strait, a mischievous stretch of water energized by all the currents that you'd expect of a narrow sea passage separating two huge land masses – Australia and New Guinea. It should have been a two-day trip, taking us through waters also negotiated under sail by Cook, Tasman and the other first Europeans who ventured here. The first day was fine; we caught a turtle, and also came across a party of Torres Strait islanders, who were feasting on a dugong, one of the last of the sea cows left in the Pacific. What we hadn't expected to encounter was the lines of reefs – four of them – which blocked our progress like underwater walls when the tide was low. Then

* Here is the Greek Hesiod, writing of the perils of sea travel in about 700 BC: 'If you are afflicted with the desire for uncomfortable travelling over the sea, then remember that the blasts of all the winds rage when the Pliades flee before the mighty strength of Orion and set in the misty deep . . . The right season for mortals to sail is fifty days after the solstice, when the burdensome days of summer come to an end. At that time you will not wreck your ship, nor will the sea destroy the men, unless the Earth-shaker Poseidon desires it or Zeus, king of the immortals, wishes to destroy them.'

came a gale from nowhere; we sheltered on a rock without any water, and ate raw shell-fish. I saw a sea snake being tossed in the waves.

After four days we did arrive safely – to be descended on by Australian customs officials who didn't believe we'd come from New Guinea, and thought we were drunk. Our eyes were red from the lashing waves, and we were incoherent – the effect, I suppose, of grimly staring at seething water for so long.

In my case, I'd always known that, should we make it, a friendly welcome – at least of sorts – would be given us on landfall. Which was not the case for Dampier, Van Diemen and many of those I've selected here. After my own little sea crossing, my heart goes out to all of the ancient mariners whose ships heaved through the centuries towards reefs and unsure lands, as helpless as our little canoe.

In the first years of the fifth century AD, Fa Hsien, a Buddhist disciple, set off from China to India in search of missing scriptures, and gives an early description of a typhoon that 'blew for thirteen days and nights' and resulted in damage to the hull. 'Then, dread-ing that the leak should gain upon them, they forthwith took their goods and merchandise and cast them overboard.' Fa Hsien contrib-uted his 'water-pitcher and his washing basin, and also other portions of his property'. In those days, as now, it was a sea thick with pirates 'who, coming on you suddenly, des-troy everything' – an indication of the quantity of trade moving back and forth, in an era when the Europeans were still clinging close to their own shores. For the Orientals, the South China Seas were well-travelled ter-ritory, yet even without the hindrance of tempest and pirate, ships drifted at times like leaves on a pond, first blown this way, then that. The sea was 'boundless in extent – it is impossible to know east or west, except by observing the sun, moon, or stars in their motions. If it is dark, rainy weather, the only

plan is to steer by the wind without a guide. During the darkness of night, one sees the great waves beating one against the other and shining like fire, whilst sea monsters of every description [surround the ship].'

The sea was a conveyor belt – of uncertain reliability – to Lands of Promise. Beyond, there were wonders, great hopes, and some-times fears; but the greatest fear of some voy-agers was that there might be nothing at all. Harald Hårdråde, a Norseman who set sail into the Atlantic half a millennium before Columbus, 'explored the expanse of the northern ocean with his ships, but darkness spread over the verge where the world falls away, and he put about barely in time to escape being swallowed in the vast abyss' – the pit where the world ends.

The Atlantic was, to some early writers – encouraged by Plato's fourth-century-BC story of Atlantis, a kingdom that had sunk beneath the sea during a cataclysmic earth-quake – a murky and impassable barrier. The Roman writer Horace in the first century BC warned of vengeance from higher powers awaiting those 'godless ships bound madly in contempt o'er channels not allowed'.

The history of sea travel, somewhat over-simplified, is this: first, the time of the Ancients, the endeavours of Phoenicians, Greeks and other classical civilizations on coast-hugging voyages – the only ocean voyages were left unrecorded, these being done in the Pacific by Polynesians in double-hulled sailing canoes, relying on the heavenly bodies and birds. Next came an era of Orien-tal mastery, when Chinese, Indian and Arab merchants conducted brisk trade throughout the East, while Europe ventured nowhere much at all. Then a Renaissance, when Euro-peans tried to circumvent their jealous Mus-lim trade rivals to gain a share of the lucrative Eastern markets: combining European and Arab design features in now fully seaworthy vessels, they headed east to India, or went the other way, going round the world westwards, thus accidentally bumping into the New World. This led to a time of dominance on the high seas by those Europeans with direct access to the Atlantic; competing with each other, these expanding European powers accurately defined the coasts of the world's land masses. And so to modern times: the sea charted but never mastered. Now the ocean blue had become a challenge in its own right, a sport.

Here, in the hope and despair of its players, is the story of the sea: the heady mix of dream and sharp reality, the vulnerability of mariners to the waves and also to their impatient sponsors waiting back home.* Here, too, are the cruel and hopeless cultural misunderstandings that came about when the pioneers at last reached distant shores – bloodstains across the so-called 'Golden Age' (the time between Henry the Navigator, a medieval prince with a passion for geography, and the eventual circling of the world by Magellan's ship). For sailing abroad was, when it came down to it, all about *acquiring* abroad. The Elizabethan seaman Frobisher makes the point: '. . . we marched through the country, with ensign displayed, as far as was thought needful, and now and then heaped up stones on high mountains and other places in token

of possession, as likewise to signify unto such as hereafter may chance to arrive there that possession is taken on the behalf of some other prince by those who first found out the country'.†

The might of all the rival nations was determined, of course, by winds and currents. To cross the Atlantic to their treasure, Spanish galleons and the cumbersome, squat merchant ships called *naos* dipped south to catch trade winds to the Caribbean, while westerlies carried them home. If wishing to trade or plunder in the Orient, mariners headed across the Atlantic towards Brazil to avoid the equatorial Doldrums, then south-east to the Cape of Africa, where they would catch the south-west trade winds up into the Indian Ocean, or risk the Roaring Forties of the southerly latitudes and continue directly east, before turning in a northerly direction towards the East Indies.

Of all the sea stories that I've quoted from here, one stands out: the story of the discovery of America by the Europeans. This was not a single event, but an innumerable series of separate discoveries, most of them long forgotten or confused in the mists of time – the trips of the Vikings, the 'legendary' voyage of the Irish monk Brendan.‡ Without

---

* Seneca, the Roman statesman and Stoic philosopher, looked forward to a future era: 'A time will come in later years,' he wrote, 'when the Ocean will unloose the bands of things, when the immeasurable earth will lie open, when seafarers will discover new countries, and Thule will no longer be the extreme point among the lands.' Sure enough, 'Thule' became not an extreme point, but a useful stepping stone for the Norse. By the third century, Gaius Julius Solinus was writing that 'Beyond Thule wee learne is a deade and frozen Sea . . .' He also, by the way, gives us this description of an unhappy-sounding Britain: 'There are no Snakes, and fewe byrdes: the people are harbourless, and warlike. When they overcome theyr enemies, they first besmeere their faces in the blood of them that be slayne, and then drinke of it.' It was 1200 years before the Oceans unloosed 'the bands of things', and European powers truly expanded over the oceans.

† Frobisher sums up the spirit not just of his time, but of all time: the ability to cross the sea was the ability to prosper. 'As concerning ships, it is that which everyone knoweth and can say, they are our weapons, they are our ornaments, they are our strength, they are our pleasures, they are our profit; the subject by them is made rich, the Kingdom through them, strong; the Prince in them is mighty; in a word, by them, in a manner, we live, the Kingdom is, the King reigneth.'
‡ Thomas Herbert chronicles the story of another who might at a stretch have discovered America: Prince Madoc ab Owain Gwnedd. In his 1638 volume, *Some yeares travels into divers parts of Asia and Afrique*, we read: 'The yeere he set forth in, was from Adam 5140, from Christ 1170, the wind and Sea seemed to favour him (Omens of Good fortune) so as, after some patience and weeks saile due West, hee descried land, a land where he found

question the Chinese had ocean-going supremacy in the first half of the fifteenth century and it's feasible that a Chinese expeditionary fleet of 1421–3 under Admiral Zheng arrived here seventy-two years before

—

store of good victualls, sweet water, fresh ayre, gold, (and which was best) where they were a good whiles healthfull: such, as over-whelmed him with joy, but moderated when he considered how Almighty God was alike powerful and gratious in all places; his exile now turned into comfort . . . Here Madoc planted (in Florida or Canada, some part of Mexico) rais'd some fortifications for defence, left a hundred and twenty men (I follow the old Copie, in this Storie) and directly by Gods providence (the best compasse) and benefit of the Pole starre after long saile arrived safely at home: where hee recounted his marvailous successfull voyage, the fruitfulnesse of the soile, the simplicity of the Savages, the great wealth abounding there, and facility of Conquest: a discourse that fill'd them with joy and admiration; and whereby hee drew many willing minds to returne with him. In ten good Barques, loaded with all necessary provisions they advanced back, and most fortunately re-attained the same place they hoped for. Great rejoy-cing was among them at that their happinesse, but no lesse sorrow followed: for, being come to the Plantation, they found few of those they left there, living: caused by too much eating, the indisposition or Novelty of that ayre and climate, (which though never so excellent, yet causes sicknesse and alter-ation in new Inhabitants) by some trecherie of the Barbarians. Madoc digested it with a Christian for-titude and patience, and forth-with bettered the Colony, by help of Eneon and Edwall his brothers contriving every thing with so good order, that they were secure from any Enemie, and had all things conducing to ease, plenty, and contentednesse: they threw away the too indulgent thoughts of their Native homes, by this reason, that if they died there, they were in the same distance from heaven, and had as easie a journey thither . . . So that Madoc and his Company returned no more, nor did the Welsh saile thither afterward, whereby one of another in small time were in some sort forgotten and never remembered.'

Not surprisingly, the Spanish were not pleased to learn that they had been beaten to the New World. 'The Ambassador observing the Indians to have many ceremonies the Spaniards used, demanded of the King who first instructed them, who answered Cortez; that many yeeres ago a strange Nation landed there, a civill people, and from examples of piety they received them; but how they were called, or whence they came he could not satisfie him.'

Christopher Columbus; the huge junks may even have circumnavigated the globe a cen-tury before Magellan. These varied landfalls in the Americas culminated in the journeys of Columbus, whose arrival in the New World put into place the single most important piece in the world jigsaw, the greatest advance in our understanding of the form of our planet.

Even after four voyages Columbus thought he had found part of the Indies; with time, he himself became as much a legend as the sea monsters his crew feared. This was a personal tragedy of a weaver's son who rose to greatness and died in bitterness. Here's Jerome Kern's contri-bution:

They all laughed at Christopher Columbus
When he said the world was round.
But – ho, ho, ho – who's had the last laugh
*   now?*

Actually, most of the highly educated of his day would not have laughed at the idea of the world being round, although almost fatally Columbus understood the earth to be smaller and therefore not so time-consuming to travel around. But Columbus indeed had the last laugh; and it was, of course, at the expense of the natives. To Columbus the peoples of 'the Indies' were innocent, primitive and defence-less, a useful combination that handed him three splendid opportunities: firstly, for spreading the gospel; secondly, for conferring on them the assumed blessings of civilization, and thirdly, for exploiting everything they offered. This is Columbus's observation, on his first contact with the Tainos of the Carib-bean: 'The inhabitants could be made slaves, for they have no arms and are all naked and without any knowledge of war. They are fitted to be ruled and to be set to work, to culti-vate the land, and to do all else that may be necessary, and you may build towns and teach them to go clothed and to adopt our customs.'

Unlike all other terrain to be explored, the seas were a shifting medium; the winds and currents by which you made progress acted unseen, determining your fate, driving you onto rocks or unknown shores. The sea became an instrument of Providence – fair winds might bless your endeavours, or tempests might pull you asunder. You might come home rich beyond your wildest dreams, or simply not come home at all.

Even following a known coast, such were the vagaries of sea travel that the act of landfall often became tantamount to an act of deliverance by the Almighty – sailing to India, Vasco da Gama was out of sight of land for a hair-raising ninety-five days, as he avoided West Africa's unfavourable winds. It is little wonder that those who took on the greatest ventures felt endorsed by God when new lands came their way.* However, being washed up on an unknown shore might or might not mean salvation, and the interiors of landmasses began to be populated by peoples and beasts of mariners' nightmares and dreams.† Sometimes their fears were grounded in truth. Marco Polo, returning by sea from China in 1292, landed on 'Sumadra'

(Sumatra) and on the palm beaches made 'land castles of beams and of logs ... for fear of those beast-like men who eat men.' Polo had come close to meeting the Bataks, whose alleged cannibalistic rituals chilled Ida Pfeiffer some 700 years later. Another new land, South America, was furnished with headless natives, and female warriors – the Amazons. Especially promising was the story of El Dorado, the Golden One, which started as an account of an Indian chief who, as a God-King, was ceremoniously sprayed with gold dust by his subjects, and came to mean, as jungle-crazed Spaniards let their imaginations feast on the image, a city of gold.

There was little incentive to hold back on the storytelling. If pioneers were to gain finance, they had to encourage appropriate tales of danger, wonder and riches. In the state library in Rio, I once examined a manuscript dated 1753, apparently the report of a Portuguese adventurer to his sponsor,§ which describes a ruined city of magnificence, with its broken masonry inscribed with strange symbols, to be found deep in the interior, perhaps the Mato Grosso. It later lent

---

* Here's Frobisher again: '. . . at our entrance thereinto we should all, with one voice, kneeling upon our knees, chiefly thanks God for our safe arrival . . . [and] that by our Christian study and endeavour those barbarous people, trained up in paganism and infidelity, might be reduced to the knowledge of true religion and to the hope of salvation in Christ our redeemer . . .'

† 'The Monoceros, or Unicorn, I cannot say I have seen,' reported Cosmas of Alexandria in approximately AD 548. 'But I have seen four brazen figures of him set up in the four-towered palace of the King of Ethiopia. They speak of him as a terrible beast and quite invincible, and say that all his strength lies in his horn. When he finds himself pursued by many hunters and on the point of being caught he springs up to the top of some precipice whence he throws himself down, and in the descent turns a somersault so that the horn sustains all the shock of the fall, and he escapes unhurt.' Only a little less miraculous was the 'Agribous, or Wild Ox', a 'large Indian' animal: 'If his tail, it is said,

---

Ox', a 'large Indian' animal: 'If his tail, it is said, catches in a tree, he does not seek to move off but stands stock still, having a strong aversion to lose even a single hair of his tail. So the people of the place come and cut off his tail, and then the beast, having lost it all, makes his escape.'

§ The commands of the sponsors through the centuries remained extraordinarily constant. Mariners may sometimes have been sent simply to chart coastlines, but the wider picture was almost always about seeking out, or bringing back, wealth. 'Try to win them over to somewhat of traffick and useful intercourse,' wrote William Dampier, dispensing guidelines for dealing with natives – 'as there might be commodities among any of them that might be fit for trade or manufacture.' He noted: 'The desire of making discoveries obliges a man to lay hold of every circumstance that is the least promising, and to neglect nothing that may gain him a tolerable acquaintance with the coasts he visits.'

encouragement to Colonel Percy Fawcett, who was lost in 1925 while on a mysterious quest to trace a similar ancient civilization. Sad to relate, the Mato Grosso has been largely clear-felled now, and though I, and many others with more dedication, have scoured the scorched grazing lands that replaced the forest, of the city there has been no sign.

Without financial incentive, there was no exploration: in the Pacific, for example, when trade declined in the seventeenth century exploration died with it. However, exploitation of the sponsor's hopes aside, we still see the potential of far lands exaggerated time and again. An unknown hope, the possibility of a Utopia. Even today, coral beaches and waving palm trees are our symbol for the perfect 'escape': once, I saw a travel poster of such a place pinned to a nomad's felt tent in Tuva, southern Siberia – just about as far from such a scene (and indeed from the sea) as is possible on the globe. The image had been exported to another culture, and been adopted by it with alacrity.

The tropical desert island has become a metaphor for paradise. The healthy, easy climate, the seductive lick of the ceaseless ocean, is a powerful draw to us now; but how much more to the sailor of times gone by – perhaps press-ganged, his gums perhaps swollen from scurvy. The iconization is as strong today; you are master of all you survey. This is a new start, where you are liberated from the conventions, the oppressions of your society, and free to define your destiny. Yes, true, but . . .

I happen to have been cast away myself on an Indonesian island off Sumatra. It was a brief stay – only three days – but it was enough. The sand and palms gave the crew members and me sanctuary from the thumping waves, and the lee of the island stopped our trade boat, overloaded with rattan and copra, from actually sinking; but it was mis-

ery. We were soon sick of eating our way through our copra cargo and drinking coconut milk and the rainwater we gathered off leaves; we desperately set about trying to slap planks on the cracked hull of our trade boat, so that we could make our escape. We knew we might be there until we dropped dead; personally it wasn't long before I was feeling very sorry for myself indeed and promising God that, if he could only get me off the island, I'd be so much better a person in future.

The desert-island notion of paradise was encouraged by the tale of the castaway Alexander Selkirk, the model for Defoe's Robinson Crusoe. Having behaved 'indecently' in church, Selkirk had run away to sea, and eventually joined one of Dampier's ventures. He didn't enjoy his stay on an uninhabited island either – it lasted a lot longer – but came away a purer man. The island had redemptive properties.

The Selkirk case, which I relate later as part of William Dampier's story, lived on partly because Selkirk's fears, like those of Crusoe, were fears that any mariner might hold. These were fears of the unknown: cannibals and beasts. They were also fears of the known: their Spanish rivals. It was also, from a Spanish point of view, a fear of what might *become* known: the trade routes. At one point, the Spanish tried to hunt poor Selkirk down – and not just for sport, but because of the threat he posed to their lucrative business. 'He apprehended they would murder him,' wrote Rogers, an eyewitness to the rescue of Selkirk, 'or make a slave of him in the mines, for he feared they would spare no stranger that he might be capable of discovering the South Sea.'

However, the greatest 'desert island' was, of course, the New World. This was a place of possible treasure – hopefully gold – but also a new, clean living space, in which to start again. It was an Eden, a time before the Fall. Giovanni Da Verrazano (1485–1528), who in

1524 travelled across the Atlantic and was greeted near present-day Rhode Island by dozens of natives (Narragansetts) who paddled out to his ship, set the tone. 'They are the most handsome people of bronze colour, some inclining to white, others to tawny colour; the profile sharp, the hair long and black and they give great attention to its care; the eyes are black and alert and their bearing is sweet and gentle, much in the manner of older times . . .'

The dream of sweet replenishment from nature was, of course, an illusion: any 'purity' was unobtainable, if only because Europeans tarnished it immediately by bringing their old ways with them. The pattern of slavery and theft of land was the same throughout the Americas – no less a founding father than George Washington had slaves. Almost ten million were to make the journey over the Atlantic to North America, the Caribbean and Brazil. But here there was space, and so time and again you could move on, and the pioneering hymn of personal liberty could be resung, the ideal kept afloat. You just had to keep moving further into the hinterlands until the Pacific Ocean was reached. Meanwhile, up and down North and South America, countless Europeans did indeed achieve the new beginning they had been seeking.

The heroic struggles of those family men and lonely sentries with one toehold clinging onto far shores is badly served in exploration literature, which favours the more dramatic, bold crossings of seas and lands. Yet their tale is repeated around the globe: Dutch families pushing north from the South African Cape, the Welsh in Patagonia, Walter Raleigh's ill-fated colony Virginia. And 200 years ago, the Parliament of Scotland established a colony at Darien, on the Isthmus of Panama – it would be a bridge between east and west, a 'door of the seas, and the key of the universe'. There were high hopes, and a harbour 'capable of containing a thousand sail'. Over two

thousand men, women and children died on the dank, forested shore. I've tried to rectify the historical imbalance here by placing two examples of settlements among the explorers – one, in Port Essington, northern Australia, where colonists might wait a year to receive a reply to any letter home; the second, in a British colony in Sumatra – a place of unnamed fevers if ever there was one – which hung on for 140 years. I once spent a week investigating the remains of the original settlement, Fort York. Though I did find porcelain and disturbed ground, the locals now working the land knew nothing of these colonists ever having existed on that patch of forlorn grass, let alone that the British had been their governors. As I left, an abattoir was about to be built over the site, a hill for which so may lonely men had died pointlessly.

New lands were also a chance for thinkers to fathom the wider world. One element of this was a back-to-basics philosophy. Jean-Jacques Rousseau (1712–78) thought that man in his natural state was good and pure – 'Man was born free, and everywhere he is in chains', and, returning to 'nature', found the Noble Savage. In Tahiti, George Forster, on one of James Cook's voyages, found a society that 'is not loaded with that multitude of miseries which are attendant upon the married state in civilised countries'. Cook himself was a realist and saw change, once contact had been made, as inevitable. However, urban people then, as now, continued to crave an imaginary natural idyll. Gaugin went to Tahiti and found a new world – or, more accurately, following the well-established tradition, invented the one he had been hoping to find. He took off the clothes of the ladies there to achieve a situation of innocence and purity.

A new land, then, meant an escape from consequence, a chance to rule over those of lesser power or, as it might seem, of lesser consequence.

The inhabitants of one land-mass, in particular, met with almost universal disapproval, even with the Enlightenment. The Dutch found the natives of Australia 'poor and abject wretches', and Dampier labelled them 'wild, cruel savages'. Even the Africans hadn't generally been entirely naked; they had at least constructed villages. To the Europeans, the Aborigines lived an animal existence, stalking kangaroos and digging for maggots – the witchetty grubs.*

I've twice lived alone with Aborigines in the Gibson Desert, and there's much that could be said about these matters – all, of course, with the glorious benefit of hindsight, and from the perspective of a twenty-first-century liberal living in West London. I'll restrain my thoughts in favour of John Moresby (1830–1922) who gives us his first impressions of lowland New Guinea, which I know well, having undergone the 'crocodile' initiation ceremony there.

'They took pains to make us understand . . . that they had eaten the former owners of the skulls (hung up in their villages),' writes Moresby. It doesn't strike the author, as indeed it didn't strike someone as methodical as Darwin, hearing cannibal tales among the Fuegians,† that the skulls were of revered

ancestors – that the cannibalistic tales told by New Guineans might serve as a sort of in-joke (such as the one played on me decades later) or that they might usefully provoke fear so as to fend off strangers, or be something of social value, a device to separate the outsider from the cognoscenti of the tribe.

'We do not trace any sign of religious worship,' Moresby goes on; but signs would have abounded for someone prepared to see. There would have been sacred relics, emblems of gods and a spectrum of spirits represented inside special spirit houses, the power base of native communities.

The criticisms could go on but, to be fair, I should give an example of one of my many cultural blunders in New Guinea. I remember being indignant when my camera was stolen. I marched to the village spirit house, and protested to the Niowra elders, who then kindly went into action to hunt down the culprit. It took some time to find out who had pilfered (to use a Moresby word) the camera, and it was only when the whole village was assembled that I discovered that the seven different clans each had bits of the camera.

---

* Even the great scientist, Joseph Banks, who sailed with Cook in 1768–71, was unable to see anything of virtue in the Aborigines, who were 'one degree removed from the brutes.' It was left to Cook to put in a word on their behalf. They might appear 'to be the most wretched people on earth,' he said, 'but in reality they are far happier than we Europeans.' He went on, with a gentle poke at the English class system: 'They live in a tranquillity which is not disturbed by the inequality of condition.' He seems to be clear in his own mind about whether the impact of Europeans had been beneficial or not – and he asked anyone who was in any doubt to tell him 'what the natives of the whole extent of America have gained by the commerce they have had with the Europeans.'

† Darwin's observations include the following rather worryingly un-scientific anecdote: '. . . it is certainly true, that when pressed in winter by

hunger, they kill and devour their old women before they kill their dogs; the boy, being asked by Mr Low why they did this, answered, "Doggies catch otters, old women no." This boy described the manner in which they are killed by being held over smoke and thus choked; he imitated their screams as a joke, and described the parts of their bodies which are considered best to eat. Horrid as such a death by the hands of their friends and relatives must be, the fears of the old women, when hunger begins to press, are more painful to think of; we were told that they then often run away into the mountains, but that they are pursued by the men and brought back to the slaughter-house at their own fire-sides!' Though I suspect that young Darwin has fallen for nothing more than a cannibal yarn, like a thousand travellers before and after, the general idea he comes away with more or less works. 'Nature by making habit omnipotent, and its effects hereditary, has fitted the Fuegian to the climate and the productions of his miserable country.'

'Oops!' I thought. This hadn't been theft, but a sharing out of my resources; I had been through the initiation ceremony into manhood, and was expected to behave as selflessly as they would. If the Niowra had hunted a pig, they would have done the same – shared it out. So my camera batteries had been given to one clan, a lens to another, flash-gun to another, and so on. The camera was useless, but the right thing, in Niowra eyes, had been done. I was no longer selfish; I was included. I was now civilized.

As so often, problems between explorers and natives come down to unfortunate mis-understandings. If it isn't nudity and theft that travellers are complaining about throughout this book, it's dishonesty. Yet truth doesn't always come in the rational, right-or-wrong, black-and-white form that we in the West generally expect. In the Sepik region, for example, there is a value placed on entertainment, similar to the Aus-tralian outback tradition of yarning. Points are also awarded for good oratory in the spirit house – it's no coincidence that Papua New Guinea's first prime minister was from the Sepik. And we shouldn't condemn the New Guineans out of hand for that; our newspapers speak in the same florid lan-guage. In my personal experience, only about 60 per cent of newsprint is factually correct, across the board – the tabloids no less than this, they are just more colourful in expression. Yet we largely accept what we read as 'true'.

To hear the native view of life, we have to rely on those travellers who took time to put their words on paper. I've included Bronislaw Malinowski, who raised eyebrows with his *Sexual Life of Savages*, a title that was deliber-ately provocative, but pioneered an important aspect of research. 'What is it', he asked, 'that makes the boys look with entranced attention at one among a group of girls, moving rhythmically in a game or carrying baskets at harvest?' Slowly, explorers were getting round to making serious attempts at not actually prejudging.

Eventually, the role of the ship's captain increasingly came to be to deliver specialists to their destinations. Darwin's observations while on his extended voyage around the world on the *Beagle* became the bedrock of his theories of natural selection, as they were for Wallace in the Malay archipelago.* The point of view of the longsuffering bearers of these non-sailors is given by John King Davis, who carried Mawson in 1929–30 on his Antarctic voyage – and couldn't wait, we now learn, to be shot of him. Mawson felt that Davis wasn't braving the ice floes as he should; Davis resented the inference that he wasn't trying hard enough. The problem lay in their differing roles: the captain's duty was, and always will be, to maintain the safety of his ship, crew and passengers. The explorer had a duty to fulfil not at sea, but on land; he and his carefully chosen team were charged with taking risks.

With Joshua Slocum's departure, in 1895, on a voyage around the world, financed by a lecture tour en route, we enter the modern era. 'The sea is there in order to be sailed over,' he wrote. The focus of exploration was now not the lands that seas might bring you to, but the seas themselves. Crossing water had become a challenge for its own sake – like the ice that led to the Poles, it has become a

---

* At this point specialists in the arts as well as scientists come to the fore. Here's Hilaire Belloc, from *The Cruise of the Nona*: 'The sea is the consola-tion of this our day, as it has been the consolation of the centuries. It is the companion and the receiver of men. It has moods for them to fill the storehouse of the mind, perils for trial, or even for an ending, and calms for the good emblem of death. There, on the sea, is a man nearest to his own making, and in communion with that from which we came, and to which we shall return. For the wise men of very long ago have said, and it is true, that out of the salt water all things came. The sea is the matrix of creation, and we have the memory of it in our blood.'

surface on which to race. This is adventure, the degree of difficulty determined by the competitor.

Joseph Conrad warned that 'adventure by itself is but a phantom, a dubious shape without a heart', but the elusiveness of the prize seems to be part of the sea's attractiveness to the likes of modern adventurers such as H. W. Tilman. He came from a mountaineering background – just as Francis Chichester had come to the sea from aviation – and commented once on the similarity of the experiences: 'Each is intimately concerned with elemental things, which from time to time demand from men who practise those arts whatever self-reliance, prudence and endurance they may have.'

As a boy I remember the agonies of my mother, whose friend's son had elected to join Tilman on what was to be his last voyage. He knew it was an honour; he knew it was a risk. Afterwards, the long silence – his death was not presumed until April 1979 – and attempts, even with a clairvoyant, to find out where in the South Atlantic they had gone down. This anguish haunted my mother when I disappeared in the Amazon after setting out aged twenty-two on my own expedition, only four years later. I reappeared, having had to eat my dog; he didn't. But such is the way of things, and I can't help but envy anyone who might have joined Tilman, even in his eighties, as he set out towards the Antarctic Ocean. This was a man of such tenacity that age never defeated him; when climbing became too much, he simply switched to oceans, and had his tussle with nature at sea. The leader of the venture, Simon Richardson, wrote home from Rio: 'If we get no further, it will all have been worthwhile.'

I start, and in one sense finish, with Saint Brendan. He emerges out of the mythical mists of time, as a contender for the title of First European Discoverer of America; 1,500 years later Tim Severin relived his journey using an identical reconstructed vessel. Severin more recently communicated his experience of a voyage live by e-mail and video to schools. Exploration of distant shores had become as democratic as it could ever be – no longer the privilege of those who set out on behalf of others, but something even children could be involved in, while the hardy explorer battled away in the back of beyond.

BRENDAN
c.489–c.570
Look, my sons, at the great deeds of our Saviour!

According to legend, Saint Brendan travelled to the Promised Land, perhaps America, hundreds of years before the Vikings. He was born in Ireland, probably near Tralee in County Kerry, and his name is associated with the founding of several monasteries in Clare, Galway and Kerry, and on islands along the Shannon. Though he had a religious calling, he also seems to have felt a passionate desire, or need, to travel; he's surely the only explorer with his own feast day, which is 16 May.

He also lived at a time when Irish monks were leaving their land to spread the Gospel. His first journey took him to the Hebrides, Shetland and the Faroe Islands, as well as Brittany. In 561 he founded a monastery at Clonfent in County Galway – apparently where the famous tale of his extraordinary sea travels begins.

The tenth-century manuscript *Navigatio Sancti Brendani* ('The Voyage of Saint Brendan') tells us that Saint Brendan's monks 'got iron tools and constructed a light boat ribbed with wood and with a wooden frame, as is usual in those parts . . . Into the boat they carried hides for making two other boats, supplies for forty days, fat for preparing hides to cover the boat, and other things needed for human life. They also placed a mast in the middle of the boat and requirements for steering a boat. Then Saint Brendan ordered his brothers in the name of the Father, Son, and Holy Spirit to enter the boat.'

In the words of Tim Severin – who re-enacted Saint Brendan's voyage by leather boat in 1976 and 1977 – the Brendan story was 'not just a wild fairy tale, but a recurrent theme based on authentic and well-researched Latin texts dating back at least to AD 800'. He and a party of monks had sailed to a land far across the ocean in a boat made of oxhides. If this is true, he probably reached America – almost a thousand years before Columbus and 400 years before the Vikings.

The paradise of birds

When they were sailing near the island where they had spent the three days, and came to the western edge of it, they saw another island almost joining it, separated only by a small channel. There was plenty of grass on it; it had groves of trees and was full of flowers. They started circling it, looking for a landing-place. As they were sailing on its southern side they found a stream flowing into the sea and there they put the boat in to land. As they disembarked, Saint Brendan ordered them to draw the boat with ropes up along the river-bed with all their might. The width of the river was about the width of the boat. The father sat in the boat. So they carried on for about a mile, until they came to the source of the stream. Saint Brendan spoke:

'Our Lord Jesus Christ has given us a place in which to stay during his holy Resurrection.'

And he added:

'If we had no other supplies but this spring, it would, I believe, alone be enough for food and drink.'

Over the spring there was a tree of extraordinary girth and no less height covered with white birds. They covered it so much that one could scarcely see its leaves or branches. When the man of God saw this, he began to think and ponder within himself what it meant or what was the reason that such a great multitude of birds could be all collected together. He was so tormented about this that the tears poured out and flowed down upon his cheeks, and he implored God, saying:

'God, who knows the unknown and reveals all that is secret, you know the distress of my heart. I implore your majesty to have pity and reveal to me, a sinner, through your great mercy your secret that I now look upon with my eyes. I rely not on what I deserve or my worth, but rather on your boundless pity.'

When he said this within himself and had taken his seat again, one of the birds flew from the tree, making a noise with her wings like a hand-bell, and took up position on the side of the boat where the man of God was sitting. She sat on the edge of the prow and stretched her wings, as it were as a sign of joy, and looked with a peaceful mien at the holy father. The man of God immediately concluded that God had listened to his plea, and spoke to the bird:

'If you are God's messenger, tell me where these birds come from or for what reason they are congregated here.'

She replied immediately:

'We survive from the great destruction of the ancient enemy, but we were not associated with them through any sin of ours. When we were created, Lucifer's fall and that of his followers brought about our destruction also. But our God is just and true. In his great judgment he sent us here. We endure no sufferings. Here we can see God's presence. But God has separated us from sharing the lot of the others who were faithful. We wander through various regions of the air and the firmament and the earth, just like the other spirits that travel on their missions. But on holy days and Sundays we are given bodies such as you now see so that we may stay here and praise our creator. You and your brothers have now spent one year on your journey. Six still remain. Where you celebrated Easter today, there you will celebrate it every year. Afterwards you will find what you cherish in your heart, that is, the Promised Land of the Saints.'

When she said this, she lifted herself off the prow and flew to the other birds.

When the hour of vespers had come all the birds in the tree chanted, as it were with one voice, beating their wings on their sides:

'A hymn is due to thee, O God, in Zion, and a vow shall be paid to you in Jerusalem.'

They kept repeating this versicle for about the space of an hour. To the man of God and his companions the chant and the sound of their wings seemed in its sweetness like a rhythmical song.

Then Saint Brendan said to his brothers:

'Repair your bodies, for today our souls are filled with divine food.'

When supper was over they performed the divine service. When all was finished, the man of God and his companions gave repose to their bodies until midnight. Waking, the man of God aroused his brothers for the vigil of the holy night, beginning with the versicle:

'Lord, open my lips.'

When the holy man had finished, all the birds responded with wing and mouth, saying:

'Praise the Lord, all his angels; praise him, all his powers.'

So it was as for vespers – they chanted all the time for the space of an hour.

When dawn rose they chanted:

'May the radiance of the Lord, our God, be upon us!' – with the same tune and for the same length of time as at matins and lauds. Likewise at terce they chanted the versicle:

'Sing praises to our God, sing praises! Sing praises to our king. Sing praises in wisdom.'

At sext they chanted:

'Shine your countenance, Lord, upon us, and have mercy on us.'

At nones they chanted:

'How good and pleasant it is that brothers live together as one!'

In this way, day and night, the birds gave praise to the Lord. And so Saint Brendan refreshed his brothers with the feast of Easter until the octave day.

The devouring beast

The venerable father and his companions sailed out into the ocean and their boat was carried along for forty days. One day there appeared to them a beast of immense size following them at a distance. He spouted foam from his nostrils and ploughed through the waves at a great speed, as if he were about to devour them. When the brothers saw this they called upon the Lord, saying:

'Deliver us, Lord, so that that beast does not devour us.'

Saint Brendan comforted them, saying:

'Do not be afraid. You have little faith. God, who always defends us, will deliver us from the mouth of this beast and from other dangers.'

As the beast came near them he caused waves of extraordinary height to go before him right up to the boat, so that the brothers were more and more afraid. The venerable elder also raised his hands to heaven and said:

'Lord, deliver your servants, as you delivered David from the hand of Goliath, the giant. Lord, deliver us, as you delivered Jonas from the belly of the whale.'

After these three pleas asking for deliverance, a mighty monster passed near them from the west going to encounter the beast. He immediately attacked him, emitting fire from his mouth. The elder spoke to his brothers:

'Look, my sons, at the great deeds of our Saviour! See how the beasts obey their creator. Wait presently for the outcome of this affair. This battle will do us no damage. It will redound to the glory of God.'

When he had said this the wretched beast that pursued the servants of Christ was cut into three pieces before their eyes. The other returned after his victory to where he had come from.

The crystal pillar

One day when they had celebrated their Masses, a pillar in the sea appeared to them that seemed to be not far distant. Still it took them three days to come up to it. When the man of God approached it he tried to see the top of it – but he could not, it was so high. It was higher than the sky. Moreover a wide-meshed net was wrapped around it. The mesh was so wide that the boat could pass through its openings. They could not decide of what substance the net was made. It had the colour of silver, but they thought that it seemed harder than marble. The pillar was of bright crystal.

Brendan spoke to his brothers:

'Ship the oars and take down the mast and sail. Let some of you at the same time take hold of the meshes of the net.'

There was a large space, roughly about a mile, at all points between the net and the pillar, and likewise the net went down a similar distance into the sea. When they had done what they had been ordered, the man of God said to them:

'Let the boat in through one of the meshes, so that we can have a close look at the wonders of our creator.'

When they had gone in and looked around here and there, the sea was as clear to them as glass, so that they could see everything that was underneath. They could examine the foundations of the pillar and also the edge of the net lying on the sea bed. The light of the sun was as bright below as above the water.

Then Saint Brendan measured the four sides of the opening of the net: it was about six to seven feet on every side.

They then sailed throughout the whole day near one side of the pillar and in its shadow they could still feel the heat of the sun. They stayed there until three o'clock. The man of God kept measuring the one side. The measurement of each of the four sides of that pillar was the same, namely about seven hundred yards. The venerable father was engaged for four days in this way around the four angles of the pillar.

On the fourth day, however, they found a chalice, of the same substance as the net, and a paten, of the same colour as the pillar, lying in a window in the side of the pillar facing the south. Saint Brendan took hold of these vessels immediately, saying:

'Our Lord Jesus Christ has shown us this wonder, and given me these two gifts, so that the wonder be manifested to many in order that they may believe.'

Then the man of God ordered his brothers to perform the divine office and then refresh their bodies, for they had had no slack time in which to take food or drink since they had seen the pillar.

When the night was over the brothers began to row towards the north. When they had passed through an opening in the net they raised the mast and sail, while some of the brothers still held the meshes of the net until all was made ready on the boat. When the sail had been spread, a favouring wind began to blow behind them so that they did not need to row but only to hold the ropes and rudder. So their boat was borne along for eight days towards the north.

The Voyage of Saint Brendan (*Navigatio Sancti Brendani Abbatis*), trans. J. O'Meara, 1976 c.970–c.1020

They fitted out their ship and when they were ready sailed out to sea . . .

Ericsson was the son of the Eirik Thorvaldsson – Erik the Red – who had emigrated from Norway to Iceland, and after a dispute was banished, and so travelled again, in so doing discovering Greenland. Evidence for this, and what happened next, comes in the form of the Icelandic sagas – ancient chronicles passed down orally at first, but appearing in manuscripts in the thirteenth and fourteenth centuries. In one, the *Saga of Erik the Red*, Ericsson set sail from his home in Greenland, probably around 999, served King Olaf Trygvasson in Norway for a term, and was sent back to Greenland to bring Christianity to its people. On the return voyage, though, he got lost and encountered a land of salmon, vines and wheat. However, according to the *Saga of the Greenlanders* – in this matter much more reliable – the journey came about because Ericsson heard reports by Herjulfsson, another lost Viking, of a strange coast. Such journeys were not so much a quest for territory as part of a longstanding tradition of bold travel by a seafaring nation.

Leif went to investigate, and discovered a glacial 'Flatstone Land', perhaps Baffin Island; a 'Land of Forests', perhaps Labrador; and Vinland – 'Meadowland' – probably northern America. Exactly where in America has been the subject of much heated debate, but the presence of grape vines indicates somewhere comparatively far south. Ericsson spent a year in Vinland before returning to Greenland in 1001; other Vikings followed – his brother was killed by Indian arrows – but interest waned with time. Ericsson – 'big and strong, of striking appearance, shrewd, and in every respect a fair-dealing man' – seems to have become a Christian, but his father 'was slow to give up his paganism', as was most of the rest of Greenland. Leif Ericsson's skeleton is believed to be among those found beside the remains of a little church, measuring only 3½ by 2 metres, and constructed of turf.

Discovering America

Now next after this [the death of King Olaf Tryggvason, AD 1000] Bjarni Herjólfsson came over from Greenland on a visit to (Earl) Eric [a man now part ruler of Norway], who gave him a good welcome. Bjarni gave an account of the travels on which he had seen the strange countries, but he was blamed for his lack of enterprise, since he had nothing to report about these lands. Bjarni became one of the earl's officers but went out to Greenland the following summer.

There was now much talk about voyages and discovery. Leif, the son of Eric the Red, from Brattahlíð [in Greenland] went to visit Bjarni Herjólfsson, bought a ship from him and collected a crew of altogether thirty-five men. Leif asked his father still to be leader of the expedition, but Eric was reluctant, saying that he was now an old man and less able to endure all the hardships than he had been. Leif said that of all the family he was still the one who would bring the best luck, whereupon Eric gave way to him and as soon as they were ready rode from home. When he was but a short distance from the ship the horse which he was riding stumbled so that he fell off and hurt his foot: at this Eric said, 'I am not destined to discover more countries than this in which we are now living: we shall no longer keep one another company,' and he went home to Brattahlíð. But Leif went on to his ship with his companions, amongst whom was a southerner called Tyrker. They fitted out their ship and when they were ready sailed out to sea and discovered first that country which Bjarni and his men had found last. They sailed up to the land, cast anchor and, launching a boat, went ashore. They saw no grass; the interior was all great glaciers, and from these to the shore the land looked like one flat rock. The country seemed to them of no value and Lief said, 'Unlike Bjarni we have not failed to come ashore in this country and I shall now give it a name and call it Helluland ("the land of flat stone").' After this they returned on board, then on putting to sea discovered the second land. Again they sailed up to the land, cast anchor, launched a boat and went ashore. This country was level and wooded, and wherever they went were broad stretches of white sand, sloping gradually down to the sea. Leif said, 'This land shall be given a name after its nature and shall be called Markland (woodland). They then returned to the ship as quickly as possible, sailing thence to the open sea with a northeast wind, and they were out two days before they saw land, towards which they sailed. Coming to an island which lay to the north of the mainland they landed on it, and looking round – the weather being fine – saw that there was dew on the grass. It so happened that on putting their hands in the dew they carried it to their mouths and thought they had never before tasted anything so sweet. After this they went back to their ship, and sailing into the sound which lay between the island and the cape jutting out to the north from the mainland they steered west past the cape. At ebb-tide it was very shallow there and their ship running aground they soon found themselves a long way from the sea: yet they were so eager to go ashore that they could not wait for the tide to rise under their ship but hurried on land where a river flowed out of a lake. As soon as the tide rose under their ship they took the boat, rowed to the ship, moved her up the river, then into the lake, where casting anchor they carried ashore their leather sleeping bags and put up temporary shelters, but later, making up their minds to stay there for the winter, they built large houses.

There was no lack of salmon and bigger salmon than they had seen before either in the river or the lake. In their eyes the general conditions of the country seemed so favourable that the cattle would need no fodder there in the winter time. There were no winter frosts: the grass only withered a little, and day and night were more evenly divided there than in Greenland or Iceland; on the shortest day the sun was up over the marks for Nones and breakfast-time. When they had finished building their houses Leif said to his men, 'Now I propose to divide our party into two and have the land explored: one half shall stay at home by the huts, while the other explores the country. The explorers must not go farther than they can return by the evening nor separate from one another.' They did this now for a time, Leif by turns going with the explorers and staying at home by the huts. Leif was a big, strong man and most imposing in appearance: he was clever and a fine leader in every way.

It was discovered one evening that a man of their party was missing – Tyrker the southerner. Leif took this much to heart, for Tyrker had lived with Leif and his father for a long time and had been very fond of Leif as a child. Leif bitterly upbraided his companions and made ready to go in search of him accompanied by twelve others, but they had only gone a short distance from the huts when Tyrker came to meet them, and they received him joyfully. Leif soon noticed that his foster-father was in good spirits. Tyrker had a prominent forehead, roving eyes and insignificant features; he was short and unprepossessing in appearance but a skilful handicraftsman. Leif asked him, 'Why are you so late, foster-father, and what made you separate from your companions?' Tyrker answered speaking for a long time in German, rolling his eyes and making faces, and they could not understand what he was saying, but after a time he said in Norse, 'I did not go much farther than you, but I have some news to tell. I have found vines and grapes.' 'Is that true, foster-father?' asked Leif. 'Undoubtedly it is true,' said he. 'I was born where there is no lack of vines or grapes.' They went to sleep for that night and in the morning Leif addressed his crew: 'We will now do two things, and each day either gather grapes or cut down vines and fell trees for a cargo for my ship.' This plan was agreed to and it is said that their ship's boat was filled with grapes. A cargo was cut for the ship and when spring came they made ready and sailed away, and Leif gave the country a name from its products, calling it Wineland. After this they put to sea and had a fair breeze until they sighted Greenland and the mountains under its glaciers.

Narratives of the Discovery of America (ed. A. W. Lawrence and J. Young, 1931)

CHRISTOPHER COLUMBUS

c.1451–1506

In order that they would be friendly to us – because I recognised that they were people who would be better freed [from error] and converted to our Holy Faith by love than by force – to some of them I gave red caps, and glass beads which they put on their chests, and many other things of small value . . .

Columbus was not the first European to reach America, but his rediscovery of the continent reawakened European interest at a time when Europe was poised to exploit the potential of new lands.

Born in Genoa, the oldest son of a weaver, he received little formal education and started sailing at the age of fourteen. In 1477 he moved to Lisbon from where he sailed widely in the Mediterranean and Atlantic. He heard stories of how ships to the west of Cape St Vincent had more than once picked up driftwood coming from further west. There were also encouraging legends: the tale of the Lost Island of the Seven Cities, which seemed to be west of the Canaries. He might also have heard the Icelandic stories of encountering land. All this suggested that, if a captain was courageous enough to sail west, not east, he might eventually come to Asia, and thus open up trade with India and the Orient. Passage by Europeans to the east by sea was held up by the Muslim domination in that area, and by that other great obstacle, Africa.

Columbus for years searched in vain for any sponsor for his Atlantic journey, his business proposal finally ending up with the Spanish monarchy. In 1492 Queen Isabella and King Ferdinand agreed to Columbus's demands (one tenth of any precious metals found, the position of viceroy over any lands he discovered, and hereditary titles) and a consortium was established to finance the voyage.

Two months after his departure from Spain on the first of his four Atlantic journeys, Columbus sighted land, an island that he named San Salvador – Watling Island, in the Bahamas. Before uncomprehending natives, he declared Spain its rightful owner. Convinced he had reached Japan, Columbus founded a settlement on the island of Hispaniola (now the Dominican Republic and Haiti) – the first European settlement in the New World for 500 years, it was to have fatal and lasting repercussions.

It was on Columbus's third voyage that he caught sight of the mainland for the first time, landing in what is now Venezuela.* However, he was a poor governor, the colonists he'd brought were restless for the easy gold they'd been expecting, and he was arrested by the official sent to re-establish control. He was sent back to Spain in chains and, his pride hurt, refused to let anyone but the Queen undo them.† Isabella, however, was disenchanted from the outset: Columbus's returning 'treasure' consisted chiefly of slaves.

* 'If this is a continent,' Columbus wrote in his journal, 'it is a matter of great wonderment and that it is such will be considered among all learned men since from it issues a river so immense that it fills a fresh sea 48 leagues long.'
  He wrote to Ferdinand and Isabella describing the luxuriant tropical forests, and the treasures to be found there – the aromatic gum, ginger, cinnamon, pepper (not to mention, of course, copper, pearls and gold). What he had seen, he felt, was the Garden of Eden, 'because all men say that it is at the end of the Orient, and that is where we are.'
† He railed against this reduced state, writing to a friend: 'I . . . have placed under their sovereignty more land than there is in Africa and Europe, more than one thousand seven hundred islands . . . In

More problematic was the fact that the Portuguese mariner Vasco da Gama had now made a journey around Africa to Asia. In 1502 Columbus, still convinced he had reached the outlying islands of Asia, set out on his fourth crossing. Given only four worm-eaten caravels, he intended to search for a passage to China. In the Caribbean, though, Columbus found his progress curtailed by his enemies, now ensconced in power; on arrival he was refused access to the harbour at Santo Domingo, even despite an approaching hurricane. On New Year's Day 1503, Columbus anchored off Panama, unable to find any passage through and, desperate to find favour with the monarchy, he concentrated on searching for gold. He established a settlement there, but after conflict arose with the natives, not to mention mutiny by the crew,

—

seven years I, by the divine will, made that conquest.' Isabella and Ferdinand read the letter, and, with popular opinion back home swelling again in his favour, released him. However, the truth was that other explorers, such as Cabral and Vespucci, had now indicated the size and potential of the South American continent. With the Portuguese and now English probing the New World, King Ferdinand could not afford any risks.

he was forced to abandon it. Columbus set sail for home in his surviving rotting ships, only to be marooned in Jamaica for a year after they foundered. He arrived in Spain in September 1504 a broken man; he was ill and his reputation shattered. Queen Isabella was dying, and he made vain attempts to get the king to restore his privileges; he died not long after, on 20 May 1506.

Though Columbus never understood the importance of his discovery – that it was a New World, not Asia – he also made important cosmographical observations, noting magnetic variations, the difference between magnetic and 'true' north indicated by the Pole Star. However, he was socially awkward; many would have thought him a crank. He claimed to hear celestial voices, felt chosen to carry God's plan to evangelize the world, in later years took on the garb of a Franciscan monk, and even dressed as such before the monarchy. His remains were interred in Seville, then shipped to Santo Domingo, then Havana, and in 1899 finally – though this is disputed – back to Seville.

The following extract is from Columbus's diaries, abstracted in the 1530s by the Spanish priest, Bartolomé de las Casas, from a poor copy of the original.

The discovery of America – again

Wednesday 19 September: He sailed on his route and between day and night made about 25 leagues because they had light winds. He wrote down 22 [to fool his despairing crew]. On this day at the tenth hour a booby came to the ship and in the afternoon they saw another; they do not usually depart more than 20 leagues from land. Some drizzles of rain came without wind, which is a sure sign of land. The Admiral did not want to delay by beating into the wind to find out if there was land, but he considered it certain that on the north side and the south there were some islands (as in truth there were and he was going in between them), because his purpose was to continue forward as far as the Indies, and the weather was good. And, pleasing God, on the way back all would be seen. These are his words. Here the pilots revealed their estimates of position: the pilot of the *Niña* found himself 440 leagues from the Canaries, the pilot of the *Pinta*, 420, and the pilot of the ship in which the Admiral sailed, an even 400.

Thursday 20 September. This day he steered west by north and west-northwest, because the winds shifted a lot in the calm weather. They probably made no more than seven or eight leagues. Two boobies came to the ship and later another, which was a sign of being near land, and they saw much weed, although the day before they had not seen any. They caught a bird by hand which was like a tern. It was a river bird, not a seabird; it had feet like a gull's. At dawn two or three land birds came to the ship singing, and later, before sunrise, they disappeared. Later a booby came from the west-northwest and went southeast, which was a sign that it left land to the west-northwest, because these birds sleep on land and in the morning go out to sea to hunt for food and do not go farther than 20 leagues from land.

Friday 21 September. That day was mostly calm and later some wind. They made between day and night no more than 13 leagues, some of it on course and some not. At dawn they found so much weed that the sea appeared to be solid with it and it came from the west. They saw a booby. The sea was very smooth like a river, and the breezes the best in the world. They saw a whale, which is a sign that they were near land, because they always go close.

Sunday 23 September. He steered northwest and at times northwest by north and at times on his route, which was west, and they made no more than 27 leagues. They saw a dove and a booby and another small river bird and other white birds. The weed was plentiful and they found crabs in it. Since the sea had been calm and smooth the men complained, saying that since in that region there were no rough seas, it would never blow for a return to Spain. But later the sea rose high and without wind, which astonished them, because of which the Admiral says here that the high sea was very necessary for me, [a sign] which had not appeared except in the time of the Jews when they left Egypt [and complained] against Moses, who took them out of captivity . . .

Tuesday 25 September. This day there was much calm and later it blew and they went on their way west until night. The Admiral began talking to Martín Alonso Pinzón, captain of the other caravel, *Pinta*, about a chart that he had sent to him on the caravel three days before, on which the Admiral had apparently drawn certain islands in that sea; and Martín Alonso said that they were in that region and the Admiral answered that so it seemed to him, but since they had not encountered them it must have been caused by the currents which always had driven the vessels northeast and that they had not traveled as far as the pilots said. And at this point the Admiral said to send the said chart to him. And it having been sent over by means of some cord, the Admiral began to plot their position on it with his pilot and sailors. At sunset Martín Alonso went up on the poop of his vessel and with much joy called to the Admiral asking him for a reward: that he saw land. And when he heard this said and affirmed, the Admiral says that he threw himself on his knees to give thanks to Our Lord, and Martín Alonso and his men said *Gloria in excelsis deo*. The Admiral's men and those of the *Niña* did the same. They all climbed the masts and into the rigging and all affirmed that it was land, and so it appeared to the Admiral, and that it was about 25 leagues off. Until night everybody continued to affirm it to be land. The Admiral ordered the ships to leave their course, which was west, and for all of them to go southwest where the land had appeared. They had gone that day about four leagues and a half and during the night 17 leagues southeast, which makes 21, although he told the men 13 leagues, because he always pretended to the men that they were making little way so the voyage would not appear long to them. So he wrote that voyage in two ways: the shorter was the pretended; and the longer, the true. The sea became very calm, because of which many sailors went swimming. They saw many *dorados* and other fish.

Wednesday 10 October. He steered west-southwest; they traveled ten miles per hour and at times 12 and for a time seven and between day and night made 59 leagues; he told the men only 44 leagues. Here the men could no longer stand it; they complained of the long voyage. But the Admiral encouraged them as best he could, giving them good hope of the benefits that they would be able to secure. And he added that it was useless to complain since he had come to find the Indies and thus had to continue the voyage until he found them, with the help of Our Lord.

Thursday 11 October. He steered west-southwest. They took much water aboard, more than they had taken in the whole voyage. They saw petrels and a green bulrush near the ship. The men of the caravel *Pinta* saw a cane and a stick, and took on board another small stick that appeared to have been worked with iron, and a piece of cane, and other vegetation originating on land, and a small plank. The men of the caravel *Niña* also saw other signs of land and a small stick loaded with barnacles. With these signs everyone breathed more easily and cheered up. On this day, up to sunset, they made 27 leagues.

After sunset he steered on his former course to the west. They made about 12 miles each hour and, until two hours after midnight, made about 90 miles, which is twenty-two leagues and a half. And because the caravel *Pinta* was a better sailer and went ahead of the Admiral it found land and made the signals that the Admiral had ordered. A sailor named Rodrigo de Triana saw this land first, although the Admiral, at the tenth hour of the night, while he was on the sterncastle, saw a light, although it was something so faint that he did not wish to affirm that it was land. But he called Pero Gutiérrez, the steward of the king's dais, and told him that there seemed to be a light, and for him to look: and thus he did and saw it. He also told Rodrigo Sánchez de Segovia, whom the king and queen were sending as *veedor* of the fleet, who saw nothing because he was not in a place where he could see it. After the Admiral said it, it was seen once or twice; and it was like a small wax candle that rose and lifted up, which to few seemed to be an indication of land. But the Admiral was certain that they were near land, because of which when they recited the *Salve*, which sailors in their own way are accustomed to recite and sing, all being present, the Admiral entreated and admonished them to keep a good lookout on the forecastle and to watch carefully for land; and that to the man who first told him that he saw land he would later give a silk jacket in addition to the other rewards that the sovereigns had promised, which were ten thousand *maravedis* as an annuity to whoever should see it first. At two hours after midnight the land appeared, from which they were about two leagues distant. They hauled down all the sails and kept only the *treo*, which is the mainsail without bonnets, and jogged on and off, passing time until daylight Friday, when they reached an islet of the Lucayas, which was called Guanahani in the language of the Indians. Soon they saw naked people; and the Admiral went ashore in the armed launch, and Martín Alonso Pinzón and his brother Vicente Anes, who was captain of the *Niña*. The Admiral brought out the royal banner and the captains two flags with the green cross, which the Admiral carried on all the ships as a standard, with an F and a Y, and over each letter a crown, one on one side of the ✠ and the other on the other. Thus put ashore they saw very green trees and many ponds and fruits of various kinds. The Admiral called to the two captains and to the others who had jumped ashore and to Rodrigo Descobedo, the *escrivano* of the whole fleet, and to Rodrigo Sánchez de Segovia; and he said that they should be witnesses that, in the presence of all, he would take, as in fact he did take, possession of the said island for the king and for the queen his lords, making the declarations that were required, and which at more length are contained in the testimonials made there in writing. Soon many people of the island gathered there. What follows are the very words of the Admiral in his book about his first voyage to, and discovery of, these Indies. I, he says, in order that they would be friendly to us – because I recognized that they were people who would be better freed [from error] and converted to our Holy Faith by love than by force – to some of them I gave red caps, and glass beads which they put on their chests, and many other things of small value, in which they took so much pleasure and became so much our friends that it was a marvel. Later they came swimming to the ships' launches where we were and brought us parrots and cotton thread in balls and javelins and many other things, and they traded them to us for other things which we gave them, such as small glass beads and bells. In sum, they took everything and gave of what they had very willingly. But it seemed to me that they were a people very poor in everything. All of them go around as naked as their mothers bore them; and the women also, although I did not see more than one quite young girl. And all those that I saw were young people, for none did I see of more than 30 years of age. They are very well formed, with handsome bodies and good faces. Their hair [is] coarse – almost like the tail of a horse – and short. They wear their hair down over their eyebrows except for a little in the back which they wear long and never cut. Some of them paint themselves with black, and they are of the color of the Canarians, neither black nor white; and some of them paint themselves with white, and some of them with red, and some of them with whatever they find. And some of them paint their faces, and some of them the whole body, and some of them only the eyes, and some of them only the nose. They do not carry arms nor are they acquainted with them, because I showed them swords and they took them by the edge and through ignorance cut themselves. They have no iron. Their javelins are shafts without iron and some of them have at the end a fish tooth and others of other things. All of them alike are of good-sized stature and carry themselves well. I saw some who had marks of wounds on their bodies and I made signs to them asking what they were; and they showed me how people from other islands nearby came there and tried to take them, and how they defended themselves; and I believed and believe that they come here from *tierra firme* to take them captive. They should be good and intelligent servants, for I see that they say very quickly everything that is said to them; and I believe that they would become Christians very easily, for it seemed to me that they had no religion. Our Lord pleasing, at the time of my departure I will take six of them from here to Your Highnesses in order that they may learn to speak. No animal of any kind did I see on this island except parrots. All are the Admiral's words.

Saturday 13 October. As soon as it dawned, many of these people came to the beach – all young as I have said, and all of good stature – very handsome people, with hair not curly but straight and coarse, like horsehair; and all of them very wide in the forehead and head, more so than any other race that I have seen so far. And their eyes are very handsome and not small; and none of them are black, but of the color of the Canary Islanders. Nor should anything else be expected since this island is on an east–west line with the island of Hierro in the Canaries. All alike have very straight legs and no belly but are very well formed. They came to the ship with dugouts that are made from the trunk of one tree, like a long boat, and all of one piece, and worked marvelously in the fashion of the land, and so big that in some of them 40 and 45 men came. And others smaller, down to some in which came one man alone. They row with a paddle like that of a baker and go marvelously. And if it capsizes on them they then throw themselves in the water, and they right and empty it with calabashes.

Sunday 21 October. At the tenth hour I arrived here at this Cabo del Isleo and anchored, and the caravels [did] likewise; and after having eaten I went ashore, where here there was no other settlement than one house. In it I found no one, for I believe that they had fled with fear, because in it was all their household gear. I did not let any of it be touched, but went away with these captains and men to see the island; for if the others already seen are very beautiful and green and fertile, this one is much more so and with large and very green groves of trees. Here there are some big lakes and over and around them the groves are marvelous. And here and in all of the island the groves are all green and the verdure like that in April in Andalusia. And the singing of the small birds [is so marvelous] that it seems that a man would never want to leave this place. And [there are] flocks of parrots that obscure the sun; and birds of so many kinds and sizes, and so different from ours, that it is a marvel. And also there are trees of a thousand kinds and all [with] their own kinds of fruit and all smell so that it is a marvel. I am the most sorrowful man in the world, not being acquainted with them. Because I am quite certain that all of them are things of value; and I am bringing samples of them, and likewise of the plants. Thus walking around one of these lakes, I saw a serpent, which we killed; and I am bringing the skin to Your Highnesses. When it saw us it threw itself into the lake and we followed it in, because it was not very deep, until with lances we killed it. It is seven *palmos* in length. I believe that there are many similar ones here in these lakes. Here I recognized aloes, and tomorrow I have decided to have ten *quintales* [of it] brought to the ship because I am told that it is very valuable. Also, walking in search of very good water, we went to a nearby village, half a league from the place where I am anchored; and the people of it, when they heard us, took to flight and left the houses and hid their clothes and what they had in the bush. I did not allow anything to be taken, not even of the value of a pin. Later some of the men approached us, and one came up to us here. I gave him some bells and some small glass beads and he was very pleased and happy. And so that our friend-ship would increase and that something would be asked of them, I ordered that he be asked for water. And after I went on shipboard they soon came to the beach with their calabashes full and were delighted to give it to us; and I ordered that they be given other trifling little strings of glass beads and they said that in the morning they would come around. I wanted to fill here all the water jars of the ship. Then, if weather permits, I will soon depart to go around this island until I have speech with this king and see if I can get from him the gold that I hear that he wears. And afterwards I will leave for another very large island that I believe must be Cipango according to the indications that these Indians that I have give me, and which they call Colba. In it they say there are many and very large ships and many traders. And from this island [I will go to] another which they call Bohio, which also they say is very big. And the others which are in between I will also see on the way; and, depending on whether I find a quantity of gold or spices, I will decide what I am to do. But I have already decided to go to the mainland and to the city of Quinsay and to give Your Highnesses' letters to the Grand Khan and to ask for, and to come with, a reply.

Monday 22 October: All this night and today I stayed waiting [to see] if the king of this place or other persons would bring gold or something else of substance; and there came many of these people, like the others of the other islands, naked and painted, some of them with white, some with red, some with black, and so on in many fashions. They brought javelins and balls of cotton to barter, which they traded here with some sailors for pieces of broken glass cups and for pieces of clay bowls. Some of them were wearing pieces of gold hanging from their noses, and they willingly gave it for a bell of the sort [put] on the foot of a sparrow hawk and for small glass beads; but it is so little that it is no thing. For it is true that any little thing given to them, as well as our coming, they considered great marvels; and they believed that we had come from the heavens.

The Diaries of Christopher Columbus's First Voyage to America, 1492–1493 (1989 edn)

BARTOLOMEU DIAZ

c.1450–1500

King João, on their return, gave it the name of Cape Boa Esperança or Cape of Good Hope, from the hope he now had of discovering the Indies, so long desired.

A Portuguese navigator of noble birth, Diaz became interested in scientific discovery while at the royal court of Aragon, encountering among others the German Martin Behaim, creator of one of the first globes, and whose theories were at the same time influencing Columbus. In 1486, sent by João (John) II to expand on the discoveries already made by the Portuguese on the African west coast, he pushed further south than previously attained, and was then blown by a storm round the African cape, later named by the king the Cape of Good Hope, for this was surely the gateway to the wealth of Asia. His expedition was a prelude to that of Vasco da Gama, who in 1497 indeed went on to find a route through to India. Diaz outfitted that expedition, and in 1500 joined one led by Cabral, which went off course on the way to the Cape of Good Hope and instead of reaching Asia, went west and made the first European discovery of Brazil; departing the continent, he was lost in a South Atlantic storm.

The way the account below tells it, King João had heard encouraging tales of a great black king – the legendary Prester John, rumoured in the twelfth century to be a Christian of great might, and later as someone who could save the faltering crusades, thus rescuing the Holy Land from the Muslims. He never was located, though it is possible that his origin lay in none other than the very un-Christian Genghis Khan – the Mongol whose dynasty of *hordes*, or palaces, had not only devastated the Islamic world, but also had threatened to bring Christendom to its knees.

Now Prester John reappears, this time hopefully to help fellow Christians find a way to India and 'Cathay' (China). Diaz ventures forth, planting *padraos* (stone pillars) along the way to lay claim to land for Portugal, and also disembarking six African natives, who had been taken back to Lisbon by Cao, a mariner who had sailed this coastline several years earlier. It was hoped one of the men, at least, would get through to Prester John. He left a supply ship in what is now Lüderitz Bay, Namibia, south-western Africa and, continuing south, was blown out of sight of land. He next encountered Africa to the north, meaning he had rounded the Cape.

Feeling his way down unknown Africa

From the information that king John received from the ambassador of Benin, and from Joam Alfonso d'Aveiro, when he was there, it appeared that to the eastward of that country, about two hundred and fifty leagues, there lived a king, the most powerful in those parts, whom they called Ogané, and who was held by them in so high esteem, that when the king of Benin died, they sent an ambassador with a great present, to acquaint him with the death, and to pray that he would confirm the succeeding one; which he does by sending him a staff, and an head-piece of shining brass, to serve as a scepter and crown, and a cross of the same metal to wear about his neck, which is looked upon as holy, and without which insignia he would not be considered as king. This ambassador, when at the court of Ogané, never saw him, but only some silk curtains behind which he was and during the audience, he put out his foot, to shew he was there, and that he accepted the presents, and agreed to the business; and to this foot they paid a religious reverence. The ambassador also had a small cross given him to wear round his neck, which gave him a superior rank in his own country; and at that time, whenever India was spoken of, there was always mention made of a king called Prester John, who, they said, was a Christian.

It occurred to the king of Portugal, that through his means he might gain some entrance into India. Besides, he had been informed by some religious Alexis which came from Spain, and from some friars that went to Jerusalem, that this king lived above Egypt, and that his country extended as far as the south seas; and consulting his cosmographers, comparing Ptolomeus's general chart of Africa, considering the discoveries that his people had made, and reckoning two hundred and fifty leagues to the east, according to what was told him by the people of Benin of king Ogané, he concluded it could be no other than Prester John; for by the accounts, they both were always hidden behind silk curtains, and venerated the cross; and he thought that proceeding in his discoveries along the coast, they could not but at last come to the extremity of that land; he therefore both fitted out ships, and sent men to go by land, being resolved to compleat the discovery. Having fitted two ships of fifty tons each, with a tender to carry provisions, (for on these expeditions their provisions too often failed them,) in the latter end of August these vessels sailed, under the command of Bartholomew Dias, one of the knights of his houshold, who had made discoveries on this coast. The other vessel was commanded by Juan Infante, another knight, and in the tender was captain Pedro Dias, brother to the commander.

Bartholomew Dias, passing the river Congo, got as far as the cape, which he called Angra dost Saltos, or Bay of the Landing, because he there landed two blacks, which the king had ordered to be instructed, and sent back to be landed at this place. There were also four other blacks belonging to the coast; one he landed on the Angra dos Ilheos, where he first erected his stone mark; the second on the Angra dos Voltas, or the Bay of Winding; the third died: and the fourth he landed in the bay, or Angri dos Ilheos, or islands of Santa Croz, with two others that were taken fishing. These people being set on shore, well dressed with gold, silver, and other ornaments, spread about in this manner, could not fail to give all the inhabitants information of the king of Portugal and his kingdom; and as his ships were so often on these coasts, he expected it would reach the ears of Prester John, and raise his curiosity to send some of his people to meet them. He had great confidence this scheme would succeed, and many women blacks were instructed also to go as far within land as possible, and give information of what they had seen, on a supposition that women would meet with less molestation than the men.

Leaving this place the land trended to the east, and they were obliged by tempests to run thirteen days with little or no sail and as their vessels were small, and the climate cold, it was very different from what they experienced on the coast of Guinea. The storms are here also irresistible, in comparison to those on the coast of Spain but on the weather becoming more moderate, they steered east, concluding the coast lay north and south, as was generally the case, but finding nothing appear, they altered, their course, and stood to the northward. At last they fell in with a bay, which they named Vaqueiros, or Cow-herds, as they saw many cows feeding, with men attending them; but as they had no interpreter, they could get no intelligence. The people also run from them, and drove their cattle to the interior parts of the country. All they observed was that they were blacks, with woolly heads, like those of Guinea. . . .

As the people were much fatigued from the terrible weather they had gone through, they all began to complain, and begged they might not proceed, as their provisions would all be expended, and before they got back to the store ships, they should perish for want: that it was sufficient to have discovered so much coast in one voyage: and that they must have doubled some great cape, which on their return they might discover. Bartholomew Dias, to satisfy the murmurs of his people, went on shore with his officers, and required them solemnly to declare what they thought was best to be done for the honour of their king. All agreeing to sail back, he made them sign a paper; yet he begged they would indulge him with sailing a day or two more along the coast, and if they found nothing remarkable, he would immediately return, which they agreed to. In these two or three days, they discovered nothing but a river, about twenty-five leagues beyond the island of the Cross, in latitude thirty-two degrees and two-thirds: and as Juan Infante, captain of the vessel St Pantelam, was the first that put foot on shore, it took its name from him, and continues the name of Rio de Infante. He then returned to the island of the Cross, and with great regret left it, remembering with pleasure the asylum it had afforded him after the great danger they had escaped.

Leaving this island, they got sight of that great and remarkable cape, undiscovered for so many centuries, which opened to view a new world, and which, from the storms they experienced, they called Cape Tormentoso; but king John, on their return, gave it the name of Cape Boa Esperança, or Cape of Good Hope, from the hope he now had of discovering the Indies, so long desired. This name will probably be preserved as long as the world lasts. Bartholomew Dias having made his observations on it, as to the nautical part, and left a stone mark called St Felippe, had not time to go on shore on account of the bad weather, but returned to seek for his vessel that had the provisions, which he found, after having been absent from her nine months; and though he left nine men in her, only three were living. One of these men, the secretary of the ship, on seeing the ships, being very weak, died with joy; the other two gave an account of their fate, which was, that they had trusted too much to the faith of the blacks, who had put some of them to death. Having taken out what provisions they wanted, they set fire to this vessel, as they had not men to navigate her.

*A General Collection of Voyages and Discoveries made by the Portuguese
and the Spaniards*, 1789

Vasco da Gama

c.1460–1524

Henceforth let no one speak to me of putting back, for know from me a certainty, that if I do not find information of what I have come to seek, that to Portugal I do not return.

Vasco da Gama, in establishing the sea route to India, not only laid the foundation of the Portuguese empire, whose trade links reached to East Africa, south-west India and Indonesia, but in effect opened the Indian Ocean and Asia to the rest of Europe.

Born in Sines, a small port in southern Portugal, da Gama was son to a provincial governor, who was charged by João II to follow up Bartolomeu Diaz's expedition and reach India. Political problems, including conflict with Spain, delayed the voyage, but Columbus's success in reaching 'Asia' from the west for the Spanish sharpened Portuguese minds. With the death of da Gama's father, the expedition was put in his hands; now a senior naval officer, he departed Lisbon on 8 July 1497, his four ships fitted out by Diaz, and with convicts on board for more hazardous duties.

With instructions from Diaz, who piloted him for the first leg, he avoided the doldrums of the Gulf of Guinea, and in November they rounded the Cape of Good Hope and planted a *padrao*, claiming the land for Portugal. Having made contact with the Hottentots – the first Europeans to do so – they proceeded up the eastern coast of Africa and had hostile encounters with the Muslims of Mozambique, who rightly saw the arrival of the Portuguese as a threat to their trading empire. Surviving another assault at Mombasa, in present-day Kenya, the Portuguese had a stroke of luck, receiving support from the Muslim ruler at Malindi, who was seeking an alliance against the southern, rival factions. Da Gama now engaged a Muslim navigator, Ahmed Ibn Majid, who in just twenty-three days piloted the fleet across the Arabian Sea to India; on 20 May 1498 they sailed into the port of Calicut. Da Gama was soon trying to establish relations with Zamorin, the Hindu ruler, but met stiff opposition again from Muslim merchants; furthermore, he had brought trade goods which the sophisticated Arab and Indian traders thought laughable – mere trinkets. He did obtain a shipment of pepper, however, and returned home, taking three times as long, owing to unfavourable winds and scurvy. So many men were lost that they decided to reduce the fleet and burn one of their ships. The remainder of the expedition returned to Lisbon in September 1499, and da Gama was given the title Admiral of the Indian Ocean.

The following extract is a glimpse into the machinations on board da Gama's first historic voyage.

Rounding the Cape: storm and mutiny

The wind increased continually, and the sea rose greatly, for then the winter of that country was setting in . . .

Seeing the weather in this state, the pilot and master told the captain-major that they had great fear on account of the weather because it was becoming a tempest, and the ships were weak, and that they thought they ought to put in to land and run along the coast and return to seek the great river into which they had first entered, because the wind was blowing that way, and they could enter it for all that there was a storm. But when the captain-major heard of turning backwards, he answered them, that they should not speak such words, because as he was going out of the bar of Lisbon, he had promised to God in his heart not to turn back a single span's breadth of the way which he had made, that on that account they should not speak in that wise, as he would throw into the sea whomsoever spoke such things. At which the crew, in despair, abandoned themselves to the chances of the sea which was broken up with the increase of the tempest and rising of the gale, which many times chopped round, and blew from all parts, and at times fell; so that the ships were in great peril from their great labouring in the waves, which ran very high. Then the storm would again break with such fury, that the seas rose towards the sky, and fell back in heavy showers which flooded the ships. The storm raging thus violently, the danger was doubled; for suddenly the wind died out, so that the ships lay dead between the waves, lurching so heavily that they took in water on both sides; and the men made themselves fast to not to fall from one side to the other; and everything in the ships was breaking up, so that all cried to God for mercy. Before long the sea came in with more violence, which increased their misfortune, with the great difficulty of working the pumps; for they were taking in much water, which entered both above and below; so they had no repose for either soul or body, and the crews began to sicken and die of their great hardships. At this the pilots and masters and all the people poured out cries and lamentations to the captains, urgently requiring them to put back and seek an escape from death, which there they were certain of meeting with by their own will if they did not put about. To which the captains gave no other reply than that they would do no such thing unless the captain-major did it. The captain-major, seeing the clamours of his crew, answered them with brave words, saying, that he had already told them that backwards he would not go, even though he saw a hundred deaths before his eyes: thus he had vowed to God; and let them look to it that it was not reasonable that they should lose all the labours which they had gone through up to this time, that the Lord who had delivered them until now, would have mercy upon them; they should remember that they had already doubled the Cape of Storms and were in the region which they had come to seek, to discover India, on accomplishing which and returning to Portugal, they would gain such great honour and recompenses from the King of Portugal for their children; and they should put their trust in God, who is merciful, and who, from one hour to another, would come with His mercy, and give them fair weather, and that they should not talk like people who distrusted the mercy of God. But, although the captain-major always spoke to them these and other words of great encouragement, they did not cease from their loud clamour and protestations that he would give an account to God of their deaths of which he would be the cause, and of the leaving desolate their wives and children: all this accompanied by weeping and cries, and calls to God for mercy. Whilst they went on this way with their souls in their mouths, the sea began to go down a little, and the wind also, so that the ships could approach to speak one another, and all clamoured with loud cries that they should put about to seek some place where they could refit the ships, as they could not keep them afloat with the pumps. The crews of the other ships spoke with more audacity, saying that the captain was but one man, and they were many; and they feared death while the captains did not fear it, nor took any account of losing their lives. The captain-major chose that the two other ships should know his design, and he said and swore by the life of the king his sovereign that from the spot where he then was he had not to turn back one span's breadth, even though the ships were laden with gold, unless he got information of that which they had come to seek, and that even if he had near there a very good port he would not go ashore, lest some of them should retire to a certain death on shore, allowing themselves to remain there, rather than go on with the ships trusting to the mercy of God, in which they had such small reliance that they made such exclamations from the weakness of their hearts, as if they were not Portuguese: on which account he would undeceive them all, for to Portugal they would not return unless they brought word to the king of that which he had so strongly commended to them, and that he took the same account of death as did any one of them. While they were at this point a sudden wind arose, with so great a concussion of thunder and dark-ness, and a stronger blast than they had yet experienced, and the sea rose so much that the ships could not see one another, except when they were upheaved by the seas, when they seemed to be amongst the clouds; and they hung out lights so as not to part company, for the anxiety and fear which the captain-major felt was the losing one of the ships from his company, so that the seamen would put back to Portugal by force, as indeed they had very much such a desire in their hearts. But the captains took very great care of this, because Vasco da Gama, before going out of Lisbon, when conversing alone with the Jew Zaeuto in the monastery, had received from him much information as to what he should do during his voyage, and especially recommendations of great watchfulness never to let the ships part company, because if they separated it would be the certain destruction of all of them. Vasco da Gama took great care of this, personally, and by means of his servants and relations in whom he trusted: and this they attended to with much greater solicitude after they had heard the sailors say that they were many, and the captains only a few single men; and in fact they had in their minds such an intention of rising up against the captains, and by force putting back to Portugal, and they thought that if it became necessary to arrest them for this and bring them before the king, he would have mercy upon them, and should they not find mercy, they preferred rather to die there where their wives and children and fathers were, and in their native country, and not in the sea to be eat by the fishes. With such thoughts they all spoke to one another secretly, determining to carry it out, and trusting that the king would not hang them all for the good reasons which they would all give him; or else to secure their lives they would go to Castile until they were pardoned: and this was the greatest insolence they were guilty of; and so they decided upon executing their plan. In taking this decision they did not perceive the danger of death, into which they were going more than ever. In the ship of Nicolas Coelho there was a sailor who had a brother who lived with Nicolas Coelho, and was foster-brother of a son of his; and the sailor brother told this boy of what they had all determined to do. This boy being very discreet, said to his brother that they should all preserve great secrecy, so as not to be found out, for it was a case of treason, and he warned his brother not to tell any one that he had mentioned such a thing to him. The boy, on account of the affection which he had for his master Nicolas Coelho, discovered the matter to him in secret, and he at once gave the boy a serious warning to be very discreet in this matter, that they should not perceive that he had told him anything of the kind. With the firm determination which Nicolas Coelho at once formed to die sooner than allow himself to be seized upon, he became very vigilant both by day and night, and warned the boy to try to learn with much dissimulation all that they wanted to do, and by what means. The boy told him that they would not do it unless they could first concert with the other ships, so that all should mutiny: at that Nicolas Coelho remained more at ease, but was always very much on his guard for himself. As the storm did not abate, but rather seemed to increase, and as the cries and clamour of the people were very great, beseeching him to put back, Nicolas Coelho dissembled with them, saying: 'Brothers, let us strive to save ourselves from this storm, for I promise you that as soon as I can get speech with the captain-major, I will require him to put

back, and you will see how I will require it of him.' With this they remained
satisfied. Some days having passed thus with heavy storms, the Lord was
pleased to assuage the tempest a little and the sea grew calm, so that the ships
could speak one another: and Nicolas Coelho coming up to speak, shouted to
the captain-major that: 'It would be well to put about, since every moment
they had death before their eyes, and if they who were captains did not choose
to do so, and so many men who went in their company were so piteously
begging with tears and cries to put back the ships, and they did not choose to
do so, it would be well if they should kill or arrest us, and then they would put
back or go where it was convenient to save their lives; which we also ought to
do, and if we do not do it, let each one look out for himself, for thus I do for
my part, and for my conscience sake, for I would not have to give an account
of it to the Lord.' Paulo da Gama, who also had come up within speaking
distance, heard all this. When they had heard these words of Nicolas Coelho,
who, on ending his speech, at once begun to move away, the captain-major
answered him that he would hold a consultation with the pilot and his crew,
and that whatever he determined to do, he would make a signal to him of his
resolution. During this time they lay hove to in the smooth water, because the
wind never changed from its former point. Vasco da Gama, as he was very
quick-witted, at once understood what Nicolas Coelho's words meant, and
called together all the crew, and said to them that he was not so valiant as not
to have the fear of death like themselves, neither was he so cruel as not to feel
grieved at heart at seeing their tears and lamentations, but that he did not
wish to have to give account to God for their lives, and for that reason he
begged them to labour for their safety, because if the bad weather came again
he had determined to put back, but to disculpate himself with the king, it was
incumbent upon him to draw up a document of the reasons for putting back,
with their signatures. At this all raised their hands to heaven, saying that its
mercy was already descending upon them, since it was softening the heart of
the captain-major and inclining him to put back, and they said that all would
sign the great service which he would render to God and to the king by
putting back. Then the captain-major said that there was no need of the
signatures of all, but only of those who best understood the business of the
sea. Then the pilot and master named them, and they were three seamen.
Upon this the captain-major retired to his cabin, and told his servants to
stand at the door of the cabin, and put inside the clerk to draw up the
document, and ordered the three seamen to enter: and dissembling, he made
inquiries as to returning to port, and all was written down and they signed it.
He then ordered them to go down below to another cabin which he had

beneath his own for a store-cabin, and he ordered the clerk to go down also with them, and he summoned the master and pilot and ordered them below also, telling them to go and sign, as the clerk was there. Then he called up the seamen one by one, and ordered them to be put in irons by his servants in his cabin, and heavy irons for the master and pilot. All being well ironed and bound, the captain-major turned them out, and called all the men, ordering the master and pilot at once to give up to him all the articles which they had belonging to the art of navigation, or if not, that he would at once execute them; of which being greatly afraid, they gave everything up to him. Then Vasco da Gama, holding them all in his hand, flung them into the sea, and said – 'See here, men, that you have neither master nor pilot, nor any one to show you the way from henceforward, because these men whom I have arrested will return to Portugal below the deck, if they do not die before that,' (for he was aware that they had agreed amongst one another to rise up and return by force to Portugal, and on that account had cast everything into the sea), 'and I do not require master nor pilot, nor any man who knows the art of navigation, because God alone is the master and pilot who had to guide and deliver them by His mercy if they deserved it, and if not, let His will be done. To Him you must commend yourselves and beg mercy. Henceforward let no one speak to me of putting back, for know from me of a certainty, that if I do not find information of what I have come to seek, that to Portugal I do not return.' Seeing and hearing these things, the crew became much more terrified, and with much greater fear of death, which they held as certain, not having either pilot or master, nor any one who knew how to navigate a ship. Then the prisoners and all the crew on their knees begged him for mercy with loud cries; the prisoners saying that they, being ignorant men and of faint heart, had come to an understanding to put the ship about and return to the king and offer themselves for death, if he chose to give it them, and they would have taken him a prisoner, that the king might see that he was not to blame for putting back; but this was not to have been done, except with the will of all the people of the other ships: but since God had discovered this to him before they had carried it out, let him show them clemency; for well they saw that they deserved death from him, which was more than the chains which they bore. All the crew frequently called out to him for clemency, and not to put the prisoners below the decks, where they would soon die. Then the captain-major, showing that he only did it at their entreaty, and not for any need which he had of them, ordered them to remain in their cabins in the forecastle still in irons, and forbade their giving any directions for the navigation of the ship, except only for the trimming of the sails and the work of the ship. Vasco da Gama then ran alongside of the other ships and spoke them, saying that he had put his pilot and master in irons, in which he would bring them back to the kingdom, if God pleased that they should return there; and that they should not imagine that he had any need of their knowledge, he had flung into the sea all the implements of their art of navigation, because he placed his hopes in God alone, who would direct them and deliver them from the perils amongst which they were going: and on that account, since he had now made his men secure, let them secure themselves as they pleased: and without waiting for an answer he sheered off.

The Three Voyages of Vasco da Gama, and His Viceroyalty (trans. Henry E. J. Stanley, 1869)

FERDINAND MAGELLAN
c.1480–1521

Maglianes was surpriz'd with a Joy that exceeded all the common bounds and measures, for this was the happy thing he look'd for.

Born into the Portuguese upper classes, the navigator, soldier and gentleman of fortune Ferdinand Magellan enlisted in the army at the age of twenty-five and travelled to India and North Africa, where a wound left him with a permanent limp. His request for an increase in allowance was rejected by Manuel I of Portugal and he next approached King Charles I of Spain (later Holy Roman Emperor Charles V), who was anxious about Portugal's now firm hold over trade to the East Indies. Magellan was provided with a fleet of five ships and promised a share of the profits, and set out from Seville on 20 September 1519 with much aplomb to find a new westward route to the Spice Islands, or Moluccas.

They crossed the Atlantic, then followed the Brazilian coast south while looking for a strait through to the west. With winter approaching, they put into southern Patagonia for almost six months. Resuming in October, he was blown by a storm into the passage he had been searching for, the Magellan Strait, and continued through into the Pacific, the ocean so named because of the calm waters he experienced there. They sailed westward and due to the prevailing ignorance of the size of the ocean, his crew suffered terrible hardships when they could not re-supply, surviving off boiled leather, rats, and sawdust.

The fleet finally reached Guam, where they were somewhat restored, and later became the first Europeans to see the Philippines. Here Magellan formed an alliance with the ruler of Cebu, and agreed to aid him with an attack on Mactan, the neighbouring island. During the fighting, on 27 April 1521, Magellan was killed.

Only one ship of the original five completed the journey, the *Victoria* – and only eighteen crew members out of an original 241 survived. The last remaining Spanish captain, Juan Sebastian del Cano, should perhaps by rights be given the accolade of being the first man to circumnavigate the earth. He didn't keep a journal, but two of his officers wrote accounts of the voyage – one of them the navigator Antonio Pigafetta, the author of the account below, which begins with Magellan emerging into the Pacific Ocean from the Strait now named after him ('the Land on both sides high and uneven, and the Mountains cover'd with Snow').

Magellan had demonstrated that the oceans were linked – the Indian Ocean was not, after all, landlocked. The vastness of the Pacific was now known, together with the form and size of South America. The Americas were at last shown, for all practical purposes, to be a separate land-mass from Asia.

Entering the South Pacific

When they came to the end of it, and found an open passage into the great Ocean, *Maglianes* was surpriz'd with a Joy that exceeded all the common bounds and measures, for this was the happy thing he look'd for, and now he was able to demonstrate his Sailing round by the West to the Emperor. The

Point of Land from whence he first saw this most desirable sight, he call'd in memory of it *Cape Desiderato*; but it seems 'twas not so desirable to all the rest of the company, for here one of the Ships stole away and sail'd homewards by her self. They give a very good Character of the *Streights*, for affording all the conveniencies of fresh Water, Fish, grateful Herbs, Wood, secure Havens, of which there are great plenty; and they say, are almost at every Leagues end. And these Advantages are to be met with all over the *Streights*, and not in one or two particular places only; there's none of the Havens (by their report) but what will entertain you with both Food and Firing.

They entred the *Pacifick Sea*, (as they call'd it) *Nov. 28. A. D.* 1520, and in this wide rambling Ocean they fail'd 3 Months and 20 Days without sight of Land: The miseries they endured for want of Provision, a good part of this time, were such as are seldom heard of. The fresh Water they had aboard stunk and was very loathsome; all their Bread was gone, and nothing left to eat but Skins and pieces of hard Leather. Nature will make any shift, tho' ever so hard and poor, to bear herself out in a distress, when 'tis possible to be done; and the poor Seamen here, rather than starve, fell very greedily to work upon those dry tough pieces of Leather that were folded about the Ropes of their Ships. But it being impossible to eat them till they were some way soften'd and fitted for chewing, they laid them asleep in the Salt Water for somedays, and then made the best of them as long as they lasted. But then again, what with this impure sort of feeding, which was short and scanty too, and the daily impoverishment of their Spirits wanting better Recruits, their numbers lessen'd apace; some died outright, others fell into pining Sickness, others had their Gums that grew quite over their Teeth on every side; by which means, being totally unable to manage those tough solids they were forc'd to feed upon, they were past all help, and so miserably starv'd to death. Their only comfort in all these direful circumstances, was a constancy of fair and good weather: The Winds blew them smoothly and gently along, and broke out into nothing of a raging Fit, all the while they were thus expos'd; the Sea as calm and quiet too, and by this got the Celebrated name of *Pacifick*. And how happy was it to be thus at rest from the Toils of a Stormy Sea? Had Famine and Tempests come together, how quickly would they have been wearied out? Whither wou'd the shatter'd Fleet have been tost, and what wou'd have become of the Discovery of the *Moluccas*?

March 6. they came up with a parcel of Islands, being then in 12 degr. *North* Lat. and 146 degr. Lon. from their first setting out. Here they went ashore to breathe and refresh a little, after all the fatigues of their tedious Voyage thro' the *South* Sea; but the thievish People of these Islands would not let them be quiet; while they were reposing themselves ashore, the others would be pilfering and stealing things out of the Ships, so that 'twas impossible to enjoy their ease in any measure, till they had taken some course to deliver themselves from these unwearied Disturbers. So they march'd with a small Party, pretty well Arm'd, up into one of the Islands, burnt some of their Houses, and killed some few of them; but this Correction, tho' it might awe them for the present, yet could not mend their evil Temper and Disposition, but they that were Thieves would be Thieves still, and in spight of Swords and Guns, wou'd play the Knave as before, for which reason they resolv'd to make no long stay there, but find out some other place where they might Rest with more safety and quiet. As for the Character of this People and their Manners, they give us this Relation:

That there is not the least appearance of any Order or Form of Government amongst them, but every Man lives as he lists, and does what's agreeable to his own humour and inclination ... So that the general corruption of their Manners will necessarily keep them all upon a level, and establish a perpetual Anarchy amongst them. As far as appears, the Men go entirely naked, not discovering any thing of that common modesty which obtains amongst most barbarous People to bestow some covering upon the Privy Parts; that distinction indeed ceases here, all Parts being equally expos'd to view. Their hair is very black, both on their Heads and Beards, the former being generally very long, and reaching down to their Wastes. They anoint themselves all over with the Oil of the Coco, but their natural Complexion is Olive. They colour the Teeth black and red; and some of them will wear a Bonnet made of the Palm-tree upon their Heads. The Women are much better favour'd than the Men, and (as their Sex requires) more modest too; they all wear Coverings made of the inner Bark of the Palm-tree, their Hair black, thick and long; and (as they say) ready to trail upon the ground. They commend them for very careful industrious Housewives, spending their time at a much better rate than the Men do, for whilst these are pilfering abroad, the others are making Mats and Nets of the Palm-tree at home; but of both sides the Work goes to the furnishing of the House. Their Houses are built of Timber, cover'd over with Boards and large Fig-leaves, and distinguish'd into several Apartments; their Beds are the Palm-Mats laid one upon another, and the leaves of the same are instead of Sheets and Blankets. They have no weapons but Clubs and long Poles, upon which they put heads of horn. Their feeding is upon Coco's, Benana's, Figs of a hands length, Sugar Canes, Fowl and Flying Fish. Their Canoes are pretty odly contriv'd and patch'd up, that they'll fail with them at a very great rate;

the Sails of them are made of broad Date-leaves sowed together; instead of a
Rudder they use a large Board with a Staff at the top, and may, when they will,
make the Stern the Forecastle, or the Forecastle the Stern; they are always
painted over either black, or white, or red, some one colour, and some
another, as they like. These People are mightily taken with any little thing
that's new and agreeable to their childish humour: When the *Spaniards* had
wounded several of them with their Arrows; nay, pierced them almost
through and through, these being strange things to them, they wou'd pull
them out of their wounds, and hold them in their hands, staring at them till
they dropt down dead. And after all, tho' they had been so roughly handled,
yet they would follow the Ships as they were going away to gaze at them; so
that they had at one time a matter of 200 of their Canoes pressing about them,
as near as they could to behold those wonderful Contrivances.

*The Voyage of Ferdinandus Maglianes . . . taken out of Antony Pigafetta, an Italian of Vicenza,
and one that assisted in this voyage,* in *Navigantium Atque Itinerantium Bibliotheca,* 1764.

Anonymous Clerk of Ship
fl. 1653
They were punish'd by receiving 25 strokes upon their bare Buttocks
with a flat piece of Wood.

We know next to nothing of the author, save that he was Dutch. I've chosen him for this very reason: he is one of the other thousands of anonymous sailors, perhaps a runaway, perhaps press-ganged. Teeth loosening with scurvy, their lives short and cheap, they were the fodder of naval exploration. The Anonymous Clerk is a sort of Unknown Soldier of the sea.

Shipwrecked

A *Dutch* Vessel, in the year 1653, being bound from *Batavia* to *Japan*, after suffering a most violent Storm of several days continuance, springing a Leak so wide that there was no means to drain the Water that rush'd into the Hold, several that happen'd to be then under Deck were drowned before they could get up, and each Man betaking himself to his shifts, 36 (of 64 that they were in all) got ashore upon the Island of *Quelpaert*, and those too severely bruised and hurt in saving themselves from the terrible Fate of their more unfortunate Companions.

However, walking next day along the shoar, to see whether the Bodies of those that had been drowned were cast upon the Land by the Waves, they found none but that of their Captain, which they buried with as much Decency as their Circumstances could then permit.

They then made a diligent search along the Sands, to see whether any of their Provisions had been cast ashoar, but found only one Sack of Meal, a small Cask of Salt Meat, a little Bacon, and a Hogshead of Claret; which was a very acceptable piece of news to the Sick Men.

Their Shipwreck happening the *15th*, on the *16th* at night they gather'd enough of the Sails and other Ruines of the Wreck, to make them a sort of a Shelter or Tent, and on the *17th*, being discovered by the Inhabitants, there came down in the Evening an hundred Armed Men, who, after counting them, kept them inclosed all that Night.

On the *18th* in the Morning, they began to enlarge their Tent; but there coming down, about Noon, two thousand Armed Men, both Horse and Foot, who drew up in Battalia before their Tent; their Clerk, chief Pilot, with his Mate and a Boy going forth to meet them; their Commander immediately caus'd an Iron Chain with a Bell to be put about their Necks, and in that Equipage were they forced to prostrate themselves before him; upon which all his Men gave a shout, and immediately afterward those in the Tent were served in the same manner. And being afterwards made kneel, many Questions were put to them, which they could not understand; no more could the *Chinese* what they endeavour'd to make them comprehend, *viz. That they were* Dutchmen, *bound from* Batavia *to* Nangasaky *in* Japan. Upon which the Commander of the *Chinese* ordering a Cup of a certain Liquor called *Arac* to be given to each of them, sent them back to their Tent; and understanding that they had little or no Provisions, sent them an hour afterward, Rice boiled in Water, of which the *Chinese* gave them very sparingly lest it should do them harm; for they imagin'd that before they had been half starved. In the Afternoon they came with Ropes in their hands, which a little surprized the *Dutch*, till they saw that their Design was to draw what they could of the Wreck ashoar; and the Admiral of the Island coming down with the Commander, the *Dutch* presented each with a Perspective-Glass and some pots of Claret, which they fill'd out in their Captain's Silver Cup; and they, liking the Liquor very well, drank till they were pretty merry, and then returning them the Cup, with many Tokens of Friendship, return'd to the places of their Residence, and let the *Dutch* retire to their Tent.

The Governour being exactly inform'd of our Circumstances, gave us every one (during his Abode there) fresh Marks of his Bounty and Compassion; but his time being unhappily expir'd the beginning of *December* following. 'Tis almost impossible to express the Marks of Kindness and Affection he shew'd them at his Departure, giving each of them a Coat well-lin'd, two pair of Shoes, and a pair of Hose made of Skins, which was a very seasonable Present for Persons in their Circumstances.

The new Governour being of a much less Humane Temper, gave them Barley instead of Rice, and Meal instead of Flour, and us'd them in every thing with so much Harshness and Severity, that meditating their Escape, and six of them entering into a Shallop, with which they designed to put to Sea; being overtaken, they were punish'd by receiving 25 stroaks upon the bare Buttocks with a flat piece of Wood four fingers broad and an inch thick, which obliged them to keep their Beds a long time; and all the rest were more closely guarded and hardly used than before.

In the month of *May* they were sent for to Court, and being put on board of Boats, with Fetters on their Feet, were carried over from the Island to the Continent.

Account of the Shipwreck of a Dutch Vessel upon the coast of the Isle of Quelpaert . . . by the Clerk of the Ship, who was one of them that escap'd, in Navigantium Atque Itinerautium Bibliotheca, 1764

Martin Frobisher
*c.*1535–94

They eat their meat all raw, both flesh, fish and fowl . . . [And] keep certain dogs not much unlike wolves, which they yoke together as we do oxen and horses . . .

Born near Wakefield, Yorkshire, Frobisher was apprenticed as a cabin boy in 1544, his intuition and flare ensuring steady rise through the ranks. Time spent in the Indies and elsewhere as a privateer – that is, holding a commission from the government to operate a private armed vessel – was followed in 1576 by the first attempt to find the North-West Passage, a route to Asia from Europe that went north-west, over the top of America, a journey not completed until 330 years later, by Amundsen.

One of the two ships, the *Michael*, returned to England, considering the venture fool-hardy. Frobisher himself was almost lost off the coast of Greenland. He reached Labrador and a deep inlet on Baffin Island, later named after him. Shortly afterwards, he made two further attempts, during which he charted the area more carefully and claimed Baffin Island for the English crown. He gave up Arctic exploration on discovering that the 'black earth' that he had collected on his first exped-ition contained no precious metal, but only valueless iron pyrites – fool's gold.* In 1585, as vice admiral on the *Primrose*, he joined Sir

---

* In 1585, John Davis followed in his wake. A man with a keen sense of common humanity, he took along a squad of athletes so as to be able to join in the summer sports activities of the 'Esquimaux'. While they competed at high jump and wrestling, his band played English folk tunes. 'Our men did overleape them, but we found them strong and nimble, and to have skill in wrestling, for they cast some of our men that were good wrestlers.'

Francis Drake in raiding the Spanish settle-ments of the West Indies. He was knighted for his daring and skilful role in the defeat of the Spanish Armada in 1588, tried settling down in Yorkshire but was soon back at sea, commanding a fleet outfitted by Sir Walter Raleigh to intercept, pillage, and destroy Spanish vessels bringing gold from Panama. He died of wounds suffered while harrying the Spanish, this time conducting a naval attack on a fort near Brest.

The account I've chosen comes from Christopher Hall, master of the *Gabriel*, the surviving ship of Sir Martin Frobisher's 1576 expedition to discover the North-West Pas-sage. His, and other eyewitness accounts, were collected by Richard Hakluyt, an Elizabethan clergyman, diplomat and scholarly geog-rapher with a passionate interest in England's burgeoning overseas trade. His collection of documents, *The Principal Navigations, Voy-ages, Traffics and Discoveries of the English Nation*, was published some twenty-five years after this voyage into the region. Each is written in its own personal style, some semi-literate, some pious, some jocular. Here, Hall describes alighting on Baffin Island in July, when the Frobisher expedition caught sight of the inhabitants – people later known as Eskimos, 'eaters of raw meat', the name given them by other Indian groups. They called themselves simply Inuit, Yupik and so on, words meaning 'people'.

Dealings with the natives and their 'crafty allurements'

The 19th day in the morning, being calm and no wind, the Captain and I took our boat, with eight men in her to row us ashore, to see if there were there any people or no. And going to the top of the island we had sight of seven boats which came rowing from the east side toward that island, whereupon we returned aboard again. At length we sent our boat with five men in her to see whither they rowed, and so with a white cloth brought one of their boats with their men along the shore, rowing after our boat, till such time as they saw our ship, and then they rowed ashore. Then I went on shore myself, and gave every of them a threaden point, and brought one of them aboard of me, where he did eat and drink, and then carried him on shore again. Whereupon all the rest came aboard with their boats, being nineteen persons, and they spoke, but we understood them not. They be like to Tartars, with long black hair, broad faces and flat noses, and tawny in colour, wearing seals' skins, and so do the women not differing in the fashion, but the women are marked in the face with blue streaks down the cheeks and round about the eyes. Their boats are made all of sealskins, with a keel of wood within the skin. The proportion of them is like a Spanish shallop, save only they be flat in the botton and sharp at both ends.

The twentieth day we weighed and went to the eastside of this island, and I and the Captain with four men more went on shore, and there we saw their houses; and the people espying us came rowing towards our boat. Whereupon we plied toward our boat; and we being in our boat and they ashore, they called to us, and we rowed to them, and one of their company came into our boat, and we carried him aboard and gave him a bell and a knife. So the Captain and I willed five of our men to set him ashore at a rock, and not among the company which they came from; but their wilfulness was such that they would go to them, and so were taken themselves and our boat lost.

The next day in the morning we stood in near the shore and shot off a falconet and sounded our trumpet, but we could hear nothing of our men. This sound we called the Five Men's Sound, and plied out of it but anchored again in thirty fathom and ooze; and riding there all night, in the morning the snow lay a foot thick upon our hatches.

The 22nd day in the morning we weighed and went again to the place where we lost our men and our boat. We had sight of fourteen boats, and some came near to us, but we could learn nothing of our men. Among the rest, we enticed one boat to our ship's side with a bell, and in giving him the bell we took him and his boat, and so kept him; and so rowed down to Thomas Williams Island and there anchored all night . . .

After 4 days some of them showed themselves upon the firm land, but not where they were before. Our General [Frobisher], very glad thereof, supposing to hear of our men, went from the island, with the boat and sufficient company with him. They seemed very glad, and allured him about a certain point of the land, behind which they might perceive a company of the crafty villains to lie lurking; whom our General would not deal withal, for that he knew not what company they were, and so with few signs dismissed them and returned to his company.

Another time, as our said General was coasting the country with two little pinnaces whereby at our return he might make the better relation thereof, three of the crafty villains with a white skin allured us to them. Once again our General, for that he hoped to hear of his men, went towards them. At our coming near the shore whereon they were, we might perceive a number of them lie hidden behind great stones, and those 3 in sight labouring by all means possible that some would come on land; and perceiving we made no haste by words nor friendly signs, which they used by clapping of their hands, and being without weapon and but 3 in sight, they sought further means to provoke us thereunto. One alone laid flesh on the shore, which we took up with the boat-hook, as necessary victuals for the relieving of the man, woman, and child whom we had taken, for that as yet they could not digest our meat; whereby they perceived themselves deceived of their expectation for all their crafty allurements. Yet once again to make as it were a full show of their crafty natures and subtle sleights, to the intent thereby to have entrapped and taken some of our men, one of them counterfeited himself impotent and lame of his legs, who seemed to descend to the waterside with great difficulty; and to cover his craft the more, one of his fellows came down with him, and in such places where he seemed unable to pass he took him on his shoulders, set him by the waterside, and departed from him, leaving him, as it should seem, all alone; who, playing his counterfeit pageant very well, thought thereby to provoke some of us to come on shore, not fearing but that one of us might make our party good with a lame man.

Our General, having compassion of his impotency, thought good, if it were possible, to cure him thereof; wherefore he caused a soldier to shoot at him with his caliver, which grazed before his face. The counterfeit villain deliverly fled, without any impediment at all, and got him to his bows and arrows, and the rest from their lurking-holes with their weapons, bows, arrows, slings, and darts. Our General caused some calivers to be shot off at them, whereby, some being hurt, they might hereafter stand in more fear of us. This was all the answer for this time we could have of our men or of our General's letter. Their craft dealing at these three several times being thus manifest unto us may plainly show their disposition in other things to be correspondent. We judged that they used these stratagems thereby to have caught some of us, for the delivering of the man, woman, and child whom we had taken.

They are men of a large corporature and good proportion. Their colour is not much unlike the sunburnt countryman, who laboureth daily in the sun for his living. They wear their hair something long, and cut before, either with stone or knife, very disorderly. Their women wear their hair long, and knit up with two loops showing forth on either side of their faces, and the rest folded upon a knot. Also some of their women race their faces proportionally, as chin, cheeks, and forehead, and the wrists of their hand, whereupon they lay a colour which continueth dark azurine.

They eat their meat all raw, both flesh, fish, and fowl, or something parboiled with blood and a little water, which they drink. For lack of water they will eat ice that is hard frozen as pleasantly as we will do sugar-candy or other sugar. If they for necessity's sake stand in need of the premises, such grass as the country yieldeth they pluck up and eat, not daintily or salad-wise to allure their stomachs to appetite, but for necessity's sake, without either salt, oils, or washing, like brute beasts devouring the same. They neither use table, stool, or table-cloth for comeliness, but when they are embrued with blood knuckle-deep, and their knives in like sort, they use their tongues as apt instruments to lick them clean, in doing whereof they are assured to lose none of their victuals.

They frank or keep certain dogs not much unlike wolves, which they yoke together as we do oxen and horses, to a sled or trail, and so carry their necessities over the ice and snow from place to place; as the captive whom we have made perfect signs. And when those dogs are not apt for the same use, or when with hunger they are constrained for lack of other victuals, they eat them, so that they are as needful for them, in respect of their bigness, as our oxen are for us.

They apparel themselves in the skins of such beasts as they kill, sewn together with the sinews of them. All the fowl which they kill they skin, and make thereof one kind of garment or other to defend them from the cold. They make their apparel with hoods and tails, which tails they give when they think to gratify any friendship shown unto them: a great sign of friendship with them. The men have them not so side as the women.

The men and women wear their hose close to their legs, from the waist to the knee without any open before, as well the one kind as the other. Upon their legs they wear hose of leather with the fur side inward, two or three pair on at once, and especially the women. In those hose they put their knives, needles, and other things needful to bear about. They put a bone within their hose, which reacheth from the foot to the knee, whereupon they draw their said hose, and so in place of garters they are held from falling down about their feet. They dress their skins very soft and supple, with the hair on. In cold weather or winter they wear the fur side inward, and in summer outward. Other apparel they have none but the said skins.

Those beasts, fishes, and fowls which they kill are their meat, drink, apparel, houses, bedding, hose, shoes, thread, and sails for their boats, with many other necessaries whereof they stand in need and almost all their riches ...

What knowledge they have of God, or what idol they adore, we have no perfect intelligence. I think them rather anthropophagi, or devourers of man's flesh, than otherwise, for that there is no flesh or fish which they find dead, smell it never so filthily, but they will eat it as they find it without any other dressing; a loathsome thing, either to the beholders or hearers.

There is no manner of creeping beast hurtful except some spiders (which as many affirm are signs of great store of gold), and also certain stinging gnats, which bite fiercely that the place where they bite shortly after swelleth and itcheth very sore.

They make signs of certain people that wear bright plates of gold in their foreheads and other places of their bodies.

The countries on both sides the straits lie very high with rough stony mountains and great quantity of snow thereon. There is very little plain ground, and no grass, except a little which is much like unto moss that groweth on soft ground such as we get turfs in. There is no wood at all. To be brief, there is nothing fit or profitable for the use of man which that country with root yieldeth or bringeth forth. Howbeit there is great quantity of deer, whose skins are like unto asses'; their heads or horns do far exceed, as well in length as also in breadth, any in these our parts or countries. Their feet likewise are as great as our oxen's, which we measured to be seven or eight inches in breadth. There are also hares, wolves, fishing-bears, and sea-fowl of sundry sorts. As the country is barren and unfertile, so are they rude and of no capacity to culture the same to any perfection, but are contented by their hunting, fishing, and fowling, with raw flesh and warm blood to satisfy their greedy paunches, which is their only glory.

There is great likelihood of earthquakes or thunder, for that there are huge and monstrous mountains, whose greatest substance are stones, and those stones so shaken with some extraordinary means that one is separated from another, which is discordant from all other quarries.

Second Voyage of Master Martin Frobisher, made to the West and North West regions in the year 1577, with a description of the country and people

FRANCIS DRAKE
c.1540–96
Our General, contented with the spoil of the ships, left the town and put off again to sea.

The English privateer and navigator Sir Francis Drake was born near Tavistock, one of twelve children, into a Puritan family that fled from Devon to Kent in 1549 to avoid persecution by Catholics. At thirteen he was at sea, by 1565 voyaging to Guinea and the Spanish Main. He was given his first command in 1567; his ship was one of a fleet under Sir John Hawkins, on a venture to the Gulf of Mexico. It was a disaster – all but two ships were sunk by the Spanish – but Drake soon made good his losses. In 1572, with a privateer's licence from Queen Elizabeth, who quietly encouraged his bold, piratical ventures that so irritated the Spanish, he led a marauding expedition, destroying and pillaging Spanish colonies on the Isthmus of Panama, where he became the first Englishman to see the Pacific. He returned with a mass of bullion, including 30 tons of silver plundered from a mule train. His reputation riding high, he helped put down an Irish rebellion, from 1573 to 1576, then embarked on a journey that aimed to reach the Pacific he had so tantalizingly seen five years earlier.

Drake's intention was to sail round the Horn, through the strait discovered by Magellan. This was the only practicable sea route to the East Indies except via the Cape of Good Hope, which was guarded by the Portuguese. Winds and currents in the Magellan Strait were so unpredictable that some held this venture more dangerous than attempting the North-East or North-West Passage. Three ships made it through, but they were now met with a tempest. One vessel was lost and another returned home, leaving Drake to carry on alone with the *Golden Hind*. As he proceeded up the west coast of South America, he plundered Spanish colonies in Chile and Peru and captured treasure bound for Panama. To avoid being confronted by the Spanish on his return journey, Drake sailed back to Britain across the Pacific, having failed to find a strait further up the coast (i.e. the North-West Passage) that would lead him back to the Atlantic. His journey took him to the Spice Islands – the six tons of cloves he took on board almost wrecked the ship, and much had to be jettisoned when it struck a reef off the Celebes – then around the Cape of Good Hope and home. It was a financial and navigational triumph; he was knighted aboard the *Golden Hind* in 1580 by Elizabeth, who had made a 5,000 per cent profit on her investment.

Having served briefly as a member of parliament, Drake's subsequent career consisted of a string of raids on Spanish possessions. Having destroyed St Augustine in present-day Florida, he visited the ailing English colony in the New World, Roanoke Island, established by Sir Walter Raleigh off North Carolina, and brought the settlers home. In 1587 Drake destroyed much of the Spanish fleet, 'singeing the King of Spain's beard' at Cadiz, and was instrumental in defeating the invading Armada after first finishing his game of bowls in Plymouth, there being, apparently, time to 'win this game and to thrash the Spanish too' – actually a matter of having to wait for the tide. In so doing, he helped end Spanish naval supremacy, and curtailed their world exploration.

The last act of his illustrious career was a failure: with a fleet of twenty-seven ships, he attempted major incursions against the Spanish in the West Indies. They failed in both their attempt on Puerto Rico and their bid to

sack Panama. Retreating in disarray, Drake   sea, off the coast at Portobelo, a town he had
became ill with dysentery and was buried at   destroyed 24 years before.

Plundering off the South American coast

To Lima we came the 13th day of February; and, being entered the haven, we
found there about twelve sail of ships lying fast moored at an anchor, having
all their sails carried on shore; for the masters and merchants were here most
secure, having never been assaulted by enemies, and at this time feared the
approach of none such as we were. Our General rifled these ships, and found
in one of them a chest full of riyals of plate, and good store of silks and linen
cloth; and took the chest into his own ship, and good store of the silks and
linen. In which ship he had news of another ship called the *Cacafuego*, which
was gone towards Paita, and that the same ship was laden with treasure.
Whereupon we stayed no longer here, but, cutting all the cables of the ships
in the haven, we let them drive whither they would either to sea or to the
shore; and with all speed we followed the *Cacafuego* toward Paita, thinking
there to have found her. But before we arrived there she was gone from thence
towards Panama; whom our General still pursued, and by the way met with a
bark laden with ropes and tackle for ships, which he boarded and searched,
and found in her 80 lb weight of gold, and a crucifix of gold with goodly great
emeralds set in it, which he took, and some of the cordage also for his own
ship.

From hence we departed, still following the *Cacafuego*; and our General
promised our company that whosoever could first descry her should have his
chain of gold for his good news. It fortuned that John Drake, going up into
the top, descried her about three of the clock. And about six of the clock we
came to her and boarded her, and shot at her three pieces of ordnance, and
struck down her mizen; and, being entered, we found in her great riches, as
jewels and precious stones, thirteen chests full of riyals of plate, fourscore
pound weight of gold, and six-and-twenty ton of silver. The place where we
took this prize was called Cape de San Francisco, about 150 leagues from
Panama.

The pilot's name of this ship was Francisco; and amongst other plate that
our General found in this ship he found two very fair gilt bowls of silver,
which were the pilot's. To whom our General said, 'Señor Pilot, you have here
two silver cups, but I must needs have one of them', which the pilot, because
he could not otherwise choose, yielded unto, and gave the other to the steward
of our General's ships. When this pilot departed from us, his boy said thus

unto our General; 'Captain, our ship shall be called no more the *Cacafuego*, but the *Cacaplata*, and your ship shall be called the *Cacafuego*.' Which pretty speech of the pilot's boy ministered matter of laughter to us, both then and long after.

When our General had done what he would with this *Cacafuego*, he cast her off, and we went on our course still towards the west; and not long after met with a ship laden with linen cloth and fine China dishes of white earth, and great store of China silks, of all which things we took as we listed. The owner himself of this ship was in her, who was a Spanish gentleman from whom our General took a falcon of gold with a great emerald in the breast thereof; and the pilot of the ship he took also with him, and so cast the ship off.

This pilot brought us to the haven of Guatulco, the town whereof, as he told us, had but 17 Spaniards in it. As soon as we were entered this haven, we landed, and went presently to the town, and to the town-house where we found a judge sitting in judgment, being associate with three other officers, upon three negroes that had conspired the burning of the town. Both which judges and prisoners we took, and brought them a-shipboard, and caused the chief judge to write his letter to the town to command all the townsmen to avoid, that we might safely water there. Which being done, and they departed, we ransacked the town; and in one house we found a pot, of the quantity of a bushel, full of riyals of plate, which we brought to our ship. And here one Thomas Moone, one of our company, took a Spanish gentleman as he was flying out of the town; and, searching him, he found a chain of gold about him, and other jewels, which he took, and so let him go.

'The people of the country'

The 5th day of June, being in 43 degrees towards the pole arctic, we found the air so cold that our men, being grievously pinched with the same, complained of the extremity thereof; and the further we went, the more the cold increased upon us. Whereupon we thought it best for that time to seek the land, and did so, finding it not mountainous, but low plain land, till we came within 38 degrees towards the line. In which height it pleased God to send us into a fair and good bay, with a good wind to enter the same. In this bay we anchored; and the people of the country, having their houses close by the water's side, showed themselves unto us, and sent a present to our General. When they came unto us, they greatly wondered at the things that we brought. But our

General, according to his natural and accustomed humanity, courteously entreated them, and liberally bestowed on them necessary things to cover their nakedness; whereupon they supposed us to be gods, and would not be persuaded to the contrary. The presents which they sent to our General were feathers, and cauls of net-work.

Their houses are digged round about with earth, and have from the outermost brims of the circle clefts of wood set upon them, joining close together at the top like a spire steeple, which by reason of that closeness are very warm. Their beds is the ground with rushes strewed on it; and lying about the house, have the fire in the midst. The men go naked; the women take bulrushes, and comb them after the manner of hemp, and thereof make their loose garments, which being knit about their middles, hang down about their hips, having also about their shoulders a skin of deer with the hair upon it. These women are very obedient and serviceable to their husbands.

After they were departed from us, they came and visited us the second time, and brought with them feathers and bags of tobacco for presents. And when they came to the top of the hill, at the bottom whereof we had pitched our tents, they stayed themselves; where one appointed for speaker wearied himself with making a long oration, which done, they left their bows upon the hill, and came down with their presents. In the meantime the women, remaining upon the hill, tormented themselves lamentably, tearing their flesh from their cheeks, whereby we perceived that they were about a sacrifice. In the meantime our General with his company went to prayer, and to reading of the Scriptures, at which exercise they were attentive, and seemed greatly to be affected with it; but when they were come unto us, they restored again unto us those things which before we bestowed upon them.

The news of our being there being spread through the country, the people that inhabited round about came down, and amongst them the king himself, a man of a goodly stature and comely personage, with many other tall and warlike men; before whose coming were sent two ambassadors to our General, to signify that their king was coming, in doing of which message their speech was continued about half an hour. This ended, they by signs requested our General to send something by their hand to their king, as a token that his coming might be in peace. Wherein our General having satisfied them, they returned with glad tidings to their king, who marched to us with a princely majesty, the people crying continually after their manner; and as they drew near unto us, so did they strive to behave themselves in their actions with comeliness.

In the fore-front was a man of a goodly personage, who bore the sceptre or mace before the king, whereupon hanged two crowns, a less and a bigger, with three chains of a marvellous length. The crowns were made of knit work, wrought artificially with feathers of divers colours. The chains were made of a bony substance, and few be the persons among them that are admitted to wear them; and of that number also the persons are stinted, as some ten, some 12, etc. Next unto him which bore the sceptre was the king himself, with his guard about his person clad with coney skins, and other skins. After them followed the naked common sort of people, every one having his face painted, some with white, some with black, and other colours, and having in their hands one thing or another for a present, not so much as their children but they also brought their presents.

In the meantime our General gathered his men together, and marched within his fenced place, making against their approaching a very warlike show. They being trooped together in their order, and a general salutation being made, there was presently a general silence. Then he that bore the sceptre before the king, being informed by another whom they assigned to that office, with a manly and lofty voice proclaimed that which the other spoke to him in secret, continuing half an hour. Which ended, and a general Amen, as it were, given, the king with the whole number of men and women, the children excepted, came down without any weapon; who, descending to the foot of the hill, set themselves in order.

In coming towards our bulwarks and tents, the sceptre-bearer began a song, observing his measures in a dance, and that with a stately countenance; whom the king with his guard, and every degree of persons, following, did in like manner sing and dance, saving only the women, which danced and kept silence. The General permitted them to enter within our bulwark, where they continued their song and dance a reasonable time. When they had satisfied themselves, they made signs to our General to sit down; to whom the king and divers other made several orations, or rather supplications, that he would take their province and kingdom into his hand, and become their king, making signs that they would resign unto him their right and title of the whole land, and become his subjects. In which, to persuade us the better, the king and the rest, with one consent, and with great reverence joyfully singing a song, did set the crown upon his head, enriched his neck with all their chains, and offered unto him many other things, honouring him by the name of *Hioh*, adding thereunto, as it seemed, a sign of triumph; which thing our General thought not meet to reject, because he knew not what honour and profit it might be to our country. Wherefore, in the name and to the use of

Her Majesty, he took the sceptre, crown, and dignity of the said country into his hands, wishing that the riches and treasure thereof might so conveniently be transported to the enriching of her kingdom at home, as it aboundeth in the same.

Composite narrative by John Cooke and possibly William Legg, taken from Richard Hakluyt's *The famous Voyage of Sir Francis Drake into the South Sea and therehence about the whole globe of the earth, begun in the year of our Lord 1577*

WILLIAM DAMPIER
1652–1715

Though they have no Names among themselves, they love to have Names given them by the English.

William Dampier – English navigator, map-maker and buccaneer – went to sea when orphaned at sixteen. Assistant manager of a Jamaican plantation at twenty-two, he then began a career that alternated between transporting timber in Central America and being a Caribbean pirate. His next journeys, which were meticulously logged and charted, established him as a distinguished explorer and hydrographer. Dampier sailed from Virginia to Africa, then back across the Atlantic to Cape Horn in 1683; he continued west, crossing the Pacific to China, dipped south to Australia, then Sumatra and eventually reached England in 1691.

The publication of his extremely popular *New Voyage Round the World* (1697) brought him great fame and sparked wide interest in the Pacific, leading to his government appointment as leader of a naval expedition to explore the South Seas in 1699. Charting the currents and coastlines of Australia and New Guinea, he discovered that New Britain was an island, and gave it that name.

Dampier returned to the Pacific in 1703, in command of a privateering expedition, even though the previous year a court martial had found him guilty of cruelty. The voyage, an unprofitable venture that lasted four years, led to his crew laying charges of brutality, drunkenness and even cowardice against him. It was during this trip that the Scottish mariner Alexander Selkirk, the model for Defoe's Robinson Crusoe, asked to be marooned on the Juan Fernandez Islands rather than face his particularly 'leaky' ship and its inept captain.*

Dampier made only one more privateering expedition, now demoted to pilot, and in the course of it rescued Selkirk, who had now endured five years alone. Dampier died penniless, his embittered *Vindication* having failed to restore his reputation.

—

* The next British party to visit the islands included Captain Woodes Rogers, who tells how they approached the shore cautiously, sending one armed party, and – when that failed to return, another – 'for we were afraid that the Spaniards had a garrison there, and might have seized 'em.' When their rowing boat returned, they not only had with them an 'abundance of crawfish' but a strange man 'clothed in goat skins, who looked wilder than the first owners of them'.

The way Rogers tells it in his *A Cruising Voyage Around the World* (1712), we see a man who, destitute on the island, had utterly adapted to a new life. We learn that 'at first he never ate anything till hunger constrained him, partly for grief, and partly for want of bread and salt'. But soon he was making fire, 'rubbing two sticks of piemento together upon his knee, a wood which served him both for firing and candle, and refreshed him with its fragrant smell'. He then lived off goats left by passing sailors – 'He soon wore out all his shoes and clothes by running through the woods; and at last was forced to shift without them, his feet became so hard, that he ran everywhere without annoyance.' The transformation had begun: 'when his [gun-]powder failed, he took them [goats] by speed of foot; for his way of living and continual exercise of walking and running, cleared him of all gross humours so that he ran with wonderful swiftness through the woods and up the rocks and hills, as we perceived when we employed him to catch goats for us. We had a bull dog which we sent with several of our nimblest runners to help him in catching goats; but he distanced and tired both the dog and the men, catched the goats, and brought 'em to us on his back.'

Nor was his improvement merely physical. He 'employed himself in reading, singing psalms, and praying; so that he said he was a better Christian while in solitude than ever he was before, or than, he was afraid, he should ever be again.' He gained, while those who had abandoned him lost – 'the ship which left him being cast away not long after, and few of the company escaped'.

Creatures of the Galapagos Islands

The Isles of *Gallapagos* are a good Number of large Islands, situate under and on both Sides the Line, destitute of Inhabitants; the Eastermost of them being 110 Leagues from the Continent. According to their Position in the Maps, they are in the Longitude of 181, extending to the West as far as 176; according to which, the Longitude from *England* West, is 68°; though, I doubt, the hydrographical Charts have not placed them far enough to the West. The *Spaniards*, who were the first Discoverers of them, describe them to be a great Number of Isles extending North-west from the Equator to 5° North. We saw no more than fourteen or fifteen, some of which were seven or eight Leagues in Length, and three or four in Breadth, pretty high and flat; four or five of the Eastermost we found rocky and barren, without either Trees, Herbs, or Grass, except what was very near the Sea-side. These Islands produce also the Dildo-tree, a sort of a Shrub of the Bigness of a Man's Leg, and ten or twelve Feet high, but without either Fruit or Leaves, instead whereof, it has sharp Prickles from Top to Bottom. These Islands afford also some Water in Ponds, and Cavities of the Rocks. Some of the Isles are low, and more fertile, and produce Trees known in *Europe*. Some of the Westermost Isles are bigger than the rest, being nine or ten Leagues long, and six or seven broad, and afford many Sorts of Trees, especially Mammee-figs; they have also some pretty large fresh-water Rivers, and many Rivulets. As the Sea-breezes by Day, and the Night Winds, without. Intermission, refresh the Air of the Isles *Gallapagos*, so they are not so much troubled with excessive Heats, nor so unwholsome, as most other Places near the Equator: During the rainy Seasons, in *November*, *December*, and *January*, they are pestered with most violent Tempests, Thunder, and Lightning: Before and after these Months, they have refreshing Showers; and their Summer Season in *May*, *June*, *July*, and *August*, without any Rains. We anchored near several of those Islands, and found frequently the Sea Tortoises sunning themselves at Noonday (a thing not usual in most other Places). Of these we killed as many as we wanted. Captain *Davis*, at another time, came to an Anchor on the West Side of these Isles, where he and his Men fed upon Land Tortoises for three Months, and saved sixty Jars of Oil from them. He met also on that Side with divers good Chanels, and Anchorage betwixt the Isles, several fresh-water Rivulets, and Store of good Trees and Fuel. Captain *Harris* (of whom hereafter) found also in some of these Islands abundance of Mammee-trees, and divers large Rivers. The Sea, adjoining to these Islands, is well stored with good and large Fish, especially with Sharks. I took the Height of the Sun with

an Astrolabe. At the North-end of the second Isle we anchored at 28' North
from the Line.

Robinson Crusoe's island

March 24. we got in Sight of the Isle of *John Fernandez*, and soon after came to
an Anchor, in a Bay at the South End, in 25 Fathom Water, within two Cables
Length of the Shore. We sent immediately to look after a *Muskito* Man we had
been forced to leave there three Years before; and who, notwithstanding all the
Search made by the *Spaniards* after him, had kept himself concealed in the
Woods. When he was left there by Captain *Watling*, (after Captain *Sharpe* was
turned out) he had with him a Gun, a Knife, and some Powder and Shot,
which being all spent, he sawed his Gun-Barrel into small Pieces, and these he
made up into Harpoons, Hooks, and suchlike Instruments; all which, though
it may seem strange, yet is commonly practised among the *Muskito Indians*,
who make all their Instruments without either Forge or Anvil. And the other
Indians, who have not the Use of Iron from the *Europeans*, make their
Hatchets, wherewith they cut their Timber and Wood, of a very hard Stone. In
the Hollowing out of their Canoes, they make use of Fire besides. The Stone
Hatchets of the *Indians*, near *Blewfield River*, are ten Inches long, fourteen
broad, and two Inches thick in the Middle, ground away flat and sharp at both
Ends; the Handle is in the Midst, being a deep Knotch, of a Finger's Length,
which they bind round with a Withe of about four Feet long. Thus the *Indians*
of *Patagonia* head their Arrows very artificially with grounded Flints: With
these before-mentioned Instruments our *Muskito* Man used to strike Goats
and Fish for his Subsistence; his Hut being half a Mile from the Sea-side, made
of Goats-skins; as was his Bed, the same serving likewise for his Cloathing;
those he had, when he was left, being quite worn out. We had no sooner
landed, than another *Muskito*, aboard our Ship, ran to meet his Country man,
and, after he had thrown himself on his Face upon the Ground, embraced
him with all the Marks of Tenderness; which Ceremony being over, he came
to salute us his old Friends. His Name was *Will*, and the other's *Robert*: For,
though they have no Names among themselves, they love to have Names given
them by the *English*.

Captain William Dampier's first voyage round the world, collected from his own account, in
Navigantium Atque Itinerantium Bibliotheca, 1764

I treat them as a Wise man shou'd his Wife, am very complaisant in trifles, and immoveable in matters of importance.

Benjamin Bloome and Joshua Charlton founded the settlement of Benkulen, West Sumatra, in 1685; Joseph Collet arrived as the settlement's deputy governor in 1712.

By the seventeenth century European influence had spread around the globe thanks to the power of their fleets. They serviced whatever trading colonies they could defend. One such British outpost was on Sumatra. Long forgotten now, like so many other tragic little outposts of seafaring nations, the 300-mile coastal strip placed Britain in the heart of the Spice Islands for 140 years, from its settlement in 1685, when the East India Company soon discovered it was a malaria-ridden graveyard, until 1824, when it effectively closed under the administration of Sir Thomas Stamford Raffles. On 17 March that year, the British conceded all rights to the island to the Dutch; at the same time Raffles, an Oriental scholar, and founder of the London Zoo, formed a colony – without authority – in Singapore to counter Dutch influence in the region.

The Benkulen enterprise was one of the first British ventures into colonial rule in South-East Asia, and not a triumph. A bitter struggle between the Dutch and English East India Companies for control of the west Java trade in pepper was drawing them dangerously close to total conflict. The Dutch already had control of nutmeg, mace, cloves and cinnamon. In 1682 they managed to secure the elevation of a sympathetic young sultan, who in return gave them exclusive rights in his territories, which enabled them to charge extortionate rates for pepper. British officials from Madras were sent to locate sympathetic rulers elsewhere, and in

June 1685, under the terms of a treaty with Sumatran rulers, an expedition under Ralph Ord arrived in Benkulen, despite the presence of Dutch ships sent there earlier to try to forestall them.

Sickness, from malaria, dysentery and a dissolute life on a fetid coast so reduced the ranks that within three months only eleven of the settlers were strong enough to hold a musket. John Bastin, who found the correspondence I quote here, wrote, 'The Bombay proverb that two monsoons were the life of a man applied with even fewer exceptions in west Sumatra.'

The building of British defences progressed slowly and badly, not helped by the engineer dying within a few months of arrival. It soon became clear that Fort York's foundations were unsound. William Dampier, serving as a gunner, wrote that it was 'the most irregular piece' of defensive work he had ever seen and that the 'Guns often fall down into the Ditches'. Thirty years later, under the competent rule of Joseph Collet, Fort York was finally abandoned, but only after a quarter of a million pounds sterling of the British East India Company's money had been squandered on its repair. A new defensive work, Fort Marlborough, was erected two miles further south, and stands to this day.

As for the pepper itself, the signs had been promising. Supplies poured in at first, but dried up as lesser rulers demanded a part in the trade. The British felt themselves in a vulnerable position, owing to pressure from the Dutch and the depletion of the settlers due to disease, and so took firm measures. William Dampier, not the most liberal of commanders himself, in 1690 found two neighbouring rulers in stocks, 'For no other Reason but because they had not brought down to the Fort such a quantity of Pepper that the Governour had sent for'.

It wasn't until the humane and energetic Joseph Collet took over as deputy governor in 1712 that Benkulen enjoyed competent rule and good relations were established with the locals, who, he asserted, were 'not the Brutes they have been represented, they can dis-tinguish between Justice and Villany, Kind-ness and Cruelty'.

His principles were soon forgotten, how-ever. After his departure in 1716, relations deteriorated dramatically, and in 1719 a rebel-lion forced the British to flee altogether. When Benkulen was reoccupied a few years later, the treaty was substantially modified, with the pepper production obligations halved.

Letters from Benjamin Bloome and Joshua Charlton to the Madras government, October 1685

On ye 26th ye Young King came downe to wellcome us, wth whom passed little or noe Materiall discourse, save only that he enquired of us whether ye intent of our comeing was to buy Pepper onely, & soe to be gone, or to Settle here: for if yt our designe was to settle here yt then whatever Pepper was in ye Country, wee might expect to have, or othere waise ye Dutch who being soe nigh ym, I mean at Sillibar, would, after yt wee were gone, prove troub[le]some to them for Selling their Pepper to ye English. And therefore, unlesse wee would dwell & abide wth ym, none would sell us Pepper. Wee told them our Aime was to Settle if upon good termes. Hee replyed yt wee could not be soe ready to ask as hee Should bee to grant.

[*After nearly two and a half months . . .*]

Notwithstand[ing] our owne People yt have workt dayly thereon, ye work is very backward, for ever Since we have been here wee can Scarce Say yt wee have had eight dayes together wthout raine, wch hath fallen in Soe Violent a Manner that it hath soe Much hindred our designe that in four months time noe more then one bastion or bulworke to the Seaward is in any forward-nesse, wch long e'r this might have been finished, but ye raines are soe great here yt in one night they have layd even to the ground yt wch hath cost a fortnights building. Soe finding we have all this while been washing a black-moor white, have Resolved to pallassade our Selves in, for ye greater Securety, takeing in halfe ye ground Mr Fowles hath Lined out for a ffort and all ye meanes hee could invent was not enough to Make his worke wth stand ye raines, for Turffeing, wch was thought to stand against all raines, hath Sever-all times been washed away, & now at this instant ye whole bulworke, wch hath been all this tyme adoeing, will by ye first Raine be certainely all washed away, for it is wholly crackt soe yt nothing can be done wthout bricks which our people hath endeavoured to make, but ye Earth is not good, for when they come to burne them they will not abid ye fire, soe that Bricks and all other Meterialls for ye raiseing of a building of that Nature must be Sent hither, if yor Honr &c Shall think convenient yt wee here remaine and fortifie . . .

Wee Shall now give yor Honr an Accot of our wofull State and Condition, wch god grant better. Wee are by Sicknesse all become uncapable of helping one another & of ye great Number of people that came over not above thirty men [are] well. Of them yt Mr Ord left here, being black and whites, abt takeing abot 20 Souldiers & Severall black Servants along wth him: of ye English souldeirs are dead here 11: & of ye Portugueese not [a]bove 4: of ye black workmen not above 15 yt is capable of working; of them are dead abt 40 & dayly die, for he that falls it is hard for him to rise. All our Servants are Sick & dead, & at this Minute not a Cooke to gett victualls ready for those that Sett at the Compas table, and Such have been our straites yt wee many times have fasted. Ye Sick lyes Neglected, some cry for remedies but none [are] to bee had: those that could eate have none to Cooke ym victualls, soe yt I may say ye one dies for hunger & ye other for want of Remidies, soe yt wee now have not liveing to bury ye dead, & if one is sick ye other will not watch, for hee Sayes that better one then two dies, Soc that people dies & noe notice [is] taken thereof.

October 2. Ao. 1685. Mr Fowles this day died, to whome wee have Paid noe wages Since he came here, Soe humbly desire yor Honor &c will Please to pay to his widdow what will be due to him.

Letter from Joseph Collet, September 1712

As to my Progress in business here . . . I have begun with matters of the greatest Importance. I have been obliged to some severities unknown here and yet at the same time wisht for a Power to inflict greater Penalties. One I have confin'd, another I have broke for lewdness and cowardness, and shall send them both for England in the Ship this comes by, together with a couple of infamous Women.

I have also shewn favour to some that have been faulty in less Degree who profess'd their Repentance and promised amendment . . .

I find myself oblig'd to ride with a very strait rein, having already cut off three parts in four of the perquisites and proffitts arising as well from the Governour's as all other inferior Posts. You may be sure this makes the losers Uneasy . . .

Perhaps you have a mind to know the little trifles of life that are different here from my former fashions . . . About 7 I eat a good breakfast of bread and butter and Bohea Tea. And note by the way that my Butter does not come much short of yours made at Hackney. I then sett to work till Twelve, either in Councill if there be occasion to call one, or in my own Chamber. At 12 I tiff [take luncheon], that is eat a (———) of boiled Chicken or Pidgeon, Crawfish, Crabbs, or Prawns, all excellent in their kind, or some good relishing bit, and Drink a good Draught out of the Punch-bowle. Then Dinner enters which always consists of 4 or 5 Dishes. We drink moderately at Table, take a Pipe for Digesting and then to work again. If I find it possible to get so much time, I go out at 4 and either ride or walk till six. If I ride I have a Horse Guard attending me and the Union Flagg carry'd before me. I have also a foot Guard of Buggess Soldiers who generally keep way with me. If I walk, I have 4 men with Blunderbusses go before and a Guard of Buggess to bring up the rear. If I dine abroad or shou'd lye out of the Fort, which I have not yet done, the number of my Guard is encreased.

At six I come home and sitt again and then to Supper. I take a Pipe or two with a chearfull Glass and then to my Chamber, where I either sit to business or what else is proper before my going to bed. I have two servants and two slaves of my own, one of them a female too, but not a present of any king, as our friend Mr Leigh waggishly inform'd us. However to prevent scandal I keep her in another Family where she works for me, ironing, etc. but never comes into my house. And let me tell you a very little share of Virtue is sufficient to secure a man from all the Female Charms in this place. Here are but 4 White Women, two of which as I told you before come home with this. Of the other two one of them is now actually kept Dark, Blouded etc. and the other is a Woman of the most indifferent personage but yet of consummate virtue. I have not heard the lest blemish of any part of her character. The rest are all blacks and a man that ventures on them seldom fails to gett the Bencoolen feaver.

All the People that have dyed here since my arrivall which are but few, have apparently been destroy'd by Drinking or Women. There has not one of our private centinells been buried these 10 months which I ascribe to their not having the oppertunity of Drinking so deep as their betters . . .

The British in West Sumatra 1685–1825 (1965)

JAMES COOK
1728–79

The man now trembled very visibly . . . upon which Captain Cook coming up to him, took hold of his hand, and embraced him, touching the man's nose with his own, which is their mode of salutation.

Born in Cleveland, Yorkshire, the son of a farm labourer, Cook became apprentice to Whitby shipwrights and enlisted in the Royal Navy in 1755. As navigator of the *Pembroke*, his charting of the St Lawrence River contributed, perhaps decisively, to the success of General Wolfe's amphibious assault on Quebec. He subsequently spent five summers (1763–7) charting the coast of Newfoundland, his investigative rigour coming to the notice of the leading scientists, who in 1768 dispatched him in the *Endeavour* to convey a scientific expedition to Tahiti. There a makeshift observatory was erected to observe the transit of Venus across the sun; a young Joseph Banks was the leader of the botanical party. Cook also had orders to seek a southern continent – Terra Australis – that geographers had long believed might balance the globe, counteracting the land-masses of Europe and Asia. He mapped and circumnavigated the islands of New Zealand, whose first European discovery had been made by Abel Tasman in 1642, and annexed the entire eastern coast of Australia for Britain.

On his return home in June 1771, the Admiralty organized a second journey, during which Cook made the first circumnavigation of Antarctica. He left England again in July the following year, and with the *Resolution* and the *Adventure* pushed further south in the Pacific than any other European, crossing the Antarctic Circle – 'the regions of perpetual day'. The many hazards he faced – severe winds and seas, floating ice and fogs – prevented Cook from even sighting the continent, but the voyage's greatest accomplishment, from a navigational point of view, was to find nothing: he established that

any possible land-mass must be further south. Cook was the first European to see many Pacific islands – he charted Tonga and Easter Island, and discovered New Caledonia – and, moving around to the Atlantic via Cape Horn, discovered the South Sandwich Islands and South Georgia.

Equally significantly, Cook lost only one man to scurvy by his return in 1775, a remarkable feat for a journey of three years, and accomplished by serving his crew fruit and sauerkraut. Back in England, he was made captain, and elected to the Royal Society. Less than a year later he again set sail. Cook's third and final voyage of discovery, with the Whitby vessel *Resolution* this time accompanied by the *Discovery*, aimed to trace the Pacific end of the long-sought North-West Passage. He revisited many Pacific islands, discovered more, surveyed the Hawaiian group, and in March 1778 at last reached the present-day Oregon coast. He followed the coast north, finally entering the Bering Strait (which divides Asia from North America), and at 70° 44′ was forced to turn back by ice. He returned to the Hawaiian Islands, arriving at Karakakoa Bay in January 1779. The natives were friendly at first, but less accommodating when Cook returned for repairs, having a broken mast. A cutter was stolen, and when on 14 February Cook – who on this voyage had occasional fits of temper – went to investigate, he was stabbed and clubbed to death in the ensuing fracas. The expedition arrived back in England in October of 1780, having sailed again through the Bering Strait to chart the Siberian coast.

Cook's three voyages between 1768 and his death were the culmination of centuries of

European interest in the Pacific. There was much more to be done by his immediate successors George Vancouver and Matthew Flinders, but Cook's work, assisted by Harrison's chronometer (which at last gave a way of accurately determining longitude at sea), opened up vast areas that had only been tentatively probed before and charted them with extraordinary accuracy.* His insistence on a proper diet was a valuable lesson passed on to officers who sailed under him, such as Vancouver and the much slandered William

Bligh, who went on to make important voyages of their own.

Cook was a navigator of genius, and determined to try to understand, not prejudge, alien cultures. He endeavoured to see others on their own terms, a remarkable thing in such a censorious age, and unusual in travellers up until recent times.

The author of the account is George Forster (1754–94), born in Danzig. His father, Johann Reinhold Forster, was the naturalist on Cook's 1772–5 Pacific journey on the *Resolution*, and a pioneering ornithologist of Antarctica, New Zealand and the Pacific. Accompanying his father on the voyage, George proved a knowledgeable and adept observer. His elegant prose, which was loosely based on his father's journal, makes his *A Voyage Round the World* one of the finest works of eighteenth-century travel literature and an account of prime importance in the history of European contact with Pacific peoples. He went on to become a professor of natural history and a German authority on journeys of discovery.

* Until now, when out of sight of land, seafarers estimated their position with the help of an astrolabe, which measured the angle of heavenly bodies. In cloud or fog – when you most needed it – this instrument ceased to have any use. 'It is something to see the pilot,' wrote Eugenio de Salazar in the sixteenth century, 'take the astrolabe in his hand, raise his eyes to the sun, try to get the sun to shine through the openings in the astrolabe, and then give up without being able to complete his measurements properly . . . At times his estimate rises so high that it is 1000 degrees over the mark. And other times it falls so low, that one would not arrive there in a thousand years.'

Fog and scurvy, December 1772

The number of icy masses encreased around us every day, so that we numbered upwards of twenty of a vast size on the 13th in the afternoon. One of them was full of black spots, which were taken for seals by some, and for aquatic birds by others, though we could not find that they even shifted their places. However seals being hitherto looked upon as certain signs of land, we sounded in the evening with a line of one hundred and fifty fathoms, but found no bottom. The latitude we were now in, was that in which Captain Lozier Bouvet had placed his pretended discovery of Cape Circumcision, and our longitude was only a few degrees to the eastward of it: the general expectation of seeing land, was therefore very great, and every little circumstance like the preceding roused all our attention; the clouds a-head were curiously examined at every moment, since every one was eager to be the first to announce the land. We had already had several false alarms from the fallacious conformation of fog-banks, or that of islands of ice half hid in snow storms, and our consort the Adventure had repeatedly made the signals for seeing land, deceived by such appearances: but now, the imagination warmed with the idea of M. Bouvet's discovery, one of our lieutenants, after having repeatedly been up to the mast-head, (about six o'clock in the morning on the 14th) acquainted the captain that he plainly saw the land. This news soon brought up all upon deck: We saw an immense field of flat ice before us, broken into many small pieces on the edges, a vast number of islands of ice of all shapes and sizes rose beyond it as far as the eye could reach, and some of the most distant considerably raised by the hazy vapours which lay on the horizon, had indeed some appearance of mountains. Several of our officers persisted in the opinion that they had seen land here, till Captain Cook, about two years and two months afterwards (in February 1775) on his course from Cape Horn towards the Cape of Good Hope, sailed over the same spot, where they had supposed it to lie, and found neither land nor even ice there at that time. Numbers of pinguins, pintadas, fulmars, snowy and blue petrels attended this vast extent of ice, and different species of cetaceous animals spouted up the water around us: two of them, shorter than other whales, were particularly noticed, in respect of their bulk and of a white or rather fleshy colour . . .

A dead calm which succeeded on the 27th, gave us an opportunity of hoisting the boat out, and going to shoot pinguins and petrels. The chace of pinguins proved very unsuccessful, though it afforded great sport; the birds dived so frequently, continued so long under water, and at times skipped continually into and out of the water, making way with such amazing velocity in a strait line, that we were obliged to give over the pursuit. At last we came near enough to one, to wound it; but though we followed it closely, and fired above ten times with small shot, which we could observe to hit, yet we were at last obliged to kill it with ball. When we took it up, we perceived that its hard, glossy plumage, had continually turned the shot aside. This plumage is extremely thick, and consists of long narrow feathers, which lie above each other as closely as scales, and secure these amphibious birds against the wet, in which they almost constantly live. Their very thick skin and their fat seem wisely appropriated to them by nature, to resist the perpetual winter of these unhospitable climates; their broad belly, the situation of their feet far behind, and their fins, which supply the place of wings, are constructed with equal wisdom to facilitate the progress of their otherwise lumpish bodies through the water . . . We were glad to meet with subjects from whence these little reflections could be drawn. They afforded us a momentary relief from that gloomy uniformity with which we slowly passed dull hours, days, and months in this desolate part of the world.* We were almost perpetually wrapt in thick fogs, beaten with showers of rain, sleet, hail, and snow, the temperature of the air being constantly about the point of congelation in the height of summer; surrounded by innumerable islands of ice against which we daily ran the risk of being shipwrecked, and forced to live upon salt provisions, which concurred with the cold and wet to infect the mass of our blood. These severities naturally inspired a general wish for a happier change of situation and climate, though our seamen coming fresh and strong from England, were not yet dispirited amidst the numberless fatigues and inclemencies to which they were exposed. The prophylactics, with which we had been supplied, and which were regularly served to the crew, namely portable broth, and sour krout, had a wonderful effect in keeping them free from the sea-scurvy. Two or three men however, of a bad habit of body, could not resist this dreadful disease; one of them in particular, George Jackson, a carpenter, fell ill ten days after leaving the Cape; his gums were ulcerous, and his teeth so loose, as to lie sideways. A marmalade of carrots, which had been much recommended was tried, but without success, it having no other effect than that of keeping him open. Our surgeon, Mr Patton, then began the cure with fresh wort, i.e. the infusion of malt, by which he gradually recovered, and in the space of a few weeks, was perfectly cured, his teeth fast, and his gums entirely renewed. As the efficient cause of his complaint still existed, he was obliged to continue the use of wort even after his cure, and by that means was kept free from all scorbutic symptoms. The encomiums on the efficacy of malt cannot be exaggerated, and this useful remedy ought never to be forgotten on board of ships bound on long voyages . . .†

---

* The Arctic explorer Nansen points out with satisfaction the example of one of the Norse pioneers. Othar, a wanderer who around 890 AD had been at the court of Alfred the Great, of whom it had been written, he 'felt an inspiration and a desire to learn, to know, and to demonstrate how far the land stretched towards the north, and if there were any regions inhabited by man northward beyond the desert waste.' A few hundred years on, the thirteenth-century Norse text *Kongespeilet*, or Mirror of Kings, was giving the first scientific descriptions of the Arctic: 'As soon as one has traversed the greater part of the wild sea, one comes upon such a huge quantity of ice that nowhere in the whole world has the like been known.'
† Among the most remarkable of the many eighteenth-century European mariners was Thomas Forrest (c.1729–1802), who plied the seas of South-East Asia, and had his own remedy for scurvy. Whereas contemporaries such as Alexander Dalrymple, and James Rennell had cartographic agencies that championed their work, Forrest's numerous valuable charts and observations have, like those of many others, been forgotten. Forrest's essay, *Thoughts on the Best Mode of Preserving Sea Provision, or of Victualling Ships in Warm Waters*, argued the benefits of tea, coffee and chocolate over 'strong liquors and pernicious grog' and noted how effective a Bengali crew were on a diet of vegetables and fish. He called for sailors to be provided with 'onions, sour crout, French beans, and small cucumbers pickled' in place of meat – but his suggestions were never taken up.

New Zealand, April 1773

As we were returning home, we heard a loud hallooing on the rocky point of an island, which on this occasion obtained the name of Indian Island; and standing in to the shore, we perceived one of the natives, from whom this noise proceeded. He stood with a club or battle-axe in his hand, on a projecting point, and behind him, on the skirts of the wood we saw two women, each of them having a long spear. When our boat came to the foot of the rock, we called to him, in the language of Taheitee, *tayo, harre maï,* 'friend, come hither;' he did not, however, stir from his post, but held a long speech, at certain intervals pronouncing it with great earnestness and vehemence, and swinging round his club, on which he leaned at other times. Captain Cook went to the head of the boat, called to him in a friendly manner, and threw him his own and some other handkerchiefs, which he would not pick up. The captain then taking some sheets of white paper in his hand, landed on the rock unarmed, and held the paper out to the native. The man now trembled very visibly, and having exhibited strong marks of fear in his countenance, took the paper: upon which Captain Cook coming up to him, took hold of his hand, and embraced him, touching the man's nose with his own, which is their mode of salutation. His apprehension was by this means dissipated, and he called to the two women, who came and joined him, while several of us landed to keep the captain company. A short conversation ensued, of which very little was understood on both sides, for want of a competent knowledge of the language. Mr Hodges immediately took sketches of their countenances, and their gestures shewed that they clearly understood what he was doing; on which they called him *tóä-tóä,* that term being probably applicable to the imitative arts. The man's countenance was very pleasing and open; one of the women, which we afterwards believed to be his daughter, was not wholly so disagreeable as one might have expected in New Zeeland, but the other was remarkably ugly, and had a prodigious excrescence on her upper lip. They were all of a dark brown or olive complexion; their hair was black, and curling, and smeared with oil and ruddle; the man wore his tied upon the crown of the head, but the women had it cut short. Their bodies were tolerably well proportioned in the upper part; but they had remarkable slender, ill-made, and bandy legs. Their dress consisted of mats made of the New Zeeland flax-plant, interwoven with feathers; and in their ears they wore small pieces of white albatross skins stained with ruddle or ochre. We offered them some fishes and wild fowl, but they threw them back to us, intimating that they did not want provisions. The approaching night obliged us to retire, not without

promising our new friends a visit the next morning. The man remained silent
and looked after us with composure and great attention, which seemed to
speak a profound meditation; but the youngest of the two women, whose
vociferous volubility of tongue exceeded every thing we had met with, began
to dance at our departure, and continued to be as loud as ever. Our seamen
passed several coarse jests on this occasion, but nothing was more obvious
to us than the general drift of nature, which not only provided man with
a partner to alleviate his cares and sweeten his labours, but endowed that
partner likewise with a desire of pleasing by a superior degree of vivacity
and affability.

The next morning we returned to the natives, and presented them with
several articles which we had brought with us for that purpose. But so much
was the judgment of the man superior to that of his countrymen, and most of
the South Sea nations, that he received almost every thing with indifference,
except what he immediately conceived the use of, such as hatchets and large
spike-nails. At this interview he introduced his whole family to us, consisting
of two women, whom we supposed to be his wives; the young woman, a boy
of about fourteen years of age, and three smaller children, of which the
youngest was at the breast. One of the wives had the excrescence or wen on
the upper lip, and was evidently neglected by the man, probably on account of
her disagreeable appearance. They conducted us soon after to their habitation, which lay but a few yards within the wood, on a low hill, and consisted of
two mean huts, made of a few sticks thatched with unprepared leaves of the
flax-plant, and covered with the bark of trees. In return for our presents they
parted with several of their ornaments and weapons, particularly the battle-
axes, but they did not choose to give us their spears. When we were preparing
to re-embark, the man came to the water-side, and presented to Captain Cook
a dress made of the flax plant, a belt of weeds, some beads made of a little
bird's bones, and some albatross skins. We were at first of opinion that these
were only intended as a retribution for what he had received, but he soon
undeceived us by shewing a strong desire of possessing one of our boat-
cloaks.

Observations made during a Voyage Round the World, on physical geography, natural history,
and ethnic philosophy, 1778

*I was in such a temper that sooner than have made any compensation or apology
I would have suffered death with cheerfulness.*

The letters of John Pope, a junior officer on an English 'country ship', or privately owned merchant vessel, describe his travels aboard the *Princess Royal*, along a key trade route of the era, plying between Calcutta, Bombay, Macao and Canton. Opium and cotton were sold in China, or ports along the way, and the proceeds used to buy tea. Such country ships played a crucial role in extending European penetration into parts of Asia in the eighteenth century and the success of the British country trade helped pave the way for British dominance in India. In later life Pope became Mayor of Bombay and an ardent Orientalist. I include him here not for his contribution to navigation, which was almost nil, but for his evocation of a world little known even to travelled Europeans. This, when he was not getting into trouble for cussing locals, was the object of his exploration: life in the tropical waters of Southern Asia.

Rangoon, a city that 'presents nothing pleasing'

The accounts I hear of this country of Pegu have not given me the most favourable idea of it. I find I must be more circumspect in my conduct than I shall like for they tell me an abusive word or wry look is sufficient to send me to prison, among the horses, and to perhaps get some stripes. Jones returned about 8 o'clock on the following morning bringing with him an old fisherman of the name of Millet as Pilot. We got under way immediately with the flood tide and at noon we were in the river. It is covered down to the margin with wood. Its shores are very steep, no signs of cultivation or inhabitants. We saw, however, a few solitary boats and a hut or two. The river at the entrance may be two or three miles broad but when a mile or two within it scarce exceeds half a mile and some places not near so much. We were boarded by some boats from a kind of guard house called Chopey, who took down our ship's name, cargo, guns etc., in a kind of large pocket book of black paper on which they wrote with a kind of soapy stone like our slate pencil. They were all stout well limbed men of copper colour with a little of the Malay features – a wrapper of silk like a Highlander tartan is the only dress. Their hair made fast atop of their heads with a knot, and immense holes in their ears. They were very profuse in making use of the appellation Klaa, which I find means 'stranger'. They soon quitted us to forward their dispatch, I suppose. And at 5 p.m. we anchored before the city of Rangoon situated on one of the Western branches of the river. I forgot to tell you that we were attacked by a swarm of bees which absolutely bade us defiance. They kept possession of the main mast and would not let us furl our sails till next morning.

The city presents nothing pleasing. It is surrounded with a wall of huge piles, so that the houses in the inclosure are not visible, you only see them in the suburbs, which are built of wood and quite surround the city. There is likewise a town on the opposite bank of the river where there are many small pagodas. You see the top of the principal one which is about a mile and a half from the city towering over the top. It is of immense size and of beautiful workmanship (dedicated to Dagon or Bood). At breakfast the next morning both Mr J. and the Captain enjoined me to behave with propriety – told me the consequence of the most trivial breach of decorum and so lectured me that I became quite impatient and promised everything with an intention, I can assure you, of profiting by their exhortations. But I may say:

> If poor weak women go astray
> Their stars are more in fault than they.

I was sent on shore with the guns, merely to put them on the wharf and come off again. We had nearly finished when I unfortunately called one of my own lascars by the opprobious epithet of 'Hog'. A man who had stood at my elbow the whole time immediately told me in Moors that I must not abuse people in this country. I told him, when I abused him, he had liberty to resent it but in the present case he could have, nay should have, none. Whether I expressed myself with too much violence or what, I was at a loss to know for before I could look round me a couple of evil looking fellows had hold of me by the collar and in spite of my cries, entreaties and resistance they had me to a hall of Justice in a second. The Linguist was sent for, who much against my will got me released for about 20 rupees or Ticalls (which are rude lumps of silver, about the value of a Rupee). I was in such a temper that sooner than have made any compensation or apology I would have suffered death with cheerfulness. However I got out of durance only to hear the reproaches of the Captain, who declared that had he known it I should have stayed a few days longer to humble me – a pretty method of consoling a body who had under-gone the disgrace of being hauled to prison, when innocent. All my protest-ations would not convince him of that so I left him in high dudgeon and went on board, where I had the same ceremony to go through with Mr J. who was likewise sure I was in the wrong. Jones only espoused my cause for which I always shall esteem him. I did not recover from those dislocating pulls for some days.

Free Mariner: John Adolphus Pope in the East Indies, 1992

William Scoresby
1789–1857
The value of the prize . . . cannot be sacrificed to feelings of compassion.

For two decades at the beginning of the nineteenth century, Scoresby was the most successful whaler in Britain, scouring the Arctic to bring back catches. Once when his keel was ripped off by ice and he was unable to stem the leak by the usual method of fothering (blocking the flow with a sail fed in from the outside), he ordered his men to remove the ship's contents, haul the vessel on to the floe and turn it over. During the 120 hours it took to make the repair, Scoresby slept only twelve.

Though only a self-taught scientist, Scoresby's written accounts and drawings of Arctic animals, plants and the behaviour of ice floes, contain a mass of detail – often far more than those produced by people specifically funded to observe them. He examined snowflakes under a microscope, drawing pictures to reveal the hexagonal shape with which we are now so familiar. To cross frozen surfaces he invented 'ice shoes' – like skis, though he had never seen them – and a 'marine diver', an instrument with which he charted how the sea was warmer at depth; he was also the first to suggest that the colours of the Arctic Sea were due to plankton. Furthermore, his eyes seem to have possessed a certain intensity, which he did not understand, and which enabled him to calm and even tame polar bears; these he brought back to Whitby as pets for his friends. Stuck in ice off Greenland in 1818, he simply plunged into a project to make a huge magnet. Eventually, he would develop compasses better than those issued by the Admiralty. His accounts and paintings of whaling incidents convey his sensitivity to the brutality of his business.

Observations on the whale

It goes under the protection of its mother, for probably a year, or more; or until, by the evolution of the whalebone, it is enabled to procure its own nourishment. Supposing the criterion before mentioned, of the notches in the whalebone being indicative of the number of years growth, to be correct, then it would appear that the whale reaches the magnitude called *size*; that is, with a six feet length of whalebone, in twelve years, and attains its full growth at the age of twenty or twenty-five. Whales, doubtless, live to a great age. The marks of age are an increase in the quantity of grey colour in the skin, and a change to a yellowish tinge of the white parts about the head; a decrease in the quantity of oil yielded by a certain weight of blubber; an increase of hardness in the blubber, and in the thickness and strength of the ligamentous fibres of which it is partly composed.

The maternal affection of the whale, which, in other respects, is apparently a stupid animal, is striking and interesting. The cub, being insensible to danger, is easily harpooned; when the tender attachment of the mother is so manifested as not unfrequently to bring it within the reach of the whalers. Hence, though a cub is of little value, seldom producing above a ton of oil, and often less, yet it is sometimes struck as a snare for its mother. In this case, she joins it at the surface of the water, whenever it has occasion to rise for respiration; encourages it to swim off; assists its flight, by taking it under her fin; and seldom deserts it while life remains. She is then dangerous to approach; but affords frequent opportunities for attack. She loses all regard for her own safety, in anxiety for the preservation of her young; – dashes through the midst of her enemies; – despises the danger that threatens her; – and even voluntarily remains with her offspring, after various attacks on herself from the harpoons of the fishers. In June 1811, one of my harpooners struck a sucker, with the hope of its leading to the capture of the mother. Presently she arose close by the 'fast-boat;' and seizing the young one, dragged about a hundred fathoms of line out of the boat with remarkable force and velocity. Again she arose to the surface; darted furiously to and fro; frequently stopped short, or suddenly changed her direction, and gave every possible intimation of extreme agony. For a length of time, she continued thus to act, though closely pursued by the boats; and, inspired with courage and reso-lution by her concern for her offspring, seemed regardless of the danger which surrounded her. At length, one of the boats approached so near, that a harpoon was hove at her. It hit, but did not attach itself. A second harpoon was struck; this also failed to penetrate: but a third was more effectual, and held. Still she did not attempt to escape; but allowed other boats to approach; so that, in a few minutes, three more harpoons were fastened; and, in the course of an hour afterwards, she was killed.

There is something extremely painful in the destruction of a whale, when thus evincing a degree of affectionate regard for its offspring, that would do honour to the superior intelligence of human beings; yet the object of the adventure, the value of the prize, the joy of the capture, cannot be sacrificed to feelings of compassion.

Account of the Arctic Regions, 1820

CHARLES DARWIN
1809–82
Whilst beholding these savages, one asks, whence have they come?

Darwin, the English naturalist whose great achievement was to put forward a scientific explanation for how evolution might have taken place, was born in Shrewsbury, grandson of the physician and poet Erasmus Darwin and the potter Josiah Wedgwood. He studied medicine at Edinburgh and, with a view to a career in the church, entered Christ's College, Cambridge, where the botanist John Stevens Henslow recommended him for the post of naturalist aboard the naval survey ship, the *Beagle*, then about to embark for South American waters. During the long voyage (1831–6), under the captaincy of Robert Fitzroy, it visited Tenerife, the Cape Verde Islands, Tierra del Fuego, Chile, the Galapagos, Tahiti, New Zealand and other places. The journey gave him a broad knowledge of the fauna, flora and geology of many terrains, educating him for his future diverse studies. In 1839 he was elected a Fellow of the Royal Society, and in the same year married his cousin Emma Wedgwood. Left independently wealthy by his father, he was able to settle down as a country gentlemen in Downe, Kent – among his gardens, pigeons and fowls – and apply himself to what would be his life's work: a quest to understand how different species came into existence.

Using his observations from the *Beagle*, in 1842 he published *The Structures and Distribution of Coral Reefs*, which set out an explanation of the origins of coral structures still accepted today. Also that year, he drew up his first, hesitant notes offering an alternative explanation of our origin. We were not immutable, as the ancient Greeks had speculated, and as was generally held to be the case; we had evolved from earlier, simpler species. The chief mechanism for this was 'natural selection': slight differences made certain individuals of a species more suitable for an environment, therefore increasing their chances of survival long enough to reproduce, and pass on those characteristics to the next generation. Though Darwin communicated the theory to colleagues, in 1858 Alfred Russel Wallace sent him a memoir on the Malay Archipelago that proposed much the same theory, which he'd worked out independently. Sir Charles Lyell and Joseph Hooker persuaded Darwin to submit a paper of his own, and this was read to the Linnaean Society on 1 July 1858, together with Wallace's paper. Darwin then set to work on his wealth of notes, shaping them into his historic publication *The Origin of Species by means of Natural Selection* (1859). This created uproar from the clergy, who saw it as an assault on the authority of the Bible and, in particular, the doctrine of man as a unique creation. With the support of T. H. Huxley (1825–95) – whose experiences collecting and comparing myriad marine organisms on the *Rattlesnake*, off the Great Barrier Reef, would educate him much as the *Beagle* voyage had Darwin – and other prominent scientists, Darwin eventually won through; but Darwin had not discussed human evolution at all, confining himself to one sentence: 'Light will be thrown on the origin of man and his history.' It was enough. And fresh controversy arose with *The Descent of Man and Selection in Relation to Sex* (1871), which more pointedly reasoned that man and the anthropoid apes must have a common ancestor. Much of the rest of Darwin's life was spent working on supplementary theses, in which he developed his theory of sexual selection. A timid man, and dogged by ill health, he was loath to argue his ideas in public; this was left to Huxley, who enjoyed a good tussle with theologians: famously, in

1860, when the Bishop of Oxford, Samuel Wilberforce, asked Huxley whether it was through his grandfather or grandmother that he claimed descent from a monkey, he replied that he would rather be related to an ape than to a man of intelligence who used his eloquence to obscure the 'real point at issue'. Though Darwin wavered between atheism and agnosticism he still managed to gain a final burial place in Westminster Abbey.

Darwin was not the sole originator of the evolution hypothesis, but through his wide-ranging observations he was the first to achieve acceptance of the mechanism of selection among the scientific community.

Erasmus Darwin, the French naturalist Lamarck and others had developed crude models of evolution, but Charles Darwin marshalled enough scientific evidence – and supplied a specific, viable mechanism – to transform evolution from a hypothesis to a verifiable theory.

I've chosen the following extracts for Darwin's attitudes to natives. We know, of course, of his subsequent realization that man is lodged in the same interconnected web as other animals, and is subject to the same laws as beasts – seeing the impoverished natives brought this home to him clearly.

Coming ashore, Tierra del Fuego

In the morning the Captain sent a party to communicate with the Fuegians. When we came within hail, one of the four natives who were present advanced to receive us, and began to shout most vehemently, wishing to direct us where to land. When we were on shore the party looked rather alarmed, but continued talking and making gestures with great rapidity. It was without exception the most curious and interesting spectacle I ever beheld: I could not have believed how wide was the difference between savage and civilized man: it is greater than between a wild and domesticated animal, inasmuch as in man there is a greater power of improvement. The chief spokesman was old, and appeared to be the head of the family; the three others were powerful young men, about six feet high. The women and children had been sent away. These Fuegians are a very different race from the stunted, miserable wretches farther westward; and they seem closely allied to the famous Patagonians of the Strait of Magellan. Their only garment consists of a mantle made of guanaco skin, with the wool outside; this they wear just thrown over their shoulders, leaving their persons as often exposed as covered. Their skin is of a dirty coppery red colour.

The old man had a fillet of white feathers tied round his head, which partly confined his black, coarse, and entangled hair. His face was crossed by two broad transverse bars; one, painted bright red, reached from ear to ear and included the upper lip; the other, white like chalk, extended above and parallel to the first, so that even his eyelids were thus coloured. The other two men were ornamented by streaks of black powder, made of charcoal. The party altogether closely resembled the devils which come on the stage in plays like Der Freischutz.

Their very attitudes were abject, and the expression of their countenances distrustful, surprised, and startled. After we had presented them with some scarlet cloth, which they immediately tied round their necks, they became good friends. This was shown by the old man patting our breasts, and making a chuckling kind of noise, as people do when feeding chickens. I walked with the old man, and this demonstration of friendship was repeated several times; it was concluded by three hard slaps, which were given me on the breast and back at the same time. He then bared his bosom for me to return the compliment, which being done, he seemed highly pleased. The language of these people, according to our notions, scarcely deserves to be called articulate. Captain Cook has compared it to a man clearing his throat, but certainly no European ever cleared his throat with so many hoarse, guttural, and clicking sounds.

They are excellent mimics: as often as we coughed or yawned, or made any odd motion, they immediately imitated us. Some of our party began to squint and look awry; but one of the young Fuegians (whose whole face was painted black, excepting a white band across his eyes) succeeded in making far more hideous grimaces. They could repeat with perfect correctness each word in any sentence we addressed them, and they remembered such words for some time. Yet we Europeans all know how difficult it is to distinguish apart the sounds in a foreign language. Which of us, for instance, could follow an American Indian through a sentence of more than three words? All savages appear to possess, to an uncommon degree, this power of mimicry. I was told, almost in the same words, of the same ludicrous habit among the Caffres: the Australians, likewise, have long been notorious for being able to imitate and describe the gait of any man, so that he may be recognized. How can this faculty be explained? is it a consequence of the more practised habits of perception and keener senses, common to all men in a savage state, as compared with those long civilized?

When a song was struck up by our party, I thought the Fuegians would have fallen down with astonishment. With equal surprise they viewed our dancing; but one of the young men, when asked, had no objection to a little waltzing. Little accustomed to Europeans as they appeared to be, yet they knew and dreaded our fire-arms; nothing would tempt them to take a gun in their hands. They begged for knives, calling them by the Spanish word 'cuchilla.' They explained also what they wanted, by acting as if they had a piece of blubber in their mouth, and then pretending to cut instead of tear it.

I have not as yet noticed the Fuegians whom we had on board. During the former voyage of the Adventure and Beagle in 1826 to 1830, Captain Fitz Roy seized on a party of natives, as hostages for the loss of a boat, which had been stolen, to the great jeopardy of a party employed on the survey; and some of these natives, as well as a child whom he bought for a pearl-button he took with him to England, determining to educate them and instruct them in religion at his own expense. To settle these natives in their own country, was one chief inducement to Captain Fitz Roy to undertake our present voyage; and before the Admiralty had resolved to send out this expedition, Captain Fitz Roy had generously chartered a vessel, and would himself have taken them back. The natives were accompanied by a missionary, R. Matthews; of whom and of the natives, Captain Fitz Roy has published a full and excellent account. Two men, one of whom died in England of the small-pox, a boy and a little girl, were originally taken; and we had now on board, York Minster, Jemmy Button (whose name expresses his purchase-money), and Fuegia Basket. York Minister was a full-grown, short, thick, powerful man: his disposition was reserved, taciturn, morose, and when excited violently passionate; his affections were very strong towards a few friends on board; his intellect good. Jemmy Button was a universal favourite, but likewise passionate; the expression of his face at once showed his nice disposition. He was merry and often laughed, and was remarkably sympathetic with any one in pain: when the water was rough, I was often a little sea-sick, and he used to come to me and say in a plaintive voice, 'Poor, poor fellow!' but the notion, after his aquatic life, of a man being sea-sick, was too ludicrous, and he was generally obliged to turn on one side to hide a smile or laugh, and then he would repeat his 'Poor, poor fellow!' He was of a patriotic disposition; and he liked to praise his own tribe and country, in which he truly said there were 'plenty of trees,' and he abused all the other tribes: he stoutly declared that there was no Devil in his land. Jemmy was short, thick, and fat, but vain of his personal appearance; he used always to wear gloves, his hair was neatly cut, and he was distressed if his well-polished shoes were dirtied. He was fond of admiring himself in a looking-glass; and a merry-faced little Indian boy from the Rio Negro, whom we had for some months on board, soon perceived this, and used to mock him: Jemmy, who was always rather jealous of the attention paid to this little boy, did not at all like this, and used to say, with rather a contemptuous twist of his head, 'Too much skylark.' It seems yet wonderful to me, when I think over all his many good qualities, that he should have been of the same race, and doubtless partaken of the same character, with the miserable, degraded savages whom we first met here. Lastly, Fuegia Basket was a nice, modest, reserved young girl, with a rather pleasing but sometimes sullen expression, and very quick in learning anything, especially languages. This she showed in picking up some Portuguese and Spanish, when left on shore for only a short time at Rio de Janeiro and Monte Video, and in her knowledge of English. York Minster was very jealous of any attention paid to her; for it was clear he determined to marry her as soon as they were settled on shore.

Although all three could both speak and understand a good deal of English, it was singularly difficult to obtain much information from them, concerning the habits of their countrymen: this was partly owing to their apparent difficulty in understanding the simplest alternative. Every one accustomed to very young children, knows how seldom one can get an answer even to so simple a question as whether a thing is black *or* white; the idea of black or white seems alternately to fill their minds. So it was with these Fuegians, and hence it was generally impossible to find out, by cross-questioning, whether one had rightly understood anything which they had asserted. Their sight was remarkably acute: it is well known that sailors, from long practice, can make out a distant object much better than a landsman; but both York and Jemmy were much superior to any sailor on board: several times they have declared what some distant object has been, and though doubted by every one, they have proved right, when it has been examined through a telescope. They were quite conscious of this power; and Jemmy, when he had any little quarrel with the officer on watch, would say, 'Me see ship, me no tell.'

Why they aren't civilized

The different tribes have no government or chief; yet each is surrounded by other hostile tribes, speaking different dialects, and separated from each other only by a deserted border or neutral territory: the cause of their warfare appears to be the means of subsistence. Their country is a broken mass of wild rocks, lofty hills, and useless forests: and these are viewed through mists and endless storms. The habitable land is reduced to the stones on the beach; in search of food they are compelled unceasingly to wander from spot to spot, and so steep is the coast, that they can only move about in their wretched canoes. They cannot know the feeling of having a home, and still less that of domestic affection; for the husband is to the wife a brutal master to a laborious slave. Was a more horrid deed ever perpetrated, than that witnessed on the west coast by Byron, who saw a wretched mother pick up her bleeding dying infant-boy, whom her husband had mercilessly dashed on the stones for dropping a basket of sea-eggs! How little can the higher powers of the mind be brought into play: what is there for imagination to picture, for reason to compare, for judgment to decide upon? to knock a limpet from the rock does not require even cunning, that lowest power of the mind. Their skill in some respects may be compared to the instinct of animals; for it is not improved by experience: the canoe, their most ingenious work, poor as it is, has remained the same, as we know from Drake, for the last two hundred and fifty years.

Whilst beholding these savages, one asks, whence have they come? What could have tempted, or what change compelled a tribe of men, to leave the fine regions of the north, to travel down the Cordillera or backbone of America, to invent and build canoes, which are not used by the tribes of Chile, Peru, and Brazil, and then to enter on one of the most inhospitable countries within the limits of the globe? Although such reflections must at first seize on the mind, yet we may feel sure that they are partly erroneous. There is no reason to believe that the Fuegians decrease in number; therefore we must suppose that they enjoy a sufficient share of happiness, of whatever kind it may be, to render life worth having. Nature by making habit omnipotent, and its effects hereditary, has fitted the Fuegian to the climate and the productions of his miserable country.

The Voyage of The Beagle, 1845

We had a visit from four ladies yesterday. One was a very fine girl about 15, as full of fun and roguery as need be, and the gentlemen of the party seemed to keep a very sharp look on her . . .

These letters were written by early settlers at Port Essington, on Australia's northern coastline, established in 1838 – a spot so isolated that replies from England could take the best part of a year to reach them. By 1845 it was clear that the settlement would not survive.

The letters express the optimism and enthusiasm of the outpost's founders, and articulate the dangers they faced as they explored the islands nearby, opening up trading posts and planting the flag.

Captain Sir Gordon Bremer to Captain Francis Beaufort, Hydrographic Office, London

HMS Alligator, Victoria, 9 December 1838

My dear friend

It is with sincere pleasure that I take up my pen to address you from hence. You feel so lively an interest in the expedition that I am sure you will be gratified at hearing of us . . .

It is a very pretty spot, and will speedily improve in appearance as the land is cleared. There is no very elevated land around this port, but it is sufficiently diversified by green hills and valleys to give it a highly picturesque and pleasing aspect. The more I see of this splendid harbour, the better I am satisfied and delighted with it. There is sufficient space for a whole navy to ride in perfect security, and the land is so rich and good that I am convinced spices, pepper, cotton, and rice may be cultivated most successfully. We find the nutmeg very good, although it is not the *true* nut of the Moluccas. The tree cotton is also abundant. Of animals, the kangaroo is numerous as are also opossums, and the kangaroo rat. The birds are geese, ducks, curlew, snipe, partridge, quail, pigeons, and an infinite variety of the parrot tribe, some of which are exceedingly beautiful – there are also some exquisite small birds.

You will be glad to hear that our intercourse with the poor natives is most friendly. Some of them are constantly with us, and have brought their women and children into the settlement without the least fear. They seem to be a kind and really well disposed people although they are doubtless like all savages easily irritated and borne away by their passions. They are certainly very fond of their children, and next to hatchets, their desire is to obtain handkerchiefs or other cloth for the pickaninies (the name they have taken from some Europeans). We had one child about 6 months old, as fine an infant as I ever saw. The mother was about 18 years of age and not bad looking. The Father was our friend Mala Maya who described the position of the fresh water lake to Mr Stewart. We had a visit from four ladies yesterday. One was a very fine girl about 15, as full of fun and roguery as need be, and the gentlemen of the party seemed to keep a very sharp look on her.

Captain Sir Gordon Bremer to Secretary of the Admiralty, London

HMS Alligator, Sydney, 31 July 1839

Sir

I have the greatest satisfaction in acquainting their Lordships that the report of an Englishman being on Timor Laut ... A young man, by the name of Joseph Forbes, who was a boy in the 'Stedcombe' schooner when she was cut off by the natives, has been recovered by the activity, zeal, and humanity of Mr Thomas Watson, Master of the schooner 'Essington'.

About 2.30 PM two canoes were observed making towards us, and in one of them, by means of a glass, we were able to distinguish the features of a European equipped as a native. . . .

The appearance of this Englishman at the time we received him on board was in the highest degree remarkable, and such as was calculated to draw forth the strongest sympathies from the bosom of any human being whose composition was not entirely void of compassionate feelings. He appeared, as far as one judge from his looks, as well as from the length of time he must have been on the island, to be about 26 years of age, of a remarkably fair complexion, notwithstanding the effects of a tropical climate. There was also a delicacy of frame about him seldom to be met with in a person of his years. His hair, which was of a lightish yellow colour, had been allowed to grow long, and was triced up after the native custom with a comb made of bamboo; its length was from 18 to 20 inches, and its texture very much resembled the finest silk in its raw state. His only garments were a sort of waistcoat without sleeves, and a blue and white dungaree girdle around his loins. There was a peculiar vacancy in his countenance, which I am at a loss how to describe, but I can compare it to nothing more aptly than to that remarkable aspect which is observable in many deaf and dumb people, and besides this there was a remarkable expression of agony in his face which no doubt from continued

suffering had become habitual. His body was much emaciated and covered
with numberless scars – the indisputable evidence of those savage tortures
which he had endured; and at the time to which this history refers his legs
were thickly studded with foul ulcers, and the sinews about the knee joint was
so much contracted as to prevent him extending his legs and consequently
rendering him unable to walk. His ears had been perforated after the custom
of the natives and the hole in the lobe of each is large enough to admit of his
wearing a piece of bamboo of at least one inch in diameter, indeed he did
wear such a piece at the time he was brought off. Nor does the catalogue of
this poor fellow's misfortunes end here – for he was found to have been much
injured in the genitals, and on being questioned about it he said that it was
caused by the bite of the native wild pig.

As might have been expected from having been on the island 16 years, he
had almost entirely forgotten his native language. He could however with
some little difficulty make himself intelligible. He gave the following account.
His name was Joseph Forbes, and that he belonged to the schooner 'Stedcombe' which had gone from Melville Island to Timor Laut to procure live
stock . . . The vessel being moored off the village of Louron, Mr Bastell [the
Mate] and the crew proceeded on shore, leaving on board the steward, a boy
named John Edwards, and himself, Joseph Forbes, in charge of the ship, and
from some cause or other when they were on shore the natives murdered
them all. As Mr Bastell and crew did not return, he (Joseph Forbes) took the
glass and saw the bodies stretched out upon the beach, the head being severed
from each. He then states that a canoe was coming towards the schooner and
expecting that the natives would deal with them on board as they had done
with those on shore, he proposed to the steward and John Edwards to arm
themselves with muskets, and to fire in case the people in the canoe attempted
to board, but to this the steward would pay no attention. He next proposed
that as he and John Edwards knew the compass; and the steward knew a little
of navigation, the[y] should punch one of the bolts out of the cable, and
liberate the schooner from her moorings and stand out to sea. This was
agreed to, and they were in the act of carrying it into effect when the canoe
came alongside, and the natives (among whom was the Orang Kaire who had
been our prisoner) boarded the vessel. They immediately surrounded the
steward and one of them seizing an axe which was lying on the deck cut off
his head on the spot. The two boys, expecting to share the same fate, betook
themselves to the rigging and were only induced to descend upon repeated
promises that they should not be injured. The natives then plundered the
vessel of her stores and removed them together with the boys to the shore.

After they had got everything which they considered worth having they set fire to the schooner.

From this time the two boys were kept in the capacity of ordinary slaves, until about four years ago, when, he says, John Edwards died, and since that time he has been unable to go about or do anything owing to the bad state of his legs. He attributes his forgetfulness of his native tongue to the death of his companion in slavery, for he remarks that since John died, he had no one to talk to. How far he is correct as to the time when John died I cannot say, but I may observe that his ideas of time appear to be very erroneous for he says he has been on the island only ten years, whereas the 'Stedcombe' was cut off in 1823 [actually 1825] which proves him to have 16. The treatment which he received during the period of his bondage appears to have been barbarous, and worthy only of a savage race for one of the common modes of punishment adopted towards him whenever he had incurred displeasure, was taking hot embers and placing them upon some part of his body until it was severely burnt. When questioned as to the way in which the different Orang Kaire behaved to him his general answer is 'Tiada Bergouse' implying 'very bad', although there are one or two to whom he applied the term 'Bergouse' 'very good' . . . Speaking of the Orang Kaire of Louron he says 'Louron cuts me down to the ground' which we construe to mean that he frequently flogged him, or knocked him down, and he also says that he used to bind him hand and foot whenever a vessel hove in sight and keep him bound as long as the vessel remained in sight. We asked him what he thought when he first saw the schooner with English colours hoisted, his answer was simple, but at the same time very expressive; viz. 'Joe see schooner – Joe no eat – Joe's belly full' evidently implying that the sight of the schooner had such an effect on his mind that he could not eat.

Letters from Port Essington, 1838–1845 (1999)

EDMUND KENNEDY
1818–48
No Jackey, those blacks are very friendly.

Born in Guernsey, Kennedy arrived in Sydney in 1840 and joined the Surveyor-General's Department as an assistant to Sir Thomas Mitchell. After a number of expeditions to open up Queensland, in 1848 he left with twelve men to map Queensland's eastern coast to Cape York, where they would be picked up by the *Ariel* at Port Albany. Though the expedition was well provisioned, swamps, thick undergrowth and tropical rains forced them to abandon their carts; their horses, exhausted by the creepers, mud and leeches, now had to carry all the supplies. To add to the men's woes, they were also being stalked by hostile Aborigines. In November, after six months, they reached Weymouth Bay; here, Kennedy left behind eight men who were too weak to go further, and two horses for them to eat. At Shelburne Bay, Kennedy left behind a further three ailing men, one of whom had accidentally shot himself. Kennedy now made a last bid for the Cape, accompanied by only Jackey Jackey, an Aborigine guide. Of the two, only Jackey Jackey was to survive – Kennedy having been speared by native inhabitants only 20 km from Cape York. Finally, having attracted the attention of the *Ariel*, Jackey Jackey was rescued and gave his account. The ship immediately went south in search of survivors. No trace of the three left at Shelburne Bay was found; two men were recovered from Weymouth Bay, the other six having died of starvation.

Statement of Jackey Jackey, an Aboriginal survivor

The next day we went a good way; Mr Kennedy told me to go up a tree to see a sandy hill somewhere; I went up a tree, and saw a sandy hill a little way down from Port Albany. That day we camped near a swamp; it was a very rainy day. The next morning we went on, and Mr Kennedy told me we should get round to Port Albany in a day; we travelled on all day till twelve o'clock (noon), and then we saw Port Albany; then he said, 'There is Port Albany, Jackey – a ship is there – you see that island there,' pointing to Albany Island; this was when we were at the mouth of Escape River; we stopped there a little while; all the meat was gone; I tried to get some fish but could not; we went on in the afternoon half a mile along the river side, and met a good lot of blacks, and we camped; the blacks all cried out 'powad powad,' and rubbed their bellies; and we thought they were friendly, and Mr Kennedy gave them fish-hooks all round; every one asked me if I had any thing to give away, and I said, no; and Mr Kennedy said, give them your knife, Jackey; this fellow on board was the man I gave the knife to; I am sure of it; I know him well; the black that was shot in the canoe was the most active in urging all the others on to spear Mr Kennedy; I gave the man on board my knife; we went on this day, and I looked behind, and they were getting up their spears, and ran all round the camp which we had left; I told Mr Kennedy that very likely those black fellows would follow us, and he said, 'No, Jackey, those blacks are very friendly;' I said to him 'I know these black fellows well, they too much speak;' we went on some two or three miles and camped; I and Mr Kennedy watched them that night; taking it in turns every hour all night; by-and-by I saw the black fellows; it was a moonlight night; and I walked up to Mr Kennedy, and said to him, there is plenty of black fellows now; this was in the middle of the night; Mr Kennedy told me to get my gun ready; the blacks did not know where we slept, as we did not make a fire; we both sat up all night after this, daylight came, and I fetched the horses and saddled them; then we went on a good way up the river, and then we sat down a little while, and we saw three black fellows coming along our track, and they saw us, and one fellow ran back as hard as he could run, and fetched up plenty more, like a flock of sheep almost; I told Mr Kennedy to put the saddles on the two horses and go on, and the blacks came up, and they followed us all the day; all along it was raining, and I now told him to leave the horses and come on without them, that the horses made too much track. Mr Kennedy was too weak, and would not leave the horses. We went on this day till towards evening, raining hard, and the blacks followed us all the day, some behind, some planted before; in fact, blacks all around following us. Now we went on into a little bit of a scrub, and I told Mr Kennedy to look behind always; sometimes he would do so, and sometimes he would not look behind to look out for the blacks. Then a good many black fellows came behind in the scrub, and threw plenty of spears, and hit Mr Kennedy in the back first. Mr Kennedy said to me, 'Oh! Jackey, Jackey! shoot 'em, shoot 'em.' Then I pulled out my gun and fired, and hit one fellow all over the face with buck shot; he tumbled down, and got up again and again and wheeled right round, and two blackfellows picked him up and carried him away. They went away then a little way, and came back again, throwing spears all around, more than they did before; very large spears. I pulled out the spear at once from Mr Kennedy's back, and cut out the jag with Mr Kennedy's knife; then Mr Kennedy got his gun and snapped, but the gun would not go off. The blacks sneaked all along by the trees, and speared Mr Kennedy again in the right leg, above the knee a little, and I got speared over the eye, and the blacks were now throwing their spears all ways, never giving over, and shortly again speared Mr Kennedy in the right side; there were large jags to the spears, and I cut them out and put them into my pocket. At the same time we got speared, the horses got speared too, and jumped and bucked all about, and got into the swamp. I now told Mr Kennedy to sit down, while I looked after the saddle-bags, which I did; and when I came back again, I saw blacks along with Mr Kennedy; I then asked him if he saw the blacks with him, he was stupid with the spear wounds, and said 'No;' then I asked where was his watch? I saw the blacks taking away watch and hat as I was returning to Mr Kennedy then I carried Mr Kennedy into the scrub: he said, 'Don't carry me a good way;' then Mr Kennedy looked this way, very bad (Jackey rolling his eyes). I said to him, 'Don't look far away,' as I thought he would be frightened; I asked him often 'Are you well now?' and he said, 'I don't care for the spear wound in my leg, Jackey, but for the other two spear wounds in my side and back,' and said, 'I am bad inside, Jackey.' I told him blackfellow always die when he got spear in there (the back); he said, 'I am out of wind, Jackey;' I asked him, 'Mr Kennedy, are you going to leave me?' and he said, 'Yes, my boy, I am going to leave you;' he said, 'I am very bad, Jackey; you take the books, Jackey, to the captain, but not the big ones, the Governor will give anything for them;' I then tied up the papers: he then said, 'Jackey, give me paper and I will write;' I gave him paper and pencil, and he tried to write, and he then fell back and died, and I caught him as he fell back and held him, and I then turned round myself and cried. I was crying a good while until I got well; that was about an hour, and then I buried him; I digged up the ground with a tomahawk, and covered him over with logs, then grass, and my shirt and trowsers; that night I left him near dark; I would go through the scrub, and the blacks threw spears at me, a good many, and I went back again into the scrub; then I went down the creek which runs into Escape River, and I walked along the water in the creek very easy, with my head only above water, to avoid the blacks, and get out of their way; in this way I went half a mile; then I got out of the creek, and got clear of them, and walked on all night nearly, and slept in the bush without a fire; I went on next morning, and felt very bad, and I spelled for two days; I lived upon nothing but salt water; next day I went on and camped one mile away from where I left, and ate one of the pandanus fruits; next morning I went on two miles, and sat down there, and I wanted to spell a little there, and go on; but when I tried to get up, I could not, but fell down again very tired and cramped, and I spelled here two days; then I went on again one mile, and got nothing to eat but one nonda; and I went on that day and camped, and on again next morning, about half a mile, and sat down where there was good water, and remained all day. On the following morning, I went a good way, went round a great swamp and mangroves, and got a good way by sundown; the next morning I went and saw a very large track of blackfellows; I went clear of the track and of swamp or sandy ground; then I came to a very large river, and a large lagoon; plenty of alligators in the

lagoon, about ten miles from Port Albany. I now got into the ridges by sundown, and went up a tree and saw Albany Island; then next morning at four
o'clock, I went on as hard as I could go all the way down, over fine clear
ground, fine iron bark timber, and plenty of good grass; I went on round the
point (this was towards Cape York, north of Albany Island) and went on and
followed a creek down, and went on top of the hill, and saw Cape York; I knew
it was Cape York, because the sand did not go on further; I sat down then a
good while; I said to myself this is Port Albany, I believe inside somewhere; Mr
Kennedy also told me that the ship was inside, close up to the main land; I
went on a little way, and saw the ship and boat; I met close up here two black
gins and a good many piccanninies; one said to me 'powad, powad;' then I
asked her for eggs, she gave me turtle's eggs, and I gave her a burning glass;
she pointed to the ship which I had seen before; I was very frightened of
seeing the black men all along here, and when I was on the rock cooeying, and
murry murry glad when the bout came for me.

   Mr E. B. Kennedy's Exploration of the Cape York Peninsula, in John MacGillivray, *Voyage of
   HMS Rattlesnake*, 1852

BRONISLAW KASPER MALINOWSKI
1884–1942

The love-sick Trobriander . . . taught by custom to be direct in amorous pursuits,
proceeds at once to the approved methods of approach . . .

Malinowski, a Polish anthropologist considered the founder of modern social anthropology, was born in Kraków, Poland, into an academic and wealthy family. He studied physics and mathematics in Poland, but reading James Frazer's *The Golden Bough* inspired him to learn more about the roots of our cultural and social behaviour; he went on to study Sociology at the London School of Economics and Political Science, where a department of anthropology had just been established.

When the First World War broke out, Malinowski had just begun a research project in Australia, but now found himself confined on the Trobriand Islands, off the eastern tip of New Guinea. Over a period of four years he studied the peoples who lived there, developing the observational skills that were to have such an influence on his future students and on the progress of anthropology itself. He learned the language of the 'tribe' and participated in their ceremonies and daily rituals. Through his studies he claimed to disprove Freud's theories of the Oedipus complex with evidence that indicated individual psychology depends on cultural context.

In 1920, Malinowski returned to London and seven years later he held the first chair in Social Anthropology at the LSE. He combined work as a professor with the continuation of his field work, and during the 1930s became particularly interested in the peoples of eastern and southern Africa. Malinowski's fluency in tribal languages as well as Russian, French, English, German, Spanish and Italian doubtless contributed to his understanding of human nature.

He was a strong advocate of the school of functionalism, that sees all human cultural activities as fulfilling a need. This need can be physical, such as the need for food; instrumental, such as the need for law and order; or integrative and psychological, such as the need for creativity and art. At the heart of functionalism lies the idea that all components of society are linked together in a balanced system.

Malinowski's obituary in the *New York Times* described him as an 'integrator of ten thousand cultural characteristics'.

The love-sick Trobriander

The love-sick Trobriander . . . [is] taught by custom to be direct in amorous pursuits, proceeds at once to the approved methods of approach.

The simplest of these is direct personal solicitation . . . we know that there are numerous opportunities for a boy to express his desire, or for a girl to induce him to do so. This is perfectly easy within the same village community. When the two belong to different villages, certain festivals bring them together; they can speak to each other, and indulge in the preliminaries of love during games and dances, and in crowds; also they can arrange a future meeting. After that, by the *ulatile* and *katuyausi* customs, the meetings can be repeated, or one of the lovers may move to the other's village.

Another method is that of solicitation by an intermediary (*kaykivi*). This is used when the two communities are distant and, owing to the season, no personal approach is possible. A mutual friend, male or female, is begged to express the boy's admiration and to arrange for a rendezvous. The *kaykivi* is not, as a rule, lightly set in motion, for its failure, if this becomes public, draws down considerable ridicule on the solicitor. But if direct approach and the *kaykivi* are both for some reason impossible, the lover uses the most powerful way of wooing, that of magic, as the first step in his attack. It is sufficient to say in this place that almost all final success in love is attributed to magic, that both men and women believe in it deeply and trust it completely, and that, because of this psychological attitude, it is very efficacious . . .

Thus there is nothing roundabout in a Trobriand wooing; nor do they seek full personal relations, with sexual possession only as a consequence. Simply and directly a meeting is asked for with the avowed intention of sexual gratification. If the invitation is accepted, the satisfaction of the boy's desire eliminates the romantic frame of mind, the craving for the unattainable and mysterious. If he is rejected, there is not much room for personal tragedy, for he is accustomed from childhood to have his sexual impulses thwarted by some girls, and he knows that another intrigue cures this type of ill surely and swiftly.

Scent and colours in love-making

We know by now how a Trobriand girl and boy are first attracted to each other, how they come together, how their intrigue develops, leading to separation or marriage; but we know little as yet of the way in which two lovers spend their time together and enjoy each other's presence . . .

The word *kwakwadu* is a technical term which signifies something like 'amorous transactions' or 'being together for purposes of love'. It would be easier perhaps to express it in German, as *erotisches Beisammensein*, or by the American colloquialism 'petting party' or 'petting session'. English speech habits are, unfortunately, refractory to stereotyped terminology, except in matters of morality. The *kwakwadu* has a wide meaning. It signifies a collective excursion, or party of several couples setting out on a love picnic; the being together of two people who are in love with each other – a sort of erotic *tête-à-tête*; the caresses and approaches before the final union. It is never used euphemistically to designate the sexual act. At a collective picnic some of the games described in the previous chapter are first played in common, and afterwards the lovers seek solitude two by two. We shall attempt to reconstruct the behaviour of a pair who have left such a party, or else started off alone in order to enjoy each other's company in some favourite spot.

The scrub surrounding the village, which is periodically cut for gardens, grows in a dense underbush and does not everywhere offer a desirable resting place. Here and there, however, a large tree, such as the *butia*, is left behind for the sake of its perfumed flowers, or there may be a group of pandanus trees. Pleasant shady places, too, can be found under an old tree in one of the groves which often mark the site of a deserted village, whose fruit trees, coco-nut-palms, and big banyans make an oasis within the stunted tropical under-growth of recent cultivation. On the coral ridge (*raybwag*) many spots invite a picnic party. Cavities and hollows in the coral, rocks of queer or attractive shape, giant trees, thickets of fern, flowering hibiscus make the *raybwag* a mysterious and attractive region. Especially delightful is the part which over-looks the open sea towards the east, towards the islands of Kitava, Iwa, and Gawa. The roar of the breakers on the fringing reef, the dazzling sand and foam and the blue sea, provide the favourite surroundings for native love making, and also constitute the scene in which the mythical drama of incestuous love has been laid by native imagination.

In such places the lovers enjoy the scent and colour of the flowers, they watch the birds and insects, and go down to the beach to bathe. In the heat of the day, or during the hot seasons, they search for shady spots on the coral ridge, for water-holes and for bathing places. As the cool of the evening approaches they warm themselves on the hot sand, or kindle a fire, or find shelter in some nook among the coral rocks. They amuse themselves by col-lecting shells and picking flowers or scented herbs, to adorn themselves. Also they smoke tobacco, chew betel-nut, and, when they are thirsty, look for a coco-nut-palm, the green nut of which yields a cooling drink. They inspect each other's hair for lice and eat them – a practice disgusting to us and ill-associated with love making, but to the natives a natural and pleasant occupa-tion between two who are fond of each other, and a favourite pastime with children. On the other hand, they would never eat heavy food on such occa-sions and especially would never carry it with them from the village. To them the idea of European boys and girls going out for a picnic with a knapsack full of eatables is as disgusting and indecent as their *kwakwadu* would be to a Puritan in our society.

All such pleasures – the enjoyment of landscape, of colour and scent in the open air, of wide views and of intimate corners of nature – are essential features in their love making. For hours, sometimes for days, lovers will go out together gathering fruits and berries for food and enjoying each other's company in beautiful surroundings. I made a point of confirming these particulars from a number of concrete instances; for, in connection with the question of romantic love already discussed, I was interested to know whether love making had direct satisfaction only for its object, or whether it embraced a wider sensory and æsthetic enjoyment. Many of the pleasures which enter into general games, amusements, and festivities, also form part of personal *kwakwadu*.

Of course, love is not made only in the open air; there are also special occasions for bringing lovers together in the village . . . In the village, however, privacy is almost impossible except at night, and the activities of lovers are much more curtailed. They lie next to each other on a bunk and talk, and when they are tired of this, proceed to make love.

How lovers behave

Let us now observe the behaviour of two lovers alone on their bunk in the *bukumatula*, or in a secluded spot in the *raybwag* or jungle. A mat is usually spread on the boards or on the earth, and, when they are sure of not being observed, skirt and pubic leaf are removed. They may at first sit or lie side by side, caressing each other, their hands roaming over the surface of the skin. Sometimes they will lie close together, their arms and legs enlaced. In such a position they may talk for a long time, confessing their love with endearing phrases, or teasing each other (*katudabuma*). So near to each other, they will rub noses. But though there is a good deal of nose-rubbing, cheek is also rubbed against cheek, and mouth against mouth. Gradually the caress becomes more passionate, and then the mouth is predominantly active; the tongue is sucked, and tongue is rubbed against tongue; they suck each other's lower lips, and the lips will be bitten till blood comes; the saliva is allowed to flow from mouth to mouth. The teeth are used freely, to bite the cheek, to snap at the nose and chin. Or the lovers plunge their hands into the thick mop of each other's hair and tease it or even tear it. In the formulæ of love magic, which here as elsewhere abound in over-graphic exaggeration, the expressions, 'drink my blood' and 'pull out my hair' are frequently used. This sentence, volunteered by a girl's sweetheart, describes his erotic passion:

Binunu	*vivila*	*dubilibaloda,*	*bigadi;*	*tagiyu*	*bimwam.*
She sucks	woman	lower lip (ours),	she bites	we spit,	she drinks.

Erotic scratches are an even more direct way of hurting and of drawing blood. We have already spoken of these as the conventional invitation of a girl to a boy. We also described their place in tribal festivities. But they are also a part of intimate love making, and a mutual expression of passion:

Tayobobu,   tavayauli,   takenu deli;   bikimali   vivila
We embrace,   we rub noses,   we lie together;   she scratches   woman
otubwaloda,   ovilavada   sene   bwoyna,   tanukwali,
on back (ours),   on shoulders (ours);   very much   good,   we know,
bitagwalayda   senela.
she loves us   very much indeed.

On the whole, I think that in the rough usage of passion the woman is the more active. I have seen far larger scratches and marks on men than on women; and only women may actually lacerate their lovers . . . The scratching is carried even into the passionate phases of intercourse. It is a great jest in the Trobriands to look at the back of a man or a girl for the hall-marks of success in amorous life. Nor have I ever seen a comely girl or boy without some traces of *kimali* in the proper places. Subject to general rules of good taste and specific taboo, the *kimali* marks are a favourite subject for jokes; but there is also much secret pride in their possession.

Another element in love making, for which the average European would show even less understanding than for the *kimali*, is the *mitakuku*, the biting off of eyelashes. As far as I could judge from descriptions and demonstrations, a lover will tenderly or passionately bend over his mistress's eyes and bite off the tip of her eyelashes. This, I was told, is done in orgasm as well as in the less passionate preliminary stages. I was never quite able to grasp either the mechanism or the sensuous value of this caress. I have no doubt, however, as to its reality, for I have not seen one boy or girl in the Trobriands with the long eyelashes to which they are entitled by nature. In any case, it shows that the eye to them is an object of active bodily interest. Still less enthusiasm will probably be felt by the romantic European towards the already mentioned custom of catching each other's lice and eating them. To the natives, however, it is a pastime, which, while pleasant in itself, also establishes an exquisite sense of intimacy.

The following is [the translation of], a condensed description of the whole process of love making, with several characteristic incidents, given me by my friend Monakewo:

'When we go on a love making expedition we light our fire; we take our lime gourd (and chew betel-nut), we take our tobacco (and smoke it). Food we do not take, we would be ashamed to do so. We walk, we arrive at a large tree, we sit down, we search each other's heads and consume the lice, we tell the woman that we want to copulate. After it is over we return to the village. In the village we go to the bachelors' house, lie down, and chatter. When we are alone he takes off the pubic leaf, she takes off her fibre skirt: we go to sleep . . .

'When I sleep with Dabugera I embrace her, I hug her with my whole body, I rub noses with her. We suck each other's lower lip, so that we are stirred to passion. We suck each other's tongues, we bite each other's noses, we bite each other's chins, we bite cheeks and caress the armpit and the groin. Then she will say. "O my lover, it itches very much . . . push on again, my whole body melts with pleasure . . . do it vigorously, be quick, so that the fluids may discharge . . . tread on again, my body feels so pleasant." '

The same informant gave me the following samples of a conversation which would occur after the act, when the two rested in each other's arms:

'Am I thy sweetheart?' 'Yes, thou art my sweetheart; I love thee very much; always, always we shall cohabit. I love thy face very much; it is that of a cross-cousin (the right woman for me).' 'I do not desire that thou shouldest take a new woman; just thou and I.'

I was informed that sexual relations between married people would be on the same lines, but, from the following [translated] text, it is clear that passion ebbs with time.

'Newly married people sleep together in one bed. When matrimony has matured, when it has become old, she sleeps in one bed, and we (i.e. the husband) sleep in another. When they feel sexually vigorous they want to cohabit; then they lie together, they bite their eyelashes, they rub their noses, they bite each other.'

Here my informant, Tokulubakiki, a married man, tries to convey the idea that even long-married persons can behave at times as lovers.

The Sexual Life of Savages, 1932

John King Davis
1884–1967

*One just drops into a kind of morass which like the great war has only
one bright spot, its conclusion.*

The (unsung) contribution of the British
navigator John Davis to Antarctic exploration
was enormous: between 1907 and 1930 he
made seven Antarctic voyages, navigating the
hazardous ice-strewn waters with exceptional
skill, landing expedition parties, relieving
them and collecting them safely for the
homeward journey.

Davis's romantic attachment to ships
began on his first sea voyage on the *Celtic
Chief*. At the age of sixteen he ran away to join
her, remaining with the same vessel as an
apprentice for the following four years.

His first taste of Antarctica was at the age
of twenty-three as First Mate on Shackleton's
1907–9 expedition ship, *Nimrod*. This was a
huge career leap for the young man, but he
proved himself more than worthy of the post
and his two seasons in the Ross Sea earned
him an enthusiastic tribute from Shackleton –
and in due course the nickname 'Gloomy
Davis' from the crew, for his pessimistic outlook, dry sense of humour and stern
approach to discipline.

In 1911, while Scott and Amundsen were
pursuing the South Pole, he was captain of
the *Aurora* and second in command of
Mawson's Australasian Antarctic expedition,
whose aim was to chart west of Victoria Land.
To do this Mawson relied on Davis to tackle
the daunting Adelie Land ice pack, to land
him and then to steer through treacherous
unknown waters for 1,500 miles as far as
Queen Mary Land. On his return three years
later Davis's reputation as an exceptional ice
navigator was firmly established; he won an
RGS medal in recognition of his oceano-
graphical research, and Mawson invited him
to be best man at his wedding.

When Shackleton made his bid to cross the

Antarctic contintent, he was Shackleton's first
choice of captain for the *Endurance* (but was
unavailable) and was commissioned in 1917 to
rescue Shackleton's Ross Sea support party,
which had been marooned for two years on
the other side of the continent.

His last Antarctic voyage was in 1929–30 as
Mawson's number two, acting as captain of
the *Discovery*, Scott's old ship, for the British,
Australian and New Zealand Antarctic
Research Expedition (BANZAR). This time,
relations between the two men became
strained. Essentially, the tension was over
control of the ship: as Mawson saw it, Davis's
approach was over-cautious, as he navigated
ice-laden waters. Davis was a professional
seaman, responsible for the safety of ship and
crew, Mawson a professional adventurer, with
a duty to sponsors to take risks to push
frontiers.

However, sharing as they did an obsession
with Antarctica, they worked amicably
together into old age on various committees
connected with research in the far south.
Davis was awarded a CBE in 1964 and died
aged eighty-three in Australia. He barred publication of his diaries for twenty years, no
doubt aware that his criticism of Mawson
would cause upset. The diaries, quoted here,
have only recently been published for the first
time.

The first extract deals with the 1916–17
expedition to rescue the party of Shackleton's
men left on the far side of Antarctica, after the
crushing of the *Endurance*. Despite obstruction from the British, Australian and New
Zealand governments, who were more concerned with the First World War, the
Discovery had finally been sent to rescue
Shackleton's party on Elephant Island – but

too late, because, on his third attempt, Shackleton had effected his own rescue in a Chilean vessel ('I have done it: damn the Admiralty,' he wrote to his wife). Efforts were then concentrated on saving the Ross party, still marooned on the other side of the Pole, and Shackleton's favoured navi-

gator, Davis, headed south with the *Aurora*.

Davis's diaries are not fluent: here is the uncensored inner mind of a fraught and thwarted leader – lonely, troubled by burdensome responsibility, and the exasperating nature of the mechanics of exploration.

The rescue of Shackleton's Ross Sea party

January 9th 1917: 8 p.m. Continued southward all last night through occasional streams of loose ice, fine clear weather. Mts Erebus and Terror were sighted at noon today at a distance of 130 miles, in fine clear weather. Both of these Mts appear from this distance to have more snow on them than usual, but this may be the effect of distance . . .

There appears to be more ice than usual South of Coulman Island, which gives one grounds for hoping that the ice has been blown out of McMurdo Sound. If this is the case we should be in communication with Cape Evans before tomorrow evening, provided the wind remains moderate and the weather fine . . . There is a very noticeable absence of Bergs.

We are sending the wireless message to the Ross Sea Party in the hopes that it may possibly reach them.

'Ross Sea Party, Cape Evans.
Aurora is now within 100 miles of Cape Evans, Hope you are all well and that ice will allow us to communicate with you shortly. Davis'

9 p.m. Beaufort Island has just been sighted and we are steering towards it in an ice free sea. What conditions will tomorrow bring forth? Shall we meet ice and be held off outside the sounds, 30 miles from Cape Royds, as we were in the *Nimrod* or shall we be able to steam right up to Cape Evans as the *Terra Nova* did on Jan[uary] 4th in 1911 . . .

It will be a glad day for the Ross Sea Party if we are able to communicate tomorrow. They have been down here now just two years and under trying circumstances. I always have been anxious about the parties who were away sledging, but the party at the Hut should be all right.

January 10th: . . . at 10.20 [a.m.] we were off Cape Royds and met the fast ice which extends Southward . . . Cape Evans is visible but there is no sign of life. We fired a rocket distress signal, hoping to rouse someone out of Shackleton's old hut. As this was unsuccessful we came alongside the ice foot and I sent a party of three men with Sir E. to visit the hut and look for some record.

11.55 [a.m.] Party returned on board with a record found at the hut stating that the Ross Sea Party were based at Cape Evans. Just before their arrival on board, a black patch was seen to the southward which was, later on, made out to be a party of six approaching, as from C[ape] Evans, with a sledge or dog team.

Sir E. Shackleton, Moyes, Middleton went out to meet the party and it was arranged before they left that they should signal to us, whether all hands were there, when they met. The parties rapidly approached each other and we anxiously watched for this signal when they met. The news they received was, apparently, that 3 of the party had not survived. We were able to see that something serious had occurred.

Bringing the ship to the edge of the floe again we put out an anchor and I went over the ice to meet the party, who were not close at hand. They looked very unkempt and dishevelled and smelt strongly of blubber. In a few seconds we learned that the whole of the party out sledging in 1915 had been at Hut P[oin]t for nearly 5 w[ee]ks before the ship blew away. The entire party wintered at C[ape] Evans and during the summer 1915–16, [an] extensive depot laying journey was made to the southward, reaching Mr Hope Jan[uary] 9th 1916. On the return journey the various parties were attacked by scurvy but all managed to reach Hut Pt on March 31st 1916 after great hardships, with the exception of Rev A.P. Spencer Smith who died on the Barrier 18 miles from Hut P[oin]t on March 9th 1916.

This party were now cut off by open water from C[ape] Evans and remained at Hut Point slowly recovering from the effects of scurvy. On May 8th 1916, Capt Mackintosh and Hayward decided to try and walk over to C. Evans. The ice at the time is reported to have been only 4″ thick. The weather had been fine for the two previous days and it is assumed that this party counted on its continuance. At 8 p.m. on May 8th a blizzard sprang up and nothing more has been heard of either of them. They were totally without equipment and there is no doubt that they perished, owing to the breaking up of the sea ice over which they were travelling, during the blizzard.

The party who were left behind at the Hut report that when the weather cleared up on May 10th 1916, they followed the tracks of this party over the sea ice towards Cape Evans, until they were abruptly terminated by open water. As however, this party had no reason to believe that Capt Mackintosh and his companion had not reached C[ape] Evans, though they were naturally anxious about them, they remained at Hut P[oin]t until a period of full moon,

July 15th 1916, when they returned to Cape Evans and learned that Capt Mackintosh had not arrived. A search was then carried out but no traces of any kind were discovered.

The crossing of the sea ice, during the darkness of winter, is a terribly risky undertaking, and taken in conjunction with the fact that this sea ice was only 4" thick, make it difficult to understand why they should have attempted it at all. With the exception of this regrettable tragedy, the rest of the party seem to have come through a very severe ordeal remarkably well.

During the afternoon a party left for C[ape] Evans and brought off some gear. I have been endeavouring to obtain from various individual members of the party a coherent account of what happened, in order to decide whether there is any possibility of Mackintosh and his companion having survived, with the result that one is reluctantly compelled to admit that there is now no hope of ever seeing them again. It is now eight months since they are missing; they were totally unprovided with equipment, it was practically mid winter when they went adrift; the bergs and islands surrounding C[ape] Evans have been searched; and even if they had drifted to the Western shore of the Sound, they could not have lived without food, shelter or sleeping bags.

Sir E. Shackleton is obtaining {from} [for] me a written report as to this occurrence, and when one has had an opportunity to analyse it carefully it may be possible to glean a few more details. Naturally the party we have relieved are labouring under considerable excitement, and [it] is just a little difficult to obtain a coherent statement, other than to the effect that they had given these people up long ago.

With Mawson, 1930

March 3rd 1930: 8 p.m. The wind gradually moderated last night . . . There was a faint aurora visible last night at 8.30 [p.m.]; some streamers of yellow greenish light radiating from about S×W up to the Zenith. We are now steering for Albany but like all our movements, our destination seems still uncertain. However it is a good thing to be homeward bound . . .

I have been trying to set out clearly the result[s] of our work in Kerguelen which affect seamen who will visit the place in future. Hurley has taken a great number of photographs which would help this job a good deal . . . I am convinced that we could have done a good deal of valuable work there, but for the fact that there is no general recognition of the fact that such work is specialist work, and should be provided for in selecting the staff for a scientific expedition going to uncharted places. We have an officer called a survey officer but he has no experience and so far has not produced anything, nor do I think he has ever been instructed to do any one job. He goes ashore with the only theodolite every time the launch makes a landing, but how one can do any work this way towards making a correct plan of one locality is difficult to see . . .

March 4th: Have been busy completing the notes and amendments for the sailing directions dealing with Kerguelen. Have tried to get photos of positions I asked Hurley to take. He is too busy so we have to do the best we can without them. I cannot conceive a more haphazard enterprise than this one. Nothing is really ever finished completely, and one just drops into a kind of morass which like the great war has only one bright spot, its conclusion.

March 5th: 8.20 p.m. . . . At 2 p.m. it was decided to start trawling and until 4.30 p.m. wire was paid out over the stern. It is now being hove in slowly <u>in the dark</u> with a good deal of difficulty. Those of the party who are inclined to work are all busy with M. The rest of them are just <u>busy</u> until the unpleasantness is over. I suppose one should not be critical but it is all so hopelessly muddled . . . Instead of starting this job at 6 a.m. and getting it done during the daylight, we are working in the dark and will be lucky if someone is not hurt before the trawl is on board.

I shall be very thankful to get to Australia. Fortunately I have a good lot of officers and a most docile and good humoured ship's company, or there would have been lots of trouble in this. M himself works hard but he will not do his own job, which I feel is to organise the work and get the best out of everyone. He messes about with everything from the food to the storage of the holds. The mate is exasperated and no wonder. I have to find excuses for him and endeavour to pretend that I like the ship being reduced to a bedlam, or there would be friction which I wish to avoid. . . . I hope I shall never have the bad luck to be associated with a scientific man as leader of a marine expedition. They are not qualified to control such an undertaking.

March 6th: 9 p.m. The dredge was on board at 10.30 p.m. with the frame broken and the net torn [and] very little in it. Too much wire had been paid out and the ship kept going while they were heaving it in. I did not interfere as one just gets into an argument with one of the experts, and so they are all rather quiet today . . .

I realise after reading my journal for the last two days there is something about this show which is missing. It is what I would call the Shackleton touch which made the ward room a brighter spot as soon as one went into it. . . . The good spirit is not there which seemed to exist on our way out from England and I hoped would persist. There are two distinct parties, the ship and the scientists, and the two seem never to have merged into one body, the members of the expedition . . .

We set all sail again and are getting along at 6 knots towards Australia . . . Byrds Expedition is due at Wellington tomorrow so I expect they are a happy crowd on board the *City of New York*. Of Wilkins we hear very little.

Have just about completed notes on Kerguelen; and Colbeck, who has turned out quite a neat draughtsman, has just finished putting our tracks on the chart. He has stuck to the job well and will make a good navigating officer, as he has brains and can do a job well when he is left alone . . .

March 7th: 8.30 p.m. . . . Have just been handed Press by the wireless man which contains a paragraph emanating from Canberra

'Mawson Antarctic Expedition now returning in *Discovery* which is expected to reach Adelaide about March 21st.'

I have no idea whether this is settled or not but I hope that the necessary arrangements will be made for dealing with the question of the future of the *Discovery*. I am quite prepared to take the vessel home if they decide to send her there, but I could not undertake to make another trip South in her . . .

M and I have totally different methods and it has only been possible to avoid friction by continually giving way, until the ship is just running herself . . . With an ordinary crew in this ship it would be impossible to maintain any discipline at all . . . A man who knows his own job should hesitate to take on anything where he will be subordinate to laymen at sea. It is and always will be a mistake to suppose it can be successful. Fortunately it has had no consequences in our case such as the loss of the *Proteus* as M and I are both sensible enough to keep our tempers. But nevertheless I shall be glad to finish my job here, and quite unwilling to go again.

March 10th: 9 p.m. . . . At 2 p.m. we went slow for tow netting and this went on until 6.15 [p.m.]. I am afraid it does not interest me enough, as I want to get on with our voyage and feel that these spasmodic efforts are not really as important as is assumed. We laboured in the last expedition to get such work done and it was supposed to be of great importance, yet the results of the work are still in the bunker room somewhere after sixteen years! . . .

Byrd's expedition has arrived and they have been accorded a great public welcome according to reports. One tires a bit of all the humbug that is associated with such enterprises. How can we judge at this time [that] what they have done [is] worth while.

March 11th: 8.30 p.m. . . . . We are steering for Albany which was 1102 miles off at noon today.

The temperature of the air has gone up, and there is a summer feeling about this fine weather that we have not enjoyed since leaving the Cape . . . Some of the party may indulge in a wash. There is plenty of water but I have never, even in the aft deck, sat down to food with people as dirty as some of our party. I spoke to M about it but he said it was because they worked so hard. I pointed out that no one worked harder than the Engineers who were always clean when they appeared at meals. I wonder if Scott, who looks down from the head of our ward table, thinks the new tenants of his old ward room an uncouth lot . . .

Trial by Ice: The Antarctic Journals of John King Davis (1997)

THOR HEYERDAHL

1914–2002

*And after all, that was just the object of our voyage, to follow the sun in its path,
as we thought Kon-Tiki and the old sun-worshippers must have done . . .*

Born in Larvik, Norway, Heyerdahl was from childhood an ardent nature-lover; he was encouraged in this by his mother, who ran the local museum. After specializing in zoology and geography at the University of Oslo, he travelled to Polynesia, where he and his bride were adopted by the Chief of Tahiti, Terreroo, in 1937. Living a Polynesian life for a year, he observed how his friends struggled with easterly winds and currents on fishing trips and he gradually became more and more sceptical of the existing theory: that the inhabitants owed their origin to stone-using migrants from South-East Asia. He began to believe they must have come from the west, by means of the ocean currents, just as much flora and fauna did.

Losing interest in zoology, Heyerdahl focused more and more on the origin of Polynesian peoples. Working at the museum of British Columbia, he published his theories of settlement patterns, but was interrupted by the war, returning to Norway to serve in the Free Norwegian Forces, where he eventually joined a parachute regiment.

After the war, Heyerdahl tested his theory: in 1947 he and five colleagues sailed a replica aboriginal balsa-wood raft – named the *Kon-Tiki* – from Callao, Peru, to Raroia atoll, Tuamotu Archipelago, in the South Pacific. They had journeyed 8,000 km (4,300 nautical miles) in 101 days. Despite continued resistance from the academic world to his theory, he had proved that such a journey was possible, even with a traditional raft. His feat had also captured the world's imagination.

In 1952, his expedition to the Galapagos Islands found pre-Inca ceramics, showing for the first time that South Americans spread their influence into the Pacific; his expedition

to Easter Island (1955–6) made the first subterranean excavations, revealing that the inhabitants had de-forested the island and planted South American species, such as water-reeds. Evidence for his theory of eastern migration was accumulating.

With the *Ra* expedition, he switched his attention to navigation by papyrus boats, setting out to prove that ancient Mediterranean people could have crossed the Atlantic to America well before Columbus. He bought 12 tons of papyrus – long believed to grow waterlogged after more than a week in open sea – and worked with experts to fashion a vessel, which he launched from what was once the Phoenician port of Safi (in present-day Morocco). *Ra* sailed 5,700 km (2,700 nautical miles), but broke up after fifty-six days owing to storms. He, and his seven-man crew (picked from seven nationalities symbolically to represent co-operation) were a week short of Barbados.

Just under a year later, Heyerdahl tried again in a shorter, modified craft, *Ra II*, and this time reached Barbados in fifty-seven days – showing the journey was indeed possible, and that both the ancient navigators and their vessels had been underestimated.

His subsequent journey (1977–8) in the reed vessel *Tigris* hoped to show that ancient mariners could not only travel with the wind but against it, and so complete journeys both ways through the Persian Gulf and Arabian Sea. Regional political conflict and oil pollution led him to burn the *Tigris* in protest at the journey's end, Djibouti.

Even well into his eighties, he was still energetically participating in archaeological digs, and acting as an ambassador of co-operation between peoples.

At a recent function in his honour, John Julius Norwich suggested his key achievement was his ideas: 'By all means knock them down, but *have ideas.*' This will be his lasting contribution – an original mind that doggedly followed its thoughts through, not easily diverted by those comfortable in how they see the world.

The Kon-Tiki expedition

By the late afternoon the trade wind was already blowing at full strength. It quickly stirred up the ocean into roaring seas which swept against us from astern. Now we fully realised for the first time that here was the sea itself come to meet us; it was bitter earnest now, our communications were cut. Whether things went well now would depend entirely on the balsa raft's good qualities in the open sea. We knew that from now onwards we should never get another on-shore wind or chance of turning back. We had got into the real trade wind, and every day would carry us farther and farther out to sea. The only thing to do was to go ahead under full sail; if we tried to turn homewards we should only drift farther out to sea stern first. There was only one possible course, to sail before the wind with our bows towards the sunset. And, after all, that was just the object of our voyage, to follow the sun in its path, as we thought Kon-Tiki and the old sun-worshippers must have done when they were chased out to sea from Peru.

We noted with triumph and relief how the wooden raft rose up over the first threatening wave-crests that came foaming towards us. But it was impossible for the steersman to hold the oar steady when the roaring seas rolled towards him and lifted the oar out of the thole-pins, or swept it to one side so that the steersman was swung round like a helpless acrobat. Not even two men at once could hold the oar steady when the seas rose against us and poured down over the steersman aft. We hit on the idea of running ropes from the oar-blade to each side of the raft, and, with other ropes holding the oar in place in the thole-pins, it obtained a limited freedom of movement and could defy the worst seas if only we ourselves could hold on.

As the troughs of the sea gradually grew deeper it became clear that we had got into the swiftest part of the Humboldt Current. This sea was obviously caused by a current and not simply raised by the wind. The water was green and cold and everywhere about us; the jagged mountains of Peru had vanished into the dense cloud-banks astern. When darkness crept over the sea our first duel with the elements began. We were still not sure of the sea; it was still uncertain whether it would show itself a friend or an enemy in the intimate proximity we ourselves had sought. When, swallowed up by the

darkness, we heard the general noise from the sea around us suddenly deaf-
ened by the hiss of a roller close by, and saw a white crest come groping
towards us on a level with the cabin roof, we held on tight and waited uneasily
to feel the masses of water smash down over us and the raft. But every time
there was the same surprise and relief . . .

We clung like flies, two and two, to the steering oar in the darkness, and felt
the fresh sea water pouring off our hair while the oar hit us till we were tender
both behind and before, and our hands grew stiff with the exertion of hanging
on. We had a good schooling those first days and nights; it turned landlubbers
into seamen. For the first twenty-four hours every man, in unbroken succession, had two hours at the helm and three hours' rest. We arranged that every
hour a fresh man should relieve the one of the two steersmen who had been at
the helm for two hours. Every single muscle in the body was strained to the
uttermost throughout the watch to cope with the steering. When we were
tired out with pushing the oar we went over to the other side and pulled, and
when arms and chest were sore with pressing, we turned our backs, while the
oar kneaded us green and blue in front and behind. When at last the relief
came, we crept half dazed into the bamboo cabin, tied a rope round our legs,
and fell asleep with our salty clothes on before we could get into our sleeping
bags. Almost at the same moment there came a brutal tug at the rope; three
hours had passed, and one had to go out again and relieve one of the two men
at the steering oar.

The next night was still worse; the seas grew higher instead of going down.
Two hours on end of struggling with the steering oar was too long; a man was
not much use in the second half of his watch, and the seas got the better of us
and hurled us round and sideways, while the water poured on board. Then we
changed over to one hour at the helm and an hour and a half's rest. So the first
sixty hours passed, in one continuous struggle against a chaos of waves that
rushed upon us, one after another, without cessation. High waves and low
waves, pointed waves and round waves, slanting waves and waves on the top
of other waves. The one of us who suffered the worst was Knut. He was let off
steering watch, but to compensate for this he had to sacrifice to Neptune and
suffered silent agonies in a corner of the cabin. The parrot sat sulkily in its
cage and hung on with its beak and flapped its wings every time the raft gave
an unexpected pitch and the sea splashed against the wall from astern. The
Kon-Tiki did not roll so excessively. She took the seas more steadily than any
boat of the same dimensions, but it was impossible to predict which way the
deck would lean next time, and we never learned the art of moving about the
raft easily, for she pitched as much as she rolled.

The sea contains many surprises for him who has his floor on a level with the surface, and drifts along slowly and noiselessly. A sportsman who breaks his way through the woods may come back and say that no wild life is to be seen. Another may sit down on a stump and wait, and often rustlings and cracklings will begin, and curious eyes peer out. So it is on the sea too. We usually plough across it with roaring engines and piston strokes, with the water foaming round our bows. Then we come back and say that there is nothing to see far out on the ocean.

Not a day passed but we, as we sat floating on the surface of the sea, were visited by inquisitive guests which wriggled and waggled about us, and a few of them, such as dolphins and pilot fish, grew so familiar that they accompanied the raft across the sea and kept round us day and night.

When night had fallen, and the stars were twinkling in the dark tropical sky, the phosphorescence flashed around us in rivalry with the stars, and single glowing plankton resembled round live coals so vividly that we involuntarily drew in our bare legs when the glowing pellets were washed up round our feet at the raft's stern. When we caught them we saw that they were little brightly shining species of shrimp. On such nights we were sometimes scared when two round shining eyes suddenly rose out of the sea right alongside the raft and glared at us with an unblinking hypnotic stare – it might have been the Old Man of the Sea himself. These were often big squids which came up and floated on the surface with their devilish green eyes shining in the dark like phosphorus. But sometimes they were the shining eyes of deep water fish which only came up at night and lay staring, fascinated by the glimmer of light before them. Several times, when the sea was calm, the black water round the raft was suddenly full of round heads two or three feet in diameter, lying motionless and staring at us with great glowing eyes. On other nights balls of light three feet and more in diameter would be visible down in the water, flashing at irregular intervals like electric lights turned on for a moment . . .

Sometimes, too, we went out in the rubber boat to look at ourselves by night. Coal-black seas towered up on all sides, and a glittering myriad of tropical stars drew a faint reflection from plankton in the water. The world was simple, stars in the darkness. Whether it was 1947 B.C. or A.D. suddenly became of no significance. We lived, and that we felt with alert intensity. We realised that life had been full for men before the technical age also – indeed, fuller and richer in many ways than the life of modern man. Time and evolution somehow ceased to exist; all that was real and all that mattered were the same to-day as they had always been and would always be; we were swallowed up in the absolute common measure of history, endless unbroken darkness under a swarm of stars. Before us in the night the *Kon-Tiki* rose out of the seas to sink down again behind black masses of water that towered between her and us. In the moonlight there was a singular atmosphere about the raft. Stout shining wooden logs fringed with seaweed, the square pitch-black outline of a Viking sail, a bristly bamboo hut with the yellow light of a paraffin lamp aft – the whole suggested a picture from a fairy tale rather than the actual reality. Now and then the raft disappeared completely behind the black seas; then she rose again and stood out sharp in silhouette against the stars, while glittering water poured from the logs.

When we saw the atmosphere about the solitary raft, we could well see in our mind's eye the whole flotilla of such vessels, spread in fan formation beyond the horizon to increase the chances of finding land, when the first men made their way across this sea. The Inca Tupak Yupanqui, who had brought under his rule both Peru and Ecuador, sailed across the sea with an armada of many thousand men on balsa rafts, just before the Spaniards came, to search for islands which rumour had told of out in the Pacific. He found two islands, which some think were the Galapagos, and after eight months' absence he and his numerous paddlers succeeded in toiling their way back to Ecuador. Kon-Tiki and his followers had certainly sailed in a similar formation several hundred years before, but having discovered the Polynesian islands, they had no reason for trying to struggle back.

Reaching Polynesia

I shall never forget that wade across the reef towards the heavenly palm island that grew larger as it came to meet us. When I reached the sunny sand beach, I slipped off my shoes and thrust my bare toes down into the warm, bone-dry sand. It was as though I enjoyed the sight of every footprint which dug itself into the virgin sand beach that led up to the palm trunks. Soon the palm-tops closed over my head, and I went on, right in towards the centre of the tiny island. Green cocoanuts hung under the palm-tufts, and some luxuriant bushes were thickly covered with snow-white blossoms, which smelt so sweet and seductive that I felt quite faint. In the interior of the island two quite tame terns flew about my shoulders. They were as white and light as wisps of cloud. Small lizards shot away from my feet, and the most important inhabitants of the island were large blood-red hermit crabs, which lumbered along in every direction with stolen snail-shells as large as eggs adhering to their soft hinder-parts.

I was completely overwhelmed. I sank down on my knees and thrust my fingers deep down into the dry warm sand.

The voyage was over. We were all alive. We had run ashore on a small uninhabited South Sea island. And what an island! Torstein came in, flung away a sack, threw himself flat on his back and looked up at the palm-tops and the white birds, light as down, which circled noiselessly just above us. Soon we were all six lying there. Herman, always energetic, climbed up a small palm and pulled down a cluster of large green cocoanuts. We cut off their soft tops, as if they were eggs, with our machete knives, and poured down our throats the most delicious refreshing drink in the world – sweet, cold milk from young and seedless palm fruit. On the reef outside resounded the monotonous drumbeats from the guard at the gates of paradise.

'Purgatory was a bit damp,' said Bengt, 'but heaven was more or less as I'd imagined it.'

We stretched ourselves luxuriously on the ground and smiled up at the white trade wind clouds drifting by westward up above the palm-tops. Now we were no longer following them helplessly; now we lay on a fixed, motionless island, really in Polynesia.

And as we lay and stretched ourselves, the breakers outside us rumbled like a train, to and fro, to and fro all along the horizon.

Bengt was right; this was heaven.

The Kon-Tiki Expedition, 1950

HAROLD WILLIAM TILMAN
1898–1977
We were in a situation that the prudent mariner does his best to avoid.

Born in Wallasey, Cheshire, Tilman served as an artillery officer on the Western Front, and then worked as a coffee planter in East Africa, where he began climbing with Eric Shipton, and later in the Himalayas and Karakoram. He took to the sea in his fifties, navigating waters that few people, and no amateur-crewed sailing boats, had seen.

He made the first ascents of Midget Peak on Mount Kenya (1930) and Nanda Devi in the Himalayas (1936) – the highest summit achieved by man at the time – and was naturally chosen to lead the 1938 attempt on Everest. After the Second World War, in which he fought in France, in the Western Desert and behind the lines with partisans in northern Italy and Albania, he made important explorations through China, Nepal, Kashmir and the fringes of the Gobi Desert, filling in blanks on the map, often with Shipton, for which he was awarded the 1952 Founder's Medal of the RGS. Whereas the Victorian explorers of Asia had avoided the peaks, Tilman aimed for them. He attempted important Himalayan summits such as Rakaposhi and Muztagh Ata. The Tilman–Shipton creed was that any worthwhile expedition could, if you had a tight-knit team, be planned 'on the back of an envelope' – a philosophy contrary to the siege mentality of, for example, the huge, successful Everest expedition of 1953.

Disenchanted with the increasingly crowded Himalayas, and feeling – in his fifties – that he was too old for peaks over 20,000 feet, in 1953 he took to the sea. For the next quarter-century, with various old cutters, he headed for both the Arctic and Antarctic, sailing some 114,000 miles before the loss of his first boat, the *Mischief*. He circumnavigated South America, leaving his boat to walk over the ice-cap of Patagonia, and also circled Africa (1957–8). On 1 November 1977 he set sail in *En Avant* from Rio for the Falklands, en route to the South Shetland Isles, but was never seen again.

On his sailing expeditions, Tilman took no life-raft, insurance, or radio. His feeling was that 'every herring should hang by its own tail'. But his fearlessness was an intelligent one: he didn't bluff it out or bungle along; he knew mountains and seas, and embraced their dangers lustily.*

Tilman has been called a literary master-craftsman, having written fifteen books – largely forgotten by the general public. Belonging as he does to the English tradition of the picaresque, his wry humour is also cultured, his lightness setting him apart from the earnest tones of his Edwardian contemporaries.

* 'There is something in common between the arts of sailing and of climbing,' Tilman wrote, having made the transition between the two arts. 'Each is intimately concerned with elemental things, which from time to time demand from men who practise those arts whatever self-reliance, prudence and endurance they may have. The sea and the hills offer challenges to those who venture upon them and in the acceptance of these and in the meeting of them as best he can lies the sailor's or mountaineer's reward . . . An essential difference is perhaps that the mountaineer usually accepts the challenge on his own terms, whereas once at sea the sailor has no say in the matter and in consequence may suffer more often the salutary and humbling emotion of fear.'

Advertising for a crew

The advertisement I had used for an earlier voyage merely said: 'Hands wanted for long voyage in small boat; no pay, no prospects, not much pleasure.' The advertising manager who, more than anyone, I should have thought, must have daily dealings with the lunatic fringe, was rude enough to query both the advertisement and my good faith. Even so, when it finally appeared, the response was far too hearty to be dealt with in conscientious fashion.

For the present cruise the advertisement ran: 'Cook wanted for cold voyage in small boat; five mouths to feed for five months.' This, too, was well received but it did not get me anyone. One promising candidate whom I interviewed, having agreed to come, wrote a letter and posted it the same evening to say he had changed his mind; and another, a young flautist, badly wanted to come but would not dream of cooking. But I had let myself in for a lot of trouble by omitting the words 'men only', a mistake that obliged me to write at least a dozen letters of regret to all the women who applied. My regrets were sincere, too, since some of these applicants would have filled the bill admirably had I been able to overcome my fear of having a woman on board for so long in such inescapable circumstances. 'Discord,' as yet another Chinese sage has remarked, 'is not sent down from heaven, it is brought about by women.' One of these women had crossed the Atlantic cooking for a crew of five men and from the way the letter was worded I gathered that these poor fish might consider themselves lucky to have had her with them. Shrinking hastily away from this seafaring Amazon, I hesitated long before refusing another who wrote less stridently to say she had cruised in several yachts in the Mediterranean, cooking the meals and arranging the flowers, and that she was a *cordon bleu*. Flowers we should have to forgo, but my mouth watered at the thought of the meals we might have. So much for the advertisement – guineas thrown away. Roger Tufft, who had sailed in *Mischief* on the Crozet venture and who still corresponded with me in desultory fashion, knew what was afoot but kept me for a long time in suspense. He is a man who sits loosely in any sedentary job, his usual occupation during his brief stays in England being that of teaching. At length, however, the temptation proved too strong and he wrote to say that he would come. Moreover, failing anyone else, he offered to try his hand in the galley. He was a great acquisition. We knew each other and he was a mountaineer as well as an experienced hand; added to that he was as strong as a horse, able to carry a load or kick steps until further orders. Instead of having time to sit about on stones, as on the last Greenland trip, I should find myself always toiling in the rear. The fact that he knew the boat and the way things were done would be valuable when starting with a strange crew, and there are few men, not excluding some of the rummer birds who have sailed in *Mischief*, with whom Roger would not be able to cope.

Ice, fog and a Christmas pudding

As we sailed on through the mist it became obvious that we were in a situation that the prudent mariner does his best to avoid. We had little idea how near we were to some unknown part of a rock-bound and probably ice-bound coast towards which we were sailing in fog, surrounded by scattered icebergs. If we went about, as caution advised, we could steer only south. So we carried on and at four o'clock that afternoon our boldness or rashness had its unmerited reward. A vast berg looming up ahead obliged us to alter course to clear it and at that moment the fog rolled away. After a month at sea the dullest coast looks exciting, but a more dramatic landfall than the one we now made, both as to its suddenness and its striking appearance, could scarcely be imagined. Two or three miles ahead, stretching away on either hand, lay a rocky coast thickly fringed with stranded icebergs and backed by high, barren mountains. Beyond the mountains and over-topping them was the faintly glistening band of the Greenland ice-cap. To identify any particular part of this strange, wild coast was hardly possible, but we guessed that a bold cape a few miles westwards might be Cape Desolation at the western end of Julian-nehaab Bight. An evening sight for longitude confirmed this. But on our making towards the cape the fog closed in again and we stood out to sea. Fog or no fog, the novelty of sailing in smooth water, the luck of our landfall, its magnificent aspect, all combined to give us a feeling of elation. From a hidden source Charles dug out a Christmas pudding and took elaborate pains over concocting a rum sauce to help it down – pains that are wasted on this kind of sauce for they merely serve to adulterate the main ingredient . . .

Unlike pack-ice, which moves generally with the wind, the movement of bergs is affected almost entirely by currents because of the far greater proportion of ice below water than above. The amount submerged varies with the type of berg. A solid block-like berg with sheer sides floats with only about one fifth above the surface, while a so-called 'picturesque' berg, pinnacled and ridged like a miniature mountain, might have one third or even as much as a half above water. We saw some great blocks of bergs 100ft. high and covering an acre or more of sea in the waters west of Cape Farewell . . .

We never tired of looking at bergs. At first we counted and logged all those in sight but north of Disko Island they became too numerous to count. If some particularly vast or grotesquely-shaped monster hove in sight we some-times went out of our way to have a closer look at him. According to the light their colour varied from an opaque dazzling white to the loveliest blues and greens. Some had caves or even a hole clean through them in which the blue colour was intense and translucent. When passing a berg it is best to keep on the windward side on account of the number of bergy bits or growlers which break away and litter the sea to leeward. In fog or at night, in waters where there is no reason to expect ice floes, the presence of these bits of ice would indicate a berg in the vicinity. If it is rough waves may be sometimes heard breaking against the berg, but no reliance can be placed upon detecting changes of air or sea temperature in its vicinity or of receiving echoes from it from a fog-horn. Radar would pick up a large berg but would probably fail to show a 'growler' quite big enough to sink a ship. The only certain method is to see it. That a good look-out all round even in daylight is essential was impressed on me the day after we made our landfall. The wind had dropped and there was nothing in sight, no land, no ice. We handed the sails and motored for some eight hours, for most of the time in fog. When the boom and mainsail are resting on the gallows the helmsman's vision is obscured on one side unless he stands up on the cockpit seat and steers with his foot, or has a line round the tiller. For one reason or another I was standing in the cockpit, peering intently ahead into the fog. Happening to bend down and glance under the boom to the port side I was startled by the sight of the large, luminous mass of an iceberg less than fifty yards away.

Mischief in Greenland, 1964

BERNARD MOITESSIER
1925–96
I found something more. A kind of indefinable state of grace.

Born in Hanoi, Indochina, the Frenchman Moitessier gained much of his sailing knowledge from the fishermen of the Gulf of Siam. He wrote four books describing his seagoing adventures in Tahiti, the Antilles and New Zealand and spent his life sailing the oceans of the world, always seeming to be running away from something.

In 1968 he was one of nine men to set out on the 'Golden Globe' race to be the first to sail single-handed non-stop around the world – Francis Chichester, recently returned from his own circumnavigation, had stopped at the mid-point. The race was won by Robin Knox-Johnston, a 'tinned sausages and corned-beef man' who ploughed on slowly and steadily through the waves while better and faster boats, or their captains, cracked up. Moitessier, probably the most talented of all the competitors, knew his boat backwards – what

it could do, and what it could not: in his hands it was a delicate instrument – but instead of winning the race, after rounding Cape Horn he chose not to turn north for Plymouth to collect the prize, but sailed on around the world again. 'You do not ask a tame seagull why it needs to disappear from time to time toward the open sea. It goes, that's all.'

Moitessier's writing presents an enormous contrast to Chichester's, who was ever the disciplinarian, adding up and checking to keep his mind alert. The Frenchman's mind, however, is in joyous free fall, blending with the ocean environment to which he is so attuned. His 'state of grace' with the elements was the product of his sensibility, but also his time – the culmination of three thousand years or more of seafaring, of learning the sea's form, and how to ride it without fear.

'Anything is possible'

It really is a fine year, such as must be rare on this southern route. I remember the little plastic bags we used to fasten at our ankles with rubber bands to protect our precious double-thick wool socks from the always wet cabin floor. Woolen gloves inside, mittens and leather gloves for handling sail, chapped fingers, the essential boots, the few clothes we would dry every day above the stove. Even the blankets were more or less damp and covered with salt.

Now . . . the temperature in the unheated cabin is 55° at dawn, 75° at noon. My supply of plastic bags is untouched. I am almost always barefoot on deck, and my clothes are as dry as when I left.

On the other hand, these two months of fair weather must have surely caused an early break-up of the ice in the far south, and I would not be surprised to learn that the icebergs went beyond their normal limit this year. In any case. I have absolutely no idea. I am wool-gathering as usual, as I often do when everything is for the best, and all you have to do is breathe peacefully and thank heaven for its gifts. Anyway, it is likely that the break-up of the pack that sets the icebergs adrift is more closely linked to seismic shocks and heavy gales than to the sun . . . There I go again, my thoughts wandering off in every direction. Not out of anxiety though; far from it. I feel joyful, surrounded by something very imminent in the air around me. I call it 'my eldest brother', the way you call your friends in the Far East. I talk to him a lot: I feel that we agree, but he does not answer. He must have his hands full keeping lows away. Or maybe he thinks I should figure things out for myself, alone with my solitude, so vast and so full.

My hair has grown a lot; it is almost down to my shoulders. My beard is so long I have to trim it around my lips every week, so as to eat my morning porridge without smearing it all over. My last complete soaping dates back to a rain squall in the doldrums, months ago . . . yet I do not have a single pimple on my skin.

Joshua is half way to the Horn. For five days in a row I have done my yoga exercises completely naked in the cockpit, before the meridian sight. I feel the sun entering into me, giving me its power. When there is no sun, or toward the end of the afternoon, I keep a sweater and wool trousers on, and the power comes from the air I breathe.

Physical and mental balance after five months at sea still comes as a surprise, when I look at the long, long curve on the little globe. Certainly I knew it was possible when I left. Anything is possible . . . it's a matter of attitude and instinctive adaptation. But I never thought it possible to attain such fullness of body and mind after five months in a closed system, with a stomach ulcer I have been dragging around for the last ten years.

The moon is gone. She will be back in a few days, like a smile, very shy at first, then bigger and bigger. The barometer is falling now, but life goes on at its normal pace, even with the threat of a gale. How long will it last, this peace I have found at sea? It is all of life that I contemplate – sun, clouds, time that passes and abides. Occasionally it is also that other world, foreign now, that I left centuries ago. The modern, artificial world where man has been turned into a money-making machine to satisfy false needs, false joys . . .

I am really fed up with false gods, always lying in wait, spider-like, eating our liver, sucking our marrow. I charge the modern world – that's the Monster. It is destroying our earth, and trampling the soul of men.

'*Yet it is thanks to the modern world that you have a good boat with winches. Tergal sails, and a solid metal hull that doesn't give you any worries.*'

'*That's true, but it is because of the modern world, because of its so-called "civilization" and its so-called "progress" that I take off with my beautiful boat.*'

'*Well, you're free to split, no one is stopping you; everyone free here, so long as it doesn't interfere with others.*'

'*Free for the moment . . . but before long no one will be free if things go on. They have already become inhuman. So there are those who go to sea or hit the road to seek the lost truth. And those who can't, or won't anymore, who have lost even hope. "Western civilization" is almost completely technocratic now, it isn't a civilization anymore.*'

'*If we listened to people like you, more or less vagabonds and barefoot tramps, we would not have got beyond the bicycle.*'

'*That's just it; we would ride bikes in the cities, there wouldn't be those thousands of cars with hard, closed people all alone in them, we would see youngsters arm in arm, hear laughter and singing, see nice things in people's faces; joy and love would be reborn everywhere, birds would return to the few trees left in our streets and we would replant the trees the Monster killed. Then we would feel real shadows and real colours and real sounds; our cities would get their souls back, and people too.*'

God created the sea and He painted it blue to make it nice for us. And here I am, at peace, the bow pointed toward the East, when I could be heading north with an unsuspected drama deep inside.

The weather is good, the wake gently spins out astern. Sitting crosslegged in the cockpit, I watch the sea, listening to the song of the bow. And I see a little seagull perched on my knee.

I don't dare move, I don't dare breathe, for fear she will fly away and never come back. She is white all over, almost transparent, with a slender beak and very large black eyes. I did not see her draw near, I did not sense the faster beating of her wings as she landed. My body is naked under the sun, yet I do not feel her on the bare skin of my knee. Her weight cannot be felt.

Slowly, I reach out my hand. She looks at me, preening her feathers. I reach closer. She stops smoothing her feathers and watches me, unafraid. Her eyes seem to speak . . .

For ten days the breeze remains weak, with calms at times, aside from a moderate SE gale, taken hove-to at first, then closehauled when the wind eased. Then more calms and light airs. Very often the sun sets red.

Two more days perhaps, and we will be off Cape Town, with Table Mountain rising straight above us. I listen to the note singing in the bow. There is another muted, rumbling one, because of the light SE swell left by the last gale. I do not listen to the rumbling note, I hear only the one that sings like a clear stream, I have chosen the best part.

Of course I will continue toward the Pacific. I can't remember who it was who said, 'There are two terrible things for a man: not to have fulfilled his dream, and to have fulfilled it.'

Maybe I will be able to go beyond my dream, to get inside of it, where the true thing is, the only really precious fur, the one that keeps you warm forever, Find it, or perhaps never return.

The Long Way, 1974

TIM SEVERIN
1940–
*Now, like the original monks, it was time to put to sea to look
for our way to the Promised Land.*

In a similar vein to Thor Heyerdahl, Severin has undertaken what he has termed 'practical experiments in archaeology' to test the feasibility of journeys said to have been done by ancient travellers; and for these endeavours, always scrupulously researched, in 1986 he was awarded the Gold Medal of the Royal Geographical Society.

His 1976–7 voyage across the Atlantic in a small oxhide boat proved that the sixth-century Irish traveller Saint Brendan's legendary voyage (see page 13) could indeed have carried him to America.

The extracts below are from his account of that journey. Severin aimed to do exactly as the Irish monks seem to have done; a stickler for detail, he covered the wood frame of their boats with 'oxhides tanned with the bark of oak', as the manuscript specified, obtaining 57 'butts' (oxhides trimmed of their upper shoulder and leg skin), which were then oiled with cod oil and dried. Then, because the *Navigatio* talked of the original being 'smeared ... on the outside with fat', he dressed the skins – after experimenting with fats and greases of the medieval era: tallow, beeswax, fish-oil, and wool grease – with raw wool greases. However, too much made the leather limp; too little didn't make it watertight. With twenty-three miles of flax thread he stitched the oxhides together; two miles of leather thong treated with tallow and fish-oil (a method in use since Roman times) served to pull the ash and oak vessel together.

It was a hazardous expedition – ice at one stage ripped though the leather hull, which required a crew member to lean over the side and stitch on a patch through restless, almost-freezing water. Over the course of two summers, they sailed a route north to Iceland, then west to Greenland and on to Newfoundland. Gradually, Severin linked together all the places mentioned in the medieval text: the Faroes must have been the 'Island of Sheep'; Mykines or Vagar, also in the Faroes, he identified as the 'Paradise of Birds'; southern Iceland was the region of the Fiery Mountain and the slag-throwing 'Island of Smiths'; the icebergs explained the 'Column of Crystal' and the northern whales the 'Great Fish Jasconius'. Each element turned up in 'logical progression around the North Atlantic, using the wind patterns of the summer sailing season'.

To succeed in his mission, Severin had to prove the journey was practicable, but also test the validity of the manuscript in the first place: this document was peppered with medieval symbolism, even when it specifically quantified progress in time and space – three to reflect the Trinity, twelve the apostles and, of course, the vague 'forty days' to represent 'a long time'.

After the strenuous voyage, Severin was left in no doubt. 'The author of the *Navigatio* obviously knew – as we now know – what it was like to be in an ocean-going curragh. He knew it was impossible to row upwind in a boat which sits so high in the water, and that a foul wind blows you down on a hostile shore, however much you want to get clear.'

The launch of *Brendan*

It was much too stormy and cold to risk *Brendan* at sea, so one of Paddy
Glennon's giant timber lorries trundled her up to the shallow lakes of the
River Shannon for trials. We stepped the masts, hung the steering paddle over
the starboard quarter, and pushed off to see what happened under sail. It was
an idyllic morning. A gentle breeze filled *Brendan*'s two square sails; the hull
canted slightly in response, and the long slim boat glided over the peaty
brown Shannon water. We were deep in the countryside with not a house in
sight. The broad river curved past deep green meadows. Swans took off before
our bows, paddling with their feet and undulating their long necks to gain
speed and height as they left behind the powerful rushing sound of their
wings. Clouds of ducks rose from the winter-brown reeds on each side of the
river, and a cart horse that had been grazing in the water-meadow came
galloping down to stop and stare in amazement at the strange, silent gliding
craft before it suddenly wheeled and galloped away with soft sucking splashes
in the mud, halting again at a safe distance and turning to watch the boat once
more. The whole scene – the square white sails moving silently over the brown
reeds – had an unreal air.

We glided into Lough Corry, scarcely more than an embayment in the
river's course. A puff of wind struck us, and suddenly everything became
alive. The boat heeled more steeply; the water began to surge against the
steering oar; a rope jerked adrift from its cleat; suddenly there was chaos. Each
sail needed four ropes to control it, and each rope developed a life of its own.
When one rope escaped, the others began to wriggle and slat. The heavy
crossyard swung over; the sail slapped against the mast; and without warning
we found ourselves grabbing at unidentified ropes and hauling in hopefully,
trying to discover which rope would quell the riot. But the wind had got
stronger, a good solid puff, and *Brendan* shot forward. The crew clung on,
ropes burning their hands. *Brendan* whizzed forward and the far bank of the
little lake loomed up. I leaned hard on the steering oar, and *Brendan* began to
turn. But it was too late. With a splintering of dry stalks, we went hurtling
spectacularly into the reed beds and found ourselves condemned to half an
hour of prodding oars into the peat bottom to punt *Brendan* free.

A dozen times a day we crashed into the reeds, which served as handy
buffers, and gradually we got to know the boat. *Brendan*, we discovered, had
her limitations. With only four oarsmen on board she was too unwieldly to
row against the wind, because her bows were blown downwind and we hadn't
the strength to get her back on course. More ominous was the fact that when

left to her own devices, *Brendan* lay broadside to the wind at a dangerously exposed angle. We dropped marker buoys in the lough, and by sailing between them learned that *Brendan* refused to go against the wind like an ordinary yacht. She pointed her bows bravely enough to the wind, but lacking a keel she slid sideways across the water like a tea tray. On the other hand she was far more stable than we had anticipated, and running with the wind astern she went famously. She twisted and turned at a touch of the great steering paddle so that I was reminded of surf boats.

This was how *Brendan* would be at sea, a one-way exhilarating ride with the wind on the stern. A pair of ash shovel handles extended the breadth of our main crossyard so we could carry more sail; and after a day on which it snowed, we rigged the two tent structures that would give us shelter on the voyage. We practiced hauling *Brendan* up onto the bank, and we covered her with a thick layer of wool grease like a long-distance swimmer. And always we watched the leather hull for signs of leaks. We knew that 30,000 stitches pierced the hull, most of them made by amateur leather-workers. Any of them could leak with dire results.

Crack . . . crack . . . crack. There it came again, something weird was happening, a strange snapping noise, this time much louder. George was right. The noise was coming from the hull. George was back on his feet, peering into the darkness, trying to see a few yards in the pitch black. Hastily I began to put on my outer clothes again, knowing by instinct that we had a crisis on our hands.

'It's ice!' George suddenly shouted. 'We're running into ice! I can see lumps of it all around.' Crack . . . crack . . . crack, we heard the sound again and realized without looking what it was. *Brendan* was hitting lumps of ice at speed, and they were swirling and bumping along her flanks so hard that they rattled and crackled along the oxhide skin.

'Drop the sails,' I yelled. 'If we collide with heavy ice at this speed, we'll knock her to pieces. Our only chance is to stop and wait for daylight.'

George moved into action. By the time I had struggled into my oilskins, he had lowered the mainsail and scampered forward over the icy tarpaulins, and already had the headsail halfway down. I went forward to help him secure the sodden canvas. It was perishingly cold. In an instant our bare fingers were numb as we secured the lashings on the sails. Neither George nor I said a word as we worked frantically. We could glimpse indistinct shapes in the water, and felt under our feet that *Brendan*'s hull juddered softly against unseen obstacles. We hurried back to the helm and took out the two most powerful hand torches. They were the only spot-lights we had. We switched them on,

one each side of *Brendan*, and shone them over the water. Their beams penetrated only fifty yards through the spray and sleet which hissed down in white
streaks through the shafts of light. But fifty yards was far enough to reveal a
sight which brought the adrenalin racing. All around us floated chunks and
lumps and jagged monsters of ice . . .

Painfully, we wallowed past them, heaving on the tiller, and silently hoping
that *Brendan* would respond in time. Smaller floes bumped and muttered on
her leather skin; and out of the darkness we heard the continuous swishing
sound of the waves breaking on ice beyond our vision.

George hoisted himself on the steering frame to get a clearer view. 'There's
a big floe dead ahead,' he warned. 'Try to get round to port.' I pulled over the
tiller as far as it would go. But it was not enough. I could see that we were not
going to make it. 'Get the foresail up,' I shouted. 'We've got to have more
steerage way.' George clipped on his lifeline and crawled forward along the
gunwale. Reaching the foremast, he heaved on the halliard to raise the sail. It
jammed. A loose thong had caught in the collar that slid up and down the
mast. 'Trondur!' shouted George. 'Quick, pass me up a knife.' Trondur's berth
was right beside the foremast, and he began to emerge like a bear from
hibernation. But it was too late. With a shudder from the top of her mast to
the skid under her, *Brendan* ran her bow into the great lump of sea ice. It was
like hitting a lump of concrete. The shock of the impact made me stagger.
'That will test medieval leather – and our stitching,' I thought. Thump! We
struck again. Thump! Once more the swell casually tossed *Brendan* onto the
ice. Then ungracefully and slowly, *Brendan* began to pivot on her bow, wheeling away from the ice floe like a car crash filmed in slow motion. Thump! The
boat shivered again. We had a feeling of total helplessness. There was nothing
we could do to assist *Brendan*. Only the wind would blow her clear. Thump!
This time the shock was not so fierce. *Brendan* was shifting. Scrape. She was
clear. 'Is she taking water?' George called back anxiously. I glanced down at
the floorboards. 'No, not as far as I can see back here,' I replied. 'Try to clear
the jammed headsail. I'll get Boots up as well. This is getting dodgy.'

Scarcely had I spoken than a truly awesome sight loomed up out of the
dark just downwind of us – the white and serrated edge of a massive floe,
perhaps the dying shard of an iceberg, twice the size of *Brendan*, and glinting
with malice. This apparition was rolling and wallowing like some enormous
log. Its powerful, squat shape had one great bluff end which was pointing like
a battering ram straight at *Brendan*, and it was rocking backward and forward
with ponderous certainty to deliver a blow of perhaps a hundred tons or so at
the fragile leather.

George took one look at this monster and leapt up the foremast to try to clear the jammed sail and give us steerage way. It was a slim hope. 'Hang on tight!' I bellowed at him as the swell gathered up *Brendan* and pushed her at the great ice lump which heaved up ponderously to greet her. Crack! Thump! The whole boat shook as if she had struck a reef, which indeed she had, but a reef of ice. The impact flung George backward from the mast. 'Christ, he's going to fall between *Brendan* and the ice floe, he'll be crushed,' I thought, horrified. But George still had the jammed halliard in his hand, and clutched at it desperately. The rope brought him up short, and for a heart-stopping moment he dangled backward over the gap like a puppet on a string. Now the wind was pinning *Brendan* against the great block of ice so that she was nuzzling up to it in a deadly embrace. The next impact was different. This time the ice floe rocked away from *Brendan* as the swell passed beneath us. *Brendan* swung over a broad spur of a wave-cut ledge projecting from the floe. The spur rose under us, caught *Brendan* with a grating sound, and began to lift and tip the boat. 'We're going to be flipped over like a fried egg,' I thought, as *Brendan* heeled and heeled. Then, with another grating sound of leather on ice, *Brendan* slid sideways off the ice spur and dropped back into the water.

Crash. The next collision was broadside, halfway down the boat's length. The leeboard took the impact with the sound of tortured wood.

This can't go on much longer, I wondered. Either *Brendan* will be blown clear of the floe, or she will be smashed to smithereens. As I watched, *Brendan* jostled forward another six feet on the next wave, and there was a chance to gauge the rhythm of destruction. It was obvious that the next blow would strike the steering paddle and snap its shaft. That would be the final problem: to be adrift in the pack ice with our steering gear smashed. Now the great floe was level with me where I stood at the tiller bar. The face of the floe stood taller than I did and in the light cast by my torch, the ice gleamed and glowed deep within itself with an unearthly mixture of frost white, crystal, and emerald. From the water-line a fierce blue-white reflected up through the sea from the underwater ice ledge. And all the time, like some devouring beast, the floe never ceased its constant roar and grumble as the ocean swell boomed within its submarine hollows and beat against its sides.

Here comes the last blow, I thought, the final shock in *Brendan*'s ordeal. I felt a wave lift the leather hull, saw the bleak edge of glistening ice swing heavily toward me and – feeling slightly foolish – could think of nothing else to do but lean out with one arm, brace against the steering frame, and putting my hand on the ice floe I pushed with all my strength. To my astonishment, *Brendan* responded. The stern wagged away and forward from the ice wall, and instead of a full-blooded sideswipe, we received a glancing ice blow that sent a shiver down the hull, but left the steering paddle intact. One wave later, the great floe was rolling and grumbling in our wake. It had been a very close call ...

Bump, slither, swing sideways, charge at the gap, don't think about the quarter inch of leather between yourself and the icy sea, ignore the rows of stitching offered up to the constant rubbing of ice along *Brendan*'s flanks; fend off with the boat hook. Helm up, helm down, search for the space between ice floes ahead; calculate, calculate. Wind, leeway, current, ice movement. For hour after the hour the ordeal continued, until by dusk, with the wind still blowing half a gale, the ice seemed to be thinning out. And this time we really did seem to be nearing the edge of the pack.

Then Brendan Luck finally ran out.

We were in sight of relatively open water and passing through a necklace of ice floes when two large floes swung together, closing a gap *Brendan* had already entered. The boat gave a peculiar shudder as the floes pinched her, a vaguely uncomfortable sensation which was soon forgotten in the problem of extricating her from the jaws of the vise. Luckily the two floes eased apart enough for *Brendan* to over-ride one ice spur, and slip free. Five minutes later, I heard water lapping next to the cooker and glanced down. Sea water was swirling over the floorboards. She was leaking. *Brendan* had been holed.

There was no time to attend directly to the leak. The first priority was still to get clear of the pack ice while there was enough daylight to see a path. Otherwise we would find ourselves in the same predicament as the previous evening, blundering into ice floes in the darkness. 'One man on the bilge pump, one at the helm; one forward controlling the headsails; and the fourth at rest,' I ordered, and for two more hours we worked *Brendan* clear of the pack until there was enough open water to run a fairly easy course between the ice floes, and set the mainsail, double reefed. The helmsman still needed to be vigilant, but the man at the headsail could at last be spared; and after twenty-four hours of sustained effort, we could revert to our normal two-man watch-keeping system. The risk, it seemed to me, was as much a question of human exhaustion as of the frailty of our damaged boat.

'We can't tackle the leak tonight,' I said. 'There's not enough light to trace it, and then to try to make a repair. Besides, we are all too tired. But it's vital to learn more about the leak. I want each watch to work the bilge pump at regular intervals and record the number of strokes needed to empty the bilge and the time it takes to do so. Then at least we will know if the leak is getting worse and gaining on us. If we've torn the stitching somewhere, then more stitches may open as the thread works itself loose, and the rate of leakage will go up.'

Trondur tapped the leather at the gunwale. 'I think stitching is broken by ice,' he said calmly.

'It's very possible,' I replied 'but we can't be sure. We've simply got to find out all we can.'

'Ah well,' said Arthur cheerily, 'that's what the right arm is for – pumping. It's our watch, Trondur, I'd better get to work. And he crawled forward to get to the bilge pump. It was none too soon. Even as we had been talking, the water level on the floor by the cooker had risen noticeably. The water slopped back and forth around our boots, and would soon be lapping into the lee side of the shelter.

Pump, pump, pump. It took thirty-five minutes of non-stop pumping to empty the bilge. *Brendan*'s bilge, though shallow, was broad and relatively flat in profile and so held a great deal of water. Just fifteen minutes after being pumped out, the water level was as bad as ever, and threatening to get worse. Pump, pump, pump. 'How many strokes to empty her?' I asked. 'Two thousand,' Arthur grunted as he collapsed, exhausted. I did a rapid sum. Two thousand strokes every hour was within our physical limit, but only temporarily. One man could steer, while his partner pumped and kept *Brendan* afloat. But this system would work only while our strength lasted, or, more likely, we ran into bad weather, and waves began once again to break into the boat. Then we would no longer have the capacity to keep emptying *Brendan* fast enough. It was a tricky situation: In slanting out of the pack ice and clawing to seaward, I had brought *Brendan* out a full two hundred miles from land, and even then the nearest land was the thinly inhabited coast of Labrador, from which little help could be expected . . .

And if we were lucky enough to trace the leak, what then? Suppose we had cracked the skid keel under the boat when *Brendan* rode upon an ice floe, or pulled its fastenings through the leather hull? At sea we could neither refasten nor mend the skid. And what if we had gashed the leather skin or ripped the flax stitching? Then, I feared, we would be in an even worse way. I could not imagine how we would ever stitch on a patch under water, it would be impossible to reach far below the hull, and equally impossible to work on the inside because there was not enough space between the wooden frames and stringers to put in a row of stitches. The more I thought about our straits, the gloomier I felt. It seemed so futile if *Brendan* were to sink so close to the end of her mission. She had already proved to her crew that an early medieval Irish skin boat could sail across the Atlantic. But how could people be expected to believe that fact if *Brendan* sank two hundred miles off Canada? It would be no good to say that there was less pack ice off Canada and Greenland in early Christian times, and that the Irish monks would probably not have faced the same problems. To prove the point about the early Irish voyages, *Brendan* had to sail to the New World.

To clear my mind, I took up a pen and made a summary of our position:

1. *Brendan* is leaking fast. We can keep her afloat for two days, or less, in bad weather; indefinitely in fair weather but at great physical cost.
2. First priority is find the leak – skid fastening? Burst stitches? Hull gash?
3. If we cannot trace and mend a leak, the Coast Guard may get a motor pump to us. Do they have a suitable pump? Can their plane find us? This will depend on visibility and sea state.
4. No pump – we MAYDAY and abandon ship.

It was a grim scenario, and the situation did not become any more cheerful during that night. Driving rain reduced visibility to a few yards, and with an increase in wind strength, the helmsman no longer had the option to dodge potential growlers in the water. *Brendan* could only flee directly downwind, and we trusted to luck that we did not hit isolated pieces of ice, or worse yet an iceberg recently set free from the pack . . .

As I sat by the pump, waiting for George to drink his coffee so that we could begin our search, I wondered where we should commence our hunt – aft, under the shelter? But this meant shifting all our personal gear. By the foremast? But this was where we had put the heavy stores like the anchors and water cans. Then, quite unconnected, a thought occurred to me. Last night, while pumping in the dark, the flashes of phosphorescence over the gunwale had been repeated almost simultaneously *inside* the boat and in the bilge pump tube. I knew nothing of the physical properties of phosphorescence, but imagined some sort of electrical connection was required. If so, then the phosphorescence had traveled directly from outside the hull to inside the hull, apparently by a direct link – the leak.

With a faint stir of interest I abandoned pumping and traced the line of the bilge pipe to its intake amidships on the port side. At that point I peeled back the tarpaulin and hung head first over the gunwale. There, just on the water line, was the most encouraging sight of the day – a sizeable dent in the leather hull. The dent was about the area and shape of a large grapefruit, an abrupt pock-mark in the curve of the leather. With growing excitement I scrambled back inside the hull and began shifting away the food packs which had been stored there. As soon as I had uncovered the hull, I saw the grapefruit-shaped

pocket and the cause of our trouble: Under tremendous pressure from outside, the leather had buckled inward into the gap between two wooden ribs,
and opened a tear about four inches long. The force of the pressure had been
so great that it had literally split the leather. The skin had not been cut or
gashed. Despite a tensile strength of two tons per square inch, the leather had
simply burst. Now, whenever *Brendan* wallowed, a great gush of sea water
spurted through the tear and into the bilge. Jubilant, I poked my head up over
the tarpaulin and called 'Great news! I found the leak. And it's in a place
where we can mend it.' The others glanced up. There was relief on all their
faces. 'Finish your breakfast,' I went on, 'while I check that there are no other
leaks.' Then I went round the boat, hanging over the gunwale to see if there
was any more damage. In fact, apart from that single puncture the leather was
still in excellent condition. Indeed it was scarcely scratched by the ice. The
other floes had simply glanced off the curve of the hull or skidded on the wool
grease.

Except that one puncture. There, a combination of the curve of the hull, the
wider gap between the ribs at that point, and the nipping between the two
floes had driven a knob or sharp corner of ice through *Brendan*'s hull. By the
same token, however, we also had room to wield a needle between the ribs and
could sew a spare patch of leather over the gash. George and Trondur came
forward. 'The patch had better go on from the outside,' I told them, 'where
the water pressure will help squeeze it against the hull. First we'll make a
pattern, then cut the patch, and stitch it in place.'

'We must cut away some wood,' suggested Trondur, examining the ash ribs.

'Yes, whatever's needed to get at the work properly.'

'I'm going to put on an immersion suit,' George announced. 'This is going
to be a cold job.'

He was right. George and Trondur in their immersion suits now had three
hours of bone-chilling work. First they cut a patch of spare leather to size,
then George hung down over the gunwale, his face of few inches above the
water, and held the patch into position. Trondur poked an awl through the
hull and the patch, followed by a long nine-inch needle and flax thread.
George reached for the needle with a pair of pliers, gripped, tugged and
pulled, and eventually hauled it through. Then he took over the awl, stabbed
from the outside of the hull, groped around until he could poke in the tip of
the needle, and Trondur gathered it up from the inside.

It was a miserable chore. The top row of stitching was difficult enough,
because it lay just above water level, so that each time the boat rolled on a
wave, George was lucky if he went into the water only up to his elbows. With

the heaviest waves, his head went right under, and he emerged spluttering and gasping. Each large wave then went on to break against the hull, and drenched Trondur who was crouching in the bilge, stitching on the inside. All this was done in a sea temperature of about zero degrees Centigrade, with occasional ice floes and icebergs in the immediate vicinity, and after nearly two days without proper rest. Inch by inch the stitching progressed, and a pancake of wool grease and fiber was stuffed between the hull and the patch to serve as a seal. Then the last row of stitches went in. This last row was completely under water, and George had to use the handle of a hammer to press in the needle.

Finally it was done. The two men straightened up, shivering with cold. George wiped the last of his protective wool grease from his hands and they had a well-earned tot of whiskey in their coffee. Even Trondur was so exhausted that he went off to curl up in his sleeping bag.

The Brendan Voyage, 1978

PART II
Plains and Foothills

*

*It is here that the huge snakes are found – and lions, elephant, bears, asps
and horned asses, not to mention dog-headed men, headless men with eyes
in their breasts . . . wild men and wild women and a great many other
creatures by no means of a fabulous kind . . .*
Herodotus, *The Histories*

Think of the word 'explorer' and we tend to think of a man in a hat sweating along with guides through the vegetation. Most likely he's wearing khaki; probably he's in the tropics, and probably a Victorian. Certainly he's a white man.

It's the image used in humorous cartoons: he hacks through the undergrowth and, the joke is, ends up trussed up by natives, and then, if really unlucky, thrown into the cooking pot. The depiction is shorthand, but we know what the cartoonist means. The white man, carried along by the scientific age, is pushing back the jungle, clearing away the mystery. The image works for us; and if I'm asked to give a speech about my own expeditions, I too find audiences half-expecting me to turn up wearing this sort of archaic tropical outfit.

This image of an explorer, which has now evolved into someone more like Indiana Jones – an adjustment that fits better in this, the Global, or perhaps American, Age – is branded on our subconscious. He arises from a time when whole swathes of continent were revealed to newly literate populations.

The Victorian explorers were the heroes of their day. The Industrial Revolution had empowered the Christian world. Now the pioneers could set forth with confidence in their superiority, and spread enlightenment. They did this romantically, tragically and – best of all – far away. Saving the child chimney sweeps and the legions of street urchins and prostitutes raised awkward questions about the real cost of industrialization. Saving a savage from the darkness of his benighted continent – and hopefully a Muslim slaver – was much more attractive. Furthermore, all this was happening against an awe-inspiring backdrop. In the endless thorn-tree-studded plains of Africa, the imagination was free to roam.

It's a powerful image, a defining image – and, as a portrayal of a typical explorer, an incorrect image. Though white scientists and missionaries were the leading investigators of the last centuries, there were a great many others of different races and eras who were key to world exploration. In short, the Victorians were extremely late on the scene.

The first explorers of the fertile lowlands were the unrecorded scouts who ventured ahead of their people in search of fresh lands and possibilities. There are Native American myths that recount the exploratory migration of people across the Bering Strait into areas of North America 30–40,000 years ago. For example, this song comes from the Pima tribe of North America's south-west.

This is the white land;
we arrive singing,
head-dresses waving in the breeze.
We have come! We have come!
The land trembles with our dancing and
*   singing.*

Similarly, Europe – like perhaps every other major land-mass except Antarctica – was first explored by prehistoric people, whose accounts of these expeditions were passed on orally and subsequently lost. When medieval Europeans at last did venture forth towards the east, what they found threw them into confusion. They had been expecting to encounter backward peoples, but it was they themselves who were lagging behind.

Until then, though the ancient Chinese

royal courts had sent missions westward to
investigate Europe, the Europeans, swathed in
the obscurity of their Dark Age, were in no
position to send anyone anywhere. The
Roman Empire had never extended much
beyond the Euphrates, beyond which were
deserts, mountains and hostile nomads; with
the rise of Islam, any communication eastward was completely blocked. Our ancestors
remained in utter ignorance of much of Asia
– for them it was inhabited by a pantheon of
monsters. Then, in 1209, from Central Asia
came the Mongol invasions. For the insular
Europeans, it was as if they were being
attacked by Martians. Their maps, such as
they were, didn't have a place for Mongolia,
and the Mongols were regarded as the offspring of Gog and Magog, two giants who
feasted on humans. The Mongol nomads –
equipped with an advanced bow and formidable war machine, the resilient and sturdy
Mongol horse, and led by arguably the greatest general of all time, Subedei – made swift
work of Eastern Europe, and laid waste the
Islamic world. In time, their empire even
incorporated Korea and China.

It's worth underlining all this, because
travellers to this day have failed to get the
message. Again and again they have set out to
explore Asia, feeling their contribution was
important, somehow forgetting the centuries
of civilization that had already preceded them
there: take James Bruce, who claimed to have
found the source of the Blue Nile, a 'spot
which had baffled the genius, industry, and
enquiry of both ancients and moderns, for
the course of near three thousand years'. Well,
yes – though the spot wasn't the ultimate
source of the Nile, as he thought – but, put
another way, his claim indicates nothing
more than the narrowness of European
experience, which was simply unaware of
Middle Eastern trading knowledge or
scholarship.

Wherever the Europeans went in the Middle East and Asia, the area had generally been

documented hundreds of years before. And
Asia was a third of the planet's total land area.

Let me pursue the example of the Mongols,
because it's a culture familiar to me. Making
their way across Central Asia, travellers
through the centuries would come across
nomads, living a humble life on the great
Siberian and Mongol steppes. Even the great
nineteenth-century Russian traveller Przhevalsky saw them as lacking all higher qualities:
'The first thing which strikes the traveller in
the life of a Mongol is his excessive dirtiness.'* The sixteenth-century Englishman
Jenkinson saw them as lacking in everything:
'town or house they have none, but live in the
open fields'.

I spent seven and a half months as a lone
foreigner with Mongol nomads; the *ger*, or
felt tent, is indeed simple, and the life of the
shepherd austere. However, if you are able to
look further, there is something distinctly not
of the peasant here.

Each time I would walk into a *ger*, having
tied up my exasperating camels outside, I'd
find myself immediately allocated half of the
space, the left side. The wife of the household
would put on some salty tea, and flick in a
slab of yak butter; the husband would kneel
before me, and from his silk *dell*, or gown,
draw a jade snuff container. As a visitor, I was
expected to do the same, and we'd swap our
containers in our palms, an intimate and gracious act that speaks loud and clear: you are
welcome, you are an equal.

This isn't just a quaint exchange of country
folk. It's an expression of perfect democracy.
Whether you are the President of Mongolia
or, like me, a passing stranger, you are
accorded the same civil treatment. As long as

---

* 'The Mongol is a slave to habit,' Przhevalsky
wrote in 1876. 'He has no energy to meet and overcome difficulties; he will try and avoid, but never
overcome them. He wants the elastic, manly spirit
of the European, ready for any emergency, and willing to struggle against adversity and gain the victory in the end. He is the stolid conservatism of the
Asiatic: passive, lifeless.'

you stay, half the *ger* is yours, and all is conducted across this central line dividing the host's home, face to face. As a visitor to a *ger*, you never even knock on a door – which would be to question the spirit of open-handed hospitality. This is about more than decency; it is survival: the Mongols rely on each other to maintain their herding life. This is their social-security system – their population, spread thinly over the poor land, is interconnected – but the roots are old, dating from a time when the Mongol Empire embraced Arabia, China and the great civilizations of the globe. Each simple felt tent I visited, out in the steppe, carried this extraordinary pedigree of high culture. And this is not just something of interest to geographers specializing in human settlement patterns. The Mongols did no less than shape our understanding of the world; for their empire reached around the known lands of the globe, as Columbus did in reaching across the Atlantic. Under the Mongols, the elements of Asia were unified, giving birth to the notion of there being one world.

Such was the antiquity and sophistication of so many eastern civilizations, their inhabitants often centred the world around themselves: the holy cities of Islam, the Middle Kingdom of China, the Himalayas, whose waters and peaks were sacred to the Hindu and (later Buddhist) tradition. Phei Hsui completed an eighteen-sheet map of China in AD 267, drawn according to a rectangular grid pattern, with ching and wei co-ordinates.

Those Europeans arriving one and a half millennia later had the same self-belief, carried by an extraordinary self-confidence in Western civilization; sometimes they were hardly able to see anything other than what they had come to see: something to confirm their sense of superiority. 'Our obstinacy was not to be overcome,' wrote Evariste Régis Huc (1813–60), having insisted on adopting the colour of garments worn only by the imperial family, 'and the mandarins submitted – as

they ought to do.' Missionaries will be missionaries but their attitudes were typical of travellers of the age. 'They appear in many districts to look upon us as a species of fools,' complained Alexander Williamson (1829–90) indignantly; and to the Chinese, the Europeans must have seemed just that: the Yung Lo Ta Tien encyclopaedia, a work of 11,000 volumes, contained 'all the knowledge in the world'. When the Hanlin Academy in Peking was burnt down in the Boxer Rebellion, it was a greater loss than the destruction of the Library of Alexandria. Put another way, the Mongol hordes of the Middle Ages had stopped short of wiping out Europe partly because the Great Khan Ogedei had died just at that vital moment, but also because the West offered them little. Compared to the richness of Persia, we were very poor pickings indeed; and the Chinese were developing striking clocks by then. The Mongols didn't want us, even as slaves.

In short, the Europeans who headed east were recorders, not explorers. It was no coincidence that local rulers saw their expeditions as espionage missions – after all, these visitors had a lot to learn, and their hosts had a lot to lose. So, in the selection of travellers that follows I've tried to represent Europeans not just as discoverers, as they are conventionally portrayed, but also as objects of discovery. Documented by the Persians, Greeks, Romans and others, we see ourselves alongside, for example, Africans in grass huts; we have all been 'backward' peoples who were intruded upon and judged. There is, for example, the mission undertaken by Priscus, in AD 448, on behalf of the Roman Empire, to Attila the Hun – the 'Scourge of God' and as strange a creature as they could expect: 'Attila just had some meat on a wooden platter, for this was one aspect of his self-discipline.'

With time, Europeans did venture forth to document the world, the scientific movement gathering steam after the founding of the Royal Society with the support of Charles II.

The late seventeenth and early eighteenth centuries saw a gradual interest by learned men across the Western nations in natural phenomena, particularly in plants and animals. Just as scientific understanding had expanded with astronomy in the time of Copernicus, now understanding of fauna and flora saw great breakthroughs. Expeditions to Asia and the New World brought knowledge of new forms of life; the disciplines of botany and zoology evolved; *The System of Nature* by the Swedish naturalist Carolus Linnaeus (1707–78) became the bedrock of classification; there was now a science of life: biology. Others of a more religious calling, such as Revd Gilbert White – whose *Natural History of Selborne* was published in 1789 – now took time to note down local curiosities to demonstrate the glory of God. White's musings represent a dawning of a philosophical form in life science, leading to the great thinkers of the next era, the philosopher Herbert Spencer (1820–1903), the biologist Thomas Huxley (1825–95), Darwin, and Charles Lyell – whose *Geological Evidences of the Antiquity of Man* (1863) gave support, from a different science, to Darwin's evolutionary theories.

The gentle observations of a quiet country parson, Revd Gilbert White, do not measure up to those of his contemporary, Erasmus Darwin, whose speculations on evolution paved the way for his grandson Charles. Take his ponderings on the fate of swallows and house martins in the winter: 'As to their hiding, no man pretends to have found any of them in a torpid state in the winter. But with regard to their migration, what difficulties attend that supposition! that such feeble bad fliers (who the summer long never flit but from hedge to hedge) should be able to traverse vast seas and continents in order to enjoy milder seasons amidst the regions of Africa!' Coleridge, in his copy of the book, scribbled, 'Surely from Dover to Calais, and from Gilbraltar to the coast of Barbary, cannot be called a traverse of *vast seas*.'

The importance of such documentation lies not in any discovery but in the technique of simple, first-hand observation, and for this reason he's included here. Place White in the tropics, and this would have been deemed an account of an explorer – as indeed he was, but on our own, unscrutinized turf.

Meanwhile, other learned men were setting out for more distant lands to interpret them. Soon the British were ahead of the game, and in 1851 they showed this to the world by staging the Great Exhibition, a collection of objects brought from far and wide. The explorers had gathered curiosities, just like Revd White pottering about Selborne Hanger; the difference was that the lands they had studied were now open for colonialization.

In the public imagination, the faraway lands were theatres of engagement, each with its own character. There was Dark Africa; there were the Lands of Promise; there was the early, enduring myth of the great 'Southern Continent' – which shrank and shrank as mariners searched in vain for it. And all the while, the march inland was spurred on by rivalry between competing European powers: in Central Asia Britain and Russia vied for political advantage; in the New World the Spanish jealously guarded their discoveries in South and Central America; the French competed with the British in North America.

While the new colonies – each glittering with the hope of a new future – were gradually settled, writers continued their task of helping the people back home assess their place in the scheme of things. As the hinterlands were opened, Other Peoples were laid out on display for us.*

* Here Georg August Schweinfurth is tussling over how to judge the contrasting African peoples he's encountered: 'But in this dread of witches, the whole superstition of the Bongo culminates and exhausts itself; and we Europeans may well ask what real right have we, with all our advancement in knowledge, to presume to reproach them? We cannot resist the impression that these poor Bongo are infinitely more free from hundreds of

In Africa, inhabitants rarely agreed with Victorian notions of dignity or civilization. Joseph Thomson, who is actually one of the most endearing of African adventurers, broke the tension, when meeting hostility, by removing his false teeth, and took pride in never causing bloodshed. Yet he saw no reason to shy away from condemnation – in a way that we would never dare now – of the 'miserable and apathetic races' he came across. In contrast, there is his 'profound astonishment' in encountering a Masai orator, whose conduct accorded with the Victorian idea of correct behaviour: he had a 'dignity of attitude beyond all praise'.

Nowadays, we can't help but cringe a little at the superior attitudes taken by our pioneering forefathers towards the locals, and with good reason; but, in my experience, there's also a common, slightly confused belief nowadays that those living 'at one with Nature' are the ones who have somehow 'got it right'. From the standpoint of the twenty-first century, this is understandable: we have seen our science produce horrors (the capacity for biological warfare, for example) as well as wonders; our very lifestyle threatens to destroy the planet. To many, even our own religion – Christianity – doesn't seem any longer to offer the answers; and if the bedrock of our cultural beliefs doesn't, what does? That's the problem: nothing is quite certain any more. So, like Rousseau and the Romantics, who looked for inspiration in the Noble Savage,

—

superstitious fallacies than many of those who boast of their civilization; much more so, for example, than the Mohammedans of the Soudan, where the idlest of superstitions prevail in every household . . . A philosopher might fairly speculate whether this land would not have been happier if the Moslems had never set foot upon its soil. They brought a religion that was destitute of morality; they introduced contagion rather than knowledge; they even suppressed the true doctrines of Mohammed their prophet, which would have enfranchized the very people whom they oppressed, and have raised them to a condition of brotherhood, and of equality.'

many have again begun to envy the simplicity of life that non-industrialized people, untouched by all our angst, seem to have. As someone who has been many months at a time alone with 'tribal' groups around the world, I'd say that this notion is as misplaced as the superior stance taken by previous, more certain, generations. Life lived without Western medicine, for a start, can become very bleak indeed. Crossing the Amazon Basin – a seven-month journey I did with the help of Matses Indians – I soon became distressed at not being able to treat my dysentery, with which I was afflicted for a hellish six weeks. Another Amazonian trek gave me two sorts of malaria, parasites in my feet, one in my stomach, and fungi growing in aggressive colonies on my skin. In Namibia my lips bled because of the relentless sun. Yet still I'm sometimes asked whether I've ever been tempted to stay on with some community, marry and settle down, perhaps with the Matses, or the Himba in Namibia, or indeed the Masai encountered by Thomson. 'They all look so content,' is a common remark. Well, perhaps; and one reason for that is, no doubt, an existence of clearly defined roles and expectations. Life proceeds in an orderly way; you know where you are. But another reason – not so savoury – is that those who are weak die off. In other words, those 'expectations' of theirs are low. 'But they are spiritually, at least, in peace . . .' a lady once said to me from the back of an auditorium. She had trekked to the Amazon to meet a shaman, and there found a wonderful man 'in balance with Nature'. Much of this aspiration is fair enough – let's face it, we haven't got it right ourselves – but I have rarely found any Westerner keen to adopt the fear that is also an element of the spiritual life of those I've spent time with. Fear of sorcerers and curses is put aside in favour of a green philosophy that the shaman seems to offer. In New Guinea, no one would walk alone with me through the forest at night because of the 'wunjumboo', a horrible hairy fiend who, if you were unlucky enough to meet him, would offer you no spiritual benefit whatsoever. In the Gibson Desert, among the Aborigines, I'd find friends would want to walk along the middle of the road at night and risk being run over rather than risk the Featherfoot, lurking in the blackness.

Until modern times, travellers were under no such illusions – even as late as the Victorian era, death in childbirth and from tuberculosis was a common feature of life back home. So Livingstone saw no romanticism in the African lifestyle; he was doing his bit to dispel the darkness – not just what he saw in the unredeemed Africans, but what had been inflicted on the native populace by the Arab slave trade. The robust gentility of the man, going about his work as the Africans laughed at his efforts at conversion, contrasted heavily with others, like his admirer Stanley; but Livingstone himself spoke of being of a 'superior' race, and the epitaph on his tombstone in Westminster Abbey is hardly flattering about Africa: 'For 30 years his life was spent in an unwearied effort to evangelize the native races, to explore the undiscovered secrets, to abolish the desolating slave trade of Central Africa, where with his last words he wrote, "All I can add in my solitude is, may heaven's rich blessing come down on every one, American, English or Turk, who will help to heal this open sore of the world."'

In exploration terms, the meeting of Stanley and Livingstone – 'Dr Livingstone, I presume' – is not significant in the slightest, except that it captured the imagination of the public back home and, therefore, in itself had impact in the world. It reinforced the idea of Christians uniting over a helpless people to defeat darkness. It was also a meeting of two worlds: one man was there to save souls, the other to sell newspapers.

This brings us back to the explorer stereotype, that Victorian sweating along, hampered by bouts of fever. He was created in the plains of far lands, which were homes of nomads, but also of the great nations that farmed the alluvial soils along major rivers such as the Nile and the Niger and in the 'cradle of civilization', between the Euphrates and the Tigris. Here also, in the lowlands, were the relics of previous dynasties: Angkor in Cambodia, those breathtaking ruins described for us by Henri Mouhot; the ruin-heaps of Troy, which Heinrich Schliemann began investigating in 1870; and Tutankhamen's tomb, revealed by Howard Carter.

One hundred years ago an explorer could still journey to remote lands and find a lost civilization in a month. Archaeology still retains its aura of romance, its reputation for startling discoveries that can reveal something immense enough to change the way we think about themselves.

I should end by turning to the perspective of the people who bore the brunt of the European advance over the plains: the nomads and other indigenous groups that were, by and large, swept away. Those people who harnessed their social structures to Nature were classed as primitive, and few stopped to listen to them. Had they done so, they might just have heard something akin to this comment from one north-east coast Native American:

Thou sayest of us that we are the most miserable and unhappy of all men, living without religion, without any rules, like the beasts in our woods and our forests, lacking bread, wine and a thousand other comforts . . . we are very content with the little that we have. Thou deceivest thyself greatly if thou thinkest to persuade us that thy country is better than ours. For if France as thou sayest is a little terrestrial paradise, art thou sensible to leave it?

Old World

HERODOTUS
c.484–c.425 BC

I have not seen a phoenix myself, except in paintings, for it is very rare and visits the country . . . only at intervals of 500 years, on the occasion of the death of the parent-bird.

A Greek dubbed the 'Father of History', Herodotus is our single most important information source on the journeys of the Ancients. He gives us our only record of the first Saharan explorers and (though he is sceptical) of Pharaoh Necho II's Phoenician fleet circumnavigating Africa (c.600 BC). Alexander the Great used Herodotus's writings as a geographical reference, and when in the eighteenth century Sir Joseph Banks founded his Association for Promoting the Discovery of the Interior Parts of Africa, and sought to determine the flow of the Niger (sending out Mungo Park, and others), Herodotus was consulted for clues. Likewise, his story of 'four fountains' giving birth to a river in central Africa was thought by many Victorians to equate to the source of the Nile (and perhaps the 'Mountains of the Moon' drawn on the AD 150 map of the greatest geographer of the Ancients, Ptolemy); the matter of solving the age-old mystery of the true Nile source was the great spur for Burton, Speke and company.

The philosophical premise of the Greeks was symmetry; it therefore followed that the earth was a shpere, the most symmetrical form – and Aristotle and other scholars made observations to prove this. Thus Herodotus thought that the world was balanced around the Mediterranean, the Nile to the south matching the Danube of the north. This con-cept helped give rise to the idea of a great southern continent which would balance Europe and Asia – a myth persisting until James Cook reached as far as the Antarctic Circle and still saw no land-mass.

Herodotus's nine-part *Histories* was the longest account written in prose at that time; in it he not only describes the struggle that culminated in the defeat of the invading Persians (490 and 480 BC), but also includes a detailed study of all the different peoples, countries and cultures he encountered on various travels throughout his life.

Most of what we know of Herodotus is derived from his own *Histories*, few other biographical references having survived. He states that he was born in Halicarnassus, Asia Minor – highly significant, because his work and outlook draw on both Asiatic and Greek cultures. Herodotus favoured the freedom, reason and self-motivation of Greek democracy over the slavery, disorder and submission on which Persian rule was based. However, like a modern historian, he tries to put events into context, describing great achievements by men on both sides. He wrote the *Histories* in order that, he says, 'human achievements may not become forgotten in time, and great and marvellous deeds – some displayed by Greeks, some by barbarians – may not be without their glory'.

The concept of 'History' was developed in Asia by the Ionian philosophers, and involved posing a question, seeking out relevant information, and then drawing conclusions. From what we do know of Herodotus' life, it was suited to that form of research: periods of extensive travelling freed him from the insular outlook of most Greek city-states. Whilst Aristotle called him a *mythologos* – and he did indeed have a love of storytelling – he also acutely observed places, people and events from his own time, while posing pertinent questions to gain information about past exploits and fables passed down over generations.

It is thought that he was exiled from Halicarnassus at a young age by the tyrant Lygdamis, but later returned to help restore constitutional government. Particularly during his twenties and thirties, Herodotus is thought to have travelled as far north as the Black Sea, west to Libya, and east to Babylon. In Egypt he explored Memphis and travelled far up the Nile.

Following his return to Halicarnassus, Herodotus soon fell out of favour and left again, this time permanently. Eventually, he joined Thurii, a pan-Hellenic colony in southern Italy, where he died, and was buried in the market place.

Egypt: cats and the crocodile

The following is an account of the crocodile. During the four winter months it takes no food. It is a four-footed, amphibious creature, lays and hatches its eggs on land, where it spends the greater part of the day, and stays all night in the river, where the water is warmer than the night-air and the dew. The difference in size between the young and the full-grown crocodile is greater than in any other known creature; for a crocodile's egg is hardly bigger than a goose's, and the young when hatched is small in proportion, yet it grows to a size of some twenty-three feet long or even more. It has eyes like a pig's but great fang-like teeth in proportion to its body, and is the only animal to have no tongue and a stationary lower jaw; for when it eats it brings the upper jaw down upon the under. It has powerful claws and a scaly hide, which on its back is impenetrable. It cannot see under water, though on land its sight is remarkably sharp. One result of its spending so much time in the water is that the inside of its mouth gets covered with leeches. Other animals avoid the crocodile, as do all birds too with one exception – the sandpiper, or Egyptian plover; this bird is of service to the crocodile and lives, in consequence, in the greatest amity with him; for when the crocodile comes ashore and lies with his mouth wide open (which he generally does facing towards the west), the bird hops in and swallows the leeches. The crocodile enjoys this, and never, in consequence, hurts the bird. Some Egyptians reverence the crocodile as a sacred beast; others do not, but treat it as an enemy. The strongest belief in its sanctity is to be found in Thebes and round about Lake Moeris; in these places they keep one particular crocodile, which they tame, putting rings made of glass or gold into its ears and bracelets round its front feet, and giving it special food and ceremonial offerings. In fact, while these creatures are alive they treat them with every kindness, and, when they die, embalm them and bury them in sacred tombs. On the other hand, in the neighbourhood of Elephantine crocodiles are not considered sacred animals at all, but are eaten. In the Egyptian language these creatures are called *champsae*. The name crocodile – or 'lizard' – was given them by the Ionians, who saw they resembled the lizards commonly found on stone walls in their own country.

Of the numerous different ways of catching crocodiles I will describe the one which seems to me the most worthy to report. They bait a hook with a chine of pork and let it float out into midstream, and at the same time, standing on the bank, take a live pig and beat it. The crocodile, hearing its squeals, makes a rush towards it, encounters the bait, gulps it down, and is hauled out of the water. The first thing the huntsman does when he has got the beast on land is to plaster its eyes with mud; this done, it is dispatched easily enough – but without this precaution it will give a lot of trouble.

What happens when a house catches fire is most extraordinary: nobody takes the least trouble to put it out, for it is only the cats that matter: everyone stands in a row, a little distance from his neighbour, trying to protect the cats, who nevertheless slip through the line, or jump over it, and hurl themselves into the flames. This causes the Egyptians deep distress. All the inmates of a house where a cat has died a natural death shave their eyebrows, and when a dog dies they shave the whole body including the head. Cats which have died are taken to Bubastis, where they are embalmed and buried in sacred receptacles; dogs are buried, also in sacred burial-places, in the towns where they belong. Mongooses are buried in the same way as dogs; field-mice and hawks are taken to Buto, ibises to Hermopolis. Bears, which are scarce, and wolves (which in Egypt are not much bigger than foxes) are buried wherever they happen to be found lying dead.

A price range for mummification

The embalmers, when a body is brought to them, produce specimen models in wood, painted to resemble nature, and graded in quality; the best and most expensive kind is said to represent a being whose name I shrink from mentioning in this connexion; the next best is somewhat inferior and cheaper, while the third sort is cheapest of all. After pointing out these differences in quality, they ask which of the three is required, and the kinsmen of the dead man, having agreed upon a price, go away and leave the embalmers to their work. The most perfect process is as follows: as much as possible of the brain is extracted through the nostrils with an iron hook, and what the hook cannot reach is rinsed out with drugs; next the flank is laid open with a flint knife and the whole contents of the abdomen removed; the cavity is then thoroughly cleansed and washed out, first with palm wine and again with an infusion of pounded spices. After that it is filled with pure bruised myrrh, cassia, and every other aromatic substance with the exception of frankincense, and sewn up again, after which the body is placed in natrum, covered entirely over, for seventy days – never longer. When this period, which must not be exceeded, is over, the body is washed and then wrapped from head to foot in linen cut into strips and smeared on the under side with gum, which is commonly used by the Egyptians instead of glue. In this condition the body is given back to the family, who have a wooden case made, shaped like the human figure, into which it is put. The case is then sealed up and stored in a sepulchral chamber, upright against the wall. When, for reasons of expense, the second quality is called for, the treatment is different: no incision is made and the intestines are not removed, but oil of cedar is injected with a syringe into the body through the anus which is afterwards stopped up to prevent the liquid from escaping. The body is then pickled in natrum for the prescribed number of days, on the last of which the oil is drained off. The effect of it is so powerful that as it leaves the body it brings with it the stomach and intestines in a liquid state, and as the flesh, too, is dissolved by the natrum, nothing of the body is left but the bones and skin. After this treatment it is returned to the family without further fuss.

The third method, used for embalming the bodies of the poor, is simply to clear out the intestines with a purge and keep the body seventy days in natrum. It is then given back to the family to be taken away.

When the wife of a distinguished man dies, or any woman who happens to be beautiful or well known, her body is not given to the embalmers immediately, but only after the lapse of three or four days. This is a precautionary measure to prevent the embalmers from violating the corpse, a thing which is said actually to have happened in the case of a woman who had just died. The culprit was given away by one of his fellow workmen.

The Histories (trans. Aubrey de Sélincourt, 1996 edn)

XENOPHON

c.431–354 BC

One of the soothsayers then proposed making a sacrifice to the wind.

The Greek gentleman and soldier Xenophon, charismatic leader of 'the ten thousand' – the Greek mercenaries who made the gruelling trek overland back to Athens from Persia – is known for his fluent accounts of contemporary events. He crossed 2,000 miles of territory unknown to the Greeks, through Turkey, Kurdistan, Iraq, Armenia, Georgia and Albania. Seventy years later, his record was used by Alexander the Great, who retraced much of Xenophon's route and in a decade founded more than 70 cities and covered 20,000 miles.

Xenophon was born an Athenian country gentleman, one of the wealthy class of the Knights, in about 431 BC, the year in which the Peloponnesian war between Athens and Sparta broke out. The Knights had always been distrustful of democracy and, while serving in the Athenian cavalry, Xenophon was sympathetic to the right-wing revolutionaries who grabbed power for short spells in 411 and 414. When democracy was restored in Athens in 401, Xenophon, spurred on by a sense of rebellion, set out for Persia to serve as a mercenary for Prince Cyrus. The prince was intent on seizing the throne from his brother, and was backed by Sparta, which, with his help, had emerged victorious from the war against Athens. Xenophon was one of thousands of ambitious young Athenians who saw in Cyrus's exploits the chance of challenging employment on the battlefield and the possibility of substantial reward.

All did not go as planned. Cyrus was killed on the battlefield of Cunaza and the 10,000 Greeks who supported him found themselves stranded. Either they could submit to the King, or begin the trek home from out of the heart of Persia.

The act of leading this 'march of the ten thousand' made Xenophon famous by the age of thirty. In five months those who survived had covered 1,500 miles of inhospitable terrain through the Armenian highlands, negotiating rivers and slopes, defending themselves against Kurdish barbarians and an horrific winter. Xenophon's book, the *Persian Expedition*, or *Anabasis*, is a vivid account of the journey, told in the third person but leaving no doubt as to whom he believed the hero to be – Xenophon emerges as the saviour of the ten thousand, and the reader must judge to what extent this was really so. The lucidity of his style and the wide-ranging scope of Xenophon's ideas means that he has been described as the first journalist, but in the vein of commentator and critic, rather than objective reporter.

The *Anabasis* makes a clear distinction between the chaotic, wild barbarians and the ordered, united world of the Greeks, who are portrayed as employing reason to resolve conflict and reacting to adversity with fairness. However, many contemporaries considered the expedition to be an adventure carried out by a disreputable band of young men. The Athenian orator Isocrates wrote the ten thousand off in his panegyric as men 'too base to be able to make a living in their countries'. Xenophon himself was described as being 'too friendly with the men', and of 'playing the demagogue'.

Xenophon later went into service against Persia under Spartan command with a coalition of Greek city-states including Athens, and was rewarded with an estate at Scillus near Olympia; he spent a contented period entertaining, hunting and writing histories, treatises and memoirs. He returned to Athens in 365 BC, took up his old place in Athenian society, and stayed there until his death.

Marching through snow, Armenia

The third day's march was a hard one, with a north wind blowing into their faces, cutting into absolutely everything like a knife and freezing people stiff. One of the soothsayers then proposed making a sacrifice to the wind and his suggestion was carried out. It was agreed by all that there was then a distinct falling off in the violence of the wind. The snow was six feet deep and many of the animals and the slaves perished in it, as did about thirty of the soldiers. They kept their fires going all night, as there was plenty of wood in the place where they camped, though those who came up late got no wood. The ones who had arrived before and had lit the fires would not let the late-comers approach their fire unless they gave them a share of their corn or any other foodstuff they had. So each shared with the other party what he had. When the fires were made, great pits were formed reaching down to the ground as the snow melted. This gave one a chance of measuring the depth of the snow.

The whole of the next day's march from here was through the snow, and a number of the soldiers suffered from bulimia. Xenophon, who, as he com-manded the rearguard, came upon men who had collapsed, did not know what the disease was. However, someone who had had experience of it told him that it was a clear case of bulimia, and that if they had something to eat they would be able to stand up. So he went through the baggage train and distributed to the sufferers any edibles that he could find there, and also sent round those who were able to run with more supplies to them. As soon as they had had something to eat they stood up and went on marching.

On this march Chirisophus came to a village about nightfall, and found by the well some women and girls, who had come out of the village in front of the fortification to get water. They asked the Greeks who they were, and the interpreter replied in Persian and said they were on their way from the King to the satrap. The women answered that he was not there, and said that he was about three miles away. Since it was late, they went inside the fortification with the water-carriers to see the head-man of the village. So Chirisophus and as many of the troops as could camped there, but as for the rest of the soldiers, those who were unable to finish the march spent the night without food and without fires, and some died in the course of it. Some of the enemy too had formed themselves into bands and seized upon any baggage animals that could not make the journey, fighting among themselves for the animals. Sol-diers who had lost the use of their eyes through snow-blindness or whose toes had dropped off from frostbite were left behind.

It was a relief to the eyes against snow-blindness if one held something black in front of the eyes while marching; and it was a help to the feet if one kept on the move and never stopped still, and took off one's shoes at night. If one slept with one's shoes on, the straps sank into the flesh and the soles of the shoes froze to the feet. This was the more likely to happen since, when their old shoes were worn out, they had made themselves shoes of undressed leather from the skins of oxen that had just been flayed. Some soldiers who were suffering from these kinds of complaints were left behind. They had seen a piece of ground that looked black because the snow had gone from it, and they imagined that the snow there had melted – as it actually had done – this being the effect of a fountain which was sending up vapour in a wooded hollow near by. The soldiers turned aside here, sat down, and refused to go any further.

As soon as Xenophon, who was with the rearguard, heard of this, he begged them, using every argument he could think of, not to get left behind. He told them that there were large numbers of the enemy, formed into bands, who were coming up in the rear, and in the end he got angry. They told him to kill them on the spot, for they could not possibly go on. Under the circumstances the best thing to do seemed to be to scare, if possible, the enemy who were coming up and so prevent them from falling upon the soldiers in their exhausted condition. By this time it was already dark, and the enemy were making a lot of noise as they advanced, quarrelling over the plunder which they had. Then the rearguard, since they had the use of their limbs, jumped up and charged the enemy at the double, while the sick men shouted as hard as they could and clashed their shields against their spears. The enemy were panic-stricken and threw themselves down through the snow into the wooded hollows, and not a sound was heard from them afterwards. Xenophon and his troops told the sick men that a detachment would come to help them on the next day, and he then proceeded with the march. However, before they had gone half a mile they came across some more soldiers resting by the road in the snow, all covered up, with no guard posted. Xenophon's men roused them up, but they said that the troops in front were not going forward. Xenophon then went past them and sent on the most able-bodied of the peltasts to find out what was holding them up. They reported back that the whole army was resting in this way; so Xenophon's men posted what guards they could, and also spent the night there, without a fire and without supper. When it was near daybreak Xenophon sent the youngest of his men back to the sick with instructions to make them get up and force them to march on. At this point Chirisophus sent a detachment from his troops in the village to see what was happening to the troops in the rear. Xenophon's men were glad to see them and handed over the sick to them to escort to the camp. They then went on themselves and, before they had marched two miles, got to the village where Chirisophus was camping. Now that they had joined forces again, it seemed safe for the troops to take up their quarters in the villages. Chirisophus stayed where he was, and the other officers drew lots for the villages which were in sight, and each went with his men to the one he got.

On this occasion Polycrates, an Athenian captain, asked leave to go on independently and, taking with him the men who were quickest on their feet, ran to the village which had been allotted to Xenophon and surprised all the villagers, with their head-man, inside the walls, together with seventeen colts which were kept there for tribute to the King, and the head-man's daughter, who had only been married nine days ago. Her husband had gone out to hunt hares and was not captured in the village.

The houses here were built underground; the entrances were like wells, but they broadened out lower down. There were tunnels dug in the ground for the animals, while the men went down by ladder. Inside the houses there were goats, sheep, cows and poultry with their young. All these animals were fed on food that was kept inside the houses. There was also wheat, barley, beans and barley-wine in great bowls. The actual grains of barley floated on top of the bowls, level with the brim, and in the bowls there were reeds of various sizes and without joints in them. When one was thirsty, one was meant to take a reed and suck the wine into one's mouth. It was a very strong wine, unless one mixed it with water, and, when one got used to it, it was a very pleasant drink.

Xenophon invited the chief of the village to have supper with him, and told him to be of good heart, as he was not going to be deprived of his children, and that, if he showed himself capable of doing the army a good turn until they reached another tribe, they would restock his house with provisions when they went away. He promised to co-operate and, to show his good intentions, told them of where some wine was buried. So for that night all the soldiers were quartered in the villages and slept there with all sorts of food around them, setting a guard over the head-man of the village and keeping a watchful eye on his children too.

On the next day Xenophon visited Chirisophus and took the head-man with him. Whenever he went past a village he turned into it to see those who were quartered there. Everywhere where he found them feasting and merry-making, and they would invariably refuse to let him go before they had given him something for breakfast. In every single case they would have on the same table lamb, kid, pork, veal and chicken, and a number of loaves, both wheat and barley. When anyone wanted, as a gesture of friendship, to drink to a friend's health, he would drag him to a huge bowl, over which he would have to lean, sucking up the drink like an ox. They invited the head-man too to take what he liked, but he refused their invitations, only, if he caught sight of any of his relatives, he would take them along with him.

When they came to Chirisophus, they found his men also feasting, with wreaths of hay round their heads, and with Armenian boys in native dress waiting on them. They showed the boys what to do by signs, as though they were deaf mutes. After greeting each other, Chirisophus and Xenophon together interrogated the head-man through the interpreter who spoke Persian, and asked him what country this was. He replied that it was Armenia. Then they asked him for whom the horses were being kept, and he said that they were a tribute paid to the King. The next country, he said, was the land of the Chalybes, and he told them the way there.

Xenophon then went away and took the head-man back to his own people. He gave him back the horse (rather an old one) which he had taken, and told him to fatten it up and sacrifice it. This was because he had heard that it was sacred to the Sun and he was afraid that it might die, as the journey had done it no good. He took some of the colts himself, and gave one colt to each of the generals and captains. The horses in this part of the world were smaller than the Persian horses, but much more finely bred. The head-man told the Greeks to tie small bags round the feet of the horses and baggage animals whenever they made them go through snow, as, without these bags, they sank in up to their bellies.

The Persian Expedition (trans. Rex Warner, 1949)

Gaius Julius Caesar
100–44 BC
All the Britons . . . shave their whole bodies except the head and the upper lip.

Roman statesman who expanded Roman dominions through Gaul and emerged victorious from the civil war against Pompey to be declared 'perpetual dictator'. His measures to re-organize the empire were cut short by his assassination but he had pioneered a route through the Alps and had also brought back to Rome the first accurate records of Britain, France and other European lands.

Julius Caesar was born into a time when Roman territory was controlled by a corrupt and power-seeking governing class who had taken advantage of the dispossessed peasantry to feed their armies. Mismanagement and divisions weakened the governing structure.

The Conquest of Gaul recounts the series of military campaigns by which Caesar brought Belgium, Germany west of the Rhine, Southern Holland, most of France and Switzerland under Roman control. During this period he also invaded Britain twice. *The Conquest* comprises eight books – which he calls 'commentaries' – each one covering the events of one year. While they claim to be straightforward reportage, there is clearly a significant dose of propaganda; certain details, such as the personal fortunes that Caesar and his associates made from these wars and the fact that the campaigns in Germany and Britain were ineffectual, are tactfully omitted.*

The success of Caesar's troops was due less to being better armed or manned than the Gauls than to their effective organization, strategy and tactics. The Roman victory also owed a lot to the character of the Gauls, whom Caesar describes throughout the books as 'impulsive' and 'emotional'. These generalizations about the Gauls' character are accompanied by detailed descriptions of their materials, housing and social organization, which serve as a rare, albeit fragmented, testimony to life in Western Europe in the first century BC.

The eight years in Gaul may have been a major part of Caesar's career, and certainly of European history, but they were only a stepping stone on the way to his ultimate goal of reorganizing the Greco-Roman world – which, to some extent, he did. Caesar had the driving personal ambition that was necessary to make any headway in Roman politics at that time. In the eyes of some, he was a power-obsessed tyrant; others believe that, had he lived, he would have shifted the Roman state from one run by rapacious commanders to one that revolved around community and tolerance.

---

* Caesar was proud of his reputation for clemency – but such clemency towards the Gauls was occassionally tempered with acts of violent barbarity. Towards the end of the campaign, a rebel force stood siege until it ran out of drinking water. Caesar describes how he treated the survivors:

'Caesar saw that his work in Gaul could never be brought to a successful conclusion if similar revolts were allowed to break out; and his clemency was so well-known that no one would think him a cruel man if for once he took severe measures. So he decided to deter all others by making an example of the defenders of Uxellodunum. All who had borne arms had their hands cut off and were then let go, so that everyone might see what punishment was meted out to evildoers.'

On the British

The interior of Britain is inhabited by people who claim, on the strength of an oral tradition, to be aboriginal; the coast, by Belgic immigrants who came to plunder and make war – nearly all of them retaining the names of the tribes from which they originated – and later settled down to till the soil. The population is exceedingly large, the ground thickly studded with homesteads, closely resembling those of the Gauls, and the cattle very numerous. For money they use either bronze, or gold coins, or iron ingots of fixed weights. Tin is found inland, and small quantities of iron near the coast; the copper that they use is imported. There is timber of every kind, as in Gaul, except beech and fir. Hares, fowl, and geese they think it unlawful to eat, but rear them for pleasure and amusement . . .

By far the most civilized inhabitants are those living in Kent (a purely maritime district), whose way of life differs little from that of the Gauls. Most of the tribes in the interior do not grow corn but live on milk and meat, and wear skins. All the Britons dye their bodies with woad, which produces a blue colour, and shave the whole of their bodies except the head and the upper lip. Wives are shared between groups of ten or twelve men, especially between brothers and between fathers and sons; but the offspring of these unions are counted as the children of the man with whom a particular woman cohabited first.

The British cavalry and charioteers had a fierce encounter with our cavalry on the march, but our men had the best of it everywhere and drove them into the woods and hills, killing a good many, but also incurring some casualties themselves by a too eager pursuit. The enemy waited for a time, and then, while our soldiers were off their guard and busy fortifying the camp, suddenly dashed out of the woods, swooped upon the outpost on duty in front of the camp, and started a violent battle. Caesar sent two cohorts – the first of their respective legions – to the rescue, and these took up a position close together; but the men were unnerved by the unfamiliar tactics, and the enemy very daringly broke through between them and got away unhurt . . .

Throughout this peculiar combat, which was fought in front of the camp in full view of everyone, it was seen that our troops were too heavily weighted by their armour to deal with such an enemy: they could not pursue them when they retreated and dared not get separated from their standards. The cavalry, too, found it very dangerous work fighting the charioteers; for the Britons would generally give ground on purpose and after drawing them some distance from the legions would jump down from their chariots and fight on foot, with the odds in their favour. In engaging their cavalry our men were not much better off: their tactics were such that the danger was exactly the same for both pursuers and pursued. A further difficulty was that they never fought in very close order, but in very open formation, and had reserves posted here and there; in this way the various groups covered one another's retreat and fresh troops replaced those who were tired.

The Druids of Gaul, and the 'entirely different' Germans

The Druids [of Gaul] officiate at the worship of the gods, regulate public and private sacrifices, and give rulings on all religious questions. Large numbers of young men flock to them for instruction, and they are held in great honour by the people. They act as judges in practically all disputes, whether between tribes or between individuals; when any crime is committed, or a murder takes place, or a dispute arises about an inheritance or a boundary, it is they who adjudicate the matter and appoint the compensation to be paid and received by the parties concerned. Any individual or tribe failing to accept their award is banned from taking part in sacrifice – the heaviest punishment that can be inflicted upon a Gaul . . .

The Druids are exempt from military service and do not pay taxes like other citizens. These important privileges are naturally attractive: many present themselves of their own accord to become students of Druidism, and others are sent by their parents or relatives. It is said that these pupils have to memorize a great number of verses – so many, that some of them spend twenty years at their studies. The Druids believe that their religion forbids them to commit their teachings to writing, although for most other purposes, such as public and private accounts, the Gauls use the Greek alphabet. But I imagine that this rule was originally established for other reasons – because they did not want their doctrine to become public property, and in order to prevent their pupils from relying on the written word and neglecting to train their memories; for it is usually found that when people have the help of texts, they are less diligent in learning by heart, and let their memories rust. A lesson which they take particular pains to inculcate is that the soul does not perish, but after death passes from one body to another; they think that this is the best incentive to bravery, because it teaches men to disregard the terrors of death. They also hold long discussions about the heavenly bodies and their movements, the size of the universe and of the earth, the physical constitution of the world, and the power and properties of the gods; and they instruct the young men in all these subjects . . .

As a nation the Gauls are extremely superstitious; and so persons suffering from serious diseases, as well as those who are exposed to the perils of battle, offer, or vow to offer, human sacrifices, for the performance of which they employ Druids. They believe that the only way of saving a man's life is to propitiate the god's wrath by rendering another life in its place, and they have regular state sacrifices of the same kind. Some tribes have colossal images made of wickerwork, the limbs of which they fill with living men; they are then set on fire, and the victims burnt to death. They think that the gods prefer the execution of men taken in the act of theft or brigandage, or guilty of some offence; but when they run short of criminals, they do not hesitate to make up with innocent men.

The god they reverence most is Mercury. They have very many images of him, and regard him as the inventor of all arts, the god who directs men upon their journeys, and their most powerful helper in trading and getting money. Next to him they reverence Apollo, Mars, Jupiter, and Minerva, about whom they have much the same ideas as other nations – that Apollo averts illness, and Minerva teaches the principles of industries and handicrafts; that Jupiter is king of the gods, and Mars the lord of war. When they have decided to fight a battle they generally vow to Mars the booty that they hope to take, and after a victory they sacrifice the captured animals and collect the rest of the spoil in one spot. Among many of the tribes, high piles of it can be seen on consecrated ground; and it is an almost unknown thing for anyone to dare, in defiance of religious law, to conceal his booty at home or to remove anything placed on the piles. Such a crime is punishable by a terrible death under torture.

The Gauls claim all to be descended from Father Dis, declaring that this is the tradition preserved by the Druids. For this reason they measure periods of time not by days but by nights; and in celebrating birthdays, the first of the month, and new year's day, they go on the principle that the day begins at night. As regards the other usages of daily life, the chief difference between them and other peoples is that their children are not allowed to go up to their fathers in public until they are old enough for military service; they regard it as unbecoming for a son who is still a boy to stand in his father's sight in a public place.

When a Gaul marries he adds to the dowry that his wife brings with her a portion of his own property estimated to be of equal value. A joint account is kept of the whole amount, and the profits which it earns are put aside; and when either dies, the survivor receives both shares together with the accumulated profits. Husbands have power of life and death over their wives as well as their children. When a high-born head of a family dies, his relatives assemble, and if the circumstances of his death are suspicious, they examine his widow under torture, as we examine slaves; if her guilt is established, she is consigned to the flames and put to death with the most cruel torments. Gallic funerals are splendid and costly, for a comparatively poor country. Everything that the dead man is supposed to have been fond of, including even animals, is placed upon his pyre; and not long ago there were people still alive who could remember the time when slaves and retainers known to have been beloved by their masters were burnt with them at the conclusion of the funeral rites . . .

The customs of the Germans are entirely different. They have no Druids to control religious observances and are not much given to sacrifices. The only beings they recognize as gods are things that they can see, and by which they are obviously benefited, such as Sun, Moon, and Fire; the other gods they have never even heard of. They spend all their lives in hunting and warlike pursuits, and inure themselves from childhood to toil and hardship. Those who preserve their chastity longest are most highly commended by their friends; for they think that continence makes young men taller, stronger, and more muscular. To have had intercourse with a woman before the age of twenty is considered perfectly scandalous. They attempt no concealment, however, of the facts of sex: men and women bathe together in the rivers, and they wear nothing but hides or short garments of hairy skin, which leave most of the body bare.

The Germans are not agriculturalists, and live principally on milk, cheese, and meat. No one possesses any definite amount of land as private property; the magistrates and tribal chiefs annually assign a holding to clans and groups of kinsmen or others living together, fixing its size and position at their discretion, and the following year make them move on somewhere else. They give many reasons for this custom: for example, that their men may not get accustomed to living in one place, lose their warlike enthusiasm, and take up agriculture instead; that they may not be anxious to acquire large estates, and the strong be tempted to dispossess the weak; to prevent their paying too much attention to building houses that will protect them from cold and heat, or becoming too fond of money – a frequent cause of division and strife; and to keep the common people contented and quiet by letting every man see that even the most powerful are no better off than himself.

The various tribes regard it as their greatest glory to lay waste as much as possible of the land around them and to keep it uninhabited. They hold it a proof of a people's valour to drive their neighbours from their homes, so that no one dare settle near them, and also think it gives them greater security by removing any fear of sudden invasion. When a tribe is attacked or intends to attack another, officers are chosen to conduct the campaign and invested with powers of life and death. In peacetime there is no central magistracy; the chiefs of the various districts and cantons administer justice and settle disputes among their own people. No discredit attaches to plundering raids outside the tribal frontiers; the Germans say that they serve to keep the young men in training and prevent them from getting lazy. When a chief announces in an assembly his intention of leading a raid and calls for volunteers, those who like the proposal, and approve of the man who makes it, stand up and promise their assistance amid the applause of the whole gathering; anyone who backs out afterwards is looked on as a deserter and a traitor and no one will ever trust him again. To wrong a guest is impious in their eyes. They shield from injury all who come to their houses for any purpose whatever, and treat their persons as sacred; guests are welcomed to every man's home and table.

There was a time when the Gauls were more warlike than the Germans, when they actually invaded German territory, and sent colonists across the Rhine because their own country was too small to support its large population. It was in this way that the most fertile district of Germany, in the neighbourhood of the Hercynian forest (which I see was known to Eratosthenes and other Greeks, who call it Orcynia) was seized and occupied by the Volcae Tectosages, who remain there to this day and have a high reputation for fair dealing and gallantry. Nowadays, while the Germans still endure the same life of poverty and privation as before, without any change in their diet or clothing, the Gauls, through living near the Roman Province and becoming acquainted with sea-borne products, are abundantly supplied with various commodities. Gradually accustomed to inferiority and defeated in many battles, they do not even pretend to compete with the Germans in bravery.

The Conquest of Gaul (trans. S. A. Handford, 1951)

PLINY THE ELDER
AD 23–79

The knight Marcus Laenius Strabo was the first to introduce aviaries containing birds of all kinds . . . Thanks to him we began imprisoning creatures to which Nature had assigned the sky.

The world's first encyclopaedia, Pliny's *Natural History*, brought together a wealth of information covering everything from the galaxies to insects and human civilization. Despite its inaccuracies, it was considered the definitive authority on natural science for 1,500 years. His writings shaped Columbus's ambitions and his accounts of the interior of north and west Africa would remain influential until the Europeans penetrated the continent in the nineteenth century.

Pliny was a Roman officer and scholar born in AD 23 into an estate-owning family in Northern Italy. His family's wealth enabled him to complete his studies in Rome, where the literary world and developments in oratory, science and philosophy whetted his appetite for knowledge. However, when he was twenty-three or twenty-four years old, he was called to Germany to fulfil his military duty. Many people of a similar background managed to find an excuse, but Pliny took his status and its expectations seriously. He rose to the rank of colonel in a cavalry regiment and befriended the future Emperor Titus, to whom he later dedicated his *Natural History*.

Pliny's experiences in Germany provided inspiration for his first works: a treatise on how to throw a javelin from horseback, and a detailed history of Rome's wars against the Germans. He also found time for scientific tours around the sources of the Danube, observing his surroundings acutely and collating material that would contribute to his later work.

In the year 59 Pliny returned to Rome intending to practise law, but for some reason changed his mind and devoted himself to writing. He had been born into an era of political instability, of mutinous legions and imperial power struggles. This culminated in a civil war, from which Pliny emerged on the victorious side – that of the Emperor Vespasian. His public life became demanding, partly owing to the patronage of Titus, who was Vespasian's eldest son. Over the next six years he was sent as a procurator throughout the Empire, this again giving him the chance to gather copious material.

The *Natural History* is the first known book in encyclopaedic form, containing, according to its author, 20,000 facts, from 2,000 works by a hundred chosen authors. Actually this is a modest claim, considering that he quotes from 146 Roman and 327 foreign authors, each meticulously sourced. The *Natural History*'s thirty-seven sections reveal Pliny's insatiable curiosity about the mechanics of the world, and his belief that Nature is what mortals call God. The book's title would have seemed strange in Roman times, and Pliny explains that the book is the study 'of the Nature of things, that is, of life'.

Life certainly abounds in the book. Scientific observation and an accurate portrayal of Roman civilization, mining, agricultural and medicinal practices are combined with descriptions emerging from Pliny's belief in magic and superstition and his love of fable. Dog-headed men who bark instead of speak and a tribe who 'have only one leg and hop with amazing speed' can be found alongside accurate notes on metals and crystallography.

His nephew, Pliny the Younger, tells us that his uncle criticized him for travelling on foot instead of in a sedan chair, as it detracted from valuable study time. Pliny never married, but adopted his nephew when his brother-in-law died, and took care of his education.

On 24 August AD 79 Pliny went to investigate a mysterious cloud that had formed over the bay. The cloud had been caused by the eruption of Mount Vesuvius, and Pliny was suffocated by the volcano's sulphurous fumes, (see page 152). His momentous book, however, was circulated further and further afield, and by the Middle Ages, when encyclopaedias had become popular sources of instruction, scholars drew widely upon Pliny. He was quoted and re-quoted, and his comments were elaborated upon, regardless of their accuracy.

Niccolo Leonicent was the first person to publish an attack on Pliny's work, *Concerning the Errors of Pliny*, in 1492. His influence gradually eroded, but it was only at the end of the seventeenth century that the *Natural History* was rejected by leading scientists. The way in which it had captured the minds and imagination of so many people until then could be seen as Nature's response to the valediction with which Pliny closed his encyclopaedia: 'Greetings, Nature, mother of all creation, show me your favour in that I alone of Rome's citizens have praised you in all your aspects.'

The interior of Africa

The River Niger has the same nature as the Nile. It produces reeds, papyrus and the same animals, and rises at the same seasons. Some place the Atlas tribe in the middle of the desert and next to them the half-animal Goat-Pans, the Blemmyae, Gamphasantes, Satyrs and Strapfeet.

The Atlas tribe is primitive and subhuman, if we believe what we hear; they do not call each other by names. When they observe the rising and setting sun they utter terrible curses against it, as the cause of disaster to themselves and their fields. Nor do they have dreams in their sleep like the rest of mankind. The Cave-dwellers hollow out caves which are their houses; their food is snake meat. They have no voice but make a shrill noise, thus lacking any communication by speech. The Garamantes do not marry but live promiscuously with their women. The Augilae worship only the gods of the lower world. The Gamphasantes wear no clothes, do not fight and do not associate with any foreigner.

The Blemmyae are reported as being without heads; their mouth and eyes are attached to their chest. The Satyrs have no human characteristics except their shape. The form of the Goat-Pans is as commonly depicted. The Strapfeet are people with feet like thongs who naturally move by crawling. The Pharusi, formerly from Persia, are said to have been Hercules' companions on his journey to the Gardens of the Hesperides. I cannot think of any more to record about Africa.

The hippopotamus

The Nile produces a creature even mightier than the crocodile: the hippopotamus. It has hooves like those of oxen; a horse's back, mane and neighing sound; a turned-up snout; a boar's tail and curved tusks, although less damaging; and an impenetrable hide used for shields and helmets, unless soaked in water. The hippopotamus feeds on crops, marking out an area in advance for each day, so men say, and it makes its footprints lead out of a field so that no traps are prepared for its return.

Marcus Scaurus was the first to put a hippopotamus, together with five crocodiles, on show at Rome when he staged the games during his aedileship; they were kept in an artificial lake. The hippopotamus stands out as a teacher in one branch of medicine. For when it lumbers ashore after excessive eating – in which it indulges all the time – to look for recently cut rushes, and sees a very sharp stalk, it presses its body on to it and pierces a vein in its leg, and so, by losing blood, lightens its body, which would otherwise become ill. Then it covers up the wound again with mud.

Ravens

Let our thanks be given to the raven as is its due. During the principate of Tiberius a young raven, from a brood hatched on top of the Temple of Castor and Pollux, flew down to a shoemaker's shop near by, where it was welcome to the owner because of religious considerations. It soon learnt how to talk, and every morning flew to the Rostra facing the Forum and greeted Tiberius by name, then Germanicus and Drusus Caesar, and, after that, the people of Rome as they passed by; finally it returned to the shop. The raven was remarkable in that it performed this duty for several years.

The tenant of the next shoemaker's shop killed the bird, either out of rivalry or in a sudden fit of anger because he claimed that some droppings had spotted his shoes. This aroused such an uproar among the general public that the man was driven out of the district and subsequently lynched, while the bird's funeral was celebrated with great pomp. The draped bier was carried on the shoulders of two Ethiopians, preceded by a flautist; there were all kinds of floral tributes along the way to the pyre, which had been constructed on the right hand side of the Appian Way at the second milestone, on what is called Rediculus' Plain.

Human reproduction

Man is the only animal whose first experience of mating is accompanied by regret; this is indeed an augury for life derived from a regrettable origin. All other animals have fixed seasons during the year for mating, but man, as has been stated, has intercourse at any hour of the day or night. All other animals derive satisfaction from having mated; man gets almost none . . .

Messalina, the wife of Claudius Caesar, thinking it would be a royal triumph, chose to compete against a certain young servant girl who was a most notorious prostitute, and, over a twenty-four-hour period, beat her record by having sex with twenty-five men. In the human race males have devised every kind of sexual deviation – crimes against Nature; women, for their part, have invented abortion. How much more shameful are we in our sex life than wild animals! Hesiod records that men are keener on sexual intercourse in winter, and women in summer.

Natural History (trans. John F. Healy, 1991 edn)

PLINY THE YOUNGER
c. AD 61–113

We are always ready to make a journey and cross the sea in search of things we fail to notice in front of our eyes.

The nephew of Pliny the Elder, the younger Pliny was a diligent Roman lawyer and administrator who also found time to be a prolific letter-writer. He selected and edited his *Letters* into nine books of correspondence, ranging from epistles to friends and family, to letters to young Romans, advising them on how to advance their careers; the letters also document his personal endeavours to explore the world around him. Pliny provided one of the most vivid portrayals of life among hard-working sections of Roman society: 'We must work at our profession and not make anyone else's idleness an excuse for our own,' he wrote after a seven-hour speech in court. 'There is no lack of readers and listeners; it is for us to produce something worth being written and heard.'

Pliny married three times, but remained childless – a cause of much dismay. 'I can leave them a well-known name and an established ancestry,' he wrote, 'if only they may be born and turn our present grief to joy.' He left a legacy of a different kind, however, in the form of his insightful and lively letters.

To Cornelius Tacitus: death by volcano

Thank you for asking me to send you a description of my uncle's [Pliny the Elder] death so that you can leave an accurate account of it for posterity; I know that immortal fame awaits him if his death is recorded by you. It is true that he perished in a catastrophe which destroyed the loveliest regions of the earth, a fate shared by whole cities and their people, and one so memorable that it is likely to make his name live for ever: and he himself wrote a number of books of lasting value: but you write for all time and can still do much to perpetuate his memory. The fortunate man, in my opinion, is he to whom the gods have granted the power either to do something which is worth recording or to write what is worth reading, and most fortunate of all is the man who can do both. Such a man was my uncle, as his own books and yours will prove. So you set me a task I would choose for myself, and I am more than willing to start on it.

My uncle was stationed at Misenum [the northern arm of the Bay of Naples] in active command of the fleet. On 24 August, in the early afternoon, my mother drew his attention to a cloud of unusual size and appearance. He had been out in the sun, had taken a cold bath, and lunched while lying down, and was then working at his books. He called for his shoes and climbed up to a place which would give him the best view of the phenomenon. It was not clear at that distance from which mountain the cloud was rising (it was afterwards known to be Vesuvius); its general appearance can best be expressed as being like an umbrella pine, for it rose to a great height on a sort of trunk and then split off into branches, I imagine because it was thrust upwards by the first blast and then left unsupported as the pressure subsided, or else it was borne down by its own weight so that it spread out and gradually dispersed. Sometimes it looked white, sometimes blotched and dirty, according to the amount of soil and ashes it carried with it. My uncle's scholarly acumen saw at once that it was important enough for a closer inspection, and he ordered a boat to be made ready, telling me I could come with him if I wished. I replied that I preferred to go on with my studies, and as it happened he had himself given me some writing to do.

As he was leaving the house he was handed a message from Rectina, wife of Tascius whose house was at the foot of the mountain, so that escape was impossible except by boat. She was terrified by the danger threatening her and implored him to rescue her from her fate. He changed his plans, and what he had begun in a spirit of inquiry he completed as a hero. He gave orders for the warships to be launched and went on board himself with the intention of bringing help to many more people besides Rectina, for this lovely stretch of coast was thickly populated. He hurried to the place which everyone else was hastily leaving, steering his course straight for the danger zone. He was entirely fearless, describing each new movement and phase of the portent to be noted down exactly as he observed them. Ashes were already falling, hotter and thicker as the ships drew near, followed by bits of pumice and blackened stones, charred and cracked by the flames: then suddenly they were in shallow water, and the shore was blocked by the debris from the mountain. For a moment my uncle wondered whether to turn back, but when the helmsman advised this he refused, telling him that Fortune stood by the courageous and they must make for Pomponianus at Stabiae [four miles south of Pompeii]. He was cut off there by the breadth of the bay (for the shore gradually curves round a basin filled by the sea) so that he was not as yet in danger, though it was clear that this would come nearer as it spread. Pomponianus had therefore already put his belongings on board ship, intending to escape if the contrary wind fell. This wind was of course full in my uncle's favour, and he was able to bring his ship in. He embraced his terrified friend, cheered and encouraged him, and thinking he could calm his fears by showing his own composure, gave orders that he was to be carried to the bathroom. After his bath he lay down and dined; he was quite cheerful, or at any rate he pretended he was, which was no less courageous.

Meanwhile on Mount Vesuvius broad sheets of fire and leaping flames blazed at several points, their bright glare emphasized by the darkness of night. My uncle tried to allay the fears of his companions by repeatedly declaring that these were nothing but bonfires left by the peasants in their terror, or else empty houses on fire in the districts they had abandoned. Then he went to rest and certainly slept, for as he was a stout man his breathing was rather loud and heavy and could be heard by people coming and going outside his door. By this time the courtyard giving access to his room was full of ashes mixed with pumice-stones, so that its level had risen, and if he had stayed in the room any longer he would never have got out. He was wakened, came out and joined Pomponianus and the rest of the household who had sat up all night. They debated whether to stay indoors or take their chance in the open, for the buildings were now shaking with violent shocks, and seemed to be swaying to and fro as if they were torn from their foundations. Outside on the other hand, there was the danger of falling pumice-stones, even though these were light and porous; however, after comparing the risks they chose the latter. In my uncle's case one reason outweighed the other, but for the others it was a choice of fears. As a protection against falling objects they put pillows on their heads tied down with cloths.

Elsewhere there was daylight by this time, but they were still in darkness, blacker and denser than any ordinary night, which they relieved by lighting torches and various kinds of lamp. My uncle decided to go down to the shore and investigate on the spot the possibility of any escape by sea, but he found the waves still wild and dangerous. A sheet was spread on the ground for him to lie down, and he repeatedly asked for cold water to drink. Then the flames and smell of sulphur which gave warning of the approaching fire drove the others to take flight and roused him to stand up. He stood leaning on two slaves and then suddenly collapsed, I imagine because the dense fumes choked his breathing by blocking his windpipe which was constitutionally weak and narrow and often inflamed. When daylight returned on the 26th – two days after the last day he had seen – his body was found intact and uninjured, still fully clothed and looking more like sleep than death.

Meanwhile my mother and I were at Misenum, but this is not of any historic interest, and you only wanted to hear about my uncle's death. I will say no more, except to add that I have described in detail every incident which I either witnessed myself or heard about immediately after the event, when reports were most likely to be accurate. It is for you to select what best suits your purpose, for there is a great difference between a letter to a friend and history written for all to read.

To Clusinius Gallus: floating islands

We are always ready to make a journey and cross the sea in search of things we fail to notice in front of our eyes, whether it is that we are naturally indifferent to anything close at hand while pursuing distant objects, or that every desire fades when it can easily be granted, or that we postpone a visit with the idea that we shall often be seeing what is there to be seen whenever we feel inclined. Whatever the reason, there are a great many things in Rome and near by which we have never seen nor even heard of, though if they were to be found in Greece, Egypt or Asia, or any other country which advertises its wealth of marvels, we should have heard and read about them and seen them for ourselves.

I am a case in point. I have just heard of something (and seen it, too) which I had neither seen nor heard of before. My wife's grandfather had asked me to look at his property in Ameria. While going round I was shown a lake at the foot of the hills called Lake Vadimon, and at the same time told some extraordinary facts about it. I went down to look at it, and found it was perfectly round and regular in shape, like a wheel lying on its side, without a single irregular bend or curve, and so evenly proportioned that it might have been artificially shaped and hollowed out. It is subdued in colour, pale blue with a tinge of green, has a smell of sulphur and a mineral taste, and the property of healing fractures. It is of no great size, but large enough for the wind to raise waves on its surface. There are no boats on it, as the waters are sacred, but floating islands, green with reeds and sedge and the other plants which grow more profusely on the marshy ground at the edge of the lake. Each island has its peculiar shape and size, and all have their edges worn away by friction, as they are constantly knocking against each other and the shore. They all have the same height and buoyancy, each shallow base dipping into the water like the keel of a boat; and this has the same appearance from all sides, both the part above and the part under water. Sometimes the islands join together to look like a continuous piece of land, sometimes they are driven apart by conflicting winds, while in calm weather they are left to float about separately. The small islands often attach themselves to the larger, like small boats to a merchant ship, and both large and small sometimes appear to be racing each other; or they are all driven to one side of the lake to create a headland where they cling to the shore; they remove or restore stretches of the lake on one side or the other, so that its size is unaltered only when they all keep to the centre. Cattle are often known to walk on to the islands while grazing, taking them for the edge of the lake, and only realize that they are on moving ground when carried off from the shore as if forcibly put on board ship, and are terrified to find themselves surrounded by water; then, when they land where the wind has carried them, they are no more conscious of having ended their voyage than they were of embarking on it. Another feature of the lake is the river leading from it, which is visible for a short distance before it enters a cave and continues its course at a great depth; anything thrown in before it disappears is carried along and reappears with it.

I have given you these details because I imagine they are as new and interesting to you as they were to me; natural phenomena are always a great source of interest to us both.

The Letters of the Younger Pliny (trans. Betty Radice, 1963)

Attila the Hun, ?–AD 453

A lavish meal . . . was prepared for us and the other barbarians, but Attila just had some meat on a wooden platter, for this was one aspect of his self-discipline.

Attila was king of the Huns, the 'scourge of God', who made sweeping conquests against the Roman Empire.

Born in Thrace, Priscus was a diplomat and historian who, in AD 448, the date of the extract, was on a diplomatic mission to the court of Attila. His detailed account of the time he spent with the Huns is one of the few surviving insights into their lifestyle. It was contained in his eight-part history, of which only fragments have been preserved.

Dining with the Scourge of God

When we had returned to our tent, Orestes' father came to say that Attila invited both parties of us to dine with him about 3 o'clock that afternoon. We waited for the time of the invitation, and then all of us, the envoys from the Western Romans as well, presented ourselves in the doorway facing Attila. In accordance with the national custom the cupbearers gave us a cup for us to make our libations before we took our seats. When that had been done and we had sipped the wine, we went to the chairs where we would sit to have dinner. All the seats were ranged down either side of the room, up against the walls. In the middle Attila was sitting on a couch with a second couch behind him. I think that the more distinguished guests were on Attila's right, and the second rank on his left, where we were with Berichos, a man of some renown among the Scythians, who was sitting in front of us. Onegesios was to the right of Attila's couch, and opposite him were two of the king's sons on chairs. The eldest son was sitting on Attila's own couch, right on the very edge, with his eyes fixed on the ground in fear of his father.

When all were sitting properly in order, a cupbearer came to offer Attila an ivy-wood bowl of wine, which he took and drank a toast to the man first in order of precedence. The man thus honoured rose to his feet and it was not right for him to sit down again until Attila had drunk some or all of the wine and had handed the goblet back to the attendant. The guests, taking their own cups, then honoured him in the same way, sipping the wine after making the toast. One attendant went round to each man in strict order after Attila's personal cupbearer had gone out. When the second guest and then all the others in their turn had been honoured, Attila greeted us in like fashion in our order of seating.

After everyone had been toasted, the cupbearers left, and a table was put in front of Attila and other tables for groups of three or four men each. This enabled each guest to help himself to the things put on the table without leaving his proper seat. Attila's servant entered first with plates full of meat, and those waiting on all the others put bread and cooked food on the tables. A lavish meal, served on silver trenchers, was prepared for us and the other barbarians, but Attila just had some meat on a wooden platter, for this was one aspect of his self-discipline. For instance, gold or silver cups were presented to the other diners, but his own goblet was made of wood. His clothes, too, were simple, and no trouble was taken except to have them clean. The sword that hung by his side, the clasps of his barbarian shoes and the bridle of his horse were all free from gold, precious stones or other valuable decorations affected by the other Scythians. When the food in the first plates was finished we all got up, and no one, once on his feet, returned to his seat until he had, in the same order as before, drunk the full cup of wine that he was handed, with a toast for Attila's health. After this honour had been paid him, we sat down again and second plates were put on each table with other food on them. This also finished, everyone rose once more, drank another toast and resumed his seat.

As twilight came on torches were lit, and two barbarians entered before Attila to sing some songs they had composed, telling of his victories and his valour in war. The guests paid close attention to them, and some were delighted with the songs, others excited at being reminded of the wars, but others broke down and wept if their bodies were weakened by age and their warrior spirits forced to remain inactive. After the songs a Scythian entered, a crazy fellow who told a lot of strange and completely false stories, not a word of truth in them, which made everyone laugh. Following him came the moor, Zerkon, totally disorganized in appearance, clothes, voice and words. By mixing up the languages of the Italians with those of the Huns and Goths, he fascinated everyone and made them break out into uncontrollable laughter, all that is except Attila. He remained impassive, without any change of expression, and neither by word or gesture did he seem to share in the merriment except that when his youngest son, Ernas, came in and stood by him, he drew the boy towards him and looked at him with gentle eyes. I was surprised that he paid no attention to his other sons, and only had time for this one. But the barbarian at my side, who understood Italian and what I had said about the boy, warned me not to speak up, and said that the seers had told Attila that his family would be banished but would be restored by this son. After spending most of the night at the party, we left, having no wish to pursue the drinking any further.

   Historici Graeci Minores (in B. K. Workman, *They Saw it Happen in Classical Times*, 1964)

Hsuan Tsang
AD 602–64

In your former existence, what crime did you commit that . . . you have been born in this evil way and with this hideous body?

Hsuan Tsang, a Chinese monk who went on a sixteen-year voyage to gather Buddhist teachings in India – later translating them into Chinese – was born into a Confucian family of four sons that had over the generations produced several scholars. Hsuan Tsang developed a fascination for Buddhist scriptures. He was ordained as a monk, and studied in the Temple of Great Learning in Chang-an, a community of monks who devoted their lives to translating sacred books from India. Hsuan Tsang soon became frustrated with discrepancies in the texts and resolved that the only way he was to gain a full understanding of them was to go to India himself.

Defying an imperial order restraining citizens from leaving China, Hsuan Tsang and his horse set out on an arduous journey that was to cover 40,000 miles.* On reaching India, he devoted himself to studying – perfecting his knowledge of Sanskrit and Buddhist teachings – but also visiting the sacred sites.

* Two fellow monks gave this description of him, as he departed for the unknown: 'His colouring was delicate, his eyes brilliant. His bearing was grave and majestic, and his features seemed to radiate charm and brightness . . . His voice was pure and penetrating in quality and his words were brilliant in their nobility, elegance, and harmony, so that his hearers never grew weary of listening to him.'

Behind him, Hsuan Tsang left a wake of respect and admiration, quickly becoming renowned throughout the country and gaining the favour of King Harsa, ruler of North India, who convened a religious assembly in his honour. Hsuan Tsang, however, was not entirely happy with all he found in the subcontinent, and criticized the nakedness, filth and wayward habits of the Hindu holy men.

In 645 the monk returned to his homeland on a chariot laden with gifts from King Harsa, as well as the 700 religious books and artefacts he had collected. In contrast to his clandestine exit from China, he received a hero's welcome. The Emperor, who was delighted with the detailed insights Hsuan Tsang gave him into the cultures, climate and products of the areas he had visited, offered Hsuan Tsang a post as a minister, but he declined, wanting to devote the rest of his life to study and to translating Buddhist teachings into Chinese.

It has been said that the number of words Hsuan Tsang translated in the last five years of his life is 84 times those in the Bible. He wrote a long work called the *Treatise on the Establishment of the Doctrine of Consciousness Only*, both of which developed the concept that the world is a reflection of the human mind.

A fish monster explains himself

In days long past, when Buddha was living, there were 500 fishermen who joined in partnership to fish for and catch the finny tribes, whereupon they entangled in the river stream a great fish with eighteen heads; each head had two eyes. The fishermen desired to kill it, but Tathâgata being then in the country of Vaisâlî, with his divine sight saw what was going on, and raising within him a compassionate heart, he used this opportunity as a means for converting and directing (*men*). Accordingly, in order to open their minds, he said to the great congregation, 'In the Vṛijji country there is a great fish; I wish to guide it (*into the right way*), in order to enlighten the fishermen; you therefore should embrace this opportunity.'

On this the great congregation surrounding him, by their spiritual power passed through the air and came to the river-side. He sat down as usual, and forthwith addressed the fishermen. 'Kill not that fish. By my spiritual power I will open the way for the exercise of expedients, and cause this great fish to know its former kind of life; and in order to this I will cause it to speak in human language and truly to exhibit human affections (*feelings*).' Then Tathâgata, knowing it beforehand, asked (*the fish*), 'In your former existence, what crime did you commit that in the circle of migration you have been born in this evil way and with this hideous body?' The fish said, 'Formerly, by the merit I had gained, I was born in a noble family as the Brâhman Kapitha (Kie-pi-tha). Relying on this family origin, I insulted other persons; relying on my extensive knowledge, I despised all books and rules, and with a supercilious heart I reviled the Buddhas with opprobrious words, and ridiculed the priests by comparing them to every kind of brute beast, as the ass, or the mule, or the elephant, or the horse, and every unsightly form. In return for all this I received this monstrous body of mine. Thanks, however, to some virtuous remnants during former lives, I am born during the time of a Buddha's appearance in the world, and permitted to see his sacred form, and myself to receive his sacred instruction and to confess and repent of my former misdeeds.'

On this Tathâgata, according to the circumstance, instructed and converted him by wisely opening his understanding. The fish having received the law, expired, and by the power of this merit was born in heaven.

Hell on Earth: the prison of Asoka

At first when Aśôka (Wu-yau) râja ascended the throne, he exercised a most cruel tyranny; he constituted a hell for the purpose of torturing living creatures. He surrounded it with high walls with lofty towers. He placed there specially vast furnaces of molten metal, sharp scythes, and every kind of instrument of torture like those in the infernal regions. He selected an impious man whom he appointed lord of the hell. At first every criminal in the empire, whatever his fault, was consigned to this place of calamity and outrage; afterwards all those who passed by the place were seized and destroyed. All who came to the place were killed without any chance of self-defence.

At this time a Śramaṇa, just entered the religious order, was passing through the suburbs begging food, when he came to hell-gate. The impious keeper of the place laid hold upon him to destroy him. The Śramaṇa, filled with fear, asked for a respite to perform an act of worship and confession. Just then he saw a man bound with cords enter the prison. In a moment they cut off his hands and feet, and pounded his body in a mortar, till all the members of his body were mashed up together in confusion.

The Śramaṇa having witnessed this, deeply moved with pity, arrived at the conviction of the impermanence (*anitya*) of all earthly things, and reached the fruit of 'exemption from learning' (*Arhatship*). Then the infernal lictor said, 'Now you must die.' The Śramaṇa having become an Arhat, was freed in heart from the power of birth and death, and so, though cast into a boiling caldron, it was to him as a cool lake, and on its surface there appeared a lotus flower, whereon he took his seat. The infernal lictor, terrified thereat, hastened to send a messenger to the king to tell him of the circumstance. The king having himself come and beheld the sight, raised his voice in loud praise of the miracle.

The keeper, addressing the king, said, 'Mahârâja, you too must die.' 'And why so?' said the king. 'Because of your former decree with respect to the infliction of death, that all who came to the walls of the hell should be killed; it was not said that the king might enter and escape death.'

The king said, 'The decree was indeed established, and cannot be altered. But when the law was made, were *you* excepted? You have long destroyed life. I will put an end to it.' Then ordering the attendants, they seized the lictor and cast him into a boiling caldron. After his death the king departed, and levelled the walls, filled up the ditches, and put an end to the infliction of such horrible punishments.

Buddhist Records of the Western World, trans. Samuel Beal, 1890

Ibn Fadlan
fl.922
When one of their chiefs dies, his family asks his girls and pages,
'Which one of you will die with him?'

Ibn Fadlan was an emissary for the Caliph of Baghdad, who in 921 sent him to the Bulgars of the Middle Volga, perhaps in response to a call for help from the king. Fadlan's *risala* (the name applied to Arabic historical accounts) of his journey describes in great detail a people of Swedish origin called the Rus, who were working as traders in the Bulgar capital.

The visitor from Baghdad is accepted among the Rus, but he also views them through the critical eyes of a devout Muslim. Some historians feel that Fadlan's prejudices detract from the veracity of his account. Taking that into consideration, Fadlan still provides an insight into Viking and Russian society, including their power struggles, during the tenth century.

A Viking funeral

I was told that the least of what they do for their chiefs when they die, is to consume them with fire. When I was finally informed of the death of one of their magnates, I sought to witness what befell. First they laid him in his grave – over which a roof was erected – for the space of ten days, until they had completed the cutting and sewing of his clothes. In the case of a poor man, however, they merely build for him a boat, in which they place him, and consume it with fire.

When one of their chiefs dies, his family asks his girls and pages, 'Which one of you will die with him?' Then one of them answers, 'I.' From the time that he utters this word, he is no longer free: should he wish to draw back, he is not permitted. For the most part, however, it is the girls that offer themselves. So, when the man of whom I spoke had died, they asked his girls, 'Who will die with him?' One of them answered, 'I.' She was then committed to two girls, who were to keep watch over her, accompany her wherever she went, and even, on occasion, wash her feet. The people now began to occupy themselves with the dead man – to cut out the clothes for him, and to prepare whatever else was needful. During the whole of this period, the girl gave herself over to drinking and singing, and was cheerful and gay.

When the day was now come that the dead man and the girl were to be committed to the flames, I went to the river in which his ship lay, but found that it had already been drawn ashore. Four corner-blocks of birch and other woods had been placed in position for it, while around were stationed large wooden figures in the semblance of human beings. Thereupon the ship was

brought up, and placed on the timbers above-mentioned. In the meantime
the people began to walk to and fro, uttering words which I did not understand. The dead man, meanwhile, lay at a distance in his grave, from which
they had not yet removed him. Next they brought a couch, placed it in the
ship, and covered it with Greek cloth of gold, wadded and quilted, with
pillows of the same material. There came an old crone, whom they call the
angel of death, and spread the articles mentioned on the couch. It was she
who attended to the sewing of the garments, and to all the equipment; it was
she, also, who was to slay the girl. I saw her; she was dark, thick-set, with a
lowering countenance.

When they came to the grave, they removed the earth from the wooden
roof, set the latter aside, and drew out the dead man in the loose wrapper in
which he had died. Then I saw that he had turned quite black, by reason of the
coldness of that country. Near him in the grave they had placed strong drink,
fruits, and a lute; and these they now took out. Except for his colour, the dead
man had not changed. They now clothed him in drawers, leggings, boots, and
a *kurtak* and *chaftan* of cloth of gold, with golden buttons, placing on his head
a cap made of cloth of gold, trimmed with sable. Then they carried him into a
tent placed in the ship, seated him on the wadded and quilted covering,
supported him with the pillows, and, bringing strong drink, fruits, and basil,
placed them all beside him. Then they brought a dog, which they cut in two,
and threw into the ship; laid all his weapons beside him; and led up two
horses, which they chased until they were dripping with sweat, whereupon
they cut them in pieces with their swords, and threw the flesh into the ship.
Two oxen were then brought forward, cut in pieces, and flung into the ship.
Finally they brought a cock and a hen, killed them, and threw them in also.

The girl who had devoted herself to death meanwhile walked to and fro,
entering one after another of the tents which they had there. The occupant of
each tent lay with her, saying, 'Tell your master, "I [the man] did this only for
love of you."'

When it was now Friday afternoon, they led the girl to an object which they
had constructed, and which looked like the framework of a door. She then
placed her feet on the extended hands of the men, was raised up above the
framework, and uttered something in her language, whereupon they let her
down. Then again they raised her, and she did as at first. Once more they let
her down, and then lifted her a third time, while she did as at the previous
times. They then handed her a hen, whose head she cut off and threw away;
but the hen itself they cast into the ship. I inquired of the interpreter what it
was that she had done. He replied: 'The first time she said, "Lo, I see here my

father and mother"; the second time, "Lo, now I see all my deceased relatives sitting"; the third time, "Lo, there is my master, who is sitting in Paradise. Paradise is so beautiful, so green. With him are his men and boys. He calls me, so bring me to him."' Then they led her away to the ship.

Here she took off her two bracelets, and gave them to the old woman who was called the angel of death, and who was to murder her. She also drew off her two anklets, and passed them to the two serving-maids, who were the daughters of the so-called angel of death. Then they lifted her into the ship, but did not yet admit her to the tent. Now men came up with shields and staves, and handed her a cup of strong drink. This she took, sang over it, and emptied it. 'With this,' so the interpreter told me, 'she is taking leave of those who are dear to her.' Then another cup was handed her, which she also took, and began a lengthy song. The crone admonished her to drain the cup without lingering, and to enter the tent where her master lay. By this time, as it seemed to me, the girl had become dazed; she made as though she would enter the tent, and had brought her head forward between the tent and the ship, when the hag seized her by the head, and dragged her in. At this moment the men began to beat upon their shields with the staves, in order to drown the noise of her outcries, which might have terrified the other girls, and deterred them from seeking death with their masters in the future. Then six men followed into the tent, and each and every one had carnal companionship with her. Then they laid her down by her master's side, while two of the men seized her by the feet, and two by the hands. The old woman known as the angel of death now knotted a rope around her neck, and handed the ends to two of the men to pull. Then with a broad-bladed dagger she smote her between the ribs, and drew the blade forth, while the two men strangled her with the rope till she died.

The next of kin to the dead man now drew near, and, taking a piece of wood, lighted it, and walked backwards towards the ship, holding the stick in one hand, with the other placed upon his buttocks (he being naked), until the wood which had been piled under the ship was ignited. Then the others came up with staves and firewood, each one carrying a stick already lighted at the upper end, and threw it all on the pyre. The pile was soon aflame, then the ship, finally the tent, the man, and the girl, and everything else in the ship. A terrible storm began to blow up, and this intensified the flames, and gave wings to the blaze.

A. S. Cook, 'Ibn Fadlan's Account of Scandinavian Merchants on the Volga in 922', *Journal of English and Germanic Philology*, 1923

Timour Beg . . . said to them that he had certainly promised not to shed their blood, but that he would stifle them in those holes.

Ruy Gonzalez de Clavijo, a Spanish diplomat who travelled to Turkistan, was born in Madrid in the late 1300s. He became a chamberlain to King Henry III of Castile and Leon, and took part in the king's second ambassadorial mission to the warlord Timur, the Turkic conqueror whose court was in Samarkand, Turkistan.

The ambassadors spent five months sailing through the Mediterranean to Constantinople, where they were overawed by the glittering grandeur of the city; the men next crossed the Black Sea, battling against wild storms. During the overland journey on horseback to Turkistan, all members of the party fell ill, and one died.

Timur welcomed the Spaniards with lavish festivities and spectacles but became ill before the ambassadors left his country, and soon died, his territories then torn apart by civil war. Ruy Gonzalez reached home in 1406, and wrote an influential account that provided the Spanish with an insight into Persia and Central Asia.

The holy relics of Constantinople

On the same day the ambassadors went to see the relics in the church of St John the Baptist, which were not shown to them before, for want of the keys. When they arrived at the church, the monks robed themselves, and lighted many candles, and took the keys, singing and chaunting all the time. They then ascended to a sort of tower, where the relics were; and with them there was a knight of the emperor's household. They then came forth chaunting very mournful hymns, with lighted tapers, and many incense bearers before them, and they placed the relics on a high table covered with a silken cloth, in the body of the church. The relics were contained in a coloured chest, which was sealed with two seals of white wax, on two plates of silver. They opened it, and took out two large silver gilt plates, which were placed on the top of the relics. They then produced a bag of white dimity, sealed with wax, which they opened, and took out a small round golden casket, in which was the bread which our Lord Jesus Christ gave to Judas at the last supper, as a sign who it was who should betray him, but he was unable to eat it. It was wrapped in a red crape cover, and sealed with two waxen seals, and the bread was about three fingers in breadth.

They then took out a gold casket smaller than the first, in which there was a crystal case, which was fixed in the casket, and which contained some of the blood of our Lord Jesus Christ, which flowed from his side, when it was pierced by Longinus. They also took out another small golden casket, the top of which was pierced like a grater, and it contained the blood which flowed from a crucifix in the city of Beyrout, when a Jew once attempted to injure it. They also showed a little case of glass, which had a cover, and a little golden chain attached to it; in which was a small red crape cover containing some hairs of the beard of our Lord Jesus Christ, being those which the Jews pulled out, when they crucified him. There was also a piece of the stone on which our Lord was placed, when he was taken down from the cross. They then showed a square silver casket, two and a half *palmos* long, which was sealed with six seals made of six plates of silver, and it was opened with a silver key. They took out of it a board, which was covered with gold, and on it was the iron of the lance with which Longinus pierced our Lord Jesus Christ. It was as fine as a thorn, and of well tempered iron, and the handle was bored through, being about a *palmo* and two fingers long; and the blood on it was as fresh as if the deed which was done with it had just been committed. It was fixed on the board, which was covered with gold, and the iron was not bright, but quite dim. There was also fixed on this board, a piece of the cane which they gave our Lord Jesus Christ, when he was before Pilate. It was a *palmo* and a half long; and near it there was also a piece of the sponge with which Jesus Christ, our God, was given gall and vinegar, when he was on the cross. In the same case with this board, there was the garment of Jesus Christ, for which the knights of Pilate cast lots. It was folded, and sealed, that people who came to see it might not cut bits off, as had been done before, but one sleeve was left outside the seals. The garment was of a red dimity, like muslin, and the sleeve was narrow, and it was doubled to the elbow. It had three little buttons, made like twisted cords, like the knots on a doublet, and the buttons, and the sleeve, and all that could be seen of the skirt, seemed to be of a dark rose colour; and it did not look as if it had been woven, but as if it had been worked with a needle, for the strings looked twisted in network, and very tight. When the ambassadors went to see these relics, the people of the city, who knew it, came also, and they all cried very loudly, and said their prayers.

Punishment for a Turk

The Turk, never having heard of Timour Beg, until that time, and believing that there was no man in the world equal to himself, got into such a passion that it was quite wonderful, and sent back letters to Timour Beg, in which he said that he was astonished that there could be a man so mad and insolent as to write such great folly; that he would do what he chose against Zaratan, and against every other man in the whole universe. He further promised to come and seek for Timour Beg, and that he could not escape from falling into his hands. He also swore that he would disgrace him, by dishonoring his principal wife.

Timour Beg, being possessed of great confidence, determined to show his power, and marched from the beautiful plains of Carabaque, in Ponsia, where he had wintered that year, with a great army, straight to the city of Arsinga. Thence he advanced into the land of Turkey, and besieged the city of Sabastria. The people of Sabastria sent to the Turk, their lord, for help; and when he heard that Timour Beg was in his territory, he got into a great passion, and collected a force, which he sent against him, under his eldest son Muzulman Chalabi. The force consisted of two hundred thousand cavalry, and he intended to follow himself, with a larger army; but before the Turks could arrive, Timour had entered the city; and he did so in this manner: he fought the besieged very fiercely, so that at last they came to speak with him, and he agreed that certain men of the city should come to him; that he would cause no blood to be shed; and that they should give him a certain quantity of gold and silver.

When Timour Beg had received the tribute which he demanded, he said that he desired to tell those of the city certain things, which were much to their advantage; and that, for this purpose, the chief men should come to him. These, trusting in the safe conduct he had given them, came to him; and Timour Beg, as soon as he had got them outside the city, caused great holes to be made; and said to them that he had certainly promised not to shed their blood, but that he would stifle them in those holes; and he ordered his troops to enter the city. He buried all who had come out to him, alive, and ordered the city to be pillaged, pulled down, and destroyed.

Narrative of the Embassy of Ruy Gonzales de Clavijo to the Court of Timur at Samarkand
(trans. Clements Markham, 1859)

GILBERT WHITE
1720–93

The swallow is a delicate songster, and in soft sunny weather sings
both perching and flying.

The Rev'd Gilbert White, an English clergy-man whose diligent observations of Hampshire wildlife over two decades establish him as one of the first naturalists, was born at 'The Wakes' in Selborne, Hampshire, and was educated at Oriel College, Oxford. He took holy orders in 1747 and soon afterwards moved back to his beloved home village, where he served as a curate. White was an explorer of small things, finding limitless enchantment within the thirty-mile boundary of Selborne. On his daily walks, he patiently studied the natural world, then came home to re-create it in detailed letters to two naturalists, Thomas Pennant and Daines Barrington. These letters accumulated over a period of twenty years and were edited by White into *The Natural History and Antiquities of Selborne*, published in 1789. The book has become an English classic, widely read for its captivating descriptions and charming simplicity of style. White believed that in nature's intricacy lay proof of God's ingenuity.

Like the two Plinys, the quiet and unassuming curate found as much to be inspired and fascinated by in the local vicinity as an intrepid traveller might have found in far-off lands. Though it would be stretching a point to say he was an ecologist in the modern, scientifically rigorous sense, White's book opened people's eyes to the study of nature, encouraging them to question the hows and whys of local species, instead of accepting them as a mere backdrop to busy lives.

He conveys the subtleties of the natural world just as James Boswell did human society in his masterpiece *Life of Samuel Johnson* (1791).

Spiders with filmy threads

On *September* the 21st, 1741, being then on a visit, and intent on field-diversions, I rose before daybreak: when I came into the enclosures, I found the stubbles and clover-grounds matted all over with a thick coat of cobweb, in the meshes of which a copious and heavy dew hung so plentifully that the whole face of the country seemed, as it were, covered with two or three setting-nets drawn one over another. When the dogs attempted to hunt, their eyes were so blinded and hoodwinked that they could not proceed, but were obliged to lie down and scrape the incumbrances from their faces with their fore-feet, so that, finding my sport interrupted, I returned home musing in my mind on the oddness of the occurrence.

As the morning advanced the sun became bright and warm, and the day turned out one of those most lovely ones which no season but the autumn produces; cloudless, calm, serene, and worthy of the South of *France* itself.

About nine an appearance very unusual began to demand our attention, a shower of cobwebs falling from very elevated regions, and continuing, without any interruption, till the close of the day. These webs were not single filmy threads, floating in the air in all directions, but perfect flakes or rags; some near an inch broad, and five or six long, which fell with a degree of velocity that shewed they were considerably heavier than the atmosphere.

On every side as the observer turned his eyes might he behold a continual succession of fresh flakes falling into his sight, and twinkling like stars as they turned their sides towards the sum.

How far this wonderful shower extended would be difficult to say; but we know that it reached *Bradley, Selborne*, and *Alresford*, three places which lie in a sort of triangle, the shortest of whose sides is about eight miles in extent.

At the second of those places there was a gentleman (for whose veracity and intelligent turn we have the greatest veneration) who observed it the moment he got abroad; but concluded that, as soon as he came upon the hill above his house, where he took his morning rides, he should be higher than this meteor, which he imagined might have been blown, like *Thistledown*, from the common above: but, to his great astonishment, when he rode to the most elevated part of the down, 300 feet above his fields, he found the webs in appearance still as much above him as before; still descending into sight in a constant succession, and twinkling in the sun, so as to draw the attention of the most incurious.

Neither before nor after was any such fall observed; but on this day the flakes hung in the trees and hedges so thick, that a diligent person sent out might have gathered baskets full.

The remark that I shall make on these cobweb-like appearances, called *gossamer*, is, that, strange and superstitious as the notions about them were formerly, nobody in these days doubts but that they are the real production of small spiders, which swarm in the fields in fine weather in autumn, and have a power of shooting out webs from their tails so as to render themselves buoyant, and lighter than air. But why these apterous insects should *that day* take such a wonderful aërial excursion, and why their webs should at once become so gross and material as to be considerably more weighty than air, and to descend with precipitation, is a matter beyond my skill. If I might be allowed to hazard a supposition, I should imagine that those filmy threads, when first shot, might be entangled in the rising dew, and so drawn up, spiders and all, by a brisk evaporation into the regions where clouds are formed: and if the spiders have a power of coiling and thickening their webs in the air, as Dr *Lister* says they have, then, when they were become heavier than the air, they must fall.

Every day in fine weather, in autumn chiefly, do I see those spiders shooting out their webs and mounting aloft: they will go off from your finger if you will take them into your hand. Last summer one alighted on my book as I was reading in the parlour; and, running to the top of the page, and shooting out a web, took its departure from thence. But what I most wondered at was, that it went off with considerable velocity in a place where no air was stirring; and I am sure that I did not assist it with my breath. So that these little crawlers seem to have, while mounting, some loco-motive power without the use of wings, and to move in the air faster than the air itself.

Swallows

All the summer long is the swallow a most instructive pattern of unwearied industry and affection; for, from morning to night, while there is a family to be supported, she spends the whole day in skimming close to the ground, and exerting the most sudden turns and quick evolutions. Avenues, and long walks under hedges, and pasture-fields, and mown meadows where cattle graze, are her delight, especially if there are trees interspersed; because in such spots insects most abound. When a fly is taken a smart snap from her bill is heard, resembling the noise at the shutting of a watch-case; but the motion of the mandibles are too quick for the eye.

The swallow, probably the male bird, is the *excubitor* to house-martins, and other little birds, announcing the approach of birds of prey. For as soon as an hawk appears, with a shrill alarming note he calls all the swallows and martins about him; who pursue in a body, and buffet and strike their enemy till they have driven him from the village, darting down from above on his back, and rising in a perpendicular line in perfect security. This bird also will sound the alarm, and strike at cats when they climb on the roofs of houses, or otherwise approach the nests. Each species of hirundo drinks as it flies along, sipping the surface of the water; but the swallow alone, in general, *washes* on the wing, by dropping into a pool for many times together: in very hot weather house-martins and bank-martins dip and wash a little.

The swallow is a delicate songster, and in soft sunny weather sings both perching and flying; on trees in a kind of concert, and on chimney-tops: is also a bold flyer, ranging to distant downs and commons even in windy weather, which the other species seem much to dislike; nay, even frequenting exposed sea-port towns, and making little excursions over the salt water. Horsemen on wide downs are often closely attended by a little party of swallows for miles together, which plays before and behind them, sweeping around, and collecting all the sculking insects that are roused by the trampling of the horses feet: when the wind blows hard, without this expedient, they are often forced to settle to pick up their lurking prey.

This species feeds much on little *coleoptera*, as well as on gnats and flies; and often settle on dug ground, or paths, for gravels to grind and digest its food. Before they depart, for some weeks, to a bird, they forsake houses and chimnies, and roost in trees; and usually withdraw about the beginning of *October*, though some few stragglers may appear on at times till the first week in *November*.

Some few pairs haunt the new and open streets of *London* next the fields, but do not enter, like the house-martin, the close and crowded parts of the city.

Both male and female are distinguished from their congeners by the length and forkedness of their tails. They are undoubtedly the most nimble of all the species: and when the male pursues the female in amorous chase, they then go beyond their usual speed, and exert a rapidity almost too quick for the eye to follow ... I shall add, for your farther amusement, an anecdote or two not much in favour of her sagacity:—

A certain swallow built for two years together on the handles of a pair of garden-shears, that were stuck up against the boards in an out-house, and therefore must have her nest spoiled whenever that implement was wanted: and, what is stranger still, another bird of the same species built its nest on the wings and body of an owl that happened by accident to hang dead and dry from the rafter of a barn. This owl, with the nest on its wings, and with eggs in the nest, was brought as a curiosity worthy the most elegant private museum in *Great-Britain*. The owner, struck with the oddity of the sight, furnished the bringer with a large shell, or conch, desiring him to fix it just where the owl hung: the person did as he was ordered, and the following year a pair, probably the same pair, built their nest in the conch, and laid their eggs.

The owl and the conch make a strange grotesque appearance, and are not the least curious specimens in that wonderful collection of art and nature.

The spirit of friendship in 'brute creation'

There is a wonderful spirit of sociality in the brute creation, independent of sexual attachment: the congregation of gregarious birds in the winter is a remarkable instance.

Many horses, though quiet with company, will not stay one minute in a field by themselves: the strongest fences cannot restrain them. My neighbour's horse will not only not stay by himself abroad, but he will not bear to be left alone in a strange stable without discovering the utmost impatience, and endeavouring to break the rack and manger with his fore feet. He has been known to leap out at a stable-window, through which dung was thrown, after company; and yet in other respects is remarkably quiet. Oxen and cows will not fatten by themselves; but will neglect the finest pasture that is not recommended by society. It would be needless to instance in sheep, which constantly flock together.

But this propensity seems not to be confined to animals of the same species; for we know a doe, still alive, that was brought up from a little fawn with a dairy of cows; with them it goes a-field, and with them it returns to the yard. The dogs of the house take no notice of this deer, being used to her; but if strange dogs come by, a chase ensues; while the master smiles to see his favourite securely leading her pursuers over hedge, or gate, or stile, till she returns to the cows, who, with fierce lowings and menacing horns, drive the assailants quite out of the pasture.

Even great disparity of kind and size does not always prevent social advances and mutual fellowship. For a very intelligent and observant person has assured me that, in the former part of his life, keeping but one horse, he happened also on a time to have but one solitary hen. These two incongruous animals spent much of their time together in a lonely orchard, where they saw no creature but each other. By degrees an apparent regard began to take place between these two sequestered individuals. The fowl would approach the quadruped with notes of complacency, rubbing herself gently against his legs: while the horse would look down with satisfaction, and move with the greatest caution and circumspection, lest he should trample on his diminutive companion. Thus, by mutual good offices, each seemed to console the vacant hours of the other: so that *Milion*, when he puts the following sentiment in the mouth of *Adam*, seems to be somewhat mistaken:

Much less can *bird* with *beast*, or fish with fowl,
So well converse, nor with the ox the ape.

  The Natural History of Selborne, 1789 (1902 edn)

JAMES BRUCE
1730–94

*It is easier to guess than describe the situation of my mind at that moment –
standing in that spot which had baffled the genius, industry, and inquiry of both
ancients and modern, for the course of near three thousand years . . .*

Also known as the Laird of Kinnaird, James Bruce was the first modern European explorer of Africa: he 'discovered' the headwaters of the Blue Nile, mistakenly believing them to be the main source of the Nile. Bruce was born in Stirlingshire and studied law but, rather than pursuing a legal career, became a wine merchant. He then entered the consular service and built up sufficient medical knowledge to travel through North Africa and the Middle East as a physician.

In 1768–74 he journeyed in search of the source of the Nile from Alexandria, via the Red Sea, to Ethiopia. A large red-head, he found the desert heat oppressive. 'I call it *hot*, when a man sweats at rest, and excessively on moderate motion,' he commented. 'I call it *very hot*, when a man, with thin or little clothing, sweats much, though at rest. I call it *excessive hot*, when a man in his shirt, at rest, sweats excessively, when all motion is painful . . . I call it *extreme hot*, when the strength fails, the voice impaired, the skin dry, and the head seems more than ordinary large and light. This, I apprehend, denotes death at hand.'

Despite bouts of malaria, and getting caught up in wars and the intrigues of the Ethiopian court, he reached what he thought was the source of the Blue Nile – though on his return to London was ridiculed by Samuel Johnson, an influential figure of the time, who had translated a travelogue on Abyssinia and claimed Bruce hadn't even been there. Humiliated, Bruce retreated to Scotland. When his book was published twenty years later, the seemingly absurd descriptions of Abyssinian culture led many (again wrongly) to assume that much of it was fiction – though the book was a popular success.

He died when he fell down the stairs at his manor, Kinnaird, while attempting to help a lady to a carriage. Bruce's legacy was a rekindled European interest in the interior of Africa, especially as to the whereabouts of the elusive source of the Nile, which was discovered eighty years later by John Speke (see page 190).

The 'Source of the Nile'

It was about four o'clock in the afternoon, but the day had been very hot for some hours, and they were sitting in the shade of a grove of magnificent cedars, intermixed with some very large and beautiful cusso-trees, all in the flower; the men were lying on the grass, and the beasts fed, with the burdens on their backs, in most luxuriant herbage. I called for my herbary, to lay the rose-branch I had in my hand smoothly, that it might dry without spoiling the shape; having only drawn its general form, the pistil and stamina, the finer parts of which (though very necessary in classing the plant) crumble and fall off, or take different forms in drying, and therefore should always be secured by drawing while green. I just said indifferently to Woldo in passing, that I was glad to see him recovered; that he would presently be well, and should fear nothing. He then got up, and desired to speak with me alone, taking Aylo's servant along with him. 'Now, said I, very calmly, I know by your face you are going to tell me a lie. I do swear to you solemnly, you never, by that means, will obtain any thing from me, no not so much as a good word; truth and good behaviour will get you every thing; what appears a great matter in your sight is not perhaps of such value in mine; but nothing except truth and good behaviour will answer to you; now I know for a certainty you are no more sick than I am.' – 'Sir, said he, with a very confident look, you are right; I did counterfeit; I neither have been, nor am I at present any way out of order; but I thought it best to tell you so, not to be obliged to discover another reason that has much more weight with me why I cannot go to Geesh, and much less shew myself at the sources of the Nile, which I confess are not much beyond it, though I declare to you there is still a *hill* between you and those sources.' – 'And pray, said I calmly, what is this mighty reason? have you had a dream, or a vision in that trance you fell into when you lagged behind below the church of St Michael Sacala?' 'No,' says he, 'it is neither trance, nor dream, nor devil either; I wish it was no worse; but you know as well as I, that my master Fasil defeated the Agows at the battle of Banja. I was there with my master, and killed several men, among whom some were of the Agows of this village Geesh, and you know the usage of this country, when a man, in these circumstances, falls into their hands, his blood must pay for their blood.'

I burst out into a violent fit of laughter which very much disconcerted him. 'There, said I, did not I say to you it was a lie that you was going to tell me? do not think I disbelieve or dispute with you the vanity of having killed men; many men were slain at that battle; somebody must, and you may have been the person who flew them; but do you think that I can believe that Fasil, so deep in that account of blood, could rule the Agows in the manner he does, if he could not put a servant of his in safety among them 20 miles from his residence; do you think I can believe this?' 'Come, come, said Aylo's servant to Woldo, did you not hear that truth and good behaviour will get you every thing you ask? Sir, continues he, I see this affair vexes you, and what this foolish man wants will neither make you richer nor poorer; he has taken a great desire for that crimson silk sash which you wear about your middle. I told him to stay till you went back to Gondar; but he says he is to go no farther than to the house of Shalaka Welled Amlac in Maitsha, and does not return to Gondar; I told him to stay till you had put your mind at ease, by seeing the fountains of the Nile, which you are so anxious about. He said, after that had happened, he was sure you would not give it him, for you seemed to think little of the cataract at Goutto, and of all the fine rivers and churches which he had shewn you; except the head of the Nile shall be finer than all these, when, in reality, it will be just like another river, you will then be dissatisfied, and not give him the sash.'

I thought there was something very natural in these suspicions of Woldo; besides, he said he was certain that, if ever the sash came into the sight of Welled Amlac, by some means or other he would get it into his hands. This rational discourse had pacified me a little; the sash was a handsome one; but it must have been fine indeed to have stood for a minute between me and the accomplishment of my wishes. I laid my hand then upon the pistols that stuck in my girdle, and drew them out to give them to one of my suite, when Woldo, who apprehended it was for another purpose, ran some paces back, and hid himself behind Aylo's servant. We were all diverted at this fright, but none so much as Strates, who thought himself revenged for the alarm he had given him by falling through the roof of the house at Goutto. After having taken off my sash, 'Here is your sash, Woldo, said I; but mark what I have said, and now most seriously repeat to you, Truth and good behaviour will get any thing from me; but if, in the course of this journey, you play one trick more, though ever so trifling, I will bring such a vengeance upon your head that you shall not be able to find a place to hide it in, when not the sash only will be taken from you, but your skin also will follow it: remember what happened to the seis at Bamba.'

He took the sash, but seemed terrified at the threat, and began to make apologies. 'Come, come, said I, we understand each other; no more words; it is now late, lose no more time, but carry me to Geesh, and the head of the Nile directly, without preamble, and shew me the hill that separates me from it.' He then carried me round to the south side of the church, out of the grove of trees that surrounded it, 'This is the hill,' says he, looking archly, 'that, when you was on the other side of it, was between you and the fountains of the Nile; there is no other; look at that hillock of green sod in the middle of that watery spot, it is in that the two fountains of the Nile are to be found: Geesh is on the face of the rock where yon green trees are: if you go the length of the fountains pull off your shoes as you did the other day, for these people are all Pagans, worse than those that were at the ford, and they believe in nothing that you believe, but only in this river, to which they pray every day as if it were God, but this perhaps you may do likewise.' Half undressed as I was by loss of my sash, and throwing my shoes off, I ran down the hill towards the little island of green sods, which was about two hundred yards distant; the whole side of the hill was thick grown over with flowers, the large bulbous roots of which appearing above the surface of the ground, and their skins coming off on treading upon them, occasioned two very severe falls before I reached the brink of the marsh; I after this came to the island of green turf, which was in form of an altar, apparently the work of art, and I stood in rapture over the principal fountain which rises in the middle of it.

It is easier to guess than to describe the situation of my mind at that moment – standing in that spot which had baffled the genius, industry, and inquiry of both ancients and moderns, for the course of near three thousand years. Kings had attempted this discovery at the head of armies, and each expedition was distinguished from the last, only by the difference of the numbers which had perished, and agreed alone in the disappointment which had uniformly, and without exception, followed them all. Fame, riches, and honour, had been held out for a series of ages to every individual of those myriads these princes commanded, without having produced one man capable of gratifying the curiosity of his sovereign, or wiping off this stain upon the enterprise and abilities of mankind, or adding this desideratum for the encouragement of geography. Though a mere private Briton, I triumphed here, in my own mind, over kings and their armies; and every comparison was leading nearer and nearer to presumption, when the place itself where I stood, the object of my vain-glory, suggested what depressed my short-lived triumphs. I was but a few minutes arrived at the sources of the Nile, through numberless dangers and sufferings, the least of which would have overwhelmed me but for the continual goodness and protection of Providence; I was, however, but then half through my journey, and all those dangers which I had already passed, awaited me again on my return. I found a despondency gaining ground fast upon me, and blasting the crown of laurels I had too rashly woven for myself. I resolved therefore to divert, till I could on more solid reflection overcome its progress.

Travels to Discover the Source of the Nile, 1790

MUNGO PARK
1771–1806

The Moors are here in great proportion . . . They hissed, shouted and abused me; they even spat in my face with a view to irritate me, and afford them a pretext for seizing my baggage.

Born in Foulshiels, Mungo Park studied medicine at Edinburgh university and then trained to be a surgeon. His first voyage was to Sumatra, at the age of twenty-four, as assistant surgeon for an East India Company vessel. In 1795, the African Association singled him out to lead an expedition to determine the direction of flow of the Niger. Park's chances of a successful mission seemed small: the last man who had attempted to explore the Niger Basin, Daniel Houghton, had disappeared – believed murdered – and Park was to be travelling through West Africa at a time when feuds between tribal peoples had been intensified by the pressures of famine.

The dour Scot was undeterred, however, and left from Portsmouth in 1795. He spent six months learning the local language, Mandingo, at an English factory on the river Gambia, then departed astride a horse, wearing a top hat. He was accompanied by an interpreter and a slave called Johnson. His main obstacles were the tribal chiefs along the way, who saw Europeans as a threat to their domination of local trade. He tried his best to appease them with financial inducements and by impressing them with his medicinal skills.

Park reached Ludamar, 560 miles from his starting point, in February 1796, having ignored numerous warnings that the area was too dangerous for a European – it was the Islamic rulers of Ludamar who had taken Houghton's life four years previously. Park himself was then taken captive, accused of spying and threatened with execution, but managed to escape and in July 1796 finally reached the Niger. He continued eastwards along the river, but by now his horse was barely alive; he himself had a high fever. He

realized that it would be tempting fate to continue further, so turned back, deciding to take a slightly different route via Kamalia, to avoid further encounters with robbers. However, this route proved little better – this time he was stripped of all his possessions. Furthermore, the rainy season had set in and, owing to the recent famine, few people were prepared to offer the bedraggled-looking stranger any help.

At Kamalia a trader took Park in, promising to take him to the Gambia, from where he could get home, as soon as possible. In fact, this meant a wait of seven months, during which time Park wrote a detailed study of Kamalia's people.

Finally, back in London, Park wrote up the full story of his exploits. *Travels in the Interior Districts of Africa* was one of the first accurate accounts of African 'tribal' life, and proved to be extremely popular. He got married, and for a short spell settled down to family life in Scotland, practising as a country doctor. In 1805, however, he departed for Africa again, on a government mission to chart the river's full course.*

This time he was accompanied by two other Scotsmen, Alexander Anderson and George Scott, as well as two sailors, four

---

* Park saw himself as a gatherer of scientific information, and did indeed bring back careful first-hand observations. The truth was more complicated. Joseph Banks declared that Park had 'opened a gate into the interior of Africa, into which it is easy for every nation to enter and to extend its commerce and discovery . . . A detachment of 500 chosen troops would make that road easy, and would build embarkations upon the Joliba – if 200 of these were to embark with field pieces they would be able to overcome the whole forces which Africa could bring against them.'

carpenters (who had been released from Ports-mouth prison on condition that they built roads for the party) and thirty-five members of a Royal African Corps garrison. Despite this support, the expedition was doomed from the outset. The soldiers' clothing was totally unsuited to the heat of West Africa, the pack animals soon got stuck in quagmires and, when the rainy season began in June, fever set in. By the time Park reached the Niger river and was ready to set sail, only five of the forty-four men were still alive. Park still held out hope. 'I am afraid your lordship will be apt to consider matters as in a very hope-less state,' he wrote to Lord Camden back in England, 'but I assure you I am far from desponding . . . I shall set sail to the east with the fixed resolution to discover the termin-ation of the Niger or perish in the attempt.'

Park did perish in the attempt. His make-shift boat reached as far as Boussa, 800 miles downstream, where it was attacked by native tribesmen. Only one of Park's slaves survived to tell the tale.

No other outsider attempted the journey until Hugh Clapperton (see page 184) sixteen years later, and it wasn't until 1830 that the Niger river was found to disgorge into the Gulf of Guinea.

Sticky times with the Moors

On the afternoon of the 1st of July, as I was tending my horse in the fields, Ali's chief slave and four Moors arrived at Queira, and took up their lodging at the Dooty's house. My interpreter, Johnson, who suspected the nature of this visit, sent two boys to overhear the conversation, from which he learnt that they were sent to convey me back to Bubaker. The same evening two of the Moon came privately to look at my horse, and one of them proposed taking it to the Dooty's hut, but the other observed that such a precaution was unnecessary, as I could never escape upon such an animal. They then inquired where I slept, and returned to their companions.

All this was like a stroke of thunder to me, for I dreaded nothing so much as confinement again among the Moors, from whose barbarity I had nothing but death to expect. I therefore determined to set off immediately for Bam-barra, a measure which I thought offered almost the only chance of saving my life, and gaining the object of my mission. I communicated the design to Johnson, who, although he applauded my resolution, was so far from showing any inclination to accompany me, that he solemnly protested he would rather forfeit his wages than go any farther. He told me that Daman had agreed to give him half the price of a slave for his service, to assist in conducting a coffle of slaves to Gambia, and that he was determined to embrace the opportunity of returning to his wife and family.

Having no hopes therefore of persuading him to accompany me, I resolved to proceed by myself. About midnight I got my clothes in readiness, which consisted of two shirts, two pair of trousers, two pocket-handkerchiefs, an upper and under waistcoat, a hat, and a pair of half boots; these, with a cloak, constituted my whole wardrobe. And I had not one single bead, nor any other article of value in my possession, to purchase victuals for myself, or corn for my horse.

About daybreak, Johnson, who had been listening to the Moors all night, came and whispered to me that they were asleep. The awful crisis was now arrived when I was again either to taste the blessing of freedom, or languish out my days in captivity. A cold sweat moistened my forehead as I thought on the dreadful alternative, and reflected that, one way or the other, my fate must be decided in the course of the ensuing day. But to deliberate was to lose the only chance of escaping. So taking up my bundle, I stepped gently over the Negroes, who were sleeping in the open air, and having mounted my horse, I bade Johnson farewell, desiring him to take particular care of the papers I had intrusted him with, and inform my friends in Gambia that he had left me in good health on my way to Bambarra.

I proceeded with great caution, surveying each bush, and frequently listening and looking behind me for the Moorish horsemen, until I was about a mile from the town, when I was surprised to find myself in the neighbourhood of a korree belonging to the Moors. The shepherds followed me for about a mile, hooting and throwing stones after me; and when I was out of their reach, and had began to indulge the pleasing hopes of escaping, I was again greatly alarmed to hear somebody halloo behind me, and looking back, I saw three Moors on horseback coming after me at full speed, whooping and brandishing their double-barrelled guns. I knew it was in vain to think of escaping, and therefore turned back and met them, when two of them caught hold of my bridle, one on each side, and the third, presenting his musket, told me I must go back to Ali.

When the human mind has for some time been fluctuating between hope and despair, tortured with anxiety, and hurried from one extreme to another, it affords a sort of gloomy relief to know the worst that can possibly happen; such was my situation. An indifference about life, and all its enjoyments, had completely benumbed my faculties, and I rode back with the Moors with apparent unconcern. But a change took place much sooner than I had any reason to expect. In passing through some thick bushes, one of the Moors ordered me to untie my bundle, and show them the contents. Having examined the different articles, they found nothing worth taking except my cloak, which they considered as a very valuable acquisition; and one of them pulling it from me, wrapped it about himself. This cloak had been of great use to me; it served to cover me from the rains in the day, and to protect me from the mosquitoes in the night; I therefore earnestly begged him to return it, and followed him some little way to obtain it, but, without paying any attention to my request, he and one of his companions rode off with their prize. When I attempted to follow them, the third, who had remained with me, struck my horse over the head, and presenting his musket, told me I should proceed no further.

I now perceived that these men had not been sent by any authority to apprehend me, but had pursued me solely in the view to rob and plunder me. Turning my horse's head, therefore, once more towards the east, and observing the Moor follow the track of his confederates, I congratulated myself on having escaped with my life, though in great distress, from such a horde of barbarians.

I was no sooner out of sight of the Moor, than I struck into the woods, to prevent being pursued, and kept pushing on with all possible speed, until I found myself near some high rocks, which I remembered to have seen in my former route from Queira to Deena; and directing my course a little to the northward, I fortunately fell in with the path.

It is impossible to describe the joy that arose in my mind when I looked around and concluded that I was out of danger. I felt like one recovered from sickness; I breathed freer; I found unusual lightness in my limbs; even the desert looked pleasant, and I dreaded nothing so much as falling in with some wandering parties of Moors, who might convey me back to the land of thieves and murderers from which I had just escaped.

I soon became sensible, however, that my situation was very deplorable, for I had no means of procuring food, nor prospect of finding water. About ten o'clock, perceiving a herd of goats feeding close to the road, I took a circuitous route to avoid being seen, and continued travelling through the wilderness, directing my course, by compass, nearly east-south-east, in order to reach as soon as possible some town or village of the kingdom of Bambarra.

A little after noon, when the burning heat of the sun was reflected with double violence from the hot sand, and the distant ridges of the hills, seen through the ascending vapour, seemed to wave and fluctuate like the unsettled sea, I became faint with thirst, and climbed a tree in hopes of seeing distant smoke, or some other appearance of a human habitation, but in vain; nothing appeared all around but thick underwood, and hillocks of white sand.

About four o'clock, I came suddenly upon a large herd of goats, and pulling my horse into a bush, I watched to observe if the keepers were Moors or Negroes. In a little time I perceived two Moorish boys, and with some difficulty persuaded them to approach me. They informed me that the herd belonged to Ali, and that they were going to Deena, where the water was more plentiful, and where they intended to stay until the rain had filled the pools in the Desert. They showed me their empty water-skins, and told me that they had seen no water in the woods. This account afforded me but little consolation; however, it was in vain to repine, and I pushed on as fast as possible, in hopes of reaching some watering place in the course of the night. My thirst was by this time become insufferable; my mouth was parched and inflamed; a sudden dimness would frequently come over my eyes, with other symptoms of fainting; and my horse being very much fatigued, I began seriously to apprehend that I should perish of thirst. To relieve the burning pain in my mouth and throat, I chewed the leaves of different shrubs, but found them all bitter, and of no service.

A little before sunset, having reached the top of a gentle rising, I climbed a high tree, from the topmost branches of which I cast a melancholy look over the barren wilderness, but without discovering the most distant trace of a human dwelling. The same dismal uniformity of shrubs and sand everywhere presented itself, and the horizon was as level and uninterrupted as that of the sea.

Descending from the tree, I found my horse devouring the stubble and brushwood with great avidity; and as I was now too faint to attempt walking, and my horse too much fatigued to carry me, I thought it but an act of humanity, and perhaps the last I should ever have it in my power to perform, to take off his bridle and let him shift for himself; in doing which I was suddenly affected with sickness and giddiness, and falling upon the sand, felt as if the hour of death was fast approaching. 'Here then (thought I), after a short but ineffectual struggle, terminate all my hopes of being useful in my day and generation; here must the short span of my life come to an end.' I cast (as I believed), a last look on the surrounding scene, and whilst I reflected on the awful change that was about to take place, this world, with its enjoyments, seemed to vanish from my recollection. Nature, however, at length resumed its functions; and on recovering my senses, I found myself stretched upon the sand, with the bridle still in my hand, and the sun just sinking behind the trees. I now summoned all my resolution, and determined to make another effort to prolong my existence. And as the evening was somewhat cool, I resolved to travel as far as my limbs would carry me, in hopes of reaching (my only resource) a watering place. With this view, I put the bridle on my horse, and driving him before me, went slowly along for about an hour, when I perceived some lightning from the north-east, a most delightful sight, for it promised rain. The darkness and lightning increased very rapidly, and in less than an hour I heard the wind roaring among the bushes. I had already opened my mouth to receive the refreshing drops which I expected; but I was instantly covered with a cloud of sand, driven with such force by the wind, as to give a very disagreeable sensation to my face and arms, and I was obliged to mount my horse, and stop under a bush to prevent being suffocated. The sand continued to fly in amazing quantities for near an hour, after which I again set forward, and travelled with difficulty until ten o'clock. About this time I was agreeably surprised by some very vivid flashes of lightning followed by a few heavy drops of rain. In a little time the sand ceased to fly, and I alighted and spread out all my clean clothes to collect the rain, which at length I saw would certainly fall. For more than an hour it rained plentifully, and I quenched my thirst by wringing and sucking my clothes.

There being no moon, it was remarkably dark, so that I was obliged to lead my horse, and direct my way by the compass, which the lightning enabled me to observe. In this manner I travelled, with tolerable expedition, until past midnight; when the lightning becoming more distant, I was under the necessity of groping along, to the no small danger of my hands and eyes. About two o'clock my horse started at something, and looking round, I was not a little surprised to see a light at a short distance among the trees and supposing it to be a town, I groped along the sand in hopes of finding corn-stalks, cotton, or other appearances of cultivation, but found none. As I approached, I perceived a number of other lights in different places, and began to suspect that I had fallen upon a party of Moors. However, in my present situation, I was resolved to see who they were, if I could do it with safety. I accordingly led my horse cautiously towards the light, and heard by the lowing of the cattle, and the clamorous tongues of the herdsmen, that it was a watering place, and most likely belonged to the Moors. Delightful as the sound of the human voice was to me, I resolved once more to strike into the woods, and rather run the risk of perishing of hunger than trust myself again in their hands; but being still thirsty, and dreading the approach of the burning day, I thought it prudent to search for the wells, which I expected to find at no great distance. In this pursuit, I inadvertently approached so near to one of the tents as to be perceived by a woman, who immediately screamed out. Two people came running to her assistance from some of the neighbouring tents, and passed so very near to me that I thought I was discovered, and hastened again into the woods.

About a mile from this place, I heard a loud and confused noise somewhere to the right of my course, and in a short time was happy to find it was the croaking of frogs, which was heavenly music to my ears. I followed the sound, and at daybreak arrived at some shallow muddy pools, so full of frogs, that it was difficult to discern the water. The noise they made frightened my horse, and I was obliged to keep them quiet by beating the water with a branch until he had drank. Having here quenched my thirst, I ascended a tree, and the morning being calm, I soon perceived the smoke of the watering place which I had passed in the night; and observed another pillar of smoke east-south-east, distant twelve or fourteen miles. Towards this I directed my route, and reached the cultivated ground a little before eleven o'clock, where, seeing a number of Negroes at work planting corn, I inquired the name of the town, and was informed that it was a Foulah village, belonging to Ali, called Shrilla. I had now some doubts about entering it; but my horse being very much fatigued, and the day growing hot, not to mention the pangs of hunger which began to assail me, I resolved to venture, and accordingly rode up to the Dooty's house, where I was unfortunately denied admittance, and could not obtain even a handful of corn either for myself or horse. Turning from this inhospitable door, I rode slowly out of the town, and perceiving some low scattered huts without the walls, I directed my route towards them; knowing that in Africa, as well as in Europe, hospitality does not always prefer the highest dwellings. At the door of one of these huts, an old motherly-looking woman sat, spinning cotton; I made signs to her that I was hungry, and inquired if she had any victuals with her in the hut. She immediately laid down her distaff, and desired me, in Arabic, to come in. When I had seated myself upon the floor, she set before me a dish of kouskous, that had been left the preceding night, of which I made a tolerable meal; and in return for this kindness, I gave her one of my pocket-handkerchiefs; begging at the same time, a little corn for my horse, which she readily brought me.

Overcome with joy at so unexpected a deliverance, I lifted up my eyes to heaven, and whilst my heart swelled with gratitude, I returned thanks to that gracious and bountiful Being, whose power had supported me under so many dangers, and had now spread for me a table in the wilderness.

Travels into the Interior of Africa, 1799 (1983 edn)

Hugh Clapperton
1788–1827

I was taken through the whole of his house – & saw his favourite wife, who pretended to be much frightened at seeing a Christian . . . she was a jolly good looking black wench . . .

Hugh Clapperton, a Scottish naval officer, made two major expeditions into the West African interior, in search of a trade passage down the Niger. One of twenty-two sons of a Scottish surgeon, at the age of fourteen he was apprenticed on a trading ship and embarked on the first of several journeys between Liverpool and America. He joined the navy, and served in both the West Indies and in Canada. In 1820 the British government selected him to be part of a three-man expedition to Lake Chad and its surrounding kingdom, Bornu, with Walter Oudrey and Dixon Denham. The expedition (1824–25)

was the fourth British attempt since the end of the Napoleonic Wars to penetrate the West African interior, and trace the course of the Niger. They were prevented from reaching the river, but a second expedition (1825–27) with his servant Richard Lander (and five others, including two doctors) approached from the south, crossing Nigeria from the Bight of Benin to the Niger. Only Clapperton and Lander did not fall prey to the climate, and on reaching Sokoto Clapperton himself succumbed to dysentery. The only survivor, Lander returned to England with his master's journals.

Offering presents to the Sultan

Saturday 3rd: Cool & Clear   the Dr a little better   having early prep[ared] our present which consisted of one of our tea trays   about 10 yds red silk – an Indian palamper [bedcover]   a piece of white linen cloth with gold stripes [of] Eygepitian manufacture   a pound of Cinamon & a pound of cloves   we waited on the Sultan at 8 A.M. accompanied by Wordee to present these to the Sultan Duncowa . . . When we went in to the house of his Excellency we found no parade of armed men as at Kuka and the other towns in Bornou   Duncowa was sitting on a bench under an aw[n]ing with only 3 old men with him   we shook hands as before with his Ex[cellenc]y and seated our selves before him   he laid hold of me & wished me to sit on the ['bench' deleted, '(raised platform of clay – 6 feet square)' inserted] along side of him but this I declined   we were presented with Gooro nuts & he repeated the promises he had made yesterday – when we presented our present & Explained the use of the Tray and what it was made of he was highly gratified   asked us if we wanted slaves or what did we want – every thing that he had or could procure he would give us   we told him that with regard to slaves that a slave was unknown in England that as soon as one set his foot on our land he was free from that instant – that we endeavoured as much as possible to put a stop [to] the Abominable [slave] Trafic on the sea coast that our Master & King had given immense sums to abolish it & that every year he sent 8 large vessels to take the ships that followed that trade & set the slaves free what then do you do want we said all that we wanted was his friendship & that we wanted to collect the flowers & plants – of the country & to see its rivers – Wonderfull says he you do not want slaves you do not want horses – you do not want money you want only to see the World you must go to Beelo who is a learned & pious man & will be glad to see men who have seen as much as you have done – you shall have all & see all that is in my province & I am sure Beelo my master will procure you every thing you wish he then descended from his honour seat & sat down on the floor alongside of us & shook hands this is the greatest compliment a great man can pay to another in this country – one of their lucky Omens took place at this time my servant who had assisted in bringing the presents got up to receive the Gooro nuts the Sultan had pres[en]t[e]d to me and in rising he capsized a pot of honey which the Sultan had given us without breaking the dish the honey running out on the Floor – had the pot been broken the Omen would have been unfortunate – the Sultan was highly elated at the accident – & ordered the poor to be called in to lick it up a way of cleaning a house I had never before seen they came in rejoiced at the lucky omen for them & [went] down upon their knees & licked it up with their tongues in no time & there was not a little squabeling about it one man came ['into' deleted] of[f] with double allowance he having a long beard which he carefully Cleaned into his hand & put in his mouth after the repast on the ground was finished – we took our leave of the Sultan & returned to our tents great Nos of Men & Women came out to wait on the D$_r$ for medecine – in the evening we had meat dried & boiled with bazeen & excellent bread sent us by our friend Hameda milk from the Sultan & a live sheep from a black Sheeref who is unwell & wants medecine.

Journals of the Travels in Bornu of the Lt. Hugh Clapperton (1996 edn)

William J. Burchell
1782–1863

I read to these men various words and sentences out of my book . . . they stood
with eyes and mouth wide open . . . unable to conceive that 'the white thing in
my hand' told me what to say . . .

William Burchell's copious catalogues of the species he identified in Africa and South America were an important reference point and inspiration for future scientists. His interest in plants began early. He was the son of a nurseryman, and entered his father's profession by taking a job at Kew Gardens.

The government then sent him to St Helena as a botanist, a post he accepted with the expectation that his fiancée would come out to join him a few years later. However, on her journey there she fell in love with the ship's captain, so broke off the engagement and married him instead. Burchell seems to have decided it was time for a complete change of scene and, after five years in St Helena, he quit his post and went to South Africa.

Between 1811 and 1815 he travelled north from the Cape, penetrating deep into the interior and taking detailed notes of his findings along the way. He gathered together 63,000 objects of scientific interest, and identified two new species: the white rhino, and the zebra that bears his name. His writings are accessible, personal and marked by the attempts he makes to understand native cultures.

His second major expedition was to South America, where from 1826–1829 he tirelessly conducted research. Back in England, he settled down to write up his discoveries and organize his collections, a task that kept him occupied until the age of eighty-two, when, having immersed himself in the lives of other people, animals and plants, he took his own life.

The 'freedom of creation'

In the middle of the night I was awakened by *the roaring of a lion*; but the sound was peculiar, and very different from that which the animal usually makes. I am assured by the inhabitants of these countries, who have had opportunities of ascertaining the fact, that he produces this noise by laying his head upon the ground and uttering, as it were, a half-stifled roar, or growl, by which means the sound is conveyed along the earth. It now seemed to us very much to resemble that which we had heard in Cape Town at the moment of the earthquake: it seemed also to have a progressive movement, as if it came from the west. I instantly sprang up, and seeing that our fires were nearly out, called to the Hottentots to put on a large quantity of fuel to make a blaze, for the purpose of keeping the beasts at a distance, as they are said to be afraid of flame. But though several of them were awake, they remained without attempting to move, until I called out. As they had supposed it to be really an earthquake, and knew that by sleeping in the open air, there was nothing to fear if such had been the case, they lay very quietly wrapped up in their karosses, till I ordered them to make up the fires. From the uneasiness of the oxen, two of which broke loose from the bushes to which they had been made fast, and from other circumstances, I was convinced that it was a lion; and at length most of the people began to think the same as myself; but Speelman persisted in declaring that it was only an *earthquake*, till, on examining the ground the next morning, we found the animal's footmarks within fifty yards of the spot where we had been lying asleep. There is little doubt that the beast's intention was to have seized one of the oxen; and as little, that the timely making up our fires prevented him. His roaring was intended to strike fear into the cattle and to put them to flight; in which case, he would have pursued, and easily have secured, his prey. It was his natural fear of man, which alone withheld him from springing upon them at once, or even upon us, as we lay quite exposed upon the bare ground; for we had, as I have remarked, little or no fire burning at that time.

As far as I am enabled to judge, there is no region in any quarter of the world, which can hold competition with *Southern Africa* in number of large animals. It would be a novel and not uninstructive mode of comparing the *zoölogy* of different countries, by noting the aggregate weight of the wild animals of each country (meaning one individual of each species) divided by the total number of species. If a table of this kind were formed, I think there is little doubt that Southern Africa would be found to stand at the head of it.

Although we are taught to believe that man is the *supreme animal* of this globe; and every thing we behold, even in civilized countries, confirms that belief; yet still the mind can never derive so perfect a conviction of this truth, as when viewing a country in a state of nature, where men and multitudes of wild beasts of every class, roam unrestrained, in all the freedom of creation. Can we view animals of immense bulk and strength, either flying from man, or submitting to his domination and labouring in his immediate service, without acknowledging at once that their timidity or submission forms a part of that wise plan, predetermined by the Deity, for giving supreme power to him who is physically the weakest of them all? or can we doubt that a part of that plan was, that man should rule alone by the divine spirit of reason and superior intellect, and, at his own option and freewill, either by the exercise of these, elevate himself above the rest of the animal creation, or by the neglect of them sink himself below the beasts? For man has nought else of which to be proud, but reason and virtue: without these he is still but mere animal, his existence is useless in the great final cause of the universe, and he will surely have to answer for his voluntary deficiencies in them, to that Aweful, Good and Great, Power, who will know no other distinction among mankind than that which they themselves make by their virtuous or vicious conduct.

We were visited by a few natives: they were personally strangers, but, having long heard of our passing through their country, they came to us in the usual friendly manner. Some of them were ornamented with a fresh *necklace of twisted entrails*. This is one of the most common ornaments, not only of the Bushmen and other tribes of the Hottentot race, but also of the Bichuana nations. To imagine that these entrails are hung round their necks just in the same state in which they are taken out of the animal, would be to entertain an exceedingly false idea of them; but it is one which those persons, who do not think, in giving an account of a foreign country, that the truth is sufficiently interesting, endeavour to create, supposing that by such means they render the proverbial filthiness of Hottentots more striking and wonderful. It is a representation, not more correct, than it would be, to tell the Bushmen, that the ladies of Europe play upon a musical instrument composed of the entrails of animals, extended between three pieces of wood. These necklaces of entrails, are washed and cleansed as properly and completely as the strings of a violin or a harp; and it is only by the subsequent accumulation of grease and red-ochre, that they become, what *we* call, dirty, but which Bushmen consider as highly improved . . .

In the afternoon, three Bichuanas joined our party, and remained with us till the next day. They told me they were herdsmen to Mattīvi, and were lying at a cattle-place lower down the Makkwarin.

They had lately been at Litākun; and now reported to me that the elder brother of Mattīvi, as soon as he heard of the approach of a white-person from the Colony, and supposing that he would return immediately after visiting that place, had conceived the desire, and actually formed the resolution, of making a journey to Cape Town, of which he had heard many accounts at Klaarwater. His plan was to return thither with me, and he had therefore long been expecting my arrival with impatience; but having heard that I had finally left the Transgariepine, and had gone back to the Colony, (this report related to my journey to Graaffreynet) he had now, under great disappointment, relinquished his intention.

This story raised my curiosity and, at the same time, a wish to ascertain the truth of it. Revolving it often in my mind, I endeavoured to imagine, what might be his motive for such a journey. When I attributed it to that desire, so rare in a savage, of visiting other countries for the purpose of enlightening his mind and of acquiring a knowledge of civilized arts, I glowed with so pleasing an idea, and almost regretted that I should not have the gratification of conducting him thither, of showing to him the practical advantages of those arts, and of inspiring him with sentiments which, at his return to his own country, might stimulate him to the imitation of what he had seen, and to the civilizing of his countrymen.

But his own countrymen, as far as I could yet see, had no dreams of this nature: their thoughts embraced little beyond eating and smoking. Our visitors begged for snuff and tobacco as soon as they accosted me; and when they had obtained this and some meat, they seemed to enjoy as much happiness as man in a state of mere animal existence, probably ever attains.

I was here much amused, and perhaps gained a new idea, by observing in them the workings of an untaught mind. I had my interpreter by my side, but wishing to put to the test, what I had hitherto learnt, or rather, written down, of the Sichuana language, I read to these men various words and sentences out of my book. These were readily understood by them, who at first, supposing me to have a tolerable knowledge of that tongue, talked a great deal, to which I could give no answer; but when they at length discovered that I could speak only when I looked in the book, they stood with eyes and mouth wide open; wondering both at the book, and at myself, and unable to conceive how it could be, that 'the white thing in my hand,' told me what to say; or how, by only looking at it, I could know more than when I did not. But the most singular part of this little comedy, was performed by *Muchunka*, whose simple brain seemed not yet to contain a true idea of the nature of writing or of the real purport and utility of our evening exercises at the dictionary and vocabulary. As it would have been only a proof of my own folly to have asked him to explain the operations and conceptions of his mind on this subject, I am left to suppose that he believed I always committed to memory his answers to my questions, and that my making 'black scratches' upon the paper with my pen, was only what he had at Klaarwater seen and heard called *schryvende* (writing). He was, he said, exceedingly surprised at my remembering so well every thing he had taught me, and even those words which he had never told me but once. When I explained, that it was the marks which I had made in the book while he was in the waggon, which now showed me what I was to say, he laughed most heartily, and desired to see the very words which I was pronouncing. On pointing them out, he laughed again; and his three countrymen, whose mouth and eyes had by this time recovered from their expression of surprise, joined in the laughter; while I myself, as I shut the book, was unable to resist the impression which their ludicrous appearance and distorted countenances made upon me.

Travels in the Interior of Southern Africa, 1822

John Hanning Speke
1827–64

I saw that old father Nile without any doubt rises in the Victoria N'yanza, and, as I had foretold, that lake is the great source of the holy river which cradled the first expounder of our religious belief.

Speke was born to a well-off family from Ilminster. He served as an army officer in India, where he developed a passion for hunting that was to stay with him for the rest of his life, and define his death. In 1854 he met Richard Burton, and embarked on an expedition under him to what is now Somalia and Ethiopia. A near scrape with death when they were attacked after landing on the Somalian coast did not deter Speke from joining Burton on another venture in 1856, sponsored by the Royal Geographical Society, to investigate the river systems of Central Africa. They hoped to solve a matter that had flummoxed all previous European geographers: the whereabouts of the source of the River Nile.

The two men spent six months in Zanzibar on the east coast, where Burton learnt Swahili and immersed himself in the pleasures of Arab society. Here, not for the first time, Burton's passionate interest in Islamic culture contrasted with Speke's more superficial – but ultimately more effective – emphasis on getting on with the job in hand. Finally, they sailed to Tanzania in a naval ship loaned to them by the Sultan of Zanzibar, and they set out into the interior.

Five months and 600 miles later they learned of a great lake to the West, and in February 1858 they finally reached Ujiji, Lake Tanganyika, the second largest lake in Africa; they were the first Europeans to see it. Speke explored the lake in a dugout canoe, while Burton recovered from a jaw infection; but, half-blind from a fever himself, and deaf from an insect that had clambered into his ear and dug 'violently away' at his eardrum, he was unable to circumnavigate it and prove it had an outlet to the Nile.

They began their return journey to Zanzibar. However, halfway to the Indian coast, at the Arab slaving outpost of Tabora, they heard of a lake far bigger than Lake Tanganyika two weeks' walk to the north. Speke set off without Burton – now too ill with malaria to travel – to investigate.

On 3 August 1858 he came to what the locals called Lake Ukerewe, or the Nyanza, which he promptly called Victoria, after his own queen. He was convinced, and rightly so, that it was the source of the Nile. On meeting up with Burton again, Burton was adamant that the source lay in Lake Tanganyika, even though Speke had calculated that it was only ten feet higher than the Nile at Gondokoro, much further down in the Sudan. The two travellers' patience with one another had already grown thin, but now a major rift developed between them. Their disagreement unresolved, Speke returned to England two weeks ahead of Burton, who stayed to convalesce in Aden.

Although Speke had promised not to divulge the results of their endeavours until they were both home, he now, without waiting for Burton, related his 'findings' to the RGS. Burton was furious, but gratified to find that, even without his vociferous lobbying, others were also sceptical of his rival's claim, which was supported by no hard evidence.*

---

* The Scottish geographer James MacQueen (1778–1870), an ally of Burton, was all too happy to write a preface for an assault on his late lamented 'Nile rival' just a month or two after Speke's death. Here is his deliciously malicious commentary on Speke's conduct at the royal court of Buganda: 'Now, what would the people of England say if King Mtésa should send one of his princes, or ministers, as ambassador to the British sovereign, and wish that

The RGS donated £2,500 for Speke to set out once more and resolve the matter. He left for Africa in 1860, with a former partner in India, the zoologist and painter James Augustus Grant.

This time, Speke found an outlet at what he named the Ripon Falls (after the President of the Royal Geographical Society) and followed its course into present-day Uganda, then on to Gondokoro in the Sudan; but because of tribal wars they had to make several detours, which allowed the possibility that they were not actually following the same river's course all the way.*

Back in England, Speke's enemies – and especially the formidable Burton – were ready to pull his latest 'findings' apart. A meeting of the British Association for the Advancement of Science was called to debate the matter, but the day before the meeting Speke shot himself in what seems to have been a freak hunting accident. It was not until twelve years later that the journalist Henry Morton Stanley proved that Speke had been right all along.

For all Burton's intellectual brilliance, and a veritable campaign against Speke, it was the latter, and not Burton, who had triumphed. Speke had found both the largest lake in Africa, Lake Victoria, and also the Nile source. While not much more impressed by African culture than the Afro-phobic Burton, Speke is invariably the more accessible in his prose.

—

this minister – a 'first-rate noble, the hangman or cook' – should reside in Buckingham Palace or Windsor Castle, and be at liberty to communicate with Queen Victoria daily, without the intervention of her ministers; and further, that she should maintain Mtésa's ambassador and suite at her sole expense? Yet even more than this is what Speke demands, for he had no diplomatic character. Why, such a demand would be considered a national insult, and the insulters at once ordered about their business, and to leave the country. Mtésa ought to have served Speke in this manner.

'We are almost moved to tears at the pathetic complaints and woes of Speke, who, though living in a splendid and well-peopled palace, yet found himself so lonely, without a wife or female companion, that very frequently he could neither sleep nor eat. . . . Now, as to all this loneliness and want of female society, we find that the Commander-in-Chief of the army had, by the hand of an elderly Mganda woman, sent him a lady, with metaphorical compliments, praying that "I would accept her to carry my water," and adding that if I did not like her, or wanted one that might be thought prettier, I could have a choice of one amongst ten of all colours. "As nothing offends so much as rejecting such presents, I kept her for the time being." The Queen Dowager afterwards made him a present of two, declaring he might have more, and consequently we find she had sent him another, which Speke intimated he did not think good enough for a man of his dignity.'

* McQueen enjoys the following caustic mockery of Speke's geographical claims: 'In reference to the true source of what is now considered as the River

—

Nile, where is that, and has Captain Speke discovered it? The answer must decidedly be, CERTAINLY NOT, nor is it nor can it be where he has on second thoughts placed it, the miserable gully the Jordans, in which there is not one drop of fresh water except what comes from the clouds during the rains and from the overflowing of the lake adjoining. On the part of old Nilus we enter the most solemn and determined protest against such an absurd and thoughtless decision. Is it possible, we say, that after the venerable old gentleman has buried his head for 3,500 years from the general knowledge of the world, that it should be suffered to be dug up in a place where there is not a drop of spring water to wet and cool his aged and parched lips? Such degradation cannot be allowed in a river god so famous. We are, therefore, grateful to our facetious contemporary *Punch*, for having given us [in a satirical cartoon] something more rational, by exhibiting to our eyes, in his own droll way, the source of the Nile in a large body of water, flowing in a copious stream through two large drainingtiles, pushed under the adjoining rocks, with Speke, for so we take it to be, as the deity of the place, sitting calmly smoking his Turkish pipe, a present no doubt from the Dowager Queen of Uganda! This is surely a better and more appropriate source than Speke's; the Old Man will at least get a draught of pure water.'

A troublesome beetle

At night a violent storm of rain and wind beat on my tent with such fury
that its nether parts were torn away from the pegs, and the tent itself was
only kept upright by sheer force. On the wind's abating, a candle was lighted
to rearrange the kit, and in a moment, as though by magic, the whole
interior became covered with a host of small black beetles, evidently
attracted by the glimmer of the candle. They were so annoyingly determined
in their choice of place for peregrinating, that it seemed hopeless my trying
to brush them off the clothes or bedding; for as one was knocked aside
another came on, and then another, till at last, worn out, I extinguished the
candle, and with difficulty – trying to overcome the tickling annoyance
occasioned by these intruders crawling up my sleeves and into my hair, or
down my back and legs – fell off to sleep. Repose that night was not destined
to be my lot. One of these horrid little insects awoke me in his struggles to
penetrate my ear, but just too late: for, in my endeavour to extract him, I
aided his immersion. He went his course, struggling up the narrow channel,
until he got arrested by want of passage-room. This impediment evidently
enraged him, for he began with exceeding vigour, like a rabbit at a hole, to
dig violently away at my tympanum. The queer sensation this amusing
measure excited in me is past description. I felt inclined to act as our donkeys
once did when beset by a swarm of bees, who buzzed about their ears and
stung their heads and eyes until they were so irritated and confused that they
galloped about in the most distracted order, trying to knock them off by
treading on their heads, or by rushing under bushes, into houses, or through
any jungle they could find. Indeed, I do not know which was worst off. The
bees killed some of them, and this beetle nearly did for me. What to do I
knew not. Neither tobacco, oil, nor salt could be found: I therefore tried
melted butter; that failing, I applied the point of a penknife to his back,
which did more harm than good; for though a few thrusts kept him quiet,
the point also wounded my ear so badly that inflammation set in, severe
suppuration took place, and all the facial glands extending from that point
down to the point of the shoulder became contorted and drawn aside, and a
string of buboes decorated the whole length of that region. It was the most
painful thing I ever remember to have endured; but, more annoying still, I
could not open my mouth for several days, and had to feed on broth alone.
For many months the tumour made me almost deaf, and ate a hole between
that orifice and the nose, so that when I blew it, my ear whistled so audibly
that those who heard it laughed. Six or seven months after this accident

happened, bits of the beetle, a leg, a wing, or parts of its body, came away in the wax.

The Discovery of the Victoria N'Yanza, 1859

At the court of the Kabaka

I was requested to sit on the ground outside in the sun with my servants. Now, I had made up my mind never to sit upon the ground as the natives and Arabs are obliged to do, nor to make my obeisance in any other manner than is customary in England, though the Arabs had told me that from fear they had always complied with the manners of the court. I felt that if I did not stand up for my social position at once, I should be treated with contempt during the remainder of my visit, and thus lose the vantage-ground I had assumed of appearing rather as a prince than a trader, for the purpose of better gaining the confidence of the king. To avert over-hastiness, however – for my servants began to be alarmed as I demurred against doing as I was bid – I allowed five minutes to the court to give me a proper reception, saying, if it were not conceded I would then walk away.

Nothing, however, was done. My own men, knowing me, feared for me as they did not know what a 'savage' king would do in case I carried out my threat; whilst the Waganda, lost in amazement at what seemed little less than blasphemy, stood still as posts. The affair ended by my walking straight away home, giving Bombay orders to leave the present on the ground, and to follow me.

Although the king is said to be unapproachable, excepting when he chooses to attend court – a ceremony which rarely happens – intelligence of my hot wrath and hasty departure reached him in an instant. He first, it seems, thought of leaving his toilet-room to follow me, but, finding I was walking fast and had gone far, changed his mind, and sent Wakungu running after me. Poor creatures! they caught me up, fell upon their knees, and implored I would return at once, for the king had not tasted food, and would not until he saw me. I felt grieved at their touching appeals; but as I did not understand all they said, I simply replied by patting my heart and shaking my head, walking if anything all the faster.

On my arrival at my hut, Bombay and others came in, wet through with perspiration, saying the king had heard of all my grievances. Suwarora's hongo [tribute] was turned out of court, and, if I desired it, I might bring my own chair with me, for he was very anxious to show me great respect –

although such a seat was exclusively the attribute of the king, no one else in Uganda daring to sit on an artificial seat.

My point was gained, so I cooled myself with coffee and a pipe, and returned rejoicing in my victory, especially over Suwarora . . .

At noon Mtesa sent his pages to invite me to his palace. I went, with my guard of honour and my stool, but found I had to sit waiting in an ante-hut three hours with his commander-in-chief and other high officers before he was ready to see me. During this time Wasoga minstrels, playing on tambira, and accompanied by boys playing on a harmonicon, kept us amused; and a small page, with a large bundle of grass, came to me and said, 'The king hopes you won't be offended if required to sit on it before him; for no person in Uganda, however high in office, is ever allowed to sit upon anything raised above the ground, nor can anybody but himself sit upon such grass as this; it is all that his throne is made of. The first day he only allowed you to sit on your stool to appease your wrath.'

On consenting to do in 'Rome as the Romans do', when my position was so handsomely acknowledged, I was called in, and found the court sitting much as it was on the first day's interview, only that the number of squatting Wakungu was much diminished; and the king, instead of wearing his ten brass and copper rings, had my gold one on his third finger. This day, however, was cut out for business, as, in addition to the assemblage of officers, there were women, cows, goats, fowls, confiscations, baskets of fish, baskets of small antelopes, porcupines, and curious rats caught by his gamekeepers, bundles of mbugu, etc, made by his linen-drapers, coloured earths and sticks by his magician, all ready for presentation; but, as rain fell, the court broke up, and I had nothing for it but to walk about under my umbrella, indulging in angry reflections against the haughty king for not inviting me into his hut.

When the rain had ceased, and we were again called in, he was found sitting in state as before, but this time with the head of a black bull placed before him, one horn of which, knocked off, was placed alongside, whilst four living cows walked about the court.

I was now requested to shoot the four cows as quickly as possible; but having no bullets for my gun, I borrowed the revolving pistol I had given him, and shot all four in a second of time; but as the last one, only wounded, turned sharply upon me, I gave him the fifth and settled him. Great applause followed this *wonderful* feat, and the cows were given to my men. The king now loaded one of the carbines I had given him with his own hands, and giving it full-cock to a page, told him to go out and shoot a man in the outer court; which was no sooner accomplished than the little urchin returned to announce his success, with a look of glee such as one would see in the face of a boy who had robbed a bird's nest, caught a trout, or done any other boyish trick. The king said to him, 'And did you do it well?' 'Oh yes, capitally.' He spoke the truth, no doubt, for he dared not have trifled with the king; but the affair created hardly any interest. I never heard, and there appeared no curiosity to know, what individual human being the urchin had deprived of life.

The source of the Nile

Here at last I stood on the brink of the Nile; most beautiful was the scene, nothing could surpass it! It was the very perfection of the kind of effect aimed at in a highly kept park; with a magnificent stream from 600 to 700 yards wide, dotted with islets and rocks, the former occupied by fishermen's huts, the latter by sterns and crocodiles basking in the sun – flowing between fine high grassy banks, with rich trees and plantains in the background, where herds of the nsunnǎ and hartebeest could be seen grazing, while the hippopotami were snorting in the water, and florikan and guinea-fowl rising at our feet . . .

I marched up the left bank of the Nile at a considerable distance from the water, to the Isamba Rapids, passing through rich jungle and plantain-gardens. Nango, an old friend, and district officer of the place, first refreshed us with a dish of plantain-squash and dried fish, with *pombé*. He told us he is often threatened by elephants, but he sedulously keeps them off with charms; for if they ever tasted a plantain they would never leave the garden until they had cleared it out. He then took us to see the nearest falls of the Nile – extremely beautiful, but very confined. The water ran deep between its banks, which were covered with fine grass, soft cloudy acacias, and festoons of lilac convolvuli; whilst here and there, where the land had slipped above the rapids, bared places of red earth could be seen, like that of Devonshire; there, too, the waters, impeded by a natural dam, looked like a huge mill-pond, sullen and dark, in which two crocodiles, laving about, were looking out for prey. From the high banks we looked down upon a line of sloping wooded islets lying across the stream, which divide its waters, and, by interrupting them, cause at once dam and rapids. The whole was more fairy-like, wild, and romantic than – I must confess that my thoughts took that shape – anything I ever saw outside of a theatre. It was exactly the sort of place, in fact, where, bridged across from one side-slip to the other, on a moonlight night, brigands would assemble to enact some dreadful tragedy. Even the Wangǔana seemed spellbound at the novel beauty of the sight, and no one thought of moving till hunger warned us night was setting in, and we had better look out for lodgings.

Start again, and after drinking *pombé* with Nango . . . the march was commenced, but soon after stopped by the mischievous machinations of our guide, who pretended it was too late in the day to cross the jungles on ahead, either by the road to the source or the palace, and therefore would not move till the morning; then, leaving us, on the pretext of business, he vanished, and was never seen again. A small black fly, with thick shoulders and bullet head, infests the place, and torments the naked arms and legs of the people with its sharp stings to an extent that must render life miserable to them . . .

At last, with a good push for it, crossing hills and threading huge grasses, as well as extensive village plantations lately devastated by elephants – they had eaten all that was eatable, and what would not serve for food they had destroyed with their trunks, not one plantain or one hut being left entire – we arrived at the extreme end of the journey, the farthest point ever visited by the expedition on the same parallel of latitude as King Mtésa's palace, and just forty miles east of it.

We were well rewarded; for the 'stones,' as the Waganda call the falls, was by far the most interesting sight I had seen in Africa. Everybody ran to see them at once, though the march had been long and fatiguing, and even my sketch-block was called into play. Though beautiful the scene was not exactly what I expected; for the broad surface of the lake was shut out from view by a spur of hill, and the falls, about 12 feet deep, and 400 to 500 feet broad, were broken by rocks. Still it was a sight that attracted one to it for hours – the roar of the waters, the thousands of passenger-fish, leaping at the falls with all their might; the Wasoga and Waganda fishermen coming out in boats and taking post on all the rocks with rod and hook, hippopotami and crocodiles lying sleepily on the water, the ferry at work above the falls, and cattle driven down to drink at the margin of the lake – made, in all, with the pretty nature of the country – small hills, grassy-topped, with trees in the folds, and gardens on the lower slopes – as interesting a picture as one could wish to see.

The expedition had now performed its functions. I saw that old father Nile without any doubt rises in the Victoria N'yanza, and, as I had foretold, that lake is the great source of the holy river which cradled the first expounder of our religious belief.

Journal of the Discovery of the Source of the Nile, 1863

SAMUEL WHITE BAKER
1821–93

It is impossible to describe the triumph of that moment; here was the reward for all our labour – for the years of tenacity with which we had toiled through Africa . . .

Born in London, Samuel White Baker worked as a young man in Mauritius and Ceylon, where he set up an agricultural settlement and oversaw the construction of a railway. A patriotic, spirited character,* he set forth into Central Africa in 1862, having found companionship in the stunning Florence von Sass, whom he had allegedly bought at a slave auction in Bulgaria, and was to marry in due course. It was with Florence that he spent fourteen months exploring the Nile's tributaries before meeting up with Speke and Grant at Gondokoro. In his *The Albert*

Nyanza he describes his thrill on encountering the two famous compatriots, as they headed northwards to trace the Nile from what they had now identified was its source: 'My men rushed madly to my boat, with the report that two white men were with them who had come from the sea! Could they be Speke and Grant? Off I ran, and soon met them in reality; hurrah for old England!' One of the shots fired to salute the occasion mistakenly killed one of his donkeys.

Speke told Baker that, while they had been exploring Lake Victoria, natives had informed them of another great lake, Luta Nzige. Baker made it his mission to find this secondary prize in the Nile river system. Several escapades later he got there and christened it Albert Nyanza.

* 'By Englishmen alone is the glorious feeling shared of true, fair, and manly sport. The character of the nation is beautifully displayed in all our rules for hunting, shooting, fishing, fighting, etc; a feeling of fair play pervades every amusement.'

'This was the great reservoir of the Nile!'

That night I hardly slept. For years I had striven to reach the 'sources of the Nile.' In my nightly dreams during that arduous voyage I had always failed, but after so much hard work and perseverance the cup was at my very lips, and I was to *drink* at the mysterious fountain before another sun should set – at that great reservoir of Nature that ever since creation had baffled all discovery.

I had hoped, and prayed, and striven through all kinds of difficulties, in sickness, starvation, and fatigue, to reach that hidden source; and when it had appeared impossible, we had both determined to die upon the road rather than return defeated. Was it possible that it was so near, and that to-morrow we could say, 'the work is accomplished'?

The 14th March: The sun had not risen when I was spurring my ox after the guide, who, having been promised a double handful of beads on arrival at the lake, had caught the enthusiasm of the moment. The day broke beautifully clear, and having crossed a deep valley between the hills, we toiled up the opposite slope. I hurried to the summit. The glory of our prize burst suddenly upon me! There, like a sea of quicksilver, lay far beneath the grand expanse of water – a boundless sea horizon on the south and south-west, glittering in the noon-day sun; and on the west, at fifty or sixty miles' distance, blue mountains rose from the bosom of the lake to a height of about 7,000 feet above its level.

It is impossible to describe the triumph of that moment; here was the reward for all our labour – for the years of tenacity with which we had toiled through Africa. England had won the sources of the Nile! Long before I reached this spot, I had arranged to give three cheers with all our men in English style in honour of the discovery, but now that I looked down upon the great inland sea lying nestled in the very heart of Africa, and thought how vainly mankind had sought these sources throughout so many ages, and reflected that I had been the humble instrument permitted to unravel this portion of the great mystery when so many greater than I had failed, I felt too serious to vent my feelings in vain cheers for victory, and I sincerely thanked God for having guided and supported us through all dangers to the good end. I was about 1,500 feet above the lake, and I looked down from the steep granite cliff upon those welcome waters – upon that vast reservoir which nourished Egypt and brought fertility where all was wilderness – upon that great source so long hidden from mankind; that source of bounty and of blessings to millions of human beings; and as one of the greatest objects in nature, I determined to honour it with a great name. As an imperishable memorial of one loved and mourned by our gracious Queen and deplored by every Englishman, I called this great lake 'the Albert N'yanza.' The Victoria and the Albert lakes are the two sources of the Nile.

The zigzag path to descend to the lake was so steep and dangerous that we were forced to leave our oxen with a guide, who was to take them to Magungo and wait for our arrival. We commenced the descent of the steep pass on foot. I led the way, grasping a stout bamboo. My wife in extreme weakness tottered down the pass, supporting herself upon my shoulder, and stopping to rest every twenty paces. After a toilsome descent of about two hours, weak with years of fever, but for the moment strengthened by success, we gained the level plain below the cliff. A walk of about a mile through flat sandy meadows of fine turf interspersed with trees and bush, brought us to the water's edge. The waves were rolling upon a white pebbly beach: I rushed into the lake, and thirsty with heat and fatigue, with a heart full of gratitude, I drank deeply from the Sources of the Nile. Within a quarter of a mile of the lake was a fishing village named Vacovia, in which we now established ourselves. Everything smelt of fish – and everything looked like fishing; not the 'gentle art' of England with rod and fly, but harpoons were leaning against the huts, and lines almost as thick as the little finger were hanging up to dry, to which were attached iron hooks of a size that said much for the monsters of the Albert lake. On entering the hut I found a prodigious quantity of tackle; the lines were beautifully made of the fibre of the plantain stem, and were exceedingly elastic, and well adapted to withstand the first rush of a heavy fish; the hooks were very coarse, but well barbed, and varied in size from two to six inches. A number of harpoons and floats for hippopotami were arranged in good order, and the *tout ensemble* of the hut showed that the owner was a sportsman . . .

I procured a couple of kids from the chief of the village for some blue beads, and having received an ox as a present from the headman of Parkāni in return for a number of beads and bracelets, I gave my men a grand feast in honour of the discovery; I made them an address, explaining to them how much trouble we should have been saved had my whole party behaved well from the first commencement and trusted to my guidance, as we should have arrived here twelve months ago; at the same time I told them, that it was a greater honour to have achieved the task with so small a force as thirteen men, and that as the lake was thus happily reached, and Mrs Baker was restored to health after so terrible a danger, I should forgive them past offences and wipe out all that had been noted against them in my journal. This delighted my people, who ejaculated 'El hamd el Illah!' (thank God!) and fell to immediately at their beef.

At sunrise on the following morning I took the compass, and accompanied by the chief of the village, my guide Rabonga, and the woman Bacheeta, I went to the borders of the lake to survey the country. It was beautifully clear, and with a powerful telescope I could distinguish two large waterfalls that cleft the sides of the mountains on the opposite shore. Although the outline of the mountains was distinct upon the bright blue sky, and the dark shades upon their sides denoted deep gorges, I could not distinguish other features than the two great falls, which looked like threads of silver on the dark face of the mountains. No base had been visible, even from an elevation of 1,500 feet above the water-level, on my first view of the lake, but the chain of lofty mountains on the west appeared to rise suddenly from the water. This appearance must have been due to the great distance, the base being below the horizon, as dense columns of smoke were ascending apparently from the surface of the water: this must have been produced by the burning of prairies at the foot of the mountains . . .

Both the guide and the chief of Vacovia informed me that we should be taken by canoes to Magungo, to the point at which the Somerset that we had left at Karuma joined the lake; but that we could not ascend it, as it was a succession of cataracts the whole way from Karuma until within a short distance of Magungo. The exist of the Nile from the lake at Koshi was navigable for a considerable distance, and canoes could descend the river as far as the Madi.

They both agreed that the level of the lake was never lower than at present, and that it never rose higher than a mark upon the beach that accounted for an increase of about four feet. The beach was perfectly clean sand, upon which the waves rolled like those of the sea, throwing up weeds precisely as seaweed may be seen upon the English shore. It was a grand sight to look upon this vast reservoir of the mighty Nile, and to watch the heavy swell tumbling upon the beach, while far to the south-west the eye searched as vainly for a bound as though upon the Atlantic. It was with extreme emotion that I enjoyed this glorious scene. My wife, who had followed me so devotedly, stood by my side pale and exhausted – a wreck upon the shores of the great Albert Lake that we had so long striven to reach. No European foot had ever trod upon its sand, nor had the eyes of a white man ever scanned its vast expanse of water. We were the first; and this was the key to the great secret that even Julius Cæsar yearned to unravel, but in vain. Here was the great basin of the Nile that received *every drop of water*, even from the passing shower to the roaring mountain torrent that drained from Central Africa towards the north. This was the great reservoir of the Nile!

Albert N'yanza: Great Basin of the Nile, 1866

David Livingstone
1813–73

As the Bakwains believed that there must be some connection between the presence of 'God's Word' in their town and these successive and distressing droughts, they looked with no good will at the church-bell . . .

Born into a devout Christian family in Lanarkshire, David Livingstone was brought up in an environment of hard work, poverty and piety. Livingstone and his six siblings shared a room at the top of their tenement flat, and from the age of ten until twenty-four he worked in the local cotton mill. He was inspired to become a medical missionary upon reading pamphlets printed by British and American churches asking for Christians to come forward to serve in China; he spent two years studying Greek, theology and medicine part-time as preparation.

As it turned out, the Opium Wars meant that that destination was no longer feasible; but through the London Missionary Society he met Richard Moffat, a Scot whose mission was in Southern Africa, and his attention turned there.

Livingstone arrived in Cape Town in 1841 and, after a decade working as a missionary in Bechuanaland, where Moffat was based, moved northwards in search of populous areas to convert, educating himself in local cultures and languages as he did so. With William Oswald he crossed the Kalahari desert and discovered Lake Ngami. It was on a second expedition, to the upper reaches of the Zambezi, that he had his first encounter with the slave trade and resolved to dedicate the rest of his life to its abolition.

By now, Livingstone had married Moffat's daughter Mary, who travelled with him on several of his expeditions, until in 1852 he decided that it would be wiser for reasons of health, education and security to send her back to Britain with their four children.

Between 1853 and 1856 he made his great series of journeys from Central Africa to the west coast, then right across the continent to the east. He travelled up the Zambezi, returning again after bouts of fever to see if it might prove a passageway into the interior for trade and other outside influences, and in 1855 came across the spectacular falls he named after Queen Victoria: 'It had never been seen before by European eyes; but scenes so lovely must have been gazed upon by angels in their flight.'

The following year Livingstone arrived back in Britain to a hero's welcome. He wrote up an account of his explorations in *Missionary Travels and Researches in South Africa* (1857), which sold an extraordinary 70,000 copies – one of the century's best sellers – before touring the country for six months giving talks.

On his next expedition (1858–64), he planned to take a steamboat on the Zambezi and find a viable route into the interior, but was not so successful, and saw the loss of his wife – who had returned to Africa – and other followers. Now he was sponsored by the government rather than the London Missionary Society, who felt he spent too much of his time exploring. He was charged with 'exploring eastern and central Africa, for the promotion of Commerce and Civilisation with a view to the extinction of the slave-trade', and with him went an entourage of ten Africans and six Europeans.

He investigated the lakes Chilwa and Nyasa, but the Quebrabasa Falls blocked progress along the Zambezi itself, as did rapids further upstream. In 1863 the government recalled the expedition, and Livingstone came home.

From both economic and political standpoints, the expedition had not lived up to the high expectations that Livingstone had encouraged back in Britain. What's more, Livingstone found that his earlier discoveries had been used locally to *extend* the slave trade. His consolation was that he had collected a great deal of scientific information and created the first stepping stone towards establishing the British Central Africa Protectorate in 1893.

Prompted by the Royal Geographical Society, Livingstone returned to Africa in 1865 to resolve once and for all the debate about the source of the River Nile. He reached the lakes Bangweulu and Mweru (1867–8) and, after respite at Ujiji, again struck west and reached the Lualaba, unsure if it was the uppermost Nile, or the Congo.

Meanwhile, nothing had been heard of him back home. Then, in 1871, he was discovered ('Dr Livingstone, I presume') by H. M. Stanley, a reporter from the *New York Herald* sent by his editor to 'find Livingstone'. Livingstone was by this time ageing and ill, but was boosted by the supplies that Stanley had brought, and together they explored the northern reaches of Lake Tanganyika, proving it had no northern outlet – and that Burton's theory as to the source of the Nile was incorrect.

Stanley tried to convince Livingstone to return with him, but he was determined to have one more crack at the Nile problem, and returned instead to Lake Bangweulu. Having reached the village of Old Chitambo, he was found one morning kneeling by his bedside, as if in prayer, but stone dead. His followers buried his heart and embalmed his body with salt; then, over the course of nine months, it was carried to the coast, from where it was taken to be buried in Westminster Abbey.

As well as spreading the gospel, and increasing awareness of the slave trade, Livingstone collated valuable information on botany, zoology and geology, and navigated accurately by means of precise astronomical observations. He believed that progress had made the European race more advanced, and said as much. He wrote that he had encouraged his white assistants to act 'as members of a superior race and servants of a government that desires to elevate the more degraded portions of the human family'. However, he also viewed the African with sympathy: 'The Bakalahari, who live at Motlatsa wells, have always been very friendly to us and listen attentively to instruction conveyed to them in their own tongue. It is, however, difficult to give an idea to a European of the little effect teaching produces, because no one can realize the degradation to which their minds have been sunk by centuries of barbarism and hard struggling for the necessaries of life; like most others, they listen with respect and attention, but when we kneel down and address an unseen Being the position and the act often appear to them so ridiculous that they cannot refrain from bursting into uncontrollable laughter.'

Ultimately, he had faith in the capability of African people to rise to the challenges and innovations of modern society. His legacy, therefore, has been as much as an instigator of African nationalism as of Western imperialism.*

* H. M. Stanley, one of the pall-bearers at Livingstone's funeral, and about to become a major figure of African exploration himself, wrote, 'May I be selected to succeed him in the opening up of Africa to the shining light of Christianity!' However, he added a proviso: 'This selfish, wooden-headed world requires promptings other than the Gospel.' Stanley would do it his way.

Lion attack

I saw one of the beasts sitting on a piece of rock as before, but this time he had a little bush in front. Being about thirty yards off, I took a good aim at his body through the bush, and fired both barrels into it. The men then called out, 'He is shot, he is shot!' Others cried, 'He has been shot by another man too; let us go to him!' I did not see any one else shoot at him, but I saw the lion's tail erected in anger behind the bush, and, turning to the people, said, 'Stop a little till I load again.' When in the act of ramming down the bullets I heard a shout. Starting, and looking half round, I saw the lion just in the act of springing upon me. I was upon a little height; he caught my shoulder as he sprang, and we both came to the ground below together. Growling horribly close to my ear, he shook me as a terrier dog does a rat. The shock produced a stupor similar to that which seems to be felt by a mouse after the first shake of the cat. It caused a sort of dreaminess, in which there was no sense of pain nor feeling of terror, though quite conscious of all that was happening. It was like what patients partially under the influence of chloroform describe, who see all the operation, but feel not the knife. This singular condition was not the result of any mental process. The shake annihilated fear, and allowed no sense of horror in looking round at the beast. This peculiar state is probably produced in all animals killed by the carnivora; and if so, is a merciful provision by our benevolent Creator for lessening the pain of death. Turning round to relieve myself of the weight, as he had one paw on the back of my head, I saw his eyes directed to Mebalwe, who was trying to shoot him at a distance of ten or fifteen yards. His gun, a flint one, missed fire in both barrels; the lion immediately left me, and, attacking Mebalwe, bit his thigh. Another man, whose life I had saved before, after he had been tossed by a buffalo, attempted to spear the lion while he was biting Mebalwe. He left Mebalwe and caught this man by the shoulder, but at that moment the bullets he had received took effect, and he fell down dead. The whole was the work of a few moments, and must have been his paroxysm of dying rage. In order to take out the charm from him, the Bakaila on the following day made a huge bonfire over the carcase, which was declared to be that of the largest lion they had ever seen. Besides crunching the bone into splinters, he left eleven teeth wounds on the upper part of my arm.

A wound from this animal's tooth resembles a gun-shot wound; it is generally followed by a great deal of sloughing and discharge, and pains are felt in the part periodically ever afterwards. I had on a tartan jacket on the occasion, and I believe that it wiped off all the virus from the teeth that pierced the flesh, for my two companions in this affray have both suffered from the peculiar pains, while I have escaped with only the inconvenience of a false joint in my limb. The man whose shoulder was wounded showed me his wound actually burst forth afresh on the same month of the following year.

The art of the rain doctor

The natives, finding it irksome to sit and wait helplessly until God gives them rain from heaven, entertain the more comfortable idea that they can help themselves by a variety of preparations, such as charcoal made of burned bats ... the internal parts of different animals – as jackals' livers, baboons' and lions' hearts, and hairy calculi from the bowels of old cows – serpents' skins and vertebrae, and every kind of tuber, bulb, root, and plant to be found in the country. Although you disbelieve their efficacy in charming the clouds to pour out their refreshing treasures, yet, conscious that civility is useful everywhere, you kindly state that you think they are mistaken as to their power; the rain-doctor selects a particular bulbous root, pounds it, and administers a cold infusion to a sheep, which in five minutes afterwards expires in convulsions. Part of the same bulb is converted into smoke, and ascends towards the sky; rain follows in a day or two. The inference is obvious. Were we as much harnessed by droughts, the logic would be irresistible in England in 1857.

As the Bakwains believed that there must be some connection between the presence of 'God's Word' in their town and these successive and distressing droughts, they looked with no good will at the church-bell, but still they invariably treated us with kindness and respect. I am not aware of ever having had an enemy in the tribe. The only avowed cause of dislike was expressed by a very influential and sensible man, the uncle of Sechele. 'We like you as well as if you had been born among us; you are the only white man we can become familiar with (thoaëla); but we wish you to give up that everlasting preaching and praying; we cannot become familiar with that at all. You see we never get rain, while those tribes who never pray as we do obtain abundance.' This was a fact; and we often saw it raining on the hills, ten miles off, while it would not look at us 'even with one eye.' If the Prince of the power of the air had no hand in scorching us up, I fear I often gave him the credit of doing so.

A conversation on rain-making

Medical Doctor – Hail, friend! How very many medicines you have about you this morning! Why, you have every medicine in the country here.

Rain Doctor – Very true, my friend; and I ought; for the whole country needs the rain which I am making.

M. D. – So you really believe that you can command the clouds? I think that can be done by God alone.

R. D. – We both believe the very same thing. It is God that makes the rain, but I pray to him by means of these medicines, and, the rain coming, of course it is then mine . . .

M. D. – But we are distinctly told in the parting words of our Saviour that we can pray to God acceptably in His name alone, and not by means of medicines.

R. D. – Truly! but God told *us* differently. He made black men first, and did not love us, as he did the white men. He made you beautiful, and gave you clothing, and guns, and gunpowder, and horses, and waggons, and many other things about which we know nothing. But toward us he had no heart. He gave us nothing, except the assegai, and cattle, and rain-making; and he did not give us hearts like yours. We never love each other. Other tribes place medicines about our country to prevent the rain, so that we may be dispersed by hunger, and go to them, and augment their power. We must dissolve their charms by our medicines. God has given us one little thing, which you know nothing of. He has given us the knowledge of certain medicines by which we can make rain. *We* do not despise those things which you possess, though we are ignorant of them. We don't understand your book, yet we don't despise it. *You* ought not to despise our little knowledge, though you are ignorant of it.

M. D. – I don't despise what I am ignorant of; I only think you are mistaken in saying that you have medicines which can influence the rain at all.

R. D. – That's just the way people speak when they talk on a subject of which they have no knowledge. When we first opened our eyes, we found our forefathers making rain, and we follow in their footsteps. You, who send to Kuruman for corn, and irrigate your garden, may do without rain; *we* cannot manage in that way. If we had no rain, the cattle would have no pasture, the cows give no milk, our children become lean and die, our wives run away to other tribes who do make rain and have corn, and the whole tribe become dispersed and lost; our fire would go out.

M. D. – I quite agree with you as to the value of the rain; but you cannot charm the clouds by medicines. You wait till you see the clouds come, then you use your medicines, and take the credit which belongs to God only.

R. D. – I use my medicines, and you employ yours; we are both doctors, and doctors are not deceivers. You give a patient medicine. Sometimes God is pleased to heal him by means of your medicine; sometimes not – he dies.

When he is cured, you take the credit of what God does. I do the same. Sometimes God grants us rain, sometimes not. When he does, we take the credit of the charm. When a patient dies, you don't give up trust in your medicine, neither do I when rain fails. If you wish me to leave off my medicine, why continue your own?

The above is only a specimen of their way of reasoning, in which, when the language is well understood, they are perceived to be remarkably acute. These arguments are generally known, and I never succeeded in convincing a single individual of their fallacy, though I tried to do so in every way I could think of. Their faith in medicines as charms is unbounded.

Missionary Travels and Researches in Southern Africa, 1857

GEORG AUGUST SCHWEINFURTH
1836–1925

There, sure enough, was the strange little creature . . . Thus, at last, was I able
to veritably feast my eyes upon a living embodiment of the myths of
some thousand years.

The German botanist Georg Schweinfurth is most renowned for his 1868–71 expedition to explore the watershed between the White Nile and the Upper Congo rivers. It was during these travels that he discovered the Uele river and became the first European to meet pygmies. Pygmies had been mentioned by classical writers, such as Homer and Herodotus, and had been alluded to by a few modern travellers on the Nile. Nobody, however, had proved their existence.

Schweinfurth bartered for a pygmy by swapping him for one of his dogs, intending to take him back to England. For a year and a half the pygmy, Nsewue, travelled with Schweinfurth, and became 'almost as affectionate as a son'. Sadly, Nsewue never made it to England, dying from a bout of dysentery, 'an attack . . . originating not so much in any change of climate, or any alteration in his mode of living, as in his immoderate excess in eating, a propensity which no influence on my part was sufficient to control'.

Georg Schweinfurth lived until the age of eighty-nine. A talented draughtsman, the drawings he left behind provided a detailed and accurate record of his finds. He amassed copious notes, specimens and artefacts while he travelled; his dismay can be imagined when one day his hut burnt to the ground, taking with it all the accumulated work of his latest expedition. He lost meteorological observations that included 7,000 barometric readings, a collection of insects, examples of African art and travel journals describing the experiences of 825 days. Stoically, Schweinfurth set about recommencing his work, profiting from the period of six months he had to wait for the trading boat that could take him down the Nile. 'Gloomily, doggedly, I took up my work again, right from the very beginning, struggling more grimly than before with shortages and privation. Now, however, patience took the place of enthusiasm – and patience can overcome any misfortune.'

The Pygmy

Several days elapsed after my taking up my residence by the palace of the Monbuttoo king without my having a chance to get a view of the dwarfs, whose fame had so keenly excited my curiosity. My people, however, assured me that they had seen them. I remonstrated with them for not having secured me an opportunity of seeing for myself, and for not bringing them into contact with me. I obtained no other reply but that the dwarfs were too timid to come. After a few mornings my attention was arrested by a shouting in the camp, and I learned that Mohammed had surprised one of the Pygmies in attendance upon the king, and was conveying him, in spite of a strenuous resistance, straight to my tent. I looked up, and *there*, sure enough, was the strange little creature, perched upon Mohammed's right shoulder, nervously hugging his head, and casting glances of alarm in every direction. Mohammed soon deposited him in the seat of honour. A royal interpreter was stationed at his side. Thus, at last, was I able veritably to feast my eyes upon a living embodiment of the myths of some thousand years!

Eagerly, and without loss of time, I proceeded to take his portrait. I pressed him with innumerable questions, but to ask for information was an easier matter altogether than to get an answer. There was the greatest difficulty in inducing him to remain at rest, and I could only succeed by exhibiting a store of presents. Under the impression that the opportunity before me might not occur again, I bribed the interpreter to exercise his influence to pacify the little man, to set him at his ease, and to induce him to lay aside any fear of me that he might entertain. Altogether we succeeded so well that in a couple of hours the Pygmy had been measured, sketched, feasted, presented with a variety of gifts, and subjected to a minute catechism of searching questions.

His name was Adimokoo. He was the head of a small colony, which was located about half a league from the royal residence. With his own lips I heard him assert that the name of his nation was Akka, and I further learnt that they inhabit large districts to the south of the Monbuttoo between lat. 2° and 1° N . . .

At length, after having submitted so long to my curious and persistent questionings, the patience of Adimokoo was thoroughly exhausted, and he made a frantic leap in his endeavour to escape from the tent. Surrounded, however, by a crowd of inquisitive Bongo and Nubians, he was unable to effect his purpose, and was compelled, against his will, to remain for a little longer. After a time a gentle persuasion was brought to bear, and he was induced to go through some of the characteristic evolutions of his war-dances. He was dressed, like the Moubuttoo, in a rokko-coat and plumed hat, and was armed with a miniature lance as well as with a bow and arrow. His height I found to be about 4 feet 10 inches, and this I reckon to be the average measurement of his race.

Although I had repeatedly been astonished at witnessing the war-dances of the Niam-niam, I confess that my amazement was greater than ever when I looked upon the exhibition which the Pygmy afforded. In spite of his large, bloated belly and short bandy legs – in spite of his age, which, by the way, was considerable – Adimokoo's agility was perfectly marvellous, and I could not help wondering whether cranes would ever be likely to contend with such creatures. The little man's leaps and attitudes were accompanied by such lively and grotesque varieties of expression that the spectators shook again and held their sides with laughter. The interpreter explained to the Niam-niam that the Akka jump about in the grass like grasshoppers, and that they are so nimble that they shoot their arrows into an elephant's eye and drive their lances into their bellies. The gestures of the Akka, to which I shall have occasion again to refer, always reminded me of the pictures given by travellers to represent the Bushmen of the south.

Adimokoo returned home loaded with presents. I made him understand that I should be glad to see all his people, and promised that they should lose nothing by coming.

On the following day I had the pleasure of a visit from two of the younger men . . . After they had once got over their alarm, some or other of the Akka came to me almost every day.

'A solitary European'

It should be mentioned that I was never a witness of that abandoned cruelty and systematic inhumanity which the accounts of previous travellers in the lands of the Upper Nile might lead us to expect. A traveller to be just will take into consideration all the circumstances of the case and all the ameliorating particulars which may be alleged; but in the majority of these narratives, which make the hair almost stand on end, the judgment that is passed is not unfrequently warped and exaggerated. There is no justification for the pride with which we civilised people boast of our humanity. We have only to reflect upon the horrors that follow in the train of our wars, and if we could enfranchise ourselves from prejudice we should be compelled to allow that we are worse barbarians than all the Nubians – nay, that we are murderers by deliberate intention, and destroyers of the happiness of the homes of thousands . . .

Yes; I took my meals alone. A solitary European, as he proceeds farther and farther from his home, may see his old associations shrink to a minimum; but so much the more, with pertinacious conservatism, will he cling to the surviving remnants of his own superiority. Nothing can ever divest him of the thought as to how he may maintain the prerogative, which he takes for granted, that he is a being of some higher order. Many a misanthrope, in his disgust at the shady side of our modern culture, may imagine that to a traveller, in his intercourse with the children of Nature, the thousand necessities of daily life must seem but trifles vain and empty, to be dispensed with without a sigh. Such an one may fancy that the bonds which fasten him to the world of civilisation are weak and all waiting to be rent asunder as soon as Nature is left to assert her unfettered rights but from experience I can assure him that the truth is very different. With the fear of degenerating ever before his eyes, the wanderer from the realms of civilisation will surely fix his gaze almost with devotion on the few objects of our Western culture that remain to him, which (however trivial they are in themselves) become to him symbols little less than sacred. Tables and chairs, knives and forks, bedding, and even pocket-handkerchiefs, will assume an importance that could never have been anticipated, and it is hardly too much to aver that they will rise to a share in his affections.

The Heart of Africa: Three Years' Travels and Adventures in the Unexplored Regions of Central Africa, 1873

EVARISTE RÉGIS HUC
1813–60

He looked at us several times; then pulling the bridle of his horse . . . he left us hastily, muttering between his teeth some words which we could not exactly hear, but which we were aware did not constitute a benediction.

The French missionary Evariste Régis Huc joined the Lazarist order when he was twenty-four, and in 1839 was sent to Macao in China. For five years he lived and worked in both northern and southern China, before joining up with fellow missionary Joseph Gabet to head, illegally, into Tibet. Disguised as lamas, they travelled for two years on a circuitous route through inhospitable deserts and forests populated by panthers, bears, wolves and tigers. They arrived, in a caravan of 2,000 people and 4,000 animals, and were welcomed in Lhasa in January 1846 by the Tibetans, but their dream of setting up a mission was not to be fulfilled: the Chinese Imperial Commissioners had them expelled after two months. They were escorted back to Canton by mandarins.

It seems that there were frequent power tussles between the mandarins and the missionaries. Discarding their Tibetan furs, which smelled strongly of yak butter and mutton, the two Frenchmen had some Chinese gowns made up, causing horror when they chose colours only intended for members of the Imperial family; but Huc was adamant that the Empire's conventions should have no hold over them, as strangers: 'Our obstinacy was not to be overcome, and the mandarins submitted – as they ought to do.'*

Huc returned to Europe in 1852 and left his order the following year. He and Father Gabet were the last Europeans to openly travel within Tibet until the twentieth century.

* Huc clearly had strong reservations as to whether one could ever make good Christians of the Chinese: 'A very short residence among the Chinese is sufficient to show that their virtue is entirely external, their public morality is but a mask worn over the corruption of their manners. We will take care not to lift the unclean veil that hides the putrefaction of this ancient Chinese civilisation, the leprosy of vice has spread so completely through this sceptical society, that the varnish of modesty with which it is covered is continually falling off and exposing the hideous wounds which are eating away the vitals of this unbelieving people. Their language is already revoltingly indecent, and the slang of the worst resorts of licentiousness threatens to become the ordinary language of conversation.'

A conflict of creeds

After some days' march across the sands of the Ortous, we noticed on our way a small lamasery, richly built in a picturesque and wild situation. We passed on without stopping. We had advanced a gunshot from the place when we heard behind us the galloping of a horse. On looking round we saw a lama following us at full speed. 'Brothers,' he said, 'you have passed our *soumé* (lamasery) without stopping. Are you in such haste that you cannot repose for a day and offer your adorations to our saint?' . . . 'We never prostrate ourselves before men; the true creed of the West forbids that.' 'Our saint is not a mere man; you do not imagine, perhaps, that in our little lamasery we have the happiness to possess a *Chaberon*, a living Buddha. It is two years since he deigned to descend from the holy mountains of Thibet; he is now seven years old. In one of his former lives he was Grand Lama of a splendid lamasery in this vale, which was destroyed, according to the prayer-books, in the time of the wars of Jenghiz. The saint having reappeared a few years since, we have constructed in haste a small lamasery. Come, brothers, our saint will hold his right hand over your heads, and luck will accompany your steps!' 'The men who know the holy doctrine of the West do not believe in all these trans-migrations of the *Chaberons*. We adore only the Creator of heaven and earth; his name is Jehovah. We believe that the child you have made superior of your lamasery is destitute of all power. Men have nothing to hope or to fear from him.' When the lama heard these words, which he certainly never expected, he was quite stupefied. By degrees his face became animated, and at last exhibited indignation and anger. He looked at us several times; then, pulling the bridle of his horse, he turned short round and left us hastily, muttering between his teeth some words which we could not exactly hear, but which we were aware did not constitute a benediction.

Election of a living Buddha

The Tartars . . . would never allow themselves to entertain the slightest doubt as to the authenticity of their *Chaberons*. These living Buddhas are in large numbers, and are always placed at the head of the most important lamaseries. Sometimes they modestly begin their career in a small temple and have only a few disciples; but very soon their reputation increases around, and the small lamasery becomes a place of pilgrimage and devotion. The neighbouring lamas, speculating upon the rising fashion, surround it with their cells; the lamasery acquires development from year to year and becomes at last famous in the land.

The election and enthronization of the living Buddhas are conducted in so singular a manner as to be well worth relating. When a Grand Lama has gone – that is to say, is dead – the circumstance is no occasion of mourning in the lamasery. There are no tears, no lamentations, for everybody knows the *Chaberon* will very soon reappear. This apparent death is but the beginning of a new existence, as it were, one ring more added to the unlimited, uninter-rupted chain of successive lives – a regular palingenesis . . .

It often happens that the disciples of the defunct have no occasion to trouble themselves at all in order to discover the new birthplace of their Great Lama. He himself takes the trouble to initiate them into the secret of his transformation. As soon as he has effected his metamorphosis in Thibet, he reveals himself at an age when common children cannot yet articulate a single word. 'It is I,' he says with the accent of authority; 'it is I who am the Great Lama, the living Buddha of such a temple; conduct me to my ancient lamasery. I am its immortal superior.' The wonderful baby having thus spoken, it is speedily communicated to the lamas of the *soumé* indicated that their *Chaberon* is born in such a place, and they are summoned to attend and invite him home.

In whatever manner the Tartars discover the residence of their Great Lama, whether by the appearance of the rainbow, or by the spontaneous revelation of the *Chaberon* himself, they are always full of intense joy on the occasion. Soon all is movement in the tents, and the thousand preparations for a long journey are made with enthusiasm, for it is almost always in Thibet that they have to seek their living Buddha, who seldom fails to play them the trick of transmigrating in some remote and almost inaccessible country. Everyone contributes his share to the organization of the holy journey. If the king of the country does not place himself at the head of the caravan, he sends either his own son or one of the most illustrious members of the royal family. The great mandarins, or ministers of the king, consider it their duty and an honour to join the party. When everything is at last prepared, an auspicious day is chosen, and the caravan starts.

Sometimes these poor Mongols, after having endured incredible fatigues in horrible deserts, fall into the hands of the brigands of the Blue Sea, who strip them from head to foot. If they do not die of hunger and cold in those dreadful solitudes – if they succeed in returning to the place whence they came – they commence the preparations for a new journey. There is nothing capable of discouraging them. At last, when, by dint of energy and persever- ance, they have contrived to reach the eternal sanctuary, they prostrate them- selves before the child who has been indicated to them. The young *Chaberon*, however, is not saluted and proclaimed Great Lama without a previous exam- ination . . . He is asked the name of the lamasery of which he assumes to be the Great Lama; at what distance it is; what is the number of the lamas residing in it. He is interrogated respecting the habits and customs of the defunct Great Lama and the principal circumstances attending his death. After all these questions, there are placed before him different prayer-books, articles of furniture, teapots, cups, &c., and amongst all these things he has to point out those which belonged to his former life.

Generally this child, at most but five or six years old, comes forth victorious out of all these trials. He answers accurately all the questions that are put to

him and makes without any embarrassment the inventory of his goods.
'Here,' he says, 'are the prayer-books I used; there is the japanned porringer
out of which I drank my tea.' And so on.

No doubt the Mongols are often dupes of the fraud of those who have an
interest in making a Great Lama out of this puppet. Yet we believe that often
all this proceeds on both sides with honesty and good faith. From the information we obtained from persons worthy of the greatest credit, it appears
certain that all that is said of the *Chaberons* must not be ranged amongst
illusion and deception. A purely human philosophy will, undoubtedly, reject
such things, or put them, without hesitating, down to the account of lama
imposture. We Catholic missionaries believe that the great liar who once
deceived our first parents in the earthly paradise still pursues his system of
falsehood in the world . . .

   Travels in Tartary, Thibet and China 1844–1846, 1850

Nikolai Przhevalsky
1839–88

The first thing which strikes the traveller in the life of a Mongol is his excessive dirtiness: he never washes his body, and very seldom his face and hands . . . his clothing swarms with parasites, which he amuses himself by killing in the most unceremonious way.

The first expedition undertaken by the Russian soldier Lieutenant-Colonel Przhevalsky was to the Far East. Then, in 1870, the Imperial Geographical Society of St Petersburg sent him to explore southern Mongolia, and with just two companions he covered 7,000 miles in three years, largely over terrain that had never been charted. They ventured to the headwaters of the Yangtze River and on to Tibet, then back across the Gobi desert to Urga, enduring extremes of temperature on the Mongolian plateau that reach 40°c in the summer and plunge to almost −40°c in the winter. In total he spent nine years exploring Central Asia – mainly China, Tibet and Mongolia – covering more than 20,000 miles. He was the first European to visit Lop Nor since Marco Polo 600 years before.

On all of his major journeys, he collected zoological and botanical specimens, gathering a wealth of scientific knowledge. His most famous legacy is the discovery of the so-called Przhevalsky horse – what seems to be the last truly wild horse.

The Mongols: 'excessive dirtiness'

The first thing which strikes the traveller in the life of the Mongol is his excessive dirtiness: he never washes his body, and very seldom his face and hands. Owing to constant dirt, his clothing swarms with parasites, which he amuses himself by killing in the most unceremonious way. It is a common sight to see a Mongol, even an official or lama of high rank, in the midst of a large circle of his acquaintances, open his sheepskin or kaftan to catch an offending insect and execute him on the spot between his front teeth. The uncleanliness and dirt amidst which they live is partly attributable to their dislike, almost amounting to dread, of water or damp. Nothing will induce a Mongol to cross the smallest marsh where he might possibly wet his feet, and he carefully avoids pitching his yurta anywhere near damp ground or in the vicinity of a spring, stream, or marsh. Moisture is as fatal to him as it is to the camel, so that it would seem as if his organism, like the camel's, were only adapted to a dry climate; he never drinks cold water, but always prefers brick-tea, a staple article of consumption with all the Asiatic nomads. It is procured from the Chinese, and the Mongols are so passionately fond of it that neither men nor women can do without it for many days. From morning till night the kettle is simmering on the hearth, and all members of the family constantly have recourse to it. It is the first refreshment offered to a guest. The mode of preparation is disgusting; the vessel in which the tea is boiled is never cleansed, and is occasionally scrubbed with argols, i.e. dried horse or cow dung. Salt water is generally used, but, if unobtainable, salt is added. The tea is then pared off with a knife or pounded in a mortar, and a handful of it thrown into the boiling water, to which a few cups of milk are added. To soften the brick-tea, which is sometimes as hard as a rock, it is placed for a few minutes among hot argols, which impart a flavour and aroma to the whole beverage. This is the first process, and in this form it answers the same purpose as chocolate or coffee with us. For a more substantial meal the Mongol mixes dry roasted millet in his cup, and, as a final relish, adds a lump of butter or raw sheep-tail fat (kurdiuk). The reader may now imagine what a revolting compound of nastiness is produced, and yet they consume any quantity of it!

The gluttony of this people exceeds all description. A Mongol will eat more than ten pounds of meat at one sitting, but some have been known to devour an average-sized sheep in the course of twenty-four hours! On a journey, when provisions are economised, a leg of mutton is the ordinary daily ration for one man, and although he can live for days without food, yet, when once he gets it, he will eat enough for seven.

They always boil their mutton, only roasting the breast as a delicacy. On a winter's journey, when the frozen meat requires extra time for cooking, they eat it half raw, slicing off pieces from the surface, and returning it again to the pot. When travelling and pressed for time, they take a piece of mutton and place it on the back of the camel, underneath the saddle, to preserve it from the frost, whence it is brought out during the journey and eaten, covered with camel's hair and reeking with sweat . . .

The most striking trait in their character is sloth. Their whole lives are passed in holiday making, which harmonizes with their pastoral pursuits. Their cattle are their only care, and even they do not cause them much trouble. The camels and horses graze on the steppe without any watch, only requiring to be watered once a day in summer at the neighbouring well. The women and children tend the flocks and herds. The rich hire shepherds, who are mostly poor homeless vagrants. Milking the cows, churning butter, preparing the meals, and other domestic work, falls to the lot of the women. The men, as a rule, do nothing but gallop about all day long from yurta to yurta, drinking tea or kumiss, and gossiping with their neighbours . . .

The Mongol is so indolent that he will never walk any distance, no matter how short, if he can ride; his horse is always tethered outside the yurta, ready for use at any moment; he herds his cattle on horseback, and when on a caravan journey nothing but intense cold will oblige him to dismount and warm his limbs by walking a mile or two. His legs are bowed by constant equestrianism, and he grasps the saddle like a centaur. The wildest steppe-horse cannot unseat its Mongol rider. He is in his element on horseback, going at full speed; seldom at a foot's pace, or at a trot, but scouring like the wind across the desert. He loves and understands horses; a fast galloper or a good ambler is his greatest delight, and he will not part with such a treasure, even in his direst need. His contempt for pedestrianism is so great that he considers it beneath his dignity to walk even as far as the next yurta.

Endowed by nature with a strong constitution, and trained from early childhood to endure hardships, the Mongols enjoy excellent health, notwith-standing all the discomforts of life in the desert. In the depth of winter, for a month at a time, they accompany the tea-caravans. Day by day the therm-ometer registers upwards of −20° of Fahrenheit, with a constant wind from the north-west, intensifying the cold until it is almost unendurable. But in spite of it they keep their seat on their camels for fifteen hours at a stretch, with a keen wind blowing in their teeth. A man must be made of iron to stand this; but a Mongol performs the journey backwards and forwards four times during the winter, making upwards of 3,000 miles. As soon as you set him to do other work, apparently much lighter, but to which he is unaccustomed, the result is very different. Although as hard as nails, he cannot walk fifteen or twenty miles without suffering great fatigue; if he pass the night on the damp ground he will catch cold as easily as any fine gentleman, and, deprived of his brick-tea, he will never cease grumbling.

Mongolia, the Tangut Country and the Solitudes of Northern Tibet: Being the Narrative of Three Years' Travel in Eastern High Asia, 1876

Frederick Burnaby
1842–85
The proprietor was dressed at first sight like a European. He had a black coat; a red sash was tied around his waist; a pair of white trousers covered his legs . . . a very high, cone-shaped astrachan hat . . . much resembling an extinguisher.

Burnaby was a journalist, linguist and military man who undertook reconnaissance missions in Asia; he also made the first crossing of the English Channel in a hot-air balloon. The son of a rich Protestant minister, he joined the Royal Horse Guards at the age of sixteen but, finding no chance of active service, embarked on balloon adventures abroad – notably for the London *Times*, reporting on the Spanish Civil War of 1874. In the winter of 1875–76 he rode through the Steppes and uplands of Russian Asia, then closed to outsiders, and was able to warn Gladstone of Russia's expansionist intentions. His book *A Ride to Khiva* brought him instant fame.

By 1881 a colonel, he was fluent in French, German, Italian, Spanish and Russian. However, it was not his linguistic skills so much as his physique that first struck those who encountered Burnaby. He was six foot four inches tall, with a 45-inch chest, weighing fifteen stone. He could lift a small pony with one arm.

Described by Henry James as 'opaque in intellect, indomitable in muscle', he died in hand-to-hand fighting on the 1885 expedition to relieve General Gordon at Khartoum.

The benefits of worshipping the spirit of evil

'Here we are, sir, with the worshippers of Old Scratch!' observed Radford, as he was preparing the mid-day meal, which consisted of a freshly-killed hen, boiled with some rice. 'Mohammed has just been telling me something about them. All I know is that Old Nick has not much to complain of so far as his flock is concerned. They have been at our sugar already, and would have carried off Mohammed's tobacco if he had not been on the look out. I suppose they think it right to steal, so as to keep on good terms with their master.'

The Yezeeds' religion, if such it may be called, is based upon the following dogma: that there are two spirits – a spirit of good and a spirit of evil. Allah, the spirit of good, can do no harm to any one, and is a friend to the human race. The spirit of evil can do a great deal of harm, and he is the cause of all our woes. From this starting-point the Yezeeds have been brought to believe that it is a waste of time to worship the spirit of good, who will not hurt them, and that the proper course to pursue is to try and propitiate the spirit of evil, who can be very disagreeable if he chooses. To do so they never venture to make use of the name of the devil, as this they believe would be an act of disrespect to their infernal master.

They are visited twice a year by different high priests, when certain rites are performed. These rites are kept a great secret. The Turks who gave me some information about the Yezeeds were unable to give me any details about the nature of the ceremonies. I was informed that the Yezeeds are divided into two sects; that the one looks upon the devil as the Grand Vizier of Allah, and the other regards him as the private secretary of the good spirit. It was said that the two sects hated each other to such an extent that, if a man belonging to the one which looks upon the devil as being the Grand Vizier of Allah were to enter a village belonging to members of the rival faith, the new arrival would have a great chance of losing his life . . .

This information was given me by some Turks with whom I had conversed during my journey. I now asked my host if these statements were true. He at once repudiated them, and declared that they were inventions of the followers of Islam.

'Do you look upon the devil as the Grand Vizier of Allah?' I now inquired.

If a bombshell had exploded in the room where I was sitting, there could not have been greater consternation than that which was evinced by the members of my host's family. Springing to their feet, they fled from the building – an old woman very nearly upsetting Radford's cooking-pot in her haste to escape into the open air. The captain looked at me, and then indulged in a sort of suppressed laugh.

'What has frightened them?' I inquired.

'Effendi,' he replied, 'you mentioned the word "Shaitan" (devil). It is very lucky for you,' continued the old man, 'that there are five of us, and we are all well armed; for, if not, the Yezeeds would have attacked our party for a certainty. Any disaster which may happen in this village during the next twelve months will be put down to you. If a man's cow or camel dies, the fellow will say that it is all your fault; the sooner we continue our march the better.'

It was getting late; the inhabitants had withdrawn to some distance from their houses, they were gazing at our party with lowering brows. I would gladly have repaired the mischief that I had done; but an apology might have only made matters worse.

On Horseback Through Asia Minor, 1877

Joseph Thomson
1858–95

. . . we soon set our eyes upon the dreaded warriors that had been so long the subject of my waking dreams, and I could not but involuntarily exclaim, 'What splendid fellows!' as I surveyed a band of the most peculiar race of men to be found in Africa.

Born in Dumfriesshire, the Scottish geologist and cartographer Joseph Thomson studied at Edinburgh University and was in his early twenties when he led his first RGS expedition, from the East African coast to Lake Nyasa (Lake Malawi). He had been second in command to Keith Johnston, but shortly after the expedition left Zanzibar, Johnston died – 'one of the most promising explorers who has ever set foot on African shores, was numbered with the long list of geographical martyrs who have attempted to break through the barriers of disease and barbarism, which make the interior of Africa almost impenetrable'. Now Thomson was faced with the predicament of whether to continue or not. He was young and inexperienced, yet felt the weight of all the great explorers of Africa behind him, as well as the obligation to see Johnston's work through. So he took command of the expedition and went on to map the lakes of the Great Rift Valley and the rivers that flowed from them. Shortly afterwards, he led an unsuccessful attempt to find coal in the Rovuma river valley for the Sultan of Zanzibar.

People who met Thomson were often amazed at his 'boy scout' appearance. He was gentle and, unlike many of his European contemporaries in Africa, never, it's said, fired a shot in anger. He subsequently led several more expeditions into Africa but, at the age of only thirty-seven, succumbed to pneumonia. East Africa's most common gazelle, *Gazella thomsoni*, is named after him.

Meeting the Masai

. . . We were informed that the Masai had been holding many consultations about us, but that after much quarrelling, they had concluded to send a deputation to interview me on the morrow. Next day, therefore we were kept in an excitable and anxious condition till we learned our fate. In the afternoon this reached its climax, when from the labyrinths of the surrounding forest a fine musical chant was raised. The word was passed round that the Masai had come. Seizing our guns in one hand, and a tuft of grass in the other, in token that we were prepared to fight, but meant peace, we proceeded outside to hear our fate. Passing through the forest, we soon set our eyes upon the dreaded warriors that had been so long the subject of my waking dreams, and I could not but involuntarily exclaim, 'What splendid fellows!' as I surveyed a band of the most peculiar race of men to be found in all Africa.

After a most ceremonious greeting performed with much gravity and aristocratic dignity, their great shovel-headed spears were stuck in the ground their bullock's-hide shields rested against them on their sides, and then the oil-and-clay-bedaubed warriors assumed a sitting posture, with their knees drawn up to their chins, and their small neat kal-skin mantles enveloping them. We on our part took position opposite them, holding our guns in our hands. I, of course, as became my dignity, occupied a camp-stool.

After a few words among themselves in a low tone, a spokesman arose, leisurely took a spear in his left hand to lean upon, and then with his knob-kerry as an orator's baton, he proceeded to deliver his message with all the ease of a professional speaker. With profound astonishment I watched this son of the desert, as he stood before me, speaking with a natural fluency and grace, a certain sense of the gravity and importance of his position, and a dignity of attitude beyond all praise . . .

Two or three others of the Masai then spoke to the same effect as their leading orator – no two, however, rising at once, or if they did so, a few words between themselves settled who was to have the ear of the meeting, while not a word was said by the others beyond inarticulate expressions of assent or dissent.

Till the formal speech-making was over each one had sat with unmoved countenance, betraying by neither word nor sign a consciousness that the second white man they had ever seen in their lives was sitting before them. On the completion, however, of that necessary preliminary, their features relaxed, and they allowed themselves to show as much curiosity as their dignity as Masai El-Moran (warriors) would permit.

We now adjourned to camp on the best of terms, where, though greatly delighted with everything we showed them, they still carefully preserved their aristocratic demeanour . . .

Before noon we had all reached the ice-cold waters of the snow-fed Ngarè N'Erobi, which rises in its full volume at the base of the mountain. We camped in a sharp bend of the stream where it almost surrounds a bit of level sward. Our first care, of course, was to make the *boma*, and thoroughly fortify ourselves. So far everything had gone on swimmingly, though I was quite bewildered by my unexpected reception, and felt as if there was something portentous in the whole affair.

The news of our arrival soon spread. The Masai men and women began to crowd into camp, and we mutually surveyed each other with equal interest. The women had all the style of the men. With slender, well-shaped figures, they had brilliant dark eyes, Mongolian in type, narrow, and with an upward slant. Their expression was distinctly lady-like (for natives), and betrayed their ideas in more ways than one. Obviously they felt that they were a superior race, and that all others were but as slaves before them . . .

Tents having been pitched, and goods stacked, properly covered from peering eyes, and surrounded with a strong guard, the more serious business of
the day commenced. Wire, beads, and cloth were taken into the tent, so that
we might prepare to dole out the black mail – the 'chango' of this district, the
'hongo' of the region further south. We had not long to wait. A war-chant was
heard in the distance, and soon a party of El-Moran, in all the unctuous glory
of a new plastering of red clay and grease, appeared, marching in single file,
and keeping step to their song, their murderous spears gleaming in the sun as
they gave them now and then a rotatory movement. They carried their heavy
shields by their side, on which was seen the newly-painted heraldic device of
their particular clan . . .

The El-Moran, having laid aside their spears and shields, stand ready in a
hollow group. My men, advancing with the hongo, suddenly throw it into the
midst, and run for their lives out of the way. With a grand yell the warriors
precipitate themselves upon the articles, on the principle of 'every one for
himself and the devil take the hindmost.' A few of the boldest get the lion's
share. In other cases two have seized the same article. It may be a bunch of
beads, and the matter is settled by the strings being torn in twain, each one
carrying off a handful, leaving a large number strewed on the ground . . .

Towards evening the camp was crowded, and in response to repeated cries
for the white Lybon [medicine-man], backed up by insolent attempts to tear
open the door of my tent, I had to step out and bow my acknowledgments,
though inwardly muttering maledictions upon them, as I was still weak, ill,
and irritable from the repeated attacks of fever, the effects of which still hung
about me. Submitting to the inevitable, I sat down on a box, the cynosure of
every eye. They had now lost their calm and dignified bearing, and had
become rude and obtrusive; the Ditto (young unmarried women) being the
most insolent, and not showing the slightest trace of fear.

For some time I submitted with patience to their annoying attentions, let
them touch me on the face, feel my hair, push up the sleeve of my coat, and
examine with intense curiosity my boots. At last, however, growing bilious
and irritable, especially at the repeated attempts of one ferocious-looking
warrior to turn up my trousers to see the natural integument below, I gave
him a push with my foot. With fury blazing in his face, and presenting the
most diabolical aspect, he sprang back a few steps and drew his simè, and was
about to launch himself upon me. I slipped aside, however, and was speedily
surrounded by the guard, while some of the El-Morua laid hold of him, and,
as he would not be pacified, led him away . . .

On peeping out of the tent next morning with the bracing feeling incidental to a temperature of only 61°, I was much impressed by the sight of Sadi marching round the camp with gun held at the salute, and a white flag raised aloft, on which were written some verses of the Koran, which were supposed to have some magical influence. As he moved along in the stilted manner of an army recruit learning his paces, he recited aloud in the Masai language intimation to all whom it might concern that we had peaceable intents, but that if they stole or did us any harm, we had medicines of such a potent kind that they would not escape scathless, as disease would decimate them and their cattle, and manifold evils fall upon the country.

Taking a peep outside the camp, I got a view of Kilimanjaro – now almost due east of us – in the clear morning air. The great eastern shoulder of Shira now bulked largely in view, springing abruptly from the Sigirari plain, with black, uninhabited forest at the base and upper barren region, fluted and scaured into the appearance of a cyclopean file . . . Before the Masai cattle left their kraals, I went out and supplied our larder by shooting two fine zebras. On my return to camp after this risky step, I was thunderstruck by the unexpected news that the whole country ahead of us was up in arms to oppose our further progress . . . The young men of the surrounding country, ever ready for a bit of military excitement, flocked to join their friends, though the chiefs and soldiers of Ngarè N'Erobi were against any such action, a fortunate thing for us, as we were made aware what was going on. The comfort of my position was not enhanced by a strong suspicion which now forced itself upon me that Muhinna and Sadi were not acting in good faith, but were in fact doing their best to ruin the caravan. With bitter feelings of disappointment and chagrin, I saw no other course open to me but to retreat to Taveta. We were quite equal to any number while we were in camp; but what could we do, spread out in single file and loaded with goods before an enemy like the Masai? Then to fight at one place, even if we were successful, would mean fighting ever after, with the result of finding ourselves after a few days irretrievably *hors de combat* . . .

An ominous silence pervaded the camp, contrasting with the hubbub of the previous day. Spies were set to watch us, but we put on a bold face, and talked coolly about going on next day, declaring that if we were not allowed to pass peaceably we would try the persuasive influence of gunpowder. Prompt action, however, was required. Information was brought us that an attack would probably be made on us next day, and therefore, to avoid a fight, I resolved to anticipate them by retreating during the night. All the usual preparations were made in the way of lighting fires, cooking, &c. Nothing was disturbed till darkness set in, and the last Masai out of camp. Word was then

quietly passed round that for the first time we were about to run away, and
that all preparation was to be made without bustle. The night set in gloomy
and dark. A black pall of clouds overspread the heavens. Some rain sputtered,
and with intense satisfaction we saw that a storm was brewing.

Two hours after sunset, the word was given to pack up. Not a sound broke
the stillness as each man buckled on his belt, caught up his gun, and shouldered his load by the light of the numerous camp fires. Then, when all was
ready, more wood was thrown on the fires, and we glided out into the blackness of night. Not an object could be seen to guide our steps, so I had to take
the lead, compass in hand, and a bull's-eye lantern under my coat to enable
me to read the card. The men kept touch of each other, while Martin with the
head-men and a party of Askari brought up the rear.

The first half-mile was the most dangerous, as we had to pass close to the
kraal of Lengobè, and if our donkeys should take a notion to bray, it was
impossible to foretell the consequence. As I led the way, I got the worst of it, in
the matter of tripping over stones, tearing my legs among the thorns, or
getting sad shocks to the system, as more than once I dropped into holes. On
these occasions the word 'Mawè!' (stones), 'Miiba!' (thorns), or 'Shimo!'
(hole) passed quietly along the line, to direct those behind. The anxious
moment at last arrived when we must pass close to the kraal, and if the
caravan had been one of ghosts, it could not have moved more silently,
though now and then a half-suppressed exclamation of 'Allah!' told that a
man had fallen or got a thorn in his foot. We passed safely; and then we
stepped out quicker, though in the intense darkness our onward progress was
one of painful straining and stumbling. Now and then we stopped, to let the
men close up and make sure that all were safe, as it was now impossible to see
a yard ahead.

The amenities of the night were not enhanced by the occasional glare of
lightning and the muttering of thunder near Kibo. Game started away almost
from our very feet. Zebras thundered past in squadrons. Hyenas raised their
horrible yells, or made us feel still more 'creepy' by their laugh. We did not
know but that we might run at any moment into the very centre of a herd of
buffalo, or have to encounter the charge of some wild rhinoceros. The bull's
eye now proved of great service, and directed the men how to go. About
midnight we reached the forest we had left three days before. Here our per-
plexities became worse, and it seemed as if we would have to wait till daylight.
Rain, however, now beginning to come down, and the thunder to approach
more near, while the lightning was perfectly dazzling, we made a determined
spurt, and finally, limp, footsore, scratched and torn, we groped our way into

camp just as the storm broke with terrific violence. We crawled into any huts that came handy, feeling devoutly thankful that we had escaped such imminent danger to the lives of the men and the fortunes of the Expedition.

Through Masailand, 1885

Helen Caddick
1875–1914

Birds and animals of all kinds are shot at, wounded, and left to die in great pain. In many parts of Africa the native fauna are fast disappearing, owing to the 'sporting' proclivities of the white man.

A member of a rich Herefordshire family, Helen Caddick decided at fourteen that what she wanted to do was travel. By the end of her life she had achieved her ambition, having gone, it seems, virtually everywhere.

Her more adventurous trips include a journey of a thousand miles up the Yangtze river into the heart of China and a three-month expedition by steamer up the Zambezi.

During her travels she built up a huge collection of souvenirs and kept detailed notes on all the people and places she visited. Her destinations ranged from Palestine to Canada, Japan, Moscow, the Philippines, New Zealand and the Andes. Her diaries throw a fresh, female perspective on the male world of empire-building, evangelism and exploitation: 'We English are an odd mixture, we send out large sums for missions, and then permit and encourage such a show in London as "Savage Africa," which must thoroughly demoralize the natives and undo years of patient work.'

Caddick's own style of travel was not exactly one of intimacy with the natives either. She often made her way surrounded by the height of luxury: 'It was delightfully comfortable to lie lazily on a long cane chair on the upper deck.' She was an escorted observer, rather than a pioneer of new territories. In one sense, this makes her writing all the more remarkable: she managed to question the mores of the day, escaping the colonial bubble she travelled in to raise unquestioned issues.

'We English are an odd mixture'

A visit to the mission took up another and a most interesting day as there were so many kinds of work going … In addition to the ordinary school instruction, carpentering, printing, gardening, etc., are taught to the boys, and needlework, laundry, dairy and housework to the girls. All this instruction makes them very useful servants for us; but I sometimes wondered how much is for ourselves and how much is honestly and solely for the good of the natives. We are certainly creating in the native a desire, and even greed, for money, and with that a wish for finery and clothing such as they had not before, and that certainly is not for their good. They look far better and are healthier with only their nsaru, or loin cloth, made of native cloth, or even of the poor calico we send out to them, than when wearing old soldiers' coats, and the shabby things they are tempted to buy at the stores – clumsy boots that deform their feet and make them walk badly, and horrid old hats stuck on their heads …

Moreover, if we are teaching them many of our own industries, they are forgetting their own. The native iron and copper work was excellent, and their axes, hoes, spears and knives were all beautifully made and ornamented ... The gourds for drinking were adorned with all kinds of quaint designs, and their ntangas, or baskets for holding their possessions, were much prettier than the ugly boxes in which we keep ours. They had decidedly an idea of making their things tasteful as well as useful, and of course had plenty of time to spend on decoration. The native weaving and the bead-work, too, is dying out as, now money is earned, all these things can be obtained more cheaply at the stores ...

Architecturally, we are not improving the look of the country. Red brick houses are certainly not pretty; while the Wankonde huts at the north end of Lake Nyasa are most picturesque and beautifully clean and neat. They have a framework of bamboo, then clay pressed into different shapes is placed in patterns between the bamboo, or sometimes the bamboo is plaited in patterns and the clay is plastered on inside. Then with a good thatch, and provided with well overhanging eaves, they have a delightfully cool house and a very pretty one.

It seems a pity we cannot develop and improve all the good in the natives without having to teach them all our own fads and customs, many of which have certainly not proved entirely satisfactory at home. We English are an odd mixture, we send out large sums for missions, and then permit and encourage such a show in London as 'Savage Africa,' which must thoroughly demoralise the natives, and undo years of patient work. It would be curious to know what the natives think of a nation that goes in crowds to see a representation of such a terribly sad incident as 'Wilson's last stand,' in which possibly some of the very same natives who took part in the slaughter are being employed to act it over again, just for the amusement of Wilson's countrymen. It surely will be counted one of the disgraces of the nineteenth century that such a show was permitted and supported ...

The great hold we have over the natives in Africa is on account of the respect, and almost awe, they have for the white man, and their belief in his superiority; but such shows must lessen their respect for us, and do incalculable harm.

A bad example

The reeds on both sides of the river were full of birds of every sort, size and colour. Kingfishers, reedmartins, and tiny birds of rose, green and scarlet colours. Of larger birds there were fish eagles, African cuckoos, black and white ibis, divers, herons, saddle-billed storks, egrets, and quantities of duck and guinea-fowl. When I remonstrated with the men for shooting at the birds, I was laughed at for not liking 'sport.' Where the 'sport' of the proceeding lay I could not discover, for there was nothing of skill about the shooting. It was just like firing into a poultry yard, and when a bird was killed, it could not be picked up, as the steamer did not stop. Often a number of wounded and helpless birds were left to die. One of the men who took part in the 'sport' belonged to the 'Society for the Prevention of Cruelty to Animals' at home, and was, moreover, proud of his active work for the society.

One day another man wounded a heron. As it flew off with its broken leg dangling, the natives shrieked with laughter and began to imitate it; upon this, the man, boiling over with righteous indignation, came up to me and said he could not stand the cruelty of the natives. 'The way they enjoyed seeing anything in pain,' etc., etc. When he had finished, I told him I thought the man who shot the bird for his own amusement was infinitely more cruel than the natives, at which he looked much astonished. I discussed the subject with the captain, who seemed to think the wounding of birds and animals of very little consequence where there were so many, and it was not until I told him I should leave the boat at the next station that he promised to have the shooting stopped . . .

Among the many practices of white men out here which tend to retard the civilising of the natives, this is a prominent one. The missionaries endeavour to impress them with a sense of the gentleness and tenderness of Christianity, and yet they see professing Christians indulge in wanton cruelty of this nature. Birds and animals of all kinds are shot at, wounded, and left to die in great pain. In many parts of Africa the native fauna are fast disappearing, owing to the 'sporting' proclivities of the white man. The tendency is to pass laws for their protection, when there is no longer any to protect.

A White Woman in Africa, 1900

George Nathaniel Curzon
1859–1925
Already the mist of ages is beginning to rise and dissolve. The lineaments are losing their beautiful vague mystery of outline.

George Nathaniel Curzon's childhood was largely defined by the neglect of his aristocratic parents, by his domineering governess ('a brutal and vindictive tyrant'), and by his first schoolmaster, who was a firm believer in corporal punishment. None of this seemed to impede his studies, however, and he excelled at Eton, then at Oxford, where he became President of the Oxford Union.

Curzon entered parliament at the age of twenty-seven and showed early promise as a statesman. In 1887 he secured permission from Lord Salisbury to take time out to travel, and for seven years explored widely in Asia. The continent captivated him, and he gained insights that proved invaluable when he later became Viceroy of India, where he brought about ground-breaking reforms, reorganizing Indian administration, establishing the North-West Frontier province and overseeing the partition of Bengal. His work was underpinned by a deep sense of duty towards the Indian people. Whilst strict with the rajas and provincial governors, he also ordered the immediate punishment of any Briton who mistreated Indian nationals, and commissioned inquiries into education, the police and the civil services.

Lord Kitchener of Khartoum was made commander-in-chief of the Indian army, at Curzon's suggestion, having disregarded warnings from friends about the soldier's stubborn and fiery temperament. The two had a massive falling-out. Curzon sent a letter to the government, stating that he would maintain his position on condition that Kitchener was removed, but this worked against him; the government was wary of Curzon's adventurous agenda in India and saw it as an opportunity to force him to resign.

On his return to England, Curzon became the Chancellor of Oxford University and was later created an earl and then a marquess. He re-entered politics to serve in wartime coalition governments, and became Foreign Secretary in Lloyd George's post-war cabinet. In this role he established a short-lived protectorate in Persia and dealt with the tumultuous upheavals in post-war Europe and the Near East.

When Tory Prime Minister Bonar Law fell ill and prepared to step down from office in 1923, Curzon hoped to succeed him. He was bitterly disappointed when – because of political wrangling, compounded by reservations of having a member of the House of Lords as Prime Minister – he was passed over for a House of Commons man, Stanley Baldwin.

The setbacks in Curzon's career might not have happened had he lived a century earlier. As it was, he died a frustrated man – doubly so, as neither his first nor his second wife had borne him the son he had hoped for, to succeed where he had failed.

In Central Asia

Travelling thus Eastwards, and arrested at each forward step by some relic of a dead civilisation, or of a glorious but forgotten past, the imagination of the European cannot but be impressed with the thought that he is mounting the stream of ages, and tracing towards its remote source the ancestry from which his race has sprung. His feet are treading in an inverse direction the long route of humanity. The train that hurries him onward into new scenes seems at the same time to carry him backward into antiquity, and with every league that he advances the *mise en scene* recedes into a dimmer distance. History lies outspread before him like the page of a Chinese manuscript, to decipher which he must begin at the bottom and work his way up to the top . . .

In these solitudes, moreover, the traveller may realise in all its sweep the mingled gloom and grandeur of Central Asian scenery. Throughout the still night the fire horse, as the natives have sometimes christened it, races onwards panting audibly, gutturally, and shaking a mane of sparks and smoke. Itself and its riders are alone. No token or sound of life greets eye or ear; no outline redeems the level sameness of the dim horizon; no shadows fall upon the staring plain. The moon shines with dreary coldness from the hollow dome, and a profound and tearful solitude seems to brood over the desert. The returning sunlight scarcely dissipates the impression of sadness, of desolate and hopeless decay, of a continent and life sunk in a mortal swoon. The traveller feels like a wanderer at night in some deserted graveyard, amid crumbling tombstones and half-obliterated mounds. A cemetery, not of hundreds of years but of thousands, not of families or tribes but of nations and empires, lies outspread before him; and ever and anon, in falling tower or shattered arch, he stumbles upon some poor unearthed skeleton of the past.

Bokhara

Bokhara is still a great city, for it numbers approximately one hundred thousand souls. Of these only one hundred and fifty are Europeans, nearly all of them Russians, Germans, or Poles. The bulk of the native population are Tajiks, the aboriginal Iranian stock, who may generally be distinguished from their Tartar brethren by the clearness and often by the brightness of their complexions, by the light colour of their hair and beards, sometimes a chestnut or reddish-brown, and by their more refined features. Tajik and Uzbeg alike are a handsome race, and a statelier urban population I never saw than in the streets and bazaars of the town. Every man grows a beard and wears an abundant white turban, consisting in the case of the orthodox of forty folds, and a long robe or *khalat* of striped cotton, or radiant silk, or parti-coloured cotton and silk. Bokhara has long set the fashion in Central Asia in the matter of dress, and is the great clothes mart of the East. Here the richness of Oriental fancy has expressed itself in the most daring but artistic combinations of colour. The brightest crimson and blue and purple and orange are juxtaposed or interlaced; and in Bokhara Joseph would have been looked upon as the recipient of no peculiar favour in the gift of a coat of many colours. Too often there is the most glaring contrast between the splendour of the exterior and the poverty that it covers. Many of the people are wretchedly poor; but living is absurdly cheap, and your pauper, undaunted by material woes, walks abroad with the dignity of a patriarch and in the garb of a prince . . .

One thing impressed itself very forcibly on my mind, namely, that Bokhara is not now a haunt of zealots, but a city of merchants. It contains a peaceful, industrious, artisan population utterly unfitted for war, and as wanting in martial instinct as in capacity. The hostility to strangers, and particularly to Christians, sometimes degenerating into the grossest fanaticism, upon which earlier travellers have enlarged, has either disappeared from closer contact with civilisation, or is prudently disguised. I attribute it rather to the former cause, and to the temperate conduct of the Russians in their dealings with the natives; because not even when I wandered about alone, and there was no motive for deception, did I observe the smallest indication of antagonism or repugnance. Many a face expressed that blank and haughty curiosity which the meanest Oriental can so easily assume; but I met with no rudeness or interference. On the contrary, the demeanour of the people was friendly, and no one when interrogated declined to answer a question. An acquaintance of the previous day would salute you as you passed by placing his hand on his breast and stroking his beard. I never quite knew what to do on these occasions. For not having a beard to stroke, I feared it might be thought undignified or contrary to etiquette to finger the empty air.

I have frequently been asked since my return – it is the question which an Englishman always seems to ask first – what the women of Bokhara were like? I am utterly unable to say. I never saw the features of one between the ages of ten and fifty. The little girls ran about, unveiled, in loose silk frocks, and wore their hair in long plaits escaping from a tiny skull-cap. Similarly the old hags were allowed to exhibit their innocuous charms, on the ground, I suppose, that they could excite no dangerous emotions. But the bulk of the female population were veiled in a manner that defied and even repelled scrutiny. For not only were the features concealed behind a heavy black horsehair veil, falling from the top of the head to the bosom, but their figures were loosely wrapped up in big blue cotton dressing-gowns, the sleeves of which are not used but are pinned together over the shoulders at the back and hang down to the ground, where from under this shapeless mass of drapery appear a pair of feet encased in big leather boots . . .

For my own part, on leaving the city I could not help rejoicing at having seen it in what may be described as the twilight epoch of its glory. Were I to go again in later years it might be to find electric light in the highways. The King of Korea has it at Seoul, a surely inferior capital; the Amir of Afghanistan has it at Kabul; then why not he of Bokhara? It might be to see window-panes in the houses, and to meet with trousered figures in the streets. It might be to eat *zakuska* in a Russian restaurant and to sleep in a Russian hotel; to be ushered by a *tchinovnik* into the palace of the Ark, and to climb for fifty *kopecks* the Minari Kalian. Who can tell whether Russian beer will not have supplanted tea, and *vodka* have supplemented opium? Civilisation may ride in the Devil's Wagon, but the devil has a habit of exacting his toll. What could be said for a Bokhara without a Kush Begi, a Divan Begi, and an Inak – without its *mullahs* and *kalendars*, its *toksabas* and its *mirzabashi*, its *skabraques* and *tchapans* and *khalats*? Already the mist of ages is beginning to rise and to dissolve. The lineaments are losing their beautiful vague mystery of outline. It is something, in the short interval between the old order and the new, to have seen Bokhara, while it may still be called the Noble, and before it has ceased to be the most interesting city in the world.

Russia in Central Asia, 1889

CHARLES GODFREY LELAND
1824–1903
*These demons have the form of a hedgehog, are of yellowish colour,
and are half a yard in length . . .*

Charles Leland was born in Philadelphia into a well-off family, yet while his upbringing was one of decorous convention, his fascination with folklore and the supernatural began to develop from early childhood. From the Irish immigrant women working in his home he learned of fairies, and from the black servants he gleaned enticing insights into voodoo. 'I was always given to loneliness in gardens and woods when I could get into them,' he recalled in his memoirs, 'and to hearing words in birds' songs and the running of falling water.'

Leland moved to England in 1870, and it became his base for eighteen years. He befriended Matty Cooper, an eminent gypsy who taught him how to speak Romany. Leland rapidly immersed himself in the gypsy world, documenting the spells, cures, charms and visions of the gypsy people, who Leland said 'have always been the humble priests of what is really the practical religion of all peasants and poor people'.

Leland was exploring a culture as unknown as many encountered by others in Africa and more 'exotic' corners of the world. However, he was considerably more generous in his judgements than many. The gypsies' practice of fortune-telling, he felt, was not deceitful, as it was usually seen by outsiders, but nor was it a real ability to see into the future: instead, it relied on an acutely tuned sense of perception.

Leland felt that, at one level, his life and work served to remind people of the 'magic' all around us: 'We are all sorcerers, and live in a wonderland of marvel and beauty if we did but know it. For the seed sprouting from the ground is as strange a truth as though we saw the hosts of heaven sweeping onward in glory, or could commune with fairies. But like children who go to sleep in the grand opera, we turn aside from the endless miracle of nature to be charmed and bewildered with the petty thaumaturgy of guitars in the dark, cigarettes, and rope-tying.'

'Snails are a type of voluptuousness'

The gypsies believe that the Earth-fairies are the foes of every kind of worm and creeping insect with the exception of the snail, which they therefore call the Pçuvus-horse. *Gry-puvusengree* would in English gypsy mean the earthy-horse. English gypsies, and the English peasantry, as well as gypsies, call snails 'cattle, because they have horns.' Snails are a type of voluptuousness, because they are hermaphrodite, and exceedingly giving to sexual indulgence, so that as many as half a dozen may be found mutually giving and taking pleasure. Hence in German *Schnecke*, a snail, is a term applied to the *pudendum muliebre*. And as anything significant of fertility, generation, and sexual enjoyment was supposed to constitute a charm or amulet against witchcraft, *i.e.*, all evil influences, which are allied to sterility, chastity, and barrenness, a snail's shell forms a powerful fetish for a true believer . . . A girl can win (illicit) love from a man by inducing him to carry a snail shell which she has had for some time about her person. To present a snail shell is to make a very direct but not very delicate declaration of love to any one. I have heard of a lady who caused an intense excitement in a village by collecting about a hundred large snails, gilding their shells, and then turning them loose in several gardens, where their discovery excited, as may be supposed, great excitement among the finders.

The hedgehog demon

Next to the Nivasi and Pçuvuse, or spirits of earth and air, and human sorcerers or witches, the being who is most dreaded as injuring cattle is the *Chagrin* or Cagrino. These demons have the form of a hedgehog, are of yellowish colour, and are half a yard in length, and a span in breadth. 'I am certain,' says WLISLOCKI, 'that this creature is none other than the equally demoniac being called *Harginn*, still believed in by the inhabitants of Northwestern India . . . The *Chagrin* specially torments horses, by sitting on their backs and making water on their bodies. The next day they appear to be weary, sad, sick, and weak, bathed in sweat, with their manes tangled. When this is seen the following ceremony is resorted to: The horse is tied to a stake which has been rubbed with garlic juice, then a red thread is laid in the form of a cross on the ground, but so far from the heels of the horse that he cannot disturb it. And while laying it down the performer sings:

> All evil stay here,
> Stay in the long thread,
> In the next brook (water).
> Give thy water,
> Jump in Chagrin!
> Therein perish quickly!

Of the widely-spread and ancient belief in the magic virtues of garlic and red wool I have elsewhere spoken. That witches and goblins or imps ride horses by night and then restore them in the morning to their stalls in a wretched condition – trembling, enfeebled, and with tangled manes – is believed all the world over, and it would probably be found that the Chagrin also gallops them.

Another charm against this being consists of taking some of the hair of the animal, a little salt, and the blood of a bat, which is all mixed with meal and cooked to a bread. With this the foot of the horse is smeared, and then the empty pipkin is put into the trunk of a high tree while these words are uttered:

> Stay so long here,
> Till it shall be full!

The blood of the bat may be derived from an Oriental belief that the bat being the most perfect of birds, because it has breasts and suckles its young, it is specially adapted to magical uses. In the Tyrol he who bears the left eye of a bat may become invisible, and in Hesse he who wears the heart of a bat bound to his arm with red thread will always win at cards. The manes of the horses which have been tangled and twisted by the Chagrin must not be cut off or disentangled unless these words are spoken:

> So long live thou, long as these hairs shall live.

It is an European belief that knots of hair made by witches must not be disentangled. The belief that such knots are made intentionally by some intelligence is very natural. I have often been surprised to find how frequently knots form themselves in the cord of my eye-glass, even when pains are taken at night to lay it down so as to be free of them. *Apropos* of which I may mention that this teasing personality of the eye-glass and cord seems to have been noted by others. I was once travelling on the Nile in company with a Persian prince, who became convinced that his eye-glass was very unlucky, and therefore threw it into the river.

The Chagrin specially torments mares which have recently foaled; therefore it is held needful, soon after the birth, to put into the water which the mother drinks glowing hot coals, which are thrice taken from the fire. With these are included pieces of iron, such as nails, knives, &c., and the following words are solemnly murmured:

> Drink, and do not be sleepy!

Many readers may here observe that charcoal and iron form a real tonic, or very practical strengthening dose for the enfeebled mare. But here, as in many cases, medicine makes a cure and the devil or the doctor gets the credit.

Gypsy Sorcery and Fortune-Telling, 1891

PETER MATTHIESSEN
1927–

I can watch elephants (and elephants alone) for hours at a time . . . There is mystery behind that masked gray visage, an ancient life force, delicate and mighty, awesome and enchanted, commanding the silence ordinarily reserved for mountain peaks, great fires, and the sea.

Peter Matthiessen – an American naturalist, journalist and author of numerous books (both fiction and non-fiction) inspired by his exploration of the remoter environments of Africa, the Americas, Asia and Australia – was born in New York, and studied at Yale and the Sorbonne. In 1953 he co-founded the *Paris Review* with Harold L. Humes; they envisaged a publication that would feature original works of fiction and poetry instead of the usual 'writing about writing'.

For three years Matthiessen worked as a commercial fisherman and captain of a charter fishing boat around Long Island. He then embarked on a number of expeditions around the globe. From his years in Africa spent pursuing his two vocations – natural historian and social observer – emerged three books: *African Silences*, *Sand Rivers* and *The Tree Where Man Was Born*. The latter draws together the sound and smell of the savannah, the tangled histories of tribal peoples and the wildlife around them, all within the context of modern African politics.

Stalking elephants – and a lioness

Of all African animals, the elephant is the most difficult for man to live with, yet its passing – if this must come – seems the most tragic of all. I can watch elephants (and elephants alone) for hours at a time, for sooner or later the elephant will do something very strange such as mow grass with its toenails or draw the tusks from the rotted carcass of another elephant and carry them off into the bush. There is mystery behind that masked gray visage, and ancient life force, delicate and mighty, awesome and enchanted, commanding the silence ordinarily reserved for mountain peaks, great fires, and the sea. I remember a remark made by a girl about her father, a businessman of narrow sensibilities who, casting about for a means of self-gratification, traveled to Africa and slew an elephant. Standing there in his new hunting togs in a vast and hostile silence, staring at the huge dead bleeding thing that moments before had borne such life, he was struck for the first time in his headlong passage through his days by his own irrelevance. 'Even *he*,' his daughter said, 'knew he'd done something stupid.'

Anxious to see the great herd from the ground, I picked up George Schaller at Seronera and drove northwest to Banagi, then westward on the Ikoma-Musoma track to the old northwest boundary of the park, where I headed across country. I had taken good bearings from the air, but elephants on the move can go a long way in an hour, and even for a vehicle with four-wheel drive, this rough bush of high grass, potholes, rocks, steep brushy streams, and swampy mud is very different from the hardpan of the plain. The low hot woods lacked rises or landmarks, and for a while it seemed that I had actually misplaced four hundred elephants.

Then six bulls loomed through the trees, lashing the air with their trunks, ears blowing, in a stiff-legged swinging stride; they forded a steep gully as the main herd, ahead of them, appeared on a wooded rise. Ranging up and down the gully, we found a place to lurch across, then took off eastward, hoping to find a point downwind of the herd where the elephants would pass. But their pace had slowed as the sun rose; we worked back to them, upwind. The elephants were destroying a low wood – this is not an exaggeration – with a terrible cracking of trees, but after a while they moved out onto open savanna. In a swampy stream they sprayed one another and rolled in the water and coated their hides with mud, filling the air with a thick sloughing sound like the wet meat sound made by predators on a kill. Even at rest the herd flowed in perpetual motion, the ears like delicate great petals, the ripple of the mud-caked flanks, the coiling trunks – a dream rhythm, a rhythm of wind and trees. 'It's a nice life,' Schaller said. 'Long, and without fear.' A young one could be killed by a lion, but only a desperate lion would venture near a herd of elephants, which are among the few creatures that reach old age in the wild.

There has been much testimony to the silence of the elephant, and all of it is true. At one point there came a cracking sound so small that had I not been alert for the stray elephants all around, I might never have seen the mighty bull that bore down on us from behind. A hundred yards away, it came through the scrub and deadwood like a cloud shadow, dwarfing the small trees of the open woodland. I raised binoculars to watch him turn when he got our scent, but the light wind had shifted and instead the bull was coming fast, looming higher and higher, filling the field of the binoculars, forehead, ears, and back agleam with wet mud dredged up from the donga. There was no time to reach the car, nothing to do but stand transfixed. A froggish voice said, 'What do you think, George?' and got no answer.

Then the bull scented us – the hot wind was shifting every moment – and the dark wings flared, filling the sky, and the air was split wide by that ultimate scream that the elephant gives in alarm or agitation, that primordial warped horn note out of oldest Africa. It altered course without missing a stride, not in flight but wary, wide-eared, passing man by. Where first aware of us, the bull had been less than one hundred feet away – I walked it off – and he was somewhat nearer where he passed. 'He was pretty close,' I said finally to Schaller. George cleared his throat. 'You don't want them any closer than that,' he said. 'Not when you're on foot.' Schaller, who has no taste for exaggeration, had a very respectful look upon his face.

Stalking the elephants, we were soon a half-mile from my Land Rover. What little wind there was continued shifting, and one old cow, getting our scent, flared her ears and lifted her trunk, holding it upraised for a long time like a question mark. There were new calves with the herd, and we went no closer. Then the cow lost the scent, and the sloughing sound resumed, a sound that this same animal has made for four hundred thousand years. Occasionally there came a brief scream of agitation, or the crack of a killed tree back in the wood, and always the *thuck* of mud and water, and a rumbling of elephantine guts, the deepest sound made by any animal on earth except the whale.

I had not been in Ndala a half-hour before Iain had us in emergency. A cow-calf herd led by an old cow known as Ophelia came up the river bed to drink at a small pool at the base of the falls. The camp lies on the ascending slope of the escarpment, at the level of the falls; just below, the river levels off, flowing gradually toward Lake Manyara, and downriver a short distance, Iain has a makeshift hide or blind. From here, he thought, he could get pictures of the herd with a complex camera device of his own invention which makes double images of the subject on the same negative; using parallax, animal measurements may be made with fair accuracy without destroying the animal itself. (The animal's shoulder height is a clue to its age, and the age structure of the population – the proportion of old animals to young – is an important indication of population health: despite the density of its elephant, Manyara at present has a healthy, 'pyramid' population, with many young animals at the base.) Though the device works, it is so unwieldy that another person must be present with a notebook to record the data, and that other person was me.

We descended the steep bank under the camp and made our way downriver to the hide. The herd was busy at the pool, but I disliked our position very much. The animals were cut off; their only escape was straight back down the river past the hide, which was skeletal and decrepit, utterly worthless. And here we were on open ground, a hundred yards downriver from the steep bank leading up to the camp . . . 'They'll never scent us,' Iain decided, setting up his apparatus, an ill-favored thing of long arms, loose parts, and prisms. But scent us they did, before he could get one picture. Ophelia, ears flared, spun around and, in dead silence, hurried her generations down the river bed in the stiff-legged elephant run that is really a walk, keeping her own impressive bulk between man and herd. We didn't move. 'I don't think she's going to charge us,' Iain whispered. But the moment the herd was safely past, Ophelia swung up onto the bank, and she had dispensed with threat display. There were no flared ears, no blaring, only an oncoming cow elephant, trunk held high, less than twenty yards away.

As I started to run, I recall cursing myself for having been there in the first place; my one chance was that the elephant would seize my friend instead of me. In hopelessness, or perhaps some instinct not to turn my back on a charging animal, I faced around again almost before I had set out, and was rewarded with one of the great sights of a lifetime. Douglas-Hamilton, unwilling to drop his apparatus, and knowing that flight was useless anyway, and doubtless cross that Ophelia had failed to act as he predicted, was making a last stand. As the elephant loomed over us, filling the coarse heat of noon with her dusty bulk, he flared his arms and waved his glittering contraption in her face, at the same time bellowing, 'Bugger off!' Taken aback, the dazzled Ophelia flared her ears and blared, but she had sidestepped, losing the initiative, and now, thrown off course, she swung away toward the river, trumpeting angrily over her shoulder.

Another day we took a picnic to the Endobash River, which descends in a series of waterfalls that churn up a white froth in its pools . . . It was a lovely late afternoon, and whirling along the lake track in the open car, exalted by wine and wind, I reveled in the buffaloes and wading birds in the bright water of the lake edge, and the great shining purple baobab that stands on the lake shore between Endobash and Ndala. But just past the Ndala crossing there were two lionesses in an acacia, and one of them lay stretched on a low limb not ten feet above the road. Oria said, 'I'll take her picture as we pass underneath,' and Iain slowed the Land Rover on the bridge while she set her camera. At Manyara the tree-climbing lions are resigned to cars, and there is no danger in driving beneath one. But this animal was much closer to the road than most, and the car was wide open: Iain had removed the roof to feel closer to his elephants, and even the windshield was folded flat upon the hood. Lions accustomed to cameras and the faces in car windows see human beings in the open as a threat; when the car passed beneath her, the lioness and I scowled nervously, and I felt my shoulders hunch around my head.

Oria said she had missed the shot, and we passed beneath again, and then again, as she shot point-blank into the animal's mouth, which was now wide open. 'Once more,' she said; both Oria and Iain seemed feverish with excitement. 'Christ,' I said, scarcely able to speak. 'You people –' But already the car had been yanked around, and seeing Iain's stubborn face, I knew that any interference short of a blunt instrument would only goad him to some ultimate stupidity that might get one of us mauled. I considered jumping out, but not for long. The lioness, extremely agitated, had risen to her feet, and a man on the ground might well invite attack. Insane as it seemed, I decided I was safer in the car, which proceeded forward.

The lioness crouched, hindquarters high, pulling her forepaws back beneath her chest, and the black tuft of her heavy tail thumped on the bark. Awaiting us, she flared her teeth, and this time I saw the muscles twitch as she hitched herself to spring: Ears back, eyes flat in an intent head sunk low upon her paws, she was shifting her bony shoulders and hind feet. Apparently Iain noticed this, for when Oria murmured, 'She won't jump,' he snapped at her, 'Don't be so bloody sure.' Nevertheless he carried on – I don't think it occurred to him to stop – and a second later we were fatally committed.

The lioness hitched her hindquarters again, snarling so loudly as the threat came close that Iain, who should have shot ahead, passing beneath her, jammed on the brakes and stalled. The front of the car stopped directly under the limb, with the cat's stiff whiskers and my whey face less than a lion's length apart; I was too paralyzed to stir. Land Rover motors spin quietly a while before they start, and while we waited for that trapped lioness to explode around our ears we listened to the scrape of claws on bark and the hiss and spitting and the heavy thump of that hard tail against the wood, and watched the twitch of the black tail tassel and the leg muscles shivering in spasms under the fly-flecked hide. The intensity, the sun, the light were terrifically exciting – I hated it, but it was terrifically exciting. I felt unbearably *aware*. I think I smelled her but I can't remember; there is only a violent memory of lion-ness in all my senses. Then Iain, gone stiff in the face, was easing the car out of there, and he backed a good long way from the taut beast before turning around and proceeding homeward through the quiet woods.

Nobody spoke. When Oria pointed out more arboreal lions, we ignored her. I felt angry and depressed – angry at having our lives risked so unreasonably, and depressed because I had permitted it to happen, as if I had lacked the courage to admit fear. At camp, I said in sour tones, 'Well, you got some fantastic pictures. I'll say that much.' And Iain, looking cross himself, said shortly, 'I'll never use them – those were for her scrapbook. I can't stand pictures of frightened animals.' Two years before a friend of Iain had given him a book of mine on travels in wild parts of South America, and now he commented that I had taken a few risks myself. But calculated risks to reach a goal were quite different from risks taken for their own sake . . .

For once, Iain failed to argue. He was silent for a while, then said abruptly that he expected to die violently, as his father had, and doubted very much that he would live to see his fortieth year. Should he maintain his present habits, this romantic prediction will doubtless be borne out. 'I'd hate to die,' he said on another occasion, 'but I'd rather risk dying than live nine-to-five.' Yet people like Iain who hurl themselves at life with such generous spirit seem to rush untouched through danger after danger, as if the embrace of death as part of life made them immortal.

Months later, when his work at Manyara had ended, Iain came with Oria to America. We discussed elephants and the fine days at Ndala, arriving eventually at the adventure with the lioness. 'Those times with the elephants weren't really dangerous,' he said; he glared at Oria when she laughed. 'Honestly. I knew what I was doing. But that business with the lion was absurd.' He shrugged, and after a pause said quietly, 'We just did it out of love of life.'

The Tree Where Man Was Born, 1972

New Worlds

HERNÁN CORTÉS
1485–1547

Considering they are so barbarous . . . it is truly remarkable to see what they have achieved . . .
Cortés, conqueror of the Aztecs

They hungered for that gold like wild pigs.
Montezuma, conquered emperor of the Aztecs

Hernán Cortés, the conquistador who defeated the Aztec emperor Montezuma to bring Mexico under Spanish rule, was born into a noble yet poor family in Extramadura, Spain. The combination of resilient fighting spirit, a hunger for gold and the religious fervour of his home environment equipped him for his later campaigns in Mexico. As a child he was distinguished by his intelligence and was sent to Salamanca to study law. A family employee described the young Cortés as 'ruthless, haughty, mischievous – a source of trouble to his parents'. This soon translated itself into an independence of character and a weakness for women.

In 1504 he set sail for Santo Domingo in the Caribbean and, after seven years spent as a farmer and notary to the town council – and recovering from bouts of syphilis – he joined Diego Velázquez on his conquest of Cuba. In the Cuban capital Santiago Cortés was both ambitious and successful, and when in 1519 Velázquez had to select someone to establish a colony on the Mexican mainland, Cortés was the obvious choice. Cortés soon gathered together an army – so successfully that Velázquez was unsettled, and sought to choose a different leader. It was too late: Cortés set out with his small but determined army of 508 soldiers, 100 sailors and sixteen horses.

When they disembarked on the coast of Mexico, Cortés burned the ships, their only means of escape. He felt it would instil a sense of determination in his men. They reached the Aztec capital Tenochtitlán (the site of present-day Mexico City), which they took by guile, aided by the tendency of the natives to accept them as gods. Cortés had also been presented with an Aztec princess, who became his 'tongue' – she spoke their language and knew how Emperor Montezuma II could be manipulated, this playing a key role in helping the Spaniards take advantage of dissent among the Aztecs. Soon Cortés had won over 6,000 Indian allies and made Montezuma his prisoner and puppet ruler.

It was the jealousy of other Spaniards that proved to be Cortés' major obstacle. On 15 June 1520 he was at the coast, dealing with a force under Panfilo Narvaez (who had been sent by Velázquez), and had left Tenochtitlán in the hands of a reckless captain. The Aztecs masterminded an uprising – the bloody 'Noche Triste' – during which Montezuma was killed and the Spaniards driven out of the city.

Cortés was not one to give up easily. He rebuilt his army and returned to Tenochtitlán the following year. Street by street the Spaniards recaptured the capital, and by the time the struggle was over the magnificent city was totally destroyed.

Cortés went on to conquer the whole Aztec empire, ruling over it between 1523 and 1526. Meanwhile, he still had to contend with jealous Spanish factions and, when his ambition drove him southwards to conquer Honduras, this opposition, abetted by his weak health, eroded his powers and caused the mission to end in failure.

On his return to Mexico, he found that his property had been seized by officials and that vicious rumours were circulating about him. In 1528 he went back to Spain to plead his case with the King. He was made Captain General and Marqués del Valle but, despite a further voyage to Mexico, never overcame suspicions about his ambitions. He died poor, frustrated and disillusioned.

The Aztecs, or course, shared a worse fate. Bernal Diaz de Castillo, one of Cortés' officers, kept a journal of the Spanish venture against the Aztecs, and quoted Cortés as saying at the outset: 'This time will bring us both honour and profit, things which are very rarely found in the same bag.' When Cortés and his men first arrived at Tenochtitlán, they were taken through a market place bigger than that of Constantinople or Seville. Montezuma himself climbed with Cortés to the summit of the great temple of Huitzilopochtli where the shrines reeked of the blood of human sacrifice. From the summit of the pyramid, Cortés gazed out over a city of more than 200,000 people. He was witnessing the most elaborate of all Native American civilizations at the height of its powers.

'The pyramids and buildings rising from the crater, all made of stone, seemed like an enchanted vision,' wrote Diaz. 'Indeed, some of our soldiers asked whether it was not all a dream. I stood looking at it, and thought that no land like it would ever be discovered in the whole world.' Two years later, Tenochtitlán was a smouldering ruin, its people decimated by a brutal siege and unfamiliar diseases. Looking back after fifty years, Diaz wrote, 'Today all that I then saw is overthrown and destroyed; nothing is left standing.'

Cortés describes the Aztec capital

This great city of Temixtitan is built on the salt lake, and no matter by what road you travel there are two leagues from the main body of the city to the mainland. There are four artificial causeways leading to it, and each is as wide as two cavalry lances. The city itself is as big as Seville or Córdoba. The main streets are very wide and very straight; some of these are on the land, but the rest and all the smaller ones are half on land, half canals where they paddle their canoes. All the streets have openings in places so that the water may pass from one canal to another. Over all these openings, and some of them are very wide, there are bridges made of long and wide beams joined together very firmly and so well made that on some of them ten horsemen may ride abreast . . .

This city has many squares where trading is done and markets are held continuously. There is also one square twice as big as that of Salamanca; with arcades all around, where more than 60,000 people come each day to buy and sell, and where every kind of merchandise produced in these lands is found; provisions as well as ornaments of gold and silver, lead, brass, copper, tin, stones, shells, bones, and feathers. They also sell lime, hewn and unhewn stone, adobe bricks, tiles, and cut and uncut woods of various kinds. There is a street where they sell game and birds of every species found in this land: chickens, partridges and quails, wild ducks, fly-catchers, widgeons, turtle-doves, pigeons, cane birds, parrots, eagles and eagle owls, falcons, sparrow-hawks and kestrels, and they sell some of the skins of these birds of prey with their feathers, heads, and claws. They sell rabbits and hares, and stags, and small gelded dogs which they breed for eating . . .

They sell honey, wax, and a syrup made from maize canes, which is as sweet and syrupy as that made from the sugar cane. They also make syrup from a plant which in the islands is called *maguey*, which is much better than most syrups, and from this plant they also make sugar and wine, which they like-wise sell. There are many sorts of spun cotton, in hanks of every colour, and it seems like the silk market at Granada, except that there is a much greater quantity. They sell as many colours for painters as may be found in Spain and all of excellent hues. They sell deerskins, with and without the hair, and some are dyed white or in various colours. They sell much earthenware, which for the most part is very good; there are both large and small pitchers, jugs, pots, tiles, and many other sorts of vessel, all of good clay and most of them glazed and painted. They sell maize both as grain and as bread and it is better both in appearance and in taste than any found in the islands or on the mainland . . .

There are, in all districts of this great city, many temples or houses for their idols . . .

Amongst these temples there is one, the principal one, whose great size and magnificence no human tongue could describe, for it is so large that within the precincts, which are surrounded by a very high wall, a town of some five hundred inhabitants could easily be built. All round inside this wall there are very elegant quarters with very large rooms and corridors where their priests live. There are as many as forty towers, all of which are so high that in the case of the largest there are fifty steps leading up to the main part of it; and the most important of these towers is higher than that of the cathedral of Seville. They are so well constructed in both their stone and woodwork that there can be none better in any place, for all the stonework inside the chapels where they keep their idols is in high relief with figures and little houses, and the woodwork is likewise of relief and painted with monsters, and other figures and designs. All these towers are burial places of chiefs, and the chapels therein are each dedicated to the idol which he venerated . . . I will say only that these people live almost like those in Spain, and in as much harmony and order as there, and considering that they are barbarous and so far from the knowledge of God and cut off from all civilized nations, it is truly remarkable to see what they have achieved in all things . . .

The most important of these idols, and the ones in whom they have most faith, I had taken from their places and thrown down the steps; and I had those chapels where they were cleaned, for they were full of the blood of sacrifices; and I had images of Our Lady and of other saints put there, which caused Mutezuma and the other natives some sorrow.

Letters from Mexico (trans A. R. Pagden, 1986)

Montezuma describes the Spaniards

[The Aztecs, hearing of the arrival of the Spanish] gave them emblems of gold, banners of quetzal plumes, and golden necklaces. And when they gave them these, the Spaniards faces grinned; they were delighted, they were overjoyed. They snatched up the gold like monkeys. They were swollen with greed; they were ravenous, they hungered for that gold like wild pigs. They seized the gold standards, they swung them from side to side, they examined them from top to bottom. They babbled in a barbarous language; everything they said was in a savage tongue . . . When the Spaniards were installed in the palace, they asked Montezuma about the city's resources and reserves . . . They questioned him closely and then demanded gold. Montezuma guided them to it. They surrounded him and crowded close with their weapons. He walked in the centre, while they formed a circle around him. When they arrived at the treasure house called Teucalco, the riches of gold and feathers were brought out to them: ornaments made of quetzal feathers, richly worked shields, disks of gold, the necklaces of the idols, gold nose plugs, gold greaves and bracelets and crowns.

The Spaniards immediately stripped the feathers from the gold shields and ensigns. They gathered all the gold into a great mound and set fire to everything else, regardless of its value. Then they melted down the gold into ingots. As for the precious green stones, they took only the best of them; the rest were snatched up by the Tlaxcaltecas. The Spaniards searched through the whole treasure house, questioning and quarreling, and seized every object they thought was beautiful.

Next they went to Montezuma's storehouse, in the place called Totocalco [Place of the Palace of the Birds], where his personal treasures were kept. The

Spaniards grinned like little beasts and patted each other with delight. When they entered the hall of treasures, it was as if they had arrived in Paradise. They searched everywhere and coveted everything; they were slaves to their own greed. All of Montezuma's possessions were brought out: fine bracelets, necklaces with large stones, ankle rings with little gold bells, the royal crowns and all the royal finery – everything that belonged to the king and was reserved to him only. They seized these treasures as if they were their own, as if this plunder were merely a stroke of good luck. And when they had taken all the gold, they heaped up everything else in the middle of the patio.

The Broken Spears: The Aztec Account of the Conquest of Mexico (trans. Lysander Kemp, 1962)

Jacques Marquette
1637–75

Michael Ako, all out of countenance, told me, that if I continued to say my breviary we should all three be killed, and the Picard begged me at least to pray apart.

A French Jesuit missionary who travelled up the Mississippi and was one of the first Europeans to document the interior of North America, Father Jacques Marquette, known as Père Marquette, was born in Laon, northern France. He became a Jesuit priest and in 1666 was sent on a mission to Quebec. He spent two years learning six native American languages, then set up a new mission at Chequamegon Bay near the western end of Lake Superior. When the Huron Indians, his allies, came under attack from the Sioux, he was forced to flee with them, moving the mission to a location between Lake Huron and Lake Michigan.

Rumours about a river to the south, known by the Indians as the Mississippi ('Big River') had aroused French curiosity – it might provide a route to the Pacific. In 1673 the governor of New France sent out the fur trader Louis Jolliet to discover the direction of flow and the mouth of the river, with Marquette as the expedition's chaplain and missionary.

They discovered the upper waters of the Mississippi, and began to travel downstream. The first Indians they encountered were the Illinois, who welcomed them with open arms – indeed, gave the travellers a peace pipe to use for the rest of the journey.

They continued down the river for thousands of miles, becoming more convinced as they did so that the river flowed not into the Pacific, but into the Gulf of Mexico, which would bring them into contact with the Spanish, who were jealously guarding their sphere of influence in the south and east, around the Caribbean. Indians began warning Marquette and Jolliet that they might receive a more hostile reception ahead and, noticing traded Spanish goods among the Indians, they decided it would be wise to turn back.

The only surviving record of the journey is a short diary by Marquette, as Jolliet's journal and map were washed overboard when his canoe overturned in the Montreal rapids.

In 1674 Marquette returned to the Illinois Indians to found another mission. He was delayed mid-journey by the harsh winter and camped with his two companions; they became the first white people to stay on the site of what was to become the city of Chicago. In the spring, Marquette reached the Illinois, but soon had to return again, having fallen ill with dysentery. On his way round the east shore of Lake Michigan towards St Ignace, he died at the mouth of the river now named after him.

An encounter with Indians

Here then we are on this renowned river, of which I have endeavored to remark attentively all the peculiarities. The Missisipi river has its source in several lakes in the country of the nations to the north; it is narrow at the mouth of the Miskousing; its current, which runs south, is slow and gentle; on the right is a considerable chain of very high mountains, and on the left fine lands; it is in many places studded with islands. On sounding, we have found ten fathoms of water. Its breadth is very unequal: it is sometimes three quarters of a league, and sometimes narrows in to three *arpents* (220 yards). We gently follow its course, which bears south and southeast till the forty-second degree. Here we perceive that the whole face is changed; there is now almost no wood or mountain, the islands are more beautiful and covered with finer trees; we see nothing but deer and moose, bustards and wingless swans, for they shed their plumes in this country. From time to time we meet monstrous fish, one of which struck so violently against our canoe, that I took it for a large tree about to knock us to pieces. Another time we perceived on the water a monster with the head of a tiger, a pointed snout like a wild-cat's, a beard and ears erect, a grayish head and neck all black. We saw no more of them. On casting our nets, we have taken sturgeon and a very extraordinary kind of fish; it resembles a trout with this difference, that it has a larger mouth, but smaller eyes and snout. Near the latter is a large bone, like a woman's busk, three fingers wide, and a cubit long; the end is circular and as wide as the hand. In leaping out of the water the weight of this often throws it back . . .

At last, on the 25th of June, we perceived footprints of men by the waterside, and a beaten path entering a beautiful prairie. We stopped to examine it, and concluding that it was a path leading to some Indian village, we resolved to go and reconnoitre; we accordingly left our two canoes in charge of our people, cautioning them strictly to beware of a surprise; then M. Jollyet and I undertook this rather hazardous discovery for two single men, who thus put themselves at the discretion of an unknown and barbarous people. We followed the little path in silence, and having advanced about two leagues, we discovered a village on the banks of the river, and two others on a hill, half a league from the former. Then, indeed, we recommended ourselves to God, with all our hearts; and having implored his help, we passed on undiscovered, and came so near that we even heard the Indians talking. We then deemed it time to announce ourselves, as we did by a cry, which we raised with all our strength, and then halted without advancing any further. At this cry the Indians rushed out of their cabins, and having probably recognised us as French, especially seeing a black gown, or at least having no reason to distrust us, seeing we were but two, and had made known our coming, they deputed four old men to come and speak with us. Two carried tobacco-pipes well-adorned, and trimmed with many kinds of feathers. They marched slowly, lifting their pipes toward the sun, as if offering them to him to smoke, but yet without uttering a single word. They were a long time coming the little way from the village to us. Having reached us at last, they stopped to consider us attentively. I now took courage, seeing these ceremonies, which are used by them only with friends, and still more on seeing them covered with stuffs, which made me judge them to be allies. I, therefore, spoke to them first, and asked them, who they were; they answered that they were Ilinois and, in token of peace, they presented their pipes to smoke. They then invited us to their village where all the tribe awaited us with impatience. These pipes for smoking are called in the country calumets, a word that is so much in use, that I shall be obliged to employ it in order to be understood, as I shall have to speak of it frequently . . .

At the door of the cabin in which we were to be received, was an old man awaiting us in a very remarkable posture; which is their usual ceremony in receiving strangers. This man was standing, perfectly naked, with his hands stretched out and raised toward the sun, as if he wished to screen himself from its rays, which nevertheless passed through his fingers to his face. When we came near him, he paid us this compliment: 'How beautiful is the sun, O Frenchman, when thou comest to visit us! All our town awaits thee, and thou shalt enter all our cabins in peace.' He then took us into his, where there was a crowd of people, who devoured us with their eyes, but kept a profound silence. We heard, however, these words occasionally addressed to us: 'Well done, brothers, to visit us!'

As soon as we had taken our places, they showed us the usual civility of the country, which is to present the calumet. You must not refuse it, unless you would pass for an enemy, or at least for being impolite. It is, however, enough to pretend to smoke. While all the old men smoked after us to honor us, some came to invite us on behalf of the great sachem of all the Ilinois to proceed to his town, where he wished to hold a council with us. We went with a good retinue, for all the people who had never seen a Frenchman among them could not tire looking at us: they threw themselves on the grass by the way-side, they ran ahead, then turned and walked back to see us again. All this was done without noise, and with marks of a great respect entertained for us.

Having arrived at the great sachem's town, we espied him at his cabin-door, between two old men, all three standing naked, with their calumet turned to the sun. He harangued us in few words, to congratulate us on our arrival, and then presented us his calumet and made us smoke; at the same time we entered his cabin, where we received all their usual greetings. Seeing all assembled and in silence, I spoke to them by four presents which I made: by the first, I said that we marched in peace to visit the nations on the river to the sea: by the second, I declared to them that God their Creator had pity on them, since, after their having been so long ignorant of him, he wished to become known to all nations; that I was sent on his behalf with this design; that it was for them to acknowledge and obey him: by the third, that the great chief of the French informed them that he spread peace everywhere, and had overcome the Iroquois. Lastly, by the fourth, we begged them to give us all the information they had of the sea, and of the nations through which we should have to pass to reach it.

When I had finished my speech, the sachem rose, and laying his hand on the head of a little slave, whom he was about to give us, spoke thus: 'I thank thee, Blackgown, and thee, Frenchman,' addressing M. Jollyet, 'for taking so much pains to come and visit us; never has the earth been so beautiful, nor the sun so bright, as to-day; never has our river been so calm, nor so free from rocks, which your canoes have removed as they passed; never has our tobacco had so fine a flavor, nor our corn appeared so beautiful as we behold it to-day. Here is my son, that I give thee, that thou mayst know my heart. I pray thee to take pity on me and all my nation. Thou knowest the Great Spirit who has made us all; thou speakest to him and hearest his word: ask him to give me life and health, and come and dwell with us, that we may know him.' Saying this, he placed the little slave near us and made us a second present, an all-mysterious calumet, which they value more than a slave; by this present he showed us his esteem for our governor, after the account we had given of him; by the third, he begged us, on behalf of his whole nation, not to proceed further, on account of the great dangers to which we exposed ourselves.

I replied, that I did not fear death, and that I esteemed no happiness greater than that of losing my life for the glory of Him who made all. But this these poor people could not understand.

The council was followed by a great feast which consisted of four courses, which we had to take with all their ways; the first course was a great wooden dish full of sagamity, that is to say, of Indian meal boiled in water and seasoned with grease. The master of ceremonies, with a spoonful of sagamity, presented it three or four times to my mouth, as we would do with a little child; he did the same to M. Jollyet. For the second course, he brought in a second dish containing three fish; he took some pains to remove the bones, and having blown upon it to cool it, put it in my mouth, as we would food to a bird; for the third course, they produced a large dog, which they had just killed, but learning that we did not eat it, it was withdrawn. Finally, the fourth course was a piece of wild ox, the fattest portions of which were put into our mouths.

After this feast we had to visit the whole village, which consists of full three hundred cabins. While we marched through the streets, an orator was constantly haranguing, to oblige all to see us without being troublesome; we were everywhere presented with belts, garters, and other articles made of the hair of the bear and wild cattle, dyed red, yellow, and gray. These are their rarities; but not being of consequence, we did not burthen ourselves with them.

We slept in the sachem's cabin, and the next day took leave of him, promising to pass back through his town in four moons. He escorted us to our canoes with nearly six hundred persons, who saw us embark, evincing in every possible way the pleasure our visit had given them. On taking leave, I personally promised that I would return the next year to stay with them, and instruct them.

A bad spirit

These Indians . . . called an assembly to deliberate what they were to do with us; the two head-chiefs of the party approaching, showed us, by signs, that the warriors wished to tomahawk us. This compelled me to go to the war chiefs with one of my men, leaving the other by our property, and throw into their midst six axes, fifteen knives, and six fathom of our black tobacco, then bowing down my head, I showed them, with an axe, that they might kill us, if they thought proper. This present appeased many individual members, who gave us some beaver to eat, putting the three first morsels in our mouth according to the custom of the country, and blowing on the meat which was too hot, before putting their bark dish before us, to let us eat as we liked; we spent the night in anxiety, because before retiring at night, they had returned us our peace-calumet. Our two boatmen were, however, resolved to sell their lives dearly, and to resist if attacked; their arms and swords were ready. As for my own part, I determined to allow myself to be killed without any resistance, as I was going to announce to them a God, who had been falsely accused, unjustly condemned, and cruelly crucified, without showing the least aversion to those who put him to death. We watched in turn in our anxiety so as not to be surprised asleep.

In the morning April 12th, one of their captains named Narrhetoba, with his face and bare body smeared with paint, asked me for our peace-calumet, filled it with tobacco of his country, made all his band smoke first, and then all the others who plotted our ruin. He then gave us to understand that we must go with them to their country, and they all turned back with us; having thus broken off their voyage, I was not sorry in this conjuncture to continue our discovery with these people.

But my greatest trouble was, that I found it difficult to say my office before these Indians many seeing me move my lips said, in a fierce tone, Ouackanché; and as we did not know a word of their language, we believed that they were angry at it. Michael Ako, all out of countenance, told me, that if I continued to say my breviary we should all three be killed, and the Picard begged me at least to pray apart, so as not to provoke them. I followed the latter's advice, but the more I concealed myself, the more I had the Indians at my heels, for when I entered the wood, they thought I was going to hide some goods under ground, so that I knew not on what side to turn to pray, for they never let me out of sight. This obliged me to beg pardon of my two canoemen, assuring them that I could not dispense with saying my office, that if we were massacred for that, I would be the innocent cause of their death, as well as of my own. By the word Ouakanché, the Indians meant that the book I was reading was a spirit; but by their gesture they nevertheless showed a kind of aversion, so that to accustom them to it, I chanted the litany of the Blessed Virgin in the canoe with my book open. They thought that the breviary was a spirit which taught me to sing for their diversion, for these people are naturally fond of singing.

Discovery and Exploration of the Mississippi Valley (ed. John Gilmany Shee, 1903)

EUSEBIO FRANCISCO KINO
c.1645–1711

All this fertility and wealth God placed in California only to be unappreciated by the natives, because they are a race who live satisfied with merely eating.

Eusebio Kino was born in Italy, and educated in mathematics and astronomy in Germany. In 1665 he joined the Society of Jesus, and sixteen years later was sent as a missionary to Mexico City.

He established his first mission, then, in 1691, set off on the first of about forty expeditions in the Pimería Alta region – which comprises modern southern Arizona as well as Sonora, Mexico. During thirty years of expeditions he produced maps that were to remain standard for a century, founded two missions near Tucson – Tumacacori and San Xavier del Bac – and helped the Pima Indians to diversify their agriculture. He also explored the sources of the Rio Grande, the Gila and the Colorado; and it was in the valley of the Colorado that he stumbled across the ruins of the impressive Indian settlement known as Casa Grande.

Kino was a strong opponent of the enslavement of Indians in the northern Mexican silver mines. The treasure he was seeking was to be found in the Indians themselves, the 'precious pearls of their souls'.

Arriving in the Californias

... we crossed the sea which in that region divides these kingdoms from California, taking as the guiding star of our voyage that star of the sea, the most devoted image of the Lady of Loreto, which led us without mishap to the desired port. There, she being set up as decently as the country and our poverty would permit, we placed the undertaking in her hands, in order that, as hers, it might continue on her account, and that she, who had been so favorable a star of the sea during our voyage, might be in the land of the Californias a beneficent sun, which, with the light of her intercession, should expel the darkness of heathendom which was blinding those who were living in the shadows of death.

As soon as this brightest of suns shone in that new hemisphere, the Prince of Darkness, in order not to lose his ancient and peaceful possession of the souls of those poor people, brought it about that they should be more blinded, through the splendor of so bright a day, so that in the night of his ill-omened darkness they might worship him through the moon, which they adored. And as he blinded their understandings, they could not comprehend the words of the light which, with resplendent rays, spoke the language of heaven for their welfare, while we, upon hearing a language which we had not known, could not in ours, which they had not heard, make known to them the high purpose, for them so advantageous, which had taken us to their lands. And although we had gone to their shores solely to seek the precious pearls of their souls, to nurture them with the heavenly dew of the Divine Word, and to give them their luster in Christ, showing them the celestial shell Mary, who conceived for their good, with the gentle dew of heaven, the perfect pearl of first luster, Christ, they thought that we came like others who at other times, sometimes not without injury to their people, had landed on their shores in search of the many and rich pearls which were produced in the countless fisheries of their coasts.

With this opinion quickened at the instigation of the Devil, well-armed and in great numbers they attacked our little guard, composed of a few Spaniards who, in the protection of most holy Mary, had a well-ordered army. The barbarians made such an assault, with such fury and so thick a shower of arrows and stones that if the Lady had not constituted an army to resist it, those poor soldiers would have perished and we with them, and our purpose would have been frustrated. But in the ardor of the sovereign influence, the strength of the soldiers was so great that the multitude of barbarians was repulsed and fled in terror from their arms.

With this glorious triumph their pride was humbled, for, although barbarians, they recognized that this must be the condition upon which they would be free from the force of our arms. Some of them came to our camp, and through intercourse with them enough was learned to enable us to tell them, in their language, the purpose of our arrival in their country. They understood it well, and as a result of the report which they gave to others, many came to see us and even to thank us for the good which we were bringing them.

The Indians

All this fertility and wealth God placed in California only to be unappreciated by the natives, because they are of a race who live satisfied with merely eating. From what we have seen and heard of them, these Californians are numerous on the shores, farther inland, and much more numerous to the northward. They live in rancherías of twenty, thirty, forty, or fifty families, more or less. They do not use houses. The shade of the trees serves them to resist the scorching heat of the sun, and the branches and leaves to protect them at night from the inclemency of the weather. In the rigor of winter they live in caves which they make in the earth; and in all these shelters they dwell many together, like brutes. So far as we have seen, the men go naked. In general they wear nothing but a band, well woven, and, in default of this, a curious little net with which they encircle the front, and some well wrought figures in mother-of-pearl which they hang round the neck, which they sometimes decorate with some little round fruits, like beads. They put the same ornament on their hands. They always carry in their hands their weapons, which are the bow, arrow, and dart, sometimes for the chase, and sometimes to defend themselves from their enemies, for some of the rancherías are hostile to others. The women are more modestly clothed, being covered from the waist to the knees with little stems of reed-grass carefully woven and pressed together. Behind, in the same way, they wear deer skins, or threads well woven. Their head-dress is a little net which they obtain from grasses, or of fiber which they obtain from the agaves. These little nets are so nicely made that the soldiers tie up their hair with them. Their necklaces, which hang almost to the waist, are figures of mother-of-pearl, and little berries, stems of reed grass, and small snails, intermingled. The bracelets are of the same material.

The occupation of the men as well as of the women is the spinning of thread and fiber, fine and coarse. Of the fine they weave very close-wrought bands and the nicely-made little nets. Of the coarse they weave nets of which they make bags or reticules in which to gather their provisions, and nets for fishing. Of grasses the men make very close-woven baskets, or hampers, of different sizes. The small ones serve as jars from which to drink water, as plates for eating, and as hats for women. The large serve for gathering small fruits and other provisions, and in which to roast their small fruits, by dint of keeping them in continual motion so as not to burn them.

By nature they are very lively and alert, qualities which they show, among other ways, by ridiculing any barbarism in their language, as they did with us when we were preaching to them. When they have been domesticated they come after preaching to correct any slip in the use of their language. If one preaches to them any mysteries contrary to their ancient errors, the sermon ended, they come to the father, call him to account for what he has said to them, and argue and discuss with him in favor of their error with considerable plausibility; but through reason they submit with all docility. By these evidences of intelligence they show that they ought not to be counted among the brutes of that kingdom. Of these there are many and various, many of which serve for the palate and for sustenance, and others only to beautify the fields and woods with their variety.

Kino's Historical Memoir of Primera Alta, 1683–1717 (1919)

ALEXANDER VON HUMBOLDT
1769–1859

The eels, stunned by the noise, defended themselves by repeated discharge of their electric batteries . . .

The travels of this German botanist and geologist in South America provided him with material for one of the most ambitious scientific studies of the natural world.

Humboldt's father, who had been an officer in Frederick the Great's army, died when he was ten and he was brought up by his Huguenot and strictly Calvinist mother. After a brief spell training to be an engineer, he joined the school of mines in Freiburg, where he spent his mornings down the mines studying their geology, his afternoons in lessons and his evenings roaming the countryside in search of plants.

Desperate to venture overseas, his plans for expeditions were continually thwarted by the political upheavals of the Napoleonic Wars, until, in 1799, he obtained permission to explore the Spanish colonies in Central and South America. Until then the colonies had only been accessible to Spanish officials and Catholic missionaries and the huge interiors of the southern New World were a scientist's paradise of uncharted territory and unknown species. Thus began a five-year expedition during which Humboldt and his companion, the French botanist Aimé Bonpland, were to cover 6,000 miles on foot, horseback and by canoe.

The expedition began in Caracas and took them down the Orinoco to the Amazon. Their provisions were soon destroyed by rain and pests, leaving the men no choice but to live off cacao beans and river water. Whatever sustenance the two scientists lacked in their diets, they seemed to make up for by feeding off their daily discoveries. Nothing dimmed their enthusiasm, and it was only on their return to civilization that they succumbed to fever.

The second stage of the expedition, after a short rest in Cuba, took them down the Andes from Colombia to Peru, following what is now the Pan American Highway but at that time was no more than rugged pathways. During the journey Humboldt studied the strong, cold ocean current of South America's west coast that became known as the Humboldt Current (now the Peru Current). He also made the connection for the first time between mountain sickness, from which they both suffered, and the thinning of oxygen due to altitude.

The two men spent a year exploring Mexico before returning home with copious amounts of new information: as well as an enormous collection of plants, they had a plethora of weather readings, and statistical data about Mexico's social and economic conditions. For the next twenty-three years Humboldt lived in Paris, then the hub of scientific thinking in Europe. He processed his findings with the help of engravers, publishers and other scientists and became an influential figure in Paris's bustling social circles; the 8,000 personal letters that have survived from this time bear testimony to his interesting mind and attractive personality.

Humboldt spent the last thirty years of his life in Berlin, devoting most of them to his ambitious study of the nature of the universe, *Kosmos*. He died at the age of ninety, his mind as sharp as ever and still busily working away on the fifth volume of his book. Darwin was probably not exaggerating when he described Humboldt as 'the greatest scientific traveller who ever lived'.

The great plains of the Orinoco

In the *Mesa de Paja*, in the ninth degree of latitude, we entered the basin of the Llanos. The sun was almost at the zenith; the earth, wherever it appeared sterile and destitute of vegetation, was at the temperature of forty eight or fifty degrees. Not a breath of air was felt at the height at which we were on our mules; yet, in the midst of this apparent calm, whirls of dust incessantly arose, driven on by those small currents of air, that glide only over the surface of the ground, and are occasioned by the difference of temperature, which the naked sand and the spots covered with herbs acquire. These *sand winds* augment the suffocating heat of the air. Every grain of quartz, hotter than the surrounding air, radiates heat in every direction; and it is difficult to observe the temperature of the atmosphere, and the variable decrement in the temperature of the different strata of the air, the horizon in some parts was clear and distinct; in other parts it appeared undulating, sinuous, and as if striped. The earth there was confounded with the sky. Through the dry fog, and strata of vapour, the trunks of palm trees were seen from afar. Stripped of their foliage, and their verdant summits, these trunks appeared like the masts of a ship discovered at the horizon.

There is something awful, but sad and gloomy, in the uniform aspect of these Steppes. Every thing seems motionless; scarcely does a small cloud, as it passes across the zenith, and announces the approach of the rainy season, sometimes cast its shadow on the savannah . . .

No sooner were our instruments unloaded, and safely placed, than our mules were set at liberty, to go, as they say here, 'and search for water in the savannah'. There are little pools around the farm, which the animals find, guided by their instinct, by the [scent?] of some scattered tufts of mauritia, and by the sensation of humid coolness, caused by little currents of air amid an atmosphere, which to us appears cool and tranquil. When the pools of water are far distant, and the people of the farm are too lazy to lead the cattle to these natural watering places, they confine them during five or six hours in a very hot stable, before they let them loose. Excess of thirst then augments their sagacity, sharpening as it were the senses and their instinct. No sooner is the stable opened, than you see the horses and mules, especially the latter, the penetration of which exceeds the intelligence of horses, rush into the savannahs. Their tail raised, their head thrown back, they run against the wind, stopping from time to time as if they were exploring space; they follow less the impression of sight than of smell; and at length announce by prolonged neighing that there is water in the direction of their course . . .

We followed our mules in search of one of those pools, whence the muddy water was drawn, that had so quenched our thirst. We were covered with dust, and tanned by the sandy wind, which burns the skin still more than the rays of the Sun. We longed impatiently to take a bath, but we found only a great reservoir of feculent water, surrounded with palm-trees. The water was turbid, though to our astonishment, a little cooler than the air. Accustomed during our long journey to bathe whenever we had an opportunity, often several times in the same day, we hastened to plunge into the pool. We had scarcely begun to enjoy the coolness of the bath, when a noise, which we had heard on the opposite bank, made us leave the water precipitately. It was an alligator plunging into the mud. It would have been imprudent to pass the night in this marshy spot.

We were only at the distance of a quarter of a league from the farm, yet we continued walking more than an hour without reaching it. We perceived too late, that we had taken a false direction. Having left it at the decline of day, before the stars were visible, we had gone forward in the plain as by chance. We were, as usual, provided with a compass, and it was even easy for us to steer our course from the position of Conopus and the Southern Cross; but all these means became useless, because we were uncertain whether, on leaving the farm, we had gone toward the East or the South. We attempted to return to the spot where we had bathed, and we again walked three-quarters of an hour, without finding the pool. We sometimes thought we saw fire at the horizon; but it was the stars that were rising, and of which the image was enlarged by the vapours. After having wandered a long time in the savannah, we resolved to seat ourselves beneath the trunk of a palm-tree, in a spot perfectly dry, surrounded by short grass; for the fear of water serpents is always greater than that of jaguars in Europeans recently disembarked. We could not flatter ourselves that our guides, of whom we knew the insuperable indolence, would come in search of us in the savannah before they had prepared their food, and finished their repast.

In proportion to the uncertainty of our situation, we were agreeable affected by hearing from afar the sound of a horse advancing toward us. The rider was an Indian armed with a lance, who had just made the *rodeo* or round, in order to collect the cattle within a determinate space of ground. The sight of two white men, who said they had lost their way, led him at first to suspect some trick. We found it difficult to inspire him with confidence; he at last consented to guide us to the farm of the *Cayman*, but without slackening the gentle trot of his horse. Our guides assured us, that 'they had already begun to be uneasy about us:' and to justify this inquietitude, they gave a long enumeration of persons, who, having lost themselves in the Llanos, had been found nearly exhausted. It may be supposed, that the danger is imminent only to those who lose themselves far from any habitation; or who, having been stripped by robbers, which has happened of late years, have been fastened by the body and hands to the trunk of a palm tree.

Fishing for electric eels

Impatient of waiting, and having obtained very uncertain results from an electric eel that had been brought to us alive, but much enfeebled, we repaired to the Cano de Bera, to make our experiments in the open air, on the border of the water itself. We set off on the 19th of March, at a very early hour, for the village of *Rastro de Abaco*; whence we were conducted by the Indians to a stream, which, in the time of drought, forms a basin of muddy water, surrounded by fine trees, the dusia, the amyris, and the mimosa with fragrant flowers. To catch the gymnoti with nets is very difficult, on account of the extreme agility of the fish, which bury themselves in the mud like serpents. We would not employ the barbasco, that is to say the roots of the pisidea erithyrna, jacquinia armillaris, and some species of phyllanthus, which, thrown into the pool, intoxicate or benumb these animals. These means would have enfeebled the gymnoti; the Indians therefore told us, that they would 'fish with horses', *embarbascarcon cavallo*. We found it difficult to form an idea of this extraordinary manner of fishing; but we soon saw our guides return from the savannah, which they had been scouring for wild horses and mules. They brought about thirty with them, which they forced to enter the pool.

The extraordinary noise caused by the horses' hoofs make the fish issue from the mud, and excites them to combat. These yellowish and livid eels, resembling large aquatic serpents, swim on the surface of the water, and crowd under the bellies of the horses and mules. A contest between animals of so different an organisation furnishes a very striking spectacle. The Indians, provided with harpoons and long slender reeds, surround the pool closely; and some climb upon the trees, the branches of which extend horizontally over the surface of the water. By their wild cries, and the length of their reeds, they prevent the horses from running away, and reaching the bank of the pool. The eels, stunned by the noise, defend themselves by the repeated discharge of their electric batteries. During a long time they seem to prove victorious. Several horses sink beneath the violence of the invisible strokes, which they receive from all sides in organs the most essential to life; and stunned by the force and frequency of the shocks, disappear under the water; but a small number succeed in eluding the active vigilance of the fishermen. These regain the shore, stumbling at every step, and stretch themselves on the sand, exhausted with fatigue, and their limbs benumbed by the electric shocks of the gymnouti. In less than five minutes two horses were drowned. The eel, being five feet long, and pressing itself against the belly of the horses, makes a discharge along the whole extent of its electric organ. It attacks at once the heart, the intestines, and the plexus coeliacus of the abdominal nerves. It is natural, that the effect felt by the horses should be more powerful than that produced upon man by the touch of the same fish at only one of his extremities. The horses are probably not killed but stunned. They are drowned from the impossibility of rising amid the prolonged struggle between the other horses and the eels.

We had little doubt, that the fishing would terminate by killing successively all the animals engaged; but by degrees the impetuosity of this unequal combat diminished, and the wearied gymnoti dispersed. They require a long rest, and abundant nourishment, to repair what they have lost of galvanic force. The mules and horses appear less frightened; their manes are no longer bristled, and their own eyes express less dread. The gymnoti approach timidly the edge of the marsh, where they are taken by means of small harpoons fastened to long cords. When the cords are very dry, the Indians feel no shock in raising the fish into the air. In a few minutes we had five large eels, the greater part of which were but slightly wounded. Some were taken by the same means toward evening.

Personal Narrative of Travels to the Equinoctial Regions of the New Continent during the years 1799–1804, 1825

MERIWETHER LEWIS and WILLIAM CLARK
1774–1809/1770–1838

I walked on shore most of the day with some hunters . . . and Killed 6 Elk 2
buffalo 2 Mule deer and a bear . . . The bear was very near catching Drewyer;
it also pursued Charbono . . .

With the 'Louisiana Purchase' of 1803, the United States acquired a vast new territory west of the Mississippi. This new territory needed exploring. President Thomas Jefferson appointed Meriwether Lewis, an ex-army lieutenant, to lead an expedition through it to the Pacific, via the Missouri and the Rocky Mountains. Jefferson brought Lewis to Washington as his private secretary and trained him for the task. When the time for departure approached, Lewis chose his close friend William Clark to be his co-leader.

The two men had strikingly different temperaments that proved to be an effective combination. Lewis was solitary and subdued and, as a naturalist, was particularly interested in the flora and fauna they encountered en route. Clark was more gregarious and open, and more skilled in the practical aspects of the expedition, such as managing the boats.

The expedition set out in May 1804, with about forty men, and spent the first winter among the Mandan, a Native American agricultural people who lived in fortified villages. In the spring they continued the arduous trek up to the headwaters of the Missouri, guided by Sacagawea, a woman from the Shoshone people whose baby was born later on the journey. They continued over the eastern slopes of the Rockies and finally reached the Pacific in November 1805. The following March they set off for the return trip and arrived back six months later. They had covered 8,000 miles, making detailed maps, navigating uncharted rivers, collecting hundreds of specimens and coming into close – usually peaceful – contact with innumerable Native Americans and French, Scottish and other trappers, who often guided them on their way.

On their return, Clark was appointed Indian Agent for the Louisiana Territory, then governor of Missouri Territory and finally Superintendent of Indian Affairs for native peoples of the Missouri and Upper Mississippi. Lewis was made Governor of Louisiana, but was shot in mysterious circumstances – suicide or murder – on his way to Washington, after being accused of mismanaging public funds.

Monday June 3rd 1805: This morning early we passed over and formed a camp on the point formed by the junction of the two large rivers, here in the the day I continued my observations . . . An interesting question was now to be determined; which of these rivers was the Missouri, or that river which the Minnetares call *Amahte Arzzha* or Missouri, and which they had described to us as approaching very near to the Columbia river. To mistake the stream at this period of the season . . . and to ascend such stream to the rocky Mountain . . . and then be obliged to return and take the other stream would not only loose us the whole of this season but would probably so dishearten the party that it might defeat the expedition altogether . . .

Between the time of my A. M. and meridian [observations] Capt. C. & myself stroled out to the top of the hights in the fork of these rivers from whence we had an extensive and most inchanting view; the country in every derection around us was one vast plain in which innumerable herds of Buffalow were seen attended by their shepperds the wolves; the solatary antelope which now had their young were distributed over it's face; some herds of Elk were also seen; the verdure perfectly cloathed the ground, the weather was pleasant and fair.

Sunday August 11th 1805: The track which we had pursued last evening soon disappeared. I therefore resolved to proceed to the narrow pass on the creek about 10 miles West in hopes that I should again find the Indian road at the place, accordingly I proceeded through the level plain directly to the pass. I now sent Drewyer to keep near the creek to my right and Shields to my left, with orders to surch for the road which if they found they were to notify me by placing a hat in the muzzle of their gun. I kept McNeal with me; after having marched in this order for about five miles I discovered an Indian on horse back about two miles distant coming down the plain towards us. With my glass I discovered from his dress that he was of a different nation from any that we had yet seen, and was satisfyed of his being a Sosone; his arms were a bow and quiver of arrows, and was mounted on an eligant horse without a saddle, and a small string which was attatched to the under jaw of the horse which answered as a bridle.

I was overjoyed at the sight of this stranger and had no doubt of obtaining a friendly introduction to his nation provided I could get near enough to him to convince him of our being whitemen. I therefore proceeded towards him at my usual pace. When I had arrived within about a mile he mad[e] a halt which I did also and unloosing my blanket from my pack, I mad[e] him the signal of friendship known to the Indians of the Rocky mountains and those of the Missouri, which is by holding the mantle or robe in your hands at two corners and then th[r]owing [it] up in the air higher than the head bringing it to the earth as if in the act of spreading it, thus repeating three times. This signal of the robe has arrisen from a custom among all those nations of spreading a robe or skin for ther gests to set on when they are visited. This signal had not the desired effect, he still kept his position and seemed to view Drewyer an[d] Shields who were now comiming in sight on either hand with an air of suspicion, I wo[u]ld willingly have made them halt but they were too far distant to hear me and I feared to make any signal to them least it should increase the suspicion in the mind of the Indian of our having some unfriendly design upon him. I therefore haistened to take out of my sack some b[e]ads a looking glas and a few trinkets which I had brought with me for this purpose and leaving my gun and pouch with McNeal advanced unarmed towards him. He remained in the same stedfast poisture untill I arrived in about 200 paces of him when he turn[ed] his ho[r]se about and began to move off slowly from me; I now called to him in as loud a voice as I could command repeating the word *tab-ba-bone*, which in their language signifyes *white-man*. But lo[o]king over his sholder he still kept his eye on Drewyer and Sheilds who wer still advancing neither of them haveing segacity enough to recollect the impropriety of advancing when they saw me thus in parley with the Indian.

I now made a signal to these men to halt, Drewyer obeyed but Shields who afterwards told me that he did not obse[r]ve the signal still kept on. The Indian halted again and turned his ho[r]se about as if to wait for me, and I believe he would have remained untill I came up with him had it not been for Shields who still pressed forward. Whe[n] I arrived within about 150 paces I again repepeated the word tab-ba-bone and held up the trinkits in my hands and striped up my shirt sleve to give him an opportunity of seeing the colour of my skin and advanced leasure[ly] towards him but he did not remain untill I got nearer than about 100 paces when he suddonly turned his ho[r]se about, gave him the whip leaped the creek and disappeared in the willow brush in an instant and with him vanished all my hopes of obtaining horses for the preasent. I now felt quite as much mortification and disappointment as I had pleasure and expectation at the first sight of this indian. I fe[l]t soarly chargrined at the conduct of the men particularly Sheilds to whom I principally attributed this failure in obtaining an introduction to the natives.

We now set out on the track of the horse hoping by that means to be lead to an indian camp, the trail of inhabitants of which should they abscond we should probably be enabled to pursue to the body of the nation to which they would most probably fly for safety. This rout led us across a large Island framed by nearly an equal division of the creek in this bottom; after passing to the open ground on the N. side of the creek we observed that the track made out toward the high hills about 3 M. distant in that direction. I thought it probable that their camp might probably be among those hills & that they would reconnoiter us from the tops of them, and that if we advanced haistily towards them that they would become allarmed and probably run off; I therefore halted in an elivated situation near the creek had a fire kindled of willow brush cooked and took breakfast. During this leasure I prepared a small assortment of trinkits consisting of some mockkerson awls a few strans of several kinds of b[e]ads some paint a looking glass &c which I attatched to the end of a pole and planted it near our fire in order that should the Indians return in surch of us the[y] might from this token discover that we were friendly and white persons. Before we had finis[h]ed our meal a heavy shower of rain came on with some hail wich continued abo[u]t 20 minutes and wet us to the skin, after this shower we pursued the track of the horse but as the rain had raised the grass which he had trodden down it was with difficulty that we could follow it. We pursued it however about 4 miles it turning up the valley to the left under the foot of the hills. We pas[sed] several places where the Indians appeared to have been diging roots today and saw the fresh tracks of 8 or ten horses but they had been wandering about in such a confused manner that we not only lost the track of the hose which we had been pursuing but could make nothing of them. In the head of this valley we passed a large bog covered with tall grass and moss in which were a great number of springs of cold pure water, we now turned a little to the left along the foot of the high hills and arrived at a small branch on which we encamped for the night, after meeting with the Indian today I fixed a small flag of the U'.S. to a pole which I made McNeal carry, and planted in the ground where we halted or encamped.

Tuesday August 13th 1805: At the distance of five miles the road after leading us down a long decending valley for 2 Ms brought us to a large cheek about 10 yds. wide; this we passed and on rising the hill beyond it had a view of a handsome little valley to our left of about a mile in width through which from the appearance of the timber I conjectured that a river passed. We had proceeded about four miles through a wavy plain parallel to the valley or river bottom when at the distance of about a mile we saw two women, a man and some dogs on an eminence immediately before us. They appeared to v[i]ew us with attention and two of them after a few minutes set down as if to wait our arrival. We continued our usual pace towards them. When we had arrived within half a mile of them I directed the party to halt and leaving my pack and rifle I took the flag which I unfurled and a[d]vanced singly towards them. The women soon disappeared behind the hill, the man continued untill I arrived within a hundred yards of him and then likewise absconded, tho' I frequently repeated the word *tab-ba-bone* sufficiently loud for him to have heard it.

I now haistened to the top of the hill where they had stood but could see nothing of them. The dogs were less shye than their masters. They came about me pretty close. I therefore thought of tying a handkerchief about one of their necks with some beads and other trinkets and then let them loose to surch their fugitive owners thinking by this means to convince them of our pacific disposition towards them but the dogs would not suffer me to take hold of them; they also soon disappeared. I now made a signal for the men to come on, they joined me and we pursued the the back track of these Indians which lead us along the same road which we had been traveling. The road was dusty and appeared to have been much traveled lately both by men and horses.

We had not continued our rout more than a mile when we were so fortunate as to meet with three female savages. The short and steep ravines which we passed concealed us from each other untill we arrived within 30 paces. A young woman immediately took to flight, an Elderly woman and a girl of about 12 years old remained. I instantly laid by my gun and advanced towards them. They appeared much allarmed but saw that we were to near for them to escape by flight. They therefore seated themselves on the ground, holding down their heads as if reconciled to die which the[y] expected no doubt would be their fate; I took the elderly woman by the hand and raised her up repeated the word *tab-ba-bone* and strip[ped] up my shirt sleve to s[h]ew her my skin; to prove to her the truth of the ascertion that I was a white man for my face and ha[n]ds which have been constantly exposed to the sun were quite as dark as their own. They appeared instantly reconciled, and the men coming up I gave these women some beads a few mockerson awls some pewter looking-glasses and a little paint.

I directed Drewyer to request the old woman to recall the young woman who had run off to some distance by this time fearing she might allarm the camp before we approached and might so exasperate the natives that they would perhaps attack us without enquiring who we were. The old woman did as she was requested and the fugitive soon returned almost out of breath. I bestoed an equ[i]volent portion of trinket on her with the others. I now painted their tawny cheeks with some vermillion which with this nation is emblematic of peace. After they had become composed I enformed them by signs that I wished them to conduct us to their camp that we wer anxious to become acquainted with the chiefs and warriors of their nation. They readily obeyed and we set out, still pursuing the road down the river. We had marched about 2 miles when we met a party of about 60 warriors mounted on excellent horses who came in nearly full speed, when they arrived I advanced towards them with the flag leaving my gun with the party about 50 paces behi[n]d me. The chief and two others who were a little in advance of the main body spoke to the women, and they informed them who we were and exultingly shewed the presents which had been given them. These men then advanced and embraced me very affectionately in their way which is by puting their left arm over you[r] wright sholder clasping your back, while they apply their left cheek to yours and frequently vociforate the word *áh-hí-e, áh-hí-e* that is, I am much pleased, I am much rejoiced. Bothe parties now advanced and we wer all carressed and besmeared with their grease and paint till I was heartily tired of the national hug. I now had the pipe lit and gave them smoke; they seated themselves in a circle around us and pulled of[f] their mockersons before they would receive or smoke the pipe. This is a custom among them as I afterwards learned indicative of a sacred obligation of sincerity in their profession of friendship given by the act of receiving and smoking the pipe of a stranger, or which is as much as to say that they wish they may always go bearfoot if they are not sincere; a pretty heavy penalty if they are to march through the plains of their country.

After smoking a few pipes with them I distributed some trifles among them, with which they seemed much pleased particularly with the blue beads and vermillion. I now informed the chief that the object of our visit was a friendly one, that after we should reach his camp I would undertake to explain to him fully those objects, who we wer, from whence we had come and w[h]ither we were going; that in the mean time I did not care how soon we were in motion, as the sun was very warm and no water at hand, they now put on their mockersons, and the principal chief Ca-me-âh-wait made a short speach to the warriors. I gave him the flag which I informed him was an emblem of peace among whitemen and now that it had been received by him it was to be respected as the bond of union between us.

The Journals of Lewis and Clark (1954 edn)

GEORGE CATLIN
1796–1872

But then the 'savage cruelty of scalping'! – savage of course, because savages do it;
but where is the cruelty of scalping? . . . he is dead; it don't hurt him.

George Catlin, an American painter and writer who became one of the first champions of the Native American cause, was born in Wilkes-Barre, Pennsylvania, and from an early age was fascinated by Native Americans – his mother had once been captured by them. He trained as a lawyer, but in 1823 left his practice to devote himself to art. An Indian delegation that travelled through Pennsylvania the following year so captured his imagination that he decided that Indians would be the primary subject of his paintings. Catlin moved to St Louis in 1830 with a letter of introduction to William Clark; the famous pioneer knew how to help Catlin prepare himself for his exploration of the Indian territories.

For the next six years he spent winters earning money from his portrait-painting to fund summers immersed in the Indian way of life. He reached as far west as Utah's Great Salt Lake and as far south as Florida, tirelessly painting and sketching. He was all too aware of the fragility of the pattern of life he was witnessing.

'I have seen him shrinking from civilized approach, which came with all its vices, like the dead of night upon him,' he wrote. 'I have seen him gaze and then retreat like the fright-ened deer . . . seen him shrinking from the soil and the haunts of his boyhood, bursting the strongest ties which bound him to the earth and its pleasures. I have seen the grand and irresistible march of civilization. I have seen this splendid juggernaut rolling on and beheld its sweeping desolation, and held converse with the happy thousands, living as yet beyond its influence, who have not been crushed, nor yet have dreamed of its approach.'

In due course, Catlin travelled across America and Europe to exhibit his paintings of buffalo hunts and rituals, of chiefs and everyday village life – all these helping raise awareness of the Native Americans' plight. Later in life, he spent time among native peoples further south, in the Amazon.

Catlin's compassion might appeal to our modern tastes, but his image of the Red Indian slots too easily into a Noble Savage fantasy, an idealized people. He is less sympathetic to others: 'One of the distinguishing features of the American Indian, that stamps his character as mentally superior to that of the African and some other races, is his uncompromising tenacity for unbounded freedom.'

An Indian woman's lot

The first startling thing you will meet on entering will be half-a-dozen saucy dogs, barking, and bristling, and showing their teeth, and often times as many screaming children, frightened at your savage and strange appearance.

These hushed, you can take a look at other things, and you see shields, and quivers, and lances, and saddles, and medicine bags, and pouches, and spears, and cradles, and buffalo masques (which each man keeps for dancing the buffalo dance), and a great variety of other picturesque things hanging around, suspended from the poles of the tent, to which they are fastened by thongs; the whole presenting, with the picturesque group around the fire, one of the most curious scenes imaginable.

In front of these wigwams the women are seen busily at work, dressing robes and drying meat. The skin-dressing of the Indians, both of the buffalo and deer-skins, is generally very beautiful and soft. Their mode of doing this is curious: they stretch the skin, either on a frame or on the ground, and after it has remained some three or four days with the brains of the buffalo or elk spread over the fleshy side, they grain it with a sort of adze or chisel, made of a piece of buffalo bone . . .

The Indian woman's life is, to be sure, a slavish one; and equally so are the lives of most women equally poor in all civilized countries. Look into their humble dwellings in all cities and towns, or in the country, in civilized communities, and see the industry and the slavish labour of poor woman! She works all the days of her life, brings water, makes fires, and tends to her little children, like the poor Indian woman; and *she may* be *a slave* to an idle husband, who is spending his time and his money, as well as her own earnings, in a tap-room.

The civilized world is full of such slavery as this; but amongst the American Indians such a system does not and cannot exist; every man is a hunter and a soldier; he must supply his family with food, and help to defend his country.

The education of woman in those countries teaches her that the labours are thus to be divided between herself and her husband; and for the means of subsistence and protection, for which she depends upon his labours, she voluntarily *assumes* the hard work about the encampment, considering their labours about equally divided.

One of the distinguishing natural traits of the American Indian, that stamps his character as mentally superior to that of the African and some other races, is his uncompromising tenacity for unbounded freedom. All efforts made (and there have been many) to enslave these people, have resulted in failures; and such an abhorrence have they of the system, that they cannot be induced to labour for each other or for white men for any remuneration that can be offered, lest the disgraceful epithet 'slave' should be applied to them by their tribe.

The practice of scalping

Amongst the Indian tribes every man is a military man, a warrior, a brave, or a chief. All are armed and ready to go to war if necessary. A *warrior* is one of those who has taken one or more scalps; a *brave* is one who goes to war as a soldier, but as yet has taken no scalps, has killed no enemy . . .

But then the '*savage cruelty of scalping!*' – savage, of course, because savages do it; but where is the *cruelty* of scalping? A piece of the skin of a man's head is cut off after he is dead; it don't hurt him; the *cruelty* would be in *killing*; and in the Christian world we kill hundreds of our fellow beings in battle where the poor Indians kill one! Cutting off a small piece of the skin of a dead man's head is rather a *disgusting* thing; but let us look. What better can the Indian take? He must keep some record. These people have no reporters to follow them into battles, and chronicle their victories to the world; their customs sanction the mode, and the chiefs demand it.

If civilized warriors should treat their fallen victims thus, it would be far worse. There would be no motive or apology for it. It would be almost as bad as taking their watch, or the gold from their pockets!

But the Indians scalp the living? Yes, that *sometimes happens*, but very rarely. The scalp being only the skin with the hair, a man *might* be scalped without injuring the bone, and, of course, without destroying life; and in the hurry and confusion of battle, the wounded and fallen, supposed to be dead, have sometimes been scalped, as the Indians were rushing over them, and have afterwards risen from the field of battle and recovered. I have seen several such. These scalps, if the Indian should ever be made aware of the fact, would not be carried; but would be buried, as things which warriors would not have a right to claim, and which their superstitious fears would induce them to get rid of.

The scalp, to be a genuine one, must be *from an enemy's head*, and *that enemy dead*, and killed by the hand of him who carries and counts the scalp. An Indian may have sufficient provocation to justify him, under the customs of his country, in slaying a man in his own tribe; but he would disgrace himself in such case by taking the scalp.

Scalps are the Indian's *badges* or *medals*, which he must procure by his own hand; he can neither buy nor sell them without disgracing himself; and when he dies, they are buried in his grave with him; his sons can't inherit them; if they want scalps, they must procure them in the same way as their father got his.

Life among the Indians, 1875

George Grey
1812–98

*I sat in the fading light, looking at the beautiful scenery . . . I wondered that
so fair a land should only be the abode of savage men.*

A colonial administrator in Australia, New Zealand and South Africa who was a pivotal figure in resolving conflicts between settlers and native populations, George Grey began his military career serving for six years in Ireland. From 1837–39 he completed two expeditions in Western Australia, both of which ended in a shambles. The first, which aimed to reach the Swan River settlement (present-day Perth) from Hanover Bay, was aborted in April 1837, two months after Grey was speared by Aborigines. During the second expedition, Grey's whaleboats were wrecked, forcing the expedition to walk its way out to safety.

In 1841 Grey was appointed Governor of South Australia. In this post he helped restore the colony's economy by encouraging and supporting farming and by limiting government spending. He was notable for his competence in handling conflict between the settlers and indigenous peoples.

In 1845 he was made Governor of New Zealand, largely with the aim of helping resolve clashes between the Maoris and British over land rights. Grey employed an effective dual policy: decisive military action against the Maoris, followed up by a diplomatic assault, which meant the forging of friendly relations with the chiefs. During this time he developed a fascination for Maori culture and wrote a comprehensive study of their history and mythology, at the same time as promoting their conversion to a Western way of life.

This was followed by a seven-year period as Governor of the Cape Colony in South Africa, where again he was successful at resolving disputes, this time between the Kaffirs and the European settlers. Grey was an independent thinker and his attempts to create federate states from the British and Boer settlements angered the British government, who soon put a stop to them. From South Africa, Grey returned to New Zealand, and between 1877 and 1879 was Premier. It was not until the age of eighty-two that Grey retired from the legislature and returned to England.

'This uncouth and savage figure'

Finding that it would be useless to lose more time in searching for a route through this country, I proceeded to rejoin the party once more; but whilst returning to them, my attention was drawn to the numerous remains of native fires and encampments which we met with, till at last, on looking over some bushes, at the sandstone rocks which were above us, I suddenly saw from one of them a most extraordinary large figure peering down upon me. Upon examination, this proved to be a drawing at the entrance to a cave, which, on entering, I found to contain, besides, many remarkable paintings.

The cave appeared to be a natural hollow in the sandstone rocks; its floor was elevated about five feet from the ground, and numerous flat broken pieces of the same rock, which were scattered about, looked at a distance like steps leading up to the cave, which was thirty-five feet wide at the entrance, and sixteen feet deep; but beyond this, several small branches ran further back. Its height in front was rather more than eight feet, the roof being formed by a solid slab of sandstone, about nine feet thick, and which rapidly inclined towards the back of the cave, which was there not more than five feet high.

On this sloping roof, the principal figure which I have just alluded to, was drawn; in order to produce the greater effect, the rock about it was painted black, and the figure itself coloured with the most vivid red and white. It thus appeared to stand out from the rock; and I was certainly rather surprised at the moment that I first saw this gigantic head and upper part of a body bending over and staring grimly down at me.

It would be impossible to convey in words an adequate idea of this uncouth and savage figure . . .

The dimensions of the figure were:

	ft	in.
Length of head and face	2	0
Width of face	0	17
Length from bottom of face to navel	2	6

Its head was encircled by bright red rays, something like the rays which one sees proceeding from the sun, when depicted on the sign-board of a public house; inside of this came a broad stripe of very brilliant red, which was coped by lines of white, but both inside and outside of this red space, were narrow stripes of a still deeper red, intended probably to mark its boundaries; the face was painted vividly white, and the eyes black, being however surrounded by red and yellow lines; the body, hands, and arms were outlined in red, – the body being curiously painted with red stripes and bars. . . .

There was another rather humorous sketch, which represented a native in the act of carrying a kangaroo; the height of the man being three feet. The number of drawings in the cave could not altogether have been less than from fifty to sixty, but the majority of them consisted of men, kangaroos, &c.; the figures being carelessly and badly executed, and having evidently a very different origin to those which I have first described. Another very striking piece of art was exhibited in the little gloomy cavities situated at the back of the main cavern. In these instances some rock at the sides of the cavity had been selected, and the stamp of a hand and arm by some means transferred to it; this outline of the hand and arm was then painted black, and the rock about it white, so that on entering that part of the cave, it appeared as if a human hand and arm were projecting through a crevice admitting light . . .

After proceeding some distance, we found a cave larger than the one seen this morning; of its actual size, however, I have no idea, for being pressed for time I did not attempt to explore it, having merely ascertained that it contained no paintings. I was moving on, when we observed the profile of a human face and head cut out in a sandstone rock which fronted the cave; this rock was so hard, that to have removed such a large portion of it with no better tool than a knife and hatchet made of stone, such as the Australian natives generally possess, would have been a work of very great labour. The head was two feet in length, and sixteen inches in breadth in the broadest part; the depth of the profile increased gradually from the edges where it was nothing, to the centre where it was an inch and a-half; the ear was rather badly placed, but otherwise the whole of the work was good, and far superior to what a savage race could be supposed capable of executing . . .

We halted for the night in one of these lovely valleys; a clear stream bubbled along within about fifty yards of us, and about a mile beyond, two darkly wooded basaltic hills raised their heads, and between these and the stream, our ponies were feeding in grass higher than themselves. I sat in the fading light, looking at the beautiful scenery around me, which now for the first time gladdened the eyes of Europeans; and I wondered that so fair a land should only be the abode of savage men; and then I thought of the curious paintings we had this day seen, – of the timid character of the natives, – of their anomalous position in so fertile a country, – and wondered how long these things were to be. With so wide a field of conjecture before me, thought naturally thronged on thought, and the night was far advanced ere I laid down to seek repose from the fatigues of the day.

Journal of Two Expeditions of Discovery in North-West and Western Australia during the years 1837, 38, and 39, 1841

EDWARD JOHN EYRE
1815–1901
Finding that I did not attempt to injure him, the native stood his ground,
though tremblingly . . .

Edward John Eyre, the first European to cross Australia's arid Nullarbor Plain, was born in England and at the age of eighteen emigrated to Australia where he became a sheep farmer. Among the labourers who were assigned to him was James Hammett, one of the Tolpuddle Martyrs, a group of six farm workers who were sentenced to seven years' service in an Australian penal colony for mobilizing a trade union in their Dorset village of Tolpuddle. During his early years in Australia, Eyre made the first crossing from Sydney to Adelaide, as well as other treks inland from Adelaide and west to Streaky Bay. In 1840 he came across Australia's largest salt lake, Lake Eyre, which was renamed in his memory.

Eyre set out on what was to be his major expedition on 25 February 1841. Accompanied by three Aborigines and a European overseer called John Baxter, he left Fowler's Bay to pioneer an overland cattle route westwards from South Australia, which would involve crossing the Nullarbor Plain. A few months later, two of the Aborigines killed Baxter and ran off with the bulk of the group's provisions. Eyre and the remaining Aborigine, Wylie, continued the journey alone, skirting the Great Australian Bight and surmounting challenges along the way – at one point, rather incongruously, with the help of French whalers. They arrived at their intended destination, Albany, that July.

Eyre eventually held governorships in New Zealand, St Vincent in the West Indies and, in 1861, in Jamaica. While in this last post, however, he found himself recalled to London and suspended from his job following his ruthless response to a black uprising – he had sanctioned the execution of over 400 people. There were demands that he should be tried for murder. However, he was cleared and he died peacefully at the age of eighty-six.

'These barren miserable plains'

In the midst of these barren miserable plains I met with four natives, as impoverished and wretched looking as the country they inhabited. As soon as they saw us they took to their heels, apparently in great alarm, but as I was anxious to find out from them if there was any water near, I galloped after two of them, and upon coming up with them was very nearly speared for my indiscretion; for the eldest of the two men, who had in his hand a long, rude kind of spear with which he had been digging roots or grubs out of the ground (although I could not see the least sign of anything edible) finding that he was rather close pressed, suddenly halted and faced me, raising his spear to throw.

The rapid pace at which I had been pursuing prevented my reining in my horse, but by suddenly spurring him when within but a few yards of the native, I wheeled on one side before the weapon had time to leave his grasp, and then pulling up I tried to bring my friend to a parley at a less dangerous distance.

Finding that I did not attempt to injure him, the native stood his ground, though tremblingly, and kept incessantly vociferating, and waving me away; to all my signs and inquiries, he was provokingly insensible, and would not hear of anything but my immediate departure. Sometimes he pointed to the north, motioning me to go in that direction, but the poor wretch was in such a state of alarm and trepidation that I could make nothing of him and left him. He remained very quietly until I had gone nearly a quarter of a mile, and then thinking that he had a fair start, he again took to his heels, and ran away as fast as he could in the direction opposite to that I had taken . . .

December 5: Upon getting up early, I thought the horses looked so much refreshed, that we might attempt to take back the dray, and had some of the strongest of them yoked up. We proceeded well for two miles and a half to our encampment of the 30th November; and as there was then a well defined track, I left the man to proceed alone, whilst I myself went once more to the coast to make a last effort to procure water among some of the sand-drifts. In this I was unsuccessful. There were not the slightest indications of water existing any where. In returning to rejoin the dray, I struck into our outward track, about three miles below, where I had left it, and was surprised to find that the dray had not yet passed, though I had been three hours absent. Hastily riding up the track, I found the man not half a mile from where I had left him, and surrounded by natives. They had come up shortly after my departure; and the man, getting alarmed, was not able to manage his team properly, but by harassing them had quite knocked up all the horses; the sun was getting hot, and I saw at once it would be useless to try and take the dray any further.

Having turned out the horses to rest a little, I went to the natives to try to find out, if possible, where they procured water, but in vain. They insisted that there was none near us, and pointed in the direction of the head of the Bight to the north-west, and of the sand hills to the south-east, as being the only places where it could be procured; when I considered, however, that I had seen these same natives on the 30th November, and that I found them within half a mile of the same place, five days afterwards, I could not help thinking that there must be water not very far away. It is true, the natives require but little water generally, but they cannot do without it altogether. If there was a small hole any where near us, why they should refuse to point it out, I could not imagine. I had never before found the least unwillingness on their part to give us information of this kind; but on the contrary, they were ever anxious and ready to conduct us to the waters that they were acquainted with. I could only conclude, therefore, that what they stated was true – that there was no water near us, and that they had probably come out upon a hunting excursion, and carried their own supplies with them in skins, occasionally, perhaps, renewing this from the small quantities found in the hollows of the gum scrub, and which is deposited there by the rains, or procuring a drink, as they required it, from the long lateral roots of the same tree. I have myself seen water obtained in both these ways. The principal inducement to the natives to frequent the small plains where we were encamped, appeared to be, to get the fruit of the Mesembryanthemum, which grew there in immense quantities, and was now just ripe; whilst the scrub, by which these plains were surrounded, seemed to be alive with wallabie, adding variety to abundance in the article of food.

We were now on the horns of a very serious dilemma: our horses were completely fagged out, and could take the dray no further. We were surrounded by natives, and could not leave it, and the things upon it, whilst they were present (for many of these things we could not afford to lose); and on the other hand, we were twenty-two miles from any water, and our horses were suffering so much from the want of it, that unless we got them there shortly, we could not hope to save the lives of any one of them.

Had the natives been away, we could have buried the baggage, and left the dray; but as it was, we had only to wait patiently, hoping they would soon depart. Such, however, was not their intention; there they sat coolly and calmly, facing and watching us, as if determined to sit us out. It was most provoking to see the careless indifference with which they did this, sheltering themselves under the shade of a few shrubs, or lounging about the slopes near us, to gather the berries of the Mesembryanthemum. I was vexed and irritated beyond measure, as hour after hour passed away, and our unconscious tormentors still remained. Every moment, as it flew, lessened the chance of saving the lives of our horses; and yet I could not bring myself to abandon so many things that we could not do without, and which we could not in any way replace. What made the circumstances, too, so much worse, was, that we had last night given to our horses every drop of water, except the small quantity put apart for our breakfasts.

We had now none, and were suffering greatly from the heat, and from thirst, the day being calm and clear, and intolerably hot. When we had first unyoked the horses, I made the man and native boy lay down in the shade, to sleep, whilst I attended to the animals, and kept an eye on the natives. About

noon I called them up again, and we all made our dinner off a little bread, and
some of the fruit that grew around us, the moisture of which alone enabled us
to eat at all, our mouths were so thoroughly dry and parched.

A movement was now observed among the natives; and gathering up their
spears, they all went off. Having placed the native boy upon an eminence to
watch them, the man and I at once set to work to carry our baggage to the top
of a sand-hill, that it might be buried at some distance from the dray. We had
hardly commenced our labours, however, before the boy called out that the
natives were returning, and in a little time they all occupied their former
position; either they had only gone as a ruse to see what we intended to do, or
they had been noticing us, and had seen us removing our baggage, or else they
had observed the boy watching them, and wished to disappoint him. Whatever the inducement was, there they were again, and we had as little prospect
of being able to accomplish our object as ever. If any thing could have palli-
ated aggressive measures towards the aborigines, it would surely be such
circumstances as we were now in; our own safety, and the lives of our horses,
depended entirely upon our getting rid of them. Yet with the full power to
compel them (for we were all armed), I could not admit the necessity of the
case as any excuse for our acting offensively towards those who had been
friendly to us, and who knew not the embarrassment and danger which their
presence caused us.

Strongly as our patience had been exercised in the morning, it was still
more severely tested in the afternoon – for eight long hours had those natives
sat opposite to us watching. From eight in the morning until four in the
afternoon, we had been doomed to disappointment. About this time, however, a general movement again took place; once more they collected their
spears, shouldered their wallets, and moved off rapidly and steadily towards
the south-east. It was evident they had many miles to go to their encampment, and I now knew we should be troubled with them no more. Leaving the
boy to keep guard again upon the hill, the man and I dug a large hole, and
buried all our provisions, harness, pack-saddles, water-casks, &c. leaving the
dray alone exposed in the plains. After smoothing the surface of the ground,
we made a large fire over the place where the things were concealed, and no
trace remained of the earth having been disturbed.

We had now no time to lose, and moving away slowly, drove the horses
before us towards the water. The delay, however, had been fatal; the strength
of the poor animals was too far exhausted, and before we had gone seven
miles, one of them could not proceed, and we were obliged to leave him; at
three miles further two more were unable to go on, and they, too, were

abandoned, though within twelve miles of the water. We had still two left, just able to crawl along, and these, by dint of great perseverance and care, we at last got to the water about four o'clock in the morning of the 6th. They were completely exhausted, and it was quite impossible they could go back the same day, to take water to those we had left behind. The man, myself, and the boy were in but little better plight; the anxiety we had gone through, the great heat of the weather, and the harassing task of travelling over the heavy sandy hills, covered with scrub, in the dark, and driving jaded animals before us, added to the want of water we were suffering under, had made us exceedingly weak, and rendered us almost incapable of further exertion. In the evening I sent the man, who had been resting all day, to try and bring the two horses nearest to us a few miles on the road whilst I was to meet him with water in the morning. Native fires were seen to the north-east of us at night, but the people did not seem to have been at the water at the sand-hills for their supply, no traces of their having recently visited it being found.

December 7: After giving the horses water we put ten gallons upon one of them, and hurried off to the animals we had left. The state of those with us necessarily made our progress slow, and it was four o'clock before we arrived at the place where they were, about eleven miles from the water. The man had gone on to the furthest of the three, and had brought them all nearly together; upon joining him we received the melancholy intelligence, that our best draught mare had just breathed her last – another lay rolling on the ground in agony – and the third appeared but little better. After moistening their mouths with water, we made gruel for them with flour and water, and gave it to them warm: this they drank readily, and appeared much revived by it, so that I fully hoped we should save both of them. After a little time we gave each about four gallons of water, and fed them with all the bread we had. We then let them rest and crop the withered grass until nine o'clock, hoping, that in the cool of the evening, we should succeed in getting them to the water, now so few miles away. At first moving on, both horses travelled very well for two miles, but at the end of the third, one of them was unable to go any further, and I left the man to remain, and bring him on again when rested; the other I took on myself to within six miles of the water, when he, too, became worn out, and I had to leave him, and go for a fresh supply of water.

About four in the morning of the 8th, I arrived with the boy at the water, just as day was breaking, and quite exhausted. We managed to water the two horses with us, but were too tired either to make a fire or get anything to eat ourselves; and lay down for an hour or two on the sand. At six we got up, watered the horses again, and had breakfast; after which, I filled the kegs and proceeded once more with ten gallons of water to the unfortunate animals we had left behind. The black boy was too tired to accompany me, and I left him to enjoy his rest, after giving him my rifle for his protection, in the event of natives coming during my absence.

Upon arriving at the place where I had left the horse, I found him in a sad condition, but still alive. The other, left further away, in charge of the man, had also been brought up to the same place, but died just as I got up to him; there was but one left now out of the three, and to save him, all our care and attention were directed. By making gruel, and giving it to him constantly, we got him round a little, and moved him on to a grassy plain, about a mile further; here we gave him a hearty drink of water, and left him to feed and rest for several hours. Towards evening we again moved on slowly, and as he appeared to travel well, I left the man to bring him on quietly for the last five miles, whilst I took back to the water the two noble animals that had gone through so much and such severe toil in the attempt made to save the others. In the evening I reached the camp near the water, and found the native boy quite safe and recruited. For the first time for many nights, I had the prospect of an undisturbed rest; but about the middle of the night I was awoke by the return of the man with the woful news, that the last of the three horses was also dead, after travelling to within four miles of the water. All our efforts, all our exertions had been in vain; the dreadful nature of the country, and our unlucky meeting with the natives, had defeated the incessant toil and anxiety of seven days' unremitting endeavours to save them; and the expedition had sustained a loss of three of its best horses, an injury as severe as it was irreparable.

Journal of Expeditions of Discovery into Central Australia, 1845

It was estimated that this army of buffaloes was at least two hours in passing our encampment or fortification and immediately following them were immense gangs of wolves, making the most hideous noise . . .

In 1845 Samuel Hancock set off from his Virginian home as a member of a forty-strong wagon train that crossed the open prairies and followed the Oregon Trail to the Pacific. Penniless when he joined the wagon train, he nonetheless managed to use his skills as a wheel-maker, brick-baker and kiln-builder to earn a living.

He provides an insight into the thoughts and deprivations of the ordinary people who opened up the continent to Europeans, as others were doing in Australia, New Zealand, Southern Africa and South America, not for science or their country's political advancement, but for no other reason than to better themselves and their loved ones. In 1860, he married and settled on Whidbey Island in Puget Sound and wrote this account – found by a New York publisher 70 years later.

The buffalo plains

Early next morning everything in camp was prepared to leave, and we traveled until about one o'clock when we had to cross Platte River, while making preparations for crossing, an immense herd of buffalo came in view; in fact the whole country as far as we could see, presented a mass of buffaloes on a stampede, coming towards us; having heard of the danger of encountering these roving herds in their stampede, we immediately went to work preparing ourselves as best we could, by driving the wagons around in a circle, to make a fortification for ourselves and animals, against the approach of these formidable travelers of the Plains. Several of our company more daring than the others took a position on an eminence and keeping an incessant firing of guns and pistols, succeeded in a diversion of their route, to within two hundred yards of us, so that we shot quite a number of them. It was estimated that this army of buffaloes was at least two hours in passing our encampment or fortification and immediately following them, were immense gangs of wolves, making the most hideous noise; these 'hangers on' of the army above referred to, are not unlike in their object the 'hangers on' of some of our more civilized armies, that is seeking something to devour; they follow the buffaloes in these stampedes in the hope that some may tire, and being unable to keep up, get in the rear, when they are beset with these followers, who by the gnawing of their ham strings, render them unable to travel and an easy prey to the appetite of the wolves . . .

Next morning a small band of buffaloes came in sight and some of the company went out to meet and if possible surround them and drive them towards camp, where we were to shoot them, this arrangement succeeded admirably, as we secured two fine ones in good order, but unfortunately in passing us, they ran through the midst of our cattle which were feeding, causing them to become frightened and join the herd all leaving at full speed.

Eight or ten men started in pursuit to recover our animals, and succeeded in overtaking them but were unable to separate the cattle from the buffaloes, and were obliged to abandon them; this was rather a serious loss, as some of the company in the morning were compelled to yoke up cows as substitutes for the run away oxen . . .

We traveled on without anything very material occurring but seeing all the time abundance of game, the plains abounding with elk, deer, antelopes, buffaloes, long eared rabbits, some bears and thousands of wolves. We came to an Indian village which the inhabitants were just vacating and we were particularly impressed by their manner of transporting their effects, which was somewhat after the style of the Sioux heretofore described, other than these were employing wolves or dogs resembling them very much instead of horses. They packed large loads on the long poles, piling them high, and leaving nothing in view except the head of the animals and these huge loads attached to them. There had been fifteen or twenty loads sent off, and I discovered there was no one in attendance on these strange conveyances, the animals walking off as though they knew where to go, and the Indians seeming to have all confidence in their performance of the duties entrusted to them.

I was induced to go and inquire into this proceeding, and was told or made to understand that one of these drags had started in the direction of their travel some time ago, under the superintendence of an Indian and that the rest would faithfully follow on their trail, without further attention. An old squaw was engaged in loading one of these concerns, and I had the curiosity to examine into all the particulars and to see whether the animal was in reality a wolf or dog, but could discern no difference in appearance from the wolves we constantly saw. Upon nearing this animal he regarded me very intently for some time, and discovering I was a stranger, started at full speed strewing his unsecured burden in every direction over the prairie. The old squaw pursued him screaming with all her might in her effort to stop him but in vain; on he went, finally dispossessing himself of his shafts, and the last I saw of him he was bounding across the prairie, apparently now in his element.

This evening we encamped early and turned out our stock to graze, about dark corralling them where they remained safely and quietly until morning, as well as ourselves. Soon after we started we ascertained that a cow had strayed away from the others, and I went out in quest of her; becoming thirsty, I alighted at an inviting and beautiful little spring, expecting a cool drink of water; upon filling my mouth I was astonished and disappointed at finding it a hot spring and my mouth scalded. Procuring the cow I rejoined the train, and traveled until evening when after encampment, one of the company expressed his intention of going out in search of deer; we observed him enter a bend of the river bottom where there was a thicket of brush, and soon afterwards heard him halloo, but attached no importance to it, as no Indians had been seen in this vicinity. A sufficient length of time having elapsed for his return, we became anxious for his safety and five of us started to look for him, when to our horror we found his lifeless body on the ground divested of clothing and scalp. It was impossible to track the Indians to avenge his death, and in the morning we interred his body as decently as possible, and shedding a tear over the grave of one of our little community, we left the encampment and resumed our journey.

After a few days' travel during which nothing specially interesting occurred, we encamped in view of the Chimney Rock, and the next evening encamped close by this beacon of the plain, when after adjusting matters in camp, some of us visited this curiosity and were highly gratified. This rock towers up to the height of perhaps two hundred and fifty feet, presenting a very imposing appearance, and very much resembling a well proportioned chimney, from the base to the Summit. On this huge pillar we found inscribed the names of many who preceded us the year before in their journey across the plains, to Oregon. On our return to camp we encountered some antelopes of which we killed two.

Next morning we made an early start and after traveling a short distance, saw near us a single buffalo, two young men went out on horseback to have some sport, and if possible to kill him, when in their pursuit they ran him close by the train where he received a number of shots; he fell upon his haunches, but standing erect on his forelegs, made battle with all who came near him; finally he was shot through the heart, which ended the career of the lonely buffalo. Abundance of game could be seen throughout the day, and we encamped early, in good grass, and passed a quiet night. Thence we continued our journey for several days uninterruptedly, when we came up to an encampment of Indians who proved to be a war party of two hundred or more of the Crow Tribe, and equipped for battle. They asked us through an interpreter, whether we had seen any of the Sioux Tribe; this question we answered rather evasively, not wishing to be the bearers of any information which might lead to a difficulty; particularly when we recollected the assurances of friendship and the quiet deportment of the last party of Sioux we had seen. These Indians said the Sioux had been killing their buffalo and other game on their lands, and that they were now in search of them to obtain redress for these injuries, and they presented quite a formidable appearance. This conversation took place between a deputation of five of our company and the Indians, which was done to prevent their coming too near us, and frightening our cattle, which showed signs of alarm, though we took the precaution to drive some distance around them. Notwithstanding all this, an Indian approached a wagon in the rear, having a mule team attached, which became frightened and rushed forward, causing all the other teams to start also, and the whole train of forty wagons dashed across the plains, the drivers having no control over the frantic animals, and the women and children who were inmates of the wagons, screaming with all their voices, some of the wagons upset, thus creating a state of affairs in our midst truly alarming, and it was some time before we could again exert any control over our teams, and stop them; when we finally did, it was ascertained that we had sustained considerable injury, some of our wagons lying on one side and teams detached from them in some instances, others with the wheels broken, and the contents strewn promiscuously around, while some of our company were lying out with broken legs, and others seriously injured, the whole scene presenting a most disastrous appearance. The Indians having witnessed the entire affair, were hastening to us, prompted no doubt by curiosity; but we, entertaining no very kind feeling for them just then, sent a guard of twenty men to intercept them and request they should advance no nearer; this being accomplished, we encamped to repair our damages. Fortunately there was a grove of cotton wood in this vicinity where we could obtain wood for heating our wheel tires, and after a two days' delay we again started westward. In the evening we encamped at Fort Laramie, an American trading post, which some of us visited and found the occupants clever people who seemed pleased to see us, while we were equally glad to meet with them; a white settlement so remote from civilization seeming a kind of protection, in the midst of this wild country. Bidding adieu to these adventures we resumed our journey and traveled on very comfortably, toward evening encamping on one of the many tributaries of North Platte River about twenty miles distant from Fort Laramie in good grass.

The Narrative of Samuel Hancock 1845–1860, 1927

LUTHER STANDING BEAR
1868–1939

I would like to state that in those days it was considered a disgrace, not an honor, for a Sioux to kill a white man. Killing a pale-face was not looked upon as a brave act. We were taught that the white man was much weaker than us.

Born Ota Kte ('Plenty Kill'), the first son of the Sioux Indian Chief Standing Bear the First – who named his boy after his own ability to liquidate his enemies – and the 'most beautiful young woman among the Sioux', Pretty Face, the young Sioux in due course found himself being educated by the white man. It was then that he learned to calculate his birth date according to the white man's method: it had been 'in the month when the bark of the trees cracked', which must have been December, and in the year of 'breaking up of camp', which, counting back, must have been 1868.

From the oral history passed down to Plenty Kill – later to earn his own name, Standing Bear – he learned how, just after he was born, the Union Pacific Railroad had come across their lands: a Sioux scout had reported that 'a big snake was crawling across the prairie'. One day, a party of Indians stopped to drink water at a newly erected railway station, and found themselves shouted off what they had thought was their own land. Back home, a council was called, and a decision made to rip up a section of track, retreat and see what would happen. When the train appeared, its crew began to shoot at the Sioux, and were so busy jeering at the Indians' attempt to catch them on their horses that they didn't look ahead. The train sped off the line. It was from this wreckage that his mother obtained the 'first beads ever seen by the Sioux nation'. Prior to that, personal adornment had been porcupine quills.

Such incidents form the background to the childhood of Standing Bear, the last days of a still unconquered people. In the autumn of 1879, an event happened that changed his life for good. Playing with some friends near the government agency buildings, he saw a crowd and went over – then found himself inside, lured in by some proffered 'sticks of candy'. There he found two Sioux boys dressed up in white man's clothes. An interpreter explained that a Capt. R. H. Pratt wanted to take him east, where he would be taught 'the ways of the whiteman'. 'We could all be dressed up, as these Indian boys then were.'

The boy was excited, if only by the thought of the candy – which he was peeved he never got – and ran back to his tepee. A family conference was held. His father, perhaps sensing the end had already come for his people, said his son could go.

In time, Standing Bear – who was to became hereditary chief of his people, the Oglala clan of the Sioux – travelled not just east, but across the water, recruited into 'Buffalo' Bill Cody's circus, which took him to London and into the world of acting.

Standing Bear's *My People the Sioux* is an historical document. 'The author of this book may be a bit short of education,' apologizes film cowboy William S. Hart in the introduction; but in a sense this lack of education gives the account its strength: 'educated' means inculcated with the rationalizing outlook that is the mark of our culture. The value of Standing Bear's tale is in its simplicity. Cushioned, no doubt, for Christian ears, it is also undecorated and heartfelt. It still comes from the heart of the Sioux he remained.

How my father got his name

The Sioux tribe, to which I belong, has always been a very powerful nation. Many years ago they traveled all over the Western country, hunting, camping, and enjoying life to its utmost, in the many beautiful spots where they found the best wood and water.

It was in a cold winter, in the month when the bark of the trees cracked, in the year of 'breaking up of camp,' that I was born. I was the first son of Chief Standing Bear the First. In those days we had no calendars, no manner of keeping count of the days; only the month and the year were observed. Something of importance would, naturally, happen every year, and we kept trace of the years in that manner. After I went to school and learned how to 'count back,' I learned that that year of 'breaking camp' was A.D. 1868; the month when the bark of the trees cracked was December. Consequently I was born in December, 1868.

My mother was considered the most beautiful young woman among the Sioux at the time she married my father. Her name was 'Pretty Face.' My grandfather – my father's father – was a chief, and accounted a very brave man. He had captured many spotted horses from other tribes in their wars with one another. Therefore, when my father was born, he was given the name of 'Spotted Horse.' This he kept until he was old enough to go on the warpath and earn his own name. He once told me how he received the name of 'Standing Bear.' His story, as near as I can remember it, was as follows:

'One of our hunting scouts returned with the news that the Pawnees were on our hunting-grounds and were killing our game; so all the braves prepared themselves for war. We knew we had a hard enemy to face, as the Pawnees were very expert with the bow and arrow. If one of these Pawnees was knocked down, he was just as liable to arise with his bow in hand, or even if lying flat on his back, he would have an arrow in his bow all ready to let drive.

'We started and traveled quite a long way. When we came up over a hill, we could see the Pawnees down in the valley. They had just finished killing a lot of buffalo, and the game lay scattered here and there. Each man was busy skinning the animal he had killed. Our men rode into them as fast as they were able. I was riding a sorrel horse at this time, and he was a good runner.

'When the Pawnees saw us coming, they scattered to get their horses and leave. We gave chase after them. I took after some men who went over a hill, but they had too good a start, and I knew there was no use tiring my horse out chasing them, so I turned back. As I was nearing my own people, I observed several of them in a bunch, and I rode in close to see what was the matter.

'When I got there, the Sioux were all in a circle around one Pawnee. His horse had got away from him in the excitement and he was left on foot. But he had a bow and arrow in his hand and was defying any of the Sioux to come near. He was a big man and very brave. When our men would shoot an arrow at him and it struck, he would break the arrow off and throw it away. If they shot at him and missed, he would pick up the arrows and defy the Sioux to come on.

'Then I asked the men if any one had yet touched this enemy. They said no; that the man appeared to have such strength and power that they were afraid of him. I then said that I was going to touch this enemy. So I fixed my shield in front of me, carrying only my lance.

'The Pawnee stood all ready for me with his arrow fixed in his bow, but I rode right up to him and touched him with my lance. The man did not appear excited as I rode up, but he shot an arrow at me, which struck my shield and glanced off into the muscles of my left arm.

'Behind me rode Black Crow. The third man was Crow Dog, and the fourth man was One Ear Horse. We four men touched this enemy with our lances, but I was the first. After the Pawnee had wounded me, the other men expected to see him get excited, but he did not lose his nerve. As soon as I had passed him with an arrow through my arm, the Pawnee had a second arrow all ready for the next man.

'The second man was shot in the shoulder, and the third man in the hip. As the last man touched the enemy, he received an arrow in the back. In this manner the Pawnee shot all the four men who had touched him with their lances. We had all gained an honor, but we were all wounded. Now that four of our men had touched the enemy, he was so brave that we withdrew from the field, sparing his life.

'We were some distance away when I began to feel very sleepy. Old Chief Two Strikes and Broken Arm, my uncle, got hold of me to keep me from falling off my horse. This was a very peculiar sensation to me, and something I had never experienced before. The last I remembered was as if falling asleep, but in reality I had only fainted.

'While I was sleeping peacefully (as it appeared to me) I heard an eagle away up in the sky. He seemed to be whistling, and coming nearer and nearer, descending in a circle. Just as the eagle came very close to me, I awoke, and there I saw the medicine man running around me in a circle with one of the whistles made from the bone of an eagle's wing. It was the medicine man who had awakened me from my seeming sleep. Then Chief Two Strikes (who was a very old man) and Broken Arm helped me home.

'These men all sang my praises as we entered the village. Then a big victory dance was given, and great honor was bestowed upon me. At the next council Chief Two Strikes proposed me as a chief, because I was brave enough to face the enemy, even if that enemy was ready to shoot me. So I was accepted and elected as a chief under the name of "Standing Bear."'

That is how my father's name was changed from 'Spotted Horse' ('Sunkele Ska') to 'Standing Bear' ('Mato Najin'). In those days every warrior had to earn the name he carried.

Before my birth, my father had led his men many times in battle against opposing tribes. He was always in front; he was never known to run away from an enemy, but to face him. Therefore, when I was born, he gave me the name of 'Ota Kte,' or 'Plenty Kill,' because he had killed many enemies.

I would like to state that in those days it was considered a disgrace, not an honor, for a Sioux to kill a white man. Killing a pale-face was not looked upon as a brave act. We were taught that the white man was much weaker than ourselves.

Going East: 'the white people are like ants; they are all over – everywhere'

We had spent our summer in playing games, and now it was the fall of the year 1879. My father had his store well stocked, and we were getting along splendidly. It was about the latter part of September, and the days were nice and cool – just the time to play hard and not feel too warm.

A little boy named Waniyetula, or Winter, and I were playing between my father's store, and the agency. He was a distant cousin of mine, but we always called each other 'brother.' The agency was perhaps a quarter of a mile from our tipi.

Suddenly we observed a great many people gathered around one of the agency buildings, and our curiosity was at once aroused. I said, 'Let us go over and see what they are looking at.' So we ran as fast as we could. Reaching the building, we looked in through one of the windows and saw that the room was filled with people. Among them were several white men and we noticed one white woman.

When they saw us peeping in at the window, they motioned for us to come inside. But we hesitated. Then they held out some sticks of candy. At this, we ran away some little distance, where we stopped to talk over this strange proceeding. We wondered whether we had better go back again to see what the white people really wanted. They had offered us candy – and that was a big temptation. So we went back and peeped in at the window again. This time the interpreter came to the door and coaxed us inside. He was a half-breed named Charles Tackett. We called him Ikuhansuka, or Long Chin. We came inside very slowly, a step at a time, all the time wondering what it meant.

There we saw two Indian boys dressed in white men's clothes. They had been educated somewhere. They were both Santee Sioux, from the Mud or Missouri River. With their new clothes on they looked like white men.

Then the interpreter told us if we would go East with these white people and learn the ways of the white man, we could be all dressed up, as these Indian boys then were. He told us the white man, whose name was Captain R. H. Pratt, had asked him to tell us this.

However, all this 'sweet talk' from the interpreter did not create much impression on me. We had heard this same sort of 'sweet talk' many times before, especially when these interpreters were paid by the Government for talking.

My mind was working in an entirely different channel. I was thinking of my father, and how he had many times said to me, 'Son, be brave! Die on the battle-field if necessary away from home. It is better to die young than to get old and sick and then die.' When I thought of my father, and how he had smoked the pipe of peace, and was not fighting any more, it occurred to me that this chance to go East would prove that I was brave if I were to accept it.

At that time we did not trust the white people very strongly. But the thought of going away with what was to us an enemy, to a place we knew nothing about, just suited me. So I said, 'Yes, I will go.' Then they said I must bring my father to the agency first, as they wanted to talk the matter over with him.

In the excitement of talking to these white people, we had forgotten all about the promised candy, so we did not get any. I ran home, and when I entered, my people were all eating. My father was sitting between his two wives, and all the five children were there. So I sat down with the others and started telling my father about the white people at the agency. The children listened to what I had to say. There were my sisters, Zintkaziwin and Wanbli Koyakewin, my two brothers, Wopotapi and Nape Sni, and my little sister, Tawahukezanunpawin. As I talked, I ate but little. I was so anxious to get back to the agency again.

After the meal, my father and I went back where the white people were. They were very nice to him, and shook hands. Then they told him, through the interpreter, about the proposed trip East. Father listened to all they had to say, then he turned to me and asked, 'Do you want to go, son?' I replied, 'Yes.'

I do not remember whether I was the first boy to sign up, but they wrote my name in a big book. At that time I was entered as 'Ota Kte, or Plenty Kill, son of Standing Bear.' After my name was in the book all the white people shook hands with me and said something in the white man's language which I did not understand.

Then my father and I came away together and started for home. He never spoke a word all the way. Perhaps he felt sad. Possibly he thought if I went away with these white people he might never see me again, or else I might forget my own people. It may be he thought I would become educated and betray them; but if he felt any of these fears, he showed no sign of it.

The next day my father invited all the people who lived near by to come to his place. He got all the goods down off the shelves in his store and carried them outside. Then he brought in about seven head of ponies. When all the people were gathered there, he gave away all these things because I was going away East. I was going with the white people, and perhaps might never return; so he was sacrificing all his worldly possessions. Some of the other chiefs also gave away many things.

The day following, the agent told the Indians he had some Government teams ready to take all the children who were going away. My father said he would much rather take me himself as far as possible. Then my sister Zintka-ziwin gave herself up to go with me, doing this as an honor.

My father had a light spring wagon, and they loaded this up with a small tipi, some bedding, cooking utensils, and whatever might be needed on the trip. We were to drive to the place where a steamboat was to carry us part of the way. When we were ready to start, I looked over to the spot where my ponies were grazing. How happy they were – and I was leaving them, per-haps never to return! My heart went out to the little animals as I stood there looking at them.

Then I asked my father if I might ride one of the saddle-ponies from Rosebud Agency to Black Pole, a distance of fifty miles, where we were to board the steamboat. He gave me permission, although I knew at the end of the journey my pony and I would have to part for many a long, lonesome day.

About halfway to Black Pole we camped for the night. At this point we met many other Indian boys and girls who were also going East with the white people. Some rode in Government wagons; others came on their ponies as I had done. Many drove their own wagons.

Early the next morning we were all on the road again, my sister riding in the wagon with her mother and father. We were now making the last lap of our journey from the reservation to the steamboat, and it would be only a short time that my pony and I would be together. We did not know where we were going, only that it 'was east somewhere.'

At last we reached Black Pole. Our tipis were pitched again, as we had to wait the arrival of the boat. However, none of us were in a hurry. Here we had such a good time! We ran, shouted, and played, trying hard to crowd in all the fun possible before we were separated from our people. We waited three days, and then were told that the boat would arrive the following day.

But at this point my sister suddenly experienced a change of heart. She concluded that she did not want any white man's education. However, that really suited me very well, because I figured that she would have been a lot of extra trouble for me. I knew that I could take care of myself all right, but if she were along and anything happened to her, I would be expected, of course, to look out for her, as she was younger than I – and a girl, at that!

Finally the boat arrived. They put a little bridge way out to the shore. It was now just about sundown. Then the Indian boys and girls who were going away were lined up, and as their names were called they went on board the boat. Even at this point some of the children refused to go aboard, and nobody could compel them to. So my sister was not the only one who had 'cold feet,' as the white people say.

When my name was called, I went right on the boat without any hesitation. By the time all the children were aboard, it was getting quite dark. So they pulled in the little bridge, while the parents of the children stood lined up on the shore and began crying. Then all the children on the boat also started to cry. It was a very sad scene. I did not see my father or stepmother cry, so I did not shed any tears. I just stood over in a corner of the room we were in and watched the others all crying as if their hearts would break. And mind you, some of them were quite young men and women.

Bedtime at length came, but I did not see any nice bed to sleep in that night. We were scattered all over that big room, the boys on one side and the girls on the other. We rolled up in our blankets and tried to go to sleep; but riding in a steamboat with a paddle-wheel at the back which made lots of noise was an experience we were not used to, and it kept us awake.

Along in the night, when we were all supposed to be asleep, I overheard some big boys talking quietly. They were going to get ready to jump off the boat. When I got the drift of their conversation, I jumped up and saw three big boys going down the stairway. The boat appeared not to be moving, so I followed after the three boys to the floor below. There I saw a lot of men bringing cordwood onto the boat. The three boys were standing at the edge of the boat waiting for a chance to jump off and take to the woods.

I remained back at the foot of the stairway watching to see what they would do. Then the larger of the boys said to the others: 'Let us not try it this time. I understand they are going to put us off the boat to-morrow anyway, and if they do, we will have a good chance then.' So they started back to their blankets on the floor and I got into mine. But I could not get to sleep, because I was wondering where we were going and what was to be done with us after we arrived.

It did not occur to me at that time that I was going away to learn the ways of the white man. My idea was that I was leaving the reservation and going to stay away long enough to do some brave deed, and then come home again alive. If I could just do that, then I knew my father would be so proud of me.

About noon the next day, the interpreter came around and told us we must get ready to leave the boat. Finally it stopped close to the shore and they put out the little bridge and we all got off. We walked quite a distance until we came to a long row of little houses standing on long pieces of iron which stretched away as far as we could see. The little houses were all in line, and the interpreter told us to get inside. So we climbed up a little stairway into one of the houses, and found ourselves in a beautiful room, long but narrow, in which were many cushioned seats.

I took one of these seats, but presently changed to another. I must have changed my seat four or five times before I quieted down. We admired the beautiful room and the soft seats very much. While we were discussing the situation, suddenly the whole house started to move away with us. We boys were in one house and the girls in another. I was glad my sister was not there. We expected every minute that the house would tip over, and that something terrible would happen. We held our blankets between our teeth, because our hands were both busy hanging to the seats, so frightened were we.

We were in our first railway train, but we did not know it. We thought it was a house. I sat next to the window, and observed the poles that were stuck up alongside the iron track. It seemed to me that the poles almost hit the windows, so I changed my seat to the other side.

We rode in this manner for some distance. Finally the interpreter came into the room and told us to get ready to leave it, as we were going to have something to eat. Those who carried bundles were told to leave them in their seats. Some of the older boys began fixing feathers in their hair and putting more paint on their faces.

When the train stopped at the station there was a great crowd of white people there. It was but three years after the killing of Custer by the Sioux, so the white people were anxious to see some Sioux Indians. I suppose many of these people expected to see us coming with scalping-knives between our teeth, bows and arrows in one hand and tomahawk in the other, and to hear a great war-cry as we came off that Iron Horse. The Sioux name for railroad was Maza Canku, or Iron Road. The term 'Iron Horse' is merely a white man's name for a moving-picture play.

The place where we stopped was called Sioux City. The white people were yelling at us and making a great noise. When the train stopped, we raised the windows to look out. Soon they started to throw money at us. We little fellows began to gather up the money, but the larger boys told us not to take it, but to throw it back at them. They told us if we took the money the white people would put our names in a big book. We did not have sense enough then to understand that those white people had no way of discovering what our names were. However, we threw the money all back at them. At this, the white people laughed and threw more money at us. Then the big boys told us to close the windows. That stopped the money-throwing.

The interpreter then came in and told us we were to get off here. As we left the little house, we saw that there were lots of what we took to be soldiers lined up on both sides of the street. I expect these were policemen, but as they had on uniforms of some sort, we called them soldiers. They formed up in a line and we marched between them to the eating-place.

Many of the little Indian boys and girls were afraid of the white people. I really did not blame them, because the whites acted so wild at seeing us. They tried to give the war-whoop and mimic the Indian and in other ways got us all wrought up and excited, and we did not like this sort of treatment.

When we got inside the restaurant, there were two long tables with white covers on. There was plenty of fine silverware and all kinds of good food. We all sat down around the table, but we did not try to eat. We just helped ourselves to all the food, scooping it into our blankets, and not missing all the lump sugar. The white people were all crowded up close to the windows on the outside, watching us and laughing their heads off at the way we acted. They were waiting to see how we ate, but we fooled them, for we carried everything back to the iron road, and inside the little houses we sat down in peace and enjoyed our meal.

Then the train started up again, and we traveled all that night. The next day we reached Sotoju Otun Wake, which, translated into Sioux, means 'smoky city' or your great city of Chicago. Here we saw so many people and such big houses that we began to open our eyes in astonishment. The big boys said, 'The white people are like ants; they are all over – everywhere.' We Indians do not call the Caucasian race 'white people,' but 'Wasicun' or 'Mila Hanska.' This latter means 'long knife.'

At Chicago we waited a long time. Pretty soon they brought us in all kinds of food. They did not try to feed us at a table again. After the meal was finished, the interpreter told us we were going to have a little dance and enjoy ourselves. We had no tom-tom with us, so they brought a big bass drum from some place. We were in a big room – possibly it was the waiting-room of the station but there were no seats in it. Here the big boys had a good time, and we little fellows looked out the windows and watched the wagons going by. A few white people were allowed to come inside and watch the dance, while there was a great crowd outside.

In the evening we were all loaded on to another iron road, traveling all night, the next day and then another night came. By this time we were all beginning to feel very restless. We had been sitting up all the way from Dakota in those straight seats and were getting very tired. The big boys began to tell us little fellows that the white people were taking us to the place where the sun rises, where they would dump us over the edge of the earth, as we had been taught that the earth was flat, with four corners, and when we came to the edge, we would fall over.

Now the full moon was rising, and we were traveling toward it. The big boys were singing brave songs, expecting to be killed any minute. We all looked at the moon, and it was in front of us, but we felt that we were getting too close to it for comfort. We were very tired, and the little fellows dozed off. Presently the big boys woke everybody. They said they had made a discovery. We were told to look out the window and see what had happened while we were dozing. We did so, and the moon was now behind us! Apparently we had passed the place where the moon rose!

This was quite a mystery. The big boys were now singing brave songs again, while I was wide awake and watchful, waiting to see what was going to happen. But nothing happened.

We afterward learned that at Harrisburg, Pennsylvania, the train turned due west to Carlisle, which placed the moon in our rear. And to think we had expected to be killed because we had passed the moon.

My People the Sioux, 1928

PART III

Hot Deserts

*

The gates of the enclosed garden are thrown open, the chain at the entrance of the sanctuary is lowered, with a wary glance to right and left you step forth, and, behold! The immeasurable world. The world of adventure and of enterprise, dark with hurrying storms, glittering in raw sunlight, an unanswered question and an unanswerable doubt hidden in the fold of every hill. Into it you must go alone . . .
Gertrude Bell, *The Desert and the Sown*, 1907

Whether cold and mountainous, as in central Asia, or hot and gravelly, as with the central Sahara, deserts have presented much the same practical problems to the traveller. Since they are thinly populated and uncultivated, provisions have to be carried; locating water becomes a priority, but wells can never be relied on: they may have dried up, or become contaminated by an animal falling in. Equally, a government might kindly reveal the secret co-ordinates of wells used by its army – as happened to me, when I tried to cross the Gobi alone – and forget to tell you that they are all padlocked. Among the sand dunes of, say, Namibia and Arabia, there is an additional obstacle: the terrain is always shifting, so there are no recognizable landmarks from which to navigate. Whatever their shape or form, then, deserts have always presented problems; they were skirted around, as pioneers searched for more fertile and lucrative prospects.*

Yet, time and again, those who have explored desert landscapes have found themselves drawn back to them. Here's Wilfred Thesiger, pausing in the Hajaz mountains to look back at a waste land – a land of what should, logic dictates, be nothingness:

A stream tumbled down the slope; its water, ice-cold at 9,000 feet, was in welcome contrast with the scanty, bitter water of the sands. There were wild flowers: jasmine and honeysuckle, wild roses, pinks and primulas. There were terraced fields of wheat and barley, vines, and plots of vegetables. Far below me a yellow haze hid the desert to the east. Yet it was there that my fancies ranged, planning new journeys while I wondered at this strange compulsion which drove me back to a life that was barely possible. It would, I felt, have been understandable if I had been working in some London office, dreaming of freedom and adventure; but here, surely I had all that I could possibly desire on much easier terms.

It might seem strange that anyone should find even an ounce of interest in what is a barren, bothersome place. Yet these stark lands do have their strange attractions, as I've found myself. In the Namib Desert, after just a week alone with my three camels, the slightest sign of life became a cherished thing. Even a sidewinder snake seemed like a friend: it was on my side, the side of the living. To me, deserts are the most captivating of all environments, as if they were not empty at all but charged with vitality. Whereas in rainforest I feel oppressed, bombarded by the teeming life around me – each frog and ant with its own niche and function – in the desert I feel unmolested. It's as if I feel somehow more inclined to open up to whatever is there.

* Fa Hsien (AD 319–414) the Buddhist monk who made the first recorded overland journey from China to India, and had to face aridity in every conceivable landscape, had this to say:
'If I were to recall all which has occurred to me, then persons of unstable minds would be excited to strive how they might enter on similar dangers and encounter corresponding risks, reckless of their personal safety. For they would argue in this way, "Here is a man who has escaped all and come back safe and sound"; and so these foolish persons would set about jeopardizing their lives in lands impossible to explore, and to pass through which, not one in ten thousand could hope for.'

To put it another way: devoid of life they may be, but in these stark stretches of nothingness I haven't ever felt alone; and in this unexpected feeling, I seem to be in good company. 'Even here in the desert have I seen God and lived after my vision,' it says in Genesis; and with the passage of time in the Bible, the desert becomes a place to seek companionship in God. John the Baptist found him there, and Jesus was forty days and forty nights living off locusts and honey, talking to his Father. Across the spiritual traditions of mankind, the pattern is similar: the Native American boy sent out to be alone, to find his spiritual ally; the Aborigine on his soul quest – popularized as a so-called 'walkabout' – seeking to find a link with the Dreamtime, which is a never-ending dimension from which he and all existence spring, and to which he will return.

Here's the reaction of Freya Stark upon first seeing the desert and its most famous inhabitant, the camel:

> The great gentle creatures came browsing and moving and pausing, rolling gently over the landscape like a brown wave just a little browner than the desert that carried it. Their huge legs rose up all around me like columns; the foals were frisking about: the herdsmen rode here and there. I stood in a kind of ecstasy among them. It seemed as if they were not so much moving as flowing along, with something indescribably fresh and peaceful and free about it all, as if the struggle of all these thousands of years had never been, since first they started wandering. I never imagined that my first sight of the desert would come with such a shock of beauty and enslave me right away. But I left feeling that somehow, sometime, I must see more of the great spaces.

For Stark – and most others who've been lured back – it seems to be all about great expanses, the uncluttered, uninterrupted horizon. 'There is a certain madness comes over one at the mere sight of a good map,' she says, as if deliberately trying to lose herself. Stark indeed had a great deal in her past that she might want to lose: a broken engagement, a domineering mother and a terrible factory accident, in which she was part scalped when her hair was yanked out by machinery. The desert gave her a new environment to exist in; there, she could take life on terms that she defined. 'Everything which belongs to your everyday life is a hindrance,' she wrote in *Baghdad Sketches*. In the desert, she could be unhindered.

I think few of us would not feel this freedom, given even one night under the desert stars beside a camper van; and how much greater that feeling when you are really alone. A case in point was my three-month Namib trek. My three camels turned out to dislike even the slightest slope, my lips were soon bleeding; but towards the end of the journey, when no one in the world knew where I was, there among the rocks and sand I found immense and very deep satisfaction. I consciously revelled in this release into a void. It was a joy in liberty often spoken of by others – 'that we were far beyond any hope of assistance', writes Wilfred Thesiger, 'that even our whereabouts were unknown, I found wholly satisfying'.

To tease this 'satisfaction' apart further, you have to look at the practicalities of desert travel. Assuming you are not in a four-wheel-drive vehicle, sealed off from the desert, then you are probably reliant on a camel; and a camel doesn't need you: unlike a horse or dog, it cannot be easily bribed with water or food. The desert may be hostile to you, but to a camel it is home. As well as being adapted to the terrain, it has a photographic memory, so it can usually remember its route, and go back at any time. But a camel has one weakness, and in this lies the solution: without his

companions, he is insecure; he is a herd animal, and needs the reassurance of a leader. So,
if you become Top Camel, you have a dedicated and loyal follower.

There are tricks to this. The camel's
instincts being tuned to survival at all times, it
avoids wasting energy. To encourage my
reluctant team to follow me, I soon learned
never to show the slightest hesitation. If I so
much as sighed, tramping up a hill, they
paused, looking ahead in what seemed to be
horror. So in the end I was reduced to humming merrily as I walked up inclines; it would
have seemed ludicrous to a passing Himba
nomad (the Himba don't use camels), but it
worked. Our fortunes were linked together,
and it was in this growing partnership – they
could offer portage, I could offer them security – that my own satisfaction lay. Gradually,
with my camel friends, I began to earn the
freedom of the desert, a place that would
ordinarily have killed me; and this feeling I
would liken to the satisfaction a sailor might
have, launching out alone to cross the Atlantic. You are master of your little vessel. You
will be buffeted, and may not make it
through, but it is up to you and fate – or God.
There are few animals or people: in the desert,
you have an uninterrupted dialogue with the
elements, the same unexplainable satisfaction
we have all felt, staring into the embers of a
fire, or listening to the crashing of the waves
along a beach.

For some, like Thesiger, the desert seems to
be a haven from the conventional life in
which they cannot find a place.* He ponders
on whether the 'perverse necessity' that drove

him from his 'own land to the deserts of the
East' had its origins in an exotic childhood:
his father was British Minister in Addis
Ababa. However, deprivation commonly
seems to fulfil something deeper in the psyche
of the Western traveller, a 'hunger of the soul',
something inside that seeks out hardship, a
place of hellfire. 'The soil was waste gravel
baked hard in the everlasting drought,' wrote
Charles Doughty, describing the world surrounding him, 'and glowing under the soles
of our bare feet, the air was like a flame in the
sun.'†

This seems a darker yearning – expressed
this way by Thesiger: 'I knew instinctively that
it was the hardness of life in the desert which
drew me back there – it was the same pull
which takes men back to the polar ice, to high
mountains, to the sea.' The comparison
should not be so surprising, because the same
ingredients are there: the open vista, the
exposed nature of the traveller. And the Poles
are, of course, deserts – cold deserts.

Frequently, travellers find that through the
waste land's solitude comes solace. Away from
the business of our worldly existence, they
enter an other-worldly one. The empty landscape provides just that place sought by the
Buddhist in meditation, or the Jew, Christian
or Muslim in prayer. This is the retreat looked
for in the simple act of shutting one's eyes. In
that vastness your mind expands to fill the
vacuum. With no distractions to be had, your
own thoughts rebound around you. Here you
must face all your hopes (God) and all your

---

* 'The Empty Quarter offered me the chance to
win distinction as a traveller; but I believed that it
could give me more than this, that in those empty
wastes I could find the peace that comes with solitude, and, among the Bedu, comradeship in a hostile world. Many who venture into dangerous places
have found this comradeship among members of
their own race; a few find it more easily among
people from other lands, the very differences which
separate them binding them ever more closely. I

found it among the Bedu. Without it, these journeys would have been a meaningless penance.'
† T. E. Lawrence observed that, for a stranger, life
with the Bedouin is appallingly hard, 'a death in
life'. Thesiger's preface to his master work, *Arabian
Sands*, expands on this: 'No man can live this life
and emerge unchanged. He will carry, however
faint, the imprint of the desert, the brand which
marks the nomad; and he will have within him the
yearning to return, weak or insistent, according to
his nature. For this cruel land can cast a spell no
temperate clime can match.'

fears (the Djinn). Jesus had to conquer the temptations of Satan, who suggested he turn stone to bread. Marco Polo noted that voices lured travellers of the Gobi away from their path to their deaths – voices I was warned about even by present-day Mongols. It is a seclusion that is sought in spiritual traditions around the world – in New Guinea, for me and other initiates, in the secret confines of the Crocodile Nest from which we emerged as 'men', or in the uncomfortable isolation of the Native American sweat-lodge; the painful self-sacrifice of the Sioux sun dance; the fasts of Lent, Ramadan, Yom Kippur. In the desert, it comes to you naturally. And so it is that, for the great religious gurus, time spent away from their people became a qualification of their status; their isolation meant they had received knowledge from their maker.

Wherever I've been – the white pans of the Chalbi of Kenya, the ancient red sands of the Kalahari – this feeling re-surfaces, though usually it is far stronger with visitors than with the indigenous population. Perhaps it is because these visitors come from crowded lands; we are simply not designed to live in such cramped surroundings. Bertram Thomas found his Arab companions appalled when he told them that no one was allowed to carry weapons in his home country, England. '"What a place!" I felt them to be thinking, "Fit only for women and slaves."'

The perspective of remote indigenous peoples is, as usual, hard to include in litera-ture, simply because they have an oral, rather than a written tradition. However, in the selection below I have managed to include statements from Ramón Medina Silva, an apprentice shaman-priest of the Huichol, who bears a resemblance to the famous sorcerer Don Juan described in Carlos Castaneda's books.

Though I never met Silva – he died in the 1970s – I have spent some weeks with the Huichols, an isolated people of north-west Mexico, whose language has remained almost unchanged since the days of their distant rela-tives, the Aztecs. Furthermore, I was uniquely privileged to go on a sacred journey with them. The idea of 'going on a journey' is very much part of the Huichol tradition – in fact, they believe the world will cease to exist if they do not conduct their annual pilgrimage to honour their gods.

Though the Huichol now live up in the hills of the Sierra Madre Occidental, their origins are down in the desert. There, in the sacred land of Wirikuta, each year they take gifts to the gods that they left behind. Fur-thermore, amidst the dust and cacti, they per-form purification rituals in order to join with the gods; for the Huichol, though they don't believe in Adam and Eve, do – like adherents to the Judeo-Christian tradition – believe mankind suffered a fall from grace. They also believe that they might return to an existence in a type of Eden, if only briefly, when they eat the peyote cactus found in Wirikuta. To us an hallucinogen, peyote is for the Huichol a gateway into reality, the pure world of the immortals.

After I had negotiated for months to be allowed to join the Huichols on their pilgrim-age, the *peyoteros* loaded their mules and I tagged on to the end of the procession, led by the shamans, as they set out from the chilly escarpment. Cow horns were blown to signal to the gods that the Huichols were fulfilling their duty once more, as we began our des-cent down a track into the arid lands below. It was an arduous trek, which meant nego-tiating not just prickly cactuses, but also the barbed wire erected by the farmers who have taken the Huichol ancestral lands. We visited each of the sacred pools used by forefathers and gods, fasting, praying and purifying ourselves over two weeks – a process that, alarmingly, involved each of us confessing aloud a complete list of the lovers we'd had.

At last we were at Wirikuta itself – just a patch of scrub like any other to me, but to the Huichols something like a shrine, a special place where the gods and ancient ones might bestow favour.

After much chanting from the shamans, it was time to gather and eat the peyote. An unassuming little cactus, it defends itself not with spines but with toxins, the alkaloids which, to us in the West, give it hallucinogenic properties.

I took my dose rather gingerly; there was no other Westerner with me, and mescaline, the active ingredient, has been described by one scientific authority as 'not a friendly drug'. Sometimes, *peyoteros* begin screaming and have to be held down after eating their cactus; the Huichols account for this by saying that the *peyoteros* have not purified themselves, and that the gods are angry to find those with impure hearts in their presence.

My experience was better. Once I had managed to overcome my desire to vomit, I began to relax. Dull stones that surrounded me where I slumped now became strangely textured. Their different colours blazed out at me. Some even seemed to be alive, gently chirruping; but more than anything I found myself with an overwhelming sense of euphoria – not the clumsy feeling of well-being you might get if drunk, but a feeling of sharpness. I was in balance, I felt, with everything around me. This was what being in Paradise must be like, I thought, as I sat there in the desert scrub. This must be the harmony of Eden: no division between man and plants, plants and animals.

The interest for me here is that this extraordinary experience took place in a desert, not near the Huichol homesteads, even though peyote can be bought in the local markets. The journey through the desert was needed not just to honour the gods and ancestors, but as a means of purification and preparation.

In this regard, it seems the desert journey has a universal relevance. Whether you are a Huichol, whose roots are in the desert, or you're a Westerner, whose culture is rooted in urban life, the effect is the same. Padding through dust, sterile soil, and cactuses seems to offer a chance to withdraw from ordinary existence.

Some of the competitive character typical of explorers' business tends to surface in the desert. In the early 1930s Harry St John Philby is said to have shut himself away for a week when he was pipped at the post by the political officer Bertram Thomas, in crossing the last chunk of unexplored Arabia, the Rub' al-Khali – once translated as the 'Abode of Emptiness', now fixed in the public imagination as 'The Empty Quarter'. 'Damn and blast Thomas,' he wrote. He only felt satisfied when he had completed a more gruelling version of the same.

By and large, though, Western explorers of deserts weren't carrying the hopes of their nations. They crossed blank spaces, as did the men of the Arctic and Antarctic, but there were no great symbols like the Poles to be conquered. And far from being the Last Unknown, they were often homes to indigenous people: the Sahara is a veritable library of rock artists, the Namib strewn with ostrich-egg necklaces, and the Australian interior scattered with implements. Before Europeans ever penetrated the Middle East, not just Arabia but the entire Sahara was laced with trade routes that stretched back to the time of Rameses, as well as pilgrim routes by which Muslims made their obligatory hajj to the Holy City of Mecca. Christian visitors were unwelcome at first – there was both a religion and trade to guard. The Tuareg put paid to some early European explorers, and brigands many more. It was easy: dependent on a chain of wells, there was little any traveller could do but go along established routes.

However, indigenous peoples as usual

fared less well. Clinging to the margins of deserts, or in arid environments such as the Australian interior (not strictly speaking, a desert), they have tended to be highly nomadic, in order to eke out an existence at all.

The most unhappy situation I've witnessed was when I was living a while among the Aboriginals of Australia's Gibson Desert, in the late 1970s, when the last independent indigenous people were brought in from the bush. As with all other nomads, the odds were especially stacked against them. They relied on well-honed skills to find game and water, but these skills were not written down, and in order for them to be learned by the next generation, the desert had to be continually travelled, its clues read. There was a great void, therefore, between them and settled people like us. Accumulating property made no sense in this culture, where baggage was a hindrance to movement. There wasn't even a concept of land ownership; in fact, their existence had been so tied to the condition of the land and the life it supported – the lizards, the kangaroos – they believed they and their ancestors were part of that land. They had known, almost instinctively, when it was time to move on from a water hole.

Then the Europeans came; and, in the course of time, those natives who were still out there in the bush were given government support in the form of pensions, unemployment benefit, child allowances . . . People who had believed that they, the marsupials and everything else in the spinifex scrub were from the Dreamtime, were now thrust into the market economy. The money was spent on beer and sweet sherry. Children lay forgotten at the feet of drunken mothers; men beat each other, or their wives. Yet no one seemed to have the will to leave. These were nomads, whose ancestors had sought out water sources: now the white man had provided a never-ending well.

This was the scene when I arrived at the outpost of Wiluna – and was chased out of the community by a drunken lady with an iron bar. There were brighter times, as when elders told me to jump on to the back of a truck as they fled into the desert to rid the young of the booze that seemed to be tormenting them. Out there in the bush – where Robyn Davidson came through on her western crossing with camels – we built a fire and, one by one, the Aboriginals wandered off into the dark. It seemed to me then, as they headed in their different directions to walk in the desert for a while – perhaps guided by their totemic animals, an emu or a snake – as if they were going home; even for the young, who had never lived in the desert, it was the only peace left to them.

It was generally the Europeans who intruded on indigenous desert people, as colonial powers encouraged pioneers to open up the interior of new lands, whether in the Americas – the Atacama Desert in Chile, for example – or in southern Africa or Australia. The first business was to map, lay boundaries, and assess potential, a task carried out by those such as Charles Sturt, in the Australian interior. Naturally, early European travellers of the Middle East, such as Richard Burton or Charles Doughty, were often scholars, Arabists on an intellectual adventure and with a strong romantic urge to share in the life of the desert wanderer. Others came as political officers, traders, missionaries, spies, essayists, and formed allegiances with the Arabs who could guide them. Some of them, such as Philby, so identified with Arabia that they adopted the faith.

Many were drawn to historical mystery and, as deserts had often overrun fertile areas, leaving cities lost in the sands, the intellectuals also included archaeologists. Fa Hsien had written about the Kingdom of Khotan in AD 399, 'The country is prosperous and happy, its people are well-to-do; they have all received the faith and find their amusement in religious music. The priests number several tens of thousand.' He describes the King's Monastery, 'ornamentally carved and overlaid with gold and silver, suitably finished with all the preciosities. Behind the pagoda there is a Hall of Buddha which is most splendidly decorated. Its beams, pillars, folding doors and windows are all gilt. Besides these there are apartments for priests, also fitly decorated beyond expression in words.' Sven Hedin rediscovered the city 1,500 years later, buried in the sands of the Taklamakan. In southern Africa, Laurens Van der Post uncovered a different treasure, a relict people who became of value at last, the 'Bushman in all of us'.

Women appear prominently in this selection. Though travel through Islamic regions was all but impossible, and though they tended to cling to the outer fringes of true desert, the freedom that was such a draw for men seems to have been far more so to women, subject as they were to the strictures of conventional life. Gertrude Bell (1868–1926) left behind the safety and cosiness of her world in order to enter, in Syria, 'the world of adventure and of enterprise, dark with hurrying storms, glittering in raw sunlight, an unanswered question and an unanswerable doubt hidden in the fold of every hill'.

The desert is stimulating: among the sands you obtain a release. 'The word ecstasy is always related to some sort of discovery,' wrote Freya Stark, 'a novelty to sense or spirit, and it is in search of this word that in love, in religion, in art or in travel, the adventurous are ready to face the unknown.'

At times, the desert seems more like a sanctuary than a hostile environment. Among the travellers in my selection there are tortured creative geniuses, wanderers such as Isabelle Eberhardt – 'I am utterly *alone* on earth' – who was later killed by, of all things, a flash flood; or Bruce Chatwin, who in central Australia leafed through his notebooks hoping, it seems, that the Aboriginal would 'shed light on what is, for me, the question of all questions: the nature of human restlessness'. Chatwin had been embraced by the literary establishment – in his *In Patagonia*, he reminded us that travel writing could be literature. However, he never quite belonged with anyone: he was married, yet homosexual; took a childish delight in the new, yet wrote with maturity. As he grew seriously ill, from an AIDs-related illness, I remember that he told his parents, whom I knew, that he'd been infected by a fungus from an egg – typically, not an ordinary egg, but one, perhaps prehistoric, found in a musty cave in China.

The outcast, the wanderer, but also the inspired, such as the musician/novelist Paul Bowles – they all sought to find or lose themselves in the void. 'When this journey out of the desert ended and the company dispersed,' wrote Van der Post, 'I found myself compelled to go on another journey, into my mind and the mind of the vanished bushman.' Here we see Van der Post's connection with Carl Jung, who was a major influence on him. 'Nobody can say where man ends,' wrote Jung. 'That is the beauty of it. The unconscious of man can reach God knows where. There we are going to make discoveries.'

Whether they came to their desert as Arab scholars, government surveyors or lost mystics, all these people were united by it. Once they had been to the desert, they were forever haunted by it. Few minded suffering the roasting again, they needed to be there once more, and answer the questions that the desert provoked deep within them. As L. M. Nesbitt wrote of his time in the Danakil Desert, Ethiopia, in the slow, rising heat, 'The very taste and smell of remote and primitive territories is forced, even though it be painfully, on the observation of the traveler.'

Marco Polo

1254–1324

No man should ever on any account take a virgin to wife. For they say that a woman is worthless unless she has knowledge of many men.

The son of a Venetian tradesman, Marco Polo was seventeen when he embarked on a journey to China with his father and uncle, who had already made one journey to China and gained the favour of the Mongol Emperor Kublai Khan, whose luxuriant seat of power the poet Coleridge made famous as 'Xanadu'. The trio travelled through the Persian Gulf, Afghanistan and the Gobi Desert and reached the Khan's court in 1275, four years after leaving Venice.

Kublai Khan took a liking to Marco Polo and made him his personal 'fact-finder', sending him on missions to distant corners of the Empire. The Polos remained in the Emperor's dominions for some sixteen or seventeen years (the exact dates of the journey are not clear from surviving manuscripts). They then accompanied a Mongol princess who was to be given as consort to a Persian ruler – in fact, when they arrived, the ruler was found to have died, so she was given to his son instead. From Persia, they continued their homeward journey to Venice.

Three years after his return to Venice, Marco Polo was taken prisoner by the Genoese during a skirmish in the Mediterranean. In prison he dictated his twenty-five years of adventures to the romance writer Rustichello of Pisa, who wrote them down in Franco-Italian, a composite language that was fashionable at the time. By the end of Polo's two-year imprisonment, the book that was to become known as *Il Milione* was born, and before long it had circulated all over Italy. As there were no printing presses, each copy was rewritten by scribes, who sometimes had no qualms in altering details, misspelling place names or removing chunks of text. Now 140 different manuscripts of *Il Milione* survive.

For centuries the civilizations of Europe and the Far East had been oblivious of one another's existence, separated by an imposing wall of Muslim nations. So *Il Milione*, while immensely popular, was often taken as a work of fiction. It contained descriptions of unknown landscapes, spices, exotic plants and animals. Even coal was a novelty – 'kind of black stones which . . . maintain the fire better than wood'. However, some of his descriptions were, indeed, fantasy and some scholars even today believe he didn't actually make the journey. The problem was, Polo gave elaborate accounts not only of what he had apparently seen, but also of what he had been told. There were men with tails; there were unicorns. There were digressions to places he had never visited, from Siberia to Ethiopia, lands occupied by peoples and strange things that no one had ever seen. Some of his descriptions were exactly right, but verged on the heretical, such as his revelation that people lived below the equator, where, according to Church views of the time, there should have been nobody at all.

When, on his deathbed at the age of seventy, Polo was asked to remove the 'fables' from his book, he replied that *Il Milione* tells of only half of what he really saw, because if he had told the whole story people really would have thought he had made the whole thing up. However, as the West spread east, disbelief gave way to respect. His book was a valuable source of geographical and cultural information. Christopher Columbus, almost two hundred years later, used Polo's description of Cipangu (now in Japan) as a precise goal in his voyage towards the setting sun.

Paradise and Assassins

Mulehet, which means 'heretics' according to the law of the Saracens, is the country where the Sheikh of the Mountain used to live in days gone by. I will tell you his story just as I, Messer Marco, have heard it told by many people.

The Sheikh was called in their language Alaodin. He had had made in a valley between two mountains the biggest and most beautiful garden that was ever seen, planted with all the finest fruits in the world and containing the most splendid mansions and palaces that were ever seen, ornamented with gold and with likenesses of all that is beautiful on earth, and also four conduits, one flowing with wine, one with milk, one with honey, and one with water. There were fair ladies there and damsels, the loveliest in the world, unrivalled at playing every sort of instrument and at singing and dancing. And he gave his men to understand that this garden was Paradise. That is why he had made it after this pattern, because Mahomet assured the Saracens that those who go to Paradise will have beautiful women to their hearts' content to do their bidding, and will find there rivers of wine and milk and honey and water. So he had had this garden made like the Paradise that Mahomet promised to the Saracens, and the Saracens of this country believed that it really was Paradise. No one ever entered the garden except those whom he wished to make Assassins. At the entrance stood a castle so strong that it need fear no man in the world, and there was no other way in except through this castle. The Sheikh kept with him at his court all the youths of the country from twelve years old to twenty, all, that is, who shaped well as men at arms. These youths knew well by hearsay that Mahomet their prophet had declared Paradise to be made of such a fashion as I have described, and so they accepted it as truth. Now mark what follows. He used to put some of these youths in this Paradise, four at a time, or ten, or twenty, according as he wished. And this is how he did it. He would give them draughts that sent them to sleep on the spot. Then he had them taken and put in the garden, where they were wakened. When they awoke and found themselves in there and saw all the things I have told you of, they believed they were really in Paradise. And the ladies and damsels stayed with them all the time, singing and making music for their delight and ministering to all their desires. So these youths had all they could wish for and asked nothing better than to remain there.

Now the Sheikh held his court with great splendour and magnificence and bore himself most nobly and convinced the simple mountain folk round about that he was a prophet; and they believed it to be the truth. And when he

wanted emissaries to send on some mission of murder, he would administer
the drug to as many as he pleased; and while they slept he had them carried
into his palace. When these youths awoke and found themselves in the castle
within the palace, they were amazed and by no means glad, for the Paradise
from which they had come was not a place that they would ever willingly have
left. They went forthwith to the Sheikh and humbled themselves before him,
as men who believed that he was a great prophet. When he asked them
whence they came, they would answer that they came from Paradise, and that
this was in truth the Paradise of which Mahomet had told their ancestors; and
they would tell their listeners all that they had found there. And the others
who heard this and had not been there were filled with a great longing to go to
this Paradise; they longed for death so that they might go there, and looked
forward eagerly to the day of their going.

When the Sheikh desired the death of some great lord . . . he would take
some of these Assassins of his and send them wherever he might wish, telling
them that he was minded to dispatch them to Paradise: they were to go
accordingly and kill such and such a man; if they died on their mission, they
would go there all the sooner. Those who received such a command obeyed it
with a right good will, more readily than anything else they might have been
called on to do. Away they went and did all that they were commanded. Thus
it happened that no one ever escaped when the Sheikh of the Mountain
desired his death. And I can assure you that many kings and many lords paid
tribute to him and cultivated his friendship for fear that he might bring about
their death. This happened because at that time the nations were not united in
their allegiance, but torn by conflicting loyalties and purposes.

I have told you about the Sheikh of the Mountain and his Assassins. Now
let me tell you how he was overthrown and by whom. But first I will tell you
something else about him that I had omitted. You must know that this Sheikh
had chosen as his subordinates two other Sheikhs, who adopted all his practices and customs. One of these he dispatched to the neighbourhood of
Damascus, the other to Kurdistan. Let us now turn to the subject of his
overthrow. It happened about the year of Our Lord's nativity 1262 that Hul-
agu, lord of the Tartars of the Levant, knowing of all the evil deeds this Sheikh
was doing, made up his mind that he should be crushed. So he appointed
some of his barons and sent them against this castle with a powerful force. For
fully three years they besieged the castle without being able to take it. Indeed
they never would have taken it so long as the besieged had anything to eat, but
at the end of the three years they had no food left. So they were taken, and the
Sheikh, Alaodin, was put to death with all his men. And from that time to this

there have been no more of these Sheikhs and no more Assassins; but with him there came an end to all the power that had been wielded of old by the Sheikhs of the Mountain and all the evil they had done.

Let us now change the subject.

Crossing the Gobi

This desert is reported to be so long that it would take a year to go from end to end; and at the narrowest point it takes a month to cross it. It consists entirely of mountains and sand and valleys. There is nothing at all to eat. But I can tell you that after travelling a day and a night you find drinking water – not enough water to supply a large company, but enough for fifty or a hundred men with their beasts. And all the way through the desert you must go for a day and a night before you find water. And I can tell you that in three or four places you find the water bitter and brackish; but at all the other watering-places, that is, twenty-eight in all, the water is good. Beasts and birds there are none, because they find nothing to eat. But I assure you that one thing is found here, and that a very strange one, which I will relate to you.

The truth is this. When a man is riding by night through this desert and something happens to make him loiter and lose touch with his companions, by dropping asleep or for some other reason, and afterwards he wants to rejoin them, then he hears spirits talking in such a way that they seem to be his companions. Sometimes, indeed, they even hail him by name. Often these voices make him stray from the path, so that he never finds it again. And in this way many travellers have been lost and have perished. And sometimes in the night they are conscious of a noise like the clatter of a great cavalcade of riders away from the road; and, believing that these are some of their own company, they go where they hear the noise and, when day breaks, find they are victims of an illusion and in an awkward plight. And there are some who, in crossing this desert, have seen a host of men coming towards them and, suspecting that they were robbers, have taken flight; so, having left the beaten track and not knowing how to return to it, they have gone hopelessly astray. Yes, and even by daylight men hear these spirit voices, and often you fancy you are listening to the strains of many instruments, especially drums, and the clash of arms. For this reason bands of travellers make a point of keeping very close together. Before they go to sleep they set up a sign pointing in the direction in which they have to travel. And round the necks of all their beasts they fasten little bells, so that by listening to the sound they may prevent them from straying off the path.

A marriage custom in Tibet

This desolate country, infested by dangerous and wild beasts, extends for twenty days' journey, without shelter or food except perhaps every third or fourth day, when the traveller may find some habitation where he can renew his stock of provisions. Then he reaches a region with villages and hamlets in plenty and a few towns perched on precipitous crags. Here there prevails a marriage custom of which I will tell you. It is such that no man would ever on any account take a virgin to wife. For they say that a woman is worthless unless she has knowledge of many men. They argue that she must have displeased the gods, because if she enjoyed the favour of their idols then men would desire her and consort with her. So they deal with their womenfolk in this way. When it happens that men from a foreign land are passing through this country and have pitched their tents and made a camp, the matrons from neighbouring villages and hamlets bring their daughters to these camps, to the number of twenty or forty, and beg the travellers to take them and lie with them. So they choose the girls who please them best, and the others return home disconsolate. So long as they remain, the visitors are free to take their pleasure with the women and use them as they will, but they are not allowed to carry them off anywhere else. When the men have worked their will and are ready to be gone, then it is the custom for every man to give to the woman with whom he has lain some trinket or token so that she can show, when she comes to marry, that she has had a lover. In this way custom requires every girl to wear more than a score of such tokens hung round her neck to show that she has had lovers in plenty and plenty of men have lain with her. And she who has most tokens and can show that she has had most lovers and that most men have lain with her is the most highly esteemed and the most acceptable as a wife; for they say that she is the most favoured by the gods. And when they have taken a wife in this way they prize her highly; and they account it a grave offence for any man to touch another's wife, and they all strictly abstain from such an act. So much, then, for this marriage custom, which fully merits a description. Obviously the country is a fine one to visit for a lad from sixteen to twenty-four.

The Travels of Marco Polo (1938 edn)

IBN BATTUTA
1304–77

A remarkable thing which I saw in this country was the respect shown to women
by the Turks, for they hold a more dignified position than the men.

Ibn Battuta, a Moroccan berber, is commonly referred to as the greatest Muslim traveller – and even simply the greatest traveller – of all time. He managed 75,000 miles, in an age when pestilence, robbers and violence threatened all progress.

At the age of twenty-one Ibn Battuta (whose name means 'duckling's son') set out from Tangiers intending to go on a pilgrimage to Mecca, but developed an insatiable taste for travel. He did not return home for another twenty-four years. During this time he visited Egypt, Shiraz, Aden, East Africa, Syria – where he narrowly escaped the Black Death – Siberia, Constantinople, and Delhi, where the Sultan commissioned him as an envoy and sent him on into China.

When he returned to Morocco in 1349, the Sultan provided him with a secretary to record an account of his travels. Two years later he travelled again, this time over the Atlas Mountains to the Niger – which he believed to be the Nile – via major trading centres for gold and salt. He returned to settle in Fez and finish his book, the convincing, vivid and amusing *Rihlah* (now evolved into *Travels in Asia and Africa 1325–1354*), which became an invaluable source of reference on the geography of Muslim countries. It's a mark of how limited travel in his day – even among the great traders of the time, the Arabs – that he described the wonders of the coconut.

Ibn Battuta, whose principle was never to follow the same road twice, was perhaps the only medieval traveller to visit the lands of every Muslim ruler. He had seen more of the known world than any man before him.

Visiting the Sultan of Turkistan

A remarkable thing which I saw in this country was the respect shown to women by the Turks, for they hold a more dignified position than the men. The first time that I saw a princess was when, on leaving Qiram, I saw the wife of the amír in her waggon. The entire waggon was covered with rich blue woollen cloth, and the windows and doors of the tent were open. With the princess were four maidens, exquisitely beautiful and richly dressed, and behind her were a number of waggons with maidens belonging to her suite. When she came near the amír's camp she alighted with about thirty of the maidens who carried her train. On her garments there were loops, of which each maiden took one, and lifted her train clear of the ground on all sides, and she walked in this stately manner. When she reached the amír he rose before her and greeted her and sat her beside him, with the maidens standing round her. Skins of *qumizz* were brought and she, pouring some into a cup, knelt before him and gave it to him, afterwards pouring out a cup for his brother.

Then the amír poured out a cup for her and food was brought in and she ate with him. He then gave her a robe and she withdrew . . .

We then prepared for the journey to the sultan's camp, which was four days' march from Májar in a place called Bíshdagh, which means 'Five mountains.' In these mountains there is a hot spring in which the Turks bathe, claiming that it prevents illness. We arrived at the camp on the first day of Ramadán and found that it was moving to the neighbourhood from which we had just come, so we returned thither. I set up my tent on a hill there, fixing a standard in the ground in front of it, and drew up the horses and waggons behind. Thereupon the *mahalla* approached (the name they give to it is the *ordu*) and we saw a vast town on the move with all its inhabitants, containing mosques and bazaars, the smoke from the kitchens rising in the air (for they cook while on the march), and horse-drawn waggons transporting them. On reaching the encampment they took the tents off the waggons and set them upon the ground, for they were very light, and they did the same with the mosques and shops. The sultan's khátúns passed by us, each separately with her own retinue. The fourth of them, as she passed, saw the tent on top of the hill with the standard in front of it, which is the mark of a new arrival, and sent pages and maidens to greet me and convey her salutations, herself halting to wait for them. I sent her a gift by one of my companions and the chamberlain of the amír Tuluktumúr. She accepted it as a blessing and gave orders that I should be taken under her protection, then went on. Afterwards the sultan arrived and camped with his *mahalla* separately.

The illustrious Sultan Muhammad Uzbeg Khán is the ruler of a vast kingdom and a most powerful sovereign, victor over the enemies of God, the people of Constantinople the Great, and diligent in warring against them. He is one of the seven mighty kings of the world, to wit: our master the Commander of the Faithful, may God strengthen his might and magnify his victory! [the sultan of Morocco], the sultan of Egypt and Syria, the sultan of the Two 'Iráqs, this Sultan Uzbeg, the sultan of Turkistán and the lands beyond the Oxus, the sultan of India, and the sultan of China. The day after my arrival I visited him in the afternoon at a ceremonial audience; a great banquet was prepared and we broke our fast in his presence. These Turks do not follow the custom of assigning a lodging to visitors and giving them money for their expenses, but they send him sheep and horses for slaughtering and skins of *qumizz*, which is their form of benefaction. Every Friday, after the midday prayer, the sultan holds an audience in a pavilion called the Golden Pavilion, which is richly decorated. In the centre there is a wooden throne covered with silver-gilt plates, the legs being of pure silver set with jewels at the top. The sultan sits on the throne, having on his right the khátún Taytughli with the khátún Kebek on her right, and on his left the khátún Bayalún with the khátún Urdujá on her left. Below the throne stand the sultan's sons, the elder on the right and the younger on the left, and his daughter sits in front of him. He rises to meet each khátún as she arrives and takes her by the hand until she mounts to the throne. All this takes place in view of the whole people, without any screening.

On the morrow of my interview with the sultan I visited the principal khátún Taytughl, who is the queen and the mother of the sultan's two sons. She was sitting in the midst of ten aged women, who appeared to be servants of hers, and had in front of her about fifty young maidens with gold and silver salvers filled with cherries which they were cleaning. The khátún also had a golden tray filled with cherries in front of her and was cleaning them. She ordered *qumizz* to be brought and with her own hand poured out a cupful and gave it to me, which is the highest of honours in their estimation. I had never drunk *qumizz* before, but there was nothing for me but to accept it. I tasted it, but found it disagreeable and passed it on to one of my companions. The following day we visited the second khátún Kebek and found her sitting on a divan reading the holy Koran. She also served me with *qumizz*. The third khátún Bayalún is the daughter of the Emperor of Constantinople the Great. On visiting her we found her sitting on a throne set with jewels, with about a hundred maidens, Greek, Turkish and Nubian, standing or sitting in front of her. Behind her were eunuchs and in front of her Greek chamberlains. She asked how we were and about our journey and the distance of our native lands, and wept, in pity and compassion, wiping her face with a handkerchief that lay before her. She ordered food to be served and we ate in her presence, and when we desired to leave she said, 'Do not sever relations with us, but come often to us and inform us of your needs.' She showed great kindness to us and after we had gone sent us food, a great quantity of bread, butter, sheep, money, a magnificent robe and thirteen horses, three good ones and ten of the ordinary sort.

Bulghár, on the River Volga

I had heard of the city of Bulghár and desired to visit it, in order to see for myself what they tell of the extreme shortness of the night there and also the shortness of the day in the opposite season. It was ten nights' journey from the sultan's camp, so I requested that he would give me a guide to take me to it, and he did so. We reached it in the month of Ramadán, and when we had breakfasted after the sunset prayer we had just sufficient time for the night prayers before dawn. I stayed there three days. I had intended to visit the Land of Darkness [northern Siberia], which is reached from Bulghár after a journey of forty days, but I renounced the project in view of the difficulty of the journey and the small profit to be got out of it. The only way of reaching it is to travel on sledges drawn by dogs, for the desert being covered with ice, neither man nor beast can walk on it without slipping, whereas the dogs have claws that grip the ice. The journey is made only by rich merchants who have a hundred sledges or thereabouts, loaded with food, drink, and firewood, for there are neither trees, stones nor habitation in it. The guide in this country is the dog which has made the journey many times, and the value of one of these reaches a thousand dinars. The sledge is tied to its neck and three other dogs are yoked with it; it is the leader, the other dogs following it with the sledges, and where it stops they stop. Its owner never beats or chides it, and when food is made the dogs are served first before the men; otherwise the [lead] dog is angered and escapes, leaving its owner to perish. When the travellers have completed forty stages they alight at the Darkness. Each one of them leaves the goods he has brought there and they return to their usual camping-ground. Next day they go back to seek their goods, and find opposite them skins of sable, minever, and ermine. If the merchant is satisfied with the exchange he takes them, but if not he leaves them. The inhabitants then add more skins, but sometimes they take away their goods and leave the merchant's. This is their method of commerce. Those who go there do not know whom they are trading with or whether they be jinn or men, for they never see anyone.

Travels in Asia and Africa, 1325–1354

René-Auguste Caillié
1799–1838
If they had even left me alone in my misery, it would have been more bearable.

René Caillié – the first European to reach Timbuktu, and return alive – was born into a poor family near La Rochelle in France. He received little education, but reading *Robinson Crusoe* inspired him to become an explorer. By the age of twenty he had been to Senegal twice, and had travelled through its interior. While in Guadeloupe, on his second voyage, Caillié came across the writings of Mungo Park (see page 177), whose expedition to the Ségou on the banks of the Niger had determined that the river flowed in an easterly direction. Taking inspiration from Park, and also from the promise of a 10,000 franc prize from the Geographical Society of Paris for the first European to report first hand on Timbuktu, Caillié set his sights on the desert city, which was at this time the wealthiest in Africa, a key market on the camel trade routes, and therefore closed to foreigners – specifically Christians. The Scot Alexander Laing successfully spent five weeks there in 1826, only to be murdered just three days after his departure.

Caillié returned to Africa in 1824, where he spent three years immersing himself in the Arabic way of life, learning their language, and adopting their customs and dress. Posing as an Arab en route to Egypt, Caillié left the West African coast in March 1827, and reached Timbuktu in April of the following year, having been delayed by five months suffering from severe scurvy. Despite his euphoria at arriving safely – just – at his destination, Caillié was not impressed by what he found.*

He remained there only a fortnight, disguised as a beggar and making detailed observations of Timbuktu-ian life.†

On his return journey Caillié took a different route, across the Sahara to Morocco. He joined up with an enormous caravan of 1,200 camels, transporting slaves and merchandise. When he arrived in Tangier, the French naval authorities at first refused to believe he had made the journey, but back in France he was ultimately awarded his prize.

—

* 'On entering this mysterious city, which is an object of curiosity and research to the civilised nations of Europe, I experienced an indescribable satisfaction. How many grateful thanksgivings did I pour forth for the protection which God had vouchsafed to me, amidst obstacles and dangers which appeared insurmountable. This duty being ended, I looked around and found that the sight before me did not answer my expectations. The city presented, at first view, nothing but a mass of ill-looking houses, built of earth. Nothing was to be seen in all directions but immense plains of quicksand of a yellowish white colour. All nature wore a dreary aspect, and the most profound silence prevailed; not even the warbling of a bird was to be heard.'

† 'They did not appear in the least mortified at being exhibited in the streets for sale,' he wrote of slaves, 'but manifested an indifference which I could easily enough account for, by the state of degradations to which they had been reduced and their total ignorance of the natural rights of mankind. They thought that things should be so, and that they had come into this world to be bought and sold . . . At the time of my departure I saw several slaves affectionately bidding each other adieu. The conformity of their melancholy condition excites among them a feeling of sympathy and mutual interest. At parting, they recommended good behaviour to each other; but the Moors frequently hurry their departure and interrupt these affecting scenes which are so well-calculated to excite commiseration for their fate.' This contrasts with the treatment he received himself as a beggar. 'When I was at the mosque a middle-aged Moor stepped up to me gravely, and without saying a word slipped a handful of cowries into the pocket of my coussabe. He withdrew immediately without affording me time to thank him. I was much surprised at this delicate way of giving alms.'

Rising suspicions about the traveller

Among the rocks I found a quantity of cotton trees, with deeply indented leaves; the husks and seeds also being smaller than those of the cotton tree cultivated in our establishments in Wâlo. I took some of the seeds of these and of many other shrubs which happened to be ripe, and hid them in the corner of my pagne; I also collected some plants. In descending the hill I was met by two Moorish hunters; they looked surprised to see me, and asked me what I came to look for so far from the camp; I shewed them my plants, and told them that I came to fetch medicines for Hamet-Dou, who was ill; they appeared satisfied, shewed me some young Guinea-fowl which they had caught and left me. I climbed another of these hills, composed of flesh-coloured quartz rocks, in smaller masses than those which I had remarked on the former. I found many resembling marble; the intermediate spaces are covered with pure reddish sand.

On my return I searched the plain for cotton trees, like those I had discovered on the hill; but I could not find a single plant. The two Moors whom I had met, had arrived at the camp before me, and given an account of my excursion: the news had come to the ears of the king and awakened his suspicions. As soon as he was aware that I had returned, he sent for me, and I had not time to dispose of my seeds. When I entered, he asked me, with an air of dissatisfaction, whence I came, and why I went to a distance from the camp by myself. There were plenty of herbs, he told me, close by, without my going so far to look for them. Some of the Moors who were present, perceived that I had a knot in my pagne, and catching hold of it, they asked me what I had got there; and then, without giving me time to reply, they untied it themselves. 'What do you want with these?' said they. 'These are to take to the white men when you go back to them;' and, without waiting for an explanation, they threw away the seeds. I tried to persuade them that these seeds had medicinal virtues, and that I had gathered them for the benefit of more than one of themselves; but, not succeeding, I assured them that when I came to them, my connexion with whites had ceased, and that I could never return to their country.

In the evening, being in the tent of a marabout, who gave instruction, I took advantage of a moment when I could procure some ink, and fell to work upon my journal: I had written about a page, when the Koont sherif came in and caught me; he took the paper from me, and, amazed to see no Arabic characters, asked me what I was writing. I thought at first of saying that I had set down some prayers that I wanted to remember, but recollecting that I had not learnt prayers enough to take up a page, I told him it was a song, and I began to sing to convince him. The incredulous sherif did not appear to believe it, and he accused me of coming to spy out their ways, that I might give an account of them to the christians. It was of importance to me to drive this idea out of his head, and I succeeded, by pretending the utmost indifference as to what I had written. I put the paper into his hands again with a smile, and said, 'Go to the factory and get this paper read; you will see whether I have deserved the affront you have offered me.' This stratagem had the effect I expected; he gave me back my paper, and asked me to read another verse. I sung another couplet; the sherif appeared convinced, and left me, to my great joy, for his surmises alarmed me exceedingly. I thanked God that I had come off so well, and resolved to be more prudent in future. From that time forward, when I wanted to write, I took care to get behind a bush, and at the least noise I hid my notes and took up my beads, pretending to be saying my prayers. This feigned devotion procured me much commendation from those who surprised me; but it was painful to me to perform such a part.

For three days the wind had blown hard from the east; the pastures were nearly bare, and messengers had been dispatched to the north to see if they were more abundant in that direction. In the evening a tremendous storm came on, the thunder rolled awfully, and the rain fell in torrents; all the tents were blown over, and the utmost confusion pervaded the camp. The storm had taken every body by surprise; there had been no time to take down the tents; the very huts themselves were carried away, the briars which had been used for fences were likewise torn up, and many persons were hurt. The Moors, though accustomed to scenes of this sort, seemed very much frightened. Nothing was to be heard but men and women recommending themselves to God: the tumult was increased by the doleful lowing of the cattle, which had been torn by the briars which the wind carried off, and were now wandering about at random. This was the first storm that I had witnessed in the desert, and the general consternation which I remarked, made me suppose that there was some imminent danger; for a moment I shared the terror of the Musulmans, but the wind subsided in about three quarters of an hour, and the rain ceased soon afterwards. The people then bestirred themselves to set up the tents again, and to collect the scattered cattle; the fires which the wind had extinguished were re-lighted, and every one dried his clothes, for it is the Moorish custom to have only one suit. I had a dry pagne with which I covered myself, and more than ten people asked me for it to change themselves; but I had too urgent occasion for it myself, to lend it, which drew upon me their abuse. I observed that the king himself had been exposed to the rain like the rest of us, and that he had no more change of apparel than his subjects, for he remained all night in his wet clothes.

I have already mentioned that this storm took every body by surprise; in a general way the Moors strike their tents when they are threatened by a storm, leaving only a few small ones, which almost always resist its force, and serve to shelter the king and the royal family; all the rest remain outside exposed to the rain. On this occasion the wind was so high, that the very smallest tents were thrown down, and the princes and princesses shared the common fate.

On the 21st of September, a Trarzas marabout, from Portendik, arrived at the camp: I was called to see some articles which he brought with him from that place: he showed me a pair of pantaloons, which I thought I recognized as having belonged to M. Lacaby, who was wrecked in the Rose Virginie, on the bank of Arquin; he had also a handsome little dressing-case, and seaman's boots, which he used to protect himself from the thorns and khakhames. I should have liked to ask him a few questions, but I dared not for fear of exciting suspicions. The particulars of this shipwreck I had been acquainted with before I left Saint Louis, and I had even seen some of the sufferers.

On the 23d of September, the messengers who had been sent to look for pasture returned, and said that they had found no water in the direction in which they had been: it was then determined to move to the N. E., where we hoped for better success.

On the 24th, the camp broke up. My marabout's camel was ill, so I travelled on foot. We crossed the hills; about six miles from the place which we had left we came to a lake, called Lakhadou, surrounded by a fine plain of argillaceous soil, covered with vegetation: here we halted for several days. This lake is pleasantly shaded by *grewias*.

For the last three days, Fatmé-Anted-Moctar had omitted to send me a meal of sangleh, as she had been accustomed to do; I received nothing from her but a little milk morning and night, and was tormented with hunger. The king had told me, it is true, to ask him for every thing I wanted; but I got no more for that; and the milk, instead of satisfying me, gave me the colic, and impaired my strength.

This evening a Moor, called Moxé arrived at the camp; he is the interpreter in ordinary to the king when he goes to the coast, and speaks French perfectly well. Hamet-Dou sent for me to question me again, and I gave him the same replies as before. Moxé told me that he was come from Galam, where the agent of the commercial society had given him a piece of Guinea cloth and a gun, and that he should return very soon; he proposed that I should accompany him, adding that four or five days would be sufficient for the journey. I should have been very glad to take this trip, and alleged, as a pretext for it, the great need I had of some new clothes. I asked the king if he would lend me a camel for the journey, and he promised he would when the waters had subsided; for, he said, the roads are impassable at this season. At night he sent me a piece of mutton for supper.

On the 25th of September, while I was at prayer, I felt myself ill from exhaustion: Moxé asked me if I had a fever, and I told him the cause of my illness, adding, that I had great difficulty to support this way of living; but I hoped, nevertheless, that I should become used to it in time. After prayer the king offered me a sheep, advising me to cook it myself, because, if I trusted to the Moors, they would devour it all. I accepted the offer; but, no doubt, fearful lest I should not take his advice, and with a view to save me from the rapacity of his subjects, he took care not to send me the sheep! It is probable that I owed this good turn to Moxé; for I was told by Fatmé-Anted-Moctar, that Moxé had endeavoured to prejudice the king against me: he insinuated, as I found, that it was not the love of God, but curiosity, which had brought me among them, and that I should not be likely to remain very long. Fortunately, some of the marabouts took my part, and the king said himself, that he could not believe that curiosity alone would have induced me to come amongst them to suffer such privations, and that God must have wrought a miracle in my behalf in operating my conversion. I thought I could perceive a little jealousy in Moxé's conduct with respect to me, and he probably feared that my presence, when I should have learned Arabic, would render his own needless. No doubt this was what also induced the negro, whom I mentioned as my interpreter in the first conversation I had with the king, to tell him I had not been shipwrecked, but that I had committed some atrocious crime among the whites, who had expelled me for it. Although the king laughed at all this, it did not fail to diminish his confidence, and I could perceive from day to day that I lost something of the esteem with which I had at first inspired him . . .

On the 30th of September, the camp broke up, and we advanced nine miles to the north, over a sandy soil covered with khakham. As I wore sandals only, after the Moorish fashion, I suffered extremely from the prickles of this plant, and my feet and legs were covered with blood. I asked several of the Moors to take me up behind them on their camels, but they said that their beasts were weary, and I must apply to the king who would furnish me with one. The king was gone on before, and I had lost sight of my marabout, so I had no hope except from the pity of those who were near me. I tried again to persuade them, for I was exhausted with pain and fatigue, but in vain; I got nothing but raillery in answer to my entreaties, and I was told that I should win heaven by suffering with patience. They spoke the truth; but I am sure not one of them would have taken my place to earn heaven at this price. If they had even left me alone in my misery, it would have been more bearable; but the young princes, mounted upon their fine horses, came bounding about me, running against me, and rallying me upon my dress, which consisted only of a coussabe made of coarse blue pagne, and falling to pieces.

   Travels through Central Africa to Timbuctoo, 1830

CHARLES STURT
1795–1869
Yet, how few voyages of discovery have terminated without bloodshed!

An Indian-born British soldier who charted the river systems of most of eastern Australia and explored 4,800 km of the interior, Charles Sturt was born in Bengal, where his father was a judge, but was educated in England. At the age of eighteen he joined the army and served in the final stages of the Napoleonic Wars before being posted to Australia in charge of a convict escort. He arrived at a time when early colonists had explored the area around Sydney, but the continent's vast interior remained a mystery. Westward-flowing rivers had led to speculation about an inland sea.

Initial surveys had failed to assess the complicated river system of the south-east, and in 1828 Sturt set out with twelve men, an assortment of soldiers and convicts, to follow the Macquarie river inland. The river was soon swallowed up by swamp, but the team continued north-westward until they came across the mighty River Darling. Sturt returned to Sydney with the strong conviction that the Darling flowed inland, along with the other south-eastern rivers. His second expedition took him down the Murrumbidgee river – to discover the Murray river. The expedition reached Lake Alexandrina, near what is now Adelaide, but failed to find a route out into the Indian Ocean and had to row 1,450 miles upstream back to Sydney.

In 1844, Sturt embarked on his historic expedition into the centre of the continent. With fifteen companions he followed the Murray and Darling rivers into New South Wales. As it turned out, they had chosen a year of drought. Temperatures reached 57°C, their ink evaporated, and for six months they were stranded in a cave, which they had further dug out to escape the heat. When rain finally came and they could move on, they found not an inland sea but the stones and sand of the Simpson and Sturt Deserts (on the border between South Australia and western Queensland). Suffering from scurvy, the party returned to Adelaide in 1846, by which time Sturt was almost blind, severely burnt, and had to be carried on a stretcher. Sturt's journal, written for his wife, gives meticulous descriptions of the ferocious conditions the party endured.

'Threatened with a total failure of water'

Sunday August 17th 1845: As I was now bent on a distant excursion, my first care was to put the camp in a state of defence in the event of its being attacked during my absence by the natives. I marked out and drew the place of a stockade that I directed Mr Stuart to erect without loss of time, and I ordered that all the firearms and ammunition should be deposited in the tent in the centre of it, that on the first indication of hostility the sheep were to be driven into the stockade, and that the men were not unnecessarily to expose themselves to the spears of the natives. On the 11th some natives came to the camp who I fed well and to whom I made some trifling presents. We had not seen many, but it was clear that at times they assemble in this neighbourhood in great numbers. Having given Mr Stuart detailed instructions for his guidance, and ordered Morgan to get the boat painted and prepared in the event of her being wanted, I again left the Depôt, Dearest, on the 14th accompanied by Mr Browne with Flood, Joseph and Lewis.

I took the spring cart, 4 pack horses, and 15 weeks provisions. This journey would in truth decide the failure or the success of the Expedition. If we find water I see no reason to doubt that we shall pass into the tropics in six weeks from this date, but unless rain falls our supply of surface water will be sure to fail, indeed it is already almost exhausted, in which case we shall be beat back . . . We travelled 24 miles without seeing a drop of surface water and at length encamped by another of those muddy puddles, which circumstances alone forced us to drink, half clay and half water.

Today our road lay over a changeable region. The flats were of increased breadth and the land waves higher, but for some miles there was no scarcity of grass on the flats. They were however all subject to flood, and the piles of rubbish at the foot of ridges shews that at times they must be three or four feet under water. About noon, we crossed a polygonum flat, in which there were several fine pools of water from two to three feet deep with some of which we cleared our throats and washed ourselves. For the last 6 miles the country fell off in appearance, the flats were of a white clay without a blade of vegetation upon them, and they were full of deep holes. The view from the top of the land waves was over a most dreary region to whichever point of the compass we turned, and no poor travellers could have blanker prospects before them than we had, with a wild and difficult desert to traverse, threatened with a total failure of water, and no indication whatever of a change of weather . . . We have again halted, Dearest, without water for our horses, but having a two gallon cask with us we have some of the good water from the polygonum flat for our tea. We are living exclusively on 5 lb of flour and 2 oz of tea a week, for neither Mr Browne nor I can venture to touch salt pork. How long we shall do on such fare I don't know, but I hold out as yet tolerably. And now, Dearest Charlotte; adieu, I am writing by lamp light and it somewhat tires my eyes. God in his Mercy bless you and maybe enable me to compass my wishes, to ensure future comfort and tranquillity to you. God bless you and my dear, dear children.

Sunday August 24th 1845: I do not know why it should be so, Dearest, but my spirits have for the last few days been unusually depressed in so much that I cannot shake off the emotions that have seized me. If therefore my journal of this week should be tinged with any feeling of depression you will know that there is no apparent cause for it . . .

We started at 7 o'clock and after crossing three land waves of great height descended from the last to a plain of great extent extending to the north and south further than we could see, and about 3 miles broad. At the western extremity of this plain there was a thick line of gum trees running directly across our track, but as they were denser to the S.W. than in the direction in which we were moving, I sent Flood to examine the neighbourhood there. On reaching the trees Mr Browne and I found ourselves on the banks of a fine creek . . . Thinking that this creek might turn out to be of importance, I determined on stopping for an hour or two, and sent Mr Browne with Flood to ride some eight or ten miles up it.

In the meantime I looked about and found two native huts. At the fires near them were the claws of crayfish, similar to those on the Murray and I thought I recognised amongst the other bones the vertebrae of some fish. On Mr Browne's return he informed me that a little above where he left me the creek had no channel but spread over a grassy flat, then at 7 miles he came on a tolerably large pond of water, but that he did not think there was any water beyond, that the country to the north was very level, and the sand ridges much lower. He had seen three natives an old man and two women, the latter of whom, contrary to their usual custom, had their two front teeth punched out and the man like all the other natives we had seen was circumcised. They understood a few words Mr Browne spoke, and told him that there was both water and hills to the N.E. I did not however think possible on their information to alter my course, and as Mr Browne had had a long ride, I remained where I was for the day . . .

I continued to the north and at ½ a mile arrived at a nice clear little water hole at which we encamped. On tasting this water we found it as I suspected from its clearness to be slightly brackish but it was not disagreeable to the taste. I don't know what put it into his head but Mr Browne fancied there were fish in it, and getting Lewis to make him a pin hook, he rigged a line and went down to the water to try his fortune when he caught a dish of nice silver perch. How these fish could possibly have got into that hole I cannot imagine. They could not originally have dropped there from a cloud? There were none in the water above which was perfectly sweet, only in this brackish hole. It is one of those anomalies in this anomalous country for which I cannot see any satisfactory explanation.

Leaving this creek yesterday, Dearest, at immediately below where we had slept it spread over a plain, we ascended some hills of clay rather than of sandy formation, that continued for two miles. From these we ascended to a barren region of salt formation on which nothing but samphire and other salsolaceous plants were growing. At three miles we crossed the half dry bed of a salt lagoon and then for eight miles traversed the most desolate wilderness on earth, but at that distance we suddenly came on a line of box trees and passing through them found ourselves on the outskirts of some beautiful grassy plains studded with trees tho' surrounded by sand hills, and more like a nobleman's park than anything else. So rapid are the changes from good to bad and from bad to good in these regions. In crossing these plains we surprised 4 native women thrashing out seeds. One of them was of a jet black colour and had curly hair, and was evidently of a distinct race. Apprehensive, I suppose, that we should seize upon them, the other 3 offered us this fair damsel, but we declined the present. They were most earnest in assuring us that there was no water in the direction in which we were going but plenty in the opposite one. However, as I doubted what these ladies said, I pursued my own way and soon found out what had made them so anxious to turn us away. Their huts were close to an almost exhausted waterhole about a mile off and their little children were playing about. As soon as they saw us they crept into their huts and hid themselves, but I went round not to frighten the poor little things. I rode some way down the bed of the little creek in which the water was to find another hole that I might not encamp near them, but could not find one, and Joseph having met with an accident by cutting his eyelids in two with his whip, I was obliged to stop opposite to the native camp.

About sunset the chief came home, a fine handsome-looking fellow of about 30. He had his spears with him and other war weapons and had I suppose been to some corroborie, as he was painted all over. He was exceedingly indignant at our having taken up our quarters so near him and threatened to go and muster his tribe and to drive us away. We did everything we could to pacify him but to no purpose. On the contrary, our kindness seemed to impress him with the idea that we were afraid and as I was determined he should not entertain that notion, I soon gave him to understand that I cared very little for him and all his tribe and I soon cooled him down altho' he continued exceedingly sulky. We therefore left him to enjoy his ill-humour, intending to go back in about an hour and to give him a tomahawk, but when I did so I found he had decamped, and the only trouble it gave me was to be a little more watchful that night, or as I should have said last night but I go on writing as if I was writing of a distant past period, without reflecting that every day brings me nearer the present.

My mind, indeed, is oppressed with some weight and I fear I am making but a lame and sorry account of this, but it is for you Dearest Charlotte, and you will excuse its errors and imperfections I know.

Journal of the Central Australian Expedition, 1844–45

RICHARD FRANCIS BURTON
1821–90

Then Shaykh Abdullah, who acted as director of our consciences, bade us be good pilgrims . . . We must so reverence life that we should avoid killing game . . . nor should we scratch ourselves, save with the open palm, lest vermin be destroyed, or a hair uprooted by the nail.

Sir Richard Burton was born in Torquay of mixed English, Irish and French ancestry. With his brother and sister he was educated in France and Italy, where he began to realize his incredible facility for languages and his estrangement from his home country. He described himself as 'a waif, a stray . . . a blaze of light, without a focus'.

While studying at Oxford, his long, wild beard and passionate temperament (as evidenced in his enthusiasm for duelling) earned him the name 'Ruffian Dick'. Before long he was sent down, though for the minor offence of attending horse races. Following his father's footsteps, he joined the army and spent eight years in India. During this time he mastered Arabic, Hindi and six regional languages to add to a list that was to total twenty-nine by the end of his life – or forty, taking into account local dialects.

Working as an army intelligence officer, he ventured in disguise as a Muslim merchant into the local bazaars. He also investigated the homosexual brothels in Karachi, and his consequent report led to their closure, but also to Burton leaving the army in disgrace when a vindictive officer circulated his detailed findings among the ranks.

After a brief spell back in England Burton set about his dream of travelling to the sacred (and forbidden) Muslim city of Mecca, via Cairo, Suez and Medina. Revelling as ever in the danger of the venture, he had himself circumcised, then adopted the disguise of an Afghan pilgrim. On his eventual arrival he sketched and measured the most holy shrine of Islam, the Ka'bah. Still unsatisfied, he then organized an expedition to the equally forbidden East African city of Harar, becoming the first European to enter without being executed.

Back on the coast, he and his officer companions, including John Hanning Speke (see page 190), were attacked by Somalis. Once recovered from his injuries – he received a spear right through both cheeks – Burton volunteered for the Crimean War of 1854–6, and then, with the backing of the Royal Geographical Society and the British Foreign Office, led his famous expedition in search of the Nile's source, again with Speke. The pair reached the shores of Lake Tanganyika, the second largest lake in Africa and, though they were the first Europeans to see it, they were too sick to explore it fully. Speke did a cursory investigation by canoe, and soon after, while Burton was recovering in the Arab slaving station of Tabora, perhaps distracted again by his predeliction for Arab culture, Speke investigated an even bigger lake to the north, and claimed that this, not the Tanganyika, as Burton supposed, was the source of the Nile. Their relationship deteriorating, Speke was the first to return to England and, despite a pledge not to reveal any of their discoveries first, now claimed to have discovered the source. The rift that this created between the two explorers was never bridged; but as it happened, Burton, for all his intellect, was wrong.

In 1860 Burton visited North America, travelling by stagecoach to Salt Lake City, where he studied the Mormon community, which he made the subject of a book. The following year he joined the Foreign Office and for three years was consul in Fernando Po, a Spanish island off West Africa. His accounts of his brief exploratory trips – with their colourful descriptions of tribal fetishism, cannibalism, ritual murder and sexual practices – ruffled the sensibilities of other diplomats, yet somehow never quite sufficiently to justify his dismissal. His next placement was Santos, Brazil, followed by Damascus. This time he was dismissed, partly because of the thrill he seemed to get from upsetting the niceties of constrained Victorian society, and partly because of the unsubtle proselytizing of his devoutly Catholic wife, Isabel.

In 1872 Burton took up the consulate at Trieste, where he stayed for the remaining eighteen years of his life, writing and translating prolifically. Burton's charisma, his abiding passion for Eastern erotica, and his loathing of what he saw as the hypocrisy of polite society, notably in the 'immodest modesty' of England, are the lifeblood of his writing. His sixteen-volume translation of the *Arabian* *Nights* is considered unparalleled in both its literary skill and fidelity to the original.

Following Burton's death from a heart attack, Isabel burned almost all of his forty-year collection of journals.

Burton's rich writing style reflects his romantic fascination with an exotic culture barred to most of his kind. He shows a conscious awareness of what Europeans had lost by becoming 'civilized'. But nothing with Burton was straightforward. While eulogizing Arabic culture, the great man was unable to embrace the Africa he explored. It was a land with 'few traditions, no annals, and no ruins, the hoary remnants of past splendour so dear to the traveller and reader of travels. It contains not a single useful ornamental work of art; a canal or a dam is, and has ever been, beyond the narrow bounds of its civilization. It wants even the scenes of barbaric pomp and savage grandeur with which the student of Occidental Africa is familiar.' Was this to do with his mastery of Arabic and his inability to talk African tongues? It was the Arabs, not the Africans, who ran the slave trade.

The road to Mecca

At about half-past five p.m. we entered a suspicious-looking place. On the right was a stony buttress, along whose base the stream, when there is one, swings; and to this depression was our road limited by the rocks and thorn trees which filled the other half of the channel. The left side was a precipice, grim and barren, but not so abrupt as its brother. Opposite us the way seemed barred by piles of hills, crest rising above crest into the far blue distance: Day still smiled upon the upper peaks, but the lower slopes and the Fiumara bed were already curtained with grey sombre shade.

A damp seemed to fall upon our spirits as we approached this Valley Perilous. I remarked that the voices of the women and children sank into silence, and the loud *Labbayk* of the pilgrims were gradually stilled. Whilst still speculating upon the cause of this phenomenon, it became apparent. A small curl of the smoke, like a lady's ringlet, on the summit of the right-hand precipice, caught my eye; and simultaneous with the echoing crack of the matchlock, a high-trotting dromedary in front of me rolled over upon the sands – a bullet had split its heart – throwing the rider a goodly somersault of five or six yards.

Ensued terrible confusion; women screamed, children cried, and men vociferated, each one striving with might and main to urge his animal out of the place of death. But the road being narrow, they only managed to jam the vehicles in a solid immovable mass. At every matchlock shot, a shudder ran through the huge body, as when the surgeon's scalpel touches some more sensitive nerve. The Irregular horsemen, perfectly useless, galloped up and down over the stones, shouting to and ordering one another. The Pasha of the army had his carpet spread at the foot of the left-hand precipice, and debated over his pipe with the officers what ought to be done. No good genius whispered, 'Crown the heights.'

Then it was that the conduct of the Wahhabis found favour in my eyes. They came up, galloping their camels . . . with their elf-locks tossing in the wind, and their flaring matches casting a strange lurid light over their features. Taking up a position, one body began to fire upon the Utaybah robbers, whilst two or three hundred, dismounting, swarmed up the hill under the guidance of the Sharif Zayd. I had remarked this nobleman at Al-Madinah as a model specimen of the pure Arab. Like all Sharifs, he is celebrated for bravery, and has killed many with his own hand. When urged at Al-Zaribah to ride into Meccah, he swore that he would not leave the Caravan till in sight of the walls; and, fortunately for the pilgrims, he kept his word. Presently the firing was heard far in our rear, the robbers having fled. The head of the column advanced, and the dense body of pilgrims opened out. Our forced halt was now exchanged for a flight. It required much management to steer our Desert-craft clear of danger; but Shaykh Mas'ud was equal to the occasion. That many were not, was evident by the boxes and baggage that strewed the shingles. I had no means of ascertaining the number of men killed and wounded; reports were contradictory, and exaggeration unanimous. The robbers were said to be a hundred and fifty in number; their object was plunder, and they would eat the shot camels. But their principal ambition was the boast, We, the Utaybah, on such and such a night, stopped the Sultan's Mahmil one whole hour in the Pass.'

As we advanced, our escort took care to fire every large dry Asclepias, to disperse the shades which buried us. Again the scene became wondrous wild. On either side were ribbed precipices, dark, angry, and towering above, till their summits mingled with the glooms of night; and between them formidable looked the chasm, down which our host hurried with shouts and discharge of matchlocks. The torch-smoke and the night-fires of flaming Asclepias formed a canopy, sable above and livid red below; it hung over our heads like a sheet, and divided the cliffs into two equal parts. Here the fire flashed fiercely from a tall thorn, that crackled and shot up showers of sparks into the air; there it died away in lurid gleams, which lit up a truly Stygian scene. As usual, however, the picturesque had its inconvenience. There was no path. Rocks, stone-banks, and trees obstructed our passage. The camels now blind in darkness, then dazzled by a flood of light, stumbled frequently; in some places slipping down a steep descent, in others sliding over a sheet of mud. I passed that night crying, 'Hai! Hai!' switching the camel, and fruitless endeavouring to fustigate Mas'ud's nephew, who resolutely slept upon the water-bags. During the hours of darkness we made four or five halts, when we boiled coffee and smoked pipes; but man and beasts were beginning to suffer from a deadly fatigue.

Dawn (Saturday, Sept. 10th) found us still travelling down the Fiumara, which here is about a hundred yards broad . . . After breaking our fast joyously upon limes, pomegranates, and fresh dates, we sallied forth to admire the beauties of the place. We are once more on classic ground – the ground of the ancient Arab poets – and this Wady, celebrated for the purity of its air, has from remote ages been a favourite resort of the Maccans. Nothing can be more soothing to the brain than the dark green foliage of the limes and pomegranates; and from the base of the southern hill bursts a bubbling stream, whose *Chiare, fresche e dolci acque* flow through the gardens, filling them with the most delicious of melodies, the gladdest sound which Nature in these regions knows.

Exactly at noon Mas'ud seized the halter of the foremost camel, and we started down the Fiumara. Troops of Badawi girls looked over the orchard walls laughingly, and children came out to offer us fresh fruit and sweet water. At two p.m., travelling south-west, we arrived at a point where the torrent-bed turns to the right: and, quitting it, we climbed with difficulty over a steep ridge of granite. Before three o'clock we entered a hill-girt plain, which my companions called 'Sola'. In some places were clumps of trees, and scattered villages warned us that we were approaching a city. Far to the left rose the blue peaks of Taif, and the mountain road, a white thread upon the nearer heights, was pointed out to me. Here I first saw the tree, or rather shrub, which bears the balm of Gilead, erst so celebrated for its tonic and stomachic properties. I told Shaykh Mas'ud to break off a twig, which he did heedlessly. The act was witnessed by our party with a roar of laughter; and the astounded Shaykh was warned that he had become subject to an atoning sacrifice. Of course he denounced me as the instigator, and I could not fairly refuse assistance.

At four p.m. we came to a steep and rocky pass, up which we toiled with difficulty. The face of the country was rising once more, and again presented the aspect of numerous small basins divided and surrounded by hills . . .

We halted as evening approached, and strained our eyes, but all in vain, to catch sight of Meccah, which lies in a winding valley . . .

We again mounted, and night completed our disappointment. About one a.m. I was aroused by general excitement. 'Meccah! Meccah!' cried some voices; 'The Sanctuary! O the Sanctuary!' exclaimed others; and all burst into loud '*Labbayk*', not unfrequently broken by sobs. I looked out from my litter, and saw by the light of the southern stars the dim outlines of a large city, a shade darker than the surrounding plain . . .

[*In due course, he reaches the Ka'bah.*] There at last it lay, the bourn of my long and weary Pilgrimage, realising the plans and hopes of many and many a year. The mirage medium of Fancy invested the huge catafalque and its gloomy pall with peculiar charms. There were no giant fragments of hoar antiquity as in Egypt, no remains of graceful and harmonious beauty as in Greece and Italy, no barbarous gorgeousness as in the buildings of India; yet the view was strange, unique – and how few have looked upon the celebrated shrine! I may truly say that, of all the worshippers who clung weeping to the curtain, or who pressed their beating hearts to the stone, none felt for the moment a deeper emotion than did the Haji from the far-north. It was as if the poetical legends of the Arab spoke truth, and that the waving wings of angels, not the sweet breeze of morning, were agitating and swelling the black covering of the shrine. But, to confess humbling truth, theirs was the high feeling of religious enthusiasm, mine was the ecstasy of gratified pride.

Narrative of a Pilgrimage to El Madinah and Mecca, 1893

Attack, after the return from Harar

Between 2 and 3 a.m. of 19 April I was suddenly aroused by the Balyuz, who cried aloud that the enemy was upon us. Hearing a rush of men like a stormy wind, I sprang up, called for my sabre, and sent Lt. Herne to ascertain the force of the foray. Armed with a 'Colt', he went to the rear and left of the camp, the direction of danger, collected some of the guard – others having already disappeared – and fired two shots into the assailants. Then finding himself alone, he turned hastily towards the tent; in so doing he was tripped up by the ropes, and as he arose, a Somali appeared in the act of striking at him with a club. Lt. Herne fired, floored the man, and rejoining me, declared that the enemy was in great force and the guard nowhere. Meanwhile, I had aroused Lts. Stroyan and Speke, who were sleeping in the extreme right and left tents. The former, it is presumed, arose to defend himself, but, as the sequel shows, we never saw him alive. Lt. Speke, awakened by the report of fire-arms, but supposing it the normal false alarm – a warning to plunderers – he remained where he was: presently hearing clubs rattling upon his tent, and feet shuffling around, he ran to my Rowtie [tent], which we prepared to defend as long as possible.

The enemy swarmed like hornets with shouts and screams intending to terrify, and proving that overwhelming odds were against us: it was by no means easy to avoid in the shades of night the jobbing of javelins, and the long heavy daggers thrown at our legs from under and through the opening of the tent. We three remained together: Lt. Herne knelt by my right, on my left was Lt. Speke guarding the entrance, I stood in the centre, having nothing but a sabre. The revolvers were used by my companions with deadly effect: unfortunately there was but one pair. When the fire was exhausted, Lt. Herne went to search for his powder-horn, and that failing, to find some spears usually tied to the tent-pole. Whilst thus engaged, he saw a man breaking into the rear of our Rowtie, and came back to inform me of the circumstance.

At this time, about five minutes after the beginning of the affray, the tent had been almost beaten down, an Arab custom with which we were all famil-iar, and had we been entangled in its folds we should have been speared with unpleasant facility. I gave the word for escape, and sallied out, closely followed by Lt. Herne, with Lt. Speke in the rear. The prospect was not agreeable. About twenty men were kneeling and crouching at the tent entrance, whilst many dusk figures stood further off, or ran about shouting the war-cry, or with shouts and blows drove away our camels. Among the enemy were many of our friends and attendants: the coast being open to them, they naturally ran away, firing a few useless shots and receiving a modicum of flesh wounds.

After breaking through the mob at the tent entrance, imagining that I saw the form of Lt. Stroyan lying upon the sand, I cut my way towards it amongst a dozen Somal, whose war-clubs worked without mercy, whilst the Balyuz, who was violently pushing me out of the fray, rendered the strokes of my sabre uncertain. This individual was cool and collected: though incapacitated by a sore right-thumb from using the spear, he did not shun danger, and passed unhurt through the midst of the enemy: his efforts, however, only illustrated the venerable adage, 'defend me from my friends'. I turned to cut him down: he cried out in alarm; the well-known voice caused an instant's hesitation: at that moment a spearman stepped forward, left his javelin in my mouth, and retired before he could be punished. Escaping as by a miracle, I sought some support: many of our Somal and servants lurking in the darkness offered to advance, but 'tailed off' to a man as we approached the foe. Presently the Balyuz reappeared, and led me towards the place where he believed my three comrades had taken refuge. I followed him, sending the only man that showed presence of mind, one Golab of the Yusuf tribe, to bring back the Aynterad craft from the Spit into the centre of the harbour.

Again losing the Balyuz in the darkness, I spent the interval before dawn wandering in search of my comrades, and lying down when overpowered with faintness and pain: as the day broke, with my remaining strength I reached the head of the creek, was carried into the vessel, and persuaded the crew to arm themselves and visit the scene of our disasters.

Meanwhile, Lt. Herne, who had closely followed me, fell back, using the butt-end of his discharged six-shooter upon the hard heads around him: in so doing he came upon a dozen men, who though they loudly vociferated, 'Kill the Franks who are killing the Somal!' allowed him to pass uninjured.

He then sought his comrades in the empty huts of the town, and at early dawn was joined by the Balyuz, who was similarly employed. When day broke he sent a Negro to stop the native craft, which was apparently sailing out of the harbour, and in due time came on board. With the exception of sundry stiff blows with the war-club, Lt. Herne had the fortune to escape unhurt.

On the other hand, Lt. Speke's escape was in every way wonderful. Sallying from the tent he levelled his 'Dean and Adams' close to his assailant's breast. The pistol refused to revolve. A sharp blow of a war-club upon the chest felled our comrade, who was in the rear and unseen. When he fell, two or three men sprang upon him, pinioned his hands behind, felt him for concealed weapons – an operation to which he submitted in some alarm – and led him towards the rear, as he supposed to be slaughtered. There, Lt. Speke, who could scarcely breathe from the pain of the blow, asked a captor to tie his hands before, instead of behind, and begged a drop of water to relieve his excruciating thirst. The savage defended him against a number of the Somal who came up threatening and brandishing their spears, he brought a cloth for the wounded man to lie upon, and lost no time in procuring a draught of water.

Lt. Speke remained upon the ground till dawn. During the interval he witnessed the war-dance of the savages – a scene striking in the extreme. The tallest and largest warriors marched in a ring round the tents and booty, singing, with the deepest and most solemn tones, the song of thanks giving. At a little distance the grey uncertain light disclosed four or five men, lying desperately hurt, whilst their kinsmen kneaded their limbs, poured water upon their wounds, and placed lumps of dates in their stiffening hands. As day broke, the division of plunder caused angry passions to rise. The dead and dying were abandoned. One party made a rush upon the cattle, and with shouts and yells drove them off towards the wild, some loaded themselves with goods, others fought over pieces of cloth, which they tore with hand and dagger, whilst the disappointed, vociferating with rage, struck at one another and brandished their spears. More than once during these scenes, a panic seized them; they moved off in a body to some distance; and there is little doubt that had our guard struck one blow, we might still have won the day.

Lt. Speke's captor went to seek his own portion of the spoil, when a Somali came up and asked in Hindustani, what business the Frank had in their country, and added that he would kill him if a Christian, but spare the life of a brother Moslem. The wounded man replied that he was going to Zanzibar, that he was still a Nazarene, and therefore that the work had better be done at once – the savage laughed and passed on. He was succeeded by a second, who, equally compassionate, whirled a sword round his head, twice pretended to strike, but returned to the plunder without doing damage. Presently came another manner of assailant. Lt. Speke, who had extricated his hands, caught the spear levelled at his breast, but received at the same moment a blow from a club which, paralysing his arm, caused him to lose his hold. In defending his heart from a succession of thrusts, he received severe wounds on the back of his hand, his right shoulder, and his left thigh. Pausing a little, the wretch crossed to the other side, and suddenly passed his spear clean through the right leg of the wounded man: the latter, 'smelling death', then leapt up, and taking advantage of his assailant's terror, rushed headlong towards the sea. Looking behind, he avoided the javelin hurled at his back, and had the good fortune to run, without further accident, the gauntlet of a score of missiles. When pursuit was discontinued, he sat down faint from loss of blood upon a sandhill. Recovering strength by a few minutes' rest, he staggered on to the town, where some old women directed him to us. Then, pursuing his way, he fell in with the party sent to seek him, and by their aid reached the craft, having walked and run at least three miles, after receiving eleven wounds, two of which had pierced his thighs. A touching lesson how difficult it is to kill a man in sound health!

First Footsteps in East Africa, 1856

WILLIAM JOHN WILLS
1834–61
Day, beautifully warm and pleasant . . . nothing now but the greatest good luck can save any of us.

Devon-born Wills travelled to Australia in 1853 with his father and brother. After working as a shepherd and helping out with his father's medical practice, he studied surveying. At the age of twenty-six he joined an expedition to cross Australia from south to north, first as the expedition's surveyor and later as second in command when the original appointee, George Landells, was dismissed. The expedition, led by Robert O'Hara Burke, was set up by the government of Victoria as part of a competition between the Australian states in order to find the best route for an overland telegraph. Messages were taking three months to travel between Australia and England; the overland telegraph was to link up with an underwater cable that would speed up communications, and therefore Australia's progress. Burke's hope was to beat a rival bid by John McDouall Stuart, an experienced explorer sponsored by South Australia.

Burke, who had been a police superintendent in Ireland, was appointed as a result more of personal patronage than of his abilities as a pioneer. He was no more experienced than Wills, a stickler for military discipline, moody and impulsive – not an easy man to work under. Fortunately, John Wills' intelligence and steadfastness helped make him a patient and effective lieutenant, able to cope with the whimsical decisions and mood-swings of his superior.

Fourteen men in total set out from Melbourne in August 1860 with twenty-three horses and about thirty camels that had been especially shipped over from India. At the halfway point, Cooper's Creek in Queensland, the expedition established a depot and waited in vain for further supplies to arrive.

Then the party split up. William Brahe was left at the Creek, awaiting relief supplies, to be fetched by William Wright, who'd been an expedition guide. Burke, Wills, John King and Charles Gray headed on northwards. Burke's instructions were that Brahe should wait for their return for three months.

It took two months for the northbound party to even arrive at the Gulf of Carpentaria – swamps prevented them from reaching the shore, but the salt water and the tide was evidence enough that they had reached the sea.

On their journey there, the weather had been acutely hot and dry. On the return journey, however, they were plagued by incessant rain. Their rations diminishing, on 17 April Gray died – perhaps of starvation, though days earlier Burke had beaten him up for cheating on rations. They spent a day burying Gray, and four days later reached Cooper Creek to find that Brahe had left. Having waited a whole month longer than asked, he'd finally departed only eight hours earlier. The day that Burke, Wills and King spent disposing of Gray's body had proved fatal.

Burke overruled the opinions of Wills and King, who wanted to catch Brahe. He was, after all, starting out afresh. They would instead try for Adelaide via Mount Hopeless, where they hoped to meet up with Sturt.

Burke, Wills and King headed in a southerly direction, but were soon weakening. From Aborigines they received some help in the form of fish and nardoo (a grass seed), but this proved insufficient, at least for Wills and Burke. Both starved to death, still wandering the interior, Wills first, while the others were desperately looking for Aborigines to save them – his last diary entry was

29 June. Burke died two days later. King was cared for by Aborigines, who burst into tears, seeing the sorry corpse of Burke. They fed King until a rescue party came along.

Meanwhile, Brahe had encountered William Wright, who was bringing the long-awaited supplies. Wright arrived at Cooper's Creek on 8 May, but saw no sign of Burke, Wills and King, who had removed all traces of their presence to stop Aborigines moving a note for any rescue party. Wright didn't think to dig up the supplies he had earlier buried for the others beneath the tree labelled 'DIG', but instead, seeing no obvious fresh sign, headed back again. As it happened, Burke, Wills and King were still only a few miles away. The note they left on 22 April ended with the words: 'Greatly disappointed at finding the party here gone.' Burke signed the note and added, 'P.S. The camels cannot travel, and we cannot walk, or we should follow the other party. We shall move very slowly down the creek.' A combination of misjudgement and bad luck had made this the most tragic expedition in the history of Australia's settlement. Wills' diaries, which display a commendable lack of self-pity, were compiled by his father, who gave them the ironic title *A Successful Exploration Through the Interior of Australia*. Yet despite the young deaths it entailed, the Burke–Wills expedition had in many ways been successful. They had proved once and for all that there was no inland sea on the Australian continent and were the first to have crossed it from south to north.

The overland telegraph was built just ten years later, following the route discovered by the rival expedition, led by John McDouall Stuart.

'I may live three or four days if the weather continues warm'

Monday, 6th May, 1861: . . . The present state of things is not calculated to raise our spirits much; the rations are rapidly diminishing; our clothing, especially the boots, are all going to pieces, and we have not the materials for repairing them properly; the camel is completely done up and can scarcely get along, although he has the best of feed and is resting half his time. I suppose this will end in our having to live like the blacks for a few months.

Tuesday, 7th May, 1861: Breakfasted at daylight; but when about to start found that the camel would not rise even without any load on his back. After making every attempt to get him up, we were obliged to leave him to himself.

Mr Burke and I started down the creek to reconnoitre; at about eleven miles we came to some blacks fishing; they gave us some half a dozen fish each, for luncheon, and intimated that if we would go to their camp we should have some more and some bread. I tore in two a piece of macintosh stuff that I had, and Mr Burke gave one piece and I the other. We then went on to their camp about three miles farther. On our arrival they led us to a spot to camp on, and soon afterwards brought a lot of fish, and a kind of bread which they call nardoo. The lighting a fire with matches delights them, but they do not care about having them. In the evening various members of the tribe

came down with lumps of nardoo and handfuls of fish, until we were posi-
tively unable to eat any more. They also gave us some stuff they call bedgery
or pedgery; it has a highly intoxicating effect when chewed even in small
quantities. It appears to be the dried stems and leaves of some shrub.

Wednesday, 8th May, 1861. Left the blacks' camp at 7.30, Mr Burke returning to
the junction, whilst I proceeded to trace down the creek. This I found a
shorter task than I had expected, for it soon showed signs of running out, and
at the same time kept considerably to the north of west. There were several
fine waterholes within about four miles of the camp I had left, but not a drop
all the way beyond that, a distance of seven miles. Finding that the creek
turned greatly towards the north, I returned to the blacks' encampment, and
as I was about to pass they invited me to stay; I did so, and was even more
hospitably entertained than before.

Thursday, 9th May, 1861: Parted from my friends, the blacks, at 7.30, and
started for Camp No. 9.

Friday, 10th May, 1861: Mr Burke and King employed in jerking the camel's
flesh, whilst I went to look for the nardoo seed for making bread: in this I was
unsuccessful, not being able to find a single tree of it in the neighbourhood of
the camp. I, however, tried boiling the large kind of bean which the blacks call
padlu; they boil easily, and when shelled are very sweet, much resembling in
taste the French chestnut; they are to be found in large quantities nearly
everywhere.

Saturday, 11th May, 1861: To-day Mr Burke and King started down the creek to
the blacks' camp, determined to ascertain all particulars about the nardoo. I
have now my turn at the meat jerking, and must devise some means for
trapping the birds and rats, which is a pleasant prospect after our dashing trip
to Carpentaria, having to hang about Cooper's Creek, living like the blacks.

Sunday, 12th May, 1861: Mr Burke and King returned this morning having
been unsuccessful in their search for the blacks, who it seems have moved over
to the other branch of the creek . . .

Thursday, 16th, 1861: Having completed our planting, etc., started up the creek
for the second blacks' camp, a distance of about eight miles: finding our loads
rather too heavy we made a small plant here of such articles as could best be
spared.

Nardoo, Friday, 17th May, 1861: Started this morning on a blacks' path, leaving the creek on our left, our intention being to keep a south-easterly direction until we should cut some likely looking creek, and then to follow it down. On approaching the foot of the first sandhill, King caught sight in the flat of some nardoo seeds, and we soon found that the flat was covered with them. This discovery caused somewhat of a revolution in our feelings, for we considered that with the knowledge of this plant we were in a position to support ourselves, even if we were destined to remain on the creek and wait for assistance from town.

Friday, 24th May, 1861: Started with King to celebrate the Queen's birthday by fetching from Nardoo Creek what is now to us the staff of life; returned at a little after two p.m. with a fair supply, but find the collecting of the seed a slower and more troublesome process than could be desired.

Monday, 27th May, 1861: Started up the creek this morning for the depot, in order to deposit journals and a record of the state of affairs here. On reaching the sandhills below where Landa [one of the camels] was bogged, I passed some blacks on a flat collecting nardoo seed. Never saw such an abundance of the seed before. The ground in some parts was quite black with it. There were only two or three gins [native women] and children, and they directed me on, as if to their camp, in the direction I was before going; but I had not gone far over the first sandhill when I was overtaken by about twenty blacks, bent on taking me back to their camp, and promising any quantity of nardoo and fish. On my going with them, one carried the shovel, and another insisted on taking my swag in such a friendly manner that I could not refuse them. They were greatly amused with the various little things I had with me. In the evening they supplied me with abundance of nardoo and fish, and one of the old men, Poko Tinnamira, shared his gunyah with me.

Tuesday, 28th May, 1861: Left the blacks' camp, and proceeded up the creek; obtained some mussels near where Landa died, and halted for breakfast. Still feel very unwell.

Wednesday, 29th: Started at seven a.m., and went on to the duckholes, where we breakfasted coming down. Halted there at 9.30 a.m. for a feed, and then moved on. At the stones saw a lot of crows quarrelling about something near the water; found it to be a large fish, of which they had eaten a considerable portion. As it was quite fresh and good, I decided the quarrel by taking it with me. It proved a most valuable addition to my otherwise scanty supper of nardoo porridge . . .

Sunday, 2nd June, 1861: Started at half-past six, thinking to breakfast at the blacks' camp below Landa's grave. Found myself very much fagged, and did not arrive at their camp until ten a.m., and then found myself disappointed as to a good breakfast, the camp being deserted. Having rested awhile and eaten a few fishbones, I moved down the creek, hoping by a late march to be able to reach our own camp; but I soon found, from my extreme weakness, that that would be out of the question. A certain amount of good luck, however, still stuck to me, for on going along by a large waterhole I was so fortunate as to find a large fish, about a pound and a half in weight, which was just being choked by another which it had tried to swallow, but which had stuck in its throat. I soon had a fire lit, and both of the fish cooked and eaten: the large one was in good condition. Moving on again after my late breakfast, I passed Camp No. 67 of the journey to Carpentaria, and camped for the night under some polygonum bushes.

Monday, 3rd June, 1861: Started at seven o'clock, and keeping on the south bank of the creek was rather encouraged at about three miles by the sound of numerous crows ahead; presently fancied I could see smoke, and was shortly afterwards set at my ease by hearing a cooey from Pitchery, who stood on the opposite bank, and directed me round the lower end of the waterhole, continually repeating his assurance of abundance of fish and bread. Having with some considerable difficulty managed to ascend the sandy path that led to the camp, I was conducted by the chief to a fire where a large pile of fish were just being cooked in the most approved style. These I imagined to be for the general consumption of the half-dozen natives gathered around, but it turned out that they had already had their breakfast. I was expected to dispose of this lot – a task which, to my own astonishment, I soon accomplished, keeping two or three blacks pretty steadily at work extracting the bones for me. The fish being disposed of, next came a supply of nardoo cake and water until I was so full as to be unable to eat any more; when Pitchery, allowing me a short time to recover myself, fetched a large bowl of the raw nardoo flour mixed to a thin paste, a most insinuating article, and one that they appear to esteem a great delicacy. I was then invited to stop the night there, but this I declined, and proceeded on my way home.

Tuesday, 4th June, 1861: Started for the blacks' camp intending to test the practicability of living with them, and to see what I could learn as to their ways and manners.

Wednesday, 5th June, 1861: Remained with the blacks. Light rain during the greater part of the night, and more or less throughout the day in showers. Wind blowing in squalls from south.

Thursday, 6th June, 1861: Returned to our own camp: found that Mr Burke and King had been well supplied with fish by the blacks. Made preparation for shifting our camp nearer theirs on the morrow.

Friday, 7th June, 1861: Started in the afternoon for the blacks' camp with such things as we could take; found ourselves all very weak in spite of the abundant supply of fish that we have lately had. I myself, could scarcely get along, although carrying the lightest swag, only about thirty pounds. Found that the blacks had decamped, so determined on proceeding to-morrow up to the next camp, near the nardoo field.

Saturday, 8th June, 1861: With the greatest fatigue and difficulty we reached the nardoo camp. No blacks, greatly to our disappointment; took possession of their best mia-mia and rested for the remainder of the day.

Sunday, 9th June, 1861: King and I proceeded to collect nardoo, leaving Mr Burke at home.

Monday, 10th June, 1861: Mr Burke and King collecting nardoo; self at home too weak to go out; was fortunate enough to shoot a crow . . .

Wednesday, 12th June, 1861: King out collecting nardoo; Mr Burke and I at home pounding and cleaning. I still feel myself, if anything, weaker in the legs, although the nardoo appears to be more thoroughly digested . . .

Friday, 14th June, 1861: Night alternately clear and cloudy; no wind; beautifully mild for the time of year; in the morning some heavy clouds on the horizon. King out for nardoo; brought in a good supply. Mr Burke and I at home, pounding and cleaning seed. I feel weaker than ever, and both Mr B. and King are beginning to feel very unsteady in the legs . . .

Sunday, 16th June, 1861: We finished up the remains of the camel Rajah yesterday, for dinner; King was fortunate enough to shoot a crow this morning . . .

Thursday, 20th June, 1861: Night and morning very cold, sky clear. I am completely reduced by the effects of the cold and starvation. King gone out for nardoo; Mr Burke at home pounding seed; he finds himself getting very weak in the legs. King holds out by far the best; the food seems to agree with him pretty well.

Finding the sun come out pretty warm towards noon, I took a sponging all over; but it seemed to do little good beyond the cleaning effects, for my weakness is so great that I could not do it with proper expedition.

I cannot understand this nardoo at all – it certainly will not agree with me in any form; we are now reduced to it alone, and we manage to consume from four to five pounds per day between us; it appears to be quite indigestible, and cannot possibly be sufficiently nutritious to sustain life by itself.

Friday, 21st June, 1861: Last night was cold and clear, winding up with a strong wind from N.E. in the morning. I feel much weaker than ever and can scarcely crawl out of the mia-mia. Unless relief comes in some form or other, I cannot possibly last more than a fortnight.

It is a great consolation, at least, in this position of ours, to know that we have done all we could, and that our deaths will rather be the result of the mismanagement of others than of any rash acts of our own. Had we come to grief elsewhere, we could only have blamed ourselves; but here we are returned to Cooper's Creek, where we had every reason to look for provisions and clothing; and yet we have to die of starvation, in spite of the explicit instructions given by Mr Burke – 'That the depot party should await our return'; and the strong recommendation to the Committee 'that we should be followed up by a party from Menindie.'

Saturday, 22nd June, 1861: There were a few drops of rain during the night, and in the morning, about nine a.m., there was every prospect of more rain until towards noon, when the sky cleared up for a time.

Mr Burke and King are out for nardoo; the former returned much fatigued. I am so weak to-day as to be unable to get on my feet.

Sunday, 23rd June, 1861: All hands at home. I am so weak as to be incapable of crawling out of the mia-mia. King holds out well, but Mr Burke finds himself weaker every day.

Monday, 24th June, 1861: A fearful night. At about an hour before sunset, a southerly gale sprung up and continued throughout the greater portion of the night; the cold was intense, and it seemed as if one would be shrivelled up. Towards morning it fortunately lulled a little, but a strong cold breeze continued till near sunset, after which it became perfectly calm.

King went out for nardoo in spite of the wind, and came in with a good load; but he himself terribly cut up. He says that he can no longer keep up the work, and as he and Mr Burke are both getting rapidly weaker, we have but a slight chance of anything but starvation, unless we can get hold of some blacks.

Tuesday, 25th June, 1861: Night calm, clear, and intensely cold, especially towards morning. Near daybreak, King reported seeing a moon in the east, with a haze of light stretching up from it; he declared it to be quite as large as the moon, and not dim at the edges. I am so weak that any attempt to get a sight of it was out of the question; but I think it must have been Venus in the Zodiacal Light that he saw, with a corona around her.

26th. Mr Burke and King remain at home cleaning and pounding seed; they are both getting weaker every day; the cold plays the deuce with us, from the small amount of clothing we have: my wardrobe consists of a wide-awake, a merino shirt, a regatta shirt without sleeves, the remains of a pair of flannel trousers, two pairs of socks in rags, and a waistcoat, of which I have managed to keep the pockets together. The others are no better off. Besides these, we have between us, for bedding, two small camel pads, some horsehair, two or three little bits of rag, and pieces of oilcloth saved from the fire.

The day turned out nice and warm.

Wednesday, 27th June, 1861: Mr Burke and King are preparing to go up the creek in search of the blacks; they will leave me some nardoo, wood, and water, with which I must do the best I can until they return. *I think this is almost our only chance.* I feel myself, if anything, rather better, but I cannot say stronger: the nardoo is beginning to agree better with me; but without some change I see little chance for any of us. They have both shown great hesitation and reluctance with regard to leaving me, and have repeatedly desired my candid opinion in the matter. I could only repeat, however, that I considered it our only chance, for I could not last long on the nardoo, even if a supply could be kept up.

Friday, 29th June, 1861: Clear, cold night, slight breeze from the east, day beautifully warm and pleasant. Mr Burke suffers greatly from the cold and is getting extremely weak; he and King start to-morrow up the creek to look for the blacks; it is the only chance we have of being saved from starvation. I am weaker than ever, although I have a good appetite and relish the nardoo much; but it seems to give us no nutriment, and the birds here are so shy as not to be got at. Even if we got a good supply of fish, I doubt whether we could do much work on them and the nardoo alone. Nothing now but the greatest good luck can save any of us; and as for myself I may live four or five days if the weather continues warm. My pulse is at forty-eight, and very weak, and my legs and arms are nearly skin and bone. I can only look out, like Mr Micawber, 'for *something to turn up*', starvation on nardoo is by no means very unpleasant, but for the weakness one feels, and the utter inability to move one's self; for as far as appetite is concerned, it gives the greatest satisfaction.

[*Burke died two days after leaving Wills; King, returning to Wills, found him dead.*]

A Successful Exploration through the Interior of Australia, 1863

JOHN KING
1841–72
They appeared to feel great compassion for me when they saw
I was alone on the creek.

Of the four members of the Burke–Wills expedition which successfully made the first crossing of Australia from south to north by Europeans, King was the sole survivor. He owed his life to a group of Aborigines who cared for him for the three and a half months before help arrived. He returned to Melbourne and was rewarded with a life pension.

'The whole party wept bitterly'

Before leaving him [Mr Wills], however, Mr Burke asked him whether he still wished it, as under no other circumstances would he leave him; and Mr Wills again said that he looked on it as our only chance. He then gave Mr Burke a letter and his watch for his father, and we buried the remainder of the field-books near the gunyah. Mr Wills said that, in case of my surviving Mr Burke, he hoped that I would carry out his last wishes, in giving the watch and letter to his father.

In travelling the first day, Mr Burke seemed very weak, and complained of great pain in his legs and back. On the second day he seemed to be better, and said that he thought he was getting stronger, but, on starting, did not go two miles before he said he could go no further. I persisted in his trying to go on, and managed to get him along several times, until I saw that he was almost knocked up, when he said he could not carry his swag, and threw all he had away. I also reduced mine, taking nothing but a gun and some powder and shot, and a small pouch and some matches. On starting again, we did not go far before Mr Burke said we should halt for the night, but, as the place was close to a large sheet of water, and exposed to the wind, I prevailed on him to go a little further, to the next reach of water, where we camped. We searched about, and found a few small patches of nardoo, which I collected and pounded, and, with a crow which I shot, made a good evening's meal. From the time we halted Mr Burke seemed to be getting worse, although he ate his supper. He said he felt convinced he could not last many hours, and gave me his watch, which he said belonged to the committee, and a pocket-book, to give to Sir William Stawell, and in which he wrote some notes. He then said to me, 'I hope you will remain with me here till I am quite dead – it is a comfort to know that some one is by; but when I am dying, it is my wish that you should place the pistol in my right hand, and that you leave me unburied as I die.' That night he spoke very little, and the following morning I found him speechless, or nearly so; and about eight o'clock he expired. I remained a few hours there, but as I saw there was no use in remaining longer, I went up the creek in search of the natives. I felt very lonely, and at night usually slept in deserted wurleys, belonging to the natives. Two days after leaving the spot where Mr Burke died, I found some gunyahs, where the natives had deposited a bag of nardoo, sufficient to last me a fortnight, and three bundles containing various articles. I also shot a crow that evening, but was in great dread that the natives would come and deprive me of the nardoo.

I remained there two days, to recover my strength, and then returned to Mr Wills. I took back three crows; but found him lying dead in his gunyah, and the natives had been there and had taken away some of his clothes. I buried the corpse with sand, and remained there some days; but finding that my stock of nardoo was running short, and being unable to gather it, I tracked the natives who had been to the camp by their footprints in the sand, and went some distance down the creek, shooting crows and hawks on the road. The natives, hearing the report of the gun, came to meet me, and took me with them to their camp, giving me nardoo and fish. They took the birds I had shot and cooked them for me, and afterwards showed me a gunyah, where I was to sleep with three of the single men. The following morning they commenced talking to me, and putting one finger on the ground, and covering it with sand, at the same time pointing up the creek, saying, 'Whitefellow,' which I understood to mean that one white man was dead. From this I knew that they were the tribe who had taken Mr Wills's clothes. They then asked me where the third white man was, and I also made the sign of putting two fingers on the ground and covering them with sand, at the same time pointing up the creek. They appeared to feel great compassion for me when they understood that I was alone on the creek, and gave me plenty to eat. After being four days with them I saw that they were becoming tired of me, and they made signs that they were going up the creek, and that I had better go downwards; but I pretended not to understand them. The same day they shifted camp, and I followed them; and, on reaching their camp, I shot some crows, which pleased them so much that they made me a breakwind in the centre of their camp, and came and sat round me until such time as the crows were cooked, when they assisted me to eat them. The same day, one of the women, to whom I had given part of a crow, came and gave me a ball of nardoo, saying that she would give me more only she had such a sore arm that she was unable to pound. She showed me a sore on her arm, and the thought struck me that I would boil some water in the billy and wash her arm with a sponge. During the operation the whole tribe sat round, and were muttering one to another. Her husband sat down by her side, and she was crying all the time. After I had washed it, I touched it with some nitrate of silver, when she began to yell and ran off, crying out, 'Mokow! mokow!' (Fire! Fire!) From this time, she and her husband used to give me a small quantity of nardoo both night and morning, and whenever the tribe were about going on a fishing excursion, he used to give me notice to go with them. They also used to assist me in making a gourley, or breakwind, whenever they shifted camp. I generally shot a crow, or a hawk, and gave it to them in return for these little services. Every four or five days the tribe would surround me, and ask whether I intended going up or down the creek; at last I made them understand that if they went up I should go up the creek, and if they went down I should also go down, and from this time they seemed to look upon me as one of themselves, and supplied me with fish and nardoo regularly. They were very anxious, however, to know where Mr Burke lay; and one day when we were fishing in the waterholes close by I took them to the spot. On seeing his remains the whole party wept bitterly, and covered them with bushes. After this they were much kinder to me than before; and I always told them that the white men would be here before two moons; and in the evenings, when they came with nardoo and fish, they used to talk about the 'whitefellows' coming, at the same time pointing to the moon. I also told them they would receive many presents and they constantly asked me for tomahawks, called by them 'Bo-mayko'. From this time to when the relief party arrived – a period of about a month – they treated me with uniform kindness, and looked upon me as one of themselves. The day on which I was released, one of the tribe who had been fishing came and told me that the whitefellows were coming, and the whole of the tribe who were then in camp sallied out in every direction to meet the party, while the man who had brought the news took me across the creek, where I shortly saw the party coming down.

Ernest Scott, *Australian Discovery*, 1929

Arminius Vámbéry
1832–1913

It is a horrible sight to see the father hide his store of water from the son; and brother from brother; each drop is life, and when men feel the torture of thirst, there is not, as in the other dangers of life, any spirit of self-sacrifice, or any feeling of generosity.

Arminius Vámbéry, a Hungarian writer and linguist who travelled in disguise with a pilgrim's caravan through Central Asia, was born in Hungary and at the age of twelve was apprenticed to a dressmaker; but he had wider ambitions, and later took up teaching. In 1857 he travelled to Constantinople, where he spent six years studying languages and immersing himself in Turkish culture.

In 1863, following an eight-month wait at the Turkish embassy in Tehran for a suitable caravan to appear, he joined a group of pilgrims who were returning to eastern Turkistan from Mecca. Disguised as a Dervish and on several occasions coming close to being revealed as an impostor, Vámbéry studied the people, customs and languages he encountered along the way. He crossed the Caspian Sea and finally left the caravan at Samarkand, before returning to Tehran.

The following year he published an exuberant account of his journey, *Travels and Adventures in Central Asia*, which often expands with a lightness of touch beyond the confines of the terrain he is exploring.

> Joy and sorrow are undoubtedly the mirror in which not only is the character of a people clearly reflected, but which likewise offers the most faithful image of their manners and customs. In joy and sorrow every sign of dissimulation vanishes, man shows himself in his true colours, and the lights and shades of his temperament become at once apparent . . . And nowhere is a better opportunity offered for studying the various features of joy and sorrow than at a birth, marriage, and death, those three stages in the great family of mankind.

Vámbéry then worked as a professor of Oriental languages in Budapest until 1905, and published works on the Altaic languages, the ethnology of the Turks and other Oriental subjects. It is also thought he provided Bram Stoker with material that was later woven into *Dracula*.

Bloody punishments in Khiva

I was ordered to take a seat, and after having been offered tea and bread, the Khan invited me to converse with him. The subject to-day was exclusively political. To remain true to my Dervish character, I forced them to press every word out of me. The Mehter watched each expression, wishing to see the confirmation of his suspicions. All his trouble was fruitless. The Khan, after graciously dismissing me, ordered me to take the money for my daily support from the treasurer.

On my saying that I did not know where he dwelt, they then gave me a Yasaul for escort, who had also other commissions to execute; and terrible indeed is the recollection of the scenes to which I was witness in his presence. In the last court I found about three hundred Tchaudors, prisoners of war, covered with rags; they were so tormented by the dread of their approaching fate, and by the hunger which they had endured several days, that they looked as if they had just risen from their graves. They were separated into two divisions, namely, such as had not yet reached their fortieth year, and were to be sold as slaves, or to be made use of as presents, and such as from their rank or age were regarded as Aksakals (grey beards) or leaders, and who were to suffer the punishment imposed by the Khan. The former, chained together by their iron collars in numbers of ten to fifteen, were led away; the latter submissively awaited the punishment awarded. They looked like lambs in the hands of their executioners. Whilst several were led to the gallows or the block, I saw how, at a sign from the executioner, eight aged men placed themselves down on their backs upon the earth. They were then bound hand and foot, and the executioner gouged out their eyes in turn, kneeling to do so on the breast of each poor wretch; and after every operation he wiped his knife, dripping with blood, upon the white beard of the hoary unfortunate.

Ah! cruel spectacle! As each fearful act was completed, the victim liberated from his bonds, groping around with his hands, sought to gain his feet! Some fell against each other, head against head; others sank powerless to the earth again, uttering low groans, the memory of which will make me shudder as long as I live . . .

A treatment of prisoners such as I have described is indeed horrible; but it is not to be regarded as an exceptional case. In Khiva, as well as in the whole of Central Asia, wanton cruelty is unknown; the whole proceeding is regarded as perfectly natural, and usage, law, and religion all accord in sanctioning it. The present Khan of Khiva wanted to signalise himself as a protector of religion, and believed he should succeed by punishing with the greatest severity all offences against it. To have cast a look upon a thickly-veiled lady, sufficed for the offender to be executed by the Redjm according as religion directs. The man is hung, and the woman is buried up to the breast in the earth near the gallows, and there stoned to death. As in Khiva there are no stones, they use Kesek (hard balls of earth). At the third discharge, the poor victim is completely covered with dust, and the body, dripping with blood, is horribly disfigured, and the death which ensues alone puts an end to her torture.

Travels and Adventures in Central Asia, 1864

SVEN HEDIN
1865–1952
This death-camp was the unhappiest I lived through in all my wanderings in Asia.

Sven Anders Hedin, a Swedish geographer who made punishing journeys across Central Asia, was born in Stockholm and had already recognized his vocation as an explorer by the age of twelve. 'Happy is the boy who discovers the bent of his life-work during childhood,' he wrote. 'That, indeed, was my good fortune.'

He embarked on his first Asian expedition when he was twenty. 'Fate', he later wrote, 'led me toward Asiatic highways; and as the years went by my youthful dreams about the North Pole gradually faded. And for the rest of my life I was to be held by the enchanting power that emanates from the largest continent in the world.'

His first scientific expedition, from 1893 to 1897, was particularly ambitious, aiming to cross Asia from west to east. He travelled to Tashkent in atrocious winter conditions, crossed the Pamirs through modern Kyrgyzstan and explored Mount Mustagh Ata, climbing to heights of 20,000 feet. On 23 April 1894 he embarked on a horrendous crossing of the Taklamakan, the largest waterless area on the planet. Hedin seems to have been undeterred by the risk of extreme danger, his apparent bravery – or recklessness – often costing the lives of both his animal and human companions. Later Hedin was to traverse the Taklamakan again, and the Ordos and Gobi Deserts.

In 1900 and 1901 Hedin made two unsuccessful attempts to reach Lhasa. Three years later the Viceroy of India, Lord Curzon, apologized to Hedin for 'destroying the virginity of the bride to which you aspired, viz. Lhasa', after the Younghusband expedition had flooded the Tibetan capital with British troops. Hedin was, however, the first European to explore Tibet's Trans-Himalaya mountain range and to prepare a detailed map of the country.

During the First World War Hedin's pro-German sympathies lost him some influential friends and the trust of the Russian, Indian and Chinese governments. However, he did set up and lead an important expedition that between 1927 and 1933 explored the Lop Nor Desert and the nearby Silk Road oasis of Lou-lan. The area had been thought forever barren, but Hedin discovered evidence of a thriving culture, dependent on hunting and fishing, that had survived until the fourth century. He was the first Westerner to see the ruins later studied in depth by Aurel Stein – notably at Dandan-oilik and Karadong – and brought back relics for specialists, having little idea himself what they were.

He also solved the puzzle of Lop Nor's changing basins, which were caused by the shifting lower course of the Tarim river. This and subsequent journeys in Tibet, written up copiously and for the most part entertainingly, brought Hedin widespread acclaim, but again his political convictions (to be precise, suspected Nazi ones) damaged his reputation.

Crossing the Taklamakan

After a while we saw the last tamarisks, and passed the last spots of even clay soil. There was nothing now but fine yellow sand. As far as the eye could reach only high dunes, quite bare of vegetation, were visible. Strange that I should not be amazed at this sight, and that it did not make me halt. It should have occurred to me that the season was too far advanced and that the risk was too great. If ill luck prevailed I might lose everything. But I did not hesitate for a moment. I had determined to conquer the desert. No matter how many weary steps I might have to take to the Khotan-daria, I would not retrace a single step of my trail. I was swept away by the irresistible *desiderium incogniti*, which breaks down all obstacles and refuses to recognize the impossible . . .

As I rolled myself in a blanket and lay down on my rug, the camels were still lying at the well, waiting in vain for water, patient and resigned, as always.

Having discarded such superfluous belongings as tent-rugs, tent-cot, stove, etc., we set out early on April 27. I went on foot, in advance. The dunes were now only thirty feet high. My hopes rose. But again the dunes mounted to double and treble size, and again our situation seemed hopeless . . .

Steel-blue rain-filled clouds appeared in the west before sunset. Our hopes revived again. The clouds expanded and approached. We kept the last two empty tanks, placed all the bowls and jugs on the sand, and spread the tent-covering on the surface of the dune. It grew dark! We took the tent-covering by the corners and stood ready to collect Life, the rescue which was to come from the sky. But when close upon us the clouds thinned out gradually. One man after another let go the cloth and walked away sadly. The clouds vanished without trace, as though the aqueous vapour had been annihilated in the warm desert-air. Not a drop reached us.

In the evening I listened to the conversation of the men. Islam said: 'The camels will collapse first, one by one; then it will be our turn.' Yolchi, the guide, thought that we had come in for *telesmat*, or witchcraft.

'We only imagine that we are walking straight ahead, but in reality we are walking in a circle all the time. We exhaust ourselves uselessly. We might just as well lie down to die anywhere.'

'Haven't you noticed the regular course of the sun?' I asked. 'Do you think that one walks in a circle when one has the sun at one's right every day at noon?'

'We only think so; it is *telesmat*,' he insisted, 'or the sun itself has gone mad.'

Thirsty, after the two miserable cups of water which was our dole for the whole day, we again went to rest . . .

That night I wrote what I supposed were to be my last lines in my diary: 'Halted on a high dune, where the camels dropped. We examined the east through the field-glasses; mountains of sand in all directions, not a straw, no life. All, men as well as camels, are extremely weak. God help us!'

May Day, a spring-time feast of joy and light at home in Sweden, was for us the heaviest day on our *via dolorosa* through the desert.

The night had been quiet, clear and cold (36°); but the sun was hardly above the horizon when it grew warm. The men squeezed the last drops of the rancid oil out of a goatskin and gave them to the camels. The day before I had not had a single drop of water, and the day before that, only two cups. I was suffering from thirst; and when by chance I found the bottle in which we kept the Chinese spirits for the Primus stove, I could not resist the temptation to drink some of it. It was a foolish thing to do; but nevertheless I drank half the bottle. Yoldash heard the gurgling sound and came toward me, wagging his tail. I let him have a sniff. He snorted and went away sadly. I threw the bottle away and the rest of the liquid flowed out into the sand.

That treacherous drink finished me. I tried to rise but my legs would not support me. The caravan broke camp but I remained behind. Islam Baï led, compass in hand, going due east. The sun was already burning hot. My men probably thought I would die where I lay. They went on slowly, like snails. The sound of the bells grew fainter and finally died away altogether. On every dune-crest the caravan reappeared like a dark spot, smaller and smaller; in every hollow between the dunes it remained concealed for a while. Finally I saw it no more. But the deep trail, with its dark shadows from the sun, which was still low, reminded me of the danger of my situation. I had not strength enough to follow the others. They had left me. The horrible desert extended in all directions. The sun was burning and blinding; there was not a breath of air.

Then a terrible thought struck me. What if this was the quiet preceding a storm? At any moment, then, I might see the black streak across the horizon in the cast, which heralded the approach of a sand-storm. The trail of the caravan would then be obliterated in a few moments, and I would never find my men and camels again, those wrecks of the ships of the desert.

I exerted all my will-power, got up, reeled, fell, crawled for a while along the trail, got up again, dragged myself along, and crawled. One hour passed, and then another. From the ridge of a dune I saw the caravan. It was standing still. The bells had ceased tinkling. By superhuman efforts I managed to reach it . . .

The sun was now glowing like an oven. 'When the sun has gone down,' I said to Islam, 'we will break camp and march all night. Up with the tent!' The camels were freed from their burdens and lay in the blazing sun all day. Islam and Kasim pitched the tent. I crawled in, undressed completely, and lay down on a blanket, my head pillowed on a sack. Islam, Kasim, Yoldash and the sheep went into the shade, while Mohammed Shah and Yolchi stayed where they had fallen. The hens were the only ones to keep up their spirits.

This death-camp was the unhappiest I lived through in all my wanderings in Asia.

It was only half-past nine in the morning, and we had hardly traversed three miles. I was absolutely done up and unable to move a finger. I thought I was dying. I imagined myself already lying in a mortuary chapel. The church bells had stopped tolling for the funeral. My whole life flew past me like a dream. There were not many hours left me on the threshold of eternity. But most of all, I was tormented by the thought of the anxiety and uncertainty which I would cause my parents and brother and sisters. When I should be reported missing Consul Petrovsky would make investigations. He would learn that I had left Merket on April 10. All traces after that, however, would then have been swept away; for several storms would have passed over the desert since then. They would wait and wait at home. One year would pass after another. But no news would come, and finally they would cease hoping.

About noon the slack flaps of the tent began to bulge, and a faint southerly breeze moved over the desert. It blew stronger, and after a couple of hours it was so fresh that I rolled myself up in my blanket.

And now a miracle happened! My debility vanished and my strength returned! If ever I longed for the sunset it was now. I did not want to die: I *would not* die in this miserable, sandy desert! I could run, walk, crawl on my hands and feet. My men might not survive, but I had to find water!

The sun lay like a red-hot cannon-ball on a dune in the west. I was in the best of condition. I dressed and ordered Islam and Kasim to prepare for departure. The sunset-glow spread its purple light over the dunes. Mohammed Shah and Yolchi were in the same position as in the morning. The former had already begun his death-struggle; and he never regained consciousness. But the latter woke to life in the cool of the evening. With his hands clenched he crawled up to me and cried pitifully: 'Water! Give us water, sir! Only a drop of water!' Then he crawled away.

'Is there no liquid here, whatever?' I said.

'Why, the rooster!' So they cut off the rooster's head and drank his blood. But that was only a drop in the bucket. Their eyes fell on the sheep, which had followed us as faithfully as a dog without complaining. Everyone hesitated. It would be murder to kill the sheep to prolong our lives for only one day. But Islam led it away, turned its head toward Mecca and slashed its carotids. The blood, reddish-brown and ill-smelling, flowed slowly and thickly. It coagulated immediately into a cake, which the men gulped down. I tried it, too; but it was nauseous, and the mucous membrane of my throat was so dry that it stuck there, and I had to get rid of it quickly.

Mad with thirst, Islam and Yolchi collected camel's urine in a receptacle, mixed it with sugar and vinegar, held their noses, and drank. Kasim and I declined to join in this drinking-bout. The two who had drunk this poison were totally incapacitated. They were overcome with violent cramps and vomiting, and lay writhing and groaning on the sand . . .

Our progress was desperately slow. Every step was an effort for the camels. Now one, then the other stopped, and had to rest for a while. Islam suffered from fresh attacks of vomiting and lay writhing on the sand like a worm. In the faint light from the lantern I lengthened my stride, and went on ahead . . .

At eleven o'clock I struggled up on to a flat sandy ridge, to listen and to reconnoitre. The Khotan-daria *couldn't* be far away. I scanned the east, hoping to detect the fire of a shepherd's camp; but everything was pitch-dark. Only the stars shone. No sound interrupted the silence. I placed the lantern in a position to serve as a beacon for Islam and Kasim, laid myself on my back, and pondered and listened . . . After I had waited for what seemed like eternity, the four camels stood forth like phantoms. They came up to me on the ridge and lay down right away. They probably mistook the lantern for a camp-fire. Islam staggered along, threw himself on the sand, and whispered labouredly that he could go no farther. He would die where he was. He made no answer when I tried to encourage him to hold out.

On seeing that the game was up, I decided to forfeit everything except my life. I even sacrificed diaries and records of observations, and took along only what I always carried in my pockets, namely, a compass, watch, two chronometers, a box of matches, handkerchief, pocket-knife, pencil, a piece of folded paper, and, by the merest chance, ten cigarettes.

Kasim, who still bore up, was happy when I told him to come with me. Hurriedly he took the shovel and pail, but forgot his cap. Later on he used my handkerchief to protect himself against sunstroke. I bade farewell to Islam and told him to sacrifice *everything*, but try to save himself by following our track. He looked as if he were going to die and made no answer.

After a last look at the patient camels I hurried away from this painful scene, where a man was fighting death, and where the veterans of our erstwhile proud caravan would end their desert journey for good. I caressed Yoldash, and left it to him to decide whether he would stay or go with us. He stayed, and I never saw the faithful dog again. It was midnight. We had been shipwrecked in the middle of the sea and were now leaving the sinking ship.

The lantern was still burning beside Islam, but its light soon died out behind us . . .

Thirst did not torment us, as it had done during the first days; for the mouth-cavity had become as dry as the outside skin, and the craving was dulled. An increasing feebleness set in instead. The functioning of all the glands was reduced. Our blood got thicker, and flowed through the capillaries with increasing sluggishness. Sooner or later this process of drying-up would reach its climax in death . . .

At sunrise, Kasim caught me by the shoulder, stared, and pointed east, without saying a word.

'What is it?' I whispered.

'A tamarisk,' he gasped.

A sign of vegetation at last! God be praised! . . .

About ten o'clock, we found another tamarisk; and we saw several more in the east. But our strength was gone. We undressed, buried ourselves in the sand, and hung our clothes on the branches of the tamarisk to make shade.

We lay in silence for nine hours . . . At seven o'clock, we dressed and continued onward. We went more slowly than ever. After three hours' walk in the dark, Kasim stopped short, and whispered: 'Poplars!' . . .

We took hold of the spade, intending to dig a well; but the spade slipped from our hands. We had no strength left. We lay down and scratched the ground with our nails, but gave up the attempt as useless . . .

The night was coming to an end; and the sun, our worst enemy, would soon rise again above the dunes on the eastern horizon, to torment us anew. At four on the morning of May 4 we started off, stumbling along for five hours. Then our strength gave out. Our hope was again on the decline. In the east there were no more poplars, no more tamarisks, to stimulate our dying vitality with their verdure. Only mounds of sand, as far as the eye could reach.

When the new day dawned, on May 5, we rose heavily, and with difficulty. Kasim looked terrible. His tongue was white and swollen, his lips blue, his cheeks were hollow, and his eyes had a dying glassy lustre. He was tortured by a kind of death-hiccup, which shook his whole frame. When the body is so completely dried up that the joints almost creak, every movement is an effort.

It grew lighter. The sun rose. From the top of a dune, where nothing obstructed the view towards the east, we noticed that the horizon, which for two weeks had revealed a row of yellow saw-teeth, now disclosed an absolutely even, dark-green line. We stopped short, as though petrified, and exclaimed simultaneously: 'The forest!' And I added: 'The Khotan-daria! Water!'

Again we collected what little strength we had left and struggled along eastward. The dunes grew lower, we passed a depression in the ground at the bottom of which we tried to dig; but we were still too weak. We went on. The dark-green line grew, the dunes diminished, stopped altogether, and were replaced by level soft ground. We were but a few hundred yards from the forest. At half-past five we reached the first poplars, and wearied, sank down in their shade. We enjoyed the fragrance of the forest. We saw flowers growing between the trees, and heard the birds sing and the flies and gadflies hum.

At seven o'clock we continued. The forest grew thinner. We came upon a path, showing traces of men, sheep, and horses, and we thought it might lead to the river. After following it for two hours, we collapsed in the shade of a poplar grove . . .

At seven p.m. I was able to get up. I hung the iron spade-blade in the crotch of a tree and used the wooden handle for a cane. The blade would serve to mark the way, in case we returned with some shepherds to rescue the three dying men and recover the lost baggage. But it was four whole days since we had deserted the men. They were sure to be dead already. And it would take us several days more to reach them. Their situation was clearly hopeless.

Again I urged Kasim to accompany me to the river to drink. He signalled with his hand that he could not rise, and he whispered that he would soon die under the poplars.

Alone I pulled myself along through the forest . . . I rested frequently, crawled part of the way on all-fours, and noticed with anxiety how the darkness grew denser in the woods. Finally the new night came – the last one. I could not have survived another day.

The forest ended abruptly, as though burnt by a fire. I found myself on the edge of a six-foot-high terrace, which descended almost perpendicularly to an absolutely even plain, devoid of vegetation. The ground was packed hard. A withered leafless twig was sticking out of it. I saw that it was a piece of driftwood, and that I was in the river-bed of the Khotan-daria. And it was dry, as dry as the sandy desert behind me . . .

Like the beds of all desert-rivers in Central Asia, that of the Khotan-daria is very wide, flat and shallow. A light haze floated over the desolate landscape. I had gone about one mile when the outlines of the forest on the eastern shore appeared below the moon. Dense thickets of bushes and reeds grew on the terraced shore. A fallen poplar stretched its dark trunk down towards the river-bed. It looked like the body of a crocodile. The bed still remained as dry as before. It was not far to the shore where I must lie down and die. My life hung on a hair.

Suddenly I started, and stopped short. A water-bird, a wild duck or goose, rose on whirring wings, and I heard a splash. The next moment, I stood on the edge of a pool, seventy feet long and fifteen feet wide! The water looked as black as ink in the moonlight. The overturned poplar-trunk was reflected in its depths.

In the silent night I thanked God for my miraculous deliverance. Had I continued eastward I should have been lost. In fact, if I had touched shore only a hundred yards north or south of the pool, I would have believed the entire river-bed to be dry . . .

I sat down calmly on the bank and felt my pulse. It was so weak that it was hardly noticeable – only forty-nine beats. Then I drank, and drank again. I drank without restraint. The water was cold, clear as crystal, and as sweet as the best spring-water. And then I drank again. My dried-up body absorbed the moisture like a sponge. All my joints softened, all my movements became easier. My skin, hard as parchment before, now became softened. My forehead grew moist. The pulse increased in strength; and after a few minutes it was fifty-six. The blood flowed more freely in my veins. I had a feeling of well-being and comfort. I drank again, and sat caressing the water in this blessed pool. Later on, I christened this pool Khoda-verdi-kol, or 'The Pool of God's Gift.'

My Life as an Explorer, 1926

MARK AUREL STEIN

1862–1943

Protected by accumulated drift sand, these masses of manuscript had lain undisturbed for centuries.

Sir Mark Aurel Stein was born in Hungary, but in 1904 became a British citizen. In 1900 he began the first of four expeditions that traced the ancient trade routes, popularly known as the Silk Road, of Central Asia. En route, he collected important information on little-known regions, documents, and artefacts.

His most dramatic discovery was that of the Caves of the Thousand Buddhas, a series of temples in the Taklamakan, filled with early Buddhist manuscripts that had lain there since the seventh century. Many were documents brought back by Hsuan Tsang, the Chinese Buddhist monk and pilgrim, from his travels in India. The work of extracting the documents from their dark resting place was nerve-racking; at any moment local officials might discover this plundering, or else the temple priest, who had let him into the rock chamber, might think better of it. 'Would not the timorous priest, swayed by his worldly fears and possible spiritual scruples, be moved to close down his shell before I had been able to extract any of the pearls?' But these fears were not realized and Stein succeeded in transferring the majority of the documents to the British Museum. He received strong criticism from many who said they should not have been taken, but the documents that he did leave have all since been stolen or destroyed.

Stealing for the British Museum

Late at night Chiang groped his way to my tent in silent elation with a bundle of Chinese rolls which Wang Tao-shih had just brought him in secret, carefully hidden under his flowing black robe, as the first of the promised 'specimens'. The rolls looked unmistakably old as regards writing and paper, and probably contained Buddhist canonical texts; but Chiang needed time to make sure of their character. Next morning he turned up by daybreak and, with a face expressing both triumph and amazement, reported that these fine rolls of paper contained Chinese versions of certain 'Sutras' from the Buddhist canon which the colophons declared to have been brought from India and translated by Hsuan-tsang himself. The strange chance which thus caused us to be met at the very outset by the name of my Chinese patron saint, and by what undoubtedly were early copies of his labours as a sacred translator, struck both of us as a most auspicious omen. Was it not 'T'ang-seng' himself, so Chiang declared, who at the opportune moment had revealed the hiding-place of that manuscript hoard to an ignorant priest in order to prepare for me, his admirer and disciple from distant India, a fitting antiquarian reward on the westernmost confines of China proper?

Of Hsuan-tsang's authorship, Wang Tao-shih in his ignorance could not possibly have had any inkling when he picked up that packet of 'specimens'. Chiang-ssu-yeh realized at once that this discovery was bound to impress the credulous priest as a special interposition on my behalf of the great traveller of sacred memory. So he hastened away to carry the news to the Tao-shih, and, backed up by this visible evidence of support from the latter's own cherished saint, to renew his pleading for free access to the hidden manuscript store. The effect was most striking. Before long Chiang returned to report that the portent could be trusted to work its spell. Some hours later he found the wall blocking the entrance to the recess of the temple removed, and on its door being opened by the priest, caught a glimpse of a room crammed full to the roof with manuscript bundles. I had purposely kept away from the Tao-shih's temple all the forenoon, but on getting this news I could no longer restrain my impatience to see the great hoard myself. The day was cloudless and hot, and the 'soldiers' who had followed me about during the morning with my cameras were now taking their siesta in sound sleep soothed by a good smoke of opium. So accompanied only by Chiang I went to the temple.

I found the priest there evidently still combating his scruples and nervous apprehensions. But under the influence of that quasi-divine hint he now summoned up courage to open before me the rough door closing the narrow entrance which led from the side of the broad front passage into the rock-carved recess, on a level of about four feet above the floor of the former. The sight of the small room disclosed was one to make my eyes open wide. Heaped up in layers, but without any order, there appeared in the dim light of the priest's little lamp a solid mass of manuscript bundles rising to a height of nearly ten feet, and filling, as subsequent measurement showed, close on 500 cubic feet. The area left clear within the room was just sufficient for two people to stand in. It was manifest that in this 'black hole' no examination of the manuscripts would be possible, and also that the digging out of all its contents would cost a good deal of physical labour.

A suggestion to clear out all the bundles into the large cella [main area] of the cave-temple, where they might have been examined at ease, would have been premature; so much oppressed at the time was Wang Tao-shih by fears of losing his position – and patrons – by the rumours which any casual observers might spread against him in the oasis. So for the present I had to rest content with his offer to take out a bundle or two at a time, and to let us look rapidly through their contents in a less cramped part of the precincts . . .

It was clear to me from the first that the deposit of the manuscripts must have taken place some time after the middle of the ninth century. But until we could find dated records among the manuscripts themselves there was no other indication of the lower date limit than the style of the frescoes which covered the passage walls . . . On various grounds it seemed improbable that they could be later than the period of the Sung dynasty, which immediately preceded the great Mongol conquest of the thirteenth century.

So there was evidence from the first to encourage my hopes that a search through this big hoard would reveal manuscripts of importance and interest. But the very hugeness of the deposit was bound to give rise to misgivings. Should we have time to eat our way through this mountain of ancient paper with any thoroughness? Would not the timorous priest, swayed by his worldly fears and possible spiritual scruples, be moved to close down his shell before I had been able to extract any of the pearls? There were reasons urging us to work with all possible energy and speed, and others rendering it advisable to display studied insouciance and calm assurance. Somehow we managed to meet the conflicting requirements of the situation. But, I confess, the strain and anxieties of the busy days which followed were great.

The first bundles which emerged from that 'black hole' consisted of thick rolls of paper about one foot high, evidently containing portions of canonical Buddhist texts in Chinese translations. All were in excellent preservation and yet showed in paper, arrangement, and other details, unmistakable signs of great age . . . Mixed up with the Chinese bundles there came to light Tibetan texts also written in roll form, though with clearly marked sections, as convenience of reading required in the case of a writing running in horizontal lines, not in vertical columns like Chinese. I could not doubt that they contained portions of the great canonical collections now known as the Tanjur and Kanjur . . .

All the manuscripts seemed to be preserved exactly in the same condition they were in when deposited. Some of the bundles were carelessly fastened with only rough cords and without an outer cloth wrapper; but even this had failed to injure the paper. Nowhere could I trace the slightest effect of moisture. And, in fact, what better place for preserving such relics could be imagined than a chamber carved in the live rock of these terribly barren hills, and hermetically shut off from what moisture, if any, the atmosphere of this desert valley ever contained? Not in the driest soil could relics of a ruined site have so completely escaped injury as they had here, in a carefully selected rock chamber where, hidden behind a brick wall and protected by accumulated drift sand, these masses of manuscripts had lain undisturbed for centuries.

How grateful I felt for the special protection thus afforded when, on opening a large packet wrapped in a sheet of stout coloured canvas, I found it full of paintings on fine gauze-like silk and on linen, ex-votos in all kinds of silk and brocade, with a mass of miscellaneous fragments of painted papers and cloth materials. Most of the paintings first found were narrow pieces from two to three feet in length, and proved by their floating streamers and the triangular tops provided with strings for fastening to have served as temple banners. These mountings made them look much more imposing when hung up. Many of them were in excellent condition, and all exactly as they had been deposited, after longer or shorter use. . . . The silk used for these pictures was almost invariably a transparent gauze of remarkable fineness. As these banners floated in the air they would allow a good deal of light to pass through – an important point, since in order to be properly seen these paintings would have to be hung up across or near the porches through which alone the cellas of the temple caves would receive their lighting . . .

Nor was there time for any closer study, such as I should have loved to give there and then to these delicate, graceful paintings. My main care was how many of them I might hope to rescue from their dismal imprisonment and the risks attending their present guardian's careless handling. To my surprise and relief he evidently attached little value to these beautiful relics of pictorial art in the T'ang times. So I made bold to put aside rapidly 'for further inspection' the best of the pictures on silk, linen, or paper I could lay my hands on, more than a dozen from the first bundle alone. I longed to carry away all its contents; for even among the fragments there were beautiful pieces, and every bit of silk would have its antiquarian and artistic value. But it would not have been wise to display too much *empressement*. So I restrained myself as well as I could, and put the rest away, with the firm resolve to return to the charge as soon as the ground was prepared for more extensive acquisitions.

To remains of this kind the priest seemed indifferent. The secret hope of diverting by their sacrifice my attention from the precious rolls of Chinese canonical texts or 'Ching' made him now more assiduously grope for and hand out bundles of what he evidently classed under the head of miscellaneous rubbish . . .

Flushed as I was with delight at these unhoped-for discoveries, I could not lose sight of the chief practical task, all-important for the time being. It was to keep our priest in a pliable mood, and to prevent his mind being overcome by the trepidations with which the chance of any intrusion and of consequent hostile rumours among his patrons would fill him. With the help of Chiang-ssu-yeh's genial persuasion, and what reassuring display I could make of my devotion to Buddhist lore in general and the memory of my patron saint in particular, we succeeded better than I had ventured to hope. I could see our honest Tao-shih's timorous look changing gradually to one of contentment at our appreciation of all this, to him valueless, lore. Though he visibly grew tired climbing over manuscript heaps and dragging out heavy bundles, it seemed as if he were becoming resigned to his fate, at least for a time.

When the growing darkness in the cave compelled us to stop further efforts for the day, a big bundle of properly packed manuscripts and painted fabrics lay on one side of our 'reading room' awaiting removal for what our diplomatic convention styled 'closer examination'. The great question was whether Wang Tao-shih would be willing to brave the risks of this removal, and subsequently to fall in with the true interpretation of our proceeding. It would not have done to breathe to him unholy words of sale and purchase; it was equally clear that any removal would have to be effected in strictest secrecy. So when we stepped outside the temple there was nothing in our hands or about our persons to arouse the slightest suspicion . . .

It was late at night when I heard cautious footsteps. It was Chiang who had come to make sure that nobody was stirring about my tent. A little later he returned with a big bundle over his shoulders. It contained everything I had picked out during the day's work. The Tao-shih had summoned up courage to fall in with my wishes, on the solemn condition that nobody besides us three was to get the slightest inkling of what was being transacted, and that as long as I kept on Chinese soil the origin of these 'finds' was not to be revealed to any living being. He himself was afraid of being seen at night outside his temple precincts. So the Ssu-yeh, zealous and energetic as always, took it upon himself to be the sole carrier. For seven nights more he thus came to my tent, when everybody had gone to sleep, with the same precautions, his slight figure panting under loads which grew each time heavier, and ultimately required carriage by instalments. For hands accustomed only to wield pen and paper it was a trying task, and never shall I forget the good-natured ease and cheerful devotion with which it was performed by that most willing of helpmates . . .

But my time for feeling true relief came when all the twenty-four cases, heavy with manuscript treasures rescued from that strange place of hiding, and the five more filled with paintings and other art relics from the same cave, had been deposited safely in the British Museum.

Ruins of Desert Cathay, 1912

Charles Montagu Doughty
1843–1926

A pleasure it is to listen to the cheerful musing Bedouin talk, a lesson in the traveller's school of mere humanity . . .

Doughty, an Arabist, writer and poet whose *Travels in Arabia Deserta* has been hailed by some as the finest travel account in the English language, was born at Theberton Hall in Suffolk into a parson's family. He was orphaned at the age of six. Of frail health, he seemed unlikely material for a desert adventurer. He failed to get into the Navy owing to a stammer that mysteriously disappeared during his later travels in Arabia, only to reappear when he was back in England.

On leaving Cambridge University, Doughty began to travel, not least to stimulate his development as a poet. He made his way to Damascus, where he learned Arabic before joining a pilgrim caravan heading south to Mecca, in 1876. He soon left the caravan to spend three months studying ancient Nabataean monuments and their inscriptions. He then set his sights on the oasis of Khaibar, taking his chances with the uncompromising Bedouin living thereabouts. He spent months living among them, sometimes as an honoured guest, but often uncomfortably dependent on their unpredictable patronage. His devout Christian faith did little to help amidst these strongly Islamic people and he endured insult, alienation, spasmodic beatings and imprisonment. Amongst this hostility, however, he also found kindness and chivalry. By the time he reached the safety of Jeddah, after two hard years of poverty and desert travel, his health was failing. Several years passed before he built up the strength to write the account of his travels.

Despite the many important geographical and anthropological observations in *Travels in Arabia Deserta*, his primary concern was to create a literary monument. He wrote in a majestic and lyrical style that lost him readership at the time but was later considered to be in tune with his remote and lonely wanderings. 'The book has no date and can never grow old,' T. E. Lawrence, another great Arabist, enthused. 'It is the first and indispensable work upon the Arabs of the desert . . .' The book, which brims with lively observations of human character, opened European eyes to the Arabian desert – not least those of Gertrude Bell, and later Wilfred Thesiger, who were both profoundly influenced by it.

Horseman and horse

Here passing, in my former journeys, we saw Aarab horsemen which approached us; we being too many for them, they came but to beg insolently a handful of tobacco. In their camps such would be kind hosts; but had we fallen into their hands in the desert we should have found them fiends, they would have stripped us, and perchance in a savage wantonness have cut some of our throats. These were three long-haired Beduins that bid us *salaam* (peace); and a fourth shock-haired cyclops of the desert, whom the fleetness of their mares had outstripped, trotted in after them, uncouthly seated upon the rawbone narrow withers of his dromedary, without saddle, without bridle, and only as an herdsman driving her with his voice and the camel-stick. His fellows rode with naked legs and unshod upon their beautiful mares' bare backs, the halter in one hand, and the long balanced lance, wavering upon the shoulder, in the other. We should think them sprawling riders; for a boast or warlike exercise, in the presence of our armed company, they let us view how fairly they could ride a career and turn: striking back heels and seated low, with pressed thighs, they parted at a hand-galop, made a tourney or two easily upon the plain; and now wheeling wide, they betook themselves down in the desert, every man bearing and handling his spear as at point to strike a foeman; so fetching a compass and we marching, they a little out of breath came gallantly again. Under the most ragged of these riders was a very perfect young and startling chestnut mare, – so shapely there are only few among them. Never combed by her rude master, but all shining beautiful and gentle of herself, she seemed a darling life upon that savage soil not worthy of her gracious pasterns: the strutting tail flowed down even to the ground, and the mane (*orfa*) was shed by the loving nurture of her mother Nature.

The settled folk in Arabian country, are always envious haters of the nomads that encompass them, in their oases islands, with the danger of the desert. These with whom I journeyed, were the captain of the haj road at Maan and his score of soldiery, the most being armed peasantry of the place, which came driving a government herd of goats, (the unwilling contribution of the few unsubmitted Idumean villages) to sell them at *Nablûs* (Sichem). Shots were fired by some of them in the rear in contempt of the Beduw, whose mares, at every gunfire, shrank and sprang under them, so that the men, with their loose seats were near falling over the horses' heads. 'Nay Sirs!' they cried back, 'nay Sirs, why fray ye our mares?' The Beduw thus looking over their shoulders, the peasantry shot the more, hoping to see them miscarry; he of the beautiful filly sat already upon his horse's neck, the others were almost dislodged. So the Officer called to them, 'Hold lads!' and 'have done lads!' and they 'Our guns went off, wellah, as it were of themselves.' And little cared they, as half desperate men, that had not seen a cross of their pay in sixteen months, to obey the words of their scurvy commander. They marched with a pyrrhic dancing and beating the tambour: it is a leaping counter and tripping high in measure, whilst they chant in wild manner with wavings of the body and fighting aloft in the air with the drawn sword. Those Beduins roughly demanded concerning me 'And who is he?' It was answered 'A Nasrâny,' – by which name, of evil omen, the nomads could only understand a calamity in their land: and they arrogantly again in their throats 'Like to this one see ye bring no more hither!' As I heard their word, I shouted 'Arrest, lay hands on them!' They thought it time to be gone, and without leave-taking they turned from us and were quickly ridden under the horizon.

The cost of the Haj pilgrimage

I saw one fallen in the sand, half sitting half lying upon his hands. This was a religious mendicant, some miserable derwish in his clouted beggar's cloak, who groaned in extremity, holding forth his hands like eagles' claws to man's pity. Last in the long train, we went also marching by him. His beggar's scrip, full of broken morsels fallen from his neck, was poured out before him. The wretch lamented to the slow moving lines of the Mecca-bound pilgrimage: the many had passed on, and doubtless as they saw his dying, hoped inwardly the like evil ending might not be their own. Some charitable serving men, Damascenes, in our company, stepped aside to him; *ana mèyet*, sobbed the derwish, I am a dying man. One then of our crew, he was also my servant, a valiant outlaw, no holy-tongue man but of human deeds, with a manly heartening word, couched, by, an empty camel, and with a spring of his stalwart arms, lifted and set him fairly upon the pack saddle. The dying derwish gave a weak cry much like a child, and hastily they raised the camel under him and gathered his bag of scattered victuals and reached it to him, who sat all feeble murmuring thankfulness, and trembling yet for fear. There is no ambulance service with the barbarous pilgrim army; and all charity is cold, in the great and terrible wilderness, of that wayworn suffering multitude.

After this there died some daily in the caravan: the deceased's goods are sealed, his wayfellows in the night station wash and shroud the body and lay in a shallow grave digged with their hands, and will set him up some wild headstone by the desert road side. They call any pilgrims so dying in the path of their religion, *shahûd*, martyrs. But the lonely indigent man, and without succour, who falls in the empty wilderness, he is desolate indeed. When the great convoy is passed from him, and he is forsaken of all mankind, if any Beduw find him fainting, it is but likely they will strip him, seeing he is not yet dead. The dead corses unburied are devoured by hyenas which will follow the ill odour of the caravan. There is little mercy in those Ageyl which ride after; none upon the road, will do a gentle deed 'but for silver.' – If we have lived well, we would fain die in peace; we ask it, a reward, of God, in the kind presence of our friends. – There are fainting ones left behind in every years' pilgrimage; men of an old fibre and ill-complexion, their hope was in Ullah, but they living by the long way only of unwilling men's alms, cannot achieve this extreme journey to Mecca. The fallen man, advanced in years, had never perhaps eaten his fill, in the Haj, and above two hundred miles were passed under his soles since Muzeyrîb. How great is that yearly suffering and sacrifice of human flesh, and all lost labour, for a vain opinion, a little salt of science would dissolve all their religion!

'Our homely evening fire'

Pleasant, as the fiery heat of the desert daylight is done, is our homely evening fire. The sun gone down upon a highland steppe of Arabia whose common altitude is above three thousand feet, the thin dry air is presently refreshed, the sand is soon cold; wherein yet at three fingers' depth is left a sunny warmth of the past day's heat until the new sunrise. After a half hour it is the blue night, the clear hoary starlight in which there shines the girdle of the milky way, with a marvellous clarity. As the sun is setting, the nomad house-wife brings in a truss of sticks and dry bushes, which she has pulled or hoed with a mattock (a tool they have seldom) in the wilderness; she casts down this provision by our hearthside, for the sweet-smelling evening fire . . .

At this first evening hour, the Beduw are all *fi ahl-ha*, in their households, to sup of such wretchedness as they may have; there is no more wandering through the wide encampment, and the coming in then of any persons, not strangers, were an unseemly 'ignorance.' The foster-camels lie couched, before the booth of hair: and these Beduins let them lie still an hour, before the milking. The great feeble brutes have wandered all day upon the droughty face of the wilderness, they may hardly crop their fills, in those many hours, of so slender pastures. The mare stands tethered before the booth at the woman's side, where there is not much passage. Such dry wire-grass forage as they find in that waste, is cast down beside her. When the Arabs have eaten their morsel and drunken léban of the flock, the few men of our menzil begin to assemble about the sheykh's hearth, where is some expectation of coffee. The younger or meanest of the company, who is sitting or leaning on his elbow or lies next the faggot, will indolently reach back his hand from time to time for more dry rimth, to cast on the fire, and other sweet resinous twigs, till the flaming light leaps up again in the vast uncheerful darkness. The nomads will not burn the good pasture bushes, *gussha*, even in their enemies' country. It is the bread of the cattle. I have sometimes unwittingly offended them, until I knew the plants, plucking up and giving to the flames some which grew in the soil nigh my hand; then children and women and the men of little under-standing blamed me, and said wondering, 'It was an heathenish deed.'

Glad at the fall of the empty daylight, the householders sit again to make talk, or silent and listless, with the drooping gravity of brute animals. Old men, always weary, and the herdmen, which were all day abroad in the sun, are lying now upon an elbow (this is the right Aarab posture, and which Zeyd would have me learn and use), about the common fire. But the reposing of the common sort at home is to lie heels out backward, about the hearth, as the spokes of a wheel, and flat upon their bellies (which they even think appeases the gnawing of hunger); and a little raising themselves, they discourse staying upon their breasts and two elbows: thus the men of this lean nation will later sleep, spreading only their tattered cloaks under them, upon the wild soil (béled), a posture even reproved by themselves. Béled, we saw in the mouth of the nomads, is the inhabited soil of the open desert and also of the oasis; they say of the dead, 'He is under the béled.' Dîra, the Beduin circuit, is heard also in some oases for their town settlement. – I asked Zeyd, 'Then say ye the béled is our mother?' – 'Ay well, and surely, Khalîl; for out of the ground took God man and all return thither.' They asking me of our custom, I said 'You are ground-sitters, but we sit high upon stools like the Tûrk.' – The legs of chair-sitters to hang all day they thought an insufferable fatigue. 'Khalîl says well,' answered Zeyd, who, a sheykh of Aarab, had been in high presence of pashas and government men at Damascus; and he told how he found them sitting in arm-chairs and (they are all cross-leg Orientals) with a leg crossed over the other, a shank or a foot: a simple crossed foot is of the under functionaries: but to lap a man's shin, (Zeyd showed us the manner,) he said to be of their principal personages. The Arabs asked me often, if we sat gathered in this kindly sort about our evening fires? and if neighbours went about to neigh-bour byût, seeking company of friends and coffee-drinking? . . .

A pleasure it is to listen to the cheerful musing Beduin talk, a lesson in the travellers' school of mere humanity, – and there is no land so perilous which by humanity he may not pass, for man is of one mind everywhere, ay, and in their kind, even the brute animals of the same foster earth – a timely vacancy of the busy-idle cares which cloud upon us that would live peaceably in the moral desolation of the world. And pleasant those sounds of the spretting milk under the udders in the Arabs' vessels! food for man and health at a draught in a languishing country. The bowl brought in foaming, the children gather to it, and the guest is often bidden to sup with them, with his fingers, the sweet forth orghra or roghrwa, irtugh: or this milk poured into the sour milk-skin and shaken there a moment, the housewife serves it forth again to their suppers, with that new gathered sourness which they think the more refreshing.

Travels in Arabia Deserta, 1888

It is desert pride and desert law to give generously to-day to the passing guest, and to-morrow to know hunger and be without the means of appeasing it.

When in his mid-thirties Thomas was posted to 'Arabia Felix' ('Happy Arabia') – the old Roman name for southern Arabia – to serve as the wazir, or financial adviser, to the Sultan of Muscat and Oman. It was while carrying out this post in the small, sweltering, coastal city of Muscat that Thomas decided he would become the first Westerner not only to venture into the middle of the great expanse of the Rub' al-Khali, the Empty Quarter – the inhospitable desert sea of southern Arabia – but also to cross it, despite the fact that T. E. Lawrence had said, 'Nothing but an airship can do it.'

He set out from Muscat in October 1926. He had not told the Sultan of his plans so was convinced that the day after his departure 'the news of my disappearance would startle the bazaar and a variety of fates would doubtless be invented for me by imaginations of oriental fertility'. In a town in southern Oman he recruited the rest of the members of his expedition – a party of Rashid Bedouin who swore loyalty to him – then set off northwards. The impression Thomas left on his Bedouin companions and on the nomads he met along the way was to remain imprinted on their minds until Thesiger's crossing of the Empty Quarter sixteen years later; this contributed to Thesiger's acceptance by the Bedu people, who considered him 'of the same tribe' as his forerunner.

Some way into the journey Thomas's guides pointed to the ground and told him: 'Look, sahib . . . there is the road to Ubar.' Thomas had heard people speak of the ancient city of Ubar that now lay buried beneath the sands. Limited water supplies and his determination to make a complete crossing of the Empty Quarter meant that Thomas had to will himself away from the temptation of following the route to Ubar. Instead, he took careful bearings of where the route lay and noted it on the extremely accurate route map of his journey that he prepared for the Royal Geographical Society.

It was sixty-seven days before they reached Doha, on the Persian Gulf. T. E. Lawrence wrote in the foreword to Thomas's book:

> Few men are able to close an epoch. We cannot know the first man who walked the inviolate earth for newness' sake: but Thomas is the last; and he did his journey in the antique way, by pain of his camel's legs, single-handed, at his own time and cost. He might have flown an aeroplane, sat in a car or rolled over in a tank. Instead, he has snatched, at the twenty-third hour, feet's last victory and set us free . . . All honour to Thomas.

The end of the journey

The following day our course, a shade to east of north, had taken us through more of this quarry-like wilderness, when, after a six-mile march, I beheld before me a large silver lake. I had learnt from my Badawin that we should pass on our right hand a certain Sabkha Amra, and had naturally supposed that it would be a dry salt-plain, like the *sabkhas* of the recent marches. Wherefore a lake some seven miles in length, and perhaps a mile and a half wide, came as a pleasant surprise. As we approached its southern end I picked up two large sea-shell fossils. Thence our course lay in a low flinty plain that edged its north side, its south shore appearing to be low sandhills.

While I photographed it, which I must needs do, straight into the sun under a yellow cloudy sky, my Badawin collected from its margin large chunks of rock salt, which they would use in cooking their rice.

The border, some twenty feet broad, had a snow-like appearance, and at a distance it was impossible to see where the salt ended and the water began. Within some six feet of the water's edge ran a line of dead white locusts – desiccated specimens probably of the large red variety that is an Arab delicacy. The wretched creatures swarm from the desert in the spring and take a suicidal plunge into the first water they meet. The position suggested that the edge of the lake had receded during the year, but no explanation was vouchsafed by the two Murras, who alone of my party had been here before. The slope was so slight that a little rain, or summer evaporation, would account for the change of level.

After leaving the lake a more north-easterly course towards the hog-backed Jabal 'Udaid led us through a plain sown with jagged splintered stones to another spacious salt plain, here called Amra. It is said to stretch westwards past the ancient sites of Iskak, Salwa and Mabak to the shores of Qatar Bight. Lake salt, and recent shell evidences and aneroid readings suggest that the base of the Qatar Peninsula was at no very distant time depressed below the sea, Qatar making an island like neighbouring Bahrain, but many times bigger.

My companions had halted in the plain for afternoon prayer. As I came up, Ugaba, my camel, decided the place suited her. She refused to be urged on ahead alone and sat bellowing for bint Riman, her usual companion on the march – an irreverent accompaniment to the audible supplications of the Faithful. I was taken to task afterwards for making an elementary mistake, that of giving her the wrong signal. She had been taught to rise to a tap of the stick on her quarters, and my tapping her neck kept her couched. An unwilling camel is provoking, but no Badu will ever be seen laying a stick about her for fear of spoiling what good qualities she has. If annoyed with her, he will shout:

'Hai! (nasal) Come to thee kharash' – a wasting disease.

'Hai! Come to thee death, lawful or unlawful.'

'Hai! Come to thee a great burden.'

But in his heart he means nothing of the kind. He has a genuine attachment for her which he knows is not reciprocated. And so when she stumbles, it is more likely to be:

'Hai! thy deliverance.'

'Hai! Allah deliver thee from evil.'

Even when he has tramped for miles in pursuit of his straying camel, he approaches her with the words:

'Hai! God bless thee,' or

'*Ya hai b'ish fulana*' – greeting her by name.

Fresh marks of camels identified with the Manasir tribe induced us to press on, for Hamad, the Murri, was in no mood to meet them.

A few distant grazing camels against the sky caused alarmist exchanges among my party. Talib, who was *persona grata* with local Manasir, rode ahead to spy out the land and conceal the constitution of our party if necessary, while we made a detour to avoid them.

'There is one thing I want from you when we arrive, Sahib,' said Sahail.

'What is that?'

'Tobacco.'

'But this is the Fast of Ramadhan.'

'Tobacco is the one thing I cannot do without, Sahib. I fast from everything but tobacco.'

'But is it not a sin?'

'By God it is, but what shall a man do? – and it is only this Ramadhan, in no previous year have I drunk tobacco.'

Formalists would doubtless hold that Sahail had broken the fast by smoking, so that there was no virtue in the rest of his abstinence. Sahail, however – he was the only smoker in my escort – did not avail himself of the lawful privilege of the traveller to break the fast altogether. He was fasting in the spirit, though had any fanatic rebuked him he would doubtless have taken it humbly.

'God have mercy on me,' I heard him mutter as I pushed on ahead.

Talib our *rabia*, who had trotted off to investigate the unknown camels, now came riding back towards us. While yet a hundred yards off he was shouting:

'Have you prayed? Have you prayed?'

'Yes, God be glorified!' my companions shouted back.

He came closer to cry:

'*Ya haiyakum, ya haiyakum*, good news! if God wills,' and my party crowded round him for the latest gossip of the desert.

A few minutes later Shaikh Salih dropped back to ride by my side.

'Good news!' he said.

'God be praised.'

''Abdul 'Aziz bin Sa'ud is in Riyadh. The governors – a reference also to Bin Jaluwi of Hasa – are in their towns; still they rule!' (The significance of this was that my Rashid and Murra companions felt secure from one another and from the Manasir.)

'Thank God,' said a third.

'And in Jafura is life' (*i.e.* pastures from recent rains).

'God be praised,' came a chorus of Badawin, for fresh pastures at hand would let them turn aside on their return journey to rest and fatten their mounts for some weeks preparatory to the long march back to the southern sands.

Rain was indeed falling where we halted for prayer. Close by on a stone an owl sat blinking, and allowed a Badu to creep up within thirty yards of it, seeming to know how difficult a target it made, for the shot having missed, it calmly perched itself within close range of another rifle, and only took clumsily to wing when that shot also went wide.

My companions remarked the footmarks of asses an hour later when we passed the six-fathom water-hole of Zurga, the water supply of the well-to-do of Doha. Following the beaten track at a sluggish pace, we saw in the distance a large herd of camels grazing – sign that hereabouts were probably the most favoured pastures in the neighbourhood. Talib was sent ahead again to investigate, while my companions talked hopefully of a milk dinner. Unrealised hope – though Talib brought back a large clod of dates from the single slave herdsman he had found in charge of the Qatar camels. To me it seemed likely that he had deprived the poor wretch of the bulk of his food supply – the dates sufficed for the whole of my party that night – but it is desert pride and desert law to give generously to-day to the passing guest, and to-morrow to know hunger and be without the means of appeasing it.

It was a bleak, bitter evening; no stick of firewood anywhere availed, only miserable fires of dung were possible. Drizzling rain fell through the night, and I woke to find my blankets drenched; so that to breakfast in the dry I lay under my camp table. But it was to be my last breakfast in the desert, and so whatever the conditions, they could be supported cheerfully.

We were arriving. The Badawin moved forward at a sharp pace, chanting the water chants. Our thirsty camels pricked up their ears with eager knowingness. The last sandhill was left behind. After the next undulation we saw in the dip of the stony plain before us Na'aija, where we had planned a final watering, and beyond it the towers of Doha silhouetted against the waters of the Persian Gulf. Half an hour later we entered the walls of the fort. The Rub' al Khali had been crossed.

Arabia Felix: Across the Empty Quarter of Arabia, 1932

HARRY ST JOHN PHILBY
1885–1960
I had schooled myself to silent endurance of his all-pervading presence.

Harry St John Philby was born in Ceylon, and after education in Britain in 1907 joined the Indian Civil Service. During the First World War he was political officer in Baghdad, then in charge of the British Political Mission to Central Arabia – this giving him the chance to explore the Arabian deserts. He crossed Arabia by camel from Uqayr to Jedda, and became the first European to visit the Nejd, for which the Royal Geographical Society awarded him their Gold Medal.

Philby's sympathies with the Sauds caused quarrels with the British government, and despite returning to work in Mesopotamia and Trans-Jordan with the civil service, he resigned and in 1925 became adviser to the Arabian King Ibn Saud. Steadily he slipped deeper and deeper into Arab culture, and converted to Islam in 1930.

In 1932, soon after Bertram Thomas had crossed the Empty Quarter from south (Salālah) to North (Doha), Philby made an epic crossing himself. This was an alternative route to that taken by Thomas, and – he was anxious to point out – a more arduous one.

Like other explorers of the Empty Quarter, he kept his eyes peeled for signs of the lost city of Ubar,* which according to legend had been destroyed by the wrath of God and then covered over by sand. 'He had waxed wanton with his horses and eunuchs and concubines in an earthly paradise until the wrath came upon him with the west wind,' wrote Philby of the unfortunate city's king, 'and reduced the scene of his riotous pleasures to ashes and desolation.'

Having crossed from north to south, straight through the Empty Quarter from Hufhuf, Philby trekked 360 miles across it to as-Sulayyil in the west. The first attempt failed owing to the camels' exhaustion, but a second, for which Philby carefully selected eleven men and fifteen camels, succeeded, thus completing the first crossing of the Empty Quarter from east to west. The expedition had travelled light, but Philby had allowed himself the luxury of a tin of peppermints to 'suck on thirsty days'.

Between 1932 and 1937 Philby mapped the Yemen highlands, and then, in 1937, travelled back from the Empty Quarter to the Hadhramaut, a journey he described in *Sheba's Daughters*. Philby remained in Arabia until his death.

---

* Philby did not see the city, but the journey was not without its moments. One of these was sliding down a dune, which created a resonant humming: 'Quite suddenly the great amphitheatre began to boom and drone with a sound not unlike that of a siren or perhaps an aeroplane engine – quite a musical, rhythmic sound of astonishing depth. The conditions were ideal for the study of the sand concert, and the first item was sufficiently prolonged, perhaps four minutes, for me to take in every detail. The men working at the well started a rival and less musical concert of ribaldry directed at the Djinns (desert spirits) who were supposed to be responsible for the occurrence.'

Slave life

For the first few days of my stay I was left to fend for myself as regards companionship. Hamdani, a youth of little merit and a hang-dog countenance, was allotted by Ibrahim for my personal service to accompany me on

my walks abroad and otherwise dance attendance on me, but the wretched
fellow made no secret of his shyness of being seen with me in public, and
spent most of his time herding me along byways and little-frequented alleys,
and ever heading for home with a persistence that exasperated me. Conversation in such circumstances was impossible, and finding that I enjoyed his
company as little as he did mine, I determined to shake him off by doing
exactly the reverse of what he suggested. I led him as often as possible through
the crowded *Suq* and past the mosques just as the faithful were wending their
ways towards them for the sunset prayer. I would sit down patiently while he
prayed and, protesting that I was not hungry when he suggested that it was
time to return home for dinner, would lead him off to the Manfuha ridge or
in the direction of the Batin to watch the sunset or the coming storm. The
crisis came on the fourth evening. I had told Hamdani to call for me at five
o'clock, as I contemplated a longer excursion than usual; he failed to appear at
the appointed hour, and I waited patiently till dinner-time, when Ibrahim,
coming in to share my meal, found himself the innocent victim of my pent-
up wrath and was told that I never wished to see Hamdani again. Next
morning I scandalised Riyadh by walking abroad alone; through the *Suq* I
went and out by the Dhuhairi gate, whence I wandered round the whole
circuit of the walls, compass and note-book in hand. My conduct – for I was
not supposed to leave the palace without escort – must have been reported to
Ibn Sa'ud, for the same afternoon two of the royal slaves, armed to the teeth
with sword, rifle and bandolier, appeared in my room to inform me that from
that moment, by the special command of their master, they were at my disposal morning, noon and night, to accompany me wherever I would go; that I
only had to call and they would appear; and that, should I wish to do so,
horses were always ready that I might ride. They were as good as their word;
whether I rode or walked, one or other of them or both accompanied me, and
they were untiring in their devotion. Henceforth my excursions reached to the
farthest limits of the oasis and its surroundings regardless of time and distance. Unlike the Arabs, my new friends vied with me in feats of endurance,
which provoked the wonder and admiration of Ibn Sa'ud, and most evenings
it was dark before we returned to the palace for dinner. Their conversation,
moreover, was a source of unfailing interest to me, for they loved to regale me
with stories of their own experiences from the days of their childhood in
darkest Africa, of the domestic side of the palace life, of persons and things in
general.

Manawar and 'Ata'llah were their names, the one a *Nubian*, the other a
Takarini from Sindar on the Upper Nile, both of about the same age – perhaps

about twenty years old – but full of ripe experience in many lands. 'My original home,' Manawar told me, and I give his story in his own words without comment, 'is a land called Abbisha, a year's journey or more beyond Khartum as slave journeys are reckoned, for the convoys are mostly of little children, for whose sake it is necessary to make frequent halts lest the hardships of the way should rob their pirate owners of the profits of their enterprise. We have a *Sultan* in that land and his name is Jarma; the people are *Muslims*, at least they pray and fast as we do here – *yasallun wa yasumun* – and practise circumcision, and their tongue is as the tongue of the Arabs, not the *Takarina* which is spoken by another race far off, whence also come slaves and of which is 'Ata'llah. Beyond us was another race called Janagua, who are not of our creed, whose men go naked and whose women wear nothing but a *Farwa* of sheepskin about their loins; they sleep on the bare earth, and if they see one circumcised they ask why the top of his *penis* is cut off. In those days I was a child and was tending our sheep in the desert when a band of robbers – they call the slave dealers Jallaba – came suddenly upon me and carried me off; never again did I see my three brothers or my mother, who was left to mourn me. With others in the same plight, lads and lasses of my own people, I came riding upon a donkey to Khartum and on to Suakin, whence I was carried across the seas to Jidda. May be that was fifteen or sixteen years ago. The man who brought me across took me first to Mecca to sell me in the slave-market, but none would buy me – for fear of the *Daula*, I think – and my master returned with me to Jidda, where I was circumcised and grew up in his service. He was a merchant, and in due course I was made to work as his salesman; but he accused me of appropriating his profits and beat me. Then he took to doing his own selling but prospered not, and one day I taunted him for his lack of success. He beat me again, and I sued him in the Turkish courts, but without avail; he won the case, and the next time I took the law into my hands, gave him a sound beating and fled to Mecca. He pursued me, vowing to have his revenge, but the Sharif protected me, eventually insisting on buying me from my master. Thus came I into the possession of the Sharif and abode in Mecca three years, at the end of which – that is about three years ago – my lord sent me, among other slaves, as a present to Ibn Sa'ud. In fifteen days I came *via* Sha'ra to Riyadh, and ever since I have been happy and prosperous in the palace service, accompanying Ibn Sa'ud in his military expeditions – once, two years ago, against the Murra south of the Hasa, and a second time against the Shammar last year, who fled when they saw afar off the dust of our coming. Slaves are well treated and held in high esteem here; never a foray goes forth but a slave goes with it, partly as a mark of royal authority and partly as a check on the leader, for Ibn Sa'ud trusts no man very far except the royal slaves, whose fidelity is above suspicion. Why, it is his ambition to have sufficient of us to give us a standard of our own in battle. Were it so, we would fight to the last man; but at present his male slaves number but thirty-eight, and a few others there are in Riyadh in the possession of the well-to-do. My uncle' – *ammi*, as the slaves affectionately address their master – 'gives me twenty or twenty-five dollars every month, and he gave me one of the slave girls to wife, who has borne me a little daughter. I am well here and the palace folk treat me well; but the best of them is Ibrahim, the usher, who is not too proud, as some are, to eat and talk with the '*Abid.*' Such was the life history of one of my new companions. 'Ata'llah, filched away from his home at a tenderer age, had little to tell of the country on the Upper Nile, where he was born.

It will be remembered that the League of Nations covenant, to which both Great Britain and the King of the Hijaz have put their signatures, enjoins upon its members the necessity of doing everything in their power to put down slavery and other recognised abuses; and it will be interesting to see what the practical effect of this injunction is in view of the fact that, while Great Britain effectively controls the Sudan and its ports, the route by which the slaves come down from Africa to Arabia, the King of the Hijaz has his capital at Mecca, probably the greatest slave-mart in the modern world. As I have indicated, slaves are well treated and for the most part exceedingly happy in Arabia, but that fact alone cannot be held to justify the operations of the slave-dealers, the worst part of whose business is the terrible mortality involved among the unfortunate children, filched away from their parents and compelled to make that long and arduous journey from the heart of Africa to the coast.

The Heart of Arabia, 1923

ISABELLE EBERHARDT
1877–1904

I have now been back in blessed Africa for a whole year and hope never to leave again . . . However poor, I have been able to explore uncharted places in my adopted land . . .

'I have given up hope of ever having a corner on earth to call my own; a home, a family, peace, or prosperity,' Eberhardt wrote. She was a Genevan wanderer of North Africa, an Islamist and mystic who travelled in the guise of a man, her drug addiction and promiscuity the only certainties in her life. She was born into an exiled family on the edge of Lake Geneva and had two elder half-brothers whose drug-taking proclivities no doubt induced her own. In her early twenties she travelled to North Africa, lured by the exotic images she had gleared from her reading. On her second trip she travelled destitute, falling into debt having failed to sort out her inheritances, which would have provided her with a secure income for the rest of her life. Finally, she resorted to begging.

Eventually, she converted to Islam and spent the rest of her life wandering the Sahara on horseback dressed as a man, 'Si Mahmoud'. This disguise was partly facilitated by an illness, thought to be anorexia. She was rake-thin, flat-chested and had a strange excess of body hair. From her diaries, little is painted directly of the places she visited; passages of observation serve as background to her self-absorbed reflections, which are coloured by her heaving moods and her struggle with depression. Her 'exploration' was directed inwards, but she was fascinated by the desert in which she sought solace.

Despite her conversion to Islam, her fragile existence on the fringe of all society and her ambiguous sexuality – sometimes seen as subversive by the French authorities – Eberhardt was an ardent apologist for French rule. Travelling at a time when the Algerian resistance movement was gaining momentum, she used her insider knowledge of local religious networks to act as an informant. Within fifty years, Algeria would become a bloodbath; the French, in whom she had so much faith, would at times descend into barbarity in their treatment of the Arabs.

At the age of twenty-eight, her short, agonized life – so preoccupied by death – was cut short by a flash flood in the desert that had so entranced her.

In Europe: 'utterly alone'

Cagliari, 1 January 1900: I sit here all by myself, looking at the grey expanse of murmuring sea . . . I am utterly *alone* on earth, and always will be in this Universe so full of lures and disappointments . . . *alone*, turning my back on a world of dead hopes and memories.

The torments and confusion of the last six months have tempered my soul for good, and I can now face the worst of time, even death or destruction, without turning a hair. The knowledge I have acquired of the human heart is now so keen that I know the two months ahead will only bring me more sorrow, for I simply pay no attention to anything other than the dreams that make up my *true* personality. I seem to wear a mask that bespeaks someone cynical, dissipated ... No one so far has ever managed to see through it and catch a glimpse of the sensitive soul which lives behind it.

No one has ever understood that even though I may seem to be driven by the senses alone, my heart is in fact a pure one filled with love and tenderness, and with boundless compassion for all who suffer injustice, all who are weak and oppressed ... a heart both proud and unswerving in its commitment to Islam, a cause for which I long to give my life some day.

I shall dig in my heels and go on acting the lunatic in the intoxicating expanse of desert as I did last summer, or go on galloping through olive groves in the Tunisian Sahel, as I did in the autumn.

Those silent nights again, those lazy rides on horse back through the salty plains of the Oued Righ's and the Oued Souf's white sands! That feeling, sad and blissful at once, that would fill my pariah's heart every time I struck camp surrounded by friends, among Spahis and nomads, none of whom ever considered me the despicable outcast I had so miserably become at the hands of fate.

Right now, I long for one thing only: to lead that life again in Africa ... to sleep in the chilly silence of the night below stars that drop from great heights, with the sky's infinite expanse for a roof and the warm earth for a bed, in the knowledge that no one pines for me *anywhere on earth*, that there is no place where I am being missed or expected. To know that is to be free and unencumbered, a nomad in the great desert of life where I shall never be anything but an outsider. Such is the only form of bliss, however bitter, the Mektoub will ever grant me, but then happiness of the sort covered by all of frantic humanity, will never be mine.

In North Africa

El Oued, 4 August 1900, 7 a.m.: As I finished writing in my diary at Terjen, I sat down on my bed, facing the door.

Had an indescribable sense of well-being and profound bliss at being there ... Siesta interrupted by children and goats.

Left with the mailcoach around 2.30 p.m. Intense heat. Did not feel well. Mounted the camel once more. Reached Mouïet-el-Caïd by maghreb [6 p.m.].

By 4 a.m. off to Ourmes, where we arrived by half-past seven. Crossed the biggest dune and came upon several dead camels, one of which was a recent casualty ...

Have now reached my goal at long last; now I must get to work with all the energy I can muster. As soon as I receive the money from Eugène, I must pay the rent, Habib, and buy basic necessities.

My luggage is to arrive today. As soon as I am living in less of a makeshift situation, I shall have to start writing the book about my journey, the first chapter of which will deal with Marseilles.

I am far from society, far from civilisation. I am by myself, on Muslim soil, out in the desert, free and in the best of circumstances, except for my health and even that is not too bad. The outcome of my undertaking is therefore up to me . . .

4 August 1900, 3.30 p.m. I am beginning to feel bored, for my luggage has not turned up and I cannot get on with my house and life . . .

Habib's house. A square building of unbleached toub, in one of the winding streets paved with fine sand, not far from the dune.

Off in a corner is a small dark goat with an amulet around its neck. Habib's many brothers come and go. The old man's wife, tall and slim, dressed in long white veils, a veritable mountain on top of her head: braids of black hair, braids and tassels made of red wool, and in her ears heavy iron rings held up by cords tied to the hairdo. To go out, she throws a blue veil over it all. A strange, ageless figure with a sunburnt skin and doleful black eyes.

Temperatures will soon start going down. There is already a little gust of wind from time to time.

To sum things up, I have not yet embarked upon my new way of life. Too much of it is still unsettled.

Batna, 26 April 1901, 11 p.m.: I am feeling depressed tonight in a way I cannot define. I feel lonely without Ouïha [i.e. Rouh', or Slimène Ehnni, whom she would marry], and cannot stand the boredom. Yesterday's storm has left Batna inundated, dark and freezing, and it is full of mud and filthy gutters. My poor Souf is very ill, so that I cannot even go for my strolls along the open road, or up to that desolate graveyard where damaged tombs, terrifying windows upon the spectacle of human dust, lie scattered among the fragrant tufts of grey chih near a green meadow full of purple flax, white anemones and scarlet poppies in full bloom.

The other day I wandered around among a crowd of Muslims brandishing the flags of ancient religious ceremonial occasions; to the accompaniment of tambours and flutes they prayed for rain, for an extension of their fleeting Algerian spring which already, in its haste to move on, is blending summer flowers with those of spring.

After six long days of only seeing Rouh' for brief and furtive moments by the gate of the hated barracks where he is quartered, he came to see me yesterday . . . I held him in my arms and after the first wild, almost savage embrace, tears ran down our cheeks, and each of us felt a very mysterious fear, even though neither of us had said a word or knew why.

I realised yesterday once again how honest and beautiful is my Slimène's soul, because of his joy that Augustin was making up with me and was doing justice to us both. In spite of my past, present and future misfortunes I bless God and my destiny for having brought me to this desert and given me to this man, who is my *only solace*, my only reason for happiness in this whole world.

I have often been hard on him and unfair, I have been impatient for no good reason, so insane as to hit him, although secretly ashamed because he did not strike back but merely smiled at my blind rage. Afterwards I always feel truly miserable and disgusted with myself for the injustice I might have committed.

This afternoon I went to see the police official who is without a doubt an enemy spy in charge of keeping an eye on me. *He* was the first to come out with the theory that P [a French police officer] was the one who had wanted me killed, and that the murderer was bound to go scotfree. If so, that means I am doomed to die anywhere I go in the South, which is the only place where we can live.

If the crime committed at Behima is only slightly punished or not at all, that will amount to a clear signal to the Tidjanyas. 'Go ahead and kill Si Mahmoud, you have nothing to fear.'

Yet God did stay the assassin's hand once, and Abdallah's sabre was deflected. If God wants me to die a martyr, God's will is bound to find me wherever I am. If not, the plots of all those who conspire against me will be their undoing.

I am not afraid of death, but would not want to die in some obscure or pointless way. Having seen death close up, and having felt the brush of its black and icy wings, I know that its proximity means instant renunciation of the things of this world. I also know that my nerves and willpower will hold out in times of great personal ordeals, and that I will never give my enemies the satisfaction of seeing me run in cowardice or fear.

Yet, as I think of the future, there is one thing that does frighten me: misfortunes that might befall Slimène or Augustin. Faced with those, I would have no strength whatsoever. It would be hard to imagine worse poverty than the kind I am up against right now: yet the only reason it worries me is that our debts stand to spell disaster for Slimène.

Fortunately, my enemies think I am rich. I was right to spend money the way I did two years ago, here and in Biskra, for a reputation of wealth is just as useful for our defence as actual wealth would have been. Oh, if those rascals were to know that I am utterly destitute and that the slightest humiliation could be my undoing, they would not hesitate for a moment!

It is obvious that they are afraid. Otherwise they would arrest me as a spy, or expel me.

I was right to account for the wretched way I live down here as mere eccentricity: that way, it is not too obvious that I am in fact destitute.

I have begun to make a point of going to people's houses to *eat*, for the sole purpose of keeping fit, something that would have been *anathema* in the old days, like the other thing I have been doing lately, namely going to see marabouts, just to beg them for money.

I must have an iron constitution, for my health is holding up contrary to all expectation: those frightening last days in El Oued, the injury, the shock to the nervous system and the haemorrhage in Behima, the hospital, the journey, half of which I made on foot, my poverty here, the cold and the poor diet, which mostly consists of bread, none of that has got me down. How long will I be able to hold out?

How can one explain the fact that at home, where I had warm clothes, an outstandingly healthy diet, and Mummy's idolatrous care, the slightest chill I caught would degenerate into bronchitis; whereas here, having suffered freezing temperatures at El Oued, and at the hospital as well, having travelled in all kinds of weather, while literally always getting wet feet, going around in thin clothes and torn shoes, I don't even catch a cold?

The human body is nothing, the human soul is all.

Why do I adore Rouh's eyes so? Not for their shape or colour, but for the sweet and guileless radiance in their expression, which is what makes them beautiful.

The way I see it, there is no greater spiritual beauty than fanaticism, of a sort so sincere it can only end in martyrdom.

The last journal entry

31 January 1904: I began this diary over in that hated land of exile, during one of the blackest and most painfully uncertain periods in my life, a time fraught with suffering of every sort. Today it is coming to an end.

Everything is radically different now, myself included.

I have now been back in blessed Africa for a whole year, and hope to never leave it again. However poor, I have been able to travel and explore uncharted places in my adopted land . . . My Ouïha is alive, and materially speaking, we are relatively well off . . .

This diary, begun a year and a half ago in horrible Marseilles, comes to an end today, while the weather is grey and transparent, soft and almost dreamy here in Bou-Saada, another Southern spot I used to yearn for over there!

I am getting used to this tiny room of mine at the Moorish bath; it is so much like me and the way I live. I will be living in it for a few more days before setting off on my journey to Boghar, through areas I have never seen: a poorly whitewashed rectangle, a tiny window giving out on the mountains and the street, two mats on the floor, a line on which to hang my laundry, and the small torn mattress I am sitting on as I write. In one corner lie straw baskets; in the opposite one is the fireplace; my papers lie scattered about . . . And that is all. For me, that will do.

There is no more than a vague echo in these pages of all that has happened these last eighteen months; I have filled them at random, whenever I have felt the need to *articulate* . . . For the uninitiated reader, these pages would hardly make much sense. For myself they are a vestige of my earlier cult of the past. The day may come perhaps when I will no longer record the odd thought and impression in order to make them last a while. For the moment, I sometimes find great solace in re-reading these words about days gone by.

I shall start another diary. What shall I record there, and where shall I be, the day in the distant future when I shall be closing it, the way I am closing this one today?

'Allah knows what is hidden and the measure of people's sincerity!'

[Isabelle Eberhardt was killed in a flash flood at Aīn-Sefra on 21 October 1904, nine months after this last entry.]

Passionate Normal: The Diary of Isabelle Eberhardt (trans. Nina de Voogd, 1987)

GERTRUDE BELL
1868–1926

Then and not till then did I see my hostess. She was a woman of exceptional beauty, tall and pale, her face a full oval, her great eyes like stars . . . No one sees Yûsef's wife . . . he keeps her more strictly cloistered than any Moslem woman; and perhaps after all he is right.

Gertrude Bell graduated from Oxford with a first-class degree in History at a time when it was still unusual for women to have a university education. She developed a passion for the Arab world, and between 1900 and 1914 she travelled through Syria, Turkey, Assyria and Iraq along the Euphrates. With her perceptive eye, she became an inspiration to later travellers interested in desert-dwellers, particularly after her lone journey, aged forty-five, to Ha'il in the heart of Arabia, a venture that won her a Gold Medal of the Royal Geographical Society.

As a lone female traveller, she was entitled to enter the harem, and thus provided Europeans with the first written and photographic insight into the lives of Arab women. Despite the tough conditions in which she travelled, she valued and retained her outward 'femininity' – among her letters home there are frequent requests for new clothes.

Bell's understanding of the Middle East led to her recruitment during the First World War by British Intelligence. She went on to serve in the High Commission in Baghdad and became an adviser to Iraq's first king. Later, she was able to pursue her vocation as an archaeologist when she was appointed Iraq's Director of Antiquities, in which capacity she oversaw the excavations at Ur and set up the National Museum in Baghdad.

In addition to her many books, she left an important collection of six thousand photographs, which record for posterity images of desert life and historic sites, many of which have since disappeared.

Advancing into the desert

To those bred under an elaborate social order few such moments of exhilaration can come as that which stands at the threshold of wild travel. The gates of the enclosed garden are thrown open, the chain at the entrance of the sanctuary is lowered, with a wary glance to right and left you step forth, and, behold! the immeasurable world. The world of adventure and of enterprise, dark with hurrying storms, glittering in raw sunlight, an unanswered question and an unanswerable doubt hidden in the fold of every hill. Into it you must go alone, separated from the troops of friends that walk the rose alleys, stripped of the purple and fine linen that impede the fighting arm, roofless, defenceless, without possessions. The voice of the wind shall be heard instead of the persuasive voices of counsellors, the touch of the rain and the prick of the frost shall be spurs sharper than praise or blame, and necessity shall speak with an authority unknown to that borrowed wisdom which men obey or discard at will. So you leave the sheltered close, and, like the man in the fairy story, you feel the bands break that were riveted about your heart as you enter the path that stretches across the rounded shoulder of the earth.

It was a stormy morning, the 5th of February. The west wind swept up from the Mediterranean, hurried across the plain where the Canaanites waged war with the stubborn hill dwellers of Judæa, and leapt the barrier of mountains to which the kings of Assyria and of Egypt had laid vain siege. It shouted the news of rain to Jerusalem and raced onwards down the barren eastern slopes, cleared the deep bed of Jordan with a bound, and vanished across the hills of Moab into the desert. And all the hounds of the storm followed behind, a yelping pack, coursing eastward and rejoicing as they went.

No one with life in his body could stay in on such a day, but for me there was little question of choice. In the grey winter dawn the mules had gone forward carrying all my worldly goods – two tents, a canteen, and a month's provision of such slender luxuries as the austerest traveller can ill spare, two small mule trunks, filled mainly with photographic materials, a few books and a goodly sheaf of maps. The mules and the three muleteers I had brought with me from Beyrout, and liked well enough to take on into the further journey. The men were all from the Lebanon. A father and son, Christians both, came from a village above Beyrout; the father an old and toothless individual who mumbled, as he rode astride the mule trunks, blessings and pious ejaculations mingled with protestations of devotion to his most clement employer, but saw no need to make other contribution to the welfare of the party – Ibrahīm was the name of this ancient; the son, Habīb, a young man of twenty-two or twenty-three, dark, upright and broad-shouldered, with a profile that a Greek might have envied and a bold glance under black brows. The third was a Druze, a big shambling man, incurably lazy, a rogue in his modest way, though he could always disarm my just indignation in the matter of stolen sugar or missing piastres with an appealing, lustrous eye that looked forth unblinking like the eye of a dog. He was greedy and rather stupid, defects that must be difficult to avoid on a diet of dry bread, rice and rancid butter; but when I took him into the midst of his blood enemies he slouched about his work and tramped after his mule and his donkey with the same air of passive detachment that he showed in the streets of Beyrout. His name was Muhammad. The last member of the caravan was the cook, Mikhāil, a native of Jerusalem and a Christian whose religion did not sit heavy on his soul. He had travelled with Mr Mark Sykes, and received from him the following character: 'He doesn't know much about cooking, unless he has learnt since he was with me, but he never seems to care twopence whether he lives or whether he is killed.' When I repeated these words to Mikhāil he relapsed into fits of suppressed laughter, and I engaged him on the spot. It was an insufficient reason, and as good as many another. He served me well according to his lights; but he was a touchy, fiery little man, always ready to meet a possible offence half way, with an imagination to the limits of which I never attained during three months' acquaintance, and unfortunately he had learned other things besides cooking during the years that had elapsed since he and Mr Sykes had been shipwrecked together on Lake Van. It was typical of him that he never troubled to tell me the story of that adventure, though once when I alluded to it he nodded his head and remarked: 'We were as near death as a beggar to poverty, but your Excellency knows a man can die but once,' whereas he bombarded my ears with tales of tourists who had declared they could not and would not travel in Syria unsustained by his culinary arts. The 'arak bottle was his fatal drawback; and after trying all prophylactic methods, from blandishment to the hunting-crop, I parted with him abruptly on the Cilician coast, not without regrets other than a natural longing for his tough ragoûts and cold pancakes.

Perpetual insecurity

The fortunes of the Arab are as varied as those of a gambler on the Stock Exchange. One day he is the richest man in the desert, and next morning he may not have a single camel foal to his name. He lives in a state of war, and even if the surest pledges have been exchanged with the neighbouring tribes there is no certainty that a band of raiders from hundreds of miles away will not descend on his camp in the night, as a tribe unknown to Syria, the Beni Awājeh, fell, two years ago, on the lands south-east of Aleppo, crossing three hundred miles of desert, Mardūf (two on a camel) from their seat above Baghdad, carrying off all the cattle and killing scores of people. How many thousand years this state of things has lasted, those who shall read the earliest records of the inner desert will tell us, for it goes back to the first of them, but in all the centuries the Arab has bought no wisdom from experience. He is never safe, and yet he behaves as though security were his daily bread. He pitches his feeble little camps, ten or fifteen tents together, over a wide stretch of undefended and indefensible country. He is too far from his fellows to call in their aid, too far as a rule to gather the horsemen together and follow after the raiders whose retreat must be sufficiently slow, burdened with the captured flocks, to guarantee success to a swift pursuit. Having lost all his worldly goods, he goes about the desert and makes his plaint, and one man gives him a strip or two of goats' hair cloth, and another a coffee-pot, a third presents him with a camel, and a fourth with a few sheep, till he has a roof to cover him and enough animals to keep his family from hunger. There are good customs among the Arabs, as Namrād said. So he bides his time for months, perhaps for years, till at length opportunity ripens, and the horsemen of his tribe with their allies ride forth and recapture all the flocks that had been carried off and more besides, and the feud enters on another phase. The truth is that the ghazu [raid] is the only industry the desert knows and the only game.

El Bārah: intolerable by night, beautiful by day

By this time it was growing dark; moreover a black storm was blowing up from the east, and we had an hour to ride through very rough country. We started at once, Mikhāil, Mahmūd and I, picking our way along an almost invisible path. As ill luck would have it, just as the dusk closed in the storm broke upon us, the night turned pitch dark, and with the driving rain in our faces we missed that Medea-thread of a road. At this moment Mikhāil's ears were assailed by the barking of imaginary dogs, and we turned our horses' heads towards the point from which he supposed it to come. This was the second stage of the misadventure, and I at least ought to have remembered that Mikhāil was always the worst guide, even when he knew the direction of the place towards which he was going. We stumbled on; a watery moon came out to show us that our way led nowhere, and being assured of this we stopped and fired off a couple of pistol shots, thinking that if the village were close at hand the muleteers would hear us and make some answering signal. None came, however, and we found our way back to the point where the rain had blinded us, only to be deluded again by that phantom barking and to set off again on our wild dog chase. This time we went still further afield, and Heaven knows where we should ultimately have arrived if I had not demonstrated by the misty moon that we were riding steadily south, whereas El Bārah lay to the north. At this we turned heavily in our tracks, and when we had ridden some way back we dismounted and sat down upon a ruined wall to discuss the advisability of lodging for the night in an empty tomb, and to eat a mouthful of bread and cheese out of Mahmūd's saddle-bags. The hungry horses came nosing up to us; mine had half my share of bread, for after all he was doing more than half the share of work. The food gave us enterprise; we rode on and found ourselves in the twinkling of an eye at the original branching off place. From it we struck a third path, and in five minutes came to the village of El Bārah, round which we had been circling for three hours. The muleteers were fast asleep in the tents; we woke them somewhat rudely, and asked whether they had not heard our signals. Oh yes, they replied cheerfully, but concluding that it was a robber taking advantage of the stormy night to kill some one, they had paid small attention. This is the whole tale of the misadventure; it does credit to none of the persons concerned, and I blush to relate it.

Intolerable though EI Bārah may be by night, by day it is most marvellous and most beautiful. It is like the dream city which children create for themselves to dwell in between bedtime and sleep-time, building palace after palace down the shining ways of the imagination, and no words can give the charm of it nor the magic of the Syrian spring. The generations of the dead walk with you down the streets, you see them flitting across their balconies, gazing out of windows wreathed with white clematis, wandering in palisaded gardens that are still planted with olive and with vine and carpeted with iris, hyacinth and anemone. Yet you may search the chronicles for them in vain; they played no part in history, but were content to live in peace and to build themselves great houses in which to dwell and fine tombs to lie in after they were dead. That they became Christian the hundreds of ruined churches and the cross carved over the doors and windows of their dwellings, would be enough to show; that they were artists their decorations prove; that they were wealthy their spacious mansions their summer houses and stables and out-houses testify. They borrowed from Greece such measure of cultivation and of the arts as they required, and fused with them the spirit of Oriental magnificence which never breathed without effect on the imagination of the West; they lived in comfort and security such as few of their contemporaries can have known, and the Mahommadan invasion swept them off the face of the earth.

  The Desert and the Sown, 1907

HOWARD CARTER
1873–1939

... when Lord Carnarvon ... inquired anxiously, 'Can you see anything?' it was all I could do to get out the words, 'Yes, wonderful things.'

Howard Carter's artist father trained him in the essentials of painting and drawing, but he had no intention of continuing the family business of painting portraits of pets and families, generally for local Norfolk landowners. Instead, he joined the Egyptian Exploration Fund as a tracer – the person who copies the drawings and inscriptions on archaeological remains on to paper for further study. When he was seventeen, he left for Alexandria, his first voyage outside Britain. On his first job – copying the scenes depicted on the walls of the tombs in Bani Hassan (grave site of the princes of Middle Egypt during 2000 BC) – he slept inside the tombs at night, watched over by their resident bats.

By the time he was twenty-five, Carter had proven skills as an archaeologist and was appointed Inspector General of Monuments for Upper Egypt, responsible for supervising and controlling archaeological investigations along the Nile valley. However, an incident in which tomb guards defended themselves against a drunken gaggle of French tourists led to Carter's demotion. He was despatched to the uninteresting town of Tanta, where so little archaeological work was in progress that he was soon forced to resign from the Antiquities Service.

For a few years Carter eked out a living as a commercial watercolourist and tourist guide, until in 1908 he met, and began to work for, George Herbert, the fifth Lord Carnarvon, a keen collector of Egyptian artefacts and antiquities. Excavating in the Valley of the Kings, Carter became convinced that somewhere nearby was the undiscovered tomb of Tutankhamen. His team spent five unreward-ing years methodically sifting through rubble in search of it. In 1922 Carnavon was close to calling a halt to Carter's endeavours, but Carter persuaded him to allow just one more season of excavation. On 1 November, just three days after getting back to the site, Carter's men broke through to the valley floor and found a sunken stone stairway. It was the tomb of the boy-pharoah Tutankhamen.

As described in the London *Times*, the news spread before the tomb had even been opened: 'The whole of Luxor, where everyone down to the smallest urchin is an antiquity-hunter, was agog. Great was the speculation in regard to the contents of the chamber ... Little, however, did Lord Carnavon and Mr Carter suspect the wonderful nature of the contents of the chambers – for there are more than one – as they stood outside.' And no wonder, for the tomb's priceless contents included state couches, statues of the Pharaoh, and four chariots, all of dazzling gold and studded with jewels.

Not withstanding local superstitions, intrigues, and disputes with the Egyptian government over the ownership of the antiquities, Carter continued to work on the site until 1928. During this period Lord Carnarvon died suddenly – from pneumonia or an innocuous-seeming insect bite, spreading rumours of a mummy's curse. One alleged inscription on the tomb read: 'Death Shall Come on Swift Wings To Him Who Disturbs the Peace of the King ...' However, despite the premature deaths of several people involved in the excavation, Carter himself died in his mid-sixties from natural causes.

The finding of the tomb

Hardly had I arrived on the work next morning (November 4th) than the unusual silence, due to the stoppage of the work, made me realize that something out of the ordinary had happened, and I was greeted by the announcement that a step cut in the rock had been discovered underneath the very first hut to be attacked. This seemed too good to be true, but a short amount of extra clearing revealed the fact that we were actually in the entrance of a steep cut in the rock, some thirteen feet below the entrance to the tomb of Rameses VI, and a similar depth from the present bed level of The Valley. The manner of cutting was that of the sunken stairway entrance so common in The Valley, and I almost dared to hope that we had found our tomb at last. Work continued feverishly throughout the whole of that day and the morning of the next, but it was not until the afternoon of November 5th that we succeeded in clearing away the masses of rubbish that overlay the cut, and were able to demarcate the upper edges of the stairway on all its four sides.

It was clear by now beyond any question that we actually had before us the entrance to a tomb, but doubts, born of previous disappointments, persisted in creeping in. There was always the horrible possibility, suggested by our experience in the Thothmes III Valley, that the tomb was an unfinished one, never completed and never used: if it had been finished there was the depressing probability that it had been completely plundered in ancient times. On the other hand, there was just the chance of an untouched or only partially plundered tomb, and it was with ill-suppressed excitement that I watched the descending steps of the staircase, as one by one they came to light. The cutting was excavated in the side of a small hillock, and, as the work progressed, its western edge receded under the slope of the rock until it was, first partially, and then completely, roofed in, and became a passage, 10 feet high by 6 feet wide. Work progressed more rapidly now; step succeeded step, and at the level of the twelfth, towards sunset, there was disclosed the upper part of a doorway, blocked, plastered, and sealed.

A sealed doorway – it was actually true, then! Our years of patient labour were to be rewarded after all, and I think my first feeling was one of congratulation that my faith in The Valley had not been unjustified. With excitement growing to fever heat I searched the seal impressions on the door for evidence of the identity of the owner, but could find no name: the only decipherable ones were those of the well-known royal necropolis seal, the jackal and nine captives. Two facts, however, were clear: first, the employment of this royal seal was certain evidence that the tomb had been constructed for a person of very high standing; and second, that the sealed door was entirely screened from above by workmen's huts of the Twentieth Dynasty was sufficiently clear proof that at least from that date it had never been entered. With that for the moment I had to be content.

While examining the seals I noticed, at the top of the doorway, where some of the plaster had fallen away, a heavy wooden lintel. Under this, to assure myself of the method by which the doorway had been blocked, I made a small peephole, just large enough to insert an electric torch, and discovered that the passage beyond the door was filled completely from floor to ceiling with stones and rubble – additional proof this of the care with which the tomb had been protected.

It was a thrilling moment for an excavator. Alone, save for my native workmen, I found myself, after years of comparatively unproductive labour, on the threshold of what might prove to be a magnificent discovery. Anything, literally anything, might lie beyond that passage, and it needed all my self-control to keep from breaking down the doorway, and investigating then and there.

One thing puzzled me, and that was the smallness of the opening in comparison with the ordinary Valley tombs. The design was certainly of the Eighteenth Dynasty. Could it be the tomb of a noble buried here by royal consent? Was it a royal cache, a hiding-place to which a mummy and its equipment had been removed for safety? Or was it actually the tomb of the king for whom I had spent so many years in search?

Once more I examined the seal impressions for a clue, but on the part of the door so far laid bare only those of the royal necropolis seal already mentioned were clear enough to read. Had I but known that a few inches lower down there was a perfectly clear and distinct impression of the seal of Tut.ankh.Amen, the king I most desired to find, I would have cleared on, had a much better night's rest in consequence, and saved myself nearly three weeks of uncertainty. It was late, however, and darkness was already upon us. With some reluctance I re-closed the small hole that I had made, filled in our excavation for protection during the night, selected the most trustworthy of my workmen – themselves almost as excited as I was – to watch all night above the tomb, and so home by moonlight, riding down The Valley.

Naturally my wish was to go straight ahead with our clearing to find out the full extent of the discovery, but Lord Carnarvon was in England, and in fairness to him I had to delay matters until he could come. Accordingly, on the morning of November 6th I sent him the following cable: 'At last have made

wonderful discovery in Valley; a magnificent tomb with seals intact; recovered same for your arrival; congratulations.'

My next task was to secure the doorway against interference until such time
as it could finally be re-opened. This we did by filling our excavation up again
to surface level, and rolling on top of it the large flint boulders of which the
workmen's huts had been composed. By the evening of the same day, exactly
forty-eight hours after we had discovered the first step of the staircase, this
was accomplished. The tomb had vanished. So far as the appearance of the
ground was concerned there never had been any tomb, and I found it hard to
persuade myself at times that the whole episode had not been a dream.

I was soon to be reassured on this point. News travels fast in Egypt, and
within two days of the discovery congratulations, inquiries, and offers of help
descended upon me in a steady stream from all directions. It became clear,
even at this early stage, that I was in for a job that could not be tackled single-
handed, so I wired to Callender, who had helped me on various previous
occasions, asking him if possible to join me without delay, and to my relief he
arrived on the very next day. On the 8th I had received two messages from
Lord Carnarvon in answer to my cable, the first of which read, 'Possibly come
soon,' and the second, received a little later, 'Propose arrive Alexandria 20th.'

We had thus nearly a fortnight's grace, and we devoted it to making preparations of various kinds, so that when the time of re-opening came, we should
be able, with the least possible delay, to handle any situation that might arise.
On the night of the 18th I went to Cairo for three days, to meet Lord Carnarvon and make a number of necessary purchases, returning to Luxor on the
21st. On the 23rd Lord Carnarvon arrived in Luxor with his daughter, Lady
Evelyn Herbert, his devoted companion in all his Egyptian work, and everything was in hand for the beginning of the second chapter of the discovery of
the tomb. Callender had been busy all day clearing away the upper layer of
rubbish, so that by morning we should be able to get into the staircase without any delay.

By the afternoon of the 24th the whole staircase was clear, sixteen steps
in all and we were able to make a proper examination of the sealed doorway.
On the lower part the seal impressions were much clearer, and we were
able without any difficulty to make out on several of them the name of
Tut.ankh.Amen. This added enormously to the interest of the discovery. If
we had found, as seemed almost certain, the tomb of that shadowy monarch,
whose tenure of the throne coincided with one of the most interesting periods
in the whole of Egyptian history, we should indeed have reason to congratulate ourselves . . .

On the morning of the 25th the seal impressions on the doorway were carefully noted and photographed, and then we removed the actual blocking of the door, consisting of rough stones carefully built from floor to lintel, and heavily plastered on their outer faces to take the seal impressions.

This disclosed the beginning of a descending passage (not a staircase), the same width as the entrance stairway, and nearly seven feet high. As I had already discovered from my hole in the doorway, it was filled completely with stone and rubble, probably the chip from its own excavation . . .

As we cleared the passage we found, mixed with the rubble of the lower levels, broken potsherds, jar sealings, alabaster jars, whole and broken, vases of painted pottery, numerous fragments of smaller articles, and water skins, these last having obviously been used to bring up the water needed for the plastering of the doorways. These were clear evidence of plundering, and we eyed them askance. By night we had cleared a considerable distance down the passage, but as yet saw no sign of second doorway or of chamber.

The day following (November 26th) was the day of days, the most wonderful that I have ever lived through, and certainly one whose like I can never hope to see again. Throughout the morning the work of clearing continued, slowly perforce, on account of the delicate objects that were mixed with the filling. Then, in the middle of the afternoon, thirty feet down from the outer door, we came upon a second sealed doorway, almost an exact replica of the first. The seal impressions in this case were less distinct, but still recognizable as those of Tut.ankh.Amen and of the royal necropolis . . .

Slowly, desperately slowly it seemed to us as we watched, the remains of passage debris that encumbered the lower part of the doorway were removed, until at last we had the whole door clear before us. The decisive moment had arrived. With trembling hands I made a tiny breach in the upper left hand corner. Darkness and blank space, as far as an iron testing-rod could reach, showed that whatever lay beyond was empty, and not filled like the passage we had just cleared. Candle tests were applied as a precaution against possible foul gases, and then, widening the hole a little, I inserted the candle and peered in, Lord Carnarvon, Lady Evelyn and Callender standing anxiously beside me to hear the verdict. At first I could see nothing, the hot air escaping from the chamber causing the candle flame to flicker, but presently, as my eyes grew accustomed to the light, details of the room within emerged slowly from the mist, strange animals, statues, and gold – everywhere the glint of gold. For the moment – an eternity it must have seemed to the others standing by – I was struck dumb with amazement, and when Lord Carnarvon, unable to stand the suspense any longer, inquired anxiously, 'Can you see anything?' it was all I could do to get out the words, 'Yes, wonderful things.' Then widening the hole a little further, so that we both could see, we inserted an electric torch.

I suppose most excavators would confess to a feeling of awe – embarrassment almost – when they break into a chamber closed and sealed by pious hands so many centuries ago. For the moment, time as a factor in human life has lost its meaning. Three thousand, four thousand years maybe, have passed and gone since human feet last trod the floor on which you stand, and yet, as you note the signs of recent life around you – the half-filled bowl of mortar for the door, the blackened lamp, the finger-mark upon the freshly painted surface, the farewell garland dropped upon the threshold – you feel it might have been but yesterday. The very air you breathe, unchanged throughout the centuries, you share with those who laid the mummy to its rest. Time is annihilated by little intimate details such as these, and you feel an intruder.

That is perhaps the first and dominant sensation, but others follow thick and fast – the exhilaration of discovery, the fever of suspense, the almost over-mastering impulse, born of curiosity, to break down seals and lift the lids of boxes, the thought – pure joy to the investigator – that you are about to add a page to history, or solve some problem of research, the strained expectancy – why not confess it? – of the treasure-seeker. Did these thoughts actually pass through our minds at the time, or have I imagined them since? I cannot tell. It was the discovery that my memory was blank, and not the mere desire for dramatic chapter-ending, that occasioned this digression.

The Tomb of Tutankhamen, 1923

MILDRED CABLE and FRANCESCA FRENCH
1878–1952/1871–1960
'The man is dying,' he said . . .
'Nothing will induce us to leave a dying man to his fate!' was our answer.

The daughter of a draper in Guildford, Mildred Cable felt her missionary calling from an early age, and studied science at London University with the express intention of becoming a medical worker with the China Inland Mission. In 1902 she joined the renowned missionary Eva French in Shanxi province. Together they ran a school for girls and were soon afterwards joined by Eva's sister, Francesca. In 1923 the 'trio', as they became known, were granted permission to travel in the Gobi, the first evangelists who had been allowed to do so since the sixth century.

For fifteen years they covered enormous distances, preaching to nomads. They were both challenged and inspired by the arid, indomitable land. 'Once the spirit of the desert had caught us, it lured us on and we became learners in its severe school,' wrote Cable in the prologue to her *Desert Journal* (1934). 'The solitudes provoked reflection, the wide space gave us a right sense of proportion and the silences forbade triviality.' The missionaries, who took the trouble to learn the languages of those they lived among, came to know the desert nomads intimately, and were well loved in return. They became so familiar with the terrain, they said, that they could trace a given pebble back to the spot from which it had been collected. 'Even the monotonous outlines of the desert, when better known, wore a subtly changing aspect, and landscapes which were broadly similar in outline became highly distinctive as their detail was scrutinised.'

They were observant researchers as well as missionaries and, while on leave back home, they gave lectures on their findings to scientific societies. Francesca French and Mildred Cable wrote over twenty books between them, each in a self-effacing style that plays down the extent of their hardships and conveys a lack of prejudice remarkable at the time in their missionary profession.

Finding a carter

When it became known in the *bazar* that we needed a carter for a trek across Gobi to Turfan, applications poured in and both officials and merchants sent us word concerning men who had once served them and were now out of a job. As employers we had a good name, for we always paid wages on the day they were due, but on the other hand it was often said that our rigid notions concerning the honesty and good conduct of our servants were hard to comply with . . .

The cook, who was our most responsible factotum, appeared in the living-room and announced in a low confidential tone that Carter Li, recommended by Mandarin Pu, wanted to speak about driving the cart to Turfan.

A tall, strongly built man with a long face like a mule was called into the room. His appearance bore the stamp of what is considered stylish in carter circles; he wore a good suit of black cotton with white calico socks, and the woven band which held in his trousers at the ankle was finished off with a smart knotted fringe. A length of black material was wound round his waist as a girdle, and a white kerchief was twisted round his shaved head. His trousers were well made by a good seamstress and fitted snugly round his middle. Experience enabled us to place him unfailingly in his own carter category. This was a self-respecting man, without the carter's too common vices of opium-smoking, gambling or fast living, and there would certainly be a limit to the squeezes he would expect. The beasts would never be neglected in his hands, for he would always place their requirements before the convenience of his master. His referee was reliable and his own home was only a few streets away. On the other hand, he would certainly be disobliging, unadaptable and rude, and the other servants would find him exacting and overbearing. His voice had a rasping sound like a coffee-grinder, and would inevitably shatter the harmony of caravan life, as he used it to assert his own rights or preferences. The thought of that voice rousing us at two a.m. for early starts made us unwilling to engage him, for the misery of zero hour was bad enough without hearing the grumblings of a disagreeable carter. He answered to the name of Li Kao-teh (Li of the High Virtues), but even this failed to attract us.

A few hours later the cook was back with another man whom a friend of his was prepared to personally recommend. This carter was rather short but very strongly built. He wore a suit of blue cotton much the worse for wear, there were patches on his socks and coat, and his shoes were shabby. His trousers were so baggy as to have no relation to the size of his body. He was an easy talker and there was the swing of a first-class walker in his gait. Anyone with knowledge of the breed would know that this man would be popular with fellow-servants, a jovial road companion, and liked by the innkeepers because of his easy-going ways and lavish generosity with his master's goods. His family name was Wang and he was always called by his nickname of Quick Stepper. He had been everywhere on the desert trade-routes and knew them thoroughly.

The question under consideration was which of the two carters was the least undesirable. The good-tempered, easily pleased man would certainly help himself to a share of everything which he handled, but pay back in extra service. The disagreeable grouch would do his work well but take control of his employer's team, refuse to yield an inch on his rights, and bring an atmosphere of ill-temper into the whole caravan. During this interview we might have been deceived concerning the proverb, 'There's ne'er a good one,' for the answers given to the questions we asked were so disarming as to give it the lie.

Quick Stepper assured us that he quite understood our demand for scrupulous honesty and the rule that opium-smoking and gambling were not allowed. He heartily concurred in the point of view that, the purpose of our journey being to declare the word of righteousness, it would be most inconvenient if our own people did the very things which we condemned. 'Smoke opium!' he said. 'Why, I do not even know how to smoke tobacco! Gamble?' He turned to the cook: '*You* would know if I gambled.' The cook kept a steady eye and said nothing.

As a matter of fact, the two men were being judged not so much by anything they said as by the cut of their clothes. We knew that every man with the snug fit and careful outline of Li was a disagreeable rascal, while every carter with the baggy breeches and loose coat of Wang was a pleasant rogue. The faults of each one, in turn, became so intolerable that the only relief was to engage the two kinds alternatively. Unfortunately for himself, Quick Stepper confided to the cook, at the close of the interview, that he had a small debt to pay off before leaving the town, and must therefore ask for two months' wages in advance. Experience teaches that a servant paid in advance is a perpetual nuisance; he will certainly run into debt at the inns and probably not be allowed to leave until the account has been settled, so this time Li of the High Virtues, later nicknamed Grouch, got the job.

One of the middle-man's necessary concessions to the carter he recommends is that he will call on the new employer the day before the journey should begin, and say that the man's old mother (or some other female relative for whom he is entitled to feel concern) has suddenly fallen ill and is gripped with a mysterious internal pain. It would certainly not be right for him to leave her at this crisis, and he therefore cannot fulfil his engagement. The inexperienced traveller is distressed, as he sees all his plans turned upside down. Before long the middle-man will certainly reappear, suggesting that a small rise in wages, if paid in advance, would perhaps enable the carter so to arrange home affairs that he himself could leave . . . The experienced desert hand has learnt to remain unmoved by any such tales of woe, and merely says, 'Very well, we will postpone departure, and if the old mother is not soon better I must find another man.' This evident understanding of the situation always hastens recovery far more effectively than any dose of medicine, and probably within twenty-four hours the caravan is off on its long journey and there is no further hold-up.

The Gobi Desert, 1942

ELLA MAILLART

1903–97

Everything must be re-learnt before life can be truly gauged. What life is worth is a conception we have all lost, more or less. But in contact with primitive, simple peoples, mountain dwellers, nomads, and sailors it is impossible to ignore the elemental laws. Life finds its equilibrium again.

Ella Maillart, born in Geneva, was an outstanding sportswoman and represented Switzerland in skiing, sailing and hockey until her early thirties. Meanwhile she dabbled in various professions, including acting (in Berlin), teaching French (in Wales), and working as a sculptor's model and stuntwoman. It wasn't until 1930 that she found her feet as a writer. Putting pen to paper was something she never found easy – 'You know too well that you fail to express the most important things, which are for ever elusive' – but she had a love of adventure and it gave her the chance to travel.

In 1932 she travelled in Soviet Turkistan, from Tien Shan (near the Kyrgyzstan border with China) to Kizil Kum, living among the local nomads. She published her account of this journey in *Turkestan Solo*.

Her most challenging adventure was an eight-month trek with London *Times* journalist Peter Fleming, on which they covered the 3,500 miles from Peking across the harsh Tsaidam Plateau, along the Silk Road and over the Karakoram to India. In 1939 Maillart travelled with her morphine-addicted companion Annemarie Schwarzenbach (known by Maillart as 'Christina') from Switzerland through Turkey to Afghanistan, in a Ford. Her book *The Cruel Way* describes not only their travels but also her unsuccessful struggle to free Annemarie from addiction: 'The moral torment Christina was going through made me understand that hunger or poverty can be less terrifying than mental suffering and anguish.'

Maillart spent her war years in India where she followed the teachings of various spiritual masters and began, as she put it, 'a new journey which ... will take me further than before towards the perfect life I was instinctively seeking. I began this journey by exploring the unmapped territory of my own mind.' She was one of the first European travellers into Nepal when it opened in 1949 and was organizing and accompanying cultural tours to various Asian countries well into her eighties.

At the age of eighty-three she travelled across Tibet, and at ninety-one made her last journey, to Goa. She died three years later in a commune she had set up at Chandolin, Switzerland.

'The desolation is superb!'

We begin to skirt the first of the pink-sloped humps. At our feet, parallel to that in which the Narin flows, stretches a wide valley. Carefully scrutinizing the smooth, almost unbroken surface of the slopes, we discern the pale spots of a few yurts gleaming in the sun like the eggs of flies in the crevices of a piece of meat . . .

We do not descend towards them.

For many days we travel thus, proceeding from valley to valley, from Teuz to the Ak Tach. I am always thinking something new is going to turn up: a landscape, aul, some new person . . .

The desolation is superb! As at sea, the monotony throws into extraordinary relief the slightest happenings . . .

From time to time, hugging the ground, a sort of small pulpy plant appears, bearing scarlet protuberances like veritable drops of blood.

Whenever the sun goes in, it gets so cold that I have to protect my ears with a scarf. An ancient sprain begins to hurt my ankle, as a result of having to bear my weight in the stirrups in the descents. But what troubles me most is one of my molars which broke on a piece of bread, so that when I chew it feels as if a needle were being pushed into the gum. An abscess might gather there at any time: that would be comforting!

We continue to advance, eyes glued to the play of muscles in the buttocks of the horse in front.

Troublesome thoughts take possession of one towards the end of the day, when one is tired and overcome by cold, hunger, and sleep all at the same time. At every little combe where there is grass and water for the beasts I wait expectantly for the signal to halt. But we have first to find an abandoned camp and traces of yurts, large pale circles of downtrodden grass. It is only there our fuel is to be found – horse and cow dung dried by the sun: 'kisiak.'

The men put up the tents while we pile up the cakes of dried dung in our arms. Before collecting them we turn them over with a foot to make sure they are dry beneath. We build an open hearth. They burn well, like embers, without flame, but throwing out a good deal of heat. The acrid odour of the kisiak permeates one's clothes, and it is that odour which came from every nomad that I met. One soon gets used to it, and welcomes it with pleasure when it announces the animation of an aul. Only some tourist in a hurry could have taken it for the smell of filth . . .

It freezes in the night. Luckily I have lined my flea-bag with my skirt, and the camel-hair bought in Aralskoie More.

During these nights under the tent, I come at last to a full realization of the fact that the monkeys are my brethren, in spite of all the sacrifices my parents imposed on themselves to perfect my education.

Imagine yourself comfortably settled in the dark tent, warm in your sleeping-bag, between two companions whom you touch whenever you move at all. Half asleep, you feel something worrying you, pressing into your skin like a crumb. Is it a flea or merely an old bite that still itches? No, it moves, gets under your sleeve, and then stops: another one that means to make a meal of you. But you know just where it is, in the middle of your wrist. So with the utmost caution the other hand approaches stealthily and a finger pounces on the prey, knocks it senseless, rolls it about, and seizes it with the thumb's help.

But the only way of making sure you have killed it is to cut it in two. Yet, imprisoned as you are in your bag, you cannot at every capture waken your neighbours by switching on a light. I challenge anybody in darkness to divide the hard little creature, hardly the size of a peppercorn, in two. Picture yourself alone, with the man-eater at your mercy . . . wondering as the moments pass what tactics should best be employed. All things considered, you decide the tongue and the teeth are a good deal more handy than the nails: and lo and behold! there is no longer anything to bother about: it was all very simple; the tongue seized the creature, the teeth bit it in two, and then it was spat out. Rid at last of the enemy, sleep becomes possible again.

Turkestan Solo, 1934

FREYA STARK

1893–1993

The word ecstasy is always related to some sort of discovery, a novelty to sense or spirit, and it is in search of this word that in love, in religion, in art or in travel, the adventurous are ready to face the unknown.

Both of Dame Freya Stark's parents were artists – her father was the English sculptor Rob Stark – and she was born while they were studying in Paris. By the age of five she could speak three languages, and was educated in Italy (where she also worked in a carpet factory) and at London University, where she studied literature.

Stark worked as a censor in London and a nurse on the Italian front during the First World War. Perhaps as a balm to the unhappy experiences of her adolescence – a broken engagement, a hideous accident that wrenched away much of her scalp – she began to develop an intense interest in the Arab world and, having spent some time studying Arabic in London, went to Baghdad. There she interspersed working on the *Baghdad Times* with extensive travels in Persia and the Hadhramaut.

As a traveller, she was resourceful and, as an unaccompanied woman, remarkably undaunted by the harsh, male terrain in which she wandered. At the age of twenty-five she journeyed into the 'forbidden territory' of the Syrian Druze, trekking through the Valley of the Assassins (named after the local Muslim sect renowned for committing political and religious murders) and spending some time incarcerated in a military prison.

The Valleys of the Assassins established Stark as both a writer and a traveller of little-known regions, securing her grants from the Royal Geographical Society. Several more notable literary accomplishments were to follow, each a textured carpet of vignettes. 'The sweet outof-door drowsiness wrapped me as if it were a part of the mountain darkness, and the river lisped and murmured between its invisible banks,' she wrote in *The Minaret of Djam*. 'It knows its own direction, I thought, and remembered a poem written long ago – "deep in my heart direction lies" – if we can follow that, we move safely and any road can lead us, carrying through the darkness ... our own secret climate of repose.' Such expression of the inner and outer journey is characteristic: as 'she covers the ground outwardly, so she advances inwardly,' Lawrence Durrell wrote of her. She pioneered a style of travel writing – rich, lucid descriptions of individual moments, punctuated by glimpses of her experience as a whole. 'Not the thing itself, but the sense of other and contrary things, makes reality,' she says in *The Valleys of the Assassins*. Loyal to Britain, and valued for her expertise in Arabian dialects, during the Second World War she slipped into Yemen to erode Italian attempts to make an aircraft base there, and worked for the Ministry of Information in Aden and Cairo, creating an anti-Axis propaganda network.

During Stark's travels in southern Arabia, she discovered the hitherto hidden routes of the ancient incense trade. She explored the trails taken by Alexander the Great and studied the impact made by Greek civilization on Middle Eastern nations, continuing to travel until well into her sixties. 'What I find trying', she wrote, 'is a country which you do not understand and where you can never be yourself. You are English, or Christian, or Protestant, or anything but your individual you.'

Arriving in the master's absence

It is unlucky to reach a nomad's tent in the master's absence.

The laws of hospitality are based on the axiom that a stranger is an enemy until he has entered the sanctuary of somebody's tent: after that, his host is responsible, not only for his safety, but for his general acceptability with the tribe. He is treated at first with suspicion, and gradually with friendliness as he explains himself – very much as if he were trying to enter a county neighbourhood in England, for the undeveloped mind is much the same in Lincolnshire or Luristan. From the very first, however, once he is a guest, he is safe, in every district I have ever been in except the wilder regions of Lakistan. This is the only arrangement which makes travel possible in a tribal country: but it makes the adoption of a guest a responsibility, and the master of the house or some influential representative is alone willing to undertake it.

My young accomplice, Hasan, had given me two letters, one to an uncle and one to a cousin: but both were out for the day, and we were received by a cavalier and jaunty young man with shining slanting eyes and thin lips, and a wavy moustache he was proud of, dressed in a white coat quilted in patterns, with a tobacco bag hanging at his sash, and a coloured silk turban off the back of his head.

He was, I discovered later, the daughter's fiancé, and took the leadership of affairs upon himself. He went swaggering ahead to lead us to the chief tent with an air of: 'We'll think what to do with you later,' which distressed my Philosopher, unprepared for so cool a welcome from his own people. 'The young generation have no manners,' I almost thought he was going to say; he was, however, wiser, and said nothing at all, but squatted under the tent awning and concentrated his mind on pouring loose tobacco into the little paper tubes he smoked all day long.

A funeral had taken away our hosts, and no one of any importance was left of the little tribe. A few retainers and cattle-men gathered around, while the women came out from the seclusion of their screens and joined in the general curiosity. Shah Riza, still looking down at his tobacco, and treating the topic with the detached manner of diplomacy, explained that I travelled for pleasure and learning, and that I was one of the great ones of Baghdad. I had a passport, he added, and the police had allowed it to pass too, apparently an unusual distinction. I had letters to carry me anywhere. I wished to find old cities, and cross the river to Lakistan.

The lady of the tent, still young but with a middle-aged, disillusioned manner, sat smoking a short clay pipe, and looked sceptically at the ground.

She had a nose tilted prettily under her turban, and a smile that gave a charming gaiety to her sulky little face. She presently undid a corner of her head-dress and produced tea, tied up there in a knot: she handed it to the household with one hand while she held her pipe in the other and began a Kurdish oration, telling Shah Riza, as far as I could gather, that we were only on sufferance till the master returned.

This female eloquence appeared to produce a certain uneasiness among the men, inclined to be more tolerant. Her daughter, a shy and beautiful creature of fourteen, looked at me with timid friendly smiles. The young man, in his offhand manner, made our tea: the ladies retired: the humbler visitors grew talkative and friendly. There would be no difficulty for Lakistan, they said: men with relatives on the other side could take us, and knew how to find out the day before where the bandits might be, and how to avoid them. It was constantly being done. All the routes are used by smugglers. Did Shah Riza think I could be induced to smuggle across some opium when I returned to Iraq? I could not do that, said I decidedly: Shah Riza had already made use of my saddle-bag to get through twelve boxes of matches and innumerable packets of cigarette paper without my knowing it. I had no wish to find opium there; I hoped to have plenty of crimes of my own to organize by that time. Opium, I observed, was an immoral thing to sell or buy. The tribesmen, who are not given to this vice, agreed with me, and grew more friendly still. But I was tired by this time: I took my *abba*, wrapped myself in it from head to foot, and went to sleep with my head on the saddle-bag.

The capacity for sleeping in public is one of the most useful things one can acquire, and takes a certain amount of practice: an *abba* is a help: in the midst of a crowded tent it will secure you privacy; and after a time, the murmur of voices, discussing you over the fire, becomes no more disturbing than the sound of running water to dwellers by a stream.

A police escort – then solitude

I rode with a leisureliness exasperating to the policemen, whose horses were much better than mine. The lieutenant offered to change my mount at intervals: but I was anxious to take some bearings later on, and had no objection to going slowly, and soon to make him tired enough to leave me, either to rest behind me or to trot on ahead.

The valley was as hot and waterless as before, but less uninhabited, for people were ploughing here and there. They gave drinks from their water-

skins to our police, who never appeared to travel with so necessary an equipment as a water-bottle in this arid land . . .

We met the first advance guards of the tribes moving to winter quarters: a
trail of tired people, donkeys and small black oxen laden with cooking-pots,
carpets, and tents, and a few chicken on the top of all. Women, their long
gowns catching them at every step, walked half bent with small children on
their backs. The daily stage for a tribe on the move must be a very slow one;
and one can realize why, a year or two ago, when some Lurs, settled by force in
eastern Persia, wanted to break their way home across the hostile land, they
eliminated the worst of the impedimenta by massacring their own families
before the march.

Shah Riza had of course forgotten the merely terrestrial matter of lunch,
though he had been reminded in good time.

'How wicked,' said he, without a moment's hesitation when I asked him;
'how wicked is the wife of Mahmud to let a guest depart without food for the
wilderness.'

'She forgot,' said I, 'but it is only once, and you forget every day. Now what
are you going to do?'

'*Khanum*,' said he, with an appearance of gentle reasonableness, 'by the
Majesty of God, can I produce food in an uninhabited land?'

I gave up the effort to cope with my Philosopher and turned to the police.
They were taking me where I had never planned to come; the least they could
do was to feed me. This, I must say, they were more than willing to do, though
I suspect them of very rarely paying for what we consumed. When the matter
of lunch was broached, the lieutenant sent a man on ahead to the upper mill
of Garau, above our former camping-place, while we followed slowly.

The lieutenant was waiting for news from Husainabad. He had, I guessed,
sent a messenger as soon as he came upon me, and was still waiting for
instructions as to his next proceeding. Just as we turned off the main track
into a little side valley, where the mill lay low under the spikes of Walantar by
a clear diminutive stream, a party was sighted coming down the valley. The
lieutenant rode to meet it, while I continued towards the mill, delighting in
the little watercourse in the shade; a built-out pier made of dry walling carried
it into a hollow where the mill stood, like a truncated pyramid, about fifteen
feet high by ten square at the base, like all the mills of Luristan.

Here two policemen spread carpets in a shady place and the inhabitants
of three poor tents gave us a timid, very doubtful welcome. And presently
the rest of the party, arriving, filled the hollow with the noise of their
cavalcade.

The head of the visiting party was a young customs officer from Husaina-bad, with blue eyes and a black and grey European suit and an intelligent expression. He spent his time in collecting taxes and catching smugglers, knew the country well, and gave me details of the castles and ruins in the district of Shirwan, which I told him I hoped to visit.

'There is a castle there called Shirawan,' said he, 'which stands on a rock, and its watercourses, brought up from far below, are still to be seen. And in the city of Nushirvan itself, which is Shirwan, you can see the water conduits running among the houses.'

He was now on his way to collect taxes, and was waiting for an additional bodyguard to join him for this unpopular sort of tour. He had five riflemen already, Delivand tribesmen from Saidmarreh, which is the headquarters of this corps. They are volunteers, and get a small amount of money and some land given to them in exchange for their services when required: they were fine-looking men, with bushy moustaches and good fighting faces, and they wore white woollen *abbas* tied back over their shoulders, turbans, sashes, two knives stuck in front of them, and their guns slung behind them. Their chief was a weedy little city specimen in a *Pahlevi* hat, very young, whose father got a lump sum from government for providing a fixed number of these people.

The Army and the Civil Service had lunch by themselves beside another tent, discussing no doubt the matter of my capture, for they threw glances in my direction now and then. I slept, until roused by a message from the lieutenant who was suddenly attacked by fever and dysentery and looked very ill indeed. I sent him quinine and opium pills, and hoped he might not die on my hands in this particularly lonely stretch of our journey. When I woke again, the volunteers from Saidmarreh were setting off as an advance guard: they were going down by the way we had come up. They were as friendly as could be when the officers were not about, and rode away looking fine against the skyline and as unlike the average figure of a tax-collector as can well be imagined.

I thought I too might be moving: I was anxious to have some leisure at the Milleh Penjeh Pass at the valley head, so as to take bearings and link up my map. I had had more than enough of the lieutenant and the police in general; and Shah Riza had irritated me by declaring that his matches were packed among my clothes in the saddle-bag, where, as he said ingenuously, no one would look for contraband, and whence he was now extracting them to the great disorder of what was left of my wardrobe. I left him, therefore, sur-rounded by chaos and protesting, while I walked away. As she saw me go, the old woman of the tent also protested. The police, she said, had not paid for my chicken, nor would ever do so. I handed over fourpence, the regular price, feeling like a guest no longer, but an intruder . . .

I set off at two-thirty, and walked for an hour along a delightful path that kept by ups and downs through open fields and glades on the higher level of the valley, where the sharp spires of Walantar run down in foothills. The valley bottom, with the stream and the main path from the Milleh Penjeh, lay all in sight below. A yellow domed tomb and the ploughed stubble-land was all the sign of humanity about, for there are no tents between the mills of Garau and the first Aftab camps, about six hours away. The upper part of the valley gradually clothed itself in a thick garment of oak trees, fair-sized and dappled with sunlight, and the low pass rose under them to a gentle skyline ahead. The silence and solitude lay pleasantly around in a delightful peace.

Solitude, I reflected, is the one deep necessity of the human spirit to which adequate recognition is never given in our codes. It is looked upon as a discipline or a penance, but hardly ever as the indispensable, pleasant ingredient it is to ordinary life, and from this want of recognition come half our domestic troubles. The fear of an unbroken *tête-à-tête* for the rest of his life should, you would think, prevent any man from getting married. (Women are not so much affected, since they can usually be alone in their houses for most of the day if they wish.) Modern education ignores the need for solitude: hence a decline in religion, in poetry, in all the deeper affections of the spirit: a disease to be *doing* something always, as if one could never sit quietly and let the puppet show unroll itself before one: an inability to lose oneself in mystery and wonder while, like a wave lifting us into new seas, the history of the world develops around us. I was thinking these thoughts when Husein, out of breath and beating the grey mare for all he was worth with the plaited rein, came up behind me, and asked how I could bear to go on alone for over an hour, with everyone anxious behind me.

The Valleys of the Assassins, 1934

WILFRED THESIGER

1910–

I thought how desperately hard were the lives of the Bedu in this weary land, and how gallant and how enduring was their spirit. Now, listening to their talk and watching the little acts of courtesy which they instinctively performed, I knew by comparison how sadly I must fail, how selfish I must prove.

The solitary travels of Wilfred Thesiger in central Africa, Asia and especially the Middle East have established him as one of the great explorers of the twentieth century, a reputation reinforced by his evocative books: *Arabian Sands* is a literary masterpiece.

Thesiger was born into a military and diplomatic family in Addis Ababa, where his father was the minister in charge of the British legation. On his death – when Wilfred, the eldest of four sons, was nine – the family returned to England. The extraordinarily exotic world to which he had been exposed at such a young age seems to have left him feeling somewhat isolated when plunged into the confines of boarding school; conversely, his education at Eton, then Oxford, instilled into him the manners of the privileged English that were to be his hallmark, even when travelling in remote cultures.

While still at Oxford, Thesiger was invited back to Abyssinia for the coronation of Ras Tafari as Emperor Haile Selassi and, following a trek among Danakil tribesmen, resolved to return there, having completed his degree. Now aged twenty-three, he embarked on his first long expedition: to cross Danakil country. Two Italian groups, not to mention the Egyptian army, had attempted this and been slaughtered; their testicles had been collected as trophies. Thesiger became the first European to emerge on the other side intact, as well as having solved the mystery of the Awash. This river arose in the mountains to the west of Addis Ababa, flowed to the east, but seemed never to reach the sea. Thesiger discovered that it reached a salt lake, and

there petered out.

After an interlude working as district commissioner for the Sudan political service, he did wartime service in North Africa and Syria with the SAS. With the conflict over, he embarked on travels through the Rub' al Khali, or 'Empty Quarter', that 'bitter, desiccated land which knows nothing of gentleness or ease'. Only two Europeans had ventured into it before him.

Initially under the pretext of hunting for the breeding grounds of the desert locust for the Middle East Anti-Locust Unit, Thesiger spent the next five years immersed in the way of life of the Bedouin, for whom he developed a deep respect. He considered their lives more complete, more noble, than those lived by our materialist societies, and regretted the encroachment of the oil industry that came to dominate the region. The symbol of our destructive 'progress' was, for Thesiger, the motor car. 'It is not the goal but the way there that matters,' he writes in *Arabian Sands*, 'and the harder the way the more worthwhile the journey. Perhaps this was one reason why I resented modern inventions; they made the road too easy.'

On his return years later, Thesiger found 'the values of the desert' had vanished; 'all over Arabia the transistor has replaced the tribal bard'. Once the statement 'I am a Bedu' was 'a proud boast, their answer to every challenge'. Now the term 'Bedu' was 'a term of abuse shouted by pedestrians at careless drivers'.

The tougher the lives of the Bedouin, the more Thesiger was impressed by their behaviour. Once, after a day without water, Thesiger reached a well with his Bedu companions, only to sit and wait for another five hours, refusing to drink until the rest of the party had arrived. Their chivalry coincided well with the values inculcated into him as an Edwardian public-school boy; and like theirs, his had been a predominantly male upbringing. Although close to his mother, Thesiger's progression from boy's boarding school to men's college, then to the desert and the army, had allowed no room for women.

Having made two crossings of the Empty Quarter, he spent the next seven years among the Marsh Arabs of southern Iraq, with summer interludes in Kurdistan, Pakistan and Afghanistan. When the 1958 revolution forced Thesiger to leave, he returned to Ethiopia, where he explored the Simien mountain range. Then, in 1968, he moved to Maralal, in the northern frontier district of Kenya, where he spent the next twenty-six years living among the Samburu. He had hoped to remain there until his death, but failing eyesight prompted his return to England, and eventually a nursing home.

A craving for privacy

I climbed to the summit of the dune and lay peacefully in the sun, four hundred feet above the well. A craving for privacy is something which Bedu will never understand; something which they will always instinctively mistrust. I have often been asked by Englishmen if I was never lonely in the desert, and I have wondered how many minutes I have spent by myself in the years that I have lived there. It is true that the worst loneliness is to be lonely in a crowd. I have been lonely at school, and in European towns where I knew nobody, but I have never been lonely among Arabs. I have arrived in their towns where I was unknown, and I have walked into the bazaar and greeted a shopkeeper. He has invited me to sit beside him in his shop and has sent for tea. Other people have come along and joined us. They have asked me who I was, where I came from, and innumerable questions which we should never ask a stranger. Then one of them has said, 'Come and lunch', and at lunch I have met other Arabs, and someone else has asked me to dinner. I have wondered sadly what Arabs brought up in this tradition have thought when they visited England; and I have hoped that they realized that we are as unfriendly to each other as we must appear to be to them . . .

The sun was getting low. Bin Kabina was still asleep. I touched him to wake him, and in one movement he was on his feet with his dagger drawn. I had forgotten that to touch a sleeping Bedu is usually to jerk him awake ready instinctively to fight for his life. I raced him down the dune face, floundering through the avalanching sand, and then we walked across to the well where the others had filled the water-skins ready for our departure in the morning.

The journey's end

We mounted our camels. My companions had muffled their faces in their
head-cloths and rode in silence, swaying to the camels' stride. The shadows on
the sand were very blue, of the same tone as the sky; two ravens flew northward, croaking as they passed. I struggled to keep awake. The only sound was
made by the slap of the camels' feet, like wavelets lapping on a beach.

To rest the camels we stopped for four hours in the late afternoon on a long
gentle slope which stretched down to another salt-flat. There was no vegetation on it and no salt-bushes bordered the plain below us. Al Auf announced
that we would go on again at sunset. While we were feeding I said to him
cheerfully, 'Anyway, the worst should be over now that we are across the Uruq
al Shaiba.' He looked at me for a moment and then answered, 'If we go well
tonight we should reach them tomorrow.' I said, 'Reach what?' and he replied,
'The Uruq al Shaiba', adding, 'Did you think what we crossed today was the
Uruq al Shaiba? That was only a dune. You will see them tomorrow.' For a
moment, I thought he was joking, and then I realized that he was serious, that
the worst of the journey which I had thought was behind us was still ahead.

It was midnight when at last al Auf said, 'Let's stop here. We will get some
sleep and give the camels a rest. The Uruq al Shaiba are not far away now.' In
my dreams that night they towered above us higher than the Himalayas.

Al Auf woke us again while it was still dark. As usual bin Kabina made
coffee, and the sharp-tasting drops which he poured out stimulated but did
not warm. The morning star had risen above the dunes. Formless things
regained their shape in the first dim light of dawn. The grunting camels
heaved themselves erect. We lingered for a moment more beside the fire; then
al Auf said 'Come', and we moved forward. Beneath my feet the gritty sand
was cold as frozen snow.

We were faced by a range as high as, perhaps even higher than, the range we
had crossed the day before, but here the peaks were steeper and more pronounced, rising in many cases to great pinnacles, down which the flowing
ridges swept like draperies. These sands, paler coloured than those we had
crossed, were very soft, cascading round our feet as the camels struggled up
the slopes. Remembering how little warning of imminent collapse the dying
camels had given me twelve years before in the Danakil country, I wondered
how much more these camels would stand, for they were trembling violently
whenever they halted. When one refused to go on we heaved on her head-
rope, pushed her from behind, and lifted the loads on either side as we
manhandled the roaring animal upward. Sometimes one of them lay down

and refused to rise, and then we had to unload her, and carry the water-skins and the saddle-bags ourselves. Not that the loads were heavy. We had only a few gallons of water left and some handfuls of flour.

We led the trembling, hesitating animals upward along great sweeping ridges where the knife-edged crests crumbled beneath our feet. Although it was killing work, my companions were always gentle and infinitely patient. The sun was scorching hot and I felt empty, sick, and dizzy. As I struggled up the slope, knee-deep in shifting sand, my heart thumped wildly and my thirst grew worse. I found it difficult to swallow; even my ears felt blocked, and yet I knew that it would be many intolerable hours before I could drink. I would stop to rest, dropping down on the scorching sand, and immediately it seemed I would hear the others shouting, 'Umbarak, Umbarak'; their voices sounded strained and hoarse.

It took us three hours to cross this range.

On the summit were no gently undulating downs such as we had met the day before. Instead, three smaller dune-chains rode upon its back, and beyond them the sand fell away to a salt-flat in another great empty trough between the mountains. The range on the far side seemed even higher than the one on which we stood, and behind it were others. I looked round, seeking instinct-ively for some escape. There was no limit to my vision. Somewhere in the ultimate distance the sands merged into the sky, but in that infinity of space I could see no living thing, not even a withered plant to give me hope. 'There is nowhere to go', I thought. 'We cannot go back and our camels will never get up another of these awful dunes. We really are finished.' The silence flowed over me, drowning the voices of my companions and the fidgeting of their camels.

We went down into the valley, and somehow – and I shall never know how the camels did it – we got up the other side. There, utterly exhausted, we collapsed. Al Auf gave us each a little water, enough to wet our mouths. He said, 'We need this if we are to go on.' The midday sun had drained the colour from the sands. Scattered banks of cumulus cloud threw shadows across the dunes and salt-flats, and added an illusion that we were high among Alpine peaks, with frozen lakes of blue and green in the valley, far below. Half asleep, I turned over, but the sand burnt through my shirt and woke me from my dreams.

Two hours later al Auf roused us. As he helped me load my camel, he said, 'Cheer up, Umbarak. This time we really are across the Uruq al Shaiba', and when I pointed to the ranges ahead of us, he answered, 'I can find a way through those; we need not cross them.' We went on till sunset, but we were going with the grain of the country, following the valleys and no longer trying to climb the dunes. We should not have been able to cross another. There was a little fresh *qassis* on the slope where we halted. I hoped that this lucky find would give us an excuse to stop here for the night, but, after we had fed, al Auf went to fetch the camels, saying, 'We must go on again while it is cool if we are ever to reach Dhafara.'

We stopped long after midnight and started again at dawn, still exhausted from the strain and long hours of yesterday, but al Auf encouraged us by saying that the worst was over. The dunes were certainly lower than they had been, more uniform in height and more rounded, with fewer peaks. Four hours after we had started we came to rolling uplands of gold and silver sand, but still there was nothing for the camels to eat.

A hare jumped out from under a bush, and al Auf knocked it over with his stick. The others shouted 'God has given us meat.' For days we had talked of food; every conversation seemed to lead back to it. Since we had left Ghanim I had been always conscious of the dull ache of hunger, yet in the evenings my throat was dry even after my drink, so that I found it difficult to swallow the dry bread Musallim set before us. All day we thought and talked about that hare, and by three o'clock in the afternoon could no longer resist stopping to cook it. Mabkhaut suggested, 'Let's roast it in its skin in the embers of a fire. That will save our water – we haven't got much left.' Bin Kabina led the chorus of protest. 'No, by God! Don't even suggest such a thing'; and turning to me he said, 'We don't want Mabkhaut's charred meat. Soup. We want soup and extra bread. We will feed well today even if we go hungry and thirsty later. By God, I am hungry!' We agreed to make soup. We were across the Uruq al Shaiba and intended to celebrate our achievement with this gift from God. Unless our camels foundered we were safe; even if our water ran out we should live to reach a well.

Musallim made nearly double our usual quantity of bread while bin Kabina cooked the hare. He looked across at me and said, 'The smell of this meat makes me faint.' When it was ready he divided it into five portions. They were very small, for an Arabian hare is no larger than an English rabbit, and this one was not even fully grown. Al Auf named the lots and Mabkhaut drew them. Each of us took the small pile of meat which had fallen to him. Then bin Kabina said, 'God! I have forgotten to divide the liver', and the others said, 'Give it to Umbarak.' I protested, saying that they should divide it, but they swore by God that they would not eat it and that I was to have it. Eventually I took it, knowing that I ought not, but too greedy for this extra scrap of meat to care . . .

Next day, after seven hours' travelling we reached Khaur Sabakha on the edge of the Dhafara sands. We cleaned out the well and found brackish water at seven feet, so bitter that even the camels only drank a little before refusing it. They sniffed thirstily at the water with which al Auf tried to coax them from a leather bucket, but only dipped their lips into it. We covered their noses but still they would not drink. Yet al Auf said that Arabs themselves drank this water mixed with milk, and when I expressed my disbelief he added that if an Arab was really thirsty he would even kill a camel and drink the liquid in its stomach, or ram a stick down its throat and drink the vomit. We went on again till nearly sunset.

The next day when we halted in the afternoon al Auf told us we had reached Dhafara and that Khaba well was close. He said that he would fetch water in the morning. We finished what little was left in one of our skins. Next day we remained where we were. Hamad said that he would go for news and return the following day. Al Auf, who went with him, came back in the afternoon with two skins full of water which, although slightly brackish, was delicious after the filthy evil-smelling dregs we had drunk the night before.

It was December 12th, fourteen days since we had left Khaur bin Atarit in Ghanim.

In the evening, now that we needed no longer measure out each cup of water, bin Kabina made extra coffee, while Musallim increased our rations of flour by a mugful. This was wild extravagance, but we felt that the occasion called for celebration. Even so, the loaves he handed us were woefully inadequate to stay our hunger, now that our thirst was gone.

The moon was high above us when I lay down to sleep. The others still talked round the fire, but I closed my mind to the meaning of their words, content to hear only the murmur of their voices, to watch their outlines sharp against the sky, happily conscious that they were there and beyond them the camels to which we owed our lives.

For years the Empty Quarter had represented to me the final, unattainable challenge which the desert offered. Suddenly it had come within my reach. I remembered my excitement when Lean had casually offered me the chance to go there, the immediate determination to cross it, and then the doubts and fears, the frustrations, and the moments of despair. Now I had crossed it. To others my journey would have little importance. It would produce nothing except a rather inaccurate map which no one was ever likely to use. It was a personal experience, and the reward had been a drink of clean, nearly tasteless water. I was content with that.

Looking back on the journey I realized that there had been no high moment of achievement such as a mountaineer must feel when he stands upon his chosen summit. Over the past days new strains and anxieties had built up as others eased, for, after all, this crossing of the Empty Quarter was set in the framework of a longer journey, and already my mind was busy with the new problems which our return journey presented.

Arabian Sands, 1959

LAURENS VAN DER POST
1906–96

We need primitive nature, the First Man in ourselves, it seems, as the lungs need air and the body food and water, yet we can only achieve it by a slinking, often shameful, back-door entrance.

The thirteenth of fifteen Afrikaner children, Sir Laurens Van der Post was born in the Orange Free State, and in his late teens became a journalist on a Durban newspaper, working his way up to the position of shipping correspondent. He then travelled to London, where he forged close ties with members of the Bloomsbury set, in particular John Maynard Keynes. His profession as a writer and farmer was disrupted by the war, during which a three-year stint in a Japanese prisoner-of-war camp seeded his profound – but elusive – personal philosophy.

Van der Post's close friendship with the psychoanalyst C. G. Jung is echoed in one element intrinsic to his thinking. Once the war was over he reflected: 'In the debris of war and disaster . . . men had lost their capacity to dream . . . I knew that somehow the world had to be set dreaming again.' He shared Jung's notion of there being a 'collective unconscious' shared by the world, and to this he appended his own concept of a split between the 'black' aspects of our psyche (the non-rational, intuitive, imaginative and creative aspects) and the 'white' (the reasoned and rational aspects). An individual needs a balance of both of these, he maintained, just as society itself does in order to remain healthy. Life in the 'developed' world was suffocating the 'black' side of our beings, and this was the root of the modern malaise.

Following the war, Van der Post went on several expeditions into the southern African interior. His first novel, *In a Province*, had been an indictment of South African racism, but now he explored the desert life of the San Bushmen of the Kalahari, with whom he had forged links as a child – a woman whose mother had been San had nursed him from birth. In 1957 he led an expedition across the Kalahari in search of the surviving remnants of these, the original inhabitants of southern Africa. For Van der Post, the Bushmen were the gatekeeper to the unconscious.*

Van der Post's command of language, mystical leanings and concern for the environment fuelled his work both as a spiritual and political adviser, as a conservationist and as a philosopher. Influential figures as diverse as Margaret Thatcher and Prince Charles have drawn inspiration from his work. 'I feel myself to have become a kind of improvised footbridge across the widening chasm between Europe and Africa,' he once said. But a footbridge of what reliability?

Three years after his death, his biographer, J. D. F. Jones, in *The Many Lives of Laurens Van der Post*, finds a less inspirational man: 'Time after time, the storyteller's tales about himself were inaccurate, embellished, exaggerated, distorted or invented. Put more bluntly, he was a constant liar.' He claims that this 'compulsive fantasist' misrepresented his wartime career (he was an acting captain, not a lieutenant-colonel) and, continued the deception in private, writing to Ingaret Gifford (who was to become his second wife)

* 'I sought to understand imaginatively the primitive in ourselves, and in this search the Bushman has always been for me a kind of frontier guide. Imagination shifts, and passes, as it were, through a strange customs post on the fateful frontier between being and unrealised self, between what is and what is to come. The questions that have to be answered before the imagination is allowed through are not new, but have to be redefined because of their long neglect and the need for answers to be provided in the idiom of our own day.'

'long, fictitious' descriptions of his wartime exploits in Abyssinia. To top it all, Jones goes on, almost all the tales supposedly told him in the Kalahari by the San, his African inspiration, were in fact drawn from the research of the nineteenth-century scholar Dr Wilhelm Bleek. The biographer argues that Van der Post even occasionally admitted to himself that 'untruth became the pattern of his life'. In *A Walk with a White Bushman*, he wrote: 'This is one of the problems for me: stories in a way are more completely real to me than life in the here and now. A really true story has transcendent reality for me which is greater than the reality of life.'

However, Van der Post is to be judged by history – Jones even argues that Van der Post had a hatred of Nelson Mandela – he will undoubtedly remain a guru to many. His books dispelled the notion of the continent being 'dark' and his sympathetic outlook towards the Bushmen is rare in the exploration of Southern Africa, whether undertaken by European or African settlers.

Cave paintings

The night did not appear to have improved the mood of the hills and I was not surprised when the bush itself came suddenly to a shuddering halt, leaving a clear space between itself and the base of the central hill as if centuries before it had learnt the importance of keeping a respectful distance from such reserved and imperious beings. Beneath the hills the shadows were cool and heavy, but, far above, the ragged, jagged shark's tooth edges of the purple crags were lined with warm sunlight. However, below the bright hem of that still morning one saw other cuts, wounds, and scars in the steep surfaces that from a distance looked so impervious. There was hardly a face that was not torn, pock-marked, pitted, and wrinkled as if with incredible suffering and struggling. Everywhere great fragments had broken away to lie in massive splinters in the sand at the base, or to balance precariously on the edge of an abyss. Now one understood better the stern mood of the place, because one was looking on an entire world of rock, isolated and without allies of any kind, making a heroic stand against disintegration by terrible forces of sand, sun, and time. It was an awesome spectacle, because neither the rock nor the forces deployed against it would give or accept quarter. As I was looking sombrely into those stony faces I heard an almost reproachful exclamation from Samutchoso at my side: 'Master, but do you not see?'

Both his voice and pointing finger were trembling with emotion. Over the scorched leaves of the tops of the bush conforming to a contour nearby, and about a hundred feet up, was a ledge of honey-coloured stone grafted into the blue iron rock. Above the ledge rose a smooth surface of the same warm, soft stone curved like a sea-shell as if rising into the blue to form a perfect dome. But it curved upwards thus for only about twenty feet and then was suddenly broken. I had no doubt I was looking at the wall and part of the ceiling of what had once been a great cave in the hills, safe above the night-prowl of the bush, and with an immense view into the activities of the flat Kalahari beyond. Some yellow stone from the dome of the cave was tipped precariously on the edges of the ledge, other fragments were toppled into the red sand at the base. But what held my attention still with the shock of discovery was the painting that looked down at us from the centre of what was left of the wall and dome of the cave. Heavy as were the shadows, and seeing it only darkly against the sharp morning light, it was yet so distinct and filled with fire of its own colour that every detail stood out with a burning clarity. In the focus of the painting, scarlet against the gold of the stone, was an enormous eland bull standing sideways, his massive body charged with masculine power and his noble head looking as if he had only that moment been disturbed in his grazing. He was painted as only a Bushman, who had a deep identification with the eland, could have painted him. Moreover, it seemed that he had been painted at a period before the Bushman's serenity was threatened, for the look of calm and trustful inquiry on the eland's face was complete. I was greatly moved because it seemed to me that this was the look with which not only the eland but the whole of the life of Africa must have regarded us when first we landed there. On the left of the bull, also deep in scarlet, was a tall female giraffe with an elegant Modigliani neck. With the tenderness of a solicitous mother she was looking past the eland towards a baby giraffe standing shyly in the right of the picture. In the same right-hand corner of the canvas below them the artist had signed this painting on the high wall with a firm impress of the palms of both hands, fingers extended and upright. The signature was marked so gaily and spontaneously that it brought an instant smile to my face. It looked so young and fresh that it mocked my recollection that rock-paintings signed in this manner are among the oldest in the world.

'How old is it, Samutchoso?' I asked.

'I do not know, Master,' he replied. 'I only know it was like this when my grandfather found it as a boy, and from what he told me and what I have seen myself it never gets older.'

'You mean the colours do not fade?'

'No! The colours do not fade, Master,' he answered, and would, I think, have said more if our party, one by one, had not been forming round us. They, too, fell silent when they saw the painting of the bull and his two companions standing there so serenely in that quiet viaduct of time.

The song of the rain

The sun had long ceased to be a friend, and the scorched earth which had daily shrunk back into its last reserve of shade had steadily darkened until at noonday the leaves of the gallant thorn trees looked as if they were about to crumble to ashes, and greeted the sunset with a sigh of relief that was echoed in our own exhausted senses. Often at noon I would see Nxou and his companions throw themselves down beside us in shade that was little more than a paler form of sunlight and instantly go to sleep, more weary with heat than with distances run. This was perhaps the most moving of all their gestures, this instant act of trust between them and the harsh desert earth which, though too harsh for us, had been kinder to them in its pagan heart than we had ever been. They lay there, securely clasped to the earth and nourished with sleep at its unfailing bosom. But when they woke they instantly stood up to scan the sky for cloud and other signs of rain as if even in their deep sleep they had felt the Mother Earth exclaim: 'Dear God, will such dryness never end?'

Daily too, on our far-hunting round, we noticed that the surface of the desert became more churned and pitted where buck and other animals had dug, with hoof and claw, to get at the roots and tubers which could give them the relief of moisture that the heavens increasingly denied. No European can know how deep this need and anxiety of the waste-land of Africa enters into the blood and mind of its children. Here at the sip-wells it was no laughing matter. Nxou and his people did not fear for their store of water supply, which was deep in the sand and protected against the sun. But they feared what the lack of rain would do to the grasses and the game on which they lived. They alone knew what kind of disaster could come if the rains failed. I am certain many a Bushman community has perished from drought and famine in the Kalahari unknown to anyone, with only a vortex of vultures in the blue to mark the place of their going, and only the hyaena and jackal to sing their funeral song. Daily the shadow of this deep fear lengthened in our awareness as sun after sun went down without a cloud in the sky; and night upon night came and went without the hope-giving flicker of lightning below the star-uneasy horizon.

One night round the fire, all of us obsessed with this discharge of disquiet in our blood, Ben told us something which perhaps shows how deeply contained is the natural Bushman in the rhythms of the seasons, and how much he is a part of their great plans. Ben told us that the little man's womenfolk would become sterile during periods of drought and, until the rains broke, would cease to conceive. He knew this from his own experience and from that of great hunters before him. That was one reason why the Bushman had such small families. Had we not noticed, he asked, that there were no pregnant women around? Where else in Africa would we see so many married and vigorous young women and not one in the family way? Yet this fear of drought went even deeper than that. If a woman had conceived in a fall of rain that was not maintained and bore a child in a period of drought which threatened the survival of all, immediately at birth the child was taken from her, before, as Dabe confirmed, 'it could cry in her heart', and was killed by the other women. The anguish and bitterness with which those who loved children performed this deed, Ben said, proved how necessary it was. Also he thought it would silence those who condemned them from their armchairs of plush and plenty. We went to bed with a new dimension added to our view of the dark necessities among which this rare flame of Stone Age life burned.

But on this particular morning there was a first real promise of rain in the air. The atmosphere was silver-dim with sudden moisture and heavy with electricity and heat. Soon after breakfast a cloud no larger than the Old Testament's hand of man appeared with a flag of wind at its head. It was soon followed by others, and all morning long we watched with growing excitement cloud upon cumulus cloud piling up like towers and palaces over some enchanted *Tempest* island. Were we to be privileged to celebrate the hunter's fulfilment not only with meat that was the food of his gods, but also with the water that was wine to his earth? As the day wore on the answer seemed likely to be positive. Yet even so I, who had seen so many promises of rain snatched away at the last moment from the cracked lips of the African earth, was afraid to hope until, at long last, the thunder began to mutter on a darkening horizon. By the time the first dancers started coming into our camp the rumble of thunder was constant and rolling slowly nearer like noise of a great battle. Suddenly it made our small camp look puny and exposed. Yet it added to the jubilation of the dancers in the clearing we had made for them.

How lovely they looked! The women had rubbed some fat into their skins and their bodies were a-glitter. Their jewellery, too, seemed to have been polished and flashed in the sun which moved on, undismayed, to grapple with the giant cloud rising in the west. The women walked towards us already attuned to the music, humming, quivering, and swaying with its rhythm and song. As they arrived they quickly collected on the edge of the clearing and began singing aloud, beating time with their feet and hands. Occasionally one of the older women would run out into the open, her arms stetched wide like the wings of a bird, her mincing steps and jeering song mocking the men who had not yet appeared from the bush, for their tardiness.

The men, however, held back out of sight, obedient to their own part in the overall pattern of the dance to come. They seemed, deliberately, to provoke the women to a greater and greater frenzy of singing and longing. When at last they came it was because they could no longer keep away and were compelled almost against their will. Then a moan as of great pain broke from them. Arms stretched out, feet ceaselessly pounding and re-pounding the earth, they came bounding out of the bush with that cry of theirs: 'Oh, look, like birds we come!'

When this happened the triumph in the women's voices soared like a star in the night and brought about a new intensity of passion to their singing. The men became so drawn into the mood of the music that it was nearly impossible to recognize their individuality. An archaic mask sat on all faces as they began to sing and dance the theme of the Eland. I have seen many primitive dances. They are invariably communal affairs and tend to have a bold, often violent, and fairly obvious pattern. But this music was rich, varied, tender, and filled with unworldly longing. It had a curious weave and rhythm to it, some deep-river movement of life, turning and twisting, swirling and eddying back upon itself in order to round some invisible objects in its profound bed as it swept on to the sea.

In this manner they danced their way into the life of their beloved eland and their mystical participation in his being. They danced him in the herd, his cows, heifers, and children around him. They danced him in his courting right up to the moment where, fastidious animal that he is, he vanishes alone, with his woman, for his love-making in the bush. They danced him grown old, challenged, and about to be displaced by the young bulls in the herd. Quite naturally the older men became the challenged, the younger the chal- lengers. The movements of the dancers, the expression on their faces, and the voices crying 'Oh!' from far down in their throats and straight from the source where the first man had his being, greatly moved us. We saw the lust for battle in the young faces; the look of perplexity in the eyes of the women torn between loyalty to a former lord and obedience to the urge of new life within them, we saw the agony of impending defeat in the expression of the old bulls. And we saw life decide the battle; the old cast out from the herd while the young, with unbelievable tenderness, put an arm around the shoul- ders of a woman become suddenly still with the acceptance of her fate, and so move inexorably together towards the oncoming night.

The darkness fell quickly because of the rising storm, and the dance of the

Eland naturally made way for the greatest of all the Bushman dances: The Fire Dance. Here the women, without a pause, grouped themselves singing in the centre of the clearing. Quickly they piled a fire there, lit it the classical way, and then an uncle of Nxou's led the men in a ring dancing around the fire. They danced the first Bushman soul setting out in the darkness, before mind or matter, to look for substance for fire. They looked in vain for its spoor in the sand as if fire were some subtle animal. Hour after hour they went round and round in the same circle without finding it. They called on the sun, moon, and stars to give them fire. Then we saw them leading the blind companions who, in some prehistoric period of the quest, had gone too near the scorching flames. Because it was a sacred dance we noticed how in the progress of his search the seeker now acquired the power of healing. Suddenly he would break off his dancing to stand behind a moaning woman and, with trembling hands draw out of her the spirit that was causing her unrest, emitting in the process the cry of the animal with which the alien invader was identified. That done, he would return to join the magic circle still dancing in search of fire. How the dancers found the power to go on ever faster and faster, hour after hour, seemed beyond explanation or belief. They danced so hard and long that the circle in the sand became a groove, then the groove a ditch high up to their calves. Long before the end they seemed to pass over into a dimension of reality far out of reach of my understanding, and to a moment and a place which belonged only technically to the desert in which we were all gathered. Indeed, so obsessed did the men become by this search for fire that they were drawn nearer and nearer to the flames beside which the women sat. Then, suddenly, they halved the circle and went dancing with their bare feet through the middle of the flames. But even that was not the end of the quest. Now, the longing became so intense that two of the older women were kept constantly busy preventing some fire-obsessed man from breaking out of the circle and hurling himself head first straight into the flames, like a moth overcome by excess of longing for the light. Indeed one man did break through, and before he could be stopped had scooped up a handful of burning coals and attempted to swallow them whole.

All the while, in the ebb of the music rising and falling like a tide around us, the noise of the thunder rose louder in our ears. The lightning began to play incessantly overhead and to wash the dancers yellow in a Nibelungen gold. It sounded as if the whole of nature was being mobilized to participate in this expression of man's first and still unfulfilled quest. The jackals, hyaenas, the shriek owls, the male ostriches booming, all seemed stirred to howl and scream as never before, and beyond the sip-wells the lions roared back deeply and most strangely at them, at us, and at the storm. Towards the end the men's feet together were beating the earth so fast and regularly that it was difficult to believe that the noise was made by the feet of many men and not by a single automatic piston.

At last, here and there, a dancer began to fall in his tracks. The two older women would pick him up and carry him aside where he lay moaning in a trance of fatigue in the darkness. Then, almost on the second of midnight, the hero of the dance, Nxou's slender and comely uncle, suddenly found fire the way it was meant to be found. He knelt down reverently beside it, the singing died away in one last sob of utter exhaustion, the dancers sank to the earth while the man picked up the coals in his naked hands and arose to scatter them far and wide for all the world to share. He stood there swaying on his feet, the sweat of an unimaginable exertion like silk tight upon his skin, dazed with the anguish of near-disaster in doom of eternal darkness as well as by the climax of deliverance. Swaying, he made a gesture and uttered words of prayer to the night around him. What the words were I never knew, except that Dabe said they were too ancient for him to understand. All I do know is that I myself felt very near the presence of a god and my eyes seemed blinded as if by sudden revelation. In the darkness beyond the sip-wells, on the high dunes at the back of the heroic dancer, the lightning struck with a savage, kriss-like cut at the trembling earth, so near that the crackle of its fire and the explosion of the thunder sounded simultaneously in my ear. And at that moment the rain fell.

It rained all night. I thought I had never heard a sweeter sound than it made on the tarpaulin over my head and in the sand within reach of my hand. So close had my search in the past few weeks brought me to the earth, its elements, and its natural children that throughout the rest of the eventful night in my half-waking condition I felt I had re-discovered the first language of all things and could hear plainly the deep murmur of the earth taking the rain into her like a woman taking a lover into her arms, all the more ardently because secretly she had doubted that he would ever come. I went on lying there in the darkness as if in the presence of Gods and Titans. All around me the voice of the thunder, now deafening with nearness, now solemn with distance, was like the voice Moses heard on his mountain-top in the desert of Sinai. When the dawn broke it was still raining heavily, and already there was a bloom of quickening new life in leaf, grass, and mark.

The Lost World of the Kalahari, 1958

PAUL FREDERIC BOWLES
1910–99

Here in this wholly mineral landscape lighted by stars like flares, even memory disappears; nothing is left but your own breathing and the sound of your heart beating.

Paul Bowles was born in New York, an only child. By the age of seventeen he had already published two surrealist poems in the international literary review *Transition*. He left college, and two years later travelled to Paris, intending to establish himself in the literary world, but rejected the idea after Gertrude Stein told him that he was not 'a real poet'.

He returned to New York and, during the 1930s, was taught by the composer Aaron Copland, with whom he also travelled to Berlin, Paris and Tangier. Over the next twenty years he gained a reputation as a composer of incidental music and of scores for ballet and the theatre, producing work for such recognized figures as Tennessee Williams and William Saroyan. In 1938 he married the playwright and novelist Jane Auer who, through her own dedication to her work, quickly became an inspiration for Bowles.

Before long he became an even more successful writer than composer, publishing fiction, poetry, and essays. The couple travelled widely and in 1947 went to North Africa, eventually settling in Tangier. His first novel, *The Sheltering Sky* (1949), was later made into a film by Bernardo Bertolucci. In the novels that followed – *The Delicate Prey*, *Let it Come Down* and *The Spider's House* – Bowles situated American characters in African surroundings. Their spiral of decline into a world of drugs and violence explored the breakdown not just of 'modern' individuals, but of modern life itself. His travel writing included *Their Heads Are Green and Their Hands Are Blue*; his sparse style and original eye bequeathed to us a unique exploration of modern Morocco, the Sahara and Mexico unnoticed by other Western visitors.

Jane Bowles died from a protracted illness in 1973; Paul lived for another twenty-six years and is buried, as he requested, back in America, in the same grave as his mother.

A baptism of solitude

Immediately when you arrive in the Sahara, for the first or the tenth time, you notice the stillness. An incredible, absolute silence prevails outside the towns; and within, even in busy places like the markets, there is a hushed quality in the air, as if the quiet were a conscious force which, resenting the intrusion of sound, minimizes and disperses it straightaway. Then there is the sky, compared to which all other skies seem faint-hearted efforts. Solid and luminous, it is always the focal point of the landscape. At sunset, the precise, curved shadow of the earth rises into it swiftly from the horizon, cutting it into light section and dark section. When all daylight is gone, and the space is thick with stars, it is still of an intense and burning blue, darkest directly overhead and paling toward the earth, so that the night never really grows dark.

You leave the gate of the fort or the town behind, pass the camels lying outside, go up into the dunes, or out onto the hard, stony plain and stand a while, alone. Presently, you will either shiver and hurry back inside the walls, or you will go on standing there and let something very peculiar happen to you, something that everyone who lives there has undergone, and which the French call *le baptême de la solitude*. It is a unique sensation, and it has nothing to do with loneliness, for loneliness presupposes memory. Here, in this wholly mineral landscape lighted by stars like flares, even memory disappears; nothing is left but your own breathing and the sound of your heart beating. A strange, and by no means pleasant, process of reintegration begins inside you, and it remains to be seen whether you will fight against it, and insist on remaining the person you have always been, or whether you will let it take its course. For no one who has stayed in the Sahara for a while is quite the same as when he came . . .

With an area considerably larger than that of the United States, the Sahara is a continent within a continent – a skeleton, if you like, but still a separate entity from the rest of Africa which surrounds it. There are plains, hills, valleys, gorges, rolling lands, rocky peaks and volcanic craters, all without vegetation or even soil. Yet, probably the only parts that are monotonous to the eye are regions like the Tanezrouft, south of Reggan, a stretch of about five hundred miles of absolutely flat, gravel-strewn terrain, without the slightest sign of life, nor the smallest undulation in the land, to vary the implacable line of the horizon on all sides. After being here for a while, the sight of even a rock awakens an emotion in the traveller; he feels like crying: 'Land!'

The oasis

The size of an oasis is reckoned by the number of trees it contains, not by the number of square miles it covers, just as the taxes are based on the number of date-bearing trees, and not on the amount of land. The prosperity of a region is in direct proportion to the number and size of its oases. The one at Figuig, for instance, has more than two hundred thousand bearing palms, and the one at Timimoun is forty miles long, with irrigation systems that are of an astonishing complexity.

To stroll in a Saharan oasis is rather like taking a walk through a well-kept Eden. The alleys are clean, bordered on each side by hand-patted mud walls, not too high to prevent you from seeing the riot of verdure within. Under the high waving palms are the smaller trees – pomegranate, orange, fig, almond. Below these, in neat squares surrounded by narrow ditches of running water, are the vegetables and wheat. No matter how far from the town you stray, you have the same impression of order, cleanliness, and insistence on utilizing every square inch of ground. When you come to the edge of the oasis, you always find that it is in the process of being enlarged. Plots of young palms extend out into the glaring wasteland. Thus far they are useless, but in a few years they will begin to bear, and eventually this sun-blistered land will be a part of the green belt of gardens.

There are a good many birds living in the oases, but their songs and plumage are not appreciated by the inhabitants. The birds eat the young shoots and dig up the seeds as fast as they are planted, and practically every man and boy carries a slingshot. A few years ago I travelled through the Sahara with a parrot; everywhere the poor bird was glowered at by the natives, and in Timimoun a delegation of three elderly men came to the hotel one afternoon and suggested that I stop leaving its cage in the window; otherwise there was no telling what its fate might be. 'Nobody likes birds here,' they said meaningfully.

Their Heads Are Green and Their Hands Are Blue, 1963

Donald Johanson
1943–

Dry silent places are intensifiers of thought, and have been known to be since early Christian anchorites went out in the desert to face God and their own souls.

American palaeoanthropologist who discovered the 3.5 million-year-old skeleton of one of the earliest known hominids, the diminutive 'Lucy', and completed his PhD in human palaeontology in 1974 at the University of Chicago and dedicated his life thereafter to the search for our human origins. His research has taken him to Ethiopia, Tanzania, Yemen, Saudi Arabia, Egypt and Jordan. It was in the Afar desert, in Ethiopia, that he made one of the most dramatic fossil discoveries of the twentieth century, on 30 November 1974.

The initial discovery was of a group of small bones from a possible human ancestor; further excavations uncovered hundreds of pieces, which together made up 40 per cent of a skeleton. These have been dated to around 3.5 million years ago, a time when our ancestors were walking upright, it's argued, but not yet making stone tools. Classified as *Australopithecus afarensis*, she was nicknamed Lucy after the Beatles' song 'Lucy in the Sky with Diamonds' which was being played in the camp the night of her discovery.

Johanson initiated a long-term exploration of the area but by 1976 political unrest in Ethiopia had put a hold on all further excavations.

In Tanzania ten years later, Johanson found a partial skeleton of the first toolmaker, *Homo habilis*, dated as 1.8 million years old; more recent excavations in Ethiopia have uncovered ancestral fossils that continue to paint a more accurate picture of human evolution and help us understand such puzzles as why we began to walk upright, and why we have developed such advanced mental powers.

Though Richard Leakey and other palaeontologists disagree with the status Johanson gives Lucy and co. in the human story, Johanson's finds remain important in the story of our origins. At the time of writing, a skull dated at almost 7 million years old has been found in Chad but claims it is hominid have been rejected by some scientists.

Dawn breaks in the Afar Desert

For most of the Americans in camp this was the best part of the day. The rocks and boulders that littered the landscape had bled away most of their heat during the night and no longer felt like stoves when you stood next to one of them. I stepped out of the tent and took a look at the sky. Another cloudless day; another flawless morning on the desert that would turn to a crisper later on. I washed my face and got a cup of coffee from the camp cook, Kabete. Mornings are not my favorite time. I am a slow starter and much prefer evenings and nights. At Hadar I feel best just as the sun is going down. I like to walk up one of the exposed ridges near the camp, feel the first stirrings of evening air and watch the hills turn purple. There I can sit alone for a while, think about the work of the day just ended, plan the next, and ponder the larger questions that have brought me to Ethiopia. Dry silent places are intensifiers of thought, and have been known to be since early Christian anchorites went out into the desert to face God and their own souls.

Tom Gray joined me for coffee. Tom was an American graduate student who had come out to Hadar to study the fossil animals and plants of the region, to reconstruct as accurately as possible the kinds and frequencies and relationships of what had lived there at various times in the remote past and what the climate had been like. My own target – the reason for our expedition – was hominid fossils: the bones of extinct human ancestors and their close relatives. I was interested in the evidence for human evolution. But to understand that, to interpret any hominid fossils we might find, we had to have the supporting work of other specialists like Tom.

'So, what's up for today?' I asked.

Tom said he was busy marking fossil sites on a map.

'When are you going to mark in Locality 162?'

'I'm not sure where 162 is,' he said.

'Then I guess I'll have to show you.' I wasn't eager to go out with Gray that morning. I had a tremendous amount of work to catch up on. We had had a number of visitors to the camp recently. Richard and Mary Leakey, two well-known experts on hominid fossils from Kenya, had left only the day before. During their stay I had not done any paperwork, any cataloguing. I had not written any letters or done detailed descriptions of any fossils. I *should* have stayed in camp that morning – but I didn't. I felt a strong subconscious urge to go with Tom, and I obeyed it. I wrote a note to myself in my daily diary: *Nov. 30, 1974. To Locality 162 with Gray in AM. Feel good.*

As a paleoanthropologist – one who studies the fossils of human ancestors – I am superstitious. Many of us are, because the work we do depends a great deal on luck. The fossils we study are extremely rare, and quite a few distinguished paleoanthropologists have gone a lifetime without finding a single one. I am one of the more fortunate. This was only my third year in the field at Hadar, and I had already found several. I know I am lucky, and I don't try to hide it. That is why I wrote 'feel good' in my diary. When I got up that morning I felt it was one of those days when you should press your luck. One of those days when something terrific might happen.

Throughout most of that morning, nothing did. Gray and I got into one of the expedition's four Land-Rovers and slowly jounced our way to Locality 162. This was one of several hundred sites that were in the process of being plotted on a master map of the Hadar area, with detailed information about geology and fossils being entered on it as fast as it was obtained. Although the spot we were headed for was only about four miles from camp, it took us half an hour to get there because of the rough terrain. When we arrived it was already beginning to get hot.

At Hadar, which is a wasteland of bare rock, gravel and sand, the fossils that one finds are almost all exposed on the surface of the ground. Hadar is in the center of the Afar desert, an ancient lake bed now dry and filled with sediments that record the history of past geological events. You can trace volcanic-ash falls there, deposits of mud and silt washed down from distant mountains, episodes of volcanic dust, more mud, and so on. Those events reveal themselves like layers in a slice of cake in the gullies of new young rivers that recently have cut through the lake bed here and there. It seldom rains at Hadar, but when it does it comes in an overpowering gush – six months' worth overnight. The soil, which is bare of vegetation, cannot hold all that water. It roars down the gullies, cutting back their sides and bringing more fossils into view.

Gray and I parked the Land-Rover on the slope of one of those gullies. We were careful to face it in such a way that the canvas water bag that was hanging from the side mirror was in the shade. Gray plotted the locality on the map. Then we got out and began doing what most members of the expedition spent a great deal of their time doing: we began surveying, walking slowly about, looking for exposed fossils.

Some people are good at finding fossils. Others are hopelessly bad at it. It's a matter of practice, of training your eye to see what you need to see. I will never be as good as some of the Afar people. They spend all their time wandering around in the rocks and sand. They have to be sharp-eyed; their lives depend on it. Anything the least bit unusual they notice. One quick educated look at all those stones and pebbles, and they'll spot a couple of things a person not acquainted with the desert would miss.

Tom and I surveyed for a couple of hours. It was now close to noon, and the temperature was approaching 110. We hadn't found much: a few teeth of the small extinct horse *Hipparion*; part of the skull of an extinct pig; some antelope molars; a bit of a monkey jaw. We had large collections of all these things already, but Tom insisted on taking these also as added pieces in the overall jigsaw puzzle of what went where.

'I've had it,' said Tom. 'When do we head back to camp?'

'Right now. But let's go back this way and survey the bottom of that little gully over there.'

The gully in question was just over the crest of the rise where we had been working all morning. It had been thoroughly checked out at least twice before by other workers, who had found nothing interesting. Nevertheless, conscious of the 'lucky' feeling that had been with me since I woke, I decided to make that small final detour. There was virtually no bone in the gully. But as we turned to leave, I noticed something lying on the ground partway up the slope.

'That's a bit of a hominid arm,' I said.

'Can't be. It's too small. Has to be a monkey of some kind.'

We knelt to examine it.

'Much too small,' said Gray again.

I shook my head. 'Hominid.'

'What makes you so sure?' he said.

'That piece right next to your hand. That's hominid too.'

'Jesus Christ,' said Gray. He picked it up. It was the back of a small skull. A few feet away was part of a femur: a thighbone. 'Jesus Christ,' he said again. We stood up, and began to see other bits of bone on the slope: a couple of vertebrae, part of a pelvis – all of them hominid. An unbelievable, impermissible thought flickered through my mind. Suppose all these fitted together? Could they be parts of a single, extremely primitive skeleton? No such skeleton had ever been found – anywhere.

'Look at that,' said Gray. 'Ribs.'

A single individual?

'I can't believe it,' I said. 'I just can't believe it.'

'By God, you'd better believe it!' shouted Gray. 'Here it is. Right here!' His voice went up into a howl. I joined him. In that 110-degree heat we began jumping up and down. With nobody to share our feelings, we hugged each other, sweaty and smelly, howling and hugging in the heat-shimmering gravel, the small brown remains of what now seemed almost certain to be parts of a single hominid skeleton lying all around us.

'We've got to stop jumping around,' I finally said. 'We may step on something. Also, we've got to make sure.'

'Aren't you sure, for Christ's sake?'

'I mean, suppose we find two left legs. There may be several individuals here, all mixed up. Let's play it cool until we can come back and make absolutely sure that it all fits together.'

We collected a couple of pieces of jaw, marked the spot exactly and got into the blistering Land-Rover for the run back to camp. On the way we picked up two expedition geologists who were loaded down with rock samples they had been gathering.

'Something big,' Gray kept saying to them. 'Something big. Something *big*.'

'Cool it,' I said.

But about a quarter of a mile from camp, Gray could not cool it. He pressed his thumb on the Land-Rover's horn, and the long blast brought a scurry of scientists who had been bathing in the river. 'We've got it,' he yelled. 'Oh, Jesus, we've got it. We've got The Whole Thing!'

That afternoon everyone in camp was at the gully, sectioning off the site and preparing for a massive collecting job that ultimately took three weeks. When it was done, we had recovered several hundred pieces of bone (many of them fragments) representing about forty percent of the skeleton of a single individual. Tom's and my original hunch had been right. There was no bone duplication.

But a single individual of what? On preliminary examination it was very hard to say, for nothing quite like it had ever been discovered. The camp was rocking with excitement. That first night we never went to bed at all. We talked and talked. We drank beer after beer. There was a tape recorder in the camp, and a tape of the Beatles song 'Lucy in the Sky with Diamonds' went belting out into the night sky, and was played at full volume over and over again out of sheer exuberance. At some point during that unforgettable evening – I no longer remember exactly when – the new fossil picked up the name of Lucy, and has been so known ever since, although its proper name – its acquisition number in the Hadar collection – is AL 288–1.

Lucy: The Beginnings of Humankind, 1981

RAMÓN MEDINA SILVA
c.1925–71

Why do we honor the one who is and is not of this world, whom we call Tatewarí, the one who is called The Fire? . . . Tatewarí, Our Grandfather . . . is there in the dark, making it light, making one warm, guarding one.

Ramón Medina Silva, also known as Uru Temay ('Newly Made Arrow'), was a shaman of the Huichol. He was born in the sierra between the indigenous communities of San Sebastián Teponahuaxtlan and Santa Catarina. As a Huichol, he was a member of perhaps the most traditional – that is, culturally intact – people of the northern Americas, a people who have resisted all attempts by the outside world to adapt even their language, as white settlers have taken their lands in the five centuries since the arrival of the Spanish.*

A peasant farmer, harvesting a meagre maize crop from the arid hill soil much like any other Huichol, Silva also possessed a genius for recounting the Huichol histories, and his considerable repertoire became an

* The Huichols – or Wixárika, as they know themselves – are a small group of Indians in Mexico numbering only 20,000. Despite century after century of Catholic pressure and of losing their land to the mestisos (the mixed-blood descendants of Conquistadors, Spanish settlers, and conquered Indian groups), they have successfully resisted the dominant faith. Though they have incorporated some important facets of the century of the 'Spanish' (as they still often call outsiders), such as metal tools and domestic animals, the majority of Huichols still live according to the body of spiritual and practical knowledge handed down through the generations by the 'divine ancestors'. It seems that the Huichols were once lowland people, who lived a nomadic existence as hunter-gatherers, but – while not much adjusting their nomadic, desert culture – gradually retreated towards the highlands, the Sierra Madre Occidental. With the incursions of the Spanish this process accelerated; to this day, with the continued loss of their lands to farmers, they have been retreating further. The sierra acts as a last bastion; they are extremely suspicious of outsiders, who are not always welcome.

invaluable source for the writer Fernando Benitez, who compiled a five-volume work on Mexican Indians.

As his reputation as an authority on Huichol customs grew, Silva became frustrated with his backbreaking existence eking out a life from the hills and, with the help of a Franciscan priest, moved to Guadalajara, Mexico's second largest city, in 1962. At the same time Silva, a man of much inner torment and varied human frailties, began to answer a spiritual calling of a Huichol kind. He would become the Huichol version of a shaman – not something a Huichol would normally welcome, because it entailed an arduous training and spiritually dangerous life – charged by the gods with the duty of conveying their will accurately to the community.

From 1965 he and his wife Guadalupe de la Cruz Ríos ('Lupe') began working with the anthropologists Barabara G. Myerhoff and Peter T. Furst, who for six years recorded a great number of what we would call 'myths', the chronicles of the Huichol people. At the same time, Silva also developed as what we would call an 'artist', expressing normal life intermixed with the invisible spiritual dimension in pictures made of yarn. He was pioneering a form based on the traditional *puros adornos* decorations, but with symbolic content.

In July 1971, just as Silva began to realize his potential as an artist, an advocate of his abused people, and an apprentice *cantador* (the Huichol shaman-singer or priest), he was murdered – shot dead in a drunken fight with a cousin over a woman.

Fans of Carlos Castaneda, a fellow student

of Myerhoff, whose adventures with 'Don Juan', a 'Yaqui sorcerer', resulted in seven books that brought him fame and fortune in the sixties and seventies (when mind-altering drugs and the exploration of other realities struck a chord), might note the odd similarity between the two men. Don Juan Matús now seems to have been largely a fictional character. However, though the work of Myerhoff and Furst surely made its way into Castane-da's writings, his earliest manuscript (1962–3) emerged before the two anthropologists, and Casteneda himself, had met the Huichol shaman.

That Silva's is an authentic voice – or at least one more authentic than Don Juan's – makes his written legacy valuable. He is almost unknown, yet surely for his people as great an explorer as the white men who encroached upon the Huichol desert lands.

Journeying with peyote

The first time one puts peyote into one's mouth, one feels it going down into the stomach. It feels very cold, like ice. And the inside of one's mouth becomes dry, very dry. And then it becomes wet, very wet. One has much saliva then. And then, a while later, one feels as if one were fainting. The body begins to feel weak, it begins to feel faint. And one begins to yawn, to feel very, very tired. And after a while one feels very light. The whole body begins to feel light, without sleep, without anything.

And then, when one takes enough of this, one looks upward and what does one see? One sees darkness. Only darkness. It is very, very dark, very black. And one feels drunk with the peyote, very drunk. And when one looks up again it is total darkness except for a little bit of light, a tiny bit of light, brilliant yellow. It comes there, a brilliant yellow. And one looks into the fire. One sits there, looking into the fire, which is Tatewarí. One sees the fire in colors, very many colors, five colors, different colors. The flames divide into colors.

It is not yellow, that flame, it is not red, that flame. It is many colors, all brilliant, very brilliant and beautiful. The beauty is very great, very great. It is a beauty as one never sees it without the peyote. The flames come up, they shoot up, and each flame divides into those colors, and each color is multi-colored. Blue, green, yellow, all those colors. The yellow appears on the tip of the flames as the flame shoots upward. And on the tips one can see little sparks in many colors coming out.

And the smoke which rises from the fire, it also looks more and more yellow, more and more brilliant. Then the fire turns to yellow, a brilliant, brilliant yellow, very bright. One sees the offerings there, many arrows with feathers and they are full of color, shimmering, shimmering.

That is what one sees, many things like that. And one sees Tatewarí, if one is mara'akáme, if one is the chief of those who go to hunt the peyote, then one sees Tatewarí. And one sees Tayaupá, one sees the Sun. One sees the mara'akáme venerating the Fire and one hears those prayers, like music. One hears praying and singing and chanting.

All this is to understand, to comprehend, to have one's life. So that we can understand what Tatewarí lets go from his heart, what the Fire lets go from his heart. One goes understanding all that which he lets go from his heart.

That is when we understand all that, when we find our life over there.

How Huichol souls travel to the Land of the Dead

. . . Well, when they die, whoever brought them into this world, those great ones, they say to her, 'Look, why did you want so many of the men's things?' And then that Old One puts out his arms, or if it is one of Our Mothers, she puts out her arms, and they show the amount of men's things she has taken pleasure with. To commit so many errors! And the poor woman has to carry all that. The poor woman, the life of that woman, goes tired, tired, saying, 'Oh, how tired I am, having to carry so many things.' And they say to her, 'Well, that is your pleasure. That is what you wanted to do over there where you lived.' They say, 'Well, look, why did you want so many things? You kept at it, you kept at it. Now you must take the whole bunch.'

That is how they speak to her. They say to her, 'You used to say over there that you were never going to get tired of men's things. So that is your pleasure now. There goes that poor woman's life, carrying all that. And the mara'akáme, he follows her. So that he can catch that soul.'

It is all the same, for the woman and for the man. They have to carry all the things they took pleasure with. They walk and walk, carrying it all. If it is a woman, she arrives there at the place of the black rocks. She arrives very tired. And she gathers together a bunch and throws them down there. But they tell her not to throw them away. If it is a man, he tries to throw it all away, just like the woman. But they tell him, 'No, do not throw that away. It was your pleasure, gather them up.' So they gather them up. That woman picks them up one by one. She puts them in her cape. It is the cape which Huichol women wear. Thirsty, hungry, they have to carry these things until they arrive over there.

Well, the life of the man walks there with all those vaginas. All those women he has enjoyed. And the woman walks there with all those penises. All those that they have taken pleasure with her . . .

Well, that life goes on walking, thirsty, tired, very thirsty, very tired. Very hungry. If it is a woman, always with her hands full of those things, those men's things she carries. And with the man it is the same.

Well, that life comes over there where they are waiting for them. And he yells, that life, he yells and he calls out to those others who have died before him. That is where the tree is, that large tree, that which is called *xápa*. It is the wild fig tree. They are *béwixi*, ancient, ancient people. They are waiting there for that life. They have souls just as we have but they are the ancient ones, those that have gone over there before. They are as they are. That is what they are there for, waiting there to make those ceremonies with that life.

So that life calls out, 'Brothers, sisters, I, too, am coming where you are. I am going over there.' Then those others there become happy. They say, 'Oh, fine, here comes my brother. My brother is coming.' And they say, 'Ah, it is my sister who is coming.' Whichever it may be, that is how they call out: 'My brother, my sister, they are coming.'

They are shouting, 'Ah, now we are going to eat! Ah, now we are going to eat those fruits that are on that tree!'

Then someone plays his violin, if he has such a thing. He plays this song that those others over there can hear it. They hear and they say, 'Oh, he is coming now. Now let us go and eat. We are very hungry. Surely he is coming, surely we are going to eat now.'

Very well. Then after taking five steps he comes to the tree which is a large wild fig tree. Then that man who is carrying the vaginas of the women he enjoyed tells his brothers, 'Yes, my brothers, now we are going to eat.' If it is three women he enjoyed in his life, or four, or five, however many it may be, he has these things with him. He carries them all in his hand. He says, 'Yes, my brothers, now I am going to throw these women's things into the tree.' He says to them all, 'I am going to throw them as one throws a stone. I will throw one up there to see how many of those fruits will fall down from that tree.'

So he speaks. He says to them, 'Ah yes, now I do have something to throw at those fruit, something I can throw up there.' And then he throws those things at the fruit. He strikes the tree with those vaginas and then they start to fall. Many fruit fall down there. After throwing the first vaginas, he throws the rest to one side. He leaves them there, all in one heap. There where the others have thrown them, those that came before. There is a pile of them there, some dressed, some without a thing on, some well covered – well, there is this pile of vaginas. He leaves them there, lying where he threw them down.

Well, that woman, the life of that woman, she arrives there in the same manner. There where the tree is, where they are waiting. It is very large, that tree, very high, with five branches and five roots. It has many fruits, that tree. There where she arrives, that woman's life makes a sound. It is a sound like that made by the dove. She calls out, 'Kukurukú, kukurukú!' And the boys with whom she had taken pleasure hear her and they clap their hands and say, 'She has come now.' All those that are over there hear her and they say, 'Ah, our sister, she has come.'

Then she takes the man's thing and she throws it at the tree. She throws it at those fruits and as the thing is very big, many fruits fall down. She says, 'Ah, this was good. It throws down much.' Then she says, 'And here is another one. And another and another.' Five throws with strong sticks, those men's things. The woman throws them up there. And the others she throws away. They remain there. There is that pile, that pile of men's things. Where the tree is.

And all those who are waiting there, they shout, 'Ah, now we are going to eat!' And they eat there, they eat those fruits which have fallen down from the tree. The life of that man, and of that woman, they have knocked down those fruits. Now they all eat there together.

Well, then. They arrive where they are dancing, those who have died before. They are dancing there to the music of the Huichol violin. He arrives and there are many pretty Huichol girls there, fully adorned, very well painted on their faces. All are dancing around Tatewarí, some drinking, some already drunk. Some are already wanting to fight because théy have drunk so much. And the one who is playing for them, his hand almost breaking from playing so much. And the one who is singing there, drunk from having drunk so much, he is close to Tatewarí, very close, because he does not know where he is going from having drunk so much.

And that life arrives over there, and his brothers embrace him. They say to him, 'Come, brother, let us go dance, let us follow the dancing.' So he gives five turns around the fire, dancing there in a circle around the fire as one does on this earth.

And that woman, that girl, in the same manner. She arrives and all embrace her, her brothers, her sisters, all of them just as we do here. In the same manner over there. She asks, 'You there, did you come first?' He says, 'Well, yes.' She says, 'Come and embrace me. You know I am yours and you are mine.' And he says, 'Well, then, if that is how it is.' And he says, 'Come let us go dance.' They go dancing, dancing, dancing, to the music of the Huichol violin.

Stacy Schaefer and Peter Furst, eds., *People of the Peyote: Huichol Indian History, Religion, and Survival* (1995)

BRUCE CHATWIN
1940–89

If this were so; if the desert were 'home'; if our instincts were forged in the desert . . . then it is easier to understand why greener pastures pall on us; why possessions exhaust us . . .

Bruce Chatwin, born in Sheffield, became a porter at Sotheby's auctioneers and in his early twenties was promoted to Director of the Impressionist Department, having, it is said, spotted a 'Picasso' in the sales room as a fake. When his eyesight suddenly faltered after eight years at the auctioneers, Chatwin, on a doctor's suggestion that the distant horizons of the desert would help to sharpen his vision again – a typically poetic explanation – took off for the Sudan. Perhaps one of the side effects of this recuperation was a traveller's restlessness; certainly it remained with Chatwin for the rest of his life.

He worked for the *Sunday Times* between 1972 and 1975, then slipped off abroad with, it's said, no more explanation than a telegram saying, 'Gone to Patagonia for six months.' From this trip emerged his first book, *In Patagonia*, based on wanderings in Argentina, which scooped up the Hawthornden Prize and the E. M. Forster Award. Several other travel-induced books followed, among them *The Viceroy of Ouidah* (on the early slave trade and inspired by travels in Dahomey and Brazil), *On the Black Hill*, a novel set on a remote Welsh hill farm occupied by twins, and *The Songlines*, a lyrical portrayal of the nomadic life of Australian Aborigines – and an opportunity to empty his famous moleskin notebooks, by then littered with his musings on the nomadic state.

Chatwin's books, like his life, rest on the frontier between fact and fiction. Although even his friends had to accept it was never very clear where fact gave way to fancy, his depictions remain powerful, and never more so than when exploring the tension between settler and nomad – what you might call the impossibility of 'permanence', as we have come to see it.

In *An Anatomy of Restlessness*, a collection of his writings published after his early death, Chatwin continues his thesis that nomadism, though not accepted as a form of modern lifestyle, is natural to us and offers an explanation for our wandering instinct.

Flynn, an Aboriginal ex-monk

The ex-Benedictine was holding court to half a dozen people in the darker part of the garden. The moonlight shone on his brow-ridges: his face and beard were swallowed up in the darkness. His girlfriend sat at his feet. From time to time, she would stretch her lovely long neck across his thigh and he would reach out a finger and tickle her.

He was, there was no denying it, difficult. When Arkady crouched beside the chair and explained what I wanted, I heard Flynn mutter, 'Christ, not another!'

I had to wait a full five minutes before he deigned to turn his head in my direction. Then he asked in a flat, ironic voice, 'Is there anything I can do to help you?'

'There is,' I said, nervously. 'I'm interested in the Songlines.'

'Are you?'

His presence was so daunting that whatever one said was sure to sound silly. I tried to interest him in various theories on the evolutionary origins of language.

'There are linguists', I said, 'who believe the first language was in song.'

He looked away and stroked his beard.

I then tried another tack and described how Gipsies communicate over colossal distances by singing secret verses down the telephone.

'Do they?'

Before being initiated, I went on, a young Gipsy boy had to memorize the songs of his clan, the names of his kin, as well as hundreds and hundreds of international phone numbers.

'Gipsies', I said, 'are probably the best phone-tappers in the world.'

'I cannot see', said Flynn, 'what Gipsies have to do with our people.'

'Because Gipsies', I said, 'also see themselves as hunters. The world is their hunting ground. Settlers are "sitting-game". The Gipsy word for "settler" is the same as the word for "meat".'

Flynn turned to face me.

'You know what our people call the white man?' he asked.

'Meat,' I suggested.

'And you know what they call a welfare cheque?'

'Also meat.'

'Bring a chair,' he said. 'I want to talk to you.'

I fetched the chair I had been sitting on and sat down beside him.

'Sorry I was a bit sharp,' he said. 'You should see the nutters I have to deal with. What are you drinking?'

'I'll have a beer,' I said.

'Four more beers,' Flynn called to a boy in an orange shirt.

The boy went eagerly to get them.

Flynn leaned forward and whispered something in Goldie's ear. She smiled and he talked.

White men, he began, made the common mistake of assuming that, because the Aboriginals were wanderers, they could have no system of land tenure. This was nonsense. Aboriginals, it was true, could not imagine territory as a block of land hemmed in by frontiers: but rather as an interlocking network of 'lines' or 'ways through'.

'All our words for "country"', he said, 'are the same as the words for "line".'

For this there was one simple explanation. Most of Outback Australia was arid scrub or desert where rainfall was always patchy and where one year of plenty might be followed by seven years of lean. To move in such landscape was survival: to stay in the same place suicide. The definition of a man's 'own country' was 'the place in which I do not have to ask'. Yet to feel 'at home' in that country depended on being able to leave it. Everyone hoped to have at least four 'ways out', along which he could travel in a crisis. Every tribe – like it or not – had to cultivate relations with its neighbour.

'So if A had fruits,' said Flynn, 'and B had duck and C had an ochre quarry, there were formal rules for exchanging these commodities, and formal routes along which to trade.'

What the whites used to call the 'Walkabout' was, in practice, a kind of bush-telegraph-cum-stock-exchange, spreading messages between peoples who never saw each other, who might be unaware of the other's existence.

'This trade', he said, 'was not trade as you Europeans know it. Not the business of buying and selling for profit! Our people's trade was always symmetrical.'

Aboriginals, in general, had the idea that all 'goods' were potentially malign and would work against their possessors unless they were forever in motion. The 'goods' did not have to be edible, or useful. People liked nothing better than to barter useless things – or things they could supply for themselves: feathers, sacred object, belts of human hair.

'I know,' I interrupted. 'Some people traded their umbilical cords.'

'I see you've done your reading.'

'Trade goods', he continued, should be seen rather as the bargaining coun-ters of a gigantic game, in which the whole continent was the gaming board and all its inhabitants players. 'Goods' were tokens of intent: to trade again, meet again, fix frontiers, intermarry, sing, dance, share resources and share ideas.

A shell might travel from hand to hand, from the Timor Sea to the Bight, along 'roads' handed down since time began. These 'roads' would follow the line of unfailing waterholes. The waterholes, in turn, were ceremonial centres where men of different tribes would gather.

'For what you call corroborees?'

'*You* call them corroborees,' he said. 'We don't.'

'All right,' I nodded. 'Are you saying that a trade route always runs along a Songline?'

'The trade route *is* the Songline,' said Flynn. 'Because songs, not things, are the principal medium of exchange. Trading in "things" is the secondary consequence of trading in song.'

Before the whites came, he went on, no one in Australia was landless, since everyone inherited, as his or her private property, a stretch of the Ancestor's song and the stretch of country over which the song passed. A man's verses were his title deeds to territory. He could lend them to others. He could borrow other verses in return. The one thing he couldn't do was sell or get rid of them.

Supposing the Elders of a Carpet Snake clan decided it was time to sing their song cycle from beginning to end? Messages would be sent out, up and down the track, summoning song-owners to assemble at the Big Place. One after the other, each 'owner' would then sing his stretch of the Ancestor's footprints. Always in the correct sequence!

'To sing a verse out of order', Flynn said sombrely, 'was a crime. Usually meant the death penalty.'

'I can see that,' I said. 'It'd be the musical equivalent of an earthquake.'

'Worse,' he scowled. 'It would be to un-create the Creation.'

Wherever there was a Big Place, he continued, the chances were that the other Dreamings would converge on it. So at one of your corroborees, you might have four different totemic clans, from any number of different tribes, all of whom would swap songs, dances, sons and daughters, and grant each other 'rights of way'.

'When you've been around a bit longer,' he turned to me, 'you'll hear the expression "acquiring ritual knowledge".'

All this meant was that the man was extending his song-map. He was widening his options, exploring the world through song.

'Imagine two Blackfellows', he said, 'meeting for the first time in an Alice pub. One will try one Dreaming. The other will try another. Then something's sure to click . . .'

'And that', Arkady piped up, 'will be the beginning of a beautiful drinking friendship.'

Everyone laughed at this, except for Flynn, who went on talking.

The next point, he said, was to understand that every song cycle went leap-frogging through language barriers, regardless of tribe or frontier. A Dreaming-track might start in the north-west, near Broome; thread its way through twenty languages or more; and go on to hit the sea near Adelaide.

'And yet,' I said, 'it's still the same song?'

'Our people', Flynn said, 'say they recognize a song by its "taste" or "smell" . . . by which, of course, they mean the "tune". The tune *always* stays the same, from the opening bars to the finale.'

'Words may change,' Arkady interrupted again, 'but the melody lingers on.'

'Does that mean', I asked, 'that a young man on Walkabout could sing his way across Australia providing he could hum the right tune?'

'In theory, yes,' Flynn agreed.

Around 1900, there was the case of an Arnhemlander who had walked across the continent in search of a wife. He married on the south coast and walked the bride back home with his new-found brother-in-law. The brother-in-law then married an Arnhemland girl, and marched her off down south.

'Poor women,' I said.

'Practical application of the Incest Taboo,' said Arkady. 'If you want fresh blood, you have to walk to get it.'

'But in practice,' Flynn went on, 'the Elders would advise the young man not to travel more than two or three "stops" down the line.'

'What do you mean by "stop"?' I asked.

A 'stop', he said, was the 'handover point' where the song passed out of your ownership; where it was no longer yours to look after and no longer yours to lend. You'd sing to the end of your verses, and there lay the boundary.

'I see,' I said. 'Like an international frontier. The road signs change language, but it's still the same road.'

'More or less,' said Flynn. 'But that doesn't get the beauty of the system. Here there are no frontiers, only roads and "stops".'

'The nature of human restlessness'

When I woke, I started rearranging the caravan as a place to work in.

There was a plyboard top which pulled out over the second bunk to make a desk. There was even a swivelling office chair. I put my pencils in a tumbler and my Swiss Army knife beside them. I unpacked some exercise pads and, with the obsessive neatness that goes with the beginning of a project, I made three neat stacks of my 'Paris' notebooks.

In France, these notebooks are known as *carnets moleskines*: 'moleskine', in this case, being its black oilcloth binding. Each time I went to Paris, I would buy a fresh supply from a *papeterie* in the Rue de l'Ancienne Comédie. The pages were squared and the end-papers held in place with an elastic band. I had numbered them in series. I wrote my name and address on the front page, offering a reward to the finder. To lose a passport was the least of one's worries: to lose a notebook was a catastrophe.

In twenty-odd years of travel, I lost only two. One vanished on an Afghan bus. The other was filched by the Brazilian secret police, who, with a certain clairvoyance, imagined that some lines I had written – about the wounds of a Baroque Christ – were a description, in code, of their own work on political prisoners.

Some months before I left for Australia, the owner of the *papeterie* said that the *vrai moleskine* was getting harder and harder to get. There was one supplier: a small family business in Tours. They were very slow in answering letters.

'I'd like to order a hundred,' I said to Madame. 'A hundred will last me a lifetime.'

She promised to telephone Tours at once, that afternoon.

At lunchtime, I had a sobering experience. The headwaiter of Brasserie Lipp no longer recognized me, 'Non, Monsieur, il n'y a pas de place.' At five, I kept my appointment with Madame. The manufacturer had died. His heirs had sold the business. She removed her spectacles and, almost with an air of mourning, said, 'Le vrai moleskine n'est plus.'

I had a presentiment that the 'travelling' phase of my life might be passing. I felt, before the malaise of settlement crept over me, that I should reopen those notebooks. I should set down on paper a résumé of the ideas, quotations and encounters which had amused and obsessed me; and which I hoped would shed light on what is, for me, the question of questions: the nature of human restlessness.

Pascal, in one of his gloomier *pensées*, gave it as his opinion that all our miseries stemmed from a single cause: our inability to remain quietly in a room.

Why, he asked, must a man with sufficient to live on feel drawn to divert himself on long sea voyages? To dwell in another town? To go off in search of a peppercorn? Or go off to war and break skulls?

Later, on further reflection, having discovered the cause of our misfortunes, he wished to understand the reason for them, he found one very good reason: namely, the natural unhappiness of our weak mortal condition: so unhappy that when we gave to it all our attention, nothing could console us.

One thing alone could alleviate our despair, and that was 'distraction' (*divertissement*): yet this was the worst of our misfortunes, for in distraction we were prevented from thinking about ourselves and were gradually brought to ruin.

Could it be, I wondered, that our need for distraction, our mania for the new, was, in essence, an instinctive migratory urge akin to that of birds in autumn?

All the Great Teachers have preached that Man, originally, was a 'wanderer in the scorching and barren wilderness of this world' – the words are those of Dostoevsky's Grand Inquisitor – and that to rediscover his humanity, he must slough off attachments and take to the road.

My two most recent notebooks were crammed with jottings taken in South Africa, where I had examined, at first hand, certain evidence on the origin of our species. What I learned there – together with what I now knew about the Songlines – seemed to confirm the conjecture I had toyed with for so long: that Natural Selection has designed us – from the structure of our brain-cells to the structure of our big toe – for a career of seasonal journeys *on foot* through a blistering land of thorn-scrub or desert.

If this were so; if the desert were 'home'; if our instincts were forged in the desert; to survive the rigours of the desert – then it is easier to understand why greener pastures pall on us; why possessions exhaust us, and why Pascal's imaginary man found his comfortable lodgings a prison.

The Songlines, 1987

PART IV

Cold Deserts

*

Tramping over the plateau, where reigns the desolation of the outer worlds, in solitude at once ominous and weird, one is free to roam in imagination through the wide realm of human experience to the bounds of the great Beyond. One is in the midst of infinities – the infinity of the dazzling white plateau, the infinity of the dome above, the infinity of the time past since these things had birth, and the infinity of the time to come before they shall have fulfilled the Purpose for which they were created . . .
Mawson, *The Home of the Blizzard*, (1915)

Once, when I was twenty-one and just graduating, I went with half a dozen student friends to investigate a glacier in northern Iceland. To be honest, we weren't exactly well prepared – in fact, we only had one ice axe between us, and hardly knew when, and when not, to put on crampons.

Up on to the nose of the glacier we went, clambering enthusiastically over the blue ice. On either side of us, the steep, forbidding slopes of the valley, carved out by the ice of previous, colder millennia as the glacier had worked downslope. Up ahead, the glacier as it was now, perched at the head of the valley, which rose abruptly in a series of vicious, weather-shattered blocks, each armoured with what Sven Hedin, elsewhere in the world, called a 'coat of ice-mail'.

It was a formidable but exciting scene, a landscape full of drama. We marched on, slowing only as we approached the beginnings of a crevasse field. We roped ourselves together, and proceeded again, relishing the novel excitement of having to veer to the left and right of the cracks, great blue slits that gapped with apparent menace around us. Then, with no warning, snow began to fall. It came down lightly at first, and we thought little of it. We carried on, deeper into the crevasse field. Then the wind picked up. The snow was suddenly coming at us horizontally, right into our faces. It stung as it struck us and soon we were forced to shield our eyes. We walked on a few paces, but now bent to the blinding wind – then abruptly stopped. Now, we couldn't see anything. Whether we looked ahead, behind, or to the sides, it was the same: whiteness. We couldn't see each other; we could barely even see our feet. This was a proper 'white-out'. I remember feeling a strange sensation of floating. With the ground invisible, everything around us invisible, I felt detached from the world, as if suspended in a cloud. What to do now? A few steps in any direction might mean us slipping into oblivion. This was a world with no context – no sound (lost to the wind), no sight, no smell. All we knew was that our boots were, for now, planted on something that was apparently solid. Other than that, we only had each other, our teammates to whom we were (rather casually) tied.

As it happened, the crisis passed in minutes, and before long we were smiling wryly at the crevasse gashes around us that had been invisible moments before. Next thing, we were striding our way up the valley, the incident over; but the memory of that brief moment on an Icelandic crevasse-field stayed with me, working like a warning in the back of my mind as I went on to embark on much more serious expeditions. Our lives had been, for those minutes, in the hands of capricious Arctic winds – the same ones that soon again delivered us clear skies and sun. The natural elements had seemed to show a side normally hidden from us in this urban age, if we don't challenge them – something like an occasional flash of temper; as if we had dared, in our innocence, to advance up a remote glacier into the realms of a goddess, and thus provoked her.

I recalled this little incident again when re-reading for this book Douglas Mawson's 1913 trek through Antarctica with Mertz and Ninnis, both of whom fell victim to the icy wastes, the latter disappearing down a crevasse with a complete dog team and most of the expedition's food, the former from eating too many dog livers, in an attempt to survive. Many of the themes of my Icelandic expedition are echoed throughout this section – and here I'm thinking not so much of the great heroism of Scott and others, as of the helplessness of man in a place so devoid of life, yet so highly charged with natural danger.

The Arctic was a busier place than the Antarctic. Early European navigators sailed north into the Arctic during the sixteenth and seventeenth centuries looking for commercial opportunities – cod and whaling grounds – as well as searching for new passages to the riches of the East, a trade route to China that would supersede the Silk Route. As well as bids for these north-east and north-west passages, there were the native peoples to investigate, such as the Inuit 'Eskimo' and Chukchi reindeer herders, and comparatively abundant wildlife, ranging from polar bears to the varied migratory flocks of Alaska and Siberia. The first accounts of the Arctic tend to be like factual reports, written for commercial sponsors, rather than for the general public, or observations by characters like the whaler William Scoresby, not charged with a duty to explore at all. The first witnesses of the Antarctic came along later, interest in the faraway region having waned after Cook established there to be no giant southern continent to balance Asia in the northern hemisphere. As for the Poles themselves, the furthest points north and south, they had no people and comparatively little flora and fauna. There were other more fruitful places to go.

When interest returned, it was because these inhospitable spaces were firmly established in the public consciousness as the last unknowns. Now they assumed a symbolic significance: they were platforms on which the best of any given generation might display their prowess. Individuals could, on these huge stages, shine before the whole world, as

they battled onward through the cold: 'Man can only do his best, and we have arrayed against us the strongest forces of nature.' Left without supplies in the rainforest, you might last a week or so. In the Sahara, a few days. In high latitudes, only hours – or a few minutes, if you fall into the icy water and suffer a heart attack. The line between success and disaster, comfort and death, is thin indeed. Speaking from personal experience again, this was brought home to me only this year, while alone on the frozen sea in the Bering Strait with my own dog team. All seemed well: the dogs were obeying my commands and we were progressing systematically through the pressure ridges – the buckled-up ice. Then I left the dogs and sledge so as to scout ahead a little bit. Only five minutes later, I turned around, and was about to retrace my steps. However, I now found that the wind had blown my tracks away. I couldn't find my dogs, or the supplies on the sledge with them. 'No great panic,' I thought; like Peary and Amundsen, I had the great benefit of wearing native skins – in my case, the reindeer skins favoured by the Chukchis, the herders of north-east Siberia. Any temperature above minus 15°C and I'd even sweat. I also carried a survival kit, and curled into a survival blanket to use as a night shelter with a view to renewing my search in the morning. Then things really went wrong. I tried to light my emergency stove, and found that someone had put dirty petrol in it. Without a stove, I couldn't cook up anything warm; nor could I drink. Dehydration, not cold, was the problem – and it was this lack (and atrocious weather) that so weakened Robert Scott, on the return leg from the Pole. There was water everywhere around, but it was frozen solid, unavailable. As it happened, in my case the night was warm – minus 20°C – and the wind dropping. I found the dogs in the morning; but it wouldn't have taken much more to tip the balance – a snowstorm, a wolf or bear scaring the dogs; or simply me losing a glove.

The extreme north and south of our planet, then, offer a different degree of physical difficulty from anywhere else. In terms of tenacity, bravery and stoicism, there is little to beat the explorers of either Pole. The greatest of them reveal much about human nature in adversity, as they battle against the elements and also, as we'll see, against their inner demons.

As world focus gradually sharpened on the Poles themselves as objectives, there was more at stake than rivalry between competitive individuals. Just as, much later, the superpowers would be engaged in a race into space to show their supremacy, so at the turn of the century both races for the Poles were chances for England and America to display theirs; and, while America triumphed at the North Pole, 'England – a dying empire – failed to reach the South Pole first, losing out to Norway,' as one anonymous editor to an edition of Shackleton's writings put it.

Nor was it a question of explorers only having to satisfy the nation whose hopes they carried; it was a question of satisfying sponsors. The high latitudes were the most expensive of all exploration arenas: at the very least, you needed a ship to get you there. So here, more than on any other terrain, it was necessary to be noticed; you might not want make a splash in the newspapers, but your paymaster did. So, to please his sponsors, Nansen, for example, dressed in Dr Jaeger's 'Sanitary Woollen Clothing' – at least when at home.

There were greater repercussions than the woolly items of clothing you were forced to display. The feud that developed between Commander Robert Peary and Dr Frederick A. Cook over the first arrival at the North Pole – Cook claimed to have got there almost exactly a year before, on 21 April 1908 – was a feud between their sponsors.

Ultimately [Beau Riffenburgh writes in his *Myth of the Explorer*] the attainment of the North Pole resulted in no imperial gain, it achieved no great scientific aim, it realised no commercial coup, and it lacked any essential benefit to mankind. Yet it was widely considered one of the most significant triumphs of its time. Why was there such commotion over an achievement lacking every attribute except personal priority? Part of the reason was that the claiming of the Pole was the culmination of centuries of exertion in exploration ... Equally important was that the claims of Cook and Peary, and their rivalry, were turned into the media event of the year.

The *New York Herald* had backed Cook, the *New York Times* had backed Peary. Forget exploration; this was a circulation war.

Cook in the end lost, not helped by his spurious claim to have made a first ascent of Mount McKinley, the highest summit in America, in 1906, using as evidence a photo of the summit that was clearly of an 8,000-foot peak some twenty miles away. His credibility was further damaged when he was imprisoned in 1923 for business fraud. He died, still claiming to have reached the Pole: 'I felt the glory which the prophet feels in his vision, with which the poet thrills in his dream. About the frozen plains my imagination evoked aspects of grandeur – I saw silver and crystal palaces, such as were never built by man, with turrets flaunting ... the shifting mirages seemed like the ghosts of dead armies, magnified and transfigured, huge and spectral.' Though President Franklin D. Roosevelt pardoned Cook shortly before his death, he never cleared his name.

Peary had meanwhile been given the title by default, supported by the National Geographic Society, which was not altogether impartial, having set the Pinkerton Detective Agency on to Cook. Doubts over Peary's claim have also mounted over the decades, particularly about his speed of progress, and his questionable findings on earlier expeditions, which featured a non-existent 'Jesup

Land' on his 1898–1902 expedition, followed by the equally illusive 'Crocker Land' in 1906.*

There was more to come. Recently, we have also had access to Peary's innermost thoughts on this, his final polar bid. In November 1984, Wally Herbert, who had made the first surface crossing of the Arctic, via the North Pole, was invited to examine Peary's private journal of the great feat. It had been unavailable for scrutiny by polar historians for seventy-six years – Peary had even refused the Congressional subcommittee of 1911, which was examining his claim, anything more than a superficial examination. 'I do not care to let it out of my possession,' he said. 'It has never been.' Only after renewed claims that Cook did in fact reach the Pole were the Peary family persuaded to release the diary from the vaults; and, as Herbert soon discovered, Peary's dairy self-evidently wasn't written with publication in mind. It was simply a log of observations and memos, including 'thoughts that it is astonishing that Peary should have taken the risk of committing to paper, let alone his diary'. He plots, he

* Anyone wondering what type of person willingly endures suffering in the extreme cold for months on end, might find Peary's state of mind illuminating. Here was a man who, from boyhood, had set himself the task of getting to the Pole – and before anyone else. 'Now a maimed old man,' he writes, describing himself in his diary entry of 24 May 1902, following one of his earlier attempts on the Pole, 'unsuccessful after the most arduous work, away from wife and child, mother dead, one baby dead. Has the game been worth the candle? And yet I could not have done otherwise than stick to it.' Here is a trapped character, and not at all the man he presented to the world after his eventual success. 'The discovery of the North Pole stands for the inevitable victory of courage, persistence, endurance, over all obstacles. In the discovery of the North Pole is written the final chapter of the great geographical stories of the western hemisphere which began with the discovery of the New World by Columbus. Here is the cap and climax, the closing of the book on four hundred years of history . . . The splendid frozen jewel of the North, for which through centuries men of every nation have struggled, and suffered and died, is won at last, and is to be worn for ever, by the Stars and Stripes.'

schemes, he denigrates his rivals: 'Was he ashamed to go back after so short an absence?' he asks, regarding his rival Nansen, whose attempt on the Pole still stands as what Herbert, discussing his finding in his *The Noose of Laurels*, rightly calls 'one of the most inspiring examples of courageous intelligence' in the history of exploration. 'Or', Peary goes on, 'did he go off for Franz Joseph Land from sensational motives and business reasons?' Peary's craving for fame veers between the gently deluded and the maddened: 'Faced with marble or granite,' he writes, pondering the type of mausoleum that would be fitting for his final resting place. 'Statue with flag on top, lighted room at base for two sarcophagi?'

More damaging still, the log of his progress to the North Pole weakens, rather than strengthens his claim to the Pole. Herbert found in Peary's diaries 'one of the most hazardous and amazing journeys ever made by man. It spoke to me of incredible courage and of a passionate, almost half-crazed need to succeed.' He read on, hoping to understand 'that self-destructive craving for fame which produced in Peary the tragic delusion that fame is the proof of true greatness'. As for whether Peary completed the journey or not, Herbert found inconsistencies in the diary throughout: a strange fluidity in handwriting, as if he'd written up his experiences in the comfort of his ship, strange blank pages as if left for filling-in anything missed out, and an incredible lack of navigational observations: there was not a single indication that a sighting for longitude was made on his outward journey, to check the extent to which he had strayed off-course owing to winds and sea currents carrying the ice. On the final four and a half days, the last 133 nautical miles, he made not one check of latitude, longitude, or compass variation. He simply made a solar observation on 6 April, and – some miracle this – found himself only three miles short of the Pole. Discovering this after all these years,

Herbert felt an 'angry frustration that Peary had left us with only his word and a few pencil marks scratched on a pad'. He could so easily have brought back a mass of acceptable proof that he and his five courageous companions had finally succeeded in reaching the Pole. 'But incredibly, Peary had simply not bothered.' He'd simply offered as proof of his claim the sort of simple calculations that Herbert and his companions, trudging over the Arctic Ocean, 'used to work out in a matter of seconds by scratching the numbers with the point of a ski stick on a smooth patch of wind-packed snow'.

Herbert gave no definitive conclusion about Peary's claim – and, as Herbert was the only serious contender to the title, that was as generous as it was wise – but the evidence is fairly clear. In 1997 American researcher Robert M. Bryce again pointed out that the pages of Peary's diary were far too pristine – they weren't, for example, soiled with walrus fat (as my own diary was after two months of trekking with dogs through the Arctic) – and concluded that neither Peary nor Cook made it to the Pole. Today, the National Geographic Society still endorses Peary, repeating again this year that he and his companion Matthew A. Henson are 'generally credited' with the achievement. However, Herbert was, surely, at least first to the exact position of the Pole.

The governments and speculators who paid for the polar ventures did so for gain of some kind – political, financial, scientific – and it was the job of the explorer, whatever his personal motive for going, to exploit those desires. Like others before him, Robert Scott received a sympathetic reaction to his proposed second, 1910–13 Terra Nova expedition, not least because of a supportive national mood: politicians wanted their countrymen to be the first to the South Pole. Richard Byrd helped raise money for his 1928 solo winter sojourn in Antarctica by an appeal to science: he'd be undertaking systematic weather observations.

Personal motives tended to merge with national ones when it came to this, almost the last great geographical prize. It's true that, in the Heroic Age, there was your duty to be done – to your men, to your country – but that should not obscure the fact that personal rewards could also be very substantial.

A torpedo lieutenant, Scott's promotion had been slow. His family circumstances were comparatively modest: polar exploration was an opportunity for professional and financial advancement. Certainly he was a man of honour, but also surely regretted the hero's welcome he knew, having failed to reach the Pole first, he would not receive. 'Well, we have turned our back now on the goal of our ambition and must face over 800 miles of solid dragging – and goodbye to most of the daydreams!'

For Shackleton, who had made his own bid for the Pole, financial reward played a part: 'I have had offers amounting to £60,000 for a book and lectures if I reach the Pole,' he wrote to Elspeth Beardmore on 3 May 1907. Years on, his endeavour having paved the way for Scott, and the ultimate victor Amundsen, he set out again, this time to cross Antarctica through the Pole. Now he was aged forty; it was a last chance at glory. 'In the *Endurance* I had centred ambitions, hopes and desires. Now, straining and groaning, her timbers cracking and her wounds gaping, she is slowly giving up her sentient life . . .'

National rivalry centred on attaining the South Pole grew, of course, when, the North Pole apparently reached by Peary, Amundsen (a protégé of the great fellow-Norwegian, Arctic explorer Nansen) set himself the other great prize in the south. Suddenly, too late in the day, Scott and the British found they had a serious rival. The irony was, Amundsen's early inspiration had been John Franklin, another doomed Brit: 'Strangely enough the thing in Sir John's narrative that appealed to me most strongly was the suffering he and his men endured. A strange ambition burned within me to endure those same sufferings.'

As it was, such was his professionalism, Amundsen's team suffered little on their journey to the Pole. 'Pride and affection shone in the five pairs of eyes that gazed upon the flag, as it unfurled itself with a sharp crack, and waved over the Pole,' he wrote of his arrival, evoking a calm scene of efficiency, which, as Roland Huntford – whose dissection of the Scott myth, *Scott and Amundsen*, caused such a rumpus among Scott admirers in 1979 – noted was in contrast with the confusion often surrounding the British effort.

Much has been made by Huntford and others of Scott's lack of rigour in planning for the unexpected, but Scott, trekking to the Pole several weeks behind Amundsen, did also receive a freak blast of bad weather. Scientist Susan Solomon, who did a stint at the American Antarctic base, McMurdo Station, and then spent thirteen years ploughing through meteorological data and eye-witness testimonies, has recently concluded that it was simply 'bad luck' that killed Scott and his men. 'Modern records prove that only once, in 1988, have comparable temperatures been found in March.' Just staying alive became hard, and the texture of the snow changed, so that now, instead of gliding over snow, the sledge runners dragged, as if being hauled through sand.

Despite, or perhaps because of, their defeat – and most certainly because of the emotive brilliance of Scott's diary writings, helped along by the expedition's cameraman, Ponting, and his fervent desire to sell the film record he'd made – the expedition earned immortality and a posthumous knighthood for Scott. After some judicial editing – excluding such lines as 'I cannot help feeling disgusted because Amundsen's action is secret and deliberate,' (written after hearing that the Norwegians were down in the Antarctic with

them and parked in the Bay of Whales) – his writings were used to inspire soldiers in the First World War, and again in the Second. 'It was a disappointment to my party that we could not go to the Pole,' Teddy Evans wrote in 1943, of the moment his support team gave three rousing cheers, and waved goodbye to the southern party, 'a great disappointment, but we had been brought up to treat misfortunes with a smile and successes with a cheer.' Inspiring stuff, and just what the nation wanted; but, freak weather notwithstanding, Scott had cut things too fine, and not for the first time. He also made several fatal errors, such as in his limited use of dogs. How much greater tribute to him, then, that Evans still remained loyal to the 'brave sailor and fine leader'. The southern party, Evans concluded, pushed forward with 'a fine perseverance', and when Oates couldn't go on, 'This very gallant gentleman, realising that the salvation of the party depended on his self-sacrifice, deliberately walked out of the tent during a cruel blizzard and strove through the snows until he dropped and died in his tracks . . .' The bald truth was less romantic. Oates knew there was little hope of salvation for anyone. He had said, just before setting out on the march, that a revolver should be available 'so that if anyone broke down, he should have the privilege of using it'. Though he was, just like Teddy Evans, dutiful and loyal to the end, this could also be seen – though I personally think uncharitably – as a simple act of suicide.

This was not the story Britain wanted, as I said, and it's not the story they got in 1913 with the publication of *Scott's Last Expedition*. One way or another, we are all fairly familiar with Scott's tale, so why have I bothered quoting the last days of his journals almost in their entirety here? To me they remain some of the most compelling non-fiction literature in English. 'These rough notes and our dead bodies must tell the tale,' Scott wrote as he died; and tell the tale they brilliantly do – and though not the whole tale, they are the tale of his era. As a modern explorer, Scott could not match the efficiency of Amundsen, but in his heroic struggle against fate and the elements he eclipsed every traveller of his time.

Scott holds the power to inspire, to this day. Even his rival Shackleton recognized great qualities in him. 'He is the most daring man I ever met,' he told Kathleen, Scott's wife, while her husband was staggering south through blizzards, 'extraordinarily brave'. In her notebook, she recorded the conversation for Scott's return. 'I said,' she wrote, ' "Yes, he's brave morally as well as physically," and he said, "Yes, indeed, I agree." '

Given the severity of conditions, Polar expeditions tended towards the military, and it was the officer class who led the ventures, and therefore determined the official record. So, for example, generally speaking we know about the epic journey to rescue the crew of the *Endurance*, sunk by ice, through Shackleton's words. For this reason, I've included among the extracts a hitherto unpublished piece from the private diary kept by Thomas Orde-Lees, a Marines officer and one of those left behind to await rescue by Shackleton. This is not an elegant bit of prose, but has the merit of not having been written for publication – unlike Scott's journal, for instance – and throws an unfiltered light on matters.* Another explorer, Stefansson, whose exploits in the Arctic had granted him considerable stature, was able to go further in shaping his-

tory – and controlling the perception of an entire region. 'It is the mental attitude of the Southerner that makes the North hostile,' he wrote; but this was surely being rather too generous to the Arctic. Amundsen, who knew well the hostility of northern latitudes, observed that if men set out into this 'friendly' Arctic with only a gun and ammunition, relying on finding food on the way as Stefansson suggested, 'certain death awaits them'. It's hard not to side with Amundsen. The 'snowfall is not heavy – less than that of Scotland,' Steffansson wrote enthusiastically, 'and melts in spring to give way to grassy and flowery meadows . . .' Putting aside that I, for one, have reason to remember Siberian snow falling in August, and have found his flowery meadows elusive in the extreme, that there is a healthy flora at all in this fragile landscape is simply an indication of the extreme specialization of species that are maximizing the benefit of a very brief summer. That the Arctic lowlands could support a 'large population of reindeer, musk ox, and other sturdy animals of potential economic value' was not to do with the abundance of the land, but due to the herds being constantly on the move, and to the well-honed skills of hardened indigenous peoples, who had to remain strictly nomadic in order to survive.

In 1920, still pursuing his notion of a friendly Arctic, Stefansson colonized Wrangel Island with four men and an Eskimo woman. The Eskimo alone survived.† The bickering and animal degradation to which the survivors of another Steffansson enterprise descended, when his vessel sank near Wrangel Island, is recorded for us only thanks to McKinlay.

---

* Orde-Lees saw that Shackleton, though a brilliant leader, had his limitations as an explorer. Even after his own life had been saved by skis on the first Scott expedition, and Scott's life had been lost partly by his ignorance of them on the second, Shackleton had failed to adopt their use properly on the *Endeavour* venture. Orde-Lees was the only member of Shackleton's party who was able to ski expertly, and Shackleton, like Scott before him, was taken aback by their usefulness. Orde-Lees wondered why 'he had not come to this conclusion long before', and why he had not insisted on every man 'being able to move on ski at a modest five miles an hour'.

† Stefansson explained the unhappy business away – one man died of illness, the other three must have 'come to grief by one of those accidents.' In short, as the Foreword to his book explains, the venture was 'only a simple story of quiet heroism and a sad ending.' So much then, for Stefansson's dictum: 'It is not only ignorance but also romance that retreats before the advance of knowledge. Every geographic

I've touched on how powerfully driven were those who made their way to the polar regions in the twentieth century† but while the early expeditions into these icy realms focused (of necessity) on physical endeavours only, that did not mean they were devoid of the higher spiritual or philosophical thought that has always been associated with the deserts of hotter climes. 'Here is the desert,' Thesiger wrote, of the empty Arabian sands. 'I had found all that I had asked; I knew that I should never find it again.' This sentiment would not be out of place coming from many an Antarctic traveller – Sara Wheeler, for example, who found that the 'ice-desert' provided something lacking elsewhere on the planet. 'I felt less homeless than I have ever felt anywhere ... I sensed that the icefields had something to teach me.'

The primary motivation of Polar explorers into the twenty-first century has remained strictly unspiritual. There's a practical reason for this: it is possible to stand and admire the breathtaking icy vistas, the star-studded night skies and northern lights, but, in minus 60°C windchill, that awesome feeling comes a lot less readily. That said, the cold deserts still seem to exert a pull on the psyche.

Byrd, alone in the Antarctic in 1934, writes of the effect of isolation and bleak beauty on the mind.

Presently I began to have the illusion that what I was seeing was also what I was hearing, so perfectly did the music seem to blend with what was happening in the sky. As the notes swelled, the dull aurora on the horizon pulsed and quickened and draped itself into arches and fanning beams which reached out across the sky until at my zenith the display attained its crescendo. The music and the night became one; and I told myself that all beauty was akin and sprang from the same substance.

This is classic desert stuff; and the effect of the barren land had a typically enduring effect: Byrd became one of the leading proponents for international co-operation in Antarctica.‡

---

discoverer must plead guilty to making the world poorer in romance. He does so in exact proportion as he makes it richer in knowledge.' There's an argument for the exact opposite – one that Richard Dawkins puts in *Unweaving the Rainbow*.
† Wally Herbert said, when asked why he made his great Arctic crossing: 'Those who need to ask will never understand the answer, while others who feel the answer will never need to ask.' An alternative answer is provided by *The King's Mirror*, a Norse text from thirteenth century which Nansen enjoyed quoting: 'If you wish to know what men seek in this land or why men journey thither in so great danger of their lives, then it is the threefold nature of man which draws him thither. One part of him is emulation and desire of fame, for it is man's nature to go where there is likelihood of great danger, and to make himself famous thereby. Another part is the desire of knowledge, for it is man's nature to wish to know and see those parts of which he has heard, and to find out whether they are as it was told him or not. The third part is a desire of gain, seeing that men seek after riches in every place where they learn that profit is to be had, even though there be great danger in it.'

‡ During his winter in the Antarctic, Byrd had ample chance to experience enlightenment from hardship. Often disoriented, suffering from depression and carbon monoxide poisoning, he goes out in a blizzard to make one of his weather observations. The entrance to his underground cabin jams shut, trapping him outside – a potential death sentence. But such experiences, he wrote later, were '. . . to the good. For that experience resolved proportions and relationships for me as nothing else could have done; and it is surprising, approaching the final enlightenment, how little one really has to know or feel sure about.' Byrd analyses this sentiment further. 'Perhaps this period was just the repeated pattern of my youth. I sometimes think so. When I was growing up, I used to steal out of the house at night, and go walking in Glass's woods, which were a little way up the road from our place. In the heavy shadows of the Shenandoah Valley hills, the darkness was a little terrifying, as it always is to small boys; but when I would pause and look up into the sky, a feeling that was midway between peace and exhilaration would seize me. I never quite succeeded, as a boy, in analysing that feeling, any more than I did when it used to come to me as a naval officer, in the night watches at sea, and later when, as an explorer, I first looked upon

The strange beauty to be found in these regions touched many polar travellers, despite the narrow perspective of their ambitions. Many, though intent only on gaining that polar record, encountered an unexpected contentment even while they suffered – the Arctic and Antarctic tend to sweep away less fundamental concerns, the minor irritations of modern Western life. If, as the Islamic proverb says, 'Freedom is absence of choice', then the polar regions provide this freedom in abundance. All choices are determined by the need to survive, and this becomes cleansing. Take, for example, the classic story of Apsley Cherry-Garrard, who at twenty-six was the youngest of the three men who set off to obtain emperor penguin eggs in the total darkness of the Antarctic winter, as part of the scientific programme prior to Scott's final attempt on the Pole. They each dragged a 757-pound sledge and travelled an average of one mile in a day, through blizzard and blackness. The redeeming feature of this pointless hardship and danger was its heroism. Cherry-Garrard compared the experience to that of an English officer in the Dardanelles, blinded and left for several days between English and Turkish trenches. Both sides fired at the man as he groped to and from them. 'Such extremity of suffering cannot be measured: madness or death may give relief. But this I know: we on this journey were already beginning to think of death as a friend.'

At last, safely back in their base with Scott, the egg-hunters sang, talked, smoked, and posed for photographs; they had won through and in so doing had learned self-respect, how to handle fear, and the security to be had in a tribe. These things you learn in

—

mountains and lands which no one has ever seen. No doubt it was partly animal: the sheer expanding discovery of being alive, of growing, of no longer being afraid. But there was the sense of identification with vast movements; the premonition of destiny that is implicit in every man; and the sense of waiting for the momentary revelation.'

the company of people who are more engaged in the world than afraid of it.

There is no escaping the fact, however, that the routes to the Poles had, by early in the twentieth century, become little more than race tracks, the icefields stadia for Olympian feats, and to some they have remained so to this day.†

Meanwhile, the frontiers of genuine exploration have changed. The significant advances are not to be found in heroic feats, but in writers who re-interpret the terrain for us, or in the specialist domain of the scientist, now operating from his protective base on an Arctic or Antarctic station, or from remote data, say at the Scott Polar Research Institute in Cambridge. Such a pioneer is Monica Kristensen, the Norwegian director of a team of scientists working on an environmental research programme on Svalbard, in the Arctic Ocean, who writes this about her experiences in prolonged darkness: 'The apparently everlasting winter is like an abyss of darkness – your thoughts die down and your mind becomes still – the hours stretch out towards a morning that never comes – there's an eternity of time to stare into an abyss until in the end you get the glimmer of a face, and if you are lucky, it is your own face you see.' As she became more and more engrossed in her meteorological readings, she sank deeper and deeper into this near-black world. While the other scientists – who were male 'to a man' –

† Contemporary writer Barry Lopez observes that though many see their trips north or south as a source of prestige, money or adulation, their ambition is, in time, 'tempered by a mounting sense of consternation and awe. It is as though the land slowly works its way into the man and by virtue of its character eclipses these motives. The land becomes large, alive like an animal; it humbles him in a way he cannot pronounce. It is not that the land is simply beautiful but that it is powerful. Its power flows into the tension between its obvious beauty and its capacity to take life. Its power flows into the mind from a realisation of how darkness and light are bound together within it, and the feeling that this is the floor of creation.'

slept, she studied the skies, and read. Her meal times became muddled: 'I'd be eating bread and cheese for dinner and then meat rolls for breakfast.' Her lips turned blue, to the alarm of her colleagues, while her mind turned black. 'I felt that a fight was going on in the shadows of my soul . . . I was aware of an eternity that was empty or perhaps an emptiness that lasts forever. There is a magical land on the border of the external landscape of man's mind. Only when hope and longings loom like cliffs over the grey sea of everyday life can reality turn into experience. Man is a lonely creature guarding his border of sanity.'

In my selection, of the other women who squeeze into this male habitat, Josephine Peary is included because she portrays the Arctic in a unique tone. Her voice has the chatty lightness of the unscientifically trained, but there's also a warmth in the way she paints a picture of Inuit culture – besides, she provides an insight into the behaviour of her husband, whose almost overbearing presence breathes onto each of her pages. There's also Sara Wheeler, not a scientist, but one whose penetration of an uncharted world to me makes her an explorer – though she trekked nowhere of significance at all. Her terra incognita was not formed of wind-hardened snow and spreads of ice – she chooses hardly to describe the polar landscape at all – but the Antarctic now colonized and defined by men. Like Kristensen, over-wintering at the other end of the planet, she was shunned at first by the bearded characters of the scientific research bases. Her task was to penetrate this new unknown, created by the male. Entering this strange, at times hostile, territory, she makes her way as men did when first approaching the virgin frozen waste a century ago.

JOHN FRANKLIN
1786–1847

The sudden failure in the strength of these men cast a gloom over the rest . . . We . . . ate a few morsels of burnt leather for supper.

Sir John Franklin, an English Admiral, perished in the Arctic while attempting to discover the long-sought North-West Passage – but although his ill-judged choice of equipment, reliance on naval discipline and notions of manly duty were no match for the hostile environment, his struggles were on such a heroic scale that he became elevated as one of the greats in the public imagination. Some have argued, perhaps too harshly, that it was a tradition of endeavour – in which few substantial discoveries were made, and at huge human cost – that characterized British polar exploration well into the next century. True or false, the missions that set out looking for Franklin certainly did much to explore the Canadian Arctic.

As a young man Franklin fought under Nelson at Copenhagen and Trafalgar and went on to serve on Matthew Flinders' hydrographic survey of the Australian coast; but his real interest lay in the Arctic and in his thirties he led a British Navy expedition, charting the coastline of Northern Canada. He was away for three and a half years, covering 5,000 miles in treacherous conditions over land and sea. While returning from an overland survey of the coast north of the Great Slave Lake in 1821, he was overtaken by the Arctic winter. Franklin's demoralized party survived on lichen (*tripe de roche*) and leather, and their escape remains one of the harshest journeys on record, involving cannibalism and the murder of Lieutenant Hood, followed by the summary execution of his murderer – incidents that Franklin chose to omit from his account. Those who survived owed their lives to friendly Inuit, who managed to live off the land, in stark contrast to the visitors.

A second expedition charted the Mackenzie River and Alaskan coast.

He became governor of Tasmania in 1836. Later, when nearly sixty, he undertook a search for the North-West Passage. The *Erebus* and *Terror* left England in May 1845 with a crew of 134 men, and disappeared shortly afterwards. It became clear years later that the ships had become stuck in ice near King William's Island. Franklin and twenty-three others had died by the following summer and the remainder perished during their attempt to head south to a trading post at the Great Fish River (Back River).

Five years later the graves of three of the crew were discovered. Further clues emerged in 1854, when John Rae gleaned from Inuit that they had seen white men pulling a sledge along the Great Fish River. 'Some of their bodies had been buried,' reported *The Times* on 23 October 1854, 'some were in a tent or tents; others under the boat which had been turned over to form a shelter, and several lay scattered about in different directions . . . From the mutilated state of many of the corpses and the contents of the kettles, it is evident that our wretched countrymen had been driven to the last resort – cannibalism – as a means of prolonging their existence.'

Rae's claim caused outrage in England and in 1857 Lady Franklin hired Captain Leopold McClintock to search for her husband anew. Two years later, he found a cairn containing two notes confirming the demise of Franklin that June; eventually he found a twenty-eight-foot boat that some remaining men had dragged with them, containing heavy, utterly useless things. Lead poisoning from their tinned food may well have affected their minds.

Living off leather and lichen

[*5/6 October 1821*] In the afternoon we had a heavy fall of snow, which continued all the night. A small quantity of *tripe de roche* [edible lichen] was gathered; and Crédit, who had been hunting, brought in the antlers and back bone of a deer which had been killed in the summer. The wolves and birds of prey had picked them clean, but there still remained a quantity of the spinal marrow which they had not been able to extract. This, although putrid, was esteemed a valuable prize, and the spine being divided into portions, was distributed equally. After eating the marrow, which was so acrid as to excoriate the lips, we rendered the bones friable by burning, and ate them also.

On the following morning the ground was covered with snow to the depth of a foot and a half, and the weather was very stormy. These circumstances rendered the men again extremely despondent; a settled gloom hung over their countenances, and they refused to pick *tripe de roche*, choosing rather to go entirely without eating, than to make any exertion.

The want of *tripe de roche* caused us to go supperless to bed. Showers of snow fell frequently during the night. The breeze was light next morning, the weather cold and clear. We were all on foot by day-break, but from the frozen state of our tents and bed clothes, it was long before the bundles could be made, and as usual, the men lingered over a small fire they had kindled, so that it was eight o'clock before we started. Our advance from the depth of the snow was slow, and about noon coming to a spot where there was some *tripe de roche*, we stopped to collect it, and breakfasted . . .

The distance walked to-day was six miles. As Crédit was very weak in the morning, his load was reduced to little more than his personal luggage, consisting of his blanket, shoes, and gun. Previous to setting out, the whole party ate the remains of their old shoes, and whatever scraps of leather they had, to strengthen their stomachs for the fatigue of the day's journey . . .
Three of the party decided to stay behind in a tent, while Franklin and the survivors pushed on towards Fort Enterprise.

[*7 October*] Descending afterwards into a more level country, we found the snow very deep, and the labour of wading through it so fatigued the whole party, that we were compelled to encamp, after a march of four miles and a half. Belanger and Michel were left far behind, and when they arrived at the encampment appeared quite exhausted. The former, bursting into tears, declared his inability to proceed, and begged me to let him go back next morning to the tent, and shortly afterwards Michel made the same request . . .

The sudden failure in the strength of these men cast a gloom over the rest, which I tried in vain to remove, by repeated assurances that the distance to Fort Enterprise was short, and that we should, in all probability, reach it in four days. Not being able to find any *tripe de roche*, we drank an infusion of the Labrador tea plant (*ledum palustre*), and ate a few morsels of burnt leather for supper. We were unable to raise the tent, and found its weight too great to carry it on, we, therefore, cut it up, and took a part of the canvass for a cover. The night was bitterly cold, and though we lay as close to each other as possible, having no shelter, we could not keep ourselves sufficiently warm to sleep. A strong gale came on after midnight, which increased the severity of the weather. In the morning Belanger and Michel renewed their request to be permitted to go back to the tent, assuring me they were still weaker than on the preceding evening, and less capable of going forward; and they urged, that the stopping at a place where there was a supply of *tripe de roche* was their only chance of preserving life . . .

Scarcely were these arrangements finished, before Perrault and Fontano were seized with a fit of dizziness, and betrayed other symptoms of extreme debility. Some tea was quickly prepared for them, and after drinking it, and eating a few morsels of burnt leather, they recovered, and expressed their desire to go forward; but the other men, alarmed at what they had just witnessed, became doubtful of their own strength, and, giving way to absolute dejection, declared their inability to move. I now earnestly pressed upon them the necessity of continuing our journey, as the only means of saving their own lives, as well as those of our friends at the tent; and, after much entreaty, got them to set out at ten a.m.: Belanger and Michel were left at the encampment, and proposed to start shortly afterwards. By the time we had gone about two hundred yards, Perrault became again dizzy, and desired us to halt, which we did, until he, recovering, offered to march on. Ten minutes more had hardly elapsed before he again desired us to stop, and, bursting into tears, declared he was totally exhausted, and unable to accompany us further. As the encampment was not more than a quarter of a mile distant, we recommended that he should return to it, and rejoin Belanger and Michel, whom we knew to be still there, from perceiving the smoke of a fresh fire . . .

The party was now reduced to five persons, Adam, Peltier, Benoit, Samandrè, and myself. Continuing the journey, we came, after an hour's walk, to some willows, and encamped under the shelter of a rock, having walked in the whole four miles and a half. We made an attempt to gather some *tripe de roche*, but could not, owing to the severity of the weather. Our supper, therefore, consisted of tea and a few morsels of leather . . .

Next morning [9 October] the breeze was light and the weather mild, which enabled us to collect some *tripe de roche*, and to enjoy the only meal we had had for four days. We derived great benefit from it, and walked with considerably more ease than yesterday. Without the strength it supplied, we should certainly have been unable to oppose the strong breeze we met in the afternoon . . .

[11 October] At length we reached Fort Enterprise, and to our infinite disappointment and grief found it a perfectly desolate habitation. There was no deposit of provision, no trace of the Indians, no letter from Mr Wentzel to point out where the Indians might be found. It would be impossible to describe our sensations after entering this miserable abode, and discovering how we had been neglected: the whole party shed tears, not so much for our own fate, as for that of our friends in the rear, whose lives depended entirely on our sending immediate relief from this place.

I found a note, however, from Mr Back, stating that he had reached the house two days before, and was going in search of the Indians, at a part where St Germain deemed it probable they might be found . . .

[12 October] When I arose the following morning, my body and limbs were so swollen that I was unable to walk more than a few yards. Adam was in a still worse condition, being absolutely incapable of rising without assistance. My other companions happily experienced this inconvenience in a less degree, and went to collect bones, and some *tripe de roche*, which supplied us with two meals. The bones were quite acrid, and the soup extracted from them excoriated the mouth if taken alone, but it was somewhat milder when boiled with *tripe de roche*, and we even thought the mixture palatable, with the addition of salt, of which a cask had been fortunately left here in the spring. Augustus to-day set two fishing lines below the rapid. On his way thither he saw two deer, but had not strength to follow them.

On the 13th the wind blew violently from south-east, and the snow drifted so much that the party were confined to the house. In the afternoon of the following day Belanger arrived with a note from Mr Back, stating that he had seen no trace of the Indians, and desiring further instructions as to the course he should pursue. Belanger's situation, however, required our first care, as he came in almost speechless, and covered with ice, having fallen into a rapid, and, for the third time since we left the coast, narrowly escaped drowning. He did not recover sufficiently to answer our questions, until we had rubbed him for some time, changed his dress, and given him some warm soup. My companions nursed him with the greatest kindness, and the desire of restoring him to health, seemed to absorb all regard for their own situation. I witnessed with peculiar pleasure this conduct so different from that which they had recently pursued, when every tender feeling was suspended by the desire of self-preservation. They now no longer betrayed impatience or despondency, but were composed and cheerful, and had entirely given up the practice of swearing, to which the Canadian voyagers are so addicted.

I undertook the office of cooking, and insisted they should eat twice a day whenever food could be procured; but as I was too weak to pound the bones, Peltier agreed to do that in addition to his more fatiguing task of getting wood. We had a violent snow storm all the next day, and this gloomy weather increased the depression of spirits under which Adam and Samandrè were labouring. Neither of them would quit their beds, and they scarcely ceased from shedding tears all day; in vain did Peltier and myself endeavour to cheer them. We had even to use much entreaty before they would take the meals we had prepared for them. Our situation was indeed distressing, but in comparison with that of our friends in the rear, we thought it happy. Their condition gave us unceasing solicitude, and was the principal subject of our conversation . . .

[26 October] We perceived our strength decline every day, and every exertion began to be irksome; when we were once seated the greatest effort was necessary in order to rise, and we had frequently to lift each other from our seats; but even in this pitiable condition we conversed cheerfully, being sanguine as to the speedy arrival of the Indians. We calculated indeed that if they should be near the situation where they had remained last winter, our men would have reached them by this day.

Narrative of a Journey to the Shores of the Polar Sea, 1823

IDA PFEIFFER

1797–1858

*Should death surprise me in my wanderings, I shall meet it with calmness,
thanking God from my inmost heart for the blessed, happy hours I spent in
admiring the wonders of his creation.*

Born in Vienna as Ida Reyer, she was raised in
the same way as her brothers – encouraged to
dress like them and join in strenuous outdoor
activities. Only at the age of forty-five, having
separated from her much older husband, was
she free to travel – and this she did, alone and
with little money, choosing the Holy Land as
a first destination, knowing that a 'pilgrimage' would meet with less disapproval from
family and friends. Encouraged by the success
of her trip and her published account, she
used the proceeds to finance another trip, this
time to Iceland.

The island wasn't at all to her taste. During
the six months she spent pottering about,
writing observations and bagging samples of
plants and rocks for sale to museums, she
found the locals dirty and vulgar, their fish-
and-porridge diet exceedingly bland.

Later, she made extensive travels around
the globe, continually disregarding the advice
of consuls and acknowledged experts worried
for her safety. Her greatest contribution to
ethnology stemmed from her visit to the
Bataks of northern Sumatra, who had excited
the Victorian imagination because they were
known as cannibals. Perhaps the first European to integrate with them, she brought out
the earliest report on the Batak way of life.
Her *A Lady's Second Journey Around the
World* was a best-seller.

In the following extract we find Pfeiffer
travelling unlike other visitors, alone and
on pony carts, and providing an intimate
view of the then unknown lives of ordinary
Icelanders.

A dangerous ride

My hostess, who was the widow of a wealthy peasant, presented to me her
four children, who were very good looking and neatly dressed. I begged
the mother to tell me what she called her little ones, that I might be able
to mention some Iceland names when I returned to my own country. She
was very much pleased with my request and named them to me as follows:
Sigridur, Gudrun, Ingebör and Lars.

I could have made myself very comfortable here, as I always endeavor to do,
whatever my accommodations may happen to be, if I could only have been
left alone; but to my great annoyance, every inhabitant, not only of this hut,
but of all the others in the place, gathered round me one by one; and station-
ing themselves, some in my own room and some in the adjoining one, I found
myself besieged even more closely than I had been at Krisuvick. There was
something about my appearance entirely new to the people, who stared at me

with untiring earnestness. The women soon became sufficiently familiar to touch my dress and feel every article I had on; while the children laid their dirty faces in my lap. The horrible uncleanliness of this crowd of people, their offensive perspiration, their perpetual snuff-taking (*without* pocket-handkerchiefs), their continual spitting – ah! it was truly fearful! I suffered more from these visits than from the longest fast; though that was a kind of penance to which I was often obliged to submit, for I could never taste any thing that was set before me during my travels throughout the whole country; and in fact the Iceland peasant has little to offer in the way of cookery but dried fish and sour milk, the latter often several months old; on very rare occasions they have grits, or unraised bread made of powdered Iceland moss.

I found that most of these people supposed me to possees a degree of information which is generally to be found only among men; apparently they thought the women of foreign countries must necessarily be as learned as the other sex. The priests always inquired if I spoke Latin, and seemed struck with astonishment when I replied in the negative. The common people consulted me for all manner of troubles; and once when I went into a hut during one of my solitary rambles near Reikjavick, I was led to an object which I should hardly have known for a human being; it was one of those wretched sufferers from the leprous eruption, whose whole body, as well as his head and face, was covered with sores and boils, and almost wasted to a skeleton from the effects of the disease. Such a spectacle might have been interesting to a physician, but I turned from it with horror.

Enough of this revolting picture! Let me rather describe an angel's head I saw at Kalmannstunga – a child of ten or twelve years old – so inexpressibly sweet and lovely that I could not but wish myself a painter to carry back to my native country, at least on canvas, that soft countenance, with its expressive eyes and beautiful dimples. But perhaps it is best as it is; a malicious fate might have thrown the portrait into the hands of some susceptible youth, whose too tender feelings would perhaps have prompted him to undertake a pilgrimage through the world – like Don Sylvio de Rosalba, in Wieland's Comic Novel – in search of the enchanting original. It is not probable that he would ever have turned his steps towards Iceland, for who would expect to find so perfect an object in that remote quarter of the globe? and thus the unhappy lover would have been doomed to wander forever, and be forever disappointed.

June 20th – The distance from Kalmannstunga to Thingvalla is eleven miles, and it is one of the worst and most fatiguing roads in Iceland, through dreary plains, shut in by high hills and jokuls. Wherever the traveller turns his eye it is met by a chilled and lifeless nature; he hastens anxiously through the barren wilderness, and eagerly climbs one eminence after another, in the hope of seeing some improvement in the scene, but in vain; he beholds the same waste – the same desolation – the same hills.

We found many places on the table-lands still covered with snow, which we were obliged to cross although we heard the waters rushing beneath; and the icy crusts over which we rode were often thin and soft under the horses' feet and of that light blue shade which is a symptom of danger. The horses frequently resisted with all their might before they could be driven across by hard blows. The pack-horse was cudgelled till he led the way; my guide followed, and I was the last. The poor animals often sank to their knees in the snow, and twice they went in above their saddle-girths. This was the most dangerous road I had ever travelled; my constant thought was what I should do if my guide were to sink in so deep that he could not extricate himself; I was not strong enough to offer him any assistance, and where should I turn for help in this desert? I might wander about in search of a human habitation, or in the hope of meeting with a fellow-being, till I perished with hunger, or was lost in the wilderness without a chance of escape. I approached every snow-field we were obliged to cross with feelings of intense anxiety, of which those only who have been placed in a similar situation can form any idea. If I had been in a large company my alarm would not have been so great; for, relying on the assistance of my companions, the peril would doubtless have appeared much less imminent.

This road should only be used when the snow affords a secure footing. We did not see a track of man or beast; and we were the only living creatures who traversed this region. I found great fault with my guide for having led me into so much danger; but it was then too late, for it was equally hazardous to advance or retreat.

To increase my troubles there was a change in the weather, which till to-day had been very pleasant. The heavens were clouded when we left Kalmannstunga, and we only caught an occasional glimpse of the sun; but when we reached the heights we were completely enveloped in the mists and clouds, and an icy wind from the neighboring glaciers was soon accompanied by torrents of rain. We had already ridden thirteen hours, and as we were nearly stiffened by the wet and the cold, I made up my mind to stop at the first hovel we came to; we found one, at last, about half a mile from Thingvalla; where I was under cover, it is true, though in other respects my situation was very little improved. The hut contained but a single room, with four large beds in it, which must have been occupied by the seven grown persons and three children who seemed to compose the household.

Unfortunately, a kind of influenza, called the *Kvef*, prevailed all over the country this season, and I found every inmate of this hut suffering from its effects; there was a constant hacking and coughing, and the floor was actually slippery from the incessant expectorations.

These poor people were so good as to offer me immediately one of their beds; but rather than spend the night in the midst of so much filth, I would have remained seated on the door-sill till morning. I preferred to convert the narrow passage leading from the kitchen to the dwelling-room into a sleeping apartment; it contained a rude shelf where the milk-pans were kept; and borrowing a blanket from the invalids in the next room (my own cloak being too wet to be of any service to me), I stretched myself upon it and feigned to compose myself to rest, in hopes of getting rid of the company of any curious hosts. After a while they left me alone, but I could not sleep; I was still damp and chilled from my long exposure to the storm, and the cold wind poured down upon me from the air-holes in the roof; for this little passage, among the many purposes to which it was applied, was also used as a smoke-house; and I suffered the greatest annoyance from a long pole directly over my head, where the fish were hung up to dry, and which I was apt to forget, till I had fully satisfied myself of its existence by at least half a dozen hard knocks whenever I attempted to sit up in my comfortless bed.

A Journey to Iceland, and Travels in Sweden and Norway, 1852

Kate Marsden
1859–1931

But those lepers – they suffered far more than I suffered, and that was the one thought, added to the strength which God supplied, that kept me from collapsing entirely.

Kate Marsden encountered the horrors of leprosy in Bulgaria in 1878, while tending the casualties of the Russo-Turkish war, and was so moved that in February 1891, having secured the patronage of Queen Victoria, the Princess of Wales and the Russian Tsarina Marya, she set out with dog sledges on a 2,000-mile journey across the Siberian tundra to the leper colonies in Yakutsk. Her mission was to find a herb that purportedly cured leprosy. She completed her journey in eleven months, but failed to find the herb. On her return to England she followed in the footsteps of Isabella Bird (see page 684) by delivering a lecture to the Royal Geographical Society and was elected to its fellowship; she was among the first women to earn this honour.

Her gloriously entitled, *On Sledge and Horseback to Outcast Siberian Lepers*, is surely one of the greatest accounts of any missionary traveller – a sprightly tale, with only a sprinkling of the earnest judgement that characterizes the genre. However, she later felt the need to write a 'vindication' to prove to her critics the whole journey had been worthwhile – indeed, hadn't been a complete hoax. The truth was that the arduous expedition had actually badly damaged her already poor health, and for the remainder of her life she was an invalid.

Through mosquito marshes to the lepers

More bogs and marshes for several miles; and then I grew so sleepy and sick that I begged for rest, notwithstanding our position on semi-marshy ground, which had not as yet dried from the heat of the summer sun. I was asleep in five minutes, lying on the damp ground with only a fan to shelter me from the sun.

On again for a few more miles; but I began to feel the effects of this sort of travelling – in a word, I felt utterly worn out. It was as much as I could do to hold on to the horse, and I nearly tumbled off several times in the effort. The cramp in my body and lower limbs was indescribable, and I had to discard the cushion under me, because it became soaked through and through with the rain, and rode on the broad, bare, wooden saddle. What feelings of relief arose when the time of rest came, and the pitching of tents, and the brewing of tea! Often I slept quite soundly till morning, awaking to find that the mosquitoes had been hard at work in my slumbers, in spite of veil and gloves, leaving great itching lumps, that turned me sick. Once we saw two calves that had died from exhaustion from the bites of these pests, and the white hair of our poor horses was generally covered with clots of blood, due partly to mosquitoes and partly to prodigious horse-flies. But those lepers – they suffered far more than I suffered, and that was the one thought, added to the strength which God supplied, that kept me from collapsing entirely.

Sometimes we rested all day, and travelled at night to avoid the intense heat. We passed forests, where hundreds of trees had fallen. According to popular superstition, the Yakut witches quarrelled, and met in the forest to fight out the dispute. But the spirit of the forest became so angry at this conduct that he let loose a band of inferior spirits; and then, in a moment, a tempest began and rushed through the forest, tearing up the trees and causing them to fall in the direction of those disputants who were in the right. But the true meaning of those fallen trees is yet more interesting and singular than the superstitious one. Underneath the upper soil of these forests combustion goes on, beginning in the winter. The thaw of summer and the deluge of rain seem to have little effect upon the fire, for it still works its way unsubdued. When the tempest comes the trees drop by hundreds, having but slight power of resistance. I brought home with me some of this burnt earth, intending to send it to the British Museum, should no specimen be already there.

My second thunderstorm was far worse than the first. The forest seemed on fire, and the rain dashed in our faces with almost blinding force. My horse plunged and reared, flew first to one side, and then to the other, dragging me amongst bushes and trees, so that I was in danger of being caught by the branches and hurled to the ground. After this storm one of the horses, carrying stores and other things, sank into a bog nearly to its neck; and the help of all the men was required to get it out . . .

Soon after the storm we were camping and drinking tea, when I noticed that all the men were eagerly talking together and gesticulating. I asked the tchinovnick what it all meant, and was told that a large bear was supposed to be in the neighbourhood, according to a report from a post-station close at hand. There was a general priming of fire-arms, except in my case, for I did not know how to use my revolver, so thought I had better pass it on to some one else, lest I might shoot a man in mistake for a bear. We mounted again and went on. The usual chattering this time was exchanged for a dead silence, this being our first bear experience; but we grew wiser as we proceeded, and substituted noise for silence. We hurried on, as fast as possible, to get through the miles of forests and bogs. I found it best not to look about me, because, when I did so, every large stump of a fallen tree took the shape of a bear. When my horse stumbled over the roots of a tree, or shied at some object unseen by me, my heart began to gallop. However, all our preparations were wasted, for the bear remained conspicuous by his absence; and, when the danger was passed, we all became very brave and talkative. We had a few simple devices for scaring away bears as we rode through the forest later on. The men used to sing and shout their hardest; bells were placed on some of the horses, and we had tin boxes half filled with stones in one hand, which we continually shook, thus making a great clattering noise.

I can just imagine how some brave bear-hunter will laugh in his sleeve, as he reads this simple mode of keeping off the ferocious creatures, which had just woke up ravenous from their winter's sleep. But, you see, we were not hunting for bears, but searching for lepers, which makes all the difference in the world. At one point some natives told us they had just seen eleven bears; but happily, although we noticed significant foot-marks, we saw none of the fraternity. Sometimes I almost felt I would rather be eaten by bears than endure the terrific clatter and noise made by the cavalcade.

Some of the natives in these wild parts eat the bark of trees mixed with milk, and now and then fish or birds. Bread, even black bread, to many is an unknown luxury. Milk is often sold in blocks; fish, meat – in fact everything – is frozen.

The burial of a native in winter is a long process. The ground has first to be thawed by placing fires upon it for three days and nights. Those who are buried at this season remain frozen always, and their bodies continue in good preservation for hundreds of years . . .

We passed several graves on our way, some of them containing, so I was told, the bodies of murdered people. When I looked upon those little mounds, I half wished that I, too, was at rest. There is a point of exhaustion reached at times when one wishes for nothing else than complete unconsciousness.

Whenever I was not too tired, I made rough entries in my journal before going to sleep, and sometimes suggestions, as they occurred to me, for the leper hospital or colony that I had in my heart. But when constant pain brought on fits of depression, I felt that I should never live to carry out any of my cherished plans. But these were only momentary weaknesses, for the very dangers and difficulties I was going through without serious accident proved so clearly that God's loving arm was around me, shielding and protecting me, and would surely lead me in safety to the end of my work . . .

After a long ride we came to nine more lepers, whose condition was worse than any I had seen. Two women, one man of about forty, and two children were naked, having no clothes whatever; and, with the exception of a few rags, they are in the same state in the winter. During the months of biting frost, all the covering they had was hay and rags. As I sat there amongst them, the flies were tormenting their festering wounds, and some of the outcasts writhed in agony. I do not wonder at being told that it was impossible to reach the lepers, for this was another settlement hidden away in the forest, with no path or communication of any kind to other places. There were traces of a bear here, and I began to wonder why some of these lepers did not, in their desperation, throw themselves in the way of the bears, and so end their miseries.

As we again mounted our horses, the Yakuts, who had kept far off from the lepers for fear of contagion, hurried on the animals in order to get away from the place as quickly as possible. As we rode forward in the darkness, the faces of those poor creatures haunted me; whilst now and then an owl hooted, or a savage rat darted at my horse, making him plunge and struggle. We kept stumbling into holes and over roots of trees, and it was as much as a tired, aching woman could do to keep her seat. Then two of the horses took fright; and, all the horses being tied in single file by tail and bridle, the whole cavalcade rushed along full tilt into the darkness, and we were simply at God's mercy. When we went steadily again, and silence reigned around, how my full heart was lifted up to God! When going at full speed, the horses would suddenly stop; then a wild goose would screech and flutter his wings, and on we would tear again.

At another place I found a yourta, too small even for one man, containing a man, two women, and a child. One of the women had been afflicted with leprosy in all its worst aspects for years; she was almost naked, having only a dirty strip of leather over her. By her side was her husband, who, although free from leprosy, nobly determined to share his wife's exile. Her child, too, preferred to accompany her mother rather than remain with the tribe. Neither husband nor child will ever be allowed to enter the community again. Close by was a woman who had just been confined. And there were also two children here, born of lepers, born to live amongst lepers, and doomed most likely to become lepers, either from contagion or hereditary taint. Surely some definite steps ought to be taken to alter this state of things. According to Medical Inspector Smirnoff's report, who had visited the lepers three months before me, he had ordered the separation of the men and women to be carried out. But, however, when I was there, I found them all together again.

On Sledge and Horseback to Outcast Siberian Lepers, 1893

Fridtjof Nansen

1861–1930

*Yet death must come one day, and the hour of our departure could
scarcely be more glorious.*

In 1888 the Norwegian explorers Fridtjof
Nansen and Otto Sverdrup crossed Greenland
from east to west, but Nansen is particularly
remembered for his 1893–6 expedition, an
attempt to demonstrate that currents moved
westward across the Arctic – one that resulted
in a dramatic bid for the North Pole and an
even more dramatic trek to safety afterwards.

Nansen had learnt how, after the *Jeannette*,
a vessel under the command of an American,
De Long, had sunk in 1881 near Wrangel
Island, not far from the Bering Strait, its
remains had drifted towards the North Pole
for two years, eventually appearing on the
other side, off Greenland, 2,900 nautical miles
away. 'It immediately occurred to me that
here lay the route ready to hand.' He deliberately took his ship, the *Fram*, into the pack
ice, hoping it might take him within reach of
the pole as it passed by; in March 1895 Nansen
abandoned the *Fram* and made a dash for the
Pole with one companion, Hjalmar Johansen,
and twenty-eight dogs. After twenty-three
days, they were only 240 miles from the Pole –
a farthest north record – but the ice proved
too difficult to negotiate and they were forced
to retreat. After a further four months, they
reached Franz Josef Land and dug themselves
in for the winter. They survived by using Inuit
skills, building a stone hut with tools made
out of walrus tusks, using walrus blubber for
lighting, and hunting bears for food and
clothing.

In May 1896, they set off again and soon
ran into a British expedition led by Frederick
Jackson, who got them out safely. A week after
they arrived home, having been away for
three years, the *Fram* was released from the
ice at Svalbard, having drifted near the Pole,
as Nansen had predicted.

Nansen's emphasis on adapting techniques
developed by the Inuit, whether with regard
to food provision, clothing or travel, was an
important example for later explorers; his
detailed scientific observations of temperature, flow and salinity filled six bulky volumes
and gave us a first insight into the pattern of
Arctic currents.

Later in life, Nansen became a distinguished diplomat and, in 1922, was
awarded the Nobel Peace Prize for his relief
work after the Russian Revolution. He also
became something of a mentor to all polar
explorers of the era: Amundsen borrowed his
Fram for his successful attempt on the South
Pole; Shackleton and Scott also consulted
him, the latter disregarding his advice to place
his faith in dogs, an arrogance that cost him
not only the race to the Pole, but the lives of
five men, including himself.

Nansen was unusual among the racing
polar explorers: big-hearted in his dealings
with rivals, he always had an eye for the
much wider picture. He came to think that
Western contact, and the church in particular, had a negative impact on the Inuit, and
formally left the Norwegian State Church.
Eskimo Life, a detailed look at Inuit character
and society, was also a eulogy in many ways:
'. . . Morality will then have so far developed
that men will no longer consider themselves
justified in swooping down upon the first
primitive people that come their way, in
order to satisfy their own religious vanity
and to do "good works" which shall minister
to their self-complacency, but which may or
may not be beneficial to the race in
question.'

To the accounts by Nansen I've appended
one by British-born Frederick G. Jackson

(1860–1938), leader of the three-year Jackson–Harmsworth Arctic expedition to Franz Josef Land. It was this expedition that Nansen stumbled across on 17 June 1896, after a year and a half on the ice – Jackson had been based only ninety-three miles from where Nansen had survived the long winter in his home-made blubber-heated stone shelter. It's that rare thing, an unpolished account – 'word for word from my journal' – which honestly and charmingly depicts the everyday Nansen, everyday Arctic summer and the everyday lot of an explorer – what to name those newly discovered lands, where to take those crucial publicity photos. Unknown to both, one dark cloud flickers briefly over this strange chapter.

Jackson notes that he 'strongly advised' Nansen that, should he attempt the South Pole, he should use horses. Here was a Brit steadfastly advocating an untested method to someone who had just completed one of the greatest feats in the history of polar exploration. It was almost a rehearsal for the Scott–Nansen conversation of fourteen years later. Horses were the means of transport that Robert Scott chose to rely on, despite Nansen encouraging him to use dogs.

A favourite of modern polar explorers, in his day Nansen towered over all other pioneers of the 'Heroic Age', though he himself never went 'south'. In many ways he is simply *the* polar man.

Struggling towards the Pole with dogs

After supper we generally permitted ourselves the luxury of a little extra drink, consisting of water, as hot as we could swallow it, in which whey-powder had been dissolved. It tasted something like boiled milk, and we thought it wonderfully comforting; it seemed to warm us to the very ends of our toes. Then we would creep down into the bag again, buckle the flap carefully over our heads, lie close together, and soon sleep the sleep of the just. But even in our dreams we went on ceaselessly, grinding at the sledges and driving the dogs, always northwards, and I was often awakened by hearing Johansen calling in his sleep to 'Pan,' or 'Barrabas,' or 'Klapperslangen': 'Get on, you devil, you! Go on, you brutes! Sass, sass! Now the whole thing is going over!' and execrations less fit for reproduction, until I went to sleep again.

In the morning, as cook, I was obliged to turn out to prepare the breakfast, which took an hour's time. As a rule, it consisted one morning of chocolate, bread, butter, and pemmican; another of oatmeal porridge, or a compound of flour, water, and butter, in imitation of our 'butter-porridge' at home. This was washed down with milk, made of whey-powder and water. The breakfast ready, Johansen was roused; we sat up in the sleeping-bag, one of the blankets was spread out as a table-cloth, and we fell to work. We had a comfortable breakfast, wrote up our diaries, and then had to think about starting. But how tired we sometimes were, and how often would I not have given anything to be able to creep to the bottom of the bag again and sleep the clock round. It seemed to me as if this must be the greatest pleasure in life, but our business was to fight our way northwards, always northwards. We performed our toilets, and then came the going out into the cold to get the sledges ready, disentangle the dogs' traces, harness the animals, and get off as quickly as possible. I went first to find the way through the uneven ice, then came the sledge with my kayak. The dogs soon learned to follow, but at every unevenness of the ground they stopped, and if one could not get them all to start again at the same time by a shout, and so pull the sledge over the difficulty, one had to go back to beat or help them, according as circumstances necessitated. Then came Johansen with the two other sledges, always shouting to the dogs to pull harder, always beating them, and himself hauling to get the sledges over the terrible ridges of ice. It was undeniable cruelty to the poor animals from first to last, and one must often look back on it with horror. It makes me shudder even now when I think of how we beat them mercilessly with thick ash sticks when, hardly able to move, they stopped from sheer exhaustion. It made one's heart bleed to see them, but we turned our eyes away and hardened ourselves. It was necessary; forward we must go, and to this end everything else must give place. It is the sad part of expeditions of this kind that one systematically kills all better feelings, until only hard-hearted egoism remains. When I think of all those splendid animals, toiling for us without a murmur, as long as they could strain a muscle, never getting any thanks or even so much as a kind word, daily writhing under the lash until the time came when they could do no more and death freed them from their pangs – when I think of how they were left behind, one by one, up there on those desolate ice-fields, which had been witness to their faithfulness and devotion, I have moments of bitter self-reproach.

Christmas dreams

Thursday, December 19th: −28.5° (19.3° below zero Fahr.). It has turned cold again, and is bitter weather to be out in. But what does it signify? We are comfortable and warm in here, and do not need to go out more than we like. All the out-of-door work we have is to bring in fresh and salt water ice two or three times a week, meat and blubber now and again, and very occasionally a skin to dry under the roof. And Christmas, the season of rejoicing, is drawing near. At home every one is busy now, scarcely knowing how to get time for everything; but here there is no bustle; all we want is to make the time pass. Ah, to sleep, sleep! The pot is simmering pleasantly over the hearth; I am sitting waiting for breakfast, and gazing into the flickering flames, while my thoughts travel far away. What is the strange power in fire and light that all created beings seek them, from the primary lump of protoplasm in the sea, to the roving child of man, who stops in his wanderings, makes up a fire in the wood, and sits down to dismiss all care, and revel in the crackling warmth. Involuntarily do these snake-like, fiery tongues arrest the eye; you gaze down into them as if you could read your fate there, and memories glide past in motley train. What, then, is privation? what the present? Forget it, forget yourself; you have the power to recall all that is beautiful, and then wait for the summer . . . By the light of the lamp she sits sewing in the winter evening. Beside her stands a little maiden with blue eyes and golden hair, playing with a doll. She looks tenderly at the child, and strokes her hair; but her eyes fill, and the big tears fall upon her work.

Johansen is lying beside me asleep; he smiles in his sleep. Poor fellow! he must be dreaming he is at home at Christmas time with those he loves. But sleep on – sleep and dream, while the winter passes; for then comes spring – the spring of life.

Sunday, December 22nd: The northern lights were wonderful. However often we see this weird play of light, we never tire of gazing at it; it seems to cast a spell over both sight and sense till it is impossible to tear oneself away. It begins to dawn with a pale, yellow, spectral light behind the mountain in the east, like the reflection of a fire far away. It broadens, and soon the whole of the eastern sky is one glowing mass of fire. Now it fades again, and gathers in a brightly luminous belt of mist stretching towards the south-west, with only a few patches of luminous haze visible here and there. After a while, scattered rays suddenly shoot up from the fiery mist almost reaching to the zenith; then more; they play over the belt in a wild chase from east to west. They seem to be always darting nearer from a long, long way off. But suddenly a perfect veil of rays showers from the zenith out over the northern sky; they are so fine and bright, like the finest of glittering silver threads. Is it the fire-giant Surt himself, striking his mighty silver harp, so that the strings tremble and sparkle in the glow of the flames of Muspelheim? Yes, it is harp music, wildly storming in the darkness; it is the riotous war-dance of Surt's sons. And again, at times, it is like softly playing, gently-rocking, silvery waves, on which dreams travel into unknown worlds . . .

Retreating, with kayaks

As we were paddling along through some small bits of ice my kayak suddenly received a violent shock from underneath. I looked round in amazement as I had not noticed any large piece of ice hereabouts. There was nothing of the kind to be seen either, but worse enemies were about. No sooner had I glanced down than I saw a huge walrus cleaving through the water astern, and it suddenly came up, raised itself and stood on end just before Johansen, who was following in my wake. Afraid lest the animal should have its tusks through the deck of his craft the next minute, he backed as hard as he could and felt for his gun, which he had down in the kayak. I was not long either in pulling my gun out of its cover. The animal crashed snorting into the water again, however, dived under Johansen's kayak, and came up just behind him. Johansen, thinking he had had enough of such a neighbour, scrambled incontinently on to the floe nearest him. After having waited a while, with my gun ready for the walrus to come up close by me, I followed his example. I very nearly came in for the cold bath which the walrus had omitted to give me, for the edge of the ice gave way just as I set my foot on it, and the kayak drifted off with me standing upright in it, and trying to balance it as best I could, in order not to capsize. If the walrus had reappeared at that moment, I should certainly have received it in its own element. Finally, I succeeded in getting up on to the ice, and for a long time afterwards the walrus swam round and round our floe, where we made the best of the situation by having dinner. Sometimes it was near Johansen's kayak, sometimes near mine. We could see how it darted about in the water under the kayaks, and it had evidently the greatest desire to attack us again. We thought of giving it a ball to get rid of it, but had no great wish to part with a cartridge, and besides it only showed us its nose and forehead, which are not exactly the most vital spots to aim at when one's object is to kill with one shot. It was a great ox-walrus. There is something remarkably fantastic and pre-historic about these monsters. I could not help thinking of a merman, or something of the kind, as it lay there just under the surface of the water blowing and snorting for quite a long while at a time, and glaring at us with its round glassy eyes. After having continued in this way for some time, it disappeared just as tracklessly as it had come; and as we had finished our dinner, we were able to go on our way again, glad, a second time, not to have been upset, or destroyed by its tusks . . .

[Nearing open water, the men lashed together their kayaks and rigged up a sail.]

In the evening we put in to the edge of the ice, so as to stretch our legs a little; they were stiff with sitting in the kayak all day, and we wanted to get a little view over the water to the west, by ascending a hummock. As we went ashore the question arose as to how we should moor our precious vessel. 'Take one of the braces,' said Johansen; he was standing on the ice. 'But is it strong

enough?' 'Yes,' he answered; 'I have used it as a halyard on my sledge-sail all
the time.' 'Oh, well, it doesn't require much to hold these light kayaks,' said I,
a little ashamed of having been so timid, and I moored them with the halyard,
which was a strap cut from a raw walrus-hide. We had been on the ice a little
while, moving up and down close to the kayaks. The wind had dropped
considerably, and seemed to be more westerly, making it doubtful whether we
could make use of it any longer, and we went up on to a hummock close by to
ascertain this better. As we stood there, Johansen suddenly cried: 'I say! the
kayaks are adrift!' We ran down as hard as we could. They were already a little
way out, and were drifting quickly off; the painter had given way. 'Here, take
my watch!' I said to Johansen, giving it to him; and as quickly as possible I
threw off some clothing, so as to be able to swim more easily: I did not dare to
take everything off, as I might so easily get cramp. I sprang into the water, but
the wind was off the ice, and the light kayaks, with their high rigging, gave it a
good hold. They were already well out, and were drifting rapidly. The water
was icy cold, it was hard work swimming with clothes on, and the kayaks
drifted farther and farther, often quicker than I could swim. It seemed more
than doubtful whether I could manage it. But all our hope was drifting there;
all we possessed was on board; we had not even a knife with us; and whether I
got cramp and sank here, or turned back without the kayaks, it would come to
pretty much the same thing; so I exerted myself to the utmost. When I got
tired I turned over, and swam on my back, and then I could see Johansen
walking restlessly up and down on the ice. Poor lad! He could not stand still,
and thought it dreadful not to be able to do anything. He had not much hope
that I could do it, but it would not improve matters in the least if he threw
himself into the water too. He said afterwards that these were the worst
moments he had ever lived through. But when I turned over again, and saw
that I was nearer the kayaks, my courage rose, and I redoubled my exertions. I
felt, however, that my limbs were gradually stiffening and losing all feeling,
and I knew that in a short time I should not be able to move them. But there
was not far to go now; if I could only hold out a little longer, we should be
saved – and I went on. The strokes became more and more feeble, but the
distance became shorter and shorter, and I began to think I should reach the
kayaks. At last I was able to stretch out my hand to the snowshoe, which lay
across the sterns; I grasped it, pulled myself in to the edge of the kayak – and
we were saved. I tried to pull myself up, but the whole of my body was so stiff
with cold, that this was an impossibility. For a moment I thought that after all
it was too late; I was to get so far, but not be able to get in. After a little,
however, I managed to swing one leg up on to the edge of the sledge which lay

on the deck, and in this way managed to tumble up. There I sat, but so stiff with cold, that I had difficulty in paddling. Nor was it easy to paddle in the double vessel, where I first had to take one or two strokes on one side, and then step into the other kayak to take a few strokes on the other side. If I had been able to separate them, and row in one while I towed the other, it would have been easy enough; but I could not undertake that piece of work, for I should have been stiff before it was done; the thing to be done was to keep warm by rowing as hard as I could. The cold had robbed my whole body of feeling, but when the gusts of wind came they seemed to go right through me as I stood there in my thin, wet woollen shirt. I shivered, my teeth chattered, and I was numb almost all over; but I could still use the paddle, and I should get warm when I got back on to the ice again. Two auks were lying close to the bow, and the thought of having auk for supper was too tempting; we were in want of food now. I got hold of my gun, and shot them with one discharge.

Johansen said afterwards that he started at the report, thinking some accident had happened, and could not understand what I was about out there, but when he saw me paddle and pick up two birds he thought I had gone out of my mind. At last I managed to reach the edge of the ice, but the current had driven me a long way from our landing-place. Johansen came along the edge of the ice, jumped into the kayak beside me, and we soon got back to our place. I was undeniably a good deal exhausted, and could barely manage to crawl on land. I could scarcely stand, and while I shook and trembled all over Johansen had to pull off the wet things I had on, put on the few dry ones I still had in reserve, and spread the sleeping-bag out upon the ice. I packed myself well into it, and he covered me with the sail and everything he could find to keep out the cold air. There I lay shivering for a long time, but gradually the warmth began to return to my body. For some time longer, however, my feet had no more feeling in them than icicles, for they had been partly naked in the water. While Johansen put up the tent and prepared supper, consisting of my two auks, I fell asleep. He let me sleep quietly, and when I awoke, supper had been ready for some time, and stood simmering over the fire. Auk and hot soup soon effaced the last traces of my swim. During the night my clothes were hung out to dry, and the next day were all nearly dry again.

Farthest North, 1897

Jackson's account of meeting with Nansen

Just after dinner Armitage came rushing in to tell me that through his field-glass he could see a man on the floe to the S.S.E. of Cape Flora, about four miles off. I could hardly believe it, such a thing seemed utterly impossible, and thought he had mistaken a walrus on the ice for a man; but having got a glass I could see he was correct. I could also make out somewhat indistinctly a staff or mast, with another man apparently standing near it close to the water's edge. It occurred then to me that it might be one of my own men, although they had all been at dinner a few minutes before, but I however found that all were present. I got a gun with all speed and firing off a shot on the bank to endeavour to arrest the stranger's attention, I started off to meet him coming across the ice, having placed Armitage on the roof of the hut to direct my course, as the high hummocky ice hid him from me when I got down upon the floe. On nearer approach I shouted to him and waved my cap. I thought at first that some accident had happened to the *Windward*, which had started earlier than I expected, and that this man had come off in a boat from her to communicate with us.

On our approaching each other about three miles distant from the land, I saw a tall man on ski with roughly made clothes and an old felt hat on his head. He was covered with oil and grease, and black from head to foot. I at once concluded from his wearing ski that he was no English sailor but that he must be a man from some Norwegian walrus sloop who had come to grief, and wintered somewhere on Franz Joseph Land, in very rough circumstances.

His hair was very long and dirty, his complexion appeared to be fair, but dirt prevented me from being sure on the point, and his beard was straggly and dirty also.

We shook hands heartily and I expressed the greatest pleasure at seeing him. I inquired if he had a ship? 'No,' he replied, 'my ship is not here' – rather sadly I thought – and then he remarked, in reply to my question, that he had only one companion who was at the floe edge.

It then struck me that his features, in spite of the black grease and long hair and beard resembled Nansen, whom I had met once in London before he started in 1893, and I exclaimed:

'Aren't you Nansen?'

To which he replied.

'Yes, I am Nansen.'

With much heartiness I shook him warmly by the hand and said:

'By Jove I'm d——d glad to see you,' and congratulated him on his safe arrival. Then I inquired:

'Where have you come from?'

He gave me a brief sketch of what had occurred, and replied: 'I left the *Fram* in 84° north latitude and 102° east longitude after drifting for two years, and I reached the 86° 15' parallel and have now come here.'

'I congratulate you most heartily,' I answered; 'you have made a deuced good trip of it and I am awfully glad to be the first person to congratulate you.' (Again we shook hands.)

He then gave me a brief sketch of what had occurred. How he had passed close to the New Siberian Islands; had entered the ice about the 80° north, had drifted for two years in a north-west direction to the 84° north and 102° east longitude. He had then left the ship with Lieutenant Johansen (who was taking care of two kayaks at the floe edge) and a team of dogs in March 1895. They had pushed north as far as 86° 15' 00" north latitude, 90° east longitude, and then judged it advisable to return and try to reach Spitzbergen *via* Franz Josef Land. How they had passed the previous winter on the land a little to the south of our furthest point north, reached in the spring of 1895, on an island in Cecil Rhodes Fjord (named by me). There they made a small hut of stones and walrus skins near the entrance to Gore-Booth fjord, and had come south down the British Channel and De Bruyne Sound, and round Cape Barents, and had been lying at the floe edge off here for two days . . .

I fancied by what he had said that the *Fram* was at the bottom, and that he and Lieutenant Johansen were the sole survivors. I consequently abstained from asking any further questions about the ship, and gave my fellows a hint later, not to do so, as I feared to hurt his feelings. It was not till nearly an hour had elapsed that from some remark he made I gathered that the *Fram* was all right; and that he expected her to be on her way to Norway. Owing to discrepancies in Payer's map he could not make out where he was, and they had let their watches run down, consequently could not get their longitude and tell their position. For two days they had been lying at the floe edge repairing their kayaks before we saw them.

Nansen had fancied he heard dogs barking and two gun-shots yesterday (I had fired about twenty shots at looms near the top of the talus of Cape Flora) but he had come to the conclusion that they were only noises made by the ice. He was uncertain as to the date. Finding themselves on the 80° north latitude they were pushing west, knowing that by so doing on that parallel they might hit Spitzbergen, where they hoped to fall in with a walrus sloop. After hearing the noises I have mentioned, Nansen thought he might be in the neighbourhood of Eira harbour, and that I might be there, as he knew something of my plans of going to Franz Josef Land, so he set off to walk to the nearest point to get upon an elevation to have a look round.

His first question was in reference to his wife, and his second as to the politics of Norway and 'were Norway and Sweden at war?' He was going gamely, but looks pale and anæmic and is very fat.

On approaching our hut I told him again how delighted I was to be the first to congratulate him and welcome him on his return. Nearing the hut all my party came forward on to the floe to meet us, and I introduced them all to Nansen and told them that he had come from the 86° 15′ north latitude, and called for three cheers for him, which was responded to most vigorously; this seemed to please him and he repeatedly said, 'This is splendid!'

I then sent Armitage on to tell Heyward to cook some food at once, and heat the bath water – of course I did my utmost to make him and Johansen comfortable.

On entering the hut I handed him a packet of letters I had brought from London for him. There was no letter from his wife at which he was very downcast, and I had again to assure him that she was very well when we left London in 1894, but a letter from his brother explained matters. He then had some fried looms, rice-pudding, and jam, and any little luxuries we could supply. (He and Johansen had lived almost entirely on bear and walrus meat for the last nine or ten months). He afterwards had a bath and I found him a change of clean clothes. I had sent all the party, except Heyward, with two sledges to bring up Johansen and the kayaks, and on his coming up I looked after him in the same manner as I had Nansen. Johansen was, if possible, in a dirtier condition than his leader, and was as black as a sweep with dirt and grease.

Contrary to Dr Nansen's experience, our sense of smell must have become considerably *lessened* by long absence from civilisation, for, strain our noses as we may, we fail to discover the slightest trace of the 'Monkey (or any other known) Brand' about our distinguished visitors from the North.

Johansen is a short, sturdy, muscular little chap, and looks as fit and well as he might have done had he just come off a yachting trip. He hasn't turned a hair, but looks the picture of health. He is a capital fellow. Nansen and I on meeting had fired four shots in quick succession to let Johansen know he had met some one.

My fellows on approaching Johansen and seeing the Norwegian flag hoisted to the mast of a kayak had given three cheers. Johansen told one of the party in German that they were 'lost' and did not know where they where, which is hardly surprising, for they had no means of ascertaining their whereabouts, as Payer's map north was unrecognisable, and they could not get their longitude owing to their watches having run down. They had a lump or two of evil-looking walrus meat and two or three draggled looking looms in their kayaks which was all the food they had with them, poor chaps. On the night of Nansen's arrival we sat up talking till 8 a.m. of the following day and then turned into our blankets, but we soon turned out again and renewed our conversation for hours. He said 'He didn't want to sleep he felt so happy.' I feel very pleased.

A Thousand Days in the Arctic, 1899

SALOMON AUGUST ANDRÉE
1854–97

We have . . . found everything eatable . . . bear, great seal, seal, ivory gull . . .
We must however shoot more so as to have larger rations . . .

Andrée – a Swedish engineer who died in the summer of 1897 during a second attempt to reach the North Pole by balloon – was born in Granna in Sweden, where his father was a pharmacist. On leaving high school he trained to be a mechanic and set up his own workshop. This went bankrupt, however, and Andrée went to work as a physics laboratory technician in the state technical school.

In 1882 he took part in an international scientific expedition to take meteorological and geophysical measurements in the north polar region, with the Swedish party under Nils Ekholm. In 1893 he bought a hot-air balloon, *Svea*, that could climb to 3,000 metres and with which he completed nine trips to take scientific measurements. Meanwhile, he worked on improvements to his balloon, creating a stopping mechanism and guide ropes to enable him to navigate. Andrée had set his sights on reaching the North Pole itself, and in 1894 presented a proposal for a polar voyage to the Swedish Science Academy. Alfred Nobel (the inventor of dynamite and founder of the Nobel Prize), covered half the expedition costs, and Andrée set out on the first attempt with the meteorologist and astronomer Nils Ekholm and the physician, photographer and technician Nils Strindberg. Heavy weather and an unfavourable wind soon put an end to the expedition, but in 1896 they commissioned the French designer Henri Lachambre to build a new balloon for a second attempt. On 11 July 1897 'the most daring Polar expedition ever undertaken' took off from Spitzbergen. On board were Andrée, Nils Strindberg and Knut Fraenkel with 767 kg of food supplies (enough for six months), as well as carrier pigeons and buoys to send messages back to the mainland. It was not until they were airborne that they christened the balloon *The Eagle*.

A carrier pigeon brought the last news: released at 82° north, its message read, 'All well on board.' However, we know from the dairies kept by the party that trouble had begun almost straightaway, when the guide ropes broke and the balloon was left to the mercy of the Arctic winds. A thick fog enveloped them, and the drop in temperature as the balloon passed from sunny clear skies to the shade kept forcing it down towards the ground. They managed to mend one of the guide ropes, and by the next day were navigating eastwards again; but overnight they fell from 500m to 20m, then became wedged on the ice for thirteen hours. Despite their dislodging the balloon and continuing on their way, the balloon still kept on scraping the ice, so Andrée decided to ground it and continue the rest of the journey on foot. The three men spent a week making preparations, then headed towards Cape Flora, dragging overladen sledges of supplies, which they navigated around crevices. Progress was painfully slow. They walked for a month, but on reaching White Island were forced to stop by strong winds, and they realized they would have to set up camp for the winter. They built a hut, and spent days hunting to stock up on meat to last till spring; but in the middle of the night on 2 October there was a deafening crack, the ice opened, and the hut filled with freezing water. Clinging to floating ice, the men drifted to the nearest land, and on 5 October, still not defeated, built another camp. At that point, the notebooks kept by Andrée and Strindberg break off.

For thirty years there was no trace of the expedition. Then, in August 1930, the *Bratvaag*, which carried a joint scientific and sealing expedition to Franz Josef Land, made the most of good weather to visit White Island, which was usually inaccessible owing to ice. On 6 August 1930, the crew landed on the island, and on the beach found cooking utensils, prompting a further search inland. There they discovered a canvas boat, tied to a sledge, and the remains of Andrée and Strindberg, the latter already buried. With them were notebooks, clothes and film. When the sensational news of the discovery reached the world, the editor of the Swedish newspaper *Dagens Nyheter*, Knut Stubbendorf, immediately equipped a fishing boat, the *Polar Bear*, for an expedition to White Island. Fraenkel's body was found, and the three men were taken back to Sweden for proper burial. They had clearly not died from hunger: copious amounts of food were found next to their bodies. It is assumed that either carbon monoxide poisoning from their stoves or contaminated bear meat had killed them.

Discovery of remains of the Andrée expedition in 1930

And then came the 6th August. A glittering day, with the sun shining in a cloudless heaven. A most intense silence prevailed everywhere, broken only now and then by thunder from the glacier to our north, where it sank steeply into the sea. This noise was produced by large masses of ice loosening and plunging into the water, there to continue their existence as floating icebergs until they were melted by the waves. Otherwise this was the home of the great white silence, and it was not possible to feel otherwise than slightly depressed by the deathly quiet. We were glad to begin to work. Now the sealers began their walrus-hunt, and towards midday two whaling-boats left the 'Bratvaag' in charge of the harpooners, Ole Myklebust and Sevrin Skjelten, to get their booty . . . While the hunt was going on, the walruses began to retire behind a point of land lying southwards, and the boats pursued them. Skipper Eliassen, in the motor-boat, was busy pulling the carcases up on land.

As the day went on, the skipper returned to the ship. He neared us calmly and quietly and told us that they had made a great find. *They had found Andrée!* And they had also found the canvas boat of the Expedition, filled with all kinds of equipment.

Eliassen had in his hands a book which had lain in the boat. The book was wet and heavy, and the leaves stuck together, but it could be opened in one or two places, and we saw that it was the Expedition's observation-book with detailed calculations of the astronomical observations. There was side after side with figures, with here and there a list of the supply of provisions, a bill of fare for the week, together with other memoranda. We were astonished to see how neatly and orderly everything was written. It was just as if the notes had been put down in a warm room, and yet the calculations had been made and

written during the course of a death-march across the ice. We were aware that
Nils Strindberg had been the scientific member of the Expedition, so that it
must have been he who had made the memoranda. And he must have been a
man of the right sort. On the first page we were able to read a part of the title:
'The sledge journey 1897.' There could be no doubt but that this was the
Expedition's observation-book, used after they had left the balloon, probably
far northwards among the ice. The news of the discovery made a deep impression on us all. Here on White Island, here where we now stood, consequently,
was the place where the boldest of all Polar expeditions had come to a tragic
close. We sat still a moment ere we thought of rising again. Our words were
very few, overwhelmed as we were by the discovery that had just been made.

But there was no time to lose. Provided with an iron-bar, mattocks, spades
and tarpaulings, we all started for the place where the find had been made,
and on the way Eliassen related the circumstances under which it had happened. It was the sealers, Olav Salen and Karl Tusvik, who had first made the
find . . .

We landed on the beach below Andrée's camp, stepping on shore close by a
little rock. At some distance lay the two bloody carcases of the walruses. Some
ivory gulls sat pecking at the meat. When we came they flew lazily away, but
soon came back again and continued their meal. We walked up the beach. An
end had been put to all hunting, of course, after the discovery was made, and
we could see the sealers stand round the boat that was lying in the snowdrift.
We waded across the little stream and went silently towards the camp. Behind
us the sea is calm and ice-free as far as the eye can reach. Glimmering white
icebergs lie aground in the neighbourhood of the island. We approach the
camp one by one, without exchanging many words. The excitement is great,
for in a few minutes we shall stand by Andrée's last camp.

We are here at the spot! Hither had Andrée and his comrades come, never
to leave the place again. The moment was a strange, a solemn one, and some
moments passed before we began our task. We did not speak much – for what
had we to say? – and gradually the whole truth broke upon us; the story of the
tragedy that had been acted here. Our thoughts found their way back to that
July day in 1897, when the 'Eagle' rose from Danes Island in Spitzbergen with
three men in the car, and was carried away by the wind on the most daring
Polar expedition ever undertaken. The men never came back. The last news
from them was brought by the carrier-pigeon which they had released in
latitude 82°, and in their communication there stood, too, the words: 'All well
on board.' That was their last message. Everything that happened afterwards
had, for a generation, been the object of the acutest speculations. Search

expeditions had sought for the vanished balloon-travellers of whom no trace could ever be found. Andrée and his comrades kept the secret of their disappearance, and gradually the world satisfied itself with the conclusion that the explorers had been lost on the ice or had fallen into the sea, leaving no trace behind them. Most people accepted this explanation. Probably no one ever imagined that Andrée would ever be found. And now here we had Andrée's camp before our eyes and the problem of his disappearance was solved.

From Andrée's diary

22 Sept.: Thickn. of ice of our floe (another place than the one before) 2.5–2.5–1.7–2.4–3.0–2.5 (7.25–7.25–5.6–7.9–9.9–8.25 ft) Str. shot a seal (with small shot) and in addition we got a couple of ivory gulls but we must be careful with our shooting for we miss pretty often as the seals as a rule do not come so near that we can be certain of hitting the head with a small shot. In . . . we were disturbed by hearing the floe break, as we thought right under the building. We were afraid that we had run aground but our bearings have shown that we are moving although we seem unable to get away from this island. Probably we are lying in some kind of backwater which the water-current from the north creates at the S. eastern and S. western corners of the island and its southern side, clear weather here seems to be rare, we have not yet been able to get a clear latitude-determination for ourselves and the island. The patchy black guillemots and ivory gulls are common here, we have also seen several specimens of the before-mentioned 'ivory-gull youngster.' The ordinary fulmar on the other hand is seen remarkably seldom.

23 Sept.: To-day all three of us have been working busily on the hut cementing together ice-blocks. We have got on very well and the hut now begins to take form a little. After a couple more days of such weather and work it should not take long until we are able to move in. We can probably carry our supplies in there the day after to-morrow. This is very necessary, as mortar we employ snow mixed with water and of this mass, which is handled by S. with great skill he is also making a vaulted roof over the last parts between the walls. We have now a very good arrangement of the day with 8 hours' work beginning with 2½ hours' work, thereupon breakfast 3/4 and afterwards work until 4.45 o'cl. when we dine and take supper in one meal. We have now also tried the meat of the great seal and have found that it tastes excellent. One of the very best improvements in the cooking is that of adding blood to the sauce for the steak. This makes it thick and it tastes as if we had bread. I cannot believe but that blood contains much carbohydrate, for our craving for bread is considerably less since we began to use blood in the food. We all think so. We have also found everything eatable both as regards bear, great seal, seal and ivory gull (bear-liver of course excepted). For want of time we have not yet been able to cut up and weigh our animal but I think we now have meat and ham until on in the spring. We must however shoot more so as to be able to have larger rations and to get more fuel and light.

29 Sept.: We are still lying off the south-side of N. I. The ice-sludge has closed and the seals have disappeared. On the other hand the bears are coming. The day before yesterday and yesterday we had visits from the bears at night and I tried to hunt a bear in my stocking-feet but did not succeed. This morning just as we come out F. saw a bear which we succeeded in enticing to us who were waiting behind our hut. S. shot him through the throat and he fell down at once but after some moments he rose again and began running pushing his fore-quarters in front along the snow. I then gave him my shot which laid him on his hind quarters but this induced him to fresh efforts and he began to run. F. at last got his shot into him and then at last he lay there in a pool, after which we hauled him up amid hurras. It was a big old he-bear. The night-bears seem to be a kind of thief bears; the one that visited us yesterday night dragged away our big seal twice and we should have lost it if S. had not succeeded in coming so near the bear as to frighten him and make him drop his booty.

Our floe is diminished in a somewhat alarming degree close to our hut. The ice pressings bring the shores closer and closer to us. But we have a large and old hummock between the hut and the shore and hope that this will stop the pressure. This sounds magnificent when there is pressure but otherwise it does not appeal to us.

Thickn. of ice 1.1–1.2–1.5–1.9 (3.6–3.9–4.95–6.27 ft) have been measured by a new fissure which has arisen in our floe. Yesterday evening the 28 we moved into our hut which was christened 'the home.' We lay there last night and found it rather nice. But it will become much better of course. We must have the meat inside to protect ourselves against the bears. The ice in N.I. glacier is evidently stratified in a horizontal direction. The day before yesterday it rained a great part of the day which I suppose ought to be considered extremely remarkable at this time of the year and in this degree of latitude.

The 1 Oct. was a good day. The evening was as divinely beautiful as one could wish. The water was allied with small animals and a bevy of 7 black-white 'guillemots youngsters' were swimming there. A couple of seals were seen too. The work with the hut went on well and we thought that we should have the outside ready by the 2nd. But then something else happened. At 5.30

o'cl. (local time) in the morning of the 2 we heard a crash and thunder and water streamed into the hut and when rushed out we found that our large beautiful floe had been splintered into a number of little floes and that one fissure had divided the floe just outside the wall of the hut. The floe that remained to us had a diam. of only 24 meter (80 ft) and one wall of the hut might be said rather to hang from the roof than to support it. This was a great alteration in our position and our prospects. The hut and the floe could not give us shelter and still we were obliged to stay there for the present at least. We were frivolous enough to lie in the hut the following night too. Perhaps it was because the day was rather tiring. Our belongings were scattered among several blocks and these were driving here and there so that we had to hurry. Two bear-bodies, representing provisions for 3–4 months were lying on a separate floe and so on. Luckily the weather was beautiful so that we could work in haste. No one had lost courage; with such comrades one should be able to manage under, I may say, any circumstances . . .

[State of diary deteriorates from here.]
  The Andrée Diaries, 1931

KNUD RASMUSSEN
1879–1933
Such an odour of paganism and magic incantation.

Rasmussen was a truly scientific polar explorer, attracted to the north not by the Pole itself but by the polar people – in some ways own his people, as he was the son of a Danish father and Inuit mother, and educated in both cultures. In 1902–4 he was a member of Ludwig Mylius-Erichsen's expedition to explore north-western Greenland and study Inuit customs. In 1910 he founded a settlement, Thule, at North Star Bay, and trade in furs, narwhal tusks, tobacco and the like both helped fund his future expeditions and provided the Inuit with medical services. He embarked on his greatest expedition on 7 September 1921, setting out with an Inuit couple with the aim of studying Inuit peoples right across the north of the American continent between Baffin Bay and the Bering Strait. His party having been held captive by Inuit of the Boothia Peninsula, they continued westward to King William Island, where they chanced on some skeletal remains of the Franklin expedition of 1845–7, finally arriving through the Bering Strait in spring 1924. His observa-

tions – including those of his last expedition (1932), from Thule to south-eastern Greenland – accumulated a mass of anthropological information, all the more valuable than his geographical data, since the cultures of the indigenous people are more vulnerable even than the fragile Arctic landscape. Whatever the material benefits of our technology – and, as anyone who has experienced the Arctic in severe cold knows, they are immeasurable – by Rasmussen's time 'Eskimo' culture was already being laid waste by missionaries, traders and trappers. These were only the vanguard of the Western invasion and its repercussions; and most other Arctic peoples, spread across Siberia, found themselves collectivized and centralized under Communism.

This account is one of the Rasmussen's earliest – not always what modern anthropologists would call 'culturally sensitive', but none the less depicting a lifestyle in northwest Greenland about to disappear for ever. The region described is now marked on the map as 'Knud Rasmussen Land'.

'At last! People, other people'

We had reached our goal!

But one of our number was dangerously ill, and we were powerless to relieve him; the people we had hoped to meet with at Cape York settlement had left their houses, and our famished dogs were circling madly round us; we had hardly enough food left for one good meal, even for ourselves.

The forced pace of the last two days and nights had greatly exhausted us; for the moment, however, we were so much struck by all the new sights around us, by the strange, primitive human dwellings, that we forgot our fatigue in exploring the settlement. But it was not long before we flung ourselves down by our sledges and dropped asleep.

A more careful examination of the snow huts then revealed that it could not have been long since their owners had left them. In one of them there was a large seal, not cut up, which provided our dogs with a very welcome feast.

There were numerous sledge-tracks running northward, with only a light powdering of snow upon them; consequently men could not be far away . . .

It was an odd experience, creeping through the long, low tunnel entrances into the houses; with our furs on we could hardly pass. At the end, we came to a hole up through which we had to squeeze ourselves, and then we were in the house. There was a strong smell of raw meat and fox inside.

The first time one sees a house of this description one is struck by the little with which human beings can be content. It is all so primitive, and has such an odour of paganism and magic incantation. A cave like this, skilfully built in an arch of gigantic blocks of stone, one involuntarily peoples mentally with half supernatural beings. You see them, in your fancy, pulling and tearing at raw flesh, you see the blood dripping from their fingers, and you are seized yourself with a strange excitement at the thought of the extraordinary life that awaits you in their company.

We walked round, examining all these things, which, in their silent way, spoke to us of the men and women who lived their lonely life up here. A little way from the houses, in a circle, were some large round stones, shining with stale grease. 'Here they must have had their meals,' suggested one of our Greenlanders. Already our imagination was at work.

Farther up, just under the overhanging cliff, lay a kayak with all its appurtenances, covered over with stones. Behind it was a sledge, with dead dogs harnessed to it, almost wholly hidden by the drifting snow. There, then, men lay buried with all their possessions, as Eskimo custom prescribes . . .

In the neighbourhood of Cape Atholl we discovered fresh sledgetracks, which we followed up. They led to a stone cairn, under a steep wall of rock, which cairn contained a large deposit of freshly-caught bearded seal. Ah! then we could not be far from human beings. The intense suspense of it! For it almost meant our comrade's life.

We had driven all night – some twelve hours, and a little way beyond Cape Atholl were obliged to pull up, to give the dogs a rest and breathing time. We had covered about fifty-six English miles at full gallop, and, should we be forced to drive all the way to Natsilivik, should have to make reasonable allowance for the empty stomachs of our poor animals. We flung ourselves down on the ice, discussed our prospects, ate a little butter – we simply dared not eat our biscuits – lay down on our sledges and went to sleep.

After three hours' rest we went on again.

We had only driven a little way when a black dot became visible in front. It developed and grew into a sledge.

'Jörgen!—Knud!—Jörgen!—Knud!'

We were half mad with relief and delight, and could only call out each other's names.

Speed signal! The dogs drop their tails and prick up their ears. We murmur the signal again between our teeth, and the snow swirls up beneath their hind legs. A biting wind cuts us in the face. At last! at last! people, other people, the new people – the Polar Eskimos!

A long narrow sledge is coming towards us at full speed, a whip whistles through the air, and unfamiliar dog-signals are borne on the wind to our ears. A little fur-clad man in a pair of glistening white bearskin trousers springs from the sledge and runs up to his team, urging the dogs on still faster with shouts and gesticulations. Behind him, sitting astride the sledge, sits another person, dressed in blue fox, with a large pointed hat on her head: that is his wife.

Our dogs begin to bark, and the sledges meet to the accompaniment of loud yelps. We spring off and run up to each other, stop and stare at one another, incapable of speech, both parties equally astonished.

I explain to him who we are, and where we come from.

'White men! White men!' he calls out to his wife. 'White men have come on a visit!'

We have no difficulty in understanding or making ourselves understood.

I hasten to the woman, who has remained seated on the sledge. All sorts of strange emotions crowd in upon me, and I do not know what to say. Then, without thinking what I am doing, I hold out my hand. She looks at me, uncomprehending, and laughs. And then we all laugh together.

The man's name is Maisanguaq (the little white whale skin), his wife Meqo (the feather); they live at Igfigsoq, from twelve to sixteen English miles south of our meeting-place, and we learn that three or four other families live at the same place.

In our eagerness to arrive at Agpat (Saunders Island) we had cut across outside the bay on which Igfigsoq lies.

The snow on the ice at the entrance to the bay being hard, we had not been able to detect sledge-tracks which might have led us to enter it. But when we heard that there were far more people at Agpat, and that the hunting and sealing there were particularly good, I decided to drive straight on, and, by sledge post, advise my comrades to do the same.

Maisanguaq promptly seated himself across my sledge, his wife driving theirs, and we all set off together towards Agpat, carrying on the liveliest conversation meanwhile. The two ought really to have been at home by this time, but had turned back to show us the way.

Meqo was a capital dog-driver, and wielded her long whip as well as any man. In West Greenland you never see a woman drive, so I expressed my surprise; Maisanguaq laughed out with pride, and called out to her gaily to lash hard with her whip, it amused the white men, and Meqo swung her whip, and off we dashed, she leading.

'*Tugto! tugto!*' she cried, and the dogs bounded forward, and soon we began to near the high-lying little island on which Agpat lay.

Maisanguaq then told me that 'many' people lived at Agpat: there were three stone houses and five snow huts; and the burst into peals of laughter each time he thought of the surprise he was going to witness. 'White men! White men!' he called out, whenever an instant's pause in the conversation occurred, and rubbed his hands with glee.

Suddenly he stopped short and listened, then jumped up in my sledge and looked behind. Another sledge had come in sight a long way to our rear.

'*Aulavte! aulavte!*' he called out. (That is the signal for a halt.) But my dogs did not understand him, and I had to come to the rescue by whistling to them.

Then he jumped out on the one side, and began to hop up in the air and slap himself on the legs. He continued to indulge in these extraordinary antics till he was quite red in the face from his exertions. This was an indication that something unusual was going on. The strange sledge came on at a gallop; as it approached, two young fellows sprang out and ran alongside, shouting. Maisanguaq began to yell too, and continued to flounder about like a madman.

At last the sledge came up to ours and stopped. The two young men were named Qulutana and Inukitsoq. First, of course, they wanted to know who we were, and Maisanguaq delivered himself of his lesson. Then the whole caravan drove on, laughing and shouting, towards Agpat.

Never in my life have I felt myself to be in such wild, unaccustomed sur-roundings, never so far, so very far away from home, as when I stood in the midst of the tribe of noisy Polar Eskimos on the beach at Agpat. We were not observed till we were close to the land, so the surprise and confusion created by our arrival were all the greater.

Maisanguaq recommenced his jumping antics by the side of the sledge as soon as we arrived within calling distance of the place, and then screamed out a deafening 'White men! White men!'

The people, who had been moving briskly about among the houses, stood still, and the children left off their play.

'White men! White men!' repeated the young fellows who had joined us. Our dogs drooped their tails and pricked up their ears as a many-tongued roar from the land reached us. And then, like a mountain-slide, the whole swarm rushed down to the shore, where we had pulled up – a few old grey-haired men and stiff-jointed old crones, young men and women, children who could hardly toddle, all dressed alike in these fox and bear-skin furs, which create such an extraordinarily barbaric first impression. Some came with long knives in their hands, with bloodstained arms and upturned sleeves, having been in the midst of flaying operations when we arrived, and all this produced a very savage effect; at the moment it was difficult to believe that these 'savages,' 'the neighbours of the North Pole,' as Astrup called them, were ever likely to become one's good, warm friends . . .

Jörgen and I were now conducted up to the houses. Sheltering walls of snow had been built up here and there to form cooking-places, and round these the natives clustered. A young fellow came up carrying a frozen walrus liver, raw, which was our first meal; all the men of the village ate of it with us, to show their hospitable intent. Curious youngsters gaped at us greedily from every side, and ran away when we looked at them.

When the pot had boiled, we were called in to the senior of the tribe, the magician Sagdloq ('The Lie'); the boiled meat was placed on the floor, and a knife put in our hands.

A lively conversation got under way. The people were not difficult to understand, as their dialect differed but little from the ordinary Greenlandic; they were surprised themselves at the ease with which they understood us, who yet came from such a distance.

After the meal, they immediately set about building us a snow hut.

'There is a sick man with you, so you must be helped quickly,' they said.

They hewed large blocks out of the hard snow: those were to be the walls of our new house. Then they set it up in a hollow in the snow, and in the course of half an hour it stood complete.

A sledge was sent for our comrades, and by early morning we were all together.

The reception these pagan savages gave us was affectingly cordial; it seemed that they could not do enough for us. And just as they were on our arrival – helpful as they could possibly be, and most generous with their gifts – so they remained the whole time that we spent among them . . .

The People of the Polar North: A Record, 1908

FREDERICK A. COOK
1865–1940
It was loneliness, frigid loneliness. I wondered whether men ever felt so desolately alone.

An American medical doctor, Cook's ventures to the Arctic were small-scale, and based on the resources and manpower of the Inuit. In 1909 Cook returned from an attempt on the North Pole with a remarkable story of survival – and a claim that he had attained the Pole on 21 April 1908. This was heavily disputed by Robert Peary, who had been trying to reach the Pole for years, and who made his own claim to the Pole in 1909. In the resulting investigation Cook was discredited. His reputation sank still further on receiving a fourteen-year prison sentence for defrauding investors in a petroleum company, who had been led to expect that oil was about to be found. However, no less a figure than Amundsen stood by him, even paying him visits in prison.

After several years in jail he was exonerated, but his reputation, which in his early years had been second to none, was destroyed. He died on 5 August 1940 and left a voice-recording: 'I have been humiliated and seriously hurt, but that doesn't matter any more. I'm getting old, and what does matter to me is that I want you to believe that I told the truth. I state emphatically that I, Frederick A. Cook, discovered the North Pole.' Now it seems probable that neither he nor Peary did.

Arrival at the Pole

Cracking our whips, we bounded ahead. The boys sang. The dogs howled. Midnight of April 21 had just passed. Over the sparkling snows the postmidnight sun glowed like at noon. I seemed to be walking in some splendid golden realms of dreamland. As we bounded onward the ice swam about me in circling rivers of gold. E-tuk-i-shook and Ah-we-lah, though thin and ragged, had the dignity of the heroes of a battle which had been fought through to success.

We all were lifted to the paradise of winners as we stepped over the snows of a destiny for which we had risked life and willingly suffered the tortures of an icy hell. The ice under us, the goal for centuries of brave, heroic men, to reach which many had suffered terribly and terribly died, seemed almost sacred. Constantly and carefully I watched my instruments in recording this final reach. Nearer and nearer they recorded our approach. Step by step, my heart filled with a strange rapture of conquest.

At last we step over coloured fields of sparkle, climbing walls of purple and gold — finally, under skies of crystal blue, with flaming clouds of glory, we touch the mark! The soul awakens to a definite triumph; there is sunrise within us, and all the world of night-darkened trouble fades. We are at the top of the world! The flag is flung to the frigid breezes of the North Pole! . . .

By a long and consecutive series of observations and mental tabulations of various sorts on our journey northward, continuing here, I knew, beyond peradventure of doubt, that I was at a spot which was as near as possible, by usual methods of determination, 520 miles from Svartevoeg, a spot toward which men had striven for more than three centuries — a spot known as the North Pole, and where I stood first of white men. In my own achievement I felt, that dizzy moment, that all the heroic souls who had braved the rigours of the Arctic region found their own hopes' fulfilment. I had realized their dream. I had culminated with success the efforts of all the brave men who had failed before me. I had finally justified their sacrifices, their very death; I had proven to humanity humanity's supreme triumph over a hostile, death-dealing Nature. It seemed that the souls of these dead exulted with me, and that in some substrata of the air, in notes more subtle than the softest notes of music, they sang a paean in the spirit with me.

We had reached our destination. My relief was indescribable. The prize of an international marathon was ours. Pinning the Stars and Stripes to a tent-pole, I asserted the achievement in the name of the ninety millions of countrymen who swear fealty to that flag. And I felt a pride as I gazed at the white-and-crimson barred pinion, a pride which the claim of no second victor has ever taken from me.

My Attainment of the Pole, 1911

Return from the Pole

As the sun sank, the sky over it was flushed with orange or gold. This gradually paled, and over the horizon opposite there rose an arc in feeble prismatic colours with a dark zone of purple under it. The arc rose as the sun settled; the purple spread beyond the polarized bow; and gradually the heavens turned a deep purple blue to the zenith, while the halo of the globe was slowly lost in its own shadow.

The coloured face of the earth painted on the screen of the heavens left the last impression of worldly charm on the retina. At the end of October the battle of the elements, storms attending the setting of the sun, began to blast the air into a chronic fury. By this time we were glad to creep into our den and await the vanishing weeks of ebbing day.

In the doom of night to follow, there would at least be some quiet moments during which we could stretch our legs. The bears, which had threatened our existence, were now kept off by a new device which served the purpose for a time. We had food and fuel enough for the winter. There should have been nothing to disturb our tempers, but the coming of the long blackness makes all polar life ill at ease.

Early in November the storms ceased long enough to give us a last fiery vision. With a magnificent cardinal flame the sun rose, gibbered in the sky, and sank behind the southern cliffs on November 3.

The days now came and went in short order. For hygienic reasons we kept up the usual routine of life. The midday light soon darkened to twilight. The moon and stars appeared at noon. The usual partition of time disappeared. All was night, unrelieved darkness, midnight, midday, morning or evening.

We stood watches of six hours each to keep the fires going, to keep off the bears, and to force an interest in a blank life. We knew that we were believed to be dead. Our friends in Greenland would not ascribe to us the luck which came after our run of abject misfortune. This thought inflicted perhaps the greatest pain of the queer prolongation of life which was permitted us. It was loneliness, frigid loneliness. I wondered whether men ever felt so desolately alone.

We could not have been more thoroughly isolated if we had been transported to the surface of the moon. I find myself utterly unable to outline the emptiness of our existence. In other surroundings we never grasp the full meaning of the word 'alone.' When it is possible to put a foot out of doors into the sunlight without the risk of a bear's paw on your neck, it is also possible to run off a spell of blues, but what were we to do with the torment of a satanic blackness to blind us?

With the cheer of day, a kindly nature, and a new friend, it is easy to get in touch with a sympathetic chord. The mere thought of another human heart within touch, even a hundred miles away, would have eased the suspense of the silent void. But we could entertain no such hopefulness. We were all alone in a world where every pleasant aspect of nature had deserted us. Although three in number, a bare necessity had compressed us into a single composite individuality.

There were no discussions, no differences of opinion. We had been too long together under bitter circumstances to arouse each other's interest. A single individual could not live long in our position. A selfish instinct tightened a fixed bond to preserve and protect one another. As a battle force we made a formidable unit, but there were no matches to start the fires of inspiration.

The half-darkness of midday and the moonlight still permitted us to creep from under the ground and seek a few hours in the open. The stone and bone fox-traps and the trap-caves for the bears which we had built during the last glimmer of day offered an occupation with some recreation. But we were soon deprived of this.

Bears headed us off at every turn. We were not permitted to proceed beyond an enclosed hundred feet from the hole of our den. Not an inch of ground or a morsel of food was permitted us without a contest. It was a fight of nature against nature. We either actually saw the little sooty nostrils with jets of vicious breath rising, and the huge outline of a wild beast ready to spring on us, or imagined we saw it. With no adequate means of defence we were driven to imprisonment within the walls of our own den.

From within, our position was even more tantalizing. The bear thieves dug under the snows over our heads and snatched blocks of blubber fuel from under our very eyes at the port. Occasionally we ventured out to deliver a lance, but each time the bear would make a leap for the door and would have entered had the opening been large enough. In other cases we shot arrows through the peep-hole. A bear head again would burst through the silk-covered window near the roof, where knives, at close range and in good light, could be driven with sweet vengeance.

As a last resort we made a hole through the top of the den. When a bear was heard near, a long torch was pushed through. The snow for acres about was then suddenly flashed with a ghostly whiteness which almost frightened us. But the bear calmly took advantage of the light to pick a larger piece of the blubber upon which our lives depended and then with an air of superiority he would move into the brightest light, usually within a few feet of our peep-hole, where we could almost touch his hateful skin.

Return from the Pole, 1953

ROBERT EDWIN PEARY
1856–1920
The prize of three centuries . . . mine at last!

The American naval officer Robert E. Peary led his first expedition to Greenland at the age of thirty, and went on to cross the Greenland ice cap twice from west to east and chart the north-east coast. Like so many explorers at the turn of the century, he was gripped by the idea of being the first to reach the North Pole. Indeed Peary was manically obsessed, almost from infancy – he is quoted as telling his mother, 'Remember, Mother, I must have fame and cannot reconcile myself to years of commonplace drudgery.'

In adulthood, the obsession deepened: 'I long ago ceased to think of myself save as an instrument for the attainment of that end.' On 6 April 1909, on his third attempt, he claimed success. His method was to travel without the bulky equipment favoured by others at the time; he advanced with an army of dogs and Inuit from Cape Sheridan on Ellesmere Island to Cape Columbia from where he made a 500-mile dash across the ice floes, using a series of relay parties. An entire Inuit community aided him on his journey –

the men drove the sledges, built snow houses and hunted for him; and the women had made his clothing. On the last leg, accompanied only by his African-American servant, Matthew Henson, and four Inuit, Peary ostensibly reached the Pole. His claim was almost universally accepted at the time, but his speed was so fast, his observations so scant, that doubts gradually surfaced. He became involved in a lengthy dispute with Frederick Cook, who claimed to have gained the Pole the previous year, but no one could doubt his pedigree as a formidable Arctic explorer. In the end, he more or less won through – until in recent times, when his diaries were examined by Arctic explorer Wally Herbert. Now it seems likely that Herbert himself was first to reach the North Pole overland.

A man who craved immortality, and took each and every opportunity to plot his own deification, his grandiose speech to President Roosevelt is as enlightening about him as the more widely known account of his final triumph in the Arctic.

To the American President

President Roosevelt: In behalf of the Peary Arctic Club and its president, Morris K. Jesup, I beg to express our deep appreciation of the great honour conferred by the National Geographical Society in this award of its gold medal, and the double honour of receiving this medal from your hand.

Your continued interest, Mr President, your permission to name the club's ship after you, and your name itself have proved a powerful talisman. Could I have foreseen this occasion, it would have lightened many dark hours, but I will frankly say that it would not, for it could not, have increased my efforts.

The true explorer does his work not for any hopes of reward or honour, but because the thing he has set himself to do is a part of his being, and must be accomplished for the sake of the accomplishment. And he counts lightly hardships, risks, obstacles, if only they do not bar him from his goal.

To me the final and complete solution of the Polar mystery which has engaged the best thought and interest of some of the best men of the most vigorous and enlightened nations of the world for more than three centuries, and to-day quickens the pulse of every man or woman whose veins hold red blood, is the thing which should be done for the honour and credit of this country, the thing which it is intended that I should do, and the thing that I must do.

The result of the last expedition of the Peary Arctic Club has been to simplify the attainment of the Pole fifty per cent, to accentuate the fact that man and the Eskimo dog are the only two mechanisms capable of meeting all the varying contingencies of Arctic work, and that the American route to the Pole and the methods and equipment which have been brought to a high state of perfection, during the past fifteen years, still remain the most practicable means of attaining that object.

Had the past winter been a normal season in the Arctic region and not, as it was, a particularly open one throughout the Northern hemisphere, I should have won the prize. And even if I had known before leaving the land what actual conditions were to the northward, as I know now, I could have so modified my route and my disposition of sledges that I could have reached the Pole in spite of the open season.

Another expedition following in my steps and profiting by my experience cannot only attain the Pole; but can secure the remaining principal desiderata in the Arctic regions, namely, a line of deep sea soundings through the central Polar Ocean, and the delineation of the unknown gap in the northeast coast line of Greenland from Cape Morris Jesup to Cape Bismarck. And this work can be done in a single season.

As regards the belief expressed by some that the attainment of the North Pole possesses no value or interest let me say that should an American first of all men place the Stars and Stripes at that coveted spot, there is not an American citizen at home or abroad, and there are millions of us, but what would feel a little better and a little prouder of being an American; and just that added increment of pride and patriotism to millions, would of itself alone be worth ten times the cost of attaining the Pole.

Nearest the Pole, 1907

Last steps to the Pole

Perhaps a man always thinks of the very beginning of his work when he feels it is nearing its end. The appearance of the ice-fields to the north this day, large and level, the brilliant blue of the sky, the biting character of the wind – everything excepting the surface of the ice, which on the great cap is absolutely dead level with a straight line for a horizon – reminded me of those marches of the long ago . . .

Near the end of the march I came upon a lead which was just opening. It was ten yards wide directly in front of me; but a few hundred yards to the east was an apparently practicable crossing where the single crack was divided into several. I signalled to the sledges to hurry; then, running to the place, I had time to pick a road across the moving ice cakes and return to help the teams across before the lead widened so as to be impassable. This passage was effected by my jumping from one cake to another, picking the way, and making sure that the cake would not tilt under the weight of the dogs and the sledge, returning to the former cake where the dogs were, encouraging the dogs ahead while the driver steered the sledge across from cake to cake, and threw his weight from one side to the other so that it could not overturn. We got the sledges across several cracks so wide that while the dogs had no trouble in jumping, the men had to be pretty active in order to follow the long sledges. Fortunately the sledges were of the new Peary type, twelve feet long. Had they been of the old Eskimo type, seven feet long, we might have had to use ropes and pull them across hand over hand on an ice cake.

It is always hard to make the dogs leap a widening crack, though some of the best dog drivers can do it instantly, using the whip and the voice. A poor dog driver would be likely to get everything into the water in the attempt. It is sometimes necessary to go ahead of the dogs, holding the hand low and shaking it as though it contained some dainty morsel of food, thus inspiring them with courage for the leap.

Perhaps a mile beyond this, the breaking of the ice at the edge of a narrow lead as I landed from a jump sent me into the water nearly to my hips; but as the water did not come above the waistband of my trousers, which were water-tight, it was soon scraped and beaten off before it had time to freeze.

This lead was not wide enough to bother the sledges.

As we stopped to make our camp near a huge pressure ridge, the sun, which was gradually getting higher, seemed almost to have some warmth. While we were building our igloos, we could see, by the water clouds lying to the east and south-east of us some miles distant, that a wide lead was opening in that direction. The approaching full moon was evidently getting in its work.

As we had travelled on, the moon had circled round and round the heavens opposite the sun, a disk of silver opposite a disk of gold. Looking at its pallid and spectral face, from which the brighter light of the sun had stolen the colour, it seemed hard to realize that its presence there had power to stir the great ice-fields around us with restlessness – power even now, when we were so near our goal, to interrupt our pathway with an impassable lead.

The moon had been our friend during the long winter, giving us light to hunt by for a week or two each month. Now it seemed no longer a friend, but a dangerous presence to be regarded with fear. Its power, which had before been beneficent, was now malevolent and incalculably potent for evil.

When we awoke early in the morning of April 3, after a few hours' sleep, we found the weather still clear and calm. There were some broad heavy pressure ridges in the beginning of this march, and we had to use pickaxes quite freely. This delayed us a little, but as soon as we struck the level old floes we tried to make up for lost time. As the daylight was now continuous we could travel as long as we pleased, and sleep as little as we must. We hustled along for ten hours again, as we had before, making only twenty miles because of the early delay with the pickaxes and another brief delay at a narrow lead. We were now halfway to the 89th parallel, and I had been obliged to take up another hole in my belt.

Some gigantic rafters were seen during this march, but they were not in our path. All day long we had heard the ice grinding and groaning on all sides of us, but no motion was visible to our eyes. Either the ice was slacking back into equilibrium, sagging northward after its release from the wind pressure, or else it was feeling the influence of the spring tides of the full moon. On, on we pushed, and I am not ashamed to confess that my pulse beat high, for the breath of success seemed already in my nostrils . . .

The last march northward ended at ten o'clock of the forenoon of April 6. I had now made the five marches planned from the point at which Bartlett turned back, and my reckoning showed that we were in the immediate neighbourhood of the goal of all our striving. After the usual arrangements for going into camp, at approximate local noon, on the Columbia meridian, I made the first observation at our polar camp. It indicated our position as 89° 57′.

We were now at the end of the last long march of the upward journey. Yet with the Pole actually in sight I was too weary to take the last few steps. The accumulated weariness of all those days and nights of forced marches and insufficient sleep, constant peril and anxiety, seemed to roll across me all at once. I was actually too exhausted to realize at the moment that my life's purpose had been achieved. As soon as our igloos had been completed, and we had eaten our dinner and double-rationed the dogs, I turned in for a few hours of absolutely necessary sleep, Henson and the Eskimos having unloaded the sledges and got them in readiness for such repairs as were necessary. But, weary though I was, I could not sleep long. It was, therefore, only a few hours later when I woke. The first thing I did after awaking was to write these words in my diary: 'The Pole at last. The prize of three centuries. My dream and goal for twenty years. Mine at last! I cannot bring myself to realize it. It seems all so simple and commonplace.'

Everything was in readiness for an observation at 6 pm, Columbia meridian time, in case the sky should be clear, but at that hour it was, unfortunately, still overcast. But as there were indications that it would clear before long, two of the Eskimos and myself made ready a light sledge carrying only the instruments, a tin of pemmican, and one or two skins; and drawn by a double team of dogs, we pushed on an estimated distance of ten miles. While we travelled, the sky cleared, and at the end of the journey, I was able to get a satisfactory series of observations at Columbia meridian midnight. These observations indicated that our position was then beyond the Pole.

Nearly everything in the circumstances which then surrounded us seemed too strange to be thoroughly realized, but one of the strangest of those circumstances seemed to me to be the fact that, in a march of only a few hours, I had passed from the western to the eastern hemisphere and had verified my position at the summit of the world. It was hard to realize that, on the first miles of this brief march, we had been travelling due north, while, on the last few miles of the same march, we had been travelling south, although we had all the time been travelling precisely in the same direction. It would be difficult to imagine a better illustration of the fact that most things are relative. Again, please consider the uncommon circumstance that, in order to return to our camp, it now became necessary to turn and go north again for a few miles and then to go directly south, all the time travelling in the same direction.

As we passed back along that trail which none had ever seen before or would ever see again, certain reflections intruded themselves which, I think, may fairly be called unique. East, west, and north had disappeared for us. Only one direction remained and that was south. Every breeze which could possibly blow upon us, no matter from what point of the horizon, must be a south wind. Where we were, one day and one night constituted a year, a hundred such days and nights constituted a century. Had we stood in that spot during the six months of the Arctic winter night, we should have seen every star of the northern hemisphere circling the sky at the same distance from the horizon, with Polaris (the North Star) practically in the zenith.

The North Pole, 1910

Mr Peary urged me to come into the igloo, which I did, rather to please
him than to get out of the storm.

Josephine Diebitsch married Robert Peary in 1888, and accompanied her husband on four expeditions to Greenland within the following fourteen years. It's possible that one reason for her going north with her husband was to get away from her mother-in-law. Peary's mother lived with them and even accompanied them on their honeymoon.

During her first expedition in 1891–2, she passed the winter on the north-west coast of Greenland whilst he crossed the ice to discover how far Greenland extended in the direction of the Pole. She wrote *My Arctic Journal* during this expedition.

A year later she returned to Greenland, and gave birth to a daughter less than 13 degrees from the North Pole. The baby was given the middle name 'Ahnighito' to honour the Inuit woman who made her first fur suit. Though travelling in the footsteps of her husband, Mrs Peary adds a different perspective, illuminating domestic action that's all but absent in the polar accounts of men.

Visiting an igloo

Our sledge reached the west end of Herbert Island at eight o'clock, and two hours later, having crossed over to Northumberland Island, we came upon a cantonment of four snow-igloos. These were occupied by families from different settlements, who congregated here to be near a patch of open water a short distance off, where they caught seal. The largest snow-igloo was occupied by Tahtara, his wife, his father and mother, and some small children. This was put at our disposal . . .

As the wind was blowing fiercely and the air was thick with drifting snow, Mr Peary urged me to come into the igloo, which I did, rather to please him than to get out of the storm. Now as long as I have been in this country I have never entered an Eskimo hut; hearing about the filth and vermin was quite enough for me. But Mr Peary said the snow-house was much cleaner, etc., etc., and seeing that it really made him uncomfortable to have me stay outside, I yielded. Can I ever describe it? First I crawled through a hole and along a passage, about six feet, on my hands and knees; this was level with the snow outside. Then I came to a hole at the end of the passage and in the top of it, which seemed hardly large enough for me to get my head through, and through which I could see numberless legs. Mr Peary called for me to come, so the legs moved to one side and I wedged myself into the aperture and climbed into a circular place about five feet high, the floor of which, all of snow, was about two feet higher than that of the tunnel. A platform one and a half feet above this floor, and perhaps four feet wide in the middle and two and a half feet at the sides, ran all around the walls of the igloo, except that part in which the aperture or door came up in the floor. The middle of this platform for about five feet was the bed, and it was covered with two or three took-too skins, which almost crawled away, they were so very much alive. On this bed sat Tahtara's mother, tailor-fashion, with a child on her back; another woman, younger by far and rather pretty, his wife; and two children, about six and eight years old; and on the edge, with his feet resting on a chunk of walrus, from which some hungry ones helped themselves whenever they wanted to, regardless of the fact that a number of feet had been wiped on it, and that it was not only frozen solid but perfectly raw, sat Tahtara himself, smiling and saying, 'Yess, yess,' to everything that Mr Peary said to him. Mr Peary had also taken a seat on the edge of this bed, and the women immediately made room for me between them; but this was more than I could submit to, so, excusing myself by saying that my clothing was wet from the drifting snow and that I could not think of getting their bedding wet, I sat down, not without a shiver, on the edge beside Mr Peary, selfishly keeping him between the half-naked women and myself.

The sides of this platform on either side of the doorway were devoted to two ikkimers (stoves), one of which was tended by Tahtara's mother and the other by his wife. These stoves were very large and filled with chunks of blubber; over each hung a pan, made of soapstone, containing snow and water, and above these pans were racks or crates, fastened very securely, on which the inmates flung their wet kamiks, stockings, mittens, and birdskin shirts. The drippings of dirt, water, and insects fell invariably into the drinking-water. I say 'drinking-water'; they have no water for any other purpose. Mr Peary had put our Florence oil-stove on the side platform and was heating water for our tea. Fortunately our teapot had a cover on it, which I made my business to keep closed.

Besides the persons mentioned there were always as many husky visitors as could possibly pack in without standing on one another. These took turns with those unable to get in, so that after one had been in a while and gazed at the circus, he would lower himself through the trap and make way for a successor among the many crouching in the passageway behind him. This was kept up throughout the night. Of course the addition of our stove, together with the visitors, brought the temperature up rapidly, and to my dismay the Eskimo ladies belonging to the house took off all of their clothing except their necklaces of sinishaw, just as unconcernedly as though no one were present.

The odor of the place was indescribable. Our stove did not work properly and gave forth a pungent smell of kerosene; the blubber in the other stoves sizzled and sometimes smoked; and the huskies – well, suffice it to say that was a decidedly unpleasant atmosphere in which I spent the night.

I soon found that if I kept my feet on the floor they would freeze, and the only way I could keep them off the floor was to draw up my knees and rest the side of one foot on the edge of the platform and place the other upon it. In this way, and leaning on my elbow, I sat from ten at night until ten in the morning, dressed just as I was on the sledge. I made the best of the situation, and pretended to Mr Peary that it was quite a lark.

Mr Peary went out to look after the dogs several times during the night, and each time reported that the wind was still blowing fiercely and the snow drifting. In the morning the wind had subsided somewhat, and after coffee the dogs were hitched, and we resumed our journey, heading for Keati.

My Arctic Journal, 1893

APSLEY CHERRY-GARRARD
1886–1959

*Polar exploration is at once the cleanest and most isolated way of having
a bad time which has been devised.*

Assistant zoologist and one of the youngest members of Scott's ill-fated Antarctic expedition (1910–13), Cherry-Garrard accompanied Scott for the first part of the journey to the South Pole, and was among the search party that eventually discovered the frozen bodies of those who had undertaken the last leg.

The tragedy of the polar trek overshadowed some of the expedition's earlier achievements, including an arduous winter journey to the breeding grounds of the emperor penguins at Cape Crozier to collect eggs for scientific research. Antarctic winter travel was a new and risky business, one that Scott had taken some persuasion to agree to, and had allowed with questionable judgement. At best, it would weaken his team and distract from his attempt on the Pole – 'this winter travel is a new and bold adventure,' wrote Scott, 'but the right men have gone to attempt it.' However, the Scott expedition had an important scientific programme and Dr Wilson, the scientific officer, picked his companions with care. He chose 'Birdie' Bowers and the twenty-five-year-old Cherry-Garrard – the latter, on the face of it, an unlikely candidate. He was a rather frail classics scholar, extremely short-sighted and therefore heavily dependent on spectacles that kept clouding with his frozen breath; but he'd been a success from the moment the expedition set sail. The letters and diaries of Scott and Wilson refer to him as their best sledger and are full of tributes to his cheerfulness, kindness, bravery and willingness to work.

As for the penguin trip, 'No words could express its [the journey's] horror,' he commented. In the winter darkness, they man-hauled their sledges over sixty-three miles of treacherous ice and then back, struggling against gale-force winds. One night their tent blew away – on the face of it, certain death. Miraculously, they found it three days on. When they arrived back, five weeks later, carrying three eggs – Cherry-Garrard had dropped two – they were as much dead as alive.

The scientific value of this mission turned out to be minimal and perhaps it had all been rather pointless; as Cherry-Garrard said, 'It's extraordinary how often angels and fools do the same thing in this life, and I have never been able to settle which we were on this journey.' But his lasting gain was an understanding of the depths human compassion and fortitude could reach. His two companions were, to him, the greatest of men, and the discovery of their bodies, and those of the rest of the southern party a year later, stayed with him for the rest of his life. 'These two men went through the Winter Journey and lived. Later they went through the Polar Journey and died. They were gold, pure, shining, unalloyed. Words cannot express how good their companionship was . . . It is hard that often such men must go first when others far less worthy remain.' Troubled by a survivor's sense of guilt, he suffered with depression and nervous breakdowns while writing his account ten years later.

Perhaps partly out of respect for Dr Wilson, Cherry-Garrard successfully campaigned to get the Tasmanian government to ban the hunting of Antarctic penguins on Macquarie Island.

The worst journey in the world

We saw the Emperors standing all together huddled under the Barrier cliff some hundreds of yards away. The little light was going fast: we were much more excited about the approach of complete darkness and the look of wind in the south than we were about our triumph. After indescribable effort and hardship we were witnessing a marvel of the natural world, and we were the first and only men who had ever done so; we had within our grasp material which might prove of the utmost importance to science; we were turning theories into facts with every observation we made – and we had but a moment to give.

The disturbed Emperors made a tremendous row, trumpeting with their curious metallic voices. There was no doubt they had eggs, for they tried to shuffle along the ground without losing them off their feet. But when they were hustled a good many eggs were dropped and left lying on the ice, and some of these were quickly picked up by eggless Emperors who had probably been waiting a long time for the opportunity. In these poor birds the maternal side seems to have necessarily swamped the other functions of life. Such is the struggle for existence that they can only live by a glut of maternity, and it would be interesting to know whether such a life leads to happiness or satisfaction.

The men of the *Discovery* found this rookery where we now stood. They made journeys in the early spring but never arrived early enough to get eggs and only found parents and chicks. They concluded that the Emperor was an impossible kind of bird who, for some reason or other, nests in the middle of the Antarctic winter with the temperature anywhere below seventy degrees of frost, and the blizzards blowing, always blowing, against his devoted back. And they found him holding his precious chick balanced upon his big feet, and pressing it maternally, or paternally (for both sexes squabble for the privilege) against a bald patch in his breast. And when at last he simply must go and eat something in the open leads near by, he just puts the child down on the ice, and twenty chickless Emperors rush to pick it up. And they fight over it, and so tear it that sometimes it will die. And, if it can, it will crawl into any ice-crack to escape from so much kindness, and there it will freeze . . .

But interesting as the life history of these birds must be, we had not travelled for three weeks to see them sitting on their eggs. We wanted the embryos, and we wanted them as young as possible, and fresh and unfrozen, that specialists at home might cut them into microscopic sections and learn from the previous history of birds throughout the evolutionary ages. And so Bill and Birdie rapidly collected five eggs, which we hoped to carry safely in our fur mitts to our igloo upon Mount Terror, where we could pickle them in the alcohol we had brought for the purpose. We also wanted oil for our blubber stove, and they killed and skinned three birds – an Emperor weighs up to 6½ stones . . .

Meanwhile a whole procession of Emperors came round under the cliff on which I stood. The light was already very bad and it was well that my companions were quick in returning: we had to do everything in a great hurry. I hauled up the eggs in their mitts (which we fastened together round our necks with lampwick lanyards) and then the skins, but failed to help Bill at all. 'Pull,' he cried, from the bottom: 'I am pulling,' I said. 'But the line's quite slack down here,' he shouted. And when he had reached the top by climbing up on Bowers's shoulders, and we were both pulling all we knew, Birdie's end of the rope was still slack in his hands. Directly we put on a strain the rope cut into the ice edge and jammed – a very common difficulty when working among crevasses. We tried to run the rope over an ice-axe without success, and things began to look serious when Birdie, who had been running about prospecting and had meanwhile put one leg through a crack into the sea, found a place where the cliff did not overhang. He cut steps for himself, we hauled, and at last we were all together on the top – his foot being by now surrounded by a solid mass of ice.

We legged it back as hard as we could go: five eggs in our fur mitts, Birdie with two skins tied to him and trailing behind, and myself with one. We were roped up, and climbing the ridges and getting through the holes was very difficult. In one place where there was a steep rubble and snow slope down I left the ice-axe half-way up; in another it was too dark to see our former ice-axe footsteps, and I could see nothing, and so just let myself go and trusted to luck. With infinite patience Bill said: 'Cherry, you *must* learn how to use an ice-axe.' For the rest of the trip my wind-clothes were in rags.

We found the sledge, and none too soon, and now had three eggs left, more or less whole. Both mine had burst in my mitts: the first I emptied out, the second I left in my mitt to put into the cooker; it never got there, but on the return journey I had my mitts far more easily thawed out than Birdie's (Bill had none) and I believe the grease in the egg did them good. When we got into the hollows under the ridge where we had to cross, it was too dark to do anything but feel our way. We did so over many crevasses, found the ridge and crept over it. Higher up we could see more, but to follow our tracks soon became impossible, and we plugged straight ahead and luckily found the slope down which we had come. All day it had been blowing a nasty cold wind with a temperature between −20° and 30°, which we felt a good deal. Now it began to get worse. The weather was getting thick and things did not look very nice when we started up to find our tent. Soon it was blowing force 4, and soon we missed our way entirely. We got right up above the patch of rocks which marked our igloo and only found it after a good deal of search.

I have heard tell of an English officer at the Dardanelles who was left, blinded, in No Man's Land between the English and Turkish trenches. Moving only at night, and having no sense to tell him which were his own trenches, he was fired at by Turk and English alike as he groped his ghastly way to and from them. Thus he spent days and nights until, one night, he crawled towards the English trenches, to be fired at as usual. 'Oh God! what can I do!' someone heard him say, and he was brought in.

Such extremity of suffering cannot be measured: madness or death may give relief. But this I know: we on this journey were already beginning to think of death as a friend. As we groped our way back that night, sleepless, icy, and dog-tired in the dark and the wind and the drift, a crevasse seemed almost a friendly gift.

'Things must improve,' said Bill next day, 'I think we reached bed-rock last night.' We hadn't, by a long way.

'Bill, Bill, the tent has gone,' was the next I remember – from Bowers shouting at us again and again through the door. It is always these early morning shocks which hit one hardest: our slow minds suggested that this might mean a peculiarly lingering form of death. Journey after journey Birdie and I fought our way across the few yards which had separated the tent from the igloo door. I have never understood why so much of our gear which was in the tent remained, even in the lee of the igloo. The place where the tent had been was littered with gear, and when we came to reckon up afterwards we had everything except the bottom piece of the cooker, and the top of the outer cooker. We never saw these again. The most wonderful thing of all was that our finnesko were lying where they were left, which happened to be on the ground in the part of the tent which was under the lee of the igloo. Also Birdie's bag of personal gear was there, and a tin of sweets.

To get that gear in we fought against solid walls of black snow which flowed past us and tried to hurl us down the slope. Once started nothing could have stopped us. I saw Birdie knocked over once, but he clawed his way back just in time. Having passed everything we could find in to Bill, we got back into the igloo, and started to collect things together, including our very dishevelled minds.

There was no doubt that we were in the devil of a mess, and it was not altogether our fault. We had had to put our igloo more or less where we could get rocks with which to build it. Very naturally we had given both our tent and igloo all the shelter we could from the full force of the wind, and now it seemed we were in danger not because they were in the wind, but because they were not sufficiently in it. The main force of the hurricane, deflected by the ridge behind, fled over our heads and appeared to form by suction a vacuum below. Our tent had either been sucked upwards into this, or had been blown away because some of it was in the wind while some of it was not. The roof of our igloo was being wrenched upwards and then dropped back with great crashes: the drift was spouting in, not it seemed because it was blown in from outside, but because it was sucked in from within: the lee, not the weather, wall was the worst. Already everything was six or eight inches under snow.

Very soon we began to be alarmed about the igloo. For some time the heavy snow blocks we had heaved up on to the canvas roof kept it weighted down. But it seemed that they were being gradually moved off by the hurricane. The tension became well-nigh unendurable: the waiting in all that welter of noise was maddening. Minute after minute, hour after hour – those snow blocks were off now anyway, and the roof was smashed up and down – no canvas ever made could stand it indefinitely . . .

We did all we could to stop up the places where the drift was coming in, plugging the holes with our socks, mitts and other clothing. But it was no real good. Our igloo was a vacuum which was filling itself up as soon as possible: and when snow was not coming in a fine black moraine dust took its place, covering us and everything. For twenty-four hours we waited for the roof to go: things were so bad now that we dare not unlash the door.

Many hours ago Bill had told us that if the roof went he considered that our best chance would be to roll over in our sleeping-bags until we were lying on the openings, and get frozen and drifted in.

Gradually the situation got more desperate. The distance between the taut-sucked canvas and the sledge on which it should have been resting became greater, and this must have been due to the stretching of the canvas itself and the loss of the snow blocks on the top: it was not drawing out of the walls. The crashes as it dropped and banged out again were louder. There was more snow coming through the walls, though all our loose mitts, socks and smaller clothing were stuffed into the worst places: our pyjama jackets were stuffed between the roof and the rocks over the door. The rocks were lifting and shaking here till we thought they would fall.

We talked by shouting, and long before this one of us proposed to try and get the Alpine rope lashed down over the roof from outside. But Bowers said it was an absolute impossibility in that wind. 'You could never ask men at sea to try such a thing,' he said. He was up and out of his bag continually, stopping up holes, pressing against bits of roof to try and prevent the flapping and so forth. He was magnificent.

And then it went.

Birdie was over by the door, where the canvas which was bent over the lintel board was working worse than anywhere else. Bill was practically out of his bag pressing against some part with a long stick of some kind. I don't know what I was doing but I was half out of and half in my bag.

The top of the door opened in little slits and that green Willesden canvas flapped into hundreds of little fragments in fewer seconds than it takes to read this. The uproar of it all was indescribable. Even above the savage thunder of that great wind on the mountain came the lash of the canvas as it was whipped to little tiny strips. The highest rocks which we had built into our walls fell upon us, and a sheet of drift came in.

Birdie dived for his sleeping-bag and eventually got in, together with a terrible lot of drift. Bill also – but he was better off: I was already half into mine and all right, so I turned to help Bill. 'Get into your own,' he shouted, and when I continued to try and help him, he leaned over until his mouth was against my ear. '*Please*, Cherry,' he said, and his voice was terribly anxious. I know he felt responsible: feared it was he who had brought us to this ghastly end.

The next I knew was Bowers's head across Bill's body. 'We're all right,' he yelled, and we answered in the affirmative. Despite the fact that we knew we only said so because we knew we were all wrong, this statement was helpful. Then we turned our bags over as far as possible, so that the bottom of the bag was uppermost and the flaps were more or less beneath us. And we lay and thought, and sometimes we sang.

I suppose, wrote Wilson, we were all revolving plans to get back without a tent: and the one thing we had left was the floor-cloth upon which we were actually lying. Of course we could not speak at present, but later after the blizzard had stopped we discussed the possibility of digging a hole in the snow each night and covering it over with the floor-cloth. I do not think we had any idea that we could really get back in those temperatures in our present state of ice by such means, but no one ever hinted at such a thing. Birdie and Bill sang quite a lot of songs and hymns, snatches of which reached me every now and then, and I chimed in, somewhat feebly I suspect. Of course we were getting pretty badly drifted up. 'I was resolved to keep warm,' wrote Bowers, 'and beneath my debris covering I paddled my feet and sang all the songs and hymns I knew to pass the time. I could occasionally thump Bill, and as he still moved I knew he was alive all right – what a birthday for him!' Birdie was more drifted up than we, but at times we all had to hummock ourselves up to heave the snow off our bags. By opening the flaps of our bags we could get small pinches of soft drift which we pressed together and put into our mouths to melt. When our hands warmed up again we got some more; so we did not get very thirsty. A few ribbons of canvas still remained in the wall over our heads, and these produced volleys of cracks like pistol shots hour after hour. The canvas never drew out from the walls, not an inch. The wind made just the same noise as an express train running fast through a tunnel if you have both the windows down.

I can well believe that neither of my companions gave up hope for an instant. They must have been frightened, but they were never disturbed. As for me I never had any hope at all; and when the roof went I felt that this was the end. What else could I think? We had spent days in reaching this place through the darkness in cold such as had never been experienced by human beings. We had been out for four weeks under conditions in which no man had existed previously for more than a few days, if that. During this time we had seldom slept except from sheer physical exhaustion, as men sleep on the rack; and every minute of it we had been fighting for the bed-rock necessaries of bare existence, and always in the dark. We had kept ourselves going by enormous care of our feet and hands and bodies, by burning oil, and by having plenty of hot fatty food. Now we had no tent, one tin of oil left out of six, and only part of our cooker. When we were lucky and not too cold we could almost wring water from our clothes, and directly we got out of our sleeping-bags we were frozen into solid sheets of armoured ice. In cold temperatures with all the advantages of a tent over our heads we were already taking more than an hour of fierce struggling and cramp to get into our sleeping-bags – so frozen were they and so long did it take us to thaw our way in. No! Without the tent we were dead men.

And there seemed not one chance in a million that we should ever see our tent again. We were 900 feet up on the mountain side, and the wind blew about as hard as a wind can blow straight out to sea. First there was a steep slope, so hard that a pick made little impression upon it, so slippery that if you started down in finnesko you never could stop: this ended in a great ice-cliff some hundreds of feet high, and then came miles of pressure ridges, crevassed and tumbled, in which you might as well look for a daisy as a tent: and after that the open sea. The chances, however, were that the tent had just been taken up into the air and dropped somewhere in this sea well on the way to New Zealand. Obviously the tent was gone.

Face to face with real death one does not think of the things that torment the bad people in the tracts, and fill the good people with bliss. I might have speculated on my chances of going to Heaven; but candidly I did not care. I could not have wept if I had tried. I had no wish to review the evils of my past. But the past did seem to have been a bit wasted. The road to Hell may be paved with good intentions: the road to Heaven is paved with lost opportunities.

I wanted those years over again. What fun I would have with them: what glorious fun! It was a pity. Well has the Persian said that when we come to die we, remembering that God is merciful, will gnaw our elbows with remorse for thinking of the things we have not done for fear of the Day of Judgement.

And I wanted peaches and syrup – badly. We had them at the hut, sweeter and more luscious than you can imagine. And we have been without sugar for a month. Yes – especially the syrup.

Thus impiously I set out to die, making up my mind that I was not going to try and keep warm, that it might not take too long, and thinking I would try and get some morphia from the medical case if it got very bad. Not a bit heroic, and entirely true! Yes! comfortable, warm reader. Men do not fear death, they fear the pain of dying.

And then quite naturally and no doubt disappointingly to those who would like to read of my last agonies (for who would not give pleasure by his death?) I fell asleep.

In the early hours of Monday there was an occasional hint of a lull. Ordinarily in a big winter blizzard, when you have lived for several days and nights with that turmoil in your ears, the lulls are more trying than the noise: 'the feel of not to feel it'. I do not remember noticing that now. Seven or eight more hours passed, and though it was still blowing we could make ourselves heard to one another without great difficulty. It was two days and two nights since we had had a meal.

We decided to get out of our bags and make a search for the tent. We did so, bitterly cold and utterly miserable, though I do not think any of us showed it. In the darkness we could see very little, and no trace whatever of the tent. We returned against the wind, nursing our faces and hands, and settled that we must try and cook a meal somehow. We managed about the weirdest meal eaten north or south. We got the floor-cloth wedged under our bags, then got into our bags and drew the floor-cloth over our heads. Between us we got the primus alight somehow, and by hand we balanced the cooker on top of it, minus the two members which had been blown away. The flame flickered in the draughts. Very slowly the snow in the cooker melted, we threw in a plentiful supply of pemmican, and the smell of it was better than anything on earth . . .

It was still dark and we lay down in our bags again, but soon a little glow of light began to come up, and we turned out to have a further search for the tent. Birdie went off before Bill and me. Clumsily I dragged my eider-down out of my bag on my feet, all sopping wet: it was impossible to get it back and I let it freeze: it was soon just like a rock. The sky to the south was as black and sinister as it could possibly be. It looked as though the blizzard would be on us again in a moment.

I followed Bill down the slope. We could find nothing. But, as we searched, we heard a shout somewhere below and to the right. We got on a slope, slipped, and went sliding down quite unable to stop ourselves, and came upon Birdie with the tent, the outer lining still on the bamboos. Our lives had been taken away and given back to us.

We were so thankful we said nothing.

The Worst Journey in the World, 1922

Robert Falcon Scott

1868–1912

We all hope to meet the end with a similar spirit.

In his early thirties, despite having no previous experience of polar travel, Scott led the British National Antarctic expedition (1901–4). From their expedition base at McMurdo Sound, he, Edward Wilson and Shackleton made the first ever extensive land journeys on the continent, reaching 82° 17′ south, 500 miles from the Pole. All three nearly died on the return journey, supplies having been too finely calculated, as they were again on Scott's next and final attempt.

Despite what was actually a near disaster, Scott's reputation was now established, and in 1910 he sailed south in the *Terra Nova* with the aim both of reaching the South Pole (a 950-mile journey from McMurdo Sound), and of carrying out a scientific programme. He had chosen to rely on horses and motorized sledges to lay his depots, and both proved unsatisfactory in the Antarctic, fatally resulting in the key 'One Ton Depot' supplies for the return journey from the Pole being placed less far south than hoped. On reaching the foot of the Beardmore Glacier, nearly the halfway point, the surviving ponies were killed for food, and the dogs sent back. The men then laboured up the 140-mile-long glacier, following the route pioneered by Shackleton's 'Farthest South' expedition (see page 520), up to the Antarctic plateau itself. On 4 January 1912, with 200 miles to go, Scott then chose the southern party for the last leg – not so much for their physical fitness, but to represent different classes and branches of the armed forces. Cavalryman 'Titus' Oates had never before set foot in the Antarctic; Edward Wilson and Edgar Evans had been with Scott on the *Discovery* expedition but, like Scott, had otherwise no cold-weather experience. At the risk of cramping the tent and confusing ration calculations, Scott now also chose an extra man, 'Birdie' Bowers, who, like Oates, was a complete novice, and had no skis. Despite inexperience with the skis they did have, and enduring – unlike Amundsen and his men – what we now know was a freak spell of particularly dire weather, the men fought through to reach the Pole two weeks later, on 16 January 1912 – only to have confirmed what they now already feared: the Norwegian team had beaten them to it.

The defeat, coupled with appalling blizzard conditions, their poor diet and the physical strain of man-hauling their sledges, began taking its toll. Edgar Evans died first, and by mid-March Oates, badly frost-bitten and not wishing to slow down his companions, walked out into a blizzard. Scott and the two others struggled on for another twenty miles; but after eight days without provisions, and in a continuing blizzard, they finally perished – eleven miles from 'One Ton Depot', having dragged along their geological samples to the end. Their watchwords were duty and manliness, and among the last sentences Scott ever scribbled were, 'How much better has all this been than lounging in too great comfort at home.' The following spring, a search party found the bodies and brought back Scott's diary, letters and geological specimens.

Many have been harsh about Scott's competency, but it's as well to remember that he was very much a man shaped by his era – Victorian – and background – naval, set firmly in the officer class. His faults were largely the faults of his time and his place. As biographers have noted, had Scott not been a man so stolidly embedded in his society, he wouldn't have received the blessing of the establishment and been able to make his attempt. Whether Scott or the abnormal weather conditions he endured were to blame for the failure of his expedition, his diaries are astounding in their evocation of place and portrayal of the human spirit. A review that appeared in *Punch* on publication of the Scott journals talked of the 'undying beauty' there. Apsley Cherry-Garrard, one of those who found Scott's body, tried to explain the 'atmosphere of hero worship into which we were all plunged' by quoting the same review: 'His humanity, his courage, his faith, his steadfastness, above all his simplicity, mark him as a man among men.' All this aside, the *Terra Nova* expedition's scientific forays into the Antarctic continent garnered data of more importance than Amundsen's, and make his expedition, in this wider context, perhaps a greater feat of exploration.

Reaching the Pole

Monday, January 15: It is wonderful to think that two long marches would land us at the Pole. We left our depot today with nine days' provisions, so that it ought to be a certain thing now, and the only appalling possibility the sight of the Norwegian flag forestalling ours. Little Bowers continues his indefatigable efforts to get good sights, and it is wonderful how he works them up in his sleeping-bag in our congested tent. (Minimum for night −27.5°.) Only 27 miles from the Pole. We *ought* to do it now.

Tuesday, January 16: Camp 68. Height 9,760. T. −23.5°. The worst has happened, or nearly the worst. We marched well in the morning and covered 7½ miles. Noon sight showed us in Lat. 89° 42′ S., and we started off in high spirits in the afternoon, feeling that tomorrow would see us at our destination. About the second hour of the march Bowers' sharp eyes detected what he thought was a cairn; he was uneasy about it, but argued that it must be a sastrugus. Half an hour later he detected a black speck ahead. Soon we knew that this could not be a natural snow feature. We marched on, found that it was a black flag tied to a sledge bearer; near by the remains of a camp; sledge tracks and ski tracks going and coming and the clear trace of dogs' paws – many dogs. This told us the whole story. The Norwegians have forestalled us and are first at the Pole. It is a terrible disappointment, and I am very sorry for my loyal companions. Many thoughts come and much discussion have we had. Tomorrow we must march on to the Pole and then hasten home with all the speed we can compass. All the day-dreams must go; it will be a wearisome return. Certainly we are descending in altitude – certainly also the Norwegians found an easy way up.

Wednesday, January 17: Camp 69. T. −22° at start. Night −21°. THE POLE. Yes, but under very different circumstances from those expected. We have had a horrible day – add to our disappointment a head wind four to five, with a temperature −22°, and companions labouring on with cold feet and hands.

We started at 7.30, none of us having slept much after the shock of our discovery. We followed the Norwegian sledge tracks for some way; as far as we make out there are only two men. In about three miles we passed two small cairns. Then the weather overcast, and the tracks being increasingly drifted up and obviously going too far to the west, we decided to make straight for the Pole according to our calculations. At 12.30 Evans had such cold hands we camped for lunch – an excellent 'week-end one'. We had marched 7.4 miles. Lat. sight gave 89° 53' 37". We started out and did 6½ miles due south. Tonight little Bowers is laying himself out to get sights in terrible difficult circumstances; the wind is blowing hard, T. −21°, and there is that curious damp, cold feeling in the air which chills one to the bone in no time. We have been descending again, I think, but there looks to be a rise ahead; otherwise there is very little that is different from the awful monotony of past days. Great God! This is an awful place and terrible enough for us to have laboured to it without the reward of priority. Well, it is something to have got here, and the wind may be our friend tomorrow. We have had a fat Polar hoosh in spite of our chagrin, and feel comfortable inside – added a small stick of chocolate and the queer taste of a cigarette brought by Wilson. Now for the run home and a desperate struggle. I wonder if we can do it.

Thursday morning, January 18: Decided after summing up all observations that we were 3.5 miles away from the Pole – one mile beyond it and three to the right. More or less in this direction Bowers saw a cairn or tent.

We have just arrived at this tent, two miles from our camp, therefore about 1½ miles from the Pole. In the tent we find a record of five Norwegians having been here, as follows;

>Roald Amundsen
>Olav Olavson Bjaaland
>Hilmer Hanssen
>Sverre H. Hassel
>Oscar Wisting.

>16 Dec. 1911

The tent is fine – a small compact affair supported by a single bamboo. A note from Amundsen, which I keep, asks me to forward a letter to King Haakon!

The following articles have been left in the tent: three half bags of reindeer containing a miscellaneous assortment of mits and sleeping-socks, very various in description, a sextant, a Norwegian artificial horizon and a hypsometer without boiling-point thermometers, a sextant and hypsometer of English make.

Left a note to say I had visited the tent with companions. Bowers photographing and Wilson sketching. Since lunch we have marched 6.2 miles S.S.E. by compass (i.e. northwards). Sights at lunch gave us half to three-quarters of a mile from the Pole, so we call it the Pole Camp. (Temp. Lunch −21°.) We built a cairn, put up our poor slighted Union Jack, and photographed ourselves – mighty cold work all of it – less than half a mile south we saw stuck up an old underrunner of a sledge. This we commandeered as a yard for a floorcloth sail. I imagine it was intended to mark the exact spot of the Pole as near as the Norwegians could fix it. (Height 9,500.) A note attached talked of the tent as being two miles from the Pole. Wilson keeps the note. There is no doubt that our predecessors have made thoroughly sure of their mark and fully carried out their programme. I think the Pole is about 9,500 feet in height; this is remarkable, considering that in Lat. 88° we were about 10,500.

We carried the Union Jack about three-quarters of a mile north with us and left it on a piece of stick as near as we could fix it. I fancy the Norwegians arrived at the Pole on the 15th Dec. and left on the 17th, ahead of a date quoted by me in London as ideal, viz Dec. 22. It looks as though the Norwegian party expected colder weather on the summit than they got; it could scarcely be otherwise from Shackleton's account. Well, we have turned our back now on the goal of our ambition and must face our 800 miles of solid dragging – and goodbye to most of the day-dreams!

'Assuredly the end is not far'

Sunday, March 11: Titus Oates is very near the end, one feels. What we or he will do, God only knows. We discussed the matter after breakfast; he is a brave fine fellow and understands the situation, but he practically asked for advice. Nothing could be said but to urge him to march as long as he could. One satisfactory result to the discussion; I practically ordered Wilson to hand over the means of ending our troubles to us, so that any one of us may know how to do so. Wilson had no choice between doing so and our ransacking the medicine case. We have 30 opium tabloids apiece and he is left with a tube of morphine. So far the tragical side of our story.

The sky completely overcast when we started this morning. We could see nothing, lost the tracks, and doubtless have been swaying a good deal since – 3.1 miles for the forenoon – terribly heavy dragging – expected it. Know that six miles is about the limit of our endurance now, if we get no help from wind or surfaces. We have seven days' food and should be about 55 miles from One Ton Camp tonight, $6 \times 7 = 42$, leaving us 13 miles short of our distance, even if things get no worse. Meanwhile the season rapidly advances.

Monday, March 12: We did 6.9 miles yesterday, under our necessary average. Things are left much the same, Oates not pulling much, and now with hands as well as feet pretty well useless. We did four miles this morning in 4 hours 20 min – we may hope for three this afternoon, $7 \times 6 = 42$. We shall be 47 miles from the depot. I doubt if we can possibly do it. The surface remains awful, the cold intense, and our physical condition running down. God help us! Not a breath of favourable wind for more than a week, and apparently liable to head winds at any moment.

Wednesday, March 14: No doubt about the going downhill, but everything going wrong for us. Yesterday we woke to a strong northerly wind with temp. $-37°$. Couldn't face it, so remained in camp till two, then did 5¼ miles. Wanted to march later, but party feeling the cold badly as the breeze (N.) never took off entirely, and as the sun sank the temp. fell. Long time getting supper in dark.

This morning started with southerly breeze, set sail and passed another cairn at good speed; half-way, however, the wind shifted to W. by S. or W.S.W., blew through our wind clothes and into our mits. Poor Wilson horribly cold, could [not] get off ski for some time. Bowers and I practically made camp, and when we got into the tent at last we were all deadly cold. Then temp. now midday down $-43°$ and the wind strong. We *must* go on, but now the making of every camp must be more difficult and dangerous. It must be near the end, but a pretty merciful end. Poor Oates got it again in the foot. I shudder to think what it will be like tomorrow. It is only with greatest pains rest of us keep off frostbites. No idea there could be temperatures like this at this time of year with such winds. Truly awful outside the tent. Must fight it out to the last biscuit, but can't reduce rations.

Friday, March 16 or Saturday 17: Lost track of dates, but think the last correct. Tragedy all along the line. At lunch, the day before yesterday, poor Titus Oates said he couldn't go on; he proposed we should leave him in his sleeping-bag. That we could not do, and we induced him to come on, on the afternoon march. In spite of its awful nature for him he struggled on and we made a few miles. At night he was worse and we knew the end had come.

Should this be found I want these facts recorded. Oates' last thoughts were of his mother, but immediately before he took pride in thinking that his regiment would be pleased with the bold way in which he met his death. We can testify to his bravery. He has borne intense suffering for weeks without complaint, and to the very last was able and willing to discuss outside subjects. He did not – would not – give up hope till the very end. He was a brave soul. This was the end. He slept through the night before last, hoping not to wake; but he woke in the morning – yesterday. It was blowing a blizzard. He said, 'I am just going outside and may be some time.' He went out into the blizzard and we have not seen him since.

I take this opportunity of saying that we have stuck to our sick companions to the last. In case of Edgar Evans, when absolutely out of food and he lay insensible, the safety of the remainder seemed to demand his abandonment, but Providence mercifully removed him at this critical moment. He died a natural death, and we did not leave him till two hours after his death. We knew that poor Oates was walking to his death, but though we tried to dissuade him, we knew it was the act of a brave man and an English gentleman. We all hope to meet the end with a similar spirit, and assuredly the end is not far.

I can only write at lunch and then only occasionally. The cold is intense, −40° at midday. My companions are unendingly cheerful, but we are all on the verge of serious frostbites, and though we constantly talk of fetching through I don't think any one of us believes it in his heart.

We are cold on the march now, and at all times except meals. Yesterday we had to lay up for a blizzard and today we move dreadfully slowly. We are at No. 14 pony camp, only two pony marches from One Ton Depot. We leave here our theodolite, a camera, and Oates' sleeping-bags. Diaries, etc., and geological specimens carried at Wilson's special request, will be found with us or on our sledge.

Sunday, March 18: Today, lunch, we are 21 miles from the depot. Ill fortune presses, but better may come. We have had more wind and drift from ahead yesterday; had to stop marching; wind N.W., force four, temp. −35°. No human being could face it, and we are worn out *nearly*.

My right foot has gone, nearly all the toes – two days ago I was proud possessor of best feet. These are the steps of my downfall. Like an ass I mixed a small spoonful of curry powder with my melted pemmican – it gave me violent indigestion. I lay awake and in pain all night; woke and felt done on the march; foot went and I didn't know it. A very small measure of neglect and have a foot which is not pleasant to contemplate. Bowers takes first place in condition, but there is not much to choose after all. The others are still confident of getting through – or pretend to be – I don't know! We have the last *half* fill of oil in our primus and a very small quantity of spirit – this alone between us and thirst. The wind is fair for the moment, and that is perhaps a fact to help. The mileage would have seemed ridiculously small on our outward journey.

Monday, March 19: Lunch. We camped with difficulty last night, and were dreadfully cold till after our supper of cold pemmican and biscuit and a half a pannikin of cocoa cooked over the spirit. Then, contrary to expectation, we got warm and all slept well. Today we started in the usual dragging manner. Sledge dreadfully heavy. We are 15½ miles from the depot and ought to get there in three days. What progress! We have two days' food but barely a day's fuel. All our feet are getting bad – Wilson's best, my right foot worst, left all right. There is no chance to nurse one's feet till we can get hot food into us. Amputation is the least I can hope for now, but will the trouble spread? That is the serious question. The weather doesn't give us a chance – the wind from N. to N.W. and −40° temp. today.

Wednesday, March 21: Got within 11 miles of depot Monday night; had to lay up all yesterday in severe blizzard. Today forlorn hope, Wilson and Bowers going to depot for fuel.

Thursday, March 22 and 23: Blizzard bad as ever – Wilson and Bowers unable to start – tomorrow last chance – no fuel and only one or two of food left – must be near the end. Have decided it shall be natural – we shall march for the depot with or without our effects and die in our tracks.

Thursday, March 29: Since the 21st we have had a continuous gale from W.S.W. and S.W. We had fuel to make two cups of tea apiece and bare food for two days on the 20th. Every day we have been ready to start for our depot 11 *miles* away, but outside the door of the tent it remains a scene of whirling drift. I do not think we can hope for any better things now. We shall stick it out to the end, but we are getting weaker, of course, and the end cannot be far.

It seems a pity, but I do not think I can write more.

R. Scott

[Last entry.]
For God's sake look after our people.

[Wilson and Bowers were found in the attitude of sleep, their sleeping-bags closed over their heads as they would naturally close them.

Scott had died later. He had thrown back the flaps of his sleeping-bag and opened his coat. The little wallet containing the three notebooks was under his shoulders and his arm was flung across Wilson.]

Letters found in Scott's tent

My dear Mrs Wilson [Mrs E. A. Wilson],

If this letter reaches you Bill and I will have gone out together. We are very near it now and I should like you to know how splendid he was at the end – everlastingly cheerful and ready to sacrifice himself for others, never a word of blame to me for leading him into this mess. He is not suffering, luckily, at least only minor discomforts.

His eyes have a comfortable blue look of hope and his mind is peaceful with the satisfaction of his faith in regarding himself as part of the great scheme of the Almighty. I can do no more to comfort you than to tell you that he died as he lived, a brave, true man – the best of comrades and staunchest of friends.

My whole heart goes out to you in pity,

Yours,

R. SCOTT.

My dear Barrie [Sir J. M. Barrie],

We are pegging out in a very comfortless spot. Hoping this letter may be found and sent to you, I write a word of farewell . . . More practically I want you to help my widow and my boy – your godson. We are showing that Englishmen can still die with a bold spirit, fighting it out to the end. It will be known that we have accomplished our object in reaching the Pole, and that we have done everything possible, even to sacrificing ourselves in order to save sick companions. I think this makes an example for Englishmen of the future, and that the country ought to help those who are left behind to mourn us. I leave my poor girl and your godson, Wilson leaves a widow, and Edgar Evans also a widow in humble circumstances. Do what you can to get their claims recognised. Goodbye. I am not at all afraid of the end, but sad to miss many a humble pleasure which I had planned for the future on our long marches. I may not have proved a great explorer, but we have done the greatest march ever made and come very near to great success. Goodbye, my dear friend,

Yours,

R. SCOTT.

We are in a desperate state, feet frozen, &c. No fuel and a long way from food, but it would do your heart good to be in our tent, to hear our songs and the cheery conversation as to what we will do when we get to Hut Point.

Later. – We are very near the end, but have not and will not lose our good cheer. We have four days of storm in our tent and nowhere's food or fuel. We did intend to finish ourselves when things proved like this, but we have decided to die naturally in the track.

As a dying man, my dear friend, be good to my wife and child. Give the boy a chance in life if the State won't do it. He ought to have good stuff in him . . . I never met a man in my life whom I admired and loved more than you, but I never could show you how much your friendship meant to me, for you had much to give and I nothing.

Scott's Last Expedition: The Journals, 1913

ROALD AMUNDSEN
1872–1928

I figured out exactly the precise day on which I planned to kill each dog as its usefulness should end for drawing the diminishing supplies on the sleds and its usefulness should begin as food for the men.

Between 1903 and 1906 the Norwegian Roald Amundsen became the first to navigate the entire length of the North-West Passage – with six others in a small fishing smack, the *Gjöa*. He next intended to tackle the North Pole and borrowed Nansen's Arctic ship, the *Fram* for the purpose. Peary's 'successful' attempt forestalled him, and instead he secretly turned his attention south. Taking the British – and even his own team – by surprise, he headed to the Antarctic and overtook Scott's expedition, making a two-month dash with dog sleds and skis from the Bay of Whales, where he overwintered, up the Axel Heiberg Glacier to the Antarctic plateau. He reached the Pole on 14 December 1911, one month before Scott, and, thanks to his superior preparation, and altogether better weather, had an easier time of it. He covered the 1,860 miles to the Pole and back in ninety-nine days. He remained bemused for many years that Scott's failed attempt to conquer the South Pole overshadowed his own success. He had seen the Pole as a physical challenge, pure and simple, not to be confused with distracting scientific experiments.

In succeeding years, he focused on air travel, then still in its infancy. In 1924 he joined Lincoln Ellsworth in an attempted crossing of the North Pole by seaplane, but they were forced into Arctic seas and nearly died. Two years later, together with the Italian explorer General Nobile (see page 550), he flew over the Pole from Spitzbergen to Alaska in a dirigible balloon. In 1928, Amundsen lost his life when his seaplane crashed into the polar sea during an attempted rescue of Nobile, whose airship had crashed on to the ice days earlier.

Beyond Shackleton's flag

We had a great piece of work before us that day: nothing less than carrying our flag farther south than the foot of man had trod. We had our silk flag ready; it was made fast to two ski-sticks and laid on Hanssen's sledge. I had given him orders that as soon as we had covered the distance to 88° 23′ S., which was Shackleton's farthest south, the flag was to be hoisted on his sledge. It was my turn as forerunner, and I pushed on. There was no longer any difficulty in holding one's course; I had the grandest cloud-formations to steer by, and everything now went like a machine. First came the forerunner for the time being, then Hanssen, then Wisting, and finally Bjaaland. The forerunner who was not on duty went where he liked; as a rule he accompanied one or other of the sledges. I had long ago fallen into a reverie – far removed from the scene in which I was moving; what I thought about I do not remember now, but I was so preoccupied that I had entirely forgotten my surroundings. Then suddenly I was roused from my dreaming by a jubilant shout, followed by ringing cheers. I turned round quickly to discover the reason of this unwonted occurrence, and stood speechless and overcome.

I find it impossible to express the feelings that possessed me at this moment. All the sledges had stopped, and from the foremost of them the Norwegian flag was flying. It shook itself out, waved and flapped so that the silk rustled; it looked wonderfully well in the pure, clear air and the shining white surroundings. 88° 23′ was past; we were farther south than any human being had been. No other moment of the whole trip affected me like this. The tears forced their way to my eyes; by no effort of will could I keep them back. It was the flag yonder that conquered me and my will. Luckily I was some way in advance of the others, so that I had time to pull myself together and master my feelings before reaching my comrades. We all shook hands, with mutual congratulations; we had won our way far by holding together, and we would go farther yet – to the end.

We did not pass that spot without according our highest tribute of admiration to the man, who – together with his gallant companions – had planted his country's flag so infinitely nearer to the goal than any of his precursors. Sir Ernest Shackleton's name will always be written in the annals of Antarctic exploration in letters of fire. Pluck and grit can work wonders, and I know of no better example of this than what that man has accomplished . . .

Every step we now took in advance brought us rapidly nearer the goal; we could feel fairly certain of reaching it on the afternoon of the 14th. It was very natural that our conversation should be chiefly concerned with the time of arrival. None of us would admit that he was nervous, but I am inclined to think that we all had a little touch of that malady. What should we see when we got there? A vast, endless plain, that no eye had yet seen and no foot yet trodden; or—No, it was an impossibility; with the speed at which we had travelled, we must reach the goal first, there could be no doubt about that. And yet – and yet—Wherever there is the smallest loophole, doubt creeps in and gnaws and gnaws and never leaves a poor wretch in peace . . .

The weather during the forenoon [of the 13th] had been just as fine as before; in the afternoon we had some snow-showers from the south-east. It was like the eve of some great festival that night in the tent. One could feel that a great event was at hand. Our flag was taken out again and lashed to the same two ski-sticks as before. Then it was rolled up and laid aside, to be ready when the time came. I was awake several times during the night, and had the same feeling that I can remember as a little boy on the night before Christmas

Eve – an intense expectation of what was going to happen. Otherwise I think we slept just as well that night as any other.

On the morning of December 14 the weather was of the finest, just as if it had been made for arriving at the Pole. I am not quite sure, but I believe we despatched our breakfast rather more quickly than usual and were out of the tent sooner, though I must admit that we always accomplished this with all reasonable haste . . . We advanced that day in the same mechanical way as before; not much was said, but eyes were used all the more . . .

At three in the afternoon a simultaneous 'Halt!' rang out from the drivers. They had carefully examined their sledge-meters, and they all showed the full distance – our Pole by reckoning. The goal was reached, the journey ended. I cannot say – though I know it would sound much more effective – that the object of my life was attained. That would be romancing rather too bare-facedly. I had better be honest and admit straight out that I have never known any man to be placed in such a diametrically opposite position to the goal of his desires as I was at that moment. The regions around the North Pole – well, yes, the North Pole itself – had attracted me from childhood, and here I was at the South Pole. Can anything more topsy-turvy be imagined?

We reckoned now that we were at the Pole. Of course, every one of us knew that we were not standing on the absolute spot; it would be an impossibility with the time and the instruments at our disposal to ascertain that exact spot. But we were so near it that the few miles which possibly separated us from it could not be of the slightest importance. It was our intention to make a circle round this camp, with a radius of twelve and a half miles (20 kilometres), and to be satisfied with that. After we had halted we collected and congratulated each other. We had good grounds for mutual respect in what had been achieved, and I think that was just the feeling that was expressed in the firm and powerful grasps of the fist that were exchanged. After this we proceeded to the greatest and most solemn act of the whole journey – the planting of our flag. Pride and affection shone in the five pairs of eyes that gazed upon the flag, as it unfurled itself with a sharp crack, and waved over the Pole. I had determined that the act of planting it – the historic event – should be equally divided among us all. It was not for one man to do this; it was for *all* who had staked their lives in the struggle, and held together through thick and thin. This was the only way in which I could show my gratitude to my comrades in this desolate spot. I could see that they understood and accepted it in the spirit in which it was offered . . .

One gets out of the way of protracted ceremonies in those regions – the shorter they are the better. Everyday life began again at once. When we had got the tent up, Hanssen set about slaughtering Helge, and it was hard for him to have to part from his best friend. Helge had been an uncommonly useful and good-natured dog; without making any fuss he had pulled from morning to night, and had been a shining example to the team. But during the last week he had quite fallen away, and on our arrival at the Pole there was only a shadow of the old Helge left. He was only a drag on the others, and did absolutely no work. One blow on the skull, and Helge had ceased to live. 'What is death to one is food to another,' is a saying that can scarcely find a better application than these dog meals. Helge was portioned out on the spot, and within a couple of hours there was nothing left of him but his teeth and the tuft at the end of his tail. This was the second of our eighteen dogs that we had lost. The Major, one of Wisting's fine dogs, left us in 88° 25′ S., and never returned. He was fearfully worn out, and must have gone away to die. We now had sixteen dogs left, and these we intended to divide into two equal teams, leaving Bjaaland's sledge behind.

Of course, there was a festivity in the tent that evening – not that champagne corks were popping and wine flowing – no, we contented ourselves with a little piece of seal meat each, and it tasted well and did us good. There was no other sign of festival indoors. Outside we heard the flag flapping in the breeze. Conversation was lively in the tent that evening, and we talked of many things. Perhaps, too, our thoughts sent messages home of what we had done.

The South Pole, 1912

Assessment of Scott's fatal mistakes

All my experience in Polar work had convinced me that dogs were the only practicable draught animals for use in snow and ice. They are quick, strong, sure-footed, intelligent, and able to negotiate any terrain that man himself can traverse. Scott, on the other hand, had come South equipped with motor sledges, which had immediately demonstrated their impracticability over the surface of ice and snow. He had brought also – and to these he pinned his fate finally – a number of Shetland ponies. I was confident that this was a fatal mistake, and much to my sorrow it was in part the cause of Scott's tragic end...

Our choice of a site for our base camp on the barrier was an essential factor in our success, just as Scott's choice of a site on the mainland to the west was an essential factor in his inability to return in safety from the Pole. In the first place, the air currents in the Antarctic regions make the weather much more

severe on the land than on the ice. At best the climate in the Antarctic is about
the worst in the world, chiefly because of the terrific intensity of the gales
which blow almost incessantly in those regions. These gales are of almost
unbelievable velocity. Scott encountered them several times of such force that
it was nearly impossible to stand erect. In his winter camp, Scott and his
companions were harassed through the weary waiting months with almost
uninterrupted bad weather – something which not only lowered the spirits of
the party but also seriously hampered their work of preparation for the final
dash. Our camp on the ice, however, was favoured with infinitely better weather, and at no time were we subject to any discomfort. Our experience of the
past in preparing an absolutely windproof shelter, and in solving the problem
of ventilating such a shelter, provided us with fairly comfortable winter
quarters.

The ice barrier – so much described in all works on Antarctic exploration –
is in reality nothing but a gigantic glacier pressing down from the heights of
the Antarctic mountains to the sea. This glacier is hundreds of miles in width
and from one to two hundred feet high. Like all glaciers, at its lower end this
one was constantly breaking off into icebergs. The idea, therefore, of making a
permanent camp on the barrier itself, though often considered, had always
been dismissed as too dangerous.

I had, however, carefully read and long pondered the works of the earlier
explorers in the Antarctic. In comparing their records, I had been greatly
struck with the discovery that the Bay of Whales, notwithstanding that it was
merely a bay whose shores were the icy walls of the glacier, had not substantially changed its shore line since its first discovery by Sir James Ross in
1842 . . .

Our location on the Bay of Whales gave us several advantages in trying to
reach the Pole. In the first place, it was somewhat nearer to the Pole than
Scott's camp, and, as the event proved, the path southward which it forced us
to take was much the more favourable for travel.

Above all of these things, however, the one which was most essential to our
success was our use of dogs. The reason briefly is this: Our method of attacking the Pole was to make repeated trips from the permanent camp southward,
setting up shelters and making caches of provisions one after the other at
several days' travel apart, so that we should be able to make the return trip
from the Pole without having to carry all our supplies there and back. Obviously, we could set up this series of caches very quickly, and at each we could
safely leave the minimum weight of supplies for the return trip. In making
my calculations for the distances between these stations and the amount of

provisions which should be left in each, I was able to reduce the weight of provisions to be carried by calculating the flesh of the dogs which carried it as part of the food supply of us men. As there are about fifty pounds of edible food in the carcass of an Eskimo dog, it was quite probable that every dog we took south with us meant fifty less pounds of food to be carried and cached. In my calculations before the start for the final dash to the Pole, I figured out exactly the precise day on which I planned to kill each dog as its usefulness should end for drawing the diminishing supplies on the sleds and its usefulness should begin as food for the men. This schedule worked out almost to the day and the dog. Above everything else, it was the essential factor in our successful trip to the Pole and our safe return to the base camp.

Scott and his companions died on their return from the Pole, not from broken hearts over our earlier arrival, but from actual starvation, because of their inability to provide adequately for food on the return trip. This difference between the two expeditions was exactly the difference between dogs and other means of transportation . . .

Nobody could hold a higher admiration than myself for the gallant courage of our brave English competitors, for nobody else so well as we can understand the fearful dangers of the trip.

Scott was a splendid sportsman as well as a great explorer. I cannot, however, say as much for many of his countrymen. Just as in times of war it may be observed that the soldiers on the opposing sides retain a high respect for their foes in arms, while the noncombatants at home seem to feel obligated to indulge in hymns of hate against their enemies, just so in exploration it often happens that the men in the field retain a high regard for their competitors, while their effortless compatriots at home seem to feel obligated to detract from the success of an explorer just because he is not of their own nation. Meaning that the following comment shall be read in the light of the preceding sentence, I feel justified in saying that by and large the British are a race of very bad losers.

My Life as an Explorer, 1927

ERNEST SHACKLETON
1874–1922

I must look at the matter sensibly and consider the lives of those who are with me.

A British merchant-naval officer born in County Kildare, Ireland, Sir Ernest Shackleton was a member of Scott's first expedition to the Antarctic (1901–4) and in 1907 led his own expedition there, sailing for the Ross Sea in the whaler *Nimrod*. One party climbed Mount Erebus and reached the Southern Magnetic Pole. Another, which he led himself, found a route up the Beardmore Glacier to the 10,000-foot Antarctic plateau and headed south to the Pole. He reached a point 88° degrees 23′ south, ninety-seven miles from the Pole, before blizzards and lack of food forced his sledge party to turn back. The return was a race with death: only a few cups of cocoa and a little pony maize were left when their base was reached. Notwithstanding, his 'Farthest South' expedition brought him fame, huge popularity and a knighthood.

With both Poles subsequently conquered by others, Shackleton set his sights on a 1,800-mile sledge crossing of Antarctica from the Weddell to the Ross Sea. In 1914 he set off with twenty-seven men in a 300-ton wooden barquentine, naming it the *Endurance*, after his family motto: 'By endurance we conquer.' Soon after reaching the Weddell Sea, she was caught in ice, and the current took her nearly 600 miles before she broke up eleven months later. The expedition members were forced into small boats and eventually reached the inhospitable Elephant Island after a fearful journey.

To get help, Shackleton and five others then set off in a tiny open-topped boat, the *James Caird*, 'jumping like a flea' through some of the roughest waters in the world, Captain Frank Worsley navigating, astoundingly, to South Georgia 800 miles away. They landed on the uninhabited south-west coast within a remarkable sixteen days. Shackleton and two others then crossed the mountainous interior and reached a whaling station at Stromness Bay, from where they effected the rescue of the remainder of the party. Though none of the expedition's goals were achieved, a victory, of sorts, had been achieved from defeat.

Shackleton shared his rival Scott's habit of cutting things fine, and a strange inability to learn from others' and his own mistakes, but he was by nature an unconventional adventurer – which was, in part, why Clements Markham and the Royal Geographical Society backed the more stoutly Victorian Scott. However, with the 1914–17 *Endurance* expedition he had again proved himself a remarkable and courageous leader – shown in his care for his men, who affectionately called him 'Boss', and his calm determination, which was capable of inspiring a loyalty that is at times very moving. John King Davis, arguably the greatest ship's captain of this age of Antarctic discoveries, once wrote in his diary of a stint with Mawson, 'There is something about this show which is missing. It is what I would call the Shackleton touch, which made the ward room a brighter spot as soon as one went into it.'

In 1921 Shackleton set forth on his third Antarctic expedition, but died on the voyage south of a heart attack, and now lies buried on South Georgia.

'The Farthest South'

January 2: Terribly hard work to-day. We started at 6.45 a.m. with a fairly good surface, which soon became very soft. We were sinking in over our ankles, and our broken sledge, by running sideways, added to the drag. We have been going uphill all day, and to-night are 11,034 ft. above sea-level. It has taken us all day to do 10 miles 450 yards, though the weights are fairly light. A cold wind, with a temperature of minus 14° Fahr., goes right through us now, as we are weakening from want of food, and the high altitude makes every move-ment an effort, especially if we stumble on the march. My head is giving me trouble all the time. Wild seems the most fit of us. God knows we are doing all we can, but the outlook is serious if this surface continues and the plateau gets higher, for we are not travelling fast enough to make our food spin out and get back to our depot in time. I cannot think of failure yet. I must look at the matter sensibly and consider the lives of those who are with me. I feel that if we go on too far it will be impossible to get back over this surface, and then all the results will be lost to the world. We can now definitely locate the South Pole on the highest plateau in the world, and our geological work and meteorology will be of the greatest use to science; but all this is not the Pole. Man can only do his best, and we have arrayed against us the strongest forces of nature. This cutting south wind with drift plays the mischief with us, and after ten hours of struggling against it one pannikin of food with two biscuits and a cup of cocoa does not warm one up much. I must think over the situation carefully to-morrow, for time is going on and food is going also . . .

January 4: The end is in sight. We can only go for three more days at the most, for we are weakening rapidly. Short food and a blizzard wind from the south, with driving drift, at a temperature of 47° of frost, have plainly told us to-day that we are reaching our limit, for we were so done up at noon with cold that the clinical thermometer failed to register the temperature of three of us at 94° . . .

January 6: This must be our last outward march with the sledge and camp equipment. To-morrow we must leave camp with some food, and push as far south as possible, and then plant the flag. To-day's story is 57° of frost, with a strong blizzard and high drift; yet we marched 13 geographical miles through soft snow, being helped by extra food. This does not mean full rations, but a bigger ration than we have been having lately. The pony maize is all finished. The most trying day we have yet spent, our fingers and faces being frost-bitten continually. To-morrow we will rush south with the flag. We are at 88° 7′

South to-night. It is our last outward march. Blowing hard to-night. I would fail to explain my feelings if I tried to write them down, now that the end has come. There is only one thing that lightens the disappointment, and that is the feeling that we have done all we could. It is the forces of nature that have prevented us from going right through. I cannot write more.

January 7: A blinding, shrieking blizzard all day, with the temperature ranging from 60° to 70° of frost. It has been impossible to leave the tent, which is snowed up on the lee side. We have been lying in our bags all day, only warm at food time, with fine snow making through the walls of the worn tent and covering our bags. We are greatly cramped. Adams is suffering from cramp every now and then. We are eating our valuable food without marching. The wind has been blowing eighty to ninety miles an hour. We can hardly sleep. To-morrow I trust this will be over. Directly the wind drops we march as far south as possible, then plant the flag, and turn homeward. Our chief anxiety is lest our tracks may drift up, for to them we must trust mainly to find our depot; we have no land bearings in this great plain of snow. It is a serious risk that we have taken, but we had to play the game to the utmost, and Providence will look after us.

January 8: Again all day in our bags, suffering considerably physically from cold hands and feet, and from hunger, but more mentally, for we cannot get on south, and we simply lie here shivering. Every now and then one of our party's feet go, and the unfortunate beggar has to take his leg out of the sleeping-bag and have his frozen foot nursed into life again by placing it inside the shirt, against the skin of his almost equally unfortunate neighbour. We must do something more to the south, even though the food is going, and we weaken lying in the cold, for with 72° of frost the wind cuts through our thin tent, and even the drift is finding its way in and on to our bags, which are wet enough as it is. Cramp is not uncommon every now and then, and the drift all round the tent has made it so small that there is hardly room for us at all. The wind has been blowing hard all day; some of the gusts must be over seventy or eighty miles an hour. This evening it seems as though it were going to ease down, and directly it does we shall be up and away south for a rush. I feel that this march must be our limit. We are so short of food, and at this high altitude, 11,600 ft., it is hard to keep any warmth in our bodies between the scanty meals. We have nothing to read now, having depoted our little books to save weight, and it is dreary work lying in the tent with nothing to read, and too cold to write much in the diary.

January 9: Our last day outwards. We have shot our bolt, and the tale is latitude 88° 23′ South, longitude 162° East. The wind eased down at 1 a.m., and at 2 a.m. we were up and had breakfast. At 4 a.m. started south, with the Queen's Union Jack, a brass cylinder containing stamps and documents to place at the furthest south point, camera, glasses, and compass. At 9 a.m. we were in 88° 23′ South, half running and half walking over a surface much hardened by the recent blizzard. It was strange for us to go along without the nightmare of a sledge dragging behind us. We hoisted Her Majesty's flag and the other Union Jack afterwards, and took possession of the plateau in the name of His Majesty. While the Union Jack blew out stiffly in the icy gale that cut us to the bone, we looked south with our powerful glasses, but could see nothing but the dead white snow plain. There was no break in the plateau as it extended towards the Pole, and we feel sure that the goal we have failed to reach lies on this plain. We stayed only a few minutes, and then, taking the Queen's flag and eating our scanty meal as we went, we hurried back and reached our camp about 3 p.m. We were so dead tired that we only did two hours' march in the afternoon and camped at 5.30 p.m. The temperature was minus 19° Fahr. Fortunately for us, our tracks were not obliterated by the blizzard; indeed, they stood up, making a trail easily followed. Homeward bound at last. Whatever regrets may be, we have done our best.

  The Heart of the Antarctic, 1910

The *Endurance* is attacked by ice

During the concluding days of September the roar of the pressure grew louder, and I could see that the area of disturbance was rapidly approaching the ship. Stupendous forces were at work and the fields of firm ice around the *Endurance* were being diminished steadily. September 30 was a bad day. It began well, for we got two penguins and five seals during the morning. Three other seals were seen. But at 3 p.m. cracks that had opened during the night alongside the ship commenced to work in a lateral direction. The ship sustained terrific pressure on the port side forward, the heaviest shocks being under the forerigging. It was the worst squeeze we had experienced. The decks shuddered and jumped, beams arched, and stanchions buckled and shook. I ordered all hands to stand by in readiness for whatever emergency might arise. Even the dogs seemed to feel the tense anxiety of the moment. But the ship resisted valiantly, and just when it appeared that the limit of her strength was being reached the huge floe that was pressing down upon us cracked across and so gave relief . . .

The pack was rather closer on Sunday the 17th October. Topsails and head-sails were set in the afternoon, and with a moderate northeasterly breeze we tried to force the ship ahead out of the lead; but she was held fast. Later that day heavy pressure developed. The two floes between which the *Endurance* was lying began to close and the ship was subjected to a series of tremen-dously heavy strains. In the engine room, the weakest point, loud groans, crashes, and hammering sounds were heard. The iron plates on the floor buckled up and overrode with loud clangs . . .

The next attack of the ice came on the afternoon of October 18th. The two floes began to move laterally, exerting great pressure on the ship. Suddenly the floe on the port side cracked and huge pieces of ice shot up from under the port bilge. Within a few seconds the ship heeled over until she had a list of thirty degrees to port . . . The lee boats were now almost resting on the floe. The midship dog kennels broke away and crashed down on to the lee kennels, and the howls and barks of the frightened dogs assisted to create a perfect pandemonium. Everything movable on deck and below fell to the lee side, and for a few minutes it looked as if the *Endurance* would be thrown upon her beam ends. Order was soon restored. I had all fires put out and battens nailed on the deck to give the dogs a foothold and enable people to get about. Then the crew lashed all the movable gear. If the ship had heeled any farther it would have been necessary to release the lee boats and pull them clear, and Worsley was watching to give the alarm. Hurley meanwhile descended to the floe and took some photographs of the ship in her unusual position. Dinner in the wardroom that evening was a curious affair. Most of the diners had to sit on the deck, their feet against battens and their plates on their knees. At 8 p.m. the floes opened, and within a few minutes the *Endurance* was nearly upright again . . .

On Sunday, October 24, there came what for the *Endurance* was the begin-ning of the end. The position was lat. 69° 11′ S., long: 51° 5′ W. We had now twenty-two and a half hours of daylight, and throughout the day we watched the threatening advance of the floes. At 6:45 a.m. the ship sustained heavy pressure in a dangerous position . . . The onslaught was all but irresistible. The *Endurance* groaned and quivered as her starboard quarter was forced against the floe, twisting the stern post and starting the heads and ends of planking. The ice had lateral as well as forward movement, and the ship was twisted and actually bent by the stresses. She began to leak dangerously at once.

I had the pumps rigged, got up steam, and started the bilge pumps at 8 p.m. The pressure by that time had relaxed. The ship was making water rapidly aft, and the carpenter set to work to make a coffer dam astern of the engines. All hands worked, watch and watch, throughout the night, pumping ship and helping the carpenter. By morning the leak was being kept in check . . .

The roar of pressure could be heard all around us. New ridges were rising, and I could see as the day wore on that the lines of major disturbance were drawing nearer to the ship. The *Endurance* suffered some strains at intervals. Listening below, I could hear the creaking and groaning of her timbers, the pistol-like cracks that told of the starting of a trenail or plank, and the faint indefinable whispers of our ship's distress. Overhead the sun shone serenely; occasional fleecy clouds drifted before the southerly breeze, and the light glinted and sparkled on the million facets of the new pressure ridges. The day passed slowly. At 7 p.m. very heavy pressure developed, with twisting strains that racked the ship fore and aft. The butts of planking were opened four and five inches on the starboard side, and at the same time, we could see from the bridge that the ship was bending like a bow under titanic pressure. Almost like a living creature, she resisted the forces that would crush her; but it was a one-sided battle. Millions of tons of ice pressed inexorably upon the little ship that had dared the challenge of the Antarctic. The *Endurance* was now leaking badly, and at 9 p.m. I gave the order to lower boats, gear, provisions, and sledges to the floe and move them to the flat ice a little way from the ship.

The working of the ice closed the leaks slightly at midnight, but all hands were pumping all night. A strange occurrence was the sudden appearance of eight emperor penguins from a crack 100 yds. away at the moment when the pressure upon from the ship was at its climax. They walked a little way towards us, halted, and after a few ordinary calls proceeded to utter weird cries that sounded like a dirge for the ship. None of us had ever before heard the emperors utter any other than the most simple calls or cries, and the effect of this concerted effort was almost startling.

Then came a fateful day – Wednesday, October 27. The position was lat. 69° 5′ S., long. 51° 30′ W. The temperature was −8.5° Fahr., a gentle southerly breeze was blowing and the sun shone in a clear sky. After long months of ceaseless anxiety and strain, after times when hope beat high at times when the outlook was black indeed, the end of the *Endurance* has come. But though we have been compelled to abandon the ship, which is crushed beyond all hope of ever being righted, we are alive and well, and we have stores and equipment for the task that lies before us. The task is to reach land with all the members of the Expedition. It is hard to write what I feel. To a sailor his ship is more than a floating home, and in the *Endurance* I had centered ambitions hopes, and desires. Now, straining and groaning, her timbers cracking and her wounds gaping, she is slowly giving up her sentient life at the very outset of her career. She is crushed and abandoned after drifting more than 570 miles in a northwesterly direction during the 281 days since she became locked in the ice. The distance from the point where she became beset to the place where she now rests mortally hurt in the grip of the floes is 573 miles, but the total drift through all observed positions has been 1186 miles, and probably we actually covered more than 1500 miles. We are now 346 miles from Paulet Island, the nearest point when there is any possibility of finding food and shelter. A small hut built there by the Swedish expedition in 1902 is filled with stores left by the Argentine relief ship. I know all about those stores, for I purchased them in London on behalf of the Argentine Government when they asked me to equip the relief expedition. The distance to the nearest barrier west of us is about 180 miles, but a party going there would still be about 360 miles from Paulet Island and there would be no means of sustaining life on the barrier. We could not take from here food enough for the whole journey; the weight would be too great.

This morning, our last on the ship, the weather was clear, with a gentle south-southeasterly to south-southwesterly breeze. From the crow's nest there was no sign of land of any sort. The pressure was increasing steadily, and the passing hours brought no relief or respite for the ship. The attack of the ice reached its climax at 4 p.m. The ship was hove stern up by the pressure, and the driving floe, moving laterally across the stern, split the rudder and tore out the rudder post and stern post. Then, while we watched, the ice loosened and the *Endurance* sank a little. The decks were breaking upwards and the water was pouring in below. Again the pressure began, and at 5 p.m. I ordered all hands on to the ice. The twisting, grinding floes were working their will at last on the ship. It was a sickening sensation to feel the decks breaking up under one's feet, the great beams bending and then snapping with a noise like heavy gunfire. The water was overmastering the pumps, and to avoid an explosion when it reached the boilers I had to give orders for the fires to be drawn and the steam let down. The plans for abandoning the ship in case of emergency had been made well in advance, and men and dogs descended to the floe and made their way to the comparative safety of an unbroken portion of the floe without a hitch. Just before leaving, I looked down the engine room skylight as I stood on the quivering deck, and saw the engines dropping sideways as the stays and bed plates gave way. I cannot describe the impression of relentless destruction that was forced upon me as I looked down and around. The floes, with the force of millions of tons of moving ice behind them, were simply annihilating the ship.

South: The Endurance Expedition, 1919

THOMAS ORDE-LEES
1879–1958
Men all out of tobacco . . . they sit about moping and cursing

German-born but educated in England, as a Captain in the Royal Marines Orde-Lees was in charge of the motor-sledges on Shackleton's 1914–17 *Endurance* expedition. He was something of an eccentric – some thought him rather a prima donna – and, along with the expedition's carpenter, was at the centre of some of the disruptions on the ship and on Elephant Island, where the men awaited rescue.

His diary, of which this is an unedited portion, copied from the pencilled original and never before published, gives us a window into the gruelling daily goings-on of the *Endurance* party who awaited rescue on Elephant Island.

On his return to duty, he became interested in aviation and entered the balloon service, also playing a part in the development of parachutes during the First World War. In later years he was a lecturer at Kobe University and *The Times* correspondent for Japan; he also taught flying to the Japanese air force in the 1930s, this spell in Japan making him *persona non grata* in England after the War.

Life, while waiting for salvation

15th June: Mild but wet 31 degrees. Blackborrow has toes amputated. All hands except doctors, Wild and Hurley remain outside for 3 hours taking shelter in cave. Bakewell cuts hair. Very dull and monotonous in bags. Able to read for an hour or two at noon. Very full [dull?] menu.

16th: Still mild and wet, rain in night thawing everywhere. In bags all day. Very monotonous.

17th: Very mild 30 degrees some snow. S.E. wind much pack but no swell. All rather weak through the lying in bags so much. Daylight 9am–3pm. Open water visible from hill. Great craving for carbohydrates.

18th: Beautiful day. 2 hours sunshine. All exchanges stopped. I am ordered to surrender all further claim on the sugar for which I had paid N F. By this order I am a loser. There is a clique against me to whom Wild gives too much heed. I am called a Jew.

June 29th: Cold calm both bays full of very loose pack. We kill a young elephant [seal]. Much scarred blubber underneath. Meat only enough for one day. 2 paddies. Another seal in water.

30th: S.W. blizzard. In bags all day. 16 penguins up. Not killed, weather too severe.

July 1st: Beautiful sunny day but very cold. Both bays clear but much pack on E.horizon drifting in. Penguins leave in morning by W. bay, very unusual. 11 penguins come up in E. bay in afternoon. 7 only killed. Skin, heart and liver only kept. Breast and legs thrown away with carcasses. Wild says we have fuel to mid August and too much meat. 13 degrees.

2nd: Wet and gloomy but able to read in hut until 3 pm by light reflected from fresh snow at door and through wet walls.

July 3rd: Terribly monotonous and weakening lying in bags so much. Get quite bed ridden. Vitiated air caused headache. Smoke from stove injures eyes. Food, rubbish etc fall on me all day long. Piece of old tent affords me some protection. Anxiety re Sir E. We invent ideas to suit events and now expect Aurora to relieve us about August 1st. Blackborrow progressing well. Hudson rather ill with pain in his back. 25 penguins up but weather too bad to kill. W. Blizzard and all men cold and wet.

Blizzard of 7th July turned my lump sugar Venesta box upside down scattering contents and shaking strap off. I find the lid 100 yards away down by N.W. rocks.

On 8th about 150 shags on N.W. rocks. Wild says Aurora will have been very quick if she gets here before end of July and that he will not get uneasy until middle of Aug. I say I shall not be anxious until end of Sept. Wild also says that the spit will be free from snow by middle of August with subsequent cold snaps. I say middle of September. My berth in hut once considered the worst is now much envied owing to its proximity to stove and facilities for cooking, warming up hoosh and running down oil from penguin fat. I exchanged places with Kerr two months ago. Hither too have had no lamp now Wild has granted me the use of nightlight directly after supper.

July 9th: Strong S.W. wind in night. 31 degrees cold but fine. Light increasing noticeable. I am able to day to write this by daylight reflected from snow through open door at 8.30 am. No ice in sight and few bergs. E bay quite clear. Some glacier brash in W Bay.

Men all out of tobacco makes them very irritable and impertinent. They sit about moping and cursing. Wild kindly gives them a small piece each which they immediately consume. Wild tells me that they have been very improvident but as they are always being told that 'the ship' will be here tomorrow it is hardly to be wondered at that they have not put any tobacco by. My snoring is very bad, it quite exasperates Wild who pulls string attached to my arm unmercifully swears at me.

July 10th: 30 degrees but very wet snow all day. In bags all day. Yesterday the water in E bay was wonderfully clear and no ice in sight. Today both bays full of brash ice. No penguins up.

July 11th: Heavy surf during night. Many falls from glacier. Ice gradually goes out of bay during day. Beautiful weather. Bright sunshine. No wind 27 degrees. Much thaw in hut, very wet under my bed. 31 penguins killed (one an Adelie).

July 15th: Mild both bays full of loose pack some of it very heavy. A tremendous glacier fall creates 40 foot wave which would have overwhelmed us but for its being damped by the loose brash in bay. 1 penguin up and killed.

July 16th: Beautifully fine, quite warm in sun 28 degrees. 1 penguin up, not killed.

17th: I catch and eat snow petrel. Very tough. We cut legs off frozen carcasses of penguins throwing away the 46 carcasses with *breasts* on! = 4 days food. I work for an hour with pick axe and get quite hot and tired digging out the penguin carcasses which shows how comparatively weak one is. Hudson and Blacborrow having complained that my feet touch theirs at night. Wild orders me to reverse my bag. This enables me to disperse with my 'halter' which has been a d—d nuisance for I think I was often awakened out of pique and not because my snoring was keeping either Wild or McIlroy awake, for both of them often sit up and read for an hour during the night and sleep in the afternoons. 24 degrees no penguins. Very fine. Much ice.

Unpublished diary

DOUGLAS MAWSON
1882–1958

When comrades tramp the road to anywhere through a lonely blizzard-ridden land . . . ties and fates of each are interwoven in a wondrous fabric of friendship and affection.

An Australian geologist, Mawson spent much of his career at the University of Adelaide. However, at the age of twenty-six he joined Shackleton's 'Farthest South' expedition of 1907–9 as a scientist, being part of the team that first climbed Mount Erebus and reached the Magnetic South Pole. Four years later, Mawson led the Australasian Antarctic Expedition, sailing through 1,500 km of pack ice to the Antarctic coast. He entitled his memoirs of this expedition *The Home of the Blizzard* on account of the 300-kilometre-an-hour winds that blew his men off their feet. In November 1912, he set off east with Dr Xavier Mertz and Lieutenant Ninnis, travelling over 1000 km in appalling weather conditions to map the coastline and collect geological specimens. Just five weeks into the journey, Ninnis disappeared down a crevasse with a team of dogs and the sledge carrying most of the food. The others turned back, but resorted to eating the remaining huskies in order to survive. Mertz then fell ill and died, probably owing to poisonous levels of vitamin A from the dogs' livers. Mawson too was in a dreadful state, with his skin falling away and his feet bloody, and he nearly gave up when he fell down a crevasse, writing later that he had been tempted to cut the rope that held him. His diary mentions his frequent sense of a guiding spirit, which helped him find the strength to continue. He eventually made it back to base, travelling alone over 160 km. His expedition discovered George V Land and

Queen Mary Land and made a huge contribution to our understanding of Antarctica. On his return home, Mawson received a knighthood. To some, Sir Douglas's expedition, judged by the magnitude of both its scale and its achievements, was the greatest, most consummate expedition that ever sailed to Antarctica.

During 1929–31 he led two more expeditions to the Antarctic, during which time he discovered Mac Robertson Land and Princess Elizabeth Land. Thanks to these expeditions Australia was able to claim 42 per cent of Antarctica as Australian territory. He argued, way before his time, that increased scientific understanding of ecosystems would lead to better management of natural resources, and advocated international controls on whaling, sealing and penguin slaughter.

He led from the front, like Scott and Shackleton, expecting to have the last word in each and every decision. This inevitably brought tension with the captains of the ships transporting them, as John King Davis, master of Mawson's *Discovery*, soon discovered (see page 94), for they had their own concerns: namely, the safety of the ship and crew. When it came to the expedition itself, there was no room for a questioning of commands; once you had elected to join, your fate was in the hands of your leader, and you followed him whatever – as the following extracts indicate in the extreme.

The loss of Ninnis

When I next looked back, it was in response to the anxious gaze of Mertz who had turned round and halted in his tracks. Behind me, nothing met the eye but my own sledge tracks running back in the distance. Where were Ninnis and his sledge?

I hastened back along the trail thinking that a rise in the ground obscured the view. There was no such good fortune, however, for I came to a gaping hole in the surface about eleven feet wide. The lid of a crevasse had broken in; two sledge tracks led up to it on the far side but only one continued on the other side.

Frantically waving to Mertz to bring up my sledge, upon which there was some alpine rope, I leaned over and shouted into the dark depths below. No sound came back but the moaning of a dog, caught on a shelf just visible one hundred and fifty feet below. The poor creature appeared to have broken its back, for it was attempting to sit up with the front part of its body while the hinder portion lay limp. Another dog lay motionless by its side. Close by was what appeared in the gloom to be the remains of the tent and a canvas tank containing food for three men for a fortnight.

We broke back the edge of the névé lid and took turns leaning over secured by a rope, calling into the darkness in the hope that our companion might be still alive. For three hours we called unceasingly but no answering sound came back. The dog had ceased to moan and lay without a movement. A chill draught was blowing out of the abyss. We felt that there was little hope.

Why had the first sledge escaped the crevasse? It seemed that I had been fortunate, because my sledge had crossed diagonally, with a greater chance of breaking the snow-lid. The sledges were within thirty pounds of the same weight. The explanation appeared to be that Ninnis had walked by the side of his sledge, whereas I had crossed it sitting on the sledge. The whole weight of a man's body bearing on his foot is a formidable load and no doubt was sufficient to smash the arch of the roof.

By means of a fishing line we ascertained that it was one hundred and fifty feet sheer to the ledge on which the remains were seen; on either side the crevasse descended into blackness. It seemed so very far down there and the dogs looked so small that we got out the field glasses, but could make out nothing more by their aid.

All our available rope was tied together but the total length was insufficient to reach the ledge and any idea of going below to investigate and to secure some of the food had to be abandoned.

Stunned by the unexpectedness of it all and having exhausted the few
appliances we carried for such a contingency, we felt helpless. In such
moments action is the only tolerable thing, and if there had been any
expedient however hazardous which might have been tried, we should have
taken all and more than the risk. Stricken dumb with the pity of it and
heavy at heart, we turned our minds mechanically to what lay nearest at
hand.

There were rations on the other sledge, and we found that there was a bare
one and a half weeks' food for ourselves and nothing at all for the dogs. Part
of the provisions consisted of raisins and almonds which had been taken as
extras or 'perks,' as they were usually called.

Among other losses there were both spade and ice-axe, but fortunately a
spare tent-cover was saved. Mertz's burberry trousers had gone down with the
sledge and the best substitute he could get was a pair of thick Jaeger woollen
under-trousers from the spare clothing we possessed.

Later in the afternoon Mertz and I went ahead to a higher point in order to
obtain a better view of our surroundings. At a point two thousand four
hundred feet above sea-level and three hundred and fifteen and three-quarter
miles eastward from the Hut, a complete observation for position and magnetic azimuth was taken . . .

We returned to the crevasse and packed the remaining sledge, discarding
everything unnecessary so as to reduce the weight of the load. A thin soup was
made by boiling up all the old food-bags which could be found. The dogs
were given some worn-out fur mitts, finnesko and several spare raw hide
straps, all of which they devoured.

We still continued to call down into the crevasse at regular intervals in case
our companion might not have been killed outright and, in the meantime,
have become conscious. There was no reply.

A weight was lowered on the fishing line as far as the dog which had earlier
shown some signs of life, but there was no response. All were dead, swallowed
up in an instant.

When comrades tramp the road to anywhere through a lonely blizzard-ridden
land in hunger, want and weariness the interests, ties and fates of each are
interwoven in a wondrous fabric of friendship and affection. The shock of
Ninnis's death struck home and deeply stirred us.

He was a fine fellow and a born soldier – and the end:

> Life – give me life until the end,
> That at the very top of being,

> The battle spirit shouting in my blood,
> Out of very reddest hell of the fight
> I may be snatched and flung
> Into the everlasting lull,
> The Immortal, Incommunicable Dream.

At 9 p.m. we stood by the side of the crevasse and I read the burial service. Then Mertz shook me by the hand with a short 'Thank you!' and we turned away to harness up the dogs.

The loss of Pavlova

Pavlova was killed and we made a very acceptable soup from her bones. In view of the dark outlook, our ration of food had to be still further cut down. We had no proper sleep, hunger gnawing at us all the time, and the question of food was for ever in our thoughts. Dozing in the fur bags, we dreamed of gorgeous 'spreads' and dinner-parties at home. Tramping along through the snow, we racked our brains thinking of how to make the most of the meagre quantity of dogs' meat at hand.

The supply of kerosene for the primus stove promised to be ample, for none of it had been lost in the accident. We found that it was worth while spending some time in boiling the dogs' meat thoroughly. Thus a tasty soup was prepared as well as a supply of edible meat in which the muscular tissue and the gristle were reduced to the consistency of a jelly. The paws took longest of all to cook, but, treated to lengthy stewing, they became quite digestible . . .

At this time we were eating largely of the dogs' meat, to which was added one or two ounces of chocolate or raisins, three or four ounces of pemmican and biscuit mixed together, and, as a beverage, very dilute cocoa. The total weight of solid food consumed by each man per day was approximately fourteen ounces. Our small supply of butter and glaxo was saved for emergency, while a few tea-bags which remained were boiled over and over again.

The march commenced on December 28 at 3 a.m. in a thirty-mile wind accompanied by light drift. Overhead there was a wild sky which augured badly for the next few days. It was cold work raising the sail, and we were glad to be marching.

Our faithful retainer Ginger could walk no longer and was strapped on the sledge. She was the last of the dogs and had been some sort of a help until a few days before. We were sad when it came to finishing her off.

On account of the steep up grade and the weight of Ginger on the sledge, we camped at 7.15 a.m. after only four miles one thousand two hundred and thirty yards.

We had breakfast off Ginger's skull and brain. I can never forget the occasion. As there was nothing available to divide it, the skull was boiled whole. Then the right and left halves were drawn for by the old and well-established sledging practice of 'shut-eye,' after which we took it in turns eating to the middle line, passing the skull from one to the other. The brain was afterwards scooped out with a wooden spoon.

On sledging journeys it is usual to apportion all foodstuffs in as nearly even halves as possible. Then one man turns away and another, pointing to a heap, asks 'Whose?' The reply from the one not looking is 'Yours' or 'Mine' as the case may be. Thus an impartial and satisfactory division of the rations is made.

The Home of the Blizzard: The Story of the Australasian Antarctic Expedition 1911–1914, 1915

VILHJALMUR STEFANSSON
1879–1962

These simple, well-bred, and hospitable people were the savages whom we had come so far to see.

A Canadian anthropologist of Icelandic extraction, Stefansson travelled widely over the Arctic ice floes, studying and adopting the Inuit way of life. His ventures culminated in his expedition of 1913–18, when he remained north of the Arctic Circle for an unbroken five years. Sponsored by the Canadian government, he headed up through the Bering Strait and eastward into the Beaufort Sea, where he made sightings of several uncharted islands, some while adrift on ice floes.

His book *The Friendly Arctic*, which proposed that Westerners could live in polar regions 'into which Eskimos were unwilling to go because they believed them devoid of resources', consolidated his fame. No less a man than Peary, now ailing, defied doctor's orders to present Stefansson with the Hubbard Medal, the highest honour of the National Geographical Society. He had 'added more than 100,000 square miles to the maps.'

Such, then, is a typical thumbnail sketch of his contribution. However, the full picture that has now emerged is rather more complicated. A few years before his death, in 1983, William Laird McKinlay (see page 539) decided to publish his own account of part of the 1913–18 expedition, viewed from the perspective of someone whom Stefansson effectively abandoned, with the other members of the inexperienced *Karluk* party, to an uncertain fate. Amundsen, lauded in public as the great guru of everything in the far north, had ridiculed Stefansson's claims of the Arctic being 'friendly'. Sure enough, lives were again lost in the 1920s, when Stefansson pursued his philosophy to its logical conclusion and colonized Wrangel Island, north of the Siberian coast, incidentally creating an international dispute with Russia, after deciding to claim the land for Britain, and then afterwards for Canada.

The extract I've chosen is from his journey along the coast of Alaska and western Canada, Point Barrow to Coronation Gulf (1908–12).

When Eskimo strangers meet

On May 9th, nineteen days out from Langton Bay, we came upon signs that made our hearts beat faster . . . The beach was strewn with pieces of driftwood, and on one of them we found the marks of recent choppings with a dull adze. A search of the beach for half a mile each way revealed numerous similar choppings. Evidently the men who had made them had been testing the pieces of wood to see if they were sound enough to become the materials for sleds or other things they had wished to make. Those pieces which had but one or two adze marks had been found unsound; in a few places piles of chips showed that a sound piece had been found there and had been roughed down for transportation purposes on the spot . . .

>

The night after this discovery we did not sleep much. The Eskimo were more excited than I was, apparently, and far into the morning they talked and speculated on the meaning of the signs. Had we come upon traces of the Nagyuktogmiut 'who kill all strangers'? Fortunately enough, my long-entertained fear that traces of people would cause a panic in my party was not realized. In spite of all their talk, and in spite of the fact that they were seriously afraid, the curiosity as to what these strange people would prove to be like – in fine, the spirit of adventure, which seldom crops out in an Eskimo – was far stronger than their fears. We were therefore up early the next morning, and soon out on the road.

All that day we found along the beach comparatively fresh traces of people, chiefly shavings and chips where the hewing and shaping of wood had taken place. None seen that day were of the present winter, though some seemed to be of the previous summer; but the next morning, just east of Point Young, we found at last human footprints in the crusted snow and sled tracks that were not over three months old. That day at Cape Bexley we came upon a deserted village of over fifty snow houses; their inhabitants had apparently left them about midwinter, and it was now the 12th of May.

The size of the deserted village took our breath away. Tannaumirk, the young man from the Mackenzie River, had never seen an inhabited village among his people of more than twelve or fifteen houses. All his old fears of the Nagyuktogmiut 'who kill all strangers' now came to the surface afresh; all the stories that he knew of their peculiar ways and atrocious deeds were retold by him that evening for our common benefit . . .

In the present case our task was simplified by the fact that the group we were following had not moved straight ahead north, but had made their fourth camp west of the second. Standing on the roofs of the houses of the second camp, we could see three seal-hunters a few miles to the west, each sitting on his block of snow by a seal-hole waiting for the animal to rise.

The seal-hunters and their camp were up the wind, and our dogs scented them. As we bore swiftly down upon the nearest of the sealers the dogs showed enthusiasm and anticipation as keen as mine, keener by a great deal than did my Eskimo. As the hunter was separated from each of his fellow-huntsmen by a full half-mile, I thought he would probably be frightened if all of us were to rush up to him at the top speed of our dogs. We therefore stopped our sled several hundred yards away. Tannaumirk had become braver now, for the lone stranger did not look formidable, sitting stooped forward as he was on his block of snow beside the seal-hole; he accordingly volunteered to act as our ambassador, saying that the Mackenzie dialect (his own) was probably nearer the stranger's tongue than Natkusiak's. This seemed likely, so I told him to go ahead. The sealer sat motionless as Tannaumirk approached him; I watched him through my glasses and saw that he held his face steadily as if watching the seal-hole, but that he raised his eyes every second or two to the (to him) strange figure of the man approaching. He was evidently tensely ready for action. Tannaumirk by now was thoroughly over his fears, and would have walked right up to the sealer, but when no more than five paces or so intervened between them the sealer suddenly jumped up, grasping a long knife that had lain on the snow beside him, and poising himself as if to receive an attack or to be ready to leap forward suddenly. This scared our man, who stopped abruptly and began excitedly and volubly to assure the sealer that he and all of us were friendly and harmless, men of excellent character and intentions.

I was, of course, too far away to hear, but Tannaumirk told me afterward that on the instant of jumping up the sealer began a monotonous noise which is not a chant nor is it words – it is merely an effort to ward off dumbness, for if a man who is in the presence of a spirit does not make at least one sound each time he draws his breath, he will be stricken permanently dumb. This is a belief common to the Alaska and Coronation Gulf Eskimo. For several minutes Tannaumirk talked excitedly, and the sealer kept up the moaning noise, quite unable to realize, apparently, that he was being spoken to in human speech. It did not occur to him for a long time, he told us afterward, that we might be something other than spirits, for our dogs and dog harness, our sleds and clothes, were such as he had never seen in all his wanderings; besides, we had not, on approaching, used the peace sign of his people, which is holding the hands out to show that one does not carry a knife.

After what may have been anything from five to fifteen minutes of talking and expostulation by Tannaumirk, the man finally began to listen and then to answer. The dialects proved to differ about as much as Norwegian does from Swedish, or Spanish from Portuguese. After Tannaumirk had made him understand the assurance that we were of good intent and character, and had showed by lifting his own coat that he had no knife, the sealer approached him cautiously and felt of him, partly (as he told us later) to assure himself that he was not a spirit, and partly to see if there were not a knife hidden somewhere under his clothes. After a careful examination and some further parley, he told Tannaumirk to tell us that they two would proceed home to the village, and Natkusiak and I might follow as far behind as we were now; when they got to the village we were to remain outside it till the people could be informed that we were visitors with friendly intentions . . .

When we approached the village every man, woman, and child was out-doors, waiting for us excitedly, for they could tell from afar that we were no ordinary visitors. The man whom we had first approached – who that day acquired a local prominence which still distinguishes him above his fellows – explained to an eagerly silent crowd that we were friends from a distance who had come without evil intent, and immediately the whole crowd (about forty) came running toward us. As each came up he would say: 'I am So-and-so. I am well disposed. I have no knife. Who are you?' After being told our names in return, and being assured that we were friendly, and that our knives were packed away in the sled and not hidden under our clothing, each would express his satisfaction and stand aside for the next to present himself. Some-times a man would present his wife, or a woman her husband, according to which came up first. The women were in more hurry to be presented than were the men, for they must, they said, go right back to their houses to cook us something to eat.

After the women were gone the men asked us whether we preferred to have our camp right in the village or a little outside it. On talking it over we agreed it would be better to camp about two hundred yards from the other houses, so as to keep our dogs from fighting with theirs. When this was decided, half a dozen small boys were sent home to as many houses to get their fathers' snow-knives and house-building mittens. We were not allowed to touch a hand to anything in camp-making, but stood idly by, surrounded continually by a crowd who used every means to show how friendly they felt and how wel-come we were, while a few of the best house-builders set about erecting for us the house in which we were to live as long as we cared to stay with them. When it had been finished and furnished with the skins, lamp, and the other things that go to make a snow house the coziest and most comfortable of camps, they told us they hoped we would occupy it at least till the last piece of meat in their storehouses had been eaten, and that so long as we stayed in the village no man would hunt seals or do any work until his children began to complain of hunger. It was to be a holiday, they said, for this was the first time their people had been visited by strangers from so great a distance that they knew nothing of the land from which they came.

These simple, well-bred, and hospitable people were the savages whom we had come so far to see. That evening they saw for the first time the lighting of a sulphur match; the next day I showed them the greater marvels of my rifle . . .

My Life with the Eskimo, 1913

WILLIAM LAIRD McKINLAY
1888–1983
Life went on. While I was digging Breddy's grave . . . Hadley and Kuraluk were hunting as usual.

McKinlay was a Scottish schoolteacher who, aged twenty-four, was invited by the distinguished anthropologist Vilhjalmur Stefansson (see page 535) to join his 1913 Arctic expedition as a magnetician and meteorologist. Though he wouldn't be paid, McKinlay was more than happy to join Stefansson, who had already made many daring Arctic journeys and written pioneering studies of the Eskimo.

Before the expedition was even properly under way, the leading ship, the *Karluk*, was trapped by ice. Stefansson left to hunt game and, finding himself cut off by open water, never returned. Instead of fetching help for his team – many of them young scientists who had never experienced cold climes before – he continued his explorations, which lasted five years. The *Karluk* drifted for months in pack ice, was crushed and sunk. The ship's commander, Robert Bartlett, who had captained Peary's ship on his final attempt on the North Pole, led the party of twenty-five, composed of crew, scientists and a family of Inuit, over the ice to Wrangel Island, then made a 700-mile journey south to Siberia and thence to Alaska to fetch help. By the time help came, six months later, eight men had died trying to reach land over the buckled ice, one man had shot himself and two had died of malnutrition. The survivors owed their lives not just to Bartlett, but to the skills of the Inuit couple, Kuraluk and his wife Kiruk (soon known as 'Auntie'), and their two daughters Helen, five, and Mugpi, three. After the expedition, McKinlay served on the Western Front, later returned to Scotland to teach, and only in his late eighties released the full story as he saw it.

The forthcoming venture

I was beginning to form a picture, as I steamed back to Glasgow on the night train, of the man to whom I was entrusting my life for the next three or four years.

Vilhjalmur Stefansson was thirty-four, the son of Icelandic parents who had emigrated to Canada. He was an anthropologist by profession, and the main reason for his explorations in the Arctic up till now had been to learn everything he could about the Eskimos. He had already made two expeditions (1906–7 and 1908–12) from which he had returned with a report of a 'new race of men', the so-called 'Blond Eskimos', and with more than fifty-thousand specimens, including species of caribou (reindeer) hitherto unknown, and more skulls of Barren Ground grizzlies than were in the possession of the scientific museums of the world. He also came back with a firm conviction that the unexplored regions around the North Pole, into which even the Eskimos refused to travel, were not the white wilderness that men imagined, but probably rich in minerals, such as copper, and that it was possible for men to live off the wild life of the Arctic by using the hunting skills of the Eskimo. This was the basis of Stefansson's great theory of the 'friendly Arctic', and perhaps it was just as well for my peace of mind that I was unaware of the great Amundsen's opinion that if men tried to take advantage of this 'friend-liness' and adventured into the Arctic regions equipped only with a gun and some ammunition, 'certain death awaits them'.

I was well on my way to the Arctic before our leader started sending dispatches which declared that:

... the attainment of the purposes of the expedition is more important than the bringing-back safe of the ship in which it sails. This means that while every reasonable precaution will be taken to safeguard the lives of the party, it is realised both by the backers of the expedition and the members of it, that even the lives of the party are secondary to the accomplishment of the work ... that the expedition is thoroughly equipped is all that we can say of it at present. The character of its management will develop from day to day, and it will only be some years from now, if no disaster overtakes us, that it will be possible to decide the relative value of the factors that make for its success for failure.

Looking back I can see in statements like these foreboding of the disasters to come, but that night as I was setting out on my great adventure, there was nothing to shake my confidence in the ability of this great man, Stefansson, to take our expedition to the Arctic and bring us all safely home again. All I read were eulogies of him, such as the one from his great friend, the conqueror of the North Pole, Admiral Peary: 'In personality and from training and experi-ence, Stefansson is especially fitted for this work; his courage and control of untoward circumstances have been proved in the six years he has already put in on Arctic investigations, and he has shown executive ability and judgement in his plans for organisation of the new expedition.'

I learned that our leader was 'a man of middle height, strong of frame, with no superfluous flesh ... he tells you frankly he makes no pretensions as an athlete. He never walks where it is possible to ride, takes little or no exercise of any description. Yet his powers of endurance seem phenomenal, and far in excess of those of the trained athlete in hard condition.' With all this added to his training as an anthropologist and his 'qualities of a dreamer', Admiral Peary felt that he must congratulate the scientific world and the Canadian Government that Stefansson 'has stepped forth to do a man's work in Arctic exploration'.

With such stirring sentiments ringing in my head, I stepped off the train in Glasgow on Friday morning, with thirty-six hours left to sailing time.

Goodbye, Stefansson

On 9 August the ice relaxed its hold and we were able to nose our way slowly to the east. Indeed, at times we had enough open water to allow us to go full speed ahead, and two more such days would have seen us at Herschel Island. But the ice was slowly tightening up again. Little or no steering could be done by the compass; the look-out in the 'barrell' followed the leads, to keep clear of the floes, with the result that the course was continually changing, and at times we appeared to be going around in circles . . .

Captain Bartlett examined the stem of the ship and found that already two of the brass stem-plates were gone and several bolts loosened on those that remained. All the *Karluk* could do was to follow open lanes and go where they led – as Stefansson described it, 'threading our way between the ice cakes and occasionally ramming to break a way'.

Soon it was very evident that we had reached our eastern limit. Snow began to fall, the temperature dropped to 17° Fahrenheit and young ice began to form in the small openings between the floes, cementing the pack into one impenetrable mass. We were motionless; so was the ice. Then, in the last week of August, the ice started moving in a solid pack, slowly, to the west, taking us with it about twenty miles a day, sometimes faster . . .

Now followed weeks of monotony and frustration. Murray alone of the scientific staff was able to carry on with the work he had come to do. He worked assiduously, day in, day out, dredging and collecting from all depths of the ocean. One single haul brought in some polychoete worms, a sea mouse, some ophyurids, two species of gastropods, two species of lamelli-branchiata (one yellow, one white), some holothurians, cirripedia, polyzoa (lace coral), a pecten, some schizopods, a shrimp with exceptionally long legs, some small red amphipods . . . When he was not busy in the ice-holes, he was busy in the laboratory, preserving his specimens in bottles, labelling them, writing notes. I wish I had thought of duplicating his notes, so that some record might have survived of many months of unremitting labour.

The rest of us had to relieve the monotony as best we could. There were some days when open lanes of water gave us the opportunity to go hunting for birds and seals, but we were not very good at it. When we killed birds they would fall in the water where we could not retrieve them; if we shot a seal it invariably sank. The Eskimos, on the other hand, were highly skilled in the use of the *manak*, which consisted of a lead weight of about six pounds at the end of a long line; a foot or so above the weight a cluster of four large hooks was fixed. Holding the line coiled like a lariat, the Eskimo cast the weight a little beyond the seal and then pulled the line. The hooks caught in the carcass, which could then be dragged to the edge of the ice.

Thanks to the Eskimos, especially Kuraluk, we now had seal meat at every meal. It was dark in appearance, smelled strong and tasted fishy. The liver, particularly of a young seal, was extremely tasty, and one sometimes got a really succulent steak. Seal steak-and-kidney pie was on our menu once a week.

The steady drift of the ice-pack continued, but for some days around the middle of September we were at a standstill, locked to the far distant land in a wedge of ice. According to the captain, Stefansson had finally made up his mind that all hope of progress for this year was ended. He was becoming worried about the prospects of getting sufficient fresh meat in the area, although our Eskimos were building up a stock which we had no difficulty in keeping fresh. The entire ice pack around us was a huge natural refrigerator. But Stefansson was not satisfied, and on the evening of 19 September he announced that he was going ashore on a caribou hunt, with Wilkins, McConnell, and the two Eskimos, Jimmy and Jerry. This came as a surprise to some of us, because not long before he had told us that in northern Alaska the caribou (North American reindeer) was practically extinct. A little later that evening he added Jenness to the party 'to give him a chance to begin his study of the Eskimo'. I have never ceased to wonder why he did not include Beuchat for the same reason . . .

Stefansson did not return to the ship in ten days. He did not return ever. Two days after he left, the wind which had been blowing moderately from the east increased to a gale, and next morning the ice had split between the ship and the shore. We were being carried away from the land in the grip of the gale-swept ice-pack, moving west at the rate of thirty miles a day, leaving an ever widening expanse of Arctic sea between us and our leader.

Marooned on Wrangel Island

One of Clam's big toes had become gangrenous. It would have to be amputated, at the first joint at least. We had no surgical instruments, only a skinning knife, and a pair of tin shears which we used to make cooking pots out of empty gasoline tins. Engineer Williamson volunteered to act as surgeon. It was a gruesome operation. Two of us held Clam's arms; a third kept his head turned away. Williamson applied pressure to the shears with his knee until they cut through the joint. There still remained some gangrenous matter to be cut away, but this would have to wait until Clam could stand it. I have never known anyone who lived up so well to his nickname; his lips remained tightly closed; there was never a murmur, only a slight twitching of the face muscles. For sheer guts it was incomparable.

Munro and Chafe were still crippled, and it looked as if they, too, might need some surgery, but not immediately. Just to round off a grizzly day, we were all laid low by an outbreak of diarrhoea. The bear meat was blamed. It happened at the end of a four-day spell of wonderful weather, which had done more than anything to help my recovery. It is impossible to exaggerate the uplift it was to our spirits to be able to desert our squalid quarters and be outside in the health-giving fresh air, in glorious sunshine. I remained outside all day and every day. I was still very, very weak, and even when we had only very light breezes I suffered intensely from the cold. But when the air was calm, with bright sunshine, there was a sensation of heat which permeated every fibre of my being. I did all the cooking. I walked up and down for exercise. I took a sledge and hauled it along for about a mile, collected a load of driftwood and built a large blazing fire, round which we sat and drank tea. That became my daily routine. Every step was an effort, every slight exertion exhausting. I wondered when I would ever regain my strength, but my spirit remained high . . .

Although I never lost my feeling of inner calm and hopefulness, there were times when the longing to be anywhere but there in that miserable, squalid camp was almost overpowering. I wanted to be alone, and yet, even in the company of all the others, I felt lonely, dreadfully lonely. It might have been better if I could have been with my scientist colleagues, discussing our work, exchanging ideas on subjects of common interest; or even just talking about roses with the Captain. Maybe the 'them scientists' attitude of some of my camp mates was to blame, perhaps some flaw in myself. Certainly whatever was lacking in our relationship was in no way the result of any sense of superiority on my part, for never in my life have I felt as deeply and devoutly humble as I did then. When you're sick, hungry, and freezing in the middle of the Arctic, it's no time to put on airs . . .

On the morning of 25 June I woke about 6.30 am when Hadley was going out of the tent. I must have fallen asleep again, because I was suddenly wakened by the sound of a shot. I stuck my head out of the tent, thinking Hadley had fired at a duck or something. But then I looked round and saw that Hadley was lying in his usual place in the tent. Then I heard Williamson shout, 'Clam! Call Hadley! Breddy has shot himself!'

I was up and out in a flash, before Clam was out of his tent, and I was followed by Hadley and Kuraluk. Breddy was dead. He was lying in his tent, the Mauser revolver beside him. Clam and Williamson were asleep, they said, and were awakened by the shot; Chafe was away hunting. The bullet had entered the right eye, penetrated the brain, and emerged on the left side of the head, a little above the ear, and higher than the point of entry.

Was it an accident? Did he commit suicide? If he did, then what had gone on in the other tent to drive him to such a desperate action? Or was it just that he could not face the prospect of many more weeks, perhaps another winter on the island? We would never know the answers.

We carried Breddy outside, and in the presence of everyone, Williamson went through his effects. All the articles that had been taken from my bag were there, including my compass, which was hidden in a sock. During the day Kuraluk and I did our best to dig a grave at the top of a small hill behind the camp, using an axe to break up the frozen earth and a piece of board for a shovel. After supper Hadley, Kuraluk and I improvised a stretcher out of three poles and a piece of canvas and carried Breddy up the hill. His body had swollen so much that the grave was not deep enough. It was extremely difficult to get down any deeper without proper tools, because we were now down to the permafrost, which was much harder than the frozen surface earth. I spent the next day at the deepening, and at last we were able to lay Breddy to rest, covering him with a heap of driftwood, over which we laid skins and piled soil and moss, to keep out animals.

Life went on. While I was digging Breddy's grave at the top of the hill Hadley and Kuraluk were hunting as usual. Hadley missed a seal, and then sat at the hole all day, waiting in vain for him to show again. But Kuraluk brought in a seal he had shot two days before, and we had a really satisfying meal of blood soup, made in the Eskimo way and quite different from the concoctions we had previously been calling blood soup. Auntie's way was to cook the seal meat and remove it from the pot, but leave the pot on the fire so that the liquid kept on boiling. Blood was then carefully and slowly trickled in so that the pot never went off the boil, and all the time stirring had to be kept up continuously. When enough blood had been added the boiling and stirring were kept up for a little longer. Then the pot was taken from the fire and the soup allowed to cool slightly. The result was fairly thick, rich and highly palatable. Slept soundly after that, and even managed a smile when

Williamson woke me in the middle of the night to ask me to make a cup of tea for him and Clam.

Hadley had taken custody of the Mauser and the Winchester rifle, which were his own personal property, and also of the ammunition belonging to them. Only twenty-four revolver cartridges remained, and three of the original hundred rounds of ammunition for the rifle. As he put them away, Hadley remarked that he wasn't going to have any more accidents. Chafe had been out at the cliffs and returned with two birds, both of which Williamson at once handed over to us. He admitted that they had been cheating on birds. For example, the previous Wednesday Chafe had reported two eggs and four birds when, in fact, he had six eggs and five birds. Williamson also admitted that Breddy had stolen birds from our store. I was tempted to tell them how the American explorer, Greely, handled the situation at Cape Sabine when twenty-four of them had to face a winter of 250 days with only forty days' rations; he had not hesitated to sign the warrant for the execution of one man caught stealing seal thongs, which were all they had to eat.

Rescue

September opened fine and fair, with clear skies, bright sun and a very light southerly air. Kuraluk killed thirty crowbills with his throwing stick. Hadley sat at a seal hole for hours and was just about to give up when the seal's snout appeared. He killed it, but it sank like a stone, and Kuraluk refused to try to find it. Hadley tried to grapple for it himself and he managed to bring the seal to the surface, but before he could get his hands on it, it slipped off the hook and disappeared.

It was bitterly cold next day, but Hadley sat at a seal hole all day, and the day after, becoming more and more despondent. Sitting beside a hole for six hours on end with nothing happening was a depressing occupation. There was not a sign of any living thing, except the odd young fox. There were several of these around from time to time, quite unafraid and very inquisitive. They would sit watching us at a distance of not more than ten feet. If we made any move towards them they would trot off, stop when we stopped, then turn and resume their watching. Williamson fired thirteen shots at one little fox with his Colt .45, and at the end of the barrage the fox was still sitting staring at him.

We were hungry, almost desperately hungry. Our birds were finished, our dried meat was gone, and sealskin could do no more than stave off starvation. We caught one young fox in a trap, but it merely proved tantalizing. Hadley said that foxes were not usually eaten, because they were too rank in flavour, but I could find no fault with that little fellow. I kept busy making and setting traps, not just for meat, but also for skins. I was optimistic enough to think I might get enough to make a fur shirt for the winter.

We were now having heavy snow again, and we were all doing what we could to improve our clothing, though some of us had little hope of keeping warm. Kuraluk went along the beach and cut off a large slab of whalebone from part of a skeleton he found. With this he intended to shoe a sledge which he would build during the winter for use on our long journey to Siberia in the spring. What optimists we were!

By 6 September we had decided that there was no prospect of bigger game in the area and we would move next day to our new camp site and start building a hut for the winter. That afternoon Hadley and Kuraluk returned dragging a seal. It was a mere infant, not more than enough to provide one main meal. Unashamedly we gorged on seal meat and blood soup, stifling our conscience with the excuse that we would be fitter for the strenuous work of moving house next day. And we finished off the banquet with a helping of fish, the first we had caught during our stay on the island. Auntie and Helen had seen these small tomcod, about fifteen inches long, in a crack in the beach ice, and caught them by 'jigging' for them. The jig was merely a bent pin fastened to a length of sinew. This was lowered into the crack and held stationary until a fish swam over it. Then, with an upward jerk, the fish was impaled on the pin. They caught about two dozen, and they were so delicious that we decided to get up early next morning and go 'jigging' for our breakfast before the big move.

So, at daybreak on 7 September everybody in our tent was out with a bent pin on the end of a line, and the tomcod catch was slowly piling up. After a few hours we three men returned to the tent to get on with preparations for the removal. Then Kuraluk went out to find a piece of wood to make a spear for Hadley. He was hardly outside when he startled us with a mighty shout:

'*Umiakpik kunno!*' ('Maybe a ship!')

Hadley and I tumbled out, and I got my glasses on the object which was causing Kuraluk's excitement. It was three miles off to the east, at the edge of the ice which filled the bay and beyond. And without any doubt it was a ship, a small schooner. She seemed to be steaming northwest, and we could not tell whether she was a relief ship, or just a walrus-hunter chasing the large herd we had seen on the ice a few days before.

When we saw her hoist her sail our hearts missed a beat. She wasn't looking for us! She was on her way north! As one man we started shouting, and the noise must have scared every seal in the Arctic, though I doubt if anyone heard it three miles away on the ship. Hadley blazed away precious ammunition with his revolver, and we sent Kuraluk racing over the ice in the hope of heading her off.

Then we saw her lower her sail, and as we watched, hardly able to believe our eyes, a party of men disembarked on the ice and began walking towards the beach. We were saved! Captain Bartlett had got through!

We were in a daze. Stupefied by shock and disbelief, we could only think of one thing – food. We called to Auntie and the kids and found that they had collected about two pounds of tomcod. Keeping our camp routine to the last, we traded some of the fish with Williamson for tea tablets. As our rescuers were crossing the ice to reach us we were putting on the pots for a meal of fish and tea, determined to eat our tomcod before we left. We didn't rush out with glad cries to meet the men who trudged up to our tents. We were shy and too dazed to speak. It was all so unreal, like a dream.

Karluk (1976 edn)

Reaching the Siberian mainland – Bartlett's story

About two o'clock in the afternoon we could make out black objects some distance ahead of us; as we drew nearer we could see that they were moving. Kataktovick had been ahead, while I drove the dogs; now he stopped, came back and said, 'Eskimo igloo.'

'*Ardegar*,' I replied, and told him to go on.

He set his face eastward again and I urged the dogs harder than ever. Ordinarily he was a good walker but now he seemed to be lagging a little and dropping back, nearer and nearer the dogs. I asked him what the matter was.

'Eskimo see me, they kill me,' he said. 'My father my mother told me long time ago Eskimo from Point Barrow go to Siberia, never come back, Siberian Eskimo kill him.'

I told him that he was mistaken and repeated what I had said the day before about the hospitality of the Siberian Eskimo. Our troubles were at an end, I said; we should now have a place to dry our clothes and get them mended, or perhaps get new ones. 'Maybe,' I added, 'we get tobacco.'

Kataktovick was still reluctant, even though I told him that perhaps we could get some dogs, or even persuade some of the Eskimo to travel along with us.

We could now make out that the objects ahead of us were human beings and that they were running about, apparently very much excited by our approach. Kataktovick hung back near the dogs. At length I said, 'You drive the dogs now and I will go ahead.' He did so with evident relief and so we went on until I was within ten yards of the Eskimo [actually Chukchi]. Then I put out my hand and walked towards them, saying in English, 'How do you do?' They immediately rushed towards us and grasped us each warmly by the hand, jabbering away in great excitement. I could understand nothing of what they were saying, nor could Kataktovick. I tried to make them understand who we were and where we had come from but they were as ignorant of my language as I was of theirs.

There could be no doubt, however, that they were glad to see us and eager to show their hospitality, for the first thing we knew they had unharnessed our dogs and were feeding them, had taken our sledge into the outer part of their house and put it, with everything still on it, up on a kind of scaffold where it would be away from the dogs and sheltered from the weather. Then an old woman caught me by the arm and pushed me into the inner inclosure and on to a platform where three native lamps were going, one at each end and the other in the middle. The roof was so low that my head touched it, so I sat down. The woman brushed the snow off my clothes with a snow-beater shaped like a sickle and thinner than ours, placed a deerskin on the platform for me to sit on, pulled off my boots and stockings and hung them up to dry. Then she gave me a pair of deerskin stockings, not so long as ours, because, as I could see, the trousers that these Siberians wore were longer than ours. After that she took off my parka or fur jacket and hung it up to dry, while I pulled off my undershirt. Others were waiting upon Kataktovick in the same way and here we were, when we had hardly had time to say, 'Thank you,' clad only in our bearskin trousers and seated comfortably about a large wooden dish, filled with frozen reindeer meat, eating sociably with twelve or fourteen perfect strangers to whom, it might be said, we had not been formally introduced. Never have I been entertained in a finer spirit of true hospitality and never have I been more thankful for the cordiality of my welcome. It was, as I was afterwards to learn, merely typical of the true humanity of these simple, kindly people . . .

[*At length, Bartlett reached Alaska across the Bering Strait, and set out by ship for Wrangel Island. Ahead of him was the* King and Winge, *which also stood a chance of spotting survivors.*]

As soon as dawn broke September 8, we went on full speed ahead, through the loose ice; some distance away, on our port bow, we could see that the ice was close-packed. By early afternoon we had made more than fifty miles and were about seventy-five miles from our goal. Luncheon was just finished and I was standing in the chart-room, when we saw a schooner dead ahead, running before the wind. The glasses were soon trained on her and we saw that she was the *King and Winge*. I hoped and was inclined to believe that she had been to the island, or she would hardly be coming back so soon. Then I began to fear that perhaps she had broken her propeller and was now taking advantage of the favoring wind to put for Bering Strait and Alaska.

I watched her as she drew nearer and nearer; then she hove to and we were soon alongside. I looked sharply at the men on her deck; her own crew was fairly large, but soon I could pick out Munro and McKinlay and Chafe, and of course the Eskimo family, and I knew that our quest was over. A boat was lowered from the *Bear*, with Lieutenant Miller in charge; I obtained permission from the captain to go along and was soon on board the *King and Winge*, among the *Karluk* party.

'All of you here?' was my first question.

McKinlay was the spokesman. 'No,' he answered; 'Malloch and Mamen and Breddy died on the island.'

There was nothing to be said. I had not really expected to see the mate's party or the Mackay party, for I had long since ceased to believe that there was any reasonable chance that they could have got through to a safe place, but though it was hard to be forced to what appeared the inevitable conclusion in their case, it was an especially sad and bitter blow to learn that three of the men whom I had seen arrive at Wrangell Island had thus reached safety only to die.

The Last Voyage of the Karluk, 1915

UMBERTO NOBILE
1885–1978
Nothing to be done! A painful confession for men of action.

In 1926, with Norwegian Roald Amundsen and American Lincoln Ellsworth, the Italian aeronautical engineer Nobile flew his airship *Norge* from the Spitzbergen to Alaska, becoming the first to cross from Europe to America via the North Pole by air. Two years later, he attempted another trans-Arctic air crossing in the *Italia*, but in May 1928, after circling the Pole, they crashed. Nobile and the other survivors were rescued a month later, having endured freezing temperatures, lack of food and the threat of attack by polar bears. Amundsen, who set off in search of Nobile on hearing of the crash, died when his own plane crashed into the Arctic Ocean.

Too close to the Pole

Towards ten o'clock there was an unexpected change in the sky, which until then had been blue all over. In front of us, an hour or two away, a barrier of cloud over 3,000 ft. high rose from the horizon, standing out against the azure of the sky above. With its weird outlines it looked like the walls of some gigantic fortress.

That band of cloud, dark and compact, had a menacing aspect which struck my imagination. 'There's no getting through that!' I thought. 'We shall be bound to turn back.'

At 10.30 we encountered a bank of thick cloud. And as at that moment it did not suit us to lose sight of the sun – height measurements being more than ever necessary – we rose above the fog, to about 2,400 ft.

We were then at 88° 10′. Another 54 miles and we should be at the Pole.

Meanwhile the Naval officers were making their solar observations. We were getting nearer and nearer to the goal, and the excitement on board was growing.

Twenty minutes after midnight, early on May 24th, the officers who were observing the sun with a sextant cried: 'We are there!'

The *Italia* was at the Pole.

We had covered 425 miles from Cape Bridgmann at an average speed of 62 m.p.h.

I had the engines slowed down and ordered the helmsman to steer in a circle.

It was impossible, alas! to descend on the pack, but we had a promise to keep: to deposit on the ice of the Pole the Cross entrusted to us by Pius XI, and by its side the Italian flag. We prepared ourselves in religious silence to carry out this gesture – so simple and yet so solemn. I ordered Alessandrini to get ready.

Then I had the engines accelerated once more, to pass under the fog. It was 12.40. Twenty minutes later we were in sight of the pack. We went on circling round at a reduced speed until the preparations were completed. I had had a large tricolour cloth fastened to the Cross, to catch the wind and guide it down.

At 1.20 a.m. I leaned out of the cabin and let fall the Italian flag. Then followed the *gonfalone* of the City of Milan, and a little medal of the Virgin of the Fire, given me by the inhabitants of Forli. For the second time our tricolour spread itself over the ice of the Pole. Beside the flag we dropped the Cross. It was 1.30, and we were about 450 ft. up.

At the moment when these rites were completed, I felt a thrill of pride. Two years after the *Norge* flight we had come back to the Pole, and this time the bad weather, from Italy onwards, had made it much more difficult.

Inside the cabin, now that the engines were almost still, a little gramophone was playing an old folk-song: 'The Bells of San Giusto', bringing back memories, taking us all of a sudden to Italy, to our homes. We were all moved: more than one had tears in his eyes. Zappi cried: 'Long live Nobile!' I was grateful to him, as I was to Malmgren, when he came and said, clasping my hand: 'Few men can say, as we can, that we have been twice to the Pole.'

Few men indeed: six Italians and one Swede . . .

We were flying between 600 and 900 ft. up. The dirigible was still light, so to keep it at the proper height we had to hold the nose down.

At 10.30 I again ordered a speed measurement. When this had been taken I walked to the front of the cabin and looked out of the right-hand porthole, between the steering-wheel and the elevator. To test the height, I dropped a glass ball full of red liquid, and stood there, timing its fall with a stop-watch.

While I was attending to this, I heard Cecioni say excitedly: 'We are heavy!'

I turned with a start to look at the instruments.

The ship was right down by the stern, at an angle of 8 degrees to the horizon; nevertheless, we were rapidly falling.

The peril was grave and imminent. A short distance below us stretched the pack. I at once gave the orders which had to be given, the only ones that could save the ship in this emergency – if that was possible: to accelerate the two engines, start the third, and at the same time lift the nose of the dirigible still higher. I hoped by these means to overcome the unexpected heaviness.

Simultaneously, I shouted to Alessandrini to run out on the top of the ship and inspect the stern valves, as I thought gas might be escaping – the only explanation that occurred to me at the moment of this serious and rapid increase in weight.

Meanwhile, the mechanics had carried out my orders. Pomella and Caratti had speeded their engines up to 1,400 revolutions and Ciocca, with surprising promptness, had started his own. The ship began to move faster, and tilted at an angle of 15 or 20 degrees.

The dynamic lift obtained in this way must certainly have represented several hundredweight.

But unfortunately we went on falling. The variometer – on which my eyes were fixed – confirmed it; in fact, we seemed to be dropping even faster.

I realized that there was nothing more to be done. The attempt to combat the increased weight by propulsion had failed . . . A crash was now inevitable; the most we could do was to mitigate its consequences.

I gave the necessary orders: to stop the engines at once, so as to avoid fire breaking out as we crashed; and to drop the ballast-chain. Sending Cecioni to do this, I put Zappi in his place.

It was all that could have been ordered; it was ordered promptly and with absolute calm. The perfect discipline on board was unbroken, so that each man carried out my orders as best he could, in the vertiginous rapidity of the event.

In the meantime the pack was approaching at a fearful speed. I saw that Cecioni was finding it difficult to untie the rope which held the chain. 'Hurry up! Hurry up!' I shouted to him. Then noticing that the engine on the left, run by Caratti, was still working, I leaned out of a porthole on that side, and at the top of my voice – echoed, I think, by one of the officers – repeated the order: 'Stop the engine!' At that moment I saw the stern-boat was only a few tens of yards from the pack. I drew back into the cabin.

The recollection of those last terrible instants is very vivid in my memory. I had scarcely had time to reach the spot near the two rudders, between Malmgren and Zappi, when I saw Malmgren fling up the wheel, turning his startled eyes on me. Instinctively I grasped the helm, wondering if it were possible to guide the ship on to a snow-field and so lessen the shock . . . Too late! . . . There was the pack, a few yards below, terribly uneven. The masses of ice grew larger, came nearer and nearer . . . A moment later we crashed.

There was a fearful impact. Something hit me on the head, then I was caught and crushed. Clearly, without any pain, I felt some of my limbs snap. Some object falling from a height knocked me down head foremost. Instinctively I shut my eyes, and with perfect lucidity and coolness formulated the thought: 'It's all over!' I almost pronounced the words in my mind.

It was 10.33 on May 25th.

The fearful event had lasted only 2 or 3 minutes . . .

When I opened my eyes I found myself lying on the ice, in the midst of an appalling pack. I realized at once that others had fallen with me.

I looked up to the sky. Towards my left the dirigible, nose in air, was drifting away before the wind. It was terribly lacerated around the pilot-cabin. Out of it trailed torn strips of fabric, ropes, fragments of metal-work. The left wall of the cabin had remained attached. I noticed a few creases in the envelope.

Upon the side of the crippled, mutilated ship stood out the black letters ITALIA. My eyes remained fixed on them, as if fascinated, until the dirigible merged in the fog and was lost to sight.

It was only then that I felt my injuries. My right leg and arm were broken and throbbing; I had hurt my face and the top of my head, and my chest seemed all upside down with the violence of the shock. I thought my end was near.

Suddenly I heard a voice – Mariano's – asking: 'Where is the General?' And I looked around me.

I had never seen such a terrible pack: a formless, contorted jumble of pointed ice-crags, stretching to the horizon.

Two yards away on my right, Malmgren was sitting, and a little farther off lay Cecioni, moaning aloud. Next him was Zappi. The others – Mariano, Behounek, Trojani, Viglieri, and Biagi – were standing up. They appeared unhurt, except for Trojani, whose face was stained by a few patches of blood.

Here and there one could see wreckage – a dreary note of grey against the whiteness of the snow. In front of me a strip of bright red, like blood which had flowed from some enormous wound, showed the spot where we had fallen. It was the liquid from the glass balls.

I was calm. My mind was perfectly clear. But now I was feeling the seriousness of my injuries – worst of all, a terrible convulsion in my chest. Breathing was a great effort. I thought I had probably sustained some grave internal injury. It seemed that death was very near – that maybe I had only 2 or 3 hours to live.

I was glad of this. It meant that I should not have to watch the despair and slow death-agony of my comrades. What hope was there for them? With no provisions, no tent, no wireless, no sledges – nothing but useless wreckage – they were lost, irremediably lost, in this terrible wilderness of ice.

I turned towards them, looking at them with an infinite sadness at heart. Then I spoke: 'Steady, my lads! Keep your spirits up! Don't be cast down by this misfortune.' And I added: 'Lift your thoughts to God!'

No other words, no other ideas, came to me in those first unforgettable moments when death seemed imminent. But suddenly I was seized by strong emotion. Something rose up from my soul – from the depths of my being: something stronger than the pain of my tortured limbs, stronger than the thought of approaching death. And from my straining breast broke out, loud and impetuous, the cry: '*Viva l'Italia!*'

My comrades cheered.

My Polar Flights, 1961

RICHARD BYRD
1888–1957

When I tumbled into the light and warmth of the room, I kept thinking,
How wonderful, how perfectly wonderful.

When injury halted his career in the American navy in 1916, Richard Byrd turned his attention to aviation and, in 1926, with Floyd Bennett, claimed to be among the first men to fly a fixed-wing aircraft over the North Pole. Two years later, he led the largest and best-equipped expedition that had ever set out for the Antarctic, during which he undertook the first flight over the South Pole. He became a rear-admiral in 1930 and during the next three decades led three more extensive Antarctic expeditions, conducting scientific research and using aircraft to map the continent; he discovered Marie Byrd Land – named after his wife. By the end of his life he was a prominent figure in Antarctic exploration and died championing a treaty aimed at promoting international co-operation on the continent.

Here is an extract from his record of a four-and-a-half-month stint alone in a 12 foot by 9 foot hut, 125 miles south of the Ross Ice Shelf, from March to August 1934.

Trapped outside in a blizzard

It is a queer experience to watch a blizzard rise. First there is the wind, rising out of nowhere. Then the Barrier unwrenches itself from quietude; and the surface, which just before had seemed as hard and polished as metal, begins to run like a making sea. Sometimes, if the wind strikes hard, the drift comes across the Barrier like a hurrying white cloud, tossed hundreds of feet in the air. Other times the growth is gradual. You become conscious of a general slithering movement on all sides. The air fills with tiny scraping and sliding and rustling sounds as the first loose crystals stir. In a little while they are moving as solidly as an incoming tide, which creams over the ankles, then surges to the waist, and finally is at the throat. I have walked in drift so thick as not to be able to see a foot ahead of me; yet, when I glanced up, I could see the stars shining through the thin layer just overhead . . .

Even so, I didn't have any idea how really bad it was until I went aloft for an observation. As I pushed back the trapdoor, the drift met me like a moving wall. It was only a few steps from the ladder to the instrument shelter, but it seemed more like a mile. The air came at me in snowy rushes; I breasted it as I might a heavy surf. No night had ever seemed so dark. The beam from the flashlight was choked in its throat; I could not see my hand before my face . . .

The wind was blowing hard then. The Barrier shook from the concussions overhead; and the noise was as if the entire physical world were tearing itself to pieces. I could scarcely heave the trapdoor open. The instant it came clear I was plunged into a blinding smother. I came out crawling, clinging to the handle of the door until I made sure of my bearings. Then I let the door fall shut, not wanting the tunnel filled with drift. To see was impossible. Millions of tiny pellets exploded in my eyes, stinging like BB shot. It was even hard to breathe, because snow instantly clogged the mouth and nostrils. I made my way toward the anemometer pole on hands and knees, scared that I might be bowled off my feet if I stood erect; one false step and I should be lost for ever.

I found the pole all right; but not until my head collided with a cleat. I managed to climb it, too, though ten million ghosts were tearing at me, ramming their thumbs into my eyes. But the errand was useless. Drift as thick as this would mess up the contact points as quickly as they were cleared; besides, the wind cups were spinning so fast that I stood a good chance of losing a couple of fingers in the process. Coming down the pole, I had a sense of being whirled violently through the air, with no control over my movements. The trapdoor was completely buried when I found it again, after scraping around for some time with my mittens. I pulled at the handle, first with one hand, then with both. It did not give. It's a tight fit, anyway, I mumbled to myself. The drift has probably wedged the corners. Standing astride the hatch, I braced myself and heaved with all my strength. I might just as well have tried hoisting the Barrier.

Panic took me then, I must confess. Reason fled. I clawed at the three-foot square of timber like a madman. I beat on it with my fists, trying to shake the snow loose; and, when that did no good, I lay flat on my belly and pulled until my hands went weak from cold and weariness. Then I crooked my elbow, put my face down, and said over and over again, You damn fool, you damn fool. Here for weeks I had been defending myself against the danger of being penned inside the shack; instead, I was now locked out; and nothing could be worse, especially since I had only a wool parka and pants under my windproofs. Just two feet below was sanctuary – warmth, food, tools, all the means of survival. All these things were an arm's length away, but I was powerless to reach them.

There is something extravagantly insensate about an Antarctic blizzard at night. Its vindictiveness cannot be measured on an anemometer sheet. It is more than just wind; it is a solid wall of snow moving at gale force, pounding like surf. The whole malevolent rush is concentrated upon you as upon a personal enemy. In the senseless explosion of sound you are reduced to a crawling thing on the margin of a disintegrating world; you can't see, you can't hear, you can hardly move. The lungs gasp after the air sucked out of them, and the brain is shaken. Nothing in the world will so quickly isolate a man.

Half-frozen, I stabbed toward one of the ventilators, a few feet away. My mittens touched something round and cold. Cupping it in my hands, I pulled myself up. This was the outlet ventilator. Just why, I don't know – but instinct made me kneel and press my face against the opening. Nothing in the room was visible, but a dim patch of light illuminated the floor, and warmth rose up to my face. That steadied me.

Still kneeling, I turned my back to the blizzard and considered what might be done. I thought of breaking in the windows in the roof, but they lay two feet down in hard crust, and were reinforced with wire besides. If I only had something to dig with, I could break the crust and stamp the windows in with my feet. The pipe cupped between my hands supplied the first inspiration; maybe I could use that to dig with. It, too, was wedged tight; I pulled until my arms ached, without budging it; I had lost all track of time, and the despairing thought came to me that I was lost in a task without an end. Then I remembered the shovel. A week before, after levelling drift from the last light blow, I had stabbed a shovel handle up in the crust somewhere to leeward. That shovel would save me. But how to find it in the avalanche of the blizzard?

I lay down and stretched out full length. Still holding the pipe, I thrashed around with my feet, but pummelled only empty air. Then I worked back to the hatch. The hard edges at the opening provided another grip, and again I stretched out and kicked. Again no luck. I dared not let go until I had something else familiar to cling to. My foot came up against the other ventilator pipe. I edged back to that, and from the new anchorage repeated the manœuvre. This time my ankle struck something hard. When I felt it and recognized the handle, I wanted to caress it.

Embracing this thrice-blessed tool, I inched back to the trapdoor. The handle of the shovel was just small enough to pass under the little wooden bridge which served as a grip. I got both hands on the shovel and tried to wrench the door up; my strength was not enough, however. So I lay down flat on my belly and worked my shoulders under the shovel. Then I heaved, the door sprang open, and I rolled down the shaft. When I tumbled into the light and warmth of the room, I kept thinking, How wonderful, how perfectly wonderful.

Alone, 1939

Wally Herbert
1934–

*For myself, I hardly ever do exercises. I find exercise as a sport unbearable. I much
prefer to set off and suffer during the first few weeks of a journey.*

Herbert was in all likelihood the first person
to reach the geographic North Pole overland.
His career is distinguished by a catalogue of
North and South Pole achievements.

Herbert has covered more than 23,000
miles in his forty years of polar travel by
sledge and open vessels, more than half
through untrodden territory. He spent much
of his twenties in Antarctica, during which
time he mapped an enormous amount
(46,000 square miles) of new country and got
to within 200 miles of achieving his ambition
of reaching the South Pole by dog sledge.
However, more followed: a sixteen-month
journey in which he and three companions
made the first surface crossing of the Arctic
Ocean – what the British Prime Minister
Harold Wilson called 'a feat of endurance and

courage which ranks with any in polar history'. They set out with dog sledges from
Alaska, trekked via the North Pole and arrived
at Spitzbergen sixteen months later, having
covered 3,800 miles. If Peary's navigation was
'faulty', as many now think, they achieved the
first overland journey to the Pole. Herbert has
received a string of honours and has had both
a mountain range in the Antarctic and a
mountain in the Arctic named after him.
However, he was knighted only in 1999 – and
then thanks to a long campaign led by Ranulph Fiennes, who called him 'the greatest
polar explorer of our time'. He now lives in
Scotland, and is an accomplished artist.

The passages below are typical of the simple, notebook style with which he describes
the potentially deadly.

When polar bears become a menace

It had been a perfect day with not a cloud in the sky except those clouds on
the horizon in the direction of land. It was also the first day we were bothered
by polar bears. A couple of polar bears came up behind us whilst we were
sledging and were effectively shooed away. But from then onwards we
encountered polar bears all the way to the landfall. They were becoming a
menace. Every day we saw at least two, and we were also meeting at that time a
lot more broken ice than we had met previously. The floes were pretty cracked
up with the pressure building up. The surface was also getting bad by that
time and there was quite a lot of slush around. So it was almost touch and go
whether we were going to get on to land anyway. The sledging season was
quickly ending and we were journeying then as fast as we possibly could. But
we were only making about eight to ten miles a day.

The land was taking a long time to get closer and there were many white-
outs. When the weather cleared we always expected to see the land much
closer, but it seemed just as far away. We seemed to be travelling and travel-

ling but making no progress. The distraction, however, was the polar bears and we killed three during those three days. Sometimes they would come down-wind, but usually they approached us from behind and they just kept coming. There was one occasion when a polar bear came in sight and Fritz was in an awkward position: he was trying to cross a stretch of very tricky ice, weak, sloppy ice, with rotten small pans of ice in the middle of it, and suddenly a polar bear came along. The dogs of course took off and dragged the sledge into the water. The sledge didn't go right down but it rocked into the water. It was pulled out with a great deal of difficulty. And all this time the polar bear kept on coming, and Fritz didn't know what to do: whether to shoot it with a gun, shoot it with a camera, or try and rescue the sledge. All the other dog teams were going berserk and it was absolute chaos. We had only three guns, so one of us had no means of self-defence, myself on this occasion. I had the camera with a telephoto lens and was taking pictures as fast as I could. But the polar bear was approaching the lead sledge from ahead, and Fritz and Ken were up by the dogs in front. Allan was just behind with his dogs, keeping them under control, and I was at the back taking pictures of the whole scene. Fritz and Ken fired a couple of shots, but it wouldn't go away. It just kept coming. It didn't actually attack – it just kept walking. You've got to shoot them sometimes otherwise they would come right on and hit you, and there is no way of knowing how close they will come before they turn round and walk away – if they do walk away at all.

To kill a polar bear, you had first to knock him over. We never went for a head shot in these situations. We would always have at least two guns aimed at him at the same time, or even three, and we didn't take any chances. This wasn't a sport, this was the real thing. We were killing to protect ourselves and the dogs, and also for dog food – but that was a very secondary motive because we had plenty of food at that time.

Polar bears normally travel on all fours. They will rise up on their hind legs occasionally, when they are some distance off, just to look over the pressure ridges. They are very fearsome but very beautiful, too. When they are some distance off, they are magnificent beasts, but when they come closer and closer, they do become very menacing. They just amble towards you with a completely fearless expression on their faces. Almost casually, they look over their shoulders and don't seem particularly interested in you at all, but they keep heading in your direction. They don't look you straight in the eye and come towards you; they casually close the distance. The previous summer a polar bear had come right in amongst the dogs and taken a few swipes at them. A couple of other times when they were heading for the dogs we had driven them off.

We couldn't take chances, and we dropped this particular one about fifteen feet away. That's as close as I want to be to a polar bear, and from that time on we decided that we would shoot all polar bears that came within twenty feet, though we always tried to scare them off. We tried several techniques. There was one occasion when all four of us, with three guns between us, walked towards the polar bear, making a lot of noise and shouting and so on. But he kept coming. As we were walking towards him, we were closing the distance that much quicker. It was ridiculous. We should really have been going the other way.

The polar bears seemed unused to humans and dogs. Most of them travel all over the ice cap but this was an area where they appeared to concentrate all along the coast of North-East Land. Probably most of the hunting is done in the summer off the north-west coast of Spitzbergen in the open water. But that is farther along the coast and there's pack ice round there and boats can't get that far.

It seemed a shame, having shot a polar bear, even in self-defence, to leave it there, so we felt obliged to chop it up for dog food. It took about a couple of hours and was very hard work for all four of us. But the dogs now began to associate the walking polar bear with the meat and, from that time on, it was impossible to hold them whenever a polar bear came in sight. They just went wild and were very difficult to control.

Across the Top of the World: The British Trans-Arctic Expedition, 1969

SARA WHEELER
1961–
But I heard the still small voice. I had never heard a certainty like it.

Born in Bristol, Sara Wheeler lives in Central London. She read Classics and Modern Languages at Oxford, and is the author of *An Island Apart: travels in Evia* and *Travels in a Thin Country*, about Chile, which was nominated for the Thomas Cook Travel Book Award. She co-edited *Amazonian: The Penguin Book of Women's New Travel Writing* with travel writer Dea Birkett. *Terra Incognita* is her account of her visits in the mid-1990s to Antarctica, sponsored by the American National Science Foundation and British Antarctic Survey. She has recently published *Cherry*, a biography of Apsley Cherry-Garrard, a stalwart of Scott's final expedition. His *Worst Journey in the World* she cites as 'the best book of exploration of all time'.

Many would say Wheeler doesn't qualify as an 'explorer' – but she has documented more new ground than many of the great polar-trekkers. The world she was exploring was the one created by men, who had so long dominated the continent. She set about interpreting the place afresh. Without compunction she offers us this rather unexpected description of the Antarctic: 'shaped roughly like a cross section of the human brain, with a grossly misplaced finger tapering towards South America'. On another note, one telling remark about the Scott myth expands beyond the flawed man to the national myths that sustained the Empire: 'The perfect hero of the great English myth never existed, just as our national emblems, the lion and the unicorn, never roamed the South Downs.'

She became determined to investigate Antarctica in 1991, after looking south over the ice fields from Chile – 'it was as if I was seeing the earth for the very first time'. Three years later, she was there, and entangled in an intimate relationship with the continent.

Looking the beast in the eye

In Antarctica I experienced a certainty amid the morass of thoughts and emotions and intellectual preoccupations seething inside my balaclava'd head. It was what I glimpsed out of the corner of my eye. It wasn't an answer, or the kind of respite offered by a bottle of calamine lotion on sunburn. It was something that put everything else – everything that wasn't Antarctica – in true perspective. I felt as if I was realigning my vision of the world through the long lens of a telescope. It emanated from a sense of harmony. The landscape was intact, complete and larger than my imagination could grasp. It was free of the diurnal cycle that locked us earthlings into the ineluctable routine of home. It didn't suffer famines or social unrest. It was sufficient unto itself, and entirely untainted by the inevitable tragedy of the human condition. In front of me I saw the world stripped of its clutter: there were no honking horns, no overflowing litter bins, no gas bills – there was no sign of human intervention at all.

You might ask why I didn't go to the Yorkshire moors or the Nevada desert if 'all' I wanted was pristine nature. It would have been a lot easier. I had been to those places, and many others, but it was the scale, the unownedness, and the overpowering beauty that made Antarctica different and diverted the Nomadic Thoughts. It wasn't a permanent diversion. I knew I would meet my demons again and again before my life ended. Still, I glimpsed a world in which everything made sense. God didn't appear to me in any particular shape or form – if anything he became even more nebulous. But I heard the still small voice. I had never known certainty like it. I felt certain that a higher power exists, and every soul constitutes part of a harmonious universe, and that the human imagination can raise itself beyond poverty, social condemnation and the crushing inevitability of death. For the first time in my life, I didn't sense fear prowling around behind a locked door inside my head, trying to find a way out. It was as if a light had gone on in that room, and I had looked the beast in the eye.

It happened in a second. I've noticed that it is often the seconds which matter. They can be far more important than the hours. Reason is too lumbering a faculty to operate in seconds, and it leaves the way clear for instinct, or for nothing at all except a bit of psychic energy flying across a synapse. The glimpse left me with a deep and warm sense of calm and mental well-being, like the cosmic glow after some astronomical phenomenon.

Rothera Base

I had not expected banners welcoming me to Rothera but I had assumed that the base commander would send someone out to meet me, if only to avoid having to deal with the removal of my frozen corpse from the airstrip. Eventually I spotted a sno-cat trundling around the edge of the apron. I flagged it down, and smiled weakly at the Beard at the wheel.

'Any chance of a lift to the main building?' I asked.

He nodded, and I climbed up, slinging my bag into the space behind the seats. The Beard was silent. I wondered if he often passed hitch-hikers.

We lurched to a standstill in front of a long, pale green building. It had two storeys, and was separated from the runway by an expanse of gravel and ice. Open water was visible a few hundred yards from each end, and behind the base a ridge of gentle hills, only partially ice-clad, afforded some protection against the wind. The Beard looked at me expectantly. 'Thanks,' I said, dragging the bag down after me. There was only one entrance to the building, so I went through it.

Finding myself in a cramped lobby, I engaged in more loitering and took off my parka. Men were coming and going along the corridors, engaged in a variety of activities but united by the fact that they all ignored me. Short of erecting a sign outside the base saying 'GO AWAY', they couldn't have made it clearer that I was unwelcome. Eventually a balding but youngish radio operator called Stu took me upstairs for a cup of tea. Everyone was crowding round a table of new mail in an institutional canteen-style dining room. Stu consulted a wall-chart and found the number of my pitroom. I was relieved to see my name written up there, for it meant at least they knew I was coming and were not about to send me back, though in reality they could not have done so as there was no means of getting back.

The pitroom was like my room at Scott Base – small, windowless and comfortable – except that there were two sets of bunks rather than one and it was painted in repulsive shades of brown and orange. Each bunk had curtains round it, which meant you could create a separate little box for yourself and hide in it. My morale faltered when I realised from the absence of belongings that I was to be alone in this room, for it meant I was the only woman on base. This late in the season there was no hope of any new ones arriving. Outside the door, someone belched like the volcanic lake in Cameroon which emitted gases so poisonous that hundreds died. I sat on my bunk and burst into tears.

Later, Stu reappeared. 'Do you need anything?' he asked.

'No, I'm fine,' I lied. 'But thanks – thanks for asking.'

'On Saturday nights we have a bit of a special dinner – tablecloths and lots of courses, that sort of thing. We get kind of dressed up.' He thought for a moment. 'Why not come and meet everyone at the bar at seven-thirty?'

'Great,' I said, the tone of my voice indicating that I did not believe it to be great at all. 'Thanks.'

'No worries,' said Stu cheerily. 'See you later.'

'Getting kind of dressed up' was a challenging concept. At halfpast seven I made the best of a clean shirt and a half-clean pair of jeans, and sallied forth. There were about thirty-five people in the bar when I got there, and they were all talking loudly or guffawing with laughter. About eight of them were wearing ties. I introduced myself to a man in a sports jacket that was too small for him, but he immediately turned his back on me. Through careful observation, in the manner of a secret service agent, I gathered that purchasing a drink involved entering a tick in a column next to one's name on a special chart which was being tossed around chummily from hand to hand. I looked over a shoulder at this chart.

'I don't expect your name will be there,' said the Beard who had given me a lift. But it was.

The meal was delicious. I sat next to a field assistant.

'What exactly does a field assistant do?' I asked him.

'Babysit the scientists,' he said.

It was difficult to make yourself heard over the permanent dull roar of badinage that characterised social events at Rothera. They practised a kind of chain-joking. A brief food fight broke out during the cheese course. Here were British men doing what they did best . . .

The next morning, before anyone else got up, I had a look round the base. Labs, the radio room, the doctor's surgery, the boot room . . . Antarctic bases were starting to look awfully familiar. Rothera was about the same size as Scott Base and Terra Nova Bay, and it was about one twentieth of the size of McMurdo. The building was still, and silent, like a museum after closing time. I ran the palm of my hand over a smooth white wall. Then I heard a woman laughing faintly. I stood very still, trying to detect where this promising sound came from. Slowly, I padded along a narrow corridor until I was standing outside an unmarked door. A woman was talking very softly. I held an ear to the door. There was something . . . familiar about the voice. Several minutes passed. Suddenly, an orchestra struck up. I pushed the door open quietly. There was the night watchman, slumbering peacefully in an armchair, and on the video screen in front of him Julie Andrews was leaping down an Austrian mountainside followed by a row of rosy-cheeked von Trapp children. He had fallen asleep watching *The Sound of Music.*

Meeting the emerging 'winterers'

On the plane to Christchurch I began to read a book by a clinical psychologist called Glin Bennet. It was called *Beyond Endurance* and one chapter was about 'the intellectual inertia' of wintering in Antarctica. To demonstrate the way groups can disintegrate, Bennet quoted the story of a meteorologist arriving at an Antarctic base in the fifties, just as winter ended. Nobody came out of the hut to greet him and his party, and they slowly realised that the group had collapsed during the long months of darkness. 'We discovered, in the different rooms', the meteorologist wrote, 'little animal dens where, as base life had broken down and they had become no longer on speaking terms with one another, each man had retired to make himself a little corner in the wreck of his personality.'

Academics had had a field day with the psychology of the Antarctic winter . . .

The Eskimos could have saved them the trouble of their research – they know all about the depression of the long night. They call it *perlerorneq*, which means 'to feel the weight of life'.

Just as 'the long, dark night of the soul' is a popular literary metaphor for spiritual turmoil, so the polar winter perfectly mirrors the inner darkness which seems to have fallen so often. Frederick Cook, one of the first to over-winter in the pack ice, wrote in his diary in 1898, 'The curtain of blackness which has fallen over the outer world of icy desolation has also descended upon the inner world of our souls . . . The night soaks hourly a little more colour from our blood.'

A cart grated past my seat, followed by a cheery stewardess propelling it down the narrow aisle. She laid trays on the fold-down tables above our knees as the sun spilled through the pebble window. I carried on with Cook. 'The grayness of the first days of the night', he wrote, 'has given way to a soul-despairing darkness, broken only at noon by a feeble yellow haze on the northern sky. I can think of nothing more disheartening, more destructive to human energy, than this dense, unbroken blackness of the long polar night.'

I wondered what in the world I was going to find . . .

The sky was streaked with angry apricot flashes when we landed, and the ice had absorbed a gloomy purple light. A mist was hanging at the feet of the Transantarctics so that the peaks appeared to be suspended between ice and sky. Once again, I felt as if I had come home. That no longer seemed bizarre – it was a comfortable feeling. When I caught sight of myself in someone else's glacier glasses, I saw that I was smiling.

Three days before I arrived, on 20 August, the sun had risen over Ross Island for the first time since 24 April. Already, for a few hours in every twenty-four the residents of McMurdo were enjoying a dusky daylight, though they had not yet seen the sun, as from McMurdo it was obscured behind Mount Erebus. My physiological clock had responded to total light by urging me not to go to bed. I wondered if so much darkness would have the reverse effect . . .

The first person I saw had tied a knot in his beard, but everyone looked healthy enough after their 'weary spell of darkness'. They were fish-belly white, of course, and they all caught colds from us and diarrhoea from the freshies our planes brought them. Most of them weren't sure how they felt. When I sat down to breakfast on the first day, the woman opposite me burst out, 'Wow, it's so good to see new faces!', yet posters appeared in the dorms saying '*Coming soon to a room near you: the roommate from hell, Winfly 1995*' next to a screaming Munch-like face and a bemused individual standing in a doorway holding a suitcase. I didn't need a poster to tell me I had entered staked-out territory – it was obvious. They had been padding the corridors and battling along the windy walkways for six months without seeing a single new creature.

'I felt the futility of my existence,' the woman at breakfast told me when I asked her how she had found the winter isolation. 'Nothing mattered. And the hopelessness of the world surviving. It lingers still.'

It was like watching a whole community coming out of hibernation. I trod very carefully. The experience put me in mind of an extremely ancient uncle in the west country who was apprenticed as a printer at the age of fourteen. On his first day he had boarded the bus to the factory at six in the morning, clutching a packet of corned-beef sandwiches. All was well until a group of hoary old printers got on the bus a mile or two later. One of them stopped alongside my young uncle and thundered: 'That's my seat, lad.'

I was allocated a bed in a room in the same dark corridor as the Corner Bar, the latter no longer under the supervision of Mike the carpenter, as he had retired to ply his trade in the north during the austral winter. It had been left in the hands of his henchman John, its only regular social gathering Coffee at ten o'clock on a Sunday morning.

'Come along,' said John when he passed me in the gloomy corridor.

Outside the window, daylight lingered like a promise. Six people were lounging around the low smoked-plexiglass table, which was spread with coffee mugs, plates of muffins and bottles of liquor. The Budweiser clock and target-practice penguin were there. When the six people saw me, they fell silent and stared as if I had been wearing no parka, no jeans, no layers of thermals, no boots nor socks and no underwear. It was as if I had walked in stark naked.

'I guess it was like waking up to find a total stranger in the bedroom,' one of them said later.

The winterers stood alone, as they always had. I envied them. Charles Laseron, Mawson's assistant biologist, put it like this. 'As the first rounding of the Horn is to the sailor, so a winter in the ice is to a polar explorer. It puts the hallmark on his experience. Having successfully emerged from the embryonic stage, he is now fully fledged, and can take his place in the select fraternity.'

Frozen-Sausage Bill was back, his eyes still the colour of cornflower hearts. He was preparing to whip pork products out of boots at safety lectures. Just as the same names cropped up in the history books, so I saw the same faces back on the ice. J. M. Barrie, who only travelled south vicariously, noted from his leather armchair that everyone who went to Antarctica came back vowing that nothing in heaven or earth would tempt them to go near polar regions again – and at the end of six months they were on their knees in front of whoever might be able to get them there.

It was certainly cold; typically about thirty below, and in those first few days the sun didn't rise until shortly before midday, and it set two hours later. When a storm came in, ropes were strung up between the dorms and the galley, so we had something to cling to. But when it was clear, the skies were diaphanous, frosting the Transantarctics in pastel pinks and blues, the slopes of each speak as sharply defined as the faces of a diamond. Each morning was lighter than its predecessor. It seemed as if summer were rushing in at unnaturally high speed, like one of those long-exposure natural history films of a flower opening.

Terra Incognita: Travels in Antarctica, 1997

PART V

Forests

*

We had certainly seen forests before, but this scene was an epoch in our lives ever to be remembered for its bitterness; the gloom enhanced the dismal misery of our life; the slopping moisture, the unhealthy reeking atmosphere, and the monotony of the scenes; nothing but the eternal interlaced branches, the tall aspiring stems, rising from a tangle through which we had to burrow and crawl like wild animals, on hands and feet.
H. M. Stanley, *Through the Dark Continent*, (1878)

We all know that feeling of being just one face in a crowd, of not mattering, of not belonging. In the forest you can feel just as isolated and insignificant. Only, it may be worse: it's not just that there's a mass of vegetation blocking your light, crowding you in; the problem is that the forest really is 'out to get you'.

I was forcibly reminded of this on my very first independent expedition, aged twenty-two, when things all went wrong and I ended up almost possessionless, sitting on the bank of a remote Amazon tributary. I'm still not clear how long it took me to walk out to safety – whether it was two weeks or three weeks, it was undoubtedly far too long. I think the distance was only sixty-five miles; but, as I got out my meagre little survival kit and began walking, cutting a notch on a stick every hundred or so paces to measure my progress – I was very soon thinking to myself that it might as well have been a thousand.

There are various reasons why tropical rainforest is not easy to survive in, the most important being that ground cover is sparse for lack of light. Most food is a hundred feet up in the tree canopy; but I had lived with the Warao and other Indian groups and knew that I could eat the tips of ferns, the hearts of palms. I could scoop little fish from pools with socks, and in turn use them as bait to catch piranhas with a hook – having remembered to reinforce the fishing line with wire against the piranha's impressive teeth.

I survived quite well for a few days; but the problem was that this highly competitive ecosystem just wasn't my home: I didn't belong there. I didn't know the rules, how to fit in. After a week or so, fungi were beginning to colonize my skin. I began to go down with malaria, and dysentery. My body seemed to be falling apart – like my clothes, which were rotting. Much of this process might have begun months before, when I had first entered the forest with Indian guides; but back then they had kept me on the right side of the survival line. Now I was alone, and it seemed the forest had me on the run.

A lot of my problem was psychological, no doubt; but I've had years of experience of tropical forest since, and the feeling I and others get is always much the same. In the sweltering darkness of the forest floor, you begin to feel the odd one out; and that is because you are. In the forest you are soon reminded that Nature operates on a principle of the 'survival of the fittest', and that you, as a human being, do not fit. Sit down on a log, and scouting ants come to investigate you: you are a potential food source. Sit there for long enough, and you'll eventually be consumed by a rat, or other scavenger; shockingly, in the rainforest even butterflies might feast off your remains.

So, sitting there in the Amazon rainforest, wondering if I would see my mother, father, sister and brother again, it was very lonely indeed; and just as when you're a stranger in a big city, sitting in your bedsit and hearing the chatter of people getting on with their own busy lives around you, it's hard not to take it personally. You begin to feel like prey – as if it's only a matter of time before something will get you. Your mind turns inward; there are no horizons to aim for, nothing on which to fix a compass bearing.

No animal has yet been domesticated that

can help you in this environment. In the deserts there are camels; in the plains there are horses; in arid mountains you can choose between mule, pack horse, llama and yak. In the forests, you are on your own. The explorers of old might have been able to roam the earth, conquering nations and meeting the occasional obstructive wild animal, but they couldn't rule plants and animals massed together like this – not without destroying the forest bit by bit.

Obviously, I did survive that first Amazon expedition – I haven't mentioned that I had an Indian dog with me, and sadly had to kill it for something to eat, in order to see home again; but I am far from alone in feeling a little haunted by tropical rainforest. This is the Western concept of Jungle. The seething mass of life that composes the Amazon Basin, Borneo and Congo have become for us the very epitome of the impenetrable and mysterious – and with good reason. Tropical rainforests are highly competitive ecosystems, vast equatorial hot-houses which, generally speaking, are ancient (the Amazon is 80 million years old). Having enjoyed a stable climate for so long, species have been able to evolve a more and more specialized existence. There are frogs that carry tadpoles on their backs, harmless bugs disguised as stinging wasps, butterflies that swoop like birds – and they all are battling it out for survival.

What about the Indians? They live there happily, don't they? Well yes . . . and no. The truth is, native populations have usually lived in clearings along rivers. Fish provide protein, gardens the necessary carbohydrates. The river is transport, and makes it easier to wash and stop fungal growth on the skin. However, it's necessary to move on after a few years, as gardens tire and houses become infested with pests.

Rarely would even they venture into the forest alone and typically they guard against the unknown by creating myths about its inhabitants. The Kalapalo of the Xingu talked about a snake with the girth of a tree, or giant black cats that would eat them. So, though many hundreds of indigenous groups have developed a system for working the forest, many fewer truly live within the forest. These – people like the Penan of Borneo, say, or the Waorani of the Ecuadorian Amazon – are specialized nomads who survive by constantly moving on to seek out new resources.

Historically, forests were an obstruction; like deserts and mountains they were to be avoided if possible. Alexander Mackenzie had the following formula for tackling the wilds of North America: '. . . a kettle of wild rice, sweetened with sugar . . . with their usual regale of rum, soon renewed that courage which disdained all obstacles . . .' A major part of our planet's lowlands was once forested, including most of Europe; but as man changed from being a nomadic hunter – who valued the forest as a living resource – to being a cultivator and herder, forests were put to use as a source of building materials or cleared for planting. As further waves of settlers followed on the heels of the pioneers, they were further destroyed.

In time, the forests became relicts, and thus were a sanctuary for species, and ideas. The titles of the books on my shelves give the general idea. To Julian Duguid the forest was a *Green Hell*; to Hanbury-Tenison a vulnerable sanctuary and something most had lost, a *Fragile Eden*; to Albert Schweitzer – *On the Edge of the Primeval Forest* – a place of origins, ancient and primitive. Gradually there in the tropics, we non-forest people have deposited all our hopes and fears. It was a place of innocence or evil – of pure, unspoiled people on one hand, or cannibals on the other; of nature in all its glory, with miracle cures for cancer, or of horrors: piranhas, snakes and spiders.

There were other types of great forest – the taiga of Siberia and North America, for example – but these cold, northern climes were sparsely inhabited, on the way to nowhere, and badly served in literature. The sweltering foliage of the tropics so came to be seen as the place where strange people and species might lurk, threaten or hide. In response to the impressive assembly of threatening creatures and bewilderingly complex, oppressive vegetation, torrents of purple prose gushed effortlessly from the explorers' pens.

For H. M. Stanley (1841–1904), passing through the unknown Congo with his huge army of guides and porters, the local inhabitants became an extension of the aggressive forest they lived in: 'I confessed my impotence to charm the savage soul,' he writes of a young boy he meets. Stanley battles his way on through the primeval lowlands, keeping a tally of other encounters: 'We have attacked and destroyed 28 large towns and three or four score villages, fought 32 battles on land and water' – and he has chosen a formidable enemy in the Congo forest: 'A violent death will be preferable to death by starvation,' he writes, as he fails to win co-operation from the natives, who see the forest as their provider. 'The constant slush and reek which the heavy dews caused in the forest through which we had travelled the last ten days had worn my shoes out, and half of the march I travelled with naked feet. I had then to draw out of my store my last pair of shoes. Frank was already using his last pair. Yet we were still in the very centre of the continent. What should we do when all were gone? was a question which we asked of each other often.'*

When the time came for explorers to write up their adventures, the forest never failed to appeal to readers. True, the bleak polar landscape would always win as a dramatic backdrop, with lone heroic figures stumbling along in a blizzard. However, the forest had at least one winning quality: mystery. In the 'primeval jungle', there was always something more, still undiscovered. It was only a matter of time before the hero would succumb, the reader was led to believe, to the jaguars, snakes or ants – or to their own fears, as they cracked up: 'the horror, the horror'.

So when Sir Walter Raleigh needed to get back in favour with Queen Elizabeth – he had had to withdraw from court life in 1591 after having bedded one of the Queen's maids of honour, Mistress Throckmorton – he set his sights on the forests of South America. Surely, from that steaming vegetation he could pull something out of the hat. What he was able to return with was, in actual fact, very little; but that didn't prevent him from writing *The Discoverie of the Large, Rich and Beautiful Empyre of Guiana, with a Relation of the Great and Golden City of Manoa (which the Spaniards call El Dorado).*

Raleigh had been spurred on to El Dorado by an account of a great Indian prince (perhaps in modern Colombia), in 1541. The central attraction, El Dorado, was originally not a place at all but a person, 'the Golden One'.

They tell me [wrote Raleigh] that what they have learned from the Indians is that this great lord or prince goes about continually covered in gold dust as fine as ground salt . . . He anoints himself every morning with a certain gum or resin that sticks very well; the powdered gold adheres to that unction. His entire body is covered from the soles of his feet to his head. He looks as resplendent as a gold object worked by the hands of a great artist . . . he washes away at night what he puts on each morning so that it is discarded and lost . . . and he does this every day of the year . . . I would rather have the sweepings of the chamber of this Prince than the great meltings of gold there have been in Peru.

---

* Stanley, for all his high-impact approach to discovery, is a journalist who describes well how the forest affects him: 'The walk to Mnazi-Moya will compel the traveler to moralise and meditate pensively. Decay speaks to him and from the moment he leaves the house to the moment he returns, his mind is constantly dwelling upon mortality.'

The El Dorado story usually made mention of the royal figure ritually bathing in a lake, and there is some archaeological evidence for some such ritual taking place in or near Guatavita and other lakes. However, whatever the exact ceremony, it had certainly died out before the first European arrival; it was already only a memory.

The tropical forest tends not to draw the spiritual out in the explorer, perhaps because, surrounded by myriad species, man is no longer special; or perhaps it's just the sapping humidity. The forests did, however, become an attraction for the fervently religious, which is a quite different thing. For the forest was, above all, a place for seekers; and in the forest there was treasure to be found in people's souls, which could be usefully saved for Jesus. There was also treasure to be found in lost cities; Colonel Fawcett was seeking one of these, we think, when he disappeared in Mato Grosso in 1925.

For naturalists, the forests were a treasure trove indeed: from the tidal mangroves, up through the slopes to cloud forests, the Victorians busied away, bottling and skinning.

When Charles Waterton (1782–1865) published his *Wanderings in South America*, some of his descriptions were received with a storm of derision, in particular his accounts of the sloth – a creature whose mode of living seemed bizarre beyond belief – and, above all, of his ride on the back of a cayman. However, an early reviewer of his book, Sidney Smith, explained that Waterton 'appears in early life to have been seized with an unconquerable aversion to Piccadilly, and to that train of meteorological questions and answers which forms the great staple of polite conversation'. Waterton belonged to the great Spirit of Enquiry, and the forests provided more than enough scientific questions to be answered.*

The forests were a honey pot for the intellectually curious. Boffins of all sorts piled into the undergrowth. Richard Spruce (1817–92) made his *Notes of a Botanist on the Amazon and Andes*; Alexander von Humboldt and Henry Bates, with Waterton, all explored the forests of South America; Wallace was there and also in the Malay Archipelago. They were all collecting evidence to make order out of 'jungle'. Nowadays, we all know the wealth of rainforest species: the British Museum (Natural History) asked me to bottle some insects in Brunei once, and I did it rather casually, popping the little things into a test tube in total ignorance, only to discover later that I'd discovered seven new species of fig wasp. Such a thing was startling to me then, even as someone quite well versed in ecology; for the Victorians, making such discoveries every day by the hour, it must have been all the more astounding. Perhaps this explains the fervour of some of the great collectors – those such as poor Wallace, who lost all of his Amazon collection, so painstakingly accumulated over years, when his ship went down.

Each specimen collected was also a piece of potential evidence, as the great thinkers of the age grappled with theories that would explain the mechanism by which Nature operated. In *The Malay Archipelago*, we see Wallace edging towards his theory of evolution (at the same time as Darwin), and are tempted to think, as we read the account of him playing with an adopted orang-utan orphan, that he is pondering on man's relationship with the apes. One of the most astounding pieces in his

—

* This is a typical example of his hands-on approach – fishing for a vampire bat with his toes: 'I had often wished to have been once sucked by the vampire in order that I might have it in my power to say it had really happened to me. There can be no pain in the operation, for the patient is always asleep when the vampire is sucking him; and as for the loss of a few ounces of blood, that would be a trifle in the long run. Many a night have I slept with my foot out of the hammock to tempt this winged surgeon, expecting that he would be there; but it was all in vain; the vampire never sucked me, and I could never account for his not doing so, for we were inhabitants of the same loft for months together.'

book is the assault Wallace makes on our society – 'the wealth and knowledge and culture of *the few* do not constitute civilisation . . .' In this case, travel did broaden the mind.

I have already mentioned that forests are refuges. The lowland forests were the last retreats of indigenous populations. Mountains also provided a bolt-hole, but unless covered in rich forest they were comparatively barren, and never provided the range of cover afforded by lowland forest, with its attendant swamps and swirling rivers.

Wherever indigenous people were accessible to outsiders, they had always been vulnerable. William Balfour Baikie (1825–64), who explored the Niger and Benue rivers, while not always sympathetic to West African culture, could see that it was being steadily weakened. 'I have been careful to note any traditions regarding the early history of the different tribes, as though at present they are of comparatively little value, the time will come when these apparently trifling stories will be sought after with as much avidity as the historical antiquary of our own country . . .'* Elsewhere, Margaret Brooke, wife of

the Raja of Sarawak, proudly describes the way her mini-kingdom dispensed justice: 'Very often the trial of more serious crimes lasted some days.' She saw no irony in the fact that an Englishman back home might, even if a pessimist, expect a minimum of a few weeks of trial and legal preparation, especially if facing execution.

Other Europeans were more interested in expanding their spiritual kingdom. Here's Albert Lloyd, who came through West Africa in the 1890s only a generation after Stanley: 'Their blood will surely be upon us as a nation if we, knowing their state, seek not to break their age-bound chains of heathenism, and "proclaim liberty to the captives, and the opening of the prison to them that are bound."'

Another explorer I've included in this section is Mary Kingsley, (1862–1900), who was travelling in West Africa before Lloyd. She objected to imperialism in all its forms and would, you feel, have given his sort of talk pretty short shift. 'As it is with the forest,' she wrote, 'so it is with the minds of the natives . . . At first you see nothing but confused stupidity and crime, but when you get to see – well! As in the other forest, you see things worth seeing.'

Modern-day missionary Elisabeth Elliot found little worth seeing in native culture: 'Among the Jivaros, witchcraft and sorcery, hate and murder take deep roots early in life', she writes. As a rule, missionaries were trying to lay down their own moral code – and there are 150 laws in Leviticus alone. Elliot's first task in Ecuador was with the Quichua

---

* Baikie goes on: 'It is hoped the present work . . . will satisfy any anxiety which may be felt about the once dreaded "Nigers", or concerning the rude natives around; and if it serves in any degree to excite a warmer feeling towards the ill-treated African to claim a small degree of attention for rich but neglected regions, or to stimulate further enquiries and explorations, the writer will consider his labours not to have been altogether in vain.' He also has this to say, by way of explanation of native aggression: '. . . we did not wish to have it recorded that the first visit of Europeans to these wild regions had been marked by quarrelling and by bloodshed, as such an event would have tended to convince these savages that our advent was not that of friends as we called ourselves, but of foes. Much may be said of the behaviour of these poor wretches. Accustomed to visits from none but enemies, there arrived unannounced at their village a party of strangers whose complexions were fair and resembled those of the Pulbe whom they so dreaded. Actuated by no sense of honour, not

restrained by any high moral or religious sentiment, they merely saw in us a weak handful whom they thought they could crush, and in our clothes and instruments, inviting objects which they, as the stronger party, might appropriate. That was the only chain of reasoning in their savage minds; they were powerful, we seemed to be weak; the temptation was too strong for them, they made the attempt, and, fortunately for us, they failed.'

Indians: '. . . the Gospel message was getting through to these sons of the jungle . . . I closed in prayer, inviting those who were really repentant to go into the back room of the school, where I could deal more carefully with them. Twelve came. We encouraged and exhorted them and arranged for a believers' meeting on Friday afternoon. Several others are very close. What joy! This is what we came here for.'

The greatest testament to the effectiveness of her work, however, were the Auca, another west Amazon group. They too, were apparently once a lost cause: 'There are those, however, who have not [accepted] and will not accept this verdict as final – those who cannot rest in peace while generations of Aucas remain beyond the frontiers of Christianity.' Such a one was her husband, Jim Elliot, who, with others, approached the Aucas with a view to replacing their religious beliefs – and paid with his life. Elisabeth Elliot stayed on in South America, steadily bringing the Aucas who had killed her husband to Jesus.

Forests being hiding places, anthropologists as well as missionaries find them attractive places in which to graze. So in this section we also find Margaret Mead scribbling in her field notebook, trying not to interfere in the lives of her subjects but systematically to interpret and classify. Napoleon Chagnon, though a controversial figure, did a thorough job of debunking the 'noble savage' idea, at least. As a keen twenty-six-year-old fieldworker arriving in his first Yanomamö village, he nervously hopes they will adopt him: 'There are a few problems, however, that seem to be universal among anthropological fieldworkers, particularly those to do with eating, bathing, sleeping, lack of privacy and loneliness or discovering that primitive man is not always as noble as you originally thought.'

One result of the anthropologist's work has been to level the playing field: we are forced to see people not as 'pygmies' or 'innocent', or even as all that 'tribal'. We're all much the same in the end: we are human beings, with a full range of experiences in life. The fact that an Amazon Indian may have a 'primitive' lifestyle – spearing fish in the river all day, and wearing only a bark loincloth – might suggest simplicity to us, but this is hardly the true picture. There are belief systems of so-called tribal peoples that we have failed even to begin to document. Take that most misunderstood of all religions, voodoo, in Haiti. Though by reputation superstitious and haunted by zombies, the Haitians actually carry with them an amalgam of West African beliefs that include a highly complex array of gods and spirits. There's Ogou, a god of fire; Ezili, a fertility goddess; Azaka, an agricultural god; and so it goes on – an extended family of deities that answers an infinite variety of needs. No anthropologist has come near to recording them all; nor is this possible, because the gods in this hidden, parallel world are ever changing, adapting to the changing circumstances of society. Once, you might have prayed to Ogou, the fire god, to help you keep warm; nowadays, you might pray to him if your car breaks down, because he is in charge of spark plugs.

Whatever the motives of explorers through the years, our image of the tropical forests, and those who live there, remains larger than life. We, back home, really seem to want it that way. I've travelled seven and a half months across the Amazon Basin, and thousands of miles through rainforest elsewhere, very often alone. In my books there are no snake attacks, no deaths via the teeth of piranhas, for the simple reason that they've never happened. I have seen bites from vampire bats, but only once. Yet the images, if not the stories, persist. It seems we don't want the rational dish the scientific explorer serves up to us; we need to set a place aside for mystery, a place that will give us hope, a Utopia we can aspire to. Perhaps we also want there to be some place that is really bad, inhabited by natives who believe in false gods and die early, so making us feel better about our own lot in life.

Some anthropologists have recently argued that the ultimate bogeyman of the forest, the cannibal, has never even existed, though several of the accounts I've selected below talk of him. Personally, while undergoing a New Guinea ritual, I found myself having to eat the powdered bones of a revered ancestor. But a few dusty old bones are one thing, of course, and the steaming flesh of an enemy is another, and I remain doubtful about the standard cannibal traveller tale. In Irian Jaya, I visited an 'uncontacted' group of people called the Obini. It was a short visit – I fled with my guides after a couple of days partly because they suspected that we were cannibals. They may or may not have had grounds for being wary; their neighbours were the Asmat, who were once famously accused of eating Michael Rockerfeller, the tycoon's art-collector son. However, it struck me, as I ran away through the forest, that the Obini, one of the remotest peoples on earth, were the same as we were: we all peopled the Unknown with cannibals.

Believing in the savagery of indigenous people helped the first Europeans entering the Americas, Africa and the East to justify both the slaughter of natives, and the subjugation of them. However, the myths have given ground with time. It has been a battle between two components of Western thought, the Greek concept of *mythos* conceding to *logos* – what we might think of as science, the rational, the logical. Our fantasies about far lands will gradually shrink, just as those nearer to home have done. Once, our own forests were populated by huge mythical peoples and powerful gods. As the importance of these forest entities decreased, so they were miniaturized. Eventually, they were just fairies and pixies; and now we have nothing at all.

Francisco de Orellana and Gonzalo Pizarro
c. 1511–46/c. 1502–48
A foul deed (what else can such treason be called?).

Orellana and Pizarro were Spanish colonizers whose expedition inland from Quito in Ecuador led to the first European navigation of the whole of the River Amazon.

In 1541 Gonzalo Pizarro, the youngest of the four half-brothers of the conquistador Francisco Pizarro, set out from Quito in search of the 'land of cinnamon', a region that, according to certain Indians, was brimming with that much coveted spice. Gonzalo Pizarro had taken part in the conquest of Peru and was working as Governor of Quito and its surrounding region when Francisco commissioned him for the expedition. Gonzalo had also heard rumours of 'The Golden One', El Dorado, and this became another object of the journey – Gonzalo was the first of many adventurers who would search in vain for the source of the legend. With him were 220 Spaniards, 4,000 Indians, a herd of pigs for food and a pack of hunting dogs to terrorize natives who put up any resistance.

Meanwhile another Spaniard, Francisco de Orellana, was gathering together a group of twenty-nine Spaniards and some Indians to join Pizarro's expedition. Orellana had been born in Trujillo and was a family friend of the Pizarros. At the age of sixteen he had travelled to the West Indies to seek his fortune, and had fought in the battles of the conquest of Peru, but then settled in Ecuador's Puerto Viejo, in Guayaquil, where he was governor.

Orellana and his men joined Pizarro in the valley of Zumaco in northern Ecuador and Orellana was made second in command of the expedition. They continued inland for seven months until they reached the Upper Coca river, where cinnamon trees were indeed growing, but in nothing like the abundance they had imagined. Meanwhile, in

this sparse land, food supplies were running out. Pizarro sent Orellana with a group of fifty-six men downstream by boat in search of an Indian village. He was ordered to return within twelve days.

The current carried Orellana and his men quickly downriver. They reached a village called Aparia that could supply them with large quantities of food, but Orellana made the decision not to return upstream and continued onwards, into the River Marañon, the 'maze'. This decision was to lead Orellana and his men to achieve the first recorded crossing of the South American continent: on 28 July 1552 they reached the tidal basin of the Amazon and, rigging sails made from blankets, continued towards the river's mouth, reaching the Atlantic Ocean on 26 August after an eight-month journey covering 2,000 miles. On the way they had fought off attacks by Indians, including one by what seemed to be pale-skinned female warriors. Friar Carvajal, whose eyewitness account is the most detailed record of the expedition, likened these women to the Amazons of Greek legend, and it was this that gave the river its name. It was possible, however, that they were just long-haired Indians – or simply invented, to add to the wonder of the land he now needed royal patronage to explore.

Meanwhile, Pizarro and his men had given up waiting for food and made the demoralizing trek back to Quito; on arrival only eighty of the Spaniards were still alive and nearly all the Indians had perished. Pizarro learned of the assassination of his half-brother Francisco in Lima the year before, and spent the next six years trying to seize control of the country – Francisco had named Gonzalo his successor, but Spain had appointed a different viceroy. He was finally defeated in 1548 and soon afterwards was executed in Cusco.

Orellana, meanwhile, had been charged with desertion by Gonzalo, but having sailed up the coast of South America he wisely decided to return to Spain, and was rewarded instead for his achievements. King Charles I commissioned him to lead a colonizing mission to claim the whole of the Amazon region – or New Andalusia, as it had been named – as Spanish territory. The journey back to South America was a shambles, and Orellana lost two of his four ships on the way. He spent the rest of his life exploring the Amazon estuary in search of the river's main channel, until his death in 1546 from tropical disease.

The extract comes from the *Royal Commentaries of the Incas* (*Comentarios Reales de los Incas*), written by Garcilaso de la Vega, the mestizo chronicler. The son of a Spanish nobleman and an Inca princess, de la Vega was one of the first known Peruvian mestizos (of mixed Spanish and indigenous blood). He learned the native Indian language, Quechua, as well as Spanish, later moving to Spain, where he wrote histories of his homeland that have become Peruvian classics.

To the land of cinnamon

In this province of Quijos, which is north of Quito, many warlike Indians sallied forth against Gonzalo; but when they beheld the multitude of Spaniards and horses, they quickly retired, and were seen no more. A few days afterwards there was such an earthquake, that many houses, in the village where Gonzalo's party were resting, were thrown down. The earth opened in many places; there was lightning and thunder, insomuch that the Spaniards were much astonished: at the same time such torrents of rain fell, that they were surprised at the difference between that land and Peru. After suffering these inconveniences for forty or fifty days, they commenced the passage of the snowy cordillera, where the snow fell in such quantities, and it was so cold, that many Indians were frozen to death, because they were so lightly clad. The Spaniards, to escape from the cold and snow of that inclement region, left the swine and provisions behind them, intending to seek some Indian village. But things turned out contrary to their hopes, for, having passed the cordillera, they were much in want of provisions, as the land they came to was uninhabited. They made haste to pass through it, and arrived at a province and village called Sumaco, on the skirts of a volcano, where they obtained food. But, during two months, it did not cease to rain for a single day; so that the Spaniards received great injury, and much of their clothing became rotten.

In this province, called Sumaco, which is on the equinoctial line, or very near it, the trees, which they call cinnamon, grow, and of which the Spaniards were in search. They are very tall, with large leaves, like a laurel; and the fruit grows in clusters, and resembles an acorn. Many of these trees grow wild in the forests, and yield fruits; but they are not so good as those which the

Indians get from the trees, which they plant and cultivate for their own use, and for that of their neighbours, but not for the people of Peru. The latter never wish for any other condiment than their *uchu*, which the Spaniards call *aji*, and in Europe pepper . . .

In Sumaco, and its neighbourhood, the Spaniards found that the Indians went naked, without any clothes; the women having a little cloth in front for the sake of modesty. They go naked because the country is so hot, and it rains so much that clothes would become rotten, as we have before said.

In Sumaco, Gonzalo Pizarro left behind the greater part of his men; and taking with him the most active, he went in search of a road, if any could be found, to pass onwards; because all the country they had as yet traversed, which was nearly one hundred leagues, was dense forest, where in many parts they had to open a road by main force, and with the blows of hatchets. The Indians, whom they took as guides, deceived them, and led them through uninhabited wilds, where they suffered from hunger, and were obliged to feed on herbs, roots, and wild fruits.

Suffering these hardships, and others which can be more easily imagined than described, they arrived at a province called Cuca, where they found supplies. The chief received them well, and gave them food. Near this place a great river passes, which is supposed to be the largest of those streams, which unite to form that river which some call the Orellana, and others the Marañon.

Here they waited nearly two months for the Spaniards who were left at Sumaco. Having been joined by them, and recovered from their fatigue, they all proceeded together along the banks of that great river; but for more than fifty leagues they found neither ford nor bridge by which they might pass over, for the river was so broad as not to admit either the one or the other.

At the end of this long journey, they came to a place where the river precipitates itself over a rock, more than two hundred feet high; and makes so great a noise, that the Spaniards heard it at a distance of six leagues before they arrived at it. They were astonished to see a thing so great and so strange; but much more did they wonder, forty or fifty leagues lower down, when they saw that the immense volume of water, contained in this river, was collected into a channel made by another enormous rock.

The channel is so narrow, that there are not more than twenty feet from one bank to the other; and the rock is so high, that from the top (where these Spaniards presently passed over) to the water was another two hundred feet, the same height as the fall. Certainly it is a marvellous thing that in that land should be found things so great and wonderful as those two rapids, and many others.

Gonzalo Pizarro and his captains, thinking that they might not find so easy a way of crossing the river again, to see what was on the other side, because all they had yet seen was a sterile and unprofitable land, bethought themselves of making a bridge over the chasm; but the Indians on the other side, though few in number, defended the pass bravely. The Spaniards were thus obliged to fight with them, a thing which they had not yet done with any Indians of that region. They fired their arquebusses, and killed a few, and the rest retired about two hundred paces, astonished at so strange a sight. They were terrified at the bravery and ferocity of that race, which they said brought lightning, rain, and thunder, to kill those who did not obey them. The Spaniards, seeing the passage clear, made a bridge of wood; and it must be considered what an undertaking it was to place the first beam across a chasm, at such a height above the water, that even to look down was an act of rashness. And so it proved to a Spaniard, who, wishing to look at the furious rush of water from the top of the rock, became giddy and fell in. On beholding the misfortune which had befallen their companion, the others were more careful; and with much labour and difficulty placed the first beam, and with help of it, as many more as were necessary. Thus they made a bridge, by which men and horses safely passed over. They left it as it was, in case it should be necessary to return by it. They journeyed down the course of the river, through such dense forests, that it was necessary in many places to cut a road with hatchets.

Suffering these hardships, they reached a land called Guema, as poor and inhospitable as the most sterile of those they had passed; and they met few Indians, while even those, on seeing the Spaniards, entered the forests, and were seen no more.

The Spaniards, and their Indian followers, supported themselves on herbs and roots. Owing to hunger, and fatigue, and the heavy rains, many Spaniards and Indians fell sick and died; but, in spite of these disasters, they advanced many leagues, and arrived at another land, where they found Indians, a little more civilized than those they had seen before; who fed on maize bread, and dressed in cotton clothes. Gonzalo Pizarro then sent people in all directions, to see if they could find any open road, but all returned in a short time with the same story, that the land was covered with dense forest, full of lagoons and swamps, which could not be forded. On this account they determined to build a brigantine, in which they might pass from one side of the river to the other, the river being nearly two leagues broad. They accordingly set up a forge for making nails, and burnt charcoal with great trouble, because the heavy rains prevented the tinder from taking fire. They also made roofed huts to burn the wood in, and defend it from the rain. Some of the nails were made from the shoes of horses, which had been killed as food for the sick, and the rest of the iron they had brought with them. They now found it more valuable than gold.

Gonzalo Pizarro, as became so valiant a soldier, was the first to cut the wood, forge the iron, burn the charcoal, and employ himself in any other office, so as to give an example to the rest, that no one might have any excuse for not doing the same. For tar, for the brigantine, they used resin from the trees; for oakum, they had blankets and old shirts; and all were ready to give up their clothes, because they believed that the remedy for all their misfortunes would be the brigantine. Thus they completed and launched her, believing that on that day all their troubles would come to an end. (But in a few days their hopes were destroyed, as we shall presently see.)

Orellana 'deserts' – and discovers the Amazon

They put all their gold on board the brigantine, amounting to more than one hundred thousand dollars, with many fine emeralds, also the iron, the forge, and everything else of value. They also sent the sick on board, who were unable to travel by land. Thus they started from this place, having journeyed already nearly two hundred leagues; and began the descent of the river, some by land, others on board the brigantine, never being far from each other, and every night they slept close together. They all advanced with much difficulty; for those on shore had to open the road in many places, by cutting with axes; while those on board had to labour hard to resist the current, so as not to get far from their comrades. When they could not make a road on one side of the river, owing to the dense nature of the forest, they passed to the other side in the brigantine, and four canoes. Having gone on in this way for more than two months, they met some Indians who told them by signs, and by means of some words understood by their own Indians, that ten days journey from the place where they then were, they would find an inhabited land; well supplied with provisions, and rich in gold, and in all other things which they wanted. They also told them, by signs, that that land was on the banks of another great river which joined the one down which they were now travelling. The Spaniards rejoiced at this news. Gonzalo Pizarro selected, as captain of the brigantine, his lieutenant, Don Francisco de Orellana, with fifty soldiers; and ordered him to proceed to the place indicated by the Indians, (which would be distant about eighty leagues); and, having arrived at the point where the two rivers meet, to load the brigantine with provisions, and return up the river, to relieve the people, who were so afflicted with hunger, that each day there died several men, Spaniards as well as Indians. Of four thousand who started in this expedition, two thousand were already dead.

Francisco de Orellana continued his voyage, and in three days, without oar or sail, he navigated the eighty leagues, but did not find the supplies which had been promised; and he considered that if he should return with this news to Pizarro, he would not reach him within a year, on account of the strong current, though he had descended in three days; and that if he remained where he was, he would be of no use either to the one, or to the other. Not knowing how long Gonzalo Pizarro would take to reach the place, without consulting with any one, he set sail, and prosecuted his voyage onwards, intending to ignore Gonzalo, to reach Spain, and obtain that government for himself.

Many of his crew objected to this, suspecting his evil intentions; and they declared that it was not right to go beyond the orders of his captain general, nor to desert him in his great necessity. A monk named Fray Gaspar de Carbajal, and a young cavalier named Hernan Sanchez de Vargas, a native of Badajos, whom the malcontents took for their chief, also dissented. Francisco de Orellana, however, appeased them for the time with fair speeches; though afterwards, when he had reduced them to obedience, he broke his word, and told the good monk that if he would not follow him, he would leave him behind, like Hernan Sanchez de Vargas. That he might suffer a more cruel death, he did not kill Hernan Sanchez, but left him in that dreary place, surrounded on one side by the dense forest, on the other by a mighty river, so that he could neither escape by water nor land, and thus he would perish of hunger.

Francisco de Orellana continued his journey; and soon, to render his intention more clear, he renounced his obedience to Gonzalo Pizarro, and elected himself a captain of His Majesty, independent of any one else. A foul deed (what else can such treason be called?) such as has been done by other worthies in the conquest of the New World . . .

Francisco de Orellana, in descending the river, had some skirmishes with the Indians inhabiting that shore, who were very fierce, and in some parts the women came out to fight, with their husbands. On this account, and to make his voyage the more wonderful, he said that it was a land of Amazons, and besought His Majesty for a commission to conquer them. Further down the river, they found more civilized Indians, who were friendly, and were astonished to see the brigantine, and such strange men. They made friends with them, and gave them food, as much as they wished. The Spaniards stayed with them some days; and then they sailed down to the sea, two hundred leagues to the Isle of Trinidad, having suffered the hardships that have been described, and many great dangers on the river. In that island Orellana bought a ship, with which he went to Spain, and besought His Majesty to give him a commission to conquer that country, magnifying his discovery, by saying it was a land of gold and silver, and precious stones, and demonstrating his assertions by the fine show of these things, which he brought with him. His Majesty gave him power to conquer the land, and to govern it. Orellana then collected more than five hundred soldiers, many of them distinguished and noble cavaliers, with whom he embarked at San Lucar, and died at sea, his people dispersing in different directions. Thus this expedition met an end, in conformity with its evil beginning.

Garcilaso de la Vega, *Royal Commentaries of the Incas*, in *Expeditions into the Valleys of the Amazons*, 1859

Adriaan Van Berkel
*fl.*1690
*They entertained him genteelly with food and drink so he might go
hearty to death.*

In October 1670 Adriaan Van Berkel left from Vlissingen in Holland on board the *Nassau*. He was heading for Berbice, the Dutch colony in what was to become Guyana, which was settled by Abraham Van Pere in 1627. Van Berkel had been put in charge of trade there, and stayed for three years, during which he made four journeys to Essequibo, another Dutch colony, to establish its border with Berbice. One of these trips was by sea and the others were overland from Fort Nassau in Berbice along Indian footpaths to Demerara, then down the Essequibo river in canoes to the Fort Kijk Overal (Fort Look Everywhere).

Van Berkel's book, *Travels in South America between the Berbice and Essequibo Rivers and Surinam, 1670–1689*, gives a lively account of his adventures but more importantly provides us with observations – perhaps fantastical – on the Arawak Indians who then had had little or no direct exposure to European culture. He also describes the lifestyle of plantation owners and their treatment of Negro slaves, and the wildlife they passed as they travelled downstream. According to Alexander von Humboldt, Van Berkel was the first person to provide a description of the electric eel.

The second part of his book covered the period 1680–89, when Van Berkel was supposedly working as a plantation manager in Surinam; however, there are suspicions that he did not visit Surinam at all, offering a plagiarized account of Warren's *An Impartial Description of Surinam* (1667) instead.

Treatment of prisoners

The fleet of which we have just spoken brought with them on their return two youths from the enemy vanquished. They travelled at night silently past the Fort and had the same so well looked after, that there was not the slightest chance of escape. These unfortunate wretches who had thus been captured on a fighting expedition were confined and shackled for about three weeks, during which time they were provided with good food and drink. In the interval, to while the time away somewhat in this miserable state, they plait a pegall or little basket used locally for a box. The prisoners are guarded by night, and in view of the fact that somebody is going to be burnt, the women prepare a quantity of drink called Pernou whereof we have spoken elsewhere and of the qualities of which we will later on give a circumstantial account.

On the day before he is to die, I have on more than one occasion seen with my own eyes, that they entertained him genteelly with food and drink so that he might yet go hearty to his death. After mid-day, everybody sneers at him as they take him from house to house, on which occasion he may receive unexpectedly a blow on the head, from which the blood will flow, accompanied with the remark: 'Your friends have done just the same to ours.' When the sun is about to set, a captain enquires whether he can see the sun all right, whereupon, having answered 'Yes,' the captain says – 'You shall never see it again.' This is his condemnation. I have seen them leading to execution one who being sufficient proud not to lose heart by any threats or fear of subsequent torture, gave the reply to the captain who passed sentence on him with a heroic and disdainful countenance: 'It is true that Fate is at present against me: but my friends will likewise at some time come to your people, and demand a reckoning for the torture you are about to inflict on me. Life is not so attractive to me that I cannot easily leave it: though I am troubled at having to die without being able to take vengeance for my death,' etc.

At evening they give him as much as he requires to eat and drink: each one bringing him something. Now they tie his hands behind his back, and to each foot a long rope. In the meantime those who have been invited have repaired there, each provided with some Maquarys, a sort of torch streaked with a certain stuff which has the quality of pitch, so that it may burn the better. In the evening about seven o'clock they start kindling fires around and within the house, after which the prisoner being placed in the middle of his enemies is bawled at in a loud voice by the oldest captain, making a big hubbub: 'Your people have caught my friends, and treated them thus.' Hereupon he thrusts the burning Maquary into his skin: after which every one, who can but reach him, attacks him. One sticks it in his face, another about the genitals, a third upon another of the tenderest spots, at the same time that he is being dragged hither and thither by the ropes. If with all his punishment he begins to get faint, they pause a while from time to time, so as to make his sufferings last the longer: because they want to sport as much as possible. In the interval they drink again with one another, just as if they were good friends: and the sufferer being thus somewhat refreshed, the business is started again. This lasts until the morning, about a short hour before sunrise, because they have then to make an end of it, which is done by a captain who crashes the miserable prisoner's head with a wooden sword. Everybody now falls upon term with a knife: one cuts him a piece out of the buttock, another out of the thigh, a third rips up another spot: to put it shortly, each to get what he can. The cut-off flesh after boiling, is put into the pepper-pot and eaten for good food. I have spoken to two whites who had tried it and maintained that it tasted very sweet. The bones are buried in the earth, except a few small ones out of which they know how to make flutes.

Amongst all this bustle, the women sing at their ease: the song consisting of the relation of the tortures suffered by their own friends who had fallen into the hands of the enemy, together with the praises of their valiant men who are calling for vengeance for their deaths in the way described.

Travels in South America between the Berbice and Essequibo Rivers and in Surinam 1670–1689
(1948)

DANIEL BOONE
1734–1820

*No populace city, with all its varieties of commerce and stately structures,
could afford so much pleasure to my mind as the beauties of nature
I found in this country.*

The American frontiersman and folk hero Daniel Boone was born in Pennsylvania into a family of English Quakers, who moved when he was young to the North Carolina frontier. He had little formal schooling, but was able to read and write. He could also hunt and trap, though at this time relations between the settlers and the local Cherokee Indians were far from stable and the Boones were forced to abandon their home temporarily in 1759. Subsequently, Boone fought in the war against the Cherokees that continued until peace was signed in 1761.

During the 1760s he made several hunting expeditions into the largely unexplored region of Kentucky to the west, encroaching on Cherokee land in defiance of established treaties. Between 1769 and 1771 he and five others were engaged to explore even further west. During this expedition he was twice captured by Shawnee Indians, but escaped and investigated the Ohio river before returning home, fired up by the prospect of settling this new region.

Two years later Boone left with a colonizing expedition of eight families, including his own, towards Kentucky. An Indian attack that cost the life of Boone's eldest son, among others, put paid to his progress; but in 1775 he started out again, this time on behalf of a Carolina trading company that wanted to forge a route by which colonists could get to Kentucky. Accompanied by well-armed men, they took a trail through the Cumberland Pass (in the Appalachian Mountains) that was to become known by the thousands who eventually migrated west along it as the 'Wilderness Road'. He reached the Kentucky river and set up the first of several fortified settlements at Boonesborough, where his family later joined him.

Boone spent the next decade leading land-hungry settlers to this new region and defending them from Indian attacks, which now took the life of his brother and another son. Boone himself was captured by Indians and was adopted as a son of the Shawnee chief, Blackfish; he lived with him for four months, then escaped.

Despite his success as a leader, Kentucky did not offer all that Boone had hoped for, and many of his land claims came to nothing. Following the American Revolution he worked as a surveyor along the Ohio river, then in 1798 moved on and settled in Missouri, where he died at the age of eighty-five. By that time he had already risen to legendary status, and when, in 1823, Lord Byron devoted seven stanzas of his poem *Don Juan* to him, his fame spread worldwide.

Life and death on the frontier

On the 22nd December, John Stuart and I had a pleasant ramble; but fortune changed the day at the close of it. We passed through a great forest in which stood myriads of trees, some gay with blossoms, others rich with fruits. Nature was here a series of wonders and a fund of delight. Here she displayed her ingenuity and industry in a variety of flowers and fruits, beautifully coloured, elegantly shaped, and charmingly flavoured; and we were favoured with numberless animals presenting themselves perpetually to our view. In the decline of the day, near Kentucky river, as we ascended the brow of a small hill, a number of Indians rushed out of a cane brake and made us prisoners. The Indians plundered us and kept us in confinement seven days. During this we discovered no uneasiness or desire to escape, which made them less suspicious; but in the dead of night, as we lay by a large fire in a thick cane brake, when sleep had locked up their senses, my situation not disposing me to rest, I gently awoke my companion. We seized this favourable opportunity and departed, directing our course toward our old camp, but found it plundered and our company destroyed and dispersed.

About this time, as my brother with another adventurer who came to explore the country shortly after us, was wandering through the forest, they accidentally found our camp. Notwithstanding our unfortunate circumstances, and our dangerous situation, surrounded with hostile savages, our meeting fortunately in the wilderness gave us the most sensible satisfaction.

Soon after this, my companion in captivity, John Stuart, was killed by the savages, and the man who came with my brother (while on a private excursion) was soon after attacked and killed by the wolves. We were now in a dangerous and helpless situation, exposed daily to perils and death, among savages and wild beasts, not a white man in the country but ourselves.

Although many hundred miles from our families in the howling wilderness, we did not continue in a state of indolence, but hunted every day, and prepared a little cottage to defend us from the winter. On the 1st of May, 1770, my brother returned home for a new recruit of horses and ammunition, leaving me alone, without bread, salt or sugar, or even a horse or a dog. I passed a few days uncomfortably – the idea of a beloved wife and family, and their anxiety on my account, would have disposed me to melancholy if I had further indulged the thought.

One day I undertook a tour through the country, when the diversity of beauties of nature I met with in this charming season expelled every gloomy thought. Just at the close of the day, the gentle gales ceased; profound calm ensued; not a breath shook the tremulous leaf. I had gained the summit of a commanding ridge, and looking around with astonishing delight beheld the ample plains and beauteous tracks below. On one hand I surveyed the famous Ohio rolling in silent dignity, and marking the western boundary of Kentucky with inconceivable grandeur. At a vast distance I beheld the mountains lift their venerable brows and penetrate the clouds. All things were still. I kindled a fire near a fountain of sweet water, and feasted on the line [*sic*] of a buck which I had killed a few hours before. The shades of night soon overspread the hemisphere, and the earth seemed to gasp after the hovering moisture. At a distance I frequently heard the hideous yells of savages. My excursion had fatigued my body and amused my mind. I laid me down to sleep, and awoke not until the sun had chased away the night. I continued this tour, and in a few days explored a considerable part of the country, each day equally pleasing as the first; after which I returned to my old camp, which had not been disturbed in my absence. I did not confine my lodging to it, but often reposed in thick cane brakes to avoid the savages, who I believe frequently visited my camp, but fortunately for me, in my absence. No populous city, with all its varieties of commerce and stately structures, could afford so much pleasure to my mind as the beauties of nature I found in this country.

Until the 27th July I spent my time in an uninterrupted scene of sylvan pleasures, when my brother, to my great felicity, met me, according to appointment, at our old camp. Soon after we left the place and proceeded to Cumberland river, reconnoitring that part of the country, and giving names to the different rivers.

In March 1771 I returned home to my family, being determined to bring them as soon as possible, at the risk of my life and fortune, to reside in Kentucky, which I esteemed a second Paradise.

On my return I found my family in happy circumstances. I sold my farm on the Yadkin and what goods we could not carry with us, and on the 25th September, 1773, we took leave of our friends and proceeded on our journey to Kentucky, in company with five more families, and forty men that joined us in Powell's Valley, which is 150 miles from the new settled parts of Kentucky; but this promising beginning was soon overcast with a cloud of adversity.

On the 10th October the rear of our company was attacked by a party of Indians, who killed six and wounded one man. Of these my oldest son was one that fell in the action. Though we repulsed the enemy, yet this unhappy affair scattered our cattle and brought us into extreme difficulty – we returned forty miles to the settlement on Clench river. We had passed over two mountains, Powel's and Walden's, and were approaching Cumberland mountain, when this adverse fortune overtook us . . .

On the 1st April [1775] we began to erect the fort of Boonsborough, at a salt lick, sixty yards from the river on the south side. On the 4th the Indians killed one of our men. On the 14th June, having completed the fort, I returned to my family on the Clench, and whom I soon after removed to the fort – my wife and daughter were supposed to be the first white women that ever stood upon the banks of Kentucky river.

On the 24th December an Indian killed one of our men and wounded another; and on the 15th July, 1776, they took my daughter prisoner – I immediately pursued them with eight men, and on the 16th overtook and engaged them; I killed two of them and recovered my daughter.

The Indians having divided themselves into several parties, attacked in one day all our infant settlement and forts, doing a great deal of damage – the husbandmen were ambushed and unexpectedly attacked while toiling in the fields. They continued this kind of warfare until the 15th April, 1777, when nearly 100 of them attacked the village of Boonsborough, and killed a number of its inhabitants. On the 19th Col. Logan's fort was attacked by 200 Indians – there were only thirteen men in the fort, of whom the enemy killed two and wounded one . . .

On the 7th February, 1778, while on a hunting expedition alone, I met a party of 102 Indians and two Frenchmen, marching to attack Boonsborough – they pursued and took me prisoner, and conveyed me to Old Chelicothe, the principal Indian town on little Miami, where we arrived on the 18th February, after an uncomfortable journey. On the 10th March I was conducted to Detroit, and while there was treated with great humanity by Governor Hamilton, the British commander at that port, and Intendant for Indian affairs.

The Indians had such an affection for me, that they refused 100*l.* sterling offered them by the Governor if they would consent to leave me with him, that he might be enabled to liberate me on my parole. Several English gentlemen then at Detroit, sensible of my adverse fortune, and touched with sympathy, generously offered to supply my wants, which I declined with many thanks, adding that I never expected it would be in my power to recompense such unmerited generosity.

On the 10th April the Indians returned with me to Old Chelicothe, where we arrived on the 25th. This was a long and fatiguing march, although through an exceeding fertile country, remarkable for springs and streams of water. At Chelicothe I spent my time as comfortable as I could expect; was adopted according to their custom, into a family where I became a son, and had a great share in the affection of my new parents, brothers, sisters and friends. I was exceedingly familiar and friendly with them, always appearing as cheerful and contented as possible, and they put great confidence in me. I often went a-hunting with them, and frequently gained their applause for my activity at our shooting matches. I was careful not to exceed many of them in shooting, for no people are more envious than they in this sport. I could observe in their countenances and gestures the greatest expressions of joy when they exceeded me, and when the reverse happened, of envy. The Shawanese king took great notice of me, and treated me with profound respect and entire friendship, often entrusting me to hunt at my liberty. I frequently returned with the spoils of the woods, and as often presented some of what I had taken to him, expressive of duty to my sovereign. My food and lodging was in common with them, not so good indeed as I could desire, but necessity made every thing acceptable.

I now began to mediate an escape, and carefully avoided giving suspicion. I continued at Chelicothe until the first day of June, when I was taken to the salt springs on Sciotha, and there employed ten days in the manufacturing of salt. During this time I hunted with my Indian masters, and found the land for a great extent about this river to exceed the soil of Kentucky.

On my return to Chelicothe 150 of the choicest Indian warriors were ready to march against Boonsborough; they were painted and armed in a frightful manner. This alarmed me, and I determined to escape.

On the 16th June, before sun-rise, I went off secretly, and reached Boonsborough on the 20th, a journey of 160 miles, during which I had only one meal. I found our fortress in a bad state, but we immediately repaired our flanks, gates, posterns, and formed double bastions, which we completed in ten days. One of my fellow prisoners escaped after me, brought advice that on account of my flight, the Indians had put off their expedition for three weeks . . .

About this time I returned to Kentucky with my family; for during my captivity my wife, thinking me killed by the Indians, had transported my family and goods on horses through the wilderness, amidst many dangers, to her father's house in North Carolina.

On the 6th of October, 1780, soon after my settling again at Boonsborough, I went with my brother to the Blue Licks, and on our return, he was shot by a party of Indians. They followed me by the scent of a dog, which I shot and escaped. The severity of the winter caused great distress in Kentucky, the enemy during the summer having destroyed most of the corn. The inhabitants lived chiefly on Buffaloe's flesh.

In spring, 1782, the Indians harassed us. In May they ravished, killed, and scalped a woman and her two daughters near Ashton's station, and took a negro prisoner. August 8th two boys were carried off from Major Hoy's station. Our affairs became more and more alarming. The savages infested the country and destroyed the woods as opportunity presented.

August 18th Colonels Todd and Trigg, Major Harland and myself, speedily collected 176 men well armed, and pursued the savages. They had marched beyond the Blue Licks, to a remarkable bend of the main fork of Licking River, about 43 miles from Lexington, where we overtook them on the 19th. The savages, observing us, gave way, and we, ignorant of their numbers, passed the river. When they saw our proceedings (having accordingly the advantage in situation) they formed their line of battle from one end of the Licking to the other, about a mile from the Blue Licks. The engagement was close and warm for about fifteen minutes, when we, being overpowered by numbers, were obliged to retreat, with the loss of 67 men, 7 of whom were taken prisoners. The brave and much lamented Colonels Todd and Trigg, Major Harland, and my second son were among the dead.

When General Clark, at the falls of Ohio, heard of our disaster he ordered an expedition to pursue the savages. We overtook them within two miles of their towns, and we should have obtained a great victory had not some of them met us when about two hundred poles from their camp. The savages fled in the utmost disorder, and evacuated all their towns. We burned to ashes Old Chelicothe, Peccaway, New Chelicothe, and Wills Town; entirely destroyed their corn and other fruits; and spread desolation through their country.

In October a party atacked Crab Orchard, and one of them being a good way before the others, boldly entered a house, in which were only a woman and her children and a negro man. The savage used no violence, but attempted to carry off the negro, who happily proved too strong for him, and threw him on the ground, and in the struggle the woman cut off his head with an axe, whilst her little daughter shut the door. The savages instantly came up and applied their tomahawks to the door, when the mother putting an old rusty gun barrel through the crevices, the savages immediately went off.

From that time till the happy return of peace between the United States and Great Britain, the Indians did us no mischief. Soon after this the Indians desired peace.

Two darling sons and a brother I have lost by savage hands, which have also taken from me 40 valuable horses and abundance of cattle. Many dark and sleepless nights have I spent, separated from the cheerful society of men, scorched by the summer's sun, and pinched by the winter's cold, an instrument ordained to settle the wilderness.

The Life and Adventures of Colonel Daniel Boone, 1823

Alexander Mackenzie
1764–1820

The Indians, when they saw our deplorable situation, instead of making the least effort to help us, sat down and gave vent to their tears.

Mackenzie, a Scottish fur-trader, was the first European known to have crossed North America, and his exploratory journeys greatly encouraged European settlement of the Northwest.

He was born in Scotland, though his father took him to New York when his mother died. His first expedition, in 1789, was undertaken on behalf of the fur company in which he was a partner, and aimed to find a water route to the Pacific. He set out from Fort Chipewyan with a party of Indians and Canadians in birch-bark canoes. They travelled to the Great Slave Lake and then down the river that was later named after him; however, the expedition found itself emerging at not the Pacific, but the Arctic, and Mackenzie gave the river

the alternative name, River of Disappointment. After travelling 2,990 miles in 102 days, he returned home to Fort Chipewyan.

Three years later he made a second attempt. This time he set out from Lake Athabasca in Alberta and headed west along the Peace river. The expedition crossed the Great Divide in 1793 and travelled down the Fraser and Bella Coola rivers, eventually reaching the Pacific at Dean Channel. They became the first men to cross the continent north of Mexico. Both of his journeys made a significant contribution to the European settlement of the American Northwest.

Mackenzie was knighted in 1802 and then returned to Scotland in 1808.

Coaxing information from scared natives

We perceived a smell of fire; and in a short time heard people in the woods, as if in a state of great confusion, which was occasioned, as we afterwards understood, by their discovery of us. At the same time this unexpected circumstance produced some little discomposure among ourselves, as our arms were not in a state of preparation, and we were as yet unable to ascertain the number of the party. I considered, that if there were but few it would be needless to pursue them, as it would not be probable that we should overtake them in these thick woods; and if they were numerous, it would be an act of great imprudence to make the attempt, at least during their present alarm. I therefore ordered my people to strike off to the opposite side, that we might see if any of them had sufficient courage to remain; but, before we were half over the river, which, in this part, is not more than an hundred yards wide, two men appeared on a rising ground over against us, brandishing their spears, displaying their bows and arrows, and accompanying their hostile gestures with *loud* vociferations. My interpreter did not hesitate to assure them, that they might dispel their apprehensions, as we were white people, who meditated no injury, but were, on the contrary, desirous of demonstrating every mark of kindness and friendship. They did not, however, seem disposed to confide in our declarations, and actually threatened, if we came over before they were more fully satisfied of our peaceable intentions, that they would discharge their arrows at us. This was a decided kind of conduct which I did not expect; at the same time I readily complied with their proposition, and after some time had passed in hearing and answering their questions, they consented to our landing, though not without betraying very evident symptoms of fear and distrust. They, however, laid aside their weapons, and when I stepped forward and took each of them by the hand, one of them, but with a very tremulous action, drew his knife from his sleeve, and presented it to me as a mark of his submission to my will and pleasure. On our first hearing the noise of these people in the woods, we displayed our flag, which was now shown to them as a token of friendship. They examined us, and every thing about us, with a minute and suspicious attention. They had heard, indeed, of white men, but this was the first time that they had ever seen an human being of a complexion different from their own. The party had been here but a few hours; nor had they yet erected their sheds; and, except the two men now with us, they had all fled, leaving their little property behind them. To those which had given us such a proof of their confidence, we paid the most conciliating attentions in our power. One of them I sent to recal his people, and the other, for very obvious reasons, we kept with us. In the mean time the canoe was unloaded, the necessary baggage carried up the hill, and the tents pitched.

Here I determined to remain till the Indians became so familiarized with us, as to give all the intelligence which we imagined might be obtained from them. In fact, it had been my intention to land where I might most probably discover the carrying-place, which was our more immediate object, and undertake marches of two or three days, in different directions, in search of another river. If unsuccessful in this attempt, it was my purpose to continue my progress up the present river, as far as it was navigable, and if we did not meet with natives to instruct us in our further progress, I had determined to return to the fork, and take the other branch, with the hope of better fortune.

It was about three in the afternoon when we landed, and at five the whole party of Indians were assembled. It consisted only of three men, three women, and seven or eight boys and girls. With their scratched legs, bleeding feet, and dishevelled hair, as in the hurry of their flight they had left their shoes and leggins behind them, they displayed a most wretched appearance: they were consoled, however, with beads, and other trifles, which seemed to please them;

they had pemmican also given them to eat, which was not unwelcome, and in our opinion, at least, superior to their own provision, which consisted entirely of dried fish.

When I thought that they were sufficiently composed, I sent for the men to my tent, to gain such information respecting the country as I concluded it was in their power to afford me. But my expectations were by no means satisfied: they said that they were not acquainted with any river to the Westward, but that there was one from whence they were just arrived, over a carrying-place of eleven days march, which they represented as being a branch only of the river before us. Their ironwork they obtained from the people who inhabit the bank of that river, and an adjacent lake, in exchange for beaver skins, and dressed moose skins. They represented the latter as travelling, during a moon, to get to the country of other tribes, who live in houses, with whom they traffic for the same commodities; and that these also extend their journies in the same manner to the sea coast, or, to use their expression, the Stinking Lake, where they trade with people like us, that come there in vessels as big as islands. They added, that the people to the Westward, as they have been told, are very numerous. Those who inhabit the other branch they stated as consisting of about forty families, 'while they themselves did not amount to more than a fourth of that number; and were almost continually compelled to remain in their strong holds, where they sometimes perished with cold and hunger, to secure themselves from their enemies, who never failed to attack them whenever an opportunity presented itself.

This account of the country, from a people who I had every reason to suppose were well acquainted with every part of it, threatened to disconcert the project on which my heart was set, and in which my whole mind was occupied. It occurred to me, however, that from fear, or other motives, they might be tardy in their communication; I therefore assured them that, if they would direct me to the river which I described to them, I would come in large vessels, like those that their neighbours had described, to the mouth of it, and bring them arms and ammunition in exchange for the produce of their country; so that they might be able to defend themselves against their enemies, and no longer remain in that abject, distressed, and fugitive state in which they then lived. I added also, that in the mean time, if they would, on my return, accompany me below the mountains, to a country which was very abundant in animals, I would furnish them, and their companions, with every thing they might want; and make peace between them and the Beaver Indians. But all these promises did not appear to advance the object of my inquiries, and they still persisted in their ignorance of any such river as I had mentioned, that discharged itself into the sea.

Journal of a Journey through the North-West Continent of America, 1801

CHARLES WATERTON
1782–1865
. . . the kind-hearted will be sorry to hear of an unoffending animal doomed to death.

The English naturalist Charles Waterton came from a strict Catholic and Royalist family living in Yorkshire. Soon after leaving school, and already a budding naturalist, he travelled to Malaga, in Spain. He was there during an outbreak of plague; although he didn't catch the disease he was far frailer on his return to England and, in order to recover, set off again for a warmer climate. He spent 1804–12 managing his uncle's sugar plantations in Georgetown, British Guiana.

Over the following twelve years Waterton made four journeys into the interior of Guiana, using the Demerara and Essequibo rivers, and made invaluable studies of plants and animals, especially bird life.

Waterton was a strong believer in obtaining close, first-hand observations of the animals he studied: 'I went expressly to look for wild beasts,' he wrote, 'and, having found them, it would have been impossible for me to have refrained from coming into actual contact with them.' His methods of preserving animal skins constituted a significant advance in the art of taxidermy.

The devout faith of Waterton's upbringing remained with him throughout his life and marked many of his observations, including his scientific papers. He gave generously to the poor, nor did he mind forgoing creature comforts himself, as he revelled in the rich fauna and flora: 'This delightful scenery of the Essequibo made the soul overflow with joy,' he wrote, 'and caused you to rove in fancy through fairyland.' Even after a long stretch in the jungle he was content, on his return to his estate – now inherited from his father – to sleep on bare boards with a block of oak for a pillow. He walled-in the estate grounds and forbade anyone from disrupting the wildlife within.

It was while wandering his land that Waterton met his end, when he sustained an internal injury at the age of eighty-three by stumbling over a briar root.

The use of Wourali poison

Wishful to obtain the best information concerning this poison, and as repeated inquiries, in lieu of dissipating the surrounding shade, did but tend more and more to darken the little light that existed, I determined to penetrate into the country where the poisonous ingredients grow, where this pernicious composition is prepared, and where it is constantly used. Success attended the adventure; and the information acquired made amends for one hundred and twenty days passed in the solitudes of Guiana, and afforded a balm to the wounds and bruises which every traveller must expect to receive who wanders through a thorny and obstructed path.

Thou must not, courteous reader, expect a dissertation on the manner in which the wourali-poison operates on the system; a treatise has been already written on the subject, and after all, there is probably still reason to doubt. It is supposed to affect the nervous system, and thus destroy the vital functions; it is also said to be perfectly harmless, provided it does not touch the blood. However, this is certain, when a sufficient quantity of it enters the blood, death is the inevitable consequence; but there is no alteration in the colour of the blood, and both the blood and flesh may be eaten with safety.

All that thou wilt find here is a concise, unadorned account of the wourali-poison. It may be of service to thee some time or other, shouldst thou ever travel through the wilds where it is used. Neither attribute to cruelty, nor to a want of feeling for the sufferings of the inferior animals, the ensuing experiments. The larger animals were destroyed in order to have proof positive of the strength of a poison which hath hitherto been doubted, and the smaller ones were killed with the hope of substantiating that which has commonly been supposed to be an antidote.

It makes a pitying heart ache to see a poor creature in distress and pain; and too often has the compassionate traveller occasion to heave a sigh as he journeys on. However, here, though the kind-hearted will be sorry to read of an unoffending animal doomed to death, in order to satisfy a doubt, still it will be a relief to know that the victim was not tortured. The wourali-poison destroys life's action so gently, that the victim appears to be in no pain whatever; and probably, were the truth known, it feels none, saving the momentary smart at the time the arrow enters.

A day or two before the Macoushi Indian prepares his poison, he goes into the forest in quest of the ingredients. A vine grows in these wilds, which is called Wourali. It is from this that the poison takes its name, and it is the principal ingredient. When he has procured enough of this, he digs up a root of a very bitter taste, ties them together, and then looks about for two kinds of bulbous plants, which contain a green and glutinous juice. He fills a little quake, which he carries on his back, with the stalks of these; and lastly, ranges up and down till he finds two species of ants. One of them is very large and black, and so venomous, that its sting produces a fever; it is most commonly to be met with on the ground. The other is a little red ant, which stings like a nettle, and generally has its nest under the leaf of a shrub. After obtaining these, he has no more need to range the forest.

A quantity of the strongest Indian pepper is used; but this he has already planted round his hut. The pounded fangs of the Labarri snake, and those of the Counacouchi, are likewise added. These he commonly has in store; for when he kills a snake, he generally extracts the fangs, and keeps them by him.

Having thus found the necessary ingredients, he scrapes the wourali vine and bitter root into thin shavings, and puts them into a kind of colander made of leaves: this he holds over an earthen pot, and pours water on the shavings: the liquor which comes through has the appearance of coffee. When a sufficient quantity has been procured, the shavings are thrown aside. He then bruises the bulbous stalks, and squeezes a proportionate quantity of their juice through his hands into the pot. Lastly, the snakes' fangs, ants, and pepper are bruised, and thrown into it. It is then placed on a slow fire, and as it boils, more of the juice of the wourali is added, according as it may be found necessary, and the scum is taken off with a leaf: it remains on the fire till reduced to a thick syrup of a deep brown colour. As soon as it has arrived at this state, a few arrows are poisoned with it, to try its strength. If it answer the expectations, it is poured out into a calabash, or little pot of Indian manufacture, which is carefully covered with a couple of leaves, and over them a piece of deer's skin, tied round with a cord. They keep it in the most dry part of the hut; and from time to time suspend it over the fire, to counteract the effects of dampness.

The act of preparing this poison is not considered as a common one: the savage may shape his bow, fasten the barb on the point of his arrow, and make his other implements of destruction, either lying in his hammock, or in the midst of his family; but, if he has to prepare the wourali-poison, many precautions are supposed to be necessary.

The women and young girls are not allowed to be present, lest the Yabahou, or evil spirit, should do them harm. The shed under which it has been boiled is pronounced polluted, and abandoned ever after. He who makes the poison must eat nothing that morning, and must continue fasting as long as the operation lasts. The pot in which it is boiled must be a new one, and must never have held anything before, otherwise the poison would be deficient in strength: add to this, that the operator must take particular care not to expose himself to the vapour which arises from it while on the fire.

Though this and other precautions are taken, such as frequently washing the face and hands, still the Indians think that it affects the health; and the operator either is, or, what is more probable, supposes himself to be, sick for some days after.

Thus it appears that the making the wourali-poison is considered as a gloomy and mysterious operation; and it would seem that they imagine it affects others as well as him who boils it; for an Indian agreed one evening to make some for me, but the next morning he declined having anything to do with it, alleging that his wife was with child!

Here it might be asked, are all the ingredients just mentioned necessary, in order to produce the wourali-poison? Though our opinions and conjectures may militate against the absolute necessity of some of them, still it would be hardly fair to pronounce them added by the hand of superstition, till proof positive can be obtained.

We might argue on the subject, and, by bringing forward instances of Indian superstition, draw our conclusion by inference, and still remain in doubt on this head. You know superstition to be the offspring of ignorance, and of course that it takes up its abode amongst the rudest tribes of uncivilized man. It even too often resides with man in his more enlightened state . . .

If, then, enlightened man lets his better sense give way, and believes, or allows himself to be persuaded, that certain substances and actions, in reality of no avail, possess a virtue which renders them useful in producing the wished-for effect; may not the wild, untaught, unenlightened savage of Guiana add an ingredient which, on account of the harm it does him, he fancies may be useful to the perfection of his poison, though in fact it be of no use at all? . . .

It is natural to imagine that, when a slight wound only is inflicted, the game will make its escape. Far otherwise; the wourali-poison almost instantaneously mixes with blood or water, so that if you wet your finger, and dash it along the poisoned arrow in the quickest manner possible, you are sure to carry off some of the poison. Though three minutes generally elapse before the convulsions come on in the wounded bird, still a stupor evidently takes place sooner, and this stupor manifests itself by an apparent unwillingness in the bird to move. This was very visible in a dying fowl . . .

The flesh of the game is not in the least injured by the poison, nor does it appear to corrupt sooner than that killed by the gun or knife. The body of this fowl was kept for sixteen hours, in a climate damp and rainy, and within seven degrees of the equator; at the end of which time it had contracted no bad smell whatever, and there were no symptoms of putrefaction, saving that, just round the wound, the flesh appeared somewhat discoloured.

The Indian, on his return home, carefully suspends his blow-pipe from the top of his spiral roof; seldom placing it in an oblique position, lest it should receive a cast.

Wanderings in South America, 1825

HENRY BATES
1825–92
The feeling of inhospitable wildness which the forest is calculated to inspire . . .

Bates was born in Leicester and worked as a hosier's apprentice, then as a clerk at a brewery in Burton-upon-Trent, while developing his interest in entomology. In 1848 he travelled to Brazil with his friend Alfred Wallace, and spent a total of eleven years enthusiastically gathering data and collecting species throughout the Amazon region, most of the time working on his own, and carrying on in spite of tropical disease. While in Para, in Brazil, he caught yellow fever, at a time when 12,000 of the state's 16,000 residents were suffering from either that disease or smallpox.

Bates covered over 1500 miles to the upper reaches of the Amazon, and collected 14,712 species. Eight thousand of them were previously unknown to science. A contemporary, Tom Sterling, gives us this description of Bates at work:

The sprightly little ex-hosier's apprentice travelled tirelessly up and down the river and through the surrounding forests, fortified by an almost childish love of nature and a belief that nothing would happen to him. His adventures were seldom heroic,

but they were charged with his own strong sense of humanity which he extended, somehow, to all creature-life . . . He crawls through the jungle litter looking for blind ants; anacondas wake him in the middle of the night, arousing no emotion but curiosity; he is sympathetic to bats . . . he takes baths with alligators. Somehow he makes one feel that these activities were not only normal, but humdrum.

Ill health finally got the better of Bates in 1889 and he returned to England, where he catalogued his collection and wrote notes on the insects that comprised it. One of his best-known discoveries was the phenomenon of mimicry, by which one species, typically an edible insect, mimics the appearance of another which is perhaps dangerous to its predator. His two-volume work *The Naturalist on the River Amazons* (1863) combines observations of flora and fauna with those on the human beings he encountered.

Bates became the first salaried Secretary of the Royal Geographical Society, a position he held until his death.

The wild man of the forest

We often read, in books of travels, of the silence and gloom of the Brazilian forests. They are realities, and the impression deepens on a longer acquaintance. The few sounds of birds are of that pensive or mysterious character which intensifies the feeling of solitude rather than imparts a sense of life and cheerfulness. Sometimes, in the midst of the stillness, a sudden yell or scream will startle one; this comes from some defenceless fruit-eating animal, which is pounced upon by a tiger-cat or stealthy boa-constrictor. Morning and evening the howling monkeys make a most fearful and harrowing noise, under which it is difficult to keep up one's buoyancy of spirit. The feeling of inhospitable wildness which the forest is calculated to inspire, is increased tenfold under this fearful uproar. Often, even in the still hours of midday, a sudden crash will be heard resounding afar through the wilderness, as some great bough or entire tree falls to the ground. There are, besides, many sounds which it is impossible to account for. I found the natives generally as much at a loss in this respect as myself. Sometimes a sound is heard like the clang of an iron bar against a hard, hollow tree, or a piercing cry rends the air; these are not repeated, and the succeeding silence tends to heighten the unpleasant impression which they make on the mind. With the native it is always the Curupíra, the wild man or spirit of the forest, which produces all noises they are unable to explain. For myths are the rude theories which mankind, in the infancy of knowledge, invent to explain natural phenomena. The Curupíra is a mysterious being, whose attributes are uncertain, for they vary according to locality. Sometimes he is described as a kind of orang-otang, being covered with long shaggy hair, and living in trees. At others he is said to have cloven feet and a bright red face. He has a wife and children, and sometimes comes down to the roças to steal the mandioca. At one time I had a mameluco youth in my service, whose head was full of the legends and superstitions of the country. He always went with me into the forest; in fact, I could not get him to go alone, and whenever we heard any of the strange noises mentioned above, he used to tremble with fear. He would crouch down behind me, and beg of me to turn back; his alarm ceasing only after he had made a charm to protect us from the Curupíra. For this purpose he took a young palm leaf, plaited it, and formed it into a ring, which he hung to a branch on our track.

Spider monkeys

The Coaitás are called by zoologists spider-monkeys, on account of the length and slenderness of their body and limbs. In these apes the tail, as a prehensile organ, reaches its highest degree of perfection; and on this account it would, perhaps, be correct to consider the Coaitás as the extreme development of the American type of apes. The tendency of Nature here has been, to all appearance, simply to perfect those organs which adapt the species more and more completely to a purely arboreal life; and no nearer approach has been made towards the more advanced forms of anthropoid apes, which are the products of the Old World solely. The flesh of this monkey is much esteemed by the natives in this part of the country, and the Military Commandant of Obydos, Major Gama, every week sent a negro hunter to shoot one for his table. One day I went on a Coaitá hunt, borrowing a negro slave of a friend to show me the way. When in the deepest part of a ravine, we heard a rustling sound in the trees overhead, and Manoel soon pointed out a Coaitá to me. There was something human-like in its appearance, as the lean, dark, shaggy creature moved deliberately amongst the branches at a great height. I fired, but unfortunately only wounded it in the belly. It fell with a crash, headlong, about twenty or thirty feet, and then caught a bough with its tail, which grasped it instantaneously, so that the animal remained suspended in mid-air. Before I could reload it recovered itself, and mounted nimbly to the topmost branches, out of the reach of a fowling-piece, where we could perceive the poor thing apparently probing the wound with its fingers. Coaitás are more frequently kept in a tame state than any other kind of monkey. The Indians are very fond of them as pets, and the women often suckle them when young at their breasts. They become attached to their masters, and will sometimes follow them on the ground to considerable distances. I once saw a most ridiculously tame Coaitá. It was an old female, which accompanied its owner, a trader on the river, in all his voyages. By way of giving me a specimen of its intelligence and feeling, its master set to and rated it soundly, calling it scamp, heathen, thief, and so forth, all through the copious Portuguese vocabulary of vituperation. The poor monkey, quietly seated on the ground, seemed to be in sore trouble at this display of anger. It began by looking earnestly at him, then it whined, and lastly rocked its body to and fro with emotion, crying piteously, and passing its long gaunt arms continually over its forehead; for this was its habit when excited, and the front of the head was worn quite bald in consequence. At length its master altered his tone. 'It's all a lie, my old woman; you're an angel, a flower, a good affectionate old creature,' and so forth. Immediately the poor monkey ceased its wailing, and soon after came over to where the man sat . . . The natives of the Upper Amazons procure the Coaitá, when full grown, by shooting it with the blowpipe and poisoned darts, and restoring life by putting a little salt (the antidote to the Urarí poison with which the darts are tipped) in its mouth. The animals thus caught become tame forthwith. Two females were once kept at the Jardin des Plantes of Paris, and Geoffroy St. Hilaire relates of them that they rarely quitted each other, remaining most part of the time in close embrace, folding their tails round one another's bodies. They took their meals together; and it was remarked on such occasions, when the friendship of animals is put to a hard test, that they never quarrelled or disputed the possession of a favourite fruit with each other.

The Naturalist on the River Amazons, 1863

Alfred Russel Wallace
1823–1913

. . . in their ignorance they accepted my operations as worthy of all respect, although utterly beyond their comprehension.

Alfred Russel Wallace had been interested in plants from a young age, but it was on meeting the British naturalist and entomologist Henry Walter Bates that he became interested in insects. Together they embarked on a voyage to Brazil that would be a turning point in his life.

Once in South America, the two naturalists split up in order to cover a larger area. Wallace spent four years exploring the Amazon alone and in 1852 he set sail for England in a trading vessel with his invaluable collection. The boat caught fire and, although no lives were lost, all of his collections – both those for the museum and his own, together with his journals, his sketches and notes – went down with the ship. 'I began to think,' he said with commendable self-restraint, 'that almost all the reward of my four years of privation and danger was lost.'

Back in England Wallace, though bereft of all his records – 'I had not one specimen to illustrate the unknown lands I had trod, or to call back the recollection of the wild species I had beheld!' – he published his *Narrative of Travels on the Amazon and Rio Negro* before setting out, in 1854, on a voyage to South-East Asia. For eight years he toured the Malay Archipelago, and there he formulated his concept of natural selection. For a period of ten years 'the question of how changes of species could have been brought about was rarely out of my mind,' he said later. It was during a bout of malaria that, while dwelling on human evolution, Wallace remembered reading *Principles of Population* by Thomas Malthus: 'There suddenly flashed upon me, the idea . . .' He thought out and drafted the theory in just one evening, spent the following two evenings writing it up, and then sent it to Darwin, who was amazed at the similarities between the young naturalist's findings and his own. Excerpts from the manuscripts of both scientists were published jointly in July 1858, with Wallace's contribution entitled *On the Tendency of Varieties to Depart Indefinitely from the Original Type*.

Wallace conceptually divided the Malay Archipelago into two halves, the western group of islands (Borneo and Bali), whose wildlife had Oriental characteristics, and the eastern group (Celebes and Lombok) which had Australian characteristics – the boundary between these is now known as the Wallace Line. The many years he spent on the islands convinced Wallace that the benefits of industrialized society were an illusion. They are enjoyed by precious few people, with the result that the majority of people 'are worse off than the savage in the midst of his tribe'.

The collector at work

When I sat down in the afternoon to arrange my insects, the house was surrounded by men, women, and children, lost in amazement at my unaccountable proceedings; and when, after pinning out the specimens, I proceeded to write the name of the place on small circular tickets, and attach one to each, even the old Kapala, the Mahometan priest, and some Malay traders could not repress signs of astonishment. If they had known a little more about the ways and opinions of white men, they would probably have looked upon me as a fool or a madman, but in their ignorance they accepted my operations as worthy of all respect, although utterly beyond their comprehension.

The next day (October 16th) I went beyond the swamp and found a place where a new clearing was being made in the virgin forest. It was a long and hot walk, and the search among the fallen trunks and branches was very fatiguing, but I was rewarded by obtaining about seventy distinct species of beetles, of which at least a dozen were new to me, and many others rare and interesting. I have never in my life seen beetles so abundant as they were on this spot. Some dozen species of good-sized golden Buprestidæ, green rose-chafers (Lomaptera), and long-horned weevils (Anthribidæ), were so abundant that they rose up in swarms as I walked along, filling the air with a loud buzzing hum. Along with these, several fine Longicorns were almost equally common, forming such an assemblage as for once to realize that idea of tropical luxuriance which one obtains by looking over the drawers of a well-filled cabinet. On the under sides of the trunks clung numbers of smaller or more sluggish Longicorns, while on the branches at the edge of the clearing others could be detected sitting with outstretched antennæ ready to take flight at the least alarm. It was a glorious spot, and one which will always live in my memory as exhibiting the insect-life of the tropics in unexampled luxuriance. For the three following days I continued to visit this locality, adding each time many new species to my collection – the following notes of which may be interesting to entomologists. October 15th, 33 species of beetles; 16th, 70 species; 17th, 47 species; 18th, 40 species; 19th, 56 species – in all about a hundred species, of which forty were new to me.

'A state of barbarism'

We should now clearly recognize the fact, that the wealth and knowledge and culture of *the few* do not constitute civilization, and do not of themselves advance us towards the perfect social state. Our vast manufacturing system, our gigantic commerce, our crowded towns and cities, support and continually renew a mass of human misery and crime *absolutely* greater than has ever existed before. They create and maintain in lifelong labour an ever-increasing army, whose lot is the more hard to bear by contrast with the pleasures, the comforts, and the luxury which they see everywhere around them, but which they can never hope to enjoy; and who, in this respect, are worse off than the savage in the midst of his tribe. During the last century, and especially in the last thirty years, our intellectual and material advancement has been too quickly achieved for us to reap the full benefit of it. Our mastery over the forces of nature has led to a rapid growth of population, and a vast accumulation of wealth; but these have brought with them such an amount of poverty and crime, and have fostered the growth of so much sordid feeling and so many fierce passions, that it may well be questioned, whether the mental and moral status of our population has not on the average been lowered, and whether the evil has not overbalanced the good. Compared with our wondrous progress in physical science and its practical applications, our system of government, of administering justice, of national education, and our whole social and moral organization, remains in a state of barbarism. And if we continue to devote our chief energies to the utilizing of our knowledge of the laws of nature with the view of still further extending our commerce and our wealth, the evils which necessarily accompany these when too eagerly pursued, may increase to such gigantic dimensions as to be beyond our power to alleviate.

   The Malay Archipelago: The Land of the Orang-utan and the Bird of Paradise (1880)

Henry Morton Stanley
1841–1904

How can I enforce them to their duty . . . ? I have publicly expressed a desire to die by a sharp quick death, which I think just now would be a mercy compared to what I endure daily.

Famed for his mission to 'find' David Livingstone in Africa, the American journalist H. M. Stanley led several subsequent expeditions which earned him a knighthood and made substantial contributions to the charting and colonizing of the continent.

He was born in Denbigh, North Wales, as John Rowlands. He spent his early years in a workhouse, then worked for a haberdasher and a butcher before running away to sea in 1857, disembarking in New Orleans, where he worked for the cotton broker Henry Hope Stanley, who became his benefactor. In due course, Rowlands decided to adopt Stanley's name.

At the close of the Civil War he travelled to Turkey and Asia as a newspaper correspondent, and between 1867 and 1868 was special correspondent for the *New York Herald*. In the following year James Gordon Bennett Jr, the editor, asked him to search for the missing Scottish missionary David Livingstone, last heard of in Central Africa investigating the source of the Nile. Rather than head straight into the heart of the continent, however, Stanley travelled via Egypt, (where he covered the opening of the Suez Canal), the Crimea (where he reported on the war), Baghdad and India. Finally, in 1871, he arrived in Zanzibar.

Hearing reports of a white man on the east shore of Lake Tanganyika, he assembled an army of porters, guides, hunters and pack animals and headed off inland. It was 236 days and 700 miles later that he finally found Livingstone in Ujiji, greeting him, famously, with the words: 'Doctor Livingstone, I presume?' He spent some months exploring the northern end of the lake with Livingstone

before returning to write his account: *How I Found Livingstone*. The book had all the heroic and wild ingredients that appealed to the imagination of Victorian England and became hugely popular.

Inspired by Livingstone, and also by this taste of adventure, Stanley resolved to complete the exploration of central Africa, and in 1874 travelled to Zanzibar, whence he set out to chart the region's great lakes. He circumnavigated Victoria Nyanza (Lake Victoria), confirming that Speke was right to claim it was a major Nile source, and carried on west across the continent, tracing – with great loss of life to his companions and bearers, not to mention locals – the Congo river down to its mouth. To cross Africa (complete with 356 assorted followers), from the east to west proved a formidable challenge – not least because the Africa seen by Burton and Speke had gone. It was now decimated by slavery, bitter wars of reprisal, and the presence of imported guns. Stanley chose to fight his way through and, though impressed by the rapport Livingstone had achieved with the Africans, saw this loss of life as an unpleasant, but necessary, by-product of exploration. 'The savage only respects force, power, boldness, and decision,' he commented.

In the Congo between 1880 and 1885, he sought suitable colonies for Leopold II of Belgium, mounting expeditions that were the first to 'prove that the Congo natives were susceptible of civilisation and that the Congo basin was rich enough to repay exploitation'. This revelation led to the setting up of a large trading venture and to the founding of the Congo Free State.

His last expedition, ten years later, was a relief mission to the Governor of southern Sudan's Equatorial province, Emin Pasha (in peril from the armies of the Mahdi), whom he reached after half of the 700 members had died. Although acrimonious and controversial, the expedition made some important discoveries: it established the link between Lakes Albert and Edward, and reported the extent of the Ruwenzori mountains. The mystery of the sources of the Nile was effectively solved. In 1882 he settled in England and became a British subject, serving in the House of Commons from 1895 until the turn of the century and was knighted in 1899.

Finding Livingstone

We push on rapidly, lest the news of our coming might reach the people of Bunder Ujiji before we come in sight, and are ready for them. We halt at a little brook, then ascend the long slope of a naked ridge, the very last of the myriads we have crossed. This alone prevents us from seeing the lake in all its vastness. We arrive at the summit, travel across and arrive at its western rim, and – pause, reader – the port of Ujiji is below us, embowered in the palms, only five hundred yards from us! At this grand moment we do not think of the hundreds of miles we have marched, of the hundreds of hills that we have ascended and descended, of the many forests we have traversed, of the jungles and thickets that annoyed us, of the fervid salt plains that blistered our feet, of the hot suns that scorched us nor the dangers and difficulties, now happily surmounted. At last the sublime hour has arrived! – our dreams, our hopes, and anticipations are now about to be realized! Our hearts and our feelings are with our eyes, as we peer into the palms and try to make out in which hut or house lives the white man with the grey beard we heard about on the Malagarazi.

We were now about three hundred yards from the village of Ujiji, and the crowds are dense about me. Suddenly I hear a voice on my right say,

'Good morning, sir!'

Started at hearing this greeting in the midst of such a crowd of black people, I turn sharply around in search of the man, and see him at my side, with the blackest of faces, but animated and joyous – a man dressed in a long white shirt, with a turban of American sheeting around his woolly head, and I ask:

'Who the mischief are you?'

'I am Susi, the servant of Dr Livingstone,' said he, smiling, and showing a gleaming row of teeth.

'What! Is Dr Livingstone here?'

'Yes, sir.'

'In this village?'

'Yes, sir.'

'Are you sure?'

'Sure, sure, sir. Why, I leave him just now . . .

'Now, you Susi, run, and tell the Doctor I am coming.'

'Yes, sir,' and off he darted like a madman . . .

Soon Susi came running back, and asked me my name; he had told the Doctor that I was coming, but the Doctor was too surprised to believe him, and, when the Doctor asked him my name, Susi was rather staggered.

But, during Susi's absence, the news had been conveyed to the Doctor that it was surely a white man that was coming, whose guns were firing and whose flag could be seen; and the great Arab magnates of Ujiji – Mohammed bin Sali, Sayd bin Majid, Abid bin Suleiman, Mohammed bin Gharib, and others – had gathered together before the Doctor's house, and the Doctor had come out from his veranda to discuss the matter and await my arrival.

In the meantime, the head of the Expedition had halted, and the *kirangozi* was out of the ranks, holding his flag aloft, and Selim said to me, 'I see the Doctor, sir. Oh, what an old man! He has got a white beard.' And I – what would I not have given for a bit of friendly wilderness, where, unseen, I might vent my joy in some mad freak, such as idiotically biting my hand, turning a somersault, or slashing at trees, in order to allay those exciting feelings that were well-nigh uncontrollable. My heart beats fast, but I must not let my face betray my emotions, lest it shall detract from the dignity of a white man appearing under such extraordinary circumstances.

So I did that which I thought was most dignified. I pushed back the crowds, and, passing from the rear, walked down a living avenue of people, until I came in front of the semicircle of Arabs, in the front of which stood the white man with the grey beard. As I advanced slowly towards him I noticed he was pale, looked wearied, had a grey beard, wore a bluish cap with a faded gold band round it, had on a red-sleeved waistcoat, and a pair of grey tweed trousers. I would have run to him, only I was a coward in the presence of such a mob – would have embraced him, only, he being an Englishman, I did not know how he would receive me; so I did what cowardice and false pride suggested was the best thing – walked deliberately to him, took off my hat, and said:

'Dr Livingstone, I presume?'

'YES,' said he, with a kind smile, lifting his cap slightly.

I replace my hat on my head, and he puts on his cap, and we both grasp hands, and I then say aloud:

'I thank God, Doctor, I have been permitted to see you.'

He answered, 'I feel thankful that I am here to welcome you.'

I turn to the Arabs, take off my hat to them in response to the saluting chorus of 'Yambos' I receive, and the Doctor introduces them to me by name. Then, oblivious of the crowds, oblivious of the men who shared with me my dangers, we – Livingstone and I – turn our faces towards his *tembe*. He points to the veranda, or, rather, mud platform, under the broad overhanging eaves; he points to his own particular seat, which I see his age and experience in Africa has suggested, namely, a straw mat, with a goatskin over it, and another skin nailed against the wall to protect his back from contact with the cold mud. I protest against taking this seat, which so much more befits him than me, but the Doctor will not yield: I must take it.

We are seated – the Doctor and I – with our backs to the wall. The Arabs take seats on our left. More than a thousand natives are in our front, filling the whole square densely, indulging their curiosity, and discussing the fact of two white men meeting at Ujiji – one just come from Manyuema, in the west, the other from Unyanyembe, in the east.

How I Found Livingstone, 1872

Attack from cannibals

In these wild regions our mere presence excited the most furious passions of hate and murder, just as in shallow waters a deep vessel stirs up muddy sediments. It appeared to be a necessity, then why should we regret it? Could a man contend with the inevitable?

At 2 p.m., heralded by savage shouts from the wasp swarm, which from some cause or other are unusually exultant, we emerge out of the shelter of the deeply wooded banks in presence of a vast affluent, nearly 2000 yards across at the mouth. As soon as we have fairly entered its waters, we see a great concourse of canoes hovering about some islets, which stud the middle of the stream. The canoe-men, standing up, give a loud shout as they discern us, and blow their horns louder than ever. We pull briskly on to gain the right bank, and come in view of the right branch of the affluent, when, looking up stream, we see a sight that sends the blood tingling through every nerve and fibre of the body, arouses not only our most lively interest, but also our most lively apprehensions – a flotilla of gigantic canoes bearing down upon us, which both in size and numbers utterly eclipse anything encountered hitherto! Instead of aiming for the right bank, we form in line, and keep straight down river, the boat taking position behind. Yet after a moment's reflection, as I note the numbers of the savages, and the daring manner of the pursuit, and the desire of our canoes to abandon the steady compact line, I give the order to drop anchor. Four of our canoes affect not to listen, until I chase them, and threaten them with my guns. This compelled them to return to the line, which is formed of eleven double canoes, anchored 10 yards apart. The boat moves up to the front, and takes position 50 yards above them. The shields are next lifted by the non-combatants, men, women, and children, in the bows, and along the outer lines, as well as astern, and from behind these, the muskets and rifles are aimed.

We have sufficient time to take a view of the mighty force bearing down on us, and to count the number of the war-vessels which have been collected from the Livingstone and its great affluent. There are fifty-four of them! A monster canoe leads the way, with two rows of upstanding paddles, forty men on a side, their bodies bending and swaying in unison as with a swelling barbarous chorus they drive her down towards us. In the bow, standing on what appears to be a platform, are ten prime young warriors, their heads gay with feathers of the parrot, crimson and grey: at the stern, eight men, with long paddles, whose tops are decorated with ivory balls, guide the monster vessel; and dancing up and down from stem to stern are ten men, who appear to be chiefs. All the paddles are headed with ivory balls, every head bears a feather crown, every arm shows gleaming white ivory armlets. From the bow of the canoe streams a thick fringe of the long white fibre of the Hyphene palm. The crashing sound of large drums, a hundred blasts from ivory horns, and a thrilling chant from two thousand human throats, do not tend to soothe our nerves or to increase our confidence. However, it is 'neck or nothing.' We have no time to pray, or to take sentimental looks at the savage world, or even to breathe a sad farewell to it. So many other things have to be done speedily and well.

As the foremost canoe comes rushing down, and its consorts on either side beating the water into foam, and raising their jets of water with their sharp prows, I turn to take a last look at our people, and say to them:

'Boys, be firm as iron; wait until you see the first spear, and then take good aim. Don't fire all at once. Keep aiming until you are sure of your man. Don't think of running away, for only your guns can save you.'

Frank is with the *Ocean* on the right flank, and has a choice crew, and a good bulwark of black wooden shields. Manwa Sera has the *London Town* – which he has taken in charge instead of the *Glasgow* – on the left flank, the sides of the canoe bristling with guns, in the hands of tolerably steady men.

The monster canoe aims straight for my boat, as though it would run us

down; but, when within fifty yards off, swerves aside, and, when nearly opposite, the warriors above the manned prow let fly their spears, and on either side
there is a noise of rushing bodies. But every sound is soon lost in the ripping,
crackling musketry. For five minutes we are so absorbed in firing that we take
no note of anything else; but at the end of that time we are made aware that
the enemy is reforming about 200 yards above us.

Our blood is up now. It is a murderous world, and we feel for the first time
that we hate the filthy, vulturous ghouls who inhabit it. We therefore lift our
anchors, and pursue them up-stream along the right bank, until rounding a
point we see their villages. We make straight for the banks, and continue the
fight in the village streets with those who have landed, hunt them out into the
woods, and there only sound the retreat, having returned the daring cannibals
the compliment of a visit . . .

This last of the twenty-eight desperate combats which we had had with the
insensate furies of savage-land began to inspire us with a suspicion of everything bearing the least semblance of man, and to infuse into our hearts
something of that feeling which possibly the hard-pressed stag feels when,
after distancing the hounds many times, and having resorted to many stratagems to avoid them, wearied and bathed with perspiration, he hears with
terror and trembling the hideous and startling yells of the ever-pursuing pack.
We also had laboured strenuously through ranks upon ranks of savages, scattered over a score of flotillas, had endured persistent attacks night and day
while straggling through them, had resorted to all modes of defence, and yet
at every curve of this fearful river the yells of the savages broke loud on our
ears, the snake-like canoes darted forward impetuously to the attack, while
the drums, and horns, and shouts raised fierce and deafening uproar. We were
becoming exhausted. Yet we were still only on the middle line of the continent! We were also being weeded out by units and twos and threes. There were
not thirty in the entire Expedition that had not received a wound. To continue
this fearful life was not possible. Some day we should lie down, and offer our
throats like lambs to the cannibal butchers . . .

Next day we clung to the channel; but as the islands lay sometimes diagonally across the stream, we finally emerged in view of the Bemberri, too late
to return. Immediately they called up their people to war, with a terrible racket
of drums; and about fifteen large canoes dashed out to meet us. But after the
Aruwimi flotilla this number was contemptible; we drove them away, followed
them to their villages, and compelled them to seek shelter in the woods. Then
the word was given that every man should provide himself with bananas and
cassava. This was done, and we re-embarked. Before, however, we could find

another opening amongst the islands, other villages discovered us, and again a terrific dinning rose, which inspired even fishing-boys to acts of ferocious valour. These we permitted to exhibit for our benefit the utmost rage they were capable of, except actually to throw their spears. Whenever they threatened to launch their weapons, a furious demonstration with our long oars was sufficient to send them skimming away. They followed us three or four miles, sending out every now and then wailing notes, which, from the frequent recurrence of the word *meat*, we understood to be expressions of regret that they were unable to secure the 'meat' which was running away from them.

Through the Dark Continent, 1878

'This pit of misery in which I am plunged neck deep'

March 4th [1877]: Halt at Chumbiri, Uyanza.

The king after saying he would give me guides as far as the Cataract for 5 *doti*, changed his mind and the extent of what he finally received after a tedious chatter was 6 cloths for himself, one coil of wire, 100 cowries. Three cloths for his sons and 960 cowries for the paddlers, besides the return of 2 goats he had given me yesterday.

He is, though old and of a kindly aspect, a prodigious liar, and his people are cunning beyond description. Their merit lies in the kind reception they give to strangers.

March 5th: Halt.

A native accused of witchcraft was drowned according to doom today: arms tied behind, and a wooden gag in his mouth, thrown into a canoe and paddled into the river and tossed overboard. As he was tossed, the executioner cried out to him: 'If you are a Magician, cause this river to dry up and save yourself.' After a few seconds he rose again and was carried down the stream about half a mile. A huge crocodile, fat with prey, followed him slowly and then rushed on him and we saw him no more . . .

March 9th: Voyage continues.

Today the 32nd fight occurred on this river, without any cause further than the savage wilfulness of the natives. In this fight we had 3 wounded in the boat and one in the canoe . . .

June 10th: Zinga Falls. Halt.

Today is the 17th day we have expended since we first saw the Mowa Falls, and our canoes are only at Massassa yet and not descended.

The Wangwana try me exceedingly. Since I have lost Frank, I am unable to leave camp to superintend the men at their work. Consequently, they play behind me. If I leave camp, the Chiefs will steal the monies left under one pretence or another. If I send messengers to hurry Manwa Sera up, the messengers idle their time on the road. We have had an instance of this today. Kacheche, the ever faithful express, the detective, knowing how anxious I was about the safety of the men and canoes, was sent before daylight to carry a message and to take three idlers to their work. Two hours afterwards a messenger left camp and overtook them, though the distance is only 3 miles. What could I say? How can I enforce them to their duty, when they are so far from me? I have publicly expressed a desire to die by a quick sharp death, which I think just now would be a mercy compared to what I endure daily. I am vexed each day by thieves, liars, and unconquerable laziness of the Wangwana. I am surrounded by savages who from some superstitious idea may rise to fight at a moment's notice. Weeks are passing swiftly away and the goods are diminishing, until we have but little left, and at the rate we are going, 6 weeks will suffice to bring us at death's door from starvation.

Should any loss happen to me, I earnestly implore my Executors – the proprietors of the *Daily Telegraph* and *New York Herald* or their Agents, when they call up the people to receive their pay, to reflect well what they are doing. The full story of my sufferings and vexations are not told in this journal, but is locked in my breast. The Wangwana deserve to have their wages carefully reckoned and not a cent more than their legitimate due ought to be paid them. They are faithless, lying, thievish, indolent knaves, who only teach a man to despise himself for his folly in attempting a grand work with such miserable slaves. Slavery is abhorrent to my very soul, and all men engaged in the trade should be doomed to instant death, but these men make me regard myself every day as only a grade higher than a miserable slave driver. Ah Frank! You are happy, my friend. Out of this dreadful mess. Out of this pit of misery in which I am plunged neck deep.

The Exploration Diaries of H. M. Stanley (1961)

Approaching the West Coast

After my dinner – three fried bananas, twenty roasted ground-nuts, and a cup of muddy water, my usual fare now – by a lamp made out of a piece of rotten sheeting steeped in a little palm-butter I wrote the following letter:

Village of Nsanda, August 4, 1877.

[*To any Gentleman who speaks English at Embomma.*]

Dear Sir,
I have arrived at this place from Zanzibar with 115 souls, men, women and children. We are now in a state of imminent starvation. We can buy nothing from the natives, for they laugh at our kinds of cloth, beads, and wire. There are no provisions in the country that may be purchased, except on market days, and starving people cannot afford to wait for these markets. I, therefore, have made bold to despatch three of my young men, natives of Zanzibar, with a boy named Robert Feruzi, of the English Mission at Zanzibar, with this letter craving relief from you. I do not know you; but I am told there is an English-man at Embomma, and as you are a Christian and a gentleman, I beg you not to disregard my request. The boy Robert will be better able to describe our lone condition than I can tell you in this letter. We are in a state of the greatest distress; but if your supplies arrive in time, I may be able to reach Embomma within four days. I want three hundred cloths, each four yards long, of such quality as you trade with, which is very different from that we have; but better than all would ten or fifteen man-loads of rice or grain to fill their pinched bellies immediately, as even with the cloths it would require time to purchase food, and starving people cannot wait. The supplies must arrive within two days, or I may have a fearful time of it among the dying. Of course I hold myself responsible for any expense you may incur in this business. What is wanted is immediate relief; and I pray you to use your utmost energies to forward it at once. For myself, if you have such little luxuries as tea, coffee, sugar, and biscuits by you, such as one man can easily carry, I beg you on my own behalf that you will send a small supply, and add to the great debt of gratitude due to you upon the timely arrival of the supplies for my people. Until that time I beg you to believe me,
Yours sincerely,
H. M. STANLEY,
Commanding Anglo-American Expedition for Exploration of Africa.

P.S. You may not know me by name; I therefore add, I am the person that discovered Livingstone in 1871. – H. M. S.

The chiefs and boat's crew were called to my tent. I then told them that I had resolved to despatch four messengers to the white men at Embomma, with letters asking for food, and wished to know the names of those most likely to travel quickly and through anything that interposed to prevent them;

for it might be possible that so small a number of men might be subjected to delays and interruptions and that the guides might loiter on the way, and so protract the journey until relief would arrive too late.

The response was not long coming, for Uledi sprang up and said, 'Oh, master, don't talk more; I am ready now. See I will only buckle on my belt, and I shall start at once, and nothing will stop me. I will follow on the track like a leopard . . .

On the 6th we roused ourselves for a further effort, and after filing through several villages separated from each other by intervals of waste land, we arrived at 9 A.M. near Banza Mbuko. Haggard, woe-begone invalids, with bloated faces, but terribly angular bodies, we sought a quiet spot a mile beyond the outermost village of the settlement. Mbinda's wooded ridge was in view, and Ikungu's bearded summits were fast receding into distance and obscurity. Banza Mbuko seemed prosperous; the inhabitants appeared to be well fed, but, as though we were denizens of another world, nothing of warm sympathy could I detect in the face of any one of all those that gazed on us. Ah! in what part of all the Japhetic world would such a distressed and woful band as we were then have been regarded with such hard steel-cold eyes? Yet not one word of reproach issued from the starving people; they threw themselves upon the ground with an indifference begotten of despair and misery. They did not fret, nor bewail aloud the tortures of famine, nor vent the anguish of their pinched bowels in cries, but with stony resignation surrendered themselves to rest, under the scant shade of some dwarf acacia or sparse bush. Now and then I caught the wail of an infant, and the thin voice of a starving mother, or the petulant remonstrance of an older child; but the adults remained still and apparently lifeless, each contracted within the exclusiveness of individual suffering. The youths, companions of Uledi, and the chiefs, sat in whispering groups, removed from the sick and grieving, and darkly dotted the vicinity of the tent; the childless women were also seen by twos and threes far apart, discussing, no doubt, our prospects, for at this period this was the most absorbing topic of the camp.

Suddenly the shrill voice of a little boy was heard saying, 'Oh! I see Uledi and Kachéché coming down the hill, and there are plenty of men following them!'

'What! – what! – what!' broke out eagerly from several voices, and dark forms were seen springing up from amongst the bleached grass, and from under the shade, and many eyes were directed at the whitened hill-slope.

'Yes; it is true! it is true! La il Allah il Allah! Yes; el hamd ul Illah! Yes, it is food! food! food at last! Ah, that Uledi! he is a lion, truly! We are saved, thank God!'

Before many minutes, Uledi and Kachéché were seen tearing through the grass, and approaching us with long springing strides, holding a letter up to announce to us that they had been successful. And the gallant fellows, hurrying up, soon placed it in my hands, and in the hearing of all who were gathered to hear the news I translated the following letter:

EMBOMMA,   6.30 A.M.,
ENGLISH FACTORY.   BOMA, 6th August, 1877.

H. M. STANLEY, Esq.

DEAR SIR,

Your welcome letter came to hand yesterday, at 7 P.M. As soon as its contents were understood, we immediately arranged to despatch to you such articles as you requested, as much as our stock on hand would permit, and other things that we deemed would be suitable in that locality. You will see that we send fifty pieces of cloth, each 24 yards long, and some sacks containing sundries for yourself; several sacks of rice, sweet potatoes, also a few bundles of fish, a bundle of tobacco, and one demijohn of rum. The carriers are all paid, so that you need not trouble yourself about them. That is all we need say about business. We are exceedingly sorry to hear that you have arrived in such piteous condition, but we send our warmest congratulations to you, and hope that you will soon arrive in Boma (this place is called Boma by us, though on the map it is Em-bomma). Again hoping that you will soon arrive, and that you are not suffering in health,

Believe us to remain,
Your sincere friends,
HATTON & COOKSON.

(Signed)   A. DA MOTTA VEIGA.
                                                 J. W. HARRISON.

Through the Dark Continent, 1878

Mary Kingsley
1862–1900

Polygamy is the institution which above all others governs the daily life of the native . . . All the missionaries have set their faces against it . . . [so] many men are excluded from the fold who would make quite as good Christians as those within it.

Mary Kingsley, the first European to visit several parts of West Africa, was the daughter of the doctor, naturalist and writer George Kingsley, and many of her father's interests became her own. She was self-taught, using her father's library to study natural history and ethnology, and when her father began to study 'primitive' societies, particularly sacrificial rites, Mary worked for him, gathering together accounts of travellers. She spent her twenties tied to the house, nursing her sick parents; but when she reached thirty, they died within six weeks of each other. The following year (1893) Kingsley joined a cargo ship bound for West Africa.

The ship sailed along the coast from Freetown in Sierra Leone to a Gulf of Guinea port on the coast of what is now Nigeria, from where she travelled inland at a time when a woman simply did not travel alone anywhere: 'A quest for fish and fetish' is how she described her journey. While exploring the lower Congo river she studied African religious practices and collected insects and freshwater fish for the British Museum.

Rather than march along as an 'intrepid explorer', Kingsley merged quietly into the areas she visited – in contrast to Stanley, travelling in West Africa less than two decades before – all the while observing.*

* Rudyard Kipling said of her: 'Being human, she must have been afraid of something, but one never found out what it was.' She herself admitted: 'I can confidently say I am not afraid of any animal – until I see it – and then – well I will yield to nobody in terror.' On falling into an animal trap containing long spikes, she remarked that 'it is at these moments you realise the blessings of a good thick skirt'.

African culture did not cease to impress her and she compared it with the 'thin veneer of rubbishy white culture' that British officials and some missionaries were trying to impose. 'As it is with the forest,' she wrote, 'so it is with the minds of the natives. Unless you live among the natives, you never get to know them. If you do this, you gradually get a light into the true state of their mind and forest. At first you see nothing but confused stupidity and crime, but when you get to see – well! As in the other forest, you see things worth seeing.' Though she did not chart rivers or disclose the existence of a single hill range, she was in at least one way more significant than other explorers: she was a freethinker, exceptionally untainted by the cultural prejudice of her time or compatriots.

In 1899 Kingsley left Britain for a third time, intending to continue her exploration of West Africa, but with the outbreak of the Boer War found herself travelling to South Africa instead. She worked in Cape Town as a journalist and nurse, caring for Afrikaner prisoners of war, but at the age of thirty-eight she caught typhoid fever and died.

The Mary Kingsley Society of West Africa, later renamed the African Society, was established in her memory. She is remarkable not just for her spirited travels, but also for her defence of the African peoples against the destructive influences of Western civilization: 'Nothing strikes one so much, in studying the degeneration of these native tribes, as the direct effect that civilisation and reformation has in hastening it. The worst enemy to the existence of the African tribe, is the one who comes to it and says: Now you must civilise, and come to school, and leave off all those awful goings-on of yours, and settle down quietly.'

Spirit charms for every occasion

Charms are made for every occupation and desire in life – loving, hating, buying, selling, fishing, planting, travelling, hunting, &c., and although they are usually in the form of things filled with a mixture in which the spirit nestles, yet there are other kinds; for example, a great love charm is made of the water the lover has washed in, and this, mingled with the drink of the loved one, is held to soften the hardest heart. Of a similar nature is the friendship-compelling charm I know of on the Ivory Coast, which I have been told is used also in the Batanga regions. This is obtained on the death of a person you know really cared for you – like your father or mother, for example – by cutting off the head and suspending it over a heap of chalk, as the white earth that you find in river beds is called here, then letting it drip as long as it will and using this saturated chalk to mix in among the food of any one you wish should think kindly of you and trust you. This charm, a Bassa man said to me, 'was good too much for the white trader,' and made him give you 'good price too much' for palm oil, &c., and that statement revived my sympathy for a friend who once said to me that when he used first to come to the Coast he had 'pretty well had the inside raked up out of him' from the sickness caused by the charms that his local cook administered to him in the interest of the cook's friends. That man keeps an Accra cook now, and I trust lives a life of healthy, icy, unemotional calm.

Some kinds of charms, such as those to prevent your getting drowned, shot, seen by elephants, &c., are worn on a bracelet or necklace. A new-born child starts with a health-knot tied round the wrist, neck, or loins, and throughout the rest of its life its collection of charms goes on increasing. This collection does not, however, attain inconvenient dimensions, owing to the failure of some of the charms to work.

That is the worst of charms and prayers. The thing you wish of them may, and frequently does, happen in a strikingly direct way but other times it does not. In Africa this is held to arise from the bad character of the spirits; their gross ingratitude and fickleness. You may have taken every care of a spirit for years, given it food and other offerings that you wanted for yourself, wrapped it up in your cloth on chilly nights and gone cold, put it in the only dry spot in the canoe, and so on, and yet after all this, the wretched thing will be capable of being got at by your rival or enemy and lured away, leaving you only the case it once lived in.

Finding, we will say, that you have been upset and half-drowned, and your canoe-load of goods lost three times in a week, that your paddles are always breaking, and the amount of snags in the river and so on is abnormal, you judge that your canoe-charm has stopped. Then you go to the medicine man who supplied you with it and complain. He says it was a perfectly good charm when he sold it you and he never had any complaints before, but he will investigate the affair; when he has done so, he either says the spirit has been lured away from the home he prepared for it by incantations and presents from other people, or that he finds the spirit is dead; it has been killed by a more powerful spirit of its class, which is in the pay of some enemy of yours. In all cases the little thing you kept the spirit in is no use now, and only fit to sell to a white man as 'a big curio!' and the sooner you let him have sufficient money to procure you a fresh and still more powerful spirit – necessarily more expensive – the safer it will be for you, particularly as your misfortunes distinctly point to some one being desirous of your death. You of course grumble, but seeing the thing in his light you pay up, and the medicine man goes busily to work with incantations, dances, looking into mirrors or basins of still water, and concoctions of messes to make you a new protecting charm.

Human eye-balls, particularly of white men, I have already said are a great charm. Dr Nassau says he has known graves rifled for them. This, I fancy, is to secure the 'man that lives in your eyes' for the service of the village, and naturally the white man, being regarded as a superior being, would be of high value if enlisted into its service. A similar idea of the possibility of gaining possession of the spirit of a dead man obtains among the Negroes, and the heads of important chiefs in the Calabar districts are usually cut off from the body on burial and kept secretly for fear the head, and thereby the spirit, of the dead chief, should be stolen from the town. If it were stolen it would be not only a great advantage to its new possessor, but a great danger to the chief's old town, because he would know all the peculiar ju-ju relating to it. For each town has a peculiar one, kept exceedingly secret, in addition to the general ju-jus, and this secret one would then be in the hands of the new owners of the spirit. It is for similar reasons that brave General MacCarthy's head was treasured by the Ashantees . . .

Concerning polygamy

Now polygamy is, like most other subjects, a difficult thing to form an opinion on, if, before forming that opinion, you go and make a study of the facts and bearings of the case. It is therefore advisable to follow the usual method employed by the majority of people. Just take a prejudice of your own, and fix it up with the so-called opinions of people who go in for that sort of prejudice too. This method is absolutely essential to the forming of an opinion on the subject of polygamy among African tribes, that will be acceptable in enlightened circles. Polygamy is the institution which above all others governs the daily life of the native; and it is therefore the one which the missionaries who enter into this daily life, and not merely into the mercantile and legal, as do the trader and the government official, are constantly confronted with and hindered by. All the missionaries have set their faces against it and deny Church membership to those men who practise it; whereby it falls out that many men are excluded from the fold who would make quite as good Christians as those within it. They hesitate about turning off from their homes women who have lived and worked for them for years, and not only for them, but often for their fathers before them. One case in the Rivers I know of is almost tragic if you put yourself in his place. An old chief, who had three wives, profoundly and vividly believed that exclusion from the Holy Communion meant an eternal damnation. The missionary had instructed him in the details of this damnation thoroughly, and the chief did not like the prospect at all; but on the other hand he did not like to turn off the three wives he had lived with for years. He found the matter was not even to be compromised, by turning off two and going to church to be married with accompanying hymns and orange-blossoms with number three, for the ladies held together; not one of them would marry him and let the other two go, so the poor old chief worried himself to a shammock and anybody else he could get to listen to him. His white trader friends told him not to be such an infernal ass. Some of his black fellow chiefs said the missionary was quite right, and the best thing for him to do would be to hand over to them the three old wives, and go and marry a young girl from the mission school. Personally they were not yet afflicted with scruples on the subject of polygamy, and of course (being 'missionary man' now) he would not think of taking anything for his wives, so they would do their best, as friends, to help him out of the difficulty.

Travels in West Africa, 1897

ALBERT B. LLOYD
1871–1946

Surely the time has come when we in this civilised land of ours . . . should stretch out our hands to these poor ignorant cannibals, and seek to lift them out of their darkness and gross superstition . . .

Albert Lloyd spent ten years working for the Church Missionary Society in parts of the Uganda Protectorate. He did not take the usual homeward route, via Lake Victoria Nyanza and Mombasa, but through the Great Aruwimi Forest, down the Congo, to the west coast of Africa. His encounters with groups such as the so-called pygmies, and also with the Bangwa, are presented in his *In Dwarf Land and Cannibal Country*.

As the book's title suggests, he saw Africa as backward and soulless. 'It was called and rightly so the Dark Continent,' he wrote. Three outside forces were now 'making tremendous bids for the soul of the country': first, Islam, 'by the very nature of her propaganda'; secondly, the modern civilization of 'more enlightened nations'; thirdly, and most importantly, the 'power of Christianity'.

Lloyd's favourite pursuit seems to have been hunting antelope, but he also had brushes with a lion, a leopard and elephants (which he hunted with his .303 rifle). A classic figure in the colonial missionary mode, he was of the opposite inclination and viewpoint to Mary Kingsley, who travelled in the region in the previous decade. Albert B. Lloyd was just the sort of person she was warning about. 'As I see it . . .' he wrote in his autobiography, *A Life's Thrills*, 'there is but one hope for Africa, as there is but one hope for the whole world – namely, a spiritual awakening – a turning to God.'

The Bangwa – a better class of cannibal

The next few days we passed through the wildest cannibal country to be found anywhere, and every day we saw dozens of villages inhabited by the Bangwa. They are a splendid race of people; I was very much taken with them. I have seldom seen such physical development and such symmetry of figure; they are upright as a dart, with heads erect, and bright, intelligent faces. These men came up to me with the greatest confidence – not as the cringing savage who will grovel at your feet before your face, and put a spear into you when your back is turned. The cannibal was straightforward and brave, and his character could be read in his actions and bearing, and one could see at once that here were the materials for the making of a fine race of people . . . His cannibalism is most pronounced, and, unlike many others, he does not seem to mind being known as a cannibal; generally speaking, he devours the bodies of his enemies, but a woman is seldom, if ever, eaten by the Bangwa. The women, however, join in the feast, not sitting with the men, but in a separate group by themselves.

It would be difficult to say whether the cannibalism of the Bangwa is practised merely from pleasure or from some superstitious idea about the strength of the enemy entering into themselves. As far as I could make out this latter is the more general belief. It is for the same reason that some tribes of Eastern Africa will eat the liver of a dead leopard that they may imbibe its strength – as the Bangwa warrior devours his enemy. On several occasions I saw them engaging in their feasts, and most ghastly were the sights, too horrible indeed to mention. Sometimes one would see part of a limb roasting over the fire, or else in a cooking pot, boiling, while the warriors sit round watching eagerly until it was cooked. But still, not withstanding the fact of there being a superstitious idea in connection with this cannibalism, there is no doubt a depraved appetite. I have seen the wild, exciting feast, where spirit dances and invocations have been the principal items, and I have seen the warriors in all soberness sit down to a 'joint of man' in exactly the same way as they would do to a piece of forest antelope. Once, when told by a European that the practice of eating human flesh was a most degraded habit, the cannibal answered, 'Why degraded? you people eat sheep and cows and fowls, which are all animals of a far lower order, and we eat man, who is great and above all, it is *you* who are degraded!' Thus will the cannibal defend the practice.

In Dwarf Land and Cannibal Country, 1900

Henri Mouhot
1826–61

... what riches and treasures of art will remain for ever buried beneath these ruins; how many distinguished men – artists, sovereigns, and warriors – whose names are worthy of immortality, are now forgotten.

French naturalist and archaeologist, Mouhot was the first European to document the great city ruins of Angkor in Cambodia.

Born in Montbeliard, Mouhot was originally a professor of French language and literature, but was driven by a desire to contribute something new to human knowledge. In his own words, he was someone who, 'with the sole object of being useful to his fellow-men, or of discovering some insect, plant or unknown animal, or verifying some point of latitude, crosses the ocean, and sacrifices family, comfort, health, and too often, life itself'. Before long, sadly, he had sacrificed all these things. Mouhot explored the tributaries of the Mekong river in Siam (Thailand), Laos, and Cambodia. It was while in Cambodia in early 1860 that he came across the ruined city of Angkor, which had been the capital of Cambodia's ancient Khmer civilization between the ninth and fifteenth centuries. In 1430 the Cambodians had fled from Angkor owing to the threat from neighbouring Thais,

relocating their capital further south for greater security. For a while it had survived as a centre of Buddhist pilgrimage, but by the time Mouhot arrived, the jungle had taken over.

Mouhot spent three weeks at the site, documenting his find and drawing sketches. A seventeenth-century English missionary had visited Angkor before him, but it was Mouhot's discovery that led to its excavation. In October 1861, while travelling through northern Laos on another expedition, Mouhot died from fever. He was buried in Laos where, in 1867, the French erected a memorial. He had continued to write until his death, and his servant forwarded his diary to the French consul in Bangkok, whence it was taken to France and published, preserving a vivid account that reveals Mouhot's deep (reciprocated) respect for the peoples of Indo-China – and reveals much about French colonial mentality.

The ruins of Angkor

There are, on the banks of the Mekon . . . ruins of such grandeur, remains of structures which must have been raised at such an immense cost of labour, that, at the first view, one is filled with profound admiration, and cannot but ask what has become of this powerful race, so civilised, so enlightened, the authors of these gigantic works?

One of these temples – a rival to that of Solomon, and erected by some ancient Michael Angelo – might take an honourable place beside our most beautiful buildings. It is grander than anything left to us by Greece or Rome, and presents a sad contrast to the state of barbarism in which the nation is now plunged.

Unluckily the scourge of war, aided by time, the great destroyer, who respects nothing, and perhaps also by earthquakes, has fallen heavily on the greater part of the other monuments; and the work of destruction and decay continues among those which still remain standing, imposing and majestic, amidst the masses of ruins all around.

One seeks in vain for any historical souvenirs of the many kings who must have succeeded one another on the throne of the powerful empire of Maha-Nocor-Khmer. There exists a tradition of a leprous king, to whom is attributed the commencement of the great temple, but all else is totally forgotten. The inscriptions, with which some of the columns are covered, are illegible; and, if you interrogate the Cambodians as to the founders of Ongcor-Wat, you invariably receive one of these four replies: 'It is the work of Pra-Eun, the king of the angels;' 'It is the work of the giants;' 'It was built by the leprous king;' or else, 'It made itself.'

The work of giants! The expression would be very just, if used figuratively, in speaking of these prodigious works, of which no one who has not seen them can form any adequate idea; and in the construction of which patience, strength, and genius appear to have done their utmost in order to leave to future generations proofs of their power and civilisation.

It is remarkable that none of these monuments were intended for habitations; all were temples of Buddhism. The statues and bas-reliefs, however, curiously enough, represent entirely secular subjects – monarchs surrounded by their wives, their heads and arms loaded with ornaments such as bracelets and necklaces, the body being covered with a narrow *langouti*. On a sort of esplanade is a statue, said to be that of the leprous king. It is a little above the middle height, and the prince is seated in a noble and dignified attitude. The head, particularly, is a *chef-d'œuvre*, the features perfectly regular, and possessing a manly beauty of a description seen now in very rare instances, and only amongst Cambodians of unmixed race, living in seclusion at the foot of the mountains, where the unhealthiness of the climate condemns them to a solitary existence; or among the savage mountaineers who occupy the border country separating Siam and Cambodia from the kingdom of Annam . . .

What strikes the observer with not less admiration than the grandeur, regularity, and beauty of these majestic buildings, is the immense size and prodigious number of the blocks of stone of which they are constructed. In this temple alone are as many as 1532 columns. What means of transport, what a multitude of workmen, must this have required, seeing that the mountain out of which the stone was hewn is thirty miles distant! In each block are to be seen holes 2½ centimetres in diameter and 3 in depth, the number varying with the size of the blocks; but the columns and the sculptured portions of the building bear no traces of them. According to a Cambodian legend, these are the prints of the fingers of a giant, who, after kneading an enormous quantity of clay, had cut it into blocks and carved it, turning it into a hard and, at the same time, light stone by pouring over it some marvellous liquid.

All the mouldings, sculptures, and bas-reliefs appear to have been executed after the erection of the building. The stones are everywhere fitted together in so perfect a manner that you can scarcely see where are the joinings; there is neither sign of mortar nor mark of the chisel, the surface being as polished as marble. Was this incomparable edifice the work of a single genius, who conceived the idea, and watched over the execution of it? One is tempted to think so; for no part of it is deficient, faulty, or inconsistent. To what epoch does it owe its origin? As before remarked, neither tradition nor written inscriptions furnish any certain information upon this point; or rather, I should say, these latter are as a sealed book for want of an interpreter; and they may, perchance, throw light on the subject when some European savant shall succeed in deciphering them . . .

On the one side you gaze upon the wooded plain and the pyramidal temple of Ongcor, with its rich colonnades, the mountain of Crome, which is beyond the new city, the view losing itself in the waters of the great lake on the horizon. On the opposite side stretches the long chain of mountains whose quarries, they say, furnished the beautiful stone used for the temples; and amidst thick forests, which extend along the base, is a pretty, small lake, which looks like a blue ribbon on a carpet of verdure. All this region is now as lonely and deserted as formerly it must have been full of life and cheerfulness; and the howling of wild animals, and the cries of a few birds, alone disturb the solitude.

Sad fragility of human things! How many centuries and thousands of generations have passed away, of which history, probably, will never tell us anything: what riches and treasures of art will remain for ever buried beneath these ruins; how many distinguished men – artists, sovereigns, and warriors – whose names were worthy of immortality, are now forgotten, laid to rest under the thick dust which covers these tombs!

Travels in the Central Parts of Indo-China, 1864

FRANK HURLEY

1885–1962

I pointed at three fine specimens of stuffed human heads and in the language of signs . . . intimated that I wanted them and would pay six steel axes therefor. Six Axes! Six Axes!

The Australian photographer and film-maker Frank Hurley is known primarily for his images of Shackleton's *Endurance* expedition. He ran away from home at the age of fourteen to work in the Sydney docks. Three years later, he got hold of his first camera, a fifteen-shilling Kodak, which he paid for at the rate of a shilling a week, and began working in the postcard business. At the age of twenty-six he secured a job as the expedition photographer on Douglas Mawson's Antarctic expedition of 1911–13 (see page 530). At the time, photographers were a particularly important part of any expedition, not only because they could document it, but also because the sale of rights to images helped to cover the expedition's costs. Hurley's expedition photographs and documentary film *Home of the Blizzard* established his reputation; soon afterwards Ernest Shackleton employed him to record his attempt to cross Antarctica (see page 520).

Hurley's diaries of this expedition reflect his toughness and determination during the two-year ordeal – and his occasional impatience with those who showed signs of cracking under the strain.*

* Fellow expedition member Thomas Orde-Lees described him as one of the hardest workers – as a metalworker he had skills of great importance to the expedition – but apparently he was not the easiest person to get along with. He was 'rather too free with his tongue to be an ideal companion and a little inclined to let his prejudices run riot . . . His interest in the expedition, on his own admission, is mainly a commercial one so it is sometimes a case of "one for you and two for me" but he never really lets this stand in the way of his zeal for the general efficiency of the expedition. Occasionally he gets on my nerves rather, banging doors and talking loudly to anyone about when he is on nightwatch. In fact, I don't reckon to get much sleep when he is on watch.'

His artistic approach to expedition photography was innovative. Rather than take routine images of posing explorers, he created dramatic scenic compositions that documented the expedition. He went to extreme lengths to get a good shot – climbing masts, braving terrible weather conditions – and even dived into the Antarctic water to save his negatives as the expedition ship, the *Endurance*, sank. Lionel Greenstreet, First Officer of the *Endurance*, said of him: 'Hurley is a warrior with his camera and would go anywhere or do anything to get a picture.' The impact of his images on his return home was enormous: he had captured haunting images of the crushing of the *Endurance* by ice, men camping on the ice floes of the Weddell Sea and everyday scenes on Elephant Island, where the men awaited rescue. 'Hurley was an interesting character,' wrote Orde-Lees. 'He is Australian – very Australian . . . As a photographer he excels and I doubt if his work would be equalled even by Ponting.'

It was during the time on Elephant Island, where the party spent seven months sheltering under an upturned boat, that a plan to explore New Guinea was conceived. As Hurley wrote: 'At night we went to sleep hungry, to dream of delicious banquets. Likewise we went to bed cold and dreamed of a country so hot that the water steamed . . . In the daytime, we talked of nothing but the tropics and the palm trees and while the wind blew ninety miles an hour and the snow covered our shelter, our party planned an expedition into New Guinea the moment we were rescued.'

However, the war years, which Hurley spent as a front-line photographer, saw most of the original party either killed, too shaken, or too badly disabled to live out this dream. Only Hurley made it to Papua New Guinea. He gathered together a party of natives and five white men, and found the contrast he had been seeking: a land of swamps, steaming lakes and headhunters. During this expedition he discovered people with apparently Semitic features living deep in the interior around Lake Murray – people he referred to as 'one of the Lost Tribes' in the film he made about them.

Hurley went on to photograph, film and write about Tasmania and parts of his homeland, Australia, and also produced some fictional film work. He returned to Antarctica with Mawson in 1929–31 and continued to work until his death at the age of seventy-six.

Bargaining for 'three fine specimens of stuffed human heads'

In these uncharted waters, every precaution was necessary; so after we had heaved anchor and turned our course back into the lake, I kept a strict lookout from a small platform built high on the mainmast. Scarcely had we progressed two miles when I noticed through the glasses a pair of canoes, one being paddled by eight men. The other seemed to be towed. The *Eureka* began rapidly to gain and I noticed the two canoes begin to draw apart. One appeared to be abandoned while the other rowed frantically for the bank so as to escape up one of the countless shallow reaches. As we drew close to the abandoned canoe, I observed it to be filled with stuffed heads, stone axes, bows, arrows, and all the sundries appertaining to the Lake Murray village. The *Eureka* was drawn alongside the prize and anchor cast.

Meanwhile I remained on the platform waving frantically a piece of yellow fabric which in 'Daru days' had served as a quarantine flag, and calling out as loudly as I could the word, 'Sambio! Sambio!' After much deliberation the canoe began to row slowly toward us, while both the paddlers and myself continued to shout, 'Sambio! Sambio!' [Peace! Peace!] to reassure each other.

I admired the prowess of these men immensely. They put down their bows and arrows and approached us, knowing neither their fate nor our intentions, but relying solely upon the honour of that magic word, 'Sambio!' Perhaps they were just as eager to ascertain what sort of creatures we were as we were eager to see them. Perhaps the tales of the white man and his implements of steel were lures worth risking even life. How strange! We keenly desirous of securing their primitive weapons and they anxious to possess the products of modern civilization!

The strange people when they came alongside fulfilled all the grotesque and fanciful ideas we had formed of them. Truly indeed they were prehistoric creatures – practically nude, covered by the hideous sipuma skin, and having the most amazing features. Their voices, strange to say, were pleasantly euphonious and comparable to the mountain folk of Maifulu and Ononghe, whom I consider the most musical of all the Papuan tribes. The canoe impressed me greatly. It was shaped with a long 'clipper' taper, bow and stern finely excavated, and devoid of outrigger. One measured no less than fifty-five feet! The rowers stood erect and paddled their craft with very long paddles, the shafts of which terminated in large flat blades. The work of making these paddles from a solid piece of timber with only adzes of stone must be laborious and lengthy.

The cast of features of these people is amazingly Hebraic. Indeed, were it not for the deep bronze of their skins, they might have passed for one of the Lost Tribes. They coincided accurately with historians' description of the lost tribes of Israel and might well pass for bronzed Babylonian Jews. The hair is shorn off close in the front; but the back extends in a long cluster of luxuriant pigtails which are increased in length by plaiting them with fibre.

Speedily we made friends, or rather appeared to, with these people and began active trading. I demonstrated the power of the rifle and its accuracy. At the report most of them jumped overboard in terror. What astonished them more than the actual report or the carrying distance of the bullet was the echo. It reverberated for fully thirty seconds and it was clear that they thought it was the shot still travelling. Matches, the taste of salt and of sugar, alike astonished and pleased them; but what they clamoured for were the empty tins which we had saved for the purpose – empty oil and benzine tins. These primitive folk are entirely destitute of utensils of any description beyond bamboo and a few water baskets made by folding the sheath of the Goru palm.

For a few tins we purchased a bundle of arrows, while the same currency bought paddles, stone clubs and other implements. They were also eager to secure axes and knives which we exchanged, securing great value for our tools. After trading profitably and to our advantage and their satisfaction, they directed us with great zeal to their village. On this trip we took the canoe in tow, an event which caused among the paddlers the greatest hilarity and delight. All the way they jabbered among themselves in their unknown dialect.

The village (reminiscent of Bairnsfather) comprised a large, flat-roofed house about one hundred feet long and thirty-five feet wide. It appeared identical to that discovered a week ago, except that the big house was open at each end and had no small entrances from the outside. It is interesting to observe that throughout all Papua there are seldom two villages in which the customs and the architectural features are precisely the same.

Our new friends pressed us warmly with much jabbering and animated pantomime to go ashore, and at length I yielded and with McCulloch and four natives set out in the dinghy.

We found the foreshores heavily overgrown with water-weeds and reeds, difficult to force the dinghy into and still more difficult to push out of in case of attack. I noted carefully that our friends were hysterically excited and I sensed trouble. A dozen over-willing hands rushed out to haul the dinghy up high and dry, in which case we would have been completely helpless in case of attack. I accordingly waved them back and made for another point where there was a clear landing and an easy get-away could be effected in case of attack. I hailed Bell to bring the vessel in as close as possible to cover us with weapons in case of danger. We landed to a wild song and dance to which the warriors beat time on drums and benzine tins, while others shook violently stuffed human heads which emitted a not unpleasant rattling . . .

There were some fifty warriors but to my consternation neither women nor children. This is ever an ominous sign and presages trouble. As we loitered on the foreshore the chief seemed to sense the reason for my hesitancy and motioned the warriors away. As they departed into the jungle immediately behind the village, I noticed them snatch up bows and arrows from the concealment of the grass. With rifles at the ready we followed the chief in single file along a narrow track towards the house. McCulloch drew my attention to numbers of arrows half concealed in the grass which had been pushed into the ground with the point directed to the house. In the event of a retreat through the grass one must inevitably become impaled on the terrible points. We were now on the threshold of the house which I observed was precisely similar to those visited previously but larger.

The chief motioned us to enter but I felt that he was a decoy to entice us into the trap. My native bodyguard warned me against this ruse saying that it was one used by their fathers. Once inside the darkness of the Dubu, a signal would have brought the warriors from their concealment, we would have been surrounded and clubbed to death.

One thinks quickly in these times, for only twenty yards away I knew fifty bowmen were excitedly waiting the signal. We could hear their suppressed whispers coming from the jungle. It was some hundred paces back to the dinghy which latter was fortunately just beyond arrow range. The retreat would have to be made diplomatically and so as not to arouse suspicion.

I pointed to three fine specimens of stuffed human heads and in the language of signs, which these people understood perfectly, intimated that I wanted them and would pay six steel axes therefor. Six axes! Steel axes! I noticed the Hebraic shrewdness for a bargain sparkle in his eyes. Such a bargain could not be refused. I also intimated by signs that we would return after the axes were brought from the vessel. So he was going to get six axes in addition to six heads! The shrewd old man called something back to his followers and carried the heads back along the track to the dinghy. He would wait on the foreshore for our return which I indicated would be immediately.

So heartily thankful for once, that even the savage breast can know that most repulsive of all traits – greed, we clambered aboard and Bell started up the engine and we headed out into the stream. The old man saw he was outwitted and shaking a bundle of arrows defiantly, hurled back in contemptuous breath the words 'Sambio! Sambio!'

The escape, I am convinced, was a narrow one and a sound lesson. From then on we decided not to land but to do our work from the vessel. This was, in fact, the only safe course remaining. The only means of landing involved some way of terrifying the people and this I had no desire to do. As if nothing had happened, the canoes put off from the shore the next morning and paid us a visit. I paid over the axes and this served to inspire confidence and to renew the friendship.

The manner in which they regarded us is as excusable as our curiosity toward them. They were much puzzled by our whiteness, by the medio-colour of our half-caste engine room assistant, the dark bronze of the others, and by the almost black of Ironi who came from one of the Kaimari villages. During their visit alongside Bell happened to have been shaving and this process roused the greatest interest. In some way they associated the white lather with the whiteness of our skin and by pantomime begged to examine the soap-suds. Bell placed a large quantity in the hands of one of the savage paddlers who tasted it, got it into his eyes (a thing which caused him to rub them violently) and rubbed it over his skin, expecting clearly that it would have the magic effect of turning him white.

Vaieki, who has the astuteness and cunning of a true cannibal, informed me that he had seen the natives in conversation and that the ruse of friendliness was to be displayed when we went ashore. After that they would lure us to the big house and kill the party. But the best laid plans of mice and cannibals 'gang aft agley.'

Pearls and Savages: Adventures in the Air, in Land and Sea in New Guinea, 1924

PERCY FAWCETT
1867–?1925

The demons of the Amazonian rivers were abroad, manifesting their presence in lowering skies, downpours of torrential rain and sombre forest walls.

Lieutenant-Colonel Percy Harrison Fawcett, DSO, made several historically insignificant expeditions into the Amazon and Mato Grosso, but achieved fame by mysteriously disappearing there. He was born in Torquay, Devon, and joined the Royal Artillery at the age of nineteen. He served for several years in Ceylon, where he met and married his wife; he also worked in Hong Kong and North Africa. While in Asia and Africa, he had begun to develop an interest in the archaeology of ancient civilizations, and would hack through seemingly impenetrable undergrowth in search of ruins. To those who expressed surprise at this tolerance of jungle hardship, he replied that he much preferred the company of savages to that of 'civilised bores'. In 1906, with the support of the Royal Geographical Society, Fawcett travelled to Bolivia to work for the Boundary Commission, demarcating the Bolivian–Brazilian border in order to facilitate the smooth running of rubber plantations.

The Amazon worked its magic on him, and he dedicated most of the rest of his life to its exploration. After three years his boundary work was terminated, but he continued to explore alone, financed by newspapers and business interests – alone, but (as someone with a powerful mystic streak) accompanied in spirit by earlier travellers: 'The forest in these solitudes is always full of voices, the soft whisperings of those who came before,' he wrote.

Fawcett's writings describe a string of flirtations with death, and a compulsion to continue ever onward despite serious threats from people, animals and hostile terrain. There is little room for the ordinary in Fawcett's prose: snakes have gleams in their eyes; there are 'bat people'; his river pilot ends up with not one, two or three arrows in him but forty-two. Fawcett's ambitions were not ordinary either; he became more and more intrigued by ancient reports of a ruined civilization in the rainforest.

The First World War forced a break in Fawcett's adventures, but he returned soon afterwards, and continued his research into the tales of a lost city, one of them perhaps founded by survivors of Atlantis who had spread to the farthest-flung corners of the world to re-establish themselves. Much of what he really thought of such fables is speculation, because Fawcett became increasingly secretive. Some said he was really looking for gold or oil; his daughter told me that the lost city idea was all 'a smokescreen', but refused to say what his true objective was. We know he examined a document dated 1753 in the National Library, Rio de Janeiro, purporting to describe an opulent city deep in the Brazilian rainforest: dripping with gold, surrounded by imposing walls and with 'great arches, so high that none could read the inscriptions on them'. Fawcett named this city – or whatever objective he really had – 'Z', and spent his remaining years trying to get there.

In 1925 he embarked on an expedition to 'Z' with his son Jack, and Raleigh Rimell, Jack's friend, and porters. There were no rivers leading along their intended route and the terrain was too dense for pack animals; the porters turned for home. The party carried on alone, carrying everything they felt they needed on their backs. Fawcett had asked that no search party come looking for the expedition, and his last recorded words, on a note given to the porters to hand to his wife, were: 'You need have no fear of any failure.'

This was the last anyone heard of Fawcett or his two companions. His disappearance has led to fifteen investigative expeditions (including one of my own, to record the Indians' perspective), and to more and more speculation. There have been 'sightings' of a bewildered Englishman, a mixed-race child – said to be the result of the expedition living intimately with the Indians (it turned out to be an albino) – and even the actual buried remains of the three men in the Xingu forest. Nothing much has been substantiated, and the cause of his disappearance is still not known.

The Abuna River, 1906–7

'You'd better look out for yourselves on the Abuna!' was the warning everybody seemed to enjoy giving us. 'The fever there will kill you – and if you escape that, there are the Pacaguaras Indians. They come out on the banks and make a boat run the gauntlet of poisoned arrows!'

'A German engineer was attacked there the other day, and three of his men killed,' said someone. Another nodded confirmation ponderously and shook a finger at us.

'Not so long ago forty-eight men went up the Rio Negro – that's an affluent of the Abuna – in search of rubber. Only eighteen came out, and one of them was stark, staring mad from the experience!'

Had we listened to all the grim warnings we should have got nowhere. By this time I was beginning to form my own opinions, and was not prepared to believe all the tales I heard about savages.

It was one of the gloomiest journeys I had made, for the river was threatening in its quiet, and the easy current and deep water seemed to promise evils ahead. The demons of the Amazonian rivers were abroad, manifesting their presence in lowering skies, downpours of torrential rain and sombre forest walls.

Before reaching the confluence of the Rapirran we stopped at the *barraca* of a Tumupasa Indian called Medina, who had made a fortune in rubber. In this filthy place Medina had a daughter who was one of the prettiest blonde Indians I have seen – tall, with delicate features, small hands, and a mass of silky golden hair. Beautiful enough to grace a royal court, an asset to any European ballroom, this superb girl was destined to join the harem of the manager at Santa Rosa and languish as the fifth member of that enterprising Frenchman's seraglio. I took several photographs of her, but together with all those of the Abuna, except a few developed at Santa Rosa, they were destroyed by the constant damp . . .

We were drifting easily along on the sluggish current not far below the confluence of the Rio Negro when almost under the bow of the *igarité* there appeared a triangular head and several feet of undulating body. It was a giant anaconda. I sprang for my rifle as the creature began to make its way up the bank, and hardly waiting to aim smashed a .44 soft-nosed bullet into its spine, ten feet below the wicked head. At once there was a flurry of foam, and several heavy thumps against the boat's keel, shaking us as though we had run on a snag.

With great difficulty I persuaded the Indian crew to turn in shorewards. They were so frightened that the whites showed all round their popping eyes, and in the moment of firing I had heard their terrified voices begging me not to shoot lest the monster destroy the boat and kill everyone on board, for not only do these creatures attack boats when injured, but also there is great danger from their mates.

We stepped ashore and approached the reptile with caution. It was out of action, but shivers ran up and down the body like puffs of wind on a mountain tarn. As far as it was possible to measure, a length of forty-five feet lay out of the water, and seventeen feet in it, making a total length of sixty-two feet. Its body was not thick for such a colossal length – not more than twelve inches in diameter – but it had probably been long without food. I tried to cut a piece of the skin, but the beast was by no means dead and the sudden upheavals rather scared us. A penetrating, foetid odour emanated from the snake, probably its breath, which is believed to have a stupefying effect, first attracting and later paralysing its prey. Everything about this snake is repulsive.

Such large specimens as this may not be common, but the trails in the swamps reach a width of six feet and support the statements of Indians and rubber pickers that the anaconda sometimes reaches an incredible size, altogether dwarfing that shot by me. The Brazilian Boundary Commission told me of one they killed in the Rio Paraguay exceeding *eighty* feet in length! In the Araguaya and Tocantíns basins there is a black variety known as the *Dormidera*, or 'Sleeper', from the loud snoring noise it makes. It is reputed to reach a huge size, but I never saw one. These reptiles live principally in the swamps, for unlike the rivers, which often become mere ditches of mud in the dry season, the swamps always remain. To venture into the haunts of the anaconda is to flirt with death.

'Savages!'

The cry came from Willis, who was on deck watching the approach to Tambaqui Rapid. Dan and I tumbled out of the shelter and looked in the direction the negro was pointing. Several Indians were standing on the bank, their bodies painted all over with the red juice of the *urucu*, a bean common in the forest. Their ears had pendulous lobes, and quills were thrust from side to side through their nostrils, but they wore no feather head-dresses. It was my first sight of these people, whom I took to be Karapunas.

'We'll stop and make friends with them,' I said; but before the order to put into the bank could be given our Indian crew had spotted them. There were cries of alarm and the paddles moved at a frenzied rate.

Shouts came from the savages, and loosing their great bows they shot some arrows in our direction. We couldn't see them coming, but one ripped through the side of the boat with a vicious smack – through wood an inch and a half in thickness, and right through the other side as well! The force behind that arrow amazed me, and without seeing for myself I would never have credited such penetrating power. Why, a rifle could scarcely do more!

It was the custom of these savages to come out two or three hundred strong on the banks, and give any passing boat a hot reception. The middle of the river was within range from either side, so there was no escaping them. I knew an instance on another river of a steamer being attacked in the same way. An arrow transfixed an Englishman through both arms and chest, and pinned him to the deck with such force that it took some time to release him.

The *igarité* slid through the water at so lively a clip that we soon came up to the Tambaqui Rapid and rushed it without mishap, the crew still paddling furiously in their fear of more arrows. It was not a very formidable rapid – by no means as bad as the next one, Fortaleza, which had a ten-foot fall, and of which the noise alone was frightening. The water rushed with a flurry of foam over an outcrop of the same granite that is to be found in the Madeira and all rivers to the east of it between eight and ten degrees South Latitude – the significance of which I came to recognize later, when studying the geology of the ancient continent. The boat had to be portaged past this fall, hauled overland on rollers made from tree trunks – a labour that left us well-nigh exhausted, so short-handed were we.

On the bank lay the half-dried body of a dead anaconda, its hide nearly an inch thick. Possibly when quite dry it may have shrunk to less than that, but even so the fine tough leather would equal in quality that of the tapir.

Four hours below Fortaleza we reached the confluence with the Madeira River, so wide that it seemed like an ocean after the narrow Abuna . . .

At the mouth of the Abuna *charque* and rice were the only foodstuffs. No one bothered to fish or hunt, or even to dress, and sweating in their filthy rags they sang their drunken catches or groaned in the throes of sickness, as the case might be. No medicines were available, and even if any had been, there was no mind clear enough to administer them. The only healthy person was a young German who came in on his way up river, a cheerful and wholesome youth who made no bones about Anglo-German relations. The burning desire of Germany, he said, was for war, in order to damage the commercial prosperity of her rivals and secure colonies.

After eight days in this vile place we managed to obtain passage aboard *batelónes* with freight for Villa Bella, a port at the mouth of the Mamoré and half-way back to Riberalta. As we pushed out into the river there came to us like a dirge of farewell the tinkle of the guitars and drone of voices ...

In the smooth stretches the crew of twenty Indians paddled; but where the water was swift and broken the boat had to be swung round rocks at the end of a long rope. Great skill was needed to avoid the ever-present dangers, and by nightfall the crew were utterly exhausted. The moment they threw themselves down on the hot rocks beside the river they were fast asleep, and in consequence pneumonia was rife amongst them – so much so that sometimes a whole crew would be carried off by it, and the boat forced to await the arrival of a fresh crew before it could go on.

Four of the men in our boat died during the first half of the voyage. Any man who fell ill became the butt of the rest, and when he died there was tremendous hilarity. The staring corpse was tied to a pole, and sparsely covered in a shallow trench scraped out with paddles on the river bank, his monument a couple of crossed twigs tied with grass. For funeral there was a drop of *kachasa* all round, and ho for the next victim!

The river here was over half a mile wide, but full of rocks, and the swift current made navigation difficult. The dangerous little rapids of Araras and Periquitos were passed without difficulty, but the more formidable one of Chocolatal took three days to negotiate. Life here was far from dull. The pilot went out to inspect the road where the *batelónes* would be portaged to by-pass the rapid, and was shot by Indians not half a mile from the boat. We found him with forty-two arrows in his body.

Brian Fawcett, ed., *Exploration Fawcett*, 1953

*Oshogu are large grubs . . . They eat the wood of trees and are believed,
partly by magic . . . to improve wounds, which do or do not contain splinters
of wooden spears.*

Margaret Mead, perhaps the best-known anthropologist of the twentieth century, was born in Philadelphia and studied anthropology at Columbia University, where she was taught by the German–American anthropologist Franz Boas. In 1925 she travelled to Samoa, where her fieldwork became the subject of her book *Coming of Age in Samoa* and established Mead as a household name.

Mead found that Samoans, reared in a totally different family structure from that of the West, do not suffer the adolescent disturbances considered natural in Western societies. Childhood and adolescence, the cultural conditioning of sexual behaviour, and cultural change became some of her specialist areas. She later travelled to New Guinea and Bali to study the lives of adolescent girls. She was a firm believer in the patient, unobtrusive study of people, aiming to assume 'a responsive, listening attitude' towards informants, and always remembering the importance of 'awareness of one's own temperament and character'.

Many of her findings have since been challenged – critics cite weak methodology, her placing too much trust in her informants – but she remains one of the great pioneers of anthropology. Between 1964 and 1969 she was curator of ethnology at the American Museum of Natural History, and she also served on US government commissions, becoming a popular and controversial lecturer on social issues.

The following extracts are from Mead's paper on the culture of the Arapesh people of the Sepik-Aitape district of New Guinea, where she spent eight months in 1931–2. The passages give an idea of an anthropologist's methodology in the field, as Mead tries not to contaminate her informant's words with her own bias. This, incidentally, also gives us a chance to hear a New Guinean voice direct. We learn what the speaker, Unabelin, has to say, judging his meaning just as she did. The footnotes are hers.

A man who was sorcerized

[Unabelin:] There was a man named Sinara of *Suabibis* [gens]. He was sorcerized. He came to our place. He built a platform around a big tree, a *sarabok* tree. He cut it [the tree]. My father heard the sound of the adze. My father called my brother. They took spears. They crept through the bush. They ambushed him from both sides. My father poised his spear in his hand. Before my father called his [gens] brother [Sinara] 'enemy.' He [Sinara] got up. My father wounded him with a big spear. My brother wounded him in the shoulder* with his spear.

---

* This detail is part of the accurate accounting that is kept of the nature, location, and sequence of all wounds in one of these intra-group fracases.

Now he ran away. My father took a club. My brother took a spear. They hid beside the road. They ambushed him. They hit him in the neck. He was a big man. He was a fighter. If he had lived, he would have killed us.† He fell down. He cried out. My father took his club. He [my father] broke his head open. He was dead. My father came up to the village. He kept the killer's watch.‡ He sat up under§ a house. He did not sleep. Had he slept, the ghost [of the dead man] would have gotten him. All¶ those who had killed men came and sat. If he wished to sleep, they wakened him. It was dawn. He went and washed. He came back and sat down. They decorated him with blackII paint. He sat in the plaza.** It was night. He washed. He cut his penis. He lost blood. The ghost left him. This is something which only men know about.†† He sat. It was night [again]. He did not sleep. He washed again. Then he slept. He counted the days, one to five days, complete. On the the sixth day he walked about [freely].

A bad man

[I asked him to describe a bad man:]

A bad man! He it is who when visitors come says: 'Now who is going to feed these people?' He and his wife sit down. Smoke issues from their house. They eat. He eats until his skin is stretched tightly [over his belly]. He wipes the grease from his lips with the back of his hand. He goes and sits down with the visitors and makes empty talk. If he has killed meat, he hides it. If his wife is good and says: 'Let's give a little of this to a friend,' he says: 'No.' If the wife is really good, she will run away from such a man. When friends come when he is not there, she will give to the friends and later conceal it from her husband. If a man is good and his wife is not, he can beat her. If a man is bad and his wife is good, she can run away. If both are no good, they are offal, that is all.

---

† This rounds out the ethical statement which began with 'He was sorcerized.' The reasoning runs: he must have been sorcerized or he would not have come in this insane way, noisily cutting a tree in the neighborhood of someone with whom he was on bad terms. Being sorcerized – and so out of his mind – he was dangerous. Killing him was an act of self-preservation, originally induced by sorcery.
‡ Called literally 'to sit up with the dog,' a purificatory ceremony enjoined on those who have killed.
§ The interior of the dwelling house is protected against contact with those who are in need of purification.
¶ This is the sort of statement that lends itself to the interpretation that the village was filled with ex-murderers, but it can equally well be interpreted as a cliché, especially as in Alitoa there was said to be only one living man who had performed this ceremony.
II The paint used in mourning.
** He had now passed from the period of purification and uncleanness to the period of exhibitionistic display.
†† Refers to the ritual blood letting, a subject not discussed with women. Unabelin used to pay lip service to the sex dichotomy when he referred to any aspect of the males' sacra.

The yams in their garden they themselves eat.‡‡ The sago which they work, they themselves alone boil and eat. The ripe coconuts which they gather, they themselves will scrape and eat. If he receives a pig, he and his wife will eat a whole leg.§§ If he distributes meat at a feast, he will break it into bits like this [indicates cubes about 1¼ inches square]. If a man is good, he gives an arm's length of meat. If he is bad, he gives a piece of skin only.

When he builds a house, if he calls on others to help him, men will not go. They will say: 'When he had yams, he alone ate them. When he killed meat, he alone ate it.' If he is harvesting and needs help, they will say: 'What, is he a good man, that we should help him!' When he works sago, they will say: 'What, should we help him cut that which he will boil and eat himself, he and his wife, only!' To him and his wife, they will say: 'You two can stay there. You can eat and copulate.¶¶ We will not help you.' If he dies, will men go bury him? They will say: 'What, was he a good man! Let the women go and weep, we will not go.' If it is time to make a clearing for a new garden and the women are sorry for himIIII and ask the men to help him, they will say to their women: 'What! did he give you food! He is mere human offal.' For he is a worthless man.

The Mountain Arapesh, v (Anthropological Papers of the American Museum of Natural History, 1949)

‡‡ It is taboo to eat yams one has grown.
§§ As opposed to redividing and redistributing it among kin who did not attend the original distribution.
¶¶ This alleged direct comment on copulation to a married couple is very abusive language.
IIII This expectation of greater softness from women is unusual and more likely to be heard from young men who have not yet full-grown wives and who are still dependent upon their mothers.

COLIN TURNBULL
1924–94

. . . the girls and their attendants cast shy glances at the young men who always drew close to watch and listen. They whispered and laughed among themselves, and when they stood up to dance they often made it very clear with their gestures which boy had taken their fancy.

After taking a degree at Oxford, the British ethnologist Colin Turnbull went to graduate school in India, where he was one of the few Westerners to study with the two Indian gurus Sri Anandamayi Ma and Sri Aurobindo. It was with this mixed educational background of Eastern and Western values that he travelled to the Ituri Forest in the Belgian Congo (now Zaire) to contact the Mbuti pygmies.

Other Europeans had been in contact with the pygmies before, but always through local intermediaries. Turnbull was the first to be fully accepted by them, and spent a total of three years during the early 1950s living with them in the forest. Turnbull believed the Mbuti, whose outlook was directly opposed to the selfishness and aggression that he felt dominated in the West, represented the positive features of humanity. His account of this experience, *The Forest People*, in which the forest plays just as important a role as its inhabitants, became widely admired, and he was made curator of African ethnology at the American Museum of Natural History in New York.

In 1965–6 Turnbull worked in Uganda among the Ik ('eek'), a group of 2,000 hunters who faced starvation and possible extinction. His findings could not have differed more from those he gleaned in the Congo. His book *The Mountain People* portrays a community plunged into turmoil: some characters snatch possessions from the bodies of their dead relatives, while youths steal food from the elderly. Turnbull's proposed solution was as radical as it was controversial in the anthropological world: he suggested saving the Ik by breaking up their society, and relocating its members in isolated groups.

Turnbull's next major project was a study of the ethical and legal issues of the death penalty in America, and he became friends with several death-row inmates. He dedicated the later part of his life to Buddhist studies and in 1992 the Dalai Lama ordained him as a Buddhist monk in India.

Female initiation

The *elima* is concerned with the arrival of a young girl at the age of maturity, her transition from girlhood to the full flowering of womanhood. This coming-of-age is marked more dramatically for girls than with boys by the physical changes that take place. Both pygmies and villagers recognize the significance of the first appearance of menstrual blood, and both celebrate it with a festival which they call '*elima*'. But here the similarity ends.

My ex-girl friend, Amina, told me a great deal about the *elima* among the BaBira, and I learned more from older women in different villages that I lived in from time to time. Everywhere, right through to the very edge of the forest, I found the same story among the villagers. Blood of any kind is a terrible and powerful thing, associated with injury and sickness and death. Menstrual blood is even more terrible because of its mysterious and constant recurrence. Its first appearance is considered, by the villagers, as a calamity – an evil omen. The girl who is defiled by it for the first time is herself in danger, and even more important she has placed the whole family and clan in danger. She is promptly secluded, and only her mother (and I suspect one or two other close and senior female relatives) may see her and care for her. She has to be cleansed and purified, and the clan itself has to be protected by ritual propitiation from the evil she has brought upon them. At the best, the unfortunate girl is considered as a considerable nuisance and expense.

It is generally assumed that the girl was brought into this condition by some kind of illicit intercourse, and her mother demands of her who is responsible. This is the girl's chance to name the boy of her choice, whether or not she has even so much as spoken to him. He is then accused, and has to make suitable offerings which are not only necessary to help in the protection of the girl and her family, but also for his protection, since he had been linked with her verbally, however untruthfully. He may then deny the charge, and there may be some litigation if the girl's parents think he would make a suitable husband. Or else they may consider him unsuitable, and let the matter drop. If he likes the girl, and accepts the responsibility, this constitutes the first step towards official betrothal. If he disclaims all responsibility, then the girl has to try again, as until she has a husband the danger is thought to remain.

The period of seclusion varies from tribe to tribe, and even from village to village. Sometimes it is just for a week or two, sometimes it lasts a month or more. And sometimes it lasts until the girl is betrothed and can be led from her room of shame to be taken away by her husband. At the final wedding ritual she is ceremonially cut off from her family, and told that she is now her husband's responsibility and must fend for herself and not come running home every time she gets beaten. The point being, of course, that if she does this then her husband can claim back the wealth he will have already paid over in the expectancy of her fidelity and success as a wife and bearer of children. And by the time the disaster occurs her family will almost certainly have spent the money to obtain a bride for one of her brothers.

The whole affair is a rather shameful one, in the eyes of the villagers, as well as a dangerous one. It is something best concealed and not talked about in public. The girl is an object of suspicion, scorn, repulsion and anger. It is not a happy coming-of-age.

For the pygmies, the people of the forest, it is a very different thing.

To them blood is, in the usual context in which they see it, equally dreadful. But they recognize it not only as being the symbol of death, but also of life. And menstrual blood to them means life. Even between a husband and wife it is not a frightening thing, though there are certain restrictions connected with it. In fact they consider that any couple that really wants to have children should 'sleep with the moon'.

So when a young pygmy girl begins to flower into maturity, and blood comes to her for the first time, it comes to her as a gift, received with gratitude and rejoicing; rejoicing that the girl is now a potential mother, that she can now proudly and rightfully take a husband. There is not a word of fear or superstition, and everyone is told the good news.

The girl enters seclusion, but not the seclusion of the village girl. She takes with her all her young friends, those who have not yet reached maturity, and some older ones.

In the house of the *elima* the girls celebrate the happy event together. Together they are taught the arts and crafts of motherhood by an old and respected relative. They learn not only how to live like adults, but how to sing the songs of adult women. Day after day, night after night, the *elima* house resounds with the throaty contralto of the older women and the high, piping voices of the youngest. It is a time of gladness and happiness, not for the women alone but for the whole people. Pygmies from all around come to pay their respects, the young men standing or sitting about outside the *elima* house in the hopes of a glimpse of the young beauties inside. And there are special *elima* songs which they sing to each other, the girls singing a light, cascading melody in intricate harmony, the men replying with a rich, vital chorus. For the pygmies the *elima* is one of the happiest, most joyful occasions in their lives.

Coming out of the forest for the first time

As we got to the top of the first incline, there was a flat stretch and then a steep rise. Half-way up this the car sank down into the mud and would not move. Henri and Kenge got out and started pushing, and after half an hour of hard work we reached the top. Once the wheels began gripping I did not stop but kept going until I was at the very crest. There I stopped the engine and waited for the other two who came running up the hill after me, joking and shouting, covered from head to foot with smelly black slime.

When Kenge topped the rise, he stopped dead. Every smallest sign of mirth suddenly left his face. He opened his mouth, but could say nothing. He moved his head and eyes slowly and unbelievingly. Down below us, on the far side of the hill stretched mile after mile of rolling grasslands, a lush, fresh green, with an occasional shrub or tree standing out like a sentinel into a sky that had suddenly become brilliantly clear. And beyond the grasslands was Lake Edward – a huge expanse of water disappearing into the distance – a river without banks, without end. It was like nothing Kenge had ever seen before. The largest stretch of water he had ever seen was when we had stood, like Stanley, and marvelled at the confluence of the Lenda and the Ituri. On the plains, animals were grazing everywhere; a small herd of elephant to the left, about twenty antelopes stared curiously at us from straight ahead, and way down to the right was a gigantic herd of about a hundred and fifty buffalo. But Kenge did not seem to see them.

As he turned around to look behind, I turned with him, and even I was overcome with the beauty of what we saw. It was one of those rarest of moments that come perhaps once or twice a year, and may last for only a few seconds, when a violent storm clears the air completely and the whole mighty range of the Ruwenzori mountains is exposed in a wild and glorious harmony, of rock and snow. The lower slopes shone green with the dense forest; the upper slopes rose in steep, jagged cliffs, and above them the great snow-capped peaks rose proudly into the clearest possible sky. There was not a cloud to match the pure whiteness of the snow. Kenge could not believe they were the same mountains that we had seen from the forest – there they had seemed just like large hills to him. I tried to explain to him what the snow was – he thought it was some kind of white rock. Henri said that it was water that turned that colour when it was high up, but Kenge wanted to know why it didn't run down the mountain-side like any other water. When Henri told him it also turned solid at that height Kenge just gave him a long, steady look and said, '*Bongo yako!*' – 'You liar!'

With typical pygmy philosophy, even though he could not understand it he accepted it, and turned his back on the mountains to look more closely at what lay all around him. He picked up a handful of grass, tasted it and smelled it. He said that it was bad grass and that the mud was bad mud. He sniffed at the air and said it was bad air. In fact, as he had stated at the outset, it was altogether a very bad country. The guide pointed out the elephants, hoping to make him feel more at home. But Kenge was not impressed – he asked what good they were if we were not allowed to go and hunt them. Henri pointed out the antelopes, which had moved closer and were staring at us as curiously as ever. Kenge clapped his hands together and said that they would give food for months and months. And then he saw the buffalo, still grazing lazily several miles away, far down below. He turned to me and said, 'What insects are those?'

At first I hardly understood, then I realized that in the forest vision is so limited that there is no great need to make an automatic allowance for distance when judging size. Out here in the plains, Kenge was looking for the first time over apparently unending miles of unfamiliar grasslands, with not a tree worth the name to give him any basis for comparison. The same thing happened later on when I pointed out a boat, in the middle of the lake. It was a large fishing boat with a number of people in it. Kenge at first refused to believe it. He thought it was a floating piece of wood.

When I told Kenge that the insects were buffalo, he roared with laughter and told me not to tell such stupid lies. When Henri, who was thoroughly puzzled, told him the same thing, and explained that visitors to the park had to have a guide with them at all times because there were so many dangerous animals, Kenge still didn't believe, but he strained his eyes to see more clearly and asked what kind of buffalo they were that they were so small. I told him they were sometimes nearly twice the size of a forest buffalo, and he shrugged his shoulders and said he would not be standing out there in the open if they were. I tried telling him they were possibly as far away as from Epulu to the village of Kopu, beyond Eboyo. He began scraping the mud off his arms and legs, no longer interested in such fantasies.

The road led on down to within about half a mile of where the herd was grazing, and as we got closer, the insects must have seemed to get bigger and bigger. Kenge, who was now sitting on the outside, kept his face glued to the window, which nothing would make him lower. I even had to raise mine to keep him happy. I was never able to discover just what he thought was happening, whether he thought the insects were changing into buffalo, or whether they were miniature buffalo growing rapidly as we approached; his only comment was that they were not real buffalo, and he was not going to get out of the car again until we left the park.

The Forest People, 1961

ELISABETH ELLIOT
1926–

*A converted Indian, formerly a notorious drinker, came to me one day
and said, '. . . How will they hear of Jesus?'*

Elisabeth Elliot was born in Brussels, where her American parents were working as missionaries. After studying Greek in Chicago she travelled to Ecuador as a missionary, and in 1958 married a former classmate, Jim Elliot, with whom she worked on translating the New Testament into the language of the Quichua Indians.

Their conversion of a local Quichua group was largely successful; a remoter people of the lowland forests of Ecuador were the next objective – 'the great challenge of the dread Aucas'. The Aucas had a formidable reputation, especially with the Shell Oil Company, which was prospecting on their land in the 1940s. Many workmen lost their lives, victims of 'hostile Indians', as an executive put it. Jim Elliot was undaunted. He felt sure that God had brought him to South America with the purpose of using him to bring the Gospel to the Aucas; 'expendable for God', he gratefully accepted this task. Around this period, Dayuma, an Auca teenager who had escaped from a bloody family feud, turned up among the Quichuas; and with her, of course, came all the key words and phrases that the missionaries might need to make contact with her people. 'Operation Auca' began.

Communication was initially established through the acrobatic manoeuvrings of the aircraft of the Missionary Aviation Fellowship, an organization that supports evangelicals ministering to the 'unreached' in jungles and deserts across the globe. They air-dropped presents such as knives, axes and even kettles over three months. Finally, having familiarized the Aucas with their little Piper Cruiser by dropping a model of it in their midst, five missionaries, including Jim Elliot, entrusted their lives to God – 'we go not forth alone' – and landed on the forested bank of the Curaray river. There, they effected a rendezvous with a small band of individuals, including one they nicknamed 'George' whom they had seen from the air. Quite quickly it all went wrong. Their radio transmissions ceased, and when a pilot flew over the forest to investigate, he saw that Jim Elliot's plane had been deliberately smashed up; a body was lying face down in the water. When the rescue party arrived, the worst fears of Elisabeth Elliot and the other missionary wives, were confirmed. The five evangelists, including Jim Elliot, had been 'martyred'.

Elisabeth Elliot, who had waited five and a half years to marry Jim, and been married to him for only two, remained in Ecuador with her ten-month-old baby; she evangelized among the Quichuas and eventually the Aucas. On her return to America she married again, but her second husband died of cancer in 1973, and she has since remarried. Traditional family values are central to her beliefs: 'when women go home they must be submissive to their husbands'. She has expounded her values as a broadcaster, as a speaker and in over twenty books.

She is philosophical about the losses she has suffered in her life. 'Whatever the problems or hurts, each one of them has been covered by the blood of Jesus and there is nothing we can or need do.'

The missionaries make contact

Three Aucas stepped out into the open. They were a young man and two women – one about thirty years of age, the other a girl of about sixteen – naked except for strings tied about the waist, wrists, and thighs, and large wooden plugs in distended ear-lobes. The missionaries, temporarily struck dumb by the surprise appearance, finally managed to shout simultaneously, in Auca: 'Puinani! . . . Welcome!'

The Auca man replied with a verbal flood, pointing frequently to the girl. His language was unintelligible, but his gestures were plain. 'He's offering her for trade,' exclaimed Pete, 'or maybe as a gift.'

When it seemed that the Aucas wanted someone to come across, Jim peeled to his shorts and began wading over to them. The others cautioned him to go slow. Jim hesitated and the Aucas were slightly hesitant, but as Jim gradually approached, the girl edged towards the water and stepped off a log. The man and the other woman followed shortly. Jim seized their hands and led them across.

With broad smiles, many 'puinanis' and much reference to their phrase-books, the five conveyed the idea that their visitors had 'come well' and need not be afraid. The Aucas' uneasiness fell from them, and they began jabbering happily to themselves and to the men, 'seemingly with little idea that we didn't understand them'.

Roj brought out some paring knives, which they accepted with cries of delight. Nate presented them with a machete and model airplane. The others, suddenly remembering the guns in the cook-shack and tree-house, went back to hide the weapons beneath their duffel. They dug out cameras and shot dozens of photos, while the women looked through a copy of Time magazine, and the man was being doused with insecticide to demonstrate civilisation's way of dealing with the swarming pests. The group spontaneously began referring to him as 'George'.

Presently the girl – the men called her 'Delilah' – drifted over towards the Piper, rubbing her body against the fabric, and imitating with her hands the plane's movement. She seemed 'dreamy', wrote Pete, 'while the man was natural and self-possessed, completely unafraid. They showed neither fear nor comprehension of the cameras.'

Pete continued: 'Soon the fellow began to show interest in the plane and we guessed from his talk that he was willing to fly over the village to call his comrades. We put a shirt on him (it's cold up high), and he climbed into the plane with no sign of any emotion except eagerness to do his part. He acted out how he was going to call and repeated the words. Nate taxied down the strip and took off while 'George' shouted all the way. After circling and shouting briefly Nate landed again, thinking to give the fellow a rest before making the flight to his village. Nothing doing! He was ready to go right then.'

Up they went again, this time to circle Terminal City. What must have been the thoughts of that primitive man as he peered down at the tree-tops and at the green sea below him, and suddenly recognised a familiar clearing, with familiar figures in it? 'George' chortled with delight, and leaned out to wave and yell at his fellow villagers. 'The woman at the Old Man's house,' wrote Nate, '– her jaw dropped on seeing "George" . . . expression of delight on the face of the young man on the platform.'

Back on the sand strip, 'George' leaped out, clapping his hands. The five men immediately gave thanks to God, with heads up to try to show their visitors that they were addressing their Heavenly Father. As Ezekiel said, 'The Word was in my bones as a living fire,' and for these men the drive to deliver to the Aucas the message of redemption through the blood of Jesus was blocked only by the language barrier. If only they might suddenly leap over the barrier and convey to the Indians one hint of the love of God!

The missionaries demonstrated for their guests such modern marvels as rubber bands, balloons, and a yo-yo; served them lemonade and hamburgers with mustard, which they evidently enjoyed. Then they tried to get across the idea that an invitation to visit the Auca village would not be scorned. For this notion 'George' displayed no enthusiasm.

'Why is it he's so reluctant whenever we broach the subject?' one of the five demanded.

Another replied: 'Maybe he lacks the authority to invite us on his own.'

'At 4.15,' Nate wrote, 'we decide to fly again. "George" decides to go along. We say "no". He puts his machete and envelope of valuables in the plane and looks at Pete as though he had already said it was okay and climbs in. On the way over we finally get Marj on the radio. Great rejoicing.

'Back on Palm Beach we held a strategy meeting; talked of going over to Auca houses if a delegation of, say, six Aucas arrive and seem happy to escort us. After that, every effort would be bent towards building an airstrip in their valley. The fellows tried to explain to "George" how an airstrip should be cleared in his village.'

At first he did not understand their word for trees. When he finally got it, he corrected their pronunciation. They stuck sticks in the sand to represent trees; then, with one of the model planes, Nate showed 'George' how the airplane would crash and tumble among the trees. With the model lying on its back among the sticks in the sand, the fellows all shook their heads and moaned in evident distress. The scene was then re-enacted, only this time the fellows took machetes and cut down all the trees (sticks) and smoothed the sand carefully. The model airplane approached for a smooth landing, accompanied by great rejoicing.

As the day wore on, 'Delilah' showed signs of impatience. Once when Jim Elliot left the group to climb up to the tree house, she leaped up and followed. When he then turned and rejoined the others, she seemed downcast.

Later, as Nate and Pete got ready to return to Arajuno, 'George' seemed to understand that he could not accompany them. Before the airplane took off the fellows carefully gathered all of the exposed film and everything that had been written to fly it out for safe keeping. If something unforeseen should happen, they did not want the record lost.

After the martyrdom

Thousands of people in all parts of the world pray every day that 'the light of the knowledge of the glory of God' may be carried to the Aucas, a people almost totally unheard of before. How can this be done? God, who led the five, will lead others, in His time and way.

From among the Quichuas with whom Jim, Ed, and Pete worked, several have surrendered their lives to God for His use, to preach to their own people – or even to the Aucas, if He chooses. They have carried on the work begun by the missionaries, speaking to their relatives of Christ, reading the Scriptures that have been translated for them, travelling sometimes in canoes and over muddy trails to teach the Bible to others who do not know its message. A converted Indian, formerly a notorious drinker, came to me one day and said, 'Señora, I lie awake at night thinking of my people. "How will I reach them?" I say. "How will they hear of Jesus?" I cannot get to them all. But they *must know*. I pray to God, asking Him to show me what to do.' In the little prayer meetings the Indians never forget to ask God to bless their enemies: 'O God, You know how those Aucas killed our beloved Señor Eduardo, Señor Jaime, and Señor Pedro. O God, You know that it was only because they didn't know You. They didn't know what a great sin it was. They didn't understand why the white men had come. Send some more messengers, and give the Aucas, instead of fierce hearts, soft hearts. Stick their hearts, Lord, as with a lance. They stuck our friends, but You can stick them with Your Word, so that they will listen, and believe.'

Through Gates of Splendour: The Martyrdom of Five Missionaries in the Ecuador Jungle, 1957

JANE GOODALL
1934–

The soft pressure of his fingers spoke to me not through my intellect but through a more primitive emotional channel: the barrier of untold centuries which has grown up during the separate evolution of man and chimpanzee was, for those few seconds, broken down.

Jane Goodall, a British primatologist dedicated to the study and conservation of chimpanzees, left school at eighteen, then worked as a secretary and film production assistant. On a trip to Kenya in 1957 she met the anthropologist and palaeontologist Dr Louis Leakey, who was struck by her obvious devotion to animals and her patient determination to find out more about them. Leakey had already felt that an understanding of chimpanzee behaviour would teach us more about human evolutionary history, and saw that a mind such as Goodall's, which had not been cluttered by scholarship, might bring a breath of fresh air to this work. His contemporaries were inclined to disagree and thought Goodall wouldn't last three weeks; she soon dispelled their doubts.

Having spent some time working with Leakey, in 1960 Goodall went to the Gombe National Park, now in Tanzania, where, in the dense forests by Lake Tanganyika, she documented chimpanzee behaviour in more detail than had been done before. One of her major discoveries was that chimps made and used tools – for example fishing termites from their nests with straws. This ability had been considered one of the distinguishing features of humans. She also found that chimpanzees were omnivorous, not vegetarian, as previously thought.

In 1964 Goodall married the Dutch photographer Hugo van Lawick (they later divorced), and the following year Cambridge University awarded her a PhD in ethnology; she was one of the few candidates ever to have received a doctorate without first taking an undergraduate degree. On her return to Tanzania she set up the Gombe Stream Research Centre – still important today as a base for the study of chimpanzees – and she and her family stayed in Gombe until 1975. Goodall has written various books and articles on her studies, notably *In The Shadow of Man*.

In 1977 she founded the Jane Goodall Institute for Wildlife Research, in Maryland, an organization that promotes primate habitat conservation and environmental awareness. She has received numerous accolades, including a CBE and the National Geographic Society's Hubbard Medal.

'David Greybeard' uses a tool

I had had a frustrating morning tramping up and down three valleys with never a sign or sound of a chimpanzee. Hauling myself up the steep slope of Mlinda Valley, I headed for the Peak, not only weary but soaking wet from crawling through dense undergrowth. Suddenly I stopped, for I saw a slight movement in the long grass about sixty yards away. Quickly focusing my binoculars, I saw that it was a single chimpanzee – just then he turned in my direction, and I recognized David Greybeard.

Cautiously I moved round so that I could see what he was doing. He was squatting by the red earth mound of a termite nest, and, as I watched, I saw him carefully push a long grass stem down into a hole in the mound. After a moment he withdrew it and picked something from the end with his mouth. I was too far away to make out what he was eating, but it was obvious that he was actually using a grass stem as a tool.

I knew that on two occasions casual observers in West Africa had seen chimpanzees using objects as tools: one had broken open palm nut kernels by using a rock as a hammer, while a group of chimps had been observed pushing sticks into an underground bees' nest and licking off the honey. But somehow I had never dreamed of seeing anything so exciting myself.

For an hour David feasted at the termite mound and then he wandered slowly away. When I was sure he had gone I went over to examine the mound. I found a few crushed insects strewn about, and a swarm of worker termites sealing the entrances of the nest passages into which David had, obviously, been poking his stems. I picked up one of his discarded tools and carefully pushed it into a hole myself. Immediately I felt the pull of several termites as they seized the grass, and when I pulled it out there was a number of worker termites and a few soldiers, with big red heads, clinging on with their mandibles. There they remained, sticking out at right angles to the stem, with their legs waving in the air.

Before I left I trampled down some of the tall dry grass and constructed a rough hide – just a few palm fronds leant up against the low branch of a tree and tied together at the top. I planned to wait there the next day. But it was another week before I was able to watch a chimpanzee 'fishing' for termites again. Twice chimps arrived, but each time they saw me and moved off immediately. Once a swarm of fertile winged termites – the princes and princesses as they are called – flew off on their nuptial flight, their huge white wings fluttering frantically as they carried the insects higher and higher. Later I realized that it is at this time of year, during the short rains, that the worker termites extend the passages of the nest to the surface, ready for these emigrations. Several such swarms emerge between October and January. It is principally at this time of year that the chimpanzees feed on termites.

On the eighth day of my vigil David Greybeard arrived again, together with Goliath, and the pair worked there for two hours. I could see much better: I observed how they scratched open the sealed-over passage entrances with a thumb or forefinger. I watched how they bit the ends off their tools when they became bent, or used the other end, or discarded them in favour of new ones. Goliath once moved at least fifteen yards from the heap to select a firm-looking piece of vine, and both males often picked three or four stems, whilst they were collecting tools, and put the spares beside them on the ground until they wanted them.

Most exciting of all, on several occasions they picked little leafy twigs and prepared them for use by stripping off the leaves. This was the first recorded example of a wild animal not merely *using* an object as a tool, but actually modifying an object and thus showing the crude beginnings of tool-*making*.

Previously man had been regarded as the only tool-making animal – indeed, one of the clauses commonly accepted in the actual definition of man was that he was a creature who 'made tools to a regular and set pattern'. The chimpanzees, of course, had not made tools to any set pattern: nevertheless, my early observations of their primitive tool-making abilities convinced a number of scientists that it was necessary to redefine man in a more complex manner than before. Or else, as Louis Leakey put it, we should, by definition, have to accept the chimpanzee as Man!

Our closest relative kills

As I watched I saw that one of them was holding a pink-looking object from which he was, from time to time, pulling pieces with his teeth. There was a female and a youngster and they were both reaching out towards the male, their hands actually touching his mouth. Presently the female picked up a piece of the pink thing and put it to her mouth: it was at this moment that I realized the chimps were eating meat.

After each bite of meat the male picked off some leaves with his lips and chewed them with the flesh. Often, when he had chewed for several minutes on this leafy wadge, he spat out the remains into the waiting hands of the female. Suddenly he dropped a small piece of meat and, like a flash, the youngster swung after it to the ground. But even as he reached to pick it up, the undergrowth exploded and an adult bushpig charged towards him. Screaming, the juvenile leapt back into the tree. The pig remained in the open, snorting and moving backwards and forwards. Presently I made out the shapes of three small striped piglets. Obviously the chimps were eating a baby pig. The size was right, and later, when I realized that the male was David Greybeard, I moved closer and saw that he was indeed eating piglet.

For three hours I watched the chimps feeding. David occasionally let the female bite pieces from the carcass, and once he actually detached a small piece of flesh and placed it in her outstretched hand. When he finally climbed down there was still meat left on the carcass; he carried it away in one hand, followed by the others . . .

Previously scientists had believed that, whilst these apes might occasionally supplement their diet with a few insects or small rodents and the like, they were primarily vegetarians and fruit eaters. No one had suspected that they might hunt larger mammals.

How the chimpanzee broke down barriers

For me, of course, the saddest loss was when David Greybeard died. For David was the first chimpanzee to accept my presence and permit me to approach him closely. Not only did he provide me with my early observations of meat-eating and tool-using and thus help to ensure further funds were available for my work, but he was the first to visit my camp, to take a banana from my hand, to permit a human hand to touch him . . .

But I do not regret my early contact with David Greybeard; David, with his gentle disposition, who permitted a strange white ape to touch him. To me it represented a triumph of the sort of relationship which man can establish with a wild creature. Indeed, when I was with David I sometimes felt that our relationship came closer to friendship than I would have thought possible with a completely free wild creature, a creature who had never known captivity . . .

One day, as I sat near him at the bank of a tiny trickle of crystal-clear water, I saw a ripe red palm nut lying on the ground. I picked it up and held it out to him on my open palm. He turned his head away. But when I moved my hand a little closer he looked at it, and then at me, and then he took the fruit and, at the same time, he held my hand firmly and gently with his own. As I sat, motionless, he released my hand, looked down at the nut, and dropped it to the ground.

At that moment there was no need of any scientific knowledge to understand his communication of reassurance. The soft pressure of his fingers spoke to me not through my intellect but through a more primitive emotional channel: the barrier of untold centuries which has grown up during the separate evolution of man and chimpanzee was, for those few seconds, broken down.

It was a reward far beyond my greatest hopes.

In the Shadow of Man, 1971

NAPOLEON A. CHAGNON
1938–

For the most part, my own 'fierceness' took the form of shouting back at the Yąnomamö as loudly and as passionately as they shouted at me . . .

The American anthropologist Chagnon's first encounter with the Yąnomamö of the Amazon was in 1964, as part of a study for the Human Genetics Department at the University of Michigan. He had chosen the Yąnomamö because they were one of the few large Indian groups that had little contact with the outside world. The 27,000 Yąnomamö were spread over an area the size of Texas that overlapped Venezuela and Brazil; Chagnon reasoned that if either country had a messy revolution, he would be able to study in the other.

Over the next three decades he made over twenty-five field trips, often living with the Yąnomamö for long periods and chronicling their life in scientific journals, in documentary films, and in his book *Yąnomamö: The Fierce People*. The good-natured mischief (as he put it) which was a feature of their early treatment of him developed into a warm and more intimate relationship.

One of his motives was to record the Yąnomamö for posterity: 'I found it sobering to realise that the twentieth century would witness the end – the extinction – of particular varieties of culture that had endured for thousands of years, that tribal culture was an endangered and vanishing social species, and that I had some sort of professional and personal responsibility to record and document what I could before it was altered or destroyed by our culture.'

Ironically, he has been accused himself of contributing to the Yąnomamö's demise, having portrayed them, it's been argued, as fiercer than they are. Yąnomamö territory was invaded during a Brazilian gold rush, and tribal and human rights organizations such as Survival International maintained that the depiction of the Yąnomamö as bloodthirsty helped swing public opinion in favour of the gold prospectors. During the 1980s an estimated 20 per cent of the Brazilian Yąnomamö population died from diseases introduced by miners. Loggers and others also invaded their lands, and neither government did much to protect them.

Chagnon defended his assertion that aggression was a central feature of Yąnomamö culture: they 'live in a state of chronic warfare', he wrote. As for the subtitle of his book, the words 'fierce people' were appropriate, he said, because 'that is the most accurate single phrase that describes them. That is how they conceive themselves to be, and that is how they would like others to think of them.' This description has been upheld by the sociologist John Peters, who spent ten years living with them. Chagnon explains that, according to one of the Yąnomamö myths, 'it is in the nature of man to fight . . . because the blood of "Moon" spilled on this layer of the cosmos, causing men to become fierce.' In an article published in *Science* in 1988 he claimed that 25 per cent of adult male deaths within the tribe resulted from violence.

Arriving in Bisaasi-teri village

The excitement of meeting my first Indians was almost unbearable as I duck-waddled through the low passage into the village clearing.

I looked up and gasped when I saw a dozen burly, naked, filthy, hideous men staring at us down the shafts of their drawn arrows! Immense wads of green tobacco were stuck between their lower teeth and lips making them look even more hideous, and strands of dark-green slime dripped or hung from their noses. We arrived at the village while the men were blowing a hallucinogenic drug up their noses. One of the side effects of the drug is a runny nose. The mucus is always saturated with the green powder and the Indians usually let it run freely from their nostrils. My next discovery was that there were a dozen or so vicious, underfed dogs snapping at my legs, circling me as if I were going to be their next meal. I just stood there holding my notebook, helpless and pathetic. Then the stench of the decaying vegetation and filth struck me and I almost got sick. I was horrified. What sort of a welcome was this for the person who came here to live with you and learn your way of life, to become friends with you? They put their weapons down when they recognized Barker and returned to their chanting, keeping a nervous eye on the village entrances.

We had arrived just after a serious fight. Seven women had been abducted the day before by a neighboring group, and the local men and their guests had just that morning recovered five of them in a brutal club fight that nearly ended in a shooting war. The abductors, angry because they lost five of the seven captives, vowed to raid the Bisaasi-teri. When we arrived and entered the village unexpectedly, the Indians feared that we were the raiders. On several occasions during the next two hours the men in the village jumped to their feet, armed themselves, and waited nervously for the noise outside the village to be identified. My enthusiasm for collecting ethnographic-curiosities diminished in proportion to the number of times such an alarm was raised. In fact, I was relieved when Mr Barker suggested that we sleep across the river for the evening. It would be safer over there.

[*Having settled in.*] The thing that bothered me most was the incessant, passioned, and aggressive demands the Indians made. It would become so unbearable that I would have to lock myself in my mud hut every once in a while just to escape from it: Privacy is one of Western culture's greatest achievements. But I did not want privacy for its own sake; rather, I simply had to get away from the begging. Day and night for the entire time I lived with the Yąnomamö I was plagued by such demands as: 'Give me a knife, I am poor!'; 'If you don't take me with you on your next trip to Widokaiya-teri I'll chop a hole in your canoe!'; 'Don't point your camera at me or I'll hit you!'; 'Share your food with me!'; 'Take me across the river in your canoe and be quick about it!'; 'Give me a cooking pot!'; 'Loan me your flashlight so I can go hunting tonight!'; 'Give me medicine . . . I itch all over!'; 'Take us on a week-long hunting trip with your shotgun!'; and 'Give me an axe or I'll break into your hut when you are away visiting and steal one!' And so I was bombarded by such demands day after day, months on end, until I could not bear to see an Indian.

It was not as difficult to become calloused to the incessant begging as it was to ignore the sense of urgency, the impassioned tone of voice, or the intimidation and aggression with which the demands were made. It was likewise difficult to adjust to the fact that the Yąnomamö refused to accept 'no' for an answer until or unless it seethed with passion and intimidation – which it did after six months. Giving in to a demand always established a new threshold; the next demand would be for a bigger item or favor, and the anger of the Indians even greater if the demand was not met. I soon learned that I had to become very much like the Yąnomamö to be able to get along with them on their terms: sly, aggressive, and intimidating.

Had I failed to adjust in this fashion I would have lost six months of supplies to them in a single day or would have spent most of my time ferrying them around in my canoe or hunting for them. As it was, I did spend a considerable amount of time doing these things and did succumb to their outrageous demands for axes and machetes, at least at first. More importantly, had I failed to demonstrate that I could not be pushed around beyond a certain point, I would have been the subject of far more ridicule, theft, and practical jokes than was the actual case. In short, I had to acquire a certain proficiency in their kind of interpersonal politics and to learn how to imply subtly that certain potentially undesirable consequences might follow if they did such and such to me. They do this to each other in order to establish precisely the point at which they cannot goad an individual any further with-out precipitating retaliation. As soon as I caught on to this and realized that much of their aggression was stimulated by their desire to discover my flash point, I got along much better with them and regained some lost ground. It was sort of like a political game that everyone played, but one in which each individual sooner or later had to display some sign that his bluffs and implied threats could be backed up. I suspect that the frequency of wife beating is a component of this syndrome, since men can display their ferocity and show others that they are capable of violence. Beating a wife with a club is considered to be an acceptable way of displaying ferocity and one that does not expose the male to much danger. The important thing is that the man has displayed his potential for violence and the implication is that other men better treat him with respect and caution . . .

For the most part, my own 'fierceness' took the form of shouting back at the Yąnomamö as loudly and as passionately as they shouted at me, especially at first, when I did not know much of their language. As I became more proficient in their language and learned more about their political tactics, I became more sophisticated in the art of bluffing. For example, I paid one young man a machete to cut palm trees and make boards from the wood. I used these to fashion a platform in the bottom of my dugout canoe to keep my possessions dry when I traveled by river. That afternoon I was doing informant work in the village; the long-awaited mission supply boat arrived, and most of the Indians ran out of the village to beg goods from the crew. I continued to work in the village for another hour or so and went down to the river to say 'hello' to the men on the supply boat. I was angry when I discovered that the Indians had chopped up all my palm boards and used them to paddle their own canoes across the river. I knew that if I overlooked this incident I would have invited them to take even greater liberties with my goods in the future. I crossed the river, docked amidst their dugouts, and shouted for the Indians to come out and see me. A few of the culprits appeared, mischievous grins on their faces. I gave a spirited lecture about how hard I had worked to put those boards in my canoe, how I had paid a machete for the wood, and how angry I was that they destroyed my work in their haste to cross the river. I then pulled out my hunting knife and, while their grins disappeared, cut each of their canoes loose, set it into the current, and let it float away. I left without further ado and without looking back.

They managed to borrow another canoe and, after some effort, recovered their dugouts. The headman of the village later told me with an approving chuckle that I had done the correct thing. Everyone in the village, except, of course, the culprits, supported and defended my action. This raised my status.

Whenever I took such action and defended my rights, I got along much better with the Yąnomamö. A good deal of their behavior toward me was directed with the forethought of establishing the point at which I would react defensively. Many of them later reminisced about the early days of my work when I was 'timid' and a little afraid of them, and they could bully me into giving goods away.

Theft was the most persistent situation that required me to take some sort of defensive action. I simply could not keep everything I owned locked in trunks, and the Indians came into my hut and left at will. I developed a very effective means for recovering almost all the stolen items. I would simply ask a child who took the item and then take that person's hammock when he was not around, giving a spirited lecture to the others as I marched away in a faked rage with the thief's hammock. Nobody ever attempted to stop me from doing this, and almost all of them told me that my technique for recovering my possessions was admirable. By nightfall the thief would either appear with the stolen object or send it along with someone else to make an exchange. The others would heckle him for getting caught and being forced to return the item.

A chest-pounding duel

The Boreta-teri and Mahekodo-teri [different Yąnomamö groups] had returned to accept the chest-pounding challenge and entered the village, each man brandishing his axe, club, or bow and arrows. They circled the village once, feinting attack on particular men among the hosts, then grouped at the center of the village clearing. The hosts surrounded them excitedly, dancing with their weapons poised to strike, then entering into the mass of bodies. Heated arguments about food theft and gluttony developed, and the hosts and guests threateningly waved their weapons in each other's faces. Within minutes the large group had bifurcated and the chest-pounding began. The Karohi-teri aided Kąobawä and his followers, whose joint numbers were even further swelled when the Lower Bisaasi-teri rushed to the village after hearing the commotion. There were about sixty adult men on each side in the fight, divided into two arenas, each comprised of hosts and guests. Two men, one from each side, would step into the center of the milling, belligerent crowd of weapon-wielding partisans, urged on by their comrades. One would step up, spread his legs apart, bare his chest, and hold his arms behind his back, daring the other to hit him. The opponent would size him up, adjust the man's chest or arms so as to give himself the greatest advantage when he struck, and then step back to deliver his close-fisted blow. The striker would painstakingly adjust his own distance from his victim by measuring his arm length to the man's chest, taking several dry runs before delivering his blow. He would then wind up like a baseball pitcher, but keeping both feet on the ground, and deliver a tremendous wallop with his fist to the man's left pectoral muscle, putting all of his weight into the blow. The victim's knees would often buckle and he would stagger around a few moments, shaking his head to clear the stars, but remain silent. The blow invariably raised a 'frog' on the recipient's pectoral muscle where the striker's knuckles bit into his flesh. After each blow, the comrades of the deliverer would cheer and bounce up and down from the knees, waving and clacking their weapons over their heads. The victim's supporters, meanwhile, would urge their champion on frantically, insisting that he take another blow. If the delivery were made with sufficient force to knock the recipient to the ground, the man who delivered it would throw his arms above his head, roll his eyes back, and prance victoriously in a circle around his victim, growling and screaming, his feet almost a blur from his excited dance. The recipient would stand poised and take as many as four blows before demanding to hit his adversary. He would be permitted to strike his opponent as many times as the latter struck him, provided that the opponent could take it. If not, he would be forced to retire, much to the dismay of his comrades and the delirious joy of their opponents. No fighter could retire after delivering a blow. If he attempted to do so, his adversary would plunge into the crowd and roughly haul him back out, sometimes being aided by the man's own supporters. Only after having received his just dues could he retire. If he had delivered three blows, he had to receive three or else be proven a poor fighter. He could retire with less than three only if he were injured. Then, one of his comrades would replace him and demand to hit the victorious opponent. The injured man's two remaining blows would be canceled, and the man who delivered the victorious blow would have to receive more blows than he delivered. Thus, good fighters are at a disadvantage, since they receive disproportionately more punishment than they deliver. Their only reward is status: they earn the reputation of being fierce.

Yąnomamö: The Fierce People, 1977

PART VI

Mountains

*

*Even then, in 1953, I had the feeling that nothing would ever be the same again –
for me, for the Sherpas, for Solu Khumbu, for mountaineering as a sport.
And nothing was. It was not that by climbing Everest nothing was left
for the mountaineers to do. Not at all. Rather the reverse. Now there was
everything to do; nothing was beyond man's ambition and there was
plenty of that everywhere . . .*
Sherpa Norgay Tenzing, *After Everest*, (1977)

Some years ago, I headed out through the tropical lowlands of New Guinea to cross the Central Range, something the remote people I was living with had never done. The obstruction lay like a blue lizard across their forested horizon, and I'd promised to tell them what it was like up there, and what lay on the other side.

As it turned out, the mountains, which had been an awesome sight for untold centuries to the lowlander, were not too difficult – at least physically – to cross. The challenge for me lay in having neither a route up, nor the confidence of knowing that someone had ever done it before – certainly, no white man had. However, though it wasn't a great feat, it was an extraordinary one because, as it happened, my crossing point brought me through the country of the Yaifo, a hitherto 'uncontacted' people living in the misty, darkly forested foothills. The Yaifo, seeing me and my New Guinean helpers approach uphill, staggering over the greasy fallen trees and moss, performed an extremely worrying display of their power, descending to dance around us with arrows on drawn bows. Duly impressed, I decided some presents of salt might go down well.

I spent a few days with the Yaifo, jotting down in my notebooks what I could of their lifestyle. I was their first visitor from any substantial distance at all and, as it happened, within months there would be many more, for oil had been discovered nearby. The Yaifo, too, had heard rumours of wealth to come, and the helicopter they had once seen flitting through the upland cloud had, I learnt through a translator, made perfect sense to them: their age-old prophesies spoke of their ancestral spirits coming from the sky, laden with wealth. Such cargo cults are well documented from the 1930s onwards, when Australians entered the interior of New Guinea, prospecting for gold. We were now at the end of an era, I reflected, as we left to carry on upslope, into the cloud. For thousands of years great powers had sent out their explorers to define new lands, and gradually small bands of people had been brought into contact with the outside world. Now, in this mountain retreat, it was happening for one of the last times on the planet: a collision between the worlds of people known, and people unknown.

I last saw the Yaifo down below me, engaged in building what they called 'nests' to attract the helicopters down. They had talked of them as birds and – whether they were speaking poetically or not – were in great hope that, given a comfortable perch and bedding, they would be lured to ground.

The point I'm leading to is that mountains are very different things to different people. To the Niowra, the New Guinea lowland people that I had lived with for many months, the mountain range was a barrier. Forbidding enough to any casual observer, to the Niowra, in their damp, mosquito-ridden forests, it was also spiritually empowered, and usefully explained thunder, which was the thumpings of angry spirits. The mountain and its dark secrets were better left undisturbed.

For the Yaifo, though, the Central Range wasn't a spiritual threat. It was their protection, their home. To them, the threat lay in the lowlands – in people like the Niowra, who were hunting heads even in the Second World War, when Japanese soldiers wandered a little too far off the jungle paths. What stopped the Yaifo crossing the Central Range, was – apart from fear of whoever might be on the other side – the cold. Sometimes during the climb, my lowland companions had to stop to light fires to warm up their bare feet, which had gone numb. When we reached the bare crags of the ridge, we silently placed little offerings of food for whatever spirit might live there, before making the descent on the other side.

Historically, long-distance travellers of whatever race have always been lowlanders, people like us – that is, of the headhunting, rather than the retreating, kind. They spread out and reached out because they were in the ascendant; they had the might, they had the confidence – though until recent times, no motive. Plains are more fertile than mountain slopes, and have longer growing seasons; they make easier places in which to live. The lowlands favour the formation of nation states; easier communications engender cross-fertilization of ideas and trade with other peoples. Mountain people, too, have conducted trade, through passes and hidden valleys; but this has always had to be a relatively low-level matter – a question of mules, llamas and yaks, and not well-served in literature.

Mountains present their own special problems to any traveller. At higher altitudes, there are avalanches, falling rocks, crevasses; at lower altitudes, nests of bandits and lairs of wild beasts. Mountains are barriers. Bastions against human expansion: they are rock, fortified by ice fields and glaciers; they are cold deserts, but crumpled up.

It is little wonder that the first land settlers, of whatever origin, by-passed them where possible. Only the polar wastes were less accessible – this very inaccessibility making the Poles a supreme challenge to individual and national endeavour – and were the last areas to be charted. Even the thick tropical forests offered something: gold, timber, rubber and slaves; and now a gene pool.

Obstacles they might have been, but as the great European navigators arrived and colonizers spread over the lowlands, to the white man, when he finally got there, they also presented a special opportunity. They fulfilled a useful role in his psyche. Each peak was a last boundary, each pinnacle a chance to measure human endurance. Each summit was an opportunity for industrialized man to conquer nature. They were yardsticks of ability, a place for men to plonk a flag: '. . . after Everest,' wrote Sherpa Tenzing, 'nothing seemed impossible'. They were also gateways for civilization. Unfurling his flag on the top of Snow Peak in the Rockies, American explorer John Fremont sees 'a solitary bee winging his flight from the eastern valley and lit on the knee of one of the men. It was a strange place, the icy rock and the highest peak of the Rocky Mountains, for a lover of warm sunshine and flowers; and we pleased ourselves with the idea that he was the first of his species to cross the mountain barrier – a solitary pioneer to foretell the advance of civilization' (from Fremont's report of his 1842 expedition).

To the great civilizations of the plains, the highlands remained largely unknown; and, being unknown, they were feared – not only because they were a hideaway for groups hostile to lowlanders. Supernatural beings of various kinds were to be found in all unfrequented spots – and mountains were the least frequented of all. The great summits were the closest points on Earth to the heavens – ever since man could look upwards they have been seen as the preserve of the gods, the appropriate setting for divine manifestations, the proper place for sacred and terrible mysteries. Moses received his tablets of law on Mount Sinai; Christ led his disciples up a mountain to be transfigured; Mohammed received the Koran in a mountain cave. The Classical world was similar; Zeus, after all, dwelt on Mount Olympus.

With time, the spiritual perception of the mountain retreat gradually gave way to a physical one: here was no longer a place for the Other, but for the Self. In the mountains you could pit yourself against the elements, break through literal and metaphorical barriers. At times, the physical and spiritual allure of mountains have, however, accommodated one another. In 1955 four English climbers stopped just short of the summit of Kanchenjunga at the request of the Sikkimese government, because it was considered too sacred for human feet to trample on; and it is rare that mountaineers remain unmoved by what they have fought so long to surmount. Having climbed Chomolungma, or 'Mother Goddess of the Earth' – renamed by the British 'Everest' – Tenzing lays out food offerings. Then Hillary enters into the spirit of things, after taking photos of his climbing partner, by adding the crucifix he's especially brought – 'symbolical at least of the spiritual strength and peace that all peoples have gained from the mountains'.

It's worth examining why mountains provoke feelings of mystery in us even today. It used to be an old travelling adage that natives didn't like their photos being taken because they thought it would capture their souls. The idea has become something of a backpacker myth; I've talked a lot about this with rainforest peoples who'd never seen cameras before mine, and they've explained that it was the threatening 'aim and shoot' operation that was so worrying. Indeed, giving them my camera, they invariably took photos of me with no regard to the horizontal; all that mattered was a precise aim on the subject, just as if you were shooting a monkey. That said, there was a perceived threat not just to the body, but also to the soul. And this is not just superstition. For don't the photographs we bring back 'capture' of the subject? We all know that mystery lends power; and in the same way as the village shaman keeps aloof, knowing that mystery gives his job potency,

the mountains, unconquered, maintain their majesty.

Sometimes in the writings of travellers – in this section as elsewhere – the local guides are glimpsed doing more than lugging the loads of their paymasters; in the selection I've chosen below, they are sometimes seen quietly placing their offerings.

The missionary Charles New was sanitized by locals on his descent from Kilimanjaro for whatever spiritual disturbance his climb might have caused. In Hawaii, Isabella Bird found she was intruding on the home of the Goddess of the Crater. Throughout these extracts, the theme is recurrent: indigenous people in the background paying homage to what the West is, necessarily, reducing.

Western culture has been eroding the mountain mystique for a long time. We all know the story of Hannibal crossing the Alps with his elephants. For centuries, such feats remained occasional, though by the Middle Ages exceptional or eccentric individuals were embarking on modest climbs. Late in the thirteenth century King Peter III of Aragon claimed the solitary ascent of Canigou (9,144 feet) in the Pyrenees; he reported that he had roused a dragon by throwing a stone into a lake at the top, though we now know there is no lake near the top.

In 1358 the knight Rotario d'Asti made the first recorded climb of a snow peak when, in fulfilment of a vow, he carried a triptych to the summit of Rocciamelone (11,605 feet), a southern outpost of the Graians. The triptych can still be seen in the cathedral at Susa.

In the New World, when Cortés was advancing on Montezuma's capital in 1519, his route took him between Popocatapetl and Iztaccihuatl. In order to show the Indians that 'no achievement was beyond the dauntless daring of his followers', he encouraged some of his officers to attempt Popocatapetl (17,888 feet). Now a picnic resort near Mexico City, it was then still an active volcano. They did not reach the summit, being 'nearly blinded and suffocated by the volumes of smoke, sparks and cinders which were belched forth'.

The story of mountaineering proper – that is, mountain travel with the intention of reaching a summit – seriously gets under way in the late eighteenth century when men of a scientific mind started to investigate the rivers of ice that flowed from the Alps. Climbing became a fashionable pastime after the ascent of Mont Blanc in 1786 by a local doctor, Michel-Gabriel Paccard, who had studied the mountain with his telescope and completed his mission with only one porter, Jacques Balmat. After mastering the highest Alpine peaks, the mountaineer had to find new challenges. The Alps were the natural cradle of mountaineering, being located in the heart of densely populated Europe. All the great ranges of more remote regions had to await the arrival of the voracious Westerner, as he advanced across far plains.

It would be a mistake to think of mountaineering as the story of conquest. It is also the story of the conquered – by which I don't mean those who have failed. Having spilt a considerable amount of other people's blood on his way into Lhasa, the soldier Younghusband had what amounted to a revelation on a slope behind the Tibetan capital: '. . . here on the quiet mountain-side . . . I seemed in touch with the wide Universe beyond this Earth as well'. The Himalayas were simply too big; all his adult life having been a soldier, he gave up wanting to fight. 'I seemed in tune with all the world and all the world seemed in tune with me.' There was more to come. 'The whole world seemed in a blaze of love, and men's hearts were burning to be in touch with one another.'

The mountains, these untrammelled places, for many such Westerners became sanctuaries from the cares of the world. 'What a pity', wrote Roerich, 'to descend out of the unpeopled spaces to the whirl of the human crowd.' I think anyone who escapes from their town to have a walk in the countryside feels this to a degree. How much more so in the most formidable mountain chain in the world. As Roerich went on: 'The very air of the Himalayas is penetrated with spiritual tension . . .'

The hidden valleys – occupied by resilient, pragmatic peoples hardened to the misfortunes that come the way of all upland peoples, subject as they are to sudden and vicious weather changes – become enchanted havens. The journeys over high passes, through thin, dry air, begin to take on the status of pilgrimages.

The mystic Alexandra David-Neel, wrote of her arrival in Lhasa: 'unforgettable spectacle which alone repaid me for my every fatigue and the myriad dangers that I had faced to behold it!' These hidden kingdoms become Shangri-Las, sacred because we have sullied ourselves in the dirty, hard-fought, moneyed plains. 'Happy people!' exclaimed the botanist Frank Kingdon-Ward in the heights of Central Asia. 'What do they know of the strife and turmoil of the Western world?' There to gather specimens for the West to add to the rationalizing body of science, he too succumbed to feelings of otherworldliness: 'Everything in that light was ethereal, almost spiritualized; and presently when I heard the sound of distant song I was not very surprised . . .'

It was a very literal sanctuary that Heinrich Harrer sought in Tibet, in the Second World War, escaping internment by the British. He also found another existence, one far removed from the conflict that raged across the rest of the world: 'One cannot close one's heart to the religious fervor which radiates from everyone.' Buddhism, with its concern for the balance of things, and the undying nature of the reincarnated soul, lent a quality to the Himalayas that was more gently felt elsewhere – in the Atlas, in the Rockies. The chants and dances of any manner of different shamans had here evolved into a philosophy, a lifestyle guided by holy tenants. At the centre of all sacred things was the Dalai Lama, who was only a boy when Harrer met him. 'We kept saying to ourselves, "It is only a child." A child, indeed, but the heart of the concentrated faith of thousands, the essence of their prayers, longings, hopes.' Interestingly, this child was the physical embodiment of former Dalai Lamas – the one, for example, met by Thomas Manning when he arrived in Lhasa in 1811. 'The Lama's beautiful and interesting face and manner engrossed almost all my attention. He was at that time about seven years old: had the simple and unaffected manners of a well-educated princely child. His face was, I thought, poetically and affectingly beautiful. He was of a gay and cheerful disposition; his beautiful mouth perpetually unbending into a graceful smile, which illuminated his whole countenance.'

Some explorers sought mountain retreats not because they valued them but because they wished to expose them to other influences. I've also included in this section extracts from the diary kept by a missionary, Annie Taylor. Having served in China, she felt called to carry the Christian faith – 'God will direct our path' – to Tibet and, though not well known, survived a journey through cold and robbers on a par with any other of the trekkers here. That she was the first European woman to enter Tibet doesn't qualify her for entry in the book; but her exposure to Tibetan mountain life, and her unadorned depiction of it does.

It was the natural environment, not God, that Kingdon-Ward sought to unravel. 'Most lovely of all, hiding shyly within the dark bamboo groves, was a meadow-rue, its large white flowers . . . like snowflakes floating through a forest of ferns. I called it the snowflake meadow-rue – there is none more beautiful.' For Hiram Bingham, seeking the Inca ruins in the Andes, it was also a search for the hidden: 'Above all, there is the fascination of finding here and there under swaying vines, or perched on top of a beetling crag,

the rugged masonry of a bygone race . . .'

In the selection I've also included Odette Keun, the quality of whose writing for me expresses more than many of those celebrating manly feats. 'We ascended . . . we felt everything falling away before us; never till then had I had such a sense of being cut off from all support. And yet we ascended – the tongue of rock narrowed, drew itself out like the materializing of an intangible force, and when we halted at its extreme point, it had raised us, with itself, high above the world.'

Eric Shipton, though a highly focused climber – indeed, a pioneer of the small scale, 'Alpine' style of climbing, who broke through many of the traditions that had restricted expeditions – talks in the same language. 'Each corner held some thrilling secret to be revealed for the trouble of looking.' The mountain gives, but only if she chooses, and only – only – if you give of yourself. Then, if you are not sacrificed on what seems at times a very bloody altar, you may be safely released: 'Return to civilisation was hard, but, in the sanctuary of the Blessed Goddess we had found the lasting peace which is the reward of those who seek to know high mountain places.'

What is the motivation of Shipton and this strange, specialist breed, these mountaineers driven to summits at almost any cost? Traditionally they are not included among the fold of 'explorers' – mountaineering is regarded as a sport; but it is more than a challenge, a vertical race track. Each extract I've chosen reads like a journey to a rendezvous with something overwhelming – they are about to meet their destiny, a shattered-open piece of Nature. The mountain climb becomes a form of self-expression, and even prayer. In the tension of the struggle upwards, all distractions are lost; time and the world itself are left behind in the duel between what the mountaineer can draw out of his inner being, and the wind, ice and rock.

The amateurism of Edward Whymper and

others has given way to the expertise of the specialists – those like Frank Smythe, perhaps the first to make a living out of the climbing process. Later came the likes of Chris Bonington, the great professionals of the post-war era. Also represented here, Ranulph Fiennes, who is more famous for his formidable polar hikes. In the extract I've chosen he is in Norway, in 1970, and the planning and execution of the expedition are like those of a covert army operation. This incorporated what the *Sunday Times* billed 'The World's Toughest Jump'. It is all very Alistair Maclean; this close-knit team thrives on all the adrenalin of a platoon probing a far mightier enemy for inner weaknesses.

I am a non-mountaineer, but know what it is to have damaged fingers, frostbite that's painful for weeks on end because you have to handle ropes and toggles, the agony of which you are prepared to endure because the rewards of attaining your goal are far greater. Explaining that you go 'because it's there' is not helpful to anyone who doesn't feel this urge, though a restless personality and that germ of curiosity that we all share are perhaps all you need. The mountaineer Wilfred Noyce tried to get to the bottom of the matter, dissecting explorer types in *The Springs of Adventure*. Among his classifications are 'the Scientific Man', 'the do-ers of good', the 'Escape simple'. Whatever it is, the mountaineers have more than the usual amount of the ingredient, call it drive, the will to go on, the determination to make it back. As Noyce wrote of one mountaineer: 'He knew little now, having passed beyond conscious thought, but that he must go on.'

Once their goal is reached, these mountaineers seem satiated – for a while: 'I felt a quiet glow of satisfaction spread through my body,' wrote Hillary, of his arrival on the top of Everest, 'a satisfaction less vociferous but more powerful than I had ever felt on a mountain top before.' Messner talks of being recharged in the mountains, as if, pitted against them, you are slowly worn down to your essential elements, and then find a strength in unity with those raw forces you have come to know. 'And besides,' wrote Roerich, 'these dangers of nature are essentially so joyous, so greatly awaken the vigor and unify the consciousness.'

Chris Bonington once said to me that he'd never go on a mountain with someone who wasn't afraid. Fear, of course, is not a weakness but a great defence. But even so, it seems to me that about one in three mountaineers of the top rank pay with their lives. Among Bonington's British climbing mates, four names immediately spring to mind: Mick Burke (lost on Everest, climbing alone to the summit), Nick Escourt (swept away by an avalanche on K2), Pete Boardman and Joe Tasker (both vanished on Everest's north-east ridge).

Whatever demons or aspirations drive them personally, mountaineers often seem to thrust on upwards, even when without hope of a prize. 'I've hardly the dimmest hope of reaching the top,' wrote Mallory, 'but of course we shall proceed as though we meant to get there.' After a disaster, rather than vowing never to put themselves in those traumatic situations again, many mountaineers acquire a sense of invincibility. This drives them back again, as if they've been branded by the mountain in these intensely lived moments, and it now owns them. 'Victory over fear,' wrote Messner, 'that is also a happiness in which I am close to myself.'

One intriguing dichotomy runs through this mountaineering business. On the one hand, there's a need for co-operation within a team, as embodied in the rope that often connects climbers; and on the other hand, by definition there's an extreme competitiveness felt between teams. In its extreme, this is depicted by Whymper and companions – dressed, you feel, in tweeds – who scrambled up the Matterhorn in a race with the Italians. Ironically, on this expedition the rope became not a life-saver but a destroyer, several climbers tragically pulling each other off the cliff.

Tenzing alludes to the trouble that followed his Everest feat, when press and politicians tried to split him from Hillary – back home, the climbers were regarded by their people as their champions. Messner has a refreshing disdain for this kind of national rivalry, and even for the idea of conquering. When asked for which nation he would be carrying a flag on one assault, he muttered his stock reply: 'I am my own homeland and my handkerchief is my flag . . .' The relationship he has with the mountain is personal. 'In order to experience this feeling of oneness with the world, I must go to the limits of my physical ability.'

The extracts I've chosen begin some time ago, when mountains allowed no sport, when there were no specialists to slay these dragons. With time, they would become benchmarks of human endeavour; but what happens when there's nowhere higher to climb? Messner has already rewritten the rule book, by climbing Everest alone, and without oxygen. 'The summit we have reached is no longer the summit,' wrote Lucien Devies, President of the French Himalayan Committee. 'The fulfilment of oneself – is that the true end, the final answer?'

*I my selfe also, by the goodnesse of Almightie God, twice escaped the most
dreadful danger of the foresaid Snow . . .*

Leo Africanus was an Islamic diplomat who spent many years in Rome following his capture by pirates, and his writings revealed much of the Muslim world for Christendom. He was born in Grenada as Al Hassan Ibn Mohammed Al Wezzani, a Moor of noble stock, soon after the city had fallen to the Catholic forces of Spain. Although this was long before the ruthless expulsion of Muslims and Jews from Spain during the Inquisition, Hassan's family moved when he was still young down to Morocco, where he received a strict Islamic education in Fez.

After leaving university he became a diplomat, travelling on missions for the Wattaside Sultan in Fez that took him to Constantinople, Arabia, sub-Saharan Africa and Egypt. In addition to the usual diplomatic task of monitoring Spanish and Portuguese activites on the Moroccan coast, the Sultan also needed Al Hassan to keep an eye on a new political rival; he often sent envoys south to sniff out these Saadian advances and measure his own vulnerability to attack. Al Hassan chronicled his journeys in journals that became a definitive source of information about Islam even into the nineteenth century.

In 1518 Al Hassan was sailing back from Constantinople when he was captured by a band of pirates, members of the Knights of St John. Deducing from the maps and books he had on board that Al Hassan was a man of learning, they took him to Rome. The object was to give him as a slave to Pope Leo X, who had a fascination for all things Oriental.

The Pope, however, was impressed by Al Hassan's intelligence, and granted him freedom on condition that he convert to Christianity. On 6 January 1520, two years after his arrival in Rome, Al Hassan was baptized and given the name of his sponsor, Pope Leo. Owing to his expertise on Africa – he claimed to have crossed the Sahara to Timbuktu twice and visited fifteen Sudanese kingdoms – he was now dubbed 'Leo Africanus'. Christendom had never before read about Africa from the viewpoint of a native. His work – particularly his famous *Cosmographia Del Africa* – gave a rare view of the world from the perspective of the Islamic sphere of influence.

It is thought that Leo Africanus returned to Africa before his death, where he converted back to Islam.

Snow in the Atlas Mountains

The Mountaines of Atlas are exceeding cold and barren, and bring forth but small store of Corne, being woody on all sides, and engendring almost all the Rivers of Africa. The Fountaines of Atlas are even in the midst of Summer extremely cold; so that if a man dippeth his hand therein for any long space, he is in great danger of losing the same. Howbeit the said Mountaines are not so cold in all places: for some parts thereof are of such milde temperature, that they may be right commodiously inhabited: yea, and sundry places thereof are well stored with inhabitants . . . Those places which are destitute of Inhabitants be either extremely cold, as namely, the same which lie over against Mauritania: or very rough and unpleasant, to wit, those which are directly opposite to the Region of Temesna. Where notwithstanding in Summer time they may feed their great and small Cattell, but not in Winter by any meanes. For then the North wind so furiously rageth, bringing with it such abundance of Snow, that all the Cattell which till then remaine on the said Mountaines and a great part of the People also are forced to lose their lives in regard thereof ... Those Merchants which bring Dates out of Numidia for the use and service of other Nations, set forth usually upon their Journey about the end of October: and yet they are oftentimes so oppressed and overtaken with a sodaine fall of Snow, that scarcely one man among them all escapeth the danger of the tempest. For when it beginneth to snow over night, before the next morning not only Carts and Men, but even the very Trees are so drowned and overwhelmed therein, that it is not possible to finde any mention of them. Howbeit the dead Carkasses are then found, when the Sunne hath melted the Snow.

I my selfe also, by the goodnesse of Almightie God, twice escaped the most dreadful danger of the foresaid Snow; whereof, if it may not be tedious to the Reader, I will here in few words make relation. Upon a certaine day of the foresaid moneth of October, travelling with a great companie of Merchants towards Atlas, wee were there about Sunne going downe weatherbeaten with a most cold and snowy kind of Hayle. Here we found eleven or twelve Horsemen (Arabians to our thinking) who perswading us to leave our Carts and to goe with them, promised us a good and secure place to lodge in. For mine owne part, that I might not seeme altogether uncivill, I thought it not meet to refuse their good offer; albeit I stood in doubt lest they went about to practise some mischiefe. Wherefore I bethought my selfe to hide up a certaine summe of gold which I had as then about me. But all being readie to ride, I had no leisure to hide away my Coyne from them; whereupon I fained that I would goe ease my selfe. And so departing a while their companie, and getting me under a certaine Tree, whereof I tooke diligent notice, I buried my money between certaine stones and the roote of the said Tree. And then we rode on quietly till about mid-night. What time one of them thinking that he had stayed long enough for his Prey, began to utter that in words which secretly he had conceived in his mind. For he asked whether I had any money about me or no? To whom I answered, that I had left my money behind with one of them which attended the carts, and that I had then none at all about me. Howbeit they being no whit satisfied with this answer, commanded me, for all the cold weather, to strip my selfe out of mine apparell. At length when they could find no money at all, they said in jesting and scoffing wise, that they did this for no other purpose, but only to see how strong and hardy I was, and how I could endure the cold and tempestuous season.

Well, on we rode, seeking our way as well as wee could that darke and dismall night; and anon we heard the bleating of Sheepe, conjecturing thereby that wee were not farre distant from some habitation of people. At length after many labours, wee found Shepheards in a certaine Cave: who, having with much paines brought their Cattell in there, had kindled a lustie fire for them-selves, which they were constrained, by reason of the extreme cold, daily to sit by. Who understanding our companie to be Arabians, feared at the first that we would doe them some mischiefe: but afterward being perswaded that we were driven thither by extremitie of cold, and being more secure of us, they gave us most friendly entertainment. For they set bread, flesh, and cheese before us, wherewith having ended our Suppers, we laid us along each man to sleep before the fire. All of us were as yet exceeding cold, but especially my selfe, who before with great horrour and trembling was stripped starke naked. And so we continued with the said shepheards for the space of two days: all which time we could not set forth, by reason of continual Snow. But the third day, so soone as they saw it leave snowing, with great labour they began to remove that Snow which laybefore the doore of their Cave. Which done, they brought us to our Horses, which wee found well, provided of Hay in another Cave. Being all mounted, the shepheards accompanied us some part of our way, shewing us where the Snow was of least depth, and yet even there it touched our Horse bellies . . .

At length entring into a certaine Village neere unto Fez, wee understood, that our Carts which passed by, were overwhelmed with the Snow. Then the Arabians seeing no hope of recompence for all the paines they had taken (for they had defended our Carts from Theeves) carryed a certaine Jew of our Companie with them as their Captive, (who had lost a great quantitie of Dates, by reason of the Snow aforesaid) to the end that he might remayne as their Prisoner, till he had satisfied for all the residue. From my selfe they took my Horse, and committed me unto the wide World and to Fortune. From whence, riding upon a Mule, within three daies I arrived at Fez, where I heard dolefull newes of our Merchants and Wares, that they were cast away in the Snow. Yea, they thought that I had beene destroyed with the rest; but it seemed that God would have it otherwise.

A Geographical Historie of Africa (1600)

Francisco Pizarro
1476–1541

First came a squadron of Indians dressed in a livery of different colours, like a chess board. They advanced, removing the straws from the ground, and sweeping the road. Next came three squadrons in different dresses, dancing and singing. Then came a number of men with armour . . . Among them was Atabaliba [the Inca Emperor Atahuallpa] in a litter lined with plumes of macaws' feathers, of many colours, and adorned with plates of gold and silver . . .

The Conquistador who defeated the Incas and founded the city of Lima was born in Trujillo, a small town to the south of Madrid, the illegitimate son of Captain Gonzalo Pizarro and Francisca González. He fought in local wars, then in 1502 went to Hispaniola (now Haiti and the Dominican Republic) with the new governor of the Spanish colony. Restless with sedentary colonial life, Pizarro took part in an expedition to Colombia; then, in 1513, he was captain to an expedition led by Vasco Núñez de Balboa to settle Panama – they became the first Europeans to reach the Pacific. For four years he was mayor and magistrate of the newly founded town of Panama, where he built up a small fortune.

In the early 1520s Pizarro heard rumours of the magnificent and wealthy Inca Empire to the south. Cortés had recently shown, in Mexico against the Aztecs, what a handful of Spaniards were able to achieve against a whole empire; Pizarro became determined that the Inca empire would be his. His first expedition towards Peru in 1524 was discouraging, but in 1527 Pizarro had reached the city of Tumbes and returned with gold, silver and other evidence of an advanced civilization. The following year Pizarro returned to Spain to secure permission from the King to settle Peru, and was appointed 'Governor' of Peru in advance. He set sail for the north coast of Peru in late 1530, accompanied by only 170 men, including his four brothers,

and from there they began their ascent into the unknown Andean massif.

The Inca Empire stretched over 2,000 miles down the spine of the Andes from modern Colombia to southern Chile and from the Pacific coast to the eastern foothills of the Andes. But at the time of Pizarro's advance, it was weakened and greatly preoccupied with a struggle over the succession to the throne. The Spaniards marched effortlessly towards Cajamarca, where the successful usurper of the Inca throne, Atahuallpa, was based. They descended into Cajamarca's fertile valley in late 1532 and found, to their horror, an encamped army of 30,000 men. Shaken, but still determined, the Spanish rode their messengers into the encampment and invited Atahuallpa to meet with Pizarro in the city the next day. Few of the Spaniards slept that night. Many went to confession and wrote last letters home. However, despite Atahuallpa's enormous entourage, the Spanish managed to seize him, using his rejection of their faith – not knowing what the Bible was, he threw it on to the ground in the main plaza – as a pretext to attack. The Spanish, bewildering the Incas with their horses and guns, killed – it's said – about 7,000 men and injured perhaps 10,000 more.

Atahuallpa was then held to ransom. Having extorted enormous amounts of gold (13,420 lbs) and silver (26,000 lbs) over six months, the Spaniards nonetheless accused

Atahuallpa of plotting to overthrow them, and executed him by garotting.*

Francisco Pizarro went on to conquer the Inca capital at Cuzco and the plundering continued throughout the Empire. Having consolidated his control, and established Manco Capac as a puppet ruler in Cuzco, he founded a new capital city, Lima, in 1535. He

was eventually assassinated, in 1541, by supporters of a former Spanish rival, Almagro, whom he had defeated and executed three years earlier.

His chronicles were written up by Francisco de Xeres, his personal secretary, who wrote an eyewitness account of the early days of the conquest by order of his master.

* The version included here is the more official one: Atahuallpa was actually given a mock trial, in which the man translating for the Emperor was said to have a 'malignant spite' against him. Of the ten witnesses that were examined, seven were 'servants of the Spanish'. They were asked twelve questions, including the following: 'Had Atahuallpa many concubines?' 'Was Atahuallpa an idolater,

and did he enforce human sacrifice?' Pedro (as opposed to Francisco) Pizarro wrote, 'Atabalipa wept, and said that they should not kill him, that there was not an Indian in the land who would move without his orders, and that, he being prisoner, what could they fear? I saw the Marquis weep with sorrow, at not being able to spare his life, by reason of the risk of his escaping.'

The Inca Emperor is held to ransom

[Pizarro] told them that though, for every Christian, there were five hundred Indians, yet they must have that reliance which good men find on such occasions, and they must trust that God would fight on their side. He told them that, at the moment of attacking, they must come out with desperate fury and break through the enemy, taking care that the horses do not hinder each other. These and similar exhortations were made by the Governor and Captain-General to the Christians, to raise their spirits, and they were more ready to come forth than to remain in their lodgings. Each man was ready to encounter a hundred, and they felt very little fear at seeing so great a multitude.

When the Governor saw that it was near sunset, and that Atabaliba did not move from the place to which he had repaired, although troops still kept issuing out of his camp, he sent a Spaniard to ask him to come into the square to see him before it was dark. As soon as the messenger came before Atabaliba, he made an obeisance to him, and made signs that he should come to where the Governor waited. Presently he and his troops began to move, and the Spaniard returned and reported that they were coming, and that the men in front carried arms concealed under their clothes, which were strong tunics of cotton, beneath which were stones and bags and slings; all which made it appear that they had a treacherous design. Soon the van of the enemy began to enter the open space. First came a squadron of Indians dressed in a livery of different colours, like a chess board. They advanced, removing the straws from the ground, and sweeping the road. Next came three squadrons in different dresses, dancing and singing. Then came a number of men with armour, large metal plates, and crowns of gold and silver. Among them was Atabaliba in a litter lined with plumes of macaws' feathers, of many colours, and adorned with plates of gold and silver. Many Indians carried it on their shoulders on high. Next came two other litters and two hammocks, in which were some principal chiefs; and lastly, several squadrons of Indians with crowns of gold and silver.

As soon as the first entered the open space they moved aside and gave space to the others. On reaching the centre of the open space, Atabaliba remained in his litter on high, and the others with him, while his troops did not cease to enter. A captain then came to the front and, ascending the fortress near the open space, where the artillery was posted, raised his lance twice, as for a signal. Seeing this, the Governor asked the Father Friar Vicente if he wished to go and speak to Atabaliba, with an interpreter? He replied that he did wish it, and he advanced, with a cross in one hand and the Bible in the other, and going amongst the troops up to the place where Atabaliba was, thus addressed him: 'I am a Priest of God, and I teach Christians the things of God, and in like manner I come to teach you. What I teach is that which God says to us in this Book. Therefore, on the part of God and of the Christians, I beseech you to be their friend, for such is God's will, and it will be for your good. Go and speak to the Governor, who waits for you.'

Atabaliba asked for the Book, that he might look at it, and the Priest gave it to him closed. Atabaliba did not know how to open it, and the Priest was extending his arm to do so, when Atabaliba, in great anger, gave him a blow on the arm, not wishing that it should be opened. Then he opened it himself, and, without any astonishment at the letters and paper, as had been shown by other Indians, he threw it away from him five or six paces, and, to the words which the monk had spoken to him through the interpreter, he answered with much scorn, saying: 'I know well how you have behaved on the road, how you have treated my Chiefs, and taken the cloth from my storehouses.' The Monk replied: 'The Christians have not done this, but some Indians took the cloth without the knowledge of the Governor, and he ordered it to be restored.' Atabaliba said: 'I will not leave this place until they bring it all to me.' The Monk returned with this reply to the Governor. Atabaliba stood up on the top of the litter, addressing his troops and ordering them to be prepared. The Monk told the Governor what had passed between him and Atabaliba, and that he had thrown the Scriptures to the ground. Then the Governor put on a jacket of cotton, took his sword and dagger, and, with the Spaniards who were with him, entered amongst the Indians most valiantly; and, with only four men who were able to follow him, he came to the litter where Atabaliba was, and fearlessly seized him by the arm, crying out *Santiago*. Then the guns were fired off, the trumpets were sounded, and the troops, both horse and foot, sallied forth. On seeing the horses charge, many of the Indians who were in the open space fled, and such was the force with which they ran that they broke down part of the wall surrounding it, and many fell over each other. The horsemen rode them down, killing and wounding, and following in pursuit. The infantry made so good an assault upon those that remained that in a short time most of them were put to the sword. The Governor still held Atabaliba by the arm, not being able to pull him out of the litter because he was raised so high. Then the Spaniards made such a slaughter amongst those who carried the litter that they fell to the ground, and, if the Governor had not protected Atabaliba, that proud man would there have paid for all the cruelties he had committed. The Governor, in protecting Atabaliba, received a slight wound in the hand. During the whole time no Indian raised his arms against a Spaniard. So great was the terror of the Indians at seeing the Governor force his way through them, at hearing the fire of the artillery, and beholding the charging of the horses, a thing never before heard of, that they thought more of flying to save their lives than of fighting. All those who bore the litter of Atabaliba appeared to be principal chiefs. They were all killed, as well as those who were carried in the other litters and hammocks. One of them was the page of Atabaliba, and a great lord, and the others were lords of many vassals, and his Councillors. The chief of Caxamalca was also killed, and others; but, the number being very great, no account was taken of them, for all who came in attendance on Atabaliba were great lords. The Governor went to his lodging, with his prisoner Atabaliba, despoiled of his robes, which the Spaniards had torn off in pulling him out of the litter. It was a very wonderful thing to see so great a lord taken prisoner in so short a time, who came in such power. The Governor presently ordered native clothes to be brought, and when Atabaliba was dressed, he made him sit near him, and soothed his rage and agitation at finding himself so quickly fallen from his high estate. Among many other things, the Governor said to him: 'Do not take it as an insult that you have been defeated and taken prisoner, for with the Christians who come with me, though so few in number, I have conquered greater kingdoms than yours, and have defeated other more powerful lords than you, imposing upon them the dominion of the Emperor, whose vassal I am, and who is King of Spain and of the universal world. We come to conquer this land by his command, that all may come to a knowledge of God, and of His Holy Catholic Faith; and by reason of our good object, God, the Creator of heaven and earth and of all things in them, permits this, in order that you may know him, and come out from the bestial and diabolical life you lead. It is for this reason that we, being so few in number, subjugate that vast host. When you have seen the errors in which you live, you will understand the good we have done you by coming to your land by order of his Majesty. You should consider it to be your good fortune that you have not been defeated by a cruel people, such as you are yourselves, who grant life to none. We treat our prisoners and conquered enemies with kindness, and only make war on those who attack us, and, being able to destroy them, we refrain from doing so, but rather pardon them. When I had a Chief, the lord of an island, my prisoner, I set him free that henceforth he might be loyal; and I did the same with the Chiefs who were lords of Tumbez and Chilimasa, and others who, being in my power, and deserving death, I pardoned. If you were seized, and your people attacked and killed, it was because you came against us with so great an army, having sent to say that you would come peacefully, and because you threw the Book to the ground in which is written the words of God. Therefore our Lord permitted that your pride should be brought low, and that no Indian should be able to offend a Christian.'

After the Governor had delivered this discourse, Atabaliba thus replied: 'I was deceived by my Captains, who told me to think lightly of the Spaniards. I desired to come peacefully, but they prevented me, but all those who thus advised me are now dead. I have now seen the goodness and daring of the Spaniards, and that Malcabilica lied in all the news he sent me touching the Christians.'

As it was now night, and the Governor saw that those who had gone in pursuit of the Indians were not returned, he ordered the guns to be fired and the trumpets to be sounded to recall them. Soon afterwards they returned to the camp with a great crowd of people whom they had taken alive, numbering more than three thousand. The Governor asked whether they were all well. His Captain-General, who went with them, answered that only one horse had a slight wound. The Governor, with great joy, said: 'I give thanks to God our Lord, and we all, gentlemen, ought to give thanks for the great miracle we have wrought this day.

Inca civilisation

The road over the mountains is a thing worth seeing, because, though the ground is so rugged, such beautiful roads could not in truth be found throughout Christendom. The greater part of them is paved. There is a bridge of stone or wood over every stream. We found bridges of network over a very large and powerful river, which we crossed twice, which was a marvellous thing to see. The horses crossed over by them. At each passage they have two bridges, the one by which the common people go over, and the other for the lords of the land and their captains. The approaches are always kept closed, with Indians to guard them. These Indians exact transit dues from all passengers. The chiefs and people of the mountains are more intelligent than those of the coast. The country is populous. There are mines in many parts of it. It is a cold climate, it snows, and there is much rain. There are no swamps. Fuel is scarce. Atabaliva has placed governors in all the principal towns, and his predecessors had also appointed governors. In all these towns there were houses of imprisoned women, with guards at the doors, and these women preserve their virginity. If any Indian has any connection with them his punishment is death. Of these houses, some are for the worship of the Sun, others for that of old Cuzco, the father of Atabaliva. Their sacrifices consist of sheep and *chicha* [fermented drink from maize], which they pour out on the ground. They have another house of women in each of the principal towns, also guarded. These women are assembled by the chiefs of the neighbouring districts, and when the lord of the land passes by they select the best to present to him, and when they are taken others are chosen to fill up their places. These women also have the duty of making *chicha* for the soldiers when they pass that way. They took Indian girls out of these houses and presented them to us. All the surrounding chiefs come to these towns on the roads to perform service when the army passes. They have stores of fuel and maize, and of all other necessaries. They count by certain knots on cords, and so record what each chief has brought. When they had to bring us loads of fuel, maize, chicha, or meat, they took off knots or made knots on some other part; so that those who have charge of the stores keep an exact account.

Francisco de Xeres, Salamanca, A True Account of the Province of Cuzco, called New
Castille, Conquered by Francisco Pizarro, Captain to His Majesty The Emperor,
our Master, 1547

GEORGE EVEREST
1790–1866

To the north, south and west the eye wandered over one uninterrupted mass of foliage . . . the whole expanse seemed marked out for eternal solitude.

Sir George Everest, a British East India army officer who completed the trigonometrical survey of India, on which depended the accurate mapping of the subcontinent, was born in Greenwich – whence grew, perhaps, his interest in precise measurement through such techniques as astronomical observation. When he was sixteen, Everest joined the East India Company as an army lieutenant. In 1814 Stamford Raffles appointed him to survey the island of Java, which had been captured from the French, and three years later he became assistant to William Lambton, who had started the Great Trigonometrical Survey of India in 1806.

Everest led his first surveying mission into a densely forested region of south-central India in 1819. Twice his party was struck by malaria and had to delay their work. 'Buoyed up hitherto with the full vigour of youth and a strong constitution I had spurned . . . thoughts of being attacked by sickness, against which I foolishly deemed myself impregnable . . .'

During a year-long recuperation, Everest mulled over the lessons learnt from this arduous mission and devised a more practical method of surveying. Rather than working all year round, the Survey was to work only during the cold and dry seasons, avoiding the wet season when, although the air was clearest and so best for observations, the malarial mosquito was abundant. To overcome the problem of poor vision during these other seasons, he undertook his measuring at night using flares.

Everest took advantage of a five-year leave in London to make much-needed improvements to his equipment – his theodolite was in a poor state and his Ramsden 100-foot steel chain had not been calibrated in twenty-five years. Now he had the most accurate surveying equipment of the day.

When, in June 1830, he returned, it was as Surveyor General of India. He continued work on the 78th meridian, by connecting two baselines in the Himalayas, one at Dehra Dun and one at Sironj. Between them lay 400 miles of plain; in order to take measurements across this plain, the team built fourteen masonry towers up to 21 metres high. It was a cumbersome operation, involving some 700 labourers travelling on foot, thirty horses for the military officers, forty-two camels for supplies and equipment, and four elephants to carry the principals. By the time these measurements were complete, Everest had fallen ill and had to hand over command to his assistant Andrew Waugh. Waugh completed a re-measurement of the central Indian baseline at Bidar in 1841; the skeleton of the survey was complete.

Not only had Everest set in place a framework for the surveying of the whole subcontinent, but he had also completed the direct measurement of more than 20 degrees of a meridian arc, giving rise to a whole new level of accuracy in geodesy – the study of the shape of the Earth. In 1843 he retired to England, married and had six children. Meanwhile, following Everest's technique, the surveying of the Himalaya's peaks was under way, though some measurements were taken from distances of 160 miles away because the Survey was not allowed to enter Nepal. Six separate measurements were made of peak XV, establishing its height to be 8,839 metres (29,002 feet). Andrew Waugh announced this measurement at a meeting of the Asiatic Society in Calcutta, with the words: '. . . here is a mountain, most probably the highest in the world, without any local name that I can discover ... [I propose] to perpetuate the memory of that illustrious master of geographical research ... Everest.'

The Survey's measurements were not far off: the accepted figure for the height of Everest today is still contested but more-or-less 8,848 metres (29,028 feet).

Native insurrection

The infliction of corporal punishment is an odious task; but in this case there was really no choice between that and giving up the operations. . . . I took an opportunity about a month after leaving Hyderabad to chastise one of these defaulters with some severity; in consequence of which the whole body, about forty in number, burst into open mutiny, seized the native gentleman whom the minister had deputed as their chief, and declared they would quit my camp and carry him back with them.

It was in a grove of mangoe trees surrounded by a ditch and bank that they had selected their spot of encampment. There sat the Daroga [headman], surrounded by the mutineers, some with their swords drawn, others looking on. It . . . became my duty to assert my authority, or give the matter up entirely as hopeless.

With the Great Trigonometrical Survey of India there has always been an escort of regular sepoys . . . not belonging to the standing army. Colonel Lambton had detached twelve of these under my orders. I drew up a small party of eight men with loaded muskets in front of the grove where the rebellious Juwans (young soldiers) were lording over their superior, and declared my intention of firing a volley into the midst of them unless they immediately laid down their arms. Their resolution quailed before this decisive step, and they now became as meanly humble as they had been audaciously insolent. So, having deprived them of their weapons, and placed them under the surveillance of my sepoys, I made a severe example of three of the principal offenders by publicly flogging them and turning them out of camp with ignominy . . .

Threats of vengeance buzzed around me for some weeks after this occurrence, and it was necessary to be armed and well prepared to resist assault on my person. But the natives of India are not a malice-bearing race and, finding when they knew me better that good behaviour was a perfect security against all unkindness, they became at last willing, obedient, and obliging as I could desire.

Releasing boulders

In those gloomy days when the mists descend and obscure the horizon, it was the chief relaxation of Mr Voysey and myself . . . to employ our followers with handspikes and ropes in tearing off the loose masses of granite, and letting them find their way to the bottom of the hill. Certain it was a magnificent spectacle to see an enormous mass, seven or eight feet high, descending along the slippery side of the spheroid and striking fire in the progress – yet cautiously at first, and as if afraid to venture – suddenly, when it met with some hindrance, it would bound up and roll over like a planet in free space, and, lastly, when it attained the limits of the jungul, it would tear down large trees, and make the welkin roar again as it tumbled into the abyss below. Doubtless all this may be very childish, but . . . the French academician, De la Condamine . . . and his companions resorted to precisely the same methods of amusing themselves . . . We did not continue the pastime during the night for fear of injury to my followers; but if our amusement was by accident prolonged a little beyond twilight it is inconceivable how grand the sight became, for wherever the rock slid along the bare side of the hill it was accompanied by a dense train of such enduring sparks as we see emitted from the impact of the hoofs of the pampered coachhorse on the London pavement; and the light emitted when it struck any obstacle was sufficient to enable us to trace its progress, and make it resemble a whirling mass of phosphoric matter.

The work of surveying

It took me about three weeks to run southward along one side of the series, and to return northward by the other side of Hydershahipett. Nothing whatever having been heard of my detached parties, great apprehensions were entertained by me for their safety; but at last a gap began to break open in the black mountain . . . and after a fortnight's further waiting I had sufficient daylight behind to distinguish the colours of the Great Trigonometrical Survey flying on one spot, and a signal mark on the other. The secret of the delay now came out. The station of Hydershahipett was on the verge of the great forests of teak and ebony, far into the depths of which was situated this elephant mountain, called Punch Pandol. The access to it was by a circuitous route, unknown to any but the few struggling natives who lived in those forests, in a state closely bordering on savage life.

The nearest village was Poomrarum, about five miles from the summit, from which it was necessary to cut a road for the instruments and tents . . .

and how my unfortunate flagmen could have had perseverance enough to go through with such a task, how they could have coaxed any uninterested persons to accompany them; how, after having pierced through a forest of teak trees, seventy, eighty and even ninety feet high, thickly set with underwood, and infested with . . . tigers and boa constrictors, without water or provisions and with jungle fever staring them in the face . . . utterly passes my comprehension.

I had, indeed, been warned months before, that these junguls were the seat of the most deadly fever, which attacked men's mental as well as corporeal faculties . . . and how by means of conciliating treatment and prompt payment, my people had managed to collect a sufficient body of hatchet men to clear away every tree that in the least obstructed the horizon over a surface of nearly a square mile . . .

I was now far advanced into this terra incognita . . . to the eastward and northward no sign of humanity could be seen. Yet it was necessary to pierce far deeper into the forest to meet the Godavery, and, having fixed on a station which I judged to occupy it. Day after day having elapsed without hearing of them, I detached a second party, and some days afterwards a third under one of my sub-assistants [Rossenrode], but still no progress was made. At last came a melancholy letter from my sub-assistant telling me that he was ill and going to die; and then as a last resort, I despatched my principal sub-assistant Mr Joseph Olliver . . . and to my great delight I at last saw my flag flying on the selected hill, and received written intelligence of the name of the nearest hamlet Yellapooram . . . and of my former parties, many of whom began to suffer from the effects of the climate . . .

The eminence was most fortunately situated, and seemed to have been placed there on purpose to accommodate me, for, had it been a hundred yards to the north, the ray to my western station of Kotaajpoor must have been obstructed . . . Three parties were immediately detached to occupy the three peaks . . . and I hoped in . . . a few days to complete the observations . . . in which, had success attended me, I should, to use Colonel Lambton's words 'have performed a very magnificent work indeed to start with!' . . .

From Yellapooram hill . . . to the north, south and west the eye wandered over one uninterrupted mass of foliage, ornamented with all the different shades of green and yellow. Not a vestige of a human habitation or of cultivated land was anywhere to be seen, and the whole expanse seemed to be marked out for eternal solitude.

J. R. Smith, *Everest: The Man and the Mountain*, 1999

. . . the lava, from all parts of the lake, slid centrewards and downwards . . .
Always changing, always suggesting force which nothing could repel,
agony indescribable, mystery inscrutable, terror unutterable, a thing of
eternal dread . . .

Isabella Lucy Bird's first real taste of travel was as a convalescent. Born in Yorkshire, she had suffered throughout her childhood from insomnia, severe headaches and, above all, a spinal problem (which tormented her throughout her adult life as well). Aged twenty-three, she took off on doctor's orders to the New World, making her way through Novia Scotia and around the Great Lakes.

Travel transformed Bird, stimulating her mind, helping her to sleep and relieving her pain. On her return to England she wrote up her experiences in *The Englishwoman in America*, but suppressed what she regarded as a self-indulgent desire to travel for the next twenty years. It wasn't until the late 1860s, by which time both her parents had died and her ailments were plaguing her badly, that she allowed herself to go off again, commencing the first of three round-the-world journeys.

Bird headed to Australia and New Zealand, and by 1871 had reached the Sandwich Islands (Hawaii). There she investigated volcanoes – their sulphurous and steaming craters both fascinated and appalled her. She camped at the 14,000-foot peak of Mauna Loa, and relished the freedom of climbing others,

such as Mauna Kea, without the assistance of companions or guides.

She sailed on to San Francisco, travelled by train into the Sierra Nevada, then set out on horseback towards the Rocky Mountains, reaching Colorado after four months.

After her next expedition to Japan, China and Malaya, now aged fifty, she married Dr John Bishop, and lived in Edinburgh; he said he had 'only one formidable rival in Isabella's heart, and that is the high Table Land of Central Asia'. Thus, when Bishop died after only five years, Bird took a short course in nursing, then headed off to trek thousands of miles through Central Asia and the Far East with a military geographical expedition. By now a renowned traveller, in 1892 she became the first woman to be elected a member of the Royal Geographical Society.

In time, Isabella Bird returned to Korea and China, where she founded several hospitals, and to Japan, where she set up an orphanage. She embarked on her final journey, through Morocco, aged seventy, and died later that year.

The extracts are taken from letters to Isabella Bird's sister, written while on the Sandwich Islands, in 1871.

Visiting a volcano

I have no room in my thoughts for anything but volcanoes, and it will be so for some days to come. We have been all day in the crater, in fact, I left Mr Green and his native there, and came up with the guide, sore, stiff, bruised, cut, singed, grimy, with my thick gloves shrivelled off by the touch of sulphurous acid, and my boots nearly burned off. But what are cuts, bruises, fatigue, and singed eyelashes, in comparison with the awful sublimities I have witnessed today? The activity of Kilauea on 31 January was as child's play to its activity today: as a display of fireworks compared to the conflagration of a metropolis. *Then*, the sense of awe gave way speedily to that of admiration of the dancing fire fountains of a fiery lake; *now*, it was all terror, horror, and sublimity, blackness, suffocating gases, scorching heat, crashings, surgings, detonations; half-seen fires, hideous, tortured, wallowing waves. I feel as if the terrors of Kilauea would haunt me all my life, and be the nemesis of weak and tired hours . . .

The whole region vibrated with the shock of the fiery surges. To stand there was 'to snatch a fearful joy', out of a pain and terror which were unendurable. For two or three minutes we kept going to the edge, seeing the spectacle as with a flash, through half-closed eyes, and going back again; but a few trials, in which throat, nostrils, and eyes were irritated to torture by the acid gases, convinced us that it was unsafe to attempt to remain by the lake, as the pain and gasping for breath which followed each inhalation threatened serious consequences.

With regard to the north lake we were more fortunate, and more persevering, and I regard the three hours we spent by it as containing some of the most solemn, as well as most fascinating, experiences of my life. The aspect of the volcano had altogether changed within four months. At present there are two lakes surrounded by precipices about eighty feet high. Owing to the smoke and confusion, it is most difficult to estimate their size even approximately, but I think that the diameter of the two cannot be less than a fifth of a mile.

Within the pit or lake by which we spent the morning, there were no fiery fountains, or regular plashings of fiery waves playing in indescribable beauty in a faint blue atmosphere, but lurid, gory, molten, raging, sulphurous, tormented masses of matter, half-seen through masses as restless, of lurid smoke. Here, the violent action appeared centripetal, but with a southward tendency. Apparently, huge bulging masses of a lurid-coloured lava were wallowing the whole time one over another in a central whirlpool, which occasionally flung up a wave of fire thirty or forty feet. The greatest intensity of action was always preceded by a dull throbbing roar, as if the imprisoned gases were seeking the vent which was afforded them by the inward bulging of the wave and its bursting into spray. The colour of the lava which appeared to be thrown upwards from great depths was more fiery and less gory than that nearer the surface. Now and then, through rifts in the smoke, we saw a convergence of the whole molten mass into the centre, which rose wallowing and convulsed to a considerable height. The awful sublimity of what we did see was enhanced by the knowledge that it was only a thousandth part of what we did not see, mere momentary glimpses of a terror and fearfulness which otherwise could not have been borne.

A ledge, only three or four feet wide, hung over the lake, and between that and the comparative *terra firma* of the older lava there was a fissure of unknown depth, emitting hot blasts of pernicious gases. The guide would not venture on the outside ledge, but Mr Green, in his scientific zeal, crossed the crack, telling me not to follow him, but presently, in his absorption with what he saw, called to me to come, and I jumped across, and this remained our perilous standpoint.

Burned, singed, stifled, blinded, only able to stand on one foot at a time, jumping back across the fissure every two or three minutes to escape an unendurable whiff of heat and sulphurous stench, or when splitting sounds below threatened the disruption of the ledge, lured as often back by the fascination of the horrors below: so we spent three hours.

There was every circumstance of awfulness to make the impression of the sight indelible. Sometimes dense volumes of smoke hid everything, and yet, upwards, from out 'their sulphurous canopy' fearful sounds rose, crashings, thunderings, detonations, and we never knew then whether the spray of some hugely uplifted wave might not dash up to where we stood. At other times the smoke, partially lifting, but still swirling in strong eddies, revealed a central whirlpool of fire, wallowing at unknown depths, to which the lava, from all parts of the lake, slid centrewards and downwards as into a vortex, where it mingled its waves with indescribable noise and fury, and then, breaking upwards, dashed itself to a great height in fierce, gory gouts and clots, while hell itself seemed opening at our feet. At times, again, bits of the lake skinned over with a skin of a wonderful silvery, satiny sheen, to be immediately devoured; and as the lurid billows broke, they were mingled with misplaced patches as if of bright moonlight. Always changing, always suggesting force which nothing could repel, agony indescribable, mystery inscrutable, terror unutterable, a thing of eternal dread, revealed only in glimpses!

The Hawaiian Archipelago, 1875

ANNIE TAYLOR

1855–c.1920

I thank God for giving me the lives of those with me. One man was killed on the spot, and ten others were wounded.

Annie Taylor was born at Egremont in Cheshire, the second of ten children. She was a frail child and suffered from a string of ailments such as a weak heart and chronic bronchitis. As a result, she received little schooling, and was largely left to her own devices; but when, at the age of thirteen, she chose to commit herself to God, her decision was met with strong disapproval from the family, especially her adventurous and well-travelled father. She set her heart on a missionary life after hearing a talk in Richmond given by the son of Doctor Moffat about his father's work in Africa. She began visiting the sick in Brighton; when her allowance was cut off, she sold some of her possessions to fund a medical training course at a London hospital.

Reconciliation with her family came when her mother turned to God after an experience in a Sicilian chapel, and by the time Taylor travelled to China in 1884 with the China Inland Mission, she had the moral, if not the financial, support of her family.

Taylor spent three years doing medical work in China, where her contemporaries found her tricky to get along with owing to her obstinately independent spirit. While there, she began to agitate about visiting Tibet, the forbidden land that had fired her imagination as a child and was now even more alluring, as its snowy peaks seeming almost within sight. She first visited Tibet in 1887 and spent some years living near its border with India, switching sides in accordance with the reactions of the Tibetan authorities. Then, in 1892, she set out on what proved to be an intrepid and at times life-threatening seven-month journey through Tibet. She entered the country in the north of China and

travelled almost as far as Lhasa before returning by a different route, covering a total distance of 1,000 miles.

No Western woman had ventured through Tibet before, and Taylor was dependent on her unwavering faith to keep her going. She was convinced that God had sent her there and would therefore watch over her. 'I am God's little woman and he will protect me', she wrote in the diary that meticulously chronicles each day of the journey, and was published eight years after her return to China. Despite the hardships she encountered, her unadorned account is punctuated with a steadfast cheerfulness and optimism – on Christmas Day she made a pudding with suet and dried fruit that she had brought all the way with her.

Travelling with her were her old friend the Tibetan convert Pontso, a Chinese man (Noga) and his Tibetan wife, and two other men to help her with her ten saddle and pack horses. Pontso remained faithfully by her side throughout the journey; but of the other three men, one turned back through fear, another died en route, and the third made an attempt on her life. Taylor wore traditional Tibetan dress and shaved her head like a Tibetan nun. She travelled light – even lighter once two attacks from bandits had stripped her of most of her possessions, including her tent, clothing, cooking utensils and a box containing 'presents for chiefs'.

As Taylor approached Lhasa, Noga began to demand money, and on her refusal betrayed her to Chinese officials, leading to her arrest. There were fifteen days of preliminary hearings before a 'chief' arrived from another part of the country to resolve the matter. A large tent was erected, in which cross-legged, tea-drinking leaders mulled over her fate against a backdrop of huddled soldiers and servants, while Taylor's slight form sat calm and determined in the middle. Her indomitable personality won through. She was forbidden from continuing to Lhasa, but instead of throwing her into jail, the authorities provided her with escort horses and a tent and provisions with which to make her way back to China.

She appeared at Ta-chien-lu on 13 April 1893, and soon afterwards news of her adventures reached England, where they were discussed at Church meetings and inspired the 'Tibetan Pioneer Mission'. Under this name a group of fourteen men set sail for India to work under her leadership. ('Pioneer' was in fact a misleading term, because Moravians had been working on the borders of Tibet for the previous thirty-seven years, carrying out conversions, translating the scriptures and preparing books.) Taylor was perhaps too self-sufficient after her travels: within a few months the mission was dissolved and its members spread throughout China. Taylor asked for more female recruits to be sent out, but over the twenty years that remained of her work in Tibet and China she was usually alone, save for the company of the Tibetan convert Pashto.

Attacked by brigands

September 9: Started early and joined a company of Mongols. They had been to Siberia to sell their wool and buy barley-flour, etc. Their caravan consists of fifty yaks, all laden, as well as a few horses. Most of the men rode on horses, but some on yaks. They were nearly all armed, and, with our own escort of about twenty men, we made a brave show.

We stopped just for a short time at noon, and had tea near a stream, then pushed on quickly, the country being infested with brigands. Now and then the escort would scatter to see whether any were hiding behind the hills. We saw numbers of deer and other animals, and the soldiers amused themselves by hunting a fine wild goat.

We were going along quietly enough, when, all of a sudden, two of those in front came galloping back to say the robbers were upon us. We looked up, and saw numbers of them coming over the crest of the hill, all armed and many of them leading an extra horse. We went back a little, but were shut up in a hollow surrounded by hills. Ten of our men advanced to meet the robbers, but, on seeing their numbers, returned. We kept close to the yaks, looking to see which way to go. By this time robbers were seen on the tops of the hills all round, and they were closing in upon us. There was nothing to do but to stand still. Then they fired on us from all sides. Men and horses fell down dead or wounded. Bullets were flying. There was hardly a sound to be heard except the guns and the cries of fear from the Lhasa women. The firing was so hot that one of the lamas asked Noga to go and tell them we would surrender. He went towards them, making peaceful signs; but as soon as he got near they took hold of his horse, and, after a scuffle, captured his gun and sword. Erminie shrieked when she saw her husband unhorsed, thinking he was killed. The Mongols shouted that they surrendered, and the brigands rushed to take the yaks. Erminie, Pontso, Nobgey, and I ran towards a gorge in the mountains, which the lama pointed out, telling us to be quick, and crying out to the robbers that we were women. We did not know whether they would come after us or not. Two Mongols, badly wounded, were galloping away in front of us, and we followed them. When we got over the crest of the hill, Nobgey went back to see how it fared with the rest. Leucotze, with two of the pack-horses, was surrounded by the robbers, and Nobgey brought us word that he feared they had killed him. Nothing could be seen of Noga.

We then went on again in the track of the wounded men. Large herds of deer started at our flight, and soon we lost all signs of the path. Finally, an encampment came in sight, and we were most thankful to reach it. The people at first received us coldly; but on hearing that we were with the party attacked they were most kind, bringing us tea and barley-flour, and helping to unload the horses. Numbers of armed men were already galloping from all sides to the scene of the fight, for our Mongol companions belong to this encampment. They gave us plenty of jo (yak-dung) to make a fire, and also some tea, and lent us a large pan to make it in. We put our things together as best we could, and with the felt mats that covered the loads I made a bed and lay down to rest. The others were sitting by the fire wrapped in their fur cloaks. Nobgey again returned to get news of our missing ones.

September 10: At daybreak all was astir, and a man brought us word that our comrades were well and most of the loads had been saved. But about midday they appeared *without* the loads. The horses had been captured as well as the goods, and only two bags of barley-flour were saved. Leucotze was guarding the horses, but two robbers with drawn swords had compelled him to dismount, and had taken possession of the loads. All my clothes and the camp-bed and my bedding were gone. Noga had a scar on his neck, which he said was made by a stroke from the back of a sword, whether by mistake or of purpose we cannot tell; but I thank God for giving me the lives of those with me. One man was killed on the spot, and ten others were wounded. Our escort all fled, leaving the Mongols with the yaks. Seven horses were killed, and one yak; and the principal man of the Mongols was taken prisoner.

The brigands proved too strong for those who went out from the encampment on hearing the shots. There are said to be two hundred of them.

Noga has friends in the encampment; so we moved to where they were, they lending us a black tent and a cooking pan, as we had now none of our own. They also made us a present of a sheep, which Leucotze set to work to kill and dress. Noga had a long talk with the people, to whom he seems to be well known. They are all bandits, and go out in companies to attack unwary travellers; so I think he must have been a robber, too. He has decided to pay a visit to the camp of our assailants, as he knows one of their chiefs, and see whether he can recover some of the stolen goods.

September 11: Noga asked for something to offer the chief, and I went to the box in which articles for presentation had been put, but found that he had stolen most of them before starting from China, and left them in his house. He admitted having done this, and did not seem at all ashamed. About ten o'clock he went off with some others, taking Leucotze with him. He was angry and rude because I would not let Pontso go as well. We have to settle down for some time now in our tent. It is made of yak's hair, not very closely woven, so that when it rains the water comes in . . .

Onward into Tibet

September 17: In the evening the lama paid us a visit. He said that our stars were good, and that by means of dice the gods had told him Noga would arrive to-day; and therefore he had come expecting to see him. After we had lain down for the night, and it was raining fast, we heard a noise, the dogs barked, and then Noga and Leucotze appeared. Noga has recovered three of the horses, my bed, and a few of my clothes, and also a little of my bedding, but *all* his own things, though none of Pontso's. He had pretended to be a servant of Ser Gon Lama Hu Tu Tuk of Cho Per Che, a great man in these parts. He is a general to whom the emperor of China has given a lot of land. The people expect that he will some day be king of Tibet. He says that in a former birth he was once emperor of China, and before that a big European chief. Noga got an old passport of his from one of his servants, and he trades on that. I found that he was wearing one of my flannel jackets.

September 18: I asked Noga in the morning to give me the jacket, as Pontso and I had no more clothing, and charged him with taking the two fur gowns. He got into a rage; and, coming over to where I was lying down, attempted to strike me. Pontso and the servant prevented him; and I ran out, going into one of the Mongol tents for refuge. The people were most kind, giving me milk to drink. I sent for the lama to help me. He came and spoke to Noga, and another of the Mongols took my part. They put up my tent for me, and I said that I must return to Tau-chau, as I could not go on with such a man. All day long they talked, but it was to no purpose. Noga quarrelled with the lama. The lama was most kind . . .

September 22: Our guide has got one horse lent him, but he has to pay twelve taels for the other as deposit. He wanted me to pay this for him. He apologized for what he did, and promised to behave in the future. I would not listen for a long time, but at last let him have five taels. A letter of agreement between us is to be written.

This afternoon a large pack of gray wolves trotted along the hills. The Mongols feared these would attack their sheep, but they passed on. Yesterday there were several large deer with long black horns. The people said that some Chinese merchants had killed one lately, and that is the reason there is so much rain now.

September 23: This morning a lama with feathers in his hair, and wearing a mask, was driving away some of the yaks; they were supposed to be bewitched, and he was frightening the devil out of them. All the people followed him, and consulted him about their cattle.

November 16: We had to cross a mountain which tried our tired horses severely. The ranges are great masses of bare rock and most grotesque in shape. As we were getting ready to start, ten armed men were seen on the other side of the river. Three crossed over. We quietly got our packs on the horses. They came up to the Chinese merchants and spoke to them. We went on in front. One followed us. Two more crossed the river, joining the other two. They eyed us very much, and we feared they were brigands. Our party had only three guns; but God would, I knew, make all end for the best. The bitter wind got up again in the afternoon.

Although my horses are all knocked up, Noga will not give them barley-flour, which he gives to his own horses. I gave out some tea for the little white pony. Noga took half of it, and gave it to his pony. He takes everything.

November 17: The way lay downhill, and the climate got much milder. There was even green grass. My black pony went on with difficulty. We came at about two o'clock to a temple, Pang Gen Gumpa. The yaks all left their loads there, and we had to put the things on our tired horses. The way led by a river with high rocky mountains on the other side. The hills were covered with bushes and stunted pine-trees. It was getting on in the afternoon when we reached the encampment . . .

November 20: The horses are in so bad a condition that the Chinese will not take two in exchange for one. I went to them and asked them to do so, but they found it would not pay. However, they spoke to the chief, and I think he will give me one. He is a lama.

I have got so thin and am so exhausted that it looks as if I could not go on without a good horse. God will provide one for me. Pontso has been crying to-day. We expect to start to-morrow.

The chief gave me some butter and other things.

November 21: Before we started, the chief let me have a good horse in place of two of my bad ones, for he pitied me, as I am not strong enough to walk. God will remember him for all his kindness.

We went through a deep gorge with perpendicular rocks on both sides. Three women who are on their way to Lhasa, tramping it with packs on their backs (one of them carrying a little baby four months old in her bosom), have joined our party. The women here wear their hair in a fringe, but plait it round the forehead. They are much fairer than those I have seen before.

November 22: The rock scenery is very grand, but the mountains are trying. We have been crossing mountains all day.

The chief, who is with us, takes great care of me, getting his men to give me hot water for tea, and making a fire for me to get warm by. It is such a treat after the rough way I have been treated by Noga, who will not let Pontso warm water for me.

In the afternoon Erminie rode beside the chief and told him that I was English; so in the evening, after we had pitched the camp, he spoke to Noga about it. Noga shouted at the top of his voice that I was English and that after to-morrow he would go no further with me. He used a lot of abusive language. I left it all with Jesus, and had perfect peace.

Adventures in Tibet, 1901

Charles New
1840–75

Travelling, like poverty, makes a man acquainted with strange bed-fellows. That night I lay in the midst of a dozen savages, of whom I knew nothing ...

Ten years after a failed German bid for the higher slopes of Mount Kilimanjaro in 1862, the British missionary Charles New managed to reach the snow line on the mountain's saddle – the first European to do so. However, owing to bad weather, he was unable to continue.

In 1875 New returned, but this time a local 'chief', who had already tried to dissuade him from climbing the mountain, stole all his equipment. On a dismal return trip, New became ill and died before reaching Mombasa on the coast. In *Life, Wanderings and Labours in Eastern Africa* he not only describes his earlier attempt, but also offers his own commentary on the cultures he encountered, including his disapproval of the slave trade. Observing a caravan of chained slaves being shipped to Zanzibar's slave market, he noted that some were in such a bad way that they 'met the fate of all damaged goods by being allowed to go to waste'.

'What a profound solitude!'

Onward and upward we pushed our way through this jungle for an hour and a half, and then emerged upon the top of a grass-covered hill, whence we obtained a splendid view. The whole of the country, east, south, and west, lay outspread before us ... If I had not gone a step farther I should not have regretted having taken some pains to secure to myself the opportunity of ascending the mountain. Already its wonders began to dawn upon me as they could not have done from below. Impressions were made upon my mind which will never be effaced. The view gave me a knowledge of the country such as I could not have obtained in any other way. It impressed itself upon my brain in an instant, and I can see it all now as plainly as I saw it then ...

The forest upon which we had now entered was a vast belt of the densest vegetation, which encircles the whole mountain, and is called by the Wachaga 'Msudu.' Its growths are for the greater part of a gigantic kind, with a thick undergrowth of smaller trees, saplings, creepers, and plants innumerable, which would make it quite impassable but for the existence of the elephant, whose paths traverse it, within certain limits, in all directions. It is probably as old as the creation, and it wears an aspect of great antiquity. Upwards from the roots – trunks, branches, twigs, leaves, creepers, bush-ropes – all are moss-covered and moss-hung, forming an impenetrable covering scarcely admitting a single sunbeam. Yet flowers exhibiting all the colours of the rainbow peeped at us from all sides below.

Through this forest we pressed our way forward and upward, without much complaining from any one till noon. Up, up, up we toiled till we reached the region of the clouds. Now, enveloped in cold, heavy, drizzling mist, a 'change came over the spirit of our dream', the porters hung behind; they complained of benumbed hands and feet, at which they looked piteously as if they thought the demon of the forest had already taken possession of them; 'presaging tears began to fall,' and even Mange muttered that 'hundreds of dollars would not bring him to such a place again.'

From one of the loftiest elevations in this region I turned to take a retrospect of the country over which we had passed. No wonder that the atmosphere was so clear, for we were far above the region of the clouds. Down rolled the mountain from our feet till all was hidden, and the eye rested upon illimitable fields of snowy clouds . . .

At four p.m. we came to a large overhanging rock, forming a kind of cave, and here our Wachaga advised that we should put up for the night . . .

Sadi greatly amused us, he was so nervous. The rocks echoing our every word, he thought there were other beings up on the mountain beside ourselves. All the stories of elves, goblins, ghosts, ghouls, and spirits of all sorts he had ever heard of regarding the occupants of Kilima Njaro, now came home to him and greatly distressed him. When he lay down, he thought he felt the shock of an earthquake. 'There!' he exclaimed, starting up; 'what was that? The very earth moves! there! there!'

Travelling, like poverty, makes a man acquainted with strange bed-fellows. That night I lay in the midst of a dozen savages, of whom I knew nothing, and who for many reasons were not a desirable party to sleep with. One of my neighbours woke me up in the middle of the night by tugging at my blanket, and when I tugged it back he made such pitiful complaints about 'mbeho' (cold) and 'ku komeka' (dying), that I could not deny him the use of it . . .

Commencing our toils early, at eight a.m. we reached a heap of rocks, among which grew a solitary tree, where we sat down to rest. The Wachaga said this was as far as they dared to go. 'We have come,' they continued, 'farther than any one ever came before, and this is all we can do. There is Kibó very near now; if you wish to go on, you can do so, and we will wait here till you come back,' I expected this. Tofiki, however, though he was feeling the cold severely, declared his determination to go with me to the last. Every encumbrance was now laid aside, for we had our work to do. For a climbing stick I borrowed a spear, while Tofiki relieved a bow of its string, and took that. Now, leaving the rest of the party over the fires which they had kindled in the centre of the group of rocks, where they were well sheltered from the cutting winds, Tofiki and I went on alone . . .

Over the rocks we ascended, ridge after ridge, to find that there was yet another. It *was* wearisome work. At length the rocks gave place to clear tracts of loose dry sand, in which we sank up to our ankles, and now we began to find it difficult to respire. It was as if there was no breath in the atmosphere. A distance of twenty or thirty yards exhausted us; my lips were cracking, the veins in my head felt like bursting, my head swam, and, I was going to say, my very wits seemed wandering. Great changes were coming over Tofiki. He could not keep up with me, though I urged him constantly to do so. 'Pole, pole (slowly, slowly), Buana,' he gasped out, and I slackened my pace. Still he remained behind; he was fast failing. When we paused for breath and rested, he rather fell than sat down. His efforts to speak were mere sputterings. At length he mustered courage to say, 'The ascent of this mountain is nothing to me, but I do not want *you* to be beaten. I fear, however, I cannot go much farther.' Now, nothing but the sternest necessity could have elicited this confession from him. I did not wish to try him too severely; still, as we were so near the goal, I cheered him on. I got him from one stage to another, till, falling to the earth and gasping for breath, he stammered out, 'Buana, I cannot go on; but if you have strength, try alone, never mind me; I should not like you to be beaten; I will wait here for you. If you come back, well and good; if not, I shall not move from this spot, but shall die here!' and the good, faithful fellow meant every word he said. I would not have sacrificed him for all the 'eternal snows' in the world, but I could not give up yet. If I could only reach the snow so as to touch it, I should be content, and it now really seemed within my reach . . .

I went on, but it was hard work, breathing being so difficult that I had to pause at every few steps for breath. The sensations, too, which came over me at the idea of the profound solitude, of standing on heights to which no human being had ever before ascended, were overpowering. The situation was appalling, there was a grandeur and a magnificence about the surroundings which were almost too much for me; instead of exhilarating, they were oppressive.

I had not gone far, however, before I came to a tremendous gulf, dropping almost sheer down between myself and the patch of snow to which I hoped I was making my way. This gulf was all that now remained between myself and it, but what an *all*! The snow was on a level with my eye, but my arm was too short to reach it. My heart sank, but before I had time fairly to scan the position my eyes rested upon snow at my very feet! There it lay upon the rocks below me in shining masses, looking like newly washed and sleeping sheep!

Hurrah! . . . I thought of Tofiki! Returning a short distance, I called to him at the top of my voice, and in a little while he made his appearance, looking horrified. What had I seen? Strengthless as he was, my cries went through him like an arrow, and gave him new vigour. He expected to find me in the hands of some monster, about to be tossed into some abysmal depth! Reaching the spot where I had seen the snow, he exclaimed, 'There is snow! What more do you want, Buana?' 'Nothing,' I observed; 'but we must carry some of it away.' It was frozen as hard as the rock itself, but with the spiked end of the spear I carried, I broke off several large masses. Tofiki put them into his blanket, slung them over his shoulders, and away we went down hill in triumph! I made the more haste as my head was so giddy that I was afraid of swooning; Tofiki, too, looked wild and strange; and besides this, as noon was approaching, the mists would soon come sweeping up the mountain and make it difficult for us to find our party. As it was, we followed down our footprints in the sand, and coming to the rocky region, steered our course by the smoke which rose from the fires of our people. Reaching our party, they looked at us enquiringly, as much as to say, 'Well, what success?' Tofiki threw down the burden of snow, saying, 'There's the white stuff; look at it; Kibó is beaten at last!' When I took the snow and began crunching it, as if it were the greatest delicacy, the men looked at each other as much as to say, 'What uganga is the Mzungu up to now?' while some said, 'Who ever saw a man eating stones before?' Mtema stared and gaped, looked first at the snow and then at me, but remained dumb with astonishment. 'Luma (eat) yourself,' I said. He looked afraid, but after a while, putting it to his mouth, he instantly shouted, 'Mringa! mringa! (water! water!) Let us take it to the mange!' 'Yes,' said my guide, 'and I shall take some to the coast, where I shall sell it for medicine! Everybody will want a piece of the white stuff that came from Kilima Njaro!' I told them it would melt before we could reach Moche, but they smiled incredulously, saying, 'Who ever heard of stones melting?' It was broken up and put into one of the calabashes. Tofiki and I were feeling all right again now; no sooner had we entered the lower stratum of the atmosphere than our strength returned to us, and we felt quite new men.

Life, Wanderings and Labours in Eastern Africa, 1873

EDWARD WHYMPER
1840–1911
At 1.40 p.m. the world was at our feet, and the Matterhorn was conquered. Hurrah!

At the age of twenty, London-born Edward Whymper was commissioned to sketch scenes in the French Alps for a British publisher. He had had childhood ambitions of becoming an Arctic explorer, but on this trip to the Alps set his heart on mountaineering. He resolved to become the first to climb the 4,478-metre (14,692 foot) Matterhorn, the third-highest mountain in Europe, which had a fearsome reputation among the climbing fraternity.

For the rest of the summer of 1860 Whymper practised mountaineering skills with a group of English climbers, then the following year returned to tackle his mountain. However, that, and a further six attempts up the south-western face over the next few years, ended in failure. This was accompanied by success on other mountains, however: he reached the summits of Mont Pelvoux and Les Ecrins, which were the second highest and highest peaks in the French Dauphiné Alps.

In 1865 Whymper decided to attempt the Matterhorn up its eastern face, a route that had always been considered impossible. He set out with a large party at the same time as an Italian group who were deter-mined to beat Whymper to the top from the north side. Whymper's expedition arrived first, on 14 July 1865, whereupon they built a cairn and spent an hour relishing their achievement.

On the way back down, however, one member of the expedition, Douglas Hadow, lost his footing and knocked over the Swiss guide Michael Croz. These two climbers pulled another two with them (the Reverend Charles Hudson and the nineteen-year-old mountaineer Lord Francis Douglas). Their rope snapped, and all four plunged to their deaths over the North Face. Whymper survived and went on to make two more ascents of the Matterhorn, in 1874 and 1895.

Although the conquest of the Matterhorn is the achievement for which Whymper is most remembered, in 1880 he became the first to scale Ecuador's Mount Chimborazo, took part in two expeditions within Greenland, and led three others in the Canadian Rockies, pulling off the first ascents of the mountains Storm and Whymper (named in his honour).

His book *Scrambles Amongst the Alps*, containing his own illustrations, became a classic of climbing literature.

Ascending the Matterhorn

We started from Zermatt on the 13th of July 1865, at half-past five, on a brilliant and perfectly cloudless morning. We were eight in number – Croz, old Peter [Taugwalder] and his two sons, Lord F. Douglas, Hadow, Hudson, and I. To ensure steady motion, one tourist and one native walked together. The youngest Taugwalder fell to my share, and the lad marched well, proud to be on the expedition, and happy to show his powers. The wine-bags also fell to my lot to carry, and throughout the day, after each drink, I replenished them secretly with water, so that at the next halt they were found fuller than before! This was considered a good omen, and little short of miraculous . . .

Before twelve o'clock we had found a good position for the tent, at a height of 11,000 feet. Croz and young Peter went on to see what was above, in order to save time on the following morning. They cut across the heads of the snow-slopes which descended towards the Furggengletscher, and disappeared round a corner; but shortly afterwards we saw them high up on the face, moving quickly. We others made a solid platform for the tent in a well-protected spot, and then watched eagerly for the return of the men. The stones which they upset told us that they were very high, and we supposed that the way must be easy. At length, just before 3 p.m., we saw them coming down, evidently much excited. 'What are they saying, Peter?' 'Gentlemen, they say it is no good.' But when they came near we heard a different story. 'Nothing but what was good; not a difficulty, not a single difficulty! We could have gone to the summit and returned to-day easily!'

We passed the remaining hours of daylight – some basking in the sunshine, some sketching or collecting; and when the sun went down, giving, as it departed, a glorious promise for the morrow, we returned to the tent to arrange for the night. Hudson made tea, I coffee, and we then retired each one to his blanket-bag – the Taugwalders, Lord Francis Douglas, and myself occupying the tent; the others remaining, by preference, outside. Long after dusk the cliffs above echoed with our laughter and with the songs of the guides; for we were happy that night in camp, and feared no evil.

We assembled together outside the tent before dawn on the morning of the 14th, and started directly it was light enough to move . . . The whole of this great slope was now revealed, rising for 3,000 feet like a huge natural staircase. Some parts were more and others were less easy; but we were not once brought to a halt by any serious impediment, for when an obstruction was met in front it could always be turned to the right or to the left.

[After a steady climb . . .] A long stride round a rather awkward corner brought us to snow once more. The last doubt vanished! The Matterhorn was ours! Nothing but 200 feet of easy snow remained to be surmounted!

You must now carry your thoughts back to the seven Italians who started from Breuil on the 11th of July. Four days had passed since their departure, and we were tormented with anxiety lest they should arrive on the top before us. All the way up we had talked of them, and many false alarms of 'men on the summit' had been raised. The higher we rose, the more intense became the excitement. What if we should be beaten at the last moment? The slope eased off, at length we could be detached, and Croz and I, dashing away, ran a neck-and-neck race, which ended in a dead heat. At 1.40 p.m. the world was at our feet, and the Matterhorn was conquered. Hurrah! Not a footstep could be seen.

It was not yet certain that we had not been beaten. The summit of the Matterhorn was formed of a rudely level ridge, about 350 feet long, and the Italians might have been at its farther extremity. I hastened to the southern end, scanning the snow right and left eagerly. Hurrah again – it was untrodden! 'Where were the men?' I peered over the cliff, half doubting, half expectant, and saw them immediately – mere dots on the ridge, at an immense distance below. Up went my arms and my hat. 'Croz! Croz! come here!' 'Where are they, Monsieur?' 'There – don't you see them – down there!' 'Ah! the *coquins*, they are low down.' 'Croz, we must make those fellows hear us.' We yelled until we were hoarse. The Italians seemed to regard us – we could not be certain. 'Croz, we *must* make them hear us; they *shall* hear us!' I seized a block of rock and hurled it down, and called upon my companion, in the name of friendship, to do the same. We drove our sticks in, and prized away the crags, and soon a torrent of stones poured down the cliffs. There was no mistake about it this time. The Italians turned and fled . . .

The others had arrived, so we went back to the northern end of the ridge. Croz now took the tent-pole, and planted it in the highest snow. 'Yes,' we said, 'there is the flag-staff, but where is the flag?' 'Here it is,' he answered, pulling off his blouse and fixing it to the stick. It made a poor flag, and there was no wind to float it out, yet it was seen all around. They saw it at Zermatt – at the Riffel – in the Val Tournanche. At Breuil the watchers cried, 'Victory is ours!' They raised 'bravos' for Carrel and 'vivas' for Italy, and hastened to put themselves *en fête*. On the morrow they were undeceived. 'All was changed; the explorers returned sad – cast down – disheartened – confounded – gloomy.' 'It is true,' said the men. 'We saw them ourselves – they hurled stones at us! The old traditions *are* true – there are spirits on the top of the Matterhorn!'

We agreed that it would be best for Croz to go first, and Hadow second; Hudson, who was almost equal to a born mountaineer in sureness of foot, wished to be third; Lord Francis Douglas was placed next; and old Peter, the strongest of the remainder, after him. I suggested to Hudson that we should attach a rope to the rocks on our arrival at the difficult bit, and hold it as we descended, as an additional protection. He approved the idea, but it was not definitely settled that it should be done. The party was being arranged in the above order whilst I was sketching the summit, and they had finished, and were waiting for me to be tied in line, when some one remembered that our names had not been left in a bottle. They requested me to write them down, and moved off while it was being done.

A few minutes afterwards I tied myself to young Peter, ran down after the others, and caught them just as they were commencing the descent of the difficult part. Great care was being taken. Only one man was moving at a time; when he was firmly planted the next advanced, and so on. They had not, however, attached the additional rope to rocks, and nothing was said about it. The suggestion was not made for my own sake, and I am not sure that it even occurred to me again. For some little distance we two followed the others, detached from them, and should have continued so had not Lord Francis Douglas asked me, about 3 p.m., to tie on to old Peter, as he feared, he said, that Taugwalder would not be able to hold his ground if a slip occurred.

A few minutes later a sharp-eyed lad ran into the Monte Rosa hotel, to Seiler, saying that he had seen an avalanche fall from the summit of the Matterhorn on to the Matterhorngletscher. The boy was reproved for telling idle stories; he was right, nevertheless, and this was what he saw.

Michel Croz had laid aside his axe, and in order to give Mr Hadow greater security, was absolutely taking hold of his legs, and putting his feet, one by one, into their proper positions. So far as I know, no one was actually descending. I cannot speak with certainty, because the two leading men were partially hidden from my sight by an intervening mass of rock, but it is my belief, from the movements of their shoulders, that Croz, having done as I have said, was in the act of turning round, to go down a step or two himself; at this moment Mr Hadow slipped, fell against him, and knocked him over. I heard one startled exclamation from Croz, then saw him and Mr Hadow flying downwards; in another moment Hudson was dragged from his steps, and Lord F. Douglas immediately after him. All this was the work of a moment. Immediately we heard Croz's exclamation, old Peter and I planted ourselves as firmly as the rocks would permit: the rope was taut between us, and the jerk came on us both as on one man. We held; but the rope broke midway between Taugwalder and Lord Francis Douglas. For a few seconds we saw our unfortunate companions sliding downwards on their backs, and spreading out their hands, endeavouring to save themselves. They passed from our sight uninjured, disappeared one by one, and fell from precipice to precipice on to the Matterhorngletscher below, a distance of nearly 4,000 feet in height. From the moment the rope broke it was impossible to help them.

So perished our comrades! For the space of half an hour we remained on the spot without moving a single step. The two men, paralyzed by terror, cried like infants, and trembled in such a manner as to threaten us with the fate of the others. Old Peter rent the air with exclamations of 'Chamounix! Oh, what will Chamounix say?' He meant, Who would believe that Croz could fall? The young man did nothing but scream or sob, 'We are lost! we are lost!' Fixed between the two, I could neither move up nor down. I begged young Peter to descend, but he dared not. Unless he did we could not advance. Old Peter became alive to the danger, and swelled the cry, 'We are lost! we are lost!' The father's fear was natural – he trembled for his son; the young man's fear was cowardly – he thought of self alone. At last old Peter summoned up courage, and changed his position to a rock to which he could fix the rope; the young man then descended, and we all stood together. Immediately we did so I asked for the rope which had given way, and found, to my surprise – indeed to my horror – that it was the weakest of the three ropes. It was not brought, and should not have been employed, for the purpose for which it was used. It was old rope, and, compared with the others, was feeble. It was intended as a reserve, in case we had to leave much rope behind, attached to rocks. I saw at once that a serious question was involved, and made him give me the end. It had broken in mid-air, and it did not appear to have sustained previous injury.

For more than two hours afterwards I thought almost every moment that the next would be my last; for the Taugwalders, utterly unnerved, were not only incapable of giving assistance, but were in such a state that a slip might have been expected from them at any moment. After a time we were able to do that which should have been done at first, and fixed rope to firm rocks, in addition to being tied together. These ropes were cut from time to time, and were left behind.* Even with their assurance the men were afraid to proceed, and several times old Peter turned with ashy face and faltering limbs, and said, with terrible emphasis, '*I cannot!*'

About 6 p.m. we arrived at the snow upon the ridge descending towards Zermatt, and all peril was over. We frequently looked, but in vain, for traces of our unfortunate companions; we bent over the ridge and cried to them, but no sound returned. Convinced at last that they were neither within sight nor hearing, we ceased from our useless efforts, and, too cast down for speech, silently gathered up our things, and the little effects of those who were lost, preparatory to continuing the descent; when, lo! a mighty arch appeared, rising above the Lyskamm, high into the sky. Pale, colourless, and noiseless, but perfectly sharp and defined, except where it was lost in the clouds, this unearthly apparition seemed like a vision from another world; and, almost appalled, we watched with amazement the gradual development of two vast crosses, one on either side. If the Taugwalders had not been the first to perceive it, I should have doubted my senses. They thought it had some connection with the accident, and I, after a while, that it might bear some relation to ourselves. But our movements had no effect upon it. The spectral forms remained motionless. It was a fearful and wonderful sight; unique in my experience, and impressive beyond description, coming at such a moment.

Scrambles Amongst the Alps in the Years 1860–69, 1871

FRANCIS YOUNGHUSBAND
1863–1942

After the high tension of the last fifteen months, I was free to relax. So I let it open itself out without restraint . . . I had a curious sense of being literally in love with the world.

Born at a hill station on the North-West Frontier, and educated in Britain, Sir Francis Younghusband left Sandhurst at nineteen, commissioned into the Ist King's Dragoon Guards. The son of a British army major in India, he was what Lord Curzon, the Viceroy, saw as shaped by the 'frontier school of character' – a perfect candidate to play an important part in the 'Great Game', the strategic manoeuvrings of Britain and Russia for control of the area. The Tsarist empire seemed intent on expanding into Afghanistan, western China and the independent kingdoms on India's northern frontier, so threatening Britain's hold on the subcontinent.

On his first reconnaissance missions – to the mountainous region between Kashmir and Afghanistan – Younghusband soon gathered a reputation for initiative and daring. He also had a gift for handling the Asians, for whom he had a deep respect.

Still in his early twenties, in 1887 Younghusband – then on leave in Peking – volunteered to travel overland back to India, in order to assess western China's defences against a possible Russian incursion. This seven-month journey took him across a stretch of the Mongolian Gobi through which no European had ventured, along one of the Silk Roads and on to India by way of the 19,000-foot Mustagh Pass, long since fallen into disuse. Back in England, he presented his observations to the Royal Geographical Society, who in due course awarded him their coveted Gold Medal in 1890.

In 1903, Younghusband was chosen to lead a military expedition into the mysterious kingdom of Tibet, establish relations with the Dalai Llama, and edge out the Russian presence. Typically, he had once proposed disguising himself as a Turkic trader in order to slip into the forbidden city of Lhasa; but his proposal had been turned down. This adventure, though, was an altogether different thing.

Departing as a newly promoted colonel, Younghusband led his expedition into a disaster – an impulsive act by a Tibetan general prompted a general massacre of his troops, a bloodbath that left one of the worst stains of the century on the British military. Furthermore, on arrival, it now became evident that there was no Russian presence after all. It was not Younghusband's fault: everyone agreed that he led with his usual panache and brilliance, in what were trying conditions; but the ineptitude of the British cabinet has resulted in him being remembered for ever as a blood-thirsty imperialist, an image that is very far from just.

On his last evening in Lhasa, Younghusband, who had always had something of a mystical streak, rode up into the mountains to take a final look at it from above, and experienced a moment of spiritual enlightenment that marked a turning point in his life: 'I felt I was seeing deep into the true heart of things . . .'

He retired from the Indian government service at the age of forty-seven and dedicated the rest of his life to spiritual matters. In 1936 he founded the World Congress of Faiths, which aimed to bring together Christians, Buddhists, Muslims, Hindus and Jews – as it still does. Six years later he died, aged seventy-nine. Carved on his tombstone is a relief depicting the holy city of Lhasa.

In tune with nature

It was a heavenly evening. The sun was flooding the mountain slopes with
slanting light. Calm and deep peace lay over the valley below me – the valley
in which Lhasa lay. I seemed in tune with all the world and all the world
seemed in tune with me. My experiences in many lands – in dear distant
England; in India and China; in the forests of Manchuria, Kashmir, and
Sikkim; in the desert of Gobi and the South African veldt; in the Himalaya
mountains; and on many an ocean voyage; and experiences with such varied
peoples as the Chinese and Boers, Tibetans and Mahrattas, Rajputs and
Kirghiz – seemed all summed up in that moment. And yet here on the quiet
mountain-side, filled as I was with the memories of many experiences that I
had had in the high mountain solitudes and in the deserts of the world away
from men, I seemed in touch with the wide Universe beyond this Earth as
well.

After the high tension of the last fifteen months, I was free to let my soul
relax. So I let it open itself out without restraint. And in its sensitive state it
was receptive of the finest impressions and quickly responsive to every call. I
seemed to be truly in harmony with the Heart of Nature. My vision seemed
absolutely clear. I felt I was seeing deep into the true heart of things. With my
soul's eye I seemed to see what was really in men's hearts, in the heart of
mankind as a whole and in the Heart of Nature as a whole.

And my experience was this – and I try to describe it as accurately as I can. I
had a curious sense of being literally in love with the world. There is no other
way in which I can express what I then felt. I felt as if I could hardly contain
myself for the love which was bursting within me. It seemed to me as if the
world itself were nothing but love. We have all felt on some great occasion an
ardent glow of patriotism. This was patriotism extended to the whole Universe. The country for which I was feeling this overwhelming intensity of love
was the entire Universe. At the back and foundation of things I was certain
was love – and not merely placid benevolence, but active, fervent, devoted love
and nothing less. The whole world seemed in a blaze of love, and men's hearts
were burning to be in touch with one another.

It was a remarkable experience I had on that evening. And it was not merely
a passing roseate flush due to my being in high spirits, such as a man feels who
has had a good breakfast or has heard that his investments have paid a big
dividend. I am not sure that I was at the moment in what are usually called
high spirits. What I felt was more of the nature of a deep inner soul-
satisfaction. And what I saw amounted to this – that evil is the superficial,

goodness the fundamental characteristic of the world; affection and not animosity the root disposition of men towards one another. Men are inherently good not inherently wicked, though they have an uphill fight of it to find scope and room for their goodness to declare itself, and though they are placed in hard conditions and want every help they can to bring their goodness out. Fundamentally men are consuming with affection for one another and only longing for opportunity to exert that affection. They want to behave straightly, honourably, and in a neighbourly fashion towards one another, and are only too thankful when means and conditions can be found which will let them indulge this inborn feeling of fellowship. Wickedness, of course, exists. But wickedness is not the essential characteristic of men. It is due to ignorance, immaturity, and neglect, like the naughtinesses of children. It springs from the conditions in which men find themselves, and not from any radical inclination within themselves. With maturity and reasonable conditions the innate goodness which is the essential characteristic will assert itself. This is what came to me with burning conviction. And it arose from no ephemeral sense of exhilaration, nor has it since evaporated away . . .

An additional ground I have for believing it to be true is that on that mountain-side near Lhasa I had a specially favourable opportunity of looking at the world from, as it were, a proper focal distance. And it is only from a proper focal distance that we can see what things really are. If we put ourselves right up against a picture in the National Gallery we cannot possibly see its beauty – see what the picture really is. No man is a hero to his own valet. And that is not because a man is not a hero, but because the valet is too close to see the real man. Cecil Rhodes at close quarters was peevish, irritable, and like a big spoilt child. Now at a distance we know him, with all his faults, to have been a great-souled man. Social reformers near at hand are often intolerable bores and religious fanatics frequently a pestilential nuisance. We have to get well away from a man to see him as he really is. And so it is with mankind as a whole . . .

The conclusion I reach from this experience is that I was, at the moment I had it, intimately in touch with the true Heart of Nature. In my exceptionally receptive mood I was directly experiencing the genius of Nature in the very act of inspiring and vitalising the whole. I was seeing the Divinity in the Heart streaming like light and heat through every part of Nature, and with the dominating forcefulness of love lifting each to its own high level.

And my experience was no unique experience. It was an experience the like of which has come to many men and many women in every land in all ages. It may not be common; but it is not unusual. And in all cases it gives the same certainty of conviction that the Heart of Nature is *good*, that men are not the sport of chance, but that Divine Love is a real, an effectively determining and the dominant factor in the processes of Nature, and Divine fellowship the essence of the ideal which is working throughout Nature and compelling all things unto itself.

The Heart of Nature, 1921

HIRAM BINGHAM
1876–1956

Suddenly we found ourselves standing in front of the ruins of two of the finest and most interesting structures in ancient America. Made of beautiful white granite . . . The sight held me spellbound.

Hiram Bingham, the American historian who found Machu Picchu, the most famous archaeological site in South America, was born and brought up in Hawaii, where his missionary father taught him mountaineering skills that would later prove invaluable to his exploration of the Andes.

The expedition for which he is most remembered was the Yale Peruvian Expedition in 1911, in search of the lost city of the Incas, Vilcabamba. This had been established by Manco, the former puppet ruler set up by Pizarro and his men, when he fled Cuzco after an unsuccessful rising against the Spaniards. From Vilcabamba the Incas led resistance against the Spaniards for another thirty years. Spanish missionaries who had heard about it reported that it was 'the chief town and the one in which was the university of idolatry, the professors of witchcraft and teachers of abominations'.

Bingham had become enchanted with the idea of discovering this secret capital of the Incas, which even the conquistadors had been unable to find, buried as it was in the heart of the Peruvian Andes. Vilcabamba was surrounded not just by severe slopes and matted vegetation, but also by legend. It was unlikely to be found without difficulty.

On 24 July Bingham's expedition, guided by an eleven-year-old local boy, emerged on a ridge below a peak known as Machu Picchu and they found themselves confronted with terraces, steps and walls of astounding quality. The ruins were overgrown with jungle, but remarkably preserved – Bingham immediately saw the similarity between one structure and the Temple of the Sun, in Cuzco. Whatever was here among the vegetation, it had surely once been a place of great importance to the Incas.

The expedition moved on, and the following month discovered another important Inca site, the city of Vitcos. It was not until the following year that Bingham led an expedition to excavate the Machu Picchu site and only then was its true scale revealed. It proved, however, not to be the city of Vilcabamba, the true location of which was finally established when the American Gene Savoy excavated some other ruins Bingham had found, at Espíritu Pampa.

In 1948, the same year in which his *Lost City of the Incas* was first published, the road leading to Machu Picchu was named the Hiram Bingham Highway.

Going to investigate 'very good' ruins

When Arteaga learned that we were interested in the architectural remains of the Incas, and were looking for the palace of the last Inca, he said there were some very good ruins in this vicinity – in fact, some excellent ones on top of the opposite mountain, called Huayna Picchu, and also on a ridge called Machu Picchu.

The morning of July 24th dawned in a cold drizzle. Arteaga shivered and seemed inclined to stay in his hut. I offered to pay him well if he would show me the ruins. He demurred and said it was too hard a climb for such a wet day. But when he found that I was willing to pay him a *sol* (a Peruvian silver dollar, 50 cents, gold), three or four times the ordinary daily wage in this vicinity, he finally agreed to go. When asked just where the ruins were, he pointed straight up to the top of the mountain. No one supposed that they would be particularly interesting. And no one cared to go with me. Our naturalist said there were 'more butterflies near the river!' and he was reasonably certain he could collect some new varieties. Our surgeon said he had to wash his clothes and mend them. Anyhow it was my job to investigate all reports of ruins and try to find the Inca capital.

So, accompanied only by Sergeant Carrasco, I left camp at ten o'clock. After a walk of three quarters of an hour Arteaga left the main road and plunged down through the jungle to the bank of the river. Here there was a primitive bridge which crossed the roaring rapids at its narrowest part, where the stream was forced to flow between two great boulders. The 'bridge' was made of half a dozen very slender logs, some of which were not long enough to span the distance between the boulders, but had been spliced and lashed together with vines!

Arteaga and the sergeant took off their shoes and crept gingerly across, using their somewhat prehensile toes to keep from slipping. It was obvious that no one could live for an instant in the icy cold rapids, but would immediately be dashed to pieces against the rocks. I frankly confess that I got down on my hands and knees and crawled across, 6 inches at a time. Even after we reached the other side I could not help wondering what would happen to the 'bridge' if a particularly heavy shower should fall in the valley above. A light rain had fallen during the night and the river had risen so that the bridge was already threatened by the foaming rapids. It would not take much more to wash it away entirely. If this should happen during the day it might be very awkward. As a matter of fact, it did happen a few days later and when the next visitors attempted to cross the river at this point they found only one slender log remaining.

Leaving the stream, we now struggled up the bank through dense jungle, and in a few minutes reached the bottom of a very precipitous slope. For an hour and twenty minutes we had a hard climb. A good part of the distance we went on all fours, sometimes holding on by our fingernails. Here and there, a primitive ladder made from the roughly notched trunk of a small tree was placed in such a way as to help one over what might otherwise have proved to be an impassable cliff. In another place the slope was covered with slippery grass where it was hard to find either handholds or footholds. Arteaga groaned and said that there were lots of snakes here. Sergeant Carrasco said nothing but was glad he had good military shoes. The humidity was great. We were in the belt of maximum precipitation in Eastern Peru. The heat was excessive; and I was not in training. There were no ruins or *andenes* of any kind in sight. I began to think my companions had chosen the better part.

Shortly after noon, just as we were completely exhausted, we reached a little grass-covered hut 2,000 feet above the river where several good-natured Indians, pleasantly surprised at our unexpected arrival, welcomed us with dripping gourds full of cool, delicious water. Then they set before us a few cooked sweet potatoes. It seems that two Indian farmers, Richarte and Alvarez, had recently chosen this eagles' nest for their home. They said they had found plenty of terraces here on which to grow their crops. Laughingly they admitted they enjoyed being free from undesirable visitors, officials looking for army 'volunteers' or collecting taxes . . .

Without the slightest expectation of finding anything more interesting than the ruins of two or three stone houses such as we had encountered at various places on the road between Ollantaytambo and Torontoy, I finally left the cool shade of the pleasant little hut and climbed further up the ridge and round a slight promontory. Melchor Arteaga had 'been there once before', so he decided to rest and gossip with Richarte and Alvarez. They sent a small boy with me as a 'guide'. The sergeant was in duty bound to follow, but I think he may have been a little curious to see what there was to see.

Hardly had we left the hut and rounded the promontory than we were confronted with an unexpected sight, a great flight of beautifully constructed stone-faced terraces, perhaps a hundred of them, each hundreds of feet long and 10 feet high. They had been recently rescued from the jungle by the Indians. A veritable forest of large trees which had been growing on them for centuries had been chopped down and partly burned to make a clearing for agricultural purposes. The task was too great for the two Indians so the tree trunks had been allowed to lie as they fell and only the smaller branches removed. But the ancient soil, carefully put in place by the Incas, was still capable of producing rich crops of maize and potatoes.

However, there was nothing to be excited about. Similar flights of well-made terraces are to be seen in the upper Urubamba Valley at Pisac and Ollantaytambo, as well as opposite Torontoy. So we patiently followed the little guide along one of the widest terraces, where there had once been a small conduit, and made our way into an untouched forest beyond. Suddenly I found myself confronted with the walls of ruined houses built of the finest quality of Inca stone work. It was hard to see them for they were partly covered with trees and moss, the growth of centuries, but in the dense shadow, hiding in bamboo thickets and tangled vines, appeared here and there walls of white granite ashlars carefully cut and exquisitely fitted together. We scrambled along through the dense undergrowth, climbing over terrace walls and in bamboo thickets, where our guide found it easier going than I did. Suddenly, without any warning, under a huge overhanging ledge the boy showed me a cave beautifully lined with the finest cut stone. It had evidently been a royal mausoleum. On top of this particular ledge was a semi-circular building whose outer wall, gently sloping and slightly curved, bore a striking resemblance to the famous Temple of the Sun in Cuzco. This might also be a temple of the sun. It followed the natural curvature of the rock and was keyed to it by one of the finest examples of masonry I had ever seen. Furthermore it was tied into another beautiful wall, made of very carefully matched ashlars of pure white granite, especially selected for its fine grain. Clearly, it was the work of a master artist. The interior surface of the wall was broken by niches and square stone-pegs. The exterior surface was perfectly simple and unadorned. The lower courses, of particularly large ashlars, gave it a look of solidity. The upper courses, diminishing in size towards the top, lent grace and delicacy to the structure. The flowing lines, the symmetrical arrangement of the ashlars, and the gradual gradation of the courses, combined to produce a wonderful effect, softer and more pleasing than that of the marble temples of the Old World. Owing to the absence of mortar, there were no ugly spaces between the rocks. They might have grown together. On account of the beauty of the white granite this structure surpassed in attractiveness the best Inca walls in Cuzco, which had caused visitors to marvel for four centuries. It seemed like an unbelievable dream. Dimly, I began to realize that this wall and its adjoining semicircular temple over the cave were as fine as the finest stonework in the world.

It fairly took my breath away. What could this place be? Why had no one given us any idea of it? Even Melchor Arteaga was only moderately interested and had no appreciation of the importance of the ruins which Richarte and Alvarez had adopted for their little farm. Perhaps after all this was an isolated small place which had escaped notice because it was inaccessible.

Then the little boy urged us to climb up a steep hill over what seemed to be a flight of stone steps. Surprise followed surprise in bewildering succession. We came to a great stairway of large granite blocks. Then we walked along a path to a clearing where the Indians had planted a small vegetable garden.

Suddenly we found ourselves standing in front of the ruins of two of the finest and most interesting structures in ancient America, Made of beautiful white granite, the walls contained blocks of Cyclopean size, higher than a man. The sight held me spellbound.

Each building had only three walls and was entirely open on one side. The principal temple had walls 12 feet high which were lined with exquisitely made niches, five high up at each end, and seven on the back. There were seven courses of ashlars in the end walls. Under the seven rear niches was a rectangular block 14 feet long, possibly a sacrificial altar, but more probably a throne for the mummies of departed Incas, brought out to be worshipped. The building did not look as though it had ever had a roof. The top course of beautifully smooth ashlars was left uncovered so that the sun could be welcomed here by priests and mummies. I could scarcely believe my senses as I examined the larger blocks in the lower course and estimated that they must weigh from ten to fifteen tons each. Would anyone believe what I had found? Fortunately, in this land where accuracy in reporting what one has seen is not a prevailing characteristic of travellers, I had a good camera and the sun was shining.

The principal temple faces the south where there is a small plaza or courtyard. On the east side of the plaza was another amazing structure, the ruins of a temple containing three great windows looking out over the canyon to the rising sun. Like its neighbour, it is unique among Inca ruins. Nothing just like them in design and execution has ever been found. Its three conspicuously large windows, obviously too large to serve any useful purpose, were most beautifully made with the greatest care and solidity. This was clearly a ceremonial edifice of peculiar significance. Nowhere else in Peru, so far as I know, is there a similar structure conspicuous for being 'a masonry wall with three windows'. It will be remembered that Salcamayhua, the Peruvian who wrote an account of the antiquities of Peru in 1620, said that the first Inca, Manco the Great, ordered 'works to be executed at the place of his birth, consisting of a masonry wall with three windows'. Was that what I had found? If it was, then this was not the capital of the last Inca but the birthplace of the first. It did not occur to me that it might be both.

Lost City of the Incas, 1948

FRANK KINGDON-WARD
1885–1958

The land leeches, however, were terrible . . . There is nothing more horribly
fascinating than to see the leaves of the jungle undergrowth, during the
rains, literally shaking under the motions of these slender, bloodthirsty,
finger-like creatures . . .

Frank Kingdon-Ward's father was a distinguished botanist, and by the end of his short life had become a professor at Cambridge. However, Frank's own success in the profession soon outshone that of his father, despite – the story goes – his having wanted, as a child, to become a cab driver.

Soon after leaving university Kingdon-Ward accepted a teaching post in Singapore, but a commission to collect plants from Tibet for planting in gardens back in England gave him the opportunity to concentrate on botany. He returned from this trip with 200 different species, twenty-two of which were new to science, including the famous Blue Poppy.

His second solo trip (1913) was frustrated by bad weather and by the refusal of the Chinese to allow him into Tibet, but in early 1924 he embarked on an expedition in search of the Tsangpo waterfalls, to which magical qualities were attributed in Tibetan legend. Travelling from the Brahmaputra, he and his companion, Lord Cawdor, penetrated the Tsangpo gorges further than any previous Westerner. They discovered several impressive waterfalls along the way, though none that matched the description of the legendary ones, which were finally discovered seventy-four years later by Ken Storm, Ian Bakerk and Hamid Sadar less than a mile upstream from where Kingdon-Ward and Cawdor had turned back. Kingdon-Ward returned from this trip laden with plants, including nearly a hundred species of rhododendron, that were shown at horticultural shows back in England. Many of the plants discovered by Kingdon-Ward can still be seen in the herbarium at Kew.

The rocky Mekong gorge

This was the last we were destined to see of the great Mekong river. I was scarcely sorry to say goodbye, for the Mekong gorge – one long ugly rent between mountains which grow more and more arid, more and more savage as we travel northwards (yet hardly improve as we travel southwards) – is an abnormality, a grim freak of nature, a thing altogether out of place. Perhaps I had not been sufficiently ill-used by this extraordinary river to have a deep affection for it. The traveller, buffeted and bruised by storm and mountain, cherishes most the foe worthy of his steel. Nevertheless there was a strange fascination about its olive-green water in winter, its boiling red floods in summer, and the everlasting thunder of its rapids. And its peaceful little villages, some of them hidden away in the dips between the hills, others straggling over sloping alluvial fans or perched up on some ancient river-terrace where scattered blocks of stone suggest the decay of a ruined civiliza-tion – all these oases break the depressing monotony of naked rock and ill-nourished vegetation, delighting the eye with the beauty of their verdure and the richness of their crops.

Happy people! What do they know of the strife and turmoil of the western world? We wear ourselves out saving time in one direction that we may waste it in another, hurrying and ever hurrying through time as if we were disgusted with life, but these people think of time not in miles an hour but according to the rate at which their crops grow in the spring, and their fruits ripen in the autumn. They work that they and their families may have enough to eat and enough to wear, living and dying where they were born, where their offspring will live and die after them, as did their ancestors before them, shut in by the mountains which bar access from the outer world.

On leeches

The land leeches, however, were dreadful.

These little fiends are about an inch long and, at a full stretch, no thicker than a knitting needle. They progress similarly to a looper caterpillar, though they are not, of course, provided with legs. Fixing one end, which is expanded into a bell-shaped sucker, the leech curves itself over into a complete arch, fixes the other extremity in the same way and, releasing the rear end, advances it till a close loop is formed. The process is then repeated, the creature advancing with uncanny swiftness in a series of loops. From time to time it rears itself up on end and sways about, swinging slowly round in larger and larger circles as it seeks blindly, but with a keen sense of smell, its prey; then suddenly doubling itself up in a loop, it continues the advance with unerring instinct. There is nothing more horribly fascinating than to see the leaves of the jungle undergrowth, during the rains, literally shaking under the motions of these slender, bloodthirsty, finger-like creatures, as they sway and swing, then start looping inevitably towards you. They have a trick, too, of dropping on to the traveller from above into his hair and ears, or down his neck. Cooper says there are three kinds of leeches in Assam, including the red or hill leech, and the hair leech. I do not recollect coming across either of these last two on the North-East Frontier but I have no doubt that if they are found in Assam they are also found in the Burmese hinterland.

Poor little Maru [his puppy] suffered most of all. I halted continuously to relieve him, on one occasion pulling six off his gums, two from each nostril, several from inside his eyelids, and others from his belly, neck, flanks, and from between his toes. Sometimes his white coat was red with blood, or rather with a mixture of blood and mud.

As for me, leeches entered literally every orifice except my mouth, and I became so accustomed to the little cutting bite, like the caress of a razor, that I scarcely noticed it at the time. On two occasions leeches obtained such strategic positions that I only noticed them just in time to prevent very serious, if not fatal, consequences. I also ran them down in my hair, under my armpits, inside my ears – in fact everywhere. My feet and ankles were by this time covered with the most dreadful sores, the scars of which I carry to this day.

The Darus of the Adung valley

The rain ceased. A party of Darus arrived, and we sent them up the valley with boxes of stores, tents, and equipment. They were the wildest and most uncouth-looking tribe I had ever seen in Upper Burma. The men were naked except for a belt composed of a number of cane rings about the thickness of packing thread round the waist, over which was draped a small square of cotton cloth, and a blanket round the shoulders against the cold. Every man wore a short hunting-knife in a half-sheath of wood supported by a string round the waist. Most of them carried crossbows. The shock of hair was long and unkempt, but trimmed all round the head. Women and girls wore short skirts and a blanket wrapped round the body. They all smoked pipes incessantly, but did not chew *pan* like the down-river tribes. Their teeth, though not discoloured by *pan*, were foully dirty, probably owing to the miscellaneous zoological diet in which they indulge . . .

The Darus are a vanishing race, doomed to extinction. Wild men need protection when encroached on by a higher civilization, just as wild birds and wild animals do, and the Darus are not protected. Not that anyone wishes to exterminate them, but everyone wishes to exploit them, and they cannot defend themselves. So they will perish. Call them, if you will, one of Nature's unsuccessful experiments; but Nature has allowed them to survive for a time in a region where no man survives for long. Encompassed on all sides by more powerful tribes, driven relentlessly deeper and deeper into the slums of the jungle, the Darus must presently fade into the *Ewigkeit*, vanish away as though they had never been. They have bored their way into the heart of the mountains, and they can go no farther. There at present they survive, in isolation, regularly venturing forth on their own initiative, but on the whole ignored, neglected, and perhaps contented.

Riddle of the Tsangpo Gorges, 1926 (quoted in J. Whitehead, ed., *Himalayan Enchantment: An Anthology*, 1990)

ODETTE KEUN
1888–1978

It was desolation triumphant. All free and spontaneous life had ceased in this universe of congealed mineral ruled by an all-powerful and ferocious law.

After a rebellious youth and an eventful young-adulthood – in Turkey, France and Algiers – in 1920 Keun travelled through Georgia on horseback with a group of soldiers. Her first escort shot himself, and to avoid scandal she married her second, a Georgian prince. *In the Land of the Golden Fleece* describes her experiences, for example among the Khevsurs, or 'men of the passes', a fiercely independent clan. The resilience of the Khevsur women particularly impressed her: they gave birth in isolated huts, with no support from their friends or family. Even in sub-zero temperatures they would be left alone to cope with their pain. 'When the mother's cries tell that the confinement is a difficult one,' Keun wrote, 'the husband, who wanders round the hut but on no pretext can rejoin his wife, encourages the sufferer by firing shots from his gun.'

When the Red Army invaded Georgia in 1921, the Bolsheviks allowed her to stay; however, this counted against her when, later in the same year, she was arrested by the British in Constantinople on suspicion of spying. She was deported to the Crimea, and there the local police arrested her, believing her to be spying – this time for the British.

Finally, still hounded by police, Keun moved to France, and through her account of her political experiences and beliefs, *Sous Lénine*, began a correspondence with the author H. G. Wells, whose lover she eventually became. Later she returned to Algiers, attempting to set up medical missions. From 1939 she lived in England, and died at the age of eighty-nine in a Worthing nursing home.

Khevsouretia: 'with trembling hands I touch this adorable tapestry'

Not a bird stirred, not a stream trickled among the flat, bare rocks. It was desolation triumphant. All free and spontaneous life had ceased in this universe of congealed mineral ruled by an all-powerful and ferocious law. All around, the enormous masses reared themselves heavily, violently jagged and brutally misshapen without order or symmetry. Rising in bristling, cyclopean peaks and in sharp pointed ridges, they surrounded the inanimate landscape like motionless battalions. Nothing was to be seen except their straight, close ranks, immovable, patient, unvarying, darkening the air, stretching on in a silence so mysterious, an endurance so inflexible, that one's nerves give way at last, and the illusion supervenes of being one of a band of damned souls wandering in a world extinct for ever, hemmed in by this procession of mournful rocks, these dark victorious ramparts from which only death could walk abroad.

Still we ascended – through an indefinite field of snow, white, or grey, or pink, but tarnished in each shade by dark stains of mineral substance. The impenetrable clouds now rose like walls before and behind us, on every side and low overhead. It seemed to me that this new entombment was more hideous than the other, more menacing, hiding more ignoble dangers, as this matter without consistence or colour, but real, opaque and in ceaseless motion, plunged downwards like a drowned body, or lifted ambiguously with a crafty glimmer. Heavy and viscous, it filled all the horizon, engulfing the mountains, pressing upon us in a grim embrace, its impalpable contact piercing the clothing to the flesh itself; nothing can fight against it, a sense of suffocation comes, and the thick, pale stillness seems to conceal a gulf into which, trying to escape it one plunges ever more deeply.

We ascended – the hillside had now become a summit; without discerning anything clearly, we felt everything falling away before us; never till then had I had such a sense of being cut off from all support. And yet we ascended – the tongue of rock narrowed, drew itself out like the materializing of an intangible force, and when we halted at its extreme point, it had raised us, with itself, high above the world.

We remained a long time on this summit – arguing, for even the guides no longer knew the route. The descent was so rough that some of the militiamen refused to expose their horses to it, and went back. Then, hour after hour, we pushed forward into the fog, sinking in the snow, or sliding on its frozen surface. The streams of slate pierced our boots, and launched us on a tumultuous descent. (In fact, from one end of Khevsouretia to the other, the schists saved us the trouble of walking; they formed an infamous, unmanageable moving pavement, and hardly had we set foot on the slope that they covered than we found ourselves at the bottom, bruised and terrified, listening with inexpressible fervour to the echo of each other's blasphemies.) But whether the road was covered with snow or with slate, it kept winding between undulating masses of grey fog, and when you turned your head to see what had become of the rest, the men and horses following each other on the narrow thread of path only half a yard away, looked like livid phantoms, moving parcels of fog incessantly issuing from and re-entering the oozing walls of mist. Then furtive beginnings of life appeared. Little streams trickled over the black slate; painfully, obstinately, they escaped from the fissures of the granite, and pushed their way, translucent as jewels, among the flat slabs that they fringed with the foam of their feeble wrath. After the unbroken silence of the summits, which had seemed endless, the song of these little streams strangely moved and comforted my heart; and we took them now for our guide. The woolly-white walls thinned around us, the angular ridges of the mountains and their discoloured sides became visible; in frozen tunnels under formidable vaults of ice, the imprisoned water had made a mighty effort and, bursting its solid shroud, rushed out through every opening, as if with bugle calls, into the sombre light. One of the finest sights of that journey was the Tsirtsloviss-Tskhali struggling with its monstrous shell: I have a photograph of it under my eyes as I write, and only to look at this smudged paper brings back something of the profound emotion I felt as I was taking it. The black side of the mountain falls sheer down in a single mass; thrown across it obliquely on one side is the petrified avalanche of the glacier; against that, with a frightful tumult, the white stream, which higher up had been freed, beats in a demented whirl, as if, having already tasted liberty, it was determined that not one of its particles should ever be captured again.

Lower down there was a new and exquisite note of colour, clusters of the large Caucasian rhododendron, fed and burnished by abundant water. They have to interlace themselves in order to survive in that bitter climate; there is not a finger's breadth between the plants; the roots are knotted together, the leaves form a dark green network, and the flowers a trellis of orange yellow. With trembling hands I touch this adorable tapestry, and the little corollas, so fresh and lustrous, efface the gloom that the mountains had cast. Still lower, a long rivulet of clear grass spreads over the ground, like a smile passing over a stern face, and we turn to each other with a cry of passionate delight for, at last, at last, we have come back into the sun . . .

In the Land of the Golden Fleece, 1924

George Leigh Mallory
1886–1924

It was not only that no European had ever been here before us, but we were penetrating a secret . . .

'Because it's there' was George Leigh Mallory's famous explanation for wishing to climb Everest – one that apparently gave him ample motivation. He became the only climber to take part in all three of the 1920s summit bids.

Mallory's passion for climbing had begun when he was a boy: his sister described how he would scramble up any tree or, in the absence of trees, any building that stood in his path. While at Cambridge studying English, he spent all of his holidays mountaineering in the Alps. His first Alpine expedition was at the age of eighteen, and in 1911 he climbed Mont Blanc. 'One must conquer, achieve, get to the top,' he said afterwards. 'One must know the end to be convinced that one can win the end – to know that there's no dream that mustn't be dared.'

Mallory became a teacher and during the First World War was a gunner. Subsequently he was invited to join two Everest expeditions – though now he was married with three young children, and he would be leaving his family for two six-month periods, or perhaps never to return at all.

The 1921 Everest expedition succeeded in its aim of mapping the north face of Everest, but was cut short following the death of one member of the team, and through general exhaustion. The next year Mallory returned with a stronger climbing team. They ascended higher than anyone before – to 27,000 feet – but this was still 2,000 vertical feet below Everest's summit.

Mallory decided to make one more attempt to reach the summit by way of the mountain's North Col before the expedition headed home, but fresh snow had just fallen and nine team members were swept away by an avalanche. Seven of them – all sherpas – died.

In 1924 Mallory made one more attempt to reach the top. The other member of the summit team was Andrew Irvine, whom Mallory described as 'one to rely on, for everything except conversation'. On 8 June 1924 the two men set out, and were last seen 'going strong for the top'. They never came down.*

Mallory's body was not found for another seventy-five years, 2,000 feet below the summit. Irvine's body is still missing. Whether they had reached the summit and died on their way back down, or whether

---

* Noel Odell, another member of the expedition, went to the top camp alone the day after Mallory and Irvine were last seen, and when he climbed to 27,000 feet he realised the hopelessness of his exhausting search: 'Then, closing up the tent . . . I glanced up at the mighty summit above me, which ever and anon deigned to reveal its cloud-wreathed features: It seemed to look down with cold indifference on me, a mere puny man, and howl derision at my petition to yield up its secret – the mystery of my friends. The summit pyramid of Everest is one of the most inhospitable spots on the face of the earth when the wind whistles across the gloomy flanks of the mountain. And how cruel that wind is when each step it hinders concerns lost friends . . . He who approaches close must ever be led on, and oblivious of all obstacles seek to reach that most sacred and highest place of all. It seemed that my friends must have been thus enchanted also: for why else would they tarry.'

Somervell, at around this time, was noting in his diary: 'Mallory and Irvine dead. That is the sad certainty. Have all our exertions and sacrifices been in vain? No, the loss of these splendid men is part of the price that has been paid to keep alive the spirit of adventure. But nobody can hold that lives lost in fighting Nature's greatest obstacles in the name of adventure and exploration are thrown away.'

they died on the way up, is still contested. In 1995 George Mallory's grandson (also called George Mallory), climbed to the summit, where he buried a photograph of his grandfather.

Assault on the North Col

The scene was peculiarly bright and windless, and as we rarely spoke, nothing was to be heard but the laboured panting of our lungs. This stillness was suddenly disturbed. We were startled by an ominous sound, sharp, arresting, violent, and yet somehow soft like an explosion of untamped gunpowder. I had never before on a mountainside heard such a sound; but all of us, I imagine, knew instinctively what it meant, as though we had been accustomed to hear it every day of our lives. In a moment I observed the surface of the snow broken and puckered where it had been even for a few yards to the right of me. I took two steps convulsively in this direction with some quick thought of getting nearer to the edge of the danger that threatened us. And then I began to move slowly downwards, inevitably carried on the whole moving surface by a force I was utterly powerless to resist. Somehow I managed to turn out from the slope so as to avoid being pushed headlong and backwards down it. For a second or two I seemed hardly to be in danger as I went quietly sliding down with the snow. Then the rope at my waist tightened and held me back. A wave of snow came over me and I was buried. I supposed that the matter was settled. However, I called to mind experiences related by other parties; and it had been suggested that the best chance of escape in this situation lay in swimming. I thrust out my arms above my head and actually went through some sort of motions of swimming on my back. Beneath the surface of the snow, with nothing to inform the senses of the world outside it, I had no impression of speed after the first acceleration – I struggled in the tumbling snow, unconscious of everything else – until, perhaps, only a few seconds later, I knew the pace was easing up. I felt an increasing pressure about my body. I wondered how tightly I should be squeezed, and then the avalanche came to rest.

My arms were free; my legs were near the surface. After a brief struggle, I was standing again, surprised and breathless, in the motionless snow. But the rope was tight at my waist; the porter tied on next me, I supposed, must be deeply buried. To my further surprise, he quickly emerged, unharmed as myself. Somervell and Crawford too, though they had been above me by the rope's length, were now quite close, and soon extricated themselves. We subsequently made out that their experiences had been very similar to mine. But where were the rest? Looking down over the foam of snow, we saw one group of porters some little distance, perhaps 150 feet, below us. Presumably the others must be buried somewhere between us and them, and though no sign of these missing men appeared, we at once prepared to find and dig them out. The porters we saw still stood their ground instead of coming up to help. We soon made out that they were the party who had been immediately behind us, and they were pointing below them. They had travelled further than us in the avalanche, presumably because they were nearer the centre, where it was moving more rapidly. The other two parties, one of four and one of five men roped together, must have been carried even further. We could still hope that they were safe. But as we hurried down we soon saw that beneath the place where the four porters were standing was a formidable drop; it was only too plain that the missing men had been swept over it. We had no difficulty in finding a way round this obstacle; in a very short time we were standing under its shadow. The ice-cliff was from 40 to 60 feet high in different places; the crevasse at its foot was more or less filled up with avalanche snow. Our fears were soon confirmed. One man was quickly uncovered and found to be still breathing; before long we were certain that he would live. Another whom we dug out near him had been killed by the fall. He and his party appeared to have struck the hard lower lip of the crevasse, and were lying under the snow on or near the edge of it. The four porters who had escaped soon pulled themselves together after the first shock of the accident, and now worked here with Crawford and did everything they could to extricate the other bodies, while Somervell and I went down into the crevasse. A loop of rope which we pulled up convinced us that the other party must be here. It was slow work loosening the snow with the pick or adze of an ice-axe and shovelling it with the hands. But we were able to follow the rope to the bodies. One was dug up lifeless; another was found upside down, and when we uncovered his face Somervell thought he was still breathing. We had the greatest difficulty in extricating this man, so tightly was the snow packed about his limbs; his load, four oxygen cylinders on a steel frame, had to be cut from his back, and eventually he was dragged out. Though buried for about forty minutes, he had survived the fall and the suffocation, and suffered no serious harm. Of the two others in this party of four, we found only one. We had at length to give up a hopeless search with the certain knowledge that the first of them to be swept over the cliff, and the most deeply buried, must long ago be dead. Of the other five, all the bodies were recovered, but only one was alive. The two who had so marvellously escaped were able to walk down to Camp III, and were almost perfectly well next day. The other seven were killed.

This tragic calamity was naturally the end of the third attempt to climb Mount Everest. The surviving porters who had lost their friends or brothers behaved with dignity, making no noisy parade of the grief they felt. We asked them whether they wished to go up and bring down the bodies for orderly burial. They preferred to leave them where they were. For my part, I was glad of this decision. What better burial could they have than to lie in the snow where they fell.

'The Third Attempt', in C. G. Bruce et al., *The Assault on Mount Everest 1922*, 1923

Last letters home

Base Camp, 16 May 1924

George to Ruth

I must tell *you* that, with immense physical pride, I look upon myself as the strongest of the lot, the most likely to get to the top, with or without gas. I may be wrong, but I'm pretty sure Norton thinks the same. He and I were agreeing yesterday that none of the new members, with the possible exception of Irvine, can touch the veterans, and that the old gang are bearing everything on their shoulders . . . It *is* an effort to pull oneself together and do what is required high up, but it is the power to keep the show going when you don't feel energetic that will enable us to win through if anything does.

Irvine . . . has been wonderfully hard-working and brilliantly skilful about the oxygen. Against him is his youth (though it is very much for him, some ways) – hard things seem to hit him a bit harder – and his lack of mountaineering training and practice, which must tell to some extent when it comes to climbing rocks or even to saving energy on the easiest ground. However, he'll be an ideal companion, and with as stout a heart as you could wish to find. If each of us keeps his strength as it is at present, we should go well together.

Somervell seems to me a bit below his form of two years ago; and Norton is not particularly strong, I fancy, at the moment. Still, they're sure to turn up a pretty tough pair. I hope to carry all through now with a great bound . . . Howard and I will be making the way to Chang La again, four days hence; and eight days later – who can tell? Perhaps we shall go to the top on Ascension Day, May 29th.

Base Camp, 16 May 1924

George to his mother
Irvine is the star of the new members. He is a very fine fellow, has been doing excellently up to date, and should prove a splendid companion on the mountain. I should think the *Birkenhead News* – is it? – ought to have something to say if he and I reach the top together . . .

Last notes

G.M. to Noel Odell
We're awfully sorry to have left things in such a mess – our Unna cooker rolled down the slope at the last moment. Be sure of getting back to IV tomorrow in time to evacuate before dark as I hope to. In the tent I must have left a compass – for the Lord's sake rescue it; we are without. To here on 90 atmospheres for the two days – so we'll probably go on two cylinders – but it's a bloody load for climbing. Perfect weather for the job.

G.M. to John Noel
We'll probably start early tomorrow (8th) in order to have clear weather. It won't be too early to start looking for us either crossing the rock band or going up skyline at 8:00 p.m. [= a.m.]

   D. Robertson, *George Mallory*, 1969

ALEXANDRA DAVID-NEEL
1868–1969

All sights, all things which are Lhasa's own beauty and peculiarity, would have to be seen by the lone woman explorer who had had the nerve to come to them from afar, the first of her sex.

Alexandra David-Neel was the daughter of a French teacher and political activist, and an associate of Victor Hugo. As a child and teenager she was restless, and often ran away: 'I cried bitter tears more than once, having the profound feeling that life was going by, that the days of my youth were going by, empty, without interest, without joy. I understood . . . that I was losing hours that could have been beautiful.'

Her first trip to Asia was in 1889, when an inheritance enabled her to travel by ship from France to Ceylon, then to India, which she explored by train until her money ran out. Back in France she began a career as an opera singer, but was soon yearning after the space of the Himalayas. On tour in Tunis she met and married Phillipe-François Neel, stayed there a while – working some of the time in a casino – but seems to have grown restless again, and not long afterwards they agreed to go their separate ways. Alexandra spent a few years studying and travelling in Europe, then in 1911 left for India. This time she was to stay in Asia for fourteen years.

She became the first European woman to meet the Dalai Lama, who was in Darjeeling, in exile from Tibet. Her fascination for Buddhism grew, and the following year she travelled to Sikkim, where she developed a close friendship with the king of the small state and visited the great monasteries to deepen her Buddhist understanding. It was in one of these monasteries in 1914 that David-Neel met Aphur Yongden, who became her devoted travelling companion, assistant and finally her officially adopted son. Together they spent over two years in a cave retreat in northern Sikkim, where David-Neel was taught by a well-known *gomchen* (hermit), and mastered the art of *thumo reskiang*, the practice of raising body temperature through meditation. While there, she also had two opportunities to slip illegally over the border into Tibet. She did not reach Lhasa, but on the second occasion got as far as Jigatze, a large city in the south.

She and Yongden travelled through Burma, Japan, Korea, and western China, where they remained for three years, staying in monasteries. In 1923 they entered Mongolia and crossed the Gobi Desert, reaching the Tibetan border via the 21,000-foot Kokura Pass, never before traversed by a European. At last, disguised as a Tibetan pilgrim – her hair dyed, her face rubbed with charcoal – she became the first European woman to reach Lhasa, the holy capital of Tibetan Buddhism.

On a later expedition at the age of sixty-six, David-Neel returned to Tibet, having travelled from Europe on the trans-Siberian railway, and stayed there for the duration of the Second World War. She retired in France, at her meditative retreat in Digne, describing the nearby mountains to curious journalists as her Lilliputian Himalayas. Although thirty years her junior, Yongden 'had the impudence' as she put it, to die before her. David-Neel lived to the age a hundred, and even renewed her passport after her hundredth birthday.

Lhasa at last

We were now in Lhasa territory, but still far from the city itself. Yongden once more repressed my desire to rejoice, even in a whisper. What could he still fear? Had we not reached our goal? And now, nature itself gave us a token of her maternal complicity.

As on the night of our starting, when we disappeared in the Kha Karpo forests, 'the gods lulled the men to sleep and silenced the dogs.' A miracle seemed to protect our entrance into Lhasa.

No sooner had we landed than the air, till then so calm, became agitated. All of a sudden a furious storm arose, lifting clouds of dust high into the sky. I have seen the simoon in the Sahara, but was it worse than this? No doubt it was. Yet, that terrible, dry lashing rain of dust gave me the impression of being once more in the great desert.

An immense yellow curtain of whirling sand was spread before the Potala, blinding its guests, hiding from them Lhasa, the roads leading to it, and those who walked upon them. I interpreted it as a symbol promising me complete security, and the future justified my interpretation. For two months I was to wander freely in the lamaist Rome, with none to suspect that, for the first time in history, a foreign woman was beholding the Forbidden City.

'The gods threw a veil over the eyes of his adversaries and they did not recognise him.' So went an old Thibetan tale which I had heard long ago in the Land of Grass.

At that time of the year, a large number of people from all the provinces of Thibet congregate in the capital to enjoy the various festivals and merry-makings, which take place there . . . I could have gone from door to door for hours, in quest of a lodging, without any other result than showing myself to a number of householders of both sexes and being compelled to answer a lot of questions. Fortunately, I was spared the trouble and danger of this.

The storm abated as suddenly as it had arisen. Newcomers, unacquainted with the city, we stood a little at a loss amid the crowd without knowing where to go. Unexpected help came again to me in the shape of a young woman.

'You want a room, Mother?' she said. 'You come from very far. You must be exceedingly tired. Follow me. I know a place where you will be all right.'

I only smiled at her, uttering thanks. I felt rather astonished. Obliging people are many in Thibet, and the kindness of the unknown woman was not altogether extraordinary, but how did she know that 'I had come from very far'? This puzzled me a little, but no doubt she had gained that idea from the sight of my pilgrim staff, and I was lean enough, after so many fasts and so much fatigue, to inspire compassion.

Our guide was not communicative. We followed her like sheep, a little bewildered by the noise and the traffic after months spent in the solitudes, and perhaps still more bewildered by our good luck. She led us outside the town to a place from which one enjoyed an extended view of most beautiful scenery, including the Potala. This detail struck me particularly; for all along the road I had wanted to get a lodging from which I could see it.

I was granted the use of a narrow cell, in a ramshackle cottage occupied by beggarly people. This was indeed the best hostelry one could have wished for the security of my incognito. The idea of looking there for a foreign lady traveller would not have occurred to anybody; and the poor beggars who frequented the place never suspected my identity.

The woman went away smiling after a brief farewell. All had happened so quickly that it seemed a dream. We never saw our guide again.

In our hovel that evening, lying on the ground amongst our miserable luggage, I said to my faithful companion: 'Do you allow me now to say that we have won the game?'

'Yes,' he said, and he shouted in a suppressed, yet most triumphant tone: '*Lha gyalo. De tamche pam!* We are at Lhasa!'

I was in Lhasa. No doubt I could be proud of my victory, but the struggle, with cunning and trickery as weapons, was not yet over. I was in Lhasa, and now the problem was to stay there. Although I had endeavoured to reach the Thibetan capital rather because I had been challenged than out of any real desire to visit it, now that I stood on the forbidden ground at the cost of so much hardship and danger, I meant to enjoy myself in all possible ways. I should really have felt ashamed of myself had I been caught, locked up some-where, and taken back to the border, having only had a superficial and brief glance at the exterior of the palaces and temples. This should not be! No! I would climb to the top of the Potala itself; I would visit the most famous shrines, the large historical monasteries in the vicinity of Lhasa, and I would witness the religious ceremonies, the races, and the pageants of the New Year festival. All sights, all things which are Lhasa's own beauty and peculiarity, would have to be seen by the lone woman explorer who had had the nerve to come to them from afar, the first of her sex. It was my well-won reward after the trials on the road and the vexations by which for several years various officials had endeavoured to prevent my wanderings in Thibet. This time I intended that nobody should deprive me of it.

My Journey to Lhasa, 1927

Eric Shipton
1907–77

After the first joy in victory came a feeling of sadness that the mountain had succumbed, that the proud head of the goddess was bowed.

Eric Earle Shipton was born in Ceylon, where his parents ran a tea plantation. He was educated in Britain, then at the age of nineteen went to work on a coffee plantation in Kenya, where he met the mountaineers Percy Wyn-Harris and Bill Tilman (see page 107) and was inspired to take up climbing. Shipton developed a close climbing partnership with Tilman, the pair together making the first ascent of Nelion, the secondary peak of Mount Kenya, and made the first crossing from Nelion to the main peak, Batian. A three-month Himalayan trek with Tilman and three sherpas set the style of his future expeditions: all team members were treated as equals, and strove to live off the land where possible. For this reason, and his belief in using simple mountaineering techniques, he instilled great respect among his sherpas.

In 1931 Shipton was asked to join an expedition in Uttar Pradesh in northern India, where he climbed Kamet (7,756 metres), the highest peak ever climbed at that time. His next major expedition was to Everest, where he reached an altitude of 8,500 metres (27,900 feet). This, three further explorations of Everest's north face and, most importantly, his 1951 expedition (which established a route up the mountain's southern side) did a great deal to pave the way for the Hillary-Tenzing ascent to the summit in 1953.

Shipton was disgruntled at not having been asked to lead this expedition, but his philosophy of simplicity in climbing, and of favouring small, unencumbered expeditions, clashed with the prevalent views of mountaineers at the time – the 1953 expedition was large, with complex logistics.

Shipton valued mountaineering for its treasured individual experiences, rather than for the possibility of fame that resulted from achieving what no man had achieved before, and this sentiment punctuates his many books. 'My most blissful dream as a child,' he once wrote, 'was to be in some such valley, free to wander where I liked, and discover for myself some hitherto unrevealed glory of Nature.'

The ascent of Nanda Devi

Cold and wet, we huddled under the lee of the cliff rising from the little strip of shore by the water's edge. A few sodden pieces of wood lay about the beach, having been deposited there when the river was in flood. With the aid of a couple of candles and a good deal of patience we got some sort of a fire started, and 'smoked ourselves' until, towards evening, the snow slackened.

On the opposite side of the river there was a wider strip of shore, on which grew a small clump of stunted birches. There was also a fair-sized cave. It was obviously the ideal base from which to tackle the final section of the upper gorge, and the sooner we got there and made ourselves snug, the better, so as soon as the snowstorm had abated we collected all the loads at the water's edge, and prepared for the crossing.

There were ten loads to be carried across. The river appeared to be slightly swollen but, as the snow had been melting as it fell, this was only to be expected. We did not anticipate that the difficulties would be much greater than they had been before.

Fastening an end of the rope to my waist and shouldering a load, I paddled up the edge of the stream, probing with my ice-axe and searching for the best place to begin the crossing. Then I started to wade slowly out into the raging waters. I soon realised that, although the river appeared only slightly higher than it had been before, it confronted us with an obstacle twice as formidable. The force of the current was terrific. As I moved a foot forward, it would be whirled sideways, and it was only by shuffling along that I could make any headway. My legs were slashed by stones swept down by the force of the river, but soon the numbing cold robbed my lower limbs of all sensation. The whirling motion of the water made me giddy, and I was hard put to it to keep my balance. In mid-stream the water was nearly up to my waist; had it been an inch higher it must have carried me away, but by a desperate effort I kept my feet. I tried to turn round, but found that the current was impossible to face, so I had to go on, and at length emerged with bleeding legs upon the opposite beach.

Tilman was a short way behind me. Being shorter, he was having an even tougher struggle. Pasang and Angtharkay were already well in the water, holding on to each other, and on to the rope which was now stretched across the river. My wits must have been numbed by the cold, for I missed the brief opportunity I had of preventing them from coming any further. Too late I realised what they were in for. Pasang was carrying a load of satu, Angtharkay had a load of clothes and bedding, which came down to his buttocks. He was very slight of build and easily the shortest of the five. When he got out towards the middle of the stream, the water was well above his waist, and it was obvious that he was prevented from being swept away only by hanging on to the rope and Pasang's firm hand, which clutched him by the arm. Soon, however, his load became water-logged, and started to drag him down. How he managed to keep his feet will always remain a mystery to me for, in spite of the help afforded him by the rope, his difficulties must have been vastly greater than my own, and I knew that I had had just as much as I could cope with. But then these Sherpas have standards of their own. As they were approaching the northern bank, however, Angtharkay actually did lose his balance and, as he went in up to his neck, I thought he was lost. But he retained his hold on the rope, and Pasang, clutching frantically at his arm, dragged him ashore. They were both rather badly shaken but immediately set about the task of pitching camp and lighting a fire . . .

It was a cheerless party which sat huddled round the weakly smouldering logs under the shelter of the cave, silent save for the continuous chatter of teeth. I felt very humble indeed for having been fool enough to tackle the river in such haste. It was obvious now that a route which involved several such crossings was out of the question, and except for the fact that we had a decent camp site, we would have been much better off on the southern shore of the stream. However, one must pay for experience, and we were later to find that much was needed in dealing with these fierce glacier streams.

Tilman's pipe had been washed away out of his pocket down the river. He is a confirmed pipe-smoker, and I think that the prospect of a month without one was gloomy, to say the least. Fortunately for him, I had been travelling in Southern Tibet the previous year with Laurence Wager, who had insisted on my smoking a pipe in the evening to keep me from talking. Since then I had continued the habit, and now Tilman was able to get a smoke at the expense of an increased flow of argumentative conversation! . . .

We now commanded both sides of the river, and it was decided that Tilman and Angtharkay should explore the possibilities of the southern side, while Pasang and I tried to get through on the northern side . . .

Edging along the base of the cliffs at the water's edge, we reached another strip of sandy shore a hundred yards further upstream. From here a steeply sloping corridor led back across the face of the precipice. All the strata we had encountered in the Rishi Nala sloped from west to east in this manner, and we hoped that by following this corridor we might be able to climb on to a terrace which would at least carry us past that formidable buttress on the southern side. But the corridor became more and more difficult to follow, and finally ended in a little platform 500 feet above the river, completely isolated save for the way by which we had come. Further advance in any direction was impossible . . .

We tried places which were obviously quite ridiculous; just as one searches under the teapot or in the coal-scuttle for a lost fountain pen when one has exhausted every likely place, and I had a similar feeling of hopelessness. But after some desperate rock-climbing, we were forced to admit defeat, and returned to camp, satisfied that at least there was no route along the northern side of the gorge.

It was a cold grey afternoon, and towards evening rain began to fall gently. The gorge wore a grim and desolate aspect, which increased my dejection as I sat in the cave, waiting for the others to return and wondering what our next move would be. If we were forced to retreat from here, we would have to abandon our attempt to penetrate into the Nanda Devi Basin, as there was no other line of possibility. As the evening wore on, we began to scan the crags of the opposite side anxiously for any sign of the others. Their delay in returning gave me some hope that they might after all have found a way; but towards dark I began to fear that an accident had occurred, for they must have realised our failure, and desperation is apt to make people run unjustifiable risks. Then all at once we spotted them, descending through the mist at a seemingly reckless speed. As they approached the river I went over to the bridge to await them. Angtharkay was in front and, as he came nearer, I could see that he was in a state of great excitement; as he balanced his way precariously over the water, above the roar of the torrent I caught the words: 'Bahut achcha, sahib, bahut achcha.'

When Tilman arrived, I heard from him the glad news that they had found, 1,500 feet above the river, a break in that last formidable buttress, guarding the mystic shrine of the 'Blessed Goddess'. From where they had stood they could see that the way was clear into the Nanda Devi Basin. The last frail link in that extraordinary chain of rock-faults, which had made it possible to make our way along the grim precipices of the gorge, had been discovered; and this meant at least a certain measure of success to our undertaking.

As I lay in the mouth of the cave after our evening meal, watching the spectral shadows hover in the ghostly clefts of the opposite wall of the gorge, and listening to the mighty boom of the torrent echoing to a great height above our heads, my feeling of despondency was changed to one of deep content.

We began the long snow trudge at eight o'clock and even at that early hour and after a cold night the snow was not good and soon became execrable. The sun was now well up. After it had been at work for a bit we were going in over our knees at every step, and in places where the slope was steeper it was not easy to make any upward progress at all. One foot would be lifted and driven hard into the snow and then, on attempting to rise on it, one simply sank down through the snow to the previous level. It was like trying to climb up cotton wool, and a good deal more exhausting, I imagine, than the treadmill. But, like the man on a walking tour in Ireland, who throughout a long day received the same reply of '20 miles' to his repeated inquiries as to the distance he was from his destination, we could at any rate say, 'Thank God, we were holding our own.'

The exertion was great and every step made good cost six to eight deep breaths. Our hopes of the summit grew faint, but there was no way but to plug on and see how far we could get. This we did, thinking only of the next step, taking our time, and resting frequently. It was at least some comfort that the track we were ploughing might assist a second party. On top of the hard work and the effect of altitude was the languor induced by a sun which beat down relentlessly on the dazzling snow, searing our lips and sapping the energy of mind and body. As an example of how far this mind-sapping process had gone, I need only mention that it was seriously suggested that we should seek the shade of a convenient rock which we were then near, lie up there until evening, and finish the climb in the dark!

It is noteworthy that whilst we were enjoying, or more correctly enduring, this remarkable spell of sunshine, the foothills south and west of the Basin experienced disastrous floods . . .

We derived some encouragement from seeing East Nanda Devi sink below us and at one o'clock, rather to our surprise, we found ourselves on top of the snow rib moving at a snail's pace towards the foot of the rocks. There we had a long rest and tried to force some chocolate down our parched throats by eating snow at the same time. Though neither of us said so, I think both felt that now it would take a lot to stop us. There was a difficult piece of rock to climb; Odell led this and appeared to find it stimulating, but it provoked me to exclaim loudly upon its 'thinness'. Once over that, we were landed fairly on the final slope with the summit ridge a bare 300 ft. above us . . .

The summit is not the exiguous and precarious spot that usually graces the top of so many Himalayan peaks, but a solid snow ridge nearly two hundred yards long and twenty yards broad. It is seldom that conditions on top of a high peak allow the climber the time or the opportunity to savour the immediate fruits of victory. Too often, when having first carefully probed the snow to make sure he is not standing on a cornice, the climber straightens up preparatory to savouring the situation to the full, he is met by a perishing wind and the interesting view of a cloud at close quarters, and with a muttered imprecation turns in his tracks and begins the descent. Far otherwise was it now. There were no cornices to worry about and room to unrope and walk about. The air was still, the sun shone, and the view was good if not so extensive as we had hoped.

Odell had brought a thermometer, and no doubt sighed for the hypsometer. From it we found that the air temperature was 20 degrees F., but in the absence of wind we could bask gratefully in the friendly rays of our late enemy the sun. It was difficult to realise that we were actually standing on top of the same peak which we had viewed two months ago from Ranikhet, and which had then appeared incredibly remote and inaccessible, and it gave us a curious feeling of exaltation to know that we were above every peak within hundreds of miles on either hand. Dhaulagiri, 1000 ft. higher, and two hundred miles away in Nepal, was our nearest rival. I believe we so far forgot ourselves as to shake hands on it.

After the first joy in victory came a feeling of sadness that the mountain had succumbed, that the proud head of the goddess was bowed.

At this late hour of the day there was too much cloud about for any distant views. The Nepal peaks were hidden and all the peaks on the rim, excepting only Trisul, whose majesty even our loftier view-point could not diminish. Far to the north through a vista of white cloud the sun was colouring to a warm brown the bare and bleak Tibetan plateau.

After three-quarters of an hour on that superb summit, a brief forty-five minutes into which was crowded the worth of many hours of glorious life, we dragged ourselves reluctantly away, taking with us a memory that can never fade and leaving behind 'thoughts beyond the reaches of our souls'.

If our thoughts were still treading on air, the short steep gully, swept by the avalanche bare of steps, soon brought us to earth. We kicked slowly down it, facing inwards and plunging an arm deep into the snow for support. Followed another exhausting drag across the snow, hindered rather than helped by the deep holes we had made coming up, and then a cold hour was spent moving cautiously, one at a time, down the ice and the benumbing rocks of the long ridge above the bivouac. We paused to watch a bird, a snow pigeon, cross our ridge and fly swiftly across the grey cliffs of the ravine beneath the snow terrace, like the spirit of Nanda Devi herself, forsaking the fastness which was no longer her own.

At six o'clock we reached the tent and brewed the first of many jorums of tea. After such a day nothing could have tasted better and our appreciation was enhanced by our long enforced abstinence. There was but a pinch left and we squandered it all recklessly, saving the leaves for the morning. Food was not even mentioned.

We paid for this debauch with a sleepless night, to which no doubt exhaustion and a still-excited imagination contributed. Each little incident of the climb was gone over again and again, and I remember, in the small hours when the spark of life burns lowest, the feeling which predominated over all was one of remorse at the fall of a giant. It is the same sort of contrition that one feels at the shooting of an elephant, for however thrilling and arduous the chase, however great has been the call upon skill, perseverance, and endurance, and however gratifying the weight of the ivory, when the great bulk crashes to the ground achievement seems to have been bought at the too high cost of sacrilege.

Nanda Devi, 1936

HEINRICH HARRER
1912–

After a short time in the country, it was no longer possible for one thoughtlessly to kill a fly . . .

The Austrian mountaineer Heinrich Harrer was on the Austro-German expedition that, in 1938, made the first ascent of the north face of the Eiger. But his most spectacular feat was to come, unexpectedly, five years later. Harrer was in the Himalayas when the Second World War broke out, and was held captive by the British at Dehra-Dun, in India, for four years, until he escaped from internment camp with fellow detainee and mountaineer Peter Aufschnaiter. Together they trekked across the Changthang plateau to Tibet, a journey that would have been remarkable even for a well-equipped expedition. They travelled on foot, and slept on the ground in the open air, with virtually no money or possessions and no official papers.

They arrived in Lhasa in rags, yet received a warm welcome. Harrer stayed in Lhasa to become a friend and informal tutor of the fourteen-year-old Dalai Lama, who gave him access to ceremonies and customs that few Westerners had witnessed. With the Dalai Llama, Harrer left Lhasa in December 1950, in advance of the invading Chinese army, and his account of this period, *Seven Years in Tibet* (1953), has been translated into fifty languages.

Although Harrer's expeditions and further books cover six continents, he is destined to be remembered for his seven-year interlude in the Himalayas: 'My heartfelt wish is that my story may create some understanding for a people whose will to live in peace and freedom has won so little sympathy from an indifferent world.'

Tibetan life

The daily life of Tibetans is ordered by religious belief. Pious texts are constantly on their lips; prayer-wheels turn without ceasing; prayer-flags wave on the roofs of houses and the summits of the mountain passes; the rain, the wind, all the phenomena of nature, the lonely peaks of the snow-clad mountains, bear witness to the universal presence of the gods whose anger is manifested by the hailstorm, and whose benevolence is displayed by the fruitfulness and fertility of the land. The life of the people is regulated by the divine will, whose interpreters the Lamas are. Before anything is undertaken, they must test the omens. The gods must be unceasingly entreated, placated or thanked. Prayer-lamps burn everywhere, in the house of the noble and in the tent of the nomad – the same faith has kindled them. Earthly existence is of little worth in Tibet and death has no terrors. Men know that they will be born again and hope for a higher form of existence in the next life, earned by pious conduct in this one. The Church is the highest court of appeal, and the simplest monk is respected by the people and addressed by the title of Kusho, as if he were a member of the nobility. In every family at least one of the sons is dedicated to the cloister in token of reverence for the Church and to give the child a good start in life.

In all these years I have never met anyone who expressed the slightest doubt about the truth of Buddha's teaching. There are, it is true, many sects, but they differ only in externals. One cannot close one's heart to the religious fervour which radiates from everyone. After a short time in the country, it was no longer possible for one thoughtlessly to kill a fly, and I have never in the presence of a Tibetan squashed an insect which bothered me. The attitude of the people in these matters is really touching. If at a picnic an ant crawls up one's clothes, it is gently picked up and set down. It is a catastrophe when a fly falls into a cup of tea. It must at all costs be saved from drowning as it may be the reincarnation of one's dead grandmother. In winter they break the ice in the pools to save the fishes before they freeze to death, and in summer they rescue them before the pools dry up. These creatures are kept in pails or tins until they can be restored to their home waters. Meanwhile their rescuers have done something for the good of their own souls. The more life one can save the happier one is.

I shall never forget an experience I had with my friend Wangdüla. We went one day to the only Chinese restaurant and there saw a goose running round the courtyard apparently on its way to the cooking-pot. Wangdüla quickly took a banknote of considerable value from his pocket and bought the goose from the restaurant keeper. He then had his servant carry the goose home, and for years afterwards I used to see the lucky creature waddling about his place.

Typical of this attitude towards all living creatures was a rescript issued in all parts of the country to persons engaged in building operations – this was during the three years which the young Dalai Lama spent in meditation. It was pointed out that worms and insects might easily be killed during the work of building, and general construction of buildings was forbidden. Later on, when I was in charge of earthworks, I saw with my own eyes how the coolies used to go through each spadeful of earth and take out anything living.

It follows from this principle that there is no capital punishment in Tibet. Murder is regarded as the most heinous of crimes, but the murderer is only flogged and has iron fetters forged on to his ankles. It is true that the floggings are in fact less humane than the death penalty as it is carried out in Western hands. The victim often dies an agonising death after the penalty has been inflicted, but the religious principle has not been infringed. Criminals condemned to a life in chains are either shut up in the state prison at Shö or sent to a district governor who is responsible for their custody. Their fate is certainly preferable to that of the convicts in the prisons who are only permitted to leave their gaol on the birth- and death-day of the Buddha, when they may beg for alms in the Lingkhor chained to fellow prisoners.

The procession of the Dalai Lama

Night fell swiftly, but soon the scene was brightly illuminated with a swarm of lights. There were thousands of flickering butter-lamps and among them a few petroleum pressure-lamps with their fearful glaring light. The moon came up over the roofs to throw more light on the proceedings. The months are lunar in Tibet so it was full-moon on the 15th. Everything was ready: the stage was set and the great festival could now begin. The voices of the crowd were hushed in anticipation. The great moment had come.

The Cathedral doors opened and the young God-King stepped slowly out, supported to right and left by two abbots. The people bowed in awe. According to strict ceremonial they should prostrate themselves but today there was no room. As he approached they bowed, as a field of corn bends before the wind. No one dared to look up. With measured steps the Dalai Lama began his solemn circuit of the Barkhor. From time to time he stopped before the figures of butter and gazed at them. He was followed by a brilliant retinue of all the high dignitaries and nobles. After them followed the officials in order of precedence. In the procession we recognised our friend Tsarong, who followed close behind the Dalai Lama. Like all the nobles, he carried in his hand a smouldering stick of incense.

The awed crowd kept silent. Only the music of the monks could be heard – the oboes, tubas and kettledrums. It was like a vision of another world, a strangely unreal happening. In the yellow light of the flickering lamps the great figures of moulded butter seemed to come to life. We fancied we saw strange flowers tossing their heads in the breeze and heard the rustling of the robes of gods. The faces of these portentous figures were distorted in a demonic grimace. Then the God raised his hand in blessing.

Now the Living Buddha was approaching. He passed quite close to our window. The women stiffened in a deep obeisance and hardly dared to breathe. The crowd was frozen. Deeply moved we hid ourselves behind the women as if to protect ourselves from being drawn into the magic circle of this Power.

We kept saying to ourselves, 'It is only a child.' A child, indeed, but the heart of the concentrated faith of thousands, the essence of their prayers, longings, hopes. Whether it is Lhasa or Rome – all are united by one wish: to find God and to serve Him. I closed my eyes and hearkened to the murmured prayers and the solemn music and sweet incense rising to the evening sky.

Soon the Dalai Lama had completed his tour round the Barkhor and vanished into the Tsug Lag Khang. The soldiers marched away to the music of their bands.

As if awakened from a hypnotic sleep, the tens of thousands of spectators passed from order into chaos. The transition was overwhelmingly sudden. The crowds broke into shouts and wild gesticulation. A moment ago they were weeping and praying or sunk in ecstatic meditation, and now they are a throng of madmen. The monk-guards begin to function. They are huge fellows with padded shoulders and blackened faces to make them more terrible. They lay about them with their whips, but the crowd press frantically round the statues of butter, which are now in danger of being overturned. Even those who have been bludgeoned come back into the fray. One would think they were possessed by demons. Are they really the same people who just now were bowing humbly before a child?

Next morning the streets were empty. The butter figures had been carried away and no trace remained of the reverence or the ecstasy of the night before. Market-stalls had taken the place of the stands which had carried the statues. The brightly coloured figures of the saints had melted and would be used as fuel for lamps – or would be made up into magic medicines.

Seven Years in Tibet, 1953

EDMUND HILLARY
1919–
My first sensation was one of relief – relief that the long grind was over . . ..

Auckland-born Sir Edmund Hillary was a bee-keeper by profession, but from an early age was obsessed with mountains, gaining his first climbing experience in New Zealand's southern Alps. In 1951 he undertook his first expedition in the Himalayas, and then joined Eric Shipton's reconnaissance expedition on the southern face of Mount Everest (see page 526).

By 1953 Hillary had climbed eleven peaks over 20,000 feet high, which proved to be experience enough for him to be selected for the British Everest Expedition, led by John Hunt. Seven previous attempts to reach the summit of Everest had failed. On this one, Hillary and the sherpa Tenzing Norgay were the two chosen to make the summit bid. They reached the summit at 11.30 on 29 May 1953. When they had made their descent back down to the waiting party, Hillary's first words to his fellow New Zealander George Lowe were: 'Well, we knocked the bastard off!'

Their achievement preceded by just a few days the coronation of Queen Elizabeth II, and the new queen subsequently knighted Hillary.

It had all been very timely: the expedition was British-led, and both Tenzing and Hillary hailed from British colonies. With the Empire waning, and the British still reeling from the war, the news caused a momentary surge in national confidence.

Hillary went on to lead several more expeditions in the Himalayas, but also became increasingly involved with improving the welfare of the Nepalese. He built clinics, hospitals and seventeen schools. Sadly, the airstrips built to service these new facilities had the effect of attracting more tourists to the Nepalese Himalayas, and to counter this, and the influx of foreigners generally, Hillary began to devote more time to environmental concerns.

On the summit

It was 11.30 a.m. My first sensation was one of relief – relief that the long grind was over; that the summit had been reached before our oxygen supplies had dropped to a critical level; and relief that in the end the mountain had been kind to us in having a pleasantly rounded cone for its summit instead of a fearsome and unapproachable cornice. But mixed with the relief was a vague sense of astonishment that I should have been the lucky one to attain the ambition of so many brave and determined climbers. It seemed difficult at first to grasp that we'd got there. I was too tired and too conscious of the long way down to safety really to feel any great elation. But as the fact of our success thrust itself more clearly into my mind, I felt a quiet glow of satisfaction spread through my body – a satisfaction less vociferous but more powerful than I had ever felt on a mountain top before. I turned and looked at

Tenzing. Even beneath his oxygen mask and the icicles hanging from his hair, I could see his infectious grin of sheer delight. I held out my hand, and in silence we shook in good Anglo-Saxon fashion. But this was not enough for Tenzing, and impulsively he threw his arm around my shoulders and we thumped each other on the back in mutual congratulations.

But we had no time to waste! First I must take some photographs and then we'd hurry down. I turned off my oxygen and took the set off my back. I remembered all the warnings I'd had of the possible fatal consequences of this, but for some reason felt quite confident that nothing serious would result. I took my camera out of the pocket of my windproof and clumsily opened it with my thickly gloved hands. I clipped on the lenshood and ultra-violet filter and then shuffled down the ridge a little so that I could get the summit into my viewfinder. Tenzing had been waiting patiently, but now, at my request, he unfurled the flags wrapped around his ice-axe and standing on the summit held them above his head. Clad in all his bulky equipment and with the flags flapping furiously in the wind, he made a dramatic picture, and the thought drifted through my mind that this photograph should be a good one if it came out at all. I didn't worry about getting Tenzing to take a photograph of me – as far as I knew, he had never taken a photograph before and the summit of Everest was hardly the place to show him how.

I climbed up to the top again and started taking a photographic record in every direction. The weather was still extraordinarily fine. High above us were long streaks of cirrus wind cloud and down below fluffy cumulus hid the valley floors from view. But wherever we looked, icy peaks and sombre gorges lay beneath us like a relief map. Perhaps the view was most spectacular to the east, for here the giants Makalu and Kanchenjunga dominated the horizon and gave some idea of the vast scale of the Himalayas. Makalu in particular, with its soaring rock ridges, was a remarkable sight; it was only a few miles away from us. From our exalted viewpoint I could see all the northern slopes of the mountain and was immediately struck by the possibility of a feasible route to its summit. With a growing feeling of excitement, I took another photograph to study at leisure on returning to civilisation. The view to the north was a complete contrast – hundreds of miles of the arid high Tibetan plateau, softened now by a veil of fleecy clouds into a scene of delicate beauty. To the west the Himalayas stretched hundreds of miles in a tangled mass of peaks, glaciers, and valleys.

But one scene was of particular interest. Almost under our feet, it seemed, was the famous North Col and the East Rongbuk glacier, where so many epic feats of courage and endurance were performed by the earlier British Everest

Expeditions. Part of the ridge up which they had established their high camps was visible, but the last thousand feet, which had proved such a formidable barrier, was concealed from our view as its rock slopes dropped away with frightening abruptness from the summit snow pyramid. Inevitably my thoughts turned to Mallory and Irvine, who had lost their lives on the mountain thirty years before. With little hope I looked around for some sign that they had reached the summit, but could see nothing.

Meanwhile Tenzing had also been busy. On the summit he'd scratched out a little hole in the snow, and in this he placed some small offerings of food – some biscuits, a piece of chocolate, and a few sweets – a small gift to the Gods of Chomolungma which all devout Buddhists (as Tenzing is) believe to inhabit the summit of this mountain. Besides the food, I placed the little cross that John Hunt had given me on the South Col. Strange companions, no doubt, but symbolical at least of the spiritual strength and peace that all peoples have gained from the mountains. We made seats for ourselves in the snow, and sitting there in reasonable comfort we ate with relish a bar of mintcake. My camera was still hanging open on my chest so I decided to put it safely away. But my fingers seemed to have grown doubly clumsy. I closed the camera and did up the leather case. I suddenly realised that I was being affected by the lack of oxygen – it was nearly ten minutes now since I'd taken my set off. I quickly checked the gauges on our bottles – 1,450-lb. pressure; roughly 350 litres of oxygen; nearly two hours' endurance at three litres a minute. It wasn't much, but it would have to do. I hastily put my set on and turned on the oxygen. I felt better immediately. Tenzing had removed the flags from his ice-axe and, as there was nothing to tie them to, he thrust them down into the snow. They obviously wouldn't stay there for long. We slowly got to our feet again. We were tired all right, and all my tension and worry about reaching the summit had gone, leaving a slight feeling of anticlimax. But the smallness of our supply of oxygen filled me with a sense of urgency. We must get back to the South Summit as quickly as possible.

I took up my ice-axe, glanced at Tenzing to see if he were ready, and then looked at my watch – it was 11.45, and we'd only been on top fifteen minutes. I had one job left to do. Walking easily down the steps I'd made in the ridge I descended forty feet from the summit to the first visible rocks, and taking a handful of small stones thrust them into my pocket – it seemed a bit silly at the time, but I knew they'd be rather nice to have when we got down.

High Adventure, 1955

TENZING NORGAY
1914–86

Many years and a lot of effort had brought me a little unexpectedly to that high and lonely place in the thin air, under an incredibly blue sky, with a whole world of mountains spread out around and below us.

Born with the name Namgyal Wangdi, the achievements of Sherpa Tenzing's later life inspired his renaming by his cousin, the reincarnate lama Tenzing Norgay Norbu. 'Norgay Tenzing' means 'Fortunate Supporter of Religion' in Nepalese.

Aged eighteen, Tenzing Norgay left his Nepalese home village of Thame without his parents' permission and headed for Darjeeling. Nepal was closed to foreigners, so all attempts at climbing Everest were being made from India, and it was in Darjeeling that sherpas were being recruited. In 1935 he was enrolled on Eric Shipton's Everest expedition, and was so impressive that he easily found employment on the British Everest expeditions of 1936 and 1938.

The Second World War put organized mountaineering ventures on hold, but afterwards Tenzing found any way he could to continue his work. 'The pull of Everest was stronger for me than any force on Earth,' he wrote later. So in 1947 he joined Earl Denman on his solitary and, one is almost tempted to add, foolhardy, attempt on the summit; he also participated in the 1952 Swiss expedition under Lambert and came within 1,000 feet of the summit.

The following year he was selected to join the British Everest expedition and, with the New Zealander Edmund Hillary, reached the summit on 29 May 1953. There he made an offering of food to the dieties, for he was standing on 'Chomolungma', Mother Goddess of the Earth. 'Besides the food, I placed the little cross,' wrote Hillary. 'Strange companions, no doubt, but symbolical at least of the spiritual strength and peace that all peoples have gained from the mountains.'

Tenzing became an international celebrity and also folk hero to many Nepalese and Indians. Recently it has been claimed that he was, in fact, born in Tibet, and spent much of his childhood there, but had covered up his origins to avoid political complications. Tenzing could not travel to England after reaching Everest's summit until he had a passport, so the Indian Prime Minister Nehru hurriedly granted him an Indian one, much to the dismay of the Nepalese, who wanted to claim him as their national hero. To have revealed himself as having been born and bred Tibetan would have enabled China to pride itself on his achievement; Tenzing would have felt this was not doing justice to India, where he had learnt his sherpa skills and gained the opportunity to climb Everest in the first place.

In 1954 Tenzing studied at a mountaineering school in Switzerland, then, on returning to Darjeeling, became the first Field Director of the Himalayan Institute of Mountaineering, a position he held for twenty-two years. When Tenzing died in 1986 his funeral cortège stretched for almost a mile.

'Nothing would ever be the same again'

Many years and a lot of effort had brought me a little unexpectedly to that high and lonely place in the thin air, under an incredibly blue sky, with a whole world of mountains spread out around and below us. I was nearly forty years of age. It was my seventh expedition to the mountain and the fulfilment of a dream. It was also the fulfilment of the efforts of a whole generation and more of climbing men, who in their own ways had had the same dream as mine, so if the achievement created a sensation it is not surprising . . .

The news of our success was only broadcast in Britain some days later, on Coronation Day, 2 June. But we had a long march back and everyone knew about the ascent of Everest long before we returned to civilisation. Then in Nepal and in India people went crazy. Politically-minded men rushed in to gain some benefit from my own part in the climb, invented stories about it and twisted the truth, proclaiming me the hero of Nepal, of India, or of the East, and so on, simply because I had been lucky enough and persistent enough to reach the top of the world and the headlines of the newspapers too.

This was a difficult time for everybody in the expedition. I could not help being pleased at this personal reception; anyone would be. But the attempt to split me from Edmund Hillary and the rest of the expedition and to create trouble amongst us was really frightening and it has left a dark mark on my memory of our victory. Also the frenzy of the crowds was almost terrifying, even before we got to Kathmandu, though worse afterwards, and so were the mobs of excited pressmen who never left us for a moment . . .

Even then, in 1953, I had the feeling that nothing would ever be the same again – for me, for the Sherpas, for Solu Khumbu, for mountaineering as a sport. And nothing was. It was not that by climbing Everest nothing was left for the mountaineers to do. Not at all. Rather the reverse. Now there was everything to do; nothing was beyond man's ambition and there was plenty of that everywhere. The sport grew as never before, especially in the Himalaya because they offered the most ambitious and the most varied climbing of any range in the world. And in growing it gave me a career I would not have thought about a few years earlier. The great Himalayan and Karakorum summits that had not so far been climbed – they were many – began to fall one after the other to expeditions from many lands: Kangchenjunga, Makalu, Pumori, K2, Dhaulagiri, Cho Oyu, Nuptse, Lhotse, Manaslu, Broad Peak . . . The list of those that were climbed in the next few years is very long indeed, and of course there were casualties, many casualties, among the Sherpas too. In a year or two few of the really famous main summits remained unclimbed, though there are to this day numbers of mountains still unclimbed – secondary summits, of course, but still very big ones. Anyway, after Everest nothing seemed impossible.

After Everest: An Autobiography, 1977

MAURICE HERZOG
1919–

That brown rock . . . that ridge of ice – were these the goals of a lifetime? Or
were they, rather, the limits of man's pride?

Maurice Herzog was born in Lyon and trained as an engineer, but after his early Alpine climbs he became more intent on mountaineering, and by 1939 had completed several dangerous ascents. During the war he served with the artillery and the Chasseurs Alpins, for which he was awarded the Croix de Guerre; he was an obvious choice to lead the 1950 French Himalayan expedition.

So far there had been twenty-two attempts at climbing the world's fourteen mountains over 8,000 metres (all of which are in the Himalayas), but not one had succeeded. Herzog's team was to tackle the mighty Annapurna, the tenth highest mountain in the world at 8,091 metres (26,493 feet). If any expedition had a chance of success it was this one; it included the highly experienced French mountaineers Louis Lachenal, Lionel Terray and Gaston Rebuffat. But no Westerners had ever even approached Annapurna, and maps of the region were inaccurate. It took almost two months of wandering through valleys just to gain access to the mountain.

They finally reached the deep gorge formed by the Miristi Khola river, working their way through it to emerge beneath the mountain's north face. Herzog offered a place on the summit team to Ang Tharkey, the head sherpa, but, as his feet were already numb with cold, he declined. Setting off at 6 a.m. on the morning of 3 June 1950, Herzog and Lachenal climbed alone in silence up towards the summit. 'Each of us lived in a closed and private world of his own,' Herzog later wrote. At 2 p.m. they reached the summit, where Herzog was overwhelmed with emotion and for a while could not understand Lachenal's impatience to turn back. Night might fall before they made it back to their camp, and the monsoon season was fast approaching.

They reached camp just in time, but not soon enough to save Herzog's fingers and toes. On the way down he had watched stupefied as his gloves slid down the side of the mountain. Forgetting that he had a spare pair of socks he could have used as a substitute, he continued barehanded, and by the time he got to the camp his fingers were violet and white, and rock solid. After the harrowing few weeks of the return journey, most of his digits had to be amputated.

In hospital, Herzog dictated his account of the expedition. *Annapurna* sold 11 million copies, and was acclaimed for its portrayal of the teamwork and the boundless optimism that had driven the expedition to the summit.

Some have said *Annapurna* does not tell the full story – suspicions that were not helped by the fact that the other team members had been made to sign a pact not to publish anything about the expedition for five years. The mountaineer David Roberts delved deeper in his book *True Summit: What Really Happened on the Legendary Ascent of Annapurna*, but by then Herzog was the only surviving member of the expedition, and much of the detail remains shrouded in mystery. Whether criticism of Herzog's book is valid or not, it has inspired many, whether mountaineers or otherwise.

The gaining of Annapurna

Stopping at every step, leaning on our axes, we tried to recover our breath and to calm down our hearts, which were thumping as though they would burst. We knew we were there now, and that no difficulty could stop us. No need to exchange looks – each of us would have read the same determination in the other's eyes. A slight détour to the left, a few more steps – the summit ridge came gradually nearer – a few rocks to avoid. We dragged ourselves up. Could we possibly be there?

Yes!

A fierce and savage wind tore at us.

We were on top of Annapurna! 8,075 metres, 26,493 feet.

Our hearts overflowed with an unspeakable happiness.

'If only the others could know . . .'

If only everyone could know!

The summit was a corniced crest of ice, and the precipices on the far side, which plunged vertically down beneath us, were terrifying, unfathomable. There could be few other mountains in the world like this. Clouds floated half way down, concealing the gentle, fertile valley of Pokhara, 23,000 feet below. Above us there was nothing!

Our mission was accomplished. But at the same time we had accomplished something infinitely greater. How wonderful life would now become! What an inconceivable experience it is to attain one's ideal and, at the very same moment, to fulfil oneself. I was stirred to the depths of my being. Never had I felt happiness like this – so intense and yet so pure. That brown rock, the highest of them all, that ridge of ice – were these the goals of a lifetime? Or were they, rather, the limits of man's pride?

'Well, what about going down?'

Lachenal shook me. What were his own feelings? Did he simply think he had finished another climb, as in the Alps? Did he think one could just go down again like that, with nothing more to it?

'One minute, I must take some photographs.'

'Hurry up!'

I fumbled feverishly in my sack, pulled out the camera, took out the little French flat which was right at the bottom, and the pennants. Useless gestures, no doubt, but something more than symbols – eloquent tokens of affection and goodwill. I tied the strips of material – stained by sweat and by the food in the sacks – to the shaft of my ice-axe, the only flag-staff at hand. Then I focused my camera on Lachenal.

'Now, will you take me?'

'Hand it over – hurry up!' said Lachenal.

He took several pictures and then handed me back the camera. I loaded a colour-film and we repeated the process to be certain of bringing back records to be cherished in the future.

'Are you mad?' asked Lachenal. 'We haven't a minute to lose: we must go down at once.'

And in fact a glance round showed me that the weather was no longer gloriously fine as it had been in the morning. Lachenal was becoming impatient.

'We must go down!'

He was right. His was the reaction of the mountaineer who knows his own domain. But I just could not accustom myself to the idea that we had won our victory. It seemed inconceivable that we should have trodden those summit snows.

It was impossible to build a cairn; there were no stones, and everything was frozen. Lachenal stamped his feet; he felt them freezing. I felt mine freezing too, but paid little attention. The highest mountain to be climbed by man lay under our feet! The names of our predecessors on these heights chased each other through my mind: Mummery, Mallory and Irvine, Bauer, Welzenbach, Tilman, Shipton. How many of them were dead – how many had found on these mountains what, to them, was the finest end of all?

My joy was touched with humility. It was not just one party that had climbed Annapurna today, but a whole expedition. I thought of all the others in the camps perched on the slopes at our feet, and I knew it was because of their efforts and their sacrifices that we had succeeded today. There are times when the most complex actions are suddenly summed up, distilled, and strike you with illuminating clarity: so it was with this irresistible upward surge which had landed us two here . . .

'Come on, straight down,' called Lachenal.

He had already done up his sack and started going down. I took out my pocket aneroid: 8,500 metres. I smiled. I swallowed a little condensed milk and left the tube behind – the only trace of our passage. I did up my sack, put on my gloves and my glasses, seized my ice-axe; one look round and I, too, hurried down the slope. Before disappearing into the couloir I gave one last look at the summit which would henceforth be all our joy and all our consolation.

Lachenal was already far below; he had reached the foot of the couloir. I hurried down in his tracks. I went as fast as I could, but it was dangerous

going. At every step one had to take care that the snow did not break away
beneath one's weight. Lachenal, going faster than I thought he was capable of,
was now on the long traverse. It was my turn to cross the area of mixed rock
and snow. At last I reached the foot of the rock-band. I had hurried and I was
out of breath. I undid my sack. What had I been going to do? I could not say.

'My gloves!'

Before I had time to bend over, I saw them slide and roll. They went further
and further straight down the slope. I remained where I was, quite stunned, I
watched them rolling down slowly, with no appearance of stopping. The
movement of those gloves was engraved in my sight as something ineluctable,
irremediable, against which I was powerless. The consequences might be most
serious. What was I to do?

'Quickly, down to Camp V.'

Rébuffat and Terray should be there. My concern dissolved like magic. I
now had a fixed objective again: to reach the camp. Never for a minute did it
occur to me to use as gloves the socks which I always carry in reserve for just
such a mishap as this.

On I went, trying to catch up with Lachenal. It had been two o'clock when
we reached the summit; we had started out at six in the morning; but I had to
admit that I had lost all sense of time. I felt as if I were running, whereas in
actual fact I was walking normally, perhaps rather slowly, and I had to keep
stopping to get my breath. The sky was now covered with clouds, everything
had become grey and dirty-looking. An icy wind sprang up, boding no good.
We must push on! But where was Lachenal? I spotted him a couple of hundred yards away, looking as if he was never going to stop. And I had thought
he was in indifferent form!

The clouds grew thicker and came right down over us; the wind blew
stronger, but I did not suffer from the cold. Perhaps the descent had restored
my circulation. Should I be able to find the tents in the mist? I watched the rib
ending in the beak-like point which overlooked the camp. It was gradually
swallowed up by the clouds, but I was able to make out the spearhead tib
lower down. If the mist should thicken I would make straight for that rib and
follow it down, and in this way I should be bound to come upon the tent.

Lachenal disappeared from time to time, and then the mist was so thick
that I lost sight of him altogether. I kept going at the same speed, as fast as my
breathing would allow.

The slope was now steeper; a few patches of bare ice followed the smooth
stretches of snow. A good sign – I was nearing the camp. How difficult to find
one's way in thick mist! I kept the course which I had set by the steepest angle

of the slope. The ground was broken; with my crampons I went straight down
walls of bare ice. There were some patches ahead – a few more steps. It was the
camp all right, but there were *two* tents.

So Rébuffat and Terray had come up. What a mercy! I should be able to tell
them that we had been successful, that we were returning from the top. How
thrilled they would be!

I got there, dropping down from above. The platform had been extended,
and the two tents were facing each other. I tripped over one of the guy-ropes
of the first tent; there was movement inside – they had heard me. Rébuffat
and Terray put their heads out.

'We've made it. We're back from Annapurna!' . . .
Rébuffat and Terray received the great news with excitement and delight.

'But what about Biscante?' asked Terray anxiously.

'He won't be long. He was just in front of me! What a day – started out at
six this morning – didn't stop . . . got up at last.'

Words failed me. I had so much to say. The sight of familiar faces dispelled
the strange feeling that I had experienced since morning, and I became, once
more, just a mountaineer.

Terray, who was speechless with delight, wrung my hands. Then the smile
vanished from his face: 'Maurice – your hands!' There was an uneasy silence. I
had forgotten that I had lost my gloves: my fingers were violet and white, and
hard as wood. The other two stared at them in dismay – they realized the full
seriousness of the injury. But, still blissfully floating on a sea of joy remote
from reality, I leant over towards Terray and said confidentially, 'You're in
such splendid form, and you've done so marvellously, it's absolutely tragic
you didn't come up there with us!'

'What I did was for the Expedition, my dear Maurice, and anyway you've
got up, and that's a victory for the whole lot of us.'

I nearly burst with happiness. How could I tell him all that his answer
meant to me? The rapture I had felt on the summit, which might have seemed
a purely personal, egotistical emotion, had been transformed by his words
into a complete and perfect joy with no shadow upon it. His answer proved
that this victory was not just one man's achievement, a matter for personal
pride; no – and Terray was the first to understand this – it was a victory for us
all, a victory for mankind itself.

'Hi! Help! Help!'

'Biscante!' exclaimed the others.

Still half intoxicated and remote from reality, I had heard nothing. Terray
felt a chill at his heart, and his thoughts flew to his partner on so many

unforgettable climbs; together they had so often skirted death, and won so many splendid victories. Putting his head out, and seeing Lachenal clinging to the slope a hundred yards lower down, he dressed in frantic haste.

Out he went. But the slope was bare now; Lachenal had disappeared. Terray was horribly startled, and could only utter unintelligible cries. It was a ghastly moment for him. A violent wind sent the mist tearing by. Under the stress of emotion Terray had not realized how it falsified distances.

'Biscante! Biscante!'

He had spotted him, through a rift in the mist, lying on the slope much lower down than he had thought. Terray set his teeth, and glissaded down like a madman. How would he stop? How would he be able to brake, without crampons, on the wind-hardened snow? But Terray was a first-class skier, and with a jump turn he stopped beside Lachenal, who was concussed after his tremendous fall. In a state of collapse, with no ice-axe, balaclava, or gloves, and only one crampon, he gazed vacantly round him.

'My feet are frost-bitten. Take me down . . . take me down, so that Oudot can see to me.'

'It can't be done,' explained Terray regretfully. 'Can't you see we're in the middle of a storm . . . It'll be dark soon.'

But Lachenal was obsessed by the fear of amputation. With a gesture of despair he tore the axe out of Terray's hands and tried to force his way down, but soon saw the futility of his action, and resolved to climb up to the camp. While Terray cut steps without stopping, Lachenal, ravaged and exhausted as he was, dragged himself along on all fours.

Meanwhile I had gone into Rébuffat's tent. He was appalled at the sight of my hands and, as rather incoherently I told him what we had done, he took a piece of rope and began flicking my fingers. Then he took off my boots, with great difficulty, for my feet were swollen, and beat my feet and rubbed me. We soon heard Terray giving Lachenal the same treatment in the other tent.

For our comrades it was a tragic moment; Annapurna was conquered, and the first 'eight-thousander' had been climbed. Every one of us had been ready to sacrifice everything for this. Yet, as they looked at our feet and hands, what can Terray and Rébuffat have felt?

Outside the storm howled and the snow was still falling. The mist grew thicker and darkness came. As on the previous night we had to cling to the poles to prevent the tents being carried away by the wind. The only two air-mattresses were given to Lachenal and myself while Terray and Rébuffat both sat on ropes, rucksacks and provisions to keep themselves well off the snow. They rubbed, slapped and beat us with a rope; sometimes the blows fell on the living flesh, and howls arose from both tents. Rébuffat persevered; it was essential to continue, painful as it was. Gradually life returned to my feet as well as to my hands, and circulation started again. It was the same with Lachenal.

Now Terray summoned up the energy to prepare some hot drinks. He called to Rébuffat that he would pass him a mug, so two hands stretched out towards each other between the two tents and were instantly covered with snow, The liquid was boiling though at scarcely more than 60% Centigrade (140° Fahrenheit). I swallowed it greedily and felt infinitely better.

The night was absolute hell. Frightful onslaughts of wind battered us incessantly, while the never-ceasing snow piled up on the tents.

Now and again I heard voices from next door – it was Terray massaging Lachenal with admirable perseverance, only stopping to ply him with hot drinks. In our tent Rébuffat was quite worn out, but satisfied that warmth was returning to my limbs.

Lying half-unconscious I was scarcely aware of the passage of time. There were moments when I was able to see our situation in its true dramatic light, but the rest of the time I was plunged in an inexplicable stupor with no thought for the consequences of our victory.

Annapurna, 1952

REINHOLD MESSNER
1944–

Once more I must pull myself together. I can scarcely go on. No despair, no happiness, no anxiety. I have not lost the mastery of my feelings, there are actually no more feelings.

Messner was brought up in the south Tyrol, and was introduced to climbing aged five by his father, in the nearby Alps and Dolomites. By the age of twenty he had been on hundreds of climbing trips and was now an advocate of rapid, lightweight climbing, 'the Alpine approach', which relied on fitness and flexibility, not the steady, slow, siege mentality hitherto the norm.

On Messner's first expedition to the Himalayas – an ascent of Nanga Parbat up its south face – his brother Gunter was killed by an avalanche. Undeterred, Messner went on to live a life of 'firsts', one of which was to become the first man to climb the world's

fourteen mountains over 8,000 metres. Messner climbed Everest in 1978 with the Austrian Peter Habeler; they were the first two people to do so without the use of additional oxygen. In 1980, he climbed Everest again, this time alone, and in the monsoon season. Asked for which country he had made this second attempt, he said, 'I am my own homeland and my handkerchief is my flag.'

In the late eighties Messner began turning his attention away from climbing, and in 1990 he became the first person to cross the Antarctic continent on foot without the assistance of dogs or machines.

Climbing Everest alone

Half an hour later I am again in the tent with Nena. Already absent in spirit I prepared my body for the days of utmost exertion. I drink and eat, and sleep in between. In the tent the temperature is pleasant. The ventilation flap and entrance are open.

This time I have myself under control. I give fear no chance from the outset. The most dangerous part of the route, the ascent to the North Col, I know already, and as far as that is concerned I could only get stuck in the snow or lose myself in the mist, but not perish. The weather is fine, there will be no mist! My self-control costs energy. I sense how keyed-up my whole body is. Even during the night I have to force myself to lie quietly. Only twice do I look out at the weather. It is fine but the air is too warm. In the blue of the night Mount Everest stands over me like a magic mountain. No pondering, no asking why, I prepare myself with every fibre of my being for the big effort.

When it is time to get up I pick up socks, boots, breeches and top clothes like a sleep-walker. Each movement is quick and sure as if I had practised them a hundred times. No wasted movement.

In front of the tent I stretch myself, sniff the night air. Then I continue my ascent of the previous day. I am soon well up. Nena has remained down below. I reach the ice hollow and pick up the rucksack.

[*Nena:*] 18 August 1980. Yes, he has gone! A tender kiss on the lips was all. Just once. When Reinhold kisses me it is full of meaning. I call after him: 'I shall be thinking of you!' He didn't hear me properly or didn't want to hear me. His voice sounded absent-minded, as he asked back: 'What?' He was a bit disturbed because the night had been warmer than usual. He was much afraid that the snow would have become too soft. So what I called after him in the still morning must for him have been irrelevant. So as not to hold him up any more I said simply: 'Bye, bye'. And back comes his answer: 'Bye, bye!' Empty words hanging in the air. What experiences will he have? What sort of change will take place in him, in me?

[*1,300 metres higher*] The snow suddenly gives way under me and my headlamp goes out. Despairingly I try to cling on in the snow, but in vain. The initial reaction passes. Although it is pitch-dark I believe I can see everything: at first snow crystals, then blue-green ice. It occurs to me that I am not wearing crampons. I know what is happening but nevertheless remain quite calm. I am falling into the depths and experience the fall in slow-motion, strike the walls of the widening crevasse once with my chest, once with the rucksack. My sense of time is interrupted, also my perception of the depth of the drop. Have I been falling only split seconds or is it minutes? I am completely weightless, a torrent of warmth surges through my body.

Suddenly I have support under my feet again. At the same time I know that I am caught, perhaps trapped for ever in this crevasse. Cold sweat beads my forehead. Now I am frightened. 'If only I had a radio with me' is my first thought. I could call Nena. Perhaps she would hear me. But whether she could climb the 500 metres up to me and let a rope down to me in the crevasse is more than questionable. I have consciously committed myself to this solo ascent without a radio, and discussed it many times before starting.

I finger my headlamp and suddenly everything is bright. It's working! I breathe deeply, trying not to move at all. Also, the snow surface on which I am standing is not firm. Like a thin, transparent bridge it hangs fragile between both walls of the crevasse. I put my head back and see some eight metres above the tree trunk sized hole through which I have fallen. From the bit of black sky above a few far, far distant stars twinkle down at me. The sweat of fear breaks from all my pores, covers my body with a touch which is as icy as the iridescent blue-green ice walls between which I am imprisoned. Because they converge obliquely above me I have no chance of climbing up them.

With my headlamp I try to light up the bottom of the crevasse; but there is no end to be seen. Just a black hole to the left and right of me. The snow bridge which has stopped my fall is only one square metre large.

I have goose-pimples and shiver all over. The reactions of my body, however, are in stark contrast to the calm in my mind: there is no fear at the prospect of a new plunge into the bottomless depths, only a presentiment of dissolving, of evaporation. At the same time my mind says, that was lucky! For the first time I experience fear as a bodily reflex without psychological pain in the chest. My only problem is how to get out again. Mount Everest has become irrelevant. I seem to myself like an innocent prisoner. I don't reproach myself, don't swear. This pure, innocent feeling is inexplicable. What determines my life at this moment I do not know. I promise to myself I will descend, I will give up, if I come out of this unhurt. No more solo eight-thousanders!

My sweaty fear freezes in my hair and beard. The anxiety in my bones disappears the moment I set my body in motion, as I try to get my crampons out of the rucksack. But at each movement the feeling of falling again comes over me, a feeling of plunging into the abyss, as if the ground were slowly giving way.

Then I discover a ramp running along the crevasse wall on the valley side, a ledge the width of two feet in the ice which leads obliquely upwards and is full of snow. That is the way out! Carefully I let myself fall forward, arms outstretched, to the adjoining crevasse wall. For a long moment my body makes an arch between the wedged snow block and the slightly overhanging wall above me. Carefully I straddle across with the right foot, make a foothold in the snow which has frozen on the ledge on this crevasse wall on the downhill side. I transfer weight to the step. It holds. The insecure spot I am standing on is thus relieved. Each of these movements I instinctively make as exactly as in a rehearsed ballet. I try to make myself lighter. Breathing deeply my whole body identifies itself with the new position, I am for a moment, a long, life-determining moment, weightless. I have pushed myself off from the snow bridge with the left foot, my arms keep me in balance, my right leg supports my body. The left foot can get a grip. Relieved deep-breathing. Very carefully I move – face to the wall – to the right. The right foot gropes for a new hold in the snow, the left boot is placed precisely in the footstep which the right has vacated a few seconds before. The ledge becomes broader, leads obliquely upwards to the outside. I am saved!

In a few minutes I am on the surface – still on the valley side to be sure – but safe. I am a different person, standing there rucksack on my shoulders, ice axe in my hand as if nothing had happened. I hesitate for a moment longer, consider what I did wrong. How did this fall happen? Perhaps my left foot, placed two centimetres above the underlying edge of the crevasse, broke through as I tried to find a hold with the right on the opposite wall.

Down below in the crevasse I had decided to turn round, give up, if I got out unharmed. Now that I am standing on top I continue my ascent without thinking, unconsciously, as if I were computer-programmed . . .

Higher up above, I know from experience, it will be only willpower that forces the body from complete lethargy for another step. This sort of snail's pace compels me to rest now for some minutes every 30 paces, with longer rests sitting down every 2 hours. As the air up here contains only a third of the usual quantity of oxygen I climb as the Sherpas do. I climb and rest, rest and climb. I know that I shall feel comparatively well as soon as I sit down but put off this compelling feeling minute by minute. I must be careful to avoid any harsh irritation of the respiratory tracts. The bronchial tubes and throat are my weakest points. I know it. And already I sense some hoarseness. So I am doubly glad that on this windy mountain hardly a breeze is blowing today. A steep rise now costs me more energy than I thought. From below, going over it by eye, I supposed it would require 5 rest stops. Meanwhile it has become 8 or 9 and I am still not on top. There, where it becomes flatter, something like deliverance awaits me. I don't want to sit down until I am over the rounded top . . .

While climbing I watch only the foot making the step. Otherwise there is nothing. The air tastes empty, not stale, just empty and rough. My throat hurts. While resting I let myself droop, ski sticks and legs take the weight of my upper body. Lungs heave. For a time I forget everything. Breathing is so strenuous that no power to think remains. Noises from within me drown out all external sounds. Slowly with the throbbing in my throat will power returns.

Onwards. Another 30 paces. How this ridge fools me! Or is it my eyes? Everything seems so close, and is then so far. After a standing rest stop I am over the top. I turn round, let myself drop on the snow. From up here I gaze again and again at the scenery, at the almost endless distance. In the pastel shades of the ranges lies something mystical. It strenghens the impression of distance, the unattainable, as if I had only dreamed of this Tibet, as if I had never been here. But where I am now, I have been already, that much I know . . .

The forward-thrusting impulse in climbing is often referred to as aggression; I prefer to call it curiosity or passion. Now all that has gone. My advance has its own dynamic force, 15 paces, breathe, propped on the ski sticks which are inwardly and upwardly adjusted. With the knowledge that God is the solution. I confess that in moments of real danger something acts as a defense mechanism; it aids survival, but evaporates as soon as the threat is past. I am not at this moment under threat. It is all so peaceful here around me. I am not in any hurry. I cannot go any faster. I submit to this realization as to a law of Nature . . .

What disquiets me is the weather. No wind. The sun burns. Clouds press in from the south. Like wedges they push their grey white masses northwards. Yes, there is no doubt; the monsoon storms are sending out their scouts . . .

I am on the best route to the summit. The going is at times tiring, at times agony, it all depends on the snow conditions. The downward-sloping slabs luckily lie buried beneath a layer of névé and up to now I have been able to go round all the rock outcrops. I can see the North-East Ridge above me, but know that at the moment nothing of the pioneers can be found there. Mallory and Irvine climbed along this ridge, exactly on its edge. That is no guess. I am convinced that Odell saw them on the 'first step', on that knob which rises out of the line of the ridge. I know now that they failed on the 'second step'. In the deep trough above me Mallory and Irvine lie buried in the monsoon snow. This hunch absorbs me like an old fairytale and I can think about it without dread . . . 'First' and 'second step' now lie above me. There Mallory and Irvine live on. The fate of the pair is now free from all speculation and hopes. It is alive in me. I cannot tell whether I see it as on a stage or in my mind's eye. At all events it is happening in my life – as if it belonged to it . . .

I am there. The ridge is flat. Where is the summit? Groaning I stand up again, stamp the snow down. With ice axe, arms and upper body burrowing in the snow, I creep on, keeping to the right. Ever upwards.

When I rest I feel utterly lifeless except that my throat burns when I draw breath. Suddenly it becomes brighter. I turn round and can see down into the valley. Right to the bottom where the glacier flows. Breathtaking! Automatically I take a few photographs. Then everything is all grey again. Completely windless.

Once more I must pull myself together. I can scarcely go on. No despair, no happiness, no anxiety. I have not lost the mastery of my feelings, there are actually no more feelings. I consist only of will. After each few metres this too fizzles out in an unending tiredness. Then I think nothing, feel nothing. I let myself fall, just lie there. For an indefinite time I remain completely irresolute. Then I make a few steps again.

At most it can only be another 10 metres up to the top! To the left below me project enormous cornices. For a few moments I spy through a hole in the clouds the North Peak far below me. Then the sky opens out above me too. Oncoming shreds of cloud float past nearby in the light wind. I see the grey of the clouds, the black of the sky and the shining white of the snow surface as one. They belong together like the stripes of a flag. I must be there!

Above me nothing but sky. I sense it, although in the mist I see as little of it as the world beneath me. To the right the ridge still goes on up. But perhaps that only seems so, perhaps I deceive myself. No sign of my predecessors.

It is odd that I cannot see the Chinese aluminium survey tripod that has stood on the summit since 1975. Suddenly I am standing in front of it. I take hold of it, grasp it like a friend. It is as if I embrace my opposing force, something that absolves and electrifies at the same time. At this moment I breathe deeply . . .

Like a zombie, obeying an inner command, I take some photographs. A piece of blue sky flies past in the background. Away to the south snow cornices pile up, which seem to me to be higher than my position. I squat down, feeling hard as stone. I want only to rest a while, forget everything. At first there is no relief. I am leached, completely empty. In this emptiness nevertheless something like energy accumulates. I am charging myself up.

The Crystal Horizon: Everest, The First Solo Ascent, 1989

RANULPH FIENNES
1944–

'They are all sweating,' I thought with quick satisfaction, 'their adrenalin is pumping away ten to the dozen and they feel like vomiting just as I do.'

Sir Ranulph Twistleton-Wykeham-Fiennes, whose title is hereditary and whose family motto is: 'Look for a brave spirit,' has led over twenty-two expeditions. He was educated in South Africa and at Eton, and joined the Royal Scots Greys, where he taught outdoor skills. These skills have served him well on his notably arduous expeditions, which were to lead the *Guinness Book of Records* in 1984 to dub him the 'World's Greatest Living Explorer'.

His early expeditions included journeys up the White Nile by hovercraft and through remote British Colombia by inflatable boat. Fiennes also led the expedition in Oman that finally uncovered the city of Ubar, described by T. E. Lawrence as the 'lost Atlantis of the Sands'. One of his most dramatic ventures, the Transglobe Expedition – a circumnavigation of the world through both Poles with Charlie Burton, following the 0° and the 180° meridians – took seven years to plan and three years (1979–82) to complete.

In 1993 Fiennes returned to Antarctica with Dr Michael Stroud and made the first unassisted crossing of the continent, an exhausting trek that took ninety-seven days and was the longest unsupported polar journey in history. Seven years earlier Fiennes and Stroud had had to abandon their fourth attempt to walk unsupported to the North Pole when they were only eighty-nine miles away from their goal.

Fiennes' expeditions now also raise money for charity; so far they have garnered over £4 million. He is proud of their scientific value – of particular interest is just how much his body can keep enduring – and successfully sued a publication for casting doubt on the value of his expeditions.

Jumping onto a mountain glacier

The Cessna's rear doorway was an upright oblong and from it we peered fascinated, almost mesmerised, at the successive vistas which flashed by as though the doorway were a cinema screen and we the cramped spectators. The fuselage was a small tube stripped of chairs and other accessories so that we sat on the smooth floor gripping one another's legs or the chair anchor-hooks to keep our heavily-laden bodies from sliding through the open doorway. Only Don stood, his back bent along the ceiling, trying no doubt to recall the route we had followed three years earlier to reach the black horn of the Lodalskåpa. Once this peak, the highest point of the Jostedalsbre, was sighted, the pilot would work out the relative position of our ice-field target and begin his climb into the thin air four thousand feet above the ice.

From time to time Don stooped to run a practised hand over our parachute packs, checking each nylon knot and metal toggle. It was a tight squeeze, so any quick movement against the fuselage might cause damage to our parachute fastenings and later result in a malfunction of the rip-cord.

The pilot knew these mountains well, and squeezed his Cessna between towering buttresses whence waterfalls poured in slow motion over glistening granite and steaming beds of dank lichen; blotting paper to the pulsating sheen of spray. Not more than fifty metres beneath us the rock had vanished: in its place a maze of serrated ice flanked the plateau. The lips of each crevasse were well delineated by a shimmering azure blue. These were the incredible fissures about which we had been warned: some were over a hundred feet in depth and would digest a parachutist complete with canopy, leaving no visible trace.

No one spoke as we watched – our hands were cold as sin; those of us without gloves shoving them between their legs for the warmth there. 'However cold it is,' I mused, 'it doesn't warrant the danger of gloves. How can I possibly feel the thin red handle, when I want it, with thick woollen gloves muting the perception of my questing fingers.'

An aromatic, almost sensual odour of body sweat tinged the cold metal smell of our temporary cabin. 'They are all sweating,' I thought with quick satisfaction, 'their adrenalin is pumping away ten to the dozen and they feel like vomiting just as I do.' I smiled at Don: he grinned down at me, sensing perhaps the confidence he exuded. I glanced at Peter. His mouth smiled but his eyes remained distant and his knuckles were white where he gripped the pilot's seat. Perhaps we were all thinking of the cliffs and the fissures, noticing how small was the white patch of the ice-field and knowing that it would be smaller yet when viewed from over ten thousand feet. There would be little margin for error . . .

Our pilot finally raised a gloved hand: he too had located our dropping zone and now circled above it to give Don a chance to appraise its limitations. Don showed the pilot two fingers – denoting the height of ascent he required. The Cessna shuddered with increased throttle and the floor lurched as we climbed.

Levelling out at two thousand feet over the Lodalskåpa, the pilot set a circular course which traversed the landing area on its upwind run . . .

Don moved back from the door suddenly and beckoned us urgently to get ready.

Awkwardly, and careful not to brush the 'chutes against one another, we levered ourselves into kneeling positions facing the maw.

This was the moment of truth from which there could be 'no honourable withdrawal,' as the military books put it. I knew not to look down or, indeed,

out into space. To the very last minute I must look at my watch-strap, the
fuselage or even a stud on the doorway – for my single ungovernable fear was
not so much the act of jumping itself; it was the fearful thought that one
glimpse of the ice, of the black peaks below, would bring alive all the latent
terrors of the dream world: the nightmarish feeling of cartwheeling away into
nothingness, mouth frozen open in a silent retching scream. To let one nig-
gling thought of that nature through the gate of the mind would be fatal – for
a flood of irrepressible apprehension might follow, and who really trusts the
strength of his own will?

Not I, so I concentrated fiercely on the solid objects within the fuselage and
mentally rehearsed the robot-like actions which make up the perfect exit,
remembering the raucous commands of the Netheravon instructors.

'Head well back as you jump . . . look at the doorway.' (This was a pipe-
dream in my case for I invariably screwed my eyes tight shut for the seconds
of leaving the aircraft.)

'Shove that stomach forward . . . spread all your limbs like you was jumping
for joy!'

And Don's last warning – specific to the Cessna. 'She's not a Rapide, so
don't treat her like one. You must jump outwards away from the plane not
just backwards in the normal fashion.'

I imagined my reaction should the 'chute not deploy when I pulled its rip-
cord. Exactly where would I find that little reserve handle which I normally
forgot about?

Then I felt a rough hand shake my shoulder. Don was shouting at me with
urgency and pointing out meaningfully.

But something was wrong. I had been subconsciously awaiting the dreaded
sound of the engines cutting back; the necessary preliminary to any free-fall
jump which slows the plane down to just above its stalling speed, minimising
the power of the slipstream past the fuselage. The Cessna was still at maximum speed. I pointed at the pilot desperately but Don gestured, very firmly,
out of the door. There was no arguing and I forced an arm through the
bucketing slipstream to grip the wing-strut, then with some effort the other
arm. This was ridiculous – I would never get into a reasonable, safe position
on the float with this roaring sucking force tearing me away.

I shall never quite know what happened next. Three years ago at the vital
moment, one of the team had lost his nerve and Don had helped him on his
way with a friendly and well-timed push. I was fearful lest he should think I
too was hesitating and give me an ignominious shove. Perhaps for this reason
I was too hurried, for, gripping the wing-strut – as a drowning man clutches a

branch – I lurched my legs towards the float below. Rubber boots scrabbling on the wet metal for a hold and hands – numb with the biting cold – gradually losing their grip on the strut, the wind force took full hold of my body. Much in the manner of an unseen squid sucking a shellfish from rock, the slipstream tore me loose and flung me away, a puppet with no strings. Unable therefore to jump outwards, my body passed close by the fuselage and a sharp pain in my hand as it struck the float side registered briefly.

'One thousand and one, one thousand and two . . .' Netheravon training had sunk in, for my disembodied voice was chiming out the seconds automatically and I opened my eyes. 'It's so very cold – I will freeze solid in this ridiculous position,' I remember thinking. Then there was that insidious feeling that my body was going into a spin. Fearfully I stretched my arms wider and pushed forward my stomach. 'One thousand and five, one thousand and six . . .' But the spin was becoming more pronounced. I glanced down at my legs and knew why; the left one was kicking desperately, convulsively, like a dying rabbit. I suppose it was instinctively trying to kick me back into a stable position but was in fact having an adverse effect. It had seemingly acquired a mind of its own and only with a great effort of will could I control it and force the whole leg outwards, 'One thousand and nine . . .'

The world was suddenly a peaceful, silent, faraway place above which my body floated, chanting its numerical litany, with absolutely no sense of movement or urgency. But only for fleeting seconds, for I was now flying at close on a hundred and thirty miles an hour and every limb must be perfectly positioned to remain stable at this speed.

They weren't however, for my head must still have been slightly inclined after watching the antics of my leg. Slowly, almost imperceptibly, its angle had caused the inverted saucer-shape of the falling body to tilt forwards. 'One thousand and twelve . . .' I was going into a dive and the sudden realisation caused panic. Both arms snapped inwards to the rip-cord, searching for the cold feel of it – but a ciné-camera was loose inside my anorak having slipped down and was pressed by the wind over the handle bar. Now my position was bunched and haywire. Grovelling in the folds of the anorak, as for gold dust, I found the red handle and ripped it away viciously, arms returning to the star position to halt a rapidly materialising somersault.

Perhaps two seconds later the crack, as of a whip, and the breathtaking arrest of the securing harness had me dangling happily beneath a full orange canopy . . .

Looking down between my legs, there were streamers of mist blowing before the wind and below them thousands of feet of dark void – most uninviting; but to the left the jagged white edge of the table top not more than a thousand feet below. My boots seemed to be moving fast along a parallel course to the glacier's flank, which was not reassuring since I must be descending at a good twenty miles an hour. After a hard tug on the left-hand toggle, the canopy turned and tacked across the wind making slow but sure progress to the south.

Now the great angled fissures of the ice-fringe passed beneath my limp legs – God forbid landing amongst that lot – then the crevasses grew narrower, more like thin blue veins. Directly ahead a lone black outcrop of curious fragmentation: surely, that was the Braeniba. Then it was past to the left and the wind was sighing as I swung like a pendulum. Everything now was close and white. The ice must be rushing up to meet me but there was no perspective, no way of telling how far away was the white mass nor precisely when I would crash into it. I braced my legs, knees bent, for the impact . . . 'head and elbows tucked in and boots below bottom'.

A fleeting glimpse of orange to the right – someone else was already down – and the slightly suffocating jolt of a beautifully soft landing – not on ice but packed snow. Wiping some from my mouth and nose, I got up to look around but was dragged over again as a strong surface wind caught the billowing canopy and pulled it along like an ice-yacht. By pulling in several lengths of a single 'chute cord, I collapsed the material and ran round to the leeward side before removing the harness.

The others were carefully restacking their 'chutes within their retaining packs; an irritating task for it was important to keep all moisture from the canopy panels before folding them. The nylon would otherwise rot with damp in time – and all our expensive 'chutes would eventually have to return to Netheravon for use by many other aspiring free-fallers.

We were shivering slightly by the time a faint rhythmic drone announced the Cessna's return, for there was no cover or sheltering nook on the sloping ice-field. Once the plane was visible to the north-west, Patrick lit two flares. It had said 'BLUE' on the army tins but they were burning away an unashamed white, slightly fluorescent, which might well go unnoticed by the plane. But the pilot evidently had a definite bearing on the dropping zone this time and soon saw us, waggling his wings before climbing to 10,500 feet for the second drop. My anorak was rippling, smacking loose folds against its canvas belt, for the wind was more persistent now. 'Eighteen knots,' I thought, 'possibly stronger from time to time.' Then for a period it would drop away almost entirely – very awkward weather for a parachutist and stronger than during the first drop . . .

'Something's come loose,' Peter was pointing at one of the pink canopies floating high above us. The kit-drop was under way and, sure enough, a dark object had parted company with one bundle and was falling towards us. It smashed into the packed snow not a hundred yards away; one of the larger radios. Initial inspection disclosed no apparent damage, but it had landed at close on eighty miles an hour and its innards must have suffered a severe jolt. Later we fitted batteries to it and were not surprised that the set was dead as a doornail.

We were certainly too far south for any light effects of the Aurora Borealis but, as twilight drew nigh, the view from our perch on the sloping plateau was striking and not easily forgotten. It must have been well past eight o'clock and the setting sun played games of visual fantasy with our world of ice. A vast and gentle swathe of violet shot with orange ruffles outlined the eastern horizon and over all the shimmering fields of prehistoric ice lay the moon shadow of the Lodalskåpa. Its ugly, almost phallic horn rose gloomy from a host of lesser peaks, glimmering faintly in outline through the haze of dusk . . .

The last 'chute away, the Cessna dived low and 'buzzed' us, wings waggling, before turning north over the valleys of Nordfjord to be lost in the spiralling gullies of Bödal.

We would have to spend the night in the shelter of the Braeniba rocks close by, so all hands were set to the loading of sledges with the heavier items – the rubber boats and 600-foot rope coils – and the tents were pitched amongst the haphazard mass of centralised items under a sheer granite cliff. Blocks of snow were shovelled into makeshift walls round each tent and tiny metal cookers were soon blazing away beneath tins of dehydrated curry or beef broth. Climbing through the entrance hole of the mini-tent I shared with Patrick, I was shocked to see – by the light of a flickering candle – that he had been wearing a pair of woman's full-length pantees under his ski-trousers. This was a revelation: poking my head out of the tent again to find some willing ears to hear this damning news, I saw to my horror that Roger – standing some distance from his tent to answer nature's call – was clad in similar black pantees.

'Aren't you cold?' I asked him.

'Not at all, they're fantastically warm. Bob Powell's wife gave some of us a pair before we left Newcastle.'

Ice Fall in Norway, 1972

CHRIS BONINGTON
1934–

I know my life will be a constant search for Annapurnas and, having found one,
I shall feel forced to seek the next.

Sir Christian Bonington was born in Hampstead and, after leaving school, trained for the army at Sandhurst. He spent three years in charge of tank troops in Germany, then worked at an army outward-bound centre from where he was able go on mountaineering expeditions in the Alps. In 1960 he was invited to join the British–Indian–Nepalese expedition to Annapurna II, and reached the summit.

His next Himalayan mission was to scale the south face of Annapurna – 12,000 feet of ice wall, like the north face of the Eiger, but on a grander scale – leading to a 26,545-foot peak. He reached the summit on 27 May 1970, and though the achievement was marred by the loss of one climber, it was a landmark in the history of mountaineering – for the aficionados, as important as the first ascent of Everest, and one of the pivotal moments of twentieth-century mountaineering.

Two years later he attempted the south-west face of Everest. Though his party were forced back by bad weather, he returned to lead the British Everest Expedition in which Doug Scott and Dougal Haston reached the summit. Also with Doug Scott, Bonington made the first ascent of the Ogre in the Karakorams. During the six-day descent the pair had to fight against a driving blizzard, Scott crawling down (having broken both legs) and Bonington in pain from a broken rib.

Several more challenging climbs followed: Mount Kongor in West Xinjiang (1981); the north-east ridge of Everest without oxygen, during which two of his climbing companions disappeared (1982); Mount Vinson, the highest peak in Antarctica; and in 1985, now having reached his fifties, with the Norwegian Everest Expedition he at last achieved another ambition, that of climbing Everest himself.

Death on Annapurna

In the morning I started writing the account of our success, to be radioed back to our committee of management. From time to time I went out and looked up at the Face through the binoculars. Tom and Mick should be down at Camp III by this time; the others would be at the foot of the long gully.

I remember Martin saying, 'Relax, Chris, it's all over. Nothing can happen now.'

'I don't think I'll be really happy till everyone is down.'

I very much doubt if this was premonition, for I have always been nervous on any descent after a hard climb, never relaxing until I get down to ground level.

I had returned to my typewriter when I heard someone rush up to the tent calling, 'Chris, Chris!' and the rest was incomprehensible. I ran out and found Mike sitting on the grass, head between knees, sucking in the air in great, hacking gasps. He looked up, face contorted with shock, grief and exhaustion.

'It's Ian. He's dead; killed in an ice avalanche below Camp II.'

Everyone had run out of their tents on hearing Mike's arrival; they just stood numbed in shocked, unbelieving silence for about five minutes as Mike gasped out his story; Mike is one of the most emotionally restrained and balanced people that I know, but that morning he was crying. I held him, my arm round his shoulder, barely restrained my own tears as I tried to find out exactly what had happened.

Mike, Ian and Dave Lambert had decided not to wait for Mick Burke and Tom, but set out from Camp III early that morning, hauling down as much gear as they could manage. We had arranged for the Sherpas at Camp I to come up to the now cleared site of Camp II to meet them.

Mike and Ian reached the site of Camp II at around 9.30, and since the Sherpas had not yet come up they decided to press on down. Ian suggested that they stopped for a rest and something to eat, but Mike was impatient to get off the mountain and pointed out that they would be down at Camp I in half an hour if they pushed on quickly.

And so they carried on down the side of the glacier, into a narrow corridor between some small ice towers and then out onto the start of the ramp which led across the ice cliffs. This was the spot that we had always realized was dangerous, but the most obvious threat had been removed earlier on in the expedition when the Sword of Damocles had fallen. There was still an element of risk, for there were some ice towers farther up the glacier, but their threat was not so obvious and it seemed unlikely that these would collapse in the space of the few seconds it took to cross the danger zone. Even so, we all tended to hurry across this section of the glacier.

Ian was in front and Mike immediately behind. Dave Lambert was about five minutes behind them. They had just come out of the narrow, enclosed corridor that led down to the ramp and they could see the five Sherpas, who were coming up to meet them, resting on a small mound just short of the sérac wall.

There was practically no warning, just a thunderous roar and the impression of a huge, dark mass filling the sky above. Mike ducked back into the side of the ice wall where a small trough was formed. He thought that Ian, slightly farther out than he, had tried to run away from the avalanche, down the slope. But Ian hadn't a hope and was engulfed in the fall.

'It went completely dark,' Mike told me later. 'I thought I'd had it; just lay there and swore at the top of my voice. It seemed such a stupid way to die.'

The fall seemed to last for several minutes, though it was probably considerably less. Mike was buried in small ice blocks but had been protected by the wall at his side from the torrent of huge blocks that had come pouring directly over him.

When the cloud of ice particles had settled and the last grating rumble had died away into the silence of the glacier, the survivors picked themselves out of the debris. The Sherpas had had to run for their lives, but fortunately had been sufficiently far from the base of the cliff to get out of the direct line of fall. Even so, Mingma had been hit by an ice block, though he was not injured.

They then started to search for Ian and found him near the foot of the avalanche debris, his body protruding from it. Death must have been instantaneous. The accident had occurred at 10 a.m. and Mike had run straight down to warn us, leaving Dave and the Sherpas with the body. They had a walkie-talkie set with them and he had told Dave to open up on the hour.

Back at Base Camp it was now just after mid-day and I opened the set. Dave came on the air and told me that they had managed to get Ian's body clear of the ice.

I immediately decided that we should carry him back to Base Camp and bury him there. The Rognon was somehow too bleak a place, and I felt that we should try to have some kind of ceremony as a tribute to so close a friend of us all. At this stage we were all numbed by the very unexpectedness, the enormity of the accident. In a strange way it would have been easier to come to terms with during the actual course of the ascent, but now, the whole climb seemed to have been over, success achieved, the risk passed. And then this.

I couldn't help having a feeling of guilt, that if I'd brought everyone off the mountain the accident might never have happened. I could dismiss this on logical grounds for the sérac could have collapsed at any point of time during the expedition and presented the type of risk that climbers face as a matter of course in the Alps. If it had fallen one minute earlier, Ian would be alive now; but equally, if it had collapsed two minutes later, Mike and all five Sherpas could also have been engulfed. It was a risk that we all knew and had accepted – you must accept this type of risk if you go climbing on any Himalayan peak – but the knowledge of this did not make the tragedy, when it occurred, any easier to understand or accept.

But the risks were not over. Mick and Tom were still on the mountain, probably somewhere below Camp III, we still had to carry Ian's body back across the lower glacier below the Rognon, another place that was fraught with peril. I could not bring myself to just sit and wait for the rest of my expedition to get back to Base Camp and therefore, taking Nick Estcourt with me, set out to meet the carrying party, and to find Mick Burke and Tom Frost.

I met them just starting across the glacier. It was terribly difficult to believe that the inanimate bundle tied in a tarpaulin, strapped to a ladder, had only an hour or so before been an active, living person. Pasang Kami had taken charge and was directing the Sherpas and Gurkha porters with a cool competence, as they manoeuvred the makeshift stretcher through the chaotic icefall. One could not help being aware of the ice cliffs frowning above. At this stage Mick Burke and Dave Lambert arrived down, but Tom Frost was still on his way. They had left Rob, one of our London Sherpas, to wait for him, but I felt I had to go back up the Rognon to assure myself that he was all right. I plodded up through the mist, my mind a mixture of grief and shock; still no sign of Tom; could something else have happened? I was nearly at Camp I and heard a rattle of stones below; they had nearly passed me in the cloud. I set off back to Base Camp with them; at least we had now got everyone else off the mountain.

That night everyone was subdued and silent, buried in their own thoughts and reaction to the tragedy. Next morning, the 30th, our porters were due to arrive from Pokhara to carry out all our gear. We buried Ian about a hundred feet above Base Camp, at the foot of the slab of rock where he had spent so much time teaching the TV team and our Sherpas and cookboys how to jumar and abseil. I said a few words of tribute; Tom said a prayer and we filled in the grave. It was a very short, simple ceremony and yet it had a beauty and dignity, enhanced by the depth of feeling of all who were present.

The Sherpas placed a wooden cross at the head of the grave and decked it with wreaths made from alpine flowers collected by the porters. The tents had been pulled down, the porters were waiting with their loads and all that was left of two months' occupation, with all its struggle, drama and laughter, were a few piles of empty tins and the lone grave of a close friend.

We turned our backs on the South Face of Annapurna and set foot, for the first time in nearly ten weeks, on the glacier below Base Camp. When we had walked up it everything had been hidden by a mantle of snow, but now that the bare bones of rubble were exposed, a dusty path worn through it, it reminded me of a vast junkyard. And then we reached the other side of the glacier, dropped down into the shallow valley at the side of the lateral moraine through lush meadows sprinkled with an ever widening variety of flowers. I don't think any of us felt regret at leaving Annapurna as we turned down into the gaping jaws of the Modi Khola gorge. We had been there too long and had given too much, and yet we had known some of the most exciting climbing of our lives, had reached a level of unity and selflessness that had made success possible. As we walked down the Modi Khola we felt a mixture of grief at the death of a friend and an extraordinary elation, not solely from our success, but also because we had managed to become such a close-knit team.

I can't attempt to evaluate the worth of our ascent balanced against its cost in terms of the loss of a man's life, of the time devoted to it or the money spent on it. Climbing, and the risks involved, are part of my life and, I think, of those of most of the team – it was certainly a very large part of Ian's life. It is difficult to justify the risks once one is married with a family, and I think most of us have stopped trying. We love climbing, have let a large part of our lives be dominated by this passion, and this eventually led us to Annapurna.

Maurice Herzog, in his story of the first ascent of Annapurna, finishes up his book with the words: 'There are other Annapurnas in the lives of men.' This is still true today, both in the realm of mountaineering and in one's own progress through life. Our ascent of Annapurna was a breakthrough into a new dimension of Himalayan climbing on the great walls of the highest mountains in the world – this represents the start of an era, not the end. Climbers will turn to other great faces, will perhaps try to reduce the size of the party, escape from the heavy siege tactics that we were forced to employ and make lightweight assaults against these huge mountain problems.

And then, on a personal level, each one of us who helped to climb the South Face will find new challenges. For Don and Dougal it is the South Face of Everest; for Tom Frost, it is living within the moral code of his Mormon faith; for Mick Burke, perhaps carving out a career in films; for myself – I know not, at the moment, but I know my life will be a constant search for Annapurnas and, having found one, I shall feel forced to seek the next.

Annapurna South Face, 1971

New Frontiers: Outer Space, Inner Mind, Underwater, Underground

*

We still have better maps of the surface of the moon than of the sea floor.
Edwin E. 'Buzz' Aldrin, and Julian Partridge, *The Blue* (1999)

In going about our investigation of the world, major terrains were left aside, either because they were economically or symbolically unimportant, or because we lacked the ability to penetrate them. Even today these realms – whether underwater, underground, or in outer space – remain relatively unknown; and although, strictly speaking, they are outside the scope of this book – which is essentially about how man stretched out around our planet's surface to see what was there – these other terrains deserve a mention. For although the further exploration of previously discovered places and peoples around the globe will continue, these other habitats are completely new arenas of discovery and perhaps point the way forward. There is also another, fourth environment where great advances are being made – within ourselves. It's one of the great ironies of exploration, of course, that we have set out to discover far lands without ever having really got to grips with the workings of our minds, the behaviour of our own cells.

Physically and intellectually, these four zones could not be more different – from the antics of a cave diver, who grapples through rib-crushing tunnels beneath the earth, to the intellectual journey Sigmund Freud took through the convoluted minds of his patients; from Neil Armstrong stepping out on the moon to Richard Dawkins exploring the driving mechanisms of life: 'They are in you and in me; they created us, body and mind; and their preservation is the ultimate rationale for our existence . . . they go by the name of genes, and we are their survival machines.'

There's something else that separates the new explorers from the ones we've so far seen: they lack a full sensual awareness of the environment they are exploring. 'One becomes, effectively, blind,' wrote the cave diver Martyn Farr, describing what it feels like to inch through water in the subterranean blackness, unable to see, smell or hear. Underground passages have been left unexplored until now perhaps because there were other more glamorous, and certainly more obvious, feats to be done on the earth's surface. But these subterranean arenas should not be ignored – to date, the caver Andrew Eavis has made his way through some 500 kilometres of underground networks around the world, which means that he has discovered more terrain on land than any other explorer alive. Michael Ray Taylor, also underground, has encountered lakes whose purity is beyond the measurement of today's technology. By wriggling his way down into our earth's crust, sometimes up to a mile beneath us, he has been able to retrieve some of the oldest-known life forms. The caves themselves are libraries of information about our planet on subjects ranging from climate change to the origin of life itself. Taylor makes a connection between the so-called 'extremophiles' – bacterial and other organisms that form ecosystems in volcanic deposits or hot springs, or without the help of sunlight, or in subterranean corridors dripping with sulphuric acid – and the nanobacteria fossils that were, just plausibly, discovered on a Martian meteorite in 1996. In *Dark Life* (1999) he records his reaction as he peers with a research scientist through an electron microscope to scan a rock sample from a thermal spring:

' "Oh my God," said the young scientist.

'Chains and clusters and loops of cells were everywhere. Some were clearly frozen in the act of cell division. Tiny filaments linked some of the spherical objects to larger cells, like a line of ducklings trailing their mother. The largest of the cells before us was the approximate diameter of a large virus, such as HIV. Viruses, however, are not technically "alive." They borrow the reproductive machinery of host cells in order to make copies of themselves, which is the only thing viruses can do (often with disastrous consequences for the host cells). They cannot eat, digest, excrete, grow, attack invaders, or carry on any of the regular functions of living beings. But these cells looked nothing like viruses. They looked exactly like textbook illustrations of living bacteria, except that quite a few of them were much, much smaller than anything science had definitively classified as life.

'We were looking at something important. Any surviving remnants of my journalistic objectivity took flight and vanished. I sat staring at images that were in themselves news, at a new reality, and I felt a hunger to learn, study, and explore this dark life. I no longer was content merely to report on the birth of a new science – I wanted to join its front ranks. I wanted to show the things before us to the world and prove that they lived.'

Many of these new theatres of exploration have been neglected because we previously lacked either the technology or the intellectual framework to tackle them. Now, discovery has become a matter not of overcoming raw nature, but raw data. The plains and fissures of the deep sea, unlike those of the Africa crossed by Stanley, or the America crossed by MacKenzie, are being explored not by adventurers striding along, gun tucked under arm, but by scientists in front of computer monitors using remote imaging. Even today, the great majority of the ocean floor remains unvisited: Robert D. Ballard has explored the Mid-Atlantic Ridge, and also found deep-sea life at hydrothermal vents in the Pacific, but there's much, much more waiting besides. Here's the zoologist Julian Partridge describing with Buzz Aldrin (in *The Blue*, 1999) both this environment and the strategies evolved by deep-water species for coping with little or no sunlight:

'Between the mid-ocean ridges and the continental slopes that rise to our more familiar terrestrial world are monotonous grey-brown abyssal plains that stretch for millions of square kilometres. In places, towering volcanoes reach from the sea floor towards the surface as sea-mounts and flat-topped guyots, only occasionally breaking through the waves to emerge as oceanic islands. Elsewhere the abyssal plains plunge downwards to become oceanic trenches, the deepest plummeting to a depth close to 11 kilometres, some 2.5 kilometres greater than the height of Mount Everest . . .

At a depth of 1,000 metres, where even the most sensitive fish eye cannot see light from the sun, the blackness pervades. Fish here, such as the elongate, huge-mouthed gulper eel and the black dragon fish, have bodies like black velvet. In contrast, shrimps at these depths are red; a strategy that only works because there is no red light at all and so they too are effectively black. In the absence of sunlight many animals turn to other senses, particularly to detect small vibrations in the surrounding darkness. Fish such as the fangtooth or the ridgehead have skins pock-marked with pores leading into canals containing cells sensitive to water movements. Other fish have skins studded with protruding bumps and nail-like outgrowths or, in the case of some angler fish, are even covered with elongated "hairs". These delicate structures confer keen sensitivity to the vibrations around; vital in a world where a wafted movement in the darkness may indicate a potential meal.

Although there is little or no sunlight in this realm there is light in the deep sea. This bioluminescence is produced by the animals themselves and their pinpoint pulses of light break the darkness intermittently. Blue flashes in the black void signify interactions that we can only guess at: territorial squabbling perhaps, sexual signalling, or the frantic engagement of prey and predator. Most animals in the deep sea are bioluminescent . . .

We can only speculate how some of these lights are used, such is our ignorance of animal behaviour in the deep, but in other cases we can guess. A tiny copepod flashes brilliantly when attacked – a call for help that may bring in predators of the assailant; others discharge tiny bioluminescent fireworks to distract, scare and confuse. A shrimp spews sticky glowing fluid towards its attacker, perhaps as a glowing decoy or perhaps fatally to mark the aggressor for the ravages of larger predators. A dull red medusa is transformed from drifting stillness to a pulsating whirl of blue light, certainly to scare or startle. In contrast, other animals, such as the black and ominous-looking angler fish, use light to attract; their fishing rods and dangling chin barbells are luminescent lures held dangerously close to their cavernous and ever-ready mouths.'

While scientists are mapping the sea's depths – which form, incidentally, the earth's largest habitat, and one that is 'home to the least understood members of the web of life' (as Partridge reminds us), others have been charting space. This story starts with the pioneer aviators, the first to try their might against gravitational pull. Then, in no time, man was in orbit – Orville Wright (who died in 1948), the person credited with being the first to fly a plane, could in theory have met the first to walk the moon, Armstrong (who was born in 1930).

Before being capable of venturing into space, an explorer needed a highly sophisticated flying capsule, and, to assist him, a whole army of physicists and technicians back at mission control. John Glenn was the first American to orbit earth, Alan Shephard the first American in space, but both were beaten by the Russian Yuri Gagarin (1934–1968) – for (as we've seen repeatedly in this book) there was more than geographical discovery at stake. Here was the race for spice trade routes, the race to the Poles, all over again. Human beings had always known caves, had always dived below the sea surface – and seen other mammals go deeper. But nothing, no eagle, no stone, had ever escaped the bounds of the earth. And with Apollo 11, man was about to do that. A million spectators were camped around the launch site: the world was watching.

The first lunar landing in 1969 captured our imagination as no other event, and to many people this moment is the pinnacle of man's achievement in exploration. 'Because of what you have done,' President Nixon told the astronauts, as they sat in their lunar module, 'the heavens have become a part of man's world.'

Despite all the technological infrastructure around them, the astronauts experienced the emotions of all venturers faced with the unknown. Here again is the wonder of Howard Carter in Egypt opening a Pharaoh's tomb, the fear and tension of Cortés in Mexico setting eyes on the great Aztec capital. Michael Collins, describing in *Carrying the Fire* (1974) the moment before take-off from earth, wrote:

'I am everlastingly thankful that I have flown once before, and that this period of waiting atop a rocket is nothing new. I am just as tense this time, but the tenseness comes mostly from an appreciation of the enormity of our undertaking rather than from the unfamiliarity of the situation. If the two effects, physical apprehension and the pressure of awesome responsibility, were added together, they might be too much to handle without making some ghastly mistake. As it is, I am far from certain that we will be able to fly this mission as planned. I think we will escape with our skins, or at least I will escape with mine, but I wouldn't give better than even odds on a successful landing and return. There are just too many things that can go wrong.'

As the earth receded, the moon loomed nearer and nearer:

'The moon I have known all my life, that two-dimensional, small yellow disk in the sky, has gone away somewhere, to be replaced by the most awesome sphere I have ever seen. To begin with, it is huge, completely filling our window. Second, it is three-dimensional. The belly of it bulges out towards us . . . I almost feel I can reach out and touch it, whilst its surface obviously recedes towards its edges. It is between us and the sun, creating the most splendid lighting conditions imaginable. The sun casts a halo around it, shining on its rear surface and the sunlight which comes cascading around its rim serves mainly to make the moon itself seem mysterious and subtle . . .'

Neil Armstrong and Buzz Aldrin separate off, leaving Collins alone in space while they descend to the moon. Then a computer system fails, and, for all the advanced technology around them, Armstrong is suddenly having to steer his way by hand, in the manner of navigators since the dawn of exploration. With almost unimaginable nerve, using his pilot's instinct and judgement, he heads beyond a 'blocky-rim crater' and seeks out a soft, even surface. After the mapping scientists back on earth have located where in the Sea of Tranquillity they are, the astronauts are at last in a position to think about opening the hatch. Armstrong prepares to descend the steps and walk on the moon (*First on the Moon*, 1970):

ARMSTRONG: You need more slack, Buzz?
ALDRIN: No, hold it just a minute.

ARMSTRONG: Okay.

ALDRIN: Okay, everything's nice and straight in here.

ARMSTRONG: Okay, can you pull the door open a little more?

HOUSTON (McCandless): Neil, this is Houston. You're loud and clear. Break, break. Buzz, this is Houston. Radio check and verify TV circuit breaker in.

EAGLE (Aldrin): Roger. TV circuit breaker's in. LMP reads loud and clear.

HOUSTON (McCandless): And we're getting a picture on the TV.

EAGLE (Aldrin): Oh, you got a good picture. Huh?

HOUSTON (McCandless): Okay, Neil, we can see you coming down the ladder now.

EAGLE (Armstrong): Okay, I just checked – getting back up to that first step, Buzz, it's not even collapsed too far, but it's adequate to get back up ... It takes a pretty good little jump ... I'm at the foot of the ladder. The LM [Lunar Module] footpads are only depressed in the surface about one or two inches. Although the surface appears to be very, very fine-grained, as you get close to it. It's almost like a powder. Now and then, it's very fine ... I'm going to step off the LM now ... THAT'S ONE SMALL STEP FOR A MAN, ONE GIANT LEAP FOR MANKIND.

Meanwhile, Collins was spinning some sixty miles above them, on his lonely vigil. He made seven orbits in total, and, having to just sit there in space, had time for reflection. Despite all the technology, in the human achievement of space flight there is still that strange chemistry of the inner journey intermingling with the outward one which has always been a feature of pushing through frontiers:

'I don't mean to deny a feeling of solitude. It is there, reinforced by the fact that radio contact with the earth abruptly cuts off at the instant I disappear behind the moon. I am alone now, truly alone, and absolutely isolated from any known life. I am it. If a count were taken, the score would be three billion plus two over on the other side of the moon, and one plus God knows what on this side. I feel this powerfully – not as fear of loneliness but as awareness, anticipation, satisfaction, confidence, almost exultation. I like the feeling. Outside my window I can see stars – and that is all. Where I know the moon to be, there is simply a black void: the moon's presence is defined solely by the absence of stars.'

Where does the adventurer go, now that he roughly knows his home patch, the planet, and must hand over detailed research to the specialist? He looks to himself: 'The final frontier may be human relationships themselves,' wrote

Buzz Aldrin. 'Our real challenge is to understand why we humans continually want to combat each other and why we're obsessed with our own satisfaction at the expense of fellow humans. We can see and understand what we can touch, but what we think and judge and reason is much more difficult to comprehend.'

As the explorers within this book have shown us time and again, competition has been a great spur of pioneers through the ages: Aldrin's Apollo mission didn't plant the American flag on the moon just for decoration. But, as I noted in the Introduction, there's also an inner impulse that we can all appreciate, if only by remembering the wonder we felt on discovering birds' nests, rock pools or fossils as children. James Cook, who perhaps revealed a larger area of the globe than anyone, spoke of 'the pleasure which naturally results to a man from being the first discoverer, even was it nothing more than sand and shoals.' In the case of Cook – someone who wouldn't, I suspect, have felt out of place training for a space mission – his particular ambition was 'not only to go farther than anyone had been before, but as far as it is possible for a man to go.'

There are no 'final' frontiers of exploration. We will never know everything and there will never be an end in sight. How much do we know even about the humble ant? Not nearly enough, biologist Edward O. Wilson tells us: for a start, it isn't quite as humble as it might seem. 'The truth is,' he writes in *In Search of Nature* (1997), 'that we need invertebrates but they don't need us. If human beings were to disappear tomorrow, the world would go on with little change . . . But if invertebrates were to disappear . . . within a few decades the world would return to a state of a billion years ago, composed primarily of bacteria, algae, and a few other very simple multicellular plants.'

We don't yet know our planet, and, as Aldrin said, we don't yet know ourselves. 'By what magic,' asks the contemporary neuroscientist Vilayanur S. Ramachandran in *Phantoms in the Brain* (1998), while discussing how our brain interprets the world around us, 'is matter transmuted into the invisible fabric of feelings and sensations?' We can't really quite say. 'Not the animal world, not the plant world, not the miracle of the spheres but man himself is now the crucial mystery,' wrote the mythologist Joseph Campbell, in *The Hero with a Thousand Faces* (1949), applying the idea of a Jungian collective unconscious to connect the different myths of humanity's varied societies, and so explain our universal 'inner' needs.

We are making perhaps more dramatic advances when it comes to our genetic makeup: the Human Genome Project (an international effort begun in October 1990 to identify the genes in our DNA) announced in June 2000 that scientists now had a working draft of the entire genome sequence. But these are early days, and there's more to human beings than codified information anyway. Or is there?

Take the idea – mentioned in Richard Dawkins' *The Selfish Gene* (1976) – that our culture is driven not by ourselves but by replicating bundles of information called 'memes', just as our biological evolution is driven by replicating genes. These memes are, like genes, embroiled in a battle for the survival of the fittest, using vehicles such as our brains, books, television, radio, the internet and religion to propagate. If we believe in these self-serving bodies, then, according to Susan Blackmore – exploring the subject further in *The Meme Machine* (1999) – 'The answers to two big questions are now obvious, and the same. What is the big brain for? What is the function of language? – To spread memes.'

If we are still, today, investigating the workings of our brain size and language, then we are at an early stage of our understanding indeed. Instead of the great days of exploration being over, in future centuries humans will look back in wonder at our present ignorance of ourselves and nostalgically reflect on this as a Golden Age of discovery, when so many simple questions were wide open – as they were for Columbus, who set out to India without knowing even how far he had to go before he got there. At the start of another millennium, we can still set out on voyages and stumble across whole New Worlds lying in the way.

However, although the frontiers of knowledge are an infinite distance ahead, the speed at which we progress towards them varies. There have been times in history when societies have thought outwardly, added to the sum of scientific knowledge and challenged home-grown values – and other times when humans have shrunk back, clinging to home shores, taking refuge in what they think they already know. Then we have retreated to another Dark Age.

The value of those who have appeared in the pages of this book is that they have reached out to include the public in their findings. The problem, as the cosmologist and mathematician Stephen Hawking points out (while musing in *A Brief History of Time* on the biggest questions of all), is that in recent times the cutting-edge of discovery has become considerably more distant from our everyday understanding. This threatens the relationship of trust between pioneers and ordinary people, and, crucially, this in turn undermines the value we place on making fresh discoveries:

'Up to now, most scientists have been too occupied with the development of new theories that describe *what* the universe is to ask the question *why*. On the other hand, the people whose business it is to ask *why*, the philosophers, have not been able to keep up with the advance of scientific theories. In the eighteenth century, philosophers considered the whole of human knowledge, including science, to be their field and discussed questions such as: did the universe have a beginning? However, in the nineteenth and twentieth centuries, science became too technical and mathematical for the philosophers, or anyone else except a few specialists. Philosophers reduced the scope of their enquiries so much that Wittgenstein, the most famous philosopher of this century, said, "The sole remaining task for philosophy is the analysis of language." What a comedown from the great tradition of philosophy from Aristotle to Kant!

'However, if we do discover a complete theory, it should in time become understandable in broad principle by everyone, not just a few scientists. Then we shall all, philosophers, scientists and just ordinary people, be able to take part in the discussion of the question of why it is that we and the universe exist. If we find the answer to that, it would be the ultimate triumph of human reason – for then we would know the mind of God.'

Acknowledgements

I would like to express my heartfelt thanks to John Hesling for gathering together an assemblage of explorers and books for me to build from, and for all his wide-ranging and perceptive comments – not to mention his unfailing, and very often single-handed, support during the 'Icedogs' Siberia project (which occurred in the middle of all this). My thanks also to the others who helped with research, particularly Annabel Short for her diligent and systematic work on biographies, and also Paul Cronin, Norman Jones, Diana Maclean, Catriona Howatson, and Belinda Wilkinson.

I owe an enormous debt to Shane Winser, who cast her expert eye over the manuscript to help pick up many of my factual errors – those errors that remain are very much my fault. I would also like to express my appreciation to the Royal Geographical Society as a whole and particularly to Nigel Winser, and also to librarians Eugene Rae and Janet Turner for giving me so much of their experience and time. Professor Richard Dawkins kindly offered his thoughts on contemporary key scientists, Professor Robert May gave advice on animal and plant populations, and Professor Peter Wadhams very generously helped out with polar ice and currents. I would also like to express my gratitude to Bob Headland and the Scott Polar Research Institute for letting me quote from the diary of Hans Orde-Lees.

Sincere thanks also to Robin Hanbury-Tenison and the other contemporary explorers mentioned in the Introduction for allowing me to quote their remarks, and to the distinguished caver Andrew Eavis and marine zoologist Julian Partridge, who went out of their way to help me illustrate a much bigger section on modern-day exploration than space in the event allowed.

Finally, I'd like to mention those at Faber and Faber, who, with my agent Vivien Green, have so patiently waited for me to produce this material – particularly, Walter Donohue, Charles Boyle and Chris McLaren – and also Alyn Shipton of Basil Blackwell, who commissioned me to write a critique of exploration literature some twelve years ago. The book never saw the light of day – I couldn't sit still in Britain long enough – but the research I did then, assisted by Jay Scrivener-Hall, Huisha and Anna Rawlinson, helped me navigate my way through all those innumerable explorers in the years since.

B.A.

The editor and publishers gratefully acknowledge permission to reprint copyright material in this book as follows: ANONYMOUS: from *Letters From Port Essington, 1838–1845*, edited by J. M. R. Cameron (Historical Society of the Northern Territory, 1999), reprinted by permission of Professor David Carment; LUTHER STANDING BEAR: from *My People the Sioux* (Williams & Norgate, 1928), reprinted by permission of A. & C. Black (Publishers); HIRAM BINGHAM: from *Lost City of the Incas* (Phoenix House, 1951), reprinted by permission of the Orion Publishing Group; CHRIS BONINGTON: from *Annapurna South Face* (Cassell & Co., 1971), reprinted by permission of the author and Curtis Brown Ltd; PAUL BOWLES: from *Their Heads Are Green* (Peter Owen, 1963), reprinted by permission of the publisher; RICHARD BYRD: from *Alone* (Putnam & Co., 1939); MILDRED CABLE & FRANCESCA FRENCH: from *The Gobi Desert* (Hodder & Stoughton, 1942), reprinted by permission of the publisher; JULIUS CAESAR: from *The Conquest of Gaul*, translated by S. A. Handford (Penguin Classics, 1951), © The Estate of S. A. Handford, 1951, reprinted by permission of the publisher; HOWARD CARTER: from *The Tomb Of Tutankhamen: discovered by the late Earl of Carnarvon and Howard Carter* (Cassell & Co., 1923); NAPOLEON CHAGNON: from *Yanomamo: The Fierce People* (Holt, Rinehart & Winston, 1977); BRUCE CHATWIN: from *The Songlines* (Jonathan Cape, 1987), reprinted by permission of the Random House Group; APSLEY CHERRY-GARRARD: from *The Worst Journey in the World* (Constable, 1922), © Angela Mathias, 1922, 1965, reprinted by permission of Constable & Robinson Publishing; HUGH CLAPPERTON: from *Journals of the Travels in Borno of the Lt Hugh Clapperton* (January 1823–September 1824), edited by James R. Bruce Lockhart (Rudiger Koppe Verlag, 1996); CHRISTOPHER COLUMBUS: from *The Diaries of Columbus's First Voyage to America, 1492–1493*, translated and edited by Oliver C. Dunn and James E. Kelley, Jr. (University of Oklahoma Press, 1989), reprinted by permission of the publisher; HERNÁN CORTÉS: from *Letters from Mexico*, translated by A. R. Pagden (Yale University Press, 1986); from *The Broken Spears: The Aztec Account of the Conquest of Mexico*, translated by Lysander Kemp (Beacon Press, 1962), reprinted by permission of the publisher; ALEXANDRA DAVID-NEEL: from *My Journey to Lhasa* (Harper & Row, 1927), copyright 1927 by Harper & Row Publishers, Inc., renewed 1955 by Alexandra David-Neel, reprinted by permission of HarperCollins Publishers; JOHN KING DAVIS: from *Trial By Ice: The Antarctic Journals of John King Davis*, edited by Louise Crossley (Bluntisham Books & The Erskine Press, 1997), reprinted by permission of the Erskine Press; ISABELLE EBERHARDT: from *The Passionate Nomad: The Diary of Isabelle Eberhardt*, translated by Nina de Voogd (Beacon Press, 1987), reprinted by permission of Time Warner Books UK; ELISABETH ELLIOT: from *Through Gates of Splendour: The Martyrdom of Five Missionaries in the Ecuador Jungle* (Hodder & Stoughton, 1957); LEIF ERICSSON: from *Narratives of the Discovery of America*, edited by A. W. Lawrence and Jean Young (Jonathan Cape, 1931); PERCY FAWCETT: from *Exploration Fawcett*, edited by Brian Fawcett (Hutchinson, 1953), reprinted by permission the Random House Group; RANULPH FIENNES: from *Ice Fall in Norway* (Hodder & Stoughton, 1972); JANE GOODALL: from *In the Shadow of Man* (William Collins, 1971), reprinted by permission of John Sykes; HEINRICH HARRER: from *Seven Years in Tibet* (Rupert Hart-Davis, 1953); SVEN HEDIN: from *My Life As An Explorer* (Cassell & Co., 1926); WALLY HERBERT: from *Across the Top of the World: The British Trans-Arctic Expedition* (Longman, 1969); HERODOTUS: from *The Histories*, translated by Aubrey de Sélincourt, revised by John Marincola (Penguin Classics, 1954; second revised edition, 1996), translation © 1954 by Aubrey de Sélincourt; revised edition © John Marincola, 1996, reprinted by permission of the publisher; MAURICE HERZOG: from *Annapurna* (Jonathan Cape, 1952), reprinted by permission of the author; THOR HEYERDAHL: from *The Kon-Tiki Expedition: by raft across the South Seas* (George Allen & Unwin, 1950), reprinted by permission of HarperCollins Publishers Ltd; EDMUND HILLARY: from *High Adventure* (Hodder & Stoughton, 1955); FRANK HURLEY: from *Pearls and Savages, Adventures in the Air, on Land and Sea in New Guinea* (G. P. Putnam's Sons, 1924), reprinted by permission of Chrysalis Books; DONALD JOHANSON: from *Lucy: The Beginnings of Humankind* (Granada Books, 1981); ODETTE KEUN: from *In the Land of the Golden Fleece* (The Bodley Head, 1924); FRANK KINGDON-WARD: from *Himalayan Enchantment: An Anthology*, edited by John Whitehead (Serindia Publications, 1990), © Jean Rasmussen, estate of Frank Kingdon-Ward and Ella Whitehead, estate of John Whitehead, reprinted by permission of Mrs Jean Rasmussen and Ella Whitehead for Hearthstone Publications; MERIWETHER LEWIS & WILLIAM CLARK: from *The Journals of Lewis & Clark*, edited by B. Devoto (Eyre & Spottiswoode, 1954); ALBERT B. LLOYD: from *In Dwarf Land and Cannibal Country* (T. Fisher Unwin, 1899); WILLIAM LAIRD MCKINLAY: from *Karluk* (Weidenfeld & Nicolson, 1976); ELLA MAILLART: from *Turkestan Solo: One Woman's Expedition from the Tien Shan to the Kizil Kum* (Putnam, 1934); BRONISLAW MALINOWSKI: from *The Sexual Life of Savages* (George Routledge, 1932), reprinted by permission of Taylor & Francis Books; PETER MATTHIESSEN: from *The Tree Where Man Was Born* (Pan Books, 1984), reprinted by permission of the author; DOUGLAS MAWSON: from *The Home of the Blizzard: The Story of the Australasian Antarctic Expedition 1911–1914* (Heinemann, 1915); MARGARET MEAD: from 'The Mountain Arapesh. V. The Record of Unabelin with Rorschach Analyses', *Anthropological Papers of the American Museum of Natural History*, Volume 41, Part 3 (published by order of the Trustees of the American Museum of Natural History, 1949), reprinted by courtesy of the American Museum of Natural History; REINHOLD MESSNER: from *The Crystal Horizon: Everest, the First Solo Ascent* (The Crowood Press, 1989), reprinted by permission of the publisher; BERNARD MOITESSIER: from *The Long Way* (Grafton Books, 1974); UMBERTO NOBILE: from *My Polar Flights* (Frederick Muller, 1961); THOMAS HANS ORDE-LEES: from the unpublished Orde-Lees diary, held by the Scott Polar Research Institute, University of Cambridge, published by permission of the Scott Polar Research Institute; JOSEPHINE PEARY: from *My Arctic Journal* (Longmans, Green & Co., 1893); HARRY ST JOHN PHILBY: from *The Heart of Arabia: A Record of Travel and Exploration* (Constable, 1922), reprinted by permission of the Estate of Harry St John Bridger Philby; PLINY THE ELDER: from *Natural History*, translated by John F. Healy (Penguin Classics, 1991), translation © John F. Healy, 1991, reprinted by permission of the publisher; PLINY THE YOUNGER: from *The Letters of the Younger Pliny*, translated by Betty Radice (Penguin Classics, 1963), © Betty Radice, 1963, reprinted by permission of the publisher; MARCO POLO: from *The Travels of Marco Polo*, translated by Ronald Latham (Penguin Classics, 1958), © Ronald Latham, reprinted by permission of the publisher; JOHN ADOLPHUS POPE: from *Free Mariner, John Adolphus Pope in the East Indies 1786–1821*, edited by Anne Bulley (BACSA, 1992), reprinted by permission of Anne Bulley; LAURENS VAN DER POST: from *The Lost World of the Kalahari* (The Hogarth Press, 1958), reprinted by permission of the Random House Group; PRISCUS: from *Historici Graeci Minores*, in *They Saw It Happen in Classical Times* by B. K. Workman (Basil Blackwell, 1964); KNUD RASMUSSEN: from *The People of the Polar*

North: A Record (Kegan, Paul, Trench, Trubner & Co., 1908); TIM SEVERIN: from *The Brendan Voyage* (Abacus, 1996), reprinted by permission of Time Warner Books UK; ERIC SHIPTON: from *Nanda Devi* (Hodder & Stoughton, 1936), reprinted by permission of Nick Shipton; RAMÓN MEDINA SILVA: from *People of the Peyote: Huichol Indian History, Religion, and Survival*, edited by Stacy Schaefer and Peter Furst (University of New Mexico Press, 1995); J. R. SMITH: from *Everest: The Man and the Mountain* (Whittles Publishing, 1999), reprinted by permission of the publisher; FREYA STARK: from *The Valley of the Assassins* (John Murray, 1936), reprinted by permission of the publisher; VILHJALMUR STEFANSSON: from *My Life With the Eskimo* (Macmillan & Co., 1913); MARK AUREL STEIN: from *Ruins of Desert Cathay* (Macmillan, 1912); TENZING NORGAY: from *After Everest: An Autobiography* (George Allen & Unwin, 1977); WILFRED THESIGER: from *Arabian Sands* (Longman, 1959); BERTRAM THOMAS: from *Arabia Felix: Across the Empty Quarter of Arabia* (Jonathan Cape, 1932), reprinted by permission of the Random House Group; HAROLD WILLIAM TILMAN: from *Mischief in Greenland* (Hollis & Carter, 1964); COLIN TURNBULL: from *The Forest People: A Study of the Pygmies of the Congo* (Chatto & Windus, 1961), © 1961 by Colin M. Turnbull, © renewed 1989 by Colin M. Turnbull, reprinted by permission of the Random House Group and Simon & Schuster; SARA WHEELER: from *Terra Incognita: Travels in Antarctica* (Jonathan Cape, 1996), © Sara Wheeler, 1996, reprinted by permission of the Random House Group and Gillon Aitken Associates; XENOPHON: from *Persian Expedition*, translated by Rex Warner (Penguin Classics, 1949), translation copyright 1949 by Rex Warner, reprinted by permission of the publisher; FRANCIS YOUNGHUSBAND: from *The Heart of a Continent* (John Murray, 1896); from *The Heart of Nature* (John Murray, 1921); from *Wonders of the Himalaya* (John Murray, 1924), all reprinted by permission of the publisher.

Every effort has been made to trace or contact all copyright holders. The publishers would be pleased to rectify any omissions brought to their notice at the earliest opportunity.

Index

References in **bold** signify main entries.

FROM MYTH TO REALITY

Five to six millennia ago, myth and reality merged in Chinese history. Shennong, the mythical forefather of the Yan and Yellow Emperors, lived in this age. He is a legendary figure credited as the founding father of Chinese farming civilization and medicinal arts. Born with a crystal stomach, he could observe how his visceral organs reacted to different herbs through the transparent stomach to distinguish various functions of different plants. Once encountering toxins he depended on tea for detoxification. This is the earliest record of tea in Chinese civilization.

In any historical period, social trends are constantly changing. Chinese tea culture has evolved in terms of production techniques and drinking methods through the ages. Tea brewing in the Tang Dynasty, tea whisking in the Song Dynasty and tea steeping in the Ming Dynasty, make up three significant phases in this development trajectory.

In recent years, a large quantity of mysterious relics has been discovered at the underground palace of Famen Temple in the outskirts of Xi'an, once a capital in dynastic China. Among these relics, in addition to Shakyamuni's index finger bone, porcelains and colored glaze, exquisite gold and silver teaware used for tea production in the

Tang Dynasty was also unearthed. These relics which were produced over a millennium ago provide concrete reference materials to study the Tang tea ceremony as documented in "The Classic of Tea" by the Sage of Tea, Lu Yu.

By the Song Dynasty, the Chinese tea ceremony had reached unprecedented heights under the encouragement of Emperor Huizong of Song. This emperor was an incompetent ruler, but was talented and skilled in artistic domains. His reign was one of the most glorious periods for artists in Chinese history. Emperor Huizong spent all day reciting poems and singing songs with his officials, hosting one after another tea party, staging tea fights and engaging in Tea liquor painting. The Japanese matcha ceremony, which is enshrined as the quintessence of Japanese culture, evolved from the tea-whisking practice in the Song Dynasty. In some sense, it acts as a living museum to display the Song tea ceremony.

Zhu Yuanzhang, the founding emperor of the Ming Dynasty, was born into a peasant family. He appreciated a thrifty lifestyle, and stripped all the unnecessary processes in the otherwise complicated

1 "The Classic of Tea," a masterpiece in terms of content and style written in the Tang Dynasty, is the earliest treatise on tea

2 Lu Yu, author of "The Classic of Tea," was adopted by a temple and was thus familiar with tea and Zen thought since childhood, and is celebrated as the Sage of Tea

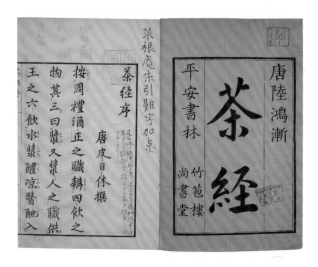

brewing methods by simply steeping tea leaves in water. The tea steeping method was popularized during his reign and survives to this day. The innovations by Emperor Taizu of Ming lowered tea production costs and simplified the drinking practice. These measures helped to popularize tea drinking among common people and make Chinese tea famous around the world.

In the Western world, Immanuel Kant compared the sense of morality in the inner world to the universe and starry sky. However, in the Chinese mindset, moral pursuits valued by Confucians and the worldview of Taoist followers are blended into an integral whole. The tea ceremony is concerned with the subtle balance between nature and virtue. Therefore, for the Chinese, tea leaves are blessings from the universe and nature. Tea is a beverage for common people, for the gentry and for those adhering to a thrifty and simple lifestyle.

1
2   3

1 The exterior of a tea house in Mount Wuyi; the bamboo slips waving in the wind are inscribed with names of tea varieties

3 A scene in a typical tea garden, the birthplace of tea leaves

2 A scene in a traditional tea store; various kinds of tea are stored in different wood cases, on which the tea's name is inscribed

CHAPTER I

Overview

Every kind of tea is marked with a distinctive property. Green tea is as energetic as the youth; Oolong is as reserved and mature as a middle-age man; black tea represents maternal love, while Pu-erh tea is an incarnation of a wise old man with a lot of stories.

1 Tea leaves vary in appearance due to
varied rolling techniques employed

2 Harvesting in a tea garden in early
spring; the earliest tea is the most
expensive. Harvest begins after the
disappearance of dew

In China—where camellia sinensis originated—the precious tea plant extends
from the south to certain regions in the north. The tea leaf tends to grow smaller as
one travels northward, shrinking from the size of an infant's palm to one as slender
as the brushstroke that defines a young girl's eyebrow in an ancient portrait. These
different regions are populated by hundreds of varieties of tea plants, and each variety
is best suited for being processed into a specific category of tea leaf. Thus there exist a
myriad of mutually distinct tea leave types.

We generally classify tea leaves by the amount of fermentation that they undergo:
green tea is not fermented; Oolong runs the gamut from lightly to highly fermented; black
tea is completely fermented; and Pu-erh should be considered "post-fermented" tea.

Young tea tips and buds are generally used to produce green tea, black tea and finer
Pu-erh, while mature leaves are used for Oolong. Various types of tea leaves are rolled
into various shapes: for Dragon Well (Lung Ching), slices resemble a sharp sword; Green
Spiral (Pi Lo Chun), soft, curvaceous spirals; Rock Tea, fluffy strips; and Iron Mercy
Goddess (Ti Kuan Yin), a semi-spherical shape.

Certain fresh blossoms, depending on their qualities, are cured with tea leaves in
order to endow them with the flower's features. The fragrance of jasmine, for instance,
is often fused with the cool, refreshing taste of green tea. Consideration is also given
as to whether tea leaves should be dry roasted, and if so, to what extent. This latter
process is applied to varieties of Oolong such as Rock Tea.

Diverse tea leaf types are thus endowed with their own unique personalities and
features. To generalize, green tea is a youth bursting with vitality; Oolong possesses
the maturity and steadiness of one at middle age; black tea represents earthly maternal
affection, and Pu-erh is a wise elder who has weathered many a storm.

Tea Production

1 After processing, dry tea leaves appear quite different from fresh leaves

2-5 After harvesting, roasting and the removal of stems, tea leaves processing is almost completed

A cup of tea is the consequence of a multitude of fortuitous factors. The cup of tea that you hold in your hand and savor is the end-result of a myriad of steps in an ongoing process, from the growth of a tea bush to the processing of tea leaves, and the brewing of the liquor.

Once a tea plant's seed has taken root and germinated, its potential is decided by the atmosphere, sunlight, rain and nature of the soil in the area where it is located, as well as how the farmer performs pruning and cuttage, adds fertilizer and protects it against insects.

But the actual processing of the plucked tea leaf is a crucial step that largely determines the special characteristics of a finished leaf. The subsequent brewing of the tea leaves revolves around diverse means intended to maximize the potential with which those leaves are endowed.

Tea production is a complex process that cannot easily be standardized. Take fermentation, for example, which has the most steps. They include: harvesting → withering → fermentation → fixation → rolling → drying →scenting/roasting. However, the processing of tea is not limited to these steps. Certain tea leaves require specific techniques. This book lists just several key functional phases. Among them, harvesting, fermentation, rolling and roasting are the principal factors that shape the "personality" of a certain kind of tea.

Harvesting [Plucking of buds or tender leaves]

Most varities of green tea are made from buds, while Oolong is generally a full-leaf tea. This is why the bottom-side of green tea leaves are still delicate and tender when brewed, while those of Oolong tea leaves are already mature. finer black tea and Pu-erh also consist mainly of buds. Green tea is only harvested in the spring, while black tea is suitable for harvest in early summer. Oolong is not only harvested in the spring but a small portion is also harvested in the winter.

Withering [Partial dehydration of fresh leaves]

Basically undertaken at the same time as fermentation; green tea does not require either withering or fermentation.

Fermentation [Using air to stimulate oxidization]

Forms tea's unique color, aroma and taste; Oolong tea has varying levels of fermentation, while the degree of fermentation of black tea approaches 100 percent.

Fixation [Using high temperature to kill leaf cells and terminate fermentation]

Suspends further alterations, "fixing" the tea in an ideal state.

Rolling [Rupturing the leaves' cell walls and shaping the leaves]

Besides releasing the tea leaves' nutrients, rolling also forms the tea leaves into different shapes such as needles (Bamboo Leaves Green), strips (Rock Tea) and round pellets (Frozen-summit Oolong). When brewed, lightly rolled tea leaves will float lightly toward the surface of the liquor. Green tea leaves are typically lightly rolled. Heavily rolled leaves will sink toward the bottom. Black tea is typically heavily rolled. Oolong tea varies from lightly to heavily rolled.

Drying [Removing excess moisture via steaming]

Stabilizes the key "properties" of the tea such as flavor.

↓

Scenting (curing, flavoring) [Causing tea leaves to absorb a floral fragrance]

The technique for scenting tea, endowing the leaves with the fragrance and properties of a given flower.

↓

Roasting [Using fire to dry-roast tea leaves]

The heavier the roasting, the more mature the fragrance, and the "cooler" the nature of the tea leaves. Only a portion of Oolong tea is roasted, such as Rock Tea.

Tea and Your Health

1 2

1-2 Tea liquor in exquisitely crafted cups

Among the world's three principal non-alcoholic beverages — coffee, cocoa and tea — the latter's effects on human health are arguably the most positive. If we momentarily disregard the various empirical observations by ancient Chinese regarding tea, we can see that modern science has employed a host of different methodologies to corroborate those insights. Scientists have accurately measured the ingredients of tea leaves and determined their clinical efficacy. The most significant ingredients for good health present in tea are vitamins, amino acids and polyphenols. In addition, tea also includes caffeine, minerals, lipopolysaccharides, carbohydrates, protein and fat.

In general, the amounts of vitamins, amino acids, polyphenols and caffeine are the highest in green tea, since these amounts drop in proportion to the degree of fermentation undergone by the tea. By contrast, green tea has the lowest mineral content, because the count increases with fermentation.

Water-soluble vitamins in tea leaves are mainly vitamin C and B-group vitamins. We are no strangers to these vitamins in our daily life, absorbing them via fruits and vegetables. But the content of these vitamins is actually higher in tea leaves than in equivalent amounts of fruits and vegetables, so drinking tea is the most healthy and convenient method of their ingestion.

In addition to vitamin C and B-group vitamins, tea also contains a variety of fat-soluble vitamins, like vitamin A whose carotene content is actually higher than an equivalent amount of carrots. But since the vitamin doesn't dissolve in brewed tea, it cannot easily be absorbed into the human body by drinking tea. But if we put the leaves in our foodstuffs and eat them, we can take advantage of the vitamin A present in tea.

Dozens of amino acids, principally thiamine, account for two to five percent of the ingredients in tea. Each type of amino acid possesses its own irreplaceable effects, but the amounts present differ widely depending upon the tea. Many of these amino acids are indispensable elements for human metabolism, and some can only be obtained through eating or drinking — the human body cannot produce them.

The main alkaloid in tea leaves is caffeine, and its role is mainly to stimulate and fortify the heart, and act as a diuretic. Our habit of drinking tea to give ourselves a lift is motivated by the fact that the caffeine — sometimes called "theine" — in tea excites the cerebral cortex.

It is particularly noteworthy that the principle behind the excitement generated by substances like alcohol, cigarettes and various stimulants is quite different than that engendered by tea. The caffeine present in tea leaves brings about a purely physiological state of excitement that is not addictive and has no major side effects. Caffeine and tea polyphenols combine chemically to form a compound that is easily discharged, and therefore the caffeine cannot readily be stored within the body.

The so-called "tea polyphenols" are catechin-based substances. Ever since tea became the object of modern scientific research, catechins have been a focal point. Research results all point to the fact that tea is highly conducive to the health of modern mankind, because it offers considerable benefits in terms of resisting the effects of carcinogenic substances, radiation and aging.

Tea contains more than forty kinds of minerals, some of which play a decisive role in maintaining the body in good health. The greatest amount is that of potassium, which is critical in maintaining osmotic pressure and blood balance, as well as the renewal of human cells. Tea also contains important elements such as manganese, selenium, zinc and calcium.

Some three percent of tea content is comprised of lipopolysaccharides that help to improve the body's ability to manufacture blood, strengthen immunity and resist the effects of radiation.

The fat content in tea is so small as to be negligible. Carbohydrate and protein contents are relatively high, but since they don't dissolve in the brewing process, tea qualifies as a "low-fat, low-sugar" beverage.

Table: Water-soluble Vitamins Available in Brewed Tea

Vitamin	Content (Micrograms / 100 grams of tea leaves)	Requirement (Micrograms)
C	100,000-500,000	60,000
B1	150-160	1,700
B2	1,300-1,700	1,800
B3	1,000-2,000	10,000
B5	5,000-7,500	20,000
B11	50-75	400
H	50-80	300

Storage of Tea

1   2   4
  3

1   Chinese art paper is commonly used to package Pu-erh tea cakes. Several small packages are placed in a bamboo basket for its good airing conditions

2   Black tea is the most suitable to be processed into tea bags

3   Loose Pu-erh leaves can be stored in bamboo baskets. An optimal airing condition ensures continuous post-fermentation

4   Pottery jars are a common choice to store tea leaves, the heavily-fermented and heavily-roasted varieties in particular

The shelf-life of tea is closely tied to its storage conditions. Under the appropriate conditions, green tea can be stored one or two years or even longer. Additionally, the greater the degree of its fermentation, the longer the tea can be stored.

Tea leaves must firstly be stored away from light, as light readily ages tea and causes flavor loss. Secondly, an airtight container is also critical for isolating the leaves from oxygen and the moisture and odors present in the air. Oxygen can easily oxidize tea and moisture can dampen the dried tea leaves, so light-resistant materials are used for packaging, and a desiccant is added. Additionally, low-temperature storage can also help maintain flavor longer.

Tea leaves themselves are exceptionally absorbent, and therefore liable to contamination by undesirable odors. This is why some tea leaves are cured with fragrant flowers, and it explains why we can use a tea sachet as a deodorizer.

We often find that teas are vacuum-packed. This is done to minimize contact with the air and the subsequent possibility that the tea will oxidize, experience moisture regain, or absorb undesirable odors. While vacuum packaging is indeed a good strategy for tea storage, it is not suitable for all varieties of tea.

Iron Mercy Goddess and Taiwanese Oolong are often vacuum-sealed, because they are heavily rolled teas that are half-rounded or in outright pellet shapes that will not break apart when air is sucked out of the container. But lightly rolled teas such as green tea and Rock Tea are shaped into a somewhat fluffier state and are thus very liable to fall apart. This would have a major negative impact on the flavor of the tea, and therefore these teas are ill-suited to vacuum packaging.

The most common tea on market today is black tea in a ready-to-steep sachet (tea-bag). This sort of packaging is appropriate because black tea is heavily rolled and often chopped in the latter stages of processing. The other reason black tea is suitable for brewing in a sachet is that the leaves absorb fairly little water and their volume does not notably increase when steeped. Just imagine if Iron Mercy Goddess or Taiwanese Oolong — which can also withstand packaging under pressure — were to be brewed in a sachet. They are highly absorbent tea leaves and the bottoms of the leaves would extend and become especially bloated. Thus directly brewing these teas in a tea bag is simply not practical. It is precisely because of the two features described above that black tea can be brewed in a convenient tea-bag, while other types of tea cannot.

Storage of Pu-erh is a somewhat special case. With the passage of time, Pu-erh ages and becomes increasingly aromatic, and this is why pricing information prominently notes how many years it's been since the tea was harvested. After Pu-erh has been produced and its shape finalized — often pressed into a cake, a brick or the shape of a bird's nest — then the "post-fermentation" process that is carried out by the air slowly gets underway.

This is why the location in which Pu-erh is stored must avoid light and odor, but it must also be well ventilated and a certain temperature and humidity maintained in order to ensure that the post-fermentation process can proceed. For these reasons, Pu-erh is often packaged in bamboo, paper, cloth and other traditional materials offering good permeability.

CHAPTER II

Green Tea

As unfermented tea, finished green tea requires the least processing and is the closest to the tea leaf in its natural state. The tea brewing process is almost like watching time move backwards: the green leaves unfold within the verdant liquid until they seem as fresh and alive as if still they were on the branch.

1-2 Chinese green tea and its Japanse counterpart are processed in different ways during the fixation process, creating different liquor colors, flavors and tastes

3 Green tea leaves unfolding in glass cups remind us of the arrival of spring

Japanese green tea (steamed)

Color: Bright green, densely colored

Aroma: Faint, neutral

Flavor: Fairly strong

Chinese green tea (pan-fried, baked and sun-dried)

Color: Yellowish green, limpid

Aroma: Fragrant

Flavor: Refreshing

As an unfermented tea, finished green tea requires the least processing and is the closest to the tea leaf in its natural state. The tea brewing process is almost like watching time move backwards: the green leaves unfold within the verdant liquid until they seem as fresh and alive as if they were still on the branch.

Differences in the production of various green tea lie principally in the way fixation and drying are carried out. Japanese green tea, for example, retains the ancient Chinese method of steaming. Processed tea leaves that have been steamed take on a dark green tint, while the liquor is vibrantly green, similar to pigments used in painting, and the aroma is faintly musty.

There are three principal types of tea in today's China: those that undergo stir fixation (pan-fried) such as Dragon Well, Green Spiral and Bamboo Leaves Green (Zhi Ye Qing); baked types such as Mount Yellow Fuzz Tip (Huangshan Maofeng), Liu'an Leaf (Liu'an Guapian) and Taiping Monkey Chief (Taiping Houkui); and sun-dried, mainly Yunnan Green Tea, and the raw ("un-ripened") tea leaves incorporated in pressed Pu-erh.

These three fixation and drying methods used in Chinese green tea ensure that each type of processed leaf possesses its own distinctive color, aroma and flavor. But overall, green tea leaves tend to be dark green, the liquor crystalline, green with a yellowish tint, and the aroma, fragrant and refreshing.

Although the production process for Green Tea is relatively the most simple, of all tea types green tea is the most difficult to brew due to the difficulty of getting the water temperature just right.

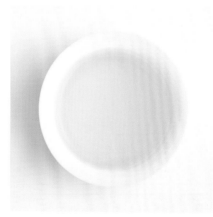 

Because the raw materials for green tea are tender tips and immature leaves, the temperature of the water used for brewing must absolutely not be too high; overly hot water not only kills some nutrients and minerals in the tea, but also renders the liquor bitter, and robs the flavor of its vitality.

Generally speaking, a temperature of eighty degrees centigrade is appropriate for infusing green tea, but when actually brewing one should take the state of the tea leaves into consideration in deciding the specific temperature. The maturity of the leaves is the principal element to consider: more tender leaves call for a slightly lower temperature, while relatively mature ones require somewhat hotter water.

In a doubtless familiar vignette from our daily lives, green tea is often brewed within a slender and elegant glass cup without a lid. The biggest advantage to choosing glass as a receptacle for brewing tea is that you can directly observe how the leaves are transformed and the liquor takes on color.

Glass is the preferred choice, but it is not the sole option. Whether you seek a bit of charm or wish to display the liquor, a lidded eggshell porcelain cup (tureen) fittingly highlights the temperament of green tea. In short, in order to accentuate the fresh and invigorating disposition of green tea, for teaware one should select high-density materials

1 White-glazed porcelain with green tea leaves drifting inside creates an appealing appearance

2 Pavilions in the grove are popular gathering points for tea drinkers

that dissipate heat rapidly. By such a standard, silver ware is an excellent choice.

Yixing clay teaware, also known as "Red Porcelain" due to the color of the clay found only in Yixing (Jiangsu), is the most widely used teaware for Chinese teas. Compared to common porcelain, Yixing clay is quite porous, and features very low density and relatively slow heat dissipation.

If green tea is brewed in a Yixing clay teapot, however, the resultant liquor will give off a rather odd, somewhat dank, smell. The aroma reminds one of the springtime in northern China which is somehow never as refreshing or cheerful as in the south.

This shows just how greatly the choice of teaware impacts the taste of the tea. Of course, the shape of the vessel also has an impact on the quality of the tea liquor. For example, the opening at the top of a typical Yixing teapot is not as large as that on a porcelain tureen, and this will also have an effect on the green tea liquor.

DRAGON WELL

1-2 Dried tea leaves and tea liquor of
Dragon Well

3-6 Branches of various forms in the
Dragon Well tea garden

Ancient Chinese poetry often likened Hangzhou's West Lake to Xishi, one of four most well-known beauties in the history of China. And it is in the vicinity of West Lake, with its enchanting mist-covered scenery interspersed with brooks, that tea leaves rivalling her beauty were first produced — Dragon Well.

Dragon Well Tea has a long history, but the roots of its fame go back to the reign of Emperor Qianlong of the Qing Dynasty, who loved to leave the capital in Beijing to travel in South China, particularly the region to the south of the Yangtze River that straddles today's Shanghai and parts of Zhejiang and Jiangsu.

The tea takes its name from a well. Legend has it that this well did not dry up even during long droughts, and people believed it to be the lair of the "Dragon that Rules the Seas," hence the name, "Dragon Well". It is said that the Chinese characters for "Dragon Well," still visible today, were inscribed on the outer wall of the well by none other than Emperor Qianlong himself, a fact that evokes a sense of nostalgia among some visitors.

Intriguingly, from older times up until today, water drawn from the Dragon Well has not just been used for steeping tea. When locals find themselves at a disadvantage in a game of mahjong, they dip their hands in Dragon Well water and apply it to their

1 Tea farmers checking on Dragon Well
tea in early summer; conservation of the
tea garden remains important even after
harvest

Lion Peak Dragon Well

Grade: 1st Grade

Harvesting Period: Pre-Qingming Festival

Raw Tea Ingredients: Lotus Heart

West Lake Dragon Well

Grade: 1st Grade

Harvesting Period: Before spring rains

Raw Tea Ingredients: Banner Spear

Zhejiang Dragon Well

Grade: 3rd Grade

Harvesting Period: After spring rains

Raw Tea Ingredients: Bird's Tongue

face, forehead and hair while praying for protection and good luck. Evidently, Dragon Well has become a cultural and folkloric symbol with great significance.

Dragon Well Tea has long had a reputation for its "Four Perfections": "jade hue, sweet scent, mellow flavor, pleasing shape." The first three are references to the liquor, while the last refers to the appearance of the tea leaves. In fact, such a description is arguably applicable to most other green tea. Nonetheless, each variety of green tea leaf does possess its own unique temperament that constitutes a recognizable point of difference.

If we disregard the human factor represented by the tea master and his or her team, and restrict ourselves just to the tea leaves, then the quality of Dragon Well is decided by three key elements.

The first decisive element is the specific location of the tea farm. The environment in this location dictates that the Lion Peak sub-region grows the finest Dragon Well.

The second decisive factor is exactly when the tea is harvested. The optimal period is in the ten days before the Qingming Festival in early April, and the next best is after Qingming but before the spring rains. Locals reflect the order of the harvest in the names given to each: "Daughter's Tea," "Wife's Tea" and "Mother-in-law's Tea." We need to note that the custom of grading and naming tea according to its harvest time is not restricted to Dragon Well.

The third decisive factor is the relative tenderness of the leaves. "Lotus Heart" Dragon Well is composed of just buds. "Banner Spear" consists of a single bud and a single leaf; the bud is tightly wrapped like a spear but expands like a banner when brewed. And the graphic "Bird's Tongue" comprises a single bud plus two leaves. These three appellations are easily pictured in the mind and memorable. When brewed, water temperature should be lowest for Lotus Heart, since it is the most delicate, warmer for Banner Spear, and hottest for Bird's Tongue.

Because the output of Lotus Heart is extremely limited, its price is very high. Most people buy the tea to present as a gift with frankly utilitarian intent. It is satirically referred to as "flattery tea," an allusion to the popular practice in today's China of making a substantial gift as a shortcut to material or professional success.

One thinks too of ancient China when the relationship between tea and men of letters was an intimate one. Besides making a gift of spring tea, much attention was also paid to presenting "a sprinkling of the finest tea leaves," because the best tea was produced in very limited amounts, and therefore quality trumped quantity.

Besides the characters for "Dragon Well" inscribed in the emperor's own evocative calligraphy, the presence of "Tiger Running Spring" near the Dragon Well and the shores of West Lake adds not a little legendary color to Dragon Well Tea. Tiger Running Stream and Dragon Well Tea are known as the perfect duo of West Lake. Infusing Dragon Well with water drawn from Tiger Running Spring is the combination of two of the finest things here on the earth.

To brew a pot of Dragon Well by the shores of West Lake ranks as a marvellous occasion in the life of a mortal. Having attained this acme, could one ask for more?

1-2 Dragon Well has transformed from the name of a tea variety to a cultural symbol. A large number of memorial arches and inscriptions themed on Dragon Well have sprung up nationwide

3 Some tea drinkers are obsessed with using Tiger Running Spring to brew tea, exemplifying the unique charm of the Third Spring in China

GREEN SPIRAL

1-2 Dried tea leaves and tea liquor of Green Spiral

3 Suzhou gardens are among the best examples of their kind, providing a perfect venue to savor Green Spiral

No matter where he or she was born in the country, each Chinese has an inexplicable attachment to the area of South China. This sentiment has come down to us over a millennium, shrouded in a magical, impenetrable fog. The famous saying in praise of the ancient sister cities in South China, "Paradise above in heaven, Suzhou and Hangzhou below on earth," captures the legends that surround the region. If Hangzhou, this paradise on earth, is made more colorful by Dragon Well Tea, then a similarly fine reputation is attached to a famous tea from Suzhou — Green Spiral.

Green Spiral is cultivated within the East and West Dongting Mountains in Taihu Lake, China's third largest fresh water lake that is dotted with ninety islands. Mist-covered mountains and waters intermingle here in an ethereal locality that has engendered many distinguished talents over the centuries.

What makes the Green Spiral plantations even more unique is the way the tea plants are planted among various types of fruit trees. The tall fruit trees shade the tea bushes in the summer and protect them from frost in the winter. Their roots and leaves intertwine like intimate lovers, scenting the tea leaves with a delightful fruity aroma.

Unlike Dragon Well Tea that is named for the place where it is grown and produced, the name Green Spiral neatly captures its color, shape and invigorating spring flavor.

The razor-thin Dragon Well leaves are shaped like the blade of a sword, while

1   A glimpse of Taihu Lake, a production
area for Green Spiral; this lake is second
only to Poyang Lake in size among all the
fresh water lakes in China

2   Green Spiral is among the most
ancient of all the tea varieties

Dragon Well	Amount of Tea: 1/4 pot
	Temperature: 80 ℃
	Steeping Time:
	1st Infusion 40 seconds
	2nd Infusion 15 seconds
	3rd Infusion 30 seconds
Green Spiral	Amount of Tea: 1/4 pot
	Temperature: 75 ℃
	Steeping Time:
	1st Infusion 20 seconds
	2nd Infusion 0 seconds
	3rd Infusion 10 seconds

Green Spiral leaves are fine and curled, and covered in tender white hairs. The amount of such fur on the underside of the tender bud is the indicator by which the "tenderness" (age) of the tea is determined.

Interestingly, like Green Spiral, Dragon Well is also very tender, but during production, those baby white hairs are rolled inward, effectively concealing them. The fact that the white fuzz is less evident to the eye does not mean that Dragon Well is necessarily less tender than Green Spiral.

The aroma of Dragon Well is as limpid as a feather-weight youth testing his mettle for the first time, or a new-born calf naively uncowed by a tiger; and its fragrance is accompanied by a subtle chill. In contrast, the flavor of Green Spiral resembles a coquettish young maiden awaiting betrothal, and thus likely to engender affection.

Green Spiral can be brewed at the same temperature as Dragon Well, or even slightly lower. But due to factors such as the way it is rolled, Green Spiral releases its essential flavor and ingredients much faster than Dragon Well, and therefore its steeping time is considerably shorter than Dragon Well's.

MOUNT MENG SWEET DEW

3 4

1 2

1-2 Dried tea leaves and tea liquor of Mount Meng Sweet Dew

3-4 The cliffs of Mount Meng are inscribed with poems and statues about tea

In an industry that is naturally classified by region of cultivation, Sichuan's share of China's tea market is hardly outstanding. It hasn't the means to compete with the green tea of the Yangtze River basin, nor is it fit to joust with the likes of Fujian's Oolong. But the historical import and unique temperament of Sichuan are irreplaceable and thought-provoking.

"Taxing are the roads of Shu, even more taxing than ascending the heavens." Thus wrote Li Bai, one of China's greatest poets, about Shu (modern-day Sichuan) back in the eighth century. These remain the basic geographical traits of Sichuan — overlapping sierras, endless crags, natural barriers and many famous mountains. Of course, famous tea flourishes amidst famous mountains. In these forested mountains covered in cloud and mist, water vapor lingers throughout the day, and there is a wealth of vegetation and animals. This is the sole place in China where the geography and environment permit the air, rain and dew to float about so divinely, endowing Sichuan tea with their unique spirituality.

Mount E'mei is the most beautiful under the sky and Mount Qingcheng the most secluded, goes an ancient Chinese saying. These two mountains have been famous for tea cultivation since ancient times, but among varieties of Sichuan tea the Meng

Green Tea Raw Material: Buds

Color: Clear liquor, green leaves

Level of Fermentation: None

Yellow Tea Raw Material: Buds

Color: Yellow liquor, yellow leaves

Processing: Unlike green tea, undergoes special "moist reheating" in a closed container.

Level of Fermentation: Some fermentation occurs during "moist reheating" phase.

Mountain is the undisputed sovereign in historical terms. Mentioning tea of Mount Meng, a famous phrase comes to mind: "Like the waters of the Yangtze River are the tea on Mount Meng."

In fact, Mount Meng tea was not only an imperial tribute tea (for presentation to the emperor and nobility) over the centuries like Dragon Well and Green Spiral, it is also the first tea to be cited in ancient documents extant today. Furthermore, the earliest documentation of managed cultivation of tea bushes by ancient Chinese also refers specifically to Mount Meng tea. Evidently Mount Meng tea has imbibed the rain and dew here over a millennium, it long ago fused harmoniously with the mountains and the forests.

Since ancient times when Mount Meng tea was classified as a tribute item, it has been processed into various types of finished tea, but Mount Meng Sweet Dew (Mengding Gan Lu) currently enjoys the greatest popularity and widest dissemination. After processing and rolling, finished Mount Meng Sweet Dew is similar in

1 | 2

1-2 An Imperial tea garden which exclusively supplied the court; Mount Meng tea was chosen as a tribute to the court in the Tang Dynasty, and was once presented to an accomplished monk in Japan by Emperor Wenzong of Tang

1 Using long-sprout teapots to make Kung Fu tea is kind of tradition in Chinese folk culture, popular in Sichuan Province. The long spout serves to lower the temperature of the tea

appearance to Green Spiral, both being tightly curled and covered in fine hairs, or silver pekoe. But the former possesses a unique aftertaste true to its name: "sweet dew", refreshing deep down with its mellow, blissful liquor.

The leaves plucked for Mount Meng Sweet Dew are no less tender than those of Green Spiral. Because both are so tender, when brewing either tea, "topping" is widely preferred among the common people, a reference to the practice of first pouring hot water into the teapot, and then adding the tea leaves on top. This method allows a "buffer" period between the time when the water is added and when the tea leaves are added, effectively lowering the actual water temperature at steeping. Since the tea leaves enter the water from the top, the leaves are not subjected to water pressure and the subsequent violent collision between the leaves and the inside of the teapot.

When brewing Mount Meng Sweet Dew, factors such as choice of utensils, water temperature, the amount of tea leaves and the timing of each infusion can mirror those for Green Spiral, but adjustments can be made as desired.

Besides Sweet Dew, since ancient times the Mount Meng tea "family" has also included another star offspring: Mount Meng Yellow Bud (Mengding Huang Ya). Only buds are used, and it classifies as a yellow, not a green, tea. Yellow and green tea processing is similar, but the former undergoes a stage when water is added and the tea leaves are baked in a closed container. Some oxidation occurs, resulting in yellowish leaves and liquor. Yellow tea is considered a non-mainstream tea, but since ancient times there has nonetheless been no shortage of famous ones such as Mount Meng Yellow Buds.

It should be noted Yellow Bud is rolled quite differently from Sweet Dew. The former is more heavily rolled, resulting in tea leaves that are flat and uniform. Besides Mount Meng Yellow Bud, other famous Chinese yellow tea includes Junshan Silver Needle (Junshan Yin Zhen), Huoshan Yellow Bud (Huoshan Huang Ya), and Beikang Mao Jian.

Mengding District is located within the disaster zone of the 5.12 Sichuan Earthquake in 2008. Originating in the region that underwent the historic changes wrought by that series of destructive tremors, Sichuan tea has taken on a new association that is a bit difficult to describe. But Mount Meng Sweet Dew now seems more precious, each tea leaf richer in sentiment.

BAMBOO LEAVES GREEN

3

1 2

1-2 The dried tea leaves and tea liquor
of Bamboo Leaves Green

3 Ink bamboo by a literati painter in the
Qing Dynasty named Zheng Banqiao.
His ink bamboos are well-proportioned,
highlighting the lofty virtues associated
with Bamboo Leaves Green

The role of bamboo in Chinese culture and the life of the Chinese people has an incomparable significance, and its impact has also deeply penetrated Japanese culture and even radiated throughout much of Asia.

And it is arguably due to scenes of bamboo groves in Southwest China — showcased in Ang Lee's "Crouching Tiger, Hidden Dragon" — that the majority of Westerners have recently acquired a certain level of appreciation for China's "bamboo culture." But in actuality, the importance of bamboo to the Chinese is far deeper than this.

Prior to the appearance of papermaking technology, Chinese characters had always been written on bamboo strips. In other words, bamboo was the medium for the recording of China's earliest civilization and history, and has been a constant theme of poetry, painting and calligraphy executed by literati and poets. Bamboo leaves boiled in water, bamboo shoots in food, utensils made of bamboo, sculptures carved from bamboo poles — bamboo is not only a link between antiquity and today, it is virtually interwoven into every layer of the life of the Chinese people.

"A diet without meat is preferable to a daily life without bamboo." In Southwest China, particularly the land occupied by the ancient State of Shu (modern Sichuan), a swathe of green bamboo typically encircles a hamlet, a popular "landscaping"

1   A glimpse of Mount E'mei, a production area of Bamboo Leaves Green; Mount E'mei provides an agreeable environment for bamboo

2   Bamboo Leaves Green drifts in water without sinking

tradition that has carried on for a millennium. Each famous mountain in Sichuan boasts its own endless sea of myriad "spears and banners" comprised of jutting bamboo poles and legions of leaves.

Bamboo branches dip much like a maiden's eyelids lowered out of shyness, or the kind demeanor of a modest gentleman. People adore the constant jade-green of bamboo throughout the four seasons, and thus the appellation Bamboo Leaves Green (Zhu Ye Qing) is much beloved. Besides being the name of the tea featured in this chapter, it is also the name of a Sichuan liquor and the name of a snake often seen in South China.

Though both are Sichuan tea, the name Bamboo Leaves Green has existed for less than half a century, and seemingly cannot be uttered in the same breath as Mount Meng tea. But that does not signify that tea production in Mount E'mei lacks history or that the moniker Bamboo Leaves Green lacks cachet. Tea grown in Mount E'mei was classified as an imperial tribute as early as the Tang Dynasty. Although its formulation occurred fairly late, Bamboo Leaves Green was christened by General Chen Yi, and thus its appellation is not without legendary color.

The superbly beautiful Mount E'mei has its own forests of verdant bamboo, and

A glimpse of a bamboo grove in southern Sichuan; legend has it that the bamboo grove and the creek within were created from the emerald silk ribbon of a deity. In the real world, bamboo groves cover an area of 4,667 hectares with sixty varieties of bamboo

this means the tea leaves grown there cannot but absorb some of the characteristics of bamboo. The name Bamboo Leaves Green, like Green Spiral, also serves to illustrate the tea's shape, color and flavor. The processed tea leaves are long strips, tapered at both ends and fuller in the middle, and shaped like bamboo leaves. When infused they hang in the liquid like needles suspended in mid-air. The leaves are bamboo green, and the liquor is pale jade as if dyed with bamboo leaves. Its aroma and flavor emulate a bamboo leaf's temperament, that is, slightly bitter with a sweet aftertaste.

If we examine it more closely, the flavor of Bamboo Leaves Green has intriguing connotations of tea and Zen (*chan* in Chinese). Before Bamboo Leaves Green was formally named, it had long been grown and produced by monks at Mount E'mei Ten Thousand Year Temple and Buddhist monasteries in the vicinity. It was reserved for imbibing during meditation.

Compared to the bracing coolness of Dragon Well's aroma or the delicate aroma of Green Spiral, if infused with equally hot water, Bamboo Leaves Green's aroma is not so pronounced. From the very first taste, that is almost void of aroma, until the tea liquor has entered the throat and a long-lasting and charming aftertaste becomes apparent, only someone in a tranquil and controlled frame of mind can experience it fully.

While it is a young and vibrant green tea, Bamboo Leaves Green also possesses a sense of detachment, a bamboo-like integrity, and understated inner strength. This tea is like the exceptional child who, when others are jumping with joy, lags just a bit behind.

Tea-tasting is an act of meditation—and this is the genuine taste of Bamboo Leaves Green.

CHAPTER III

Oolong Tea

Oolong tea is generally made of mature tea leaves, the exception being White Tip Oolong in Taiwan, which uses tender buds. The production of Oolong tea involves fermentation, heavy rolling (light-rolled Rock Tea is an exception) and roasting processes and is somewhere between non-fermented green tea and fully fermented black tea in term of fermentation.

1-5 The more heavily fermented the Oolong tea is, the redder the tea liquor in color

6 A glimpse of the tea garden on Mount Wuyi in Fujian; Rock Tea is produced in this garden

Oolong tea is generally made of mature tea leaves, the exception being White Tip Oolong in Taiwan, which uses tender buds. The production of Oolong tea involves fermentation, heavy rolling (lightly-rolled Rock Tea is an exception) and roasting processes and is somewhere between non-fermented green tea and fully fermented black tea in term of fermentation.

Predominantly made of mature leaves, Oolong tea's fermentation level is determined by tea tree variety, the required properties of the finished products and historical influence. In this way, some varieties of Oolong tea have varied in fermentation level in different historical periods, such as Iron Mercy Goddess. Some varieties observe a uniform fermention level due to their distinctive features, such as Wuyi Rock Tea and White Tip Oolong. Generally speaking, the more heavily fermented the tea is, the redder it looks, and the more challenging it is to identify the

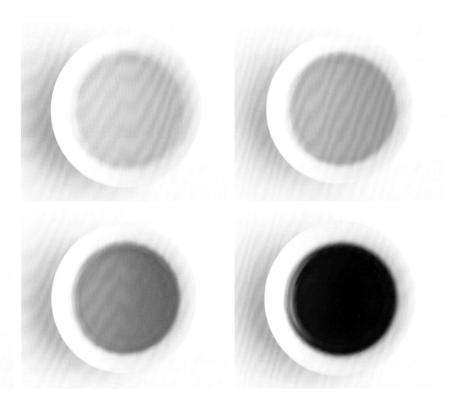

1-2 Yixing clay teaware made of coarse
clay is the best choice to brew Rock Tea

ceased, but to date no convincing conclusions have been reached.

All along, however, a considerable number of people have believed that the primordial ancestors of this Rock Tea are four ancient tea trees, still extant, located on Tianxin Cliff where the words "Big Red Robe" have been inscribed in stone.

Today, even though most of the Rock Tea available on the market proudly carries the "Big Red Robe" sobriquet, the genuine item has become virtually extinct. Some studies have concluded that the traditional so-called "Big Red Robe" was actually the result of the blending of three varieties by tea farmers. Perhaps more tellingly, the local authority found a tea that they could reasonably christen "Big Red Robe," and this has allowed the region to continue to claim the role of the flagship brand.

For this reason, among the four heavyweight Rock Teas—Big Red Robe, Golden Water Turtle, White Cockscomb and Iron Arhat — the most famous Big Red Robe is more a name for a "grade" of tea than a specific variety. It might be more realistic to say the name now represents an ideal set of qualities in Rock Tea.

"Craggy charm," a fairly high degree of fermentation and dry-roasting — such are the unchanging ingredients of Rock Tea, as well as the "solitary" flavor of Rock Tea. But in the rapidly changing China of today where all is in a state of flux, everything progresses with the times, and Oolong too undergoes frequent facelifts. The Oolong on the market today has basically done away with dry-roasting, and even its level of fermentation is lighter than in the past, changing our perception of what characteristics a traditional Oolong should have.

Among these Oolong varieties, Iron Mercy Goddess is most representative. The "greening" of Oolong — processing it like an unfermented green tea — first began on the island of Taiwan. Taiwan is also home to White Tip Oolong, an unrivalled variety once praised by the Queen of England as "Oriental Beauty." But the overall competitiveness of Taiwan's Oolong cannot be compared to that cultivated on the mainland of China in our day. Accordingly, Taiwanese tea merchants has created "light" Oolong, emphasizing its fragrance, and promoted this characteristic as a standard to be applied during formal tea-tasting.

Just when light Oolong dominates the market within Taiwan, the only tea that continues to adhere to its original character and traditional processing is Rock Tea. The reason it occupies a niche market is due to the "stringy" finished tea leaves that result from light rolling; they cannot easily be transported because they occupy a lot of space, and cannot be vacuum-packed. Even more troublesome, annual dry-roasting is required if long-term storage is desired.

Rock Tea is like a lonely hermit who lives in seclusion in deep mountains and brooks. Its temperament is similar to a forty-something male: rich in life experiences, a bit stubborn, and a tad pedantic. He disdains explaining himself and is unconcerned with changes in the material world. He simply exists in a natural state, concealing his lofty scholarly spirit.

The Neo-Confucian thinker Zhu Xi once wrote a line of verse in praise of Wuyi Rock Tea: "Frigid is the valley / Neither bee nor butterfly dally." This line prophetically captures the state of this "reclusive" tea.

1 The interior of an ancestral hall on Wuyi Mountains; a large number of ancestral halls extolling the virtue of learning the sages can be found here. Gardens attached to these halls are popular places to drink tea

2 The River of Nine Bends winds across Wuyi Mountains, one of the main production areas of Rock Tea. The production areas of famous teas are often blessed with outstanding water environments

IRON MERCY GODDESS

1 2   3 4

1-2 The dried tea leaves and tea liquor
of Iron Mercy Goddess

3 A harvest scene of Iron Mercy Goddess;
the properties of tea are influenced by how
it is harvested

4 A scene of drying Iron Mercy Goddess
Leaves in the sunit is harvested

In terms of a specific variety of tea, Iron Mercy Goddess is the undisputed market share leader in the Chinese mainland today. Both the young and the old, the elite and the commoners all enjoy Iron Mercy Goddess, comprising a tea-consuming clientele that transcends differences in location, age and class. Perhaps its popularity is mainly due to, among others, the "breadth" of the beverage's appeal as a semi-fermented "Oolong tea" (Qing Cha).

More specifically, Iron Mercy Goddess is classified between green, black and Pu-erh tea, and it is endowed with a light aroma of an unfermented tea combined with the more complex flavor of a fully fermented one. Furthermore, the "maturity" (age) of Iron Mercy Goddess's tea leaves and their degree of fermentation can be adjusted, and there is also the option of dry-roasting, and if so, for how long. It is evident that the Iron Mercy Goddess on the market in recent years is less thoroughly fermented and dry-roasted for a shorter time, than in the more distant past. The traditional practice of retaining the reddish edges during fermentation, referred to as "red-trimmed green leaves," is now considered passé. Of course, the production and tasting of tea remain subjective to the whims of fashion, and there is always a possibility that "classic" Iron Mercy Goddess may stage a comeback.

1　Emperor Qianlong bestowed the
name "Iron Mercy Goddess" on the tea
because its leaves are weighty and thick
and colored like iron, and its curved,
feminine shape and fragrance bring the
Goddess of Mercy to mind

Big Red Robe	Tea Leaf Volume: 1/3 pot
	Temperature: 95 ℃
	Steeping Time:
	1st Infusion 40 seconds
	2nd Infusion 20 seconds
	3rd Infusion 40 seconds
	4th Infusion 90 seconds
	5th Infusion 180 seconds
Iron Mercy Goddess	Tea Leaf Volume: 1/4-1/3 pot
	Temperature: 90 ℃
	Steeping Time:
	1st Infusion 60 seconds
	2nd Infusion 25 seconds
	3rd Infusion 40 seconds
	4th Infusion 70 seconds
	5th Infusion 120 seconds

Iron Mercy Goddess is cultivated in Anxi, Fujian Province. Like other tea production centers, Anxi features mist-covered peaks that host narrow swathes of land with pristine water sources. Just as when porcelain is mentioned, Jingdezhen is inevitably cited, Iron Mercy Goddess has basically become a synonym for Anxi.

The origin of the Iron Mercy Goddess moniker can claim certain uniqueness. For example, Dragon Well Tea is produced in Hangzhou's Dragon Well; Big Red Robe is a historical allusion (a Ming emperor, cured of an illness by the tea, ordered that the tea plant be draped in red robes); and Bamboo Leaves Green is named after the shape and flavor of its tea leaves. But Iron Mercy Goddess's appellation reputedly originates in the name of the plant on which it grows. However, if we look further into the past, Iron Mercy Goddess also has its own historic allusion: after he tasted Iron Mercy Goddess, the great tea and literary connoisseur Emperor Qianlong bestowed this name on the tea because its leaves are weighty and thick and colored like iron, and its curved, feminine shape and fragrance bring the Goddess of Mercy to mind.

Like the vast majority of Oolong tea, Iron Mercy Goddess utilizes freshly picked mature tea leaves. For this reason, it differs from green tea whose buds or tender leaves have not fully opened. The leaves plucked for Iron Mercy Goddess resemble the mien of a lovely woman awakening in the early morning, her beauty burgeoning — thus they are dubbed a "bare-faced harvest".

When plucked, the leaves are taken while the stems are generally discarded, unlike green tea that comprises a stem along with the leaves on it. To form the tea leaves into a semi-sphere or a somewhat looser shape, they are wrapped in a cloth and tumbled by hand. After processing, the finished tea takes on a brownish-green hue.

A porcelain or Yixing tureen or teapot are all acceptable for steeping Iron Mercy Goddess, but the choice depends upon the maturity of the leaves, and the style and ambience that the tea brewer wishes to evoke. Because Iron Mercy Goddess is less fermented and dry-roasted, the temperature of the water should be lower than for Rock Tea — no higher than 90 degrees centigrade, and preferably a bit less. The amount of tea placed in the pot should allow the leaves to expand fully upon infusion. If too numerous, the leaves at the bottom will not entirely unfold. The liquor will have an unpleasantly "stagnant" air about it.

Another Oolong tea, Rock Tea, has a stringy shape that is relatively fluffy, while

1-2 A glimpse of a Iron Mercy Goddess tea garden in Anxi County, Fujian Province; the picturesque forests are known for their tea gardens and spas

Iron Mercy Goddess is more rounded and more tightly rolled. Therefore, when placed in the tea vessel, Iron Mercy Goddess and Rock Tea will look rather different. Rock Tea requires much more space once it is infused.

The name "Irom Mercy Goddess" has its root in Buddhist vocabulary, but over time the Goddess of Mercy has evolved into the image of a compassionate and beautiful female. Intriguingly, the original Mercy Goddess was a masculine image, and "iron" accentuated this feeling of maleness. Indeed, the taste of Iron Mercy Goddess is like a determined male in his later thirties: he is mature and has made his mark in our rough-and-tumble world; he has a certain shrewdness and inscrutability; and one must spend some time to grasp his qualities. Because the characteristics of Iron Mercy Goddess are similar to someone nearing his thirties, devoted connoisseurs — especially middle-aged career civil servants — often insist that Iron Mercy Goddess has a marked "official" taste to it.

FROZEN-SUMMIT OOLONG

1 2 | 3

1-2 The dried tea leaves and tea liquor of Frozen-summit Oolong

3 Dongding Hill is the production area of Frozen-summit Ooling. Gardens producing this variety of tea have witness the cultural exchanges between the Mainland and Taiwan

A key source of tea within China, Taiwan produces the most varieties of Oolong. While Taiwanese Oolong still cannot compete with Fujian Oolong in those areas outside the island, nonetheless within the mainland, Taiwanese Oolong is recording greater market penetration year by year. This trend is not merely evidenced by rising market share or the increasing number of fans of Taiwanese Oolong who do not hail from the island; it is even more apparent that Oolong tea made in the mainland has actually taken to emulating those grown and produced on the opposite side of the Taiwan Straits.

In recent years, the level of fermentation undergone by Iron Mercy Goddess made in the mainland has dropped markedly compared to earlier times, with more emphasis placed on its aroma. Superficially, this is rooted in a "pop culture" phenomenon in which consumers are influenced by claims that green tea is "healthier." But there is also a less obvious reason for Iron Mercy Goddess's evolution: the deep-seated influence of Taiwanese Oolong whose lighter levels of fermentation and emphasis on aroma are, after all, its creative hallmarks.

Contemporary Taiwan hosts many tea cultivation regions, and the varieties of tea produced there feature a plethora of names. If we go back somewhat in

Pouchong	Rolling: Light
	Fermentation: Light
	Tea Volume: 1/2 pot
	Water Temperature: 90 ℃
	Steeping Time:
	1st Infusion 55 seconds
	2nd Infusion 25 seconds
	3rd Infusion 45 seconds
	4th Infusion 80 seconds
	5th Infusion 180 seconds
White Tip Oolong	Rolling: Mid-to-heavy
	Fermentation: Light-to-middle
	Tea Volume: 1/4-1/3 pot
	Water Temperature: 90 ℃
	Steeping Time:
	1st Infusion 60 seconds
	2nd Infusion 30 seconds
	3rd Infusion 50 seconds
	4th Infusion 90 seconds
	5th Infusion 180 seconds
Frozen-summit Oolong	Rolling: Light
	Fermentation: Heavy
	Tea Volume (pot): 1/2
	Water TempErature: 85 ℃
	Steeping Time:
	1st Infusion 50 seconds
	2nd Infusion 25 seconds
	3rd Infusion 40 seconds

history, we can divide Taiwanese tea into two major categories. One belongs to those originally introduced from Fujian Province (located directly opposite Taiwan), Frozen-summit Oolong and Wenshan Pouchong being representative of this category; and the second is a tea that is truly native to Taiwan — White Tip Oolong, also known as Pekoe Oolong. Frozen-summit Oolong and Wenshan Pouchong happen to possess the traits of Taiwan Oolong tea described above, that is, light fermentation and an emphasis on aroma.

The designation "Frozen-summit" is associated with the mountain of this name in Taiwan where it is cultivated. In standard Mandarin, the Chinese characters for this name are "Tung Ting". In Taiwanese dialect, "Tung Ting" means "to tip-toe." One had to walk on the very tips of one's toes in order to negotiate the rugged and slippery mountain paths. That's because the weather was rainy and humid year-round. The unique environmental conditions make Frozen-summit Oolong special too.

Historically, Frozen-summit Oolong introduced into Taiwan from Fujian has been produced in a manner similar to Iron Mercy Goddess grown in the mainland. Its shape in finished form is also similar to Iron Mercy Goddess, shaped somewhere between a semi-sphere and a fully rounded pellet. But traditionally Frozen-summit Oolong was less heavily fermented than Iron Mercy Goddess, and therefore was a bit less worldly-wise and a tad fresher; a little less subtle, and a bit more trenchant. The temperament of Frozen-summit Oolong lies in a certain elegance that is neither overbearing nor fawning, hidden beneath an understated maturity. This results in an admirable combination, a calm yet uninhibited "personality."

When harvested in the winter or the spring, Frozen-summit Oolong is highly soluble and its flavor at its most mellow. Plucked in the autumn, however, the tea is often judged short on body and lacking in aftertaste.

Although autumnal Frozen-summit Oolong is less mellow than the spring version, the former is somehow endowed with a fragrance — one that cannot be intentionally acquired—like the rarefied ambience of a traditional Chinese ink-wash landscape painting. It appears a bit faint and insubstantial, but it has been enriched with a noticeable spunk.

The changes between the tastes of spring and autumnal Frozen-summit Oolong are like the transition from passionate love to the cool-heartedness one gradually feels

1 A glimpse of a tea gathering; Taiwan
is known for its thriving tea culture;
various kinds of outdoor tea gatherings
are frequently held

after separation. Tea leaves plucked in different seasons fits one's mood at different times, and this is also part of the spiritual dimension of tea.

Brewing Frozen-summit Oolong in a Yixing clay teapot should highlight its personality. If you steep the tea in an eggshell tureen, besides an especially deep flavor you will also benefit from a slightly brisk sensation on your palette. And even if you infuse the tea in a blue-and-white porcelain cup in the office, simply and conveniently, this too is consistent with Frozen-summit's temperament.

Wenshan Pouchong is also known as Pouchong clear tea, and it is often treated as a "sister tea" to Frozen-summit Oolong. Wenshan Pouchong is cultivated in the Wenshan Mountains of Taiwan. As to why it is called "Pouchong," it is said that in the Qing Dynasty when sealing technology was not as developed as nowadays, this tea was tightly wrapped on the inside and outside using dual-layer bamboo paper in order to retain its aroma. This packaging was called "Pouchong," literally, "wrapped variety (of tea)."

Wenshan Pouchong is arguably the Oolong tea variety that most emphasizes tea leaves with a refreshing fragrance. The raw tea leaves used in Wenshan Pouchong are even tenderer than those in Frozen-summit Oolong, and the former is less heavily fermented as well. The degree of rolling applied is similar for both these teas, and Wenshan Pouchong forms a stringy shape that curls naturally. For these reasons, Pouchong can be brewed with water that is slightly cooler than that required for Frozen-summit Oolong.

In Taiwan, White Tip Oolong is quite heavily fermented, and in the Oolong family, it resembles black tea the most. Pouchong, on the contrary, is very lightly fermented and therefore qualifies as the closest thing to a green tea among Oolong family members.

For this reason, when brewing Pouchong clear tea, the feeling is of a tea somewhere between juvenescence and maturity, and the taste also is firmly "in between." Like a vibrant, cheerful youth just entering society, the aroma wafts lightly; like the corner of a young girl's skirt inflated by a gust of wind, or a young man's sleeves fluttering in the wind, one is tempted to approach yet hesitant to spoil the moment.

WHITE TIP OOLONG

1 2   3

1-2 The dried tea leaves and tea liquor
of White Tip Oolong

3 A glimpse of a White Tip Oolong tea
garden; such tea gardens are mainly
distributed in the north of Taiwan

White Tip Oolong is a rare variety grown only in Taiwan with few rivals anywhere in the world. It is commonly known by one of its many sobriquets: "Oriental Beauty," "Champagne Beauty," "Tri-colored Tea," "Bitten Tea," and "Boast Tea," among others. These sobriquets tell us a great deal about the unique properties of this variety.

The name, "White Tip Oolong," captures many of the significant properties of this variety. We have mentioned in the former chapter on green tea that, generally speaking, the more white tips we find in the tea, the more tender it is believed to be and the higher it will be priced. However, this rule does not normally apply to Oolong tea. The ingredients for this variety are mature tea leaves. Therefore, in most cases, we do not see white tips in Oolong tea. However, White Tip Oolong is an exception, as it is the only variety of Oolong tea that uses buds, which partly explains its uniqueness. You can try every variety of green tea but still never know what fermented tea tastes like. You can try every other variety of Oolong tea but you still have no idea of the aroma of bud tea. Taking a sip of White Tip Oolong, you will remember forever the fragrance that half-fermented bud tea can produce.

White Tip Oolong is heavily withered and fermented, and thus shares more similarities with the black tea category, which is heavily withered and fully fermented.

1 Trimmed tea gardens follow the rise
and fall of the landscape, creating a
unique view

How much tea leaves are withered can be identified by observing how much water the bottom of the tea leaves take in after brewed. In most cases, the withering level changes with the amount of fermentation that has taken place. As White Tip Oolong is a heavily fermented bud tea, it should be brewed at a water temperature between that for green tea and that for Oolong tea.

White Tip Oolong is rolled into long curled leaves, with a bud ridden with white tips, the second leaf reddish in color and the third yellowish. Therefore, it is also known as the "Tri-colored Tea." Some people maintain that one can identify white, green, red, yellow and brown colors in the dry tea leaves, and thus insist on referring to White Tip Oolong as "Five-colored Tea." Dragon Well as a variety of the green tea category is roughly divided into Lotus Heart, Banner Spear and Bird's Tongue, based on the shape of the bud leaves. However, White Tip Oolong is named as "Tri-colored Tea" or "Five-colored Tea" on basis of color variations that have taken place in the fermentation process.

Generally speaking, green tea is harvested prior to the Qingming Festival (literally translated as "Pure Brightness" and sometimes known as the Tomb Sweeping Festival) or Guyu (literally, Grain Rain), while Oolong tea can be harvested in spring, autumn or winter. However, in order to produce White Tip Oolong, farmers have to prick buds or tender leaves around the Dragon Boat Festival in summertime. The reason is quite interesting. Top-quality White Tip Oolong has a unique flavor that is believed to be a product of bites inflicted by a certain kind of grass-hopper. This explains why Taiwan is the only production area for this tea variety. Even though we can find similar geographic and climatic conditions in other parts of the world, it would be challenging and even problematic to introduce this special kind of grass-hopper along with the tea trees. This also explains why White Tip Oolong earns the name "Bitten Tea." Generally speaking, the more seriously tea leaves have been bitten, the smaller their bottoms will be, and the tougher the bottoms will turn when brewed, as few tender buds can sustain growth after being bitten by grass-hoppers. This is the magic of nature. The insect plague contributes to the distinctive aroma of White Tip Oolong: a blessing in disguise.

White Tip Oolong was highly priced due to its rarity in ancient China. Therefore, drinking White Tip Oolong was seen as a gesture of conspicuous consumption. This

1 White Tip Oolong, like the flying Apsaras
in the Mogao Grottoes, observes various
colors. For this reason, it is commonly
referred to as "Oriental Beauty"

3 Only White Tip Oolong can be blended
with wine, giving rise to the name
"Champagne Beauty"

2 A simple tea gathering for White
Tip Oolong involves the use of a small
teapot, red fruit and candles

association gives birth to the sobriquet, "Boast Tea." This anecdote is reminiscent of Dragon Well story, which was disdained as "flattery" by the general public as Dragon Well was exclusively monopolized by local officials as a tribute to please superiors. These anecdotes indicate that tea culture was already deeply ingrained in popular culture even though drinking tea remained mostly a privilege of the nobility and literati in the Tang and Song Dynasties. Those tea varieties which were unaffordable for the general population — due to their astonishingly high price — were thus denigrated with popular mockery and contempt.

The story behind the "Oriental Beauty" sobriquet is more legendary. It is said that the British Queen was so impressed by the scent and pleasing look of the tea liquor that she insisted that White Tip Oolong deserved the title of "Oriental Beauty." As this sobriquet started to gain popularity, White Tip Oolong was often compared to delicate and charming ladies. However, as "there are a thousand Hamlets in a thousand people's eyes," there is no consensus how to interpret a certain variety of tea. Therefore, we can also interpret White Tip Oolong in our own way. As a heavily-fermented tea, White Tip Oolong also encapsulates the masculinity of a sophisticated man. It has no

Wen Shan Pouchong	Fermentation Level: Light
	Withering Degree: Light
Rock Tea	Fermentation Level: Medium
	Withering Degree: Medium
White Tip Oolong	Fermentation Level: Heavy
	Withering Degree: Heavy
Black Tea	Fermentation Level: Full
	Withering Degree: Heavy

equivalent in tea, as unique as Jia Baoyu in "A Dream of Red Mansions," immersed in a female world of powder without compromising his masculinity, like a flawless jade falling into the mortal world.

The sobriquet "Champagne Beauty" can be explained in two ways. Firstly, it is said we can identify tinges of champagne in the tea liquor of White Tip Oolong. Secondly, Westerners have been known to add a drop of champagne to its tea liquor to produce a unique flavor. This practice of mixing wine and tea challenges convention. But it should be acknowledged that people can drink tea however they choose. As long as the nutrition in the tea is not compromised, we can make tea in an innovative way to express our sentiments and create a unique tea experience.

Black Tea

Black tea is actually termed as "red tea" in the Chinese language, which indicates the difference between the Chinese and Western tea culture. The Chinese term "red tea" describes the color of tea liquor, while the English term "black tea" captures the color of the dried tea leaves.

Black tea is by far the most popular tea globally in terms of yield and consumption. It must of course be understood that this conclusion is based on the inclusion of tea markets in the Western world, where black tea dominates the market. However, in China and Japan, unfermented tea and lightly fermented tea constitute the mainstay of the market. In terms of production, black tea is produced in a number of countries including China, Japan, Sri Lanka and India, among others. Of these producers, the Chinese were the first to grow black tea. Renowned black tea varieties associated with other countries, such as Darjeeling, all originated in China.

Black tea is, in fact, referred to as "red tea" in the Chinese language, illustrating one of the differences between Chinese and Western tea cultures. As with green tea, the Chinese term "red tea" is used to describe the color of the tea liquor, while in the Chinese language "black tea" refers to a variety whose liquor is black in color. In western culture, tea tends to be named after the color of the dry leaves, which explains the use of the name of "black tea." Some assert that difference in name stems from a mistaken translation. However, there is little evidence to support this interpretation.

There are also differences between Japanese and Chinese tea cultures. In contrast to Chinese tea culture which builds upon the liquor, Japanese tea culture maintains the brewing process as its core. For this reason, Japanese tea culture has divided into different schools, while Chinese tea culture has not.

What differentiates black tea leaves and the liquor of black tea is its heavily-fermented property. In black tea, fermentation occurs after the rolling process. Since it is a fully-fermented tea, the production of black tea does not involve the fixation process that terminates fermentation by killing the cells. Black tea is also made of buds or tender tea leaves. For this reason, we can spot golden tips in top-quality black tea, which turn from white to gold during the fermentation process. Also due to its fully-fermented nature, black tea can be brewed in water exceeding ninety degrees centigrade in temperature or even in boiling water. Though most Westerners prefer to use ceramics of high density to brew black tea, Yixing clay pots with low density are a great choice to preserve the strong flavor when brewing traditional unchopped Chinese black tea. In China, black tea is roughly categorized into Kung Fu Black Tea, Souchong Black Tea, and black tea fannings. The first category includes Dian Hong and Keemum Black Tea, while Lapsang Souchong is the best known among the second category. Such classifications can help the public differentiate varieties, but tells us little about the

properties of them. Taking Kung Fu Black Tea as an example, its name suggests that its production is extremely time-consuming. However, all top-quality black tea takes time to produce. For example, Lapsang Souchong requires an additional process of scenting to give the tea a hint of pine. The third category, namely, black tea fannings, is generally the most popular among Western tea enthusiasts. It needs to be chopped before it is made into tea bags. The original flavor of black tea fannings is preserved even when served in tea bags.

Unchopped black tea mostly takes the shape of long twisted leaves. The raw materials for black tea are sourced from a wide range of tea trees that are widely distributed across China, including the broad-leaved tea trees for Dian Hong, medium-leaved trees for Lapsang Souchong and small-leaved trees for Keemum. I personally believe that broad-leaved black tea such as Dian Hong and Assam in India are better choices for blending.

KEEMUM AND DIAN HONG

1-2 The dried tea leaves and tea liquor of Dian Hong

3 Keemum Black Tea is a top quality Chinese black tea, and is produced in Qimen County in Anhui and its neighborhood

Keemum Black Tea is named after its production area, where cloud-capped hills rise in elegant procession. Tea gardens on the hills are covered with reddish yellow soil, creating an agreeable condition for the growth of Black Tea. Keemum was already known as a production area of tea back in the Tang Dynasty, when green tea, rather than Black Tea, was its primary product. It was not until the Guangxu Years in the Qing Dynasty that local tea farmers started to produce Keemum Black Tea. Despite its late debut, Keemum Black Tea quickly rose to fame, winning the Gold Award at the Panama World Expo in 1915. Since then, it has been frequently presented by the Chinese government to foreign emissaries. This world famous variety is referred to as "Prince Tea" in Britain.

Dian Hong (literally, Yunnan Black Tea) is also named after its production base, within which Dian refers to the ancient name for Yunnan Province. Broad-leaved Dian Hong and small-leaved Keemum Black Tea differ in flavor and other properties due to their different production areas, but share similar production processes and brewing methods. Farmers will choose buds with one or two leaves to make black tea. The more tender the tea leaves are, the higher they will be graded. Generally, it is easier to identify gold tips in Dian Hong than in Keemum because the leaves are plucked from different varieties of tea trees.

1 | 2

1 The red soil of Yunnan is the
birthplace of Dian Hong

2 Workers are processing black tea
in a tea factory of Qimen County, Anhui
Province

It is interesting to note that the tea leaves used to make black tea can also be used to make green tea. For this reason, Keemum was once known for its high yield of green tea. Even today, a small amount of Dian Lv (literally, Yunnan Green Tea) is produced to supply a limited group of consumers. In some sense, the difference between green tea and black tea lies in the fermentation process. It should be acknowledged that both categories are imbued with unique merits. Like a piece of jade, we can choose to preserve its original shape and form without making changes, or we can leave it in the hands of a sculptor who will shape it to his own vision. However, it should be noted that not all processing produces positive effects. In some cases, changes can spoil unadorned beauty. This rule also applies to tea processing. In recent years, in the context of rapid growth in China, it is a common trend to seek novelty. In response, some bold experiments have been made using the materials for Oolong and traditional green tea to make black tea. However, every kind of tea tree has its unique properties. We must take account of these properties when tea leaves are processed. For this reason, many of these experiments with tea varieties have met a lukewarm reception with new varieties ending in failure with only a short market presence.

LAPSANG SOUCHONG

1   2 | 3

1-2   The dried tea leaves and tea liquor of Lapsang Souchong

3   Tea farms in the Preservation Area on Mount Wuyi. According to "The Classic of Tea," Lapsang Souchong originally referred to tea produced on Mount Wuyi

Tea leaves of Lapsang Souchong are somewhere between Dian Hong and Keemum Black Tea in size and, like Rock Tea, are grown in the Wuyi Mountains. Lapsang Souchong has a longer history than Keemum Black Tea and was among the first varieties introduced to the Western world. Byron, a leading figure in the Romantic Movement in the early nineteenth century, mentions Lapsang Souchong in his "Don Juan."

Lapsang Souchong stands out from the category of Souchong Black Tea not for its production area or variety of tea trees, but for its unique flavor, a product of the pine-scenting process. Mostly employed during the drying or withering process, this technique to introduce hints of pine to tea utilizes the remarkable absorptive quality of tea leaves. The combination of the lasting scent of pine and the thick aroma of Souchong Black Tea in the Wuyi Mountains produces an intoxicating atmosphere.

One thing that deserves mentioning is that there is also a variant of Lapsang Souchong which does not involve the scenting process in its production. This variant is labeled with a tag clarifying its identity as "non-scented Lapsang Souchong." In the Chinese market, black tea is usually rolled into long leaves; whereas, to target the international market, it is a common practice to chop Black Tea into fannings and package it in tea bags. Generally speaking, tea bags are usually only steeped once.

1 The production of Lapsang Souchong involves scenting tea leaves with pine branches during the drying process, which gives a distinctive flavor to the tea

2 A glimpse of a Lapsang Souchong tea garden on Mount Wuyi; it is common to make the tender leaves of Lapsang Souchong into black tea in the Chinese market

Keemum Black Tea	Size of tea leaves: Small-leaved
	Shape: Long twisted leaves
	Amount of tea: Less than 1/4 pot
	Water Temperature: Above 90 ℃
	Brewing time:
	1st Infusion 25 seconds
	2nd Infusion 5 seconds
	3rd Infusion 20 seconds

Lapsang Souchong	Size of tea leaves:Medium-leaved
	Shape: Long twisted leaves
	Amount of tea: 1/4 pot
	Temperature: Above 90 ℃
	Brewing time:
	1st Infusion 30 seconds
	2nd Infusion 5 seconds
	3rd Infusion 20 seconds

Dian Hong	Size of tea leaves: Broad-leaved
	Shape: Long twisted leaves
	Amount of tea: More than 1/4 pot
	Temperature: Above 90 ℃
	Brewing time:
	1st Infusion 45 seconds
	2nd Infusion 10 seconds
	3rd Infusion 30 seconds

Taking a two-gram tea bag as an example, the drinker need only steep it in 130 ml of boiled water for ten minutes to produce full flavored tea liquor. Tea bags are easy to carry and steep. While they provide a convenience that traditional tea-brewing methods are unable to, brewing tea in a traditional way can preserve the original flavor of tea on one hand and offer the drinker a chance to embark on a cultural journey on the other hand. On this journey, the drinker must think about the brewing methods and vessels, and how to create an overall ambience. Each journey is a unique experience.

CHAPTER V

Pu-erh Tea

Pu-erh is believed to be good company when we want to lose ourselves in deep mediation or seek inner peace. Although there is a trend that Pu-erh tea is starting to be better received among younger drinkers, Pu-erh is still much more popular among more senior consumers with conservative tastes. Pu-erh tea is not exactly about kinship, nor friendship or romance. It is concerned with a fourth kind of relationship.

1　The dry tea leaves and tea liquor of Pu-erh tea

2　Pu-erh tea is mostly compressed into tea cakes or bricks for easy storage. Drinkers break up the bricks by hand or tea knife

Before going into detail about Pu-erh Tea, we should first get a rough understanding of dark tea. Compared with green tea, Oolong and black tea, dark tea is not as widely appreciated by the public. Dark tea is a collective term to refer to post-fermented tea, and Pu-erh belongs to this category. "Post-fermented" means that the fermentation process continues after the tea leaves are processed into finished products. This also means that the fermentation process comes after the fixation process. In this sense, what sets dark tea apart from the pre-fermented cateogry such as Oolong and black tea depends on which process occurs first, fixation or fermentation. For this reason, the flavor, taste and value of dark tea actually improve with age, with the post-fermentation process gradually taking effect — a unique property of dark tea. Dark tea dates back to the Tang and Song Dynasties. In addition to Pu-erh Tea, this category includes Anhua Dark Tea in Hunan, Border-Sale Tea in Sichuan (mainly supplied to the Tibetan region), and dark tea in Hubei and Guangxi.

Pu-erh tea takes its name from its production area in Pu-erh County, Yunnan Province. It is made of broad-leaved tea, and available as loose leaves, compressed tea cakes, tea bricks of varied sizes and tea bowls. Among them, tea cakes account for the lions share. Most tea cakes weigh seven *liang*, or 350 grams each, with seven

smaller cakes bound together into a set. In China, seven is usually associated with auspicious meanings. The weight of an individual cake, the total weight of each set, and the number of cakes in each set all amount to odd numbers. This unique packaging approach expresses a wish for good fortune. It is commonly acknowledged that Yunnan Province is home to some of the most ancient tea trees in the world, while the most established production areas of Pu-erh tea are the Six Tea Mountains in Yunnan. Among the trees more than a century old, more than half are in the Six Tea Mountains. Pu-erh harvested from these centuries-old trees is of great value. An opportunity to savor tea from these trees is something to be remembered. However, although the quality of tea leaves does influence the flavor of the tea liquor, how a cup of Pu-erh tea tastes is also determined by whether the brewing process is properly handled and the drinker's subjective feelings at that moment.

Concerning the classifications of Pu-erh tea, raw Pu-erh and ripened Pu-erh are the most commonly used terms. What's the difference between the two? Actually, the notion of ripened Pu-erh did not come into being until the 1970s, when wet-piling techniques were invented. Pu-erh tea processed in a traditional way belongs to the category of

raw tea. It has to undergo a gradual process of darkening and fermentation through exposure to environmental conditions. This aging process gives it a mature aroma. In this sense, raw Pu-erh should be understood as Pu-erh Tea stored for maturity. Ripened Pu-erh involves the utilization of wet-piling techniques to accelerate the fermenation process, so that the green tea leaves turn blackish brown and taste as if they have been stored for years. However, the definitions of raw and ripened are relative terms, and might sound confounding at times. For example, raw tea that has been stored for years is already ripened, while ripened tea that has been stored for years also undergoes the natural aging process which is a defining feature for the raw tea.

It is generally agreed that ripened Pu-erh can never equal vintage raw Pu-erh in flavor and taste. However, the former still remains a popular choice for tea drinkers for two main reasons. Firstly, the latter is limited in quantity, and this rarity accounts for its high price. In addition, many consumers find it difficult to distinguish authentic raw Pu-erh from the overwhelming supply of ripened Pu-erh. Secondly, if the wet-piling process is conducted in the right way, the liquor of the former is also acceptable in

1　Tea gatherings, simple in style and
rich in Zen undertones, are suitable for
drinking Pu-erh tea

taste. More importantly, like raw Pu-erh, ripened Pu-erh can also be stored to allow for further fermentation. Generally speaking, raw Pu-erh is seldom produced as a loose leaf tea, since tea cakes or bowls are more convenient for storage.

It is widely believed that the longer Pu-erh Tea is stored, the more fragrant it will become, however little is known about this process in scientific terms. For this reason, we still have little idea whether we should store Pu-erh for decades or for centuries to maximize the benefit of the ageing process. Despite these unsolved puzzles, there are however some established norms within the industry. For example, ripened Pu-erh has to be stored for almost a decade before being categorized as "vintage Pu-erh," while it takes raw Pu-erh a decade and a half to gain this qualification. As it can be stored for decades, Pu-erh can act as a life-long companion. I myself have often given Pu-erh tea cakes as a gift to newly-wedded friends, in the hope that they can sample it every anniversary. As time passes, the tea will travel with them through life, changing with them.

In addition to the vintage year, storage condition also plays a significant role in determining the quality of Pu-erh tea. If the location is chosen badly, the tea might even deteriorate with time. To ensure the correct aging, Pu-erh should be placed in an airy location free from alien smells. It is not difficult to imagine how the tea can be damaged by unpleasant odors from the environment. However, the strong absorption ability of tea can also be used to our advantage. For example, it is a common practice to wrap Pu-erh tea with pomelo peel, which has two merits. Firstly, pomelo peel is also good at absorbing odors, and thus can help to screen the tea from other smells. Secondly, the unique scent of pomelo peel, aromatic with hints of bitterness, is a perfect match for Pu-erh tea. Therefore, Pu-erh tea packaged with pomelo peel is suffused with a surprisingly scented flavor.

In addition to ventilation, temperature and humidity are also of prime importance for the storage of Pu-erh tea. Opinions still vary concerning whether Pu-erh tea should be stored in a dry or humid environment, and it seems that experts on tea storage are not likely to reach agreement any time soon. Personally speaking, I believe that it should be stored in an environment with a relatively moist atmosphere. In my opinion, without moisture in the air, the post-fermentation process of Pu-erh tea diminishes. However, too much moisture will make it easier for bacteria to breed. Pu-erh stored in such an environment tastes as if it is already rotten. Though some consumers are fond of this

1 YiXing clay teaware is the best choice
to make Pu-erh tea. Broad tea leaves
are better to make into Pu-erh tea

rotten smell, it is thought by others that this kind of tea can be harmful to health.

When brewing Pu-erh tea, we should make a distinction between raw tea that is newly produced and ripened tea that has undergone the wet-piling process. The former shares much in common with green tea in many respects. As to loose tea, we can brew it like broad-leaved green tea. As for tea bricks or bowls, we should lengthen the brewing time based on how hard the brick or bowl has been compressed. Ripened tea can be brewed in roughly the same way as black tea, except that we should reduce the amount of water, increase the water temperature and shorten the brewing time. Compressed tea bricks should be steeped for a longer time. Vintage raw Pu-erh should be brewed by taking consideration of its properties.

Every tea variety has its unique health benefits and in recent years the benefits of Pu-erh tea have been widely promoted. As a post-fermented tea, its cooling properties are reduced to the bare minimum and for this reason, Pu-erh tea does not overly-stimulate the intestines, stomach and body. Ethnic minorities living in the plateau areas often have meat heavy diets and depend on dark tea like Pu-erh to help break down fat. For this reason, it is widely believed that Pu-erh can be an effective tool in helping lose weight.

In addition, it is also believed that Pu-erh is effective at preventing cancer and cardiovascular diseases. What deserves attention is that although its fluorine content is less than green tea and Oolong, brewing methods in the plateau area can enhance the level of fluorine, and coarse leaves generally have more fluorine than tender leaves. A proper intake of fluorine can help to strengthen tea, but too much can have a negative effect on the circulation system. Therefore, it is advised not to drink dark tea too often. Alternatively, lovers of dark tea can stop using fluorine tooth paste to counter balance their intake.

Part II

TEA CULTURE

CHAPTER VI

Principles

Before touching upon the spiritual domain of tea ceremony, we should become familiar with imbedded or related principles in tea brewing practice. The ultimate purpose of grasping these principles is to not to be constrained and stifled by them but to challenge and innovate them.

1
2

1-2 The rich connotations of the tea
ceremony require us to be selective of
the tea brewing environment

In the last part, we talked about categories of Chinese tea and detailed the brewing methods for various categories. Some readers might assume that tea brewing is just a technical thing. It simply involves choosing the right teaware, considering the temperature of water and the amount of tea leaves, and releasing the liquor from the tea leaves. It is true that the tea brewing process can be broken down to these steps in a practical sense. During this process, the brewers need to make a clear distinction between different categories in the first place. Even when encountering unknown varieties, brewers can still use the distinctive properties of tea leaves to make decisions about the teaware, amount of tea, temperature of water and length of steeping time. Besides this, experts can learn from the experience and make improvements as they see fit. In reality, tea brewing is not just concerned with technical issues; cultural and artistic aesthetics are equally important.

It is common in China that issues are often approached in a scholarly manner, with topics theorized. In this larger context, schools of thoughts contend for attention. It is widely assumed that the surging interest in tea-related theories mirror the booming of tea culture. But we should take a critical view of this assumption. However, taking a closer look at this issue, we find that this superficial boom is ridden with problems. The Japanese culture now exerts a powerful influence worldwide. Some Chinese scholars have understated the disparities between Chinese teaism and its Japanese counterpart, and presented Chinese teaism to an international audience without making sufficient distinction between the two. For this reason, we need to make a detailed investigation of how much Chinese teaism legacy has been preserved in a real sense. I firmly believe that we should at least obtain a basic understanding of tea before diving into the theoretical domain. This understanding should be based on two aspects. First, we should understand the different varieties of tea. Secondly, we should become familiar with imbedded or related principles in the tea brewing practice, which will be covered in this chapter. Before we go into detail, what we should first acknowledge is the principles exemplified in this chapter, concerned time, space and existence are of great importance, but are only parts of a whole. Secondly, the ultimate purpose of grasping these principles is to not to be constrained and stifled by them but to challenge and innovate them.

TIME

2

1

1 An old-fashioned wood table, coarse grey fabrics and old alcohol burner add to the antique flavor of the tea gathering

2 Sundials were used to keep time in ancient China. Its surface displays the Eight Diagrams

As far as tea brewing practice is concerned, time is meaningful in two senses, the first associated with the physical domain, and the second more abstract and sentimental. Physical time is concerned with how much time it takes to brew each variety of tea, how many times a certain kind of tea can be steeped, or how long the tea is expected to last. The more abstract notion is related to the properties of tea and artistic or aesthetic elements.

Harvesting time is not an essential determinant for tea properties. Instead, tea properties are predominantly determined by what happens during the fermenting, roasting, rolling and withering process. Among these, fermentation level is the most significant factor. In both daily and yearly cycles, the level of fermentation should gradually increase. To be exact, green tea is the best choice for the morning, oolong for midday, and roasted Oolong, black tea, Pu-erh for the afternoon or evening. Over the course of the year, green tea, Oolong, black tea and Pu-erh are optimal beverage for spring, summer, autumn and winter respectively. If a host wishes to offer two or more kinds of tea for a tea party, the more heavily fermented should be supplied at a later stage. This means green tea should be served first while Pu-erh tea should come

1 Tea can also be drunk in ordinary
settings. The flow of rivers outside the
window mirror the flow of time

last. As far as scented tea is concerned, it is better to drink jasmine tea in the morning or springtime, Osmanthus Oolong in the afternoon or summertime as it is efficient to relieve fatigue and prevent heatstroke, and ginseng tea in the evening or autumn and winter.

The advice above is experience-based. However, this advice is also based on health considerations and the human physiological response to tea. For example, people who seldom drink tea may become intoxicated after drinking various kinds of tea. This so-called "tea-drunkenness" is a syndrome causing dizziness, nausea or rapid heart rate. This syndrome is triggered by overstimulation by caffeine in tea liquor. This is by no means a serious condition with a light sweetmeat alleviating symptoms. However, the best way to avoid this tea-drunkenness is to start with less fermented tea and work toward heavier varieties. It is advisable to drink green tea in the morning because green tea is the most efficient to boost energy. More heavily-fermented tea is less stimulant, and thus is a better choice for later in the day. On a yearly basis, spring is suffused with the vitality with which green tea is associated. Winter is a time for seclusion, when the taste of Pu-erh tea is a perfect choice.

Different tea varieties are characterized by their unique properties and embedded connotations. In this way, people often tend to relate different tea to different groups of people. When preparing a tea party for children, green tea, as an exemplification of youth and energy, is an optimal choice. For aspirational adolescents who want to look sophisticated, lightly-fermented Oolong can capture their tastes. Similarly, roasted tea such as Rock Tea is a favorite of middle-aged males who have been around the world and learned from life. Young females often prefer scented tea; mothers are likely to serve the family black tea, while a pot of Pu-erh tea is always good company for the elderly generation.

It should be noted that these assumed associations between different tea varieties and social groups are a massive overgeneralization, and should not be taken as rules. Therefore, we should have the consciousness to defy such assumptions in the tea brewing practice. For example, if we want to hold a tea party in a bamboo grove in autumn, Bamboo Leaves Green might be a good option, because such tea is rolled into bamboo-shaped leaves and hints of bamboo can be identified in the liquor. In addition, Bamboo Leaves Green is taken to be an "autumn tea" as it tends to be identified with a tint of loneliness and desolation. When working on a tea party to celebrate the first snow fall of the year, we can choose "Snow Drifting on the Green Pond" scented by jasmine. Simply reciting its name evokes a scene in which crystal snowflakes kiss the water's surface. The jasmine fragrance is an incarnation of springtime, which implies we can anticipate the arrival of spring even in the depths of winter. When making decisions concerning which tea variety to choose, we should think in different ways. For example, when hosting a tea gathering in memory of a deceased friend, we could serve Pu-erh tea to create a solemn atmosphere or green tea in memory of them in the prime of their life, diluting sorrow with positive elements.

The practice of those conducting the tea ceremony is an important component of a tea party. In this process, tea leaves and hot water are brought together in a teapot, and tea liquor is distilled from the pot and served to guests. In addition to the tea brewing practice, the incense burning, flower arrangement and zither playing can also

1 Block printing illustrations vividly depict how people used to entertain themselves in tea houses during the Qing Dynasty

play important roles. All these elements add cultural depth to the tea party.

No matter whether we are host or guest, the experience of a party is unique and cannot be duplicated. Because at the next gathering, we will meet different people, drink different tea varieties, or have different feelings. Heraclitus, a philosopher in ancient Greece, once said, "No man steps in the same river twice." His observation also applies to the tea drinking experience. The difference lies in the fact that Heraclitus approaches the issue of the ever-changing nature of the universe from a philosophical and speculative perspective, while the uniqueness of each tea drinking experience in Chinese tea culture is based on the intangible notion of karma. Man encounters a certain man or a certain subject in a certain time and space in a predestined way. All is a product of the magical power of karma.

1 Traditional Chinese tea houses are popular entertainment venues, however, such tea houses have decreased in number

2 Old gate board, vine chair, and moss-covered pots can be used to make a tea gathering

SPACE

1 Potted plants add to the ambiance of the tea brewing practice

2 A glimpse of the study; the slender-shaped table can be used for tea brewing

The spatial elements associated with the tea brewing practice are easier to understand than the temporal elements. Whether brewing tea or attending a tea party, both must occur in a physical space. This space can be reduced to the teapot or extended to the boundless universe. All these spaces are meaningful and related to our tea brewing practice.

The most significant space for tea brewing is the so-called "tea settings." These settings include all the indispensable utensils and the space they occupy. The utensils encompass necessary teaware such as tea stove, kettle and cup, in addition to some non-functional components such as adornments to create a certain atmosphere. A typical tea setting in daily life is likely to be made up of a table, a piece of table cloth, a set of teaware, some tea snacks, as well as some artifacts, a vase or miniascape, and Chinese calligraphy or painting scroll hanging on the wall as the background. In this sense, we can understand the tea setting as the crystallization of a design concept and the designers' creativity. But an overriding principle is that the tea setting has to satisfy all the required functions and match the chosen theme.

The theme is a defining feature for a tea setting. Based on this theme, we can

choose the right tea variety and concept development method. This process can also operate the other way around. Sometimes, we have to refer to the distinctive properties of a certain tea variety to decide on the design concept and select proper components for the tea setting. In the selection phase, we have to differentiate between function and decoration. Actually, there is never a distinct boundary between the two. For example, even when selecting tea-brewing utensils, we have to consider the form, color and material of the teaware to make the tea setting pleasing to the eye. We can break down components of the tea setting into different categories, based on whether they are associated with the visual, audio, tactile, olfactory, and gustatory experience, whether it is solid or liquid, whether it has life, whether it is consumptive, as well as its texture, color and form. For example, tea cups may be solid porcelain vessels with pheasant motifs involving the utilization of under-glaze and over-glaze techniques, feeling smooth to the touch. Tea snacks may be lotus-shaped, light bluish in color, made of glutinous rice, sticky and sweet. Flowers may be added to match the overall ambiance. Of course, this is a rigid example, but it provides a certain approach to understand tea settings.

To understand tea settings in this way might give birth to a false assumption that a tea setting consists of various elements on different levels. Actually, whatever elements are included in a certain tea setting is solely based on the designer's personal choice. Sometimes, we might adopt a minimal approach and thus choose only functional elements. If a tea gathering is designed to share Pu-erh tea that has been stored for decades, perhaps a male tea ceremony performer may wear a plain gown greyish in color, without decoration; the table covered with greyish coarse table cloth; teaware of deep grey pottery or Yixing clay teapots featuring simplistic styles; on the wall hangs a calligraphy scroll in clerical script reading "the greatest aroma is aroma-less"; the setting involves no use of flowers, incense or zither, or other adornments. In the tea gathering process, attendees are to refrain from chatting. In this seemingly somber gathering, attendees can concentrate on the Pu-erh without distraction. In fact, this unadorned tea setting is defined by a unique charm. The color palette, the performer's gown, tablecloth, teaware, tea liquor and scroll create a subtle rhythm. The use of grey tones weakens the visual impact, with no sound save the rubbing of fabrics, the shifting of teaware, and the flowing of tea. In this way, the aroma and taste

1-4 Any space with a special atmosphere
can also be used for tea drinking

of the tea become the dominant factor, lingering in the tea drinkers' mind.

Tea settings can be either interior or exterior spaces. Tea houses are a typical setting. Tea gatherings are also held outdoors in the cradle of mountains and water, or in a man-made garden which strives to reproduce and encapsulate the charm of a natural landscape. Chinese tea drinkers often entertain themselves in commercial venues such as tea houses.

Tea houses and tea gardens are commonly found in Japan, where both are specifically designed and constructed, becoming established components in Japanese tea culture. In China, tea houses and tea gardens are seldom built specifically for the purpose. However, this does not mean that the Chinese attach less importance to the tea-brewing space. Instead, it indicates that they resort to a much wider range of locations for tea-brewing. Without the restriction of immobile tea houses, tea settings gain mobility in architectural space and can be carried around based on the special requirements of tea drinkers. In ancient China, where strict codes were observed to safeguard a hierarchy of social class, servants brewed tea in a room while the guests were served in another. Both private gardens in South China and imperial gardens were intended to mimic natural scenery on a reduced scale. They were not exclusively used for tea drinking activities but they were the most sought-after venues for tea gatherings. For tea drinkers in ancient China, one could not appreciate the beauty of tea drinking without taking the chance to brew and drink tea deep in the mountains or close to water. This understanding is manifested in classic Chinese paintings on tea.

1 Some exquisite elements are commonly used in tea gatherings, such as rockeries and goldfish

2-3 Chinese garden designers value the techniques of "borrowing scenery." An open window can add flavor to the indoor tea gatherings

Chinese tea houses are time-honored. They share similar niche that cafés in Western society fill, but differ from the latter in the fact that the latter is primarily concerned with serving individual consumers. In traditional Chinese tea houses, even unacquainted consumers greet each other in an amiable and friendly way, while waiters chat with customers as if well acquainted. These genial interactions serve as a cohesive force to bond all the parties in the tea house as an integral community. In addition, tea houses were also venues for traditional opera performance, another vehicle for social interaction. In contemporary China, most tea houses provide separate rooms for customers to protect their privacy, except those which are primarily intended as venues of traditional performances. Such tea houses act more like traditional arts center.

1-2 In China, tea drinking is closely
associated with gardens

EXISTENCE

1 | 2

1 Tea cups of different styles can be used in varied settings to bring out the various features of the tea liquor

2 Teaware in daily use doesn't have to make complete set. But it's better that different items share similar features

A minimal tea setting or tea brewing practice can be simplified into three components: firstly, ingredients, including dry leaves and water; secondly, people who brew the tea; and thirdly, tea utensils. Taking a closer look at the three components from the perspective of time, we find that both the first and the second will vanish with the passage of time, and only the last persists. In the micro universe of tea brewing practice, teaware will survive as cultural relics such as Stonehenge in the UK, the pyramids in Egypt and the Acropolis in Greece, while tea and tea drinkers continue to come into being and vanish, just like human civilizations.

As far as an item of teaware is concerned, if we put aside its cultural connotations, texture and form are the most important factors. Of course, on certain occasions, other factors such as color, pattern and techniques employed gain importance. Color and pattern are sometimes determined by the texture and form of the teaware, but are also an integral part of the overall subjective aesthetics. Therefore, we can take both factors into account when talking about texture and form, rather than focus on them in a separate section. Generally speaking, as long as production techniques do not affect the texture and form of the teaware, they are seldom considered due to its vague and distant association with tea brewing practice.

1-3 Glazed porcelains and colored glazed teaware excavated from the underground palace in Famen Temple, Shaanxi Province.

In the first part, when talking about tea brewing, we mentioned the texture of teaware. But all the teaware mentioned belongs to category of either pottery or porcelain, which implies they are the most ideal options for teaware. However, in addition to them, metal and glassware are also commonly used tea vessels.

In terms of metalware, tin can prevent oxidation effects on tea leaves due to its impressive sealing properties. Therefore, tin containers are often used to store tea leaves. Pig iron can optimize water quality in a special way during the boiling process. For this reason iron kettles are commonly used to heat water, especially in Japan. In terms of the steeping process, silverware is the most commonly used metalware.

The pottery and porcelain mentioned earlier are part of a larger category of earthenware finished with firing techniques. In this category, the increase in the firing temperature leads to an increase in the teaware density and a decrease in water absorption ability. Some porcelains have zero water absorption. There is one variety in particular which shares similarities with pottery and porcelain but differs from them in an important way. This variety of earthenware includes Yixing clay teaware with good water absorption and breathability. In general, Yixing clay teawar and high density porcelain are popular choices.

Teaware of different textures can influence tea liquor in different ways. In this process, density plays the most significant role. The higher the density, the faster the heat is dispersed, and the better it is to highlight the aroma and taste of unfermented tea. Similarly, it takes longer for teaware with a lower density to dissipate heat, which is more suitable to brew teas leaves with a deeper level of fermentation.

Silverware is marked with a relatively high density with good heat dissipation. Glassware and porcelains share similar density. These three kinds of teaware are good choices for green tea and can maximize its freshness and liveliness. Most tea drinkers favor porcelains with a relatively thin shell for green tea. The thinner the shell is, the less time it takes to disperse heat and the more evident the aroma of green tea. Silverware is not a popular choice. First of all, it is relatively expensive in price; secondly, to most tea drinkers, metalware does not feel as comfortable as porcelain. Glassware is widely used by modern Chinese to brew green tea. First of all, it is crystal and transparent so the way tea leaves drift and dance in the cup are visible. However, traditional tea drinkers believe that visibility compromises the sense

1-3 Similar materials can be made into different varieties of teaware, while various materials can be made into teaware of a certain kind

4 One step in the production of Yixing clay teaware; hand-made Yixing clay teaware involves complicated processes

of beauty. Therefore, they often choose porcelains over glassware. Considering the forms, lidded cups are the most suitable for green tea. Technically speaking, tea cups without lids accelerate heat dissipation. The set consisting of lid, cup and saucer is commonly known as a "Sancai cup" (literally translated as "Tri-talent cup"). The three components in the set are associated with heaven, man and earth. Traditional lidded cups are made of porcelain, but lidded glass cups are also available. Yixing clay cups with white glaze on the interior are another variety. Such ware is suffused with an antique and solemn air, suitable for green tea with its high density. The white-glazed interior of this particular variety produces an eye-pleasing appearance with green tea liquor against a white background.

Other porcelain varieties are in wide use for other purposes, but Yixing clay ware is a prime partner in tea brewing. It is often used to make teapots and other tea utensils. Also known as red porcelain, it is a local specialty of Yixing City. It can take a wide range of colors from red and purple to green. Teapots make up a dominant proportion of Yixing clay teaware. Varied techniques can produce a rich variety of teapots. Generally speaking, Yixing clay ware is less dense than common porcelains.

1 |

2 | 3

1 A pig-iron kettle is one of the best ways to heat water to brew tea, while a clay kettle is a good way to cleanse the water

3 Porcelain teapots are a good choice for a large variety of tea

2 Yixing clay teapots of various sizes, shapes and densities

THE CHINA TEA BOOK

140

Therefore, it performs well in terms of heat emission and water absorption. Based on these properties, Yixing clay teapots are a better option for brewing heavily-fermented tea, such as black tea and fermented Pu-erh tea. Considering the shape, teapots with a small mouth and a spacious belly can slow heat dissipation, and can thus enhance the strong aroma of heavily-fermented tea. In terms of texture, Yixing clay teapots occupy a dominant position in traditional teaware. From the days of dynastic China, a large variety of Yixing clay teapots survive to this day. As far as form is concerned, various classifications are used. Based largely on the relationship between handle and body, teapots can be roughly categorized into back-handled, side-handled, loop-handled, and handle-less teapots. Among them, back-handled teapots are the most typical, with side-handled teapots commonly seen in Korean and Japanese tea settings.

If we want to match different tea varieties with tea utensils of varied textures and shapes, it can be assumed that lidded cups with a thinner shell are optimal choices for green tea, while Yixing clay pots are suitable for black tea and ripen Pu-erh tea. What is the best option then, if we have to find one, for Oolong which lies between green tea and black tea in terms of fermentation level? The answer lies in porcelain teapots with a thicker shell. The porcelain texture exploits the property which Oolong shares with

1 The loop-handled kettle was invented by Su Shi in the Song Dynasty. Bamboo and other materials are used to make the handle

2 The side-handled kettle is widely used in the Japanese and Korean tea ceremonies

green tea, while the teapot shape considers its similarity with Pu-erh. What deserves attention is that no established rule exists concerning the right utensils to brew green tea and Pu-erh. Lidded cups and Yixing clay ware are suggested to inspire tea drinkers to break conventions. Which tea utensil to choose is determined by specific conditions, theme of the tea gathering and brewing methods used. For example, we can utilize lidded cups and Yixing clay teapots to capture springtime in South China and North China respectively, which impresses people in different ways. Or, we can also use lidded cups to brew Pu-erh tea to breathe vitality into the otherwise stately liquor. As to Oolong, porcelain utensils will give prominence to the fragrance, while Yixing clay utensils can incorporate cultural connotations. Which kind of teaware to select is actually determined by what tea brewers feel at that moment.

In addition to the significant components of the tea settings, some uncommon and auxiliary utensils are also used. An ancient Chinese poet once exclaimed that a scene featuring green tea leaves drifting in tea liquor against jade teapot is more than attractive. Jade teapots are time-honored artifacts in China. In Chinese culture, jade is perceived as the incarnation of gentlemanly virtue. In addition to jade, tea is also compared to gentlemanly conduct. Therefore, tea and jade teaware are a perfect match. Jade teaware is marked with a unique flavor which varies greatly from porcelain teaware. But as jade teapots are extremely expensive, consumers need to be certain jade materials are genuine as counterfeits can be harmful to health.

Auxiliary tea utensils often include wooden and bamboo ladles, scoops, tea leave containers, and funnels among other things. Wood and bamboo are closely associated with nature. They play a prominent role in Japanese tea culture. For instance, the tea whisk is not only necessary but indispensable in the matcha tea ceremony.

1 A stove unearthed from the underground palace at the Famen Temple

2 A salt shelf unearthed from the underground palace at the Famen Temple

3 Silver cooker used to bake tea cakes, unearthed from the underground palace at the Famen Temple

4 A Tang tea grinder unearthed from the underground palace at the Famen Temple

5 A Tang tea sieve unearthed from the underground palace in the Famen Temple

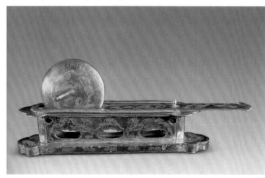

AMBIANCE

1 3
2 4

1-4 Various materials and techniques are employed in the scenting process to match tea leaves and tea gatherings

In the tea brewing practice, teaware is the most enduring. In a tea gathering, there are uncertainties as well as ever-changing and vanishing elements. For example, a tea party might involve the incense burning, a flower arrangement and zither performance. In a tea gathering, such artistic forms are only meaningful when they are associated with the theme of tea party. And their transient existence also exemplifies the uniqueness of each tea drinking experience.

It is popularly believed that incense burning, flower arrangements and zither playing, especially the first two activities, are closely related to Japanese Teaism. This belief is well-grounded, but it should be noted that these three components are not exclusive to any school of tea culture. Therefore, although we will cover these elements in this book, it is primarily concerned with Chinese tea ceremony, which is the origin of teaism.

Incense burning practices came into being in the Spring and Autumn Period and Warring States Period, but did not gain maturity until the Sui and Tang Dynasties. Later, it was introduced to Japan. Through the ages, incense burning and the tea ceremony in China have evolved to maturity through mutual influence. The former process is mostly conducted prior to the tea brewing phase and acts as a prelude to the tea party. If a party is large in scale with a large number of attendees, more than two tea varieties will be served, and the brewing process might last for a considerable length of time. If so, the organizer can stage an incense burning performance to show how to make incense and then burn the incense. On the other hand, if a tea party only involves a limited number of attendees and will not last long, finished incense products can be burnt instead, which will save time by skipping over the incense making process and avoid distraction from the tea brewing stage.

Incense takes various forms, either powder, regular or irregular shapes. Generally speaking, incense in regular shapes is chosen for tea parties. Such incense is roughly categorized into the so-called "boned incense" and "boneless incense." The first category is produced by applying scent to bamboo filaments, while the latter category includes spiral-shaped incense or incense sticks with bamboo filament removed from its core. Spiral incense is seldom chosen for a tea party due to its complicated shape and the space it takes up.

The incense burning process requires the carefully considered selection of

1 Straight incense is commonly used
and convenient

2 Decorations at a tea gathering should
not interfere with the flavor of the tea

incense and incense burners. We should make sure in the first place that incense and incense burner texture match each other. In addition, we should also take account of the theme of a given tea party, the tea to be served as well as the defining features of the teaware. For instance, if a certain tea party is concerned with Buddhist practice or recreation of court lifestyles, sandalwood incense sticks and copper tripod burner are top on the list. If green tea is served, we can choose floral-scented incense such as jasmine or chrysanthemum incense as well as a blue and white porcelain burner with a slender shape. If Pu-erh is served, eaglewood incense and a Yixing clay burner with spacious belly and narrow mouth should be chosen. Similarly, Oolong tea often goes hand in hand with flower or timber scented incense and the official Ru kiln or white-glazed porcelains with stout shape and spacious mouth. In addition to these traditional incense varieties, imported essential oil and Western incense are also occasionally used, matched with the right burner. Such utensils are suitable for a small-scale tea party with two or three participants.

It should be remembered the highlight of a tea party is tea rather than incense. Therefore, it is an overriding rule that incense chosen should not interfere with the

1 Flower arrangement is not all about flowers. Branches and shrubs put in the right pottery vessel can create a unique flavor

2 Lavish use of colors and flower blossoms infuses a Western-style romance into the tea drinking environment

tea brewing and drinking process or overwhelm the flavor of the tea. If jasmine tea is served, jasmine-scented incense should not be chosen, since it will adversely affect the dominance of tea flavor. For the same reason, if the tea is already scented with an eaglewood flavor, incense scented in the same way should not be burned. In addition, incense should be lit before the tea brewing practice to avoid its influence on tea flavor. The incense burner should not be placed in an airy location in case that the incense will disperse too rapidly. It should also not be put in a prominent position which might block the view of tea party attendees.

In contrast to incense, flower arrangement is easier to understand. Though flowers in a tea party will wither one day, they last much longer than incense. Generally speaking, flower arrangement performance should extend from the beginning to the conclusion of the tea party. It remains still in contrast to incense which drifts around in air.

Flower arrangement in China came into existence at around the same time with (or slightly later than) incense burning practice. It is likely to have evolved from Buddhist practice. Flower arrangement did not gain maturity and popularity until the Sui and Tang Dynasties. It was introduced into Japan together with the Buddhist religion. Currently, two or three thousand varied schools of flower arrangement are established in today's Japan. In Chinese history, flower arrangement underwent concurrent development with the incense burning practice and tea ceremony, and has become a significant component of the tea party or tea gathering.

When utilizing flower arrangement in a tea party, we should take some extra considerations. Firstly, we should choose flowers without strong fragrance. Incense vanishes in a short time, while flowers are present throughout the tea party. Therefore, a strong flower fragrance might steal thunder from the tea flavor. Secondly, the tea party should be themed on refined or interesting topics. Therefore, flowers flamboyant in color or large in size are not good options. But there are exceptions. For example, in court tea parties or tea gatherings with unique local flavor, flowers with gaudy names or negative associations are seldom used, while those with auspicious meanings are preferred despite their large sizes. Of course, the selection of flowers is primarily determined by the interpretations of the tea party planners.

1-2 Potted landscape fits the tea
gathering, and does not interfere with
tea flavor

3 Potted landscapes can be used in
various kinds of tea gatherings

Chosen flowers should match the theme and visual styles of the tea party, as well as the tea to be served. Though flower arrangement can constitute an independent performance, it is supposed to be related to the overriding theme of the tea party. For instance, when brewing Wuyi Rock Tea, we could select a withered branch spotted with small-sized flowers, and insert the branch into solemn-looking pottery ware as if it were sprouting out of the ware. Or, we can choose a branch of red plum blossoms whose saturated colors are consistent with the charm of Rock Tea. However, though belonging to the larger category of plum blossoms, neither wintersweet nor white-colored plum blossoms are the best choices. With red plum blossoms in winter, the heavily fermented and heavily roasted nature of Rock Tea makes it a good option to drink in winter. If green tea is brewed, we should choose light-colored flowers or newly sprouted branches in springtime, and arrange them together in light-colored porcelain without much decoration. If roses are added to the tea liquor, roses should not be chosen for flower arrangement; osmanthus Oolong should not go hand in hand with osmanthus for flower arrangement.

In addition to tea properties, we should also consider the relationship between

flower arrangement practice and the tea party from a broader perspective. For example, looking at the shape, curled Green Spiral leaves are a perfect match for vines. As for Dragon Well, we can choose sword-shaped leaves to highlight its embedded vigor. Considering the tea and flower names, Oriental Beauty should go well together with corn poppy (named Beauty Yu in China). When brewing Bamboo Leaves Green, we can select asparagus fern as adornment. When serving the Iron Buddha, we can choose podocarpus macrophyllus (also known as Buddha Pine in China). Some other associations are also common. For instance, pine branches might remind us of the hints of pine in the tea liquor of Lapsang Souchong.

Improvised musical performances are usually staged either towards the end of the tea party or between two tea varieties. The former, which acts as the conclusion of the tea party, can create a lingering memory of the tea party and tea liquor. The latter is expected to play a transitional role. The traditional zither is the best choice for the musical instrument. A time-honored instrument, zither playing stands out as an established practice for the literati in ancient China. It is challenging to play the zither well and it is a common saying in China that zither playing shares a similarity with Zen practice. In this sense, tea is the perfect companion for zither players. In addition to the zither, other musical instruments such as the four-stringed Chinese lute, flute, two-stringed bowed instrument and horse-head fiddle are all good choices. What music to play is largely determined by the theme of the tea party. In most cases, only solo performances are staged in the tea party. Sometimes, we can also hear singers chanting to the music or find Western orchestral musical in the performance.

Zither playing is primarily concerned with tea drinkers' auditory experience and works to create a peaceful atmosphere or restore inner peace in tea drinkers. The incense appreciating practice appeals to the olfactory experience, flower arrangement to the visual experience, tea liquor to the gustatory experience and teaware to the tactual experience. A tea party actually involves the participation of all senses, transforming the tea tasting practice into a comprehensive artistic experience.

CHAPTER VII

Ancient Chinese Tea Culture

Different from its Western counterpart, Chinese traditional art is primarily centered on calligraphy and painting, both of which exist as independent artistic forms. Tea-related poetry, painting and calligraphy works are common in China.

1 Brush, ink, paper and inkstone are
collectively known as "Four Treasures of
Study," and are associated with the tea
drinking habits of the literati

2 Paintings and calligraphy scrolls are
commonly used to decorate tea-drinking
venues

Western arts build upon architecture, while sculpture and painting both act as affiliation for architecture. Different from its Western counterparts, Chinese traditional arts are primarily centered on calligraphy and painting, both of which exist as independent artistic forms. As a consequence, Western sculptors and painters always have to take consideration of the spatial relationship between their works and the architecture, while Chinese calligraphers and painters never have to bother themselves with such concerns. Traditional Chinese calligraphy and painting works are either made into hanging scrolls to hang in the hall, or into handscrolls to observe at a closer distance. Each form has its unrivaled merits. The bondage with calligraphy, painting and tea is deep-seated in the Chinese culture.

For quite a long time in the Chinese history, poetry reigned over all the other literary forms, and served as sources of inspiration for calligraphers and painters. In addition to poetry, calligraphy and painting, tea became another significant factor in the life of a man of letters.

POETRY

1

1 Su Shi, Northern Song Dynasty, "Chao Ran Tai"

Most Western readers assume that "tea ceremony" is a Japanese notion. However, the truth is that China is the de facto birthplace for tea ceremony. This notion first made presence over twelve centuries ago in a poem by a Tang poet named Jiao Ran. It was not until eight centuries later that Sen no Rikyu, the hugely influential figure in Japanese tea ceremony, brought up this term. One of Jiao Ran's poems, "Drinking Tea," was improvised when the poet was savoring tea with his friend named Cui Shishi. This poem depicts the shape and color of tea leaves, the tea-brewing scene and the drinkers' personal experience. Besides, this poem has also established tea drinking practice as important as wine drinking. Jiao's poem has actually interpreted the notion of tea ceremony from three perspectives, including the tea itself, tea-drinking practice and tea-savoring enjoyment. No matter whether the definition is flawless, Jiao has made a breakthrough.

Jiao Ran has not only been recognized as an influential figure that had contributed to the definition of tea ceremony, but also known for his friendship with Lu Yu, who is respected as the Sage of Tea in China. Their profound friendship which was a product of their common passions about tea was noted in Jiao's poems and other historical documents. Some scholars have affirmed that Jiao Ran was a mentor for Lu Yu. Lu could never have finished "The Classic of Tea" without instructions and enlightments from Jiao. Both of them lived in the Tang Dynasty, which was a booming age for the Chinese tea culture. If someone is too obsessive to make a distinction between

the two, he would find that Lu Yu was more focused on the pragmatic aspects. His "The Classic of Tea" has covered systematic tea brewing methods. Jiao Ran was more interested in the spiritual domain. He maintained that the tea drinking process can be translated into a Zen-practicing ritual. However, compared with their differentiated focuses, their recognition of talents in each other and their contribution to Chinese tea culture trigger more interests among scholars, who believe that they had scored glorious accomplishments in tea-related poetry and treatise respectively. Their close relationship also exemplified how resonance between poetry and tea culture reached an unprecedented height in the Tang Dynasty.

As one of the most influential figures in Chinese poetry, Li Bai, who was celebrated as "Poet Transcendent," was also known as "Immortal of the Wine Cup," since wine seemed to be an efficient catalyst for his inspirational outbursts. Therefore, he had produced a large number of poems themed on wine. Actually, his poems on tea were equally impressive. One of his poems was intended to express his gratitude for an accomplished Buddhist monk who had gifted him cactus tea. The poem was set in a Taoist wonderland. According to the poet, the cactus tea must have been in the exclusive possession of deities, and thus has the magical power to restore the youth. Marked by a fusion of narrations and sentimental expressions, this poem is actually the first one themed on tea and also the earliest one concerning the functions, which indicates that tea culture was already established in the Chinese society back then.

Pyramid poem is one of the most interesting kinds of poetry. The whole poem takes the shape of a pyramid since each line has more Chinese characters than the previous one. A pyramid poem by the Tang poet Yuan Zhen describes the shape and color of tea leaves, and what a fun it is to brew and drink tea in floral fragrance in the moonlight. The last line of the poem argues that tea is effective to reduce the influence of alcohol. This argument is questionable in the scientific sense. In the Tang Dynasty, which was over one thousand years ago, both wine and tea were brewed in different ways from today. Therefore, tea liquor might be useful to relieve discomfort caused by excessive drinking. Nowadays, it is certain that this argument does not hold water. Scientific findings have proven that having tea after drinking wine will relieve drunkeness temporarily because tea can help accelerate excretion of alcohol from the liver. But the burden on the kidney and stimulation to the heart will increase during

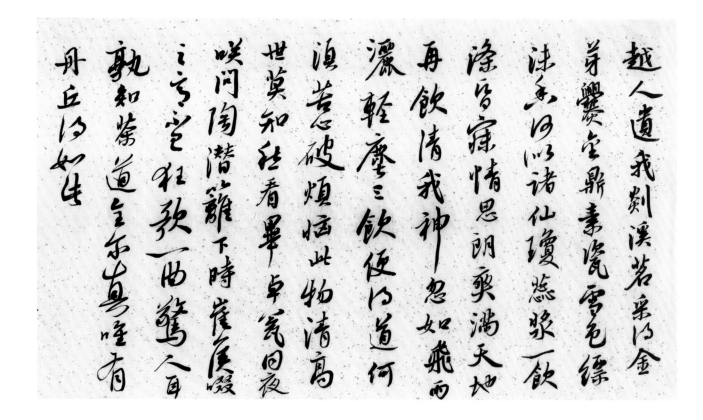

this process. Therefore, it is not a wise move to have tea while or after drinking wine.

Tang Dynasty witnessed the birth and boom of tea poems, a large proportion of which were exquisitely worded. By the Song Dyansty, tea poetry and tea fights both occupied a prominent role. In this period, tea poetry was themed on a wider range of subjects, including the spring to brew tea, tea property, the savoring process, teaware, tea party, figures and anecdotes about tea, related treatise, hills forested by tea trees, tea snacks, and production technologies.

In ancient China, it was a common practice for talents to travel around the country to live up to their aspirations. Therefore, homesickness might be the most popular subject in ancient Chinese poetry. A Song poem by Su Shi has integrated his meditation over tea with his yearnings for his hometown in a seamless way. The first part depicts what unfolded before the poet's eyes when he looked into the distance on a towering terrace in North China, while the second part makes it clear that this poem was composed following the Cold Food Festival. This traditional festival is associated with a tragic story in the Chinese history. Back in the Spring and Autumn Period, Chong'er, prince of the Jin State, was once cornered by his enemies into isolated mountains and nearly starved to death. His servant Jie cut down flesh from his own thigh to feed Chong'er. Later, Chong'er returned to the Jin State and was enthroned, while Jie retreated into a secluded life with his mother in mountains. In order to force his loyal servant to return to his side, Chong'er set the mountains on fire to drive out Jie. However, Jie still adhered to his original decisions and chose to be burnt alive with his mother under the tree. This tragedy landed Chong'er in such enormous grief that he ordered that no one was allowed to make fire on the day when Jie died in scorching flames. From then on, people had to stand cold food on that day, which explains why this festival is named Cold Food Festival. Following the Cold Food Festival is the Qingming Festival, when people have to return to their hometown and visit the graveyard to pay their respects to their lost family. Newly produced tea also starts to be supplied around this festival. However, Su could not return to his birthplace in South China. Therefore, he sighed over his own experience after drinking wine: Talking to my friends about my yearnings for my hometown would make me even more homesick. Thus, I could do nothing but console myself by brewing tea newly produced in my hometown in South China. This poem gives full expression to a life philosophy: life is ridden with sorrows; we can do nothing but seek joy amidst these sorrows.

Just like Su Shi, I myself was brought up in Sichuan, one of the most renowned tea production areas in China. Fortunately, it is much less challenging nowadays to transport spring tea from South China to North China within days, which is a great relief for me. Because I cannot feel the arrival of spring unless immersing myself in the aroma of the newly produced tea from South China. Its aroma which I can identify with my hometown thus serves as a kind of compensation. Therefore, I can totally understand what Su felt back then, since I am also one of those who relieve their homesickness with tea from hometown.

Another celebrated Northern Song poet Huang Tingjian also wrote a poem on tea. The beauty of this poem is that the poet vividly detailed the tea brewing and savoring process, and accurately captured the joy that is difficult to put to words when drinking tea. In the Song Dynasty, Dragon and Phoenix Tea Cake was a predominant category of tribute tea. Tea leaves would be compressed into cakes, sealed with wax and then stamped with motifs featuring dragon or phoenix. The first half of this poem describes the tea brewing process. The poet halved the phoenix cake and smashed it, when it suddenly occurred to him that he had just separated the couple of phoenixes on the cake. Then, he ground the smashed cake into jadelike ashes, and put them into teapot. When the boiling water sounded like the raving of pine forests, the poet poured it into the pot. The second half of the poem is concerned with the joy that surged in the poet's veins the moment he was submerged in the overwhelming fragrance which he found himself speechless when trying to describe. It was as if a friend had just returned from a long trip, but would like to talk with the poet the whole night despite his fatigue. The poet might have exhausted his words but could not find the right expressions for such a delight. The poem brilliantly related tea savoring to meeting with an old friend after a long time, which has accurately captured the feelings that thousands of tea drinkers have experienced.

In the Ming and Qing Dynasties, poetry constantly lost influence until the Chinese literary landscape was dominated by novels. However, this change should not be intepreted as a decline in literati's interests in tea. Actually, they just resorted to another form. In the novel "A Dream in Red Mansions," readers can find a lot of descriptions on tea.

In the Tang and Song Dynasties, tea was in short supply and it involved complicated processes to brew tea, when tea culture was closely associated with the court and the literati. For example, Emperor Huizong of the Song Dynasty authored "Treatise on Tea," which gives a detailed portrait of tea production industry back in the Northern Song Dynasty. By the Ming and Qing Dynasty, tea drinkers had simplified the tea brewing process, after which tea leaves were just steeped in hot water. This transformation in tea brewing methods led to the popularities of tea drinking practice — even the civilians would not find it time-consuming to brew tea. However, renowned tea varieties were still monopolized as tributes to the court. Emperor Qianlong in the Qing Dynasty wrote a poem to delimeate blossoms on the

tea trees, which was quite creative, since tea blossoms had never made presence in a Chinese poem, though tea leaves constituted a common subject.

In the Qing Dynasty, a poet brilliantly selected one line from two poems by Su Shi respectively, and made them into a poetic couplet, hanging the scrolls on the Hangzhou Tea House. The couplet means "The West Lake looks like the fair lady at her best, good tea always reminds us of pretty girls." A celebrated calligrapher and painter Zheng Banqiao also wrote a couplet on tea, exclaiming "I want to brew the newly produced tea with river water, and buy all the mountains across the country as my personal landscape screens." Both of the couplets have exemplified that the Chinese literati bear a universal interest in tea.

CALLIGRAPHY

1

1 Cai Xiang, Northern Song Dynasty,
"Jing Cha Tie"

The earlist tea poem that we can find in historical documents was written in the Tang Dynasty. In contrast, the first calligraphy works on tea were much time-honored. We could identify the Chinese character for tea on blue-glazed vessels in the Eastern Han Dynasty, though it looked different from the character in common use today. It should be noted the Chinese characters have undergone a gradual evolution in form since their birth. The "tea" character in modern Chinese language was not established until the publication of Lu Yu's "The Classic of Tea." Even after its establishment, other forms of characters for tea were still used concurrently.

Calligraphy is always of overriding importance in traditional Chinese arts. It has evolved from the oracle bone script, stone drum script, great seal script, lesser seal script, clerical script to the cursive script, regular script and running script. Chinese calligraphy builds upon the pictographic Chinese written language, encapsulates the Chinese culture and aesthetics, and transforms into a unique artistic form. The Chinese calligraphy challenges the established Western appraisal norms. To a Westerner, the value of a calligraphy work lies in how exquisitely it was manipulated. They valued the forms of letters over meanings of the words. For a Chinese calligrapher, calligraphy is based on the language, which is meaningful and functional. Therefore, the connotations of the words are also taken into account when a calligraphy work is appreciated.

It is an established practice to name the calligraphy scrolls by accomplished calligraphers after the first two Chinese characters in the text or a key word in the passage. This rule applies to the "Ku Sun Tie" by Huaisu in the Tang Dynasty. Translated into modern language, the text means "the bamboo shoots and tea are quite tasteful. You can bring me more." The text indicates that tea was a common and treasured gift in the literati class. Interpreting from the text, it is evident that this scroll was originally intended as a letter or a message, which might be the earliest on tea that has been discovered. From the artistic perspective, the work exemplifies the unrestrained calligraphy style of Huaisu.

In the Song Dynasty, calligraphy was closely related to personal edifications of the calligrapher. "Jing Cha Tie" (Jing Cha, literally translated as selected tea leaves) by Cai Xiang was named after the subject of the scroll. Cai Xiang himself was quite an expert on tea. His treatise "Notes on Tea" has crystallized his understanding and expertise of

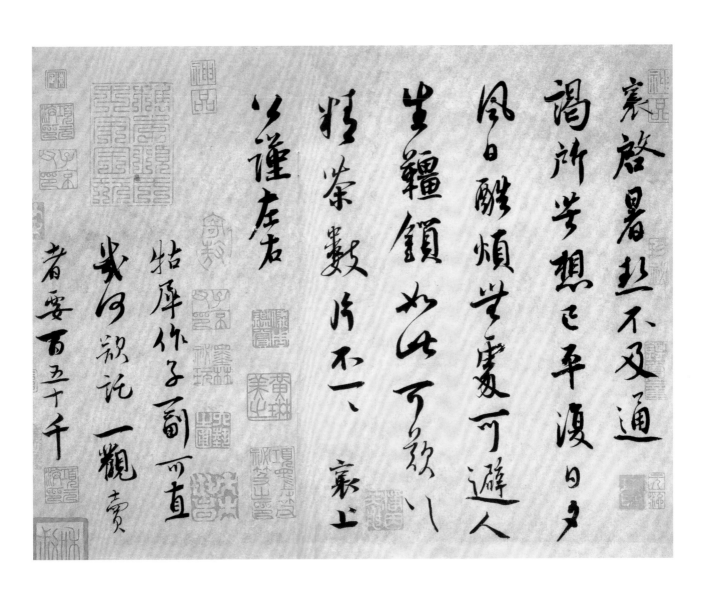

1 Xu Wei, Ming Dynasty, "Seven
Procedures to Brew Tea"

煎茶之類

一人品煎茶雜瀹
清小雜然要頂真
人與茶品相得故
其瀹海傳於高流
大隱雲霞泉石
之上軍魚蝦麋鹿之
儔

二品泉山水為之江
水次之井水又次之
井貴汲多又貴停
波之多又水倍瀹
新汲貯之陳
味藏鮮洌

三烹點烹風浩
火候湯眼鱗之
起沫湯越泊投
茗紫中一湯少
許候湯若相溲

tea. In addition, he made innovations by reducing the size of Dragon Tea Cake, which was a tribute to the emperor.

We mentioned Su Shi in the former passages. Su was also recognized for his expertise on tea. He had discovered the health care functions of tea long ago, documenting how to take care of teeth by use of tea. He was also the inventor of loop-handled teapot, which he designed for brewing tea. The legacy from Su Shi does not only include a number of tea poems, but also quite a considerable quantity of calligraphy scrolls on tea. "Yi Ye Tie" is one of them, in which Su mentioned how he gifted a friend a tea cake. His records make it clear that the custom of taking tea as treasured gift is deep-seated in the Chinese culture.

The Ming and Qing Dynasties witnessed further development of calligraphy, when there was still an impressively large quantity of calligraphy works on tea. "Seven Procedures to Brew Tea" by Xu Wei, a Ming scholar, was a gem in the Chinese calligraphy arts. The original text of this scroll was selected from a treatise by Lu Tong in the Tang Dynasty. Lin Zexu, who launched a massive campaign to eliminate opium trade in China, was also a tea lover. He once wrote a couplet, "brewing tea by using the dew crystallized on the bamboo leaves in the pine grove, reading, painting and reciting poems in the shades of phoenix tree in the rain," which expresses his personal aspirations as a typical scholar.

What deserves attention is that current research on Chinese calligraphy arts has prioritized the forms over the meanings. As far as calligraphy works on tea are concerned, tea culture and relevant information embedded in the text are in most cases slighted or even neglected. We should find a solution to this problem so that researches on Chinese calligraphy can become more fruitful and rewarding.

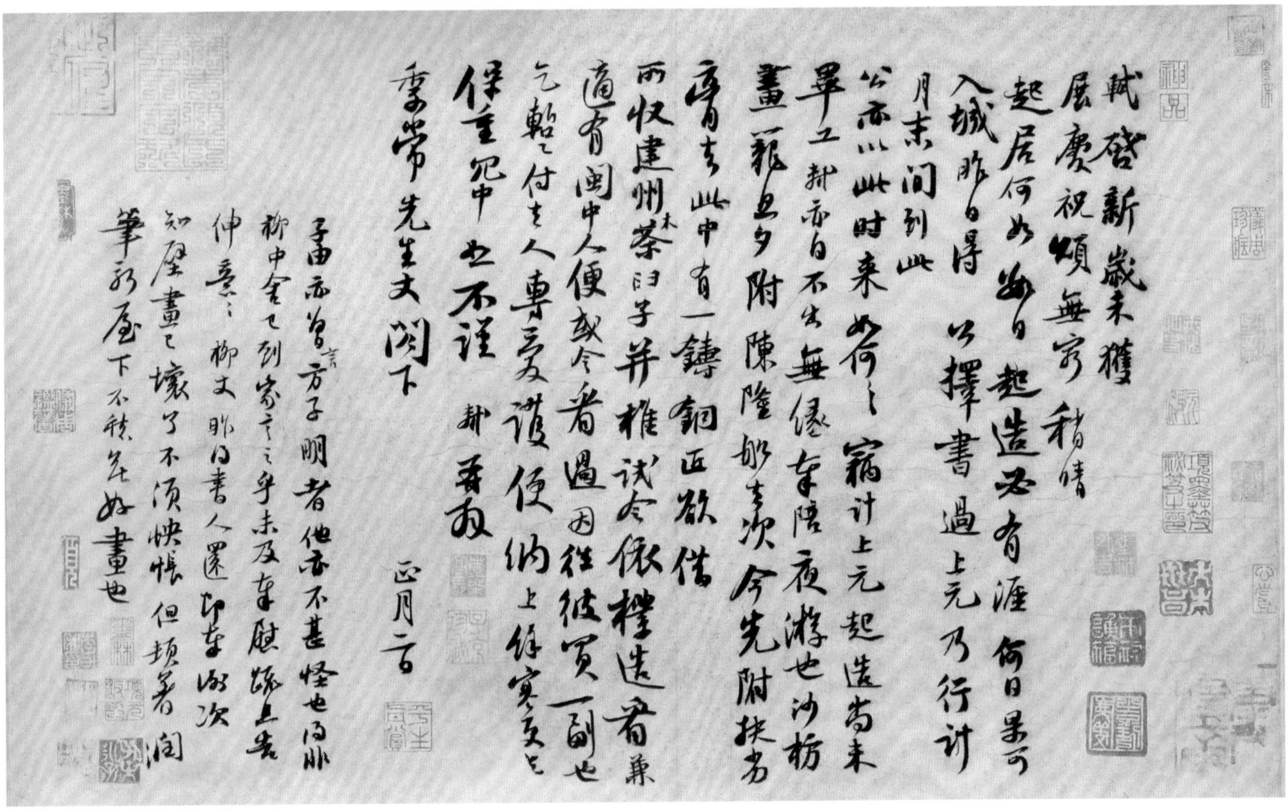

PAINTING

1

1 Zhou Fang, Tang Dynasty, "Playing the
Zither and Drinking Tea"

It is relatively challenging to identify elements of tea culture in paintings without textural messages. The researchers have to grasp a profound understanding of the social context in which the painting was crafted. Chinese paintings concerning tea can be roughly divided into two categories: the first category is centered on other subjects, but we can find some tea-related activities in it; the second category is primarily themed on tea-related activities.

In the "Scrolls of Exemplary Women," which is attributed to Gu Kaizhi in the Jin Dynasty, the vessels on the ground are believed to indicate that a tea ceremony is performed. "Xiao Yi Acquiring the Orchid Pavilion Preface by Deception" attributed to Yan Liben in the Tang Dynasty and "Playing the Zither and Drinking Tea" attributed to Zhou Fang both involve a scene of tea ceremony. The former one is concerned about an episode in which Xiao Yi took possession of a renowned calligraphy work in an indecent but impressively brilliant way. In the lower left corner of this painting, two servants are brewing tea. We can see clearly how the tea is tossed up and down in the boiling water as well as a rich variety of vessels for brewing tea and drinking tea. These vessels share a lot in common with court commissioned gold and silver teaware that was unearthed from the underground palace of Famen Temple in Shaanxi Province. The painter included these elements to imply the hospitality on part of the host. Therefore, these elements were not placed in a prominent location in the painting. "Playing the Zither and Drinking Tea" presents what a carefree and cultured life that female nobility lived by spending time playing the antique zither and drinking tea. This painting delivers a message that tea drinking used to act as a significant token of social status and aesthetic taste in the Tang Dynasty.

"Literary Gathering," by Zhao Ji, Emperor Huizong of the Song Dynasty, might have captured the most grand tea gathering in ancient China, when most gatherings were held in a quiet location with a limited number of attendees. The tea party depicted in the painting was already grand in scale. The impressively exquisite teaware on the giant table provided referential materials for historical studies. Emperor Huizong was an accomplished calligrapher and painter, and also an expert on tea. His "Treatise on Tea" showcases his brilliant and literati-oriented understandings of tea. "Preparing Tea" by Liu Songnian in the Southern Song Dynasty reflects a scene in which the servants are preparing tea to serve their master. Being a typical painting on tea ceremony, this painting is suffused with a sense of tranquility and calmness.

Zhao Mengfu in the Yuan Dynasty selected a unique subject for his "Tea Fight." Today, such activities have already evolved into appraisal and grading of various tea products. However, back in dynastic China, tea fights were primarily founded on tea brewing skills rather than the quality of tea leaves. The most renowned contest in the history is the one which was presided over by Emperor Huizong of the Song Dynasty. The contestants had to scent the tea cake, smash and grind it to ashes, toss the ashes into the tea cups, and poured water into the cups. The more foams the contestant could produce, the more skilled he had proven to be. Other skills were also recognized. Some people could take good control of the exact amount of foams produced. They could make sure that the foams rose to the same height with the bowl edge without brimming over. Others could produce a certain pattern with foams in a flash. However, the tea fight in Zhao Mengfu's painting depicts a tea-brewing competition between two rivaling groups of four tea traders in the market, who wanted to prove their products were better. The painter vividly portrayed the gestures

1 Liu Songnian, Southern Song Dynasty,
"Preparing Tea"

2 Emperor Huizong, Northern Song
Dynasty, "Literary Gathering"

and facial expressions of the characters, and also included a rich variety of teaware such as tea steamer, tea stove, teapot and tea cup commonly used among civilian tea drinkers.

Many Ming and Qing paintings are also primarily concerned with tea ceremony. "Yuchuan Brews the Tea" by Ding Yunpeng in the Ming Dynasty and "Yuchuan Brewing Tea" by Jin Nong in the Ming Dynasty both depict Lu Tong, a renowned tea expert in the Tang Dynasty, as the protagonist. The former painting was finished in brilliant colors. Yuchuan is seated in the shades of a banana tree, holding a fan in hand and with his eyes fixed on the stove. Behind him is a wide range of teaware including kettle. A servant, who carries a kettle, seems to head for the spring, while the other servant, with the tea case in hand, comes from a distance. The latter painting is marked with elegant light-toned colors, an antique flavor and a relatively simple character structure. There is a banana tree in the background. Yuchuan sits at a short desk with a stove, a pot and a bowl on top, while a servant is fetching water from a spring.

Just like poetry and calligraphy works on tea, tea-themed paintings have evolved into a complicated and thriving system, and made a unique scene in the Chinese cultural landscape. I hope that works selected in the former passages can help readers to understand tea culture from multiple perspectives.

1 Zhao Yuan, Yuan Dynasty, "Lu Yu
Brewing Tea"

山中茅屋是誰家
兀坐閒愓到日斜
俗客不來山鳥散
呼童汲水煮新茶

CHAPTER VIII

Tea and Zen

The belief in the oneness of tea and Zen equates
ordinary tea drinking practice with Zen meditation,
which exemplifies the notion that life should be
centered on Buddhist practice.

1 The oneness of tea and Zen is of overriding importance in the Zen ideas celebrated in the tea ceremony

2 Buddha statues featuring tranquility are commonly placed in the tea-brewing room to indicate the association with Zen principles

When we talk of Zen thoughts concerning tea culture, most readers will think of Japanese Teaism. It is true that the Japanese have incorporated traditional Zen Buddhism and religious practice into daily life and transformed them into established customs. In addition, Zen thoughts strongly influence how the Japanese behave. These thoughts are not only at the center of the Japanese tea ceremony, but also at the heart of Japanese flower arrangement arts and incense burning appreciation. Zen is more closely related to Japanese Teaism because the Japanese have enshrined the tea ceremony as a highlight to popularize national culture. The Japanese matcha tea ceremony actually originated from tea whisking practice in the Song Dynasty. Similarly, Japanese Zen was also introduced from China. This chapter will not attempt to approach tea ceremony in a systematic way or expound on Zen thoughts embedded in the Japanese tea ceremony, but talk generally about how Zen thoughts have influenced tea brewing practice.

The oneness of tea and Zen occupies a dominant position in Zen thought in the tea ceremony. There is a common Chinese saying which says the most indispensable daily necessities in a man's life include firewood, grain, oil, salt, sauce, vinegar and

tea, which indicates what a significant role tea plays in the daily life of the Chinese. The belief in oneness of tea and Zen equates ordinary tea drinking practice with Zen meditation, which exemplifies the notion that life should be centered on Buddhist practice.

The belief in the oneness of tea and Zen experienced constant development until gaining maturity in the Song Dynasty, when the Zen school was established as the mainstream in Chinese Buddhism. This Buddhist school valued unexpected comprehension, which means that Buddhist practitioners could spontaneously achieve enlightenment through introspection. In this process, monks relied on tea to relieve exhaustion and restore inner peace when lost in meditation. In daily life, monks also resorted to tea to dispel distraction from worldly lusts. For this reason, many elements of tea ceremony evolved from Buddhist practice. Prior to the Tang Dynasty, when "The Classic of Tea" was published, tea ceremony was already well developed, sharing a bond with Buddhism which could not be easily severed. Sage of

1

1 Candocks in Claude Monet's paintings exemplify the unique charm of the impressionist school, while lotuses in Oriental culture are closely related to Buddhist karma and Zen meditation

Tea, Lu Yu, was a Buddhist follower himself. In the Tang and Song Dynasties, the tea ceremony was introduced to Japan by two monks named Jianzhen and Eisai. Later, it was popularized by Japanese monks.

There is an oft-quoted Buddhist story concerned with the oneness of tea and Zen. It is said that a Tang Zen practitioner in Zhaozhou Prefecture had a monk visitor. The practitioner asked, "Have you ever been here before?" His visitor answered, "I have been here once." The host replied, "Go have some tea!" One day, the host asked another visitor the same question. The visitor said that he had never been there. The host's reply remained the same, "Go and have some tea." His servant, after observing his replies, asked out of curiosity, "why are you replying in the same way regardless of others' answers?" The host called his servant by name and said to him, "Go and have some tea." This anecdote is believed to be of milestone importance in the establishment of the idea of the oneness of tea and Zen. Zen thoughts can be interpreted in various ways, just like the host's replies concerning tea.

The idea of the oneness of tea and Zen is closely related to the Zen school. But if we assume the "Zen" in "oneness of tea and Zen" shares an identical meaning with the "Zen" in "Zen school," we have arrived at a false conclusion. Considering millennia-old Chinese religions and cultural customs, the former does share something in common with the latter, but the former is much more meaningful in traditional Chinese culture than the latter. To a certain extent, the beliefs of Chinese religious followers can be generalized into "Confucian thoughts are fundamental; Taoist principles are pragmatic; but the ultimate pursuit for a man lies in pursuing nothing." This generalization commits the error of overgeneralization, and does not apply to all Chinese believers in different dynasties and in different social classes. However, this generalization approximates the lifelong pursuits of traditional Chinese literati. Considering this, the oneness of tea and Zen is concerned with conflicting concepts of action and inaction, secular life and monastic life, ritual and personality, moderation and harmony as well as the relationship between man and heaven.

Zen thought in the tea ceremony is not only restricted to historical anecdotes and cultural research, but also associated with tea ceremony masters. These thoughts are present in each and every tea brewing and drinking practice in our daily life. If we seek peace and relief by experiencing the beauty of ordinary life through every practice,

then everything happening in life can be transformed into a valuable opportunity to appreciate the beauty of life.

The "let it be" mentality is a significant element of Zen thought that we should think about. Each day, we may have several cups of tea, some brewed by ourselves and some served by others. When brewing the tea by ourselves, we might inadvertently make the tea too strong because we are caught up in a business call. When served by others, we may regret that they have made black tea rather than our favorite green tea; or perhaps the tea leaves are not as good-quality as we thought. Real tea lovers will not be influenced by their personal preference and dilute the over-strong liquor with water, and might feel as if they are drinking an unfamiliar kind of tea. No matter what the conditions, they will make best use of what they have in hand and try every means to optimize their enjoyment of the tea. This mentality and behavior exemplifies the principles of Zen thought.

The "all are equal" mentality is another significant element of Zen thought. In the tea brewing process, every steeping will produce different flavors. Therefore, tea brewers are supposed to first pour tea liquor into a pitcher which is commonly known

1 Monks of Fajing Temple in Hangzhou harvesting tea leaves

2 A tea gathering in a Buddhist monastery; drinking tea is also a form of Buddhist practice for the monks

as the "Justice Cup" and then share it among different drinkers, rather than serving someone before others. If we have no justice cup in hand, we can find other solutions. For example, if two drinkers are served, we should fill the teapot with two cupfuls of water. When pouring the tea liquor, we should pour half a cup into the first cup, and a full cup into the second, and then fill the first cup. Steady hands and the continuity of movement will also help to ensure that the liquor in the two cups is of the same strength. If four drinkers are served, this rule also applies. This way of sharing crystallizes the wisdom of the ancient Chinese, and their insistence on treating everyone as equal.

In addition to "let it be" and "all are equal," other Zen thoughts are widely observed in the tea brewing practice. The key lies in whether we can understand the oneness of tea and Zen in daily life and the most ordinary things around us. For instance, the importance of ensuring balance and harmony in our lives. These elements can also be expressed in the tea brewing process through careful consideration of the amount of water and tea used, and how long the tea is brewed. In daily life, we make preparations in advance for the tasks we plan based on previous

experience. Similarly, we can learn and make adjustments to the way to prepare tea based on our own evaluation of the tea liquor. Also, the consistency and fluidity of the tea brewer's movements can help to concentrate the brewers' mind in a similar way to Zen principles. The brewer can also identify the care with which they treat their teaware as a microcosm of wider conduct in life. Even in cleansing the teaware following the brewing process, we can express gratitude for the tea and the gift of nature, a metaphor for our overall gratitude for life in general.

1-3 Zen is universal, if you keep Zen in mind. Tea, wood, leaf, or bamboo can all be related to Zen ideas

CHAPTER IX

Dissemination

Similar to its development trajectory over the ages, the geographic dissemination of tea culture is also interesting. During this process, the spirituality of the Chinese tea culture has been inherited and further developed by Japanese tea ceremony, while its practicality has been spread along the Ancient Tea Route.

1 Jianzhen, an accomplished Tang Monk, traveled to Japan to popularize Buddhist teachings. He brought tea and tea culture to Japan

2 Jasmine-scented tea is a local favorite in Beijing. It is closely associated with local history and cultural tastes

3 Chinese tea stores in Paris; there are many fans of Chinese tea all across the globe

Observing the development trajectory of tea culture through the ages is an interesting exercise. The mythical Patron of Agriculture introduced tea into people's daily life. Ever since the birth of tea culture, the Chinese have made numerous innovations to tea culture, such as steaming tea in the Tang Dynasty, whisking tea in the Song Dynasty and steeping tea in the Ming Dynasty. However, in the neighboring Japan, matcha, which is recognized as mainstream Japanese tea culture, retains a great similarity with the tea whisking practice in the Song Dynasty from which it is derived. In some sense, the Japanese ritual of senchado preserves the tea steaming practice of the Tang Dynasty while incorporating the steeping methods of the Ming Dynasty. In this sense, Chinese tea culture has experienced continuous evolution, while its Japanese counterpart adheres more strictly to tradition.

Similarly, how tea culture has been disseminated in geographic terms is also interesting. There are three examples to this story. Historically, tea was first grown in South China. At present, the northernmost tea production areas in China are Laoshan and Rizhao, where green tea named after the production areas is produced. Secondly, Beijing, the capital of several feudal regimes in dynastic China, is known for scented tea. In ancient China, due to restrictive transport and storage conditions, tea

leaves became severely oxidized on their way from South China to Beijing, and their flavors were compromised. For this reason, it was a common practice to scent the tea leaves with flowers to enhance its aroma. Flower-scented tea was thus established as a dominant tea product in the city. And finally, the third example is Indian black tea which makes up a considerable share of the world market. Of the two main varieties, Assam black tea is made from native tea trees, while Darjeeling was originally grown in China. In addition to the three important elements listed above, how Chinese tea ceremony was introduced to Japan and along the Ancient Tea Route into Tibet deserves a more detailed description.

JAPANESE TEA CEREMONY

1

1 A Japanese green tea garden at the foot of Mount Fuji

In a narrow sense, the Japanese tea ceremony refers to matcha which evolved from tea whisking in the Song Dynasty and developed into various schools and etiquettes. In a broad sense, this notion also encompasses senchado. Senchado originated from the tea-steaming practice in the Tang Dynasty, while incorporating elements of the tea steeping practice in the Ming Dynasty. Senchado arrests our attention because it shares much in common with the Chinese steeping method and is the most commonly used method in Japanese daily life.

The Japanese tea ceremony has evolved under the infuence of its Chinese counterpart. In the Heian Era, the tea brewing method of the Tang Dynasty was introduced to Japan, when the royal family, nobility, monks and other members of high society were keen to imitate tea drinking culture in China, giving rise to the popularity of tea among the nobility. In the Kamakura, Muromachi, Azuchi and Momoyama Eras, the tea whisking methods of the Song Dynasty spread to Japan, when temple tea, tea fights and academy tea gained prevalence, and the Japanese tea ceremony started to take shape. In the Edo Era, the tea steeping method of the Ming Dynasty was introduced to Japan, bringing to maturity the Japanese tea ceremony and giving birth to various schools. During the development process of the Japanese tea ceremony, three figures were influential. Among them, Murata Juko is recognized as the founder of the Japanese tea ceremony. Takeno Jōō played a transitional role, while Sen no Rikyu drew inspiration from his predecessors and became an accomplished master in the history of the Japanese tea ceremony.

It is an established practice in the scholarly world to take the birth of various schools as a signifier of the maturity of an artistic form. For instance, the Japanese tea ceremony originated in China, but developed into various schools during the localization process. In contrast, the Chinese tea ceremony which came into existence millennia ago did not evolve into distinct schools. This difference is caused by the varied emphases and priorities between the two societies. The Chinese tea ceremony is centered on the tea liquor, while its Japanese counterpart is primarily perceived as a form of spiritual expression. Therefore, "The Book of Tea" by Okakula Tensin is primarily concerned with Zen, art, meditation and philosophy. However, this book starts with tea leaves and the tea brewing practice. A wide range of reasons have led to the difference between Chinese and Japanese tea ceremonies. Firstly, there are

1-2 Matcha represents the essence
of the Japanese tea ceremony. Both
thick and thin tea can be served in a
tea gathering

3 Rites between guest and host make
up a significant part of the Japanese
tea ceremony

many tea production areas and a rich variety of tea leaves in China. Tea production technologies and tea-making methods are constantly improved to optimize the quality of tea liquor. At its earliest stage, the Japanese tea ceremony merely imitated the Chinese tea ceremony. However, in an island country, only a limited variety of tea was accessible to the Japanese. Therefore, they tended to focus on rites and the spirituality of tea. However, this acknowledgement does not mean that the Chinese tea ceremony does not rival its Japanese counterpart in artistic value and spiritual pursuit. The Japanese tea ceremony exists as an independent artistic form, whereas Chinese tea culture has made its way into all aspects of society. It is no exaggeration

1 | 3
2

1 Water container and water whisk. The joints in the bamboo and revealed thread ends are intended to highlight the natural style

3 A glimpse of a Japanese tea garden; tea gardens and tea houses are significant components of the tea ceremony

2 A tea-brewing scene in Japan

that everything in life can be associated with tea culture in China. The idea of establishing tea culture as an independent discipline as in Japan is alien in China, where tea culture permeates every aspect of daily life.

The idea of the oneness of tea and Zen was established in China through the influence of Lu Yu. The Chinese had already incorporated tea ceremony as an indispensable component of their life. The Chinese tea ceremony is not restricted by Zen, but incorporates Confucian understanding and the pragmatism valued in Taoist thought. The Japanese rejoiced in their discovery of Buddhist thought, and built their tea ceremony on their religious understandings. That's why religion occupies a dominant position in the Japanese tea ceremony. The differences in thoughts are also manifested in practice. For example, when a host shares tea with visitors, Chinese face the front of the teapot to visitors to show respect. But the Japanese will face the front to themselves out of their reverence for the teapot. Chinese tea drinkers will leave some remnants in their cups to indicate that they are not greedy and that they wish for abundant resources in life. Japanese drinkers will finish all in their cups to be grateful for the blessing from nature. Another element important in the Japanese tea ceremony is the spatial relationship between objects. In this way, a proper distance is maintained

1 Karesansui, literally translated
as the Japanese Rock Garden, is an
expression of Zen thought and the
belief in the oneness of tea and Zen

between different tea utensils, which should be arranged in an aesthetically-appealing way. In contrast, the Chinese arrange teaware in a random way as they value an unintended beauty that is not man-made. Chinese teaware adopts various styles. The court collections are always exquisitely crafted, while coarsely-produced ones are favorites of the literati. In contrast, the Japanese observe a uniform standard concerning teaware style, which places stress on a natural and unadorned beauty. They even make their napkins into irregular shapes to indicate that they are not intentionally manipulated by human effort. Chinese tea drinkers are often motivated by a quest for perfection, while the Japanese consciously preserves imperfections. For instance, in Japan, the water container must be made of timber or bamboo with scars; or the tea whisk must have its unfinished tips revealed. In short, the Chinese are less restrained in their tea ceremony, while the Japanese incorporate profound religious understandings into their tea culture. Therefore, Japanese tea ceremony approximates a form of performance arts, in which the host, guests and subjects all participate as equals. The Chinese tea ceremony is practically-oriented and prioritizes the quality of tea liquor. Besides, it is an established belief in Chinese culture that men can agree to disagree. In this way, Chinese tea ceremony exhibits a rich diversity and is not subject to the same set of established rules.

"The Book of Tea" by Okakura Tenshin was finished in the early twentieth century. The author maintains that after years of national turbulence, the Chinese had lost their passion for tea and cared about nothing but its flavor. Chinese tea was still aromatic as usual, but the romance of the Tang and Song ceremonials are not to be found in the cup. If Tenshin Okakura could see with his own eyes today's China, he might see the broader picture and see the birthplace of Japanese tea culture. The tea which the Chinese have held in hand for thousands of years not only encapsulated but enhanced the romance of the Tang, the ceremonial of the Song and the simplicity of the Ming, all of which have survived the trials of time.

ANCIENT TEA ROUTE

1 Densely compressed dark tea was a huge component of trade along the Ancient Tea Route.

2 Horses were the main vehicle to transport tea and other commodities along the Ancient Tea Route

The Ancient Tea Route is of prominent significance to the history of civilization as it facilitated foreign trade and cultural popularization. Its thriving depended on tea trading to a large extent. The route originated from exchanges between horse and tea traders following the Tang and Song Dynasties. Back at that time, horses were a rare commodity in Central China, while tea was rare in the Tibetan region. Therefore, merchants took this opportunity and their business prospered. With the birth and development of horse and tea exchanges, trade between Central China and the Tibetan region gradually stabilized and was systemized, enlarged in scale. In this context, a giant transport network with the three routes between Qinghai and Tibet, Sichuan and Tibet, and Yunnan and Tibet as arteries came into being, which was later known as the "Ancient Tea Route."

We cannot talk about the Ancient Tea Route without mentioning the Silk Road. The latter is more famed as it was an international route which started from Chang'an(today's Xi'an in Shaanxi Province), transecting Asia and Europe, and

1 Black Dragon Pond in Lijiang, Yunnan
Province; the Ancient Tea Route is
known for its picturesque scenery

finally connecting ancient Chinese civilization with its counterparts in Greece and Rome. Though the Ancient Tea Route extends to countries in South Asia, it is still primarily a route linking the Han and the Tibetan ethnic groups. The Silk Road was mainly intended for the delivery of silk, porcelain, fur, spice, jade, plants, herbs and other commodities, while the Tea Route originated from horse and tea trading, which constituted its mainstay business, though it finally encompassed other commodities. However, this does not mean that the Ancient Tea Route was inferior to the Silk Road. Archaeological findings have proven that the former is much more ancient than the latter, though it only became well-known in the Tang and Song Dynasties. In addition, the Tea Route has no rival in terms of the altitude traversed: it reached the Qinghai-Tibetan Plateau, commonly known as the Roof of the World.

The birth of the Ancient Tea Route is not only economically and culturally meaningful, but also significant to ancient China in a political and strategic sense. The central government strengthened its relationship with border areas through commodity exchanges on one hand, and obtained war horses to enhance its military powers on the other. Barter along this route allowed trade to be conducted without metal currency which could be used to produce weapons. Tea could not be locally sourced on the Chinese boundary due to the harsh natural conditions there. Ethnic groups living on the boundary primarily feed on meat, thus they needed tea to reduce fats and dispel inner heat. In a scientific sense, alkaline substances in tea can neutralize acid components in meat to restore an inner physical balance. Therefore, when ethnic groups on the borders rose up, the central government could appease them without the use of its army — they could simply impose a tea embargo.

The aforementioned facts seem to be unrelated to tea. But in reality, they exemplify the importance of tea to the Chinese economy, and the extent to which tea was seen as part of national identity. Tea that was transported along the Ancient Tea Route was predominantly made up of post-fermented tea including Pu-erh. Ethnic groups on the Chinese borders were perceived to have unruly lifestyles, which the Chinese thought was mirrored by their choices of tea. Of course, their preference for post-fermented tea was in fact due to their habit of blending tea with milk and butter. The Ancient Tea Route is not only known for its precipitousness and toughness, but also for its many anecdotes. For example, it is widely believed that the wet-piling

1 Lamas of Tibetan Buddhism drinking
buttered tea, a mainstay beverage in the
Tibetan area,It is commonly consumed
with glutinous rice cakes

2 The Ancient Tea Route also traversed
Shangri-La, which some believe James
Hilton depicted in his book "Lost Horizon."

drew inspiration from tea traders' experience on the Ancient Tea Route. During the
transportation process, moisture accidentally permeated the package of tea cakes,
accelerating the fermenting process. Though this assumption sounds well-grounded,
it has not been proven with concrete evidence.

Japan, a neighbor of China, still strictly observes the tea ceremony originally
celebrated in ancient China, Tibetan residents living along the Ancient Tea Route
have localized dark tea in an innovative way. The Japanese have also accepted the Zen
thoughts of ancient Chinese and nurtured them through preservation of the Chinese
tea ceremony, while Tibetans still adhere to their Tibetan Buddhism. It is evident that
tea culture in practice on the Ancient Tea Route is quick to adapt to local customs
and circumstances.

The China Tea Book

Author: Luo Jialin

Photographer: Han Zheng

Photo Galleries: Panoramic Photo, CFP, Dameimages

Calligrapher: Shao Ding

        (Calligraphic Works on P160, P162, P165)

Translators: Bruce Humes, Coral Yee

Copy Editor: Lee Perkins

Commissioning Team: Roaring Lion Media Co., Ltd.

Editors in Chief: Guo Guang, Mang Yu

Commissioning Editor: Ren Yuan

English Editors: Vera Pan, Fiona Wong

Designers: Peng Tao, Zhang Yuhai